A Communion of Subjects

"Indeed we must say that the universe is a communion of subjects rather than a collection of objects."

Thomas Berry

Contents

Acknowledgments xiii

Essay Abstracts xv

Heritage of the Volume
MARY EVELYN TUCKER 1

Prologue
Loneliness and Presence
THOMAS BERRY 5

Introduction
PAUL WALDAU AND KIMBERLEY PATTON 11

PART I
Animals in Religion, Science, and Ethics: In and Out of Time

"Caught with ourselves in the
net of life and time":
Traditional Views of Animals in Religion
KIMBERLEY PATTON 27

Seeing the Terrain We Walk:
Features of the Contemporary Landscape of
"Religion and Animals"
PAUL WALDAU 40

PART II
Animals in Abrahamic Traditions

Judaism

Sacrifice in Ancient Israel: Pure Bodies,
Domesticated Animals, and the Divine
Shepherd
JONATHAN KLAWANS 65

Hope for the Animal Kingdom:
A Jewish Vision
DAN COHN-SHERBOK 81

Hierarchy, Kinship, and Responsibility:
The Jewish Relationship to the Animal World
ROBERTA KALECHOFSKY 91

Christianity

The Bestiary of Heretics:
Imaging Medieval Christian Heresy
with Insects and Animals
BEVERLY KIENZLE 103

Descartes, Christianity,
and Contemporary Speciesism
GARY STEINER 117

Practicing the Presence of God:
A Christian Approach to Animals
JAY MCDANIEL 132

Islam

"This she-camel of God is a sign to you":
Dimensions of Animals in Islamic Tradition
and Muslim Culture
RICHARD FOLTZ 149

The Case of the Animals Versus Man:
Towards an Ecology of Being
ZAYN KASSAM 160

"Oh that I could be a bird and fly,
I would rush to the Beloved":
Birds in Islamic Mystical Poetry
ALI ASANI   170

PART III
Animals in Indian Traditions

Hinduism

Cows, Elephants, Dogs, and Other Lesser
Embodiments of *Ātman*:
Reflections on Hindu Attitudes Toward
Nonhuman Animals
LANCE NELSON   179

Strategies of Vedic Subversion:
The Emergence of Vegetarianism
in Post-Vedic India
EDWIN BRYANT   194

Buddhism

"A vast unsupervised recycling plant":
Animals and the Buddhist Cosmos
IAN HARRIS   207

Snake-kings, Boars' Heads,
Deer Parks, Monkey Talk:
Animals as Transmitters and Transformers in
Indian and Tibetan Buddhist Narratives
IVETTE VARGAS   218

Jainism

Inherent Value without Nostalgia:
Animals and the Jaina Tradition
CHRISTOPHER CHAPPLE   241

Five-Sensed Animals in Jainism
KRISTI WILEY   250

PART IV
Animals in Chinese Traditions

Early Chinese Religion

"Of a tawny bull we make offering":
Animals in Early Chinese Religion
ROEL STERCKX   259

Daoism

Daoism and Animals
E. N. ANDERSON AND LISA RAPHALS   275

Confucianism

Of Animals and Humans:
The Confucian Perspective
RODNEY TAYLOR   293

PART V
East Meets West:
Animals in Philosophy and Cultural
History

Human Exceptionalism
Versus Cultural Elitism:
(Or "Three in the morning, four at night")
ROGER AMES   311

Humans and Animals:
The History from a
Religio-Ecological Perspective
JORDAN PAPER   325

PART VI
Animals in Myth

A Symbol in Search of an Object:
The Mythology of Horses in India
WENDY DONIGER   335

Animals in African Mythology
KOFI OPOKU   351

"Why Umbulka Killed His Master":
Aboriginal Reconciliation and
the Australian Wild Dog
(*Canis lupus dingo*)
IAN MCINTOSH   360

PART VII
Animals in Ritual

Knowing and Being Known by Animals:
Indigenous Perspectives on Personhood
JOHN GRIM   373

Animal Sacrifice:
Metaphysics of the Sublimated Victim
KIMBERLEY PATTON   391

Hunting the Wren: A Sacred Bird in Ritual
ELIZABETH LAWRENCE   406

Ridiculus Mus:
Of Mice and Men in Roman Thought
CHRISTOPHER MCDONOUGH   413

Raven Augury from Tibet to Alaska:
Dialects, Divine Agency, and
the Bird's-Eye View
ERIC MORTENSEN   423

PART VIII
Animals in Art

On the *Dynamis* of Animals, or
How *Animalium* Became *Anthropos*
DIANE APOSTOLOS-CAPPADONA   439

PART IX
Animals as Subjects:
Ethical Implications for Science

Wild Justice, Social Cognition, Fairness,
and Morality: A Deep Appreciation
for the Subjective Lives of Animals
MARC BEKOFF   461

From Cognition to Consciousness
DONALD GRIFFIN   481

Are Animals Moral Agents?
Evolutionary Building Blocks of Morality
MARC HAUSER   505

Ethics, Biotechnology, and Animals
BERNARD ROLLIN   519

Animal Experimentation
KENNETH SHAPIRO   533

PART X
Are Animals "for" Humans?
The Issues of Factory Farming

Caring for Farm Animals:
Pastoralist Ideals in an Industrialized World
DAVID FRASER   547

Agriculture, Livestock, and Biotechnology:
Values, Profits, and Ethics
MICHAEL FOX   556

Agribusiness: Farming Without Culture
GARY VALEN   568

PART XI
Contemporary Challenges:
Law, Social Justice, and the Environment

Animals and the Law

Animal Law and Animal Sacrifice:
Analysis of the U.S. Supreme Court Ruling on
Santería Animal Sacrifice in Hialeah
STEVEN WISE   585

Animals and Social Justice

"A very rare and difficult thing":
Ecofeminism, Attention to Animal Suffering,
and the Disappearance of the Subject
CAROL ADAMS   591

Interlocking Oppressions: The Nature of
Cruelty to Nonhuman Animals and its
Relationship to Violence Toward Humans
KIM ROBERTS   605

Animal Protection and
the Problem of Religion
PETER SINGER   616

Animals and Global Stewardship

Earth Charter Ethics and Animals
STEVEN ROCKEFELLER   621

Pushing Environmental Justice
to a Natural Limit
PAUL WALDAU   629

Conclusion
A Communion of Subjects and a
Multiplicity of Intelligences
MARY EVELYN TUCKER   645

Epilogue
The Dance of Awe
JANE GOODALL   651

List of Contributors   657

Index   667

Acknowledgments

The editors wish to thank the extraordinary group of contributors to this volume; their scholarship, insight, and humanity have offered us a humbling learning experience as we worked together with them through the years on *A Communion of Subjects*. To Thomas Berry, geologian and wise teacher, thank you for providing the inspiration that drew the various sectors of this book into communion and coherence. Our deep gratitude is due to Professors Mary Evelyn Tucker and John Grim, directors of the Forum on Religion and Ecology, and to Richard Clugston of the Center for Respect of Life and the Environment (CRLE) for their vision and leadership in the area of religion and ecology, and in particular for their support of the conference on Religion and Animals at Harvard University in 1999. Thanks to Professor Tu Wei-ming of Harvard University and to the Yen Ching Institute for their sponsorship of the same conference, which was the genesis for the present book. The funds for the production editing and for many of the illustrations and permissions were generously provided by the CRLE and the Religion and Animals Institute at Tufts School of Veterinary Medicine. Leslie Bialler, our valiant copyeditor at Columbia University Press, brought intelligence, care, and humor to a harrowing task. Finally, our heartfelt thanks to the wonderful Wendy Lochner, senior editor of religion and philosophy at Columbia University Press, whose profound interest in this project has been steadfast from the beginning, and whose encouragement has sustained us to the end.

To all the creatures of the earth, human and nonhuman, thank you for bearing witness to the complexity and power of life itself, as it is expressed in so many forms and subject to so many visions: religious, scientific, and ethical.

PAUL WALDAU AND KIMBERLEY PATTON

Essay Abstracts

"A very rare and difficult thing":
Ecofeminism, Attention to Animal Suffering,
and the Disappearance of the Subject
CAROL ADAMS

This ecofeminist exploration addresses two out-of-place cows and what they teach us about several interrelated issues regarding the religious imagination and human relations with nonhumans. The first cow was fashioned by film-maker David Lynch for the "Cow Parade," a collection of artily-painted sculptured bovines scattered throughout New York City. Lynch's painted cow, which had "Eat My Fear" written across its hacked, decapitated and disemboweled body, was on display only two and a half hours, but caused children to cry and subsequently was kept under wraps in a warehouse. The other cow, an actual cow, jumped a 6-foot fence in Cincinnati in the winter of 2002 to escape a meatpacking plant and then, until she was captured, ran free in a city park for 10 days. The day after Easter, she appeared in a parade that celebrated the start of the baseball season. Now called, "Cinci Freedom," she received a key to the city as part of the city's festivities. She was then transported to an animal sanctuary to live out her natural life unmolested by meat packers, while many of the humans who celebrated her freedom headed to the ballpark to watch baseball and chomp down on some hot dogs. Ecofeminist insights offer assistance in unraveling the paradoxes concerning nonhuman suffering inherent in these stories. Specifically, these insights provide a conceptual understanding of the dualistic opposition between "humans" and "nonhumans/animals," the issues of disembodied versus embodied responses to suffering, and the positive nature of grief as a response to the death of nonhumans. This essay also reviews the fruits of ecofeminist-animal rights theory, such as found in the author's application of the concepts "absent referent" and "mass term" to the fate of nonhuman animals to be consumed as food. It concludes by recommending the cultivation of "attention" to the suffering of non-humans.

Human Exceptionalism Versus Cultural Elitism: "Three in the morning, four at night"
ROGER AMES

In classical Western thought, from Aristotle and the Stoics through Aquinas and Descartes, the notion of "human exceptionalism"—human beings are an exception to nature, both in kind and quality—has been a persistent theme. This assumption has been reinforced by theological assumptions that make the non-human world, including animals, a means to a human end. The chain of being, pathetical fallacy, and the sanctity of human life are all expressions of a world in which animals have been essentially defined, and relegated to the down side of a familiar dualism.

I want to identify and explore philosophical assumptions in East Asian philosophies broadly, that locate the animal world in a fundamentally different natural cosmology. There are several assumptions that inform this natural cosmology that seem inclusive and liberating: yin-yang correlative categories rather than exclusive dualisms, a this-world sensibility rather than a two-world "reality/appearance" dichotomy, ars contextualis ("the art of contextualizing") rather than linear teleology, bottom-up emergent harmony rather than top-down exclusive righteousness, philosophical syncretism rather than systematic philosophy, the way rather than the truth. Unless we academics are willing to allow that ideas have little determinative force, how can we reconcile such seemingly liberating sensibilities with the accusation that the Sinic cultures must take some real responsibility for being a market that fuels the depletion of endangered species?

There is a real human elitism in East Asian hierarchical thinking. Confucius, in the face of social and political turmoil, refuses to withdraw because "I cannot run with the birds and beasts. Am I not one among the people of this world?" Mencius claims that the difference between the human being and the beast is "infinitesimal," and that in the absence of culture, the human being is deplorably animal. Xunzi argues that the human being is a "super-animal" that has rescued itself from ugly animal behaviors through the creation of a moral mind. It certainly can be argued that in all three cases, the human "becoming" is a cultural achievement rather than a natural kind, but this achievement still gives the human being privilege of place within this world view.

Daoism and Animals
E. N. ANDERSON AND LISA RAPHALS

Animals are mentioned very frequently in Daoist texts, but usually in a metaphoric or instructional way; animal parables are used to illustrate points. The world reflected in these stories is largely pragmatic and rural; animals are for food and work. However, it is also a world in which imaginary and fantastic animals have a large share, and in which ordinary animals have moral, spiritual, or even shamanistic qualities. The early sources that launched the Daoist tradition use animals largely in teaching stories. Later texts, especially in the Six Dynasties period, often present Daoist figures as having special relationships with animals. They keep tame cranes and ride on them, or they can transform into various animals for certain purposes. The human and animal realms are not sharply separated. Classical Chinese has no word translating the English "animal(s)." Little explicit moral comment attaches to human use of animals. By implication, it is the human dao (and therefore natural and proper) for humans to eat animals and utilize them for work. However, both wider Daoist principles and the explicit conservation ideology of early syncretic texts seem to imply a general sense of respect for the animal world. Wanton slaughter and waste would probably be condemned.

ESSAY ABSTRACTS

On the Dynamis of Animals, Or How Animalium Became Anthropos
DIANE APOSTOLOS-CAPPADONA

This essay offers a consideration of the visual process of moving through predominantly Western art history, acknowledging that the earliest images reveal a recognition of the power and dignity of animals in their own right, followed by a gradual cultural shift toward the domestication of the animals until they become sympathetic images of the *human* condition and thereby reflect a total impingement of their individual dignity and integrity. Consequently, the animal is no longer *animalium* but *anthropos*, no longer icon but image, no longer symbol but emblem. An analogous process can arguably be detected in the humanization of religion, of religious ritual, and of (Western) culture. This is not simply the issue of the human craving identification with the animal or a form of sympathetic magic but, more important, a denigration of the beauty, power, and integrity of the animal until it is both owned and controlled by human beings, a constructed creature rather than an autonomous subject that was frequently ascribed divine powers.

"Oh that I could be a bird and fly, I would rush to the Beloved": Birds in Islamic Mystical Poetry
ALI ASANI

This essay explores the principal themes and imagery associated with birds in Islamic mystical poetry. After a brief examination of the Quranic basis for the special significance accorded to birds in Sufi poetry, it discusses bird symbolism in the poems of various Muslim authors including the Persian poet Farid ad-Din Attar (d. 1220) who composed one of the most brilliant mystical epics ever written on this theme, *The Conference of the Birds*.

Wild Justice, Social Cognition, Fairness, and Morality: A Deep Appreciation for the Subjective Lives of Animals
MARC BEKOFF

In this essay I will consider various aspects of the rapidly growing field called cognitive ethology. I will conclude with discussion of some moral implications of the study of animal cognition that I call "wild justice." I will not be directly concerned with consciousness, per se, for a concentration on consciousness deflects attention from other, and in many cases more interesting, tractable problems in the study of nonhuman animal (hereafter animal) cognition. After presenting some general background material concerning the ethological approach to the study of animal behavior, I will consider how, when, where, and why individuals from different taxa exchange social information concerning their beliefs, desires, and goals. My main examples come from studies of social play in mammals and antipredator behavior in birds. I will concentrate on nonprimates so as to give readers a taste for broad comparative discussion. Basically, I argue that although not all individuals always display behavior patterns that are best explained by appeals to intentionality, it is misleading to argue that such explanations have no place in the study of animal cognition. A pluralistic approach is needed and alternative explanations all deserve equal consideration.

Prologue: Loneliness and Presence
THOMAS BERRY

The "communion of subjects" goes beyond the obvious meanings of sharing and relation with beings outside the human race. In fact, since we cannot be truly ourselves in any adequate manner without all our companion beings throughout the earth, the larger community constitutes our greater self. Thus, our own identities can be drawn from such a connection. The presence of other, nonhuman beings—the creatures with whom we share the planet—helps us see pre-occupation with humans alone is not just debilitating, but also a betrayal of human possibility. The recognition that the universe is composed of subjects with whom to commune, not of objects to exploit, releases us from an isolated, debilitating loneliness. It promotes recovery of ancient insights about the value of all life and even of Earth itself. In such matters, religious traditions have a crucial role to play, raising awareness of ethics, daily life choices, and wider ecology.

The Emergence of Vegetarianism in Hindu Textual Sources
EDWIN BRYANT

The essay will examine the history of animals in orthodox Hindu Sanskrit textual sources in terms of their appropriateness as objects of human consumption. It will chart the development of attitudes toward meat-eating from the sacrificial culture of the oldest Vedic period to the emergence of a vegetarian ethic in later periods. The essay will explore the tension between the *hiṃsā,* "violence," constitutional to the sacrificial requirements of the Vedic age, and the *ahiṃsā,* "non-violence," essential to most *mokṣa* —"liberation-" centered religious cultures of the post-Vedic age.

Inherent Value without Nostalgia: Animals and the Jaina Tradition
CHRISTOPHER CHAPPLE

According to Jaina cosmology, the niche occupied by animal life forms is continuous with the human realm. Humans have experienced countless lifetimes as humans and, because no one can enjoy more than seven consecutive births as a human, will most likely experience animal life in the future. In the stories of the Tīrthaṅkaras, the twenty-four great teachers of the Jaina faith, animals play an important role. Jaina iconography depicts each of these Jaina leaders in as-sociation with a particular animal. When he renounced the world, Mahāvīra, the most recent Tīrthaṅkara, descended from a palanquin ornamented with animals' portraits. The tradition describes his qualities, upon his awakening, as evoking those of powerful animals. Animal tales are used throughout the tradition to inspire ethical behavior. The Jainas have established an extensive network of animal hospitals and shelters (*pinjrapoles*) for the care of aged or infirm animals. However, this compassion for animals is not sentimental. In general, because of their "live and let live" philosophy, Jainas do not keep pets, as this would be considered a form of slavery or entrapment. Furthermore, they will not engage in the practice of mercy killing of suffering animals, presuming that such action would interfere with the natural karmic process earned by the animal through past actions. Nonetheless, the Jainas have been champions of animal protection in India and revere animals for their actual and potential spiritual attainments.

Hope for the Animal Kingdom: A Jewish Vision
DAN COHN-SHERBOK

In this new millennium, serious questions are being raised about the treatment of animals. In the past, animals were viewed as provided for human use. Yet, the Jewish tradition challenges such a human-centered vision and promotes a compassionate and sympathetic regard for the animal world. This essay charts the development of such an attitude from biblical times to the present and explores its application in modern society.

A Symbol in Search of an Object: The Mythology of Horses in India
WENDY DONIGER

Most of the peoples who entered India entered on horseback and then continued to import horses into India: the people formerly known as Indo-Europeans (who brought their horses with them), the people who became the Mughals (who imported Arabian horses from Central Asia and Persia, overland and by sea) and the British (who imported Australian Walers). There is no native, village tradition of horses in India as there is among the natives of Ireland or Egypt, where the people kept horses. Yet the symbol of the horse became embedded in the folk consciousness and then stayed there even after its referent, the horse, had vanished from the scene, even after the foreigners had folded their tents and gone away. To this day, horses are worshipped all over India by people who do not have horses and seldom even see a horse, in places where the horse has never been truly a part of the land.

A Marxist might view the survival of the mythology of the aristocratic horse as an imposition of the lies of the rulers upon the people, an exploitation of the masses by saddling them with a mythology that never was theirs nor will ever be for their benefit, a foreign mythology that distorts the native conceptual system, compounding the felony of the invasion itself. But the horse-myths of non-horsey people may pose a challenge to materialist or Marxist interpretations of mythology: the symbolism has power even where there can be no actual material basis for its importance to the people. A Freudian, on the other hand, might see in the native acceptance of this foreign mythology the process of projection or identification by which one overcomes a feeling of anger or resentment or impotence toward another person by assimilating that person into oneself, becoming the other. Though there is much to be said for these interpretations, I would want to modify them in several respects. I would point out that myths about oppressive foreigners and their horses sometimes became a positive factor in the lives of those whom they conquered or dominated.

"This she-camel of God is a sign to you":
Dimensions of Animals in Islamic
Tradition and Muslim Culture
RICHARD FOLTZ

Islam, as an Abrahamic faith, has much in common with Christianity and Judaism. All three monotheistic faiths consider humans to have a special status within the hierarchy of creation, distinct from and above other animals. However, Islam offers some important differences. Most notably, animals in Islam are believed to have souls, and to differ from humans only in that they lack volition. Islamic tradition includes important references to nonhuman animals in the areas of philosophy, literature, and the sciences.

Agriculture, Livestock, and Biotechnology:
Values, Profits, and Ethics
MICHAEL FOX

The intensive production of animals on "factory farms" — the bioconcentration camps of the agribusiness food industry — have many hidden costs and serious long-term consequences for consumers, the environment, and to rural communities. The costs and consequences, now being compounded by the nascent "life science" (biotechnology) industry, are documented with two intentions: first, to demonstrate that they are the product of an outmoded, if not pathological, attitude toward life; second, to contrast this attitude with the spirit and practice of organic agriculture, which provides basic bioethical principles for a more humane, sustainable, socially just, and healthful approach to meeting the nutritional needs of a growing consumer populace.

Caring for Farm Animals: Pastoralist Ideals in an Industrialized World
DAVID FRASER

Animal agriculture in the West has traditionally been guided by a pastoralist ethic, descended from cultural traditions evident in the Bible, which focuses on the relationship between animal keepers and domestic animals in their care. Pastoralist ideals attach value to diligent care of animals, and they create an unspoken moral contract that allows people to use animals as long as appropriate care is provided. Today, this traditional value system is being severely challenged by competing industrial and market-related values. Market pressures, combined with technological innovation, have led to (1) restrictive environments for farm animals, (2) elimination of inessential amenities such as bedding and exercise, and (3) increased automation and less human–animal contact. These changes have led to widespread public concern. Critics accuse animal producers of having callously abandoned traditional animal care values. Many animal producers, however, continue to espouse traditional values, yet feel compelled by market forces to use the predominant quasi-industrial production methods. Animal producers, and society generally, urgently need a new moral vision of our relationship with animals to allow animal agriculture to proceed in a manner that is ethically satisfactory for both producers and consumers. To be effective, this new vision will have to set limits on the ability of market forces to override traditional ethical values. To be accepted, it will likely need to be compatible with traditional pastoralist values.

Epilogue: The Dance of Awe
JANE GOODALL

Based on her extensive, now famous fieldwork with the wild chimpanzees of Tanzania, this interview with Jane Goodall offers her most focused reflections to date on the possibility of a lived spiritual dimension of animal life. Scientific prejudices regarding the "impossibility" of animal consciousness and emotion, persisting throughout her education at Cambridge in the mid-twentieth century and up to this day, forced Goodall while a student to suppress what she believed to be true. Based on her encounters with chimpanzees' unique, responsive ritual dance on the occasion of heavy rainfall and even more spectacularly to a jungle waterfall, she speculates that animals may feel something akin to what we call "religious awe."

From Cognition to Consciousness
DONALD GRIFFIN

This essay proposes an extension of scientific horizons in the study of animal behavior and cognition to include conscious experiences. From this perspective animals are best appreciated as actors or active "subjects" rather than as passive objects. A major adaptive function of their central nervous systems may be simple, but conscious and rational, thinking about alternative actions and choosing those the animal believes will get what it wants, or avoid what it dislikes or fears. Versatile adjustment of behavior in response to unpredictable challenges provides strongly suggestive evidence of simple but conscious thinking. Especially significant objective data from animal thoughts and feelings are already available, once communicative signals are recognized as evidence of the subjective experiences they often convey to others. The scientific investigation of human consciousness has undergone a renaissance in the 1990s, as exemplified by numerous symposia, books, and two new journals. The neural correlates of cognition appear to be basically similar in all central nervous systems. Therefore, other species equipped with very similar neurons, synapses, and glia may well be conscious. Simple perceptual and rational conscious thinking may be at least as important for small animals as for those with large enough brains to store extensive libraries of behavioral rules. Perhaps only in "megabrains" is most of the information processing unconscious.

Knowing and Being Known by Animals: Indigenous Perspectives on Personhood
JOHN GRIM

This essay seeks to open understanding of such central symbols as the horse and buffalo in the formation of a healer among the Plains Lakota, as well as ritual modes in sub-Arctic Cree hunting divination, in which hunters speak of hunted animals using the erotic languages of human love. The essay also explores the Columbia River Plateau Salish Winter Dance, in which visionary songs reenact the knowing of animals in the acquisition of spiritual power, and being known by animals in ethical reflection upon food and responsibility to the natural world. Finally, this essay considers the embodied speech relationships of ancestors and animals among the Dogon peoples of sub-Saharan Africa. These rituals draw attention to different modes of human–animal interdependencies, or communion, such as human sovereignty in the context of animal "nations," erotic intimacies, an animal's capacity to respond to human need by transmitting cosmological forces in a song, and the ways in which animals are understood as assisting humans during the times and spaces of transitions. In four words: person, intimacy, transition, and ecstasy.

"A vast unsupervised recycling plant": Animals and the Buddhist Cosmos
IAN HARRIS

Buddhism is a two and a half thousand year old tradition that has flourished in most regions of Asia. Its heritage has been preserved in written texts, architectural structures, political systems, and village customs. Not unsurprisingly, its view of animals is complex and continually shifting. Nevertheless, there are some underlying continuities, and this essay will provide a clear overview of the following central issues:

1. Sentience in Buddhist cosmology
2. Traditional classificatory models—humankind, animals, and other beings
3. Rebirth and the conservation of sentience
4. Ethical implications
5. Hostile and exemplary animals
6. Animals in Buddhist modernism

Are Animals Moral Agents? A History of Temptation and Control
MARC HAUSER

In this essay I follow the footsteps of Immanuel Kant and look at the problem of morality the way a chemist would look at the structure of a crystal. By decomposing morality into some of its core ingredients, we can better assess the capacities of animals to engage in moral action. In particular, I begin by making a distinction between moral agents and patients, arguing that the former depends upon the capacity to take on responsibilities. I then explore the nature of animal emotion, the capacity to inhibit actions, and the ability to take into account what others believe and desire. Although animals have some of the core moral ingredients, they appear to lack the capacity for understanding what others think, have an impoverished capacity for inhibition, and appear not to make the distinction between right and wrong. In this sense, animals are not moral agents. They do, however, deserve our complete dedication as moral patients, organisms with emotion who deserve to be protected from harm.

Hierarchy, Kinship, and Responsibility:
The Jewish Relationship to the Animal World
ROBERTA KALECHOFSKY

This essay will explore two basic tenets that have guided Judaism's relationship to the animal world. The first tenet is that all animals share in and reflect God's justice and mercy. The second tenet was developed within the parameters of a hierarchy that posited the human race at the center of the moral drama and, at the same time, sustained a kinship with and responsibility for, primarily, domestic animals. The essay will demonstrate how this position gave rise to a multitude of laws (commandments or *mitzvot*) that regulated that human responsibility. This position, however, was developed between two poles of religious thought that will be examined: the belief that the animal was created "in order that good should be done to it"; and the tradition that human beings were given permission to eat meat. This permission is traditionally viewed as related to conditions in the post-flood world, as provisional, and ultimately contrary to a messianic and redeemed world. Eating meat, though tolerated, has always been viewed as morally debatable.

The Case of the Animals Versus Man:
Toward an Ecology of Being
ZAYN KASSAM

The Case of the Animals Versus Man, a tenth-century work written by a group of philosophically minded Muslim authors called the *Ikhwān al-Safā'* ("the Brethren of Purity") raises the issue of human maltreatment of animals, and whether it is at all justified for humans to marshal the bodies of beasts for their own purpose. Were animals created to serve humans as argued in sacred texts, and should they be subjected to enslavement and maltreatment as a consequence? While ultimately the text argues in favor of the first (animals were created to serve

humans), the authors nonetheless subversively draw attention to the symbiotic relationship between the world of humans and the animal kingdom and give humans pause to think on how all of God's creatures might be treated regardless of their rank in a divinely ordained ontological hierarchy.

The Bestiary of Heretics: Imaging Medieval Christian Heresy with Insects and Animals
BEVERLY KIENZLE

Twelfth-century Europe experienced a remarkable upsurge of popular heresy and a vast production of anti-heretical literature that adopted creatures such as the moth and the wolf in the search for biblical authorities to bolster its arguments. The Western church, challenged by charismatic itinerant preachers, lay apostolic movements, and the Cathar counter-church, responded with pen, pulpit, and crusade. In so doing, it relied on the learning of the "Twelfth-Century Renaissance," the flowering of cathedral schools that continued and developed patristic exegesis and crystallized various genres of books, such as bestiaries and aviaries. Medieval authors drew from biblical, ancient, and patristic sources to moralize animal lore and apply it to preaching and writing against heresy. The medieval imagination, in its inheritance of Platonism, possessed a "symbolist mentality" that transformed animate creatures into figures for heretics. From the lowly moth to the wily fox, these creatures and their behavior patterns came to symbolize dissident Christians and their conduct. This essay explores the imaging of heresy with insects and animals during this key period of European religious history and analyzes how moral consequences were drawn from descriptions of animal behavior.

Sacrifice in Ancient Israel: Pure Bodies, Domesticated Animals, and the Divine Shepherd
JONATHAN KLAWANS

Various biases, both religious and cultural, have had a negative impact on scholarship on sacrifice in the Hebrew Bible. As a result, too many analyses focus exclusively on the killing of the animal, without recognizing that these rituals had religious meaning to those who practiced them. This study will examine the sacrificial process broadly conceived, including both the preparatory rites of purification and the prerequisite rearing of the animals to be offered. When the scope is widened, it becomes much easier to imagine what these rituals meant in ancient Israel. By lording over their herds and flocks—and by selecting which animals will be given to the altar—ancient Israelites were reflecting on their own relationship to their God, whom they imagined as their shepherd.

Hunting the Wren: A Sacred Bird in Ritual
ELIZABETH LAWRENCE

The wren (*Troglodytes troglodytes*) was once the object of an annual ritual carried out in certain areas of Britain and Europe in which the bird was hunted and killed, generally around the time of the winter solstice. The seasonal slaughter of this tiny song bird at first seems paradoxical, for throughout its range the wren is generally beloved and protected by strict prohibitions against harming it. Killing the wren, however, undoubtedly originated as the solemn ritual sacrifice of a revered creature performed in order to bring about the spring return of the sun's light and warmth, ensuring the renewal of all life on earth. Over time, the original motivation for the sacrifice of the wren was lost, and new meanings were superimposed upon a ritual that continued to be carried out as an important part of popular tradition. Vestiges of the wren-hunt ritual persist today.

Analysis of the elements of the wren hunt in conjunction with consideration of the bird's salient attributes and people's reactions to those attributes sheds light on the process whereby a living creature in the natural world was transformed into a sacred being who was the object of beliefs that were expressed in an elaborate ritual. Consideration of the wren's visible characteristics that were believed to indicate the presence of invisible inner power helps to elucidate the process whereby a certain animal becomes endowed with religious significance. The wren-hunt ritual, with its various attendant ceremonies, demonstrates that the input of both animal and human in a particular human–animal interaction determines the symbolic status of that animal, which in turn influences treatment of the species in society. It is often the cognitive image of a species, not its actual biological traits, that motivates people's interactions with animals. In today's world, that image can influence the fate of the species—determining whether it will face extinction or be allowed to survive.

Practicing the Presence of God: A Christian Approach to Animals
JAY MCDANIEL

A seventeenth-century Christian monk, now known as Brother Lawrence, once spoke of Christian living as "practicing the presence of God." The subject of my essay is "practicing the presence of God" in relation to our closest biological and spiritual kin, often called "the animals."

As I use the phrase, "practicing the presence" is more than "thinking about animals" and "acting compassionately toward animals." It lies in being aware of them, in seeing them, as subjects of their own lives, as valued by God for their own sakes, and as ways through which, in humility, Christians receive divine presence. In Orthodox Christianity, this way of seeing other creatures is called "the contemplation of nature." According to Kallistos Ware, it involves an awareness of other beings in their "suchness" and also an awareness of these beings as sacramental presences through which holy light shines. This contemplation is understood to be a complement to that "contemplation of God" which occurs in silent prayer.

My thesis is that, in the contemporary setting, there are many theologies available within Christianity that can help Christians "practice the presence," ranging from Orthodox to Evangelical to Protestant. And there are several guidelines for compassionate acting in relation to animals, most specifically those developed by the Annecy Conference in France under the auspices of the World Council of Churches. But what is most needed is an emphasis on prayerful living, on fresh ways of seeing, that can complement and support such thinking and acting. I will discuss such ways of seeing, emphasizing their connectedness to traditions of contemplative prayer.

Ridiculus Mus: *Of Mice and Men in Roman Thought*
CHRISTOPHER MCDONOUGH

Although the ominous significance of the mouse in the classical world was frequently noted by the ancients, no study has satisfactorily explained why in particular the mouse should be so reckoned. Of great significance in understanding the foreboding status of the mouse is the widespread belief in its autochthonous origin. As a creature of the earth, the mouse was marked by tremendous fecundity, yet at the same time it was intimately associated with death. The appearance of mice in several Etruscan tombs is especially noteworthy in this context. Likewise important is the association of mice with domestic architecture: it was a sign of a house's imminent collapse when mice deserted it, thus indicating the connection of mouse and house. The mouse, living as it does within the walls of the house, is easily seen as a creature

of borders, crossing without difficulty between the realms of public and private, just as it passes over the boundary of life and death. As a marginal entity, the mouse poses a problem for the Roman religious system, which prefers definite categories to ambiguity. This inability to fit into traditional Roman taxonomy of thought brings the mouse's ominous status more sharply into focus. While we might smile along with Horace at the *ridiculus mus,* its liminality was a source of Roman cultural anxiety, surely no laughing matter.

"Why Umbulka Killed His Master": *Aboriginal Reconciliation and the Australian Wild Dog (*Canis Lupus Dingo*)*
IAN MCINTOSH

Its origins are a mystery. About four thousand years ago, the dingo appears in Australia and eradicates the thylacine (zebra-striped native dog). By the time of European colonization in 1788, the Tasmanian Tiger, as the thylacine was known, was a memory in northern Australia. The only evidence of its former presence was in ancient Aboriginal rock paintings in places like Kakadu National Park. Yet despite this demise, the new invader inspired a richness and variety of narratives almost unparalleled in Aboriginal cosmology. Apart from the perhaps the water snake or rainbow serpent, there is no other totemic symbol of such power and import. This essay looks at the ways in which Aborigines make reference to this animal in narratives that convey a profound message about themselves and their relationships with others—a nationwide movement of shared ideas that reached its fullest expression at the time of first contact with non-Aborigines.

Raven Augury from Tibet to Alaska: Dialects, Divine Agency, and the Bird's-Eye View
ERIC MORTENSEN

Ravens (*Corvus corax*), through their speech and behavior, serve as divinatory messengers in Tibet and Mongolia, and among religious cultures as diverse within Central Asia as the Naxi to the Tuvinians. The morphology of raven folklore across the various cultural regions of northeastern Asia and northwestern native North America, across the Bering Strait, witnesses the raven becoming a deity, a mischievous creator, a transformer. How and why and when did the raven come to be seen and heard, religiously, in such differing ways? Historical migration of peoples, transmission of folklore, and the diffusion of diverse religions, all conspire to complicate a lucid analysis of the changing role of the raven. Nevertheless, upon close scrutiny of textual and oral evidence, we find that the distinction between medium and divinity is itself inexact and malleable. This essay scrutinizes the shifting role of the raven, postulating that the speech and behavior of the bird informs its diverse religious roles. Furthermore, given raven intelligence, communication, and active participation in the construction of human religious traditions, can we wonder about the raven's divine agency? Can ritual, with a syntax, reactivate myth?

Cows, Elephants, Dogs, and other Lesser Embodiments of Ātman: Reflections on Hindu Attitudes toward Nonhuman Animals
LANCE NELSON

This essay will explore dominant Hindu attitudes toward nonhuman animals as revealed in major Sanskrit texts of classical Hinduism, such as the Hindu law books (*dharmaśāstras*), the epics, the Purāṇas, and the literature of Yoga and Vedānta, as well as in other sources. It will be shown that, from the point of view of contemporary ecological and animal-rights paradigms, the Hindu material is ambivalent, particularly in terms of its notions of hierarchy.

Animals in African Mythology
KOFI OPOKU

The mythology of Africa is the product of the unceasing wonder of our African ancestors who raised essentially fundamental questions about the origin and nature of the universe, human destiny, and the meaning of the many experiences we have in life. This wondering engendered a reflection on the fundamental aspects of human existence and experience. The answers to the questions that they posed came in the form of timeless stories that expressed profound and multidimensional truths, which helped them to understand their place in the cosmos and their relations with their environment, both physical and spiritual.

These timeless stories reflected a keen awareness of their environment, and since they believed themselves to be interconnected with, and interdependent on, all that existed they did not consider themselves as separate beings.

Animals, who were credited with consciousness and with whom humans could communicate, feature prominently in African mythology as agents in creation, companions of the first human beings, messengers of the spirits; and they were considered to be altogether indispensable in the human quest for meaning, which has not been rendered obsolete by humanity's increasing technological advancement. These stories continue to speak to the human condition.

Humans and Animals: The History from a Religio-Ecological Perspective
JORDAN PAPER

Humans, being animals, have been intimately interrelated with other animals from their inception as a recognizable species. For most of human history, humans understood the animals, as well as plants, on which their lives depended as superior numinous beings and related to these beings ritually. Horticulture, agriculture, herding, industrial, and postindustrial cultures led to continuing changes in the nature of the relationship. This essay analyzes the changes in these relationships between humans and animals, with a focus on ritual, from the methodology of religio-ecology.

"Caught with ourselves in the net of life and time": Traditional Views of Animals in Religion
KIMBERLEY PATTON

The recent discovery of the powerful representations of animals in the Paleolithic Chauvet Cave, particularly of predators as well as the expected range of hunted prey, has reconfirmed the enshrined symbiosis between animals and human beings. Delineating the contours of the religious nature of that ancient relationship, however, has long been an interpretive challenge. Lévi-Strauss's famous assertion about indigenous forms of cognition that "animals are good to think" can serve only as one starting point in the kaleidoscope of semantic fields traditionally played by animals in human religiousness, even the most sublimated, including cosmogony, magic, sacrifice, myth, metamorphosis, antinomianism, theriomorphism, divination, and mimesis. Animals both bear and make meaning for human beings.

Sacrifice: Metaphysics of the Sublimated Victim
KIMBERLEY PATTON

In a highly rationalistic contemporary idiom, the paradoxical ritual realm of animal sacrifice easily lends itself to caricature; rights-based approaches all too readily, without reflection, interpret animal sacrifice as a kind of cruel reification of the victim whose only role is as theologically (and anthropocentrically) exploited and ultimately ruined object. In fact, a more tex-

tured analysis of sacrificial forms reveals the animal victim, at least in the lens of the sacrificing tradition, as an elevated being whose uniqueness, active agency, and metaphysical status are guaranteed by the theurgic efficacy of the ritual itself.

Interlocking Oppressions: The Nature of Cruelty to Nonhuman Animals and Its Relationship to Violence Toward Humans
KIM ROBERTS

The idea that there is a connection between the way individuals treat animals and their treatment of fellow human beings has a long history in popular culture but a shorter history as the subject of scientific research. Recently a growing body of evidence has confirmed an association between repeated, intentional abuse of animals and a variety of antisocial behaviors including child abuse, domestic violence, and other violent criminal activities. As a result of the research and high-profile cases, animal abuse is beginning to gain recognition as an indicator of exposure to violence in the home, and a predictor of increased risk of future acts of violence.

This essay explores the interconnections between violence against animals and violence against people, using research findings and case examples and briefly discusses how we can address this connection through the development of coordinated community responses to violence.

Earth Charter Ethics and Animals
STEVEN ROCKEFELLER

The Earth Charter, the heart of which is an ethic of respect and care for Earth and all life, came out of the 1990s global ethics movement and is now receiving growing worldwide support. This essay explores how the Earth Charter views animals and how its ethic of respect and care is applied to them. The discussion of the various Earth Charter principles relevant to relations between people and animals provides brief accounts of some of the debates that influenced the wording of these principles.

Biotechnology and Animals: Ethical Issues in Genetic Engineering and Cloning
BERNARD ROLLIN

Since scientific ideology distances itself from ethics in declaring science "value-free," scientists typically do not articulate the issues emerging from new developments. The advent of genetic engineering has thus created a lacuna in social ethics that demands filling in. Following what I call "Gresham's Law for Ethics," bad ethical thinking tends to seize center stage. Prominent amongst such thinking are the claims that genetic engineering is intrinsically wrong, because it violates "God's will" or the "natural order." It is difficult to find ethical sense in such claims—they are either theological or else they devolve into consequentialist claims, and thus fail to claim intrinsic wrongness. The most difficult ethical issues emerging from biotechnology are in fact the least discussed—the fate of the animals developed by these modalities. Two such issues are the sacrifice of animal welfare for profit in commercial agriculture and the development of genetically engineered models of human disease.

Animal Experimentation
KENNETH SHAPIRO

How can we evaluate animal research? Momentarily bracketing the several ethical arguments, how effective is the strategy of developing animal models of human disorders? I present a critique of the concept and current practice of validation of animal model research. The critique is based on a published empirical study of animal models of selected psychological disorders. I argue that validation studies are rarely undertaken and, in any case, are less critical than assessment of the degree to which the research is productive of further understanding and/or advances in treatment. I suggest that such productive generativity is a broader and more relevant criterion than validation for assessing animal model research. In addition to some practical suggestions for animal care committee members and investigators, I conclude that the limited generativity found in the models evaluated strongly suggests the need to reexamine the strategy of animal model research itself. The primary theological implication of this project—"the devil is in the details"—is discussed.

Animal Protection and the Problem of Religion
PETER SINGER

I argue that the Judeo-Christian tradition is, to its core, biased against giving equal consideration to the interests of nonhuman animals. Attempts to reinterpret religion in a manner more favorable to animals may do some good, but the historical record suggests that, in the West, the status of animals has been advanced more by the decline in religious belief than by the reinterpretation of religious traditions.

Descartes, Christianity, and Contemporary Speciesism
GARY STEINER

It is well known that Descartes considered animals to be organic machines and that as such they may be used as resources in the general endeavor to render human beings "the masters and possessors of nature." What led Descartes to this conception of the moral status of animals? In order to get to the ethical roots of Descartes's views about animals, we must consider not only his conception of mechanism but also the extent to which his conception of moral rights and obligations regarding animals is influenced by ancient and medieval philosophy in the West.

Several key figures in that tradition of thought are Christian thinkers, and it turns out to be impossible to understand Descartes's views about animals without acknowledging the influence that these thinkers had on Descartes. Moreover, Descartes's desire to use animals as resources reflects a form of the "speciesism" that has dominated thinking about animals from Aristotle to the present. A reflection on the historical influences that shaped Descartes's views about animals promises to help us understand the historical genesis as well as the specific nature of contemporary speciesism.

"Of a tawny bull we make offering": Animals in Early Chinese Religion
ROEL STERCKX

This essay surveys the various roles of animals as subjects and objects in early Chinese sacrificial religion. We examine the question of zoolatry in early China, the role of animals as mediums, and the use of animal victims in sacrifice. The essay focuses on religion in practice—in other words, on the internal architecture of devotional worship, and is based on a close reading of the early Chinese ritual canon.

Of Animals and Man: The Confucian Perspective
RODNEY TAYLOR

The Confucian tradition, both in its classical phase as well as its later development in Neo-Confucianism, focuses upon the establishment of moral order within the individual and the world at large. While it has traditionally looked to a set of specific moral relations, a set of relations that excludes animals, to enact the moral transformation of individual and world, the broader agenda of Confucian learning and self-cultivation precludes no living thing. With a foundational moral injunction that no hu-

man being can bear to witness the suffering of another living thing, the tradition recognizes a unity of all life. Though priority historically has always been played upon the relation of one person to another, the tradition has also embraced the sense of Heaven, earth, and humans as a single entity. In this perspective, all people are one's brothers and sisters, and all living things are one's companions. The implications of this fundamental moral axiom for the Confucian should be apparent in how we interact with all living things.

A Communion of Subjects and a Multiplicity of Intelligences
MARY EVELYN TUCKER

Thomas Berry's theme of identity through communion with other, nonhuman subjectivities, draws upon a lifetime of work and insight. Weaving together multiple themes and, ultimately, drawing all of us, human and nonhuman alike, together into a differentiated, diverse, and sharing community, this view of the earth's living beings in concert helps us see our place in relation to our world characterized by interconnection, not separation. When we recognize that we live amidst a multiplicity of intelligences— hunting and foraging intelligences, courting and mating intelligences, flying and swimming intelligences, migrating and molting intelligences, communicating and playing intelligences—we begin to appreciate that life is displayed in particular and differentiated forms throughout the enormous array of species with whom we share our planet. It is this vision that must be activated in our consciousness and experience if the human venture is to continue. This will require a shift from an anthropocentric sense of domination to an anthropocosmic sense of communion with all life forms. The implications of this idea are richly refracted throughout this volume through the lenses of multiple disciplines.

Agribusiness: Farming Without Culture
GARY VALEN

Agriculture is an ancient relationship between humans and nature that provides sustenance and livelihood for all the generations we call civilization. The foundations of human organizations, from family units to empires, are based on the ability to produce food. Through most of history, interrelationships between animals and humans, along with soils and climate, have formed the cornerstones of agriculture.

The industrialization of food production and the emergence of agribusiness is ending the delicate balance between humans, animals, and nature in modern farming systems. Machines, technologies, and the use of animals as commodities now produce incredible profits for a few powerful conglomerates. One half of the United States' favorable balance of trade comes from the sale of agricultural products, technology, and services. If we measure success as financial, then farming and farm businesses as well as food processing and distribution are the most successful enterprises in history. Few small-scale and community-based farmers share in this economic success.

Agribusiness is flourishing now and with new technologies and factory-like systems promise to make Western nations even richer in the coming years as populations explode in places that are not blessed with fertile soils, favorable climates, masses of animals, and wealthy landowners. This is not agriculture! When viewed as a culture or special set of human relationships with Earth, agriculture weaves the elements of people, animals, plants, and land into a fabric of food production that will be passed intact to future generations. Agriculture does not abuse or destroy any of its crucial elements, for to do so would bring the end to all that agriculture holds up in human civilization.

As agribusiness gradually forces the elimination of agriculture as a special set of relationships, all people, and especially those who treasure ethics, must raise a cry of alarm that there is more to farming than profit. An agricultural production ethic must be embraced so that the culture and human relationships with Earth that produce food are once again restored to the land, the farmers and our partners, the animals.

Snake-kings, Boars' Heads, Deer Parks, Monkey Talk: Animals as Transmitters and Transformers in Indian and Tibetan Buddhist Narrative Literature
IVETTE VARGAS

Despite the complicated cross cultural transmission of Buddhism through diverse genres, Buddhists have always told a lot of stories, many containing animals. Buddhist studies constructed models of thinking about the rules of these stories in terms of portraying Buddhist doctrines. One way of thinking usually portrayed sophisticated Buddhists as employing stories to communicate Buddhist doctrine to the ordinary lay person who could not otherwise understand the teachings. The implication was that such stories could never be taken literally or as representative of real Buddhist thought. Aside from this model, an idea arose in another direction going back to the nineteenth century that interpreted narratives like the *Jātaka*s (birth stories of Buddha's previous lives) as mere childish folk tales wherein animals were anthropocentrically exploited. These views are now so embedded in the general scholarly consensus about what constitutes proper Buddhist thought and its suitable genre that it has become completely naturalized in the scholarly literature about Buddhism. However, such thinking is changing, and animals should take center stage in the enlightenment that stories are sophisticated didactic tools.

This essay draws attention to the continued presence of animal figures historically in Indian and Tibetan Buddhist literature. Animal figures and narrative literature are important partners in the spread of Buddhist doctrine cross-culturally, and it is the special quality that these figures and the genre of narrative hold that will help scholars better understand the transmission process of doctrine and practice. By studying a few select narrative genres, animals are examined for their role as active transmitters of Buddhist doctrine (transmitters of particular Buddhist philosophical movements and even moral values) and transformers in their roles as catalysts and participants of the paradoxically ontological process of transformation—one of the fundamental principles of Tibetan tantric practice. They also reflect the struggles between Buddhist and indigenous religious traditions and political identities. The works of Buddhist scholars and religious historians as well as literary theorists are consulted. Overall, this essay highlights the wide scope that animals have traditionally played in human religiousness.

Seeing the Terrain We Walk: Features of the Contemporary Landscape of "Religion and Animals"
PAUL WALDAU

There is an astonishing range of issues that come under the rubric "Religion and Animals." In this essay I survey such topics. I argue that it is important when addressing religious views of nonhuman animals to take the following considerations into account: (1) information about the realities of other animals, (2) interdisciplinary approaches to the diverse subject matter, (3) the shortcomings of scientific approaches; (4) the centrality of humans' ethical abilities; and (5) the interlocking nature of oppressions of marginalized humans and nonhuman animals. I argue further that the ability to see nonhuman animals is critically related to the social dimensions of human knowledge, and that consideration of these dimensions pushes one to engage problems of epistemology, sociology of knowl-

edge, traditional treatment of nonhuman animals, and pluralism.

Pushing Environmental Justice to a Natural Limit
PAUL WALDAU

"Environmental justice," like many prominent terms used in contemporary circles engaging problems of social justice and the expansion of ethical discourse beyond the human realm, is a term that has been used in a number of different, and sometimes contrary, ways. This essay identifies the range of uses, and then suggests terminology and concepts for these related but distinguishable concerns. The group of concerns as a whole is then related to the concerns at the center of the study of religion and nonhuman animals. Examples from within and without religious traditions are used to show that, across the history of ethical discussion, there not infrequently has been an identifiable conservativism that has limited many advocates of social and environmental justice to a surprisingly minimal expansion of the moral circle. Two points are drawn from this. First, some very prominent environmental justice advocates reflect this kind of conservativism, and thus fail to notice and take seriously issues that are illuminating for their own work. Second, at the same time, other proponents of environmental justice advocate a much broader, more holistic set of concerns also commonly called "environmental justice," but which in fact are qualitatively different from the concerns of the first set of "environmental justice" advocates. The essay concludes by reflecting on sociological studies pointing out the interlocking nature of oppressions affecting disempowered individuals, marginalized groups, and nonhuman species generally in the "developed" world.

Five-Sensed Animals in Jainism
KRISTI WILEY

This essay treats the place of five-sensed rational animals in the realm of all living beings (i.e.,
other animals and humans, excluding heavenly
beings and hell-beings). It focuses on the common experience of pleasure and pain of five-
sensed rational animals and humans, of animals
and humans as moral agents, and the basic instincts and desires that are shared by all living
beings. With this as a basis, Jain approaches to
themes of conversion, suffering, communion,
cosmology and eschatology are examined.

*Animal Law and Animal Sacrifice: Analysis of
the U.S. Supreme Court Ruling on Santería
Animal Sacrifice in Hialeah*
STEVEN WISE

This essay describes the oft-cited 1993 United
States Supreme Court case that addressed the
circumstances under which Santería practitioners could be prohibited from ritually sacrificing
nonhuman animals. This important case is often
erroneously said to hold that religious sacrifice
cannot be regulated by American law. What the
case actually means is merely that religiously
motivated killing of nonhuman animals cannot
be prohibited while comparable secular practices are permitted.

A Communion of Subjects

Heritage of the Volume

MARY EVELYN TUCKER

This unique volume on world religions and animals arose in the context of a three-year intensive conference series entitled "Religions of the World and Ecology," held at the Center for the Study of World Religions at Harvard Divinity School. The series critically examined attitudes toward nature in the world's religious traditions in addition to highlighting environmental projects around the world inspired by religious values. From 1996 to 1998 the series of ten conferences examined the traditions of Judaism, Christianity, Islam, Hinduism, Jainism, Buddhism, Daoism, Confucianism, Shinto, and indigenous religions. The conferences, organized by Mary Evelyn Tucker and John Grim, at that time of Bucknell University, in collaboration with a team of area specialists, brought together some eight hundred international scholars of the world's religions as well as environmental activists and leaders.

Recognizing that religions are key shapers of people's worldviews and formulators of their most cherished values, this broad research project has identified both ideas and practices supporting a sustainable environmental future. The papers from these conferences are published in a series of ten volumes from the Center for the Study of World Religions and Harvard University Press.

Three culminating conferences were also held at the American Academy of Arts and Sciences, at the United Nations, and at the American Museum of Natural History in New York in October 1998. These events brought representatives of the world's religions into conversation with one another as well as into dialogue with key scientists, economists, educators, and policymakers in the environmental field.[1]

This volume by Columbia University Press makes a distinctive contribution by extending the research project to include attitudes of world religions toward other species. The conference on World Religions and Animals was held at the Harvard-Yenching Institute in May 1999. It was the intention of this gathering to build on the earlier conferences involving both interreligious and multidisciplinary perspectives. *A Communion of Subjects* brings together a wide range of scholars to illustrate the varied ways in which religions have portrayed animals in myths, symbols, and rituals, as well as how such views were translated into actual practice. The original conference was highly unusual in that it was not limited to the study of religion, but also embraced multidisciplinary perspectives of religion, science, law, agriculture, social justice, and global stewardship. This volume reflects that unique breadth as the papers include those from the conferences as well as others that were specially solicited to broaden the conversation.

The intention is to suggest the movement outward of ethical concerns exclusively from the human sphere to encompass other species and the larger web of the natural world. Just as religions played an important role in creating sociopolitical changes in the twentieth century through moral challenges for the extension of human rights, so too now, in the twenty-first century, religions are contributing to the emergence of a broader environmental ethics based on diverse sensibilities regarding the sacred dimensions of the "more-than-human world."[2]

The understanding of nature, and particularly of animals as numinous realities to be reverenced, is widespread in world religions and is now being recovered. This ranges from the positions in the Western religions of Judaism, Christianity, and Islam that the earth and its species are part of divine Creation and therefore should be respected, to the views of indigenous traditions that nature and nonhuman animals are infused with a sacred presence, to the perspectives of particular Asian religions that earth and its life forms participate in ongoing creative transformations with which humans are in harmony. In many ways the recovery of these perspectives constitutes a reentry of the religions into a range of cosmological issues that has been relinquished almost entirely to the scientific disciplines.

A Communion of Subjects makes a distinctive contribution to these efforts. Its goals take on a special urgency as scientists acknowledge that we are now living amidst a sixth extinction period where an enormous, worldwide loss of species is being documented. They acknowledge as well that, unlike earlier ones, this extinction period is caused in large part by human interference with ecosystems. The implications of this massive loss of biodiversity are only beginning to be understood, at the same time as we are appreciating anew the unique kinds of intelligences that distinguish the more-than-human world. It is the subtle interactions of these intelligences that constitute what Thomas Berry has called "a communion of subjects."

Berry's keynote address at the Harvard conference on world religions and animals highlighted this theme of experiencing the world as "a communion of subjects, not a collection of objects." Berry has devoted a lifetime of thinking, writing, and teaching to articulating this perspective. As a cultural historian who began his work reflecting on Giambattista Vico's philosophy of history, he has been particularly concerned with situating our historical moment in the context of history of the earth and evolution of the universe. He is deeply committed to opening the human community to our role as participants in the larger earth community.[3]

A central aspect of Berry's project is evoking the numinous dimensions of the natural world. In doing this he calls humans to awaken to the unnumbered species with whom we share this planet. The multiple intelligences and rich emotional life of each species contributes to the larger whole and creates the grounds for communion, resonance, and relationship. Thus clearly for Berry, the more-than-human world is not simply an inert, dead world of objects to be exploited by humans, but is a vital, alive, numinous communion of subjects with which we co-inhabit the earth.

Berry's lifelong study of the world's history and religions and his particular attention to Asian cultures and indigenous traditions have given him a unique perspective from which to critique our current situation. He is particularly eager for humans to resituate themselves in communion with other species, no longer as despoilers, dominators, or manipulators. The objectification of the natural world and its many life forms has allowed for untold degradation of ecosystems and the destruction of species and their habitats. Berry is proposing a new story of the unfolding display of the evolution of the universe that awakens an understanding of our profound connection to every life form. He suggests that this comprehensive story of evolution will provide the context for healing our alienation from the natural world, from other species and from one another.[4]

As we recover again and discover anew our kinship with life, from atoms to galaxies, there will blossom forth a reinvigorated reverence for life. It is this deep feeling for life that lies at the heart of Berry's phrase, "a communion of subjects." It is this affective, feeling dimension that will help to carry us through our most difficult challenges ahead. As Berry notes, we can place our confidence in the powers that have shaped the universe through its 14 billion-year journey to sustain the human in this transformative moment:

> If the dynamics of the universe from the beginning shaped the course of the heavens, lighted the sun, and formed the earth, if this same dynamism brought forth the continents and seas and atmosphere, if it awakened life in the primordial cell and then brought into being the unnumbered variety of living beings, and finally brought us into being and guided us safely through the turbulent centuries, there is reason to believe that this same guiding process is precisely what has awakened in us our present understanding of ourselves and our relation to this stupendous process. Sensitized to such guidance from the very structure and functioning of the universe, we can have confidence in the future that awaits the human venture.[5]

NOTES

1. A major result of these conferences was the establishment of an ongoing Forum on Religion and Ecology that was announced at the United Nations press conference to continue the research, education, and outreach begun at the earlier conferences. A primary goal of the Forum is to develop a field of study in religion and ecology that has implications for public policy. Toward this end the Forum has continued to sponsor various conferences at Harvard and on the West Coast as well as workshops for high school teachers. www.environment.harvard.edu/religion

2. This term is used by David Abram in his book *The Spell of the Sensuous: Perception and Language in a More-Than-Human World* (New York: Vintage Books, 1997).

3. Berry develops these ideas further in his latest book, *Evening Thoughts: Reflecting on the Earth as Sacred Community* (Berkeley: Sierra Club Books and University of California Press, 2006).

4. He develops this perspective most fully in his book with Brian Swimme, *The Universe Story* (San Francisco: Harper San Francisco, 1992).

5. Thomas Berry, *The Dream of the Earth* (San Francisco: Sierra Club Books, 1988), p. 137.

Prologue

Loneliness and Presence

THOMAS BERRY

At the time of his treaty with the European settlers in 1854, Chief Seattle of the Suquamish tribe along the North Pacific coast is reported to have said that when the last animals will have perished "humans would die of loneliness."[1] This was an insight that might never have occurred to a European settler. Yet this need for more-than-human companionship has a significance and an urgency that we begin to appreciate in more recent times. To understand this primordial need that humans have for the natural world and its animal inhabitants we need only reflect on the needs of our children, the two-, three-, and four-year-olds especially. We can hardly communicate with them in any meaningful way except through pictures and stories of humans and animals and fields and trees, of flowers, birds and butterflies, of sea and sky. These present to the child a world of wonder and beauty and intimacy, a world sufficiently enticing to enable the child to overcome the sorrows that they necessarily experience from their earliest years. This is the world in which we all grow up, in, to some extent in reality, to some extent through pictures and stories.

The child experiences the "friendship relation" that exists among all things throughout the universe, the universe spoken of by Thomas Aquinas in his commentary on the writings of Pseudo-Dionysius the Areopagite, the mystical Christian neoplatonist of the fifth or sixth century. Indeed we cannot be truly ourselves in any adequate manner without all our companion beings throughout the earth. This larger community constitutes our greater self. Even beyond the earth we have an intimate presence to the universe in its comprehensive reality. The scientists' quest for their greater selves is what evokes their relentless drive toward an ever greater understanding of the world around them.

Our intimacy with the universe demands an intimate presence to the smallest particles as well as to the vast range of the stars splashed across the skies in every direction. More immediately present to our consciousness here on Earth are the landscapes; the sky above, the earth below; the grasses, the flowers, the forests and fauna that present themselves to our opening senses. Each in its own distinctive perfection fills our mind, our imagination, our emotional attraction.

Of these diverse modes of being, the animals in the full range of their diversity belong within our conscious human world in a special manner. A few years ago Joanne Lausch wrote a book concerned with the smaller animals, the insects. The title, *The Voice of the Infinite in the Small*, indicates that even those living forms to which we are least attracted still have their own special role in the grand design of the universe. They speak to us and must not be slighted or treated with contempt. If we assault them with chemical sprays they will mutate and defeat us time after time.

As humans we come into being as an integral part of this million-fold diversity of life expression. Earlier peoples celebrated the whole of the universe in its integrity and in its every mode of expression. From the moment of awakening consciousness, the universe strikes wonder and fulfillment throughout our human mode of being. Humans and the universe were made for each other. Our experience of the universe finds festive expression in the great moments of seasonal transformation such as the dark of winter, the exuberance of springtime, the warmth and brightness of summer, the lush abundance of autumn. These are the ever-renewing moments of celebration of the universe, moments when the universe is in some depth of communion with itself in the intimacy of all its components.

Even with this comprehensive presence of the universe to itself and to its varied components, there is a challenging, even a threatening aspect experienced in every component. Each individual life form has its own historical appearance, a moment when it must assert its identity, fulfill its role, and then give way to other individuals in the processes of the phenomenal world. In our Western tradition, this passing of our own being is experienced as something to be avoided absolutely. Because we are so sensitive to any personal affliction, because we avoid any threats to our personal existence, we dedicate ourselves to individual survival above all else. In the process of extending the limits of our own lives, we imperil the entire community of life systems on the planet. This leads eventually to failure in fulfilling our own proper role within the larger purposes of the universe.

Rather than become integral with this larger celebration-sacrificial aspect of the universe, we have elected to assert our human well-being and survival as the supreme values. For us, here in the Western world, the human becomes the basic norm of reference for good and evil in the universe. All other modes of being become trivial in comparison. Their reality and their value are found in their *use* relationship to our own well-being. In this context we lose the intimacy that originally we had with the larger community of life. We are ourselves only to the extent of our unity with the universe to which we belong and in which alone we discover our fulfillment. Intimacy exists only in terms of wonder, admiration, and emotional sympathy when beings give themselves to each other in a single psychic embrace, an embrace in which each mode of being experiences its fulfillment.

Such observations as these are needed because our reduction of the entire universe to subservience to the human has led to our present situation. As Norman Myers observes, in terms of species extinction we are in the process of creating the greatest impasse to the development of life on earth since the beginning of life almost four billion years ago.[2] Niles Eldredge suggests we are in the midst of the sixth great extinction period due to loss of species.[3]

Here we might observe an awakening to our present situation and the structuring of a new guiding vision for our Western civilization through an event that occurred in the early decades of this century. While hunting in Arizona, the forester Aldo Leopold shot a female wolf with a pup. He tells us that he reached the wolf in time to watch "a fierce green fire dying in her eyes." "I realized then, and have known ever since that there was something new to me in those eyes—something known only to her and to the mountain."[4] From then on his perspective on human relations with the natural world was utterly changed.

Our own lives too were changed, for that event and the reflections born of it have provided a new ethic—one never known previously in any formal way to the European-American people, an ethic that Aldo Leopold designated as "a land ethic."[5] His basic statement is simply that "A land ethic changes the role of *Homo sapiens* from conqueror of the land-community to plain member and citizen of it. It implies respect for his fellow-members, and also respect for the community as such."[6] This simple prosaic statement carries implications that challenge the entire range of Western civilization. It challenges all the governmental, educational, economic and religious institutions of our society as regards the ethical basis of what they are doing.

Another fascinating moment in human-animal intimacy is when, after a night's sleep on a beach, Loren Eiseley awakened in the presence of a young fox who had wandered from its den. He tells us: Here was "a wide-eyed innocent fox inviting me to play, with the innate courtesy of its two forepaws placed appealingly together, along with a mock shake of the head. Gravely I arranged my forepaws while the puppy whimpered with ill-concealed excitement. I drew the breath of the fox's den into my nostrils. ... Round and round we tumbled for one ecstatic moment."[7]

This sense of intimacy with the land has found comprehensive expression in the life of Henry David Thoreau when he became attracted to a field of special beauty in the region where he often walked. He even put down a deposit in anticipation of buying the field. Later Thoreau decided not to buy the land, realizing that he already possessed the region in its beauty and its spiritual integrity and did not really need to gain physical possession. Whoever owned it

physically could not keep him from intimacy with this region in its wonder and its beauty.

In such discussion as this we might go to the world of literature, where the deeper interpretation of our human experiences is generally found. In the *Rime of the Ancient Mariner* by Samuel Taylor Coleridge we read of the mariner who got himself, the ship, and the entire crew into an agonizing experience by his revulsion at the sight of the slimy creatures of the sea. He received a healing from his deep sorrow of soul only when he learned to bless the sea-serpents and all living beings: "A spring of love gushed from my heart, / And I blessed them unaware." The curse of the doldrums of the sea was lifted, the wind arose, the sailors came back to life: joy was theirs once again.

There are also the numerous passages in Fyodor Dostoevsky's *The Brothers Karamazov*. "Love the animals. God has given them the rudiments of thought and joy untroubled. Do not trouble them. Do not harm them, don't deprive them of their happiness, don't work against God's intent." Often Dostoevsky speaks of the innocence of the animals in contrast to the loss of innocence in humans. We need to be inspired by the birds especially: "My brother asked the birds to forgive him; that sounds senseless but it is right; for all is like an ocean, all is flowing and blending, touch in one place sets up movement at the other end of the earth. It may be senseless to beg forgiveness of the birds, but birds would be happier at your side—a little happier anyway —and children and all animals, if you yourself were nobler than you are now."

Even with all our technological accomplishments and urban sophistication we consider ourselves blessed, healed in some manner, forgiven and for a moment transported into some other world, when we catch a passing glimpse of an animal in the wild: a deer in some woodland, a fox crossing a field, a butterfly in its dancing flight southward to its wintering region, a hawk soaring in the distant sky, a hummingbird come into our garden, fireflies signaling to each other in the evening. So we might describe the thousand-fold moments when we experience our meetings with the animals in their unrestrained and undomesticated status.

Such incidents as these remind us that "The universe is composed of subjects to be communed with, not of objects to be exploited."[8] For with all the other benefits that we receive from the world about us, none can replace these deeper moments that we experience somewhere within the depths of our being. These are the moments when we are truly ourselves, when we attain a rare self-realization in the truly human mode of our being.

To me it seems that the universe as a whole and in each of its individual components has an intangible inner form as well as a tangible physical structure. It is this deep form expressed in its physical manifestation that so entrances us in these moments. When Aldo Leopold looked into those "fierce green eyes" of the dying wolf, he saw something more than the physical light reflected there. The wolf and the human came to an intimacy with each other beyond description. That is the fascination, the mystery, the immeasurable depths of the universe into which we are plunged with each of our experiences of the world about us. Such are the experiences spoken of by Aldo Leopold, Loren Eiseley, Henry David Thoreau, Samuel Taylor Coleridge, Fyodor Dostoevsky and more recently by Rachel Carson, Annie Dillard, and Terry Tempest Williams. What they experienced was something so significant in the course of human life that it would be difficult to imagine that human life would be truly satisfying in any other context.

Although this intimacy exists with the stars in the heavens and with the flowering forms of earth, this presence of humans with the other members of the animal world has a mutual responsiveness unknown to these other modes of being throughout the universe. Our relation with the animals finds its expression especially in the amazing variety of benefits they provide for us in their guidance, protection, and companionship. Beyond these modes of assistance, they provide a world of wonder and meaning for the mind—beauty for the imagination. Even beyond all these they provide an emotional intimacy so unique that it can come to us from no other source. The animals can do for us, in both the physical and the spiritual orders, what we cannot do for ourselves or for each other. These more precious gifts they provide through their presence and their responsiveness to our inner needs.

The difficulty in our relation with the animals comes from the sense of *use* as our primary relationship with the world about us. Hardly any other attitude so betrays ourselves and the entire universe in which we live. Every being exists in intimate relation with other beings and in a constant exchange of gifts to each other. But this relationship is something beyond pragmatic *use*. It is rather a mutual sharing of existence in the grand venture of the universe itself. By indigenous peoples, the universe is perceived as a single gorgeous celebration, a cosmic liturgy that humans enter through their ritual dances at those moments of daily and seasonal change, at dawn and sunset, at the equinox and solstice moments.

At such moments the human venture achieves its validation in the universe and the universe receives its validation in the human. The grand expression of wonder, beauty, and intimacy is achieved. As Henri Frankfurt, an archeologist of the Near East observed, the various modes of being of the universe were addressed as "thou" rather than "it." "Natural phenomena were regularly conceived in terms of human experience and human experience was conceived in terms of cosmic events."[9] As humans we awaken to this wonder that stands there before us. We must discover our role in this grand spectacle.

Recovery of Western civilization from its present addiction to *use,* as our primary relation to each other and to the world about us, must begin with the discovery of the world within, the world of the *psyche* as designated by the Greeks, a word translated by the term *anima* in the Latin world, or by the term *soul* in the English world.

The term *anima* is the word used to identify a living or animated or *ensouled* being from the earliest period in European thought. While the word *soul* has been abandoned by scientists lest it compromise the empirical foundations of their study, the reality of the thought expressed remains forever embedded in the very language that we use. The term *animal* will forever indicate an ensouled being. This interior world of the psyche, the anima, the soul, the spirit, or the mind provides the basis for that interior presence that we experience with each other throughout the world of the living. Simply in their physical dimensions things cannot occupy the same space while remaining their individual selves. This mutual indwelling in the same psychic space is a distinctive capacity of the transmaterial dimension of any living being. Not only can two psychic forms be present to each other in the same psychic space, but an unlimited number of forms can be present. Indeed the entire universe can be present, for as Thomas Aquinas tells us: "The mind in a certain manner is all things." Even so, this inner presence, while distinct from, is not separate from the outer experience. This capacity for indwelling each other, while remaining distinct from each other, is a capacity of soul or mind or the realm of the psyche. In this integration of both the inner and outer realms we discover our fulfillment.

To reduce any mode of being simply to that of a commodity as its primary status or relation within the community of existence is a betrayal. While the nonliving world does not have a living soul as a principle of life, each member of the nonliving world does have the equivalent as its inner principle of its being. This is an *inner form* that communicates a power, an enduring quality, and a majesty that even the living world cannot convey. In a more intimate way, the nonliving world provides the mysterious substance that transforms into life. Throughout this entire process a communion takes place that belongs to the realm of spirit. There is a spirit of the mountain, a spirit surely of the rivers and of the great blue sea. This spirit mode has been recognized by indigenous peoples everywhere, also in the classical civilizations of the past where such spirits were recognized as modes of personal presence.

Both to know and to be known are activities of the inner form, not of the outer structure of things. This inner form is a distinct *dimension of*, not a *separate reality from*, the visible world about us. To trivialize this inner form, to reduce it to a dualism, or to consider it a crude form of animism is as unacceptable as it would be to attribute the experience of sight to a refinement of the physical impression carried by the light that strikes the eye, or to reduce the communication made by a Mozart symphony to vibrations of the instruments on which it is played.

One of the most regrettable aspects of Western civilization is the manner in which this capacity for inner presence to other modes of being has diminished in these past few centuries. It would seem that the capacity for interior communion with the other-than-human modes of being has severely diminished in Western civilization. While the full expression of this diminished capacity has come in recent centuries, it is grounded in the deeper tendencies in our cultural traditions to emphasize the spiritual aspect of the human over against the so-called nonspiritual aspect of the other modes of being.

NOTES

1. [Editors' note: This story is likely apocryphal. Regarding the fact that the standard quote by "Chief Seattle" is not composed of the actual words of the historical individual Seeathl (1786–1866), a chief of the Squamish and Duwamish tribes of the northwest United States, see the explanation advanced first by Rudolph Kaiser in 1984, which is published in his essay, "Chief Seattle's

Speech(es): American Origin and European Reception," in Brian Swann and Arnold Krupat, eds., *Recovering the Word: Essays in Native American Literature* (Berkeley: University of California Press, 1987). The issue is also explained in David Suzuki and Peter Knudtson, *Wisdom of the Elders: Honoring Sacred Native Visions of Nature,* New York: Bantam, 1992, pp. xx–xxiii. Nevertheless the sentiment is surely emblematic of the Native American view —and hence of Thomas Berry's view—of an intensive web of relationship between human beings and animals, whose rupture would be fatal to both.]

2. Norman Myers, cited in E.O. Wilson, *Biodiversity* (Cambridge: Science Center, Harvard University, 1989), p. 34.

3. Niles Eldredge, *Life in the Balance: Humanity and the Biodiversity Crisis* (Princeton: Princeton University Press, 1998), p. x.

4. Aldo Leopold, *A Sand County Almanac: And Sketches Here and There* (New York: Oxford University Press, 1949, 1968), p. 138.

5. Leopold, *Almanac,* pp. 237–264.

6. Ibid, p. 240.

7. Loren Eisley, *The Unexpected Universe* (New York: Harcourt Brace Jovanovich, 1969), p. 210.

8. [Editors' note: Berry has expressed this theme in various ways. See, for example, the epigraph that prefaces this book.]

9. Henri Frankfurt, et al., *Before Philosophy: The Intellectual Adventure of Ancient Man: An Essay on Speculative Thought in the Ancient Near East* (Chicago: University of Chicago Press, 1946; Baltimore: Penguin Books, 1974).

Introduction

PAUL WALDAU AND KIMBERLEY PATTON

Who are the animals and what do they mean to us? The radical intimacy between human beings and the multiple animal worlds that surround and penetrate our own, an intimacy suggested by Thomas Berry, is both catalyst and center of meaning for this wide-ranging volume. Berry's challenge to see the world as a "communion of subjects" rather than as a "collection of objects" moves the ground for our relationship to animals away from use, away from commodification, and even away from sentimentality. If animals are, in their own right, the *subjects* of experience, beings with consciousness, emotional and moral range, ontological status, theological value, or pain comparable to our own, rather than the *objects* of human perception or usage, then we must approach the topic of animals with new lenses and new questions.

Thomas Berry is a cultural historian, or, as he is sometimes called, a "geologian"—a theologian of the earth. In our "Enlightenment-vectored" Western intellectual world, as Huston

Smith has called it, the religious dimensions of any question are often treated at best as a colorful sidebar, and at worst as features that are distorted, oppressive, polemical, romantic, or anti-rational, whose effect is to undermine the progressive evaluation of the fruits of scientific and sociological research. Rather than seeing religion as a problematic addendum to public thought about the status of animals, however, this volume uniquely takes the study of "Religion and Animals" as its principal focus. It then invites additional reflection upon its central themes from scientists, ethicists, and thinkers from related fields such as law and philosophy.

The volume's conceptual center in the theme of animals in religion is due in part to its heritage as part of the series of conferences sponsored by the Forum on Religion and Ecology, which has resulted in an important series of publications, *Religions of the World and Ecology*.[1] The conference held at Harvard University in May 1999 (described by Mary Evelyn Tucker in her essay,

"Heritage of the Volume") was the initial stage for an inspiring although sometimes strenuously difficult interchange between religionists, ethicists, and scientists around the topic of religion and animals. Our intellectual commitments are complex. This is not a book about animal rights. Nor is it a book about environmentalism. It is not a book about ritual, or about Darwinian controversies. All of these topics emerge, but they are part of a scope of enquiry ranging from the role of the horse in ancient Indian religious imagination to the social construction in science of the laboratory rat. *This is a book about the religious implications of animal subjectivities.* We use the plural form because of the diversity with which subjectivity exists in the animal realms, and the ways in which the subjectivity of each species and each individual within that species differs from that of others, and from that of human beings. What if the world is indeed "a communion of subjects"? What would that mean, and what would it require of us?

Religious traditions have, in fact, had impact in countless ways on how *each* human being now engages the worlds about us and amidst which we live. And animals, both human and nonhuman, are rich worlds unto themselves. The realm of "Religion and Animals," whether as a personal inquiry or as an academic field, seeks the intersection of these worlds. Such attempts to engage the surrounding world are both ancient and new, reflecting humans' constant urge to situate ourselves, our families, and our human, animal, and ecological communities. "Religion and Animals," then, arises directly from deep, daily concerns about who we are, who our companions are, the places in which we live, and the choices we make about the "others," human and nonhuman, in our lives.

This volume collects multiple voices speaking about this extraordinary intersection. Our authors express their concerns in many languages, various traditions of description, and vocabularies unfamiliar to many in their respective attempts to describe one facet or another of this complex tale. To some, the multiplicity will seem Babel-like, because the authors in this collection speak in so many different ways about our relationship with the rest of the world's living beings. The sheer variety, at times dissonant and at other times contrapuntal, makes obvious the essential point that this story, when well told, is the richest of songs. It is, at once, awe-inspiring, awful, astonishing, sad, elevating, and humbling. In the music is the heroic and demonic, the ethical and arrogant. Whether one hears chorus or cacophony, it will be clear to all that much still needs to be said about this extraordinary intersection of worlds. In the spirit of the Zen Buddhist counsel that the traveler who has one hundred miles to travel would do well to count ninety miles as the halfway point, we should speak humbly about the many steps we have yet to take in our attempt to describe either the ordinary or the fabulous in the matter before us.

As a collective whole our human communities, and in particular those subcommunities concerned with education and morality, are only now beginning to reveal and to consciously attend to the intersection of religion and animals. The human side of the song is often very familiar, the nonhuman side too often unfamiliar. That we have tried for so long to express this relationship bespeaks its fundamental relevance to us. That we remain at a rudimentary stage of the process, most particularly in our contemporary academic and political worlds, says much about the need for humility as we give voice to the ways in which the vast universe of religion and the equally vast world of nonhuman animals play into, and with, one another. The history of "Religion and Animals" is an engaging one. It will, no doubt, be told again and again, and this despite millennia of efforts to narrate and analyze the obvious concerns that religions have regarding views about and actions toward other living beings.

Despite the radical commitment of *A Communion of Subjects* to a multidisciplinary range of offerings, all of our authors respond to the challenge raised by Thomas Berry in his opening address to our conference: "The world is a communion of subjects, not a collection of objects." Berry's words unexpectedly electrified his scholarly audience, already alive with the tension of coming together as historians of religion, theologians, research scientists, veterinarians, ethicists, and social analysts—a very unorthodox juxtaposition in the academy. Even though they were hearing his words for the first time, speakers continued to return to "a communion of subjects" in their talks during the days that followed—in meditation, inspiration, or counter-challenge.

In revising these essays our authors were asked to reflect in a more formal and systematic way the power of Berry's naturally organizing idea. Throughout the book, we see how as living beings, animals have often been "objectified" in some forms of religion, science, ethics —how they have been construed as things of aesthetic "value" or, conversely, expendable and abusable. We also see how in realms as diverse as mythology, the legal sphere, and cognitive zoology, animals emerge not as passive objects but as actors or "subjects" in their own right—that is, as autonomous entities with consciousness, agency, or rights, as well as moral, emotional, or even devotional capabilities. We asked the authors to reflect upon the word "communion," with its overtones of profound interrelationship and participation between animals, between human beings, and between these multiple worlds. We asked them all to reflect from the standpoint of their separate disciplines on the issue of the "constructed" (or "projected") nature of animals versus their lived and living realities. Finally, we asked them to bear in mind the multiplicity of views of animals *within* particular religious traditions, ethical trajectories, social histories, or research methods. In other words, our authors confront the fact that variability in ideas about animals comes not just from different lenses, in that those lenses are not homogeneous, that is, "of a piece."

Complexities, Tensions, and Perspectival Challenges

Any account of religious traditions' engagement with other animals will swell into a multitude of complex issues. Some of the complexities stem from the well-known fact that over the millennia of their existence, religious traditions have provided an array of views and materials on virtually any general subject that believers, scholars and other interested parties might explore. This variety is made all the more challenging because even within any one religious tradition, such views and materials can be in significant tension.

A very different set of complexities arises from the fact that the living beings outside our own species can be startlingly different from one another. Many are mentally, socially, and individually very simple, but others are so mentally and socially enigmatic that we may not have the ability to understand their lived experience well, if at all. Ignorance of these differences has often led, both within and without religion, to crass oversimplifications. Indeed, many of our most familiar ways of talking about the nonhuman living beings upon the earth turn out to be, upon careful examination, coarse caricatures and profoundly inaccurate descriptions: "projections" that may go well beyond anthropomorphizing. Indeed, a number of our scientific authors demonstrate that the resistance of research methodologies to so-called "anthropomorphizing" really has at its heart a passionate ideological commitment to the difference between species, between humans and other kinds of animals. Once that blinding commitment is laid aside, as animal researchers like Jane Goodall and Donald Griffin have done in their decades of work with chimpanzees, bats, and other animals, deep affinities as well as important differences between human beings and animals emerge. As the relatively recent field of animal personality research reveals, not only creatures "higher" on the evolutionary scale but also those "lower" (e.g., invertebrates such as octopi, stickleback fish, or *drosophilia* [fruit flies]) manifest ranges of temperament. These various personalities can not only be individually differentiated within a given population but also, mirroring human types, tend to remain consistent in each individual's characteristic response to various types of stimuli. The picture is then far more nuanced. The animals, our nonhuman companions on the earth, challenge us to try to imagine their world, and to see how we have affected it, even as they continue to affect us so profoundly.

Whatever else may be said of religions in the matter of nonhuman animals, these ancient and enduring cultural, social, and transcendental systems have unquestionably driven countless human actions. In fact, religion has often been the primary source for answers to questions such as, "Which living beings really should matter to me and my community?" The answers to such questions given by, for example, the early Jains and Buddhists and the early Christians have had, in their respective milieux and beyond, great influence on how the living beings outside the human species have been understood and treated.

Symbolic Thought and Inherited Conceptions

Readers of this volume will not have turned many pages before noticing that some religious believers' perspectives on nonhuman animals have been dominated by something other than a careful engagement with the animals themselves. For example, inherited preconceptions, which often have taken the form of either idealized or dismissive generalizations found in documents held to be revealed, operate in some cases as definitive assessments of *all* nonhuman animals' nature, abilities, and moral significance. Heritages of this kind can present severe problems for historians, theologians, and believers who wish to engage readily available, empirically based evidence that contradicts, in letter or spirit, inherited views that are inaccurate or in some other way misleading.

Images of nonhuman living beings, which abound in religious art, writing, and oral traditions, have been important in myriad ways for religious believers. Animals are not marginalia in the great illuminated manuscripts of religion; they lurk not only in the woods beyond the fire, but at its very burning heart as well. As so many essays in this volume suggest, one cannot explore religious traditions adequately, nor really understand them well, without coming to terms with the diverse roles played out in their ideas about animals. Yet while some of these ideas are connected in one way or another to the animals portrayed, many are only remotely related, if at all, to the animals pictured, named, or allegorically deployed. Some studies of "Religion and Animals" are confined solely to the study of religious images of other animals, in no way raising the issue of the actual biological beings themselves. This volume is different, continually interesting itself in, for example, the relationship between Raven and raven, the mercurial trickster and the great black, canny predator who still haunts the trees of the land where his mythological forms evolved.

Ethics and Institutions: Treatment of "The Others"

Religious traditions characteristically foreground ethical concerns for "others." These others can, of course, include both humans and nonhumans. Some religious traditions insist that the universe of morally considerable beings includes all living beings. Other religious traditions have had a pronounced human-centered bias because they assert that only humans truly matter. Ironically problematizing this assertion, Paul Shepard entitled his controversial book, *The Others: How Animals Made Us Human.*[2] Note, however, that even if proponents of these competing claims differ radically as to the extent to which human caring abilities should reach outside the human species, they share the conviction that humans are characterized by extraordinary ethical abilities to care for "others."

A central question in the study of religion and animals is, "Who are the others?"

Although in many circles there is a tendency to equate religious views with factual propositions about the world, most religious traditions include the insight that actions speak louder about what one really believes than do spoken or written words. Accordingly, what religious traditions truly "think" about other animals is, at least in part, represented by believers' treatment "on the ground," as it were, of other living beings. A religion that features, say, bull worship in its temples while in no way addressing the brutal treatment of cattle in the daily world outside the temple, will, quite naturally, seem to some to have a less positive attitude toward cattle than does a religion that unequivocally prohibits harsh treatment or even killing of bulls and cows even though such animals do not appear in any places of worship or traditions of iconography.

In the official pronouncements of some organized religions, themes may be sounded that are much more one-dimensional than the nuanced behavior of believers in their everyday interactions with nonhuman living beings. Thus, even if at times anthropocentric biases dominate a modern religious institution's discourse and conceptual generalities about nonhuman animals, the tradition in question may well honor additional insights regarding which "others" are appropriate subjects for humans' considerable ethical abilities. The study of religion and animals naturally accommodates analyses of institutional ideologies, but such views can most clearly be seen enacted in the far vaster realm of individual believers' actions and perspectives toward the many lives, the multiple intelligences and subjectivities, the "parallel nations" that surround them.

It is widely recognized in contemporary social sciences that oppression of humans and oppression of other animals are often linked. The oppression of one kind of living being seems to lead to the oppression of other kinds of living beings. For this reason, the study of religion and animals can be closely tied to the powerful concern with social justice found in most (although admittedly not all) religious traditions, even when those traditions seem to be exclusively human-centered.

As vessels of meaning and educators in matters cultural, intellectual, ethical, social, and ecological, religious traditions mediate views of the world around us across time and place. It is natural then that, since nonhuman animals are truly around and with us in our ecological communities, religious traditions have had a major role in passing along basic ideas about these beings' place in, or exclusion from, our communities of concern. Understanding this feature of religion, particularly as it is a highly contextualized piece in the large puzzle of any religious tradition, is an essential task in the study of religion and animals.

The Scope and Content of this Volume

In the essays that follow, the profundity of Thomas Berry's notions of "loneliness and presence" are sounded in extraordinarily diverse ways regarding our relations to, communities with, and alienations from the rich menagerie we commonly call "animals."

Part I, "Animals in Religion, Science and Ethics: In and Out of Time," comprises two essays by the editors that we hope will offer a broad overview of what is at stake in our volume. In "Caught with Ourselves in the Net of Life and Time," Kimberley Patton writes on the mythic, ritual, and epistemological dimensions of traditional "animal worlds" historically determined by—and determinative of—lived human experience. These are the ways in which animals have added religious depth to human lives, and have been understood religiously. The animal, no longer numinous, power-bearing, swarming, or part of the intimate *habitus* of the farming or hunting family, has been assigned to sharply divided categories: beloved family pet, abandoned victim, zoo exhibit, urban pest, domesticated food unit, object of the bourgeois hunt, endangered denizen of a fragile, shrinking wilderness, and so on. Patton argues that the power of that "charged" relationship remains, despite its utilitarian suppression or rational sublimation. In a counter-challenge to the positive value of religious systems vis-à-vis animals, Paul Waldau attempts to survey "the terrain we walk"—to critically appraise in the twenty-first century the role of the worlds' religions in the landscape of human-animal relations, the ways in which animals have been treated as "others," and to ask what questions can best illumine the ethical challenges inherent in this history of religions.

Parts II–V offer focused scholarly studies of animals in many of the great religious traditions of the world. The place of various creatures in the diverse and influential Abrahamic traditions, tensions in the ancient and ethically inclusive South Asian traditions, and aspects of the complex Chinese traditions are treated. East then meets West in several broad discussions of nonhuman animals in various philosophical traditions and cultural trajectories. The place of myth in the recurring intersection of religious belief and our engagement with other animals is broached, followed by reflections on the place of the earth's other living beings in a diverse set of rituals, social thought, and arts traditions.

"Animals in Abrahamic Traditions" begins with Judaism and its ancient tradition of the ritualized slaughter of animals, traced from the Genesis account of the Lord's preference for Abel's animal offering to Cain's first fruits, up through the elaborate sacrificial cultus of the Jerusalem Temple. Jonathan Klawans considers the unexpectedly intimate, theologically allegorized relationship between the pastoralist ancient Israelites and the animals they offered for sacrifice: "By lording over their herds and flocks —and by selecting which animals will be given to the altar—ancient Israelites were reflecting on their own relationship to their God, whom they imagined as their shepherd." Rabbi Dan Cohn-Sherbok offers a different but complementary perspective in his panoramic view of Biblical and Rabbinic sources on the treatment

of animals, as well as later medieval philosophical, mystical, and commentarial traditions, all of which he argues promote compassion for animals as expressed in the ancient principle *of tsa'ar balei chayim* (forbearance of harm to living things, "kindness to animals"). Roberta Kalechofsky elaborates on the themes developed by Cohn-Sherbok by examining the principles behind Jewish legal norms up to the present, including the demythologization of animals in Israel and the age-old strand of human protective responsibility for animals as developed in *halachah;* her essay takes the reader up to the teachings of Rav Kuk and the modern Jewish vegetarian movement.

Christian attitudes to animals are thoroughly treated in the next section as Beverly Kienzle's essay, "The Bestiary of Heretics," lays out the symbolization of particular animals (moth, wolf, and cat, among others) as representations of witchcraft and heretical movements in medieval Christian Europe, as well as the dire consequences of such thought for the treatment of the actual animals whose lore was thus moralized. Gary Steiner demonstrates the Aristotelian and Christian intellectual heritage of Descartes' famous view of animals as organic machines. By way of constructive theology, Jay McDaniel draws from the history of monastic contemplative thought to offer resources within mainstream Christianity for a "Franciscan" alternative to the "instrumentalist" attitude to animals he sees as prevalent in the contemporary tradition, drawing heavily from the views of Aquinas and Descartes manifest in the previous article.

Richard Foltz opens the section on Islam with a comprehensive survey of a wide range—Qur'ānic, hadīthic, and mystical teachings on animals, as well as the contemporary tensions involved with the expression of such teachings in Muslim culture. God's providence for all living things and its corollary of human stewardship, based on the Qur'ān, echoes Jewish themes explored in **Part I**: "Everything in Creation is a miraculous sign (*aya*), inviting Muslims to contemplate their Creator ... 'This she-camel of

God is a sign of God to you; so leave her to graze in God's earth, and let her come to no harm, or you shall be seized with a grievous punishment.'" (S 7:73). The provocative tenth-century *The Case of the Animals versus Man,* written by a group known as the *Ikhwān al-Ṣafā'* ("the Brethren of Purity"), shows the animals complaining to the King of the Jinn about their enslavement and maltreatment by human beings; this fascinating text is exegeted by Zayn Kassam in light of Berry's notion of the communion of subjects. Ismā'īlī scholar Ali Asani concludes this section with an essay on the breathtakingly beautiful use of birds as metaphors for the soul and for spiritual aspiration that pervades Sufi poetry in every language from Arabic to Swahili: "Oh that I could be a bird and fly, I would rush to the Beloved."

Judaism, Christianity, and Islam all insist on the ontological and moral gulf between humans and the rest of earth's living beings. This is why some animal rights activists and scholars often dismiss these traditions as "bad for animals," and why, conversely, animal rights rhetoric often does not reach or affect traditional monotheistic religious agendas, standing as it does, as David Carlin points out, in the "long tradition of trying to narrow the gap between humans and lower animals." Carlin attributes the motive behind this move to "a strong animosity toward the view of human nature taken both by biblical religions and by the great classical schools of philosophy. ... To reduce human nature to nothing more than its biological status is to attack this ancient and exalted conception of human nature."[3] *A Communion of Subjects* reveals the problems with Carlin's critique: major sources in the biblical and classical western traditions, like many animal protectionists, often condemned human arrogance, and for their part many animal protectionists find it abhorrent to "reduce human nature to nothing more than its biological status." But there can be no question that, for better or for worse, classical monotheistic theologies grow out of hierarchical valuation: in keeping with the Genesis account of creation

of human beings in the *tselem* of God (the divine image), these theologies say that we human beings *are* infinitely more valuable than animals—just as is true in the Buddhist or Jain systems of thought, although there, driven by the metempsychotic principle, for highly different reasons.

Pace both sides of the debate, often both entrenched as well as unfairly parodied by each other, we try to show in the essays we present here that dwelling on the primacy of humanity in Judaism, Christianity, and Islam is not heuristically useful in comprehending the theological status and religious significance of animals. Nor, for that matter, is such a principle any more helpful in exegeting the same issue in the Eastern traditions. The Abrahamic traditions are not classically "anthropocentric" in the sense by which they are so often indicted. Instead, there is a way in which the Abrahamic traditions rather might be understood as *theocentric,* that is, they place God, not man—the God of Abraham and Sarah and Hagar, the God who created the Earth, who gave the Law, and who then spoke in history through His prophets, the final and greatest one of whom according to Islam was Muḥammad; God, the uncreated light, the source of all being—at the center of their cosmological construction. All other forms of meaning thus derive from this source, despite the deep tensions that arise as a result.

In their various recombinations of the doctrine of *saṃsāra,* religious traditions which have their origins in South Asia add a special dimension to the framing of the universal moral order as a divine-human-animal hierarchy: through karmic dictate, the human being can face an animal rebirth; indeed, as the *Jātakamālas* narrate, even the Buddha himself experienced countless prior animal lives.[4] **Part III, "Animals in Indian Traditions,"** includes essays on Hinduism, Buddhism, and Jainism. In a provocative essay, Lance Nelson invites the reader to reflect upon the frequent gulf in Hindu India between, on the one hand, religious or mythological ideals concerning animals, and, on the other, lived practice, which frequently appears to undermine those ideals. Continuing the theme of internal tensions, Edwin Bryant in an important and original study traces the history of the emergence of a vegetarian ethic in Hindu Sanskrit textual sources, showing the development of attitudes toward the consumption of meat, starting with the early Vedic sacrificial culture up to the later affirmation of the liberation-centered post-Vedic ethic of *ahiṃsā*, "nonviolence," with particular attention to caste-based dietary expectations.

Animal, human, divine, and demonic beings oscillate between bodies in the Buddhist cosmos, "a vast unsupervised recycling plant in which unstable but sentient entities circulate from one form of existence to the next," as described by Buddhologist Ian Harris, and by standard Mahāyāna teaching: "All beings throughout the six realms can be considered as our father and mother." The implications of this for Buddhist ethics, in particular for the practice of *mettā* ("loving-kindness"), are drawn out and brought into a discussion of contemporary issues of Buddhist values vis-à-vis animal and environmental protection in Asia; perhaps not surprisingly, the tensions between ideal and praxis are similar to those described by Lance Nelson in Hinduism. Picking up on the "stigma of animal rebirth" ingrained in the Buddhist wheel of *karma* and *saṃsāra*, Tibetan studies scholar Ivette Vargas eloquently shows how animals nevertheless served as "vehicles" for the transmission of doctrine in Indian and Tibetan narratives and in Buddhist iconography from the earliest stages of the tradition: the lion who represents the Buddha himself, the deer who flank the wheel of Dharma, the Nāgās (great serpents) to whom the Buddha entrusts the guardianship of the *Prajñāpāramitā* ("Perfection of Wisdom") texts until they are recovered by the missionary scholar Nagarjuna in the first century, among many others.

The implications of a radically applied doctrine of *ahiṃsā* are perhaps nowhere so startling as in Jainism, as Christopher Chapple shows in his essay, "Inherent Value Without Nostalgia: Animals and the Jaina Tradition." The Jain affirmation of the purificatory process of karma, and the Jains' refusal to interfere with this sacred mechanism of ultimate salvation, results in such apparently contradictory directions as the maintenance of an extensive network of *pinjrapoles*, hospitals for aging or ill animals, throughout India, and a refusal to engage in "mercy killing" for suffering animals. Kristi Wiley further explains how Jain beliefs about "five-sensed animals" have played out in traditional texts with respect to moral agency, cruelty, and violence.

Part IV, "Animals in Chinese Traditions," turns to the religious traditions of East Asia. An ancient sacrificial liturgy in China's oldest poetry collection, *The Book of Odes* (*Shijing*) reads:

> Of a tawny bull we make offering;
> It is accepted, it is approved,
> Many blessings are sent down.

The role of animals in the religious culture of early China is the focus of Roel Sterckx's study of such phenomena as spirit mediums, oracles, healing and sacrificial rituals. Addressing Daoism in particular, E.N. Anderson and Lisa Raphals show how thoroughly the ancient Chinese knew local fauna and thus accorded other animals "a general sense of respect." Touching on animals used for work and food, imaginary animals, and ordinary animals that "have moral, spiritual, or even shamanistic qualities," Anderson and Raphals suggest that in the Daoist tradition, "The human and animal realms are not sharply separated." In "Of Animals and Man: The Confucian Perspective," Rodney Taylor reveals how the lens of the human-animal relationship can offer perspectives that reveal important—and sometimes forgotten—dimensions of religious traditions. Treating ancient and modern thinkers, Taylor challenges "the prevailing tendency to classify the Confucian ethic as just another species of humanism." A close reading of Confucian sources with an eye to the tradition's con-

cern for other living beings leads Taylor to conclude that "Confucianism does not restrict the
realm of value or the scope of moral relations to
human beings."

"East Meets West" in **Part V** as two wide-
ranging analyses look at the large issue of "Animals in Philosophy and Cultural History." Noting "the entrenched ambiguity that attends any
attempt to separate out the animal and human
worlds," Roger Ames ably weaves observations
about classical Western thinking and the modern animal rights movement in order to "recover
the philosophical assumptions that have influenced the sinitic narrative in locating animals in
a fundamentally different natural cosmology."
The interdisciplinary and cross-cultural implications of the intersection of religion and animals are broad indeed, and Jordan Paper's "Humans and Animals: The History from a Religio-
Ecological Perspective" reveals just how vast the
sweep of this field can be. His essay moves from
gathering-hunting cultures to agricultural societies to modern industrialized societies, from
Mengzi of ancient China and Aristotle to modern Canadians and the contemporary Makah
people hunting whales on the Pacific Coast of
North America. In this encompassing journey,
Paper asks the reader to consider the significance
of shifts "in the relationship between humans
and animals in different parts of the world from
a communion between related beings to constructed notions of the inferiority, subservience,
and/or enemy nature of animals to the projection of an utterly unreal anthropomorphic personality onto animals."

The chronic presence of other animals in our
human mythology is the subject of **Part VI,
Animals in Myth.** In her "The Mythology of
Horses in India," Wendy Doniger treats the potent and mutable role of animal images in myth
and religious understanding. Discussing complex shifts in horses as, in turn, a potent symbol
of political power, fertility, and beauty, Doniger observes, "The history of the mythology
of horses in India demonstrates the ways in
which the people of India first identified horses

with the people who invaded them on horseback and then identified themselves with the
horses, in effect positioning themselves as their
own exploiters." The theme of multivalent animal symbols is also sounded in Kofi Opoku's
wide-ranging review, "Animals in African Mythology." Touching on myths about the origin of
the world, of food and death, and of the sociopolitical order of human communities, Opoku
describes the centrality of nonhuman beings in
African worldviews as stemming from "an absorbing and seemingly inexhaustible fascination
with animals." Importantly, the appearance of
other living beings in mythologies is far more
than mere imagery, for Opoku returns again and
again to the interrelatedness of, on the one hand,
the roles allocated in various stories to particular animals, and, on the other hand, the named
animals' observable characteristics. Opoku concludes, "[B]y observing animals and thinking
about them, humans discovered an abundant
source of wisdom that was already there." The
theme of animals as both valued "others" and
also symbolic vehicles of cultural tensions (as in
Kienzle's contribution) pervades Ian McIntosh's
essay on aboriginal reconciliation and the Australian dingo. McIntosh addresses the complex
ways in which native Australian mythmakers
used the dingo as a symbol of a-sociality to
account for the dislocation and "intercultural
mayhem" brought on by the arrival of European
peoples.

In **Part VII, Animals in Ritual,** John Grim
takes on the challenge "to understand from a
Western intellectual perspective ... the mutuality of knowing between humans and animals"
in his "Knowing and Being Known by Animals:
Indigenous Perspectives on Personhood." Grim
masterfully explores Berry's "communion of
subjects" notion through a discussion of "personhood" as a developmental process integrally
related to the human person's encounter of nonhuman living beings. Kimberley Patton raises
fundamental questions in "Sacrifice: Metaphysics of the Sublimated Victim" about the facile representation of animal sacrifice as a one-

dimensional act that honors only human interests and thus dismisses animal victims as mere ritual objects. Patton's work reflects the importance of putting ritual acts in context by means of analysis that pays attention to their multiple aspects, approaching the ritual, at least initially, *on its own terms* before ethical judgments are made. When this is done in the case of sacrifice, the victim usually emerges, at least through the lens of the sacrificing tradition, as an active rather than a passive being, metaphysically significant—a sublimated agent rather than a degraded or exploited player in the ritual drama.

The paper that generated perhaps the most discussion during the conference was Elizabeth Lawrence's "Hunting the Wren: A Sacred Bird in Ritual." A respected veterinarian pioneer and anthropologist who to our sorrow passed away in the autumn of 2003, before the publication of this volume, Lawrence works out a riddle: why, for centuries of English history, was the familiar and beloved wren chased and killed on the day after Christmas, St. Stephen's Day, in religiously framed and sanctioned hunts? This piece reveals the potential of both tradition and metaphor for paradox, for this tiny bird attracted attention "not by means of noble or grandiose qualities, nor by fearsomeness, but rather because of its striking and idiosyncratic traits and certain characteristics that seem contradictory or incongruous." Baffling marginality and ambiguity are also the theme of Chris McDonough's scholarly historical jaunt, "*Ridiculus Mus:* Of Mice and Men in Roman Thought." This essay thoroughly engages the details of a seemingly bizarre preoccupation in the classical Mediterranean world with creatures that many of us in modern society might view as vermin, unworthy of any regard. But animal species have often held divinatory or therapeutic powers we cannot now comprehend, and exploring these values across time and place is what currently drives some of the best work in the field of religion and animals.

The exploration of divinatory ritual continues in Eric Mortensen's "Raven Augury from Tibet to Alaska: Dialects, Divine Agency, and the Bird's-Eye View," which explores the sensitivity of various religious traditions (the Naxi, Tibetan indigenous peoples, Pacific Native Americans) to the uncanny intelligence of ravens (now documented by modern scientific work). By asking why so many cultures scrupulously watched corvids and accorded them oracular significance, Mortensen grants a profound epistemological respect to the observations of other peoples. To seriously engage such accounts of animal powers in traditional religious systems is to envision better possible answers to questions about who animals are and what they can mean to us.

Part VIII, Animals in Art, complements the foregoing sections by turning to influential iconographic traditions of animals in our culture. Focusing on the important truth that "the image is the most natural and foundational form of the human question for meaning," in her "On the *Dynamis* of Animals, or how *Animalium* became *Anthropos*," Diane Apostolos-Cappadona describes an important transformation of animal images in western art history. Such images shifted gradually from an early recognition of the power and dignity of animals in their own right to images of domesticated animals, and then later to animal images as sympathetic emblems of the human condition. Apostolos-Cappadona draws the parallel between these shifts and larger Western culture's gradual "loss of awe" and denigration of the beauty, power, and integrity of nonhuman animals until they were owned and controlled by humans.

In **Parts IX–XI** we turn our gaze to the ethical implications of nonhuman animals' undeniable existential complexity for scientific traditions. The implications of these rich topics are explored by research scientists, lawyers, philosophers, scholars of social thought, and bioethicists who hold central places in the contemporary discussion of our current values, both inclusivist and exclusivist, regarding life outside our species.

Part IX, "Animals as Subjects: Ethical

Implications for Science," highlights the dual meanings of the word "subject"—both as Thomas Berry uses it (an autonomous, living entity who generates particular, individual perspective and undergoes experience) and as scientific experimentation has used it (the willing or unwilling human and nonhuman animal participants in clinical trials, i.e., far closer to "object"). In his essay, "Wild Justice," animal behaviorist and "deep ethologist" Mark Bekoff plunges into the mental "worlds" of other animals, describing what research has illumined of animal emotion: joy, grief, even depression; of animal empathy: social play, cooperation, fairness, trust, even forgiveness, both intra-species and extra-species. These are all capabilities that many contemporary human beings tend to ascribe only to our own kind, *contra* millennia of experience, and more recently, *contra* scientific observation in both artificial and natural settings. Naturalists such as John Hay have long questioned our use of consciousness as a gold standard criterion to distinguish man from beast: "Do men belabor the special nature of consciousness too much, as if it ... separated mankind from the rest of animal creation? Consciousness must be infinitely more mysterious, more connective, than any attributes we may assign it of personal distinction."[5] Substantiating Hay's protest, the late comparative zoologist David Griffin argues in one of his most important articles, "From Cognition to Consciousness," that animals do, in fact, exhibit all the features of rational, evaluative, and in some cases even self-reflective mentation that we associate with conscious thinking. Griffin further suggests that the correlation between neural features of human beings and those of animals fully supports a move into the possibility of animal *consciousness*. Issues of temptation, control, and agency ground the essay of primatologist Mark Hauser, who asks the provocative question, "Are animals moral agents?" He answers in surprising ways that highlight the necessity of our constant qualification and nuance of human categories when applied to animals. Ethical issues

raised in genetic engineering and cloning are addressed by Bernard Rollin, tracking the shift from the traditional, biblically based constraint of non-cruelty, whereby the suffering of animals deemed "normal" or "necessary" in the course of normal human economic or medical enterprise might be accepted, to a "more adequate" moral code that shifts the perspective to the animal's own: can religious institutions serve as a support for this shift? Finally, psychologist Kenneth Shapiro offers a historically based critique of the ethical, and by extension the spiritual, dimensions of animal experimentation: "the animal is a conduit, a vehicle, for the study of certain relations between brain functions, external stimuli, and movement. The animal has lost his or her integrity in that only parts of the animal are the focus of interest. The rats are 'laboratory animals' in the sense that they are *part* of the laboratory."

"Are Animals 'for' Humans?" is the problematic of **Part X,** which focuses specifically on the theological and ethical implications of factory farming in three essays by "animal agriculture specialists" David Fraser and Gary Valen and veterinarian Michael Fox. This section explores the ways in which industrial ideals and the Western high-fat, high-protein diet have co-opted the intimate, ancient practice of animal husbandry, and cross-examines the validity of Lynn White's claim that the roots of today's environmental crisis lie in Jewish and Christian scriptural claims of human mastery over nature. These essays expose the economic pressures facing small independent and large corporate producers alike who wish to adhere to "pastoralist ethics" (whose roots, Fraser argues, are every bit as biblical) whereby animals are treated with ethical sensitivity, and not only to maximize profits through the use of confinement technologies. "Only that which we regard as sacred is secure," writes Fox of global agribusiness, "and our reverence must be total, or it is not at all." "Life forms," he asserts, are not "living resources. ... In the process of transforming the *ecos* into a bio-industrialized wasteland, and transforming the *telos* of animals to serve our own ends, we will unwittingly transform ourselves into something less than human that does not recognize contempt and indifference toward life as a disease of the soul." Gary Valen's "The Soul of Agriculture" project, which attempts to revision food and fiber production in the United States, serves as a platform for difficult questions: "Does it matter how animals are treated in intensive livestock and poultry systems? Are we comfortable knowing that factory farm sows spend their lives in tiny crates on concrete- or metal-slatted floors where they must eat, sleep, eliminate, give birth, and nurse their babies in the same small space?"

Part XI turns to some of the most important contemporary challenges surrounding animals and religious issues: law, social justice, and the environment. Steven Wise, a scholar specializing in animal law, unpacks the Supreme Court ruling upholding the legality of the sacrifice of animals in private home shrines of Santería practitioners in Hialeah, Florida, as a protected form of religious expression. Carol Adams trains the lens of ecofeminist theory upon the issue of animal suffering in the food industry and elsewhere, arguing that its essential questions are those of subjectivity—in particular, "the disappearance of the subject of non-human suffering," which follows from what she calls the move of "hyper-separation" by which human beings see themselves as "not-animals": some*thing* must not be seen as having been some*one*. The religious imagination that would restore such awareness, she says, following the thought of Simone Weil, is "the capacity to recognize the possibility of relationships and bring attention to suffering." Kim Roberts of the Humane Society courageously addresses the religious and gender-based aspects of the interlocked history of violence against animals and against people, and the ways in which animal cruelty almost invariably serves as a social indicator of potential domestic abuse or even mass murder. Co-editor Paul Waldau's interview with philosopher and ethicist Peter Singer, author of *Animal Liberation,* elicits from Singer with un-

precedented clarity his views on the moral challenges posed to communities of faith and the modern animal movement. The current director of the drafting of a document for global ethics, *The Earth Charter,* Steven Rockefeller, explains in his essay the implications of this highly influential document for the lives of animals and their place in the future of the planet, including the exposition of multicultural differences raised by indigenous peoples over seemingly innocuous terms in the Charter advocating "compassion" in hunting, or the case of Jains protesting language itself protesting "wanton destruction" of living beings (for *no* destruction of living beings is acceptable in the thoroughgoing Jain applied ethic of *ahiṃsā*). Paul Waldau paints the implications of "pushing environmental justice to a natural limit" by implying that the basic moral question "who are the others?" can be illumined by religious insights.

Finally, these multiple voices are joined by two of the most profound voices of our time in this arena—of Mary Evelyn Tucker, who for years has raised awareness of the relevance of religious insights and communities to environmental issues, and Jane Goodall, the best-known primatologist in the world, who has been described as "one of the intellectual heroes of the century." In her Conclusion, Tucker links Berry's "communion of subjects" with David Abram's notion of the "more-than-human world": "In our preoccupation to identify the ways in which we as humans are distinctive among the myriad species of life, we have forgotten to highlight the ways in which we are related. ... We have thus become like a species that has lost its familiar migratory route." Tucker's hope is that "with some humility ... we may be able to participate again in the patterned and transformative life of the animal world that we share." In the book's Epilogue, Goodall speculates on the final frontier of animal subjectivity: the capacity for religious response. Describing the ritualized dance of chimpanzees before a waterfall deep in the jungle in Tanzania, which she alone has witnessed (the "waterfall display"), she says, "What I saw was an expression of what I think is a spiritual reality." Unhesitatingly affirming that, like us, animals have souls, she calls this "awe."

A Communion of Subjects, then, summons voices that collectively invite believers, non-believers, ethicists, scientists, consumers, and all other humans to meet the challenge of asking *and answering* how the two important topics of "religion" and "animals" are joined. At the very least, meeting this challenge offers the prospect of deepening our questions about our own sometimes arrogant, sometimes compassionate, and sometimes ignorant claims about the other biological beings on this planet and their worlds. All of this is, of course, a venture of a fundamentally ecological nature, for we cannot know about the lives of these fellow living beings without knowing about their communities, habitats, and wider ecological webs. Above all, though, careful answers to questions about whether and in what ways our world is a "communion of subjects" rather than a "collection of objects" offer prospects for a deeper understanding of the place of all beings within *our* cosmos.

NOTES

1. Volumes in the Religions of the World and Ecology series are published by the Harvard University Center for the Study of World Religions and distributed by Harvard University Press. They include: Mary Evelyn Tucker and Duncan Ryūken Williams, eds., *Buddhism and Ecology: The Interconnection of Dharma and Deeds* (1997); Mary Evelyn Tucker and John Berthrong, eds., *Confucianism and Ecology: The Interrelation of Heaven, Earth, and Humans* (1998); Christopher Key Chapple and Mary Evelyn Tucker, eds., *Hinduism and Ecology: The Intersection of Earth, Sky, and Water* (2000); Dieter T. Hessel and Rosemary Radford Ruether, eds., *Christianity and Ecology: Seeking the Well-Being of Earth and Humans* (2000); J.J. Girardot, James Miller, and Liu Xiaogan, eds., *Daoism and Ecology: Ways Within a Cosmic Landscape* (2001); John Grim, ed., *Indigenous Traditions and Ecology: The Interbeing of Cosmology and Community* (2001); Christopher Key Chapple, ed., *Jainism and Ecology: Nonviolence in the Web of Life* (2002); Have Tirosh-Samuelson, ed., *Judaism and Ecology Created World and Revealed World* (2002); Richard C. Foltz, Frederick M. Denny, and Azizan Baharuddin, eds., *Islam and Ecology: A Bestowed Trust* (2003). Forthcoming are Rosemarie Bernard, ed., *Shinto and Ecology* and Mary Evelyn Tucker and John Grim, eds., *Cosmology and Ecology*.

2. Paul Shepard, *The Others: How Animals Made Us Human* (Washington, D.C.: Island Press, 1996).

3. David R. Carlin, "Rights, Animal and Human," *First Things* 105 (2000): 16–17.

4. Some of the discussion in the preceding four paragraphs represents mutual revision and elaboration by the editors of ideas initially presented in a journal article by Kimberley Patton, "'He Who Sits in the Heavens Laughs': Recovering Animal Theology in the Abrahamic Traditions," *Harvard Theological Review* 93, no. (2000): 401–34.

5. John Hay, *The Great Beach* (New York: Norton [1963], 1980), p. 106.

I

ANIMALS IN RELIGION, SCIENCE, AND ETHICS: IN AND OUT OF TIME

"Caught with Ourselves in the Net of Life and Time"

Traditional Views of Animals in Religion

KIMBERLEY PATTON

In a world older and more complete than ours, they move finished and complete, gifted with extensions of the senses we have lost or never attained, living by voices we shall never hear. They are not brethren; they are not underlings; they are other nations, caught with ourselves in the net of life and time, fellow prisoners of the splendor and travail of the earth.

— Henry Beston

On the first floor of the Israel Museum in Jerusalem, the skeleton of an adult male excavated at Eynan in the Hula Valley in Galilee is on display. The remains are Natufian, and date anywhere from 10,500 to 8,300 BCE. Very close by the upper body lie the bones of a small dog. The man was buried on his side in a fetal position with his head facing, and one arm extended toward, the similarly curled skeleton of the dog. It is very difficult, if not impossible, to exegete the meaning of this particular burial arrangement, which could range from an expression of mutual affection in life to the type of sympathetic destruction known in countless funerary contexts from around the world, both prehistoric and historic. Intentional canine burials, particularly in groups, emerge in later Mediterranean archaeology, for example at Ashkelon and Sardis, as an ongoing enigma in the cultic history of these regions.[1] But it is not difficult to sense that, no matter how obscure the nuances of the relationship between this particular human being and this animal in the Galilee, it was strong and deep, leaving them entwined even in death. "Until one has loved an animal," wrote Anatole France, "a part of one's soul remains unawakened."

For most of us, it can be no mystery that in a large majority of religious traditions, animals have been of supreme signifying importance. The depth of our response to them reveals a kind of connection that is ancient and abiding. When they—animals, birds, insects—appear before or around us in huge numbers, creating a kind of re-enactment of primordial "swarming" during the earth's earlier histories, we are amazed. Mixed with our awe or horror, there is a kind of nostalgia that may have no objective correlative in any urban or suburban experience. When we encounter millions of migrating monarch butterflies, or hundreds of pink flamingoes, balancing on elegantly thin legs as they wade, or stampeding bison, or endless, majestic heaps of braying sea lions at the ocean's edge—even when we see hordes of locusts destroying months of labor in the fields in a matter of minutes—human beings think at some level, *this was how it used to be. This was what our ancestors saw: this was the world they knew.* It is no accident that such encounters sometimes give rise to metaphors of the First Time. As wildlife photographer Fred Bruemmer writes in his recent book *Glimpses of Paradise: The Marvel of Massed Animals,*[2] "Humans have multiplied prodigiously and most of the ancient animal wealth of our world has been destroyed. … But here and there, for a variety of reasons, some animal species still exist in huge numbers and convey in their multitude a vision of Eden, of a world that once existed. I have searched for paradise for more than 30 years. I've sought out those magic places where animals congregate in large numbers, places that teem with the fullness of life."[3]

Apart from their epiphanies *en masse,* individual animals have been central players in human lives in one manner or another. Their lives, idiosyncrasies, and destinies affect us deeply from the time of childhood; this is not the result of modern, wilderness-starved sentimentality, but instead, as the late human ecologist Paul Shepard argued in *The Others: How Animals Made Us Human,*[4] represents a crucial arena for our cognitive, moral, and emotional development. And when they die, if we have known and cared for them, we are shattered. My young daughter still cannot bear to talk about the crippled squirrel baby she rescued from our Samoyed at the foot of a tree over two years ago. We could not find a trace of his mother; but had she ever accepted him in the first place? In shifts, every four hours, through five long days and nights, we nursed little Shadow using a medicine dropper filled with ridiculously expensive orphaned-kitten formula. Still, one afternoon, for no apparent reason, he wrapped his tiny question-mark tail around himself in his nest of old socks and stopped crying. Using one of the nicer socks as a shroud, we buried him

in the backyard and set a concrete angel above him. This was very sad—but, as it turned out, not *over.* Now none of my family sees squirrels the same way. We know what their very young look and smell like, and what their piercing cries sound like; how they cling like burrs to sweaters and how they passionately guzzle their milk between slender clawed feet. We know because we tried to parent one of their tribe. As a result of our brief intimacy with Shadow, and our disproportionate, aching sorrow at his death, squirrels weirdly changed for us from furry pests into relatives.

Animal-loss counselors have long known and stated that the grieving we do at the death of beloved animals often runs to the same depths that it does for our human dead.[5] That this equivalency is often socially unacceptable or even unrecognized has not helped human beings to deal with such grief. Our hearts, apparently, do not honor the Darwinian degrees of evolution of which our acculturated minds are cognizant: the "categorically human self"[6] that is allegedly superior in every way to the animal's lost self is nevertheless undone by its demise. And in industrialized American and European societies, it is not only evolutionary values, but also our religious heritage that countermands such grief: "It was only a cat." (A frog, a gerbil, a parakeet.) Yet on some level, scientific and theological discriminations between species crumble when an animal we loved is lost to us. We are reminded of the etymology of "totem," from the Ojibwa "ototeman," a verbal phrase expressing membership in an exogamous group: "he is a relative of mine." In totemic societies, the animal is not merely a symbolic conveyer of identity: *he is a relative of mine.* The cat was a crabby old uncle, or a beloved little brother, or my heart's companion. The relationship was rich and real, although the relational participants were of different species. Cat's death, and the loss of the unique, irreplaceable communion between us two, is thus unbearable. *Contra* the mindless rhetoric of media and a great deal of popular psychology on tragedy, the wound left by Cat's absence will not "heal" in my lifetime, any more than will its human analogue: change, but not heal. And *contra* the well-meaning nonsense of popular wisdom, "getting another cat" will not salve the original wound any better than "getting another brother" would.

This is hard to face, and harder still to articulate given the cultural taboos that constrain full lamentation, but our souls know its inherent truth. The denial of the depth of this almost universal experience contributes to the kind of spiritual disassociation referred to by Václav Havel in 1994, when he told Philadelphians on the fourth of July, "the world of our experiences seems chaotic, disconnected, confusing. … We do not know exactly what to do with ourselves." What is missing? Havel answered his own question simply: "The awareness of our being anchored in the earth and the universe, the awareness that we are not alone nor for ourselves alone." Our inextricable relationship with animals is one of the elements of this awareness, this anchor. Relegated to sentimentality or to managed brutality, it has lost some cultural legitimacy. Yet it has not diminished in power. Hurricane Katrina's legacy of human faces twisted in grief as beloved animals named Trouble or Snowball were separated from their owners by rescuers bears witness.

How old are these associations in human religious experience? The new *locus classicus* for the contemplation of animals in primeval religion has become the Chauvet Cave, discovered in the Ardèche region in Southern France in 1995 by three local speleologists, whose initial response to what they saw within was to kneel. The Chauvet paintings represent the oldest collection of created animal images in the world, with most of the paintings radiocarbon-dated to 31,000 BCE. These fluid, astonishing images of lions, bears, horses, rhinos, aurochs, wooly mammoths and even an owl thus belong squarely in the Aurignacean period, upsetting for good the art historical chronology of Henri Breuil that had

dated such perspectival ability millennia late. The iconography and archaeology of the cave testify to an extraordinarily complex relationship between animals and human beings. The existential nature of that relationship cannot be ignored, but neither can it be satisfactorily interpreted. Theories of hunting magic do not entirely help us here; these murals show hunting as well as hunted animals. The cave contains a high percentage of depictions of carnivorous predators, as well as animals that, as far as we know, were never hunted.

Furthermore, the Chauvet cave was clearly inhabited by bears, not only before the paintings were made, as bear nests and bear claw marks on their surfaces attest, but clearly afterward as well, as claw marks scratched *over* the paintings make clear; perhaps there were even times when bears and humans were cohabitants of the cave. The presence of a figure that is half-human, half-bison portrayed on a hanging rock perpendicular to the Lion Panel in the most remote chamber of the cave, perhaps that of a human wearing ritual animal garb, seems phenomenologically comparable to the so-called "sorcerer" figure at Les Trois Frères. But are we dealing with "proto-shamanism"?[7] The leading Paleolithic archaeologist Paul Bahn cautions vehemently—and justifiably—against the reckless universal application of shamanistic models to explain prehistoric art. Nevertheless the corrective of a "literal" interpretation as the default category may be just as misleading, and what *are* we to make of this figure? Even more problematic at Chauvet is the speleologists' discovery of the so-called "bear altar." At some point in time, a bear skull was deliberately placed at the edge of a fallen stone from the ceiling of the cave next to the Panel of the Horses. At least thirty disarticulated bear skulls without skeletons seemed to have been arranged around the circumference of the stone. The French discoverers write, "This intentional arrangement troubled us because of its solemn particularity." Bahn dismisses such ideas of bear cults as fan-

ssemblage could "just as a bored child playing in ults were painting!"[8]

ave also shows a feature ... Paleolithic sites, namely the reduplication ... tures—backs, bellies, horns, or entire individuals drawn eight or nine times, for example, not just re-traced (as are Australian aboriginal petroglyphs of the Dreamtime heroes, to this day), but drawn with each new line slightly separated from its predecessor. Were the artists trying to depict a herd? Or motion, a stampede, just as animated panels use successive positions to show protracted action? Or, as paleontologist Alexander Marshack argues, does the impulse toward reduplication try to *effect* ritual renewal, so that the animal's presence as a source of food might not be exhausted?[9] Does the repeated portrait magico-religiously "re-create" or resurrect its subject, the slain animal?

We know that the Chauvet artists hunted animals. But did they love them? Fear them? Worship them? Do these murals belong to the realm of religion? If, following Geertz and Zuesse, we accept a broad definition of religion as systematic thought that orients human existential experience to metaphysical powers through external, culturally accepted forms, I think there can be no doubt on this point. The cave offers us a cognitive, spiritual map of part of the observable world: a world lost to us, but peopled by animal powers—or "powerful animals." What exactly the relationship was between the images of animals and the living, breathing animals known to the Aurignacean groups of ancient southern France remains a matter of (re-) constructive theology. As archaeologist and cognitive theorist Colin Renfrew asks of prehistoric peoples, whose ideologies are known to us only through fragmented material artifacts, "What did they think?"[10] Animals and human thought belong together, for the latter seems to require the former.

In his work *Totemism,* Claude Lévi-Strauss made a celebrated remark, explaining why certain animals but not others are chosen as to-temic signifiers. "Natural species," he wrote, "are chosen not because they are 'good to eat' but because they are 'good to think.'"[11] By this he meant that certain animals can "stand for" social arrangements, kinship relations, and modalities of thinking and interpretation. We can extend this notion of animals as a kind of cognitive language to the sphere of religion, in that they so efficaciously seem to bear ideas of, in Stanley Walens' words, "selfness and otherness that lie at the basis of human and religious thought," as well as "analogies that can represent the relationship of the human to divine."[12] We find throughout world religions a tendency for humans to define themselves, their own characteristics, their values, their laws, their immediate world and even their gods in terms of these species that are so other—so different from us and yet, so hauntingly related. Animals can carry, as psychoanalyst James Hillman says, "the shadow of the culture," like the monkey, the pig—or the dog, as David Gordon White shows in his wide-ranging historical and ideological study from Europe to Northern Africa to China: *Myths of the Dog-Man.*[13]

"Animals are good to think": this is true not only anthropologically, but apparently also developmentally; but here the process of signification collapses. In the experience of human children, animals while "good to think" stand for *themselves:* in their own right, they are peers, friends, enemies, or mysteries. They are as vitally important to children as other human beings, and the child seems almost to require their presence, both in reality and in play, in order to construct her world meaningfully. Paul Shepard traces the "profound, inescapable need for animals" as part of a critical stage in children's psychological development.[14] Children see animals without symbolism, he argues, and thus the characteristic behaviors of each appear to correspond with aspects of their own humanity. So contact with animals allows children to internally undertake a kind of matching game that allows the emerging self to be synthesized. From around our second year, we become "ecstatically absorbed with animals, not only as beings but as types with names."[15] Very young children, when they encounter a new kind of animal, intently engage in classification and perceptual discrimination, what psychology calls "cognitive mapping"—the process of making sense of what is unknown by extrapolating from what is known.[16] Later, Shepard argues, the mimicking of animals, and even the anthropomorphizing of them, is essential for the child: "By pretending that animals speak to one another, he imposes on them a pseudo-humanity which, although illusory, is the glue of real kinship." As observable, living, non-abstract co-inhabitants of the world that are like the child but also *different* from her and also *different from one another,* they help her mentally to create the cosmos, to map terrain, and to begin to establish identity.

Shepard goes on to argue that animal lives are also an appropriate metaphor for the evolving, transgressive, and ambiguous psychological state of adolescence. "Then in maturity, [animals] are the perfect tutors for ... adult realities; metamorphosis, birth, puberty, healing, courtship, fertility, and protection." Participation in animal nature, through mimesis, ritual, dance, and totemism allows for a continual interrelationship with cosmos. In contemporary industrialized societies we encourage the childhood stage of Shepard's model. The adolescent stage is lost to all but a few, such as the notorious love of adolescent girls for horses. But surely we have lost the value of animal spirituality to adult life in all but the most fetishistic forms. Dreams alone insist on adults' original orientation toward animals, and will not relinquish childhood memories:

By zealously repudiating the animal form, omitting the middle matrix, we retreat from the polymorphic ambiguity of life. The bearless cosmos deprives us of personal experience of the sacred paradigm, substituting for it an abstract, verbal exegesis. ... The carrying of a positivistic, literal attitude toward animals into the adult sphere

marks the failure of initiation and maturity in human life. ... Our dreams, however, remain true to a different world from that in which we now live.[17]

Gail Melson takes up the theme from a psychological angle, a significant amplification of her earlier investigations of the developmental impact of relationships exclusively between human beings. Ubiquity and identification had led to a kind of curious snow-blindness: "Animals were so *there* as part of the woof and web of childhood, including my own, that I had never noticed them ..."[18] Melson's research, conducted through interviews, reveals a web of attachment and identification so profound as to be often expressed by children as *deeper* than their affection for their human best friends. As she argues:

I propose a "biocentric" view of development, one that recognizes the pervasiveness of real and symbolic animals in children's lives. I argue that the study of children has been largely "humanocentric," assuming that only human relationships—with parents, siblings, relatives, friends, teachers, other children—are consequential for development. This humanocentric perspective on development is at best a seriously incomplete portrait of the ecology of children. ... animal presence in all its forms merits neither facile sentimentalizing nor quick dismissal, but serious investigation.[19]

In classic children's works such as Kenneth Grahame's *The Wind in the Willows,* animals are outrageously anthropomorphized. This trend continues unabated today, not only in books but also in Disney films and many stuffed animals; even if they are realistically made, children turn them into little people in their imaginative play. Perhaps there is a reason for this. The genre of children's literature around the world seems to reflect a kind of yearning for a lost age when animals and human beings could indeed speak the same language, and co-existed without the antagonism and complicated tensions of the predator–prey relationships that are now expected between them, both for biological and cultural reasons.[20] The child, whether as the story's protagonist or as its reader, is somehow seen as the symbolic catalyst and center of this picture of peace, as in the Isaianic vision of the wolf dwelling with the lamb and the lion with the calf, "and a little child shall lead them."[21]

The affinity between children and animals has probably contributed to a persistent tendency in the discipline of the European and American history of religions known as developmentalism. Developmentalist theory posits that religions have "evolved" from theological naïveté or crudity to theological sophistication. The bigger the role that nature, but particularly that animals, played in a given tradition, whether in the form of totemism, a belief in animal spirits or gods, or strong human ritual identification with animals, the more likely it was up until recently to be taken as literally, "childish."[22] Animal cults were and still are sometimes seen as atavisms—survivals, throwbacks to the hunting heritage, to shamanistic identification or covenant through slaughter and represented as irrational, emotional, and immoral. Partly this is very specifically due, of course, to monotheistic triumphalism. It was also strongly influenced by Freud, for whom all religious belief was the neurotic sublimation of unresolved infantile conflicts and desires. In *Totem and Taboo*, Freud called any separation from animals "still as foreign to the child as it is to the savage or primitive man."[23] The equation of childhood with "primitive" religions through the link of an ingrained affinity for animals logically leads to a developmentalist model, with this affinity serving as a kind of index of theological or philosophical sophistication. For Freud, true maturity, "outgrowing" childhood, would entail shedding our need for both gods and animals. Historically, of course, supremely advanced civilizations with theriomorphic gods like ancient Egypt stand as stark challenges to this calculus.

If, rather than Freud, we follow Shepard, Hillman, or Walens in viewing religions that "demote" animals as in some way impoverished, rather than as more differentiated, we are nevertheless left with a spectacular challenge in trying to think comparatively about animals in religion. Why do animals attract such a rich history of religious response? It is hard to avoid their special powers and their autonomy as sources of their apparent power. However socially constructed, animals are nevertheless also, always mysteriously, themselves, living lives in their own cultures that intertwine with our own to a greater or lesser extent, but are nevertheless beyond our complete control. As the cruel tsunami tore across the Indian Ocean on December 26, 2004, coastal animals everywhere somehow sensed its advent and sought higher ground. A sense of this awe-inspiring autonomy courses through Henry Beston's words. In ancient and indigenous traditions, animals seemed to be able to transcend the "net of life and time." Wild animals in particular were observed to move outside human physical constraints, and their imitation in ritual had initiatory value in that it potentially made possible a human integration of this antinomian and potent identity. Metamorphosis in myth is the temporary or permanent instantiation of this value, even when the change is punitive and represents a new social condition—as in the transformation of the Athenian sisters Procne and Philomela into, respectively, a swallow and a nightingale, after their ordeal of rape and revenge. In Gitxsan legend, a boy who will not stop shooting squirrels is returned to his family by the chief of squirrels as a skeleton hung in a tree. When sung back to life through sacrifice and fasting, the resurrected boy orders the flesh of the squirrels he hunted to be burned, thus becoming a great shaman whose name is Squirrel: "*Ia heiaha a, heia'aya negwa iaha!* I become accustomed to this side; I become accustomed to the other side."[24]

The concept of the varieties of creatures as "other nations," paralleling ours, is mirrored in the visionary traditions of northern native

Americans, as for example in the famous childhood dream, narrated in old age, of the Oglala Sioux leader Black Elk: "I was taken away from this world into a vast tipi, which seemed to be as large as the world itself, and painted on the inside were every kind of four-legged being, winged being, and all the crawling peoples. The peoples that were there in that lodge, they talked to me, just as I am talking to you."[25] But such an idea is also found in the Qur'ānic references to animal species as "communities," as in Surāh 6:38: "There is not an animal (that lives) on the earth, nor a being that flies on its wings, but (forms part of) communities (*ummam*) like you." The uncanny idea that animals have their own societies and their own relationship to the greater powers is by no means limited to nonliterate, nonurban, or animistic religious systems.

Semiotically, animal images in myth are always complex and dynamic, never one-dimensional or static. In other words, such images are like their zoological prototypes. Walens reminds us that animals, especially fantastic ones like the Australian aboriginal Rainbow Serpent, do not have a solitary meaning that can be "plugged in" on a substitutionary one-to-one basis. Rather, Rainbow Serpent undulates through a complex range of symbol domains, and mediates between other domains as well. The ecological situatedness of the animal is an invariable part of its symbolism. For example, it is not just the orca whale as static "thing" that carries symbolic value for Northwestern native peoples, but also the whale as contextualized verb, as *living subject* rising from the depths into the light of the upper world. Thus the orca, not *qua* orca, but *as it is observed to inhabit its own world* evokes the "process of emergence: insight, birth, or the supernatural intrusion into human affairs."[26]

In the interaction between "animal ethics" and that of the history of religion, the self-righteous, untextured imposition of secular ethical frameworks is seldom helpful. It is true that the hierarchical triptych in the Abrahamic traditions demarcating strict boundaries between the divine, human, and animal worlds was and is foreign to most other traditions, whether classical or indigenous. However, even here, things are more complex than they seem. One often finds that once a tradition seems clear enough with respect to where it stands on animals, a paradox, an exception, or an internal inconsistency will suddenly surface, one that threatens to invert completely one's neat judgment about whether that tradition "values" or "exploits" animals. Ritualizing cultures that sacrificed selected animals such as the Celtic or Vedic seemed to hold animals in far more awe and reverence and to have far more knowledge of them "on the ground" than many nonsacrificing cultures like our own, where some animals are cherished as pets while others, like veal calves, are raised as commodities without regard for their well-being. A text such as Genesis 1:20–28[27] that is excoriated by many as anthropocentric and unfairly oppressive to animals, may in the treatment of a conservative Christian theologian like Andrew Linzey reveal instead a divine mandate for human stewardship of nonhuman creatures.[28] Do certain Eastern traditions, because they are firm advocates of *ahiṃsā*, or the radical principle of nonviolence toward all living things, *necessarily* treat animals more compassionately than so-called Western traditions? Lance Nelson's essay on Hinduism in this volume answers negatively. Does the construction of animals as karmic agents also caught in the wheel of rebirth elevate them, or does it denigrate them by subjecting them to clearly human ethical expectations, behaviorally foreign to them? The Jain version of *ahiṃsā*, seemingly infinitely humane, may seem infinitely cruel after one has seen nonintervention in action in Jain "animal hospitals" for dying creatures, in order to allow them to suffer through their karmic residue and ultimately achieve liberation.[29]

In the case of the monotheistic traditions, Western scholars, particularly those working in feminist theology, animal theology, and deep ecology, chronically complain that these traditions are anthropocentric, that is, that they place human beings at the center of matrices of meaning and value, with animals below human beings, or on the periphery of the Creation. In fact, this is inaccurate. These traditions are *theocentric*, that is, they historically have placed at the center of their cosmological construction God, the God of Abraham who acts in history and yet is also unbound by "the net of life and time," with everything else deriving from that tenet. There is no question that we are dealing with hierarchical valuation, that is, the ideology that finds human beings infinitely more valuable than animals, just as they are in the Buddhist or Jain systems of thought, because they are capable of a moral range that animals do not possess.

However, having said this, we must search for the metaphysical animal in other highways and byways in monotheisms. And sure enough that animal emerges, perhaps even more powerful because at the periphery—in the biblical eaglehood of the Lord as she stirs her nest, giving her young no rest; in the talmudic glory of Leviathan playing with his Creator in the afternoon; in the breath of the ox, donkey, and sheep who blew on the shivering Christ child in Bethlehem barnyard animals who still, at the stroke of midnight each Christmas eve, can speak; in the Holy Spirit descending "like a dove" from the heavens over the Jordan; in the prophetic white birds who sang to the Irish saint Brendan and his monks in their circling sea-coracle in *The Voyage of St. Brendan*, in the *ḥadīth* of the spider who spun the web across the cave's mouth to save Muḥammad and Aʾisha from the hostile Quraysh as they thundered by; in the thirty birds in Farid ud-din Attar's great poem who struggle on cruel pilgrimage to find their king, discovering his shining radiance to be none other than a transfigured mirror of themselves, Simorgh: "Thirty Birds." It is true that the Abrahamic traditions do not centralize animals in their constructions of truth or Law, but neither do they peripheralize them ethically, devotionally, or in the religious imagination. Ani-

mals remain in these traditions players in their own right, with distinct and unique relationships to God.[30]

The triadic analogue ("triptych") that animals are to human beings as human beings are to gods, although useful to some extent in interpreting monotheistic forms, is inadequate as a universal principle. "Otherness" of course is philosophically fashionable, as the title of Paul Shepard's book reminds us, but closer examination of the features of many traditional thought systems reveals perhaps a far greater weight to sameness between these three realms. Bear with White Paw, a Sioux, commented in the early twentieth century, "The bear has a soul like ours, and his soul talks to mine in my sleep and tells me what to do."[31] In many traditions, animals are not merely people, but actually *metamorphosed human beings*, echoing what children in most cultures seem naturally to think. The Celtic pantheon contains deities, like Rhiannon, who spend so much of their time in animal form that the very term "metamorphosis" is probably inadequate. Furthermore, things were not always so fixed as they are now. Consider the eloquent Inuit statement transcribed in Knud Rasmussen's notes from the same time period: "In the very earliest time, when both people and animals lived on earth, a person could become an animal if he wanted to and an animal could become a human being. Sometimes they were people and sometimes animals and there was no difference. All spoke the same language. That was the time when words were like magic. The human mind had mysterious powers. A word spoken by chance might have strange consequences. It might suddenly come alive and what people wanted to happen could happen—all you had to do was say it. Nobody could explain this: That's the way it was." That this ontological fluidity between animal and human states is so closely associated with a lost performative efficacy of words cannot be accidental.

The "identification" between the hunter and the hunted animal is often far more than sympathetic imagination or guilt; instead, it is existentially construed. *They are both human.* Thus here again, the concept of "otherness" must be carefully parsed, or even set aside. A Barren Land Inuit told Raymond de Coccola, "Fish have souls like all human beings. They have to be killed in a certain way, and they have to be killed at once, or they will speak evil words to the hunter. We fear the souls of the dead—human or animal, bird or fish—for they bring starvation, sickness, and suffering. That's why we must obey the rules of taboo."[32] The *inua,* the human essence of the animal, even and especially the hunted animal, is shown in (among myriad examples of circumpolar Inuit art) Alaskan Yup'ik masks, worn in a range of ceremonial contexts.[33] Wooden doors open in the carved mask-faces of fox or bear to show the human within. By divine decree animals can also substitute more than adequately for human beings as sacrificial victims—the white hind, for example, that Artemis provides in the place of Iphigenia, daughter of Agamemnon, stretched upon the altar at Aulis, or the roan mare that appears miraculously on the Bœotian plain instead of the virgin demanded by two vengeful slain maidens in Plutarch's *Life of Pelopidas,* or the rabbinical ram caught in the thicket that begins its journey at the dawn of time to the site of the *aqedah.* This is not a matter of simple subtraction (God accepts a "lesser offering"); this bespeaks instead a ritual, or even ontological, interchangeability of human and animal, as well as the substitutionary value of the latter, no matter what relief attends the averted human sacrifice. Nuer young men are identified from the time of puberty with particular oxen; they are even given "ox-names," and their oral poetry focuses on the attributes of their individual oxen. In Nuer sacrifice, one gives *oneself* as an offering back to God (*Kwoth*); this self-giving is *best* represented by the immolation of the precious and beloved ox who, above all, bears the identity of the sacrifier. "Men and oxen have a symbolic equivalence in the logic of sacrifice," wrote Evans-Pritchard, "so that whatever sacrificed is an 'ox.' If there were enough oxen one might always sacrifice an ox, and in

symbol and by surrogate, one does so, but as there are not enough, other offerings have to take their place and oxen be kept for the greater crises."[34]

In traditions for which metempsychosis is a crucial tenet, of course, the collapse of the distinctions between human being and animal becomes even more acute, at the same time that they are upheld and theologically re-inscribed. Hindu ideas of *saṃsāra,* of the cycling successive reincarnations of a soul, renders the animal/human distinction on one level a purely external one, although not one without a critical index of spiritual merit. Animal birth always represents a moral, and ultimately a metempsychotic, regression. The same is true of Buddhism, although the *Jātaka* tales of the Buddha's previous lives as a bodhisattva in animal form make it clear that however stylized these parables, *mokśa* may still be elegantly overcome and spiritual salvation attained in the animal world —among fish, or even water buffaloes. "Once the Buddha was a monkey," begins one of the tales, and because there are so many variations on this formulaic opening one tends to forget their startling premise. A transposition of the theme into another tradition with a radically different orientation toward incarnation is all that is necessary to make the point, for therein lies heresy: "Once Jesus was a blue heron. Once Muhammad was a tiger."

Creatures mediate between divine and human realms in the myth and ritual of most traditions. Prophecy, omens, and divination are their special province; the liver of the slaughtered sheep was the forecasting device of the ancient Near East, and the carapace of the tortoise that of Bronze Age China, but living birds are ubiquitous oracles. As Eric Mortensen shows in this volume, the highly intelligent raven, for example, is credited with knowledge of the future in religious complexes from ancient Ireland to the Naxi of Tibet and across the Bering Strait to the Pacific Coast. But it is more than this; in the religious imagination, animals *are* in some sense not merely "sacred" but divine; the divine self-manifests in animal form; animals bear the god-head. Phenomenal animals are only one mani-festation of this relationship; particularly in the American continents, there was and is a strong belief, as noted by Joseph Epes Brown, in ar-chetypal "essences" appearing in animal form, that not only guard or even own real animals but are also available through dreams and vision quests. The Cree elder Raining Bird explains, "Each animal has its own Master Spirit which owns all the animals of its kind ... so all the ani-mals are the children of the Master Spirit that owns them. It is just like a large family." [35] The Mayan jaguar as iconographically represented is hypostasized, numinous; each *real* jaguar is therefore in some sense theophoric, and the cir-cumstances of its appearance and behavior are crucially important.

James Hillman speaks radically about ani-mals that appear in the human religious imagi-nation or in dreams; he says they are neither symbols of the developing self nor attributes of human qualities. They are not even "represen-tatives" of the divine.[36] In many religious tradi-tions, he recalls, animals were gods. So to dream of a pig or a wolf or a dog does not reveal the pig-gish or wolfish or doggish nature of the dreamer —that is, it does not indicate the unconscious assertion of lower, instinctual nature. In describ-ing such a dream, he remarks, both a modern child and an ancient Egyptian would say that she had been visited by an animal. "There's a pig in my room; I saw a wolf last night." That visit, instead, says Hillman, is a theophany. *The ani-mal, that is, the god, wants something:* wants to do something for or to the dreamer, or wants to communicate. "Being saved by an animal makes the dreamer feel that there's something special or holy about them." Interestingly, he also re-jects much of a difference, so cherished by many, between the "animal out there," that is, the real animal, and the animal of the religious or dream-ing imagination. He reverses the tables instead: "I would rather think that the animal out there is also a psychic fact."

Why are animals gods? Or why, in the cases of Hathor or Hanuman, are gods animals? Hill-man speculates that it is their apparent quality of eternality, their permanent and cyclic stability, their unchangeability: "Animals are always the same, always returning like the sun." He also ob-serves their autonomy, the theme that we con-sidered earlier. Animals have an apparent alle-giance to a realm other than that of human culture and response. While this self-sufficiency may have been sacred to the Egyptians, he offers that to the later Western mind, it was demonic and threatening. Against animals' independence from the human sphere, he speculates, came compensatory moves, born out of a sense of threat: the legal degradation of animals into the category of property, the theological view that animals do not have souls, and the Carte-sian view that animals are not only inferior to human beings, but also are animated objects that cannot think and are incapable of feeling pain. Hillman argues that this putative ontologi-cal difference is so collectively internalized that we react to animals at opposite ends of a bi-polar spectrum: we exterminate them, consume them, or alternatively, de-nature them and senti-mentalize them: "I think the pet has become an anthropomorphized little animal, a little freak. It's completely in the human world. That's no longer an animal as totem or fetish or familiarus or tribe member. It's like a having a eunuch, as in the middle ages." [37] People have pets as an un-conscious religious activity, as a shamanistic me-diation of the spirit world so repressed in our culture. Pet owners? "Whether they know it or not they're still in the cult."

Would Hillman say the same of Natufian man from Galilee, buried with his arm reaching to his little dog? Does this burial reflect attenu-ated affection for a "pet" or rather some vanished eschatological association between the two? It is hard to know. All that seems clear is that the deep rapport still clinging after twelve millen-nia to the bones of these two interlocked be-ings must surely be something charged, something holy, something that social construction can only partially interpret, but to which the religious imagination, with its unflinching reach into the depths of the human heart, must instead respond.

NOTES

1. E.g., excavations at Sardis in Asia Minor dating from the early fifth century BCE show a practice of killing and dismembering young puppies, then burying them in pots in honor of Hermes Kandaulas ("Dog Throttler"). See Crawford H. Greenewalt, Jr., *Ritual Dinners in Early Historic Sardis,* University of California Publications, Classical Studies, v. 17 (Berkeley, University of California Press, 1978); George M. A. Hanfmann et. al., *Sardis from Prehistoric to Roman Times: Results of the Archaeological Exploration of Sardis, 1958–1975* (Cambridge: Harvard University Press, 1983); Lawrence E. Stager, "Why Were Hundreds of Dogs Buried at Ashkelon?" *Biblical Archaeology Review* 17, no. 3 (1991): 26–42. The Hittites also apparently practiced the apotropaic sacrifice of puppies.

2. Fred Bruemmer, *Glimpses of Paradise: The Marvel of Massed Animals* (Buffalo: Firefly Books, 2002).

3. Ibid, p. 10.

4. Paul Shepard, *The Others: How Animals Made Us Human* (Washington, D.C.: Island Press, 1996).

5. See, among other studies, Wallace Sife's acclaimed *The Loss of A Pet: A Guide to Coping with the Grieving Process When a Pet Dies* (Stafford, Australia: John Wiley & Sons, Howell Publishing, 1998).

6. Gene Myers, *Children and Animals: Social Development and Our Connection to Other Species* (Boulder, CO: Westview Press, 1998), p. 165.

7. See also Neil S. Price, ed., *The Archaeology of Shamanism* (London and New York: Routledge, 2001), especially essays by Andrzej Rozwadowski, "Materiality of Shamanism as a 'World-View': Praxis, Artefacts and Landscape," and Hans Christian Gulløv and Martin Appelt, "Special Objects—Special Creatures: Shamanistic Imagery and the Aurignacian Art of South-West Germany."

8. Paul Bahn, "Foreword," in Jean-Marie Chauvet, Éliette Brunel Deschamps, and Christian Hillaire, *Dawn of Art: The Chauvet Cave,* trans. by Paul Bahn (New York: Harry N. Abrams, 1996), p. 8. The association of a religious orientation toward animals with "childishness" or with less sophisticated theological thought is one of the most prominent features of developmentalist models of human religious history.

9. Alexander Marshack, "Images of the Ice Age," *Archaeology* 48, no. 4 (1995): 28–39.

10. Colin Renfrew and Paul Bahn, "What Did They Think? Cognitive Archaeology, Art and Religion," in *Archaeology: Theories, Methods, and Practice,* 2nd ed. (New York: Thames and Hudson, 1996), ch. 10, pp. 369–402.

11. Claude Lévi-Strauss, *Totemism* (Boston: Beacon Press, 1963), p. 89.

12. Stanley Walens, "Animals," in *The Encyclopedia of Religion,* ed. Mircea Eliade (New York: Macmillan Publishing Company, 1987), vol. 1, p. 291.

13. David Gordon White, *Myths of the Dog-Man* (Chicago: The University of Chicago Press, 1991).

14. Paul Shepard, "The Ark of the Mind," *Parabola* 8, no. 2 (1983): 54–59.

15. Shepard, *The Others,* p. 44.

16. Naming is based on visible anatomical clues —less often sound, feel, and smell—an attention to parts already practiced and now ritualized. Confronted with a strange animal, the ritual unfolds as follows: there is first a silent, staring look; then a turn of the head to the caregiver who responds by saying the animal's name; then the child's repetition aloud of the name; and then further staring. It begins with isolating and naming parts of the body, pigeonholing, making 'collections' of parts—noses, tails, legs, claws, ears. These exist not only as bits of creatures but as categories, a nose being the concrete example of the abstraction 'noses.' This procedure

is little noticed by parents because they are part of it, having experienced it themselves as children, and are predisposed to fall into the pattern as adults." Shepard, *The Others,* p. 44.

17. Speaking of the substitution of the resurrected Jesus for the ceremonially hunted bear who is born again in the spring is, according to Shepard, a collective psychic disaster. He writes, "Hunger for the wild animal's significance is reflected ... in the vicarious imagery of decorative arts, virtuoso and eccentric originality, pets, and media stereotypes."

18. Gail F. Melson, *Why the Wild Things Are: Animals in the Love of Children* (Cambridge: Harvard University Press, 2001), p. 4.

19. Ibid., pp. 4–5.

20. Things do not move smoothly for a child raised in the West from "primitive" identification with animals to dispassionate Darwinian hierarchy. Melson is quick to point out that later trajectories regarding animals are determined, not "natural," and are often highly difficult for children to parse: "Cultural messages are considerably more complex than an initial fusion of child with animal, followed by a simple assertion of human supremacy at the pinnacle of the evolutionary ladder. Children grapple with a complicated, often contradictory, mix of social codes governing animals and their treatment. There are creatures incorporated as family members, stamped out as pests, saved from extinction, and ground into Big Macs. The result is that children often mirror societal unease with culturally sanctioned uses of animals." Melson, *Why the Wild Things Are,* pp. 20–21.

21. The reference is to the painting by the eighteenth century Quaker painter Edward Hicks, "The Peaceable Kingdom," which charmingly represents the vision of Isaiah 11:6 that Andrew Linzey undertakes as a literal eschatological promise, one that describes the transfigured future. It is also the cover design chosen by Gail F. Melson for *Why the Wild Things Are.*

22. Stanley Walens, s.v. "Animals" in *The Encyclopedia of Religion,* 1:292. "It was believed that the stages of increasing religious awareness could be mapped by the changing role of animals in religion."

23. Sigmund Freud, *Totem and Taboo: Some Points of Agreement between the Mental Lives of Savages and Neurotics* (New York: W. W. Norton, 1950), p. 7; cited and discussed in Melson, *Why the Wild Things Are,* p. 21 and n. 20.

24. Michael D. Blackstock, *Faces in the Forest: First Nations Art Created on Living Trees* (Montreal and Kingston: McGill-Queen's University Press, 2001), pp. 57–58.

25. Interview with Joseph Epes Brown, *Parabola* 8, no. 2 (1983), "Animals," p. 7.

26. Walens, "Animals," p. 292.

27. [20]And God said, "Let the waters bring forth swarms of living creatures, and let birds fly above the earth across the dome of the sky. [21]So God created the great sea monsters and every living creature that moves, of every kind, with which the waters swarm, and every winged bird of every kind. And God saw that it was good. [22]God blessed them, saying, "Be fruitful and multiply and fill the waters in the seas, and let birds multiply on the earth." [23]And there was evening and there was morning, the fifth day.

[24]And God said, "let the earth bring forth living creatures of every kind: cattle and creeping things and wild animals of the earth of every kind." And it was so. [25]God made the wild animals of the earth of every kind, and the cattle of every kind, and everything that creeps upon the ground of every kind. And God saw that it was good.

[26]Then God said, "Let us make humankind in our image, according to our likeness; and let them have dominion over the fish of the sea, and over the birds of the air, and over the cattle, and over all the wild animals of the earth, and over every creeping thing that creeps upon the earth."

[27]So God created humankind in his image,
   in the image of God he created them;
   male and female he created them.

[28]God blessed them, and God said to them, "Be fruitful and multiply, and fill the earth and subdue it; and have dominion over the fish of the sea and over the birds of the air and over every living thing that moves upon the earth."

28. Andrew Linzey, *Animal Theology* (Urbana and Chicago: University of Illinois Press, 1994).

29. Paul Kueferle, "Frontiers of Peace," British Broadcasting Corporation, 1986.

30. See Kimberley C. Patton, "'He Who Sits in the Heavens Laughs': Recovering Animal Theology in the Abrahamic Traditions," *Harvard Theological Review* 93, no. 4 (2000): 401–34.

31. Frances Densmore, *Teton Sioux Music,* Smithsonian Institution, Bulletin of the Bureau of American Ethnology (Washington, D.C.), 1918.

32. Raymond de Coccola and Paul King, *The Incredible Eskimo: Life among the Barren Land Eskimo* (Surrey, B.C.: Hancock House, 1987), cited in Harold Seidelman and James Turner, *The Inuit Imagination: Arctic Myth and Sculpture* (New York: Thames and Hudson, 1994).

33. See especially Anne Fienup-Rirordan, ed., *Agayuliyararput: Kegginaqutm Kangiit-llu [Our Way of Making Prayer: Yup'ik Masks and the Stories They Tell],* trans. by Marie Meade (Seattle and London: Anchorage Museum of History and Art in association with the University of Washington Press, 1996).

34. Edward E. Evans-Pritchard, "The Meaning of Sacrifice Among the Nuer," *Journal of the Royal Anthropological Institute* 84 (1954): 21–33, reprinted in Jeffrey Carter, *Understanding Religious Sacrifice: A Reader* (London and New York: Continuum, 2003), p. 200; also see the treatment of ox-human relationships, Nuer poetry, and sacrificial exegesis in the 1970 film made by the Harvard Peabody Museum, "The Nuer."

35. Verne Dusenberry, *The Montana Cree: A Study in Religious Persistence* (Acta Universitatis Stockholmiensis, Stockholm Studies in Comparative Religion, Stockholm: University of Stockholm/ Almquist & Wiksell, 1962; Norman: University of Oklahoma Press, 1998).

36. James Hillman, "Let the Creatures Be," *Parabola* 8, no. 2 (1983), "Animals," pp. 49–53.

37. Ibid., p. 53.

Seeing the Terrain We Walk

Features of the Contemporary Landscape of "Religion and Animals"

PAUL WALDAU

Though some have suggested that the topic of this volume is a new emphasis in academia, religious traditions, and general public awareness, we do not begin this discussion of religion and animals completely anew. Rather, we rely heavily on much that has already been claimed within and without religion about the nonhuman lives amidst which we live. This volume takes an additional step in a fundamental exploration that has been an ongoing project of sensitive, compassionate humans for millennia. It is the editors' and contributors' hope to engender vigorous, lucid debate, and even to birth a new kind of community, addressing the many issues arising at the intersection where concern for and about "religion" crosses our inevitable interaction with the nonhuman living beings that we generally refer to as "animals."

As the multiplicity of views stated in this volume demonstrates, such discussion and community will be dominated by a pronounced *pluralism*. The remarkably diverse perspectives on nonhuman lives found throughout human-

kind's religious traditions offer, when collected together, an unparalleled opportunity to see certain complex features of the many different topics we might reasonably collect under the heading "Religion and Animals."

The Center of the Field—Obvious Inquiries

Newly emerging fields in academia do well to answer fundamental questions about the center of the field *and* its parameters. The center of the field, so to speak, includes at least two fundamental inquiries.

The first of these central inquiries is embodied in these questions—*How have religious traditions and their believers engaged other animals? Have they promoted or prevented obvious harms to the nearby biological individuals outside human communities, or have they ignored them altogether?*

Religious traditions have played an integral role in the recurring human tendency to evaluate the world around us. At times, some religions have advanced and maintained hierarchical evaluations, while others have seen and dismantled myriad forms of human subordination of marginalized groups. Various forms of "power-over-others" have been exercised by elite groups of humans for their own benefit, and even a cursory review of history reveals that both humans and nonhumans have been marginalized by elitist groups claiming some special status.[1] How have religious traditions handled potential human power over nonhumans? Have all religions utilized the human/nonhuman hierarchy so familiar in industrialized societies today that many unreflectively hold it to be the order of nature? Or is such a hierarchical ordering of earth's lives more on the order of mere custom and social construction masquerading as natural, even metaphysical, reality?

Religious views, or at the very least opinions dressed up in language derived from religious traditions, have often been understood to be the proximate or ultimate cause of overtly violent acts affecting living beings, human and nonhuman. The political, cultural, and economic aggression known in the Christian world as the "Holy Crusades" were understood quite differently in the Islamic world, where they were seen as a paradigmatic form of human-on-human violence. Even more common than the abundant wars pitting one human group against another have been human efforts to eradicate nonhuman forms of life. Philo, the first-century Jewish historian, used the image of a *continuous* war with other animals "whose hatred is directed … towards … mankind as a whole and endures … without bound and limit of time."[2] Since both common sense and the most rigorous of empirical investigation reveal that the vast majority of nonhuman animals do *not* war against humans, Philo's distorting image can be used to point out that one peculiar form of human-on-nonhuman harm, indeed, violence—a form that has, sadly, been institutionalized to an extraordinary degree—occurs when authorities of any kind, religious or not, pass along human caricatures and ignorance of nonhuman animals' actual realities.

At the same time, religious traditions have often been the primary movers of a compassionate engagement with other lives. The possibility of such an engagement has often been thought of as an eminently religious act, although that will sound strange to many modern believers who are heirs to a version of religion that has become virtually autistic about nonhuman realities. Still, religion as a whole has an extraordinarily distinguished record of fostering the ethical abilities that are the means by which humans can and often do care about other animals.

This first of the central inquiries in the religion and animals field is, thus, about matters we generally call "ethical" or "moral."

The second of the central inquiries is embodied in this question—*What roles have religious traditions had as mediators of views of nonhuman animals?* Even a cursory review of rituals, dances, myths, folktales, songs, poetry, iconography, and canons reveals that animal images of many kinds have been and remain central features of religious expression. Hence, the study of images of nonhuman animals found so broadly in religious symbolism must be an essential feature of the study of religion and animals.

Engaging this issue of images and religions' mediating role regarding views of nonhumans is no simple matter, however. Religious traditions include an extraordinary variety of stories in which nonhuman animals are mentioned in some way, and these have great differences in tenor and purpose. Some are positive and integrating while others demean and distort. Some honor the value of nonhuman lives as fully as others justify human use of any nonhuman animal for any purpose.

Of great importance in the field of religion and animals, then, is that nonhuman animals often have been "others" whose presence was important to religious believers. Various nonhuman animals have signified meaning, mediated theologically, or have provided an important dimension within rituals. Such constructions may or may not, however, honor those nonhuman animals' own lived realities; they may even obscure or intentionally eclipse those realities.

Thus by virtue of an examination of these multiple roles played by images and stories, we can ask, *Have the realities of nonhuman animals, their daily actualities and "historicities," as it were, been seen well?* As noted above, for those who care to see other animals accurately, what amounts to a subtle but powerful form of violence occurs when worldviews or belief systems promote specific forms of misunderstanding and caricature that mislead about the verifiable realities of nonhuman animals. So it is quite natural that practitioners within this field ask again and again if religious traditions have, in fact, passed along inadequate caricatures of nonhuman others in, say, a canonical scripture, such that a religious believer would be in error when relying literally on this information.[3]

Relatedly, in sacrificial contexts the use of animals, human and nonhuman alike, has resulted in lives being intentionally extinguished for purposes that are not those of the victims involved. Is the intentional, violent killing of the sacrificial victim always and everywhere a denial of that being's importance? Can such killing in a ritual or symbolic act be an affirmation of some kind? What are the values and assumptions that underlie affirmative answers to these questions about sacrifice? If answers on these challenging questions are different for human sacrificial victims than for nonhuman victims, why is that so?

Careful work on these basic questions about the transmission of images, as well as the inherently ethical questions raised above, leads to the conclusion that religious traditions have, historically, been the *principal vehicle* by which the status of nonhuman animals was evaluated by not only believers, but also entire cultures and their institutions. This evaluative role has been taken over in crucial respects, of course, by scientific and political traditions; but the importance of religious traditions as continuing mediators of views and values regarding nonhuman animals remains one of the most obvious features of humans' contemporary assessment of their relationship to the rest of life on this earth.

Parameters of the Field—Corollary Questions

Arrayed around these basic inquiries at the heart of the field of religion and animals are critically important issues that draw on the center, but which are, in important respects, conceptually distinct. Consider how the following inquiries beg questions about the parameters of this dynamic field.

Has there been tension between, on the one hand, religious constructions of animals and, on the other, various admittedly secular views? For example, how do we treat religion-based views that are relatively less compassionate than secular engagements with other animals that are, by consensus, sensitive and compassion-driven?[4] And what of the difference between traditional religious claims about other animals and claims that rely solely on fact-based perceptions of their (that is, nonhuman animals') realities? If a religious view can be convincingly demonstrated to be inaccurate in important respects, how might that view be analyzed in its religious importance or its relevance to our ethical abilities? Given the central role that religious traditions have had, and continue to have, as mediators of ethics, worldviews, and in particular images of nonhuman animals and their place in our moral schemes, these and many other additional questions arise when one undertakes the study of religion and animals.

There are other kinds of problems as well. Can religious traditions, by virtue of their sacred histories, whether oral, written or part of a nonverbal art such as dance or iconography, be said to have "seen" any nonhuman animals well, realistically, *or in ways that empirical investigation cannot?* In general, what is the relationship between sacred history and the complex task of any human trying to grasp another animal's actual realities? Can religions, in fact, play a special role in helping humans engage nonhumans?

Scholars today are beginning to unravel in greater detail what roles, if any, concerns about nonhuman animals, and indeed the nonhumans themselves, have had within the worldviews and lives of religious communities. Detailed work on such issues produces, as so often is the case, myriad additional questions. Have animals' roles as vehicles for religious significance enhanced or weakened their status as "others" to which religious believers and communities respond? Have those instances where nonhuman animals served elevated roles ever worked to subordinate human interests? Have religious institutions treated nonhuman animals differently than have individual religious believers? In what different ways have other living beings been members of the incredibly diverse communities that religious believers have developed and nurtured? Have religious concerns about nonhumans affected the status of animals generally in *nonreligious contexts?*

While these questions and many others raise the possibility of dramatic differences existing among religious traditions on matters of humans' interaction with the living beings around us, questions often have power well beyond their answers. For example, the very asking of these questions tests both the parameters of the emerging field of religion and animals and whether past modes of inquiry were adequate to the simplest of tasks at the center of this field. Further, can religion and animals inquiries yield helpful observations about the nature of religion? Do such questions go beyond identification of boundaries for the study of religion and animals by revealing that humans' interactions with nonhumans inevitably pervade numerous fields of inquiry and cannot, therefore, be studied in any manner other than through a robust interdisciplinary approach?

Seeing the Pluralism

Even the most cursory investigation across religious traditions reveals an astonishing array of answers to the most basic questions about what the relation of humans to nonhumans has been. Some religious believers have noticed some other animals and taken them seriously even as other believers' absolute dismissal of nonhumans has dominated their local human community.[5]

If those studying religion and animals see this diversity, especially as it is manifested in various ways across different traditions of symbols, practical engagement, and stories[6] bequeathed to us by our ancestors, the differences noted can inform all of us about the vast range of human possibilities regarding the nonhuman lives around us. In fact, the plurality of views offers important opportunities to probe layers within the views each of us has inherited. In effect, awareness of the plurality of views enables one to carry out an archeological exploration, so to speak, of the scholarly, institutional, cultural, or personal claims one has inherited. For example, each inquirer was born into a particular way of talking about and treating the local nonhumans, as well as traditions of generalization about all nonhuman life. Probing that inheritance offers the possibility of seeing its peculiar strengths and limitations. Through such efforts, we can see important features of our own claims, as well as features of other, competing claims regarding humans' place on this earth relative to the place and realities of other living beings. This same exercise of personal archeology can also help us see our ideas about our place and that of others in complex ecosystems and even the Earth as a whole.

Walking This Terrain

Consider the everyday image of a human traveler negotiating a path—limited by the traveler's bipedal body, a primate's vision-dominated sensory abilities, the imagination of those who made this path, and the traveler's inherited story of why this path matters at all. Similarly, when we approach our Earth's nonhuman lives, we may take a path composed of an inherited set of symbols, practices, and stories regarding them. If so, we again negotiate the terrain before us with important constraints and limitations— we might well have inherited an entirely different set of symbols, practices, and stories. Crucially, each person's particular heritage of ideas —whatever it is—is no less constraining than the obvious limits conferred on each of us by our limited sensory abilities. Just as we can't hear humpback whales' ever-changing communications in the sea while on a terrestrial path, our forebears didn't tell us about those "songs" because our species had no detailed knowledge of these complex communications' existence in any detail until the last half of the twentieth century.[7]

Such limitations, whether of our own personal or cultural inheritance or those imposed by our natural finitudes, underscore how truly embedded humans are in their abilities and inheritances as they trod whatever paths they have chosen to take in life. We are, to use religio-ecological terms one finds in the vibrant discussion of religion and ecology, creatures of vision embedded in the land. Can our vision, physical *and* cultural, see other creatures fully? Many nonhumans negotiate their own paths with extravagantly different sensibilities, such as the exquisitely sensitive olfactory capacities of elephants and dogs or the echolocation abilities of dolphins. From our paths, it is easily discerned that dolphins live in an entirely foreign, watery world—but what, in fact, do they do with these foreign (to us) abilities and their discernibly large, complex brains? This is not easily known by land dwellers, for our paths go elsewhere.

Indeed, for each embodied creature the challenge is to negotiate one's daily terrain with genetically programmed—and limited—senses. Our eminently human challenge is to use our

eyes, our other limited senses, and our all-important ethical abilities and imagination to see the path before us—where have we walked, and where *can* we walk, in our relationship to the rest of the animal kingdom?

No matter how we may answer this central question,[8] and no matter whether our answer weights more heavily humans' obvious special abilities or our equally obvious connections and similarities to other life forms, some simple realities must ground us as we walk any path along which we try to see the field of religion and animals.

The Realities of Other Animals

Most simply, there is a pressing need to allow the realities of "animals" to be a factor in our assessment of religious views of the living beings outside our species. Traditional views may, at times and in important ways, enable us to see dimensions of nonhuman animals. But it is disingenuous to ignore that at least some traditional views have been dominated by caricature and bias, and have thereby created important limitations for believers who might opt for engaging the actual animals as honestly, fully, and fairly as possible for the human spirit.

If this simplest of needs is to be met, uncritical reliance on inherited views will be an unjustifiable tactic unless we conclude that those inherited views are responsive to the realities of nonhuman animals. And to draw this conclusion, one must in some manner or another engage competing claims about nonhuman animals, whether they be found in other religious traditions or in various traditions of empirical investigation.

The Realities of Interdisciplinary Work

Information and perspectives found in many disciplines, including all sorts of empirical investigation traditions, are of great relevance to our understanding of other animals. The animal piece, in fact, can be found throughout human life, as attested fully by the essays in this volume. But so much of great relevance to the field of religion and animals has been, traditionally, outside the purview and distinctive contributions of religious studies, theology, history of religions, sociology of religion, and anthropology of religion.

The information to be found in many life sciences is of obvious importance.[9] Equally important are the sensitive and ethically expansive perspectives found in ecological and environmental studies, social and environmental justice critiques, and the many different forms of the animal protection movement.[10]

Respecting Multiple Traditions of Empirical Observation

A full engagement with the power and diversity of religious views on nonhuman animals has interesting benefits. It can help one see better the impoverished nature of worldviews that, under the guise of being purely scientific, are instead merely "scientistic."[11] It is well known that the science establishment has had, historically, some serious shortcomings in a number of important respects, some of which have dealt with nonhuman animals. Enlightening appraisals of this important but complex history reveal extended periods of scientific investigation overdetermined by agenda-laden paradigms and distorting reductionist ideologies that admit of no other valid means of human knowledge. Analyses of this complex aspect of our scientific traditions and the occasional lack of humility in the scientific establishment come from both within and without the halls of science. Of particular relevance here are many astute observations of informed philosophers of science, theologians, and ethicists.[12]

Empirical assessments of the realities around us, including other animals, are not, of course, the province of science(s) alone. Religious tra-

ditions often hold fascinating insights that reflect empirical observations.[13] The success of both scientific empiricism and other traditions of empirical observation is grounded in the fact that each of us as an embodied individual naturally engages in empirical investigation of our surroundings.

In the midst of our highly individualized, thoroughly grounded lives as one of Earth's terrestrials, each of us can, as a moral being, consider the impacts of our actions on those "others" nearby, whether they are human or nonhuman. We are all acutely aware that we have very special capacities for insights into the value and sufferings of living beings. If we take the time to notice the living beings around us, we see much more than atomized individuals. We see, of course, individuals in *their* context—that is, amidst their families, communities, populations, species, and larger ecological webs.

Modern Western ways of talking about humans often place very high value on the importance of individuals (for example, the notion of "rights" held by individuals is often held to be the high water mark of ethical and even legal development).[14] Yet it is uncontroversial these days to assert that other ecological realities are also an essential, even if unseen, part of any individual's life. That there can be important relationships between and among species is the operative insight in Thomas Berry's eloquent observation in the Prologue, "we cannot be truly ourselves in any adequate manner without all our companion beings throughout the earth. This larger community constitutes our greater self." As Darwin showed in such detail, life is indeed a dance of many partners.

Individual mammals, for example, whether members of the human or any other species, are always individuals in *social* circumstances.[15] This all-important mutual integration of lives, often downplayed in atomized conceptualizations of "person" and "ethics," can be seen in the simplest features and basic circumstances of any individual mammal's life. Indeed, we *cannot* understand any living being's "individuality" without considering such interrelatedness within a community. Further, since all life grows and dies in a larger web, any individual, regardless of his or her species membership, is *fully* seen and understood only within that web. This interconnection is epitomized by Gary Snyder's Buddhist-inspired observation that "there is no death that is not somebody's food, no life that is not somebody's death."[16]

The discrete existence of "individuals," like the existence of different species, is one of the most striking and least disputable of biological data, but a heavy concentration on individuality alone will mislead if is not balanced against the connectedness of family, community, species, similar life forms, and, indeed, all life. And what is true of our ability to engage meaningfully the realities of individuals is also true of our comprehension of "species"—we cannot understand any individual or any species outside its larger ecological context.

These salient realities of interconnectedness in no way require those who study religion and animals to downplay claims that individuality and species are important dimensions of our understanding of biological life. But this profound and defining interconnectedness does suggest that *any* vision or account of life that focuses heavily on just individual-level phenomena or just species-level phenomena will be altogether too one-dimensional to engage the fullest range of humans' remarkable abilities to notice and care about "others."

Embracing the Breadth of Our Ethical Natures

Taking the time to notice and be serious about such realities has, of course, ethical dimensions. How can one know which individuals to consider important if one doesn't know them in context? The questions "Which individuals will be seen?" and "Will they be only humans?" beg further questions about social and ecological realities and connections. Together, these questions underscore the inherently ethical nature

of seeing beyond individuals, beyond any one species, and beyond caricatured images of "animals" advanced by any single tradition of human valuing. A moral agent, to see the world well and take responsibility for her impacts upon "others," *must* see complementary, larger biological realities that are central parts of any whole life.

Thus, if we are to honor what each culture, through its religions or other ethically sensitive views of life, has proudly asserted about humans —namely, that *we are ethical beings*—we come to this simple issue: who are the others about whom or which I *should* care? It is axiomatic that such a purely ethical question is integrally related to the very core of any religious sensibility. All versions of religious ethics, in one way or another, postulate that humans, as moral actors, have an obligation to know the consequences of their own actions. And if engaging the other lives on the earth—whether individual animals, populations, integrated parts of a web of life in a specific econiche, or the whole earth—has ethical dimensions, then refusals to take such realities into account necessarily do as well. An implication of the claim that "the larger community constitutes our greater self" is, then, that we, as ethical beings, must try to learn about the "others" in our "larger community/greater self." It is not just knowledge of others animals' realities, then, that has potential ethical implications, *but our ignorances as well.*

If so, we find ourselves in a quandary about how to handle traditional claims about nonhuman animals. Given that taking religious claims seriously is a "must" if the adherents are to be engaged, can we take each and every element of specific, dismissive claims about nonhuman animals in the same way as those adherents do? Merely passing along a view because it is traditional is risky business, for our forebears made claims that are, if used as propositional claims about the world and animals surrounding us, often demonstrably wrong. It is a commonplace in modern education that an unreflective adherence to traditional claims has often been the excuse for failing to challenge inherited prejudices. Blind allegiance to inherited values—women are inferior to men, blacks were destined by God to be the slaves of whites—was often the engine, so to speak, of the race, ethnic, and gender prejudices identified so fully in the twentieth century. These biases were often premised on an obviously fallacious reasoning process—absence of evidence was converted into evidence of absence. In other words, a refusal to admit evidence of the oppressed beings' special natures was converted into evidence that they lacked any important qualities. But it was simply the refusal to look, the failure to take these marginalized beings seriously, that created the alleged "absence of evidence." The field of religion and animals is confronted with a simple question: Has this same kind of refusal, and in particular its self-inflicted ignorance, been taking place in some religions and in education because of some humans' deep biases against members of nonhuman species? Have *we* refused to take *them* seriously or to notice *their* realities, and thus converted a manufactured absence of evidence of their moral importance into evidence of an absence of moral importance?

Seeing the Terrain's Hills and Valleys: Goals in Studying Religion and Animals

To be sure, certain well-known limitations do govern us with regard to our engagement with the lives of other animals. In one sense, humans are typical primates—vision, rather than some other sensory apparatus, dominates our terrestrial existence. But as earth's precocious animals, it is well within our abilities to go further than mere appearance even when perception of the details of nonhuman lives is notoriously difficult. Above all, if we are to live up to our important claim that we have considerable moral, religious, and philosophical abilities, we must see past our own limits and biases. This means we, as embodied, vision-dominated, ambulating animals, must get beyond earthbound inclinations

to focus on our immediate surroundings—our next step, our physical wants, our family, our limited communities of belief, race, and species. Visionaries like Thomas Berry help us "see" further, using our imagination to assess where and how our community "walks" among all living beings.

Some religious traditions are well-known for the breadth of their attempt to engage other lives—Jainism and some indigenous traditions are often cited for their regard for nonhuman lives. A few religious traditions, and in some case quasi-religions, have at one time or another advanced only the interests of a single race or a single nation. Other religious traditions have focused primarily, even exclusively, on a commitment to all *and only* humans. Yet, as familiar as it is to contemporary ears, a commitment to our own species only, challenged as "speciesism" in modern times, is not characteristic of all religions or even all subtraditions of those religions that in their mainline interpretation are dominated by this limitation.[17]

In the face of such pluralism, the journey one undertakes when exploring religion and animals is obviously multidimensional, which suggests the existence of a number of diverse goals that are needed if one is to travel very far in this exploration. Along the many paths into the emerging field of religion and animals, one encounters extraordinary ways in which any human's understanding of other living beings, whether human or nonhuman, is a product of "social construction"—that is, the images that dominate are as much or more a product of peculiar, culture-bound generalizations and presuppositions as they are an immediate and personal response to the observable realities of the animals who are being "described/constructed." The prevalence of this phenomenon is easier to discern when one looks at a large collection of views, whether from different cultures or multiple eras from a cultural tradition that has grown and evolved over long periods of time. For example, if one looks across the temporal sequence of dominant views of nonhuman animals in the Western intellectual tradition, one finds not a single story, but an accumulation of changing paradigms.[18]

Similarly, if one looks across a large number of traditions, such as those represented in this volume, one more easily can perceive and appreciate the socially constructed features of each view. Social construction is also more readily apparent if one compares a number of views dominated by the all-too-common claim that they are the *only* answer to all interesting questions pertaining to religion and animal issues. Such exclusivism happens in different subtraditions. It is sometimes found, for example, in various traditions that make claims about religious writings they deem to be infallible revelation full of propositional content about, among other things, nonhuman animals. *But exclusivism also occurs in certain scientific traditions,* such as behaviorism or other scientistic claims, that aggressively assert their own validity in ways that exclude all other human approaches to nonhuman animals' realities.

Pluralism can be, then, an ally when one is assessing one's own or others' understanding of the diverse universe of issues intuitively grouped under the umbrella we are calling religion and animals. Acknowledging both pluralism and the diversity of issues also helps one see how relevant the religion and animals field is to contemporary debates over ethics or morality. Indeed, if one looks generally at the many parts of any one complex contemporary society (take, for example, any industrialized country), it will be apparent that there are many different views of nonhuman animals, some of which are in direct conflict with others. The pluralism is, in effect, educational, and forces one to consider the origin and finitudes of any one view claiming to be exhaustive or definitive.

THE GOAL OF HONORING DISTINCTIVENESS

When one looks across human cultures in this way one becomes increasingly aware of how unique many different accounts of "animals" are. The diversity is couched in many distinct traditions of discourse (that is, ways of talking about the issue), diverse iconographic traditions, and wildly conflicting propositional claims, all of which contrast with one another so dramatically that interested observers can see more readily the dynamics and tensions of "animal views" put together by any one human society. This is as true of culturally constructed views that promote compassion as it is of dismissive caricatures framed by domination-oriented humans.

At the very least, we can, through engaging a broad collection of human stories about other animals, see more easily that each human is a tradition-based primate who grows up amidst, and thus will likely rely heavily on, a specific set of inherited views and discourse purporting to inform regarding nonhuman animals. Given the diversity of human cultures, whether any one person's inherited stories are "historicities" (here used in the sense of accounts that inform us well about other animals' realities) is a complex, humility-generating inquiry.

Simply said, humans, as a collective, have many diverse traditions of mapping the world, ourselves, and, of course, the surrounding communities of life. One goal that scholars, students, and inquiring minds of all kinds can achieve is the sorting out of these many story lines, honoring each in its own right as a meaningful narrative even if it is not, as its more literal proponents may claim it to be, an exhaustive inventory of all interesting issues. This approach need not reduce our stories to mere constructions, for it is possible to be quite sensitive to both the existential and religious importance of inherited views at the same time one assesses their culturally distinct, and relative, features.

To be sure, this is all rather humbling for the scholar, for she may not have too many clues about how to sort out these and other issues in a way that is both faithful to those who hold this story dear and at the same helpful about what such religious believers in fact know of the animals portrayed. At the very least, however, the humility can prevent the kind of arrogance too many scholars have exhibited in the past when interpreting other humans' reading of the significance of life around them, an example of which appears in the following:

> Civilization, or perhaps education, has brought with it a sense of the great gulf that exists between man and the lower animals. ... In the lower stages of culture, whether they be found in races which are, as a whole, below the European level, or in the uncultured portion of civilized communities, the distinction between men and animals is not adequately, if at all, recognized. ... The savage ... attributes to the animal a vastly more complex set of thoughts and feelings, and a much greater range of knowledge and power, than it actually possesses ... It is therefore small wonder that his attitude towards the animal creation is one of reverence rather than superiority.[19]

Here, both nonhumans *and* humans ("the savage," that is, those "below the European level") are deprecated. Surely, the arrogance of this passage reveals the risks of assuming that one's own view is the "common sense" view. Humility is needed whenever one attempts to evaluate "others," whether they be human or nonhuman. Crossing two enormously complex subjects such as religion and animals creates a paradigmatic example of the need for humility —we are humbled not only by the sheer number of different views of what "an animal" is,[20] but also by the daunting complexity and diversity of both the nonhuman world and the remarkably persistent "religious" abilities of humankind. We humans have been using our abilities to engage nonhumans for millennia, and throughout the history of this engagement there has been a stunning amount of religious speculation. Our abilities to construe realities as diverse as "animals" and "religion" are, not surprisingly, a matter of debate. Both are realms that have dimensions not immediately apparent to our limited visual abilities, and neither realm is, much to our chagrin, universally accessible to us as bipedalists.

THE GOAL OF WALKING TOGETHER, SEEING BETTER

How else, other than via insights that come through personal humility, might we "see the terrain" better? Of the utmost importance is what our collective efforts might achieve, for it is within our genius to be social and, through such togetherness, see better and walk further. Working collectively, we can see well the extraordinary diversity along a continuum of options. These options range from, on the one side, views that are radically exclusive of all others (including human others—egotism, for example), to, on the other side, views that are radically inclusive (such as certain "deep ecologies"[21]).

The extraordinary range of options along the continuum between the most exclusivist and inclusivist claims regarding any individual's relation to all other life is best explored, and thus seen better, in a collective fashion—as we do in this volume. Consider what kind of consortium might best see the features of any one culture's claims about humans' complex existential realities compared to those of all other animals. Most likely, such complexities are best seen by a cooperative consortium composed of, on the one hand, some believers and scholars who grew up within the culture in question and, on the other hand, some who were raised in other cultures but who in good faith are interested in seeing as fully as possible our target culture's construction of "religion and animals" problems.

In such a setting, we are likely to achieve a frank appraisal about what "we," that is, the human community in its collective wisdom, do and don't know of other animals' lives. Through such inquiries, we can assess whether specific claims about "our humanity" and "superiority" are overstated. Further, we can assess as well as possible whether any one interpretation is dominated by, or bereft of, the arrogance that all too often has characterized a particular culture's self-assessment in relation to either other cultures or nonhuman lives.

Note what such a foregrounding of *communal* inquiry confirms—humans are crucially important, complex beings. Such cooperative work, however, leads us to see better how assertions regarding human superiority have often been made by repudiating, caricaturing, and being arrogant about our status relative to some "others" (whether nonhuman *or* human) about whom those making the dismissive claims have been, frankly, entirely ignorant or, at least, poorly informed.

THE GOAL OF UNDERSTANDING LANGUAGE AND SYMBOLS

Working collectively also offers great possibilities for raising our own self-consciousness about the manner in which each of us has been trained to talk about these issues. Close attention to the medium of language can promote care in choosing how we will talk to one another on the subject of "animals" after we have come to some understanding about the stories and claims we have inherited from our respective religions, cultures, communities, and families.

Collective work also offers the opportunity of meeting the important challenge of achieving a better understanding of the nature and diversity of our own uses of symbols other than language. Interestingly, while at times human cultures have risen elegantly above the literal in our symbolic flights, the symbols used sometimes rely on portrayals of nonhuman animals that disable, even cripple, our imaginations by needless and ignorant repudiations of those other beings' lives. At times, the repudiations amount to nothing more or less than the trivial claims that nonhuman animals are not human, or that their lives are not meaningful in ways that our limited abilities can appreciate.

Importantly, our understandings of nonhuman animals reside in many places other than our speech and writings, for it is not our discursive and propositional claims that alone disclose our views of other animals. Of at least equal importance are the disclosures found in the rhythms and practices of our daily lives and the complex multivalencies of dances, rendered art, ritual, myth, folktale, song, poetry, and the other arts found so universally throughout our cultures.

If we become sensitive to these media, engaging as fully as we can not only what they suggest about other animals' lives but also other humans' actions toward the living beings and whole ecosystems beyond our own cultural spheres, each of us might more easily recognize our place in the surrounding realities, not to mention the strengths and limitations of our own reasoning patterns.

Walking together in this way, we will at times discover refusals to reason and investigate regarding nonhuman animals. And we will have to grapple with the tenacity with which central institutions in some traditions, not the least of which those prevalent in the Western academic world, have held the view that only humans are mentally complex and organize the world with cognitive maps. The mantra in the Western tradition has at times been something like "only humans are rational or intelligent," "only humans communicate via a language or with concepts," "only humans are concerned for others or possess social rules," "only humans are self-aware," "only humans have cultures," or "only humans are persons." Upon examination, such claims are problematic for any number of reasons. For example, "rational" and "intelligent" have meant many things,[22] and intellectually respectable academics now apply many treasured terms and concepts to some nonhuman animals.[23]

Challenges to Collective Efforts

Numerous challenges await even the best-orchestrated collective efforts. Practical and political hurdles are often severe. Traditional practices and vested economic interests can entrench dismissals, even denials, of other animals' complexities—for example, many people do not care to hear that farm animals are, by scientific or ethical measure, sentient beings that suffer, have personalities, or exhibit intelligence. Attitudes anchored in traditional practices or ways of speaking about nonhumans can develop much as did attitudes toward the enslavement or subordination of some humans—various beneficiaries of the practice assert that the practices are beyond moral challenge and even reflect, as explained below, "the order of nature." Questioning of culturally accepted ways of treating nonhumans can become, just as questioning of certain human-on-human oppressions became, challenges to vested interests that result in the marginalization of the believer or scholar who dares to inquire into the basic morality of the practice or the existence of alternatives, recalling G. K. Chesterton's observation that "Men can always be blind to a thing so long as it is big enough."[24]

Epistemological Hurdles

We are, as a species and as individuals, limited in our abilities to speak about other animals' realities. One reason is the well-known problem of determining with any certainty the inner realities of other individuals' mental lives.[25] As some authors in this volume note, there is a developed debate over the place of other animals' mental, emotional, social, and personal complexities. Many who have reviewed the empirical evidence draw the conclusion that there are some animals outside the human species that have lives incomparably richer than the caricatures one finds in various Western "authorities" such as Descartes.[26]

Without solving the complex epistemological dilemmas that plague knowing what others, including humans, are like, one can say modestly that some human learning about other species is possible. Indeed, this claim is implicit in any *dismissal* of them as much as it is in

any affirmation of them. The English philosopher S. Clark notes, "We can reason our way to understand the world and its denizens, if indeed we can, because the ways of the world are embedded in our very being."[27] Savage-Rumbaugh, on the basis of long experience with other great apes, notes that humans and chimpanzees inhabit a common perceptual world, "a sort of joint awareness that leads to joint perception and joint knowing" such that "what gains my attention is often the same as what gains theirs."[28] The obvious physical similarities have long been controversial, as evidenced by the 1747 comments of Linnaeus, the founder of modern systems used in classifying living beings:

> I demand of you, and of the whole world, that you show me a generic character ... by which to distinguish between Man and Ape. I myself most assuredly know of none. I wish somebody would indicate one to me. But, if I had called man an ape, or vice versa, I would have fallen under the ban of all ecclesiastics. It may be that as a naturalist I ought to have done so.[29]

Beyond these, psychological similarities have repeatedly been asserted in modern times, as when experiments that inflict harm on other primates are carried out for the sole purpose of understanding *human* psychopathology.[30]

Even with our limited ability to assess with absolute certainty the types of complexity in the lives of other animals, the question arises, are their lives rich enough on their own terms to merit the consideration of humans as responsible, caring, and informed moral agents? Some religious believers emphatically insist that it is the heart and soul of their religiosity to recognize that nonhuman lives command our ethical attention (think of Francis of Assisi or the historical Buddha), while other religious believers insist that only human beings should command such attention.

Getting Beyond Self-Inflicted Ignorance

Another challenge to collective efforts to see religion and animals issues clearly arises because
entire cultures remain, by choice, profoundly
ignorant of realities that are easily ascertained by
those who care to look at the daily lives of other
animals. Of relevance to the study of religious
views of nonhuman animals is the fact that caricature, ignorance, and dismissal are all too evident in many religious traditions even as some
authorities and believers within those traditions
adamantly insist that humans (or, at least, "true"
believers within their own tradition) epitomize
human ethical capabilities.

If, as has often been pointed out, ethical systems will, on the whole, be limited by the entities that individuals are prepared to notice and
take seriously,[31] then self-inflicted ignorance can
dramatically affect the ethical stances of religious believers. Ignorance has limited humans
across place and history in many areas—the oppressions of patriarchy, slavery, racism, jingo-
ism, fundamentalism, and phobias regarding
sexual preference offer many examples of one
group of humans using inherited biases based
on ignorance and caricature against other humans for the explicit purpose of excluding the
marginalized humans from the most basic of
moral protections.

The tendency to ignorance and caricature
can also be found when the issue is other animals' realities. Speciesist attitudes, which claim
only human interests need matter to the moral
agent, can be kept in place by self-inflicted ignorance. Such exclusivist attitudes can also be kept
in place by something other than myopia—in
addition, assumptions about the paradigmatic
nature of inherited cultural assumptions can do
the same. At the end of the eighteenth century, the influential theologian William Paley
focused on a common feature of our sociologi-
cally held knowledge when he took Aristotle to
task for advancing the view that some humans
are by nature, and thus should be, slaves to other
humans.

Aristotle lays down, as a fundamental and self-
evident maxim, that nature intended barbarians
to be slaves; and proceeds to deduce from this
maxim a train of conclusions, calculated to justify the policy which then prevailed. ... Nothing is so soon made as a maxim; and it appears
from the example of Aristotle, that authority and
convenience, education, prejudice, and general
practice, have no small share in the making of
them; and that the laws of custom are very apt
to be mistaken for the order of nature.[32]

Attempts to justify prevailing policies and
practices—especially those buttressed by an attitude that equates inherited, socially mediated
beliefs with the order of nature or an absolute
ethical norm—can impede collective efforts to
see religion and animals issues better, and can
inadvertently help intentionally inflicted ignorance to prevail.[33]

When a refusal to inquire into a nonhuman
animal's complexities becomes an arrogant refusal to inquire at all, this tendency impover-
ishes human ethical abilities dramatically. The
example of opinions about wolves is instructive,
for there is a remarkable shortfall between carefully pieced together information about daily
lives of wolves and the image of wolves that
dominates certain circles. Midgley, after reviewing the current state of knowledge about the
lives of real wolves, suggested how remarkably
different the actual biological beings are from
the image of a wolf "as he appears to the shepherd at the moment of seizing a lamb from the
fold." She notes that those who have taken the
time to watch wolves "have found them to be,
by human standard, paragons of steadiness and
good conduct." Summarizing, she comments,

Actual wolves, then, are not much like the folk-
figure of the wolf, and the same is true for apes
and other creatures. But it is the folk-figure that
has been popular with philosophers. They have
usually taken over the popular notion of lawless
cruelty which underlies such terms as "brutal,"
"bestial," "beastly," "animal desires," and so on,

and have used it uncriticized, as a contrast to illuminate the nature of man.[34]

Regarding our cultural forebears' use of inherited caricatures regarding wolves' and many other nonhuman animals' true abilities and traits, there is this irony—these humans claimed to be seeking knowledge even as they perpetuated the self-inflicted ignorance that they inherited from their own society at birth.

The tendency to caricatures of nonhuman animals has become a prominent feature of some of the most influential human cultural traditions in today's world. It is particularly evident in certain humans' steadfast refusal to employ constructively those very abilities that distinguish humans as excellent discoverers of the realities surrounding us. It is interesting to assess how prone to, and very capable of, rationalizations humans can be when, regarding the possibility that other animals may call upon our ethical natures, we deny the extent of our wonderful ethical abilities because we are spellbound by socially inflicted ignorance. But through continuing, intentional refusals to inquire beyond what we have inherited, caricature of other animals can remain so rampant in some groups that one is tempted to change Aristotle's optimistic "All men desire to know" (*Metaphysics* 1.980a22) into the more realistic "Most men, and many women as well, prefer the caricature whenever it serves their interest."

The Stark Realities of Present Practices

Challenges are also raised by any number of long-standing practices, such as the deceptively simple issue of "farm animals." The very phrase calls to mind bucolic images of pastures, cuds, and swishing tails. But few religious authorities in any tradition have concerned themselves with the modern phenomenon known widely as "factory farming."[35] The complex use of nonhumans as experimental subjects in "biomedical experimentation" has drawn some, though

by no means much, attention.[36] In the former, food animals are raised in conditions that are, relative to traditional husbandry techniques, extraordinarily harsh. In the latter, individual animals are intentionally harmed based on their status as experimental models for primarily human diseases.[37]

Given that, in terms of both numbers and kinds of cruelty inflicted, the present treatment of "farm animals" in the industrialized, "developed" world could be characterized as worse than at any other time or place in history, one might not unreasonably expect to hear religious voices regarding such practices. Religious traditions have at times spoken out on related phenomena such as ecological problems and globalization, and some subtraditions in religion have a distinguished history of speaking out on social and economic injustices.

But religious traditions have often been silent on the issue of nonhuman animals. This is important because religious traditions remain in the overwhelming majority of cases the principal influence on the criteria by which believers chose to value and protect, or demean and harm, living beings. Religious traditions, with their impact on worldviews and lifestyles, influence not only the way adherents think, see, and talk about the world, but also the ways they act toward "others," whether human or otherwise. Further, even if they remained unconcerned for the nonhuman animals affected by husbandry and medical experimentation practices that involve cruelty, a religious tradition's ethical authorities might nonetheless be concerned with the effect such practices might have on the development and maintenance of ethical sensitivities and character. Thus, rather than silence, one might well expect to find that religious authorities work to stay informed about what is happening in our world, thus gaining information they can use to dispel ignorance about any practice, including the current treatment of nonhuman animals.

At the very least, some religious traditions have underwritten many notions, claims, prac-

tices, and rationalizations that not only legitimize, but also justify and promote, extraordinary and often unnecessary harm to nonhuman
animals.[38] A recent example can be found in
the revised Catholic Catechism: "Animals, like
plants and inanimate things, are by nature destined for the common good of past, present and
future humanity."[39]

This is, of course, at odds with much else in
the Catholic tradition, let alone the rest of the
Abrahamic tradition and the Indic, certain Chinese, and many indigenous traditions. And, empirically speaking, it is hardly the stuff of basic
observations, as is evidenced in John Muir's
comment, "I have never yet happened upon a
trace of evidence that seemed to show that any
one animal was ever made for another as much
as it was made for itself."[40]

It is not, however, merely the lack of evidence
for such claims that calls them into question,
or pushes us as inquiring moral agents to pursue this issue further. It is also our heightened
awareness of a kind of arrogance that forms the
basis of many human claims about "superiority."
This arrogance is in tension with other, arguably more fundamental religious insights that
push one to respect life, the integrity of ecological webs, and an integration of humans into a
wider, natural world that is less anthropocentrically conceived.

Additionally, there is what might be called an
"ethics of inquiry" that characterizes our pursuit of knowledge. This is the obvious tendency
of some, though certainly not all, humans to
explore the realities amidst which we live. Such
an ethics of inquiry pushes one to state as honestly as possible what one finds in the world,
even if the discovered reality does not support
inherited views of humans, nonhumans, or human superiority.

Many of these elements—harsh realities of
present practices, self-inflicted ignorance, adamant refusals to investigate, adherence to traditional dismissals in the face of greater awareness of other animals' realities, and the appeal
of an ethics of inquiry—have driven various

ethics- and compassion-based critiques of the
treatment of nonhuman animals that are consonant with much else that is religious—personal humility, critiques of human arrogance,
and concerns for taking responsibility for one's
actions.

Role of Religious Traditions

The framing of ethical issues in many contemporary religious traditions remains overwhelmingly anthropocentric, as it is in most of academia and the secular world generally.[41] There
are signs within even the most anthropocentric
of contemporary religious traditions of a growing interest and even commitment to broader
concerns, signaled perhaps most prominently
by the emergence of ecological concerns challenging the most exclusivist forms of anthropocentrism.[42] Ignorance of the realities of nonhuman animals, however, remains profound,
complicating the ability of religious traditions
to respond. For those religious traditions that
lack mechanisms for identifying and accepting
changing information or new perspectives generated in spheres of influence outside the tradition, the very existence and implications of new
developments or information can cause them to
retreat into a conservative, even fundamentalist,
stance on relevant issues.

The Ironies of Indifference

Religious indifference to the animal protection
movement involves certain ironies, not the least
of which are the following.

There are important connections between
the risk of harms to humans that arise from and
are closely connected to the harms that some
humans do to nonhumans—this connection is
sometimes referred to as interlocking oppressions. This is an ancient concern, which has been
confirmed recently in much greater detail.[43]
Since religions have always sought involvement
in humans' social lives, when religions ignore

the stark realities of human harms to nonhuman animals, they risk at the very least also failing to see the challenge of overlapping or interlocking oppressions.

Further, for many people in the modern animal protection movement the commitment to the sacredness of life functions very much like a religion. Herzog, for example, has pointed out the parallels between conversion to, and the lifestyles of, a religious faith and animal rights activism.[44] He also points out the role of cosmologies in the lives and thinking of both animal protectionists and pro-"animal research" scientists, implicitly calling to mind the centrality of cosmology in religious views of the world.[45]

Relatedly, there is much contemporary religious imagery about issues involving nonhuman animals. In Jasper and Nelkin's history of the animal protection movement, which they refer to as a "crusade," the authors identify a threefold division in the animal protection movement: welfarists, pragmatists, and "fundamentalists."[46] The terms "crusade" and "fundamentalists" call to mind the way in which contemporary religious categories such as conversion, fundamentalism, faith, and ultimate concern illuminate some features of the commitment found among some animal protection advocates.

This same feature appears in parallels between vegetarianism and religious commitment, which are legion and have been recognized in some law courts[47] and by some philosophers.[48] Another developing connection is the manner in which references to the ongoing debate in secular philosophy over the place of nonhuman animals have made their way into some of the contemporary scholarship dealing with religious views of nonhuman animals.[49] In a recent book on zoos entitled *The Modern Ark,* various quotes echo the title's allusion to the story of Noah and the flood that operates as a paradigmatic narrative in the Abrahamic traditions.[50] Howard Kushner comments that zoos "remind us of our real place in the universe," while the former director of the largest American zoo organization refers to zoos as "cathedrals of wildlife."[51] These religio-ethical echoes are made more explicit in arguments that the nonhuman world generally and nonhuman animals specifically are necessary to our thinking and the religious imagination.[52]

Conclusion

At the beginning of the twentieth century, W. E. B. Du Bois began his remarkable *The Souls of Black Folk* with the observation, "The problem of the twentieth century is the problem of the color line."[53] Du Bois' concern was, of course, to highlight the challenge raised by the depth and character of the extraordinarily pervasive exclusions in American culture affecting marginalized humans said to be "colored."[54] At the beginning of the twenty-first century, humans' exclusions of other humans remain extremely significant problems throughout the world, as the ethnic cleansing phenomena of the 1990s so dramatically revealed.

It may be, though, that the most significant problem of the twenty-first century is the problem of the species line. This is not because all human-against-human violence has been solved. Indeed, the prevalence of civilian deaths in wars and terrorist acts at the beginning of the twenty-first century proclaim loudly that human violence against human others remains a central problem. But the problem of violence goes well beyond the species line, and in important ways the human community's violence against the nonhuman world keeps violence in our midst. Even the most rabid speciesist can recognize that *if* we work to eliminate our violence toward any and all lives generally, *then* we affirm the value of human life. Even if one remains avowedly and eminently speciesist, one might still choose to offer fundamental protection to *all* lives, reasoning, "how much more then would we underscore the value of each, unique *human* life?"

The inclusivist approach to ethics suggested by this essay, premised on a pervasive and rigorous critique of existing practices and values, offers hope for protecting more than merely marginalized "others," whether they are fellow animals of the human kind or another kind. Also included is our relationship to our local econiche, and indeed to our most immediate ecosystems and the earth itself—all of these can elicit rich responses that help us see the value of lives in community. Seeing this important connection in the web of life has been greatly advanced by the series of conferences at Harvard University that begin in the late 1990s on "Religions of the World and Ecology."[55] This groundbreaking series pushes us to consider generally what creates the possibility of changes in values and perspective within a religious tradition. While we must be wary of facile answers, one experience that moves people of conscience is direct engagement with oppression and its realities.

As Clark has noted about our ethics in *The Moral Status of Animals*, we cannot take into account what we refuse to notice or take seriously. And it is here that religious traditions have a role to play, for they remain central in the realms of moral discourse and training. If we push each other to ask, "What is the terrain we currently walk?" or, better yet, "What is the terrain we make nonhuman animals walk?", we will confront startling realities. The very asking of this question has much more power than the individual answers that are provided in the growing field of religion and animals—the question itself challenges some religious traditions' established formulation as to who and what individuals and communities matter among the webs of life surrounding us.

It is true that this emerging field asks questions that, implicitly or explicitly, suggest some specific traditions or subtraditions need an adjustment of their values, even an eclipse of certain longstanding exclusivist claims such as that evident in the Catholic Catechism passage quoted above. A counterbalance to this possible criticism is the field's strong affirmation of the inclusivist and life-affirming values already in place within religious traditions, even if these have often been subordinated to anthropocentric formulations or the harmful exclusions and values of elitist groups.

The collective work and sharing so needed in the emerging field of religion and animals is, without question, an important companion to have along on this journey. We can learn from one another, and in doing so learn that many traditions contain distinctive affirmations of values that have been submerged in many modern, industrialized, "developed" countries. This volume is thus not only an attempt to dialogue about contemporary developments, but also an attempt to reintroduce ancient perspectives to the academy and society more broadly. Given that religious traditions have been principal carriers of views of the world, they must, as providers of values and cosmology, play a central role in seeing our own exclusions better.

Yet, just as religious traditions once welcomed many who readily promoted slavery among humans as their religious right and duty, they now welcome those who renounce the relevance of nonhuman animals' realities to the issues here discussed. But, it is respectfully suggested, religious traditions are so centrally committed to ethical viewpoints that their self-inflicted ignorance about such things is inconsistent with their deepest insights about the value of life and lives. Gandhi once framed the most basic of our moral insights in a pithy aphorism about what truly discloses our beliefs— "The act will speak unerringly."[56] This important challenge can be framed in many different ways, an example of which is Hauerwas and Berkman's use of Christian terms and ideas to describe the same insight Gandhi advances.

> For our practices, more than our arguments, reveal and shape what is truly important to us. ... our practices with regard to other animals shapes our beliefs about them, ... [and it is] clear that the very consumption of animals by Christians

has shaped and continues to shape how Christians have thought about them. ... our eating of animals undoubtedly encourages a form of anthropocentrism. ... theology sometimes ends up underwriting classifications that are not intrinsic to its discourse.[57]

Hauerwas and Berkman add that the challenge is especially difficult because "avoiding implicit anthropocentric assumptions is no easy task." Yet, in light of our recurring claims about how moral or ethical humans are "by nature," or can be through sheer self-discipline, it is imperative that religious traditions examine their own past, current, and future contributions to human debates about the relationship between, and even possible community with, human and nonhuman animals.

NOTES

1. A well-known example of one culture's struggle with elitism and marginalization of humans is Howard Zinn, *A People's History of the United States* (New York: Harper & Row, 1980).

2. Philo, *De Praemiis et Poenis,* with both Greek and English text, The Loeb Classical Library Series, No. 341, trans. by F. H. Colson (London: Heinemann; Cambridge, MA: Harvard University Press, 1968), Section 85.

3. Consider this generic problem—a claim appears in a scripture held both revealed and infallible regarding certain features of the life of a particular nonhuman animal, and empirical evidence can be gathered that shows the claim not to be literally true. (A minor, though oft-cited, example of an error in fact is the claim in Leviticus 11:6 about hares chewing cud.)

4. Many of the most prominent animal protection advocates are notably negative about religious beliefs as factors in our views of nonhumans. See, for example, the works of Peter Singer and Stephen M. Wise.

5. The term "absolute dismissal" is from the opening chapter of Mary Midgley, *Animals and Why They Matter* (Athens, Georgia: University of Georgia Press, 1984), which is an informed history and philosophical discussion of the mainline Western cultural tradition's engagement with nonhuman animals.

6. As occasionally happens with the term "myth" when it is used outside religious studies contexts, the word "story" may initially be taken by some as a derogatory term. It is employed in a positive sense here, calling to mind the narratives used in human communities to evoke listeners' awareness, wonder, awe, and even participation in the subject matter of the story. For purposes of this argument, the words "story," "myth," and "narrative" are interchangeable.

7. Consider the basic information gathered in the last quarter of a century about these most complex of nonhuman communications. See, for example, the summary in Roger Payne, *Among Whales* (New York: Scribner's, 1995), chapter 4.

8. Consider whether this question is more ethical, more religious, or more scientific. The question has historically been asked in each of these ways. Can the question be asked in all three modes at once? And, if so, what might this suggest regarding the relationship of ethical, religious, and scientific enterprises?

9. The life sciences are really a bewildering forest of individual concerns and approaches that might be found under the general labels "biology" and "botany." The following list only begins to hint at how diverse these have become: agriculture, animal behavior, aquaculture, biochemistry, biotechnology, cognitive sciences, comparative developmental evolutionary psychology, conservation biology, developmental biology, entomology, environmental sciences, ethology, genetics, microbiology, molecular and cell biology, neuroscience, nutrition, paleobiology, parasitology, pharmacology, population biology, systematics, zoopharmacognosy.

10. Some of these are described in Paul Waldau, "Religion and Which Sciences? Science and Which

Community?" *The Journal of Faith and Science,* 4 (2001): 115–42.

11. The concept is raised in academic circles: for example, Ian Barbour, *Religion and Science: Historical and Contemporary Issues* (San Francisco: Harper, 1997); and Gregory R. Peterson, "Demarcation and the Scientistic Fallacy," *Zygon,* 38, no. 4 (December 2003): 751–61). It is also discussed in widely used educational tools designed to advance critical thinking: for example, Theodore Schick, Jr., and Lewis Vaughn, *How to Think about Weird Things,* 2nd ed. (Mountain View, California: Mayfield, 1999).

12. See, for example, Bernard E. Rollin, *The Unheeded Cry: Animal Consciousness, Animal Pain and Science* (Oxford: Oxford University Press, 1989); Barbour, *Religion and Science;* Keith Ward, *Defending the Soul* (Oxford: Oneworld Publications, 1992) (particularly the critique of J. Monod generally and that of Richard Dawkins' facile dismissal of religion); and, regarding sociobiology, Mary Midgley, *Beast and Man: The Roots of Human Nature,* rev. ed. (New York: Routledge, 1995).

13. It is well known, for example, that various indigenous traditions have had keen awareness of the lives and habits of nonhuman animals. Examples from the Buddhist and Christian traditions can be found in Paul Waldau, *The Specter of Speciesism: Buddhist and Christian Views of Animals,* New York: Oxford University Press, 2001) in, respectively, chapters 6 and 8.

14. A relevant study is Charles Taylor, *Sources of the Self: The Making of Modern Identity* (Cambridge: Harvard University Press, 1989). The most deliberate and systematic philosophizing about moral rights for nonhumans remains Tom Regan, *The Case for Animal Rights,* 2nd ed. (London: Routledge, 1988), and the most detailed attempt to state the basis of legal rights for some nonhuman animals is Steven M. Wise, *Rattling the Cage: Toward Legal Rights for Animals* (Cambridge, MA: Merloyd Lawrence/Perseus, 2000).

15. This is, of course, true of some nonmammals as well.

16. Gary Snyder, "Grace," *Co-Evolution Quarterly,* 43 (Fall 1984): 1.

17. "Speciesism" was coined in 1970, and used widely now by many philosophers. For an analysis, see Waldau, *Specter of Speciesism.*

18. One well-known four-part sequence is used by the environmental ethicist Hargrove: ancient, medieval (heavily symbolic), modern (representative use of animal images), and post-modern. See, Eugene Hargrove, "The Role of Zoos in the Twenty-First Century," in B. G. Norton et al., eds., *Ethics on the Ark: Zoos, Animal Welfare and Wildlife Conservation* (Washington: Smithsonian Institution Press, 1995), pp. 13–19.

19. Northcote W. Thomas, "Animals," in J. Hastings, ed., *Encyclopedia of Religion and Ethics* (Edinburgh: T. & T. Clark; New York: Scribner's, 1908), p. 1:483–535, at 483.

20. A good collection by an anthropologist is Tim Ingold, ed., *What Is an Animal?* (New York: Routledge, 1994).

21. See, for example, Bill Devall and George Sessions, eds., *Deep Ecology: Living as if Nature Mattered* (Salt Lake City: Peregrine Smith, 1985).

22. For example, as to rationality, there has been no general agreement in the history of ideas regarding what is meant by "rational." Richard Sorabji, in *Animals Minds and Human Morals: The Origins of the Western Debate* (Ithaca: Cornell University Press, 1993), pp. 65–77, argues that the concept of reason itself often varied in ancient times. Similarly, see Charles Taylor, *Sources of the Self,* p. 168, on the difference between, for example, Plato's notion of reason and modern, procedure-oriented notions of reason. "Intelligence" also has long been recognized to be many different things. A modern example pointing out the difference is Howard Gardner's *Frames of Mind: The Theory of Multiple Intelligences* (New York: Basic, 1985), which identifies seven different kinds of human intelligence.

23. Regarding language and concepts, see Sue Savage-Rumbaugh and Roger Lewin, *Kanzi: The Ape at the Brink of the Human Mind* (New York: Wiley, 1994); Sue Savage-Rumbaugh, Stuart G. Shanker, and Talbot J. Taylor, *Apes, Language, and the Human Mind* (New York, Oxford University Press, 1998); and Roger Fouts, *Next of Kin* (New

York: William Morrow, 1997); and Eileen Crist, "Can an Insect Speak? The Case of the Honeybee Dance Language," in *Social Studies of Science* 34, no. 1 (February 2004): 7–43. Re social rules, see Frans de Waal, *Good Natured: The Origins of Right and Wrong in Humans and Other Animals* (Cambridge: Harvard University Press, 1996). Regarding self-awareness, see Sue Taylor Parker, Robert W. Mitchell, and Maria Boccia, eds., *Self-Awareness in Animals and Humans: Developmental Perspectives* (Cambridge: Cambridge University Press, 1994); and Donald R. Griffin, *Animal Minds: Beyond Cognition to Consciousness* (Chicago: University of Chicago Press, 2001). On personality, individuality, and intelligence, see Sue Taylor Parker and Kathleen Rita Gibson, eds., *"Language" and Intelligence in Monkeys and Apes: Comparative Developmental Perspectives* (Cambridge: Cambridge University Press, 1990), Parker, et al., *Self-Awareness,* and the work of Fouts and Savage-Rumbaugh generally. On culture, see W. C. McGrew, *Chimpanzee Material Culture: Implications for Human Evolution* (Cambridge: Cambridge University Press, 1992), and Richard W. Wrangham et al., eds., *Chimpanzee Cultures* (Cambridge: Harvard University Press, 1994).

24. Originally published in 1918 in a series of "The Superstition of Divorce" pamphlets written for the *New Witness,* this series became a book of the same title in 1920 (London: Chatto and Windus). The quote appears in Section VI, "The Story of the Vow."

25. The problem of other minds has long been a major topic in philosophical circles. See Daniel C. Dennett, *Kinds of Minds: Toward an Understanding of Consciousness* (San Francisco: HarperCollins, 1996) for a discussion.

26. That three of the contributors to this volume are *pioneers* of this position in modern academia and science—Griffin, Goodall, and Bekoff—suggests how startlingly persistent the denial of other animals' realities has been in important educational circles.

27. Stephen R. L. Clark, *How to Think About the Earth: Philosophical and Theological Models for Ecology* (London: Mowbray, 1993), p. 32.

28. Savage-Rumbaugh and Lewin, *Kanzi,* p. 260. Similarly, see Jane Goodall (published under van Lawick-Goodall), *In the Shadow of Man* (Boston: Houghton Mifflin, 1971), p. 234.

29. Letter to J. G. Gmelin, February 14, 1747, in George Seldes, ed., *The Great Thoughts* (New York: Ballantine, 1985), p. 247.

30. See, for example, Nigel W. Bond, ed., *Animal Models in Psychopathology* (London: Academic Press, 1984), and Barbara Orlans, *In The Name of Science* (New York: Oxford University Press, 1993). Among the earliest psychological uses of primates as human models are Darwin's 1872 classic *The Expression of the Emotions in Man and Animals;* Robert Yerkes, *The Mental Life of Monkeys and Apes: A Study of Ideational Behavior* (New York: Holt, 1916); and Wolfgang Köhler, *The Mentality of Apes,* trans. from the second revised edition by Ella Winter (New York: Harcourt, 1925).

31. This is S. R. L. Clark's formulation of this general problem. See *The Moral Status of Animals* (Oxford: Clarendon, 1977), p. 7.

32. William Paley, *Principles of Moral and Political Philosophy,* 7th ed. (Philadelphia: Dobson, 1788), p. 32, discussed Aristotle's view of non-Greeks as slaves. (See also, for example, *Politics* 1.5.1254b20–21).

33. Kant used the image of a "self-inflicted" limitation in the opening lines in his famous 1784 essay "What is Enlightenment?" (The essay appears in *On History,* ed. and trans. by Lewis Beck White [New York and Indianapolis: Bobbs-Merrill company/Liberal Arts Press, 1963]). Kant understood a disability to be "self-inflicted" "whenever its cause lies not in lack of reason but in lack of resolution and courage to use it without direction from another" (p. 3). Kant went on to state a dictum that became a signature phrase of the Enlightenment, *Sapere aude!,* translated by White as "Dare to know!" As White's Footnote 1 indicates, "This was the motto adopted in 1736 by the Society of the Friends of Truth, an important circle in the German Enlightenment." (ibid.)

34. Midgley, *Beast and Man,* pp. 25–27.

35. An interesting exception to the general si-

lence of many religious institutions is a resolution passed at the General Convention of the Episcopal Church of the United States in 2003. In part, Resolution Do16 read, "*Resolved,* That the Episcopal Church encourage its members to ensure that husbandry methods for captive and domestic animals would prohibit suffering in such conditions as puppy mills, and factory-farms."

36. See, for example, Tom Regan, ed., *Animal Sacrifices: Religious Perspectives on the Use of Animals in Science* (Philadelphia: Temple University Press, 1986).

37. Descriptions of these conditions formed an essential part of Peter Singer's widely discussed *Animal Liberation: A New Ethics for Our Treatment of Animals,* rev. ed. (New York: Random House, 1992; originally published 1975), a work often referred to as the "bible" of the animal rights movement. See, for example, Deborah Blum *The Monkey Wars* (Oxford and New York: Oxford University Press, 1994), p. 115.

38. "Unnecessary" here is used in a narrow sense, to denote something *not* required for an individual's or group's immediate biological survival. Hence, slavery is "unnecessary" because the master can give it up and still have a healthy life; consuming factory farmed meat can also be "unnecessary" under this standard because, for example, many modern consumers recognize that there are alternative sources of the kinds of protein humans need to survive.

39. *Catechism of the Catholic Church 1994* (London: Geoffrey Chapman, 1994), Paragraph 2415.

40. Quoted in David Kinsley, *Ecology and Religion: Ecological Spirituality in Cross-Cultural Perspective* (Englewood Cliffs, New Jersey: Prentice Hall, 1995), which cites Roderick Frazier Nash, *The Rights of Nature: A History of Environmental Ethics* (Madison: University of Wisconsin Press, 1989), p. 40.

41. Has Jonas, *The Imperative of Responsibility: In Search of an Ethics for the Technological Age* (Chicago: University of Chicago Press, 1984), p. 4, and James Gustafson, *Theology and Ethics,* Chicago: University of Chicago, 1981), pp. 96f., make the argument that traditional ethics has been anthropocentric.

42. For a list of the many ways in which social and cultural values are in ferment regarding non-

humans, see Paul Waldau, "Will the Heavens Fall? De-Radicalizing the Precedent-Breaking Decision," *Animal Law* 7 (2001): 75–118.

43. See, for example, Randall Lockwood and Frank R. Ascione, eds., *Cruelty to Animals and Interpersonal Violence: Readings in Research and Application* (West Lafayette, Indiana: Purdue University Press, 1998).

44. Harold A. Herzog, Jr., "'The Movement is My Life': The Psychology of Animal Rights Activism," *Journal of Social Issues* 49, no.1 (1993): 103–19.

45. Harold A. Herzog, Beth Dinoff, and Jessica R. Page, "Animal Rights Talk: Moral Debate over the Internet," *Qualitative Sociology* 20, no. 3 (1997): 399–418.

46. James M. Jasper and Dorothy Nelkin, *The Animal Rights Crusade: The Growth of a Moral Protest* (New York: The Free Press, 1992)

47. In 1996, the Director of U.S. Equal Employment Opportunity Commission in San Diego, California, ruled that vegetarianism is a religious belief under Title VII Civil Rights Act of 1964, as amended.

48. See, for example, Kristin Aronson, *To Eat Flesh They Are Willing: Are Their Spirits Weak? Vegetarians Who Return to Meat* (New York: Pythagorean Publishers), and Rynn Berry, *Food for the Gods: Vegetarianism and the World's Religions* (Brooklyn, New York: Pythagorean, 1998).

49. See, for example, references to the work of the utilitarian Peter Singer and the deontologist Tom Regan in Andrew Linzey and Daniel Cohn-Sherbok, *After Noah: Animals and the Liberation of Theology* (London: Mowbray, 1997). Note, however, the absence of references to this body of work in Andrew Linzey and Dorothy Yamamoto, eds., *Animals on the Agenda: Questions About Animals for Theology and Ethics* (Chicago: University of Illinois Press, 1998).

50. Vicki Croke, *The Modern Ark: The Story of Zoos: Past, Present and Future* (New York: Scribner's, 1997), p. 103.

51. Ibid., quoting Terry Maple, former president of American Zoo and Aquarium Association.

52. The first argument is made in great detail by Paul Shepard in *The Others: How Animals Made*

Us Human (Washington, D.C.: Island Press, 1996), and the second is the substance of James Hillman's comments in an interview with Thomas Moore appearing in *Parabola* 8, no. 2 (Spring/May 1983): 49–53. Lévi-Strauss famously commented about non-human animals being "good to think" in *Totemism,* trans. by Rodney Needham (Boston: Beacon, 1963), p. 89.

53. W. E. B. Du Bois, *The Souls of Black Folk* (Reprint: New York: Signet/New American Library, 1969; originally published 1903). This comment appears in the original introduction known as "The Forethought" (at xi of the 1969 reprint); see also the beginning and conclusion of the second chapter, "Of the Dawn of Freedom," at 54 and 78 of the 1969 reprint.

54. Of course, all humans are colored, those usually denominated "white" being, generally, somewhat pink or lighter in appearance. It is interesting that "white" continues to be the description of choice for the peoples with lighter skin pigmentation. Of interest on the "superordination of whiteness to blackness" in various cultures and especially in the Christian and western intellectual traditions, see Robert Hood, *Begrimed and Black: Christian Traditions on Blacks and Blackness* (Minneapolis: Fortress, 1994).

55. Individual volumes cover Buddhism, Confucianism, Hinduism, Islam, Judaism, indigenous traditions, Christianity, Jainism, and Daoism — the details are at the website of the Forum on Religion and Ecology.

56. I am indebted to the English philosopher of religion John Hick for this quote, which is cited in Margaret Chatterjee, *Gandhi's Religious Thought* (Notre Dame, Indiana: Notre Dame University Press, 1983), p. 73. The original quote is from Mahadev Desai, *Day to Day with Gandhi* (Varanasi: Navajivan, 1968–1972), 7:111–12.

57. Stanley Hauerwas and John Berkman, "A Trinitarian Theology and the 'Chief End' of 'All Flesh,'" in Charles Pinches and Jay McDaniel, eds., *Good News for Animals? Christian Approaches to Animal Well-Being* (Maryknoll, New York: Orbis, 1993), pp. 62–74, at 62–63.

II

ANIMALS IN
ABRAHAMIC TRADITIONS

JUDAISM

Sacrifice in Ancient Israel

Pure Bodies, Domesticated Animals, and the Divine Shepherd

JONATHAN KLAWANS

An analysis of biblical sacrifice holds promise for elucidating ancient Israelite attitudes toward animals in general and toward especially those animal species that were considered most fit for sacrifice: sheep, goats, and cattle (Leviticus 1:2). But understanding sacrifice in ancient Israel is a problematic endeavor, for a good deal of what has been written on biblical sacrifice has been influenced by undue and imbalanced hostility toward a ritual that means much more than most are willing to grant.

One challenge raised by sacrifice in general is a moral one—or so it is thought. A number of theoretical works on sacrifice operate on the assumption that there is some direct relationship between the practice of sacrifice and the human proclivity for violence.[1] For such theorists, figuring out how sacrifice began allows one to understand the origin of human violence too. The first step toward appreciating what sacrifice means within any specific religious system, however, is to reject this approach outright. If sacrifice poses an ethical problem, it is because animals are killed in the process. Yet the (incomplete) elimination of ritual sacrifice from (most) contemporary religious practice has done no good for the animals. Whoever feels smug about the elimination of sacrificial altars can just visit a slaughterhouse or a laboratory: neither is a more welcome place for an animal than an ancient temple.[2] The elimination of sacrifice is not an ethical development, but an aesthetic one. The only real advance here is one of differentiation:[3] Where premoderns worshipped and consumed animals in a single process, moderns have divided the two activities by the short distance and time that separate our places of religious assembly from our refrigerators.

The imbalanced moral disgust (that scholars often don't bother to conceal) toward sacrifice in general finds two accomplices in the religious agendas of many who set out to study sacrifice in ancient Israel in particular. Christian theology predicates itself on the idea that the self-sacrifice of God's son supersedes the presumably flawed system of ancient Israelite ritual sacrifice that preceded it. Such theological suppositions are by no means absent from works on ancient Israelite sacrifice or early Christian ritual.[4] But religious opposition to ancient Israelite sacrifice is not distinctively Christian. It is less well known but no less significant that the movements of Judaism that advocate modernizing reforms (Reform, Conservative, Reconstructionist) assert with an equal determination that animal sacrifice will remain a thing of the past.[5] Because the history of modern Jewish historical scholarship is intertwined with the history of synagogue reform (in figures such as Abraham Geiger[6]) we should not be surprised that a good deal of Jewish scholarship on the Hebrew Bible or ancient Judaism operates on the assumption that sacrifice was hopelessly outmoded and meaningless.[7] While the (modernist) Jewish[8] and Christian presuppositions differ to no small extent, what they share is the common idea that biblical sacrifice is—and, by implication, always was—a morally and spiritually incomplete ritual. Because a great deal of scholarship on the Bible is carried out by those who operate with one of these perspectives (the present author included) it is no coincidence that sacrifice is often treated with disdain and disgust.

How then to approach sacrifice? Paradoxically, part of the problem has been that scholars have set their scopes, at the same time, too narrowly and too broadly. When setting out to study sacrifice in ancient Israel, there is no need to consider either where sacrifice came from or what finally happened to it. Sacrifice was an unquestioned given in the biblical world.[9] Modern scholarly concerns with how sacrifice came about in the first place or why sacrifice seems to have disappeared should be set aside. These questions are at best irrelevant to the task at hand: we cannot necessarily understand what something represents in one context by understanding how it began in some earlier era or what later happened to it closer to our own day. Too often, though, the analysis of sacrifice in ancient Israel is driven by a desire to answer these questions. When one sees Israelite sacrifice as either a vestige of things past or as sign of things to come, one can hardly understand sacrifice for what it is. Our scope is more narrow: we will remain focused on sacrifice in ancient Israel.

In a different way, however, the study of ancient Israelite sacrifice has been too confined. The analysis of sacrifice too frequently focuses exclusively on the killing of an animal, which actually constitutes only one step of a ritual process that is much broader. To understand sacrifice we must understand more than what it means to spill blood. We must endeavor to understand what it means to purify oneself for sacrifice, to own animals fit for sacrifice, and to select from among them a single sacrificial offering. What is more, we must understand what it means not only to kill the animal, but also to dissect it, to consume some parts of it and to burn other parts on the altar. As Victor Turner advised some time ago, sacrifice is to be understood as a process with several stages.[10] Turner was following Henri Hubert and Marcel Mauss, who devoted part of their classic 1898 essay to describing the processes of "sacralization" and purification that precede sacrifice.[11] This is the scope that must be widened: instead of focusing on the single element of sacrifice that causes us the most trouble, we must try to imagine the entire process of sacrifice, as an ancient Israelite experienced it.

In what follows, we will trace a number of facets of the ancient Israelite sacrificial process, and we will present a symbolic framework for tying many of these aspects together. We remain, for the present purposes, focused on ancient Israelite *animal* sacrifice, even though Israelite sacrificial worship did not always involve animals.[12] Moreover, for the present purposes, we are concerned with sacrifice in general, and will not distinguish between the disparate forms and contexts of distinct ancient Israelite sacrificial offerings.[13]

As we retrace and rethink the general contours of the ancient Israelite sacrificial process (broadly defined), we will do well to think of animals as subjects, and not as objects. Some are likely to assume that because Israelites performed animal sacrifice, they must have despised or at least objectified the animals they offered. We will proceed with a different assumption: in order to understand what it meant for them to sacrifice, we must first understand what it meant for them to act as their animals' shepherds. As we will see, the Hebrew Bible presents a good deal of evidence that the necessary preliminaries of sacrificial acts—including, especially, shepherding—had profound theological connotations. Therefore, to trace Israel's sacrificial process—and to grasp fully its symbolic meanings—we will also need to appreciate better Israel's relationship with its animal subjects.

Ritual Purity and Imitatio Dei

For ancient Israel, the sacrificial process can be said to begin with ritual purification. Ritual purity is the prerequisite of those who come to the sanctuary to offer sacrifices, of those who regularly officiate at sacrifices (priests), and of any animals that are to be offered as sacrifices. The relation between ritual purity and sacrifice is underscored in Scripture: laws concerning both are juxtaposed in the text of Leviticus.[14]

Ritual purity can be defined as being in a state free from ritual impurity. Ritual impurity results from direct or indirect contact with any one of a number of natural sources including childbirth (Leviticus 12:1–8), certain skin diseases (13:1–46; 14:1–32), fungi in clothes and houses (13:47–59; 14:33–53), genital discharges (15:1–33), the carcasses of certain impure animals (11:1–47), and human corpses (Numbers 19:10–22). Ritual impurity also comes about, paradoxically, as a byproduct of certain purificatory procedures (e.g., Leviticus 16:28; Numbers 19:8).[15] The durations of these impurities differ, as do the requisite cleansing processes—but the intricacies of these laws are not our concern at this moment. What is our concern is the fact that these impurities convey an impermanent contagion, which prevents all who are ritually impure from coming into contact with the sacred. In order to bring an offering to a sacred altar, one must be ritually pure.

A number of theories have been advanced in the attempt to account for the varied nature of the substances viewed as ritually defiling in Leviticus 11–15 and Numbers 19. One popular theory focuses on death as the common denominator of the ritual purity system. The most articulate champion of this view currently is Jacob Milgrom, who, after reviewing the sources of ritual defilement, states:

> The common denominator here is death. Vaginal blood and semen represent the forces of life; their loss—death. ... In the case of scale disease [i.e., "leprosy"], this symbolism is made explicitly: Aaron prays for his stricken sister, "Let her not be like a corpse" (Numbers 12:12). Furthermore, scale disease is powerful enough to contaminate by overhang, and it is no accident that it shares this feature with the corpse (Numbers 19:14). The wasting of the body, the common characteristic of all biblically impure skin diseases, symbolizes the death process as much as the loss of blood and semen.[16]

The importance of death as a common denominator of the avoidance regulations in priestly traditions can also be seen, perhaps, in the blood prohibition (Leviticus 17:10–14), in the elimination of carnivores from the diet of ancient Israel, and in the abhorrence of pigs, which played a role in Canaanite chthonic (underworld) worship.[17] The purpose of the system, as Milgrom elsewhere states, is to drive a wedge between the forces of death, which are impure, and the forces of life, which like God are holy.[18]

This impurity-as-death "theory"—we could just as well call it a metaphor (see below)—is by no means entirely new, and Milgrom notes that other scholars have focused on death in order to understand ritual impurity in ancient Israel.[19] This view finds *partial* corroboration in the fact that death is problematized in other purity systems, such as those of the Zoroastrians and the Greeks.[20] Yet the view of death as impure and corpses as defiling is by no means universal: some societies concerned with defilement problematize death, while others do not.[21] Just as there are no universal taboos, so too there is no universal theory of impurity.

While few scholars deny the importance of death-avoidance to the biblical purity system, some questions remain. One question concerns the relationship between death-avoidance and sex-avoidance. A second question concerns sacrifice. Indeed, the centrality of death to the ritual purity system brings us to a riddle at the heart of our concerns. Why, if the ritual purity system is concerned with keeping death out of the sanctuary, does the sacrificial system involve precisely the opposite: the killing of animals, *in the sanctuary?*[22]

Regarding the relationship between death and sex, the death-avoidance theory may well explain why individuals become ritually defiled when genital fluids are lost through nonsexual discharge from the body—surely the potential for life is lost in such situations. But it remains unclear whether or not the fear of death really explains why sex and birth *always* defile, even when no mishap occurs. Moreover, why is it that the only substances which flow from the body and defile are sexual and/or genital in nature? Even blood flowing from the veins of a dying person is not ritually defiling! A number of scholars have convincingly argued, *contra* Milgrom, that the overarching concern with death-avoidance does not fully explain the particular concern with sexual/genital discharges. Tikva Frymer-Kensky and David P. Wright, among others, emphasize the important role that attitudes toward sexuality (but not necessarily gender) play in ancient Israel's perceptions of defilement.[23] Both of these scholars argue, with different emphases, that both death *and* sex figure in the ritual purity system of ancient Israel, and that the system serves to highlight the differences between persons and God.

Because God is eternal, God does not die. As Wright puts it, "the mortal condition is incompatible with God's holiness."[24] Because God has no consort, God cannot have sex. Therefore, as Frymer-Kensky puts it, "in order to approach God, one has to leave the sexual realm."[25]

By separating from sex and death—by following the ritual purity regulations—ancient Israelites (and especially ancient Israelite priests and Levites) separated themselves from what made them least God-like. In other words, the point of following these regulations is nothing other than the theological underpinning of the entire Holiness Code: *imitatio Dei* (Leviticus 11:44–5, 19:2, 20:7, 26). Only a heightened godlike state—the state of ritual purity—made one eligible to enter the sanctuary, God's holy residence on earth. Here we come back to Hubert and Mauss, and their classic essay on sacrifice, where with regard to the process of "sacralization" they said: "All that touches upon the gods must be divine; the sacrifier is obliged to become a god himself in order to be capable of acting upon them."[26] The applicability of this observation to the priestly materials of the Pentateuch ought now be manifest.

Yet we are still left with a problem: if death is defiling (and banned from the sacred) why does killing animals find a central place within the sacred? The answer to the riddle lies, in part, in the fact that the kind of death that occurs in the sanctuary is not a natural kind of death, but a highly controlled one. Sacrifice is frequently described (or derided) as "violent"; and it certainly is, at the very least, deadly and bloody. But the violence of sacrifice is not random or indiscriminate: animal sacrifice in ancient Israel proceeds only in a very orderly and controlled way.[27] The domesticated animals fit to be offered as sacrifices have no power whatsoever to resist: "like a gentle lamb led to the slaughter" (Jeremiah 11:19).[28] That is why, at least in ancient Israel, sacrifice is very little like the hunt: the sacrificial animals chosen cannot put up much of a fight.[29]

As we will see momentarily, in ancient Israel, sacrifice involves—in part—the controlled exercise of complete power over an animal's life and death. This is precisely one of the powers that Israel's God exercises over human beings: "The Lord kills and brings to life" (1 Samuel 2:6; cf. Deuteronomy 32:39). But exercising control over the death of a subordinate being—a *subject*—is not the only aspect of sacrificial ritual that can be understood in light of *imitatio Dei*. Indeed, we will soon see that a great many facets of sacrificial ritual can be understood in this light.

Domestication and Imitatio Dei

Ritual purity is not the only prerequisite for sacrifice, nor is it the only prerequisite that may help us understand better the nature and meaning of ancient Israel's sacrificial process. Before an Israelite could offer anything as a sacrifice, the Israelite would have to acquire whatever items, animal or vegetable, are to be offered. Sacrificial rituals in ancient Israel involved select animals as well as wine, incense, grains, and bread—we will provide details as necessary, and we will remain focused, for the purposes of the present collection, on animal sacrifices. In a society such as ancient Israel in which many (if not most) were agrarians and pastoralists, it behooves us to reflect on whether we can learn something about sacrifice by understanding better the relationship between Israelites and their animals.

In his essay "The Domestication of Sacrifice," Jonathan Z. Smith offered the tantalizing suggestion that sacrifice could be understood as a "meditation on domestication."[30] Smith here is at once criticizing the theories of René Girard and Walter Burkert and offering something of an alternative. Smith points out that "animal sacrifice appears to be, universally, the ritual killing of a domesticated animal by agrarian or pastoralist societies."[31] He even entertains the possibility that animals were originally domesticated so that they could be sacrificed.[32] Leaving the question of origins aside, we wish to ask what we can learn about ancient Israelite sacrifice if

we were to meditate on the process of domestication as a prerequisite for sacrifice.

We must, however, exercise some caution when trying to make use of Smith's insights for an understanding of the Hebrew Bible. Smith offered his theory as a kind of "*jeu d'esprit*."[33] When pressed in the conversation that followed the paper, he asserted that he didn't even believe his own theory.[34] In contrast to Burkert and Girard, Smith emphatically—and very seriously—rejected altogether the enterprise of theorizing about the origins of sacrifice.[35] It is ironic, therefore—but true nonetheless—that Smith's reflections on the process of domestication and its relation to sacrifice make an important contribution to an understanding of sacrifice in the Hebrew Bible. The reason for this is obvious: not only do domesticated animals play a key role in ancient Israelite sacrifice, but metaphors comparing ancient Israelites to their domesticated animals also play a key role in ancient Israelite theologizing: "The Lord is my shepherd," the psalmist famously noted (23:1). Smith's essay—mind-game or not—points us in the direction of connecting these two phenomena.

Before we go further, some clarification is in order. What precisely is domestication? Smith provides the helpful definition: "domestication may be defined as the process of human interference in or alteration of the genetics of plants and animals (i.e., selective breeding)."[36] A useful recent work by the biologist Bruce D. Smith provides further details on this process, which as he puts it results in the "human creation of a new form of plant or animal."[37] As B. D. Smith ably demonstrates—in a manner clear even to the nonscientist—a domesticated plant or animal is "identifiably different from its wild ancestors and extant wild relatives."[38] The origins of this process are not of our concern, any more than the origins of sacrifice. What is important for us is the fact that domestication by its nature involves human control over a plant or animal's life and death. While this is true of plants (which were sown, grafted, and reaped by human farmers), it is even more dramatically true with regard to animals. By keeping animals penned up, by separating herds, by controlling and rationing their feeding, by selectively killing some and selectively allowing others to breed, the herder exercises a rather striking amount of control over the animals in his possession.[39] In light of what we have already said about ritual purity, sacrifice, controllability, and death, it is certainly worth thinking about the relationship between sacrifice and domestication in ancient Israel.

Ancient Israelites were no exception to the general rule noted by J. Z. Smith: their animal sacrifices also consisted of domesticated species. But only certain domesticated animals were allowed on the altar. Pigs of course were out of the question (Leviticus 11:7), as were the other carnivores and omnivores whose consumption was proscribed in Leviticus 11 and Deuteronomy 14. Israel's dietary rules also banned the consumption of horses, camels, and donkeys (which were nonetheless kept by them and used for transportation).[40] But Israel's altar was subject to greater restriction than Israel's table.[41] Israel's animal sacrifices came primarily from the herd and flock—cattle, sheep, and goats—but also included certain species of domesticated birds. Thus Israel's sacrificial offerings involved animals that are by nature docile, defenseless, and communal (living and reproducing in flocks and herds).

We should not be surprised that ancient Israelite literature makes generous use of metaphors involving its favorite domesticated animals.[42] As any reader of the Bible knows, these metaphors are rather prominent, and a good number of them depict God as Israel's shepherd: "for He is our God, and we are the people He tends, the flock in his care" (Psalms 95:7).[43] In the capacity of shepherd, God is depicted as protecting, guiding, feeding, and even slaying his flock.[44] Setting aside the slaughter images for the moment, the other activities mentioned constitute the necessary preliminaries to the sacrificial act. Before any animal can be sacrificed, it must first be protected when born, fed, and then

finally guided to its place of slaughter. What is more, since maimed animals are unfit for sacrifice (Leviticus 22:19–20), the careful shepherd who wishes to offer a sacrifice will keep an eye toward protecting the animals that are fit for sacrifice. The art of herding is selective breeding—choosing which males will be allowed to reproduce with which females. The good shepherd will, therefore, as a matter of course make the "life and death" decisions for his herds and flocks.

Israel's sacrificial system presumes that Israelites themselves will be doing some good tending of their herds or flocks: if they did not, there would be nothing left to offer. Israel's theologizing frequently depicts God performing precisely that role vis-à-vis Israel, tending the flock. Thus it stands to reason that, on some level, ancient Israelites understood tending their own flocks in light of this analogy: as Israel is to Israel's herds and flocks, so too is God to God's flock, Israel. The prophetic and hymnic metaphors based on this analogy—as well as other metaphors we will examine below—provide a clue as to how we can understand the ways in which ancient Israelites may have understood their rituals. More specifically, taken as a whole, these metaphors provide further confirmation of the case we are making —that the process of sacrifice can be understood as an act of *imitatio Dei*.

Imitating God in the Sanctuary of God

We have established that two preliminaries for the sacrificial process can be understood in light of *imitatio Dei*. Ancient Israelites understood the chores related to the raising and caring of domesticated animals—even though these are not rituals per se—by analogy to their relationship with God. We have also suggested that the ritual purifications which were the prerequisites for encountering the sacred can also be understood in light of the notion of *imitatio Dei*. Other preliminaries for sacrifice can similarly be understood: Jon D. Levenson, building on Mircea Eliade's temple-as-cosmos notion,[45] has argued that the biblical narratives of tabernacle (and temple) construction take on a cosmic significance. Among other evidence, Levenson notes how the language and structure of the tabernacle-construction narrative carefully recall the language and structure of Genesis 1.[46] In so doing, Levenson demonstrates that the priestly traditions understand tabernacle and temple construction as an act of *imitatio Dei*. In the remainder of this section, we will discuss other aspects of sacrificial ritual that can be understood in the same light.

Coinciding with the process of purification comes a process of selection: the offerer and/or the officiating priest for each sacrificial ritual must *select* the animal to be sacrificed. Any animal offered must be without blemish (Leviticus 1:3). When these laws are elaborated, we learn that the Israelites were prohibited from offering anything blind, injured, maimed, or deformed; there is a particular concern with the wholeness of the male animal's genitalia (Leviticus 22:17–28).

It is commonly pointed out that it is fitting that animals offered on the holy altar be perfect and whole.[47] It is equally important to recognize, however, that this stipulation does not only concern the animal: it requires the offerer to carefully examine the animal destined for sacrifice. These regulations, moreover, don't only apply at the moment of sacrifice. As we have noted, prudent shepherds will properly care for their flocks, watching for blemishes that have appeared, trying to prevent others from coming about, and perhaps even controlling the breeding of those animals born with defects. What is more, Leviticus prohibits offering an animal and its offspring on the same day (Leviticus 22:26–28). This regulation requires of all offerers of sacrifice, priestly and otherwise, to remain keenly aware of the familial relationships among the animals to be offered as sacrifices.

Even after, in accordance with these regulations, the offerer has eliminated unfit animals, presumably more than one fit animal is left in the herd or flock—and that's when the selection of the animal truly takes place.[48] The closest we come to a description of this aspect of the sacrificial process is in Exodus 12, where the Israelites' selection and watching over the animal to be consumed as a "Passover" offering (12:6) can be juxtaposed with God's guarding and watching over Israel in preparation for the tenth plague (12:42). Of course, the book of Leviticus itself more than once draws a connection between the human capacity to make distinctions and the divine power to do the same (Leviticus 10:10; 11:46–7). Clearly, the process of selection too can be understood in light of the concern to imitate God.

We have already mentioned that exercising control over the life and death of the animal can be understood in light of *imitatio Dei*. Once the animal is killed, we come to the next major step that can be understood in light of *imitatio Dei*: the dissection of the animal. After the animal has been slaughtered, the offerer and the priests look into, examine and dissect the animal's carcass. The offerer not only brings about the animal's death, he looks into the animal; he separates it into its constituent parts. He decreates it. Although the basic regulations for this process—specifying what parts belong where—are laid out in Leviticus and elsewhere, there are very few descriptions of the image of an offerer or priest looking into the innards of an animal. The only relevant passages I know of can be found in Jeremiah, the Psalms, and a few other places, which speak of God, who "examines the kidneys and heart."[49] A possibly related image can be found in Isaiah 63:1–6, which depicts God wearing a bloodstained garment— would not the priestly garments be stained with blood?[50] Indeed, other passages also depict God manipulating blood, in ways not unlike what the priests are expected to do with the blood of their sacrificial animals (see esp. Isaiah 34:6–7).[51] Can we infer from these images that the priest—by looking into the animal, and by spattering or manipulating its blood—is doing divine work?

Once the animal is dissected, various parts of

it are consumed in one way or another. While the blood of the animal is doused about parts of the altar or sanctuary, the fat, meat and organs of the animal are either consumed in the flames of the altar, or eaten by the priests. These aspects of sacrifice, too, can be well understood in light of *imitatio Dei*. A number of biblical scholars have struggled with the idea of a God who eats, and it may now come as little surprise that many argue that Israelites could not have believed in such an idea.[52]

Perhaps the biblical God doesn't rely on food the same way people do (Psalms 50:12–13), but God certainly does "consume"—and the difference between "eating" and "consuming" exists only in our translations, not in the original Hebrew. Throughout biblical narrative, God appears to the Israelites as a "consuming fire." In the context of holy war, God will travel with and before the Israelites as a "consuming fire" to devour Israel's enemies.[53] Strikingly, God also appears as a "consuming fire" in a number of sacrificial narratives. These concern the offerings of (among others) Moses, Aaron, David, Solomon, and Elijah.[54] Therefore, by "consuming" and burning elements of sacrificial offerings, the offerers of sacrifice in ancient Israel are imitating activities often attributed to God in narratives in which God's presence during a sacrifice is explicitly described.

We have seen that the typical ancient Israelite sacrifice involves the performance by Israelites and priests of a number of activities that can be understood well in the light of the concern to imitate God.[55] The process of ritual purification may well involve the separation of people from those aspects of humanity (death and sex) which are least God-like. The performance of pastoral responsibilities—caring, feeding, protecting and guiding—can easily be understood in light of *imitatio Dei,* as can the more dramatic acts of selective breeding. Closer to the altar, the selection, killing, dissection, and consumption of sacrificial animals are also activities with analogues in the divine realm. God too selects, kills, looks inside things, and appears on earth as a

consuming fire. The sacrificial process as a whole can therefore well be understood in light of the idea of imitating God.

Sacrifice and Metaphor

It is likely that some will resist the suggestion that sacrificial rituals can be better understood in light of the notion of *imitatio Dei*. It is also likely that some will resist the present analysis because of our unabashed use of images culled from the Psalms and prophetic literature in order to understand the rituals dryly laid out in Leviticus. Some might suppose that passages like Jeremiah 11:20 (in which God examines the kidneys and heart) or Isaiah 40:11 (in which God the shepherd gathers, guides and feeds his flock) do not really concern sacrifice at all because they are just metaphors. We cannot, however, be so quick to label these images as metaphors and then dismiss them from a discussion of the meaning of sacrificial rituals. First of all, it is worth keeping in mind that as long as the date of priestly strand(s) of the Pentateuch remains a debated issue, it can by no means be presumed that the (presumably metaphorical) passages in Jeremiah (or even the Psalms) are later than the (presumably literal) descriptions of sacrificial rituals in Leviticus. Of course, this observation is really only relevant if we operate under the standard assumption that metaphors involve secondary and non-literal usages which in some way extend beyond the original, literal usage of the terminology in question. The more time one spends reflecting on metaphor, however, the more one is impelled to rethink simplistic approaches.[56]

This essay began with the observation that anti-sacrificial biases in contemporary scholarship have hindered the understanding of sacrifice in ancient Israel. It can equally be said that the understanding of sacrifice has suffered because of anti-metaphorical biases in scholarship. There is a long-standing tradition in western philosophy—going back all the way to Aristotle—which disparages metaphor as something that is merely ornamental.[57] For more than forty years, however, a number of philosophers, linguists, and anthropologists have worked to rehabilitate metaphor, arguing that metaphor is cognitive, meaningful, often primary and foundational, and so pervasive as to become inescapable.[58] Nonetheless, very few works that set out to study ancient Israelite ritual in general (to say nothing of sacrifice in particular) seek to make use of biblical metaphors in their analysis.[59] In general, the study of Israelite sacrifice has suffered because anti-metaphorical biases in biblical scholarship have eliminated sacrificial metaphors from the discussion.[60]

It is no longer sound to assume that metaphor is historically secondary. Quite often, the reverse can be demonstrated, even within the Hebrew Bible.[61] One stunning example is the "dry bones" vision in Ezekiel 37. Here we find a metaphorical reference to the resurrection of the dead which by virtually all accounts precedes by hundreds of years the time when ancient Israelites literally believed in any notion of resurrection of the dead.[62]

It is also no longer methodologically sound to dismiss metaphor as merely ornamental. At the very least, metaphor—when it can be demonstrated to be in existence—must be taken seriously. It must also be recognized that metaphor, even when it can be demonstrated to be historically secondary, frequently *expands* the meanings and usages of words and concepts, thereby influencing both behavior and beliefs.[63] Consider, for instance, one of the few biblical metaphors that is generally treated properly: the prophetic comparison of God's covenant with Israel to a marriage between a man and a woman (e.g., Hosea chs. 1 and 2). This is clearly metaphorical, yet most scholars are willing to grant that this metaphor in particular *expands* our understanding of ancient Israelite perceptions of what a covenant meant. Scholars don't dismiss Hosea chapter 2 as mere metaphor, and Jeremiah 11:20 ought not be dismissed either. It is one thing to label Jeremiah 11:20 and similar

passages as metaphor—this could well be justified. It is quite another thing to go on to assume that these passages contribute nothing to our understanding of ancient Israelite sacrifice. If rituals (sacrifice included) mean anything at all, they involve metaphors, practically by definition.[64] Why dismiss one set of metaphors from the discussion of another? Considering that a fair amount of evidence can be marshaled in defense of the argument that the notion of *imitatio Dei* informed ancient Israelite approaches to sacrifice, the prophetic images which depict God in sacrificial terms or in pastoral roles ought to be looked at very seriously. These may well be root metaphors that contribute to our understanding of what sacrifice meant to ancient Israelites.

Sacrifice, then, ought to be understood *metaphorically*—and I use the term advisedly.[65] There is an analogy at the heart of sacrifice.[66] The offerer and priest play the part of God, and the domesticated animals—from the herd and the flock—play the part of the people (and particularly Israel). This analogy can be fully appreciated only when both halves receive equal consideration: As God is to people, so too—during the process of sacrifice—is the people of Israel to the domesticated animals offered for sacrifice. Indeed, one value of understanding sacrifice metaphorically is that we are encouraged to think of the roles played by both the people and the animals. Theories of sacrifice that identify the (usually innocent) animal with the (usually guilty) offerer without identifying the offerer with something or someone else—as analogy would require—can only hope to explain half of sacrifice, if even that much.

Before concluding, we need to counter two tropes in biblical scholarship—reflections on sacrifice which are based, in part, on judgments concerning Israel's attitude toward animals. The first misconception is the idea that because humans in the beginning were vegetarians, that sacrifice is therefore something that was not originally intended, or at least less than ideal.[67] It is true that Genesis 1:29–31 (cf. Genesis 9:1–

11) mandates that humans and animals are to eat only plants (even while humans are told to lord over both animals and plants in Genesis 1:28). While this diet is strictly speaking "vegetarian" and even "nonviolent," one should wonder whether these terms accurately and objectively describe the diet imagined in Genesis 1 and 2, which seems to consist exclusively of *raw* plants.[68] This diet also excludes, it would appear, dairy products, bread, and anything else that requires human effort or cooking. From a canonical perspective, agriculture begins with the expulsion from the garden (Genesis 3:17–19), and cuisine begins even later. What is more, also from a canonical perspective, animals were sacrificed by Abel (4:1–5) and Noah (8:20), before permission was granted to eat animals (9:1–3). There is therefore no direct correspondence between the permission to eat animals and the understanding that one must sacrifice them.

A second misconception concerning biblical attitudes toward animals and animal sacrifices also concerns the Genesis narratives. It is sometimes suggested that the Hebrew Bible has a stated preference for animal over vegetable offerings, reflecting the preference of herding over agriculture.[69] This is ostensibly borne out by the Cain and Abel story—where the agrarian Cain kills the pastoralist Abel after the former's sacrifice was rejected by God (Genesis 4:1–8). This is also borne out, ostensibly, by the fact that Leviticus chapters 1–2 detail sacrificial rules beginning with expensive animals and working its way down to grain. But interpretations of sacrifice that pit herders against farmers overlook two indisputable facts. First, the sacrificial rituals of the priestly traditions routinely involve offerings consisting of both animal and vegetable (e.g., Exodus 29:38–42; Leviticus 24:5–9; Numbers 28:1–8), as well as wine, oil, and other sundry products. Second, the literary and archaeological evidence for ancient Israel suggests that herders and farmers worked together: the ancient Israelite economy was neither entirely nomadic nor exclusively agricultural.[70] These two facts are two sides of

the same coin: the social life of ancient Israel involved both plants and animals, and its ritual reflects that symbiosis.

Ancient Israel and Animal Sacrifice

Those who would seek to equate the value of people and animals would find little support for their views in the literature and rituals of ancient Israel. The sacrificial rituals of the Hebrew Bible are predicated on the inequality of people and animals: the sacrificial offerings come from the animals that Israelites owned and raised, bought and sold. But this inequality is relative, not absolute. The key to understanding ancient Israelite sacrifice is to remember the analogy: as God is to Israel, so is Israel to its flocks and herds.

We do well, therefore, to think of Israel's sacrificial animals as subjects, not as objects. While it is all too easy to objectify the sacrificial carcass, to do so focuses all attention on only one aspect of a complex and meaningful process. We do better also to reflect on all the meaning implied in the fact that Israelites offered sacrifices from the herd and flock at the same time that they understood their God (to whom they sacrificed) as their shepherd. It stands to reason, therefore, that the meaning of sacrifice to ancient Israelites was informed not only by what took place at the altar, but also by what transpired in their relationships with animals before getting to the altar. The sacrificial animal must be birthed, protected, fed, and guided—all things that Israel wished for themselves from their God. The meaning of sacrifice, therefore, derives not primarily from what the animals offered Israel, but rather from what Israel provided to its domesticated animals, which parallels the care that they wished their God to provide for them.

The selective killing of animals for the sake of worshipping God will never sit well with those of us raised in modern nonsacrificing religious traditions. But the selective denigration of sacrifice by moderns who use animals without living with them should not sit well with us either. Those who approach sacrifice in ancient Israel with the presumption that sacrifice is primitive and unethical cannot help us understand what sacrificing animals meant to ancient Israel. Ancient Israel was a culture that not only lived with animals, but thought and theologized with them too. At the same time as they sacrificed their own domesticated animals, they were very likely thinking of themselves as their God's flock:

> The Lord is my Shepherd, I shall not want.
> He makes me lie down in green pastures;
> He leads me beside still waters …
>
> (Psalms 23:1–2)

> He will feed his flock like a shepherd;
> He will gather the lambs in his arms,

> and carry them in his bosom
> and gently lead the mother sheep.
>
> (Isaiah 40:11)

> I myself will be the shepherd of my sheep, and I will make them lie down, says the Lord God. I will seek the lost, and I will bring back the strayed, and I will bind up the injured, and I will strengthen the weak, but the fat and the strong I will destroy. I will feed them with justice.
>
> (Ezekiel 34:15–16)

If placing oneself in the position of another constitutes the essence of empathy, then ancient Israel had empathy to spare for their own domesticated animals, even when—or perhaps, especially when—they carefully guided them to the altar to sacrifice them to their own divine shepherd.

NOTES

1. See, especially, René Girard, *Violence and the Sacred* (Baltimore: Johns Hopkins University Press, 1977) and Walter Burkert, *Homo Necans: The Anthropology of Ancient Greek Sacrificial Ritual and Myth* (Berkeley: University of California Press, 1983). See also the essays in Robert G. Hamerton-Kelly, ed., *Violent Origins: Walter Burkert, René Girard, and Jonathan Z. Smith on Ritual Killing and Cultural Formation* (Stanford: Stanford University Press, 1987). For further bibliography and discussion of sacrifice in general and in ancient Israel in particular see Klawans, "Pure Violence: Sacrifice and Defilement in Ancient Israel," *Harvard Theological Review* 94 (2001): 133–55, and *Purity, Sacrifice, and the Temple: Symbolism and Supersessionism in the Study of Ancient Judaism* (New York: Oxford University Press, 2005). The latter presents the author's fuller treatment of the arguments presented below.

2. Cf. the comments of Marcel Detienne (p. 3) and Jean-Louis Durand (p. 88) in Detienne and Jean-Pierre Vernant, eds., *The Cuisine of Sacrifice Among the Greeks,* trans. Paula Wissing (Chicago:

University of Chicago Press, 1989). See also Mary Douglas, *Leviticus as Literature* (Oxford: Oxford University Press, 1999), pp. 66–67.

3. Cf. Mary Douglas, *Purity and Danger: An Analysis of the Concepts of Pollution and Taboo* (London: Routledge and Kegan Paul, 1966), pp. 73–93.

4. See, e.g., Gillian Feeley-Harnik, *The Lord's Table: The Meaning of Food in Early Judaism and Christianity* (Washington, D.C.: Smithsonian Institution Press, 1994) and Robert G. Hamerton-Kelly, *The Gospel and the Sacred: Poetics of Violence in Mark* (Minneapolis: Fortress Press, 1994). See Klawans, "Interpreting the Last Supper: Sacrifice, Spiritualization, and Anti-Sacrifice," *New Testament Studies* 48 (2002): 1–17, for further bibliography and discussion.

5. On the elimination of references to sacrifice (or just the restoration of sacrifice) from the traditional Jewish liturgy, see Ismar Elbogen, *Jewish Liturgy: A Comprehensive History* (Philadelphia: Jewish Publication Society, 1993), pp. 308–32. For a more comprehensive history of this phenomenon, see Jakob J. Petuchowski, *Prayerbook Reform in Eu-*

rope (New York: World Union for Progressive Judaism, 1968).

6. For Geiger's views on sacrifice and liturgical reform, see Petuchowski, *Prayerbook Reform*, pp. 33–35, 165–171.

7. See for instance the treatment in the following commentaries, meant for use in modern English-speaking synagogues: Joseph H. Hertz, ed., *The Pentateuch and Haftorahs: Hebrew Text, English Translation and Commentary* (London: Soncino Press, 1961), p. 486 (on Lev. 17:7) and pp. 560–62; W. Gunther Plaut, ed., *The Torah: a Modern Commentary* (New York: Union of American Hebrew Congregations, 1981), pp. 750–55 (comments on sacrifice by Bernard J. Bamberger) and pp. 1217–18 (comments by W. Gunther Plaut); and now also: David L. Lieber, ed., *Etz Hayim: Torah and Commentary* (New York: The Rabbinical Assembly, 2001), pp. 585–86 (comments edited by Harold Kushner), pp. 1446–50 (essay by Gordon Tucker). For the spillover of this approach into the academic realm, see Jacob Milgrom, *Leviticus 1–16: A New Translation with Introduction and Commentary* (*The Anchor Bible* 3; New York: Doubleday, 1992), pp. 440–43 and 1003.

8. Traditional (Orthodox) Judaism, by contrast, still holds out the hope for the eventual rebuilding of the temple in Jerusalem and, along with that, the restoration of sacrificial practice. But for reasons that we need not discuss here, those who hold the traditionalist Jewish views do very little academic scholarship on biblical sacrifice.

9. Some prophetic texts do state that God rejects the sacrifices of the wicked Israelites (e.g., Isa. 1:11; Jer. 6:20; Mic. 6:6–9; cf. also Prov. 15:8, 21:27). Yet it is anachronistic to understand these passages as rejections of sacrifice per se. Prophetic visions of restoration—true to their time—imagined a temple in Jerusalem and sacrifices on its altar (see, e.g., Isa. 2:1–2; Jer. 33:18; Mic. 4:1–2 and of course Ezekiel 40–48). See my fuller discussion of the prophetic approaches to sacrifice in *Purity, Sacrifice, and the Temple*, pp. 75–100.

10. Victor Turner, "Sacrifice as Quintessential Process: Prophylaxis or Abandonment?" *History of Religions* 16 (1977): 189–215.

11. Henri Hubert and Marcel Mauss, *Sacrifice: Its Nature and Functions*, trans. W.D. Halls (Chicago: University of Chicago Press, 1964), esp. pp. 19–32.

12. Ancient Israel's sacrificial worship included (among other things) offerings of grain (Lev. 2:1–16), bread (Lev. 24:5–9), and incense (Exod. 30:34–38). On the significance of the incense altar, for example, see Carol Meyers, "Realms of Sanctity: The Case of the 'Misplaced' Incense Altar in the Tabernacle Texts of Exodus," in Michael V. Fox, et al., eds., *Texts, Temples, and Traditions: A Tribute to Menaḥem Haran* (Winona Lake, IN: Eisenbrauns, 1996), pp. 33–46.

13. For a fuller summary of ancient Israelite sacrificial worship see Gary A. Anderson, "Sacrifice and Sacrificial Offerings (OT)," in David Noel Freedman, ed., *The Anchor Bible Dictionary* (New York: Doubleday, 1992), 5:870–86.

14. Leviticus treats rules of sacrifice in (roughly, and not exclusively) Leviticus chapters 1–10, and rules pertaining to ritual purity (again, roughly, and not exclusively) in Leviticus 11–15.

15. On ritual impurity in general see David P. Wright, "Unclean and Clean (OT)," in Freedman, ed., *The Anchor Bible Dictionary*, 6:729–41. See also Klawans, *Impurity and Sin in Ancient Judaism* (New York: Oxford University Press, 2000), pp. 21–42.

16. Milgrom, *Leviticus 1–16*, pp. 766–8 and 1000–1004; quote from 1002. For a critical discussion of the impurity as death theory, see Howard Eilberg-Schwartz, *The Savage in Judaism: An Anthropology of Israelite Religion and Ancient Judaism* (Bloomington: Indiana University Press, 1990), pp. 182–86, and 248, n. 16.

17. On the dietary laws in general as understood in this light, see Milgrom, *Leviticus 1–16*, pp. 704–42, esp. 732–33, and 741–42. On the pig's role in chthonic worship, see Milgrom, *Leviticus 1–16*, pp. 649–53; on the blood prohibition, see Milgrom, *Leviticus 1–16*, pp. 704–13.

18. Milgrom, *Leviticus 1–16*, pp. 732–33.

19. Milgrom, *Leviticus 1–16*, pp. 766 and 1001–2. See for instance, Emanuel Feldman, *Biblical and Post-Biblical Defilement and Mourning: Law as The-*

ology (New York: Yeshiva University Press, 1977), pp. 13–30. Regarding the ancient Israelite system, this view can be traced back at least as far as Alfred Edersheim, *The Temple: Its Ministry and Services as They Were at the Time of Jesus Christ* (London: Religious Tract Society, 1874), pp. 348–50.

20. See Anna S. Meigs, "A Papuan Perspective on Pollution," *Man* 13 (1978): 304–18, which Milgrom cites in his discussion (*Leviticus 1–16*, p. 1001). On the centrality of death to the Zoroastrian impurity system, see Jamsheed K. Choksy, *Purity and Pollution in Zoroastrianism* (Austin: University of Texas Press, 1989), pp. 16–19. Death also figures prominently in ancient Greek conceptions of impurity, see Robert Parker, *Miasma: Pollution and Purification in Early Greek Religion* (Oxford: Clarendon Press, 1983), pp. 32–73.

21. In ancient Egyptian religion, for instance, corpses were purified in order to secure their safe passage into the next world, but corpses were not considered a source of ritual defilement for the living. Indeed, corpses were brought into sanctuaries; see Aylward M. Blackman, "Purification (Egyptian)," in James Hastings, ed., *The Encyclopedia of Religion and Ethics* (New York: Scribner's, 1919), 10: 476–82.

22. This same question is also posed by Eilberg-Schwartz, *The Savage in Judaism*, p. 186.

23. Tikva Frymer-Kensky, "Pollution, Purification, and Purgation in Biblical Israel," in Carol L. Meyers and M. O'Connor, eds., *The Word of the Lord Shall Go Forth: Essays in Honor of David Noel Freedman in Celebration of his Sixtieth Birthday* (Winona Lake: Eisenbrauns, 1983), pp. 399–410, esp. p. 401; Frymer-Kensky, *In the Wake of the Goddesses: Women, Culture and the Biblical Transformation of Pagan Myth* (New York: Fawcett Columbine, 1992), esp. p. 189; Wright, "Unclean and Clean (OT)," esp. p. 739. On the more general question of the role of gender in the ritual purity system, see Eilberg-Schwartz, *The Savage in Judaism*, pp. 178–82, and Klawans, *Impurity and Sin*, pp. 38–41.

24. Wright, "Unclean and Clean," p. 739.

25. Frymer-Kensky, *In the Wake*, p. 189.

26. Hubert and Mauss, *Sacrifice*, p. 20; cf. pp. 84–85.

27. On the issue of control and its relationship to ancient Israelite ritual purity and sacrifice, see Eilberg-Schwartz, *The Savage*, pp. 186–94; cf. Klawans, "Pure Violence," pp. 144–45.

28. Biblical passages here and below are quoted from the New Revised Standard Version (NRSV), with some modifications.

29. Whether or not, as Walter Burkert maintains, sacrifice finds its origins in the domestication of primitive hunting practices, it must be kept in mind that sacrifice is generally—and certainly in ancient Israel—performed on domesticated animals by agrarians and pastoralists. See Burkert, "The Problem of Ritual Killing," in Hamerton-Kelly, ed., *Violent Origins*, pp. 149–76 and Jonathan Z. Smith, "The Domestication of Sacrifice," also in Hamerton-Kelly, ed., *Violent Origins*, pp. 191–205, esp. p. 197.

30. Smith, "Domestication," pp. 191–205, quote from p. 199.

31. Smith, "Domestication," p. 197.

32. Smith, "Domestication," p. 204; this is the thesis of Erich Isaac, "On the Domestication of Cattle," *Science* 137 (1962): 195–204; cf. also Girard, *Things Hidden Since the Foundation of the World* (Stanford: Stanford University Press, 1987), pp. 68–73.

33. Smith, "Domestication," p. 206.

34. Hamerton-Kelly, ed., *Violent Origins*, p. 213.

35. Smith, "Domestication," pp. 191–96; see also Smith's comments in the discussion that follows, esp. pp. 206–14, 224–25.

36. Smith, "Domestication," p. 199.

37. Bruce D. Smith, *The Emergence of Agriculture* (New York: Scientific American Library, 1995), p. 18. With special attention to the animals of the biblical world, see also Edwin Firmage, "Zoology (Fauna)," in Freedman, ed., *The Anchor Bible Dictionary*, 6:1111–67. Some recent research emphasizes the roles played by animals themselves in this process: see Stephen Budiansky, *The Covenant of the Wild: Why Animals Chose Domestication* (New Haven: Yale University Press, 1999). Of course, the origins of this process are not directly of concern here—for the present purposes we focus on the imbalanced relationship between shepherds and their

domesticated flocks, especially as perceived by ancient Israelite shepherds themselves.

38. B. D. Smith, *The Emergence of Agriculture*,
p. 18.

39. See Smith, *The Emergence of Agriculture*, pp.
28–33.

40. On Israel's dietary rules, see Milgrom, *Leviticus 1–16*, pp. 641–742; cf. Eilberg-Schwartz, *The Savage*, pp. 125–26, 218–21. Of course, Douglas, *Purity
and Danger*, pp. 41–57 remains important, but
Douglas herself has revisited the topic and changed
her views a number of times; see "The Forbidden
Animals in Leviticus," *Journal for the Study of the Old
Testament* 59 (1993): 3–23 and, most recently, *Leviticus as Literature*, pp. 134–75.

41. Milgrom, *Leviticus 1–16*, pp. 721–26.

42. On animal metaphors in ancient Israel, see
Eilberg-Schwartz, *The Savage*, pp. 115–40.

43. Eilberg-Schwartz, *The Savage*, pp. 120–21,
and 247 n. 5.

44. For the image of God protecting his flock,
see, e.g., Gen. 49:24; Isa. 40:11, and Jer. 31:10. For
the image of God guiding his flock see, e.g., Isa.
40:11, 49:10–11, 63:13–14; Jer. 23:3–4, 31:10, 50:19,
Ezek. 34:13; Mic. 2:12, 7:14; Ps. 23:1–3, 78:52 and
80:2. For the image of feeding see: Jer. 50:19; Ezek.
34:13–15, Hos. 4:16; Mic. 7:14 and Ps. 23:1–3. For
the image of slaughter, see Isa. 53:7; Jer. 12:3, 51:40;
Ezek. 34:16; and Ps. 44:12, 23. Other general references to God as shepherd include Jer. 13:17; Ps. 74:1,
79:13, 95:7, and 100:3. For extended passages incorporating many of the above images (and others as
well) see Ezekiel ch. 34 and Zechariah chs. 10–13. At
times, God is depicted as ruling over Israel's shepherds—dismissing Israel's failed leaders, and ap-
pointing new ones (e.g., Jer. 23:1–4, and Ezek. 34:1).
But even in these passages it is also asserted that
God too is to play the role of shepherd (Jer. 23:3–4;
Ezek. 34:10). Some have creatively argued that passages such as Psalm 23:1–3 do not mean that Israel
understood God as a shepherd: see Victor H. Matthews and Don C. Benjamin, *Social World of Ancient
Israel, 1250–587 BCE* (Peabody, MA: Hendrickson,
1993), pp. 63–64. The prevalence of these images,
however, compels us to take them seriously.

45. See Mircea Eliade, *The Myth of the Eternal
Return: Or, Cosmos and History* (Princeton: Princeton University Press, 1954), pp. 3–48.

46. Levenson, *Creation and the Persistence of Evil:
The Jewish Drama of Divine Omnipotence* (Princeton: Princeton University Press, 1988), pp. 78–99
and pp. 100–120; *Sinai and Zion: An Entry into the
Jewish Bible* (San Francisco: Harper & Row Publishers, 1985), pp. 142–45; cf. also Michael Fishbane,
*Text and Texture: Close Readings of Selected Biblical
Texts* (New York: Schocken Books, 1979), pp. 3–16.
For some observations on *imitatio Dei* relating more
directly to sacrifice, see also Levenson, *The Death
and Resurrection of the Beloved Son: The Transformation of Child Sacrifice in Judaism and Christianity*
(New Haven: Yale University Press, 1993), pp. 25–
32.

47. Douglas, *Purity and Danger*, pp. 53–54; Milgrom, *Leviticus 17–22*, p. 873.

48. See Erhard S. Gerstenberger, *Leviticus: A
Commentary* (*The Old Testament Library;* Louisville:
Westminster John Knox Press, 1996), pp. 26, 29;
and Gordon J. Wenham, *The Book of Leviticus* (*The
New International Commentary on the Old Testament;* Grand Rapids, MI: William B. Eerdmans,
1979), p. 55.

49. See Jer. 11:20, 17:10, 20:12; Ps. 7:10; Prov.
17:3; 1 Chron. 29:17. In most English editions of
the Bible, the phrase is translated figuratively, which
obscures the sacrificial nature of the metaphor. The
NJV reads "test the thoughts and the mind"; the
NRSV reads: "who try the heart and mind"; the
RSV reads: "who triest the heart and the mind."
For a more literal reading one must go back to the
KJV, which reads: "that triest the reins and heart."
The idea that ancient Israelites believed the heart
to be the center of thought (e.g., Deut. 8:5 and
1 Kings 2:44) is beside the point. The figurative
translations obscure the fact that organs being examined are, regardless of their function, organs that
figure prominently in sacrificial rituals (e.g., Lev.
3:4, 10, 15).

50. I thank Jon D. Levenson for bringing this aspect of Isaiah 63 to my attention. Note too that a
number of sacrificial terms appear in the passage:

e.g., "daub" (v. 3) and "lean" (v. 5). See also Isaiah 34–35, for similar images and usages.

51. See also Jer. 46:10 and Ezek. 39:17–20; cf. Isa. 30:27 in which God's "sifting" of the nations is described with the same term as the priestly "waving" of sacrificial offerings (e.g., Lev. 9:21).

52. For a classic articulation of this view, see Roland de Vaux, *Studies in Old Testament Sacrifice* (Cardiff: University of Wales Press, 1964), esp. pp. 38–42. For a more recent articulation of this view, see Milgrom, *Leviticus 1–16*, p. 440. For a critique of this kind of approach, see Gary A. Anderson, *Sacrifices and Offerings in Ancient Israel: Studies in their Social and Political Importance* (Atlanta, GA: Scholars Press, 1987), pp. 14–19; and "Sacrifice and Sacrificial Offerings (OT)," p. 872.

53. See, e.g., Num. 9:15; Deut. 4:24, 9:3, 32:22, and Lam. 2:3; cf. also 2 Kings 1:10–11. Generally, on the notion of holy war see, Gerhard Von Rad, *Holy War in Ancient Israel* (Grand Rapids, MI: William B. Eerdmans, 1991); Susan Niditch, *War in the Hebrew Bible: A Study in the Ethics of Violence* (New York: Oxford University Press, 1993). On sacrificial aspects of holy war ideology see Niditch, *War*, esp. pp. 28–55. The appearance of God as a consuming fire is just one of a number of phenomena common to both sacrificial and military ideologies in the Hebrew Bible. In the (priestly) wilderness traditions, God's residence finds its place in the midst of a war camp. Moreover, ritual purity is a prerequisite for holy war, just as it is for sacrifice (Deut. 23:10–15, 2 Sam. 11:11; cf. Von Rad, *Holy War*, p. 42). God is also depicted as a warrior in many of the passages (cited above) that describe God manipulating blood (e.g., Isa. 34:6–7).

54. See, e.g., Exod. 24:17; Lev. 9:24; 10:2; Num. 9:15; 1 Kings 18:38; cf. also Gen. 15:17 and 1 Chron. 21:26.

55. Of course, Israelites will perform these activities less frequently, and with less intensity, than their priests.

56. For a useful and readable survey of the complex philosophical debates on metaphor and their impact on contemporary understandings of religious language, see Dan R. Stiver, *The Philosophy of Religious Language: Sign, Symbol, and Story* (Malden, MA: Blackwell, 1996) esp. pp. 112–133. Further on philosophy and metaphor, see the helpful collection of essays in Sheldon Sacks, ed., *On Metaphor* (Chicago: University of Chicago Press, 1978), which contains seminal essays by, among others, Donald Davidson and Paul Ricoeur. For an anthropological perspective on metaphor, see, e.g., James W. Fernandez, *Persuasions and Performances: The Play of Tropes in Culture* (Bloomington: Indiana University Press, 1986) esp. pp. 3–70; and Claude Lévi-Strauss, *Totemism* (Boston: Beacon Press, 1962). For a brief survey of some of the relevant anthropological literature, with specific attention to biblical metaphors, see Eilberg-Schwartz, *The Savage*, pp. 115–40. Perhaps the most challenging (and the most readable) of contemporary philosophical work on metaphor is George Lakoff and Mark Johnson, *Metaphors We Live By* (Chicago: University of Chicago Press, 1980). Another useful and readable work that is more directly related to the Hebrew Bible is G. B. Caird, *The Language and Imagery of the Bible* (London: Duckworth, 1980). Despite the fact that this work is often confessional (e.g., p. 271) and at times offensive (e.g., p. 143, where Jewish dietary laws are described as "tyranny"), it contains helpful discussions of meaning in general (pp. 35–84) and metaphor in particular (see pp. 131–59). Thanks are due to Marc A. Cohen for providing the bibliography and for helping me to find some grounding in the philosophic and linguistic debates regarding metaphor.

57. On the anti-metaphorical bias in western philosophy, see Ted Cohen, "Metaphor and the Cultivation of Intimacy," in Sacks, ed., *On Metaphor*, esp. pp. 1–3; Lakoff and Johnson, *Metaphors We Live By*, pp. 189–92; and Stiver, *The Philosophy of Religious Language*, pp. 8–13, 112–14.

58. See especially Lakoff and Johnson, *Metaphors We Live By*. See also Fernandez, *Persuasions and Performances*, esp. pp. 32–36, 58; Lévi-Strauss, *Totemism*, esp. p. 102; and Stiver, *The Philosophy of Religious Language*, pp. 112–33. On biblical metaphors in particular, see Eilberg-Schwartz, *The Savage*, esp. pp. 117–21.

59. Eilberg-Schwartz is a notable exception.

60. This statement deserves qualification. Some sacrificial metaphors, like those we catalogue here, are systematically ignored. Other sacrificial metaphors—like the analogy between sacrifices and gifts (e.g., Num. 18:12) or between sacrifice and food (e.g., Ezek. 44:16)—receive attention. But these metaphors have been elevated arbitrarily to the level of "theory." This observation on the fluidity between "theory" and "metaphor" vis-à-vis sacrifice is based on Edmund Leach, "The Logic of Sacrifice," in *Culture and Communication: The Logic by Which Symbols are Connected* (Cambridge: Cambridge University Press, 1976), pp. 81–93.

61. Caird, *Language and Imagery*, pp. 185–97.

62. Caird, *Language and Imagery*, p. 246.

63. Generally, see Fernandez, *Persuasions and Performances*, pp. 23–24; Lakoff and Johnson, *Metaphors We Live By*, pp. 147–55. On biblical metaphors in particular, see Eilberg-Schwartz, *The Savage*, pp. 122–26.

64. On metaphor and ritual generally, see Fernandez, *Persuasions and Performances*, pp. 23–24; 41–50; and Lakoff and Johnson, *Metaphors We Live By*, pp. 233–35. With regard to the Hebrew Bible specifically, see Eilberg-Schwartz, *The Savage*, pp. 119, 122–26. Some prefer to understand rituals as metonymic. On the distinction between metaphor and metonymy, see Lakoff and Johnson, *Metaphors We Live By*, pp. 35–40. For a theory of sacrifice as metonymic, see Lévi-Strauss, *The Savage Mind* (Chicago: University of Chicago Press, 1966), pp. 222–28.

65. We follow Leach in this respect against Lévi-Strauss. Where Lévi-Strauss dismissed sacrifice as metonymic and largely nonsensical (*Savage Mind*, pp. 222–28), Leach defended sacrifice in general (and ancient Israelite sacrifice in particular) as logical, symbolic and metaphorical. See Leach, "Logic of Sacrifice."

66. Similar analogies may well be involved in other ritual structures that can be understood in light of *imitatio Dei*: e.g., Israelites resting on the recurring seventh day of the week as God rested on the eternal seventh day of creation; Israelites constructing a temple on earth as God constructed the earth itself. The notion of *imitatio Dei* has its limits: people cannot fully identify with God; they can merely aspire briefly to play on the human level roles otherwise played by God on the divine level.

67. For this approach, see J. W. Rogerson, "What was the Meaning of Animal Sacrifice?" in Andrew Linzey and Dorothy Yamamoto, eds., *Animals on the Agenda: Questions about Animals for Theology and Ethics* (Urbana: University of Illinois Press, 1998), pp. 8–17.

68. On the vagaries of the term "vegetarian," see, e.g., Catherine Osborne, "Ancient Vegetarianism," in John Wilkins, David Harvey and Mike Dobson, eds., *Food in Antiquity* (Exeter: University of Exeter Press, 1995), pp. 214–24.

69. See, e.g., Ithamar Gruenwald, *Rituals and Ritual Theory in Ancient Israel* (Leiden: Brill, 2003), pp. 40–93.

70. For literary and archaeological evidence on farming and herding in ancient Israel, see Matthews and Benjamin, *Social World of Ancient Israel*, pp. 37–66.

Hope for the Animal Kingdom

A Jewish Vision

DAN COHN-SHERBOK

Throughout its long history, Judaism has emphasized that the animal kingdom is to be respected and dealt with kindly. In the earliest writings of the tradition as well as in its later commentaries, many injunctions exist regarding each human's obligation to treat nonhuman animals well. The animals included are not only the domesticated animals that are an integral part of any community, but also animals without an owner and those belonging to non-Jews. The underlying vision of merciful treatment of all living beings is thus a central feature of Judaism's idea of a moral life, and this remains true even though humans are allowed in a number of ways to use other animals as food, laborers, and property.

As with so many things Jewish, there is debate on just how far this moral obligation extends. One can find traditional statements or comments from contemporary thinkers to the effect that life outside the human species is here for humans' benefit. But even when human uses of other animals are permitted by Judaism, such uses are highly regulated in ways that reflect the mandate to minimize as much as possible suffering of any kind.

Animals and the Torah

Because animals are part of God's creation, humanity has a special responsibility for their care. Such an idea is expressed in the Book of Genesis where God commands that both human beings and creatures should fill the earth. Humankind, he declares, is to dominate all living things:

> Then God said, "Let us make man in our image, after our likeness; and let them have dominion over the fish of the sea, and over the birds of the air, and over the cattle, and over all the earth, and over every creeping thing that creeps upon the earth." So God created man in his own image, in the image of God he created him; male and female he created them. And God blessed them, and God said to them, "Be fruitful and multi-

ply, and fill the earth and subdue it; and have dominion over the fish of the sea and over the birds
of the air and over every living thing that moves
upon the earth."

(Genesis 1:26–28)

It might be assumed that such an injunction
gives license for human beings to treat animals
in any way they wish. Scripture, however, insists
that dominance implies stewardship. Although
animals can be eaten and used for sacrifice, the
Bible insists on humane and compassionate concern for all of God's creatures. Such an attitude
is exemplified in the Torah, which lists a variety
of laws governing their treatment. The Book
of Deuteronomy, for example, states that "You
shall not muzzle an ox when it treads out the
grain." (Deuteronomy 25:4). Here the law specifies that when an ox is threshing, it should not
be prevented from eating the grain it has beaten
out; like those who work the field, working animals are entitled to the food they have labored
to produce.

Such humanitarian concern is reflected in
Deuteronomy 22:1–3 where all Israelites are
commanded to look after domestic animals that
have been lost:

You shall not see your brother's ox or his sheep
going astray, and withhold your help from them;
you shall take them back to your brother. And if
he is not near you, or if you do not know him,
you shall bring it home to your house, and it shall
be with you until your brother seeks it; then you
shall restore it to him, and so you shall do with
his ass.

Moreover, the next verse adds that if a domestic animal has fallen, one should help its
owner so as to avoid any injury to the beast:

You shall not see your brother's ass or his ox fallen
down by the way, and withhold your help from
them; you shall help him to lift them again.

(Deuteronomy 22:4)

In a parallel passage the Book of Exodus deals
with the animals of one's enemies—even in such
situations, innocent creatures are to be treated
with kindness. One's feelings about their owners should not override the principle of humane
consideration:

If you meet the enemy's ox or his ass going astray,
you shall bring it back to him. If you see the ass
of one who hates you lying under its burden, you
shall refrain from leaving him with it, you shall
help him to lift it up.

(Exodus 23:4–5)

Such kindness toward the beasts of the field
is to be extended to other creatures. Thus, Deuteronomy states that birds, too, must be treated
with mercy. Here instructions are given about
what to do with a bird's nest in which birds
or eggs are found with their mother—the law
stipulates that the mother is to be set free so she
can produce more offspring:

If you chance to come upon a bird's nest, in any
tree or on the ground, with young ones or eggs
and the mother sitting upon the young or upon
the eggs, you shall not take the mother with the
young; you shall let the mother go, but the young
you make take to yourself.

(Deuteronomy 22:6–7)

Specific legislation was also invoked to insure
that animals should be protected from harm
in a wide range of circumstances. So as to insure that in cases where animals were yoked together, Deuteronomy 22:10 prohibits the harnessing together of a strong and weak animal:
"You shall not plow with an ox and an ass together." Sabbath law similarly expresses concern
with animal welfare—just as human beings are
to rest on the Sabbath, so are beasts of the field:

Remember the Sabbath day, to keep it holy. Six
days you shall labor, and do all your work; but
the seventh day is a Sabbath to the Lord your

God; in it you shall not do any work, you, or your son, or your daughter, or your manservant, or your maidservant, or your ox, or your ass, or any of your cattle.

In a similar fashion, animals are to be cared for during the Sabbatical year—the grain produced during this period is to be eaten by the beasts of the field as well as the needy:

The Sabbath of the land shall provide food for you, for yourself and for your male and female slaves and for your hired servant and the sojourner who lives with you; for your cattle also and for the beasts that are in your land all its yield shall be for food.

(Leviticus 25:6–7)

According to Scripture, the feelings of animals should be taken into consideration. Thus Leviticus states: "And when the mother is a cow or ewe, you shall not kill both her and her young in one day." (Lev. 22:28) Such a merciful attitude is reflected in a similar prohibition against boiling a kid in its mother's milk, an injunction found in Exodus 23:19, 23:26, and Deuteronomy 14:2. The Bible, thus, provides a framework for the merciful treatment of all living things—the animal kingdom is to be respected and dealt with kindly.

The Rabbinic View

Following biblical teaching, the rabbis stressed the need for animal welfare: all living things are part of God's creation and therefore require special consideration. With regard to the basic principle that one should not inflict pain on animals, the twelfth-century Jewish philosopher Moses Maimonides and the medieval Jewish mystic Judah ha-Hasid appealed to Numbers 22:32 where the angel of God says to Balaam: "Why have you struck your ass?" In the light of such a sentiment, the *Code of Jewish Law* declares:

It is forbidden, according to the law of the Torah, to inflict pain upon any living creature. On the contrary, it is our duty to relieve the pain of any creature, even if it is ownerless or belongs to a non-Jew.[1]

Applying this rule to specific circumstances, the *Code* goes on to legislate:

When horses, drawing a cart, come to a rough rode or a steep hill, and it is hard for them to draw the cart without help, it is our duty to help them, even when they belong to a non-Jew, because of the precept not to be cruel to animals, lest the owner smite them to force them to draw more than their strength permits.[2]

Turning to the specific biblical legislation about the treatment of animals, the medieval Jewish exegete Rashbam commenting on the prohibition against boiling a kid in its mother's milk stated: "It is an unworthy act and a form of gluttony to eat the milk of the mother with (the meat of) its young, and the same principle is to be found in the laws against killing a mother and its young on the same day, and 'sending the mother bird away.' The command is intended to teach civilized behavior."[3] In a similar vein, the medieval philosopher and biblical scholar Abraham Ibn Ezra speculated about the intention of this law: "Perhaps (the reason for the command) is that it represents cruelty to cook a young goat in its mother's milk, in the same way as 'Do not slaughter a cow or a sheep and its young on the same day' and 'you must take the mother (bird) along with its young.'"[4]

In connection with the prohibition in Leviticus against killing an animal and its young, *Targum Yonatan* states: "Sons of Israel, O my people, just as I in heaven am merciful, so shall you be merciful on earth. Neither cow nor ewe shall you sacrifice along with her young on the same day."[5] The midrash *Vayikra Rabba* continues this theme; here R. Berekiah said in the name of R. Levi: "It is written, 'A righteous man cares for the needs of his animal' (Proverbs 12:10). 'Righteous man' refers to the Holy One, blessed be He, in whose Torah it is written, 'You must not take the mother along with the young.' … Another explanation is that 'A righteous man cares' applies to the Holy One, blessed be He, in whose Torah it is written, 'Whether it is a bull, a sheep or a goat, do not slaughter it and its child on the same day.'"[6]

Maimonides, too, added his reflections on this verse in the *Guide for the Perplexed:*

It is prohibited to kill an animal with its young on the same day, in order that people should be restrained and prevented from killing the two together in such a manner that the young is slain in the sight of the mother; for the pain of the animals under such circumstances is very great. There is no difference in this case between the pain of man and the pain of other living beings, since the love and tenderness of the mother for her young ones is not produced by reasoning, but by imagination, and this faculty exists not only in man but in most living beings.[7]

According to Maimonides, the same reason which applies to the prohibition against killing a dam and its young on the same day so as to spare the animal grief also applies to the law which enjoins that we should let the mother fly away when we take the young: "If the law provides that such grief should not be caused to cattle or birds, how much more careful must we be that we should not cause grief to your fellow-men."[8]

Echoing such a sentiment, the nineteenth-century scholar Samuel David Luzzatto in his *Yeshodei ha-Torah* wrote:

The Torah commanded to respect and be kind to animals or birds when they show acts of kindness, as is evident in the law concerning sparing the mother bird. For the dam sitting on the young or the eggs could have flow away and saved herself when she heard or saw a man approaching. Why did she not fly away and save herself? Because she had compassion for her chil-

dren. Had man been permitted to take her, he would get the impression that compassion is bad, foolish and deleterious. On the other hand, the prohibition of taking the dam indelibly imposes upon man the paramount importance of compassion.[9]

Such sensitivity to animal welfare is reflected in a number of incidents in which the rabbis expressed kindness to God's creatures. The great nineteenth-century Orthodox leader, Israel Salanter, for example, failed to appear on Yom Kippur (Day of Atonement) eve to chant the Kol Nidre prayer. When his congregation became concerned, they sent out a search party. After a considerable time Israel was found in the barn of a Christian neighbor. On the way to the synagogue, he had come across one of his neighbor's calves that had become entangled in the brush. When he saw that the beast was in distress, he led it home through the countryside. Such an act of compassion was perceived as equivalent to his prayers on that holy evening.[10]

Rabbi Zusya once went on a journey to collect money to ransom prisoners. When he came to an inn, he found a large cage with many types of birds in one room. He realized they wanted to fly out of the cage, and he had pity for them. He said to himself: "Here you are, Zusya, walking your feet off to ransom prisoners. But what greater ransoming of prisoners can there be than to free these birds?" He then opened the cage and set them free. When the innkeeper saw the empty cage, he was furious and asked those in the house who had let the birds go. They answered that there was a person loitering who appeared to be a fool and must have been the one who did this. The innkeeper shouted at Zusya: "You idiot! How could you rob me of my birds?" In response Zusya said: "You have often read these words in the Psalms — 'His tender mercies are over all his work.'" The innkeeper beat Zusya and threw him out of the inn, but Zusya went away content.[11]

Another story is told of Rabbi Abramtzi who was full of compassion: he was filled with sympathy for all living things. He would not walk on the grass lest he trample it; he was careful not to tread on grasshoppers or insects. If a dog came to his house, he would instruct the members of his household to feed it. In winter, he scattered the crumbs of bread and seed on his window sills. When sparrows and other birds picked at the food, his face lit up with joy. He looked after his horses better than his coachmen. Whenever his coach had to ascend a hill, he would climb out in order to lighten the load, and often he pushed the cart to help the horses. On summer days, he compelled his coachmen to stop so that the horses should rest and graze.

It happened one day that the rabbi was on the road on Friday. Due to the rain the road was muddy and the wagon could only proceed with difficulty. By midday not even half the journey had been completed; the horses were worn out. Rabbi Abramtzi told his driver to stop and feed the horses so they could regain their strength. Afterwards the journey continued, but the wagon sunk in to the mud, and the horses had difficulty maintaining their balance. The coachman scolded them, urging them on. Rabbi Abramtzi grabbed him by the elbow and exclaimed: "This is cruelty to animals, cruelty to animals!" The coachman was furious and complained: "What do you want me to do? Do you want to celebrate the Sabbath here?" "What of it," the rabbi said. "It is better that we celebrate the Sabbath here than bring about the death of these animals. Are they not God's creatures? See how exhausted they are. They do not have enough strength to take another step." "But what about the Sabbath?" asked the coachman. "How can Jews observe the Sabbath in the forest?" "My friend," Rabbi Abramtzi replied, "The Sabbath Queen will come to us also here, for her glory fills the whole world, particularly in those places where Jews yearn for her. The Lord shall do what is good in his eyes. He will look after us, supply us with our wants and guard us against all evil."[12]

Tsa'ar Ba'alei Chayim *and Religious Slaughter*

The concept of *tsa'ar ba'alei chayim* (kindness to animals) also applies to ritual slaughter. From biblical times Jews have been permitted to kill animals for food, but the process of slaughter is rigidly regulated by law. Hence the Book of Deuteronomy decrees: "you may slaughter any of the cattle or sheep that the Lord gives you, as I have instructed you." (Deut. 12:21). According to rabbinic tradition, there are three requirements for slaughter (*shechitah*): (1) a properly qualified slaughterer (*shochet*); (2) the proper instrument (*halaf*); and (3) the correct procedure.

As far as the *shochet* is concerned, he must be a pious and sensitive person who has been instructed in Jewish law. He must not be physically or mentally impaired, nor a drunkard; in addition, his hands must be steady. Before receiving a license, he must undergo rigorous training in the law. Instruction about animals, the *halaf,* and proper examination of the animal after it has been slaughtered are among the topics he must master.

The knife that the *shochet* is to use must be at least twice as along as the diameter of the animal's neck and must be sharp and clean—it must not have any imperfections, so that the animal is slaughtered as painlessly as possible. The act of *shechitah* should take no more than a second and ought to render the animal senseless immediately. In theory such scrupulous attention to detail should ensure that *shechitah* is the quickest and most painless way to kill animals.

There are five laws which are devised to insure that the act of slaughter is performed swiftly and without pain:

1. *Shechiyah*—delay. There should be no delay or interruption while slaughter takes place. The knife is to be kept in continuous movement backward and foreword. The slightest delay, even for a second, renders the animal unfit for food.

2. *Derasah*—pressing. The knife is to be drawn gently across the animal's neck without undue

exertion; it should not be pressed against the animal's neck. The least pressure renders the animal unkosher.

3. *Haladh*—digging. The knife should be drawn across the throat rather than stabbed into the neck of the animal and should be visible at all times.

4. *Hagramah*—slipping. The limit for the knife to be drawn is from the large ring of the trachea to the top of the upper lung when inflated. If the slaughter takes place anywhere else, the animal is rendered unfit for consumption.

5. *Ikkur*—tearing. If either the trachea or the esophagus is torn or removed from its normal position during the process of slaughter, the animal becomes unkosher.

Regarding the examination process, once the animal has been killed it should be allowed to bleed for a few moments. The *shochet* should then inspect the animal to determine if it had been suffering from any disease or deformity. The reason for such an inspection is to insure that no diseased meat will be consumed; further, since the act of *shechitah* is connected with the temple sacrifice, it should be unblemished just as animals which were to be sacrificed in ancient times were to be perfect.

In response to the question whether the Jewish method of slaughter is humane, Ronald L. Androphy writes in *Judaism and Animal Rights*:

Doctors and scientists, both Jewish and gentile, have attested to this time and time again. Modern medical technology has enabled us to test the validity of *shechitah*'s claim to painlessness. In all cases it was proven that *shechitah* is the swiftest and most painless method of slaughtering.

I have seen both nonkosher slaughtering as well as *shechitah,* and the difference between the two is enormous. In the nonkosher slaughtering the slaughterer shows no concern for the animal. The worker plunges the knife into the animal's neck, stabbing, hacking, and slicing through the throat. The animal shrieks in pain, its whole

body twisting in agony, its face and its eyes screwed up. Death is not only drawn out, it certainly is excruciatingly painful. The *shechitah* I witnessed was exactly the opposite. The *shochet* was quick; in less than a second he was done. The animal did not cry out. Its body and face were not contorted in agony.

Shechitah is effective for several reasons: first, the *shochet* is not a slaughterhouse worker but a specifically trained, tested, supervised and sensitive individual who knows exactly what has to be done and how to do it; second, the knife used is more than razor sharp so that the animal does not feel any pain when the *shochet* draws the knife across the animal's throat. Most importantly, the act of *shechitah* not only severs the trachea and esophagus but it also severs the jugular veins and carotid arteries. The result is a sudden and voluminous outpouring of blood and immediate acute anemia of the brain thus rendering the animal senseless instantaneously.[13]

While such a view is contested by various animal welfare organizations who maintain that pre-stunning is in fact more humane than the Jewish form of slaughter,[14] there is no doubt that this traditional procedure was intended to cause animals the least pain possible in accord with the Jewish principle of *tsa'ar ba'alei chayim.* Even the fiercest contemporary critics of *shechitah* acknowledge that for millennia the Jewish method of slaughter was the least painful form of animal killing until this century.

Animal Welfare in Modern Society

In the light of Judaism's concern for all living creatures, there are a number of areas in the contemporary world where the concept of compassion for animals needs to be applied. First, attention needs to be drawn to the inhuman conditions under which animals are raised today. Chickens, for example, are bred for slaughter in long, windowless sheds where they never experience sunlight, exercise or fresh air. In such an environment, crowding is often so great that chickens cannot even stretch their wings. Such terrible conditions often result in feather-pecking and cannibalism. Similarly, geese (and ducks) which are raised to produce pâté de foie gras are forced to endure the most terrible ordeal: the farmer generally holds down the neck of the goose between the legs and pours corn down its neck. When this procedure is no longer effective, he uses a wooden plunger. As the liver increases in size, sclerosis develops and eventually after the animal has been stupefied with pain the liver is removed.

Another example of such cruelty relates to veal calves. After being allowed to nurse for only a few days, the calf is removed from its mother, and locked in a small slotted stall without even enough space to move or lie down. To obtain the desired veal, the calf is given a high-calorie, iron-free diet. Because the calf is so starved for iron it licks the iron bars of its stall or drinks its own urine; to prevent this from occurring, its head is tethered to the stall. The stall is kept so warm that the calf drinks more of its high-calorie liquid diet than it would normally. After enduring such torture, the animal is eventually taken for slaughter. Additional cruelties are often inflicted on such animals who are first transported by rail or truck. Jammed into a confined area for hours or days, they are deprived of food, water, exercise and ventilation and are often exposed to extreme heat, cold and humidity. In past centuries such mechanized methods of farming did not exist. Instead animals were raised and killed for food without undergoing such suffering. Given Judaism's concern for avoiding cruelty, every effort must be made to abandon these modern means of animal torture.

A second issue on the moral agenda is vegetarianism. Due to Judaism's compassionate concern for the animal kingdom, an increasing number of Jews have in recent years adopted a vegetarian diet. Given Judaism's insistence that animals be treated with mercy, there is an inevitable contradiction between the quest to care for

all of God's creatures and the rules of *shechitah;* this is not a recent observation—in the tenth century this paradox was recognized by the great rabbinic scholar Sherira Gaon.[15] Vegetarianism, as a policy of refraining from eating meat, would eliminate such inconsistencies.

According to tradition, it was not part of God's original plan for meat to be eaten. After creating heaven and earth, God instructed Adam about his proper relationship with other living things: "Behold I have given to you all vegetations ... for food.'" (Gen. 1:29) According to tradition, the Garden of Eden represents the divine order of creation; it is the perfect, ideal society where only fruit and vegetables are eaten. Human beings are thus meant to be vegetarians, and just as at the beginning of time when there was no eating of meat, so at the end of time there will be a return to this original state.

> This was arguably the prophet Isaiah's
>   vision of a future society:
> The whole shall dwell with the lamb,
> and the leopard shall lie down with the kid,
> and the calf and the lion and the fatling
>   together,
> and a little child shall lead them.
> The cow and the bear shall feed;
> their young shall lie down together;
> and the lion shall eat straw like the ox ...
> They shall not hurt or destroy in all my
>   holy mountain.
>
> (Isaiah 11:6–7, 9)

Here the animal kingdom is viewed as at peace: no longer are wild beasts carnivorous, and by implication human beings would similarly desist from killing for food. Given such a utopian conception of animal and human life, there are compelling reasons for vegetarianism to be adopted in contemporary Jewish society. As Jews are not commanded to be carnivorous,[16] the practice of eating only fruit and vegetables is perfectly consistent with the principle of *tsa'ar ba'alei chayim*. Such a policy would overcome the objections currently being raised about religious slaughter—even though *shechitah* was no doubt the most humane form of killing animals in pre-modern times, it would be far more compassionate not to slaughter living creatures at all.[17]

Turning to the issue of animal experimentation, the primary Jewish source dealing with this topic is the commentary by Rabbi Moses Isserles in the *Code of Jewish Law*. In his view the laws of *tsa'ar ba'alei chayim* can be waived for medical or other significant purposes.[18] Such a principle would legitimize experimentation on animals as long as there is a clear connection between such scientific investigation and human welfare (provided that steps have been taken to eliminate unnecessary pain). Yet, much animal experimentation today has no medical or serious humane value. In this connection, Richard Schwartz writes:

> Many laboratory experiments are completely unnecessary. Must we force dogs to smoke to reconfirm the health hazards of cigarettes? Do we have to starve dogs and monkeys to understand human starvation? Do we need to cut, blind, burn and chemically destroy animals to produce still another type of lipstick, mascara, or shampoo?[19]

The principle of *tsa'ar ba'alei chayim* would rule out animal experimentation for inessential human needs, and in addition provide a framework for encouraging alternative methods of research. Increasingly scientists have argued for different research procedures to be employed such as, for example, clinical and epidemiological trials in the case of psychology and psychiatry, mathematical modeling, in-vitro screening, autopsy and biopsy study, computerized positron-emission tomography, and magnetic resonance imaging.[20] No longer should animals be perceived as the raw materials of the laboratory—instead they should be seen as part of God's creation to be valued and respected in their own right.

Such a quest to grant dignity to all living things has important implications for a Jewish view of hunting. The classical responsum on this topic was given by the eighteenth-century halakhist Yehezkel Landau:

> How can a Jew kill a living animal for no other purpose than to satisfy the cravings of his time ... (and if one attempts a rationalization and sins) it is because bears and wolves and other violent animals are liable to cause damage, (such an argument might make sense) in cases when (those animals) came into a human settlement ... but to pursue them in the forests, their place of residence, when they are wont come to a (human) settlement, is not a mitzvah and you are only pursuing the desires of your heart.[21]

Such a repudiation of hunting for sport is embedded in the rabbinic tradition. Thus, the Talmud declares: "One who sits in a stadium spills the blood."[22] On the basis of such teaching, Judaism categorically condemns all forms of hunting for pleasure including fox-hunting, bullfights, dogfights, and cockfights. In a similar spirit, the rabbis were opposed to killing animals for their pelts—for this reason the Talmud forbids associating with hunters who set dogs on the trail of hunted animals.[23] Hence the Jewish faith would condemn such horrific procedures as the use of bone-crushing leghold traps to capture wild animals, clubbing baby seals and skinning them while alive, and hanging rabbits and raccoons by their tongues so they will have scar-free pelts.

As far as keeping animals is concerned, the Jewish tradition demands that care and responsibility be exercised on behalf of the animals under human care. Thus Rabbi Eliezer ha-Kapar stated that a person is not permitted to buy cattle, beasts, or birds unless he can provide adequate food for them.[24] Similarly Rabbi Yehudah stated that one is not permitted to eat anything until after feeding one's animals.[25] For these reasons pets should be provided with good food, shelter and veterinary care. Further, if pets can no longer be housed, they should be given a good new home. Writing in this connection, Aviva Cantor advises:

Caring responsibly for an animal means not getting rid of your pet without ensuring that it has a good new home. Abandonment of pets is one of the most rampant abuses of animals today. Living in an age when everything is disposable, we increasingly encounter the tragedy of the disposable pet. People buy pets from irresponsible breeders … or adopt animals while on vacation without considering whether they can afford them financially, emotionally or logistically. Too often the pets are later simply thrown out into the street. As a result, millions of stray dogs and cats roam the streets and alleys of our cities, most of them starving and ill, the object of children's torture and often a danger to human health and well-being as well.[26]

Diverse Voices in Judaism

To be sure, passages written by respected Jewish leaders do at times exhibit an attitude to "animal issues" that seems far more humanocentric than many examples included above and, thus, seemingly less compassionate toward nonhuman lives. Consider a summary by Elijah Judah Schochet, an Orthodox Jew, regarding the place of nonhuman living beings within Judaism:

The following basic conclusion would seem to be warranted: that the world of fauna, although the authentic handiwork of God, is, in reality, far removed from its Maker's hand or concern. Man, on the other hand, emerges as a distinct entity, far superior to the animal, and standing within a special relationship to his Creator. True, man has specific obligations toward animals; he is not to abuse or mistreat them. But these obligations are relatively few, and they bespeak more accurately the relationship of a master toward his servant, or even an artisan toward his tool, than that of a living being toward his fellow living being, also fashioned by the hand of God.[27]

Such passages make it clear that Judaism, like other traditions, offers multiple voices on the place of nonhuman animals in our world. But notice that even if the tenor of Schochet's passage or others like it is less positive than some of more "animal friendly" examples given above, Schochet nonetheless clearly acknowledges that "man has specific obligations toward animals; he is not to abuse or mistreat them." This value —manifested in numerous ways—is eminently Jewish and thus appears in even those thinkers who, in a relative sense, discount life outside our species.

This emphasis on the moral significance of animals has been important historically, for as Andrew Linzey and I argued in *After Noah: Animals and the Liberation of Theology,*

It is very doubtful whether the largely Christian movement against cruelty in the nineteenth century could have emerged at all without the many long years of specifically Jewish sensitivity to suffering embodied in the rabbinic principle of tsa'ar ba'alei chayim (pain of living creatures) which prohibits the causing of unnecessary suffering to any living being.[28]

Conclusion

In summary, even though there is considerable diversity of thought within the tradition, merciful treatment of all living beings has from time immemorial been a core value of Jewish views of the proper relationship between humans and earth's nonhuman living beings. Thus, even if various uses of animals have been held to be a divinely granted prerogative, a framework of specific, detailed regulations exists to ensure that suffering be minimized. In its general features and its specific practices, then, Judaism reflects a profound moral commitment to respect the animal kingdom and to deal with its individuals in a kindly manner whenever that is feasible. In this regard, Judaism has often expressed the insight that other animals, though distinct from humans, are not a collection of objects. Rather, human and nonhuman animals, especially in their interaction, are well seen as "a communion of subjects."

NOTES

1. Richard Schwartz, "Tsa'ar Ba'alei Chayim—Judaism and Compassion for Animals" in Roberta Kalechofsky, ed., *Judaism and Animal Rights* (Marblehead, MA: Micah Publications, 1992), p. 61.

2. Ibid.

3. Rashbaum to Ex. 23:19.

4. Ibn Ezra to Ex. 23:19.

5. *Targum Yonaton*, Lev. 22:28.

6. *Vayikra Rabbah* 27:11.

7. *Guide to the Perplexed* 3:48.

8. Ibid.

9. *Yesodei ha-Torah* in Jonathan Sacks, "On Judaism and Animals" (University of Essex, 1991).

10. Schwartz, "Tsa'ar Ba'alei Chayim," p. 61.

11. Ibid.

12. Ibid., p. 66–67.

13. Ronald L. Androphy, 'Shechitah' in Roberta Kalechofsky, *Judaism and Animal Rights*, p. 76.

14. Ibid., p. 80–81.

15. Roberta Kalechofsky, "The Vegetarian Restoration," in *Judaism and Animal Rights*, p. 168.

16. Richard Schwartz, "Questions and Answers"' in *Judaism and Animal Rights*, p. 222–23.

17. See, for example, Aisha Labi, "A Stunning Debate: A Proposal to Ban Ritual Slaughter in the U.K. Forges an Unlikely Alliance of Muslims and Jews," *Time Europe* 161, no. 25 (June 23, 2003).

18. Schwartz, "Tsa'ar Ba'alei Chayim," p. 59.

19. Richard Schwartz, "Questions and Answers" in *Judaism and Animal Rights*, p. 238.

20. Murray J. Cohen, "The Irrelevance of Animal Experimentation in Modern Psychiatry and Psychology," in *Judaism and Animal Rights*, p. 301.

21. Quoted in Aviva Cantor, "Kindness to Animals," in *Judaism and Animal Rights*, p. 30.

22. *Avodah Zarah* 1.

23. Aviva Cantor, "Kindness to Animals," in *Judaism and Animal Rights*, p. 31.

24. *Yevamot* 15.

25. *Gittin* 62a.

26. Aviva Cantor, "Kindness to Animals," p. 32.

27. Elijah Judah Schochet, *Animal Life in Jewish Traditions: Attitudes and Relationships* (New York: Ktav, 1984) p. 3.

28. Andrew Linzey, and Dan Cohn-Sherbok, *After Noah: Animals and the Liberation of Theology* (London: Mowbray, 1997), p. 11.

Hierarchy, Kinship, and Responsibility

The Jewish Relationship to the Animal World

ROBERTA KALECHOFSKY

Under the biblical perspective, a change took place in the status of animals from what had prevailed in Babylonian and Egyptian cultures: animals were demythologized—as were humans. There are no animal deities in the Bible; there are no human deities in the Bible. Animal life was neither elevated nor degraded because of the demythologizing process. Animals were no longer worshipped, singly or collectively, but they were accorded an irreducible value in the divine pathos, which is expressed in the covenantal statements, in halachic decisions or laws, and in aggadic material. These three branches of Jewish expression determine the tradition known in Judaism as *tsa'ar ba'alei chayim* (cause no sorrow to living creatures). Aggadic material is made up of stories and legends, sometimes called *midrashim,* such as the story of how God led Moses to the burning bush because Moses ran to rescue a lamb who had strayed. Halachic material comprises a body of decisions regarding specific issues that have the binding effect of law. Like any body of law, these decisions rest on precedent and authoritative statements, in this case by rabbis in the Talmud, or by rabbis throughout the centuries whose decisions are called "responsa." However strong the aggadic tradition might be on any issue, halachic decisions take precedent in governing the behavior of the observant Jew, though they do not always express the underlying ethos of the tradition. As in any culture, sentiment is often stronger than law.

The biblical and Talmudic position with respect to animals is summarized in the statement by Noah Cohen:

The Hebrew sages considered the wall of partition between man and beasts as rather thin ... the Jew was forever to remember that the beast reflects similar affections and passions as himself.... Consequently he was admonished to seek its welfare and its comfort as an integral part of his daily routine and instructed that the more he considers its well being and contentment, the more would he be exalted in the eyes of his maker.[1]

The story the prophet Nathan tells David when Nathan chastises him for his behavior in stealing Bathsheba from her husband expresses the kinship the biblical Jew felt for animals, which embraced the animal as part of the family:

> There were two men in one city; the one rich and the other poor. The rich man had many flocks and herds; but the poor man had nothing, save one little ewe lamb, which he had bought and nourished up, and it grew up together with him and with his children. It ate from his own food and drank from his own cup, and lay in his bosom, and was to him like a daughter. (Samuel II, 12: 1–4)

Judaism accepts a hierarchical scheme to creation, but hierarchy did not exclude feelings of loving kinship. With respect to animals the rule might be stated as kinship yes, reverence no.

In the creation story, in the biblical terminology in the commandment of biological fruitfulness, and in the blessing of life given equally to the animals and to the human race, Rabbi Elijah Schochet sees a "unity of man and beast: since *ruach chayim* ('spirit of life') can refer to both man and beast, as can *nefesh chayah* ('living creature')." He points out that in the Book of Jonah the animals are clad in mourning sackcloth, "just like their human counterparts," and take part in the public ritual of mourning.[2] Such passages strike a modern reader as quaint, but they suggest the biblical sense of closeness between animal and human.

The other side of this relationship, which is inexplicable to the modern mind, is that retributive justice could be extended to animals: "Inherent in 'covenant' is 'responsibility,' and Scripture does not spare animals from responsibility for their deeds ... and at times animals would seem to be treated as though they were coequal

with men."[3] Inexplicable as this may seem to the modern mind, it suggests that animals had legal standing, as indeed their inclusion in the covenantal statements would make mandatory. The covenantal statements point not only to the animals' legal position, determining things that are due them such as proper food and care, but also to their position in the divine ethos and reflect the centrality of the animal in God's concern.

> "As for me," says the Lord, "I will establish My Covenant with you and with your seed after you, and with every living creature that is with you, the fowl, the cattle, and every beast of the earth with you; all that go out of the ark, even every beast of the earth."
>
> (Genesis 9:9–10)

> And in that day I will make a covenant for them with the beasts of the field and with the fowls of the heaven, and with the creeping creatures of the ground. And I will break the bow and the sword and the battle out of the land and I will make them to lie down safely.
>
> (Hosiah 2:20)

Animals are included in the covenant which establishes the Sabbath:

> The seventh day is a sabbath of the Lord your God; you shall not do any work, neither your son, nor your daughter, nor your male or female slave, nor your cattle, nor your stranger who is within your settlements.
>
> (Exodus 20:10 and Deuteronomy 5:14)

Cohen extrapolates from the covenantal statements a doctrine of equality between humans and animals. "Does not the Bible itself treat them [animals] as humans with whom the Lord can execute treaties and covenants?"[4] Voltaire, who was no friend of religion, wrote, "the deity does not make a pact with trees and with stones which have no feelings, but He makes it with animals whom He has endowed with feelings often more exquisite than ours, and with ideas necessarily attached to it."[5] Not only are the animals included in the Sabbath covenant, but also the wellbeing of the animal is considered more important than the Sabbath, and many Sabbath laws could be suspended in order to come to the aid of a stricken animal.

Jesus' observation that "God notes the fall of every sparrow," expresses this traditional divine concern for the animals. God cares for and suffers over animal life. The nineteenth-century English clergyman Humphrey Primatt, who wrote one of the earliest tracts against animal abuse, believed that "Mercy to Brutes is a doctrine of Revelation. … and Superiority of rank or station exempts no creature from the sensibility of pain, nor does inferiority render the feelings thereof the less exquisite."[6] Not only mercy to brutes but also ultimate justice that would render equity and equality to animals was a doctrine of revelation for Rabbi Avraham Kuk, whose writings on the subject have become pivotal for Jewish vegetarians and animal rights advocates. Rabbi Kuk said:

> The free movement of the moral impulse to establish justice for animals generally and the claim of their rights from mankind are hidden in a natural psychic sensibility in the deeper layers of Torah. … Just as the democratic aspiration will reach outward through the general intellectual and moral perfection … so will the hidden yearning to act justly towards animals emerge at the proper time. What prepares the ground for this state is the commandments, those intended specifically for this area of concern.[7]

Being also a nomistic religion, Judaism is rich in laws governing the relationship between humans and animals. *The Encyclopedia Judaica* provides a good summary of these laws, beginning with the observation that "moral and legal rules concerning the treatment of animals are based on the principle that animals are part of God's creation toward which man bears responsibility.

Laws and other indications in the Pentateuch make it clear not only that cruelty to animals is forbidden but also that compassion and mercy to them are demanded of man by God."[8]

These laws make the effort to balance human need against what would constitute cruelty toward animals, and they consistently reveal the scope of Jewish concern regarding animals. As James Gaffney pointed out, "the fullest and most sympathetic treatment in any comparable religiously oriented encyclopedia in English is that of the *Encyclopedia Judaica,* a reminder that the Hebrew Bible laid foundations on which it was possible and natural to build."[9] Any discussion of laws, however, inevitably involves interpretation, which itself depends upon which system of hermeneutics one uses to interpret passages in the Bible. Interpretations oscillate between whether human beings have an absolute duty to animals, or a relative duty depending upon human need, such as might be required in medical experiments or in eating meat.[10]

Furthermore, in establishing the biblical and later Jewish teaching on animals, we have from the outset the problem of interpreting the first document, Genesis: we are a long way from knowing what words such as "dominion" and "subdue" meant two and half millennia ago. Yoel Arbeitman, a scholar of Semitic languages, summarizes half a dozen meanings from other scholars of *rdh,* the Hebrew verb for "to have dominion," as "to rule or shepherd in a neutral sense," "to lead about," "lead, accompany; master, punish …" "to be governed/controlled" as in "to tame."[11] In attempting to understand with some confidence how the Bible viewed human beings vis-à-vis animals, Arbeitman parallels his effort to retrieve a final denotation of *rdh* with an effort to understand the Hebrew for "earth" (the substance Adam and other earth creatures are made from) and for "image" (*selem/salma*) the term used for the Hebrew resemblance to God. With reference to Hebrew, Syrian, Aramaic, and Assyrian texts, and gleanings from archeology and philology, Arbeitman concludes resignedly that the effort does not yield much. "And that is the sum of what the ancient biblical texts will tell us": that humans and land animals are said to have been created from the same substance (*adamah* or earth), that God breathed a special life force (personality? soul?) into humans; that the concept of the human being was modeled on that of a statue, being three dimensional, and that the result is "a benign ... patriarchal hegemony of Adam."

Since scholarship on this subject is so unyielding, interpretation and tradition become crucial. The fact that Adam names the animals in second Genesis does not suggest to Arbeitman "dominion," but "bonding," "naming is the way of establishing a *relationship* to the other —not *dominance,* but a *bond* between them!" (emphasis Arbeitman's).[12] That with which we bond, we call by name. This interpretation is reinforced by the fact that in second Genesis the animals are created prior to Eve and are regarded as helpmates to Adam. God later decides that Adam needs a helpmate who resembles him —an obvious biological necessity in order to carry out the commandment "to be fruitful and multiply," as species naturally procreate only with themselves.

However, the general drift of the Jewish attitude in Western culture toward animals from biblical times through the Middle Ages to the modern era, is that they are not co-equal, though animals still inherit a significant position from the biblical stance toward them. Moreover, the paradigm shift from the concept of hierarchy to the concept of equality within the last century makes it difficult for the modern mind to accept the biblical and Jewish values regarding animal life because they are based on quasi-equality, or even inequality. Biblical and Talmudic laws embedded in the concept of hierarchy are often seen to function as life-threatening to all but the power-elite.[13] The concept of equality has such force in modern Western thought that laws based on hierarchical systems are peremptorily judged as unjust, though the parent-child

relationship is inescapably hierarchical. (Any other relationship for the child would be life-threatening.)

Regardless of what scholars may ultimately decide *rdh* means, Biblical and Talmudic laws regarding human responsibility for animals are embedded in the concepts of "dominion" and "hierarchy" which, in their turn, were modeled on the family; in turn, the image of the "good" father was modeled on the idea of God, as expressed by Jesus in the Sermon on the Mount. God has dominion, a parent has dominion, human beings have dominion. But the dominion granted to humans in Genesis is at once severely limited by the dietary injunction to be vegetarian. Even when permission to eat meat is granted after the flood, that permission has immediate restraints placed on it. Dominion is always of limited power, and hierarchy need not and did not exclude feelings of loving kinship in the Bible, as expressed in Nathan's admonishment to David. If Nathan's story did not reflect a common sentiment at the time, it would have had no meaning for David. Other stories, such as those revolving around the relationship of the shepherd to his sheep, dictated that it was the "unprotected" creature who merited the deepest sentiment of protectiveness, as expressed by the nineteenth century rabbi, Samson Raphael Hirsch.

> There are probably no creatures who require more the protective divine word against the presumption of man than the animals, which like man have sensations and instincts, but whose bodies and powers are nevertheless subservient to man. In relation to them man so easily forgets that injured animal muscle twitches just like human muscle, that the maltreated nerves of an animal sicken like human nerves, that the animal is just as sensitive to cuts, blows, and beatings as man.[14]

Jewish law commands the righteous Jew to feed his animal(s) before he feeds himself because, the Jewish argument is, a human being can understand hunger, but an animal cannot. However, animals do understand hunger. They understand thirst, appetite, sexuality, fear, and loneliness. The commandment is hortatory for the purpose of encouraging responsibility and behavior that leads to the idea of the *imitatio Dei* with respect to animals. The *imitatio Dei* depends upon the concept of hierarchy; indeed, derives from it. However, the precept of kindness to animals for the sake of the *imitatio Dei* leads some Jewish commentators to argue that the motive for concern for animals is human moral betterment, even though the covenantal statements reflect the centrality of the animal in God's concern. The depiction of the creation of fish, fowl, and animal in Genesis, is each species with its integrity, and substantiates the view that animals were regarded as integral subjects in their own right. God's delight in these creations, stated with blessing or with simple majesty, "And it was good," does not reflect a god who created animal life to be in bondage.

Rabbi Kuk interpreted human dominion as an evolutionary process, a necessary stage in which the human identity sorts itself out from the animal world. Nevertheless "dominion," however benignly interpreted, is an omnipresent temptation to power. Hence, Rabbi Hanina cautioned, "If we deserve it, we will have dominion; if not, we will descend to the lowest depths," making "dominion" a moral issue. Aggadic tales, such as the story of creation which points out that the mosquito was created before humankind, are intended to deflect human arrogance. Dominion can be a source of evil, but within Jewish piety, the Jew was always to remember that his own position rests on God's grace and that his life is only as valuable as his behavior is moral, particularly with respect to animals.

Justice for animals in Jewish tradition flows from these two primary sources, one divine, the other human. Animals are part of the divine economy and partake of God's just world, God's blessing and delight. This justice is given to animals through God "who opens His Hand and feeds all," who has designed each creature so that he is capable of preserving his life. Justice for animals is built into the divine order of the world from the very creation of the world. God, just and merciful, did not create creatures for evil reasons or purposes, but so that "good should be done to the animal." [15] These central statements of faith posit the place of the animal within the Jewish world view and make it impossible to subtract the theoretical and theological dignity of animal life from the Jewish concept of God Who found them good.

Two tales, the first aggadic and the second biblical, enforce the centrality of the animal in the unfolding of Jewish destiny: God's choice of Moses to lead the Jewish people out of Egypt because Moses goes to rescue a lamb that leads him to the burning bush; and Eliezer's choice of Rebecca to be the wife of Isaac because Rebecca says to Eliezer, "Drink and I will also water your animal." Concern for the animal in both tales is not merely a nice sentiment or only a moral quality; it points to historic destiny.

The laws concerning animals have been summed up in many places and would be too numerous to cite here. Biblical, Talmudic, and post-Talmudic literature are replete with them, but they indicate a consistent pattern, as Noah Cohen points out in his analysis of them: "examination of the biblical, talmudic, and medieval jurisprudence concerning the lower creatures reflects a coherent system of humane legislation whose purpose is to defend the subhuman creation and to make humans more human." [16] As with any body of law, however, these laws too rest on precedent and interpretation, and the protection they afford animals may vary from time to time, not only among Jews but also among Christians. Paul allegorized the law which prohibits the muzzling of the ox when he treads out the corn in the fields (Deuteronomy 25:4), claiming that the ox was only a symbol for the human. The law which states that "If thou seest the ass of him that hateth thee lying under his burden, thou shalt forebear to pass by him; thou shalt surely release it with him," (Exodus 23:5) can be interpreted to suggest that its purpose is not the protection of the animal, but to inculcate the practice of mercy in the human being: "to make humans more human."[17] On the other hand, except for Paul, an elastic interpretation is never applied to the law concerning the muzzling of the ox. James Gaffney, in his criticism of Paul's allegorization of this law, states:

> The passage about the ox was as nonallegorical as everything else in the book of Deuteronomy, where it is found as part of the law of Moses. Like certain other passages in that same book, it is plainly intended to be read as a piece of divine legislation in behalf of animals, despite some inconvenience to human greed. ... It is indeed "for oxen that God is concerned," and to at least that extent he "does not speak entirely for our sake." The Mosaic law does envisage animal interest, does legislate animal rights, and to that extent does represent animals as moral objects.[18]

Too often the meanings and values of words, concepts, and laws retreat into the political and sociological mire of translation, while the problems of interpreting the Bible are further refracted through a myriad of disciplines such as anthropology, archeology, and philology. A common difference, for example, between Hebrew and non-Hebrew texts is in the translation of "living things" (in reference to animals) or "living beings." As Arbeitman points out, "It should be stressed that the application of non-life in the standard English renderings of 'crawling things,' 'living things,' which occur in some translations, has no basis in the Hebrew."[19] A restoration of the original intention and understanding of Torah passages concerning animals would provide a necessary clarification and a foundation for those who are concerned with what the Bible has to say about animals. The law concerning the muzzling of the ox appears in the same passage of divine legislation regarding the treatment of the poor, but no interpretation exists suggesting that concern for the poor deflects from the status of the poor as moral

objects. Torah does not make this distinction. Why should we? In both cases, compassion is dictated by how a righteous Jew should behave (compassion is embedded in righteousness), but it doesn't follow that such behavior reduces the object of compassion.

Though these laws have been variously interpreted, they continue to establish protection as can be seen in two recent rulings, based on interpretation of halakhic laws: Rabbi David Ha-Levy's decree that the manufacture of fur and the wearing of fur violates the precept of *tsa'ar ba'alei chayim,* and Rabbi Moishe Feinstein's condemnation of veal. In his *responsa,* Rabbi Feinstein does not conclude that the veal calf is non-kosher because the laws regarding what is kosher and what isn't derive from a different halachic branch from the laws regarding *tsa'ar ba'alei chayim,* but he does conclude that the raising and the eating of the veal calf is a violation of *tsa'ar ba'alei chayim:*

> It is definitely forbidden to raise calves in such a manner because of the pain that is inflicted on them. ... a person is not permitted to do anything he wants to his animals which would cause them pain, even if he would profit from these things, except for those things which are for his direct benefit such as slaughtering them for food and using them in his work.[20]

Rabbi Feinstein, as had the Reverend Humphrey Primatt, and most animal rights advocates up to the twentieth century, regarded meat as a dietary necessity and exempted the slaughtering of animals from laws pertaining to cruelty. In Judaism, the elaborate laws of *shechitah* (ritual killing) evolved so that animals would be slaughtered for food in the most humane manner possible. Up until 1906 and the passage of federal laws which required the shackling and hoisting of animals, *shechitah* was the least painful way to slaughter food animals. But the laws failed the animals (in spite of the prohibition against tying an animal's hind legs) when the rabbis accepted the federally mandated shackling and hoisting of animals, and eventually the evils of factory farming. Rabbi David Rosen has called this submission to the modern practices in rearing and slaughtering of farm animals, "a flagrant violation of the prohibition" of *tsa'ar ba'alei chayim*.[21]

Permission to eat meat is, in Eric Katz's view, the "dark thread" that runs through the millennial tradition regarding the Jewish view of animals. He laments that "It could have been otherwise: Jewish law could have commanded vegetarianism," and he sees in this refusal to "command vegetarianism," an ultimate anthropocentrism.[22] But Judaism does not command either eating meat or vegetarianism. The choice is optional, though eating meat was traditionally viewed darkly by the rabbis, and the desire to eat meat was regarded as "lust": is there a decree demanding of man that he butcher and consume the flesh of fauna? Should meat be part of his standard normal diet? Not at all. Quite the contrary. The crucial passage in Deuteronomy reads: "When the Lord thy God shall enlarge thy border, as He hath promised thee, and thou shalt say: 'I will eat flesh,' because thy soul desireth to eat flesh; thou mayest eat flesh, after all the desire of thy soul!" Now rabbinic tradition perceives in this text a clear indication that it is man's desire to eat flesh, not God's decree that he is to do so, and attributes an unflattering connotation to this lust for flesh.[23]

What Torah commands is that *if* you eat meat, then you must sacrifice the animal properly, and the laws of *shechitah* built on this. That there was only one designated temple in which a Jew could sacrifice an animal is regarded by some scholars as an effort to limit sacrifice and the eating of meat. Other scholars believe that Jews in the Diaspora, living in the Greek and Roman worlds during the late biblical centuries, may not have eaten meat at all, since there was no way for them to sacrifice their animals properly, except on the three festival occasions when they may have made a pilgrimage to the temple in Jerusalem.

As with the laws concerning animals, there is a plethora of laws concerning *kashrut* (Jewish dietary laws), which indicate that the rabbis were not comfortable with eating meat. There are Talmudic passages critical of eating meat. "Man should not eat meat, unless he has a special craving for it and then should eat it only occasionally and sparingly" (*Chulin* 84a). "A man should not teach his son to eat meat" (*Chulin* 84a). Meat is never included in the seven sacred foods of eretz Israel: pomegranates, wheat, barley, olives, dates, fig honey, and grapes. There is no special prayer for the eating of meat, as there is with wine, bread, and vegetables. The rabbis believed that the laws of *kashrut* were intended to teach us reverence for life and to refine our appetites. Even so arcane a law as the prohibition against "seething a kid in its mother's milk" was interpreted by Philo of Alexandria (first century CE) to inculcate human kindness: What, he argued, is more revolting than that an animal should be cooked in the substance that was given to its mother for the animal's life? Central to Jewish mysticism is the role that vegetarianism plays in messianic expectations: here vegetarianism functions in the concept of Jewish mystical time which chronicles human development from the vegetarian state in the Garden of Eden to the Messianic age when it is believed we will be vegetarians again. Rabbi Kuk regarded the Edenic commandment to "eat nuts, herbs and green things," as symbolic of Torah's intention of ultimate justice for the animal. In his inaugural speech as president of the Reconstructionist College, Rabbi Arthur Green prophesied that vegetarianism will be the next *kashrut* of the Jewish people, and Rabbi Arthur Hertzberg has declared that a slow but certain movement toward vegetarianism for Jews is taking place:

> Judaism as a religion offers the option of eating animal flesh, and most Jews do, but in our own century there has been a movement towards vegetarianism among very pious Jews. A whole galaxy of central rabbinic and spiritual teachers including several past and present Chief Rabbis of the Holy Land have been affirming

vegetarianism as the ultimate meaning of Jewish moral teaching. They have been proclaiming the autonomy of all living creatures as the value which our religious tradition must now teach to all of its believers. ... Jews will move increasingly to vegetarianism out of their own deepening knowledge of what their tradition commands as they understand it in this age.[24]

For Rav Kuk this development is the meaning of the Edenic diet and of that justice for animals which he lovingly and perceptively found buried in the deeper layers of Torah.

A theological/nomistic relationship flows between the laws (*halakhah*), the magisterial creation of animal life (as well as of earth) in Genesis, and the covenantal statements in the Bible, because in Judaism the laws governing responsibility to animals derive from the animal's place in the divine economy, assured by the covenantal statements, by the Jewish view of creation, and the Jewish view of a just and compassionate Creator. The stress of these laws with respect to the Jew is summed up in the question: How should the righteous (just) Jew behave toward animals, and the answer lies in the concept of the *imitatio Dei*. The just and merciful human behaves toward animals as a just and merciful Creator behaves toward humans.

NOTES

1. Noah J. Cohen, *Tsa'ar Ba'alei Hayim: The Prevention of Cruelty to Animals—Its Bases, Development, and Legislation in Hebrew Literature* (Nanuet, New York: Feldheim Publishers, 1976), p. 1.

2. Elijah Judah Schochet, *Animal Life in Jewish Tradition: Attitudes and Relationships* (New Jersey: Ktav, 1984), pp. 53–54.

3. Ibid., p. 54.

4. Cohen, *Tsa'ar Ba'alei Hayim,* p. 1.

5. Voltaire, *Treatise on Tolerance,* ch. 12, ed. Simon Harvey (New York: Cambridge University Press 2000).

6. Reverend Humphrey Primatt, *The Duty of Mercy and the Sin of Cruelty to Animals* (Edinburgh, 1834), pp. viii, 14–15.

7. Rabbi Kuk's major work on this subject, *A Vision of Vegetarianism and Peace,* still awaits a definitive translation from Hebrew to English. To date, the best translation and interpretation is in an unpublished thesis by Rabbi Jonathan Rubenstein.

8. Zvi Kaplan, "Animals, Cruelty To," *Encyclopedia Judaica* 16 vols. (Jerusalem: Keter, 1971), 3: 6. Pages 6–22 give a usefully succinct summary of these laws and a description of the biblical human/animal relationship. Also see Richard Schwartz, *Judaism and Vegetarianism* (New York: Lantern Books, 2001) pp. 19–29.

9. James Gaffney, "The Relevance of Animal Experimentation to Roman Catholic Ethical Methodology," in Tom Regan, ed., *Animal Sacrifices: Religious Perspectives on the Use of Animals in Science* (Philadelphia: Temple University Press, 1986), p. 160. For an example of such various interpretations, see in the same publications, Rabbi J. David Bleich, "Judaism and Animal Experimentation," p. 61.

10. Yoël Arbeitman, "In All Adam's Domain," in Roberta Kalechofsky, ed., *Judaism and Animal Rights: Classical and Contemporary Responses* (Marblehead: MA: Micah Publications, 1992), pp. 34–35.

11. Ibid., p. 34. For further discussion of "dominion," see Schwartz, *Judaism and Vegetarianism,* pp. 1–39.

12. Arbeitman, *Judaism and Animal Rights,* p. 34.

13. Steven Wise, *Rattling The Cage: Toward Legal Rights For Animals* (Cambridge, MA: Perseus Books 2000) suggests, in the mode of modern argumentation, that "dominion" invariably reduces the dominated creature to a "non-thing." The author defines "dominion" and "hierarchy" as responsible for the "legal vacuum" in which animals now exist, though animals in the past have occupied various combinations of status (legal/divine, semi-divine and legal/non-divine) in hierarchical cultures.

14. Samson Raphael Hirsch, *Horeb,* chap. 60, section 415 (New York: Soncino Press, 1962), p. 292.

15. An example of moral wrestling with the animal issue can be seen in Rabbi Sherira Gaon's tenth-century letter on this issue, "Sherira Gaon Defends the Rights of Animals," in Franz Kobler, ed., *Letters of Jews Through the Ages,* 3 vols. (Philadelphia: Jewish Publication Society, 1952) 1:121.

16. Cohen, *Tsa'ar Ba'alei Hayim,* p. 105.

17. For variation in interpretation, see Bleich, "Judaism and Animal Experimentation," In Tom Regan, ed., *Animal Sacrifices: Religious Perspectives on the Use of Animals in Science* (Philadelphia: Temple University Press, 1986), p. 65.

18. Gaffney, "The Relevance of Animal Experimentation, p. 151.

19. Arbeitman, *Judaism and Animal Rights,* p. 41. J.R. Hyland, *The Slaughter of Terrified Beasts: A Biblical Basis for the Humane Treatment of Animals* (Florida: Viatoris Ministries, 1988), has a detailed analysis of misinterpreted (and mistranslated) passages regarding animals.

20. Rabbi Moshe Feinstein, "Igros Moshe," *Even Ha-Ezer,* vol. 4, responsum 92 (New York: Moriah, 1963), pp. 164–65.

21. Rabbi David Rosen, "Vegetarianism: An Orthodox Jewish Perspective," in Roberta Kalechofsky, ed., *Rabbis and Vegetarianism: An Evolving Tradition,* (Marblehead, MA: Micah Publications, 1995) p. 53.

22. Eric Katz, "Sounds of Silence," *Judaism and Animal Rights,* pp. 56–59.

23. Schochet, *Animal Life in Jewish Tradition,* p. 50.

24. Rabbi Arthur Hertzberg, "The Jewish Declaration on Nature," Address on the 25th Anniversary of World Wildlife Fund. Reprint: Roberta Kalechofsky, *Vegetarian Judaism—A Guide for Everyone* (Massachusetts: Micah Publications, 1998) p. 189.

CHRISTIANITY

The Bestiary of Heretics

Imaging Medieval Christian Heresy with Insects and Animals

BEVERLY KIENZLE

Animals figure prominently in literature from the Western Middle Ages: fables, bestiaries, stories about Renard the fox, and beast poems.[1] They also play a role in ecclesiastical writings: medieval exegesis and related genres such as sermons and treatises. The dominant medieval view of nonhuman creation, grounded on Genesis 1:28, held that humans maintained dominion over animals, considered theologically, legally, and practically as property.[2] One current of thought, as exemplified in St. Francis of Assisi, held nonhuman creation in some esteem, and some later scholastic authors, ascribing to the Aristotelian and Pauline notion of the community of all creatures (Romans 8:21), debated their presence in heaven.[3] Nonetheless, non-humans served as literary property for authors who attributed moral qualities to animals and their behavior in order to illustrate or under-score a didactic message. Included among the *res* that possess hidden meaning in the Augustinian view of the universe, animals convey the moral message that textual interpreters assign to them.

While nonhuman creatures such as Renard the fox may be the foremost actors in medieval beast literature, they generally serve nonetheless as objects, vehicles for the authors' opinions.[4] As in literature from other periods, animals in medieval writings allow the authors to voice criticism of society. The appropriation of animal behavior for delivering human moral messages increased as animal encyclopedias accorded more attention to moralizations and preachers' aids of various types included animals in their repertoires.[5]

In the late twelfth century, animals played a greater role in ecclesiastical writings, including the various genres of anti-heretical literature. This essay explores the array or bestiary of non-human creatures, insects and animals, used to image heresy during the High Middle Ages and analyzes how anti-heretical writers transformed animal traits into the salient features of the heretics they attacked. This body of literature, far from the hagiography that depicted Francis and other saints embracing creation,[6] allows no communion between animals and humans. Its often

Cistercian authors lived close to nature and enriched their meditative literature with images of goodness flowing from creation; yet when they engaged in polemical battles, the creatures of nature are clearly objectified.[7]

Twelfth-century Europe experienced a remarkable upsurge of popular heresy, spurring ecclesiastical writers to produce copious polemical literature. The Western Church, challenged by charismatic itinerant preachers, lay apostolic movements such as the Waldensians,[8] and the Cathar counter-church,[9] attacked heresy with pen, pulpit, and crusade. Treatises against the dissidents furnished preachers and then inquisitors with arguments and proof texts. Preaching campaigns were launched throughout Europe, notably in southern France, and upon their failure Church and state mounted the Albigensian crusade (1209–1229). A "persecuting society" took shape and the inquisitorial process crystallized.[10]

The writers who compiled the Church's anti-heretical dossiers relied on the learning of the "Twelfth-Century Renaissance,"[11] the flowering of cathedral schools that transmitted and extended classical learning and patristic exegesis, developing various genres of books including bestiaries and aviaries. As animal literature became increasingly popular, medieval authors drew from biblical, ancient, and patristic sources to moralize animal lore and apply it to preaching and writing against heresy.

From the wily fox to the lowly moth, animals and their behavior came to symbolize dissident Christians and their conduct.

Medieval Exegesis: Typology, the Spiritual Sense, and the Symbolist Mentality

How did medieval writers make the interpretive leap from creatures of nature to contemporary people? Certainly they could have looked to established genres of animal literature, which dated back to the classical fable. More importantly, however, they were schooled in a hermeneutic that searched for a divine and Christian meaning everywhere.[12] The key method for medieval exegetes was typology: "something real and historical which announces something else that is also real and historical."[13] The type, generally a person or thing in the Old Testament, was paired with the antitype, a person or thing in the New Testament foreshadowed by the Old Testament. Sacrificial animals in the Hebrew Scriptures such as the ox, the calf or the lamb commonly represented Christ.[14]

Medieval polemicists stretched typology so that a current event became the antitype or thing foreshadowed by its scriptural type. Commentators interpreted the lived text of the present according to the past text of Scripture; a twelfth-century dissident was then viewed as the antitype of a scriptural creature such as the fox (Song of Songs 2:15). Medieval writers also manipulated typology by apocalyptic thinking, when the present occurrence or person was interpreted as both antitype, foreshadowed by scripture, and prototype, harbinger of the end of time. Thus the present is read in terms of both past and future; the animal representing a heretic typified a double menace, pointing perilously backward and forward at the same time.

Furthermore, twelfth-century exegetes inherited the patristic tradition that distinguished between the letter and the spirit, the literal and the spiritual, making the analogy between body and soul, between the word-text and the Word-God, incarnate in Jesus Christ.[15] Paul's statement in 2 Corinthians 3:6, "the letter kills, but the spirit gives life," was taken to designate the two meanings of Scripture. The great Cistercian abbot and writer Bernard of Clairvaux (1090–1153) refers to "the surface meaning of divine Scripture, which the Apostle calls the written letter that kills." Bernard says that, "the law is spiritual, according to the Apostle's testimony, and was written for us, not only to please us with the appearance of its outer surface, but also to satisfy us with the taste of its inner meanings, as with a kernel of wheat" (Deuteronomy 32:14).[16] Like the kernel of wheat, the images convey the notion that the letter is exterior and the spirit interior. One must strip away the exterior in order to arrive at the interior, hidden meaning.

While this exegetical method derives from ancient Alexandria and especially Origen (c. 185–c. 254),[17] medieval exegetes adhered closely to the theory of signification that Augustine of Hippo (354–430) developed in *De doctrina christiana,* a foundational guide to Christian hermeneutics.[18] There he defines a sign as "a thing which causes us to think of something beyond the impression the thing itself makes upon the senses." Natural signs are distinguished from conventional, which include those given by God and contained in the Scriptures.[19] Signs may be figurative or literal. A knowledge of biblical languages is important for understanding literal signs, while figurative signs require acquaintance with languages and also with things—animals, stones, plants, numbers, music, history, various practical arts, and so on.[20] For Augustine, animals and other natural elements find a place in Scripture for their didactic value; acquaintance with them illuminates the similitudes that Scripture employs and lack of knowledge impedes understanding.[21] Augustine also formulated the foundational Western patristic view on the "qualitative" difference between humans and animals, which functioned to serve human masters.[22] Animals then were objects for interpretation, theoretically excluded from communion with humans, their rational and superior interpreters.

The twelfth century inherited, transmitted, and developed these Augustinian notions of signification, including the conviction that animals could serve to illuminate higher truths. Hugh of St. Victor (c. 1096–1141) in his *Didascalion,* inspired by Augustine's *De doctrina christiana,*[23] illustrates the theory of signification with an example from 1 Peter 5:8: "Your adversary the devil prowls around like a roaring lion, seeking someone to devour." In Scripture not only the words (*verba*) but the signs (*res*) have meaning, explains Hugh. Therefore, the word "lion" designates the animal and the animal signifies

the devil.[24] While the lion generally assumed a high-ranking position in beast literature, exegetes reading 1 Peter 5:8 counted it with numerous other animals that could represent evil.[25]

The exegete shared in the "symbolist mentality" of the twelfth century, as Marie-Dominique Chenu explains it: the "conviction that all natural or historical reality possessed a *signification* which transcended its crude reality and which a certain symbolic dimension of that reality would reveal to man's mind. Giving an account of things involved more than explaining them by reference to their internal causes; it involved discovering that dimension of mystery." The word *speculum* came to refer to the world and the elements therein as a mirror or reflection of God, as the Parisian master Alan of Lille (c. 1125–1202) wrote:

> Omnis mundi creatura
> Quasi liber et pictura
> Nobis est et speculum.
>
> (Every creature of the world
> is as a book or picture,
> and also a mirror for us.)[26]

That mirror reflected not only the divine, however; figures of evil and the diabolic were also perceived in creation and stocked the image-banks of anti-heretical literature.

The value accorded animals demonstrated some ambivalence when, for example, the lion was attributed positive or negative traits depending on the author's point of view, the circumstances of the text, and the evolution of the symbol over the course of the Middle Ages.[27] However, portrayals of animals remain largely negative in that they are more often associated with vices and evil characters than with virtues or divine persons.

Medieval exegetes bent on teaching moral lessons often seem oblivious to any notion of discontinuity in the parallels they wished to establish. The symbolic moral significance outweighed all else. Hélinand of Froidmont (c. 1160?–1237), for example, unflinchingly com-

pared the Virgin Mary to an elephant in one sermon and to an ox in another when he sought
to praise the chastity represented by the pachy-
derm and the diligence embodied in the ox.[28]
This follows in line with the admonition of the
scholar bishop Ambrose of Milan (c. 340–397);
in the *Hexameron* he advises humans to imitate virtuous animal behavior, such as the ant's
industriousness.[29] Nonetheless, some creatures
could represent such extreme opposites as Christ
and the devil. Rabanus Maurus (780–856) explains that the lion of Judah signifies the King
of Kings (Revelation 5:5), and the lion as ravenous beast represents the devil (1 Peter 5:8), as in
the example above from Hugh of St. Victor.[30]

Sources for Animal Lore

For unlocking the clues to the hidden meaning in the creatures of nature,[31] twelfth-century
authors drew on ancient and medieval repositories of animal lore, broadly termed bestiaries.
The bestiary designates a corpus of animal lore
that derives from the *Physiologus,* a Greek work
dating probably from the second century C.E.,
which was translated into Latin and numerous
vernacular languages. The Latin tradition made
additions to the *Physiologus* from the *Etymologiae*
of Isidore of Seville (c. 560–636) and produced
the earliest known Western bestiary. By the first
or second quarter of the twelfth century, other
sources and moralizations had been added to
the bestiary. Further passages from the *Etymologiae* were incorporated, in addition to selections from Pliny the Elder's *Historia Naturalis,*
Solinus's *Collectanea rerum mirabilium,* and
Ambrose of Milan's *Hexameron.* Various Latin
and vernacular bestiary traditions developed
and their production increased during the
twelfth and thirteenth centuries, with a peak between approximately 1180 and 1260. Bestiaries
and their derivative sources—the *Physiologus,*
the *Etymologiae,* Pliny, Solinus—all served as
school texts and a twelfth-century author might

have drawn on any or all of those sources.[32]
A near contemporary of Hugh of St. Victor,
Hugh of Fouilloy (d. c. 1174), composed *The
Aviarium,* a work that collected many moralizations about birds and proved highly influential for subsequent preachers. More influential
was the *Historia Scholastica* of Petrus Comestor,
whose commentary on Genesis expounded on
the proper function and didactic value of animals: "Animals were created for our instruction
and for the praise of God." [33]

Exegetical and encyclopedic works beyond
the bestiary also provided material for polemical
writers. Commentaries on Scripture established
parallels between certain creatures and heretics.
Ambrose, who engaged in conflict with Arianism in his own city, drew numerous such parallels in his commentary on the Gospel of Luke.
Those were echoed by succeeding centuries that
either remained in real tension with Arianism
or perceived Arianism as the archetypal heresy.
Gregory the Great (d. 604) included many
references to animals in his extensive exegetical works. The ninth-century encyclopedist and
abbot Rabanus Maurus extended Isidore of
Seville's *Etymologiae* in the bestiary he composed with moralizations and scriptural proof
texts for a range of interpretations. These are
but a few and the best known authors whose
works the twelfth-century polemicists could
have consulted.[34]

The Bestiary of Heretics

Numerous animals and other living creatures
were adduced to represent heretics in the polemical literature of the twelfth and early thirteenth centuries: wolves, foxes, cats, dogs, fallow deer, leopards, jackals, moths, and so on.
The wolf and the fox were the types of the
heretic par excellence. Here we shall examine
briefly the wolf and the fox and then focus on
some creatures that received less attention: the
cat, the moth and the mole.

THE WOLF AND THE FOX

Many medieval characterizations of animals are negative, with animals often representing vices or evil in some form. The Second Letter of Peter may have provided Christian exegetes the connection between heresy and animals in its comparison of false teachers and prophets to animals, destined to be caught and killed (2 Peter 2:1). Whatever the initial link, numerous authors chose to represent vices and vicious behavior with animals and their traits. Among all those, the wolf and the fox probably represent evil tendencies and behavior more than any other animals. Both appear in Scripture with decidedly negative qualities, and the fox figures in the *Physiologus* as well.[35]

The wolf makes numerous appearances in Scripture, where rapacity and deceit mark its character, as they do in bestiary literature (see figure 1).[36] The wolf inspired fear in the Middle Ages not only because it preyed on valuable herds but also from the perception that it hungered for human flesh.[37] A few examples will illustrate the wolf's usual depiction in Scripture and exegesis. Matthew 7:15 warns about false prophets who are ravenous wolves in sheep's clothing. John 10:12 reads that the hireling sees the wolf coming and leaves the sheep, and that the wolf snatches and scatters them. Among later writers, Isidore of Seville relates that the wolf, rabid and rapacious, destroys all in its path. Rabanus Maurus extends the moral typing of the wolf to encompass the heretic. He explains that the wolf rarely represents anything good; at times it signifies the devil as in John 10:12b; and at times it represents heretics or deceitful people (Matthew 10:16; John 10:12a). Bernard of Clairvaux compares the rebellious dissident Arnold of Brescia to a wolf. Alain of Lille accuses the Waldensians of being wolves in sheep's clothing. Hildegard of Bingen (1098–1179) identifies an animal to represent each of five eras of temporal rule in her visionary works, *Scivias* and the *Liber divinorum operum* (*Book of Divine Works*). The fifth era, typified by the gray wolf, would bring the persecutions of Christians by the wolf-like Antichrist, after the heretics and forerunners of Antichrist pave his way in the fourth era, that of the black pig. Hence heretics precede and prepare the wolf's attack.[38]

The fox, which became the major character in later medieval beast literature,[39] counts among scriptural animals, but not as frequently as the wolf. Like the wolf, it has a reputation for deceit and destruction, as in Judges 15:4–5, where Samson ties torches to foxes' tails in order to destroy the Philistines' grain, and Song of Songs 2:15, exhorting to catch the little foxes that destroy the vineyards.[40] The animal's deceitful and destructive behavior grounds its association with heresy from the time of the Gnostic controversies. Irenaeus of Lyons recounts the story of someone who convinced simple people that a mosaic portrait of the king, rearranged to depict a fox, was in fact that of the king. The fox's image summed up both the deceitful act and the heresy to which Irenaeus compared it.[41] Other anti-heretical authors echo the fox's typing as the heretic, among them Tertullian, Philastrius, Ambrose, Jerome, Augustine, Gregory the Great, and Bede. Through their works and others, this typology passed into the extensive tradition of commentary on the Song of Songs.[42] Isidore of Seville describes the animal's predilection for twisting paths and its practice of feigning death in order to trap unsuspecting birds. Rabanus Maurus states the moral quality of the fox clearly: "the fox by allegory represents the deceitful devil, or the crafty heretic or the sinful human"; he cites Matthew 8:20, Song of Songs 2:15 and Judges 15:4–5 as proof texts.[43] The fox as the type of the heretic appears frequently as a commonplace in polemical literature of the twelfth and early thirteenth centuries, which saw the ravaged vineyard as their threatened contemporary church. Bernard of Clairvaux composed a series of sermons on the Song of Songs 2:15, the third of which replied to a Praemonstratensian abbot, Evervin of

Figure 1. Wolf in bestiary. From Hugh of Fouilloy, *De bestiis et aliis rebus: seu Columbia deaurata* [ca. 1230–1250]. Ms. Typ. 101, folio 10r, Houghton Library, Harvard College Library. By permission of Houghton Library, Department of Printing and Graphic Arts.

Steinfeld who sought his opinion on heretics in the Rhineland. Innocent III even issued the call for the Fourth Lateran Council (1215) with a 1213 bull entitled: "The Lord of Host's Vineyard."[44]

THE CAT

While cats figure in a few positive anecdotes as defenders of the faith,[45] the cat generally figures as a sign of the devil, whether object of adoration during secret gatherings of heretics, or instrument for spurring conversion by fright. Eventually the feline, which early sources like Isidore and Rabanus laud for its acute vision at night,[46] comes to symbolize the heretic (see figure 2). The famous preacher Berthold of Regensburg explains what feline quality linked the cat inextricably to the heretic. He states: "God called [the heretic] a Ketzer, because he can creep secretly where no man sees him, like the cat [Katze]."[47] Feline secrecy probably explains several references that polemicists make to cats in secret rites. Alan of Lille's *Summa contra hereticos,* one of the major polemical treatises of the late twelfth century, defamed the cat and popularized the notion that heretics conducted secret rites with felines. Alan asserted that the Cathars were named after the cat, "because they kiss the hind parts of a cat in whose form ... Lucifer appears to them."[48] Similar accusations appear elsewhere, notably in the *De nugis curialium* (*Courtier's Trifles*) composed around 1185 by Walter Map and in an *exemplum* (short anecdote) about Dominic, founder of the Dominican order. Map reports that a black cat descended a rope into nighttime gatherings of heretics and offered itself for adoration — kisses on its feet, anus, and private parts.[49]

The Dominican preacher Stephen of Bourbon compiled a collection of *exempla,* including one very similar to Walter Map's and another about the foundation of the first Dominican house in southern France. According to one *exemplum,* Dominic was preaching in the town of Fanjeaux, the heart of Cathar country, when nine women came to him at prayer, asking for a sign to help them discern whether or not to follow the Cathars. Dominic continued to pray and then instructed the women to stand bravely when the Lord showed them what lord they had been serving. A large, horrid cat leaped into their midst, with a long tongue and a short tail that exposed a foul posterior releasing horrible odors. The creature, obviously a sign of the devil, reportedly frightened the women into orthodoxy and some became the first sisters at Prouille, Dominic's first religious foundation.[50]

The power of making obscene gestures to cats received enough credibility to appear in a papal bull issued by Gregory IX in 1233 when he enjoined the archbishop of Mainz to undertake anti-heretical preaching.[51] The supposed ritual actions of cat-kissing are mirrored in the illuminations of Bibles produced in the early thirteenth century. The *Bible moralisée* depicts both heretics and Jews with cats, specifically in the act of kissing the animals below the tail. Finally, similar rituals surface in late medieval treatises against the Waldensians.[52] These accusations mirror the penalties in Burgundian law, where stealing a valuable dog incurred the penalty to kiss the dog's posterior in public.[53] Humans perceived as beast-like were assumed or forced to act like animals. Cats became closely identified with witchcraft and its rituals, to the extent that they were persecuted even up to the modern period.[54] The persecution of cats contradicts the general view, as expressed by Joyce Salisbury, that medieval Christians did not apply their symbolism and "seldom bothered to follow the logical consequences of their metaphors."[55]

MOTH AND MOLE

Several creatures from the usual fox to the less common moth and mole figure the heretic in the letters of an influential Cistercian, Henry abbot of Clairvaux (1176–1179). Henry participated in two missions to southern France in 1178 and 1181 and between those influenced legislation against heresy at the Third Lateran

Figure 2. Heretics worshipping cat. Roundel 3a from the Apocalypse fragment of the Toledo Bible of St. Louis [ca. 1227–1234]. Manuscript M 240, folio 3v, Pierpont Morgan Library. By permission of Pierpont Morgan Library, Department of Medieval and Renaissance Manuscripts.

Council (1179). Such missions before the Albigensian Crusade emphasized preaching but also established precedents and procedures for inquisition. Henry, named cardinal bishop of Albano in 1179, marked himself in 1181 as the first churchman to lead an armed expedition in a Christian land. Henry's rhetoric and images are therefore closely allied to decisive and precedent-setting action.[56]

Henry's letters, undoubtedly designed for public reading, ring with militant imagery. To portray heretics, Henry adds the moth and the mole to the conventional figures of little foxes and treacherous wolves. In a letter composed prior to the 1178 mission, Henry accentuates the dangerous qualities of his adversaries: the heretics in southern France and notably in the city of Toulouse. Intervention is required not only to exterminate the foxes in the vineyard but also to close out the gnawing moths from the clothes-chest of Solomon. Following the 1178 mission, Henry issued another letter, a highly emotional appeal for holy war that casts heresy as a new Goliath looming against God's people.[157] To represent the resistance that heretics show to their foes, Henry chooses the fox, the serpent, the leopard, hiding its colors with its spots, the fallow deer, noted for its ability to escape, the moth, and the mole.[58] Let us focus on the moth and the mole.

The moth is singled out for its destructive capabilities. In addition to the moths that gnaw Solomon's wardrobe, the creature appears in Ecclesiasticus 42:13, Job 4:19, 13:28, 27:18; Psalm 39:11; Isaiah 14:11 (maggots and worms in RSV), 50:9, 51:8; Hosea 5:12; Matthew 6:19, Luke 12:33, and James 5:2. These scriptural moths surface frequently in medieval exegesis to represent various sins that the authors conceptualize as destructive, namely envy, avarice, lust, sin in general or adversity.[59]

Christian exegetes associated the moth with heresy as early as the fourth century. Ambrose of Milan viewed the moth as a figure for the Arian and included that interpretation in his widely consulted commentary on the Gospel of Luke. Ambrose declares that the moth is the heretic, specifically Arius and Photinus; it destroys clothing as Arius tears the Word away from God. It represents knowledge of Christ without his dual nature. A spirit that does not believe that the Father and Son are one in divinity is moth-eaten. Likewise the spirit that does not believe that Christ came in the flesh is itself a moth and Antichrist. Elsewhere Ambrose comments that if one's intellect is earthly and therefore fragile, the heretical moth will destroy it and the rust of wickedness will devour it. Again he cites the moth as a type for Arius and Photinus, who rend the church's garment with their impiety by wanting to separate the dual nature of Christ.[60]

After Ambrose, Gregory the Great in his influential *Moralia in Job* interpreted the moth as a figure for the heretic. Commenting on Job 27:18: "He builds his house like the moth" in the Vulgate, Gregory remarks that teachers of heresy corrupt the minds that they seize. The moth building itself a house by destroying has no better figure for comparison than the heretic who established a place for his teaching in the minds he has corrupted.[61] The extensive allegorical compendium, *Allegoriae in universam Scripturam Sacram,* offers a similar interpretation, stating that the moth represents any heretic because the maliciousness of heretics gnaws away the conscience.[62] Bernard of Clairvaux, Henry's most famous predecessor as abbot of that monastery, does not interpret the moth as a heretic but links it nonetheless with the devil and hell. Reacting to Isaiah 14:11, the abbot exclaims: "O God, how far removed the covering of a precious stone from that of a larva, and the delights of paradise from the corrosive moth of hell!"[63]

The mole fares no better than the moth in Henry of Clairvaux's eyes, and perhaps worse. Twice it represents a stage of metamorphosis: the first from a fox and the second from a wolf. To praise and demonstrate the 1178 preaching mission's success, Henry declares that orthodox preachers forced the heretics into hiding, causing the foxes to metamorphosize into moles and go underground where they gnawed and destroyed the roots of holy plants. Subsequently Henry describes the conversion of a local heretical leader noted for holding secret meetings at his castle. The heresiarch is cast as an Arian and a mole, led out from his treacherous hole and transformed from a wolf into a sheep of Israel. Hence the mole, formerly a wolf before going underground, becomes a sheep when it emerges into the light; a sort of triple metamorphosis takes place,[64] dramatically increasing both the threatening power of fox and mole and the impact of the conversion.[65]

The mole's scriptural presence is limited to Isaiah 2:20. Exegetes target the mole for its blindness, moralized in various negative ways that seem connected to its inclusion among the unclean animals in Leviticus. Isidore of Seville sees the creature as punished by everlasting blindness and darkness. Rabanus Maurus extends the moralization to explain that the mole's inability to see figures the errant ways of the idolatrous who remain in the darkness of ignorance and foolishness. Furthermore, the mole represents heretics or false Christians deprived of the light of true knowledge and confined to the earth and the space beneath it.[66]

Conclusion

Polemical writers of the High Middle Ages use animals as objects in their verbal attack on heresy. Monastic authors celebrated nature in many of their writings and were familiar with and even somewhat responsible for the animal literature that enjoyed increasing popularity in the twelfth century.[67] Nonetheless, when defending orthodoxy against the threat of heresy, they employed centuries-old exegetical techniques such as typology to associate heretics with animals and animal-like behavior. Nature was viewed as

a vast repository of signs which, when properly interpreted, would yield understanding of divine order; that process of interpretation included the identification of evil that threatened the social order. Animals and heretics alike are objectified and demonized in this polemical literature. Animals in this context generally stand far from the wolf of Gubbio, the hare, and the birds respected by St. Francis, who exalted the communion of all creatures. Instead they are seen as participating in the diabolical not the divine. They clearly suffer from the prejudice of what Jay McDaniel calls the "Instrumentalist" tradition of Christian thought.[68] Negative attitudes reinforced by violent rhetoric led to the persecution of heretics. Animals—generally treated as property and food source—increasingly became victims of cruelty when cats were systematically persecuted because of their association with heretics and then witches. To review this history of polemic and persecution, harmful to humans and nonhumans alike, sharpens our awareness of how all creation continues to be exploited and heightens our hope and determination to achieve a true "communion of subjects."

Acknowledgments

This essay is dedicated to Kay Shanahan and Anne Brenon, whose love for animals has been inspirational, and to our five family cats: Walter, Basile, Athena, Tecla, and Cecilia, who warmed my lap as I first revised. Portions of the essay appear in B. Kienzle, "La représentation de l'hérétique par l'imagerie animale," in Anne Brenon and Christine Dieulafait, eds., *Les cathares devant l'histoire: Mélanges offerts à Jean Duvernoy* (Castelnaud La Chapelle: l'Hydre éditions 2004), pp. 181–95, and used here with permission of the editors. I am grateful to Jan Ziolkowski for helpful comments and suggestions on bibliography.

NOTES

1. For an excellent overview of medieval "beast literature," see Jan Ziolkowski, *Talking Animals. Medieval Latin Beast Poetry, 750–1150* (Philadelphia: University of Pennsylvania Press, 1993), pp. 1–14.

2. See Joyce E. Salisbury, *The Beast Within: Animals in the Middle Ages* (New York and London: Routledge, 1994), pp. 1–12; and Jay McDaniel, "Practicing the Presence of God," in this volume, and his summary of teachings in Judaism and Christianity that are prejudicial to animals. McDaniel draws on Andrew Linzey and Dan Cohn-Sherbok's analysis in *After Noah: Animals and the Liberation of Theology* (London: Mowbray, 1997), pp. 1–16.

3. See Michel Pastoreau, "L'animal et l'historien du Moyen Age," in Jacques Berlioz and Marie-Anne Polo de Beaulieu, eds., *L'animal exemplaire au Moyen Age (Ve–XVe s.)* (Rennes, Presses Universitaires, 1999), pp. 14–16. Pastoreau, p. 16, argues that attitudes toward animals improved in the Western Middle Ages, compared to classical and biblical antiquity: "Ces questions, ces curiosités, ces interrogations multiples que le Moyen Age occidental se pose souvent à propos de l'animal soulignent combien le Christianisme a été pour lui l'occasion d'une remarquable promotion. L'Antiquité biblique et gréco-romaine le négligeait ou le méprisait: le Moyen Age chrétien le place sur le devant de la scène." (These issues, curiosities, and the many questions that the Western Middle Ages asked itself so often about animals underscore how remarkably favorable toward them Christianity proved to be. Antiquity, biblical, and Greco-Roman times neglected or scorned animals: the Christian Middle Ages placed them center stage.)

4. Salisbury, *Beast Within*, p. 124, observes that Ysengrinus, protagonist of a Latin beast epic, is the first animal character to have a human name and personality. This sort of anthropomorphism increased in later medieval literature.

5. See Carolyn Muessig, "The *Sermones feriales et communes* of Jacques de Vitry: A critical edition of Sermons 10 and 11 on animals," *Medieval Sermon Studies* 47 (2003): 33–60. In *L'animal exemplaire au moyen âge*, see especially Claude Bremond,

"Le bestiaire de Jacques de Vitry (1240)," pp. 111–22; Baudoin van den Abeele, "L'allégorie animale dans les encylopédies latines du Moyen Age," pp. 123–37; Marie Anne Polo de Beaulieu, "Du bon usage de l'animal dans les recueils d'*exempla*," pp. 147–69; Franco Morenzoni, "Les animaux exemplaires dans les recueils de *Distinctiones* bibliques alphabétiques du XIIIe siècle," pp. 171–88.

6. See Ziolkowski, *Talking Animals*, p. 33, and Pierre Boglioni, "Il Santo e gli animali nell'alto medioevo," in *L'Uomo di fronte al mondo animale nell'alto medioevo*, 7–13 aprile 1983, 2 vols. (Spoleto, 1985), 2:935–94.

7. On the Cistercians' polemical writing, see Beverly Mayne Kienzle, *Cistercians, Heresy and Crusade in Occitania 1145–1229* (Woodbridge, UK: York Medieval Press and Boydell and Brewer, 2001); and on Cistercians and nature imagery, see B.M. Kienzle, "Maternal Imagery in the Sermons of Hélinand of Froidmont," in *De Ore Domini: Preacher and Word in the Middle Ages*, eds. Thomas L. Amos, Eugene A. Green, Beverly Mayne Kienzle, Studies in Medieval Culture XXVII (Kalamazoo: Medieval Institute Publications, 1989), p. 100. On the violence in early Cistercian manuscript illumination, see Conrad Rudolph, *Violence and Daily Life: Reading, Art, and Polemics in the Cîteaux Moralia in Job* (Princeton: Princeton University Press, 1997), pp. 42–62.

8. Malcolm Lambert, *Medieval Heresy, Popular Movements from the Gregorian Reform to the Reformation* 2nd ed. (Oxford/Cambridge USA: Blackwell, 1992), pp. 5–78; Jeffrey Burton Russell, *Dissent and Order in the Middle Ages: The Search for Legitimate Authority* (New York, 1992), pp. 44–47; Edward Peters, *Inquisition* (Berkeley/Los Angeles: University of California Press, 1988), pp. 47–48.

9. For an introduction to the Cathars, see Malcolm Lambert, *The Cathars* (Oxford and Malden, MA: Blackwell, 1998). Recent trends in research are presented in Anne Brenon, *Les archipels cathares* (Cahors: Dire Editions, 2000). Ironically the Cathars were distrusted because of their vegetarianism, a refusal to kill animals rooted in a disdain for prod-

ucts of coition, and for some, in the belief that animals had souls. See Brenon, "La créature animale dans la vision cathare du monde," in *Homme, Animal, Société, III, Histoire et animal,* eds. Alain Couret and Frédéric Oge, Toulouse: Presses de l'Institut d'Etudes politiques, 1989), pp. 281–91.

10. On persecution, see R. I. Moore, *Formation of a Persecuting Society* (Oxford: Blackwell, 1987). On the Albigensian crusade and polemical literature, see Kienzle, *Cistercians, Heresy, and Crusade.*

11. On the schools and literature, see Charles Homer Haskins, *The Renaissance of the Twelfth Century* (Cleveland/New York: Meridian Books, 1963); and Linda Paterson, *The World of the Troubadours. Medieval Occitan Society, c. 1100-c. 1300* (Cambridge: Cambridge University Press, 1993). On exegesis, see Beryl Smalley, *The Study of the Bible in the Middle Ages* (Oxford, 1952; reprint Notre Dame, IN: University of Notre Dame Press, 1970); *The Gospels in the Schools c. 1100-c. 1280* (London: Hambledon Press, 1985).

12. Salisbury, *Beast Within,* pp. 104–12.

13. Erich Auerbach, "Figura," in *Scenes from the Drama of European Literature* (New York: Meridian Books, 1959), p. 29.

14. Willene Clark, "Twelfth- and Thirteenth-Century Latin Sermons and the Latin Bestiary," in *Compar(a)ison* 1 (1996): 10.

15. See Henri de Lubac, *Medieval Exegesis,* I, trans. Mark Sebanc (Grand Rapids, MI/Edinburgh: Eerdmans Publishing, 1998), pp. 3–8; Smalley, *The Study of the Bible,* pp. 1–2.

16. *Sermons for the Summer Season. Liturgical Sermons from Rogationtide and Pentecost,* trans. with Introduction by B. M. Kienzle, additional translations by J. Jarzembowski *Cistercian Fathers* 53 (Kalamazoo, MI: Cistercian Publications, 1991), pp. 115–16. In *De doctrina christiana,* Augustine speaks of figurative things, whose "secrets are to be removed as kernels from the husk as nourishment for charity." 3.XII.18, *On Christian Doctrine,* trans. D. W. Robertson, Jr., (Indianapolis, 1958), p. 90.

17. H. de Lubac devotes a chapter and much more to Origen in *Medieval Exegesis,* I, pp. 142–72 and *passim.* A recent and excellent study of Origen's exegesis is Brian Daley, "Origen's *De Principiis.* A Guide to the Principles of Christian Scriptural Interpretation," in J. Petruccione, ed., *Nova et vetera* (Washington, D.C., 1998), pp. 3–21.

18. *On Christian Doctrine,* Prologue, p. 3.

19. Ibid., 2.I.1-II.3, pp. 34–35.

20. Ibid., 2.X.15-XXX.47, pp. 43–67.

21. Ibid., 2.XVI.24, pp. 50–51.

22. Salisbury, *Beast Within,* p. 2.

23. Smalley, *The Study of the Bible,* p. 103, and pp. 83–106 on Hugh of St. Victor.

24. *PL* 176: 790–91.

25. Salisbury, *Beast Within,* pp. 129–30.

26. Marie-Dominique Chenu, *Nature, Man and Society in the Twelfth Century,* ed. and trans. J. Taylor and L. K. Little (Chicago, 1968), pp. 102, 117. On the *speculum* image, see Herbert Grabes, *The Mutable Glass. Mirror-imagery in titles and texts of the Middle Ages and English Renaissance,* trans. Gordon Collier (Cambridge/ London / New York: Cambridge University Press, 1982), pp. 1–15.

27. See Pastoreau, "L'animal et l'historien du Moyen Age," pp. 23–26. Pastoreau, p. 25, argues that the symbolism of the cat, dog, and squirrel shows a large difference between the early Middle Ages and the thirteenth century.

28. See Beverly M. Kienzle, "Mary Speaks Against Heresy: An Unedited Sermon of Hélinand for the Purification, Paris, B.N. ms. lat. 14591," *Sacris erudiri* 32 (1991): 292–93.

29. Salisbury, *Beast Within,* p. 113.

30. Rabanus Maurus, *De universo,* PL 111: 217–18.

31. Chenu, *Nature, Man and Society,* pp. 104–11.

32. On the history of the bestiary, see Willene B. Clark and Meradith T. McMunn, eds., *Beasts and Birds of the Middle Ages: The Bestiary and Its Legacy* (Philadelphia: University of Pennsylvania Press, 1989), pp. 2–5.

33. See Willene B. Clark, ed., trans., and comment., *The Medieval Book of Birds: Hugh of Fouilloy's Aviarum* (Binghamton, NY: Medieval and Renaissance Texts and Studies, 1992). Petrus Comestor, *Historia Scholastica, PL* 198 1063A: "animalia ad instructionem nostram et Dei laudem creata sunt …"

34. See various works of Ambrose and Gregory the Great cited below, as well as Rabanus Maurus,

De universo, PL III: 217–26; Clark, "Twelfth- and Thirteenth-Century Latin Sermons and the Latin Bestiary," pp. 5–19, cites several sermon authors who refer to earlier sources. See also Jacques Voisenet, *Bêtes et hommes dans le monde médiéval. Le bestiaire des clercs du Ve au XIIe siècle* (Turnhout: Brepols, 2000). Voisenet, whose work I discovered after completing this article, notes many of the patristic parallels I include below but does not extend his analysis to the late twelfth century and its polemical literature.

35. *Physiologus,* trans. Michael J. Curley, (Austin/London: University of Texas Press, 1979), pp. 27–28. See Emilio Mitre Fernández, "Animales, vicios y herejías (Sobre la criminalización de la disidencia en el Medievo)," in *Cuadernos de Historia de Espana LXVIV, En memoria de don Claudio Sánchez-Albornoz* (Buenos Aires: Instituto de Historia de Espana, 1997), pp. 259–63, 272–73.

36. Wolves appear in Gen. 49:27; Eccl. 13:17; Isa. 11:6, 65:25; Jer. 5:6; Ezek. 22:27; Hab. 1:8; Zeph. 3:3; Mt. 7:15, 10:16; Lk. 10:3; Jn. 10:12; Acts 20:29. Salisbury, *Beast Within,* p. 130, notes that even in secular literature, wolves were perceived as a threat to social order.

37. Salisbury, *Beast Within,* pp. 69–70.

38. Isidore, *Etymologiae sive originum, Libri XX,* ed. W. M. Lindsay 2 vols. (Oxford: Clarendon, 1911), XII.2.23–24 (No page numbers are given in this edition); Rabanus Maurus, *De universo, PL* III: 223; Bernard of Clairvaux, *The Letters of Bernard of Clairvaux,* trans. Bruno Scott James, New Intro. by Beverly Mayne Kienzle, (Stroud, UK: Sutton Publishing, Kalamazoo, Mich.: Cistercian Publications, 1998), Letter 250 (letters 239 and 242 compare Arnold of Brescia and Peter Abelard to the dragon, the bee, Goliath, and various other images of evil); Alan of Lille, *Summa quadrapartita, PL* 210: 377; Hildegard of Bingen, *Scivias,* trans. Columba Hart and Jane Bishop; Intro. Barbara J. Newman; Preface, Caroline Walker Bynum, (New York: Paulist Press, 1990), Classics of Western Spirituality, Book III, Vision 11.6, p. 495; *Liber divinorum operum,* Part III, Vision 10.33, translated in *Hildegard of Bingen's Book of Divine Works with Letters and Songs,* ed. Matthew Fox, (Santa Fe, NM: Bear and Company, 1987),

p. 360. See the analysis of Hildegard's view of the ages in Kathryn Kerby-Fulton, *Reformist Apocalypticism and Piers Plowman* (Cambridge: Cambridge University Press, 1990), pp. 39–50, who highlights Hildegard's use of the wolf image also to represent corrupt clergy, p. 35. For additional discussion of the wolf, see Gherardo Ortalli, "Animal exemplaire et culture de l'environnement," in *L'animal exemplaire,* pp. 44–48.

39. Salisbury, *Beast Within,* p. 131.

40. The fox appears in Judg. 15:4–5, Song 2:15, Ps. 63:10 (fox in the Vulgate; jackal in the RSV); Ezek. 13:4; Lam. 5:18 (fox in the Vulgate; jackal in RSV); Neh. 4:3; Mt 8:20; Lk. 9:58, 13:32 (referring to Herod).

41. Jean-Daniel Dubois, "Polémiques, pouvoirs et exégèse. L'exemple des gnostiques anciens en monde grec," in *Inventer l'hérésie,* ed. Monique Zerner (Nice, 1998), pp. 48–49; M. Scopello, "Le renard symbole de l'hérésie dan les polémiques patristiques contre les gnostiques, in *Revue d'Histoire et de Philosophie Religieuses* 71 (1991): 73–88.

42. Among the many examples are Tertullian, *PL* 2: 47; Philastrius, *PL* 12: 1170; Ambrose, *PL* 15: 1707 1888; Jerome, *PL* 25: 109; Augustine, *PL* 37: 1040, *PL* 40: 527, Maximus of Turin, *PL* 57: 451; Gregory the Great, *PL* 79: 500; Bede, *PL* 91: 896, 92: 42, 967; *PL* 93: 923. On medieval Western exegesis of the Song of Songs, see E. Ann Matter, *The Voice of My Beloved: The Song of Songs in Western Medieval Christianity,* (Philadelphia: University of Pennsylvania Press, 1990).

43. Isidore, *Etymologiae,* XII.2.29; Rabanus Maurus, *De universo, PL* III: 225.

44. Bernard of Clairvaux, *On the Song of Songs, III,* trans. Kilian Walsh and Irene M. Edmonds, CF 31, (Kalamazoo: Cistercian Publications, 1991), pp. 179–180; *PL* 214: 823, *Epistola* 30.

45. Laurence Bobis cites the *Dialogue des créatures,* a late-fourteenth-century text where a cat preaches about cleanliness and godliness, and Luc de Tuy, *De altera vita fideique controversiis adversus Albigensium errores libri III,* where a cat pursues a heretic even after death. "Chasser le naturel … L'utilisation exemplaire du chat dans la littérature médiévale," in *L'animal exemplaire,* pp. 239–240.

46. Isidore, *Etymologiae*, XII.2.38; Rabanus Maurus, *De universo*, *PL* III: 226.

47. Berthold of Regensburg, *Vollständige Ausgabe seiner predigten* 2 vols., ed. Franz Pfeiffer (1862–1880; repr. Berlin, 1965), cited by Sara Lipton, *Images of Intolerance. The Representation of Jews and Judaism in the Bible moralisée* (Berkeley: University of California Press, 1999), p. 192, n. 35.

48. *PL* 210: 366A.

49. Walter Map, *De Nugis Curialium (Courtiers' Trifles)*, trans. Marbury Bladen Ogle and Frederick Tupper (London, 1924), pp. 72–73.

50. Etienne de Bourbon, *Anecdotes historiques. Légendes et apologues tirés du recueil inédit d'Etienne de Bourbon*, ed. A. Lecoy de la Marche (Paris 1877), pp. 34–35 (Dominic in Fanjeaux), p. 323 (Black cat in group of heretics). On cats and the devil, see L. Bobis, "Chasser le naturel," pp. 237–38; and on cats and the motif of "le diable panzooique," see Pierre Boglioni, "Les animaux dans l'hagiographie monastique," in *L'animal exemplaire*, pp. 70–71.

51. Cited in Joshua Trachtenberg, *The Devil and the Jews. The Medieval Conception of the Jew and Its Relation to Modern Antisemitism* (New Haven, 1943; rpt. with introduction by Marc Saperstein, Philadelphia: 2nd paperback edition, 1983), pp. 205–6. Sara Lipton, *Images of Intolerance*, p. 192 n. 36.

52. Lipton, *Images of Intolerance*, pp. 88–90; and on the rituals alleged in treatises against the Waldensians, p. 191 n. 34. See also Peter Biller, "Bernard Gui, Sex and Luciferanism," in *Praedicatores Inquisitore—I, The Dominicans and the Mediaeval Inquisition*. Acts of the 1st International Seminar on the Dominicans and the Inquisition, Rome February 23–25, 2002 (Rome: Istituto Domenciano, 2004), pp. 455–70.

53. Salisbury, *Beast Within*, p. 39.

54. See the discussion of folklore in chapter 2 of Robert Darnton, The *Great Cat Massacre and Other Episodes in French Cultural History* (Basic Books, 1984).

55. Salisbury, *Beast Within*, p. 132.

56. The standard work on Henry is "Yves Congar, Henry de Marcy, abbé de Clairvaux, cardinal-évêque d'Albano et légat pontifical," in *Analecta Monastica*, Series 5, *Studia Anselmiana* vol. 43 (Rome, 1958), pp. 1–90. See also Kienzle, *Cistercians, Heresy and Crusade*.

57. The letters are *Epistola* 11, from May 1178, and *Epistola* 29 from the fall of that year, *PL* 204: 223–25, 235–40.

58. The leopard appears in Eccl. 28:27, Isa. 11:6, Jer. 13:23 and Hab. 1:8. Medieval authors including Gilbert of Hoyland compare the leopard to the heretic, *PL* 176: 989 and *PL* 184: 152. The fallow deer, from Prov. 6:5 and Isa. 13:14, figures the devil for Ps.- Rabanus Maurus, *PL* 112:905, and wicked doctrine for Walafrid Strabo, *PL* 113: 1252.

59. A computer search of the *Patrologia Latina* produced 825 matches on the nominative case alone. Representative examples are found in *PL* 107: 834, III: 235, and 112: 1359.

60. *Expositio Evangelii secundum Lucam*, *PL* 15: 1538–39; *Expositio in Psalmum CXVIII*, *PL* 15: 1361; *De spiritu sancto*, *PL* 16: 741.

61. *PL* 76:51. See also *PL* 113: 826.

62. *PL* 112: 1067.

63. *PL* 183: 664. See also Garnier of St. Victor who compares the moth to heretical wickedness (*haeretica pravitas*), *PL* 193:133.

64. *PL* 204: 236–37, 239.

65. See Salisbury, *Beast Within*, p. 141, on attitudes toward changes in animals' shapes.

66. See Jerome on unclean animals, *PL* 23:311; Isidore of Seville, *Etymologiae* XII.2.5; Rabanus Maurus, *De universo*, *PL* III:226. The mole generally figures the miser. See C. Muessig, "The *Sermones feriales et communes*," p. 57; and B. van den Abeele, "L'allégorie animale dans les encylopédies latines du Moyen Age," p. 133.

67. On the monastic Latin literature that preceded the vernacular beast fables, see Ziolkowski, *Talking Animals,* and Salisbury, *Beast Within*, p. 117.

68. Jay McDaniel, "Practicing the Presence of God," in this volume. On the implications of animal insults, see Edmund Leach, "Anthropological Aspects of Language: Animal Categories and Verbal Abuse," in *New Directions in the Study of Language*, ed. Eric H. Lenneberg (Cambridge: MIT Press, 1966), pp. 23–63.

Descartes, Christianity, and Contemporary Speciesism

GARY STEINER

As enlightened as we may consider ourselves to be today on the question of animal rights and the question of the nature of animal experience, it has got to come as a surprise that our views and even the methods we employ in examining these sorts of questions are in certain respects pointedly Cartesian.[1] Descartes is widely recognized to have held the view that animals do not in any deep sense have experiences, and it is generally assumed that in one way or another this conviction led Descartes to the proposition that human beings have no moral obligations whatsoever toward animals.[2] Are we today not too enlightened to believe the sorts of things that Descartes took for granted about animals? Have we not disburdened ourselves of the sorts of prejudices that limited Descartes's perspective?

In fact we have not. Even if we might be said to be more sensitive and open to the prospect that animals are not mere machines, our entire way of life and more importantly the very ways in which we tend to *proceed in arguing* about these questions reflect some very Carte-

sian prejudices. Nowhere are the traces of these prejudices more evident than in contemporary debates about speciesism. While speciesism is a term that gets employed in a variety of ways nowadays, it always implies that one species, human beings, considers itself superior to other species simply because it is different from other species.[3] This superiority is asserted somewhat dogmatically, much in the way that racists dogmatically assert the superiority of their own race, or in the way that sexists dogmatically assert the superiority of their own sex. In each case an implicit claim is made to moral superiority, and the corollary to this claim is the proposition that the beings that claim superiority are thereby entitled to rights and privileges to which their supposed inferiors are not.

Contemporary debates about the moral status of animals very often take the form of controversies about speciesism. Curiously enough, defenders of animal rights in these debates argue in a way strangely reminiscent of Descartes. Specifically, proponents of each side of this debate tend to argue about (a) whether animals can or cannot legitimately be said to possess certain capacities or qualities that we tend to associate with being human, and (b) whether it can be *proved* that animals do or do not possess these capacities or qualities. The second of these controversies is more uniquely Cartesian than the first: for, notwithstanding the distinctive conception of mind that Descartes develops in his endeavor to capture the essence of being human, Descartes, who takes his cue primarily from Aristotle, the Stoics, Saint Augustine, and Saint Thomas Aquinas, is wholly traditional in his endeavor to deny that animals possess certain human-identified qualities. What is most distinctive from a methodological standpoint in Descartes's approach is his preoccupation with proof, a preoccupation that is best understood as a corollary of his conceptions of the mind and rational evidence.[4] Nonetheless, in its approach to each of these questions the contemporary speciesism debate shows a clear debt to Descartes.

I will briefly sketch out Descartes's views on the nature of animal experience and the moral status of animals, with some specific emphasis on the debt that Descartes's views owe to Christian conceptions of human beings and animals, and then I will return to the question of speciesism and try to pinpoint the way Descartes has influenced the contemporary debate. In the end I would like to propose that the very limits that we so easily recognize in Descartes's treatment of animals are those that confront the very conceptualization of animals and animal rights in the speciesism debate. Ultimately the endeavor to restore a sense of reverence for animal life need not depend on an acknowledgment of human-like capacities in animals such as reason or language. The key to overcoming speciesism and embracing animals as "our companion beings," an ideal sketched out by Thomas Berry in his prologue, depends not on a comparison between animal and human "natures" but instead on the recognition that both animals and human beings make their home together in the one

supreme realm of nature that the ancient Greeks characterized as *physis*. It is nature in this sense to which Thomas Berry draws our attention when he speaks of the "inner form" that lies at the core of the world, and it is nature in this sense that thinkers such as Schopenhauer, Nietzsche, and Heidegger have in mind when they seek to overcome the soul-body dualism of Christianity and Cartesian philosophy toward the prospect of a sense of humans belonging to nature. After examining the implications of Descartes's appropriation of Christian soul-body dualism for his understanding of the moral status of animals, I will briefly return to the notion of *physis* and say something about its potential for realizing the ideal of "a communion of subjects."

Descartes's Views on the Nature of Animal Experience

Descartes's reputation for hostility toward animals was secured forever when his contemporary Henry More vilified him for "the internecine and cutthroat idea that you advance in the *Method,* which snatches life and sensibility away from all the animals."[5] Twentieth-century commentators were no less harsh in their assessments; Norman Kemp Smith, for example, endorsed More's assessment when he termed Descartes's position downright "monstrous."[6] For Descartes, animals are essentially machines, completely lacking in reason and in fact in any kind of inner experience, and as such they are due no moral obligations at all; we may experiment on them, and we may kill and eat them without moral scruple. In order to support this view, Descartes advanced three basic grounds for denying that we have moral obligations toward animals, all of which return us in one way or another to the faculty of reason as the dividing line between human beings and animals.

Descartes presents the first and most fundamental of these criteria in Part 5 of the *Discourse on Method,* where he maintains that nonhuman animals lack reason and language, and hence are ultimately indistinguishable from machines.[7] Descartes takes the inability to use language in a fully meaningful way—and by this he means to exclude the chattering of magpies and the like—as a sign that animals "have no reason at all" and that "nature ... acts in them according to the disposition of their organs. In the same way a clock, consisting only of wheels and springs, can count the hours and measure time more accurately than we can with all our wisdom."[8] This account of the functioning of animals recalls Descartes's conception of the body in the *Treatise of Man* as "but a statue, an earthen machine" whose nerves function in the same way as the tubes in "the grottos and fountains in the gardens of our kings" and whose heart functions like the pipes in a church organ;[9] the difference between animal and human bodies is simply that God has united the latter with a rational soul.[10] And since the rational soul is the seat of all conscious activity, it should not be surprising that animals are incapable of rationality and language.

A simple and vivid way of understanding this complex claim about animals is to say, as is sometimes done, that for Descartes animals are essentially like trees that learned to walk. Of course there is an obvious objection to such a characterization, one originally advanced by Plutarch and later reiterated by Descartes's contemporary Pierre Gassendi. Plutarch rejected the proposition that animals lack reason and language when he suggested that when dying animals cry out they are "begging for mercy, entreating, seeking justice."[11] Gassendi slightly recasts this objection when he proposes to Descartes that animals do have a kind of "logos" of their own, even if it is not the logos of human beings:

> You say that brutes lack reason. Well, of course they lack human reason, but they do not lack their own kind of reason. So it does not seem appropriate to call them ἄλογα except by comparison with us or with our kind of reason; and in any case λόγος or reason seems to be a gen-

eral term, which can be attributed to them no less than the cognitive faculty or internal sense. You may say that animals do not employ rational argument. But although they do not reason so perfectly or about as many subjects as man, they still reason, and the difference seems to be merely one of degree. But although they do not produce human speech (since of course they are not human beings), they still produce their own form of speech, which they employ just as we do ours.[12]

In framing the objection in these terms, Gassendi is capitalizing on the rich variety of meanings contained in the Greek term *logos,* meanings that range from sentence and proposition to logic to proportion to "account." Gassendi, like Plutarch, is raising the possibility that there is a "logic" or sense to animal experience, even if it is not the same as the logic or sense of human experience. Hence Plutarch and Gassendi call on us to consider whether we are not being unduly anthropocentric in denying "logos" to animals simply because they don't speak, do mathematics, structure their lives in an explicitly teleological manner, etc.

Descartes anticipates this line of reasoning in the *Discourse* when he says that even the best trained animals such as parrots "are incapable of arranging various words together and forming an utterance from them in order to make their thoughts understood." Animals "cannot show that they are thinking what they are saying." The actions of animals are due entirely "to the disposition of their organs." Hence animals are pure mechanism, just like clocks or church organs. Descartes's direct response to Gassendi in the *Objections and Replies* to the *Meditations* is of a piece with the reasoning articulated in the *Discourse:*

> I do not see what argument you are relying on when you lay it down as certain that a dog makes discriminating judgements in the same way as we do. Seeing that a dog is made of flesh you perhaps think that everything which is in you also exists

in the dog. But I observe no mind in the dog, and hence believe there is nothing to be found in a dog that resembles the things I recognize in a mind.[13]

This is a position that Descartes maintained throughout his life; notwithstanding the suggestion of some commentators that Descartes was eventually to abandon the strict terms of the *bête-machine* hypothesis,[14] according to which animals are mere machines and nothing else, as late as one year before his death Descartes would say that "the wagging of a dog's tail is only a movement accompanying a passion, and so is to be sharply distinguished, in my view, from speech, which alone shows the thought hidden in the body."[15]

Descartes articulates a second criterion for distinguishing human beings and animals at the end of Part V of the *Discourse* and in his correspondence, namely that animals lack immortal souls. This criterion is closely related to the first, so much so that it is difficult to establish a definitive boundary between the two. Descartes says that animals have "sensitive" souls, just as Aristotle and Aquinas had maintained; but, along with Aristotle and Aquinas, Descartes argues that animals lack reason and hence "rational" souls. Along with Aquinas, Descartes identifies the rational soul as an immortal soul, and he makes a sharp distinction between the souls of rational beings and the "souls" of beings like dogs and trees. In a letter to More, Descartes outlines his views on animal souls in the following way: We cannot *prove* whether or not animals possess immortal, rational souls, but the "stronger and more numerous" arguments lie on the side of supposing that animals *lack* immortal souls; the most reasonable assumption is that animals possess a "corporeal soul" [*anima corporea*] which is "purely mechanical and corporeal," in contrast with the "incorporeal principle" that characterizes "the mind [*mentem*] or that soul [*animam*] which I have defined as thinking substance [*substantiam cogitationem*]."[16] Two earlier letters written by Descartes help to bring this conception of "corporeal soul" into relief as something very much like the Aristotelian-Thomistic conception of sensitive soul. In one he says that "the souls of animals are nothing but their blood" [*animas brutorum nihil aliud esse quam sanguinem*], and he argues that "this theory involves such an enormous difference between the souls of animals and our own that it provides a better argument than any yet thought of to refute the atheists and establish that human minds cannot be drawn out of the potentiality of matter."[17] In the other he assimilates the corporeal soul to mechanism:

> I would prefer to say with Holy Scripture (Deuteronomy 12:23) that blood is their soul [viz., the soul of animals], for blood is a fluid body in very rapid motion, and its more rarified parts are called spirits. It is these which move the whole mechanism of the body.[18]

Here Descartes follows both Aristotle, who associated logos (speech, reason, calculation, etc.) specifically with human beings; and Aquinas, who viewed the rational soul as immortal. When Descartes asserts the immortality of the human soul and the mortality of the sensitive souls of animals, he is drawing out an implication of his soul-body dualism, which asserts that all of nature is inert matter. Since animals are part of nature, and since natural things are not the sorts of beings toward which (on Descartes's and the Western philosophical tradition's view) we have obligations, we have no moral obligations toward animals—and it is then easy to see why Descartes views animals as essentially organic machines.

Descartes takes his reasoning from Aristotle by way of Aquinas. Aristotle argued that humans have "calculative" imagination (which enables us to abstract concepts from our particular experiences, and to use these concepts in linguistic formulations like assertions and deliberations), whereas nonhuman animals have only "sensitive" imagination, which means that they cannot generalize from particular experiences; calculative imagination characterizes rational souls, and sensitive imagination characterizes sensitive souls.[19] Aquinas's account differs from Aristotle's primarily in the introduction of the Christian distinction between mortal and immortal souls; for Aquinas, human, rational souls are immortal whereas the sensitive souls of animals are corruptible, i.e., mortal.[20]

For Aristotle and Aquinas, because animals are governed by the sensitive soul, they cannot discriminate between different objects of desire and make informed choices among them, but instead can only be caused to move toward the objects of their desires by the sheer presence of the objects to the animals' perception. In Aristotle's account, external objects of desire (rather than deliberation or free choice) are the causes of the actions of animals governed by the sensitive soul; similarly, in Aquinas's account, the "inclination of sensuality ... has absolutely the nature of law" in animals, whereas in human beings it is reason that has the status of law.[21] To this extent, for both Aristotle and Aquinas, animals do not "choose" in a rationally informed way, and hence it would not make sense to hold them responsible for the choices they make.

From this Aristotle and Aquinas, and Descartes along with them, argue that because animals lack moral obligations, they must also lack moral rights (or: we must have no obligations toward them, if they can have no obligations toward us or toward themselves). This principle was articulated by the Stoic philosopher Chryssipus in terms of the notion of *oikeiosis* or community: Either a being is within the sphere of moral rights and obligations, or it is not; animals are incapable of rationality, so they must lie outside the sphere of moral obligations.[22] Perhaps the most interesting corollary of the Stoic principle of *oikeiosis* is that we have *no obligations whatsoever* toward animals—*nothing* that we do to animals can properly be construed as an injustice.[23]

Descartes's treatment of animals reflects an implicit commitment to this principle. Hence it is curious that Descartes should offer his third ground for denying that we have moral obligations toward animals, namely the supposition that animals are incapable of conscious perceptual states like pain; for if Descartes truly believes that it is not wrong to inflict pain on animals, then he does not need to argue that animals are incapable of feeling pain. Why, then, does Descartes go to elaborate lengths to argue that animals are incapable of conscious perceptual states? The reason, I think, is that the terms of his metaphysical dualism require him to do so; the foundations of his physics lead him to conceive of nature in purely mechanistic, efficient-causal terms, and this leaves no room for "inner," subjective awareness on the part of beings that lack a rational soul. Perhaps unexpectedly, this way of conceptualizing the distinction between the spiritual and the earthly follows from commitments that I take to be Christian in nature; notwithstanding a great deal of contemporary scholarship that argues for a view of Descartes as a secular atheist, I believe that the best way to understand Descartes's conception of bodies as pure mechanism is to see it as an attempt, in effect, to reconcile the Thomistic distinction between material and immaterial beings with Galileo's desire to assert the autonomy of scientific explanation. In other words, Descartes is trying to preserve a Christian commitment to the moral superiority of beings with immortal, rational souls, while at the same time recognizing the tragic limitations of Aristotelian science.[24]

Given these aims, it should not be surprising that Descartes proceeds in the following way. "Perception" in animals involves no actual awareness, but instead occurs in the way in which we might imagine an infrared beam "sensing" the presence of something in the path of a closing garage door. Descartes offers the following characterization of sight in animals:

Animals do not see as we do when we are aware that we see, but only as we do when our mind is elsewhere. In such a case the images of external objects are depicted on our retinas, and perhaps the impressions they make in the optic nerves cause our limbs to make various movements, although we are quite unaware of them. In such a case we too move just like automatons, and nobody thinks that the force of heat is insufficient to cause their movements.[25]

Descartes offers the following example as an illustration of this conception of vision:

> When people take a fall, and stick out their hands so as to protect their head, it is not reason that instructs them to do this; it is simply that the sight of the impending fall reaches the brain and sends the animal spirits into the nerves in the manner necessary to produce the movement even without any mental volition, *just as it would be produced in a machine*. And since our own experience reliably informs us that this is so, why should we be so amazed that the 'light reflected from the body of a wolf onto the eyes of a sheep' should be equally capable of arousing the movements of flight in the sheep?[26]

This conception of sensation informs not only Descartes's conception of vision, but also his conception of sensations like pain:

> I do not explain the feeling of pain without reference to the soul. For in my view pain exists only in the understanding. What I do explain is all the external movements which accompany this feeling in us; in animals it is these movements alone which occur, and not pain in the strict sense.[27]

These characterizations of sense-perception point toward what Bernard Williams once called an "all or nothing" view of mental life: "either a creature has the full range of conscious powers, and is capable of language and abstract thought as well as sensation and feelings of hunger, or it is an automaton, with no experience of any kind."[28] Because animals lack reason and calculative imagination, they must lack all aspects

of mental or "inner" experience, including the capacity to feel "pain in the strict sense." Apart from his mechanistic conception of body, Descartes is quite close to Aquinas's views about the human beings and animals; hence it should not be surprising that Descartes's denial that animals can feel pain is not the basis for his denial that animals have moral worth, but instead is a mere corollary of his soul-body dualism and his mechanistic conception of body.

Against the background of this triad of criteria for distinguishing human beings and animals, it is worth considering what Descartes and his philosophical forbears say about the use of animals. Aristotle set the tone for the Western "speciesist" treatment of animals when he said that

> after the birth of animals, plants exist for their sake, and ... the other animals exist for the sake of man, the tame for use and food, the wild, if not all, at least the greater part of them, for food, and for the provision of clothing and various instruments. Now if nature makes nothing incomplete, and nothing in vain, the inference must be that she has made all animals for the sake of man.[29]

Saint Augustine was to endorse this view of animals seven centuries later in *The City of God* when he said that animals are not "related in community with us" because they lack reason; hence the biblical commandment against killing does not prohibit us from killing animals — "by the altogether righteous ordinance of the creator both their life and death are a matter subordinate to our needs."[30] Saint Thomas Aquinas was in turn to rely explicitly on the authority of Augustine almost a thousand years later when he said "hereby is refuted the error of those who said it is sinful for a man to kill brute animals; for by the divine providence they are intended for man's use according to the order of nature. Hence it is not wrong for man to make use of them, either by killing them or in any other way whatever."[31] The thread that connects Aristotle, the Stoics, Augustine, and Aquinas is the conviction that beings must be rational in order to merit membership in moral community; as Aquinas argues in the *Summa Contra Gentiles,* if there is any reason to be kind to animals, it is simply that doing so will make us more inclined to treat human beings kindly.[32]

Descartes's views on the moral status of animals bear the deep imprint of Greek and Christian tradition. In a letter to More, after asserting the purely mechanical nature of animal souls and the rational nature of the incorporeal soul of humans, and after maintaining that animal "life" consists "simply in the heat of the heart," Descartes proceeds to conclude that his view of the nature of animal experience "is not so much cruel to animals as it is indulgent to human beings since it absolves them from the suspicion of crime when they eat or kill animals."[33] This is the basis for Descartes's conviction that animal experimentation is a morally unobjectionable practice. Indeed, in several places Descartes describes with enthusiasm his own forays into vivisection. In a letter to Plemp, Descartes notes that the hearts of fish, "after they have been cut out, go on beating for much longer than the heart of any terrestrial animal"; he goes on to explain how he has refuted a view of Galen's concerning the functioning of cardiac arteries by having "opened the chest of a live rabbit and removed the ribs to expose the heart and the trunk of the aorta. ... Continuing the vivisection [*Pergens autem in hac animalis viui dissectione*], I cut away half the heart."[34] And in the *Description of the Human Body,* Descartes says that certain of Harvey's views concerning blood pressure in the heart can be corroborated "by a very striking experiment. If you slice off the pointed end of the heart in a live dog, and insert a finger into one of the cavities, you will feel unmistakeably that every time the heart gets shorter it presses the finger, and every time it gets longer it stops pressing it."[35] Descartes proceeds to discuss other observations that will need to be made in the course of this experiment, and he also suggests that there are certain advantages to be gained from performing the experiment on the heart of a live rabbit instead of a dog.[36]

Descartes's commitments concerning the use of animals follow from his well known program to use physics to "render men the masters and possessors of nature."[37] His statements manifest none of the concern or hesitation about the exploitation of nature that Saint Augustine expressed when he characterized scientific curiosity as *concupiscentia oculorum.*[38] Notwithstanding this departure from Augustine, in an important sense Descartes's views concerning the moral status of animals are substantially in line with the Christian tradition of thinking about animals, a tradition which, as we have seen, is itself deeply influenced by Aristotelian and Stoic thinking. One way to answer the question why Descartes turned to a mechanistic understanding of nature is to say that he wanted to overcome the limitations of Aristotelian substantial forms in the attempt to predict and control natural processes, and this answer is certainly compelling. But another answer, one that is entirely compatible with the first, is to say that Descartes wanted to draw out the implications for natural science of the Christian distinction between the immaterial and material (immortal and mortal) realms. This desire led Descartes to a treatment of animals as having no "inner" life whatsoever; and while it led him away from the Thomistic conception of animals as beings capable of feeling, in virtually all other respects Descartes's conception of the differences between human beings and animals is consistent with the Christian philosophical tradition.

How Descartes's Views Have Influenced the Contemporary Debate

It is interesting to recognize that the contemporary debate in Western philosophy concerning animal rights takes its bearings almost entirely from the question whether animal experience can be assimilated to human experience. The usual terms of the speciesism debate are that either animals *have* certain rights (a position taken by Tom Regan), or that they should have little or *no* rights at all (Michael P. T. Leahy and others). I would like to propose that there is something curiously Cartesian in the basic terms of this debate; specifically, some sort of Cartesian prejudices about the nature of mind, as well as the question of which beings can be said to have minds or mind-like experience, seem to lie at the center of the contemporary speciesism debate.

Consider first of all the centrality of the notions of rights and interests in the speciesism debate. Arguments against the view that animals possess a moral status equal to that of human beings tend to take the form of arguing that animals are not the kind of beings that can legitimately be said to possess "rights" to anything, and *a fortiori* that they cannot legitimately be said to have the right not to be killed, experimented upon, etc. Virtually all arguments against animal rights rely on the ancient prejudice about rationality or linguistic ability being a sign of human superiority. A good example of this approach is the work of Michael Leahy, who invokes certain Wittgensteinian notions in order to argue that it simply *doesn't make sense* to treat animals as the kind of beings toward which we ought to have moral obligations.

Wittgenstein makes a very telling move when he maintains that "our investigation is therefore a grammatical one,"[39] because this not only sets a methodological tone for everything that follows, but it also determines the outcome of anything like the speciesism debate in advance of any subsequent argumentation. This is because it reduces the resolution of all philosophical problems to "what we would say"—what *we* would say—and it thereby gives special primacy to the force of cultural and historical custom in the explication and resolution of these problems. One is reminded here of Wittgenstein's debt to Hume who, significantly if rather less famously, argued for the "grammatical" approach to the resolution of philosophical problems well over a century before Wittgenstein.[40] In doing so, Hume left us with the problem of how to justify our moral claims on the basis of anything more enduring than personal sentiment or popular opinion. So while there is some appeal to the Humean-Wittgensteinian approach as regards the effort to expose certain problems in the history of philosophy as mere pseudo-problems resulting from a simple misunderstanding of philosophical grammar, that approach suffers from the tragic limitation of reducing ethics from a *pre*scriptive to a merely *de*scriptive discipline.

Wittgenstein says that "One can imagine an animal angry, frightened, unhappy, happy, startled. But hopeful? And why not? A dog believes his master is at the door. But can he also believe his master will come the day after tomorrow?— And *what* can he not do here? . . . Can only those hope who can talk? Only those who have mastered the use of a language."[41] One is reminded here of Aristotle's distinction between calculative and sensitive imagination, and of the traditional view of animals as beings that lack a sense of past, present, and future because they lack the capacity for conceptual abstraction. Only a being that is capable of contemplating the future can meaningfully be said to "hope" for anything; and if animals lack the ability to conceptualize the future, then it would seem absurd to attribute to them the ability to have hopes.

This kind of reasoning gets used to argue that animals cannot be said to have "interests," and hence that they cannot have anything like a "life project." In turn this means that they cannot be said to suffer any kind of loss—hence the claim that it cannot be said coherently that the suffering or death of animals is a regrettable event. Leahy pursues this style of reasoning to the point of claiming that all appeals to notions such as the inherent moral value of animals are nothing but "opportunistic flights of fancy" born of a "sad and mischievous error."[42] What is of signal importance here is the *way* in which Leahy comes to this conclusion: he displays a wide variety of traditional attempts to assimilate animals to human beings on the basis of capacities like the ability to have rights or interests, and he derides appeals to animal rights on the ground that animals are not linguistic beings.

Some thinkers go so far as to draw the following analogy: Imagine a person who experiences excruciating pain, but who is given a drug that makes her/him forget the experience of the pain completely—is there any sense in which the person could be said to have suffered a misfortune? And if not, then is this not comparable to the situation of an animal that feels pain and then has no memory of it afterward? A similar line of reasoning runs in the following way: We know that Lucretius says that death cannot be said to be a misfortune even for a human being, since one must experience an event in order for it to be a misfortune, and death is an event which we precisely do not experience since we cease to exist in the instant of its occurrence;[43] is not the death or supposed suffering of an animal an event of this kind, to the extent that the animal has no sense of past or future, and hence no sense of an ongoing life project, and moreover that an animal's death cannot be considered a misfortune because it neither "experiences" nor "values" its death?[44] These sorts of arguments, whether they be based in Lucretius or Wittgenstein, are intended to distinguish animal experience from human experience in such a way as to make the proposition that animals have "experience" in a morally relevant sense seem patently absurd.

In opposition to this form of argumentation, contemporary commentators such as Joel Feinberg and Tom Regan argue that animals precisely can have interests. Contemporary proponents of animal rights take their cue from the nineteenth-century thinker H. S. Salt, who was the first to argue systematically for a "rights" approach to the problem of animal welfare;[45] and these contemporary proponents argue that in order to have rights, a being must be capable of having interests or "conative life," which includes the capacity to have beliefs, desires, goals, and the like.[46]

But such thinkers attribute capacities to animals that animals simply don't seem to have—like a sense of the future or of their being a being among other beings. Even the most animal-friendly person has to wonder about arguments like this, particularly in the light of Aristotle's insightful distinction between calculative and sensitive imagination; for however we might best characterize the nature of animal experience, it seems dubious to force terms such as "interests," "beliefs," "expectations," and the like into our characterization. Wittgenstein, in other words, seems right to say that it makes no sense to attribute a state such as hope to a dog, at least in the full-blown human sense of anticipation of anything beyond the extremely short term. For hope in this sense presupposes a capacity for conceptual abstraction that animals such as dogs seem not to possess. But as we have seen, this is quite a different matter than the question of the moral implications of denying that animals possess the capacity for language, conceptual abstraction, and the like. Hence one might argue, with H. J. McCloskey, that it makes more sense to argue for human obligations toward animals, and moreover that having an obligation toward animals need not entail that animals have corresponding rights that they may assert (or that may be asserted on their behalf) against us.[47]

This approach comes at least somewhat closer to doing justice to the moral terms of the human-animal relationship, since it avoids the mistake of attributing to animals the "at least rudimentary cognitive equipment" that a being must possess in order to be able to have interests and hence rights.[48] For as Feinberg himself admits, the idea of interests is bound up with the idea of cultivating interests in the course of a whole life, and hence with the idea of happiness; and if we think of happiness in a philosophically rich sense, namely as Aristotelian *eudaimonia* rather than as a utilitarian sum of pleasurable events, then the absurdity of attributing things such as life projects (a notion that is inseparable from the notion of interests) to animals should become readily apparent.[49]

Now what seems clear is that both sides of the argument in the speciesism controversy implicitly accept the traditional Western terms of the debate: they argue about whether animals have capacities that make them sufficiently like humans to be counted in our sense of moral community, and in particular the debate comes down to the question whether animal experience is sufficiently "mind-like" to justify treating animals as quasi-moral agents. One thinks here of just how much a part of classical liberal political theory terms such as "interests," "rights," and "duties" are; and in turn one thinks of just how indebted liberal theory, with its central notion of the autonomous individual, is to the Cartesian conception of mind.

But is there any other way to try to view the situation? E.g., might it be possible to start with a *feeling* about animals that many people seem to have, namely a feeling that the divinity of nature is expressed through the being of animals? For if we take the Cartesian/Western approach, then we begin with the presupposition that animals are objects, and we face the task of providing rational criteria for assigning moral rights to these objects. It seems to me that in the very formulation of the problem and the method for its solution, this approach makes it entirely too likely that we will fail to find animals worthy of moral respect. In part this failure will be due to the anxiety of influence we face when we try to conceive of nonrational beings as beings with moral worth, and in part it will be due to a comparable anxiety that we face in the attempt to overcome the Christian prejudice that attributes moral worth to beings on the basis of distinctions like immateriality-materiality and immortality-mortality.

Both sides of the contemporary debate seem to proceed from a kind of anthropocentrism that either denies to animals capacities such as rationality and the immateriality of mind, or attributes to them capacities such as the ability to "have interests." What is peculiar and questionable about this approach is something that the philosopher Thomas Nagel once observed about our reflections on the experience of animals, namely that because the perceptual encounter that animals have with the world is so fundamentally different from the encounter that human beings have, the nature of the perceptual encounter that animals have with the world is ultimately largely a matter of speculation.[50] Nagel's analysis suggests that if we try to hold animals to standards that are fashioned in the image of human capacities, then we should not be surprised when animals fall short of those standards; and by extension, we should not be surprised when advocates of animal rights try to argue for claims that seem a little strange, such as that animals have language, or that animals have "interests" in something like the sense in which human beings have interests, etc. It is not clear why we should need to treat animals as quasi-humans rather than treating them, say, along the lines of the Greek notion of *physis* as this notion is retrieved by philosophers such as Nietzsche and Heidegger—namely as beings that are radically "other" in relation to human experience, beings that exhibit a mystery, autonomy, and intrinsic worth that is not reducible to anthropomorphic categories and hence is as incommensurable with the terms of the contemporary debate over speciesism as it is with the categories of a thinker as traditional as a Descartes or an Aquinas.[51]

The potential benefit of viewing the question of animal rights in terms of the Greek conception of *physis* is twofold: First, it opens up the possibility of thinking through the issue of animal rights in the context of a view of nature as a space with intrinsic value, in contrast with the traditional Western view of nature as a space that is devoid of intrinsic value because it is not "rational." Here one might think of the work of Hans Jonas in *The Imperative of Responsibility* and his attempt to extend the Kantian notion of moral obligation beyond the realm of rational beings; this would open up the prospect of a model of moral respect and obligations toward an entity (namely nature) from which we demand no reciprocal duties of moral respect.[52] And in turn, viewing animal rights in terms of the Greek conception of *physis* holds the promise of helping human beings to rethink their proper place in the larger scheme of the cosmos, in accordance with the task of what Martin Heidegger conceived as a primordial ethics that seeks to overcome the hegemony of anthropocentrism and reestablish a sense of piety toward and a sense of dwelling in nature.[53]

To this extent, the task of rethinking Descartes's presuppositions about the dividing line between animals and human beings becomes the task of rethinking the notion of obligations toward an avowedly nonrational natural world and the closely related task of rethinking the human vocation of dwelling in the earth. In the end, an adequate conception of dwelling may require us to abandon altogether the juridical rights-and-obligations approach that we have inherited from liberal political theory, and to seek in its place a phenomenologically richer conception of being-in-the-midst of nature.

NOTES

1. For the sake of linguistic simplicity I shall use the term "animals" in this discussion to refer to non-human animal species; in doing so I do not intend to imply that human beings are not animals.

2. It should be noted at the outset that the interpretation of Descartes's views on animals is complicated by a widespread penchant for mythologizing, particularly but not exclusively in the direction of demonizing Descartes. For example, Jack Vrooman, Peter Harrison, and Keith Gunderson assure us that Descartes was a very kindly dog owner, while Richard Ryder insists that Descartes "proceeded to alienate his wife by experimenting upon their dog"—quite an achievement, given that Descartes was never married. See Jack Vrooman, *René Descartes: a Biography* (New York: G.P. Putnam's Sons, 1970), p. 194; Peter Harrison, "Descartes on Animals," *Philosophical Quarterly* 42 (1992): 219–27, at p. 220; Keith Gunderson, "Descartes, La Mettrie, Language, and Machines," *Philosophy* 39 (1964): 193–222, at p. 202; Richard D. Ryder, *Animal Revolution: Changing Attitudes Towards Speciesism* (Oxford: Blackwell, 1989), p. 57.

3. I take as axiomatic Tom Regan's formulation of speciesism as "the attempt to draw moral boundaries solely on the basis of biological considerations. A speciesist position, at least the paradigm of such

a position, would take the form of declaring that no [nonhuman] animal is a member of the moral community because no animal belongs to the 'right' species—namely, Homo sapiens." Tom Regan, *The Case for Animal Rights* (Berkeley/Los Angeles: University of California, 1983), p. 155. For several alternative definitions of speciesism, see Ruth Cigman, "Death, Misfortune and Species Inequality," *Philosophy and Public Affairs* 19 (1980): 47–64, at p. 48.

4. The primary focus of this paper is the first of these controversies rather than the second; for an incisive treatment of Descartes's conception of rational evidence, see Harry R. Frankfurt, *Demons, Dreamers and Madmen: The Defense of Reason in Descartes's Meditations* (Indianapolis: Bobbs-Merrill, 1970).

5. "Caeterum a nulla tuarum opinionum animus meus, pro ea qua est mollitie ac teneritudine, aeque abhorret, ac ab internecina illa & iugulatrice sententia, quam in Methodo tulisti, brutis omnibus vitam sensumque eripiens. ..." Henry More, letter to Descartes, December 11, 1648, *Oeuvres de Descartes* (hereafter AT plus volume and page number), 12 vols., eds. Charles Adam and Paul Tannery (Paris: Vrin, 1964–74) 5:243. For a translation of Descartes's correspondence with More concerning animal nature that includes the material cited here,

see Leonora D. Cohen, "Descartes and Henry More on the Beast-Machine—A Translation of Their Correspondence Pertaining to Animal Automatism," *Annals of Science: A Quarterly Review of the History of Science Since the Renaissance* 1, no. 1 (1936): 48–61.

6. See Norman Kemp Smith, *New Studies in the Philosophy of Descartes* (New York: Russell and Russell, 1963), p. 136; see also A. Boyce Gibson, *The Philosophy of Descartes* (New York: Garland, 1987), p. 214.

7. Descartes, *Discourse on Method*, AT 6:56–60, *The Philosophical Writings of Descartes* (hereafter CSM plus volume and page number), ed. John Cottingham, et al., 3 volumes (Cambridge: Cambridge University, 1984–91), 1:139–41.

8. AT 6:58f., CSM 1:140f.

9. Descartes, *Treatise of Man*, AT 11:120, 130f., 165; *Treatise of Man* (French-English ed., trans. Thomas Steele Hall, Cambridge: Harvard University, 1972), pp. 2, 21f., 71. Descartes spells out the specific terms of this mechanistic conception of animals in his letter to Reneri for Pollot, April or May, 1638 (AT 2:39–41, CSM 3:99f.); his letter to the Marquess of Newcastle, November 23, 1646 (AT 4:575f., CSM 3:303f.); and his letter to More, February 5, 1649 (AT 5:276–79, CSM 3:365f.).

10. AT 11:143, *Treatise of Man*, p. 36.

11. Plutarch, *De esu carnium* (*The Eating of Flesh*) 994E, in *Plutarch's Moralia* (Greek-English, trans. Harold Cherniss and William C. Helmbold, 15 vols., Loeb Classical Library, Cambridge: Harvard University, 1957), 12:549. It should be noted, however, that Plutarch is not entirely against using or killing animals; he says that "there is no injustice, surely, in punishing and slaying animals that are antisocial and merely injurious, while taming those that are gentle and friendly to man and in making them our helpers in the tasks for which they are severally fitted by nature." *De sollertia animalium* (*The Cleverness of Animals*) 964, in Plutarch's *Moralia*, 12:353.

12. Gassendi, "Fifth Set of Objections [to Descartes's Meditations]," AT 7:270f., CSM 2:189; cf. AT 7:262, CSM 2:183.

13. "Author's Replies to the Fifth Set of Objections," AT 7:359, CSM 2:248.

14. See for example Marjorie Grene, *Descartes* (Minneapolis: University of Minnesota Press, 1985), pp. 50f. On the nature and extent of Descartes's commitment to the bête-machine hypothesis, see Gunderson, "Descartes, La Mettrie, Language, and Machines."

15. Letter to More, April 15, 1649, AT 5:344f., CSM 3:374.

16. Letter to More, February 5, 1649, AT 5:276f., CSM 3:365f.

17. Letter to Plempius for Fromondus, October 3, 1637, AT 1:414f., CSM 3:62. See also "Author's Replies to the Sixth Objections," AT 7:426, CSM 2:288.

18. Letter to Buitendijck, 1643, AT 4:65, CSM 3:230. John Passmore is therefore wrong to conclude that Descartes believes that animals "lack ... even that sensitive soul which both Aristotle and Aquinas had allowed them." Passmore's mistake was to assume that possession of a sensitive soul entails that animals can feel, and hence that "there could be pain and suffering where there has been no sin." John Passmore, "The Treatment of Animals," *Journal of the History of Ideas* 36 (1975): 195–218, at p. 204; cf. Bernard Williams, *Descartes: The Project of Pure Enquiry* (New York: Penguin, 1978), p. 287. As should become clear below in connection with Descartes's conception of feeling in animals, there is no reason to suppose that possession of a sensitive soul entails the ability to "feel" in a sense that would pose a problem of theodicy.

19. See Aristotle, *De Anima* 3.3, 10, 11 and Gary Steiner, *Anthropocentrism and Its Discontents: The Moral Status of Animals in the History of Western Philosophy*, ch. 3 (Pittsburgh: University of Pittsburgh Press, 2005).

20. Aquinas, *Summa Theologica* I, q. 75, art. 6, resp. (*Basic Writings of Saint Thomas Aquinas*, 2 vols., ed. Anton C. Pegis, Indianapolis/Cambridge: Hackett, 1997, 1:691f.) and q. 76, art. 3, resp. (*Basic Writings of Saint Thomas Aquinas*, 1:705f.).

21. Aristotle, *De Anima* 3.10 at 433a19ff.; Aquinas, *Summa Theologica* I–II, q. 91, art. 6, resp. (*Basic Writings of Saint Thomas Aquinas*, 2:755f.).

22. See Chrysippus, *Physica* chapters 4 and 5 and

especially chapter 8, section 5, "Animalia (et plantas) propter hominum utilitatem facta esse," in volume 2 of *Stoicorum veterum fragmenta,* ed. H. von Arnim, 3 vols., Leipzig, 1903–1905, vol. 4 with indices by M. Adler, Leipzig, 1924. See also Cicero, *De Finibus bonorum et malorum* 3:66f.; Porphyry, *De Abstinentia* 1:4, 1:6, 3:1, 3:19–22; and Sextus Empiricus, *Adversus mathematicos* 9:130. For a more detailed discussion of the Stoics' views on animals, see Richard Sorabji, *Animal Minds and Human Morals: The Origins of the Western Debate* (Ithaca: Cornell University Press, 1993), ch. 10.

23. Porphyry, *De abstinentia* 3:1. This is the position that Plutarch is explicitly at pains to criticize; see *De sollertia animalium* 963f.

24. Whether this is an authentically Christian commitment has been a subject of great controversy, especially since Lynn White published "The Historical Roots of Our Ecological Crisis," *Science* 155 (March 10, 1967): 1203–1207. A discussion of White's argument and its reception goes beyond the scope of the present paper; it is worth noting, however, that if we take the pronouncements of the Fathers of the Church (particularly Augustine and Aquinas) as the measure in deciding this question, a virtually ironclad case can be made in support of White's thesis—as the passages from Augustine and Aquinas cited in the present paper should demonstrate. At the same time it should be recognized that Christianity is a complex tradition with many heterodox voices, and that these voices have often failed to find representation in the pronouncements of Church orthodoxy. From the standpoint of the orthodoxy established by the dominant philosophical voices of the Christian tradition, a sense of deep reverence for material nature as a creation with intrinsic rather than instrumental value is at best heterodox; at the extreme, reverence for nature is not really "Christian" at all, but instead is motivated by metaphysical and moral commitments that are finally incompatible with the doctrines laid down by Augustine and Aquinas. For detailed defenses of this view, see Gary Steiner, *Descartes as a Moral Thinker: Christianity, Technology, Nihilism* (Amherst, NY: Prome-theus/Humanity Books, 2004) and *Anthropocentrism and Its Discontents,* ch. 5.

25. Letter to Plempius for Fromondus, October 3, 1637, AT 1:413f., CSM 3:61f.

26. "Author's Replies to the Fourth Set of Objections," AT 7:230, CSM 2:161 (italics mine). Descartes takes the sheep-wolf example from Avicenna and Aquinas. Cf. *The Passions of the Soul,* article 16, AT 11:341f., CSM 1:335: "Thus every movement we make without any contribution from our will—as often happens when we breathe, walk, eat and, indeed, when we perform any action which is common to us and the beasts—depends solely on the arrangement of our limbs and on the route which the spirits, produced by the heat of the heart, follow naturally in the brain, nerves, and muscles. This occurs in the same way as the movement of a watch is produced merely by the strength of its spring and the configuration of its wheels." Cf. *The Passions of the Soul,* article 38, AT 11:358, CSM 1:342f.

27. Letter to Mersenne, June 11, 1640, AT 3:85, CSM 3:148.

28. Bernard Williams, *Descartes: The Project of Pure Enquiry* (Harmondsworth: Penguin, 1978), p. 284.

29. *Politics* 1:8 at 1256b14–22, in *The Complete Works of Aristotle,* ed. Jonathan Barnes (Princeton: Bollingen/Princeton University, 1995), 2:1995. Cf. 1:5 at 1254b10–21.

30. Saint Augustine, *De civitate dei* 1:20, in *The City of God Against the Pagans,* Latin with English translation by George E. McCracken (Cambridge: Harvard University Press, 1957), pp. 92f. See also Saint Augustine, *De moribus ecclesiae catholicae et de moribus manichaeorum* 2:17, in *The Catholic and Manichean Ways of Life,* trans. Donald A. Gallagher and Idella J. Gallagher (Washington, D.C.: Catholic University Press, 1966), pp. 102 and 105): "to refrain from the killing of animals and the destroying of plants is the height of superstition … there are no common rights between us and the beasts and trees …"; "… we can perceive by their cries that animals die in pain, although we make little of this since the beast, lacking a rational soul, is not related to us by a common nature."

31. *Summa Contra Gentiles* 3, chapter 112, *Basic Writings of Saint Thomas Aquinas,* 2:222.

32. *Summa Contra Gentiles* 3, chapter 112, *Basic Writings of Saint Thomas Aquinas,* 2:222. Kant would later follow this reasoning; see Immanuel Kant, *Lectures on Ethics,* eds. Peter Heath and J. B. Schneewind, trans. Peter Heath (Cambridge: Cambridge University Press, 2001), pp. 198, 212f., 434. See also Steiner, *Anthropocentrism and Its Discontents,* ch. 5, 7.

33. AT 5:276ff., CSM 3:365f.

34. Letter to Plempius, February 15, 1638, AT 1:523–527, CSM 3:80–82.

35. AT 11:241, CSM 1:317.

36. AT 11:242f., CSM 1:317f.

37. *Discourse on Method,* Part 6, AT 6:62, CSM 1:142f. (translation altered).

38. Saint Augustine, *Confessions,* book 10, section 35; cf. book 10, section 30, in *Confessions,* trans. R. S. Pine-Coffin (New York: Penguin, 1987), pp. 241, 233 (where "concupiscentia oculorum" is translated as "gratification of the eye"), and 1 John: 2:16.

39. Ludwig Wittgenstein, *Philosophical Investigations,* trans. G. E. M. Anscombe (Macmillan, 1968), section 90, p. 43.

40. David Hume, *A Treatise of Human Nature,* 2nd ed., ed. L. A. Selby-Bigge (Oxford: Clarendon, 1981), pp. 262 ("all nice and subtle questions concerning personal identity … are to be regarded rather as grammatical than as philosophical difficulties"); 490f. ("the ideas of justice and injustice; as also those of property, right, and obligation" are, like the genesis of natural languages, matters of "convention"); and 610 ("It belongs to Grammarians to examine what qualities are to be entitled to the denomination of virtue").

41. *Philosophical Investigations,* Part 2, sec. 1, p. 174. For a more complete examination of Wittgenstein's remarks on the differences between human beings and animals, see Michael P. T. Leahy, *Against Liberation: Putting Animals in Perspective* (London/New York: Routledge, 1991), chapter 5.

42. *Against Liberation: Putting Animals in Perspective,* p. 220.

43. Lucretius, *De rerum natura* 3:830, 870ff., 898ff., 1091.

44. See Cigman, "Death, Misfortune and Species Inequality," pp. 53–57.

45. H. S. Salt, *Animals' Rights Considered in Relation to Social Progress,* 2nd ed. (London: Bell, 1922; 1st edition, 1892). Salt, however, was not the first to speak of the rights of animals; see for example Arthur Schopenhauer, *On the Basis of Morality,* trans. E. F. J. Payne (Providence/Oxford: Berghahn, 1995, first published in 1839), p. 180.

46. See Joel Feinberg, "The Rights of Animals and Unborn Generations," in *Philosophy and Environmental Crisis,* ed. William T. Blackstone (Athens: University of Georgia Press, 1974, pp. 43–68), at p. 49. Tom Regan bases his view of animals as bearers of rights on the claim that animals are "subjects-of-a-life" with preferences, interests, and "a psychophysical identity over time." *The Case for Animal Rights,* p. 243. Cf. p. 279: To exclude animals from the sphere of moral rights on the grounds that they are moral patients rather than moral agents is simply "arbitrary in the extreme" and indefensible. See also Tom Regan, "Do Animals Have a Right to Life?" in *Animal Rights and Human Obligations,* ed. Tom Regan and Peter Singer (Englewood Cliffs: Prentice-Hall, 1976, pp. 197–204), p. 201.

47. H. J. McCloskey, "Rights," *Philosophical Quarterly* 15 (1965): 115–127, at 121 and 125. Cf. W. D. Ross, *The Right and the Good* (Oxford: Clarendon, 1930), ch. 2, app. 1, pp. 48–50, where Ross discusses the prospects for arguing that human beings have certain obligations toward animals even though animals have no corresponding rights that may be asserted on their behalf against human beings.

48. Feinberg, "The Rights of Animals and Unborn Generations," p. 52.

49. One contemporary thinker who seeks to attribute interests to animals while refraining from attributing rights to them is Peter Singer. Singer equates the capacity to experience feelings of pleasure and pain with sentience or consciousness, and hence with the capacity to have interests. Peter Singer, *Practical Ethics,* 2nd ed. (Cambridge: Cambridge University Press, 1993), pp. 12ff., 118ff., 277; see also Peter Singer, *Animal Liberation,* 2nd ed. (London: Jonathan Cape, 1990). For Singer, a given being's capacity to have interests is a sufficient con-

dition for our including that being in our utilitarian moral calculus; see *Practical Ethics,* p. 23.

50. See Thomas Nagel, "What is it like to be a bat?" in *Mortal Questions* (Cambridge: Cambridge University, 1979), pp. 165–80.

51. See for example Martin Heidegger, "The Question Concerning Technology," in *The Question Concerning Technology and Other Essays,* trans. William Lovitt (New York: Harper Colophon, 1977), p. 10 and Martin Heidegger, *Grundfragen der Philosophie: Ausgewählte "Probleme" der "Logik" (Gesamtausgabe* vol. 45, Frankfurt: Klostermann, 1984), pp. 121–131, 137, 178f.; cf. Heidegger's talk of "the Open" in "What are Poets For?" *in Poetry, Language, Thought,* trans. Albert Hofstadter (New York: Harper Colophon, 1975), pp. 106ff. In a lecture course from 1929–30, Heidegger devotes more than a hundred pages to a comparative analysis of the relationship that animals and human beings each have toward the world, where "world" is construed in the phenomenological terms developed in the Marburg lectures and *Being and Time.* Martin Heidegger, *Die Grundbegriffe der Metaphysik: Welt – Endlichkeit – Einsamkeit* (Gesamtausgabe vol. 29/30, Frankfurt: Klostermann, 1983, pp. 261ff., translated as *The Fundamental Concepts of Metaphysics: World, Finitude, Solitude,* trans. William McNeill and Nicholas Walker, Bloomington: Indiana University Press, 1995). The preeminent feature of this analysis is Heidegger's scrupulous effort to avoid conceiving of animal experience in (unduly) anthropomorphic terms. See Steiner, *Anthropocentrism and Its Discontents,* ch. 9.

52. Hans Jonas, *The Imperative of Responsibility: In Search of an Ethics for the Technological Age* (Chicago: University of Chicago Press, 1984), pp. 4, 8, 202. It should be noted, however, that Jonas's primary concern in this text is not nature itself but rather future generations of humanity. For a more complete discussion of Jonas's views, see Steiner, *Anthropocentrism and Its Discontents,* ch. 10.

53. See Martin Heidegger, "Letter on Humanism," in *Basic Writings* (New York: Harper and Row, 1977), p. 235. Of all modern thinkers in the Western philosophical tradition, it is probably Schopenhauer, in his critique of Kant's ethics, who comes closest to this ideal of dwelling with nonhuman beings. See Schopenhauer, *On the Basis of Morality,* pp. 96 and 175; Schopenhauer moves toward placing animals on a moral par with human beings by appealing to compassion or sympathy as the means for disclosing our inner connectedness with animals, though in the end he argues for animal rights (p. 180) and the permissibility of eating animals (p. 182). The roots of Schopenhauer's argument for our connectedness with animals are to be found in his conception of the world will; see Arthur Schopenhauer, *The World as Will and Representation,* 2 vols., trans. E. F. J. Payne (New York: Dover, 1958) and Steiner, *Anthropocentrism and Its Discontents,* ch. 8.

Practicing the Presence of God

A Christian Approach to Animals

JAY MCDANIEL

Can Christianity, "good news" for humanity as the very term "Gospel" proclaims, become good news for animals? I write as a Christian, influenced by process theology and other sources, who believes that Christianity, which has often been bad news for animals, can become good news for them in the future. I hope this essay will be of service not only to Christians who care about animals and who hope that Christianity can become more sensitive to them, but also to people of other religions or of no religion, who are hopeful that Christianity might become "good news for animals," if not for the sake of Christians themselves, then at least for the sake of animals. The essay is divided into seven sections. I outline their contents as follows, so that you might read them in whatever order you wish.

The first section suggests that the transformation of Christianity into "good news for animals" requires an encounter with the commodifying effects of consumer culture and a par-

ticipation in what one process theologian, John Cobb, calls "the Earthist movement."[1] The organizing themes of this volume, inspired by Thomas Berry, offer a similarly profound vision. In this section I also draw upon an international document, the Earth Charter, the principles of which are clear statements of Earthist sentiments.

The second section explains why, even though many Christians are now developing "ecological theologies," there is still a need to ask: "But can Christianity become good news for animals?" My argument is that ecological theologians too easily emphasize "environmental ethics" and "social justice for humans" over "compassion for individual animals," when, in fact, all three are important.[2] A responsible Christian ethic will seek to be good news for individual animals; good news for species of animals and plants; and, of course, good news for people, particularly the poor and powerless. It will try to combine animal welfare, environmental ethics, and human rights, hopeful that communities can be created in which all three are operative.

The third section considers negative and positive traditions within Christianity concerning animals, suggesting that Christians need to repent of the former and learn from the latter. This involves reclaiming what I call "the Franciscan alternative," which recognizes that individual animals have value "in and for themselves" even as they also have value for one another and for God, and that they are part of a diverse and interconnected whole which has unique value for God.

The fourth section offers more precise definitions of the words "Christianity," "animals," and "good news." I suggest that "Christianity" is not a static set of ideas, but rather a family of people "in process," and that this family is capable of growth and change, that "animals" are ensouled creatures, whose members lie within a variety of biological classes, but whose common characteristic is that they have rich capacities for feeling and goal-guided action, accompanied by intense capacities for pain, and that "good news" for animals involves treating animals kindly, protecting their species, respecting their autonomy, recognizing their independent relations with God, and seeing them as revelations of divine presence.

The final sections turn to three dimensions of Christian life in terms of which Christianity can become "good news for animals": practical action, theological understanding, and spiritual depth. By "practical action" I mean love-in-action: that is, willing responsiveness to the needs of living beings, animals included. By "theological understanding" I mean discursive insight concerning the nature of things, including the nature of animals in their relation to God. And by "spiritual depth" I mean inner availability to the Breath of Life, as exemplified in ecological contemplation.

In the fifth section I turn to practical action. I suggest that becoming "good news for animals" involves following the norms of the eco-justice movement, particularly its emphasis on solidarity with victims, and then, as a way of concretizing these norms, following the guidelines of the Humane Society of the United States.[3] I hope that these norms and guidelines are sufficient to answer the question: How should we Christians treat animals?

In the sixth section I turn to theological understanding. I note three sources which can be of service to a theology sensitive to animals: the trinitarian theology of Andrew Linzey, process theology, and feminist theology of the sort developed by the neo-Thomist theologian, Elizabeth Johnson.[4] I allude to a dialogue between Johnson and myself, in which we jointly affirm that animals are lured by God as an indwelling Spirit, albeit in a persuasive rather than coercive way; that this Spirit also shares in the suffering and joys of animals, on their own terms and for their own sakes; and that, should there be life after death for humans, it ought also to be available for animals.[5] This dialogue shows the degree to which certain forms of contemporary theology, process and feminist, are willing to move beyond anthropocentric habits of thought toward animal-sensitive understandings of God.

In the seventh section, I turn to the spiritual dimension of Christian life, and more specifically to what Johnson calls "ecological contemplation."[6] Other theologians have other names for it. The Protestant theologian Sallie McFague calls it "seeing with the loving eye;" while the Orthodox theologian Kallistos Ware calls it "the contemplation of nature."[7] Following Ware, but also in the spirit of McFague and Johnson, I suggest that contemplative seeing involves seeing all things, animals included, in their particularity, as subjects in and for themselves; combined with a recognition that, in this particularity, they reveal the light of God. I propose that, in the last analysis, it is only when Christians come to see animals in this way, as subjects of their own lives and also as holy icons, that they—we—can be good news for animals in a sustained way.

By way of conclusion, I ask the question: And how might Christians enter into this way of seeing? What kinds of spiritual disciplines are available to us? I suggest that the most important discipline will be to spend time in the presence of animals themselves, not as they appear on television screens or in cartoons, but as they appear in palpable, physical presence. We Christians can become good news for animals, only if we allow ourselves to be awed, again and again, by the sheer beauty of their mysterious presence.

I suggest further that, for the economically and temporally privileged in our world, who have the means and time to leave the city, this may involve spending time in wilderness areas. But for many in our world, spending time with animals can occur only in cities and at home. Toward this end, I recommend a form of spiritual discipline which is often considered sentimental and patronizing by environmentalists, but which may well be necessary for urban peoples if they are to develop "the loving eye" in the age of consumerism. It is spending time with companion animals: dogs and cats, for example, or dwarf hamsters or snakes. My suggestion is that, if we are to develop the loving eye with animals, it will need to begin, for many, with the loving touch—with the knowledge of the life of an animal "other" with whom were are in daily relationship.

Back, then, to the question: Can Christianity become good news for animals? I hope this essay provides an introduction to this question and offers various ways for answering, with hope and humility, "Yes."

The Earthist Movement

Christianity seeks to be good news to the world. Thomas Berry and other ecological theologians rightly argue that "the world" does not simply mean "the world of human beings." It means the earth and its creatures, including humans, and also the stars and galaxies. The "world" is that diverse whole in which God took deep delight on the seventh day of creation.

It is difficult to know how Christianity can be good news to the galaxies. Perhaps Christians, like others, are "good news" to the heavens when they are awed by the womb-like presence of a dark and starlit sky, feeling both insignificant yet included in a deeper mystery many name "God." In any case, it is clear that Christianity can be, or at least should be, good news for the earth and its creatures. This is not because Christianity is the best religion or because all people should convert to it. Each religion has its gifts and liabilities. Mass conversion to Christianity would destroy part of the world's religious diversity, which itself contributes to the deeper mystery. Rather it is because slightly less than a third of the world's population claim "Christianity" as their religion, and they will inevitably influence the world for good or ill. They can become "good news" for the earth by following the first four principles of the Earth Charter (see Steven Rockefeller, "Earth Charter, Ethics, and Animals," in this volume). They can respect the earth and all life, care for the community of life in all its diversity, strive to build free, just, participatory, sustainable, and peaceful societies and secure earth's abundance for present and future generations.[8] Should Christians decide that following these guidelines, understood as hymns of hope, is part of what it means to be a disciple of Christ, earth would indeed receive good news. Of course, if Christians follow these guidelines, they—we—ought to do so in cooperation with people of other religions, and no religion, who do the same.

In our time, there is perhaps only one religion that is almost incapable of bringing good news to the earth, because its core teachings are inherently un-ecological. That religion is Consumerism. It is an overconsuming lifestyle characteristic of about a fifth of the world's population, but aspired to by many others, as well as a set of attitudes and values, promulgated twenty-four hours a day by the media and Internet. Its priests are public policy makers who believe that the world is, or ought to be, a global market-place united by a worldwide consumer culture. Its "evangelists" are the advertisers who display the products of growth through advertisements, convincing us that we are not "happy" or "whole" unless we possess what they sell. Its holy icons are window displays in department stores. And its church is the shopping mall. One of its core teachings is that each year we are saved, or made whole, by consuming more than we did the year before.

This religion is "bad news" for earth and its creatures in several ways. It leads us to think that the planet is a stockpile of unlimited resources, there for the taking, and that we have no obligations to preserve its resources for future generations of humans and other creatures. It leads us to reduce various forms of land—wetlands and grasslands, for example—to real estate that can be bought and sold in the marketplace. And it leads us to think of plants and animals as mere commodities with no value apart from their usefulness to humans.

The Protestant theologian John Cobb suggests that consumerism is the popular expression of a recent development in world history, which he calls "Economism." This is his name for a way of structuring public life that measures almost all human interactions in economic terms, and that takes economic growth for its own sake as the central organizing principle. Cobb argues that Economism is gradually replacing Nationalism as a central organizing principle in many modern societies; just as, approximately three centuries ago, Nationalism replaced Christianism, which was the central organizing principle of the West during the Middle Ages. Economism is the public side of much modern life. Consumerist attitudes, with their commodifying tendencies, are the subjective side.

If Christianity is to live up to its ecological potential, and if it is to grow beyond its ecological liabilities, it will have to do so in the face of Economism. It will have to exercise what biblical theologian Walter Brueggemann calls "the prophetic imagination," which lies in critiquing the dominant modes of thought and practice in one's age, insofar as they are unjust and unsustainable; and opening oneself to fresh possibilities for new and hopeful futures. Such imagination was evident in Moses, Jeremiah, Isaiah, and Jesus, so Brueggemann explains, and it can be part of Christian life today.

How, then, can Christians live into this prophetic calling? One way is to understand that they are part of a larger social movement—a people's movement, if you will—which Cobb, as mentioned earlier, calls "Earthism." This is Cobb's name for a social movement, found in many different circles today under different names, which puts devotion to the earth and humanity ahead of devotion to the economy and consumer values. The spirit of this movement is found in people of many different religions and also of no religion. According to Cobb, Earthism can overcome the dominance of Economism only if it has the support of people from many traditions and communities."[9] If Christianity is to become good news for the earth, it will need to lend its support to the Earthist hope.

Environmental Ethics and Animal Welfare

Of course, Christianity has not often lived up to its ecological promise. It has not often enough been "Earthist" in orientation. Often it has fostered anthropocentric forms of thought, feeling, and action that neglect the kinship of humans with other creatures and presume that the earth and its creatures are but instruments for human use. This instrumentalist approach to the planet and nonhuman creatures has been reinforced by dualistic attitudes that elevate men over women, spirit over flesh, mind over matter, reason over feeling, urban over rural. All of this has been well-documented in theological critiques of the Christian past, particularly by feminist theologians.

For ecological theologians, feminist and otherwise, the "good news" is that this "bad news" is not "all the news." There are also traditions within the Christian past that are antidotes to anthropocentrism and can provide nourishment for a healthier future. Both sides of this equation—the bad news of unecological ways of thinking and the good news of ecological ways of thinking—have now been highlighted in many books on ecological theology. These are well summarized in the published proceedings from the Harvard Conference on Christianity and Ecology. My aim here is to extend the discussion by asking a new question: Can Christianity become good news for animals?

The question is important because, despite their good intentions, even ecologically sensitive theologians can sometimes neglect individual animals. By "individual" animals I do not mean Cartesian individuals. I am not imagining animals as disembodied souls whose relations with their own bodies and environments are external. Rather I am imagining them as relational souls, whose very selves are creative responses to bodily influences and environmental surroundings. If individual human beings are persons-in-community, then so are individual animals. They are subjects of their own lives, either consciously or unconsciously, and their subjectivity—their awareness and feeling, their creativity and intelligence—is itself a creative response to such influences.

Ecological theologies come in many forms: Orthodox, Catholic, Protestant, and Evangelical; mystical, feminist, prophetic, and philosophical. Amid their diversity, they rightly encourage a "care for the community of life in all its diversity," but then they can easily fall into one or both of two traps. Either they can so emphasize the diversity of various "species" that they forget the individual creatures who constitute the species. Or they can recognize the importance of individual animals, but then so emphasize the instrumental value of these individuals to their species and to ecosystems that

they forget the intrinsic value of these individuals in and for themselves. In these two ways, ecological theologies sometimes slide into a one-sided emphasis on "environmental ethics" at the expense of "animal welfare." They satisfy the legitimate concerns of the Sierra Club, but forget the concerns of the Humane Society.

Diverging Paths Within Christianity?

Back, then, to the question. Can Christianity become good news for animals? I use the word "become," with its future emphasis. The point is painfully obvious to many who have deep respect for animals, who find joy in their presence, who are concerned with the suffering humans too often inflict upon them, and who wish that Christianity might validate such feelings. Some of these people are Christian; others are post-Christians who long since rejected Christianity as hopelessly anti-animal. For the most disillusioned among them, the only "good news" about Christianity is that it permits, and even encourages, repentance and conversion. Their hope is that Christians will repent of their attitudes toward animals, and convert to a more compassionate approach.

THE NEGATIVE TRADITIONS

Let us begin by addressing the negative aspects of the tradition, because they have been dominant historically, before we turn to the positive traditions, which I take them to be the heart and soul of the Christian approach to the world.

Unfortunately, on the negative side, there is much of which to repent. The anti-animal aspects of the Christian past have been well documented in various books, including *After Noah: Animals and the Liberation of Theology*. The book is co-written by the most prominent of animal rights theologians, Andrew Linzey of Mansfield College at Oxford, and a professor of Judaism at the University of Wales, Dan Cohn-Sherbok, also a contributor to the present volume. These authors point to five teachings that are found in Judaism and Christianity, all of which contribute to prejudice against animals. They are: (1) that animals are "put here for us," (2) that some animals are inherently unclean, (3) that some animals are meant to be sacrificed for ritual purposes, (4) that animals are slaves to human need, and (5) that animals have no rational soul, mind, or sentience.[10] Each of these five teachings deserves extensive discussion. It is arguable, for example, that some of the sacrifice traditions involve a respect for individual animals because they recognize that animals belong to God, not to humans, and because the very idea that they are "sacrificed" presupposes their great value.[11] Nevertheless, Linzey and Cohn-Sherbok argue that all five teachings—including those which teach that animals are to be sacrificed—are morally problematic because they reduce animals to mere instruments, if not for humans, then for God.

The first four are found within biblical traditions themselves and are the common symbolic heritage of Judaism and Christianity. In Christianity, even Jesus is understood as a sacrifice, albeit the last one. He is the "lamb of God" who, once and for all, took away the sins of the world.

Equally influential within later historical Christianity, however, are the ideas that animals are "here for us" and that they are "slaves." According to Linzey, these two themes recur time and again within Christian theology, represented by notable theologians such as Augustine, Aquinas, Luther, and Calvin. The final teaching—that animals are mere machines—is a more modern and Cartesian way of thinking. In our time, this teaching is intensified by consumerist habits of thought which, as noted above, tend to reduce all living beings—plants as well as animals—into commodities for exchange in the marketplace.

As I move toward more positive contributions from Christianity, it is important for us to keep the negative tradition in mind. Perhaps two

illustrations can serve are reminders. The first is Thomas Aquinas' view, following Aristotle, that animals are here for us, and that we can use them as we wish:

> There is no sin in using a thing for the purpose for which it is. Now the order of things is such that the imperfect are for the perfect. ... It is not unlawful if man uses plants for the good of animals, and animals for the good of man as the Philosopher (Aristotle) states.[12]

We rightly note that "the order of things" to which Aquinas appeals functions as a legitimation of a certain approach to animals to which he is already committed. Here "theology" functions as a legitimation of domination.

The second illustration is Martin Luther's exegesis of Genesis 9:3, where God permits meat-eating. Luther writes:

> In this passage God sets himself up as a butcher; for with his word he slaughters and kills the animals that are suited for food, in order to make up, as it were, for the great sorrow that Noah experienced during the flood. For this reason God thinks Noah ought to be provided for sumptuously now.[13]

Apparently, even God is more interested in the gastronomic needs of Noah than the suffering of the animals. Here, too, a hermeneutics of suspicion seems appropriate.

THE POSITIVE TRADITIONS

Within historical Christianity, these negative traditions are dominant, but they are not the whole of the tradition. Christianity contains less influential traditions that serve as correctives to each of the five themes identified above. For the sake of balance, I will name five of them.

First and foremost, there are various themes within the Bible that are friendly to animals. These include the injunction to give animals rest on the sabbath; the idea that animals are subject to divine purposes which are beyond human need; and the idea that animals, no less than humans, are beneficiaries of the messianic age. John Wesley, for one, took the latter idea to suggest that individual animals, no less than humans, will enjoy life-after-death.

While many imagine the Bible to be mostly "bad news" for animals, some theologians suggest the contrary. One contemporary theologian, Lukas Vischer, has written a book on animals for the World Council of Churches in which he argues that the Bible as a whole is good news for animals, or at least better news than modernity. In his words:

> The testimony of the Bible sees humans and animals in close community. They are near to one another. Even though the special role of human beings is emphasized, scripture as a whole takes for granted that animals are part of the environment.
>
> The degradation of the status of animals to objects finds no justification in the Bible. While the cultural roots of it are in antiquity, it is essentially the product of the sequence of modern thought since Descartes (1596–1650) which has made humankind the center of the universe and has seen the outside world as subject to the human mind.[14]

If Vischer is correct, this is good news indeed, because the Bible is, of course, the single most important document of the Christian tradition. If Christians were to think more biblically, and less Cartesianly, they might be better news for animals.

Additionally, however, there are four more resources within historical Christianity that are relevant to animals. These include many stories concerning Jesus' companionship with, and kindness toward, animals in early Christian noncanonical texts, such as the Gospel of Pseudo-Matthew; the teachings of various theologians within the history of Christianity—such as John Chrysostom and John Wesley—

for whom a kindly approach to animals is a sign of Christian compassion; the examples of many a saint, who—at least in depictions to the sixteenth century—were so often presented as companions to, and protectors of, animals. Francis of Assisi is a prime example, but there are many others. Finally, the additional resources within historical Christianity include ways of feeling, celebrated by many Christians, which, if extended to animals, can be quite good news. These include empathy for the vulnerable, nonviolence, compassion, and what Kallistos Ware, has called "the contemplation of nature," as mentioned earlier.

THE FRANCISCAN ALTERNATIVE

What I am suggesting, then, is that there is a "Franciscan" alternative to the dominant tradition, which might be called the "Instrumentalist" tradition. At the heart of this alternative is a recognition that individual animals are kin to us, that they have value in and for themselves, and that they are sacramental presences in human life. Of course, for some environmentalists, it may seem as if this Franciscan alternative neglects larger ecological considerations. It may seem sentimental, short-sighted, environmentally irresponsible, and a distraction from more important concerns. And, for human rights advocates, it may seem to neglect the needs of human beings.

These suspicions are not necessary. The heart of the Franciscan alternative lies in recognizing the value of all life, human life included, as was evident in the example of Francis himself. This "Franciscan" point of view is well captured in a single sentence from a 1998 Report to the World Council of Churches. The sentence defines that the World Council calls "the integrity of creation." That "integrity" is: "the value of all creatures in and for themselves, for one another, and for God, and their interconnectedness in a diverse whole that has unique value for God."

The Franciscan alternative I recommend lies in recognizing the value of creatures "in and for themselves" as well as "for one another" and "for God" in a "diverse whole" that has "unique value" for God. Certainly human beings possess value "in and for themselves" even as they also possess value "for one another" and "for God." So do animals. And ecosystems possess value as making possible many forms of life, plant and animal. From the perspective of this report to the World Council of Churches, all of these values are contained within, and contribute to, the life of the divine.

In short, a Franciscan alternative is holistic rather than issue-dominated. It is not human-centered, animal-centered, plant-centered, or systems-centered, at the expense of these other centers; rather it is divinely centered, in a way that understands the divine life as including all life, individually and communally, within an interconnected, diverse whole.

To be sure, tradeoffs between these kinds of values are sometimes required. Honest decisions must sometimes be made between the value that some organisms—malarial mosquitoes, for example—have "in and for themselves," and the value that others—children whom they might infect—also have "in and for themselves."

A Franciscan approach, thus, cannot avoid ranking organisms, relative to context, for the sake of practical considerations. If a choice must be made between the mosquito and the child, it will probably choose the child. Just as it will chose between the tick and the dog. But the aim of a Franciscan approach is to make tradeoffs a last resort, not a first resort. The aim is to respect all life as much as possible, and then to live as lightly and gently as possible, realizing that "absolute moral purity" is an illusion, because life inevitably involves the taking of life. It is to live lovingly, and also to be honest about the reality of conflicting aims within the scope of life. If life is robbery, it involves robbing as little and as humanely as possible, with a humble realization that all life, not just human life, matters to God "in and for itself."

Back, then, to the question: Can Christianity seek to live lightly and gently with other crea-

tures? Can it become good news for animals? Let me define my terms more carefully.

Definitions

CHRISTIANITY

By "Christianity" I do not mean a static set of doctrines with a well-defined essence. Rather I mean a multicultural and multigenerational family of people, with roots in the healing ministry of Jesus, who seek to live what they call the Christian life. Among the world's Christians, 20 percent live in North America, 20 percent in Latin America, 15 percent in Africa, 30 percent in Europe, 14 percent in Asia, and 1 percent in Oceania. They represent and are influenced by many different traditions: Catholic, Protestant, Orthodox, Evangelical, Pentecostal, and African Independent Churches. In certain parts of the world, the latter two traditions are the fastest growing. This means that, if Christianity is to become good news for animals, it will not be because a single theology, emerging in the West, will be a voice for that good news. Rather it will be because the Christian life, as lived from many different points of view and in many different ways, becomes good news for animals.

Should this happen, it will not be that Christians have adopted "care for animals" as an issue among issues. Rather it will be that they will have grown deeply dissatisfied with the many problems of the world, and seek a better way of living, of which care for animals will be a part. Their "preferential option for animals" will be part of a larger "preferential option for the earth." They will call this preferential option "the Christian life."

ANIMALS

By "animals" I mean something close to what the Bible means by creatures of "the flesh," that is, creatures with fragile tissue who have inner drives akin to humans and who can suffer in ways that resemble human suffering. My point is not that such creatures are "better" than other creatures who are less like humans, but rather that we have moral obligations to these kinds of creatures that are different from our obligations to other kinds: sponges and mites, for example.

By "animals," then, I mean something more specific than is found in an ordinary biology text. I mean members of the animal kingdom, primarily but not exclusively chordates, with brains and nervous systems similar to our own, who possess four properties. I mean creatures who can feel the presence of their surroundings; who, within the limits imposed by body chemistry and environmental influences, can choose and be guided by subjective aims for "living well" in situations in which they find themselves; who can suffer pain, distress, discomfort, anxiety, and fear; and who act as "relatively unified selves" or "subjective centers of awareness," and thus who receive energy and influence from their bodies and initiate responses, much as we do.[15]

GOOD NEWS

By "good news" I mean a certain way of feeling, thinking, and behaving toward animals that include compassion, humility, and amazement. I mean treating animals—and more specifically nonhuman animals—with compassion and protecting them from cruelty and destruction, protecting the species to which they belong, such that earth is filled with biological diversity, recognizing animals as having intrinsic value quite apart from their usefulness to humans, recognizing that they have their own unique ways of being related to God, however God is understood, and recognizing that, precisely amid their uniqueness, they can reveal the mystery of divine presence to human beings.

From an animal's perspective, the first two are probably the most important. We can imagine a Christian who treats individual animals with compassion and who protects the species,

but who does so with no interest in the "intrinsic value" of the individual, or who does not think that animals have independent relations with God, or who does not think that animals can reveal God to human beings. This person would be good news for animals in a minimal sense. This good news would then be completed if, in addition to treating animals ethically, she approached them with respect, amazement, and gratitude, as expressed in the three additional sensibilities named above.

Practical Action

ECO-JUSTICE AND THE HUMANE SOCIETY

If Christianity does become good news, that news will involve all three dimensions of Christian life: practical action, theological understanding, and spiritual depth. By practical action, I mean what Christians usually mean by "discipleship." I mean moral behavior, guided by sound thinking and spiritual discernment, which promotes the well-being of animals. By "theological understanding" I mean voluntary assent to worldviews, stories, and ideas that help orient a person to the role and value of animals within the interconnected and diverse whole Christians call "creation." And by "spiritual depth" I mean preverbal and predoctrinal modes of perceiving and feeling the presence of animals in their intrinsic value. Toward this end of practical action, two sources are particularly helpful: the eco-justice movement, which is now some three decades old, but has roots in the social gospel movement, and the guidelines of the Humane Society of the United States.

THE ECO-JUSTICE MOVEMENT

"Eco-justice" names a moral perspective that is part of the worldwide ecumenical movement within Christianity. It links concerns for justice and peace with concerns for environmental well-being, so that ecology *and* justice, not ecology *or* justice, are the norm. Accordingly, as explained by Dieter Hessel, it "provides a dynamic framework for thought and action that fosters ecological integrity and the struggle for social and economic justice. It emerges through constructive human responses that serve environmental health and social equity together—for the sake of human beings and otherkind."

Hessel explains further that this perspective is grounded in four basic norms:

- Solidarity with other people and creatures—companions, victims, and allies—in each community, reflecting deep respect for creation.
- Ecological sustainability—environmentally fitting habits of living and working that enable life to flourish; and using ecologically and socially appropriate technology.
- Sufficiency as a standard of organized sharing, which requires basic floors and definite ceilings for equitable or fair consumption.
- Participation in decisions about how to obtain sustenance and to manage community life for the good in common and the good of the commons.[16]

Eco-justice advocates belong to many different Christian traditions, and they have different racial, ethnic, sexual, economic, and gender identities. But they generally emphasize these four themes in their ethical deliberations, their advocacy, and their actions. To date, according to Hessel, eco-justice ethics has become operationally significant in relation to several major problems: energy production and use, sustainable development, population policy, food security, and environmental justice. It is also relevant to thought and action on endangered species, climate change, and equitable and sustainable livelihoods. "Operational significance" involves recommending public policies (economic and political) aimed at addressing these problems and then helping to create the political will to enact and enforce those policies.

My suggestion, then, is that Christianity can become good news for animals if participants in the eco-justice movement also begin to work on issues of animal abuse. Already they are working on the preservation of species, which is part of what it means to be "good news for animals." The need is to combine such work with attention to individual animals and their suffering. In terms of sheer numbers, the most serious abuse lies in the rearing, transporting, and slaughtering of animals for "meat," particularly under factory farm conditions. The animals at issue include chickens, pigs, cows, and lambs. In the interests of the first of the four norms identified above—solidarity with the victims—an eco-justice ethic will protest against the abuse of these animals, recommend consumer boycotts, and help develop legislation to prevent future abuse. Similar attention will be given to animals used for the testing of industrial products (soaps and shampoos), animals used for recreational purposes (rodeos, bullfights), and animals that are hunted for pure sport.

At the same time, an eco-justice approach will attend to connections between the abuse of animals in these settings and the abuse of human beings: e.g., the workers in slaughter houses, who are often poor and powerless, and whose working conditions are oftentimes inhumane. And it will attend to ways in which the abuse of animals is connected to other forms of violence in the world, as is exemplified in studies that suggest linkages with domestic violence and serial killing.

In short, an eco-justice approach to animals will not compartmentalize "the abuse of animals," treating it as an issue disconnected from other forms of injustice and violence in the world, but will see this abuse as part of a larger and more destructive way of living in the world to which Christianity, and other religions as well, offer peaceful alternatives. The best hope for Christianity becoming good news for animals at an ethical level lies in eco-justice advocates adding animals to the creatures with whom they feel solidarity, and then encouraging others to do the same.

HUMANE SOCIETY OF THE UNITED STATES

To the moral perspective of eco-justice, the Humane Society of the United States adds practical guidelines for treating animals, each of which can help in the application of eco-justice norms, and each of which can guide legislation and other forms of public policy. The guidelines are stated as mandates:

- It is wrong to kill animals needlessly or for entertainment or to cause animals pain or torment.
- It is wrong to fail to provide adequate food, shelter, and care for animals for which humans have accepted responsibility.
- It is wrong to use animals for medical, educational, or commercial experimentation or research, unless absolute necessity can be found and demonstrated, and unless this is done without causing the animal pain or torment.
- It is wrong to maintain animals that are to be used for food in a manner that causes them discomfort or denies them an opportunity to develop and live in conditions that are reasonably natural for them.
- It is wrong for those who eat animals to kill them in any manner that does not result in instantaneous unconsciousness. Methods employed should cause no more than minimum apprehension.
- It is wrong to confine animals for display, impoundment, or as pets in conditions that are not comfortable and appropriate.
- It is wrong to permit domestic animals to propagate to an extent that leads to overpopulation or misery.

An eco-justice movement that takes these guidelines seriously will, in fact, be good news for animals.

Theological Understanding

Ethics cannot really be separated from theology. How we understand God in relation to animals will influence how we treat them. Thus, if Christianity is to become good news for animals, it will require that traditional Christian teachings be displayed in their relevance to animal life.

In our time, the theologian who has done the most to show this relevance is Andrew Linzey. He has developed many ideas to show how trinitarian thinking would be relevant to animals. Suffice it to say that Linzey has himself developed a theology that satisfies these very demands. For Christians interested in what he calls "Animal Theology," his own trinitarian perspective is the model.

Two additional forms of theology that can help Christians become "good news for animals" are process and feminist theologies, particularly as the latter is exemplified in the neo-Thomist perspective of Elizabeth Johnson. Process theology and the feminist neo-Thomism of Johnson have much in common. Both are forms of philosophical theology that enter into the fray of contemporary philosophical debate, recommending worldviews that can make sense not only to Christians shaped by Christian language, but also to people of other orientations: scientists, artists, politicians, and homemakers. Both recognize that too much traditional Christian theology has been wedded to particularized modes of discourse that have often grown stale and static. And both recognize that these stale modes of discourse, such as the insistence that God always be conceived as He Who Is, and never as She Who Is, have supported and valorized patriarchal habits of thought and behavior. Both seek to be postpatriarchal.[17]

Spiritual Depth

THE CONTEMPLATION OF NATURE

Theology itself can take us only so far. In the final analysis, Christians can become good news for animals only if we feel the presence of animals in fresh ways. What is needed are not simply new ways of thinking about animals, but more contemplative ways of perceiving them. In the Christian tradition, of course, the word "contemplation" does not mean thinking about things. It refers to a kind of prayer in which the mind does not function discursively but rather is relaxed and alert. In *The Orthodox Way* Kallistos Ware interprets this attention in relation to nature. He means simple, nondiscursive attention to natural world. Elizabeth Johnson calls it "ecological contemplation" and Sallie McFague calls it "the loving eye."

QUIET LISTENING TO NATURE

Ware distinguishes two aspects of such seeing. The first involves appreciating the sheer uniqueness—the "thusness" or the "thisness"—of God's creation: "We are to see each stone, each leaf, each blade of grass, each frog, each human face, for what it truly is, in all its distinctness and intensity of its specific being."[18]

In seeing an animal, for example, we "contemplate nature" when we look into her eyes, behold her face, and listen to the sounds and silences. We bracket our own subjective agendas and are simply present to her in her suchness. Ware's point is that this mindful awareness, this appreciative consciousness, can be enjoyed in relation to stones and frogs, rivers and stars, as well as people. It is prayer.

In the second aspect of contemplating nature there is also the quiet listening and inner silence. But this listening is slightly different from seeing things in their suchness. We see things as pointing beyond themselves to the one who created them, and the one who shines through them in their particularity: "we see all things, persons, and moments as signs or sacraments of God."[19]

In looking into the eyes of an animal, for example, we may be aware that there is something sacred and holy, something divine, in the animal. God's Spirit is in her, shining through her, even as she is more than the Spirit. It is as if she is a holy icon, a stained glass window, through which holy light shines. This is the second aspect of contemplation noted by Ware in his discussion of contemplating nature. If we call the first "mindful attention," we might call the second "sacramental consciousness." It is sensing others as visible signs of an invisible grace.

According to Ware, this contemplation of nature can be part of our daily lives. It does not preclude thinking and acting; we can approach life prayerfully even as we approach it thoughtfully and practically. This does not mean that we approve of all that we see. Some of what we see is tragic, some horrible, and some sinful. But it does mean that we can see things lovingly and forgivingly, gratefully and empathically, like God. Our anger over the world's injustices and tragedies can be, like God's wrath itself, the obverse side of pain. Thus, "we are to see all things as essentially sacred, as a gift from God and a means of communion with him."[20] Such is the life of prayer. It receives the world prayerfully, with a listening spirit, full of wisdom.

The question then becomes: And how can we cultivate this listening spirit? Traditionally, the answer has been: "With the help of spiritual disciplines." If Christianity is to become good news for animals, we will need such disciplines that take us into the palpable presence of animals, such that we can listen to them and be awed by them, again and again.

For the privileged among us, spending time in the presence of wild animals can help. Their very wildness bespeaks an "otherness" that is beyond self-absorption and that can have a healing effect in our lives. We appreciate them in their suchness, precisely because we do not matter to them. In our irrelevance, they help heal us of our pretensions. We realize that they have their own connections to the Mystery at the heart of the universe, and that we are not the center of things.

But most people on our planet do not have the luxury of wilderness excursions. They live in cities; they are overly busy; and their closest possibility for intimacy with animals is with companion animals. Thus, as a spiritual discipline for learning to listen to animals, I recommend "taking care of pets." Clearly the relationship in such caretaking is hierarchical, like that of a parent and a child. The parent establishes guidelines for behavior and the child lives within them. According to Sallie McFague, this is a serious problem in relation to pets. She equates owner-pet relations with parent-child relations, and deems both problematic, because they so easily lapse into subject-object relations.

However, for many people today, a relationship with their pets (or "companion animals," to use a term preferred by many), is the first way, and perhaps the only way, they can learn to listen to animals. They will enter into what Sallie McFague calls "the loving eye" by first discovering "the loving touch" of an animal they love and care for. This touch can itself be good news for the animal. Many companion animals do indeed benefit from being loved and cared for by their "owners," and in many ways, they "own their owners" in delightful and loving ways. The relationship is subject-subject, and it is mutually beneficial.

My suggestion, then, is that one kind of "spiritual discipline" which is good news for animals, because it leads to contemplative listening, is taking care of companion animals and being in their presence. This discipline is good news for animals, among other reasons, because there are so many animals who need such care. It can also lead to a wider respect for the whole of animal life, wild animals included. And it can lead one to consider the many ways in which domestic animals—chickens, pigs, and cows, for example—are inhumanely reared and slaughtered for food.

If Christianity is to become good news for animals, it will be because all three dimensions of Christian life are involved: practical action, theological understanding, and spiritual depth. And it will be because Christians in different parts of the world, some among the overconsumers of the world, and some among the poorest of the poor, grow dissatisfied with the illusions of consumer culture, seeking instead a more holistic approach to life, in the companionship of others who seek the same. I have written this essay in order to show how this transformation might occur among Christians. For many Christians, a first step will be to dwell in the presence of animals already in their midst. It will begin, not with theology, but with touch: flesh-upon-flesh, as enlivened by the Spirit. For a religion that celebrates enfleshment, supremely realized in incarnation, salvation by touch is an appropriate beginning.

NOTES

1. John B. Cobb, Jr., *The Earthist Challenge to Economism: A Theological Critique of the World Bank* (New York: St. Martin's Press, 1999).

2. Surveys of ecological theologies include: Peter W. Bakkan, Joan Gibb Engel, and J. Ronald Engel, eds., *Ecology, Justice, and Christian Faith: A Critical Guide to the Literature* (Westport, CT: Greenwood Press, 1995); Max Oeschlager, *Caring for Creation: An Ecumenical Approach to the Environmental Crisis* (New Haven: Yale University Press, 1994); *Theology for Earth Community: A Field Guide* (Maryknoll, NY: Orbis Press, 1996); Dieter T. Hessel and Stephen Bede Sharper, eds., *Redeeming the Time: A Political Theology of the Environment* (New York: Crossroad, 1998). Scharper's survey is particularly instructive vis-à-vis the issue of "environmental ethics" and "animal welfare," In his survey he treats many kinds of ecological theology: biblical, tra-

ditionalist, "new cosmology" approaches, ecofeminist, process, and liberationist, but singles out process theology as one of the few that attends to individual animals as well as collectives. An exception to Scharper's generalization is James Nash's *Loving Nature: Ecological Integrity and Christian Responsibility* (Nashville: Abingdon, 1991). Nash is well aware of the tendency among ecological theologians to emphasize "collectives" over "individuals" (pp. 179–83). For readers interested in ways in which traditional Christian doctrines might offer "firm foundations" for an ecological theology, Nash's book is without parallel. His own constructive approach includes attention to individuals and collectives.

3. For an introduction to the eco-justice movement, see Dieter Hessel, "Ecumenical Ethics for the Earth Community," *Theology and Public Policy 8*, nos. 1 and 2 (Summer and Winter 1996): 17–29. The guidelines recommended by the Humane Society of the United States appear, among other places, in Charles Birch and Lukas Vischer, *Living with the Animals The Community of God's Creatures* (Geneva: WCC Publications, 1997), pp. 80–81.

4. See Andrew Linzey, *Animal Theology* (London: SCM Press, 1995); see also Phyllis Zagano and Terrence Tilley, eds., *Things Old and New: Essays on the Theology of Elizabeth A. Johnson* (New York: Crossroad, 1999). I wrote pp. 56–80, offering a process approach to God in relation to animals, with particular attention to problems of animal suffering; pp. 110–16 are Johnson's response to process theology, in which she draws parallels from a feminist, neo-Thomist perspective.

5. See Zagano and Tilley, *Things Old and New,* especially pp. 56–80 and 110–16.

6. Elizabeth A. Johnson, *Women, Earth, and Creator Spirit* (New York: Paulist Press, 1993), p. 63.

7. Sallie McFague, *Supernatural Christians: How We Should Love Nature* (Minneapolis: Fortress Press,

1997), pp. 91–117; Kallistos Ware. *The Orthodox Way,* revised edition (Crestwood, N.Y.: St. Vladimir's Press, 1995), p. 119.

8. These are the first four principles of the Earth Charter (Benchmark Draft II).

9. Cobb, *The Earthist Challenge to Economism,* p. 82.

10. Andrew Linzey and Dan Cohn-Sherbok, *After Noah: Animals and the Liberation of Theology* (London: Mowbray, 1997) pp. 1–16.

11. For a systematic discussion of animals as unclean, see Walter Houston, "What Was the Meaning of Classifying Animals as Clean or Unclean?" in Andrew Linzey and Dorothy Yamamoto, eds., *Animals on the Agenda* (London: SCM Press, 1998), pp. 18–24. For a discussion of animals as sacrifices, see J. W. Rogerson, "What was the Meaning of Animal Sacrifice?" in ibid., pp. 8–17.

12. Linzey and Cohn-Sherbok, *After Noah,* p. 7.

13. Ibid., p. 7.

14. Vischer, *Living with the Animals,* p. 2.

15. In process theology, we call such selves "souls," and recognize that there can be degrees of soul. An embryo just after conception, for example, has less soul than an embryo in the third trimester. Moreover, we suggest that "souls" are evolutionary expressions of, not exceptions to, the kind of energetic aliveness found also in the living cells of plants, in microorganisms, and in rocks. By this definition, "souls" are natural, not supernatural. By animals, then, I mean sentient beings with souls. By this definition, humans, too, are animals.

16. Hessel, "Ecumenical Ethics for Earth Community," p. 19.

17. See Zagano and Tilley, *Things Old and New,* especially pp. 56–80 and 110–116.

18. Ware, *The Orthodox Way,* p. 119.

19. Ibid.

20. Ibid., p. 120.

ISLAM

"This she-camel of God is a sign to you"

Dimensions of Animals in Islamic Tradition and Muslim Culture

RICHARD FOLTZ

It is frequently claimed that one position or another represents "true" Islam. Nevertheless,
there exists no unified Islamic or Muslim view
of nonhuman animals. It is also important to acknowledge that, while the terms are often difficult to disentangle for those both within and
without the tradition, "Islamic" and "Muslim"
are certainly not synonymous, since attitudes
held by individuals or collectives who happen to
be "Muslim" may not be "Islamic."[1]

There are currently about 1.2 billion Muslims, and they can be found in nearly every
country. The vast majority—about 85 percent
—are not Arab but belong to other ethnic and
linguistic groups. The largest concentration of
Muslims, 33 percent, can be found in South
Asia. The nations with the largest Muslim populations are Indonesia, Bangladesh, Pakistan, and
India. By contrast the Middle East contains 25
percent of the world's Muslim population. Since
Muslim identities and worldviews are in all cases
made up of multiple sources, one would predict
that attitudes toward nonhuman animals among

Muslims of diverse cultural backgrounds would
show both similarities and differences. This indeed turns out to be the case.

Nonhuman Animals in Islamic Texts

Islam (literally, "submission"), as an ideal is understood by believers as the state God wills for
His creation (*khalq*). This is apprehended by the
Sunni majority through the revealed scripture
of the Qur'ān, the life example of the Prophet
Muḥammad (the *sunna*, as attested in ḥadīth
reports), and the *shari'a*, a comprehensive code
of life as articulated in the legal texts of the
so-called Classical period (eighth to tenth centuries CE). Shī'ītes also follow the teachings of
their Imams, and Sufis (who can be Sunni or
Shī'ī) defer to the authority of their spiritual
guides (*shaykh*s, or *pīr*s). The actual practices and
attitudes of Muslims have always been shaped
by Islamic sources in combination with extra-
Islamic cultural ones. Islamic sources tend to be

embodied in authoritative texts, while cultural sources often are not.

Much of Islam's textual tradition is originally in Arabic, which for many centuries played a role analogous to the scholarly *lingua franca* in Christian Europe. The Arabic word used in the Classical texts to refer to animals, including humans, is *hayawān* (pl. *hayawānāt*).[2] This term appears only once in the Qur'ān, however, where it refers rather to the "true" existence of the afterlife.[3] For nonhuman animals the Qur'ān instead uses the term *dabba* (pl. *dawābb*).[4]

Human beings are often described in Arabic texts as "the speaking animal" (*hayawān al-nātiq*), although the Qur'ān itself acknowledges that nonhuman animals also have speech:

> And [in this insight] Solomon was [truly] David's heir; and he would say: "O you people! We have been taught the speech of birds, and have been given [in abundance] of all [good] things: this, behold, is indeed a manifest favor [from God]!"[5]

Arabs in pre-Islamic times practiced animal cults, various meat taboos, sympathetic magic (*istimtar*) and possibly totemism. Some tribes had animal names, such as the Quraysh ("shark"), which was the tribe of the Prophet Muḥammad, and the Asad ("lion").[6] Certain animals, including camels, horses, bees, and others, were believed to carry blessing (*baraka*), while others, such as dogs and cats, were associated with the evil eye. Genies (*jinn*) were believed sometimes to take animal form.

The Qur'ān proscribed many pre-Islamic practices related to animals,[7] which nevertheless survived in some cases. Also notable is the persistence of blood sacrifices, such as that performed on the Feast of Sacrifice (Eid al-Adha) which commemorates the prophet Abraham's willingness to sacrifice his son (Isma'il, not Isaac, in Islamic tradition). Many Muslims also make blood sacrifices in fulfillment of vows (*nazr*), seven days after the birth of a child (*aqiqa*), or on the tenth day of the month of Dhu'l-hijja

in atonement for transgressions committed during the pilgrimage to Mecca (*hajj*). Also surviving are beliefs in metamorphosis (*maskh*), several examples of which occur in the Qur'ān.[8] Some heterodox Muslim groups retained a belief in metempsychosis (*tanasukh*). Six chapters of the Qur'ān are named for animals: the Cow (2), the Cattle (6), the Bee (16), the Ant (28), the Spider (29), and the Elephant (105).

Islam is what contemporary ecologists would probably call a strongly anthropocentric religion, although Muslims might prefer to see their worldview as "theocentric." Within the hierarchy of Creation, Muslims see humans as occupying a special and privileged status. The Qur'ān says, "Hast thou not seen how Allah has subjected (*sakhkhara*) to you all that is in the earth?"[9] The term *khalīfa* (lit., "successor"), which in the Qur'ān is applied to humans, is generally defined by contemporary Muslims as "vice-regent," as in the verses that state "I am setting on the earth a vice-regent (*khalīfa*)," and "It is He who has made you his vice-regent on earth."[10] According to this view, while nonhuman Creation is subjugated to human needs, the proper human role is that of conscientious steward and not exploiter.[11] The earth was not created for humans alone: "And the earth has He spread out for all living beings (*anām*)."[12] Everything in Creation is a miraculous sign of God (*aya*), inviting Muslims to contemplate the Creator. Nonhuman animals fall into this category, as in the following verse:

> ... This she-camel of God is a sign to you; so leave her to graze in God's earth, and let her come to no harm, or you shall be seized with a grievous punishment.[13]

Nevertheless, the Qur'ān specifies that certain animals were created for the benefit of humans:

> And He has created cattle for you: you derive warmth from them, and [various] other uses; and from them you obtain food; and you find beauty

in them when you drive them home in the evenings and when you take them out to pasture in the mornings. And they carry your loads to [many] a place which [otherwise] you would be unable to reach without great hardship to yourselves. And [it is He who creates] horses and mules and asses for you to ride, as well as for [their] beauty: and He will yet create things of which [today] you have no knowledge.[14]

Yet despite this hierarchy, humans are described as similar to nonhuman animals in almost all respects. Unlike in Christianity, in Islam nonhuman animals are considered to have souls (*nafs*). Some Muslim scholars have opined that nonhuman animals will be resurrected along with humans on the Day of Judgment. The Qur'ān states that all creation praises God, even if this praise is not expressed in human language.[15] The Qur'ān further says that "There is not an animal in the earth, nor a flying creature on two wings, but they are communities (*umām*, sg. *umma*) like unto you."[16] A jurist from the Classical period, Ahmad ibn Habit, even surmised from this verse that since the Qur'ān elsewhere states that "there never was a community (*umma*) without a warner [i.e., a prophet] having lived among them,"[17] then perhaps nonhuman animals also have prophets. Ibn Hazm (d. 1062) denied this, arguing that "the laws of Allah are only applicable to those who possess the ability to speak and can understand them,"[18] but his rebuttal lacks weight since the Qur'ān explicitly states that animals do speak, albeit in their own languages.

The Qur'ān emphasizes that God takes care of the needs of all living things: "There is no moving creature on earth, but Allah provides for its sustenance."[19] The world is not for humans alone: "And the earth: He has assigned to all living creatures."[20] Nonhuman animals can even receive divine revelation, as in the verse which states: "And your Lord revealed to the bee, saying: 'make hives in the mountains, and in the trees, and in [human] habitations."[21] It has thus been argued by some Islamic commen-

tators that humans are unique only in that they possess volition (*taqwa*), and are thus responsible for their actions.[22]

Meat-Eating and Slaughter

Islamic dietary laws are derived both from the Qur'ān and from the Classical legal tradition. The overwhelming majority of Muslims eat meat; indeed, meat-eating is mentioned in the Qur'ān as one of the pleasures of heaven.[23] The Qur'ān explicitly allows the eating of animal flesh, with certain exceptions:

> O you who have attained to faith! Be true to your covenants! Lawful to you is [the flesh of] every beast that feeds on plants, save what is mentioned to you [hereinafter]: but you are not allowed to hunt while you are in a state of pilgrimage. Behold, God ordains in accordance with his will.[24]

On the other hand the Qur'ān prohibits the eating of animals that have not been ritually slaughtered, as well as the eating of blood, and pigs:

> Forbidden to you is carrion, and blood, and the flesh of swine, and that over which any name other than God's has been invoked, and the animal that has been strangled, or beaten to death, or killed by a fall, or gored to death, or savaged by a beast of prey, save that which you [yourselves] may have slaughtered while it was still alive; and [forbidden to you] is all that has been slaughtered on idolatrous altars.[25]

A similar verse, however, adds an exemption in case of dire need:

> … but if one is driven [to it] by necessity—neither coveting it nor exceeding his immediate need—verily, God is much-forgiving, a dispenser of grace.[26]

Muslim jurists later expanded these restrictions, categorizing all animals in terms of whether eating them is lawful (*halal*), discouraged (*makruh*), or forbidden (*haram*). Classifications differed somewhat from one school to the next, but among the animals forbidden by the jurists are dogs, donkeys, frogs, peacocks, storks, beetles, crustaceans, and many kinds of insects (although locusts are popular among Bedouins). Some prohibitions arise from the animal's behavior, such as scavenging or eating other forbidden animals, from the unpleasant flavor of their meat, or merely because they are considered "disgusting." The eating of carnivores, monkeys, or reptiles is mostly forbidden, although the Maliki school permits the flesh of jackals, birds of prey, monkeys, and most reptiles.

Ritual (*halal*) slaughter is said to follow the principle of compassion for the animal being killed. According to the hadith literature, Muhammad said, "If you kill, kill well, and if you slaughter, slaughter well. Let each of you sharpen his blade and let him spare suffering to the animal he slaughters."[27]

Apart from condoned slaughter for purposes of human survival, Muhammad frequently reminded his companions to take the interests of nonhuman animals into consideration. The hadiths report him as saying, "For [charity shown to] each creature which has a wet heart [i.e., is alive], there is a reward."[28] In another hadith, Muhammad is said to have reprimanded some men who were sitting idly on their camels in the marketplace, saying "Either ride them or leave them alone."[29] He is also reported to have said, "There is no man who kills [even] a sparrow or anything smaller, without its deserving it, but Allah will question him about it [on the Day of Judgment],"[30] and "Whoever is kind to the creatures of God, is kind to himself."[31] The hadiths mention two contrasting stories with particular relevance to the treatment of animals. In one, a woman is condemned to hell because she has mistreated a cat;[32] in another, a sinner is saved by the grace of Allah after he gives water to a dog dying of thirst.[33] In the interpretation of G. H. Bousquet, Islam thus "condemns to hell those who mistreat animals, and . . . more importantly, accords extraordinary grace to those who do them good."[34]

The killing of some animals for any reason is forbidden on the basis of certain hadiths. Animals that Muslims are never to kill include hoopoes and magpies, frogs, ants and bees. On the other hand, Muhammad ordered the killing of certain other animals, including mottled crows, dogs, mice, and scorpions. Muslims are not allowed to kill any living thing while in a state of ritual purity, for example while praying or on pilgrimage. Animal skins may be used as prayer rugs, but only if the animal has been ritually slaughtered. Hunting for sport is forbidden on the basis of numerous hadiths, as are animal fights and other such entertainment, although Muslims have often not abided by these prohibitions.

Animal Rights in the Islamic Legal Tradition

The thirteenth-century legal scholar 'Izz al-din ibn 'Abd al-salam, in his *Qawa'id al-ahkam fi masalih al-anam* (*Rules for Judgment in the Cases of Living Beings*), has the following to say about a person's obligations toward his domestic animals:

- He should spend [time, money or effort] on it, even if the animal is aged or diseased in such a way that no benefit is expected from it. His spending should be equal to that on a similar animal useful to him.
- He should not overburden it.
- He should not place with it anything that might cause it harm, whether of the same kind or a different species.
- He should kill it properly and with consideration; he should not cut their skin or bones until their bodies have become cold and their life has passed fully away.

- He should not kill their young within their sight.
- He should give them different resting shelters and watering places which should all be cleaned regularly.
- He should put the male and female in the same place during their mating season.
- He should not hunt a wild animal with a tool that breaks bones, rendering it unlawful for eating.[35]

The legal category of water rights extends to animals through the law of "the right of thirst" (*haqq al-shurb*). A Qur'ānic basis can be found in the verse, "It is the she-camel of Allah, so let her drink!"[36] It has been noted with some irony that Classical Islamic law accords nonhuman animals greater access to water than do the "modern" laws of the United States.[37]

However, although the rights of nonhuman animals are guaranteed in the legal tradition, their interests are ultimately subordinate to those of humans. As ibn 'Abd al-salam writes:

The unbeliever who prohibits the slaughtering of an animal [for no reason but] to achieve the interest of the animal is incorrect because in so doing he gives preference to a lower, *khasīs,* animal over a higher, *nafīs,* animal.[38]

The tenth-century poet al-Ma'arri, who became a vegan late in life, was accused by a leading theologian of the time of "trying to be more compassionate than God."[39] Thus, despite the rights accorded to nonhuman animals in Islamic law, contemporary animal rights philosophers would probably conclude that Islam does not simply condone attitudes which they would label as "speciesist,"[40] but actually requires them.

Nonhuman Animals in Islamic Philosophy and Mysticism

Islamic philosophers and mystics have often used nonhuman animals in their writings. Almost invariably, however, animal figures are employed as symbols for particular human traits, or are entirely anthropomorphized actors in human-type dramas. In other words, even where nonhuman animals appear, the real message is about humans. The philosophical treatise of the so-called "Pure Brethren" (*Ikhwān al-safā*) of Basra, *The Case of the Animals versus Man Before the King of the Jinn,* and the epic poem of Farid ad-Din Attar, *Conference of the Birds* (*Mantiq al-tayr*) are two examples. Both works are treated in this volume in the two essays that follow this one, by Zayn Kassam and Ali Asani, respectively.

Islamic philosophy (*falsafa*) in the early centuries derives primarily from the Hellenistic tradition. Aristotle's *Historia animalium* was translated into Arabic in the eighth or ninth century, and Muslim mystics (Sufis) associated the "animal soul" of the philosophers with the "lower self" (*nafs*), that is, the baser instincts which the spiritual seeker must strive to overcome.

In addition to Attar's *Conference of the Birds,* many other Sufi treatises also contain animal stories and characters. Jalal ad-Din Rumi's thirteenth-century *Mathnawī al-ma'anawī,* which some Muslims have called "the Qur'ān in Persian," is one of the best-known. In most cases animal characters are used to represent human traits, such as a donkey for stubbornness. Elsewhere, however, they serve as a contrast for human weaknesses, as when Rumi emphasizes the exemplary faith of nonhuman animals in their Creator:

The dove on the tree is uttering thanks to God, though her food is not yet ready.
The nightingale is singing glory to God, saying, "I rely on Thee for my daily bread, O Thou who answerest prayer.
...

You may take every animal from the gnat
    to the elephant: they have all become
    God's dependents ...
[While] these griefs within our breasts arise
    from the vapor and dust of our existence
    and vain desire.[41]

According to Rumi, nonhuman animals even
excel humans in some qualities, particularly that
of loving devotion to which Sufis aspire:

Wolf and bear and lion know what love is: he
that is blind to love is inferior to a dog! If the
dog had not a vein of love, how should the dog
of the Cave have sought to win the heart of the
Seven Sleepers?[42]

    You have not smelt the heart in your own
kind: how should you smell the heart in wolf and
sheep?[43]

On the other hand, Rumi's vision of the mystic quest follows Aristotle's "great chain of being," in which the soul travels upward from an
inorganic state to vegetable to animal to that of
a human, before ultimately becoming lost in its
Creator:

I died to the inorganic state and became endowed with growth, and [then] I died to [vege-
table] growth and attained the animal.

    I died from animality and became Adam
[man]: why then should I fear? When have I become less for dying?[44]

So it would seem that even if nonhuman
animals possess laudable qualities, the value of
these lies mainly in their instructive potential
for humans, who are nevertheless a stage above
them in the cosmic hierarchy.

    Other Sufi stories offer lessons about com-
passion and renunciation, using the theme of
abstention from killing animals for meat. One
such story, from a hagiography compiled by Farid ad-Din 'Attar, features the eighth-century female Muslim mystic Rabi'a of Basra:

Rabi'a had gone up on a mountain. Wild goats
and gazelles gathered around, gazing upon her.
Suddenly, Hasan Basri [another well-known
early Muslim mystic] appeared. All the animals
shied away. When Hasan saw that, he was perplexed and said, "Rabi'a, why do they shy away
from me when they were so intimate with you?"
    Rabi'a said, "What did you eat today?"
    "Soup."
    "You ate their lard. How would they not shy
away from you?"[45]

'Abd al-Karim al-Qushayri (d. 1074 CE) tells
a similar story about the early Sufi Ibrahim ibn
Adham, who, it is said, liked to go hunting. One
day, as he was pursuing an antelope, he heard
a voice asking him, "O Ibrahim, is it for this
that We have created you?" Immediately he got
down from his horse, gave his fine clothes to a
shepherd in exchange for a wool tunic, and assumed the life of a wandering dervish.[46]

    A number of Sufism's well-known historical
figures have been vegetarian. An early female
Sufi, Zaynab, is said to have been persecuted
for her refusal to eat meat.[47] Most stories about
Sufi vegetarians originate in South Asia, suggesting possible Hindu or Buddhist influence.[48] On
the other hand, a few vegetarian anecdotes also
occur among the Sufis of North Africa and the
Ottoman world.[49] Generally speaking, however,
among the Sufis vegetarianism is seen as a form
of spiritual discipline intended to benefit the one
who practices it, rather than out of interest for
the animals who are spared.

Nonhuman Animals in Muslim Literature and Art

Nonhuman animals appear throughout the literary and artistic production of Muslims. As in
the philosophical and mystical texts, in poetry
and prose literature they are most often used as
embodiments of specific human traits and for
purposes of teaching moral lessons relevant to

humans. Among the animal stories popular in Muslim societies, perhaps the best-known is Ibn al-Muqaffa's ninth-century translation of *Kalila and Dimna,* a collection of fables, mainly political in nature, which came to pre-Islamic Iran from India.[50] Other works that feature animals include Warawini's thirteenth-century *Book of the Border-keeper* (*Marzbān-nāma*) and Nakhshabi's fourteenth-century *Parrot Book* (*Tūtī-nāma*). The *Thousand and One Nights* (*Alf layla wa layla*) stories also contain many animal characters.

The tradition of Muslim representational art (as opposed to "Islamic art" strictly speaking, which is nonrepresentational), which was most highly developed in Iran and spread from there to India and Turkey, is rich with animal themes, especially illustrated stories (such as *Kalila and Dimna*) and royal hunting scenes, whether in books, carpets, metalwork, ceramics, or rock engravings. Lion figures, associated in the Iranian tradition with monarchy, appear on many public buildings, even sometimes (as in the case of Samarkand's *Shīr-dār* seminary) religious ones.

Works of Muslim scientists on zoology should also be mentioned. Among these the best known is the seven-volume *Book of Animals* (*Kitāb al-hayawān*) of al-Jahiz (d. 868/9 CE).[51] As in the fable literature, al-Jahiz's use of animals is instrumental; although ostensibly a comprehensive zoological catalogue, al-Jahiz's opus aims primarily at demonstrating the magnificence of God through a study of his created beings. The later work of al-Damiri (d. 1405), *Hayat al-hayawān al-kubra,* is largely a commentary on and expansion of al-Jahiz.[52]

Contemporary Muslim Views on Vegetarianism and Animal Testing

In recent years individual Muslims have given attention to animal issues as never before. Within this emerging consciousness, extra-Islamic (mainly Western) influences are clearly present. Growing numbers of Muslim vegetarians and animal rights activists appear in most cases first to have been converted to the cause, then sought support and justification for it within their Islamic tradition. Some radical reinterpretations have been put forth as a result, although that preoccupation with the rights of nonhuman animals remains firmly outside of the mainstream in Muslim societies around the world today.

Perhaps the most prominent contemporary voice in articulating Islamic concern for nonhuman animals is the late Basheer Ahmad Masri (1914–1993), a native of India who spent twenty years as an educator in Africa before moving to England in 1961, where he became imam of the Shah Jehan mosque in Woking. Masri's stated worldview, that "life on this earth is so intertwined as an homogeneous unit that it cannot be disentangled for the melioration of one species at the expense of the other,"[53] sounds as much deep ecological as Islamic.

At first glance, Masri's views on factory farming and animal testing are not incompatible with those of today's animal rights activists. He writes, for example, that

> to kill animals to satisfy the human thirst for inessentials is a contradiction in terms within the Islamic tradition. Think of the millions of animals killed, in the name of commercial enterprises, in order to supply a complacent public with trinkets and products they do not really need. And why? Because we are too lazy or too self-indulgent to find substitutes.[54]

Yet Masri does not argue against animal testing as such, only that it should not result in pain or disfigurement to the animal.[55] Masri is careful to couch his arguments in Islamic language, and ultimately he leaves the traditional Islamic notion of human exceptionalism unchallenged.

The late Turkish Sufi master Bediuzzaman Said Nursi (1877–1960) is heralded by his followers as a model animal lover. As a result of time spent in prison, where he witnessed indiscriminate spraying of insecticides, Nursi wrote an entire treatise on the importance of flies.[56] He also claimed to be able, like Solomon, to understand animal languages, as in the following passage:

> ... one day I looked at the cats; all they were doing was eating, playing, and sleeping. I wondered, how is it these little monsters which perform no duties are known as blessed? Later, I lay down to sleep for the night. I looked; one of the cats had come. It lay against my pillow and put its mouth against my ear, and murmuring: "O Most Compassionate One! O Most Compassionate One!" in the most clear manner, as though refuting in the name of its species the objection and insult which had occurred to me, throwing it in my face. Then this occurred to me: I wonder if this recitation is particular to this cat, or is it general among cats? And is it only an unfair objector like me who hears it, or if anyone listens carefully, can they hear it? The next morning I listened to the other cats; it was not so clear, but to varying degrees they were repeating the same invocation. At first, "O Most Compassionate!" was discernible following their purring. Then gradually their purrings and meowings became the same "O Most Merciful!" It became an unarticulated, eloquent and sorrowful recitation. They would close their mouths and utter a fine "O Most Compassionate!" I related the story to the brothers who visited me, and they listened carefully as well, and said that they heard it to an extent.[57]

Another contemporary Sufi teacher, the Sri Lankan M. R. Bawa Muhaiyadeen (d.1986), enjoined his followers to practice vegetarianism, saying:

> All your life you have been drinking the blood and eating the flesh of animals without realizing what you have been doing. You love flesh and enjoy murder. If you had any conscience or any

sense of justice, if you were born as a true human being, you would think about this. God is looking at me and you. Tomorrow his truth and his justice will inquire into this. You must realize this.[58]

Still, it must be acknowledged that such perspectives remain well outside of the Muslim mainstream. In pushing the limits of Islamic tradition, Masri, Nursi, and the Bawa all go further than any of today's numerous self-proclaimed Islamic environmentalists who have written on the rights of nonhuman animals. Mawil Izzi Dien, in his recent groundbreaking book *The Environmental Dimensions of Islam,* takes due note of the rights accorded to nonhuman animals in Islamic law. Elsewhere, however, Izzi Dien makes his speciesist preferences clear, as when he offers the following justification of meat-eating:

> According to Islamic Law there are no grounds upon which one can argue that animals should not be killed for food. The Islamic legal opinion on this issue is based on clear Qur'ānic verses. Muslims are not only prohibited from eating certain food, but also may not choose to prohibit themselves food that is allowed by Islam. Accordingly vegetarianism is not permitted unless on grounds such as unavailability or medical necessity. Vegetarianism is not allowed under the pretext of giving priority to the interest of animals because such decisions are God's prerogative.[59]

While to date no Muslim legal scholar has argued (in print at least) that the permissibility of meat-eating should be reconsidered,[60] increasing numbers of Muslim vegetarians are making their views known, especially over the internet. A number of postings suggest that the Prophet Muḥammad, though an occasional eater of meat, kept mainly to a vegetarian diet.[61] Muslim doctors are recognizing the benefits of a vegetarian diet for human health.[62] The worldwide spread of factory farming techniques means that Muslims often cannot be sure that their meat is truly *halāl*, especially now that even pig remains are often mixed into livestock feed. For these and other reasons, vegetarian and animal rights societies have begun to appear all over the Muslim world.[63] Vegetarian restaurants are cropping up in some Muslim countries.

Reassessing Traditional Views of Dogs

One area of interspecies relations in which traditional Muslim attitudes differ markedly from those in Western societies is the keeping of dogs as pets. In most schools of Islamic law dogs are classified as ritually unclean (*najis*), which means, among other things, that a Muslim may not pray after being touched by a dog.[64] There is a joke about a pious man who is rushing to the mosque after hearing the prayer call. It has been raining, and a stray dog steps in a puddle and splashes him. Realizing he has no time to return home and change, the man looks the other way and says, "God willing, it's a goat."

Even Muslims who do own dogs, such as farmers who use them as guards or herders, generally will not touch them. In June 2002 Iran's formal head of state, Supreme Leader Ayatollah Ali Khamene'i, decreed a ban on public dogwalking and even the sale of dogs, as being "offensive to the sensitivities of Muslims."

When one of the most significant living legal thinkers in the Islamic world, Kuwaiti-born Khaled Abou El-Fadl, recently admitted that he is a devoted dog lover and began combing through the Classical law books to see whether Muslim anti-dog views were supported by the texts, reaction from conservative Muslims was extreme, even amounting to death threats.[65] Nevertheless, as a result of his research, Abou El-Fadl determined that the ḥadīths used to justify aversion to dogs were highly questionable and perhaps spurious.[66]

Conclusion

It can be said today that although traditional attitudes among Muslims toward nonhuman animals remain unchanged in most cases, new influences and emerging global concerns may bring about large-scale shifts in the years to come, especially as environmental protection movements raise awareness of human dependence on nonhuman actors within the earth's complex ecosystems. While the number of Muslims who think in such terms today is small, it is growing; and ways of conceptualizing human relations with nonhuman animals are emerging which are both new and relevant to contemporary needs, yet succeed in keeping within the established framework of Islamic thought.

NOTES

1. See the discussion by Marshall Hodgson in *The Venture of Islam: Conscience and History in a World Civilization, vol. 1: the Classical Age of Islam* (Chicago: University of Chicago Press, 1974), pp. 57–60.

2. The notion appears to derive from that of possessing life, *haya(t)* (cf. Hebrew *chayah*).

3. For the life (*al-hayawāt*) of this world is nothing but a passing delight and a play—whereas, behold, the realm of the hereafter is indeed the only life (*al-hayawān*). (29:64)

4. Qur'ān, 2:159, 164; 24:44–45; 31:9–10; 42:29; 43:11–12; 45:3–4; and 51:49 (Muhammad Asad version).

5. Ibid., 27:16.

6. Ch. Pellat, "Hayawān," *Encyclopedia of Islam*, new edition (Leiden: Brill, 1971–), 3:305.

7. For example, 5:102–103; 6:139.

8. Qur'ān, 5:65; 2:61, 65.

9. Ibid., 22:65.

10. Ibid., 2:30; 6:165.

11. But see the critique of the stewardship defini-

tion in Jafar Sheikh Idris, "Is Man the Viceregent of God?" *Journal of Islamic Studies* 1, no.1 (1990): 99–110.

12. Qur'ān, 55:10.

13. Ibid., 7:73.

14. Ibid., 16:5–8. I have slightly corrected Asad's translation.

15. Ibid., 17:44; 22:18; 24:41.

16. Ibid., 6:38.

17. Ibid., 35:24.

18. Ibn Hazm, *Al Fisāl fi' l-Milāl wa l-Ahwa'wa n-Nihāl,* 5 vols., (Cairo: Yutlab min Muhammad Ali Subayh, 1964), 1:69.

19. Qur'ān, 11:6.

20. Ibid., 55:10.

21. Ibid., 16:68.

22. Al-Hafiz B. A. Masri, *Islamic Concern for Animals* (Petersfield, UK: The Athene Trust, 1987), p. 4.

23. Qur'ān, 52:22, 56:21.

24. Ibid., 5:1; see also 6:145; 16:5, 66; 40:79; and elsewhere.

25. Ibid., 5:3; see also 2:173 and 6:145.

26. Ibid., 16:115; see also 2:173 and 6:145.

27. Sahīh Muslim, 2/11, "Slaying," 10:739.

28. Ibid., Bukhārī, 2:106.

29. Musnad of Ibn Hanbal. Muḥammad adds that some of these animals were better than those who rode them, since they remembered God more.

30. Nasa'i, 7:206, 239.

31. Cited in Masri, *Islamic Concern for Animals,* p. 4.

32. Sahīh Muslim, trans. A. Siddiqi, 4 vols. (Lahore: Muhammad Ashraf), 4:1215, 1381.

33. Ibid., Muslim, 4:1216.

34. G. H. Bousquet, "Des animaux et de leur traitement selon le Judaïsme, le Christianisme et l'Islam," *Studia Islamica* 9, no. 1 (1958), p. 41. These ḥadīths are retold in a recent book for Muslim children, *Love All Creatures* by M. S. Kayani (Leicester: The Islamic Foundation, 1997 [1981]).

35. 'Izz al-din ibn 'Abd al salam, *Qawā'id al-Ahkām fī Masālih al Anām* (Damascus: Dar al-Tabba, 1992); cited in Mawil Izzi Dien, *The Environmental Dimensions of Islam* (Cambridge: Lutterworth, 2000), p. 46.

36. Ibid., 91:13.

37. James L., Wescoat, Jr., "The 'Right of Thirst' for Animals in Islamic Law: A Comparative Approach," *Environment and Planning D: Society and Space* 13 (1995): 638.

38. *Qawā'id al-ahkām fī masālih al anām,* cited in Izzi Dien, *Environmental Dimensions,* p. 146.

39. Geert Jan van Gelder, *Of Dishes and Discourse: Classical Arabic Interpretations of Food* (Richmond: Curzon, 2000), p. 88. I am grateful to Jonathan Benthall for suggesting this reference.

40. Peter Singer defines speciesism as "a prejudice or attitude of bias toward the interests of members of one's own species and against those of members of other species." (Peter Singer, *Animal Liberation: A New Ethics for Our Treatment of Animals* (New York: Random House, 1975), p. 7.

41. Jalal ad-Din Rumi, *Mathnawī al-ma'anawī,* trans. R. A. Nicholson, *The Mathnawi of Jalalu'ddin Rumi,* 5 vols. (London: Luzac, 1925–40), 1:2291–6.

42. The reference is to Qur'ān, 18:17–21.

43. Rumi, *Mathnawī al-ma'anawī,* 5:2008–11.

44. Ibid., 3:3901–2.

45. Farid ad-Din 'Attar, *Tazkirat al-Awliyā,* tr. Paul Losensky and Michael Sells, in Michael Sells, *Early Islamic Mysticism* (Mahwah: Paulist Press, 1996), p. 160.

46. Qushayri, cited in Emile Dermenghem, *La culte des saints dans l'Islam Maghrebin* (Paris: Gallimard, 1954), p. 100.

47. Margaret Smith, *The Way of the Mystics* (New York: Oxford University Press, 1978), pp. 154, 162.

48. Annemarie Schimmel, *Mystical Dimensions of Islam* (Chapel Hill, North Carolina: University of North Carolina Press, 1975), pp. 348, 358.

49. Dermenghem, *La culte des saints,* pp. 97, 101.

50. Ramsey Wood, *Kalila and Dimna* (Rochester, VT: Inner Traditions, 1986).

51. Abi Uthman Amr ibn Badr al-Jahiz, *Kitāb al-hayawān,* 4 vols., (Beirut: Dar al-kutub al-'ilmiyya, 1998).

52. Muhammad ibn Musa al-Damiri, *Al-Damiri's Hayat al-hayawān al-kubra: A Zoological Lexicon,* trans. A.S.G. Jayakar (London: Luzac, 1906–1908).

53. Masri, *Islamic Concern for Animals,* p. vii.

54. Ibid., p. 17.

55. Al-Hafiz B.A. Masri, "Animal Experimentation: The Muslim Viewpoint," in *Animal Sacrifices: Religious Perspectives on the Use of Animals in Science,* ed. Tom Regan (Philadelphia: Temple University Press, 1986), p. 192.

56. Bediüzzaman Said Nursi, *Latif Nükteler* (Istanbul: Sözler Yayýnevi, 1988), pp. 5–11. English trans. in *The Flashes Collection* (Istanbul: Sözler Publications, 1995), pp. 339–43. I am grateful to Ibrahim Özdemir for alerting me to this and the following reference.

57. Nursi, *The Flashes Collection,* pp. 384–85.

58. M.R. Bawa Muhaiyadeen, *Come to the Secret Garden: Sufi Tales of Wisdom* (Philadelphia: Fellowship Press, 1985), p. 26.

59. Izzi Dien, *Environmental Dimensions,* p. 146.

60. I have suggested elsewhere, however, that in light of the many demonstrable negative effects on humans of producing meat industrially—including not only human health but also hunger, given the inefficiency of meat versus grains in making food calories available for human consumption—the Islamic emphasis on social justice has implications for meat eating that Muslims may begin to explore in the future, perhaps through applying the principle of "the public good" (*maslaha*). See Richard C. Foltz, "Is Vegetarianism Un-Islamic?" *Studies in Contemporary Islam* 3, no. 1 (2001): 53–54.

61. The site IslamicConcern.com contains links to many of these other sites.

62. Dr. Shahid Athar of Indiana University Medical School, for example, writes, "There is no doubt that a vegetarian diet is healthier and beneficial to health in lowering weight, blood pressure, cholesterol, and blood sugar." (http://www.islamicconcern.com/comments.asp)

63. A list of organizations can be found at the Islamic Concern site under the "Resources" section.

64. The Hanafi school of law, more lenient than the others in many respects, does not have this restriction.

65. Teresa Watanabe, "Battling Islamic Puritans," *Los Angeles Times* (January 2, 2002), p. A1.

66. Even a millennium ago, al-Jahiz argued that the ḥadīths about killing dogs referred to specific cases and not general ones.

The Case of the Animals Versus Man:

Toward an Ecology of Being

ZAYN KASSAM

A fascinating text that my students and I read in my Islamic Philosophy course tells of how at first, when the people of the race of Adam were few in number, they lived in fear, hiding from the many wild animals and beasts of prey. However, as the population grew they built cities and settled on the plains; they enslaved cattle and beasts and used them for their own purposes such as riding, hauling, plowing, and threshing; they "wore them out in service, imposing work beyond their powers, and checked them from seeking their own ends."[1] In presenting their case the speaker for the animals, the mule, states that humans "forced us to these things under duress, with beatings, bludgeoning, and every kind of torture and chastisement our whole lives long."[2] Some animals—the wild asses, gazelles, beasts of prey, and wild creatures and birds— were able to escape enslavement by the race of Adam by fleeing to deserts, forests and glens.

Some of the animals retreated to an island in the midst of the Green Sea. When human survivors of a shipwreck arrived, and duly set about forcing the animals into their service (for they believed that animals were their slaves) the animals appealed to the King of the Jinn, asking him to adjudicate their complaints against the humans. That adjudication will be the subject of this chapter. In keeping with the theme of this book, the text presupposes an epistemological communion of subjects in which, as Thomas Berry remarks, we once had an intimacy with "the larger community of life" in the universe. While we have now acculturated ourselves to a "use" model in our relationship to nonhuman living creatures, re-envisioning a collaborative and complementary model of mutual co-existence might entail our being able to enter into conversation with nonhuman animals. Doing so would allow us to understand more keenly the impact of our exploitative and subjugating relationships upon the self-fulfillment of all life forms that is in consonance ("our proper role") with what Berry terms the "larger purposes of the universe." To quote Berry:

We are ourselves only to the extent of our unity with the universe to which we belong and in which alone we discover our fulfillment. Intimacy exists only in terms of wonder, admiration, and emotional sympathy when beings give themselves to each other in a single psychic embrace, an embrace in which each mode of being experiences its fulfillment.

The text under consideration here imaginatively explores how the animals might make a case against the human employment of a use model; thus, while a communion of subjects characterized by intimacy is Berry's aim and, we might suppose, the aim of the animals in our tenth-century text, the epistemic communion offered by the text through which we may come to understand the animals' point of view is a step in that direction, however unsatisfying the ultimate conclusion may be to modern consciousness.

This text details the arguments put forth by the animals and the humans regarding the maltreatment the former have received at the hands of the latter, and the latter's belief that enslavement of animals was one of the privileges accorded to them. The text was authored sometime during the latter half of the tenth century by a group of thinkers whose identities are known but whose particular Muslim sectarian affiliations, if any, are still in dispute.[3] The group identifies itself simply as the Ikhwān al-Ṣafā', or the Brethren of Purity, and is famed for its encyclopedic work divided into four parts, which together number fifty-two epistles ranging in scope from discussions of mathematics, physics, psychology, law, theology, and religion. *The Case of the Animals versus Man*, the particular text under discussion here (henceforth referred to as *The Case*), is found in the eighth epistle of the second section on Physics under the title "On the Generation of Animals and their Kinds."

The Ikhwān merit our attention for several reasons. Their writings have been referred to as eclectic in their adoption of a wide-ranging

number of resources, summarized and analyzed by I. R. Netton, who investigates the adoption of Pythagorean, Platonic, Aristotelian, and Neoplatonic elements by the Ikhwān. Another extremely influential source is identified as the *Corpus Hermeticum* along with the *Saturnalia* of Macrobius (fl. c. 400 CE), and this is in part where the brilliance of the Ikhwān lies: that the writers did not feel that knowledge was the true preserve of any one civilization or culture, a remarkably modern view. Netton also investigates Christian and Jewish influences found in their work, and argues that the Ikhwān drew upon Persian, Sanskrit, Buddhist, Zoroastrian and Manichaean literatures as well. Eclectic indeed. But were they uncritical? Netton suggests that the Middle Eastern milieu in which these authors from Baṣra wrote was noted for its diversity of thought; a milieu that was multicultural, multireligious, and multilinguistic in the manner of our own time. The Ikhwān wrote their work not to advance any sectarian or particular notion of Islam, but rather to advance their own philosophy based on the universal potential of the attainment of purity (hence their name, Ikhwān al-Ṣafā', the Brethren of Purity), for which knowledge from any source could be drawn upon with appropriate modifications as necessary in order to realize the goal of eternal subsistence in a beatific state.[4] In this regard, according to their own testimony, the Ikhwān identify their sources as the following:

We have drawn our knowledge from four books. The first is composed of the mathematical and natural sciences established by the sages and philosophers. The second consists of the revealed books of the Torah, the Gospels and the Quran and the other Tablets brought by the prophets through angelic Revelation. The third is the books of Nature which are the ideas (*ṣuwar*) in the Platonic sense of the forms (*ashkāl*) of creatures actually existing, from the composition of the celestial spheres, the division of the Zodiac, the movement of the stars, and so on ... to the transformation of the elements, the production of the members of the mineral, plant and animal kingdoms and the rich variety of human industry. ... The fourth consists of the Divine books which touch only the purified men and which are the angels in intimacy with the chosen beings, the noble and the purified souls. ...[5]

While much more research needs to be undertaken with regard to the Ikhwān's sources and the mode of their appropriation of these along with their acceptance or rejection of particular ideas, it is apparent also that the identity of the texts constituting the fourth category, that of the "purified men," needs to be further explored. Suffice it here to say that the Ikhwān were ecumenical in their use of discourses not limited to those generated by Muslims and were willing to consider knowledge and its production as a divinely generated activity cutting across religious and cultural boundaries. Indeed, Seyyed Hossein Nasr goes so far as to advance the remark that the Ikhwān's attitude is that one Truth underlies all things, a remark consonant with Nasr's own position as a perennialist thinker. Nasr continues,

> ... If Scripture or angelic vision can be here a source of the knowledge of the cosmos, it is because as yet the distinction between Nature and Supernature has not been made absolute. One may say that for the Ikhwān the supernatural has a "natural" aspect, just as the natural has a "supernatural" aspect."[6]

Because there is clearly no room in this chapter to explore the many interesting dimensions of the Ikhwān's attempt to draw upon all sources at their disposal—even if we knew what these were—I will present only very briefly, and largely in expository fashion, their deliberations regarding the status of animals. In preface, we must note two lines of thought, one stemming from Platonic and Neoplatonic ontological conceptualizations that place the animal world somewhere below the mid-point in the hierarchy or chain of being that comprises ensouled creatures, and the other stemming from Scripture that gives humans domination over animals. In the first, while humans, although animals, are demarcated from other animals by virtue of their capacity for rational discourse, they are also considered to be farther along the ladder of creation and, while embodied, much closer to the angels in the hierarchy of being. Thus, animals are conceptualized in the legacy of works left behind by the Greeks as part of the natural world but inferior to human beings. In a somewhat different manner, the same point is made by religious discourses such as those found in Genesis 1:26: "Then God said, "Let us make humankind in our image, according to our likeness; and let them have dominion over the fish of the sea, and over the birds of the air, and over the cattle, and over all the wild animals of the earth, and over every creeping thing that creeps upon the earth." To this domination are coupled fear and dread as in Genesis 9:2: "The fear and dread of you shall rest on every animal of the earth, and on every bird of the air, on everything that creeps on the ground, and on all the fish of the sea; into your hand they are delivered." To these Genesis texts, one may add Qur'ān 22:36: "Thus have We made them (sacrificial camels) subject unto you, that haply ye may give thanks" as well as other verses that testify that God provides livestock for the use, shelter, and nourishment of humans. While the note of domination is struck more strongly in the Genesis texts than in the Qur'ānic texts, the "there-for-your-use" dispensation of the Qur'ān has largely been understood as a rationale for domination, albeit in a humane manner, in the Muslim traditions, commentarial, and legal (hadīth, tafsīr, and fiqh) literature.[7] Thus the decks are stacked against the animals from both the philosophical and the scriptural traditions, and while the Ikhwān are ultimately unable to overturn the rationale of domination, they do introduce into the discussion the ethics of care incumbent upon those who have need of, utility for, and dominion over other life forms, evoking Leopold's land ethic as articulated by Berry. It is to a discussion of *The Case* that we now turn.

The Case opens with the King of the Jinn requesting the speaker for the humans for evidence and proof to substantiate the human claim that all animals are their slaves. The human in his response provides both religious texts and rational proofs to substantiate his claim, referring to verses in the Qur'ān, the Torah, and the Gospels, which clearly relate that animals were created for the use of humankind, and further, that the animals were ordained to be slaves of humans. While verses from the Torah and the Gospels are not cited here, three Qur'ānic verses are:

Cattle He created for you, whence you have warmth and many benefits. You eat of them and find them fair when you bring them home to rest or drive them out to pasture.

Q 16:5–6

You are carried upon them and upon ships.

Q 23:22

… horses, mules, and asses for riding and for splendor.

Q 16:8

At this, the mule, the speaker for the beasts, responds that God, the One, the Unique, the Ever-Abiding and the Eternal, created through His divine Word, the command "Be!" The mule reports that God made a light shine forth, and from this light created the fire and water and the constellations and the stars, the firmament, the earth, the mountains, beings such as the archangels, the cherubim, the jinn, living things such as animals and plants, and humans. All these were provided as a kindness and blessing for humankind, for surely the sun, the moon, the wind and the clouds could not be considered slaves to humans! Similarly, God intended humans to live in posterity on earth, "to inhabit it, not to lay it waste, to care for the animals and profit by them, but not to mistreat or oppress them"[8] and surely, continues the mule, verses from scriptural texts say nothing about humans as masters and animals as slaves, for they point only to the kindness and blessings showered by God upon humans. Indeed, when one examines the full Qur'ānic text surrounding the quotations above, one is able to see that the point being made in all of these is God's adaptation of nature in service of human needs as a form of divine grace and generosity to humanity.[9]

Since it is clear that the two warring parties in *The Case* interpret Scripture differently, suggesting that scriptural texts such as the Qur'ān, revealed in the seventh century, were by no means considered univocal in their meaning in the tenth century, the King of the Jinn decides to admit as evidence only those claims which are grounded solidly in definite proof. This move is critical not for the removal of scriptural evidence as first appears to be the case, but rather, for the inclusion of rational discourse, preferably philosophically grounded, in the understanding of God's intentions—bearing in mind that the ninth to the twelfth centuries saw the efflorescence of the intellectual sciences in the Islamic world sparked primarily but not solely through increased familiarity with Greek philosophical works. Indeed, the Ikhwān are considered to be Neoplatonists in their inclination. We see here, then, a movement from the literal understanding of Scripture to a more informed, interpretative mode of hermeneutics that called upon the leading sciences of the day for its execution. Accordingly, the humans then claim that "Our beautiful form, the erect construction of our bodies, our upright carriage, our keen senses, the subtlety of our discrimination, our keen minds and superior intellects all indicate that we are masters and they slaves to us."[10] The animals easily dispense with this objection by claiming that from the point of view of natural science, the form of humans is better for them in order to make it easier for them to meet their own particular needs, while the forms of animals are better for them in order for them to do the same, that is, form is relative to function, and each species has a form most suitable for its ecological purpose.

So the humans move to a symbolic understanding of what it means to be upright, and the justification proffered for human superiority by argument of form is that all supralunary or celestial conditions had been rendered perfect by God on the day that Adam was created, thus resulting in a form that was the finest and had the most perfect constitution. The forms of the animals, on the other hand, are presented by the humans as being full of irregularities such as the big ears sprouted by the small-bodied rabbit, the tiny eyes of the massive elephant, and so forth. To this the animals retort that the humans have missed the beauty and wisdom inherent in the creation of animals by a wise Creator who alone knew the reason and purpose for the forms given to them.

Thus, the argument of the finest form advanced by the humans is deftly turned by the animals into an inadmissible human questioning of the wisdom of the Creator reminiscent of Job 39 and 40 where the Lord said to Job: "Is it by your wisdom that the hawk soars, and spreads its wings toward the south? ... Shall a faultfinder contend with the Almighty?" In exploration of the wisdom of the Creator, the animals advance the argument that beauty is relative to function; each species has the precise proportions and limbs it requires to make it able efficiently to seek the beneficial and shun the harmful, thereby making the point, further substantiated in the Qur'ān, that God guides all things, as reported by Moses in Qur'ān 20:52: "Our Lord who gave its nature to every thing and guided all things."

The arguments the humans make in order to justify their master-slave relationship with the animals moves on to the matter of property. The humans now furnish as evidence of their lordship the fact that they buy and sell animals, feed and water them, shelter them, protect domestic herds from wild beasts, treat their illnesses, train them, and put them out to pasture when they are old—all this, say the humans, they do out of kindness and compassion, just as masters and owners do for their servants and property.

While the kindness and compassion of masters and owners might be a laudable ideal to strive for, the animals reassure the King of the Jinn that the record shows otherwise. Greeks and Persians enslave each other when they war, they argue to the monarch; who then is master, and who slave? Is enslavement surely nothing other than the turn of fortune? And as for all the sustenance, shelter, and ministering that humans undertake on behalf of captured animals, is not all that motivated by fear of loss of profit and the many benefits that accrue to humans from the use of animals, rather than by genuine kindness and compassion? And where is the mercy and compassion of humans to be found in the brutal beatings, the heavy burdens, the separation of kids and lambs from their mothers almost at birth, the slaughtering of these for food? All of these, they argue, are in direct contradiction of the Qur'ānic injunction to "show compassion and indulgence."[11]

It is surprising to find issues such as these, which perturb us greatly today, articulated in the tenth century. Even more surprising is the lament of the ass who suggests that if physical torture were not enough, humans also insult each other by reviling their sisters with crude expressions referring to the sexual genitalia of both the ass and the woman in conjunction. Once again this resonates with our current policing of language to remove inscribed assumptions of gender and race.

The pig then proceeds to lodge his particular complaint, which is that he is confused. Some revile him, some use his meat in celebration, some consider his fecundity to be a blessing, and some use his products for medicinal purposes. To introduce such a wide-ranging understanding of the pig's stature in different societies was a remarkable commentary to place before tenth-century Muslim audiences, for whom the flesh of the pig was (and is) considered unlawful.

The assembly is adjourned at this point, and King of the Jinn takes counsel with his fellow jinn. What is to be done if the case is adjudicated in favor of the animals? Who will purchase their freedom? And how will humans, who rely so heavily on the labor and products of the animals, continue to subsist? Will that not cause further enmity between the humans and the jinn, who will be implicated in the king's finding in favor of the animals? And what if the arguments of the humans, who are eloquent by nature, overcome the objections of the animals? What will be the fate of the animals?

At this point, the King of the Jinn remarks that the beasts must have patience in captivity until the cycle of the epoch is completed, in consonance with the idea favored in circles such as those of the Ismāʿīlīs that new cycles are ushered in at every epoch.[12] The present cycle is the epoch of the Biblical Adam, which would culminate with the Mahdi, or the Guide, who would vanquish lawlessness and restore order to the world before it entered a new cycle. The previous cycle had been that before the creation of the human Adam, when the earth was inhabited by the jinn, followed by a cycle in which God sent the angels to live on earth and drive the jinn to the farthest corners, and in which Lucifer was captured by the angels and placed under their tutelage until he rose to become a chief among them. At the end of that cycle, a new cycle was ushered in during which God created the first human and prophet, Adam, and each prophet after him initiated a new mini-cycle within the larger cycle of Adam. At the end of this cycle, then, which is the mini-cycle of Muḥammad, the seal of the prophets, the animals would be brought deliverance "just as He [God] delivered the House of Israel from the oppression of the House of Pharaoh, the House of David from the tyranny of Nebuchadnezzar,"[13] and so forth.

Meanwhile discussions are taking place among the humans too. Since they cannot do without the animals, they resolve to accept only the judgment to improve the condition of the animals they have enslaved, "lighten their load, and show more kindness and compassion toward them, for they are flesh and blood like us, and they feel and suffer. We have no superiority to them in the eyes of God for which He was rewarding us when He made them subject to us,"[14] thus making the remarkable admission that the subjugation of animals to humans was not by virtue of human superiority in God's eyes, but a signal of His grace toward humans—the animals' contention precisely.

Meanwhile the animals too have gathered, and recognize that although the humans are far more eloquent and articulate than they, they must present their case clearly and fluently. They decide to ask each of the six classes of animals to present their case predicated on the principle that each kind has its own virtues. The discussions among each of the classes of animals are a veritable mine of information about each in addition to discussions of cosmology and the natural order, as well as providing moral instruction. With respect to the latter, for example, the legendary griffin relates that he uses his massive body in order to guide ships safely back to shore in his attempt to please God and to show gratitude for his great frame,[15] or in another instance, the crocodile recommends the frog, who is both an aquatic and a land animal, as best suited to represent the class of aquatic animals by virtue of his constant singing of God's praises and his intervention when Nimrod cast Abraham into the fire and the frog both quenched the fire with water and sated Abraham's thirst, or when he helped Moses against the Pharaoh.[16]

Once the animals have chosen their representatives, the combined assembly meets and the King of the Jinn calls upon humans of different climes and races to extol their virtues. The pattern is set: a human sets forth what is laudable in his clime and culture and tradition, and a member of the jinn points out a counter-argument.

It could be argued that the Ikhwān utilized the strategy of placing in the words of these humans and animals viewpoints that might not be acceptable to the orthodox and legalistically minded Muslim, in order both to instruct and to critique. Thus the Greek praises God, who sounds very much like the Neoplatonic *ontos* in the description given by the Greek: "God, who in bounty and grace caused the Active Intellect to flow forth from His goodness, source of science and mysteries, light of lights and element of all spirits. ... who produced mind from His light, and out of His Self-perception, the universal celestial soul, possessed of movements and source of all blessings and life."[17] The Greek then goes on to boast that God made his race kings because of their natural virtue, their powerful minds, their keen discernment, their deep understanding of the great many sciences and arts of medicine, astronomy, mathematics, and metaphysics to name a few.

To this an outspoken jinni pointedly asks whether the Greeks would have acquired what he boasts of had it not been for the wisdom of the Israelites and the Egyptians that the Greeks transplanted into their own land and then claimed sole credit for.[18] This by no means indicates a rejection of Greek wisdom, for the Ikhwān both appropriated and modulated Hellenistic thought for their own purposes, but is, rather, a surprisingly postmodern critique reminding those who produce hegemonic discourses that they, too, have borrowed from others.

Attention then turns to the animal representatives, whose arguments are noteworthy. The bee, representative of the swarming creatures, counters the human assumption that only humans have sciences and knowledge, thought and judgment, and the capacity to direct and govern by stating that in fact the capacity of the bees in all these arenas is far more judicious and exacting. The bee, after elaborating upon the gift of divine inspiration allotted to the bee in Qur'ān 16:68 talks about the social organization and the industriousness of swarming creatures such as the bees, the ants, and the silkworms.[19] Further, the Lord has blessed bees with skill and knowledge of the geometrical arts, which they utilize in building their dwellings; the ability to take from every flower and fruit and to produce what is healing for humankind. Further, the form of the bee, the beauty of his mores, and the excellence of his way of life are made "a sign for those who reflect."[20]

In response to the humans' contention that they are superior by virtue of their ability to partake of excellent food, such as the flesh of the fruit rather than its rind, and foods of a cooked variety, the nightingale argues that no human food is obtained without much toil on their parts, while for animals the food is procured "without toil to our bodies, trouble to our souls, or fatigue to our spirits," nor do animals suffer the consequences of disease visited upon humans who do not eat a balanced diet or are given to gluttony. Indeed, disease is visited upon animals largely as a result of contact with humans.[21]

A human, identified as a Hebrew from Iraq, then counters with the statement that the superiority of humans lies in the fact that humans have been ennobled with prophecy and inspiration, divine laws, purification, and prayer. The nightingale points out that such measures are necessary for those in error, those who dispute God's lordship, those who are oblivious of His goodness and neglectful of remembrance of Him, and those who are forgetful of their covenant with Him. The animals, however, "are free of all these things, for we acknowledge our Lord, believe in Him, submit to Him and proclaim His unity without doubt or hesitation."[22] Further arguments are submitted detailing the evil the human race visits not only on animals but on itself as well, so much so that the best of humans are forced to flee to the dwelling places of animals, not because they share their form, but because they are akin to them "in character, probity, uprightness, and blamelessness,"[23] causing the humans in the assembly to hang their heads in shame.

The point advanced thus far is that the Ikhwān have shown, through appeals to what was scientifically then known about animals and their constitutions, habitats, habits, and organization, that there is not much that humans can boast about if they wish to make a claim of superiority over the animals in order to defend their assertion of dominance and consequent enslavement. With respect to divine inspiration, high moral virtues, hymns of praise, prayers of gratitude, assistance to humans and prophets, the animals again score high points, whereas humans are guilty in every regard of neglect, error of judgment, carrying out of evil deeds, and gluttony. It sounds too good to be true, for the arguments in favor of the animals seem to hold sway in the court.

A sage from among the jinn adds the argument that God out of His mercy, compassion, and grace entrusted the angels, whose chief is the universal human rational soul, with the care and welfare of the children of Adam. This somewhat cryptic statement is rather surprising since in most contemporaneous Muslim Neoplatonic formulations the human soul is conceived to be either a trace or a particularized form of the Universal Soul (*Nafs-i Kull*) that controls the celestial spheres and all that lies beneath them, including the sublunary world. Further investigation is needed to determine whether the Ikhwān meant the individuated human soul that has as its origin the Universal Soul in their usage of the shorthand phrase "universal human rational soul." In any case, this human soul's purpose is to recollect, in a manner reminiscent of Plato, where it comes from, and the soul holds the key to eternal beatitude once it has been purified during its earthly journey and returns to its source.[24]

Both this universal rational soul and the corporeal form of humans remain in the seed of Adam and are transmitted to each succeeding generation. However, although it is by means of this soul that the children of Adam grow and develop, are held morally accountable, return to the Universal Soul, and with it will be resurrected on Judgment Day to paradise, their heedlessness and hypocritical observation of revealed guidance, through which angels communicate with humans, yields them little result.[25] Further,

adds this sage, in the larger scheme of being, humans and animals are the "least of creatures in number and the lowest in rank and status," being far outweighed both in number and status by the multiplicity of subtle spiritual creatures, the angelic presences, who dwell within the tiers of the heavens.[26]

Just when it appears that the humans have lost their case and been humbled in the process, a human orator from the Hijāz, from the sacred Muslim precincts of Mecca and Medina, announces the promise made by the divine Sovereign: that humans alone of all the species will be resurrected and reckoned with on the Day of Judgment. No, the animals protest, for you [humans] may equally go to hell as you may to paradise! In either case, says the Hijāzī, "we ... survive eternally and immortally."

The pleading of the case is now at an end. The King of the Jinn delivers his judgment: "All the animals were to be subject to the commands and prohibitions of the humans and were to be subservient to the humans and accept their direction contentedly and return in peace and security under God's protection."[27]

Disappointed as my students—and we—are with this adjudication, the outcome had been foretold when the council of Jinn could not determine pragmatically how it could be that humans could do without the animals. And it is a surprising conclusion, given the fact that as Muslims, one would have expected the Ikhwān to be intimately familiar with the Qur'ānic text that relates in 6:38: "There is not an animal in the earth, nor a flying creature flying on two wings, but they are peoples like unto you. We have neglected nothing in the Book [of our decrees]. Then unto their Lord they will be gathered," which suggests that animals will be taken up into their Lord just as humans will be. Yet, at the same time, the Hellenization of the Ikhwān brought with it an ontological scheme in which humans were perceived as positioned on the periphery between the angelic orders and the three natural kingdoms comprising the nonhuman animal, the vegetal, and the mineral.

Although at first glance it seems that the purpose of the text is fulfilled when the humans come to a heightened understanding of their responsibility toward God's creatures, while the animals, mindful of the interdependent relationship between themselves and humans come to agree among themselves to settle for human promises to treat the animals better, the matter does not end there. If *The Case* serves as a forum through which the Ikhwān communicated their teaching, then in consonance with the Ikhwān's unified ontology, according to which the domain of Nature is an act of the Universal Soul, and the study of Nature is in actuality a study of the divine providence by which the individual soul can recollect its true home, then much more has been accomplished. Along the journey of understanding, the Ikhwān, through these proceedings, have addressed the issue of what it truly means to be human: a state in which one is on intimate terms with the universe that sustains life, life which is comported with a sense of wonder, gratitude, compassion and care.

NOTES

1. Ikhwān al-Ṣafāʾ, *The Case of the Animals versus Man Before the King of the Jinn: A Tenth-century Ecological Fable of the Pure Brethren of Basra,* transl., intro., comment., Lenn Evan Goodman (Boston: Twayne Publishers, 1978) (henceforth, *The Case*), p. 51.

2. *The Case,* p. 55.

3. Lenn Evan Goodman, for example, suggests that "The Ikhwān rejected and ridiculed all forms of denominationalism and factionalism. They regarded religious sects as the expression of human ignorance and deficiency ... and sectarianism as an expression for the lust for power. They expressly state that the injection of politics into religion (no matter how necessary their collaboration may be) is the cause of religion turning from its true goal to the quest for worldly dominance" in *The Case*, p. 43. Susanne Diwald in her German translation of the third part on Soul and Intellect titled, *Arabische Philosophie und Wissenschaft in der Enzyklopadie Kitab Ikhwan as-safa': Die Lehre von Seele und Intellekt* (Wiesbaden: Otto Harrassowitz, 1975), pp. 22–27 considers the work to be of orthodox Sufi provenance although the references to the theory of imāmate puzzle her sufficiently for her to state that she will revisit the question again. Geo Widengren in his article titled, "The Gnostic Technical Language in the Rasāʾil Ikhwān al-Ṣafāʾ" in *Actas IV congresso de estudios árabes e islâmicos* (1968): 181–203, at p. 182, considers the encyclopedia to be "the expression of the true Qarmatian spirit," which he characterizes as having adapted Neo-Platonic, Pseudo-Hermetic and Sabian ideas, along with a political theory subscribing to ʿĀlī and his descendants or as having Shiʿī ideology. The authorship of the Rasāʾil has also been attributed to the Muʿtazilites, the Ismāʿīlīs, and I. R. Netton reiterates the view that cases have been made in favor of several single authors, or for a group of several authors, who lived in Baṣra. See I. R. Netton, *Muslim Neoplatonists: An Introduction to the Thought of the Brethren of Purity* (Edinburgh: Edinburgh University Press, 1991), pp. 3–4. In any case, many of the questions raised by A. L. Tibawi in 1955 have still not been resolved or adequately studied; see A. L. Tibawi, "Ikhwān al-Ṣafāʾ and their Rasāʾil: a Critical Review of a Century and a Half of Research," *Islamic Quarterly,* 2, no. 1 (1955): 28–46. See also Seyyed Hossein Nasr, *An Introduction to Islamic Cosmological Doctrines* (Albany: State University of New York Press, 1993), pp. 25–40, makes the observation that although it is difficult to resolve the problematic issues of authorship and affiliation, it is clear that the Ikhwān do not fall squarely into the realm of the rationalist theologians such as the Muʿtazilites, nor the logical Aristotelians, known as the Mashshāʾiyūn. Their import lies, rather, in the tremendous influence their works exercised over the Shīʿah, both Twelver and Ismāʿīlī, philosophers such as Ibn Sīnā, and theologian-Sufis of the stature of al-Ghazālī,

and of course, the works of the Ikhwān have continued to be read, in several languages, to the present day. It should be noted here that although Netton does not consider the Ikhwān to be Ismāʿīlī in persuasion, arguing that this is too narrow a definition for them, aside from being inaccurate, he also views Ismāʿīlī thought as having been one of the sources to which the Ikhwān appealed. See Netton, *Muslim Neoplatonists*, p. 107. The late Henry Corbin, a leading exponent of Ismāʿīlī thought, positioned the Ikhwān squarely as embodying Ismāʿīlī thought in their writings, a view that is shared by many eminent scholars in the field; however, equally prominent scholars have argued that while there may be a shared universe of ideas, the Ikhwān cannot be categorized as such.

4. See Netton, *Muslim Neoplatonists*, pp. 105–8.

5. Translation quoted by Seyyed Hossein Nasr, *An Introduction to Islamic Cosmological Doctrines*, p. 39.

6. Ibid., p. 40.

7. Although full-length studies of Muslim discourses pertaining to animal treatment are needed, websites such as *http://www.islamset.com/env/* promote both the view that animals should be treated kindly and the view that animals are created for human service.

8. *The Case*, p. 54.

9. Ibid., pp. 205–6, n. 15.

10. Ibid., p. 56.

11. Qurʾān 24:22, revealing, as Goodman remarks in his commentary, an unusual reading of the poor to whom compassion and indulgence is to be shown as referring to the animal world. *The Case*, p. 62, n. 34.

12. For a fuller exposition of this notion, see Henry Corbin, *Cyclical Time and Ismaili Gnosis* (London: Kegan Paul International, 1983).

13. *The Case*, p. 77.

14. Ibid., p. 80.

15. Ibid., p. 104.

16. Ibid., p. 107.

17. Ibid., pp. 124–25.

18. Ibid., p. 125.

19. Qurʾān 16: 68–69: "And thy Lord inspired the bee, saying: Choose thou habitations in the hills and in the trees and in that which they thatch; / Then eat of all fruits, and follow the ways of Thy Lord made smooth (for thee). There cometh forth from their bellies a drink diverse of hues, wherein is healing for humankind. Lo! Herein is indeed a portent for people who reflect."

20. *The Case*, pp. 137–138; Qurʾān 16:69.

21. Ibid., pp. 151–52.

22. Ibid., pp. 156–57.

23. Ibid., p. 165.

24. See Nasr, *An Introduction*, pp. 102–3.

25. *The Case*, pp. 170ff.

26. Ibid., pp. 198ff.

27. Ibid., p. 202.

"Oh that I could be a bird and fly, I would rush to the Beloved"

Birds in Islamic Mystical Poetry

ALI ASANI

Sufi poets, whether writing in Arabic, Persian, Urdu, Sindhi, Gujarati, or Swahili, have been fascinated by birds. Many have regarded birds as ensouled beings who have a special relationship with God. Since they are able to fly free in the heavens, birds are perceived as having easier access to the Divine Beloved than earthbound creatures such as humans, who suffer the fate of being caged in the shell of the material body, as the famous Persian poet Hafiz explains in his verses:

> Within the egg of the body
> You are a marvellous bird—
> since you are inside the
> egg; you cannot fly
> If the body's shell should
> break, you will flap your
> wings and win the spirit.[1]

Not surprisingly many Muslim mystics would agree with the sentiments of an anonymous sixteenth-century Sufi poet who wrote in Hindi:

Oh that I could be a bird and fly
I would rush to the Beloved!

Aside from looking at birds as spiritual beings in their own right, Sufis also considered them as symbols representing the soul. For them, the flight of birds in the skies is an apt image for the ascent of the soul to the highest heaven. It is certainly true that the idea of the soul as a bird-like entity is not unique to Muslim mystics, for we can find examples of this usage in other religions, dating back to ancient Egypt. However, no other tradition of mysticism has developed as elaborate a symbolism and imagery related to soul-birds as Sufism. This essay explores some of the more important aspects of this symbolism and imagery as expressed in the various Sufi poetic traditions.

Fascination with birds among Sufi circles can be partly attributed to specific references to birds in the Qur'ān. Verse 38 of chapter 6 of the Qur'ān relates that birds and animals form communities parallel to that of humans: "There is not an animal in the earth, nor a flying creature with two wings, but they are peoples like unto you." Verse 41 in chapter 24 brings to the attention of believers that everything in creation, including "birds with wings outspread," prays to and praises one and the same God. Both verses serve to remind humans that, through the act of prayer and submission to God (*islam*), they are in fact in communion with the rest of God's creation. The latter verse, moreover, goes on to declare that each species of creation possesses its own distinctive manner of prayer and mode of praising God. While ordinary humans may not be attuned to the "languages" in which other creatures pray, another Qur'ānic verse (27:16) suggests it is possible for a select few to be graced with the comprehension of the language of the birds (*mantiq ut-tayr*). According to this verse, God taught the Prophet Solomon "the language of the birds." Muslim mystics were particularly intrigued by this fact since it suggested that Solomon, like a Sufi *shaykh* (spiritual preceptor), was endowed with a special type of esoteric knowledge through which he could decipher a language that was alien to ordinary humans. Indeed, verse 18 of the same Qur'ānic chapter indicates that Solomon's spiritual wisdom and knowledge of nonhuman languages was not limited to "bird language": he could even understand an ant who complained to him about the destruction of ant colonies by the horses of his army. Not surprisingly, being able to listen to birds and beasts and discern within their cries the praise of God came to be regarded as the sign of the spiritual adept:

Last night a bird cried out till dawn,
    ravishing my mind and
patience, my strength and thoughts.
The sound of my voice must have reached
    the ear of a sincere friend
He said, "I cannot believe that a bird's call
    could drive you so crazy."
I said, "It is contrary to human nature that
    a bird sings God's praises while I remain
    silent!"[2]

Solomon's ability to comprehend the language of the birds inspired the Persian poet Sanai (d.1131) to compose a long *qasida* or panegyric poem entitled *Tasbih at-tuyur* ("The Rosary of the Birds"). In this poem, Sanai interprets the language of each bird species, particularly its way of praising God, into human language. Thus, according to Sanai, when the stork says "*lak lak*," it is in fact praising God by saying (in Arabic) "*al-mulk lak al-amr lak*," ("Kingdom belongs to You, Command belongs to You"). Following Sanai, many Persian mystics have interpreted the pigeon's constant cooing "*ku ku*" to be its way of expressing its constant longing and searching for the Divine Beloved as it proclaims (in Persian) "Where is He? Where is He?" Similarly for Muslim mystics on the Indian subcontinent, the cries of the *papiha* bird "*piu piu*" represented its calling out (in Hindi) "The Beloved, the Beloved."

For Sufis, comprehending the language of the birds was not limited simply to deciphering their calls as they engage in worship of God. Bird songs and melodies could also be understood as the expressions of spiritual experiences of beings at various stages of spiritual development. In this regard, Sufi poets were particularly intrigued by the song of the nightingale, which they interpreted to be the lament of a yearning lover. Thus arose the most famous pair of images in Persian and Persianate-influenced mystical poetry: the yearning nightingale (*bulbul*) who sings to the rose (*gul*) in the hope of gaining its love. In innumerable poems in Persian, Turkish, Urdu, and related languages, the nightingale represents the longing soul-bird who is forever bound to the rose, the symbol of divine beauty. In as far as the nightingale never tires of singing of its love for the rose and patiently endures thorn pricks, it embodies the soul longing for eternal beauty. It is this longing that inspires the creativity manifest in the nightingale's songs and melodies.[3] For many poets, the unrequited longing of the nightingale is the highest state the soul can reach. Love-in-longing results in creativity and is, therefore, far superior than union, which brings about silence and annihilation.[4] In this sense the nightingale is the paradigm of the most perfect lover. It is for this reason that Rumi writes:

> For Heaven's sake don't talk about the rose!
> Talk about the nightingale who is separated
>   from his rose![5]

The falcon also captured the imagination of Sufi poets. Unlike the nightingale that is limited to lamenting in the rose-garden, the falcon is free to soar high in the heavens, only to return to the outstretched hand of its master when it is summoned. Playing on the double meaning of *baz*, the Persian word for falcon also means "to come back" (*baz ayad*), Rumi sees the falcon as the noble soul that returns from its earthly exile to God (the falconer) when it hears the call of His drum. Like some other Sufis, he has associated the summons that the falcon-soul hears with the words of the Quranic verse 89:27, "*Irji'i*" "Return, o soul at peace!"—words by which God commands the perfectly transformed soul to return to Him:[6]

> How should the falcon not fly from the
>   hunt towards its King
> When he hears the news "Return!" when
>   the drum is beaten?[7]

Extending this image further, Rumi proclaims that once perched back upon the divine hand from which it flew away,

> The falcon rubs its wings on the King's
>   hand
> Without tongue he says "I have sinned."[8]

Besides the nightingale and the falcon, a whole range of other birds feature prominently in Islamic mystical poetry. Peacocks, parrots, swans, crows, eagles, to name a few species, populate the *'alam-i mithal*, the "world of symbols," through which the Sufi poet accesses the hidden reality that underlies existence. The most

renowned example of a Sufi poem that makes extensive use of bird imagery is the *Mantiq ut-Tayr*, an epic written in double-rhymed verse by the Persian poet Farid ad-Din 'Attar (d. 1220). Consisting of some 4,500 verses, this work has come to be regarded as one of the classic expositions of the mystical journey and spiritual development of the soul. While the title "*Mantiq ut-Tayr*," inspired by the Quranic verse 27:16, is that by which the epic came to be popularly known, 'Attar himself called the work *Zaban-i murghan*, Persian for "language of the birds" or *Maqamat-i tuyur*, the "Stations of the Birds." The work was most probably inspired by three earlier works dealing with birds: Avicenna's *Risalat at-tayr*, a philosophical treatise in which the author discusses the journey of the soul by using as an allegory the story of a bird who, once freed from its cage by other birds, flies off on a journey to the Great King; al-Ghazali's treatise by the same name, which deals with the theme of suffering on the spiritual path;[9] and Sanai's Persian panegyric, *Tasbih ut-Tuyur*, "The Rosary of the Birds," which, as already mentioned above, attempts to interpret the calls and cries of birds as forms of praising God.

The story underlying the *Mantiq ut-Tayr* is simple: the birds of the world gather to discuss the importance of having a king and the need to find someone to govern them justly. In the course of the discussion, the hoopoe bird, famed in Islamic lore as the messenger of Prophet Solomon to Queen Sheba, declares that indeed the birds do have a king—the unique and indescribable *Simurgh*, who lives beyond the distant Mount Qaf. He invites the birds to join him in a journey to seek the *Simurgh* whom few have actually seen. The hoopoe reveals that a long time ago the mysterious *Simurgh* had let one of His colorful feathers float down into China where it created quite a stir and remains as a visible sign of His presence. This is why, the hoopoe declares, a saying attributed to the Prophet Muhammad, "Seek knowledge even if it be in China," is of special significance. The hoopoe, however, warns fellow birds that the journey to the magnificent and glorious *Simurgh* is a difficult one:

> The road is long, the sea is deep—one flies
> First buffeted by joy and then by sighs;
> If you desire this quest, give up your soul
> And make our sovereign's court your only
>   goal.[10]

One by one the birds make excuses to avoid undertaking the journey but the hoopoe responds to each excuse, usually by narrating an exemplary parable or a story. In the end, a great number of birds agree to undertake the quest, and set out for the palace with the hoopoe as their leader. On their way to Mount Qaf they traverse seven valleys, each of which represents a different stage along the path. On account of the great trials and tribulations they experience as they cross these valleys, several birds drop by the wayside. Eventually only thirty birds reach the palace of the *Simurgh,* where they are finally admitted into his court. It is here that they discover, in what is one of the most brilliant puns in mystical poetry, that they, the thirty birds, *si murgh,* are collectively none other than the *Simurgh*—a clever and innovative way of describing the unity experienced by the soul in the presence of the Divine.

Attar interprets the characteristic conduct of each bird as an indication of the status of its spiritual development or an illustration of some limiting aspect of the soul. For instance, when the hoopoe first proposes to the birds that they undertake the quest for the *Simurgh,* various birds provide reasons why they cannot join in the quest. Each bird's excuses are based on behavior considered typical of its species. Attar shows how this behavior limits its perspective and can become a hindrance to its spiritual progress. Thus in the *Mantiq ut-Tayr,* the nightingale, who in the cosmos of Persian poetry is conceived as a lover of the rose, tells the hoopoe that his true beloved is the rose from whom he cannot bear to be separated for even a second:

> My love is for the rose; I bow to her;
> From her dear presence I could never stir.
> …
> My love is here; the journey you propose
> Cannot beguile me from my life—the rose.
> It is for me she flowers; what greater bliss
> Could life provide me—anywhere—than
>   this?[11]

In his response, the hoopoe points out that the nightingale's love for the rose is superficial and transitory. The beauty of the rose, he declares, lasts only as long as it is in bloom, hence it is a fickle beloved. Alluding to the expression "the laughing of a flower" used in Persian to indicate the blossoming of a flower, the hoopoe advises the nightingale:

> Forget the rose's blush and blush for shame!
> Each spring she laughs, not *for* you, as you
>   say
> But *at* you—and has faded in a day.[12]

Contrary to the conventional portrayal of the nightingale in Persian poetry as a perfect lover, Attar perceives the nightingale as representing a being who is hopelessly attached to the superficial and transitory world, a devotion that can never result in eternal happiness.

Similarly the duck represents a being who is solely concerned with outward appearances. When asked to join the quest for the *Simurgh,* the duck tells the birds:

> Now none of you can argue with the fact
> That both in this world and the next I am
> The purest bird that ever flew or swam;
> I spread my prayer-mat out, and all the
>   time
> I clean myself of every bit of grime
> As God commands. There's no doubt in my
>   mind
> That purity like mine is hard to find.[13]

The hoopoe replies to this speech by pointing out that the duck lives in an aquatic dream and that while it boasts of its physical purity he questions whether its life is as pure and meaningful as it declares. The duck performs a lifetime of rituals, such as its constant ablutions and prayers, but is heedless of the spiritual meaning behind exoteric forms. It needs to engage in a deeper search for the spiritual truth.

As we have seen, the hoopoe served as a messenger between Solomon and Sheba. Hence it is frequently identified in poetic traditions not only as a go-between but also as one who guides the lover to the beloved. In the *Mantiq ut-Tayr,* Attar stresses the hoopoe's role as a guide in the quest for the *Simurgh.* The hoopoe shows the birds the way, points out their limitations, gives advice and encourages them to persevere on the path functioning in much the same way as a Sufi *shaykh.* Like the Sufi *shaykh,* the hoopoe possesses spiritual knowledge (*ma'rifa*) and wisdom that he has acquired by his association with Solomon:

> I come as Solomon's close friend and claim
> The matchless wisdom of that mighty
> name.
> …
> I bore his letters—back again I flew—
> Whatever secrets he divined I knew
> A prophet loved me; God has trusted me
> What other bird has such dignity?[14]

Not surprisingly, the hoopoe's role as a guide to spiritual truths is one with which Attar identifies himself closely for it is through the voice of this bird that he is able to share his spiritual insights. Just as the hoopoe shares his wisdom with the birds, Attar is able to share his wisdom with humanity. Commenting on Attar's identification with the hoopoe, Dick Davis, a translator of the *Mantiq ut-Tayr* writes:

> Attar very frequently gives the impression of merging his personality with that of the hoopoe; this is aided in Persian by the absence of punctuation, in particular quotation marks; a translator has to choose whether the hoopoe or the

author is speaking, whereas Attar need not make this decision. Though the stories are ostensibly told by the hoopoe to birds they are in reality told by Attar to men.[15]

The assimilation of Attar's personal identity with that of the hoopoe is reminiscent of the identification of several Sufi poets with the nightingale. The nightingale singing songs of lament resembles the mystic: like the nightingale, the poet composes love poems expressing yearning for a distant and inaccessible beloved and like the nightingale, the poet's creativity stems from longing. It is on account of the conflation of the poet's identity with this bird that several poets chose "nightingale" as their poetic penname. A prominent example was the Persian and Urdu Sufi poet Muhammad Nasir (d. 1758) who used "*andalib,*" another term for nightingale, as his pen-name and titled his famous work on mysticism, *Nala-yi Andalib,* "The Lament of the Nightingale." He writes:

> A hundred meadows have bloomed into
> roses from the heart of my confusion
> I am the nightingale of the painted
> garden—don't ask about my
> lamentation![16]

Perhaps the most famous example of human-bird identification in modern Muslim poetry occurs in the work of the poet-philosopher Sir Muhammad Iqbal (d. 1938), commonly identified as the "spiritual father" of the nation state of Pakistan. Among the influences impacting Iqbal's thought was the rich tradition of mysticism particularly as interpreted by Rumi. A major theme in Iqbal's reformist poetry is redefining conceptions of the human self so that its noble and spiritual nature is realized. For this purpose, Iqbal's favorite symbol is the *shahiin,* falcon or eagle, a bird with which he was so enamored that among his admirers it has become an emblem of his personality.[17] For Iqbal, the falcon is the independent spirit of humanity which is able to soar to ever-increasing heights in its creativity and the development of its potential as it searches endlessly for the Infinite Beloved. In one of his poems, which incidentally provides the lyrics of one of the most popular songs played by a contemporary Pakistani rock-band *Junoon*, Iqbal declares that the human is a falcon:

There are many more worlds beyond the
stars
There are many more tests of love
These spaces are not empty of life
Here are hundreds of more caravans [on the
move]

Do not be content with the world of the
senses
There are many more meadows and many
more nests
If one nest has been lost, do not grieve
For there are many more places to sigh and
lament about
You are a falcon, and flying is your nature
Ahead of you are many more heavens
Do not get ensnared in the unrelenting
cycle of day and night
You have many more worlds and abodes
[to explore]![18]

NOTES

1. Jalal ad-Din Rumi, *Divan-i Shams-i Tabriz,* ed. B. Furuzanfar (Tehran: University of Tehran Press, 1957–67), lines 333567–68; as translated by W. Chittick, *The Sufi Path of Love* (Albany: SUNY Press, 1983), p. 29.

2. Sadi, *Gulistan,* 2:120, as quoted in Carl Ernst, *The Shambhala Guide to Sufism* (Boston, London: Shambhala, 1997), p. 181.

3. Annemarie Schimmel, *Mystical Dimensions of Islam* (Chapel Hill: University of North Carolina Press, 1975), p. 307.

4. Ibid., p. 307.

5. Jalal ad-Din Rumi, *Mathnawi-i ma'nawi,* ed. and trans. R.A. Nicholson, 8 vols (London: Luzac, 1925–40), 1: line 1802.

6. For Rumi's imagery concerning the falcon, see Annemarie Schimmel, *The Triumphal Sun: A Study of the Works of Jalaloddin Rumi* (London, The Hague: Fine Books and East-West Publications, 1978), pp. 117–18.

7. Jalal ad-Din Rumi, *Divan-i Kabir,* ed. B. Furuzanfar, 10 volumes (Tehran: University of Tehran, 1957–80), 1353/14300.

8. Rumi, *Mathnawi,* 2:334.

9. Sayyed Hossein Nasr, "The Flight of Birds to Union: Meditations on the Attar's *Mantiq ut-Tayr,*" in *Islamic Art and Spirituality,* ed. S.H. Nasr (Albany: State University of New York Press, 1987), pp. 99–100.

10. Farid ud-Din Attar, *The Conference of the Birds,* trans with an introduction by Afkham Darbandi and Dick Davis (New York: Penguin, 1984), p. 34.

11. Ibid., p. 36.

12. Ibid., pp. 36–37.

13. Ibid., p. 40.

14. Ibid., p. 33.

15. Ibid., p. 17.

16. Annemarie Schimmel, *A Two Colored Brocade: The Imagery of Persian Poetry* (Chapel Hill: University of North Carolina Press, 1992), p. 314.

17. Schimmel, *A Two Colored Brocade,* p. 394, n. 23.

18. Muhammad Iqbal, *Bal-i Jibril,* 14th ed. (Lahore: Feroze Sons, 1965), pp. 89–90.

III

ANIMALS IN INDIAN TRADITIONS

HINDUISM

Cows, Elephants, Dogs, and Other Lesser Embodiments of *Ātman*

Reflections on Hindu Attitudes Toward Nonhuman Animals

LANCE NELSON

> The wise see the same [reality] in a Brahmin endowed with learning and culture, a cow, an elephant, a dog, and an outcaste.
>
> —Bhagavad Gītā 5.18

The *Deccan Herald* of January 25, 1999, reports that, a few days earlier, in the town of Shakarapuram near the South Indian city of Bangalore, a group of devotees gathered to hear a talk on the *Bhagavad Gītā* by a famous scholar, Bannanje Govindacharya. He was visiting from Udipi, a Vaiṣṇava pilgrimage center of great sanctity. As part of the function, the *paṇḍit's* new Kanada translation of the much-loved Hindu epic the *Rāmāyaṇa* was being formally released to the public. As Govindacharya alighted from his vehicle, proceeded into the hall, and ascended the stage, an adult monkey followed close behind. The organizers tried to shoo the monkey off the platform, but it refused to budge, so they decided to let it be. When it came time to release the book, the audience of 350 watched as the monkey took the new *Rāmāyaṇa* from the author's hand, removed the ceremonial wrapping, and spent a few seconds scanning the pages. Having returned the book to its author, the monkey then descended from the platform and, while the scholar gave his talk, sat harm-lessly and unharmed in the lap of one astonished member of the audience after another. When the function was over, it departed. The human participants were most impressed. Surely, it was concluded, this was a visit from Hanumān, the famed monkey god and hero of the *Rāmāyaṇa*, who—in addition to being famed for his unmatched prowess in battle—is known for his perfect mastery of Sanskrit grammar.[1] Was he there to scrutinize the new version of the story in which he figures so prominently, and to signal his approval? As a *cirañjīvī*—a "long-lived" one, a near immortal—Hanumān is believed to appear wherever the *Rāmāyaṇa* is being read and honored. Partly because of their association with Hanumān and the *Rāmāyaṇa*, monkeys are treated as sacred everywhere in India.[2]

We are perhaps not surprised to hear such reports in connection with the Hindu tradition. After all, is not Hindu India home of the proverbial "holy cow"? Dorane Jacobson tells of a central Indian villager who was accused of "cow murder," even though the animal's death was

accidental. He was sentenced to social and religious ostracism until he could pay a substantial fine, which took him ten years to save the
money to pay. Even then, for many years after
that he was still known as "the one who murdered his calf."[3] The cow was associated with
the sacred, though not yet completely sacrosanct, in the ancient hymns of the Vedas (second to first millennium BCE). Since then, she
has undergone a gradual apotheosis, becoming
over time a key symbol of all that is sacred to,
and unifies, Hindus.[4] There is evidence of concern for giving shelter and maintenance to unproductive cattle as early as the fourth century
BCE,[5] and homes for aging and enfeebled cattle
(gośālas) are attested in India by the sixteenth
century CE.[6]

Gośālas continue to be a prominent feature
of Hindu religious institutions. Hindu faithful
refer to the cow as "our mother" (go-mātā). The
cow in Purāṇic myth is Kāmadhenu, "yielder
of the milk of all desire," source of nutriment
and prosperity.[7] She is Surabhi, "the Fragrant,"
the symbolic embodiment of the Earth; she is
Lakṣmī, the goddess of fortune. Respondents
in the holy city of Varanasi, where Brahmins
can be found who daily perform go-pūjā (cow
worship), confided, "We believe that 330 million Hindu gods live in every atom of the cow's
body," and, "We believe in going to heaven by
the aid of the cow."[8] A cow donated to Brahmins is said to carry the departing soul across
the river Vaitaraṇī, which separates the world of
the living from the world of the dead. This belief is enacted in the Vaitaraṇī ritual, in which
the worshiper clutches the tail of a cow with
both hands. In death as well as in life, human
beings thus depend upon the cow as upon their
mother.[9] The cow, further, is associated with the
world-stabilizing purity of Brahminhood, and
indeed is said to be the animal whose form is
typically inhabited by souls prior to their incarnation as Brahmins.[10] Touching a cow is a
source of good fortune and ritual purification, as
is the use of go-mātā's milk, curd, clarified butter, urine, or dung. Even more purifying is the

ritual application of these "five products of the
cow" (pañcagavya) combined, a preparation also
known as "the five-fold nectar" (pañcāmṛta). In
recent centuries, the cow has emerged as a prime
symbol of "Hindu nationhood," and the Cow
Protection Movement has become a focus of
Hindu identity vis-à-vis the Muslim and colonial British Other.[11]

Sacred monkeys and holy cows do not tell
the whole story of nonhuman animals in India.
Other species have symbolic religious value:
snakes, as emblems of fertility; lions, associated
with the Goddess Durgā; even rats, as we shall
see below. On the other hand, one should not
get the impression the Hindu world represents
a secure zone for nonhuman animals. Animal
sacrifice, for example, plays a not insignificant
role in Hindu religious history up to the present.
Animal rights activists tell the story of a woman
in Hyderabad during the 1990s, who had just received what in the United States would be called
a "career break." She had been given a part in
a Hindi film, and was on her way to name and
fame, at least on a local level. Out of thanks,
she started a small temple for animal sacrifice.
Her celebrity apparently attracted others to offer
sacrifices in search of similar boons, and the
small shrine soon became, we are told, "a foun-
tain of blood."[12] More recently, in June of 2002,
King Bir Bikram Shah Gyanendra of Nepal and
his wife, Queen Komal Rajya, stirred up controversy by flying directly from Kathmandu to
Guwahati, Assam, to perform a pañcabali, or
sacrificial offering of five animals, at the famous (for some Hindus, infamous) temple of
the Goddess Kāmākhyā. After the sacrifice, the
king and queen attended a lunch held in their
honor at the official residence of the Governor
of Assam. Unmoved by the protests of animal
rights activists, the king and queen moved on to
Kolkata (formerly Calcutta), where they offered
a goat in sacrifice to the Goddess Kālī at the Kali-
ghat temple.[13]

The attitudes toward nonhuman animals
within Hinduism are immensely complex and
often, as the incidents recounted above illus-

trate, strike the observer as antithetical. I will explore here the main outlines of Hindu thinking on the subject of the moral and spiritual status of nonhuman animals. As a thematic motif, I will take a well-known verse from the *Bhagavad Gītā* (c. 200 BCE), and explore its implications through references to Hindu legal traditions, theology, myth, and popular stories. In the process, I will give considerable attention to the *Laws of Manu* (*Mānava Dharmaśāstra*, 200 BCE–200 CE), the most important work on Brahminical concepts of *dharma* (social and religious duty).

The Sanskritic orthodoxy of the Brahmin elite has tended, as we shall see, toward a narrow, anthropocentric (one might well say, "androcentric") view of the world, one that conceptualized nonhuman animals as "lower" forms of existence and allowed for animal sacrifice. At the same time, it does contain material that undermines humanity's vision of itself as a privileged species, and, by the classical era, it had incorporated as a core value the ethics of nonviolence or noninjury (*ahiṃsā*). In addition, there have always been elements within the tradition that have criticized and even sought to subvert or reverse elements of the orthodox worldview and practice. These have to some extent provided more positive images of nonhuman life forms. I will consider them as well.

Sameness of Self and Transmigratory Journeying between Species

A number of passages in the *Bhagavad Gītā* have been cited as demonstrating an ecologically supportive ethic of respect for life in all its forms. Particularly interesting in this connection is *Gītā* 5.18, which reads: "The wise see the same [reality] in a Brahmin endowed with learning and culture, a cow, an elephant, a dog, and an outcaste (or 'Dog-Cooker,' *śvapāka*)." This verse brings to the foreground a number of important issues concerning Hindu attitudes toward nonhuman animals. I will use it as the point of departure and thematic touchstone for my remarks as we proceed.

First, *Gītā* 5.18 brings to mind the Hindu doctrine that is perhaps most fundamental to understanding the Hindu conception of the spiritual and moral value of every life-form. This is the idea, shared by nearly all of the many schools of Hindu thought, that the true spiritual Self (*ātman*) is qualitatively identical in all beings—from, as it is said, the creator god Brahmā down to a blade of grass (see *Manu* 1.50). The Vaiṣṇava commentator Rāmānuja (eleventh-twelfth century CE) explains the text:

> Although the selves (*ātmans*) are being perceived in extremely dissimilar forms, the wise know the selves to be of uniform nature. ... The dissimilarity of the forms is due to [the various] material [adjuncts], and not to any dissimilarity in the self. (*BhGR* 5.18)

There is a vigorous dispute between Hindu theists such as Rāmānuja, who believe there are many *ātmans*, one for each being, and the nondualist (*advaitin*) theologians, who hold that the Self is quantitatively as well as qualitatively identical, there being only a single, universal *ātman*. But the idea that all beings ultimately have the same spiritual potential is the same for both. So the sages here see—quite literally, since it is assumed that their mystical vision is fully awakened—all beings as endowed with a Self that is equal in potential and equal in value. On the level of spirit, at least, there is an essential equality between the Brahmin, the cow, the elephant, the dog, and the outcaste.

Extending the principle embodied in this verse, the *Gītā* itself, in certain passages, articulates a vision of universal empathy, as at 6.32, which echoes the golden rule: "When one sees the pleasure and pain in all beings as the same in comparison with self ... one is considered the highest *yogin*." The great nondualist commentator Śaṅkara (seventh century CE) takes this text as suggesting the universality of consciousness and, therefore, a reflective basis for universal compassion: "Just as for me pain is both dis-agreeable and undesired, so is it for all living be-ings" (*sarva-prāṇinām, BhGŚ* 6.32). Holding to this standard, the *Gītā* espouses as its ideal sages who "delight in the welfare of all beings" (*sarva-bhūta-hite ratāḥ,* 5.25), that is, *all* beings, not just human beings.

Perhaps equally important in determining the Hindu view of nonhuman beings is the re-lated and complementary notion of transmigra-tion or rebirth (*punar-bhāva*). It is the same con-sciousness that may appear at different times all life forms, whether Brahmin, cow, elephant, dog, or outcaste. As is well-known, Hindus be-lieve that each being, on its journey toward its ultimate goal of *mokṣa*—final beatitude in re-lease from the cycles of rebirth (*saṃsāra*)—goes through a succession of innumerable lives, dur-ing which the *ātman* undergoes a wide variety of embodiments. These embodiments may be in plants as well as animals, not to speak of gods and other beings inhabiting other, "higher" planes of existence.

An essential notion here, of course, is that each of us was once embodied in plant and ani-mal forms, and may again be, as may others who are near and dear to us. The *Yogavāsiṣṭha* suggests that we ought to be mindful, and may through yogic practice actually become aware, of our former incarnations in animal form.[14] As we shall see below, the Purāṇas contain many stories of individuals who, for various reasons, were reborn as animals. At Deshnok, Rajasthan, one may today visit the temple of Karṇī Mātā, a fifteenth-century female mystic, associated with the ruling families of Bikaner, who came to be regarded as an incarnation of the Goddess Durgā. The temple where she is now enshrined as Deity has imposing silver gates and exqui-site marble carvings, but is most famous as the "Temple of Rats," because it is filled with scurry-ing rodents who are understood to be deceased members of the clan of Karṇī Mātā. In conse-quence of a boon given to the saint, these, her relatives, never descend into the kingdom of the god of death, Yama, but wait out their time until their next human birth in the bodies of these rats, protected in this temple. Devotees bring food offerings to present to the rats; they allow the rodents to climb all over them and finish off any food the rats may leave. Eating *prasād* (offertory food) that has been nibbled or sipped by these sacred rats, and thereby consecrated, brings good fortune.[15]

The Doctrine of Noninjury

These two notions, equality in spirit and aware-ness of reincarnation, are closely associated with the well-known, though not exclusively Hindu, doctrine of *ahiṃsā* or noninjury. The *Mahābhā-rata* proclaims repeatedly, "*ahiṃsā* is the high-est duty (*dharma*)" (1.11.12, 3.198.69, etc.) and the Hindu law books teach uniformly that non-injury is the common duty (*sādhāraṇa-dharma*) of all human beings.[16] In the Hindu tradition, the *ahiṃsā* ethic is especially incumbent on as-cetics. The ritual of *saṃnyāsa* or renunciation in-volves giving a promise of "safety to all living be-ings" (6.39). "To protect living creatures," the re-nouncer "should inspect the ground constantly as he walks, by night or by day" (*Manu* 6.68). Patañjali's *Yogasūtras* (c. 400 CE), a manual for ascetic practice, requires *ahiṃsā* as the primary virtue of *yogin*s (practitioners of *yoga*). It is de-fined by the commentator Vyāsa as "the non-harming (*anabhidroha*) of all beings everywhere at all times" (*YSV* 2.30). The Yoga system en-courages *yogin*s to investigate the subtle roots of violence within their own psyches through deep meditation and counter them by developing strong waves of "contrary thought" (*pratipakṣa-bhāvana, YS* 2.33). According to Vyāsa the *yogin* should think as follows:

> Burning with the terrible fire of rebirth, I have sought refuge in the practice of *yoga* after prom-ising safety to all living beings. If I, the very per-son who had once given up perverse thoughts [of violence], were to revert to them, I would be be-having like a dog. ... One who reverts to what

has once been renounced is like a dog licking up its own vomit. (*YSV* 2.33)

The *yogin* is encouraged to thoroughly contemplate violence, its motives, and its consequences. As to the latter, Vyāsa recommends that the following be deeply pondered:

> Having robbed the victim of strength, the killer loses the vigor of his body and senses. Having caused pain he suffers pain—by being born in hell, in [the bodies of] animals, in the wombs of evil spirits, and so on. (*YSV* 2.34)

We will take up below the negative characterization of the dog in the Hindu tradition, evidenced here, as well the use of the threat of animal rebirths as a moral deterrent. The point here is that the *yogin* is engaged in a struggle to entirely uproot violence from consciousness. Ascetics who succeed in this endeavor develop the power to completely neutralize all hostility in their environment (*YS* 2.35). This includes, in yogic lore, the power to pacify dangerous animals and to cause species that are mutual enemies to live together in peaceful harmony.

An example of such a saint is Ramana Maharishi, the great twentieth-century sage of South India. Ramana was known not only for his personal realization of the highest truth of Advaita (nondualism), but also for his extraordinary affection for, and ability to communicate with, animals. He knew the habits, likes and dislikes, individual personalities and biographies, and even the inter- and intra-species politics of the various animals and animal communities that shared his *āśrama* (hermitage) with his human devotees: dogs, cats, squirrels, peacocks, crows, sparrows, monkeys, cows, snakes, and scorpions. Bhagavan (the "Blessed One"), as Ramana was known, used personal pronouns, and often individual names, when referring to these creatures, and he is said not to have discriminated between his human and nonhuman devotees. "We do not know what souls may be tenanting these bodies," he would say, "and for fin-

ishing what portion of their unfinished karma they may seek our company."[17] He is reported to have understood the language of the monkeys that lived in the environs and earned their trust to the extent that they brought their disputes to him to adjudicate.[18] Ramana refused to allow cobras and other snakes that appeared in the *āśrama* to be killed, which would have been the ordinary practice. A devotee reports that once a large green snake had taken to frequenting a *paṇḍāl*, a large pavilion built for a festival. Ramana was reluctant to have this new inmate of the *āśrama* chased away, until it was pointed out that the snake might suffer at the hands of festival-attendees, who were likely to be less tolerant of reptiles than himself. "It might be so," he responded. The account continues:

> Bhagavan thereupon looked at the snake for a while, steadfastly and graciously. Immediately after that the snake, which was remaining still all the time we were discussing, got down [from] the pandal rapidly, went into the flower garden and disappeared. There was no knowing what message he received when Bhagavan gazed at him. ... The snake was never seen afterwards.[19]

Ascetics, of course, represent only a small fraction of Hindu society. Householders, the vast majority, cannot follow the *ahiṃsā* ethic as rigorously, but neither are they expected to. Indeed, the situation of the upper-caste householder in this respect was for centuries complicated by the obligations of the ancient Vedic sacrificial cult. The practice of animal sacrifice (*paśu-bandha*, "animal-binding") was by the time of the major Hindu law books (200 BCE–200 CE) in decline. There was discomfort within the Brahminical tradition about sacrificial violence,[20] as well as anxiety regarding its possible consequences for the perpetrators;[21] in addition there was the external pressure of critiques from Buddhist and Jaina advocates of *ahiṃsā*. Nevertheless, Vedic sacrifice was supported by the prestige of antiquity and was still in vogue, and the authors of the law books take the sacrificial ideology into account. For householders, at any rate, animal sacrifice was permitted, even required (*Manu* 4.25–28). Indeed, Manu proclaims that animals were created for sacrifice, declaring, "killing in sacrifice is not killing," and that violence (*hiṃsā*) ordained by the Veda is really *ahiṃsā* (5.39, 44). Plants and animals killed in sacrifice are reborn in the "highest level of existence" (*Manu* 5.42).[22] Still, Manu shows the influence of the rising tide of *ahiṃsā*-thinking. He recognizes that even plants have consciousness and experience happiness and unhappiness (*Manu* 1.49–50). Noninjury is highly praised as the preferred ideal for the virtuous, even among householders (*Manu* 5.45–47).

Slowly, the *ahiṃsā* ethic triumphed over the ancient sacrificial *cultus*, and animal sacrifice came to be condemned as a practice no longer permissible, especially among followers of the *bhakti* (devotional) traditions.[23] The Vaiṣṇava *Bhāgavata Purāṇa* (*BhP*, eighth-ninth century) forbade the offering of meat in sacrifice and its consumption as a violation of the principle of *ahiṃsā* (*BhP* 3.25.7–8, 7.15.7–8, 10, 11.5.14). The *Purāṇa* attributes awareness of human intentions—as well as feelings of fear—to animals confronted by the threat of sacrificial death: "Seeing someone about to sacrifice with material offerings, beings are filled with dread, fearing 'This self-indulgent [human], having no compassion, will slay me'" (*BhP* 7.15.10). Starting in the tenth century, Hindu legal writings include animal sacrifice in lists of *kali-varjya*s, actions that are "prohibited in the Kali Age," the present era of moral and spiritual decline, despite their being enjoined in the ancient texts.[24] By the thirteenth century, we find the Vaiṣṇava theologian Madhva recommending across-the-board substitution of animal effigies (*piṣṭa-paśu*, or "flour-animals") for living victims in Vedic rituals.[25] This was a generalization of a practice that began in the late Vedic period[26] and may be observed today in modern reenactments of the ancient rites. Sacrifice continued, however, in the temples of the goddesses Kālī and Durgā, in tantric rites, and regional village traditions.[27]

A practice closely connected with the ethic of nonviolence, and one for which Hinduism is rightly well-known, is vegetarianism. Along with the killing of animals, the ancient sacrificial rites allowed the consumption of animal flesh, including beef, in a ritual context.[28] By the ninth century, however, vegetarianism was becoming the norm for Brahmins and followers of *bhakti* sects, especially Vaiṣṇavas, although the ruling castes—the Kṣatriyas—retained their traditions of hunting game and eating meat. As, however, the development of Hindu vegetarianism is well documented by Edwin Bryant in the next essay, I need not dwell on it here.

Hierarchy, Anthropocentrism, and Symbolic Denigration

There is a common presupposition that vedantic panentheism entails a Hindu sense of oneness with nature, seen as a manifestation of the divine. In fact, classical Hindu theology and social thought present a view of the world that is unapologetically hierarchical and anthropocentric. The idea of the superiority of human beings is justified, not on the basis of their possession of a soul, for as we have seen the same *ātman* is found in all beings. Even plants, we noted, have consciousness and experience happiness and unhappiness (*Manu* 1.49). Neither is it argued in physical or emotional terms, for as the *Hitopadeśa* tells us, "Human beings share food, sleep, fear, and sexual activity in common with animals" (*HN* 1.25). For the Brahmins who set the rules, the key distinction is rather cognitive, moral, ritual, and soteriological: only human beings have the capacity to receive and appropriate revelation (*śruti*), in the form of the Veda, and thus only human beings have access to that which comes from the Veda, namely *dharma* (correct ritual behavior and morality). "Dharma is the distinctive quality," the *Hitopadeśa* verse continues, "without which human beings are the same as animals." And in the end, only human beings, in the ordinary course of things, have access to *mokṣa* or *mukti* (spiritual liberation). To be more precise, to have full and direct access to these cosmically valenced privileges, one must—for many conservative teachers—be a "twice-born" Hindu, that is to say, a male member of the upper three castes. For some, like Śaṅkara, access to *mokṣa* requires that one be no less than a Brahmin male, and a *saṃnyāsin* (world-renouncer) to boot.[29]

As is well known, Hindu teachers, despite their many theological differences, all agree that one's station in this hierarchical universe, and the course of one's journey through *saṃsāra,* is determined by one's karma, the moral consequences of one's actions. The circumstances of one's birth, whether in human or nonhuman form, is attributed to one's karma. And it must be kept in mind that the process is not strictly linear, for one can, over the course of rebirths, fall into "lower" states of existence as well as rise to enjoy "higher" forms.

In Manu we find an interesting systematization of this hierarchical scheme, and its transmigratory consequences, articulated in terms of the theory of the *guṇa*s, the three psychophysical "qualities" or "strands" that, according to the traditional Hindu worldview, are the stuff of existence, combining to make up the entire range of phenomena, mental as well as physical. *Sattva* ("goodness," "lucidity"), the most highly valued of these constituents, is the *guṇa* of intelligence, creativity, and spirituality; *rajas* ("energy"), the *guṇa* of passion and dynamism; and *tamas* ("darkness"), of ignorance and lethargy (*Manu* 12.24–29, 38). At *Manu* 12.39–51, we learn of the postmortem transmigratory destinies of human beings who have cultivated a preponderance of each of these three qualities: "People of lucidity [*sattva*] become gods, people of energy [*rajas*] become humans, and people of darkness [*tamas*] always become animals" (*Manu* 12.40). When one considers that among the qualities associated with *tamas* Manu lists ignorance, confusion, sensuality, inability to reason, lack of intelligence, greed, sleepiness, incontinence, cruelty, atheism, and carelessness,

one begins to see that the portrait of the nonhuman world, onto which these qualities are projected, is not a very positive one. Among possible human destinies, rebirth as an animal is a frightening punishment. Thus:

> Violent men become carnivorous (beasts); people who eat impure things become worms; thieves (become animals that) devour one another... Women, too, who steal in this way incur guilt; they become the wives of these very same creatures. (*Manu* 12.59, 69)

The *Chāndogya Upaniṣad* (5.10.7–8) promises rebirth as a dog or pig to those whose conduct has been evil. Those who neglect or despise Vedic values, the text tells us, will be reborn again and again as "small creatures." Śaṅkara comments:

> They take birth as these small creatures—gadflies, mosquitoes, and other insects—which are reborn again and again.... They spend their time in mere birth and death, having opportunity for neither ritual nor enjoyment. (*CU* 5.10.8)

The fact that Hindu theologians understand the self or "soul" (*ātman*) within all living beings to be qualitatively identical—and that some, like Śaṅkara, see all selves as metaphysically one—is often cited as evidence of an egalitarian, even communitarian, spiritual outlook. The related concept of reincarnation, in which the same soul may appear in different forms, human and nonhuman, has likewise been offered as implying an "organic solidarity between humanity and nature."[30] To be sure, our text from the *Gītā* tells us that the wise see the same transcendent essence and final spiritual potential in Brahmins, cows, elephants, and dogs. But how do the sages respond to the empirical actuality of these diverse species? Here is Śaṅkara's take:

> In a Brahmin, in whom *sattva* predominates and who has the best latent mental impressions (*saṃskāra*), in an intermediate being like a cow, which

is dominated by *rajas* and is without [such] impressions, and in [beings] such as elephants, which are wholly dominated by *tamas* alone—those wise ones are "equal-visioned" whose habit is to see equally the one immutable Brahman. (*BhGŚ* 5.18)

Śaṅkara sees oneness on the level of spirit, no doubt; that is what he is known for. However, he also sees very clearly the kind of anthropocentric hierarchy we have been discussing. So does Viśvanātha Cakravartin (eighteenth century), the Gauḍīya Vaiṣnava commentator, who sees Brahmins and cows as being alike in the highest class of beings, those who are predominant in *sattva* (*sāttvika-jāti*). The elephant for him is in the middle (*madhyame*), while the dog and the outcaste Dog-Cooker (*śvapāka*) are together at the bottom, in the group dominated by *tamas* (*tāmasa-jāti*, *BhGV* 5.18). This is an interesting kind of solidarity between humans and animals, to be sure. It reflects how the nonhuman world becomes symbolically connected with the system of caste, and shows clearly the connection between oppression of nonhuman animals and the oppression of marginalized human beings. This is the symbolic set that our *Gītā* verse assumes and wants to evoke. Cows, as emblematic of all that is pure and holy, are associated with Brahmins. Dogs, on the other hand, are regarded as the Caṇḍālas or outcastes of the animal world, being stigmatized as thoroughly impure.

The orthodox tradition has held that dogs are indiscriminate in their eating habits and their sexual behavior. Designated "vomit-eaters," they haunt cremation grounds where they become eaters of carrion; they have sex with members of their own family and menstruating females. The behavior of dogs, in short, resembles that attributed to outcastes, both being utterly abhorrent to Brahmin sensibilities. Dogs, along with Caṇḍālas, pollute the food of Brahmins if they happen to glance at them while they eat; a dog pollutes sacred offerings likewise by sight

(*Manu* 3.239–42). Thus, as Doniger has pointed out, "the dog [is] to the cow in the world of beasts what the outcaste is to the Brahmin in the world of men."[31]

Animal Heroes, Animal Stories

One more set of issues must be raised. The *Bhāgavata Purāṇa*, in a passage quoted above, describes the fear experienced by animals at the prospect of facing the sacrifice. This raises the question of the moral and spiritual sensibility of animals. The theological texts, interestingly, do not really address this issue. We must look at mythic, literary, and popular narrative sources for such information. We can afford to bypass here the fables of the *Pañcatantra* and *Hitopadeśa*, which clearly intend to teach about human behavior and polity, not about animals or how we should regard them. Other treatments of animals in Hindu literature are more promising resources for our present concern.

In Kālidāsa's famous play *The Recognition of Śakuntalā*, we find the nonhuman world expressing grief in an extraordinarily poignant way when the beloved heroine must leave her father's hermitage. Says Śakuntalā's friend:

> The bitterness of parting is not yours alone;
>   look around you and see how the Holy
>   Grove grieves, knowing the hour of
>   parting from you is near:
> The doe tosses out mouthfuls of grass,
>   the peacocks dance no more;
> pale leaves flutter down
>   as if the vines were shedding their limbs.
>   (Act 4, vs. 14)[32]

In numerous passages in the *Bhāgavata Purāṇa*, all of nature is portrayed as responding in love to the beauty of Lord Krishna, the divine incarnation, and the call of his flute: deer worship, birds are dumbstruck, cows hold Krishna reverently in their minds (*BhP* 10.21.10–14). Beyond this, all of India knows of the noble Jaṭāyu, the vulture-king of the *Rāmāyaṇa*, who sacrificed his own life attempting to save Sītā, Rāma's beloved wife, from abduction by the demon Rāvaṇa. The great bird's funeral rites were performed by the very hand of the divine incarnation, Rāma, and he thereby obtained *mokṣa*. Even more beloved is the loyal, devoted, and heroic Hanumān, the monkey who led Rāma's forces in the battle to rescue Sītā. We have already encountered him in his appearance as a monkey to a group of devotees, as documented by the *Deccan Herald*.

Among the more interesting animal stories are those which show animals attaining *mukti*, or *mokṣa*, spiritual liberation. In what follows, I will observe the order of the animals of *Gītā* 5.18: cows, elephants, and dogs. Consider first the story of Lakshmi, a cow who was counted among the most faithful devotees of Bhagavan Ramana Maharshi, the twentieth-century saint whose fondness for animals has already been mentioned. Lakshmi grew up in the *āśrama* of the saint, and waited daily on Ramana, for whom she seemed to have a single-minded devotion. Devotees noticed that, while the saint was normally undemonstrative, "the open expressions of his Grace that Lakshmi used to receive from him were quite exceptional."[33] At the hour of her death, the Maharshi gave her his most tender attention, placing his hand on her head and heart in a gesture of special blessing. On Lakshmi's tomb—erected in a prominent location in the *āśrama* and graced with a statue depicting her—was engraved an epitaph composed by the saint, declaring that the cow had attained *mukti*. Asked whether "liberation" was here used figuratively, Ramana replied that the words meant what they said, actual liberation.[34] There had been much speculation as to the reason for the extraordinary attention that Ramana had given this cow. The general consensus was that she had known the master in a previous birth. A. D. Mudaliar, a devotee of the *āśrama* during Ramana's life, writes:

Although Lakshmi now wore the form of a cow, she must have attached herself to Sri Bhagavan and won his Grace by love and surrender in a previous birth. It seemed hard to explain in any other way the great solicitude and tenderness that Sri Bhagavan [Ramana] always showed in his dealings with her.[35]

It was decided that Lakshmi must be the reincarnation of Keeraipatti, an elderly woman who had rendered much devoted service to the master prior to her death in 1921. This seemed possible, as Lakshmi had arrived at the *āśrama* as a small calf in 1926. Ramana would not confirm this speculation on the cow's former human life directly, but hinted that it was the case.[36]

Returning to classical texts, in the *Bhāgavata Purāṇa* (8.2–4) we read perhaps the most famous story in the Hindu tradition dealing with animal spirituality; it focuses on the second animal mentioned in our *Gītā* verse. The story of "liberation of the elephant" (*gaja-mokṣa*, BhP 8.2–4) tells of Gajendra, the leader of a great elephant herd, who—while bathing in a lake—was caught in the jaws of a giant crocodile and found himself being dragged into the water toward his likely death. Realizing that escape was impossible, the elephant-king focused his mind, repeating mentally a Sanskrit hymn in fervent praise of Lord Viṣṇu. The Lord Himself appeared, mounted on his heavenly vehicle, the giant bird Garuḍa. With great difficulty, the elephant uttered the words, "Hail to Thee, O Nārāyaṇa [Viṣṇu], Preceptor of the Universe!" (*BhP* 8.3.32) upon which the Lord, dismounting, pulled both Gajendra and the crocodile out of the lake, split the attacker's jaw with his discus, and freed the elephant.

It turned out that the crocodile was a heavenly being, a celestial musician (*gandharva*), who had been incarnated as a crocodile as the result of a curse. Freed from his sin and this unfortunate embodiment by the touch of the Lord, he prostrated and returned to his heavenly abode. Gajendra, having been delivered from the jaws of the crocodile, was delivered also from his elephant body, being granted *mukti* by the Lord. And in his case too we learn that the animal was more than merely an animal. In his previous life he was Indradyumna, a noble king turned ascetic, who had been devoted to the Lord. It was in this former life that he had learned the rather longish (twenty-seven-verse) Sanskrit hymn he had just, as an elephant, re-membered and mentally recited to attract the Lord's solicitude. King Indradyumna, like the *gandharva*-crocodile, had also been condemned to his uncomfortable animal rebirth as the result of a curse. He had made the mistake of slighting the temperamental Brahmin sage Agastya, who uttered the following imprecation: "May this impious, malevolent, and feeble-minded fellow, who has insulted a Brahmin just now, sink into in blinding ignorance. Since he is stupid like an elephant, let him be born as one" (*BhP* 8.4.10).

In the *Caitanyacaritāmṛta,* a biography of the sixteenth-century Bengali saint Caitanya, we read of a dog who had been tagging along with a group of disciples journeying to meet their mas-ter, Lord Caitanya, at Jagannāth Purī. One of the disciples, Śivānanda Sena, had been caring for and feeding the dog. He had even gone to the trouble of bribing a boatman who had been reluctant to take the dog across a river with the party. One day as they traveled, the dog disappeared, only to turn up at Purī after the disciples had arrived. Śivānanda and his comrades were astonished to come upon the dog sitting at the feet of the master, who was feeding him. At Lord Caitanya's coaching, the dog was chanting "Kṛṣṇa! Kṛṣṇa!" Overcome at this amazing sight, Śivānanda bowed. Later, they learned that the dog's love for God had been awakened by this contact with the mas-ter, and that the dog had been liberated from his canine body into Krishna's heavenly para-dise (*CC* 3.1.12–28).[37] Commenting on this epi-sode, A.C. Bhaktivedanta Swami Prabhupada remarks, "Śivānanda Sena's attachment to the dog was a great boon to that animal," and goes

on to explain that the dog's salvation was made possible by *sādhu-saṅga,* the spiritually uplifting effect of association (*saṅga*) with holy persons (*sādhu*). "This result is possible," he concludes, "even for a dog."[38]

In the *Mahābhārata,* we read of Yudhiṣṭhira's faithfulness to a dog who was faithful to him. Marching through the Himalayas toward Mount Meru, Yudhiṣṭhira was stunned to find the god Indra appearing before him to announce that he—Indra, the king of the gods—had come to take him to heaven. Yudhiṣṭhira begged to be able to take his faithful companion, the dog, with him. Indra refused, saying "there is no place for dog-owners in heaven," and in the exchange that followed, Indra explained all the ways in which dogs are sources of pollution. Yudhiṣṭhira remained adamant; he would not abandon the dog: "People say that to abandon one who is de-voted to you is a bottomless evil equal to mur-dering a Brahmin. Therefore, great Indra, I will never, in any way, abandon him now in order to achieve my own happiness." At that point the dog, who had been listening to the con-versation, changed appearance, manifesting his true form as the god Dharma, or Righteous-ness. He blessed Yudhiṣṭhira, who was in fact the god's son. Yudhiṣṭhira then mounted Indra's divine chariot and achieved what no other had: entry into heaven with his earthly body (*MBh* 17.2–3).[39]

A number of considerations ought to be brought to bear in evaluating stories such as these. First, it must be understood that in many cases their power derives largely from their pre-senting something unexpected. The cow Lak-shmi would not in the normal course of things be considered able to attain *mokṣa,* since the or-thodox teachers proclaim only humans are eli-gible. Still, she is a cow, and cows—we have seen—are holy. So while unusual, and perhaps thought-provoking, her spirituality is perhaps not overly surprising. But animal spirituality gets more surprising, in the Hindu context, the "lower" on the conventional scale we go. By the time we get to the dog, the orthodox Brahmini-cal system of values and symbols—as decreed by Manu—is challenged, as if by a parable that sees to overthrow the established order of things. The despised species may become a profound, if un-orthodox and potentially antinomian, symbol of the inbreaking divine. Hinduism, too often judged by outsiders as trapped its own rigid and oppressive categories, here reveals itself as self-critical, even capable of the subversion of its most well-established rules.

Second, the hearer may learn from these stories—as in the cases of dogs revealed to be gods—that the divine is to be waited upon in all life forms and that the sacred can manifest itself through all beings, no matter how "lowly." This is a lesson that it is difficult to apply consistently. Indeed, in an important study Nagarajan[40] has shown that Hindus in daily life apply notions of sacrality only selectively and intermittently. Still, the lesson remains—no matter how imper-fectly appropriated—and it is an important one.

Third, and now from a more critical stand-point, one wonders here to what extent these stories, in apparently extolling the spiritual po-tential of animals, are really subordinating them to humans. As Jaini points out, the idea of a hu-man being "temporarily shackled by a lower des-tiny" is a common motif in the Hindu epics. Is it possible, as Jaini believes, that this "reduces the relevancy of the tale[s] as referring to ani-mals,"[41] except perhaps insofar as it reempha-sizes the conventional belief in the wretched nature of animal existence? I think it is. Was Lakshmi the cow liberated because, as a cow, she manifested extraordinary devotion or be-cause she incarnated devotional sensibilities pre-viously cultivated as a human? We know well that the cow is a special case in the Hindu con-text. Still, the devotees were not satisfied in their understanding of the master's behavior toward Lakshmi until they had settled on the theory that she was human, and a devotee, in her im-mediately preceding life. Again, would Gajen-dra, as an elephant, have spontaneously remem-bered the Lord if memories and tendencies from his past life as a royal ascetic had not been acti-vated? Probably not, we must conclude. Śivā-nanda Sena's dog was not a god in disguise, nor did the narrator suggest that he was re-cently born in human form. But would he, as a dog, have attained Vaikuṇṭha, the Lord's abode, were it not for the benefit of contact with hu-man devotees, and their God-intoxicated mas-ter, whose spirituality was somehow transferred to awaken the dog's fortunate heart? The story tells us in the end more about the transfor-mative power of the master's spirituality than the spiritual potential of the dog. The birds of Krishna's Vṛndāvana forest, who respond so ex-traordinarily to the Lord's beauty, are—after all, we are told—really not animals but ancient sages (ṛṣi), incarnated to enjoy the Divine play on earth. Even Hanumān, beloved as the mon-key god, is more deity than monkey, being com-monly recognized as an avatāra of Śiva and son of Vāyu, the god of the wind.

The doctrine that all beings have souls that are qualitatively equal may, as we have seen, sug-gest empathy and compassion. Lest we read too much into the Hindu view of things, however, it should be said that this doctrine in itself does not entail any developed psychic or moral life in animals. Even less does it suggest the possi-bility of any real communion between humans and nonhumans. Ātman in its transcendence is aloof, inactive, and—though a witness of things —certainly noncommunicative; no ātman-to-ātman communication is envisioned. In Hindu thinking, communion would occur, not on the level of ātman, but on the level of mind. And Hindu thought does not, as we have seen, gen-erally have a high estimate of the cognitive abili-ties of animals who, despite their possession of ātman, are dominated in their empirical being by the dullness of tamas. Hence, any powers of, or potential for, communio would be limited.[42]

Conclusion

In the Hindu context, nothing is simple; judgments must always be made cautiously after long study. We must keep in mind, whatever truth we may see in them, that critiques such as I have just offered can be pushed beyond the point of usefulness. The theologies and sacred stories of Hinduism are appropriated by Hindus from within their own mythic canopy, not from outside, and this mythic universe is still very much alive. When I complained to a Hindu friend about the reductionism that treats manifestations of extraordinary spirituality in animals as human traits explainable by reincarnation, he responded, "But then, *all* animals were once human, were they not? Just as all humans were once animals!"

Nonhuman animals are embodiments of the eternal Self that is universally present in all beings. As such they carry the infinite value of Spirit, even if its manifestation in their psychic life is limited. On another level, a notch down from ultimacy, animals may be vehicles for the consciousness of our deceased relatives or friends (however veiled), or the lively awareness of saints; or they may even be the earthly manifestations of gods. Such ideas cannot, in the Hindu context, be considered insignificant. Even on the empirical level, religious dimensionalities and resulting distinctions must be taken into account. True, nonhuman animals are in the classical tradition generally ranked low in the hierarchy of beings. But then remember the cow, sattvic in nature, whose value is tantamount to that of the Brahmin.

Brahminism itself, which sees things inevitably from the "top down," is not the only voice in the Hindu tradition. With no enforcer of orthodoxy, this is a tradition with multiple voices, a diversity of visions. "Who speaks for Hinduism?" is a constantly contested question. There are yogic exemplars like Ramana Maharshi, who collapse orthodox categories in many ways, among these their quasi-shamanic communion with animals. There are professional tellers of "God-stories" (*hari-kathā*), men and women, immensely popular, who still vividly recount puranic tales of gods, *guru*s, and animals miraculously shape-shifting back and forth across hierarchal boundaries. And there are millions of devoted Hindus for whom those stories are yet very real. In short, despite the secular trends in contemporary India, which give support on many levels to narrow human self-centeredness,[43] there is material in the Hindu tradition that may well lend itself to the emergence of a new vision of human-animal relations.

ABBREVIATIONS

Unless otherwise indicated, the translations from Sanskrit provided are my own.

BhG *Bhagavad Gītā*. See *BhGŚ*.
BhGR *Śrī Rāmānuja Gītā Bhāṣya*. Text with translation by Svami Adidevananda. Mylapore, Madras: Sri Ramakrishna Math, n.d.
BhGŚ *Śrīmadbhagavadgītā with the Śrīmat-Śāṅkarabhāṣya*. Ed. with several other commentaries by Wasudeva Laxman Sastri Pansikar. New Delhi: Munshiram Manoharlal Publishers, 1978.

BhGV *Śrīmad Bhagavadgītā with the Commentaries Sārārthavarṣiṇī of Viśvanātha Cakravartin and Gītābhāṣya of Baladeva Vidyābhūsana*. Kusumasarovar, Mathura: Kṛṣṇadasababa, c. 1966–67.
BhP *Bhāgavata Purāṇa*. Ed. J.L. Shastri. Delhi: Motilal Banarsidass, 1999.
CC *Caitanyacaritāmṛta of Kṛṣṇadāsa Kavirāja*. Trans. Edward C. Dimock. Ed. Tony Stewart. Cambridge: Harvard University Press, 1999.
CU *Chāndogya Upaniṣad* with Śaṅkara's *Bhāṣya*. In *Ten Principal Upanishads with Śaṅkarabhāṣya*.

Works of Śaṅkara in the Original Sanskrit. Vol. 1. Delhi: Motilal Banarsidass, 1964.

HN *Hitopadeśa of Nārāyaṇa.* Ed. with translation and notes by Max Müller as *The First Book of the Hitopadeśa.* London: Longman, 1864.

Manu *The Laws of Manu.* Trans. Wendy Doniger with Brian K. Smith. London: Penguin Books, 1991. (I have used Doniger and Smith's translations.)

MBh *Mahābhārata.*

YS *Yogasūtra of Patañjali with the Commentary of Vyāsa.* Ed. and trans. Bangali Baba. Delhi: Motilal Banarsidass, 1976.

YSV *Yogabhāṣya* of Vyāsa. See *YS.*

NOTES

1. *Deccan Herald,* January 25, 1999, http://www.deccanherald.com/deccanherald/jan25/ctman.htm (May 16, 1999). Also: "Monkey Steals Show During Auspicious Function," *Indian Express,* January 26, 1999, http://www.indianexpress.com/ie/daily/ 1999 0126/02652055.html (March 23, 2003).

2. According to recent reports, there are as many as 10,000 or more monkeys wandering the streets of Delhi. They occupy government buildings and create other nuisances. It even seems that a man was killed by a flower pot dropped by a monkey. Authorities are at a loss as to how to control them without offending Hindu sensibilities. See, e.g.: Daniel Lak, "Monkeys Create Havoc in Delhi," BBC News, April 14, 2000, http://news.bbc.co.uk/1/hi/world/south_asia/713151.stm (March 23, 2003); Rahul Bedi, "Indians Jail Marauding Monkeys," news.telegraph, January 12, 2002, http://www.telegraph.co.uk/news/main.jhtml?xml=/news/2002/01/12/wmonky12.xml (March 23, 2003).

3. Dorane Jacobson, "A Reverence for Cows," *Natural History* 108 (June 1999): 58, 63.

4. Frank Korom, "Holy Cow! The Apotheosis of Zebu, or Why the Cow Is Sacred in Hinduism," *Asian Folklore Studies* 59 (2000): 181–204.

5. Deryck Lodrick, *Sacred Cows, Sacred Places: Origins and Survivals of Animal Homes in India* (Berkeley: University of California Press, 1981), p. 89.

6. Peter van der Veer, *Religious Nationalism: Hindus and Muslims in India* (Berkeley: University of California Press, 1994), p. 90.

7. Madeline Biardeau, "Kāmadhenu: The Mythical Cow, Symbol of Prosperity," in *Asian Mythologies,* ed. Yves Bonnefoy (Chicago: University of Chicago Press, 1993), p. 99.

8. Deryck O. Lodrick, "On Religion and Milk Bovines in an Urban Indian Setting," *Current Anthropology* 20 (March 1979): 242.

9. van der Veer, *Religious Nationalism,* p. 87.

10. Biardeau, "Kāmadhenu," p. 99; Swami A.C. Bhaktivedanta Prabhupada, "Serve God or Serve Dog," 1976, http://www.prabhupadavani.org/web/text/236.html (February 8, 2003).

11. van der Veer, *Religious Nationalism,* pp. 86–94; Christophe Jaffrelot, *The Hindu Nationalist Movement in India* (New York: Columbia University Press, 1996), pp. 204–10.

12. Poornima Harish, "Animal Sacrifice: One Brave Woman Leads the Fight for a Total End to Ritual Killing," *Hinduism Today,* April 1999, http://www.hinduismtoday.com/1999/4/1999-4-12.html (March 23, 2003).

13. G. Vinayak, "Gyanendra visits Kamakhya Temple; 5 animals sacrificed," rediff.com, June 27, 2002, http://www.rediff.com/news/2002/jun/27 nep.htm (February 8, 2003); "Nepal King Sacrifices Animal Again," rediff.com, June 28, 2002, http://www.rediff.com/news/2002/jun/28nep.htm (February 8, 2003).

14. Swami Venkatesananda, *Vasiṣṭha's Yoga* (Albany, N.Y.: State University of New York Press, 1993), pp. 620–21.

15. See Karnimata.com, n.d., http://karnimata.com (January 18, 2003); "Deshnok Karni Mata Temple," RealBikaner.com, n.d., http://www.realbi

kaner.com/temple/deshnok/index.html (January 18, 2003); "Deshnok," Deshnok.com, n.d., http://www.deshnok.com (January 18, 2003).

16. Pandurang Vaman Kane, *History of Dharmasastra: Ancient and Medieval Religious and Civil Law India,* 6 vols, 2d ed., rev. and enlarged, Government Oriental Series; Class B, no. 6 (Poona: Bhandarkar Oriental Research Institute, 1968), 2 (pt. 1):10; 5 (pt. 2): 945.

17. Arthur Osborne, *Ramana Maharshi and the Path of Self-Knowledge* (London: Rider, 1973), p. 110.

18. T. M. P. Mahadevan, *Ramana Maharshi: The Sage of Arunacala* (London: Unwin Paperbacks, 1977), p. 55.

19. Suri Nagamma, "Letters from and Recollections of Sri Ramanasramam," Sri Ramanasram, n.d., http://www.ramana-maharshi.org/lettrec.htm (January 18, 2003).

20. Jan E. M. Houben, "To Kill or Not to Kill the Sacrificial Animal (*Yajña-Paśu*): Arguments and Perspectives in Brahminical Ethical Philosophy," in Jan E. M. Houben and Karel R. Van Kooij, eds., *Violence Denied: Violence, Non-Violence and the Rationalization of Violence in South Asian Cultural History* (Leiden: Brill, 1999), pp. 117–24.

21. A number of passages in the Brāhmaṇas express fear that, in the next world, the sacrificer will be eaten by his victim. See *Kauśītaki Brāhmaṇa* 11.3; *Śatapatha Brāhmaṇa* 11.6.1 and 12.9.1.1 and *Jaiminīya Brāhmaṇa* 1.42–44. *Manu* 5.55 warns that one who eats mean in this life will, in the next, be eaten by the same animal.

22. Cf. *Ṛgveda* 1.162.21: "You do not really die here, nor are you injured. You go to the gods on paths pleasant to go on" (quoted by Henk W. Bodewitz, "Hindu *Ahiṃsā* and its Roots," in Houben and Van Kooij, eds., *Violence Denied,* p. 24, n. 2 [Leiden: Brill, 1999]).

23. Kane, *History of Dharmasastra,* 4:424–25.

24. Houben, "To Kill or Not to Kill," p. 153.

25. Ibid., p. 156.

26. D. N. Jha, *The Myth of the Holy Cow* (London: Verso, 2002), p. 41; Michael Witzel, "The Case of the Shattered Head," *Studien zur Indologie und Iranistik* 13/14 (1987): 412.

27. Hugh B. Urban, "The Path of Power: Impurity, Kingship, and Sacrifice in Assamese Tantra," *Journal of the American Academy of Religion* 69 (December 2001): 798. A fact that may or may not comfort moderns disturbed by "animal" sacrifice in Hinduism, whether of the Vedic or Tantric variety, is that human beings have not always been excluded from the lists of animals to be offered. In the late Vedic period human sacrifice, if perhaps no longer practiced, was somewhat nervously remembered and still countenanced as, at the very least, a theoretical possibility. See Witzel, "The Case of the Shattered Head," pp. 390–92; Houben, "To Kill or Not to Kill," pp. 120–23, 127–28; Danielle Feller Jatavallabhula, "Raṇayajña: The Mahābhārata War as a Sacrifice," in Houben and Van Kooij, eds., *Violence Denied,* pp. 69–104. Tantric rites included (and perhaps occasionally still include) the ritual slaughter of humans in addition to goats and buffalo (Urban, "The Path of Power," pp. 806–9; Alex Perry Atapur, "Killing for 'Mother' Kali," *Time Asia,* July 29, 2002, http://www.time.com/time/asia/magazine/article/0,13673, 501020729-322673,00.html [February 8, 2003]).

28. Rajendralala Mitra, "Beef in Ancient India," in *Indo-Aryans: Contributions Toward the Elucidation of their Ancient and Medieval History,* vol. 1, pp. 354–88 (London, E. Stanford, 1881; reprint Delhi: Indological Bookhouse, 1969); D. N. Jha, "Myth of the Holy Cow."

29. Perhaps the most dramatic statement of this radically elitist view occurs at the opening of Śaṅkara's *Vivekacūḍāmaṇi* (vs. 2). See also *BhP* 3.29.28–34 and my "Theism for the Masses, Non-dualism for the Monastic Elite: A Fresh Look at Śaṅkara's Trans-theistic Spirituality," in *The Struggle Over the Past: Fundamentalism in the Modern World,* edited by William Shea (Latham, MD: University Press of America, 1993), pp. 61–77.

30. Rajagopal Ryali, "Eastern-Mystical Perspective on Environment," in Dave Stefferson, Walter J. Herrscher, and Robert S. Cook, eds, *Ethics for Environment: Three Religious Strategies,* pp. 47–48 (Green Bay: University of Wisconsin Press, 1973).

31. Wendy Doniger O'Flaherty, *The Origins of Evil in Hindu Mythology* (Berkeley: University of California Press, 1976), p. 173.

32. Chandra Rajan, trans., *Kālidāsa, The Loom of Time: A Selection of His Plays and Poems* (New Delhi: Penguin Books India, 1989), p. 224.

33. A. Devaraja Mudaliar, *The Cow, Lakshmi* (Tiruvannamali, India: Sri Ramanasramam, 1996), p. 11.

34. Mudaliar, *The Cow, Lakshmi,* pp. 14–15.

35. Ibid., p. 11.

36. Ibid., p. 12.

37. Edward C. Dimock, trans., *Caitanyacaritāmṛta of Kṛṣṇadāsa Kavirāja,* edited by Tony Stewart (Cambridge: Harvard University Press, 1999), pp. 782–83.

38. Swami A. C. Bhaktivedanta Prabhupada, *Śrī Caitanya-caritāmṛta of Kṛṣṇadāsa Kavirāja Gosvāmī,* Part 3, vol. 1 (New York: Bhaktivedanta Book Trust, 1975), pp. 13, 17.

39. Wendy Doniger O'Flaherty, ed. and trans., *Textual Sources for the Study of Hinduism* (Chicago: University of Chicago Press, 1988), 53–56.

40. Vijaya Rettakudi Nagarajan, "The Earth as the Goddess Bhū Devī: Toward a Theory of 'Embedded Ecologies' in Folk Hinduism," in *Purifying the Earthly Body of God: Religion and Ecology in Hindu India,* ed. Lance E. Nelson, 269–95 (Albany, N.Y.: State University of New York Press, 1998).

41. Padmanabh S. Jaini, "Indian Perspectives on the Spirituality of Animals," in David J. Kalupahana and W. G. Weeraratne, eds., *Buddhist Philosophy and Culture: Essays in Honor of N. A. Jayawickrema,* 169–78 (Colombo: N. A. Jayawickrema Felicitation Volume Committee, 1987), p. 170.

42. If we recall the identification of dogs and Caṇḍālas in the classical tradition, and that large numbers of *human* beings (low caste, untouchable/dalit, etc.) in Hindu India remain hierarchically marginalized—dare we say, like animals?—the ideal of including nonhuman animals in a world that is a communion of subjects may seem all the more remote.

43. Unquestionably the most visible animal rights campaigner in India today is Maneka Gandhi, daughter-in-law of the late Indira Gandhi, three times elected to the Lok Sabha (India's parliament), former environment minister, and lately welfare minister. A tireless campaigner for the protection of India's endangered species and such varied causes as nonviolent silk production, resistance to multinational fast food outlets, and the abolition of animal experimentation, she is a founder and current chairperson of the NGO, People for Animals. Lamenting that India nowadays seems "to measure progress in the move from vegetarianism to non-vegetarianism" (Mark Gold, "Diet for the New Century," March 1999, http://www.animalaid.org.uk/campaign/vegan/feed99.htm [March 23, 2003]), Gandhi asserts: "Hindus are seen as a gentle people coexisting and caring for all plants and animals and setting an example to the rest of the world. Perhaps that was once true, but look at us now. Today India is the largest exporter of meat in Asia with 75% exported. 37% of our crop is going to feed Europe's meat animals and over 300,000 cattle are killed in abattoirs daily. Factory farming is becoming the norm" (Maneka Gandhi, "Statement in Support of Animal Aid's 'Veggie Month, 1997,'" n.d., http://www.animalaid.org.uk/Veg98/warning.htm [May 16, 1999]).

Strategies of Vedic Subversion

The Emergence of Vegetarianism in Post-Vedic India

EDWIN BRYANT

This essay examines aspects of the history of animal slaughter in certain orthodox Hindu Sanskrit textual sources[1] by exploring the tension between the *hiṃsā,*[2] "violence," constitutional to the sacrificial requirements of the Vedic age, and the *ahiṃsā,* "nonviolence," associated with the *ātman,* or soul-based sensitivities of the post-Vedic age.[3] As the development between these two polarities evolved, animals increasingly began to be perceived as subjects, fellow souls temporarily encapsulated in nonhuman physical bodies, as opposed to disposable objects that could be utilized and sacrificed against their will in the pursuit of human needs. In this latter regard, the attitudes during the Vedic period were comparable to that in other sacrificial cultures of the ancient world that invoked scriptural authority for legitimacy in the matter of the slaughter and consumption of animals.

Where the Indian case study is noteworthy, and thus of particular interest to the comparative study of animals in the religious traditions of the world, is that a vegetarian ethic developed sometime prior to the Common Era, wherein a sense of communion between humans and animals evolved. This was based on the conviction that all living beings contained an *ātman,* or innermost conscious self. These *ātman*s were all perceived as ontologically equal irrespective of the material form, human or nonhuman, within which they were temporarily encapsulated. Such communion was further enhanced by the notion of reincarnation that emerged in the late Vedic period, which held that all souls in animal forms were eventually destined to attain human forms, while souls in human forms could potentially become animals in future births, depending on the nature of their activities during their human sojourn.

Attention will be directed here to the dissonance caused by the emergence of such an ethic to orthodox sensitivities, which were reluctantly obligated to acknowledge the legitimacy of animal slaughter in the sacrificial context, since such activities are prescribed in the sacred texts of the older Vedic period. These texts are considered *apauruṣeya,* trans-human (i.e., divinely re-vealed), and their acceptance is one of the main definitional factors of orthodoxy. This dilemma caused many orthodox Brāhmaṇas, the priestly and scholarly caste, to devise strategies of sub-version or reinterpretation of the ancient sacri-ficial injunctions, despite being constrained by the very nature of orthodoxy to stop short of ex-plicitly rejecting Vedic authority altogether. This essay explores some of the hermeneutical meth-ods adopted to accomplish these ends.

The Vedic period is the earliest era in South Asia for which we have written literary records, and provides the substratum from within which, or against which, all subsequent religious ex-pressions evolve, at least in the north of the subcontinent. The prominent religious expres-sion in this period is that of the sacrificial cult wherein items, including animals, are offered to the various gods through the medium of fire. Considerable textual detail regarding the spe-cifics of the sacrifice exists in the vast body of material that was orally transmitted and re-corded by the followers of the Vedic cult. While the Sanskritic literary tradition is voluminous, the texts containing material specific to the sac-rifice include the four Vedas, much of which consist of hymns used in the sacrificial con-text; the prose Brāhmaṇa texts (not to be con-fused with the priestly caste), which contain prescriptions and details of sacrificial specifics; the Āraṇyakas, which are a type of bridge be-tween the Brāhmaṇa and Upaniṣadic texts; the Upaniṣads, which are less concerned with sacri-fice and more with philosophical enquiry; and the various Sūtra texts, some of which contain detailed information connected with the correct performance of sacrifice. There are also various Smṛti law books principally dealing with vari-ous rules and regulations governing various as-pects of human activity, some of which also include sacrificial prescriptions. The post-Vedic period sees the emergence of the Epics such as the *Rāmāyaṇa* and *Mahābhārata,* as well as the Purāṇas. These texts consist primarily of narra-tions about Hindu gods and goddesses and their

devotees, but are also vast repositories of infor-mation on sacrifice and ritual, as well as a wide variety of subject matter that has shaped what has come to be known as Hinduism, including cosmologies, the social system, royal lineages, and esoteric and normative modes of worship.

There are numerous references as early as the *Ṛgveda,* the oldest and most revered Vedic text, to people eating meat. They enjoyed the flesh of fat sheep,[4] as well as that of the goat and the bull, and they relished the smell of meat.[5] Indra, a prominent god of the early period, boasts of having been offered more than fifteen oxen,[6] and horses, bulls, oxen, barren cows and rams were offered to Agni, the god of fire.[7] Most of the references toward meat-eating and animal slaughter in this ancient period occur within a sacrificial context. Perhaps the most famous Vedic sacrifice is the *aśvamedha,* the horse sacri-fice, wherein horse flesh is cooked in a pot and offered to the fire.[8] A dog as well as a number of other animals are also killed in the horse sac-rifice.[9] There are a number of other forms of Vedic sacrifices in addition to the *aśvamedha,* such as the *rājasūya* and the *agniṣṭoma,* in all of which animals are sacrificed. The later Śrauta-sūtra texts in particular discuss many types of animal sacrifices, some of which involved the slaughter of numerous different animals.[10] Al-though cows were *aghnyā,* "not to be killed," and despite their sacrality in later Hinduism, barren cows as well as bulls were also killed ritually.[11] It is noteworthy, given the prevalence of vege-tarianism among this class in later times, that in many of these sacrifices the meat was distributed to the Brāhmaṇas, the priestly caste (not to be confused with the Brāhmaṇa texts by the same name).[12] The animals are not simply sacrificed, their flesh is eaten: some Brāhmaṇa texts go into considerable detail discussing which parts of the slaughtered animal's anatomy was to be appor-tioned to which priest.[13]

At the same time, preliminary signs of ten-sion or unease with such slaughter are occa-sionally encountered even in the earlier Vedic period. As early as the *Ṛgveda,* sensitivity is shown toward the slaughtered beasts; for example, one hymn notes that mantras are chanted so that the animal will not feel pain and will go to heaven when sacrificed.[14] The *Sāmaveda* says: "we use no sacrificial stake, we slay no victims, we worship entirely by the repetition of sacred verses."[15] In the *Taittirīīya Āraṇyaka*, although prescriptions for offering a cow at a funeral procession are outlined in one place, this is contradicted a little further in the same text where it is specifically advised to release the cow in this same context, rather than kill her.[16] Such passages hint, perhaps, at proto-tensions with the gory brutality of sacrificial butchery, and forerun the transition between animals as objects and animals as subjects.

The same tension becomes progressively more visible in the later Vedic period — some texts are still legitimizing violence against animals, while others are opposing it, sometimes in the same text. The *Śatapatha Brāhmaṇa* has one of the earliest statements prohibiting the consumption of meat, at least that of the bull or the cow. This text states that the gods decree that these particular animals support everything in the world, therefore eating these is like eating everything and a person so doing will be reborn as a sinful being.[17] Yet, in the same breath, the verse acknowledges that Yajñavalkya, a renowned sage, eats the flesh of cows and oxen provided it is tender. The slightly later *Bṛhadāranyaka Upaniṣad* is advocating that parents should eat rice cooked with beef or veal if they want a learned son who is a knower of the Vedas,[18] but by the still slightly later *Chāndogya Upaniṣad,* we find a clear reference to refraining from killing, *sarva bhūtāni,* 'all living entities,' heralding the types of attitudes that become so typical of later Hinduism.[19]

Some ambivalence toward animal sacrifice and meat consumption is also visible in the Dharma and Gṛhya Sūtras, which are prescriptive law books. There are a variety of lists in these texts outlining creatures that are fit for human consumption that parallel the ancient dietary restrictions of other old-world cultures:

from five-toed animals, only porcupine, hare, iguana, rhinoceros, and tortoise are edible. Birds that eat by scratching with their feet and are not web-footed may be eaten, as may fishes, animals killed by beasts of prey if no blemish is visible, and animals deemed fit by the wise. Animals that can be eaten include those with a double row of teeth, too much hair, without hair, or one hoofed, as well as various birds and fish.[20] To a great extent, this genre of texts continues in the same vein as the ritualistic texts: the first food of a child should be goat or partridge meat if the parents desire boons;[21] one desiring the harmony of minds should eat calf meat mixed with some sour substance;[22] food mixed with fat satisfies the forefathers for varying periods of time — beef for a year, buffalo for longer and rhino longer again.[23] Vasiṣṭha, one of the authors of a set of Dharmasūtras, recalls that sage Agastya, during a thousand-year sacrifice, went out to hunt in order to prepare sacrificial cakes with the meat of tasty beasts and fowls.[24] This story is to reoccur as a source of authority in a number of other later texts condoning meat-consumption. Pāraskara, another such author, also delineates that those worthy of special reception were to be offered *arghya,* a preparation that had to contain flesh.[25] The author of another set of Sūtras, Āpastamba, declares that if a host feeds his guests meat, he attains merit.[26] In these texts, too, the cow is not exempt from slaughter: Vasiṣṭha's Sūtras state that milk cows and oxen may be offered,[27] and that a host may offer hospitality to a Brāhmaṇa priest by cooking a full-grown ox.[28] Just as discordant from the perspective of later Hinduism, Gautama notes in his Sūtras that even a hermit may eat meat.[29] Nor is this even always an option: if an ascetic invited to eat at a sacrifice rejects meat he shall go to hell for as many years as the slaughtered beast has hairs.[30]

All in all, in the Dharmasūtras and the early Vedic period in general, killing is clearly legitimated and even obligatory in certain situations, provided it is in sacrificial contexts; however, even then, injunctions against meat-eating do begin to surface. The Baudhāyana Dharmasūtras determine that a student is to abstain from meat-eating, since this is considered a breach of appropriate conduct.[31] For Āpastamba, a student is not to eat meat oblations even if they are offered to the forefathers.[32] While stating that the slaughter at a sacrifice is not considered slaughter, Vasiṣṭha nonetheless states that meat can never be obtained without injuring living beings, and injuring living beings does not procure heavenly bliss.[33]

It is toward the end of the Vedic period, in the Smṛti genre of law books, that we get a more overt sense of discomfort with the butchery surrounding the sacrificial cult, and increasing reference to the benefits of abstinence. While some texts unabashedly uphold the old ways, other texts, or even other sections of the same text, show signs of disquiet or even conflict. In the *Yajñavalkya Smṛti,* for example, it is stated that one can eat meat without incurring any guilt when one's life is in danger, when making offerings to the ancestors, when it has been sprinkled with water and *mantra*s recited, or when it has been offered to the gods and forefathers.[34] Yet, the verses following this allowance state that one slaying beasts outside of the ritual context dwells in hell for as many days as there are hairs on the body of the beast, and one who avoids meat-eating obtains all desires, gets the fruits of the horse sacrifice and, though living at home, becomes a sage.[35]

Nowhere is this conflict of priorities more evident than in Manu, the principal lawgiver for Hindus, and reputed author of what was to become the most authoritative legal text in Hinduism. Here again we find that killing in a sacrificial context is not considered killing,[36] and that birds and beasts recommended for consumption may be slain by Brāhmaṇas to feed their dependants on the grounds that Agastya and other sages did so in ancient times.[37] As in the older texts, Manu lists the types of creatures one can eat,[38] along with the creatures not to be eaten.[39] But Manu is much more specific about the sacrificial parameters of meat-eating: one may lawfully eat meat only when it has been sprinkled with water, when *mantra*s have been recited, when Brāhmaṇas desire one to do so, when one is performing a rite according to law, and when one's life is in danger.[40] One should not eat meat without a sacred purpose;[41] meat eating is permissible only in a sacrificial setting,[42] but within such a context, herbs, trees, cattle, birds and other animals slaughtered in sacrifice attain a higher existence in their next life along with the Brāhmaṇa priest performing the ritual.[43] Killing animals according to Vedic injunctions leads the sacrificer as well as the animal to the highest position.[44] In addition, if a man engaged in sacrifice refuses to take meat he becomes an animal for the next twenty births.[45]

With regard to the sacrificial prerogative of meat-eating, then, Manu subscribes to the injunctions and customs of his Vedic forefathers. Where he departs from them, however, is in his drastic admonitions against meat consumption outside that context: a man who slays unlawfully, that is, outside the sacrificial context, will be slain as many times as there are hairs on the body of the animal;[46] he who increases his own flesh with the flesh of others is the greatest of sinners;[47] one who injures living beings to please himself never finds happiness either living or dead;[48] one who permits the slaughter of animals, cuts them, kills them, buys them, sells them, cooks them, or serves them is himself equal to a slayer of animals;[49] one who desires to increase one's own flesh by the flesh of others, is the worst kind of sinner;[50] one should shun meat eating because meat cannot be obtained without injuring sentient beings which is detrimental to heavenly bliss;[51] one should abstain from meat eating upon considering the origin of flesh and the cruelty of fettering and slaying corporeal beings;[52] one who has an addiction to meat should—significantly—rather make a sacrificial animal out of clarified butter or flour;[53] and, again—just as significantly—an abstainer of meat gets equal merit with a performer of the prestigious Vedic horse sacrifice.[54] The Vedic sacrifice is thus not rejected; instead a nonviolent yet equally efficacious alternative is offered. It is in Manu that we find the popular etymology of the term for meat: *mām sah* "me, he" (i.e., the animal whose flesh I eat in this life will devour me in the next world;[55] see also, in this regard, *Mahābhārata, Anuśāsana Parva* 116). Manu even prescribes five sacrifices to atone for the sins incurred in the unavoidable killing of tiny entities in the five "slaughter-houses" that are a standard feature of any Hindu homestead: the grinding stone, pestle, mortar, hearth, and water vessel.

The impression one can draw from all this, I suggest, is that as a *Vaidika*, an orthodox follower of Vedic culture, Manu is obliged to defer to the sanctity of Vedic injunctions, and thereby is forced to allow the performance of animal sacrifice and the eating of meat in ritualistic contexts. But the quantity and quality of his invectives against meat-eating for the purpose of satisfying the palate suggest that were it not for such scriptural constraints, Manu would have no tolerance for the slaughter of animals. Indeed, he goes so far as to implicitly undermine normative sacrificial practices by authorizing a substitute to the sacrificial animal, one made of butter and flour, and declaring that abstinence from meat produces the same benefit as the ancient highly desired and prestigious horse sacrifice. Efficacious alternatives are thus created for the hallowed Vedic rites, and sensitivity for animals as subjects clearly emerges from such prescriptions.

The *Mahābhārata* contains some of the strongest statements against the slaughter of animals and the eating of meat. On the one hand we have the usual statements indicating that animals were eaten, at least by the Kṣatriyas, the warrior caste; the sun god, for example, promises Yudhiṣṭhira an unlimited supply of food including meat, after being worshipped by him.[56] Moreover, the sacrificial rites were still in full swing—Yudhiṣṭhira feeds ten thousand brāhmaṇas with various delicacies including the flesh of wild boars and deer,[57] and elsewhere performs an *aśvamedha* horse sacrifice in which vast num-

bers of creatures were tied to the stake, slaughtered, and cooked.[58]

But on the other hand the *Mahābhārata* has numerous stories and anecdotes glorifying the merits of nonviolence toward animals. For example, the story is recounted of a sage who was once impaled by some thieves on a pike. When the sage asked Dharma, the god of righteousness, what his offense had been to merit such a karmic reaction, he was informed that he had once pricked an insect with a blade of grass and was now suffering the karmic consequences, thereby underscoring the severe reaction involved in harming even an insect. Elsewhere, the sage Jājali allowed birds to nest on his head, refraining from stirring so as not to injure them. He stood in this condition even after the eggs had hatched, and, indeed, remained immobile until well after the birds had grown and flown off from the nest, awaiting their possible return. Another sage, Cyavana, while meditating under water, was hauled up by fishermen's nets along with a multitude of fishes. Seeing that great slaughter of fish surrounding him, the sage declared that he had lived with the fish for so long that he could not abandon them, and thus he should either die with them, or the fishermen should sell him along with the catch.[59]

Some of the strongest admonitions against meat-eating emanate from the mouth of Bhiṣma, grandsire of the Kuru dynasty. Bhiṣma explains to Yudhiṣṭhira that compassion is the highest religious principle—indeed, three entire chapters of the Epic are dedicated to the evils of meat-eating.[60] The eating of meat is compared to eating the flesh of one's son, and those who indulge in such a diet are among the vilest of human beings, and their future lives are fraught with great misery. Howsoever it is dressed, Bhiṣma notes, meat enslaves the mind and deprives the consumer of the joys of heaven —in fact, the righteous gained entrance into heaven in previous ages by giving up their own bodies to protect the lives of other creatures.[61]

Yudhiṣṭhira then posits the important question as to how, given all this, Vedic sacrifices and rites could be followed without the offering of meat to the forefathers. Although Bhīṣma nominally acknowledges that Manu had authorized the eating of meat in a sacrificial context, he reminds Yudhiṣthira that one who abstains from doing so acquires the same merit as that accrued from the performance of even a horse sacrifice. Moreover, those desirous of heaven perform sacrifice with seeds instead of animals. Bhīṣma, like Manu, thus provides an efficacious means of fulfilling Vedic sacrificial imperatives without requiring the slaughter of animals and thus he, too, implicitly undermines normative sacrificial expectations.

Bhīṣma goes on to state that discarding a meat diet is the highest form of religion, and by so doing one enjoys the confidence of all creatures and is never put in danger from other beings, even if lost in the wilderness.[62] Although flesh is the tastiest of foodstuffs, there is nothing dearer to any creature than life, and thus there is no one crueler than one who deprives creatures of their cherished life in order to increase one's own flesh at their expense.[63] One suffers similar torment oneself in various future births, where one is oneself eaten by the very animals one has eaten — one will have to suffer the exact same violence oneself in a future life, as one inflicts on other creatures in this life.[64] One who abstains from meat-eating, or recites the merits of such abstinence, attains all types of boons in life followed by heaven in the next; such a person never sees hell, even if wicked in other respects. In contrast, one who shortens the lifespan of other creatures sees one's own lifespan shortened, and is persecuted in turn as a beast of prey, and finishes up tormented in hell. Bhīṣma, echoing Manu, also notes that all those involved in the arrangements for meat consumption — the buyer, seller, and cook — are no different from meat-eaters.[65]

Despite all this, Bhīṣma is still forced to concede that animals killed in sacrifice can be eaten even though he immediately adds that any other type of meat-consumption is the way of the demon.[66] However, we begin to see statements in the *Mahābhārata* that explicitly encroach upon the inviolability of animal slaughter even in sacrificial contexts. These statements thus go further than just providing a nonviolent but equally efficacious alternative to ritualistic slaughter, as Manu does. The Brāhmaṇa Satya, for example, is described as loosing the merit he had accrued *because* he had engaged in violence at sacrifices.[67] The text also informs us that in the *satya yuga,* the golden age, animals were not killed in sacrifice. Animal slaughter was introduced in *treta yuga,* the second of the four ages, when people first began to resort to violence, and it continued thereafter. The implication here is that the slaughter of animals in sacrifice was the later development of an age that was less pure, enlightened, and compassionate. Here we see the beginning of a rewriting of the old Vedic script concerning the legitimacy of sacrifice. The Vedic prescriptions condoning and promoting animal sacrifice are not ostensibly rejected, but they are demoted to a later, more degraded period of human history when human virtue had declined. The time is ripe for more radical revisionistic exegesis of the Vedic injunctions.

A similar ambivalent and conflicted situation prevails in the Purāṇic texts. In places, meat-eating and animal sacrifice are encouraged, in others they are fiercely discouraged. On the one hand, in the *Brahmavaivarta Purāṇa,* Śiva relates to Parvatī in a laudatory tone the story about the charity of king Suyajña who used to feed millions of brāhmaṇas with meat.[68] Likewise, the Padma and the Viṣṇu Purāṇas, primary texts for the strictly vegetarian Vaiṣṇava sects, relate the story of how the demons were bewildered into desisting from the Vedic rites and the sacrifice of animals, as a result of which the gods were able to regain control of heaven.[69] Thus, desistance from animal sacrifice is portrayed in a negative light, suggesting that the sacrifice of animals continued to be an expected mode of religion in the Purāṇic age; indeed, the *aśvamedha* sacrifice, among others, is frequently mentioned in many Purāṇas.[70]

Yet, many of these same Purāṇas are also conflicted about violence against animals, despite following the pattern of being constrained by Vedic imperative to nominally accept it in sacrificial contexts. As we have seen elsewhere, tension with the sacrificial cult is evidenced within the pages of the same text: the *Kūrma Purāṇa* requires that the performer of *śrāddha,* rites to departed ancestors, is to feed Brāhmaṇas with rice and meat of various kinds prepared with the appropriate rituals,[71] and proclaims that any higher caste person not eating flesh at such sacrifices becomes like an animal for twenty-one births.[72] And yet, the same *Kūrma Purāṇa* states that Brahmā created the institution of sacrifice *without* the slaughter of animals.[73]

Like the *Mahābhārata,* in the *Skandha Purāṇa,* too, we find a revisionism of the discourse of sacrifice. We are informed that the sages were dismayed to see the violence of the sacrifice, which they stated to be against the *dharma,* religious duty, of the gods. They claimed that meat had never been eaten by the *sāttvic,* more enlightened, gods and that sacrifice is only supposed to be performed with grain or milk. When King Vasu, infamous as a sacrificer of animals, was asked by the sages whether animals or herbs were to be offered in the rites, he fell from heaven to earth for indicating the former.[74] Importantly, the *Skandha* also gives its own alternative version of the origin of Vedic sacrifice. Once, due to a Brāhmaṇa's curse, the three worlds were afflicted by famine. The common people slaughtered animals to satisfy their hunger, but the sages did not, even though dying of starvation. The sages told the people that they could sacrifice animals if their intention was to offer them to the gods rather than killing them for themselves. Consequently, gods, kings, and nonroyal mortals performed animal sacrifices and ate the meat as sanctified remnant, but, the texts hasten to add, the true *bhaktas,* devotees of God, did not indulge in such meat eating, even though they, too, were afflicted by the calamity.[75] In this narrative, the ancient Vedic sacrificial cult is presented as being a concession to

humanity on account of the specific exigencies of an emergency situation (but was nevertheless one that was not availed of by the saintly).

Along similar lines, in the *Matsya Purāṇa,* there is a dialogue on the eve of a sacrifice among sages who disapprove of the violence of sacrifices, preferring to prescribe rites involving the oblations of fruits and vegetables instead of animals.[76] As we have seen with Manu and the *Mahābhārata,* the Vedic sacrificial format is thus preserved, but the ingredients of the rites are adjusted so as to exclude slaughter. Elsewhere, the *Matsya Purāṇa* negotiates with the Vedic heritage in another way, namely, by stating that the demerit incurred by killing at sacrifices is heavier than any merit accrued therefrom.[77] Here, the boons of animal sacrifice promised by the Vedic texts are acknowledged, but they are outweighed by the negative karma incurred by such activities.

The text that perhaps goes farthest in distancing itself from the sacrificial cult is the most important Purāṇic text, the *Bhāgavata Purāṇa.* In this text, a person understanding the essence of *dharma* does not eat meat at sacred rites, for there is no satisfaction in the slaughter of animals; indeed, refraining from harming all living beings in thought, word, or deed is promoted as the highest *dharma.*[78] Even here, the text does begrudgingly acknowledge that for special rites, although not for routine ones, a king may kill just the required number of animals and no more,[79] and one with a penchant for meat may eat the remnants of animals offered in sacrifice —although the text hastens to add that such activity is by no means obligatory.[80] But, elsewhere, the *Bhāgavata* makes a point of relating the story of Prācīnabarhis who wantonly killed many animals in hunting and in sacrifices, and who was given a vision of these same animals waiting for his death so that they could inflict corresponding violence on him by cutting him with steel-like horns as his just karmic reaction.[81]

The text warns that the sin of slaying creatures cannot be removed by performing sham sacrifice just as mud cannot be cleansed by mud, and a wine-drinker cannot be purified by wine. Moreover, those who kill animals at sham sacrifices are hypocrites and fall into hell where they are tortured.[82] The way this text deals with animal slaughter is to graphically present the horrific reactions that accrue from its performance—a man cooking animals and birds is merciless and goes to *kumbhipāka* hell where he in turn is fried in boiling oil; unlawful animal killers are made the target of the arrows of the servants of Yama, the lord of death; those killing animals in sham sacrifices are themselves cut to pieces in *viśasana* hell; those harming insects and other lesser creatures go to the *andhakūpa* hell where, deprived of sleep and unable to rest anywhere, they are tortured by those very creatures.[83] In this way, while the boons promised by the old sacrificial texts are not denied, the *Bhāgavata Purāṇa* supplies the fine print of the Vedic contract—violence performed in the pretext of sacrifice produces temporary benefits, but at a horrible price.

I suggest that such tension in these post-Vedic texts can be understood in at least two ways. They could represent conflicting statements surfacing in synchronic chronological time, with different pro and con statements emanating from the individual sensitivities and inclinations of different authors juxtaposed together in the same text. Or, they could more likely reflect the passage of diachronic chronological time, with later redactions of the same texts adding invectives against meat-eating and sacrificial slaughter at a time when the sacrificial cult had already faded in appeal and authority, while simultaneously preserving older sections from earlier redactions which acknowledged or even encouraged such practices. Either way, what we seem to find in ancient India—which is perhaps unique amongst the sacrificial cultures of the old world in this regard—is the development of significant discomfort with the heritage of a divinely ordained sacrificial matrix that was heavily involved in the slaughter of nonhuman animals. Prompting this was the idea in the later Vedic period of a communion of

humans and animals as fellow beings embodying the same *ātman*, life force. Consequently, what was to become a prominent vegetarian ethic emerged as animals underwent a transformation in human perspectives from expendable objects of consumption to conscious subjects of experience. Many innovative thinkers involved in this development jettisoned the Vedic sacrificial rituals and their sources of authority, the Vedic texts, altogether. Some of them eventually became known as Jains and Buddhists. These communities retained no compunction toward Vedic authority, but could scorn the whole sacrificial culture along with the texts which sanctioned it and preach an unencumbered *ahiṃsā*, nonviolence, without the ambivalence or tension that was the lot of those remaining in the orthodox Brāhmaṇa fold.

In contrast to those who took the heterodox route, Vedic authority remained a straitjacket, compelling many orthodox Purāṇic compilers to condone or at least acknowledge sacrificial slaughter on some level or other, at least nominally. By definition, orthodoxy entails accepting the divine revelatory nature of the Vedic texts and, by extension, their injunctions. In other words, such authors were stuck with a divinely ordained sacrificial culture with all that this involved in terms of the slaughter of animals. But they nonetheless simultaneously managed to marshal all manner of ingenious arguments against animal slaughter short of jettisoning the whole sacrificial culture and, by extension, the authority of the textual sources that condoned it.

They attempted to accomplish this by rewriting the Vedic sacrificial script in a number of different ways. They argued that even though animal sacrifice is permissible—and only permissible—within the confines of the ritualistic context, only the lower gods eat meat; or only nondevotional men engage in sacrifice; or such sacrifice is the perverted development of a post–golden age; or it is the allowance of an emergency situation of famine; or fruits, seeds, or other such ingredients should be substituted for the animals; or sacrifice accrues ghastly karmic results that far outweigh any benefits gained. In short, the authors of seminal Hindu texts began to promote the view of an enlightened individual as one partaking in a communion of ultimate equality and nonviolence between all creatures (but see Lance Nelson's essay preceding this one in this volume for a problematization of this ideal). They envisioned a universe where, at least in theory, all beings were accepted as living subjects with the same rights to life as their human companions, rather than less-animate and thus disposable objects fit for sacrifice or human consumption.

That these authors were successful in their exegetical revisionism vis-à-vis the scriptural injunctions of the Vedic matrix is evidenced by the prevalence of vegetarianism among the Hindu upper castes[84] and among lower castes aspiring for upward mobility. They succeeded in undermining and reinterpreting the sacrificial texts in numerous ways without explicitly and overtly rejecting them, and, like their contemporary Jains and Buddhists, they strongly advocated the importance of nonviolence against what they perceived as fellow beings temporally encapsulated in the bodies of nonhuman animals. As such, the strategies they adopted, or, perhaps more importantly, their very willingness to contextualize and assign new meanings to the old injunctions from the perspective of these emerging sensitivities of communion and shared subjectivity, exemplify hermeneutical and attitudinal possibilities for other scriptural traditions of the world that have similarly legitimized the slaughter of animals in their ancient periods.

NOTES

1. This article will not consider the philosophical literature, since the rational response to traditional Vedic sacrifice as represented in certain philosophical texts has been covered by Jan Houben, "To Kill or Not to Kill the Sacrificial Animal (Yajna Pasu)" in J. Houben and K. Van Kooij, eds., *Violence Denied* (Leiden: Brill, 1999). Other related articles on the subject of non-violence against animals include Koshelya Walli, *The Conception of Ahiṃsā in Indian Thought* (Varanasi: Bharata Manisha, 1974), and Unto Tähtinen, *Ahiṃsā: Non-Violence in Indian Tradition* (London: Rider, 1976).

2. *Hiṃs* is the desiderative verbal form of *han*, to kill.

3. I will restrict my focus to verses explicitly referring to violence against animals in specific, as opposed to the much larger range of references to *ahiṃsā* in general.

4. *Ṛgveda* 10.27.17.

5. *Ṛgveda* 1.162.12.

6. *Ṛgveda* 10.86.14 (see also, 10.27.2).

7. *Ṛgveda* 10.91.14.

8. *Ṛgveda* 1.162.13–19.

9. *Śukla Yajurveda Adhyāya* 24.

10. E.g., *Āpastamba Śrautasūtra* 14.5.1; *Āśvalāyan* 3.7.

11. *Ṛgveda* 10.91.14; 10.27.2.

12. E.g., *Atharvaveda* 9.5.

13. See K.S. Macdonald, *The Brahmanas of the Vedas* (Delhi: Bharatiya Corp, 1979, reprint), chapter VI for discussion.

14. *Ṛgveda* 1.162.21.

15. *Sāmaveda* 1.176.

16. *Tattirīya Āraṇyaka* 6.1.2.

17. *Śatapatha Brāhmaṇa* 3.1.2.21.

18. *Bṛhadāraṇyaka Upaniṣad* 6.4.18.

19. *Chāndogya Upaniṣad* 8.15; the verse qualifies that there is an exception to this injunction, namely, "at holy places."

20. *Gautama Dharmasūtra* 17.27–38. Vasiṣṭha sanctions the same five animals mentioned above but lists hedgehog instead of rhinoceros. He further elaborates that animals having teeth in one jaw except camels can be eaten. All aquatics are acceptable except crocodile, porpoise, alligator, and crab; he is also more specific about the types of birds that eat

by scratching—these are five in number, two types of partridge, the blue-rock pigeon, the crane, and the peacock (*Vasiṣṭha Dharmasūtra* 14.39–48; see, also *Baudhāyana Dharmaśāstra* 1.6.13).

21. *Āśvalāyana Gṛhyasūtra* 1.16.1–3.

22. *Atharvavedīya Kauśika Gṛhya Sūtras* 12.8.

23. *Āpastamba Dharmasūtra* 2.7.16.24–28; 2.7.17.1–3.

24. *Vasiṣṭha Dharmaśāstra* 4.8.

25. *Pāraskara Gṛhyasūtra* 1.3.29.

26. *Āpastamba Dharmaśāstra* 2.3.7.4.

27. *Vasiṣṭha Dharmaśāstra*, 14.46–47. He notes, however, that there are conflicting statements about rhinos and wild boar.

28. *Vasiṣṭha Dharmaśāstra* 4.8.

29. *Gautama Dharmasūtra* 3.30 (Hardatta, a commentator, understands "even" to indicate in emergency situations).

30. *Vasiṣṭha Dharmaśāstra* 11.34.

31. *Baudhāyana Dharmaśāstra* 3.4.1–2.

32. *Āpastamba Dharmaśāstra* 2.2.5.16.

33. *Vasiṣṭha Dharmaśāstra* 4.7.

34. *Yajñavalkya Smṛti* 7.179.

35. *Yajñavalkya Smṛti* 7.181.

36. *Manu* 5.39.

37. *Manu* 5.22–23.

38. *Manu* 5.15–16.

39. *Manu* 5.11.

40. *Manu* 5.27.

41. *Manu* 5.34.

42. *Manu* 5.31; 5.36.

43. *Manu* 5.42; *Viṣṇu Smṛti* 51.60.

44. *Manu* 5.42.

45. *Manu* 5.35.

46. *Manu* 5.38.

47. *Manu* 5.52.

48. *Manu* 5.45.

49. *Manu* 5.51.

50. *Manu* 5.52.

51. *Manu* 5.48.

52. *Manu* 5.47–49.

53. *Manu* 5.38.

54. *Manu* 5.53.

55. *Manu* 5.55.

56. *Vana Parva* 3.52–54.

57. *Sabha Parva* 4.1–2.

58. *Aśvamedha Parva* 85; 89.

59. *Aśvamedha Parva* 50.

60. *Aśvamedha Parva* 114-116.

61. *Aśvamedha Parva* 114.

62. *Aśvamedha Parva* 115; 116.

63. *Aśvamedha Parva* 116.

64. *Aśvamedha Parva* 116.

65. *Aśvamedha Parva* 115.

66. *Aśvamedha Parva* 116.

67. *Śantiparva Parva* 272.

68. *Brahmavaivarta Purāṇa, Prakṛti Khaṇḍa* 50.14–16 (reference from K. Walli, 1974).

69. *Padma Purāṇa, Sṛṣṭikhaṇḍa* 13.

70. E.g., *Agni* 14.27.

71. *Kūrma Purāṇa* 22.54.

72. *Kūrma Purāṇa* 2.22.75.

73. *Kūrma Purāṇa* 1.29.42.

74. *Skandha Purāṇa* 2.9.6.

75. *Skandha Purāṇa* 2.9.9.

76. *Matsya Purāṇa* 143.30–32.

77. *Matsya Purāṇa* 142.12.

78. *Bhāgavata Purāṇa* 7.15.7–8.

79. *Bhāgavata Purāṇa* 4.26.6.

80. *Bhāgavata Purāṇa* 11.21.29.

81. *Bhāgavata Purāṇa* 4.25.7–8.

82. *Bhāgavata Purāṇa* 5.26.25.

83. *Bhāgavata Purāṇa* 5.26.13–25.

84. The Kṣatriya, warrior caste, is an important exception to this but a discussion of this topic is beyond the scope of this paper.

BUDDHISM

"A vast unsupervised recycling plant"

Animals and the Buddhist Cosmos

IAN HARRIS

Cosmology, Sentience and Animal Life

Buddhism has flourished in most regions of Asia, in some cases for more than two thousand years. Its heritage has been preserved in written texts, architectural structures, political systems, and village customs. Not unsurprisingly, its view of animals is complex—periodically shifting and, to a substantial extent, determined by cultural attitudes that often predate the emergence of Buddhism itself.

Given the overwhelmingly agrarian condition of Indian society in the early Buddhist period and the practice of mendicancy among the first members of the monastic order, among other factors, it is perhaps unsurprising that animals feature regularly in the writings of the canonical and classical periods of Buddhist history. This is particularly the case for the Pāli canon of Theravāda Buddhism, where animals are mentioned simply as part of the narrative background, may hold some symbolic significance, or—more rarely—may be fully charac-

terized as central figures in a narrative sequence. Their categorization also occurs quite frequently in the texts where folk taxonomies such as grass-eaters, dung-eaters, creatures born from water, beasts of the forest, footless, many-footed, etc., are quite frequent. Categories of birds and creeping things are also widely acknowledged although the notion of species, as such seemed alien to the redactors of this literature.

The early texts display a fair to good knowledge of specific animals and their habits.[1] The most commonly mentioned animal in the popular stories of the Buddha's previous lives (*Jātaka*) is the monkey[2] and the Buddha is said to have lived in the form of the monkey Nandiya (*J*.ii.199f).[3] Monkeys are often a metaphor for mischievousness and lack of wisdom but there is no evidence that they were ever regarded as having any special filiation with humans. The elephant is also well represented; twenty-four different individuals are mentioned in the *Jātaka* collection alone. Such stories demonstrate a good knowledge of these animals' natural history, although some inaccuracies may be identified. They also demonstrate a "background acceptance of captivity and instrumental" usage, perhaps unsurprising given the close connection between elephant ownership and kingship.[4] Indeed, being able to ride an elephant or a horse is said to be the sign of high merit (*A*.iii.302), and in an interesting metaphor the training of an elephant is compared to the meditative techniques associated with the four foundations of mindfulness (*M*.iii.136). However, the welfare of elephants is not ignored and some stories recognize that elephants prefer freedom to captivity, and may suffer in servitude.[5]

Some care is needed in the proper interpretation of the *Jātaka* and other animal-oriented stories. Certainly, animals are often displayed in a positive light. They are shown to be capable of tender feelings for one another; they perform acts of extreme altruism; and they may live together harmoniously.[6] As such, they provide a guide to the proper conduct of humans. However, it could be argued that the often highly anthropomorphic character of the essentially pre-Buddhist folk-tradition of these narratives is largely devoid of "naturalistic" content, thus defeating the intention of those who bring them forward as evidence in support of an authentic Buddhist environmentalist ethic. Indeed, the animals are not really animals at all, for at the end of each story the Buddha reveals that the central character was none other than himself in a former life, with his monastic companions playing the supporting roles.

From the ultimate perspective, Buddhism views the world as unsatisfactory and a place of both gross and subtle suffering. All beings within the realm of rebirths (*saṃsāra*) suffer, but the level of dis-ease endured by animals is held to be an especially gross kind. This is partially related to their position in the "natural order" where the weak are at the mercy of the strong (*M*.iii.169). Nevertheless, animals possess the faculty of thought,[7] although their ability to develop useful insights into the true nature of things is limited. Their inferiority in this regard is linked to the fact that beings living in a state of perpetual insecurity have difficulty in maintaining calm mental states. For this, and other reasons, animals may not seek admittance to the monastic order (*saṅgha*)[8] and cannot easily act upon the teachings of a Buddha. Indeed, recitation of the monastic rules in an animal's presence is an offense (*Vin*.i.135) and monks are prohibited from imitating their behavior. Thus, the Buddha condemned a monk who decided that he would graze like a cow (*Vin*.ii.134) while an ascetic who copied the manners of a dog (*M*.i.387–89) was soundly castigated. Even though they may be regarded as autonomous entities, possessing both consciousness and devotional capabilities, animals are more unfavorably oriented to the possibility of liberation than are humans and rebirth as an animal has been universally regarded in a negative light.

A lack of insight into the true nature of reality has an impact on an animal's moral status. The animal may, for example, be constitutionally disposed toward acts of violence and sexual misconduct. The commonly encountered term, *tiracchānakathā*, meaning "low conversation" but literally "animal talk," seems to point in this general direction. Animals also tend to disregard the taboos that are held to be binding on human society, particularly those connected with cannibalism or incest. Goats, sheep, chickens, pigs, dogs, and jackals are particularly blameworthy in the latter regard (*D*.iii.72). Indeed, it is not unusual for the texts to classify animals alongside human matricides, parricides, hermaphrodites, thieves, and Buddha-killers (*Vin*.i.320).

From the Buddhist perspective, beings may be reborn into one of five destinies (*gati*), i.e. gods (sometimes subdivided into the realms of the *devas* and *asuras*, or demi-gods), humans, ghosts, animals, and denizens of hell, that comprise *saṃsāra*. It is worth noting that, while humans have a *gati* to themselves, all animals are lumped together in a single category. The universe, however, is a vast unsupervised recycling plant, in which unstable but sentient entities circulate from one form of existence to the next. The number of rebirths experienced by beings is theoretically without number, and promotion or relegation from one destiny to another, solely on the basis of past actions (*karma*), is accepted doctrine in all traditional forms of Buddhism. In consequence, the Buddha taught that we have all enjoyed close kinship relations with a virtual infinity of other beings in the past: "Monks, it is not easy to find a being who has not formerly been your mother, or your father, or your brother, your sister or your son or daughter." (S.ii.189)

This mutability of individual identity implies that we are loosely related to all beings whether divine, infernal, or animal. "All beings, throughout the six realms, can be considered as our father and mother" is the standard Mahāyāna Buddhist expression of the position—the most explicit Buddhist variation on Thomas Berry's notion of the world as "a communion of subjects, not a collection of objects."

Animals in Buddhist Ethics

"I undertake the precept to abstain from the taking of life" is the first of the five ethical precepts that are theoretically binding on all Buddhists, whether they are monks or members of the laity. The precept is underlined by the Buddha's statement that:

> Putting away the killing of living things. ... (the Buddha) holds aloof from the destruction of life. He has laid the cudgel and the sword aside and ashamed of roughness and full of mercy, he dwells compassionate and kind to all the creatures that have life. (D.i.4)

The Buddha spoke against the immolation of animals in the sacrificial rites connected with the Vedic tradition (D.i.127f) and trade in living beings is one of the five modes of employment to be avoided by the Buddhist laity (A.iii.208).

Indeed, when an anthropologist invited Sinhala villagers to define what Buddhism had taught them, they replied, "not to kill animals."[9] The Theravāda *Vinaya* tells us that butchers, fletchers, hunters, fowlers, and animal tamers are all destined to suffer a horrible death. In a much later text, the *Sutra of the Remembrance of the Good Law*,[10] the eight levels of hell are described in great detail. We read that, in a region called the hell of repetition, reprobates who have killed birds and deer without any regret are forced to eat dung alive with flesh-eating worms as punishment for their misdeeds.[11]

The first precept applies to all forms of life, ranging from the most complex to the most simple, but in reality the situation is rather more complicated. All of the ancient Indian renunciant traditions accepted the existence of minuscule entities, but the Buddha's position was that "if you can't really see them, then you can't be said to have caused intentional harm." Buddhism, then, steers a middle way between the inordinate diligence of the Jains[12] and a complete lack of care. Size is another significant factor in determining the magnitude of a crime against sentiency. For Buddhism, killing an elephant is worse than killing a dog, for large animals take more effort to kill and the degree of sustained intention must be consequently greater (cf. MA.i.165f). This seems to imply that the consequences are worse when killing an elephant than a chimpanzee. As we have already noted, there is no anthropomorphic principle in Buddhism that can act as a counterbalance in this ethical equation.

We might expect that the first precept would entail the observance of a fully vegetarian diet but, as Gombrich has noted, vegetarianism is "universally admired, but rarely practiced" in Buddhist Asia.[13] In actual fact, the Buddha accepted meat and resisted the schismatic Devadatta's attempts to place the *sangha* on an exclusively vegetarian diet (Vin.ii.171–2), arguing that such practices were optional. Indeed, vegetarianism as a fully articulated ethic manifests itself only at a comparatively late stage in Buddhist history, some seven hundred years after the Buddha's death.[14]

It seems that Buddhism from its inception regarded only intentional killing as wrong, for only intentional acts are *karmically* productive. Bearing this in mind, the Buddha deemed it acceptable to receive meat[15] from lay donors, since both recipient and giver were innocent of intentional killing, and, in any case, to deny a member of the laity the opportunity for making merit was felt to be a more serious matter. The only stipulation governing the monastic consumption of most meats is that they should be pure in three respects: a monk should neither have heard or seen the slaughter, or suspected that the animal had been killed on his behalf.[16]

The rules of monastic discipline also restrict walking during the rainy season to avoid killing small creatures, but the injunction is not binding on the laity. Suppose a Buddhist peasant plows a field prior to sowing seed. It is inevitable that worms and other small creatures will be killed and injured in very large numbers. This appears contrary to the spirit of noninjury (*ahiṃsā*) on which the first precept is founded. However, since the action is deemed devoid of the intention to kill, and because food production is essential to the maintenance of society, and of course to the continuity of the *saṅgha,* whose members rely on food donations from their lay supporters, plowing is permitted for the laity. Monks, on the other hand, must studiously avoid injury to animals, as well as plants,[17] and may not engage in agricultural labor (*Vin.*iv.32–33).[18]

If a monk should dig a pit into which a human falls and is killed, he is guilty of a serious offense and should be permanently expelled from the order. But if the victim turns out to be an animal, the monk must merely expiate his crime. A monk guilty of theft from another human must also be permanently excluded, but if he releases an animal from a hunter's trap out of compassion, rather than through any desire to own the creature (*Vin.*iii.62), he is innocent of an offense. Some texts accept the possibility that

an animal may have the right of property. The collection of honey is not considered quite right in most Buddhist cultures, unless the honey is to be used as a medicament. A beast of prey can also be said to rightfully possess its quarry. Nevertheless, the rules of monastic discipline do not find it an offence if a monk were to take the quarry for himself; although why he should wish to do so is a little difficult to comprehend!

Animal protection has a long history in Buddhist Asia. When Prince Vessantara returns to his kingdom at the end of the famous *Jātaka* story he releases all animals, even cats, from servitude as a kind of thank-offering (*J.*vi.593). Indeed, the ideal king, ruling in conformity with the Buddha's teachings, ensures the harmonious ordering of the entire natural order[19] by protecting his people as well as the wild animals of the forest and birds (*migapakkhī*) (*D.*iii.58ff). In another mythological fragment Sakka, the chief of the gods, commands his charioteer, even though they are both fleeing from enemies, to drive in such a way that bird nests are not shaken from the trees since "it is better to give up one's own life than make a bird nestless" (*S.*i.224). In a final story, a devout boy (*SA.*ii.112) is told that his mother will be cured from an ailment only by eating the flesh of a hare. Catching the creature in a field, the boy subsequently repents and releases the hare. But the mother is revivified through the power of her son's rejection of violence.

This is an important theme in the edicts of the ancient Indian Buddhist king, Aśoka. Animal sacrifices were banned in his capital city during fifty-six "no-slaughter days" each year.[20] The attitude later transplanted itself easily in China. The Emperor, Wu Ti (502–550 CE) is said to have fed fish held in a monastery pond as part of his Buddhist devotions while, in 759 CE, a Tang emperor is reported to have donated a substantial sum toward the construction of eighty-one such ponds (*fang sheng chi*) for the preservation of animal life. As late as the mid-1930s, the National Buddhist Association broadcast radio lectures on the need for animal protection, particularly around the period of "animal day," a date that traditionally coincided with the Buddha's birthday festivities.[21] Even today ethnobotanical studies seem to support the notion of the monastery as nature reserve.[22]

However, not all of the evidence points in the same direction. We know that during the Tang period monasteries "engaged in multifarious commercial and financial activities"[23] that may very well have had an adverse influence on the natural environment. There is also evidence that the widespread practice of animal and bird release, as a merit-making exercise, causes great harm, not least because the creatures are caught from the wild and kept in conditions of overcrowding and starvation before recovering their freedom. When the practice of releasing fish was imported into Japan, perhaps being blended with elements of Shintō in the process, more fish died in the ritual than were in fact granted freedom.[24]

As we have already seen, the putative structure of the Buddhist cosmos underlines a sense of solidarity between humans and other forms of life. This sense is conducive to the arising of the important Buddhist virtue of lovingkindness (*mettā*): "Just as a mother would protect with her life her own son ... so one should cultivate an unbounded mind towards all beings, and loving-kindness (*mettā*) towards all the world" (*Sn.*149–50).

Mettā is the first of the four divine-abidings (*brahmavihāra*), a series of important meditative exercises. The initial stages of the practice involve the direction of loving kindness towards oneself, for he "who loves himself will never harm another" (*S.i.*75). The circle of *mettā* may then be extended toward an honored teacher, a friend, a neutral person, a foe, a dead person, etc., with the motivation, "May all beings be happy and secure, may they be happy-minded. Whatever living beings there are—feeble or strong, long, stout or medium, short, small or large, seen or unseen, those dwelling far or near, those who are born or those who await rebirth —may all beings, without exception, be happy-

minded" (*Khp.*8–9). However, only those most advanced on the path should extend *mettā* to beings that might evoke strong feelings of aversion or desire. Clearly, animals fall into this category. Indeed, when a specific animal is mentioned in connection with *mettā*, the context is, more often than not, apotropaic.[25] Thus, when the schismatic Devadatta attempts to destroy the Buddha by sending the enraged and intoxicated elephant Nālāgirigiri to trample him underfoot, the Buddha employs *mettā* to subdue the beast (*Vin.*ii.194).

The Culture / Nature Distinction

In many traditional settings it is a very bad omen for a wild animal to enter the village at night. It may bring along evil spirits in its wake. Spiro,[26] for instance, describes how monks chanted the *Ratana Sutta* (*Sn.*222–38) in a Burmese village the morning after a stag had been seen entering the settlement. Forest-dwelling monks are also particularly prone to the dangers represented by the natural world. They may be attacked by tigers or snakes, hence the importance of *mettā* as a protective mechanism.

Looked at from another perspective, the monk is subject to the depredations of many small creatures. Their cumulative effect is to make his existence in the forest distinctly uncomfortable. Insects, rats, and the like are continually attacking his limited range of possessions. Though this may be inconvenient, the monk can turn it to his advantage, for it is an example of the process of decay affecting all conditioned things.[27] Meditation on this fact can develop a deeper understanding of impermanence, insubstantiality, and suffering. The perception of danger may also be utilized on the spiritual quest. Fear is a particularly strong emotional state. Its strength and associated physical effects may become the focus of meditation that leads to the development of important insights into the functioning of the mind.[28] In conquering fear the forest-dwelling monk may also gain supernatural powers. Plenty of contemporary evidence exists to support the view that this is what, in part, defines the charismatic monk.[29]

The *Upāli Sutta* (*M.i.378*) tells of some cultivated land that is transformed back into dense forest though the agency of wicked persons. The context of the story makes it clear that wickedness is the human counterpart of wilderness while moral goodness corresponds to a physical environment under the management of human agency. In the *Vessantara Jātaka* we also hear that the wilderness may be tamed through the practice of *dharma*[30] and, in some senses, a prepared and moderately manicured version of wilderness is of more appeal to early Buddhism than nature "red in tooth and claw." Some ancient Brāhmaṇical writers appear to have shared this feeling for improved nature. Nevertheless, positive nature mysticism is not entirely absent from the early Buddhist tradition. The *Sāma Jātaka* (no. 540), for example, tells of a man who lives in harmony with his surroundings. Deer are not afraid of him and he is compared favorably with the king of Benares, who is addicted to hunting. Many verses composed by the early Buddhist saints invoke a similar sense. Speaking of his enlightened state, Mahā Kassapa sings: "With clear water and wide crags, haunted by monkeys and deer, covered with oozing moss, these rocks delight me." (*Thag*.1070)

However, such sentiments are relatively rare. The overwhelming attitude remains one of resigned pessimism about the impermanence of all conditioned things, an outlook later established as the majority position of the Mahāyāna, at least in India.

Buddhist Modernism and Animal Protection

When we survey Buddhist-inspired environmentalism in Asia today, concerns for water resource conservation and forestry are particularly prominent. In contrast, the preservation of species and other matters related to animal welfare come much further down the list of priorities. This is partly because the availability of water supplies and the adverse effects of deforestation have a more obvious impact on the lives of ordinary people. In this connection, some prominent Thai monks have recently championed the practice of ordaining trees as a way of ensuring their protection.[31] Animals, though undoubtedly important, do not seem to be so immediately relevant to the concerns of most socially engaged Buddhists.

Of course, there are exceptions to this general rule. In wealthier and more urbanized regions, like Taiwan, Buddhist-inspired organizations, such as the Life Conservationist Association (LCA) of Taipei, founded by Master Shihchaohui and Bhikkhuni Sakya Chao-Fei, campaign against the adverse effects of certain Chinese-cultural practices, such as the collection of bile from farmed bears, horse-racing, private tiger ownership, eating of bird's nests, and stray dogs.[32] A crucial point here is that the organization recognizes that traditional values, including those related to Buddhism, have not been conducive to animal welfare. The aim, then, is to replace them with a more enlightened and global ethic. It is, however, noteworthy that the LCA has established strong links with other nongovernmental organizations (NGOs), such as the World Society for the Protection of Animals.[33]

It is difficult to imagine that Tibetan communities in exile in India could flourish successfully without support from the government of India, other foreign donor countries, and a variety of NGOs. Significant financial and moral support has been made available to create employment in areas considered worthwhile by these international donors and ecologically beneficial projects of rural development have been assigned a high priority. Indeed, there is some evidence that Tibetan refugees have been specifically advised that, in embracing environmentalist credentials, they will significantly advance their ultimate cause.[34]

Since 1985, the Tibetan government-in-exile has become involved in the Buddhist Perception of Nature Project (BPNP),[35] a program of environmental awareness with a specific emphasis on education. Resources for school children have been prepared and a number of practical projects are underway.[36] The project is funded by the World Wildlife Fund (WWF)[37] and the Hong Kong and the New York Zoological Societies. It also has the blessing of H. H. Dalai Lama, who now regularly takes the opportunity to publicize his environmental credentials on the international stage.[38] This is the background to the *Five Point Plan for Tibet,* published in September 1987, in which the Dalai Lama has insisted that the Tibetan people are dedicated to environment protection (point 4). An official statement that, "prior to the Chinese invasion, Tibet was an unspoiled wilderness sanctuary in a unique natural environment"[39] nicely reinforces this position while blackening Chinese environmental and other credentials at the same time. A case of killing two political birds with one stone! The government-in-exile's recent packaging of pre-1959 Tibet as a green Shangri-la[40] draws on these motifs. But, as a little detailed investigation suggests, all is not quite as it seems. To give one example, most Tibetan-language environmentalist terms are neologisms, coined in recent times in an attempt to translate alien concepts.[41]

Concluding Remarks

Fielding's classic observation[42] that the Buddhists of early-twentieth-century Burma held an attitude of "noblesse oblige" toward animals seems to hold good for the tradition as a whole. Buddhism encourages kindness toward animals. Such kindness was, certainly, in accord with the renouncer conventions of the Buddha's own time, and he did nothing to undermine that outlook.

Traditional Buddhist cosmology instills a fellow feeling, or sense of community, with all sentient beings caught in the beginningless circle of *saṃsāra*. This general ethical principle stands at the root of the practice of loving-kindness

(*mettā*). Yet, more detailed analysis of the practice itself reveals a significant level of instrumentality in the sense that the meditation aims, at least in part, at the enhancement of the practitioner's own spiritual status rather than the alleviation of the suffering of others. Having said this, a positive approach to the natural world based on a doctrine of enlightened self-interest is better than no approach at all.

However, Buddhism's ultimate aim is to escape from the restrictions imposed by our position as beings-within-the-world. This can be accomplished only by the elimination of all negative desires. Concern for the animal kingdom can happily be taken along as baggage on the path to perfection, but at some stage it will be left at the side of the road. Indeed, from the Buddhist perspective some of the major ecological issues of our day, such as the extinction of species, are really pseudo-problems that can be straightforwardly resolved through the application of the principle of the preservation of sentiency that allows for the rebirth of beings in a variety of different destinies (*gati*) within *saṃsāra*. This is the context in which we should view some of the rather negative portrayals of the animals in canonical sources. Schmithausen has argued "that in an age where establishing ecological ethics has become imperative [such teachings] ... ought to be de-dogmatized by being relegated to their specific didactic contexts."[43] This has been the route taken by a variety of modern-engaged Buddhists both in Asia and farther afield. My only slight worry is that this tacit elimination of traditional doctrine, combined with an overdependence on intellectual and financial support from non-Buddhist sources, may tend to distort the tradition.

In the final analysis, Buddhism can contribute significant resources for the development of a global ecological ethic but it is not, in essence, an ecological religion. To quote the final words of the Buddha, "Decay is inherent in all conditioned things. Work out your salvation with diligence" (*D.ii.156*).

NOTES

1. See Florian Deleanu, "Buddhist 'Ethology' in the Pāli Canon: Between Symbol and Observation," *Eastern Buddhist* (New Series) 23, no. 2 (2000): 79–127.

2. Christopher Key Chapple, "Animals and Environment in the Buddhist Birth Stories," in Mary Evelyn Tucker and Duncan Ryūken Williams, eds., *Buddhism and Ecology: The Interconnection of Dharma and Deeds* (Cambridge: Harvard University Center for the Study of World Religions, 1997), pp. 131–48.

3. Pāli canonical sources are cited using the following abbreviations:

A.	*Aṅguttara Nikāya*
D.	*Dīgha Nikāya*
J.	*Jātaka*
Khp.	*Khuddakapāṭha*
M.	*Majjhima Nikāya*
MA.	*Papañcasūdanī*
S.	*Saṃyutta Nikāya*
SA.	*Sāratthappakāsinī*
Sn.	*Suttanipāta*
Thag.	*Theragāthā*
Vin.	*Vinaya Piṭaka*
Vism.	*Visuddhimagga*

4. Thai kings are said to have sometimes offered the gift of an auspicious white elephant to overpowerful courtiers with the intention of ruining them through the cost of the creature's upkeep; hence the English term "white elephant," meaning an unwanted gift. In a variation on the ancient Indian horse-sacrifice, Burmese kings are known to have allowed an elephant to wander unhindered about the land. A pagoda was built at each of its stopping places, thus extending that monarch's territory. See Aung Thwin, "Jambudīpa: Classical Burma's Camelot," in J. P. Ferguson, ed., *Essays on Burma,* Contributions to Asian Studies Vol. XVI (Leiden: Brill, 1981), p. 52.

5. Welfare issues are also expressed in connection with farmed animals. Cowherds are cautioned against ill treatment; they are warned not to milk their cattle dry and to tend them carefully when they are injured or troubled by flies' eggs (*A.*v.347–48).

6. A good example is the courtesy, deference, and general benevolence shared between a partridge, a monkey, and a bull elephant in *Vin.*ii. 161.

7. Buddhism makes a distinction between the realms of sentient beings and the receptacle world (*bhājanaloka*), i.e., the physical environment in which they are located. The most frequent term for an animal is *tiracchāna,* literally "going horizontally," although animals are included in the following more general categories: *sattā*—sentient beings; *pāṇā*—breathing things; *bhūtā*—born things; *jīva*—living things. Plants seem to straddle the divide between the animate and inanimate realms. Some early sources assign them a limited form of sentiency, i.e., the possession of the sense of touch.

8. *Vin.*i.87f tells the story of a snake (*nāga*) that, having taken the form of a youth, gains admission to the *saṅgha.* He reverts to his true form at night when asleep and is expelled from the order by the Buddha with the admonition, "You *nāgas* are not capable of spiritual growth in this doctrine and discipline. However ... observe the fast on the fourteenth, fifteenth, and eighth day of the half-month. Thus you will be released from being a *nāga* and *quickly attain human form*" [my italics].

9. Martin Southwold, *Buddhism in Life: The Anthropological Study of Religion and the Sinhalese Practice of Buddhism* (Manchester: Manchester University Press, 1983), p. 66.

10. Taishō 17:1–379.

11. The "hell where everything is cooked," a region of the burning hell (*tapana*), is reserved from those who have set fire to forests, while the "bird hell" in the hell of no interval (*avīci*) contains sinners who once deliberately caused famines by disrupting water supplies. For a full discussion of the Buddhist hells, see Matsunaga, Daigan, and Alicia *The Buddhist Concept of Hell* (New York: Philosophical Library, 1972).

12. The Jains scrupulously aim to avoid all injury to such beings, whether this is intentional or otherwise.

13. Vegetarianism in contemporary Sri Lanka is on the increase. Most nuns are vegetarian, according to Tessa Bartholomeusz, *Women Under the Bo Tree: Buddhist Nuns in Sri Lanka* (Cambridge: Cambridge University Press, 1994), p. 140. The practice is also recommended by the popular lay-based Sarvodaya movement, according to George D. Bond, *The Buddhist Revival in Sri Lanka: Religious Tradition, Reinterpretation and Response* (Columbia: University of South Carolina Press, 1988), p. 280. In 1985 the powerful All Ceylon Buddhist Congress lobbied the government against setting up a Ministry of Fisheries, for this was seen as an endorsement of the fishing industry (p. 118).

14. See D. S. Ruegg, "*Ahimsā* and Vegetarianism in the History of Buddhism" in S. Balasoorya, et al., eds., *Buddhist Studies in Honour of Walpola Rahula* (London: George Fraser, 1980), pp. 234–41.

15. However, monastic discipline (*Vin.*i.218ff) totally forbids ten kinds of meat. The list includes human flesh, elephant, lion, snake, tiger, etc. The reasons for the emergence of this particular list are quite complex. Some items, such as the elephant, are royal animals and protected by the king. Relatives of a dead lion have the capacity to track down and kill those who have consumed it—a powerful disincentive! A similar list of prohibited meats is found on Asoka's Pillar Edict V.

16. For further discussion of the issue, see C. S. Prasad, "Meat-eating and the Rule of *Tikotiparisuddha*," in A. K. Narain, ed., *Studies in Pāli and Buddhism* (Delhi: B. R. Publishing, 1979), pp. 289–95.

17. The eleventh expiatory offence in the Theravāda monastic code is directed toward the destruction of vegetable growth (*bhūtagāma*) (*Vin.*iv.34). For a detailed examination of the problem of plant sentiency, see Lambert Schmithausen, *The Problem of the Sentience of Plants in Earliest Buddhism*, Studia Philologica Buddhica: Occasional Paper Series VI (Tokyo: International Institute for Buddhist Studies, 1991).

18. A particularly interesting case related to this complex issue comes from Rangoon, Burma, in the late 1950s. The authorities, wishing to do something about the large population of stray dogs in the city, put down pieces of meat, only some of which were poisoned, in various locations. It was argued that the procedure would ensure that only those dogs with unfavorable *karma* would die, thus absolving anyone else of blame. See Winston L. King, *In the Hope of Nirvana: An Essay on Theravada Buddhist Ethics* (LaSalle, IL: Open Court, 1964), p. 281.

19. The establishment of a universal and hereditary monarchy as sole guarantor of harmony on a global scale fits the bill for an authentically Buddhist position on the protection of animals. However, apart from the practical difficulties of establishing such a polity, the suggestion is quaintly anachronistic and likely to be deeply unattractive, even to most contemporary inhabitants of the traditional Buddhist heartlands.

20. N. A. Nikam and R. McKeon, *The Edicts of Asoka* (Chicago: University of Chicago Press, 1959), pp. 55–56.

21. J. Prip-Møller, *Chinese Buddhist Monasteries: Their Plan and Its Function as a Setting for Buddhist Monastic Life* (Copenhagen and London: G.E.C. Gads Forlagand, Oxford University Press, 1937), pp. 161–163.

22. On the influence of Buddhist temples on the dispersal of certain plant species, see Pei Shengji, "Some Effects of the Dai People's Cultural Beliefs and Practices on the Plant Environment of Xishuangbanna, Yunnan Province, Southwest China," in Karl L. Hutterer, A. T. Rambo, and G. Lovelace, eds., *Cultural Values and Human Ecology in Southeast Asia*, Michigan Papers on Southeast Asia no. 24 (Ann Arbor: Center for South and Southeast Asian Studies, University of Michigan, 1985), pp. 321–39.

23. D. C. Twitchett, "Monastic Estates in T'ang China," *Asia Major* (New Series) 5 (1956): 123.

24. Williams, Duncan Ryüken, "Animal Liberation, Death, and the State: Rites to Release Animals in Medieval Japan," in Mary Evelyn Tucker and Duncan Ryüken Williams, eds., *Buddhism and Ecology: The Interconnection of Dharma and Deeds* (Cambridge: Harvard University Center for the Study of World Religions, 1997), pp. 149–62.

25. On the way in which Buddhist protective rituals positively support environmental concerns, see Ian Harris, "Magician as Environmentalist: Fer-

tility Elements in South and Southeast Asian Buddhism," *Eastern Buddhist* (New Series) 32, no. 2 (2000): 128–56.

26. Melford E. Spiro, *Buddhism and Society: A Great Tradition and its Burmese Vicissitudes* (2nd, expanded edition) (Berkeley: University of California Press, 1982), p. 270.

27. Writers as varied as Buddhaghosa (*Vism*.ii. 58) and Candrakīrti (*Prasannapadā* 246, 1a3 and 299, 9f) both recommend the forest with its continual fall of leaves as a practical metaphor for impermanence.

28. In this connection, see F.L. Woodward, trans., *Manual of a Mystic, Being a Translation from the Pāli and Sinhalese Work Entitled the Yogavachara's Manual* (London: Pāli Text Society, 1916).

29. On the charisma of successful forest-dwelling monks see S.J. Tambiah, *Buddhism and the Spirit Cults in Northeast Thailand* (Cambridge: Cambridge University Press, 1970) and *The Buddhist Saints of the Forest and the Cult of Amulets* (Cambridge: Cambridge University Press, 1984). Also see M. Carrithers, *The Forest Monks of Sri Lanka: An Anthropological and Historical Study* (Dehli: Oxford University Press, 1983).

30. See M. Cone and R. Gombrich, trans., *The Perfect Generosity of Prince Vessantara* (Oxford: Oxford University Press, 1977), pp. 28–29.

31. The practice may well have its origin in a widespread revival of tree-planting in Thailand in the wake of the Bangkok Bicentennial of 1982. See Kasetsart University, *Invitation to Tree Planting at Buddhamonton* (Bangkok: Public Relations Office, 1987).

32. The first edition of the Association's newsletter *Animal News Taiwan* was published in October 1994.

33. I am grateful to Oliver Yih-Ren Lin, University College, London, for supplying me with some of this information.

34. Toni Huber, "Green Tibetans: A Brief Social History," in Frank J. Korom, ed., *Tibetan Culture in the Diaspora* (Vienna: Verlag der Österreichischen Akademie der Wissenschaften, 1997), p. 109.

35. See Shann Davies, ed., *Tree of Life: Buddhism and Protection of Nature* (Hong Kong: Buddhist Protection of Nature Project, 1987). Both Thai and Tibetan strands of the project now exist. They aim to disseminate selections of the Buddhist scriptures, particularly those deemed relevant to environmental awareness, etc. In Thailand it is claimed that fifty thousand such selections have already been distributed to schools, monasteries, and other institutions. Chatsumarn Kabilsingh, a significant Thai scholar associated with the project, has published a number of works under its auspices, for example, *A Cry from the Forest: Buddhist Perception of Nature, A New Perspective for Conservation Education* (Bangkok: Wildlife Fund Thailand, 1987).

36. The impact of foreign NGOs on the development of environmentally engaged Buddhism is not restricted to the Tibetan exile community. For information on a parallel situation in Cambodia, see my "Buddhism in Extremis: The Case of Cambodia," in Ian Harris, ed., *Buddhism and Politics in Twentieth-Century Asia* (London: Pinter, 1999), pp. 54–78.

37. The first international interfaith event dealing with ecological issues from a religious perspective was held at Assisi on September 29, 1985 on the twenty-fifth anniversary of the founding of the WWF. The Dalai Lama's representative, Ven. Lungrig Namgyal, delivered one of the tradition-specific declarations. See *The Assisi Declarations: Messages on Man and Nature from Buddhism, Christianity, Hinduism, Islam and Judaism* (London: WWF, 1986).

38. My comment is devoid of any personal animosity—the Dalai Lama is clearly a man of the highest integrity. Nevertheless, as an international figure he must face in two directions at once; toward his Buddhist countrymen and toward influential international elites. An enthusiastic endorsement of the contemporary agenda of the second group, with its emphasis on the global nature of the world's problems, may be the most effective means of eliciting their support for the Tibetan people's fight to regain their homeland.

39. International Campaign for Tibet 1990, p. 50, quoted in *Five Point Plan for Tibet,* point 4.

40. For more on the modern construction of Tibet as an eco-paradise, see Donald S. Lopez, *Pris-*

oners of Shangri-La: Tibetan Buddhism and the West (Chicago: University of Chicago Press, 1988), and Peter Bishop, *The Myth of Shangri-La: Tibet, Travel Writing and the Western Creation of Sacred Landscape* (Berkeley: University of California Press, 1990).

41. *Five Point Plan for Tibet*, p. 111.

42. H. Fielding, *The Soul of a People* (London: Macmillan, 1908), pp. 257–58.

43. Lambert Schmithausen, "The Early Buddhist Tradition and Ecological Ethics," *Journal of Buddhist Ethics* 4 (1997): 22.

Snake-Kings, Boars' Heads, Deer Parks, Monkey Talk

Animals as Transmitters and Transformers in

Indian and Tibetan Buddhist Narratives

IVETTE VARGAS

In the visual and textual milieu of Buddhist traditions, animals have played a prominent role in revealing the complexities of Buddhist cosmology, doctrine, and practice while reflecting indigenous and pre-Buddhist traditional elements. As befits a religion that originated in a rural setting like India and the subsistence agriculture of the Tibetan plateau, one may find an overabundance of actual, mythical, and magical animals in Buddhist narrative art and literature. Animals like the lion, deer, elephant, yak, horse, serpent, dragon, and hybrid (animal-human) forms were often adopted from earlier pre-Buddhist motifs and transformed by the Buddhist tradition.

Yet early on, such images of animals portrayed mixed messages to Indian and Tibetan audiences. Narratives with animal characters on a visual and textual level were often seen as didactic devices intended to instruct the "unsophisticated" ordinary layperson about Buddhist teachings. Often animals were used meta-phorically to exemplify human values as evident throughout the *Jātaka* genre of literature.[1] The fifth-century Buddhist scholar Buddhaghoṣa, however, thought that such narratives frequently distorted Buddhist doctrine.[2]

Of course, not all the narrative tellings were viewed in a pejorative sense. Often oral narratives were told to a diversity of audiences in the Buddhist tradition, and they were an effective way of transmitting Buddhist doctrine (*dharma*). The metaphorical value of animals is evident in the *Jātaka* stories, for example, based on the revelations of the Buddha and his followers at the end of the stories as the animal characters. Animals also, in this and other genres, appear as capable of thinking and achieving enlightened awareness, an achievement that is not the exclusive domain of humans. Overall, there were ambivalent views about the role of animal images in the Buddhist literary and ritual traditions; thus further interpretation of these images is needed today.

As the Indian Buddhist and Tibetan Vajrayāna traditions show, narratives reflect a complexity and sophistication of ideas about animals. Animals (Sanskrit, *tiryañc;* Tibetan, '*dud 'gro*)[3] are often subjects and active agents in the process of transmission of Buddhist ideas. This essay focuses on animals not only as metaphorical tools, but also as vehicles of transmission and transformative players in some key Buddhist narratives (as reflected in art, texts, and dramatic religious performances) of India and Tibet.[4] Although the claims here do not completely shatter the view of animals as "mediated objects" (and they are not part of a comprehensive study), they also portray animals as *subjects* in the Buddhist tradition.[5] This rather tenuous yet complementary tension is fundamental to this study.

Images of Narratives and Narratives of Images: Getting Beyond the Animal Stigma

Much Buddhist thought is grounded in complex ideas of cosmology and the doctrines of karma and rebirth. Here is where the metaphorical use of animal images takes on force early in the Indian Buddhist tradition and is adopted wholeheartedly in the Tibetan case, creating an ambivalent representation of animals. A popular image in both traditions' textual and visual sources is the wheel of *saṃsāra*, the cycle of rebirth. Actual animal images on the wheel correspond to human values. This wheel of existence is often depicted throughout monastic compounds (especially on vestibules and hanging scrolls for meditation). One common depiction is of the wheel held in the mouth and claws of Yama, the deity of death, with its perimeter ringed with the twelve preconditions that create rebirth. Anthropomorphism is at play in its nave, where three animals represent human values: the cock, symbolizing desire; the snake, hatred; and the pig, delusion. These three "poisons," as they are known in the early Indian

Buddhist tradition (which are extended to five in the Tibetan case) are the propelling forces of the cycle of existence. Karmic retribution determines where on the wheel each individual will be reborn.

Depicted are six rebirth realms within the wheel; the three upper realms consist of heaven, *asura*s (warring gods), and humans; the three lower, animals, hungry ghosts, and hell. Individuals reborn as animals must suffer the cruelties to which animals are subjected. Rebirth in the lower realms makes it difficult to achieve enlightenment. Rebirth is still an impermanent state, however, so the possibility of rebirth in higher realms or even enlightenment exists. Therefore, despite negative images like these in the literature, there are also images that reflect a more positive view of animals.

As the enlightenment possibility alludes to, animals function in more capable ways than meet the eye; they are active agents. As the deer that appears in the scene of the first sermon of the historical Buddha in the town of Ṛṣipatana (modern Sarnath near Benares, India) makes us aware, animals were active witnesses to an event that marks the Buddhist tradition and were hearers of the teachings. Throughout Indian and Tibetan monastic compounds, this event is commemorated with deer depicted iconically flanking the wheel of the *dharma* (replacing the wheel of *saṃsāra*). Therefore, despite the persistence of the stigma of animal rebirths in Indian and Tibetan Buddhist narratives, there are many examples in which this thought is challenged.

The Mark of a Tradition: Lion's Roar, Elephant Thrones, and Bodhisattva Peacocks

In metaphorical terms, animals have played a key role in Indian and Tibetan Buddhist traditions. Animals often convey key Buddhist figures and events, religious doctrines, and even political ideology. Not only do animals hearken back to key narratives in these traditions, but they also reflect underlying philosophical ideas associated with the qualities of Buddhas and *bodhisattva*s.

In the Indian Buddhist tradition is the concept of Buddha families. For example, a different Buddha is the head of a "family" of Buddha figures, each of whom is associated with an animal figure depicted on thrones.[6] In general the concept of Buddha families is related to different aspects of the experience of enlightenment. Although there is some variation in the different texts,[7] these Buddhas, associated with the five directions in a *maṇḍala* (geometric representation of a Buddha universe), point to the relation of animal images with religious perceptions and India's centrality in Buddhist cosmology.

One of the central figures in the Buddhist tradition associated with the Buddha is the lion. Lions are often royal symbols in India. For example, the Sarnath lions of Aśoka are used as coat of arms. The white snow lion is depicted on the Tibetan flag symbolizing the nation of Tibet. The historical Buddha is described as a lion as reflected by his epithet, 'lion of the Śākyas' (Tibetan, Sa kya sen ge). His first sermon to the five ascetics was like hearing a "lion's roar." Countless lion thrones in sculptural art reinforce this image. In terms of the five Buddha families, two Buddhas, Vairocana (Tibetan, Rnam par snang mdzad) and Ratnasambhava (Tibetan, Rin chen 'byung gnas) are often described and depicted as having lion thrones, depending on their directional positions. The direction in which the latter Buddha and his lion throne are depicted iconographically in *maṇḍala*s may represent geographically Sinhala, the ancient name of Ceylon/Sri Lanka, literally meaning "the land of the lion."

Another very common figure that appears in both Indian and Tibetan Buddhist traditions is the elephant. In *maṇḍala* depictions of Akṣobya (Tibetan, Mi g.yo ba, Mi bskyod pa), the Buddha of the Vajra Family is supported by an elephant. This image appears again in the *Akṣobya Vyūha Sūtra* where Śakyamūni Buddha tells the

story about a Buddha called Viśalaksha in Abhirati who was faced with a monk wanting to gain enlightenment for the sake of sentient beings. Despite the warning, the monk swore not to exhibit feelings of anger and desires by undertaking a whole series of vows. He eventually became unshakable (Sanskrit, *akṣobya*, Tibetan, *mi g.yo ba*) in holding the vows and became a Buddha of that name. Iconographically, this Buddha is often depicted touching the earth with his right hand, supported by a throne with eight elephants in royal regalia. Having touched the earth (a gesture reminiscent of the historical Buddha in the Pāli narratives), he draws attention to the earth, bearing witness to the Buddha's enlightenment. The image of the elephant is often the insignia of India symbolizing royalty and supremacy.

Cosmologically, eight or sixteen elephants support the physical universe, at the center of which are India's Buddhist heartlands. It was also the exclusive privilege of a king to be carried by an elephant, and so images of the Buddha with elephants remind the reader of his own royal pedigree. Thus, this image of the eight elephants that support the throne equates Akṣobya (often depicted in the center of *maṇḍala*s of the five Buddha Families) with the continent of India (and its Buddhist tradition) as the center of the universe. In addition, the etymology of Akṣobya's name can also be equated with the nature of the elephant as unchangeable and unmoving. The elephant is known in Buddhist thought to be one of the possessions of the *cākravartin* (turner of the wheel).

Another throne image is seen in the depictions of white Vairocana, who is supported by a dragon throne. This particular animal image fits well with India's geopolitical associations in the Buddhist worldview. In *maṇḍala* representations, Vairocana is depicted in the eastern direction. Since to the east of India is China, a region often described as the land of the dragon, the symbol of the dragon throne is significant. Imperial emperors in China had dragon thrones that survived until Sun Yatsen's revolution in

1911.[8] More information on the dragon is discussed in relation to snakes in the next section.

Another example is the depiction in some *maṇḍala*s of the Buddha Amitābha (Tibetan, 'Od dpag med), the Buddha of compassion and head of the Lotus Family. Set to the west, this Buddha is supported by a peacock throne representing that area of the world west of India (perhaps Persia).[9] The peacock image evokes an Indian myth that describes peacocks as capable of swallowing poisonous snakes without coming to harm and transmuting their poison into a nourishing nectar (as the snake nourishes the peacock's beautiful plumage). On the tantric level, this symbolism of the peacock may correspond to the image of Amitābha, who can transform the poisons of human existence into something beneficial—a means of enlightenment.

This metaphorical image of the peacock resonates in the Tibetan Buddhist tradition especially in relation to the concept of transformation ('gyur ba). According to a text ascribed to the Indian teacher Dharmarakṣita, a *bodhisattva* is able to transform adversity into a beneficial experience like a peacock among poisonous plants:

In jungles of poisonous plants strut the
  peacocks,
Though medicine gardens of beauty lie
  near.
The masses of peacocks do not find gardens
  pleasant,
But thrive in the essence of poisonous
  plants.
In similar fashion, the brave Bodhisattvas
Remain in the jungle of worldly concern.
No matter how joyful this world's pleasure
  gardens,
These Brave Ones are never attracted to
  pleasures,
But thrive in the jungle of suffering and
  pain.
We spend our whole life in the search for
  enjoyment,
Yet tremble with fear at the mere thought of
  pain;

Thus since we are cowards, we are miserable
  still.
But the brave Bodhisattvas accept suffering
  gladly
And gain from their courage a true lasting
  joy.
Now desire is the jungle of poisonous plants
  here.
Only Brave Ones, like peacocks, can thrive
  on such fare.
If cowardly beings, like crows, were to
  try it,
Because they are greedy they might lose
  their lives.
How can someone who cherishes self more
  than others
Take lust and such dangerous poisons for
  food?
If he tried like a crow to use other illusions,
He would probably forfeit his chance for
  release.
And thus Bodhisattvas are likened to
  peacocks:
They live on delusions—those poisonous
  plants.
Transforming them into the essence of
  practice,
They thrive in the jungle of everyday life.
Whatever is present they always accept,
While destroying the poison of clinging
  desire.[10]

Metaphorically, the image of peacocks as *bodhisattva*s confirm the latter's role in the world, to remain in *saṃsāra* and transform its negative attributes into positive vehicles that lead to enlightenment.

Snake-Kings and Other Animals: Preservers, Controllers, and Vehicles of Transmission and Transformation

Animals have played a major role as preservers and transmitters of the Buddhist tradition (even if they needed a little coaxing through a "conversion" experience). This section provides close case-studies of how certain animals, among them the snake, are active agents of the transmission of doctrine and beliefs in Buddhist literature.

Perhaps one of the most ambivalent and fascinating figures that appear throughout Buddhist literature in Asia are *nāga*s (Tibetan, *klu*) often considered both dangerous and beneficial entities. Closely linked with the environment, the monastic institution, royalty and political institutions, and the well-being of individuals, *nāga*s have often been at the center of Buddhist traditions and their transmission. Powerful creatures that dwell in the underground or in rivers, *nāga*s control fertility and destruction through their power over rain, and are agents of diseases like leprosy and epilepsy.

They were, on the one hand, the historical Buddha's staunchest adversaries and, on the other, guardians of the Buddha and his teachings (once they were pacified).[11] Because of their potential for good as well as harm, their presence in Buddhist literature reflects an underlying concern on the part of the authors to maintain order, perhaps reflecting a tension in the relationship between the monastic institution and the society around it, or Buddhism and local traditions. Their presence reflects the underlying local or pre-Buddhist beliefs reconciling themselves to the Buddhist doctrines (or the Buddhist tradition reconciling with local beliefs in these entities). Aside from ideas about syncretism, their presence can also be conceived as being very much part of Buddhist beliefs, not necessarily a reflection of an outside belief being assimilated by another tradition.

*Nāga*s are often described or visually depicted as snake-like, in a hybrid form containing anthropoid and zoomorphic characteristics, or in completely human form, and wearing crowns (if described as kings). They also appear as an elephant in the Pāli scriptures and as dragons in China and Japan.[12] They are often described as deities and kings. Frequently connected to ponds, cisterns, trees, and underground areas,

they inhabit the unknown depths of nature. *Nāga*s are not only good to think with (about representations and power dynamics) but also their forms reflect, on the part of the Buddhist tradition, a real reverence for and ambivalence about the forces of nature.

The preoccupation on the part of the Buddhist tradition with order is specifically related to the *nāga*s' roles in the local society and in the Buddhist monastic realm and rituals. In the minds of local populations in India and Tibet even to this day, *nāga*s are providers of essential needs, whether they be rain, fertility, harvests, or protection from calamity in the form of disease, drought, flood, and attack. Alongside these environmental (and even political) powers, these entities are preservers, controllers, and vehicles of Buddhist teachings and the Buddha himself. Rituals of appeasement and the building of shrines and temples in their honor make these events possible. There are several examples from Asian literature to substantiate this view.

The view of *nāga*s as promoters of order is strongly advocated in early Buddhist literature. Lowell Bloss in his study of early Indian Buddhist stories promotes this idea by connecting the *nāga* with kingship. In several stories he describes, he notes that the sign of a successful king is one whose reign promotes prosperity and a sense of order in the kingdom (often in the form of riches, good harvest, and stable weather). In order for this to occur, however, the king oftentimes must pay tribute to the *nāga* who in turn delivers rain (a sign of his approval of the king's tribute).[13] As Bloss notes, kings themselves lack the power to control the environment without the support of the deities of the environment, much like the Chinese idea of the mandate of heaven and offerings made to local Chinese gods of the earth, rain, and so forth. Kings have lost favor if they ruled immorally or unfairly and did not continue their tribute to the gods (also closely connected to ruling morally). *Nāga*s are also associated with certain territories, so the recognition of their presence by individuals like kings was thought to lead to peace and prosperity in that particular land.

The nature of the *nāga*, however, is not always predictable and absolutely controllable, so much needs to be done to appease and please this entity. The use of snake charmers in Indian courts also substantiated the claim that *nāga*s must be appeased and subdued in order for them to deliver the help needed. A similar example is seen in China and Japan with rainmakers and the use of rainmaking scriptures directed toward these entities (in the form of dragons) to protect the nation.[14]

Richard Cohen in his study of the Ajanta cave-temple complex in India, especially those dated from the fifth century, clearly delineates that *nāga*s are intricately involved in a "reciprocal relationship" with the monastic institution, and their relationship is important to maintain a demeanor of order. Recounted in stories from the Buddhist scriptures, Buddhist monastics and the Buddha himself found themselves in a constant power play with these unpredictable creatures. In the end, a "dharmic harmony" was achieved between the sangha, the surrounding laity and patrons of the monastic cave complex, and the *nāga*s themselves.[15] Cohen argues that a domestication and localization takes place in relation to these entities. Often reconciliation of the belief systems of the local people and their own beliefs in the potential power of these entities led monastics and the Buddha himself to incorporate the *nāga*s into the Buddhist framework. One of several examples is the deal that Buddha Śākyamuni bridged with an evil *nāga* who was previously a snake charmer insulted by the lack of reverence due to him by his surrounding community. The *nāga* in turn was converted by the Buddha and agreed not to cause havoc on the population on the condition that he be allowed to harvest the crops every twelve years. Out of compassion, the Buddha allowed him this concession.[16] In other stories about the *nāga*s Apalāla and Gopāla, *nāga*s are described as disgruntled monastics from previous lives set on damaging the Buddhist teachings. The Buddha subdued them with his presence in the form of a reflection in a pond they inhabit.[17] Other stories also describe the Buddha negotiating with these entities by providing his presence in the form of relics or a shadow.[18]

It is interesting to note that *nāga*s are often mesmerized by the Buddha's presence and insist on keeping it for their own. Often described as hoarders of riches, in terms of jewels and teachings, this is not surprising. The recognition that the success of the Buddhist teaching is dependent on the forces of nature is also a relevant message here. *Nāga*s will provide stability, wealth, and well being, and they will work in conjunction with the Buddhist tradition as long as they are respected for who they are and recognized for their place within the cosmos. For example, a *nāga* appears early on in the biography of the historical Buddha in the role of the *Nāga* King Muccalinda. This serpent shelters the future Buddha from the rain (coiling himself around the Buddha seven times) as he meditates prior to his full enlightenment experience in Bodhgaya.[19] This tree is the only place that the future Buddha could obtain enlightenment. In addition, trees are also known as the residences of *nāga*s and are linked with the image of the center of the world (Mt. Meru in Indian mythology). Another interpretation of the Muccalinda story reflects the idea that the Buddha received royal authorization from the *nāga* (therefore reinforcing the Buddha's connection with divine kingship that is prevalent throughout Indian literature) to guide all people from then on.[20]

The Buddhist tradition's concern for order coupled with legitimacy is also reflected in the construction of shrines and propitiatory rites to these entities. Cave 16 in Ajanta is an example of the Buddhist tradition's accommodation to the *nāga*. According to the dedicatory inscription, the Buddha took over the home of a *nāga* who originally resided in this cave but relocated the *nāga* home further inside the cave. As Cohen states, "Cave 16's *nāga* king sat as an unblinking guardian over the entrance to this monastery and the Waghora River before it."[21] Therefore, although the image of the Buddha supplanted that of the *nāga* (perhaps he took supremacy) in this cave temple, the *nāga,* however, acts as guardian of the teachings and of the presence (in the form of an image) of the Buddha. His power is also respected by the tradition. This image of preserver and guardian is constantly reiterated in the *Mahāyāna* Buddhist tradition, where these figures are known to have been the preservers of the major texts, the *Prajñāpāramitā* (*Perfection of Wisdom*) texts. These texts were entrusted to them by the historical Buddha until recovered by Nāgārjuna, the first- or second-century Indian Buddhist scholar who spread the *Mahāyāna* teachings.

In the Tibetan tradition, the equivalent term for *nāga* is *klu. Klu* play a central role in Bon and Buddhist cosmology and rituals associated with the environment, disease, and the political structure.[22] *Klu* are believed to equally inhabit water sources, trees, and underground areas, usually ant hills, leading the way to their underground homes. In Tibetan Buddhist cosmology, *klu* appears as a central figure. *Klu* is known in this tradition as one of several hundred terms for demons or malevolent forces, *gdon* is another one. Tibetan medical texts also mention the term *klu gdon,* which is difficult to define. The universe consists of three worlds: the gods or celestial world (*Lha Yul*), the human world (*Me Yul*), and the *nāga* world (*Klu Yul*).

As in the Indian tradition, Tibetan temples for the *klu* are erected in order to appease and honor *klu* because of their potential to create havoc and calamity. The main *klu khang* (short for *Rdzong rgyab klu'i pho drang* meaning "the water spirit house behind the fortress") in Lhasa is a three-storied temple situated on an island in a lake outside of the Potala Palace. It was built around the time of the sixth Dalai Lama (Tshangs dbyangs rgya mtsho, 1683–1706?). According to Jakob Winkler, who has done extensive studies on this temple, the lake was formed as a result of the excavation of building materials

after the building of the Potala. It was believed that the *klu* were disturbed by this, and in order to pacify them, the Fifth Dalai Lama, Blo bzang rgya mtsho, promised to appease them by building a temple as a place for propitiatory rituals. Later, a temple dedicated to the *klu* was built on the island, the present-day *klu khang.* This temple eventually became a place of personal retreat for the Dalai Lamas.[23] According to doctors at the Mentsikhang (Tibetan hospital) in present-day Lhasa, patients are often sent to the *klu khang* to undergo a purification ritual and request for prayers dedicated to the *klu.* The ritual performed by *lamas* (religious practitioners) is called *tshe 'thar* (literally, life–releasing ritual). Often the symbol associated with this ritual is a frog (*sphel ba*).[24]

The connection to the environment and the Buddhist tradition's role in subjugating the forces of nature in the form of *klu* and other entities is also evident in the Tibetan tradition. Several demons (some known as *klu*) appear in the story of Padmasambhava, the great eighth century tantric meditation master who subdued the ground (*sa 'dul*) of Bsam yas (the first temple) by performing a ritual dance (*gar 'cham*). These demons are described as interfering with the newly arrived Buddhist tradition. As Mona Schrempf notes in her discussion of Padmasambhava's actions and Buddhist and Bon po dance rituals, "with that he created excellent conditions, such as pacifying the malice of the gods and demons."[25] Commemorating this event and others, rituals describe that through the generation of and identification with higher tantric deities, monk dancers subjugate what is considered to be evil and disturbing on the way to enlightenment (different classes of evil spirits and hindrances to the Buddhist *dharma*).

As mentioned earlier, the process of appeasement and negotiation by Buddhist traditions regarding these entities often has to do with the recognition of the negative aspect of these deities, especially their association with infliction of illness and hindrances of the Buddhist teachings. An example of this belief appears in the Newar tradition in Kathmandu, Nepal, concerning a pilgrimage site that houses a sacred image of a *garuda* (Indian mythical bird-like creature). At this site, a *garuda* is believed to have manifested itself from the rosary of an image of Nāgārjuna. In Indian mythology, *garuda*s are the *nāga*s' natural enemy, birds eat snakes. According to Newar tradition, at this site this *garuda* manifested itself in the summertime and devoured a *nāga* that came out of the middle of a lake. Furthermore, one text states,

> At this time, in the temple, the image of *garuda* perspires, and many people come here to moisten scarves with the exuding perspiration to gain protection from the ravages of *Nāga* spirits. ... Leprosy is the most dangerous disease inflicted by the *Nāga*s; also abscesses, consumption, ulcers, itch, sores and swelling of the limbs, and all diseases related to excessive indulgence, or lack of the element water.[26]

Just below this temple, there is a sacred pond where it is believed that the *garuda* and *nāga*-king Shankhapola, who were once at war, became friends. Once a year a sacred ruby is immersed in water and the water acts as a protection against *klu* diseases.[27]

The *nāga*s' link with disease is also pervasive throughout Tibetan medical texts, such as the *Rgyud bzhi*, which connects *klu nad* (demon or water spirit disease) with a certain number of demons or malevolent forces that cause specific diseases. In chapter 81 of the third *tantra* of the *Rgyud bzhi*, diseases like leprosy, insanity, epilepsy, and paralysis fall under the category of *klu nad*.[28] Often diseases that cannot be easily treated and healed with conventional medicine are diagnosed as having been caused by these demons. What is also interesting is the distinction made between different levels of demons, often linked with the Tibetan Bon tradition. *Klu* are directly related to the Indian

notion of a *nāga* (water spirit), while *gdon* is an evil spirit, a demon, something that can possess a human being.[29] As mentioned earlier, in present-day Lhasa, Tibet, physicians at the Mentsikhang (medical hospital) still diagnose *klu nad* and *gdon nad* and send patients to the *klu khang* despite the Chinese Communist government's perception of the religious nature of these diseases. The demons create a link between the hospital and the temple, and, in turn, they preserve Tibetan identity within a powerful institution that historically has maintained links with Buddhist and Bon teachings. The link to Tibetan indigenous traditions and Buddhist teachings is in many ways potentially threatening and politically volatile in the current Tibetan Autonomous Region of Tibet (where the main medical facilities are located and in an institution that is continually undergoing secularization and commodification because of the Chinese government's need to address the market economy).[30]

The link between *klu* and leprosy in particular appears in several biographical accounts of Tibetan teachers.[31] The biographies of the tenth-century Indian Buddhist Nun Dge slong ma Dpal mo, preserved in Tibetan texts, describe that she contracted leprosy due to her karma. The presence of the *nāga* is prevalent and had to be subdued in order for her to reveal her true nature as a Buddha figure. These texts also substantiate the claim that *nāga* are not only responsible for disease, but are also capable of being transformed into preservers of the *dharma* and therefore, heal on a much larger scale (physically, spiritually, and cosmically). One text describes that after having meditated and fasted before the *bodhisattva* Ekādaśamukha (the Eleven-faced Avalokiteśvara) for a full year, her illness "shed like the skin of a snake." She was endowed with *bodhicitta* ("enlightened attitude") and transformed obstacles and the eight *nāga*s. In fasting rituals associated with this Buddhist nun, the *klu* and other demons are hindrances of the Buddhadharma, and undergo a transformation through the power of the Buddhist teachings:

> In the *saga* month
> [at the time of the constellation] *sa ri nam mthongs,*
> the interfering demons were placed in the state of *bodhicitta.*
> [Nun Palmo's] illness, sins, and defilements were purified
> and she saw the truth of the first *bhūmi.*
> On the first day of *sa ga zla ba,*
> she witnessed the countenance of the Holy Tārā
> and [Tārā] prophesized,
> 'Buddha activities of all the Buddhas
> of the three times are consolidated in you.'
> On the eighth day,
> she witnessed the majority of the *kriyā* tantra deities
> such as five Amoghaśa deities and so forth.
> On the fifteenth day,
> she witnessed the countenance of the Eleven-faced One
> endowed with a thousand hands
> and a thousand eyes and furthermore,
> countless Buddhas in all the pores of the body,
> the hands also being the quintessence of Buddhahood.
> On the eyes on the palms of the hands,
> she witnessed a host of tantric deities.
> Since the holy one talked about the Dharma,
> inconceivable *samādhi* arose in [her].
> She saw the truth of the eighth *bhūmi.*
> Then moreover she practiced the fasting ritual
> for three months more for the sake of all sentient beings.[32]

According to this text, the eight *nāga*s were transformed (in line with Tibetan tantric ideas) into protectors of the practice of the *bodhisattva* Avalokiteśvara in his two forms, Mahākaruṇika

and Ekādaśamukha, respectively.[33] In addition, the image of the snake that appears in this text cannot be taken lightly. As a snake sheds its skin, Nun Palmo sheds her previous existence as a leprous nun and is reborn as a Buddha figure, a *sprul sku* (renunciate being), and *bodhisattva.* As mentioned earlier, snakes' link with rebirth and fertility is relevant here as well. The rain brings in new birth (reminiscent of dragons) as a snake sheds his skin.

As animals like the lion, elephant, dragon, peacock, and snake make clear, animals not only protect and preserve the Buddhist teachings but also act as literal "vehicles" of transmission of the doctrine.[34] For example, both Indian and Tibetan Buddhist literature (also evident in Hinduism) include an elaborate pantheon with deities mounted on animals (such vehicles are called in Sanskrit, *vāhana*).[35] In the Tibetan case, the mounts of guardian figures (Tibetan, *mgon po, srung ma*), for example, show animals whose actual and mythical qualities are closely linked with the powers of the deities on top of them, some are related to pre-Buddhist ideas, and others signify political and sectarian powers. The twelve female *Bstan ma bcu gnyis* ("Tenma Chunyi"), for instance, originally non-Buddhist deities of the mountains described in the *Padma Thang Yig,* the biography of the eighth-century tantric master Padmasambhava,[36] were figures who were subdued, converted, and eventually became protectors and transmitters of the Buddhist teachings.[37] Most of the figures have a different animal vehicle: a dragon, *rkyang* (a wild ass), a white snow lion (used as a symbol for the Tibetan nation), a white lipped *'brong* (wild yak), a doe, a black mule, a *garuḍa* (mythical bird in Indian mythology), black snakes (also worn), and a tiger. Often these animal figures signify a link to the tantric and ascetic natures of the deities.

In the depictions of the Buddha families in *maṇḍala*s, the Buddha Amoghasiddhi (Tibetan, Don yod grub pa)[38] of the Karma Family, rests upon a mythical bird, a *garuḍa.* A *garuḍa* (Tibetan, *kyung, mkha 'lding*) is replete with Indian symbolism—known as the mythical lord of birds and devourer of *nāgas*. The mythical *garuḍa* is associated with the Himalayan regions in the north and sometimes with the legendary horned eagle of Tibet (Tibetan, *mkha' lding*). In the Indian tradition, the *garuḍa* may be depicted as a great bird but is often in the form of a therianthropic figure (a deity with a combination of animal and human characteristics). In this case, he is in the form of a bird head and human body.

*Garuḍa*s appear in many forms in the Tibetan tradition, assuming greatest prominence in the Rnying ma and Rdzogs chen transmissions. Most often iconographically, the Tibetan tradition depicts the *garuḍa* with the upper torso and arms of a man; the head, beak, and legs of a bird; and large wings that unfold from his back. Often he has three eyes with a *nāga* in his beak, and he wears a necklace of jewels with a yak tassel. Like the peacock mentioned earlier, tantric transformation is a central concept in relation to the *garuḍa;* this figure is known to transmute poison into *amṛta* (the nectar of long life and prosperity). In the Rnying ma tradition, the *garuḍa* personifies certain wrathful forms of Padmasambhava, and in the *gter ma* (treasure) tradition, he is often the guardian of scriptural and iconic treasures. He is associated with Vajrapāṇi (Tibetan, Phyag na rdo rje) and Hayagrīva (Tibetan, Rta mgrin). Robert Beers notes in his work on Buddhist deities that according to a *sādhana* (ritual text) of Vajrapāṇi, *garuḍa*s are visualized at many different points in the body. Five *garuḍa*s represent the wisdom, elements, and qualities of the five Buddha families: "a yellow *garuḍa* stands for earth, a white one for water, a red one for fire, a black one for air, and a blue or multicolored one for space."[39] As the cases describe above, iconic animals as actual mounts are a signifying attribute of the deity, his powers and personal nature. These forms also point to animals as active agents of Buddhist doctrine while in a complex relationship with the Buddhist deity.

The therianthropic figures that appear in Buddhist texts often relate animals to their roles

as vehicles of transmission of Buddhist teachings and illustrate the character and power of enlightened beings. For example, animals appear in the narratives of the visionary experiences and dance performances (*'cham*) of lamas (monks) to protect and transmit teachings in the Tibetan tantric tradition.[40] Tibetan monks usually enact Buddhist narratives related to particular legends and doctrines in dance form whereby female and male deities and demons are represented in fearful masks with animal heads. Some of these narratives derive from stories of the former births of the Buddha (the *Jātakas*), the *Avadāna* (Tibetan, *rtogs brjo*) literature, and stories of the Mahāsiddhas. Those specific to the Tibetan tradition include biographies of Padmasambhava or that of his followers, divine female figures, as well as others, often revolving around teachings like subduing ("killing an enemy") and expulsion, and those meant to inspire and/or initiate the viewer of a vision.[41]

'Cham is a rich aspect of religious life throughout the Tibetan region and a lens through which to study the role of animals in narrative contexts.[42] One *'cham yig* (book on dancing) claims:

> Especially the precious teacher (guru Rinpoche) Chos kyi dbang phyug, the zhabs drung Rin chen phun tshogs of 'Bri khung monastery and many other discoverers of treasure books ... went in their dreams to the Zangs mdog dpal ri. Here, having seen the performance of various dances, they kept in mind the manifold body positions they had observed and also the wonderful apparitions, utilizing these for the practice of dancing.[43]

As in other tantric rituals, the meditational practice of *'cham* is based on the transformation of the body, speech, and mind of the practitioner and the space around him into the sacred realm, which involves animal figures.

In the visionary experiences of Pad ma gling pa (1450–1521), a key figure in the Pad gling sect of the Rnying ma tradition and one of the

108 gter ston ("revealers of hidden treasures"), visions of animal-headed figures are abundant. His visions of dances include those of the heavenly paradise called the Copper Colored Mountain (Tibetan, *Zangs mdog Dpal ri*) of Guru Padmasambhava and of deer-headed attendants who dance in his honor. At one time at the temple of Gtam zhing in eastern Bhutan, this dance was performed with lamas wearing animal masks for a consecration ceremony, which would be later be known as *Pad gling gter 'cham* ("the dance of the treasure discoverer of Pad ma gling pa").[44]

René de Nebesky-Wojkowitz in his classic study, *Tibetan Religious Dances*, describes the Tibetan dance work called the *Vajrakīla 'cham yig* (a work attributed to the Dalai Lama V Ngag dbang blo bzang rgya mtsho, 1617–1682) and the role of animal images. He claims that lamas who wear masks of a particular deity or groups of deities "should firmly grasp the ego or self of whatever deity in question."[45] In other words, in the performance of the dance ritual, the lama dancers voluntarily become possessed by the deified animal figures. Reminiscent of traditions of possession in Tibetan rituals, deities are invited to protect and actively take part in them. The space of the performance becomes a sacred space (a Buddha realm), much in line with Victor Turner's liminal process,[46] while the lamas themselves are, according to tantric theory, "transformed" into the deities.[47] According to R. A. Stein, the goal of 'cham (as in many tantric rituals of subjugation and possession), is to "liberate life power from the *linga* or victim, so as to use it to enhance the life of the performers themselves."[48]

As in the *Mani Rimdu* ritual, to be discussed below, "the wonderful *mudrā* dance [is] done in connection with the bskyed rim meditation."[49] *Bskyed rim* meditation is by definition a visualization of oneself as a deity of the *yi dam* class. Reminiscent of Mircea Eliade's notion that "one becomes what one displays," the lamas wearing the masks are really the mythical therianthropic

figures they portray.[50] These therianthropic figures then act out Buddhist doctrine in a performative context.

Therianthropic figures are also common in the *Mani Rimdu* rituals performed in monastic compounds in Solu Khumbu, Nepal.[51] The ceremony usually takes place over three days and includes fourteen different dances and a yak sacrifice. Yaks are prominent animals in Tibetan culture, often as pack animals and utilized in rituals. According to classic studies by Luther Jerstad and Christoph von Fürer-Haimendorff,[52] not only do animals in this ritual appear as hybrid figures exemplifying deities of Tibetan Buddhism (who transform ordinary realms into sacred Buddha realms), but they (and the qualities they embody) also become important participants of Tibetan Buddhist ritual contexts. Animals play a central role in transmitting Tibetan Buddhist ideas like subduing, destroying, and transforming negative forces, and therefore, enforcing purification rituals.

Generally, *mani rimdu* is a modification of the Tibetan term *Ma ni ril sgrub*. The first word *ma ni* often refers to the famous "wish-fulfilling jewel" held by Buddha figures.[53] The word *ril bu* means "a ball or pellet" while the verb *sgrub [pa]* means "to accomplish." According to studies of *Mani Rimdu* rituals mentioned above, the object of this ritual is to compel the cooperation of, often, indigenous deities, uncooperative spirits of the environment, and Buddhist deities (some of these not independent of one another). In practice, the pellets and the ritual around it have an apotropaic function such as ensuring rain for crops. The ritual is also meant to propitiate the mountain gods around Sherpa communities and assure long life to its inhabitants. In several rituals, there is an "attack" on a deity and a diminution of his own life force. In turn, other participants, through symbolic techniques, liberate the life force of sacrificial beings and send it to the gods by offering substances. These rituals reflect an accommodation of local indigenous ideas of the environment (that include animal spirits) and Buddhist ideology. The *Vajra-kīla 'cham* also includes an episode in which two lamas representing a wolf (*spyang ku*) and a hawk (*khra*) symbolically chase malevolent spirits and hindrances.[54]

Other examples in the Tibetan tradition of therianthropic deities include Hayagrīva ("the Horse-headed one," Tibetan, Rta mgrin)[55] and the four female *phra men ma* that point to the centrality of animals in Tibetan Buddhist ritual. The horse-headed figure, for example, is prominent in narratives throughout Asia as a god of horses, expeller of demons, or messenger of prayer (as depicted on prayer flags, Tibetan, *rlung rta*). The Buddha Ratnasambhava is also often depicted sitting on a yellow throne supported by four horses. Of great significance at the tantric level is that horses can be domesticated or at least tamed (subdued). Human desires and other negative emotions (Sanskrit, *kleśas*) are reflected in the horses' behavior and can be brought under control and refined through meditation on this Buddha.

According to Ngag dbang bstan 'dzin nor bu 'gyur med chos gyis blo gros's text describing *Mani Rimdu*, the *Bde kun las byang* (*Union of Blissful Manual*),[56] composed in 1897, Rta mgrin appears in meditation and is visualized as living within the Lord of the Dance (the central figure of the *Mani Rimdu* ritual texts). Iconographically, this deity appears in many forms, often having a small green neighing horse's head (sometimes three of them) protruding from the top of his own head. He is cloaked with a human pelt, elephant skin, a silken robe, and a tiger-skin skirt. Originally an Indian deity whose tantric practice was brought to Tibet by Padmasambhava, this figure is the protector of the Lotus family. As described in the biography of Padmasambhava, the horse's head commemorates Rta mgrin's part (along with a swine-headed deity) in the subjugation (that is, conversion) of the deity Rūdra (who appears in Vedic texts). Rta mgrin transformed himself into a horse and

entered the vast body of Rūdra by the anus forcing him to surrender.[57] Rta mgrin is also known as Excellent Horse Heruka (*Rta mchog Heruka*), Glorious Steed (*Rta mchog dpal*), and the King of Wrath (*Khro ba'i rgyal*).[58]

In the *Manual*, Rta mgrin is described in various ways relating to the ritual context as a "wild horse," as the performer of a dance in which he "dissolve[s] the three worlds in the objectless realm," as the Expeller of Demons, as Heruka, as the meditator-lama who bribes and threatens the obstructive forces gathered in the place of meditation, and as King of Wrath.[59]

Next, the *Manual* describes a group of four female figures called *phra men ma*. These figures are described as having a beautiful woman's body with the face of an animal (a raven, pig, dog, or owl). These forms are an example of a tantric Buddhist tradition of animal-headed female deities.[60] The origin of these figures is complex and likely an amalgamation of different traditions from India, Tibet, and other areas of Central Asia. In summary, the animal-headed figures relate to the directions, doors of monasteries or *maṇḍala*s, and specific independent powers.

Etymologically, the term *phra men ma* is very complex.[61] These deities are equated with several Buddhist tantric actions:

> Sorceresses who actually are the four
>   immeasurables!
> I praise you, great glorious attendants.
> Magicians! Masters of the four actions—
> who perfect the acts which summon, tie,
>   bind, and intoxicate.[62]

In the *Manual* of the *Mani Rimdu*, the four *phra men na* appear naked holding a *katvam* (a ritual knife) in their left hands and dancing ecstatically. They are similar to the *ḍākinī* (Tibetan, *mkha' 'gro ma*) in Indian and Tibetan *Mahā-yāna* traditions in appearance and function. Vaj-ravārāhī (Tibetan, Rdo rje phag mo), for example, in her biography is often described with a boar's head and the body of a woman. She appears in dancing pose with the right leg bent and holding a curved knife up in the air, the latter signifying the cutting off of ignorance in human beings. The boar's head emerging from her right ear is often interpreted as triumph over ignorance (again harkening back to early Buddhist associations of the boar with ignorance), one of the poisons depicted in the center of the wheel of *saṃsāra*.[63]

Tibetan Buddhist rituals also include the participation of real (ordinary) animals and the ordinary animals' ability to communicate with the divine (act as mediators) and be divine themselves. A ritual in Hemis monastery in Ladakh where horses, dogs, and goats are offered to the deities (perhaps as offerings reminiscent of pre-Buddhist traditions)[64] and then driven several times around the monastery is a case in point. This ritual draws attention to animals' roles as mediators. Nebesky-Wojkowitz surmises that these animals serve as scapegoats, *glud* (a common practice in Tibetan religious traditions, in which harmful forces are transferred to an object), or simply as messengers.[65]

An example of animals' awareness of the divine world is evident in other narrative contexts. In *'cham yig* texts, animals are described as being led to the scene of rituals.[66] René de Nebesky-Wojkowitz notes that the popular belief is that, at the moment animals tremble, the deities' spirits are either present or the deities are satisfied with the offerings they receive during a festival.[67] As Kimberley Patton notes,

On a phenomenological level, we might [look] at the ways in which animals are believed to possess a unique awareness of holiness, accompanied by a kind of responsive urgency: theophany cannot go uncommunicated. The animal is compelled to react to and to reveal the presence of the other world. This poignant awareness, this *gnosis*, is part of a larger spectrum of special rapport. In many religious worlds, animals can and do communicate with the divine. A mutual intelligibility obtains between God and

animals that exists outside of human perceptual ranges.[68]

In relation to animals' divine role, Tibetan consecration rituals' use of animals are another case in point. Again the *Mani Rimdu* rituals, as performed in Solu Khumbu, Nepal, provide a good example. At the very beginning of the ritual is a dedication of a yak to the mountain god.[69] As Jerstad's classic study on *Mani Rimdu* makes us aware, prayers are offered first to five long-life goddesses associated with various Himalayan peaks. The long-life goddess associated with Mt. Everest, which arises directly above Tengboche Monastery in Solu Khumbu, Nepal, is called Mi g.yo glang bzang ma or immovable good ox. Jerstad describes an offering to her:

During the chanting of the prayer ... a yak, tied to the courtyard [of the monastery], is anointed with butter and milk, and draped in silk banners by a lama and a layman. The animal's head, ears, shoulders, and tail are consecrated in symbolic offering to Mi g.yo glang bzang [-ma]. The dedication of the yak is the end of the prayer of Everest. This animal will do no more work after its consecration. It is theoretically turned loose to roam the Khumbu mountainsides as a living offering to the goddess.[70]

As is typical of a consecration ritual, the object or being (in this case, a yak) is transformed from a mundane object into a sacred being. The yak "localizes" the sacred presence of the enlightened being, making it available for human beings, who accumulate religious merit from interaction with it. A consecrated object is also regarded as a form of the emanation body of the Buddha, the form visible to ordinary beings.[71]

Animals such as the yak are often incorporated into the mythic and political ideology of a culture,[72] and in the Tibetan case, these animals are often thought of as divine beings. The yak, *Bos grunniens,* or the "grunting ox," is a shaggy animal flourishing at high altitudes in Tibet and Nepal in both wild and domestic variety.[73] A valuable pack animal and a source of dairy, the yak also has great significance in terms of the identity of the Tibetan peoples, especially in terms of royal succession and religious competition among different groups. The narratives that focus on the struggles and competition of Buddhism with local deities reflect Tibetan Buddhist views of animals' roles.

Haarh's study of the Yarlung Dynasty is a revealing case in point. In it, we get a glimpse of the connections in the stories of the reputedly first Tibetan king, Gnya' khri btsan po, and the seventh king, Gri gum btsan po. The latter king was known as the first mortal who severed the *rmu* thread, the thread that linked all previous lineage of kings to the sky. As a result of this king's act, subsequent kings began to leave corpses and so required burials. In a Tun huang document analyzed in Haarrh's study, Gri gum asks rhetorically, "'Can we fight the Enemy? Are we equal in prudence to the Yak?' One and all they answered, 'We are not.'"[74] According to this account, the first king ritually killed a red yak, which was believed to have been a "demon" creature that ruled Tibet before him, while the seventh king, who cut the thread of succession, was not successful. On the basis of these lines, Haarh contends that Gri gum failed in his ritual fight with the yak. He comments, "Preliminarily it seems strange that the Yak, which was probably the most important game and domestic animal of the Tibetans, is characterized as something to be dreaded."[75] Underlying this fear is the political significance of this animal, the yak represents a rival religious and political entity. Animals figure in narratives not on account of how good they are to eat, but how good they are to think about religious struggles and competitions among groups in a culture.

In one of the episodes of the life of Padmasambhava called the *Padma Thang Yig*, we see how animals often represent the local deities of Tibetan religion that struggle with Buddhism's first establishment in Tibet. According to Charles Toussaint's translation, for example, Padmasambhava's conversion of a yak (which

represents the ancestral spirits in theriomorphic form of the royal clan of Tibet and its sacred mountain, Yar lha sham po), is described as follows:

> Then, when he went to the valley of Shampo,
> Shampo appeared, a white yak as big as a mountain,
> Mouth and nostrils exhaling whirlwinds of snow-storms.
> By the mudra of the iron hook the Guru seized it by the snout,
> He tied it up by the mudra of the noose,
> he enchained it by the mudra of fetters,
> And by the mudra of the bell he thrashed its body and spirit.
> Now, the yak giving up the heart of its life,
> he subjugated it by an oath and entrusted to it a treasure.[76]

As is typical of Buddhist tantric texts, figures associated with non-Buddhist traditions are often subdued and converted to Buddhism and serve as protectors of the new tradition (note: the animal is entrusted a treasure, *gter ma*); often Buddhist teachings and icons are kept for future revelations.

Divine animals appear in the Tibetan Buddhist tradition in their role as creators of a whole culture. While the *bodhisattva* (prior to the historical Buddha) appears as a monkey in the *Jātaka* tales of the early Buddhist tradition, transmitting Buddhist teachings; the *bodhisattva* of compassion, Avalokiteśvara (Tibetan, Spyan ras gzigs) appears as one as well in the Tibetan tradition. The Tibetan text *Ma ni bka' 'bum* describes the *bodhisattva* incarnated as a monkey who is lured by a seductive rock demoness, a *srin mo*. Their offspring are the first Tibetans. A passage in this text explicitly attributes the compassionate qualities (that are also deeply embedded in the Tibetan character) to this paternal monkey.[77] The source of Tibetans' physical strength and courage is attributed to the demonic ancestress.

What is also striking in the Tibetan religious tradition[78] is the concept of animals as being the seat of a life power or principle. This life force (*bla*),[79] residing in the body, is connected with external objects and is generally attached to an individual, community, nation, or place like an animal, tree, or mountain. This life force can leave the body, exposing it to illness and death. Rituals for recalling it back to the body are therefore performed. Nebesky-Wojkowitz's classic study, *Oracles and Demons of Tibet*, describes *bla gnas kyi sems can* (literally "the sentient being of the site of the life force") as the "life power animal." This life power takes the form of "a tiger, a lion, an elephant, or a bear" (animals with royal connotations) and is often associated with that of a king (*rgyal po'i bla gnas*) or a noble family. Often Tibetans will regard as their life power animal "a horse, mule, sheep, ox, or yak" (representatives of domestication).[80] Because of this belief, these animals are often protected from harm. In order to endanger someone or cause death, the perpetrator would need to harm or take possession of the *bla gnas*.[81]

Conclusions

As anthropologist Michael Carrithers states, "narrative thought consists not merely in telling stories, but of understanding complex nets of deeds and attitudes."[82] Animals represent complex roles in Indian and Tibetan Buddhist narrative traditions. From the iconic animals who serve as signifying attributes of deities or as modes of transportation, to therianthropic forms that embody and protect sacred teachings and empower Buddhist rituals, and finally, to the divine beings, animals are not only, in the Lévi-Straussian sense, "good to think with" about Buddhist doctrine and practices, but are also central to the tradition. Through the lens of "animal," we have learned about religio-political rivalries, Buddhist doctrine, and ritual practices and so much more—but especially how animals are key players, transmitters, and transformers in Indian and Tibetan Buddhist traditions.

NOTES

1. See N. K. Dash, "Education in Ancient South Asia as Known from Panini," *Asian Studies* 16, no. 4 (n.d): 1–8.

2. Buddhaghoṣa was against the *Jātaka* genre in particular and especially his view of monk Sāti, who had the responsibility of reciting the *Jātaka* stories. *Jātaka* recount the previous lives of the historical Buddha. Buddhaghoṣa accused Sāti of holding heretical views. As Paul Griffiths notes in his study on the *Jātaka*s and this particular incident:

This [monk Sāti] is a reciter of the *Jātaka*s with little knowledge [of doctrine]. Reciting the stories of the Blessed One's previous births, he hears the connections made [between persons in the story and those present at the Buddha's telling of it] thus: 'Monks, at that time I was

Vessantara (or Mahosadha, or Vidhurapaṇḍita, or Senakapaṇḍita or King Mahājanaka. ...).' Then he develops the following eternalistic view: 'These [aggregates of] physical form, sensation, cognition and mental construction cease here [at death]; but consciousness continues on from this world to another and from another world to this, consciousness is reborn.'

Majjhimanikāyaṭṭhakathā (*Papañcasūdanī*) 2.305.4–10.

As Griffiths notes, in Buddhism, eternalism (Pāli, *śāsvatadṛṣṭi*), the view that there is an unchanging continuing principle underlying existence or a permanent self, is considered heretical. He states, "Buddhaghoṣa appears to have thought that a person who is not familiar, misunderstands, or is unskilled in Buddhist doctrine would likely misunderstand the identification." Paul Griffiths, "Scriptural Heresy and the Need for Proof: Reflections on Buddhist Attitudes to Karma and Personal Identity in the *Jātakas*." paper presentation (n.d.): 22.

3. *Tiryañc* derives from the Sanskrit word *tiras* meaning "being bent over, crooked, or horizontal" while the Tibetan word *dud 'gro* is divided into *dud pa:* "to incline, to bow" and *'gro ba:* "to go," together meaning "moving or going stooped over." Both indicate the mode of posture and locomotion of these creatures. These are general terms for animal in both languages.

4. Most Sanskrit terms are indicated if they are the most popular in usage. Otherwise, both Sanskrit and Tibetan equivalents are used. Some narratives are shared by both traditions.

5. The theologian Thomas Berry's idea of the "communion of subjects" is poignant here. I am especially indebted to Kimberley Patton's study of the role of animals as "theological subjects" in her article, "'He who sits in the heavens laughs': Recovering Animal Theology in the Abrahamic Traditions," *Harvard Theological Review* 93 (2000): 401–34. Having worked with Professor Patton on a course on animals and religion at Harvard University helped me revisit, become enlightened about, and develop a more nuanced understanding of the role of animals in the narratives of Buddhist traditions.

6. See F. D. Lessing and Alex Wayman, *Introduction to the Buddhist Tantric Systems* (Delhi: Motilal Banarsidass, 1978).

7. For example, in the earliest tantras such as the *Guhyasamāja* and *Hevajra Tantras*, a very precise geographical configuration is described for these Buddha Families. In the later *Kālacakra Tantra*, the colors, directions, and qualities of the Five Buddha Families are arranged in a different order. For a discussion of the iconography of these figures, see Robert Beers, *The Encyclopedia of Tibetan Symbols and Motifs* (Boston: Shambhala Publications, 1999), pp. 90–93. See also Vessantara, *Meeting the Buddhas* (Surrey: Windhorse Publications, 1993).

8. Beers, *The Encyclopedia*, pp. 90–91.

9. This image is reminiscent of the legendary "peacock throne" that survived until the deposition of the Shah of Iran.

10. *Theg pa chen po'i blo sbyong mtshon cha 'khor lo* provided by Geshe Ngawang Dhargyey, et al., trans., *A Mahayana Training of Mind: The Wheel of Sharp Weapons* (Dharamsala, India: Library of Tibetan Works and Archives, 1981), pp. 7–8.

11. In Indian mythology, *nāga* (Tibetan, *klu*) are the serpent spirits who inhabit what could be labelled as the "underworld," Lanka, or water sources like lakes, rivers, ponds, and trees. In many respects, the Buddhist *nāga* inherited much of the early Indian Hindu symbolism. In Buddhist cosmology, they are assigned to the lowest level of Mt. Meru with their *garuḍa* (mythical birds) enemies on the level above. See Richard S. Cohen, "Nāga, Yakṣinī, Buddha: Local Deities and Local Buddhism at Ajanta," *History of Religions* 37, no. 4 (May, 1998): 360–400.

12. John D. Ireland, trans., *The Udana: Inspired Utterances of the Buddha* (Kandy: Buddhist Publication Society, 1997); Brian O. Ruppert, "Buddhist Rainmaking in Early Japan: The Dragon King and the Ritual Careers of Esoteric Monks," *History of Religions* 42, no. 2 (November, 2002): 143–74; Michael Loewe, "The Cult of the Dragon and the Invocation for Rain," *Chinese Ideas about Nature and Society: Studies in Honor of Derk Bodde* (Hong Kong: Hong Kong University Press, 1987): 195–213; and Howard J. Wechsler, *Offerings of Jade and Silk: Ritual and Symbol in the Legitimation of the T'ang Dynasty* (New Haven: Yale University Press, 1985).

13. Lowell W. Bloss, "The Buddha and the Naga: A Study in Buddhist Folk Religiosity," *History of Religions* 13, no. 1 (Aug., 1973): 39–40.

14. See Ruppert, "Buddhist Rainmaking," pp. 143–74; Loewe, *Chinese Ideas about Nature and Society*, pp. 195–213; Wechsler, *Offerings of Jade and Silk*.

15. Cohen, "Nāga, Yakṣinī, Buddha," p. 400.

16. Hsüan Tsang, *Si-yu-ki: Buddhist Records of the Western World* 2, trans. Samuel Beal (London: Kegan Paul, Trench, Trübner, 1906): 320–21.

17. Cohen, "Nāga, Yakṣinī, Buddha," pp. 376–77.

18. For relic and shadow stories, see Bloss, "The Buddha and the Naga," pp. 51, 44.

19. T. W. Rhys Davids, trans., *Buddhist Birth Stories: Jātaka Tales* (Boston: Houghton, Mifflin, 1880), p. 97.

20. Bloss, "The Buddha and the Naga," p. 50.

21. Cohen, "Nāga, Yakṣiṇī, Buddha," p. 374.

22. There is some literature on this subject. One of the comprehensive studies on diverse demons in the Tibetan tradition is R. D. Nebesky-Wojkowitz, *Oracles and Demons of Tibet: The Cult and Iconography of the Tibetan Protective Deities* (Kathmandu, Nepal: Tiwari's Pilgrim's Books, 1993). *Klu* occupy a central place in the Tibetan pantheon; many ritual texts are devoted to them, including the celebrated Gshen chen klu dga', *Klu 'bum dkar nag khra gsum rgyas pa* (Dalhousie, H.P.: Damchoe Sangpo, 1983). See P. Kvaerne, "The Canon of the Tibetan Bonpos," *Indo-Iranian Journal* 16 (1974): 43, 102.

23. Jakob Winkler, "The Rdzogs chen Murals of the Klu Khang in Lhasa." *Religion and Secular Culture in Tibet*. Tibetan Studies II. Edited by Henk Blezer (Leiden: Brill, 2002), pp. 321–44.

24. This is based on interviews conducted at the Mentsikhang in Lhasa, Tibet, in July 2005.

25. Mona Schrempf, "Taming the Earth, Controlling the Cosmos: Transformation of Space in Tibetan Buddhist and Bon-po Ritual Dance," *Sacred Spaces and Powerful Places in Tibetan Culture: A Collection of Essays* (Dharamsala, India: Library of Tibetan Works and Archives, 1999), p. 198.

26. Keith Dowman, "A Buddhist Guide to the Power Places of the Kathmandu Valley," *Kailash: A Journal of Himalyan Studies* 8, nos. 3–4 (1981): 277–78.

27. I am indebted to Tibetan scholar Hubert De-Cleer for this information on November 15, 2001. He also pointed out an extract from the fourth Khams sprul Bstan 'dzin chos kyi nyi ma's (Si tu Panchen's disciple) *Kathmandu Guide* originally published by Alexander MacDonald in *Kailash* that is helpful in this regard. This was based on an edition of this text in an anthology brought out by Dudjom Rinpoche in the early 1980s.

28. *Gdon* or *gdon bgegs* is the general category for demons that cause diseases like leprosy. In the Tibetan religious system, there are many "demon-like" entities called *bgegs pa*, literally meaning "obstacles," *klu* (*nāgaœ*), *bdud*, and so forth. The *Rgyud bzhi* describes leprosy's connection to so-called "demonic forces." See G.yu thog Yon tan mgon po, *Bdud rtsi snying po yan lag brgyad pa gsang ba man ngag gi rgyud* (Lhasa: Bod ljongs mi dmangs dpe skrun khang, 1993), chapter 81 (*gza'i gdon nad bcos pa*), pages 392–400. See an image in *The Atlas of Tibetan Medicine*, a commentary on the *Rgyud bzhi*, that illustrates the seventeenth-century medical text, *The Blue Beryl* (*Vaidūrya sngon po*), which depicts various gynecological diseases along with other illnesses like leprosy, evil spirits, madness, dementia, and epilepsy. These are attributed to the action of demons. See John Avedon, et al., *The Buddha's Art of Healing: Tibetan Paintings Rediscovered* (New York: Rizzoli, 1998): plate 39, 153.

29. This information is provided by an informant I am calling Dr. Losang at the Mentsikhang in Lhasa, Tibet during an interview in July 2005.

30. These ideas arise out of my ongoing research project on the interface between religion and medicine through the study of *klu* in texts and in Lhasa, Tibet. For studies on the medical tradition and its link with the political and scholastic tradition, see Janet Gyatso, "The Authority of Empiricism and the Empiricism of Authority: Medicine and Buddhism in Tibet on the Eve of Modernity," *Comparative Studies of South Asia, Africa and the Middle East* 24, no. 2 (2004): 83–96; Kurtis R. Schaeffer, "Textual Scholarship, Medical Tradition, and Mahayana Buddhist Ideals in Tibet," *Journal of Indian Philosophy* 31 (2003): 621–41.

31. From the eleventh to thirteenth centuries, many Tibetan practitioners and teachers contracted illnesses (like leprosy) and kept the company of lepers such as Ras chung pa, Ma gcig Lab sgron (1055–1145), and Chad kha ba Ye shes rdo rje (1102–1176). See Jérôme Edou, *Machig Labdrön and the Foundations of Chöd* (Ithaca, NY: Snow Lion Publications, 1996), 133; a translation of and commentary on 'Chad kha ba's *Blo sbyong don bdun ma'i khrid yig mdor bsdus don bzang bdud rtsi'i snying po* and a brief synopsis of his life are provided by Geshe Kelsang Gyatso, *Universal Compassion: Transform-*

ing Your Life Through Love and Compassion (New York: Tharpa Publications, 2002); Ivette M. Vargas, "Falling to Pieces, Emerging Whole: Suffering, Illness and Healing Renunciation in the Life of Gelongma Palmo" (Ph.D. diss., Harvard University, 2003); Vargas, "The Life of dGe slong ma dPal mo: The Experiences of a Leper, Founder of a Fasting Ritual, and Transmitter of Buddhist Teachings on Suffering and Renunciation in Tibetan Religious History," *Journal for the International Association of Buddhist Studies* 24: 2 (2001): 157–185.

32. My translation of the Tibetan text: *sa ga sa ri nam mthongs kyi zla ba la bar du gcod pa'i bgegs rnams byang chub kyi sems la bkod/ nad dang sdig sgrib rnams byang ste/ sa dang po'i bden pa mthong/ sa ga zla ba'i tshes gcig la rje btsun sgrol ma'i zhal gzigs te/ dus gsum sangs rgyas thams cad kyi phrin las nyid la 'dus so zhes lung bstan/ tshes brgyad la don zhags lha lnga la sogs kri ya'i lha phal che ba'i zhal gzigs/ bco lnga la zhal bcu gcig pa phyag stong spyan stong dang ldan pa'i zhal gzigs shing/ de yang ba spu'i bu ga thams cad na sangs rgyas dpag tu med pa gnas pa/ phyag rnams kyang sang rgyas kyi ngo bo la/ phyag mthil gyi spyan rnams ni gsang sngags kyi lha tshogs su gzigs/ 'phags pas chos gsungs pas ting nge 'dzin bsam gyis mi khyab pa rgyud la skyes/ sa brgyad pa'i bden pa mthong ngo// de nas yang sems can thams cad kyi don du smyung gnas zla ba gsum mdzad de/* Jo gdan Bsod nams bzang po, *Smyung gnas bla ma brgyud pa'i rnam thar,* blockprint. (Lhasa: Dpal ldan Par khang, n.d.): 6a.6–7a.2.

33. Jo gdan, *Smyung gnas,* 6a.5–6: "The eight great *nāga*s pledged particularly to be the *Dharma* protectors of the Eleven-faced One." (*khyad par du klu chen brgyad kyis zhal bcu gcig pa'i sgos kyi skyong du khas blangs/*).

34. This study will focus only on some examples and is not meant to be an exhaustive list. A famous example not dealt with is the lion vehicle of the *bodhisattva* Mañjuśrī.

35. For example, the rat vehicle for Gaṇeśa in Hinduism.

36. This figure is often called the second Buddha, who brought tantric teachings to Tibet.

37. *Bstan ma bcu gnyis* often refer to the twelve female subterranean spirits who were converted by Padmasambhava to be protectors of Mount Ever-

est and were entrusted a treasure. See *Padma Bka' Thang yig,* the biography of Padmasambhava by Ye shes mtsho rgyal. O rgyan gling pa (gter ston, b. 1323), *Padma Bka' Thang yig (= O rgyan Gu ru Padma 'byung gnas kyi Skyes rabs Rnam par Thar pa Rgyas par Bkod pa Padma Bka' Thang Yig, = Padma Bka' Thang).* Kenneth Douglas and Gyendolyn Bays, trans., *The Life and Liberation of Padmasambhava,* Canto 60 (Emeryville, CA: Dharma Publishing, 1978), p. 371. For an iconographic description, see Ladrang Kalsang, *The Guardian Deities of Tibet* (Dharamsala, India: Little Lhasa Publications, 1996), pp. 57–75.

38. The significance of the first half of his name *amogha* is fearlessness and *siddhi* means an accomplishment in the *tantric* sense.

39. Beers, *The Encyclopedia,* pp. 65–68.

40. See Ellen Pearlman, *Tibetan Sacred Dance: A Journey into the Religious and Folk Traditions* (New York: Inner Traditions International, 2002).

41. See N. K. Dash, "The Avadānas and their Influence on Tibetan Drama," *The Tibet Journal* 17, no. 3 (Autumn 1992): 41–46. This performance also reflects Tibetan indigenous and Bon po traditions.

42. Classic scholarly accounts include Richard J. Kohn, *Mani Rimdu: Text and Tradition in a Tibetan Ritual* (Ann Arbor: UMI Dissertation Services, 1994); Ren de Nebesky-Wojkowitz, *Tibetan Religious Dances* (Paris: Mouton Publishing, 1976); Luther G. Jerstad, *Mani Rimdu: Sherpa Dance Drama* (Seattle: University of Washington Press, 1969); R. A. Stein, "Le Linga des danses masquées et la théorie des âmes," *Sino-Indian Studies* 5 (1957): 200–234; Matthias Hermanns, *Mythen und Mysterien der Tibeter* (Cologne: Baldwin-Pick, 1956); and, among others, Pearlman, *Tibetan Sacred Dance.*

43. Nebesky-Wojkowitz, *Tibetan Religious Dances,* p. 241.

44. See Michael Aris, *Hidden Treasures and Secret Lives: A Study of Pemalingpa (1450–1521) and the Sixth Dalai Lama (1683–1706)* (New Delhi: Motilal Banarsidass: Indian Institute of Advanced Study, 1988), pp. 60–61; Padma gling pa, *Rig 'dzin Padma gling pa yi zab gter chos mdzod rin po che [The Recovered Teachings of the Great Pema Lingpa],* 20 vols. (Thimphu, 1976); and Janet Gyatso, *Apparitions of*

the Self: The Secret Biographies of a Tibetan Visionary (Princeton: Princeton University Press, 1999).

45. *yid lha gang dang gang gi nga rgyal brtan po 'dzin cing/*. See Nebesky-Wojkowitz, *Tibetan Religious Dances,* p. 112.

46. Victor Turner, *The Ritual Process: Structure and Anti-Structure* (Chicago: Aldine, 1966).

47. According to this work, "the mental manipulation is to act inseparably from the self and clear appearance of the creation stage deity" (Tibetan text, *yid kyi bzo ni lha'i bskyed rim gyi nga rgyal gsal snang dang ma bral bas so//*). See Nebesky-Wojkowitz, *Tibetan Religious Dances,* p. 241.

48. Stein, "Le Linga," pp. 200–234.

49. The process may be divided into three parts: the creation stage (visualizing oneself as the deity), creation in front (visualizing the deity in front), and creation in the flask (visualizing the deity in a flask of water). Nebesky-Wojkowitz, *Tibetan Religious Dances,* p. 191.

50. Mircea Eliade, *Shamanism: Archaic Techniques of Ecstasy* (Princeton: Princeton University Press, 1964), pp. 179–80.

51. *Mani Rimdu,* a Sherpa variety of *'cham,* has been well documented by Jerstad (1969) and Christoph von Fürer-Haimendorff, *The Sherpas of Nepal* (New Delhi: Sterling Publishers, 1964), pp. 210–24. In addition, the empowerment section associates the female deities with the four types of action: pacifying, extending, magnetizing, and destroying.

52. Jerstad, *Mani Rimdu;* von Fürer-Haimendorff, *The Sherpas of Nepal.*

53. It also refers to anything with the prayer, "O maṇi pad me hum," a formula written on an object like stones and linked with the *bodhisattva* of compassion, Avalokiteśvara.

54. See Mona Schrempf, "Taming the Earth, Controlling the Cosmos: Transformation of Space in Tibetan Buddhist and Bon-po Ritual Dance," *Sacred Spaces and Powerful Places in Tibetan Culture: A Collection of Essays.* (Dharamsala, India: The Library of Tibetan Works and Archives, 1999), p. 208.

55. Literally meaning the "horse-necked one."

56. *Ngag dbang bstan 'dzin nor bu 'gyur med chos gyis blo gros, Thugs rje chen po bde gshegs kun 'dus kyi sgrub thabs chog khrigs zab lam gsal ba'i nyin byed ces bya ba bzhugs so/ (The Sun that Makes the Profound Path Clear: The Practice (Sādhana) of Union of the Blissful Great Compassionate One Arranged in Ritual Form)* (Rongphu: Thubten Choling, 1897).

57. Douglas and Bays, *The Life,* Canto 60, pp. 26–47.

58. Kohn, *Mani,* 27.

59. *Ngag dbang bstan 'dzin nor bu 'gyur med chos gyis blos gros, Thugs rje chen po,* 17b5. See Richard Cohen, *Mani,* pp. 27–29.

60. For information on these figures and similar animal-headed female figures, see John Ardussi and Lawrence Epstein, "The Saintly Madman in Tibet," in J. Fisher, ed., *Himalayan Anthropology* (Paris: Mouton Publishers, 1978), p. 329; A. L. Basham, *The Wonder That Was India* (New York: Macmillan, 1959), pp. 168, 318; Benoytosh Bhattacharyya, *The Indian Buddhist Iconography* (Calcutta: Firma K. L. Mukhopadyay, 1958), pp. 196, 258, 297–99, 316–17, 364; Ferdinand Diederich, *Yung Ho Kung: An Iconography of the Lamaist Cathedral in Peking with Notes on Lamaist Mythology and Cult* (Stockholm: Elanders boktrycheri aktiebolag, 1942), p. 131; Francesca Freemantle and Chögyam Trungpa, trans., *The Tibetan Book of the Dead: The Great Liberation Through Hearing the Bardo by the Guru Rinpoche According to Karma Lingpa* (Boulder: Shambhala Publishing, 1975), pp. 63, 65, 67; Antoinette Gordon, The *Iconography of Tibetan Lamaism* (Rutland, VT: Charles E. Tuttle, 1959), p. 101; Kohn, *Mani Rimdu: Text and Tradition in a Tibetan Ritual* (Ann Arbor: UMI Dissertation Services, 1994), pp. 37–38; Nebesky-Wojkowitz, *Oracles and Demons of Tibet* (Netherlands: Mouton and Co., 1956), pp. 46–47, 92, 98; Miranda Shaw, *Passionate Enlightenment: Women in Tantric Buddhism* (Princeton: Princeton University Press, 1994); David Snellgrove, *Buddhist Himālaya: Travels and Studies in Quest of the Origins and Nature of Tibetan Religion* (Oxford: Bruno Cassire, 1957), p. 232; and Vessantara (Tony McMahon), *Female Deities in Buddhism: A Concise Guide* (New Town, NSW: Windhorse, 2004).

61. For the purposes of this study, I refer to them as female deities that serve a number of functions.

They have been equated with demonesses and *mkha' 'gro ma* (the Tibetan literally meaning "sky-goer," Sanskrit, *ḍākinī*).

62. Ngag dbang bstan 'dzin nor bu 'gyur med chos gyis blo gros, *Thugs rje*, 18.3, see Kohn, *Mani Rimdu*, p. 35.

63. See Grags pa don grub, Rgyal tshab Iv (1547–1613), *Rje Dus gsum mkhyen pa'i dam lnga tshan lnga las 'phag mo lha mo'i dkyil tshigs bcad du bsgrigs pa* (*Visualization Practices Upon the Maṇḍala of the Five-fold Vajravārāhī, one of the chief Deities of the Dus gsum mkhyen pa*) (Rumtek, Sikkim: Rumtek Monastery, 1972).

64. See Dan Martin, *Unearthing Bon Treasures: Life and Contested Legacy of a Tibetan Scripture Revealer* (Leiden: Brill, 2001).

65. Nebesky-Wojkowitz, *Oracles*, p. 507; *Tibetan Religious Dances*, p. 74.

66. In the annual dances at Gantok in Sikkim, the mounts of the three chief guardian deities of Sikkim are also brought by attendants near the circle where the dancers turn.

67. Nebesky-Wojkowitz, *Tibetan Religious Dances*, p. 74.

68. Patton, "He Who Sits," pp. 413–14.

69. Tibetan Buddhist tradition focuses on sacred geography, and it often combines Buddhist and non-Buddhist elements in its ritual corpus.

70. Jerstad, *Mani Rimdu*, p. 110.

71. Of course, as Jerstad suggests in his study of the ritual, this can be construed as a substitute for animal sacrifice. As pointed out in an early study by Matthias Hermanns and anthropologist Robert Paul, a yak sacrifice is always performed at *'cham* in northeastern Tibet, where slaughtering of animals is common. See Robert A. Paul, *The Tibetan Symbolic World: Psychoanalytic Explorations* (Chicago: University of Chicago Press, 1982), p. 112; Hermanns, *Mythen und Mysterien der Tibeter*.

72. A few years ago a herpatologist told me the story that when he was about to return from the island of Puerto Rico with 22 *coquís*, native small frogs (male and female), to Harvard University to study their mating patterns, he was stopped by a customs officer at the airport in San Juan. The officer was shocked to find this species of frog, representative of the island of Puerto Rico, being taken away from the island. I thought about the political implications of U.S.-Puerto Rican relations and Puerto Rican views of being stripped of their identity, the *coquí*. Animals in this study are very much linked with the religious and political identity of a nation.

73. The Tibetan name for the wild yak is *'brong*, while the domestic animal is called *g.yag* ("yak").

74. Erik Haarh, *The Yar lung Dynasty* (Copenhagen: G. E. C. Gad's Forlag, 1969), p. 402.

75. Haarh, *The Yar lung*, p. 235.

76. Gustave Charles Toussaint, *Le Dict de Padma* (*Padma Thang Yig*) (Paris: E. Leroux, 1933), p. 245.

77. *Maṅi bka' 'bum*, Punakha redaction (New Delhi: Trayang and Jamyang Samten, 1975): chapter 34.

78. Although contained in Buddhist texts, there are non-Buddhist elements.

79. This concept has been widely studied in scholarship but as yet, its origins and function are difficult to understand. See Marion Duncan, *Customs and Superstitions of Tibetans* (London: Mitre Press, 1964), p. 249; Ferdinand Lessing, "Calling the Soul: A Lamaist Ritual," *Semitic and Oriental Studies* 11 (1951): 263–84; Samten G. Karmay, "L'âme et la Turquoise: Un Rituel Tibétain," *Rituels Himalayens*. Special Issue *of L'Éthnographie* 83 (1987): 97–103; Stan Mumford, *Himalayan Dialogue: Tibetan Lamas and Gurung Shamans in Nepal* (Madison: University of Wisconsin Press, 1989), pp. 168ff; David Snellgrove, *Himalayan Pilgrimage* (Oxford: Bruno Cassirer, 1961), p. 143; R.A. Stein, *Tibetan Civilization* (London: Faber, 1972), pp. 226–29; and Giuseppe Tucci, *The Religions of Tibet* (London: Routledge and Kegan Paul, 1980), p. 193.

80. Nebesky-Wojkowitz, *Oracles*, pp. 481–483.

81. Ibid.

82. Michael Carrithers, *Why Humans Have Cultures: Explaining Anthropology and Social Diversity* (Oxford: Oxford University Press, 1992), p. 82.

JAINISM

Inherent Value without Nostalgia:

Animals and the Jaina Tradition

CHRISTOPHER CHAPPLE

Ahiṃsā paramo dharmah—Nonviolence is the highest dharma.

Animals play a prominent role in the metaphysics and ethics of Jainism. The first section of this exploration of the place of animals in the Jaina religious tradition explains the philosophical attitude taken toward animals in Jainism, after which it discusses the hierarchy of life forms as found in primary Jaina texts such as the *Ācārāṅga Sūtra*, the *Tattvārtha Sūtra*, and some of the later narrative literature. The second section investigates the symbology of animals in Jainism, with special reference to the identification of several Jaina Tīrthaṅkaras, or religious leaders, with specific animals. The third section will discuss the Jaina tradition of establishing and maintaining animal shelters (*pinjrapoles*).

Animals in the Jaina Cosmos

According to Jainism, 8,400,000 different species of life forms exist.[1] These beings are part of a beginningless round of birth, life, death, and rebirth. Each living being houses a life force, or *jīva*, that occupies and enlivens the host environment. When the body dies, the *jīva* seeks out a new site depending upon the proclivities of karma generated and accrued during the previous lifetime. An animal that has acted virtuously may improve its prospects for return as a higher life form. If the animal has been vicious, then it will probably descend in the cosmic order, either to a lower animal form or to the level of a microorganism (*nigoda*), an elemental body dwelling in the earth; it may even return in liquid form, or in fire or air.

The taxonomy of Jainism places life forms in a ranked order starting with those beings that possess only touch, the foundational sense capacity that defines the presence of life. These include earth, water, fire, and air bodies; microorganisms; and plants. The next highest order introduces the sense of taste; worms, leeches, oysters, and snails occupy this phylum. Third-order life forms add the sense of smell; here are to be found most insects and spiders. Fourth-order beings are sighted. These include butterflies, flies, and bees. The fifth level introduces hearing. Birds, reptiles, and mammals dwell in this realm.[2]

Jaina cosmology consists of a storied universe in the shape of a female figure. The earthly realm or middle world (*manusya-loka*) consists of three continents and two oceans. The animals listed above, including humans, can be found here. Additionally, depending upon their actions, animals may be reborn in one of eight heavens or seven hells. If animals perform auspicious deeds they might be reborn in heaven.

In two remarkable stories, Jaini cites instances where animals perform deeds that guarantee themselves an elevated status. Two cobras, Dharanendra and Padmāvatī, save the life of Pārśvanatha, the twenty-third great Jaina Tīrthaṅkara. They are soon after burned to death by non-Jainas conducting a fire ritual. However, because of their good deeds, they are reborn in the heavenly abode of the Yakṣas and even today are worshipped as guardian deities.

The second story pertains to a prior birth of Mahāvīra, the twenty-fourth and most recent Tīrthaṅkara, who lived around 500 BCE. In this birth, the soul that would later become Mahāvīra was born as a lion. Two Jaina monks, who happened to notice that this lion seemed receptive to Jaina teachings, "instructed him in the value of kindness and admonished him to refrain from killing."[3] The lion was so deeply affected by their lecture that he renounced hunting and killing for food and eventually starved to death. He was reborn in heaven, and later became Mahāvīra.

Similarly, though more rare, Jaina lore includes stories of animals going to hell for their misdeeds. As P.S. Jaini has noted, citing the *Tattvārtha Sūtra*, "birds can be born no lower than the third hell, quadrupeds not below the fourth, and snakes not below the fifth; only fish (and human males) are able to be born in the seventh hell."[4]

These stories underscore the firm belief that animals act as moral agents, that they can choose between right and wrong, and that their ac-

tions will result in consequences both immediately and in terms of future births. This has led Professor Jaini to conclude that "what most clearly distinguishes them [animals] from the denizens of hell and the gods is the fact that, like humans, they are able to assume the religious vows. ... This similarity with humans may partly explain the penchant of Indians—and particularly Jainas—to consider all life as inviolable. While this is not the same as exalting animals as holy beings, as some Hindus have done, it has prompted many Indians to renounce all violence toward lesser beings and recognize the sacredness of all forms of life."[5] Because of the Jaina view of the interchangeability of life forms and because of their unique cosmological view that sees all live forms possessing five senses as hierarchically equal, Jainism establishes a truly unprecedented philosophical foundation for compassionate behavior toward animals.

However, not all the stories told about animals highlight noble qualities. The Jainas also employ a pointed dialectic to show how negative behavior results in corresponding punishment. In some instances, such stories tell of how human folly and moral shortcomings lead to disaster and disarray. In other instances, animals, following the instincts of their particular species, enmire themselves deeper and deeper in the morass of *saṃsāra*, moving from one wretched animal form to another. In the story of Yaśodhara, a former king and queen become a sequence of animals, as will be explained. However, these animals lead rather ordinary lives and follow the sometimes repugnant instincts associated with their particular birth forms. Rather than providing an inspirational tale about superior moral accomplishments, this story, like many in the Jaina story tradition, underscores the difficulty inherent in a life not formed by spiritual insight and discipline.

The story of Yaśodhara first appears in Haribhadra's *Samarāiccakahā*, an eighth-century Prakrit collection of popular Jaina tales. It was retold in Harisena's *Bṛhatkāthakośa*, a Sanskrit text written in 931, and later in Somadeva's *Yaśatilaka*. In this story, King Yaśodhara discovers his beloved principal wife committing adultery. She then poisons Yaśodhara and his mother, Candramatī, while they sacrifice a rooster made of flour to the local goddess. He is reborn as a peacock and his mother is reborn as a dog. Both end up back in the court as pets of Yaśodhara's son, Yaśomati, who is now king. One day the peacock remembers his former life as king and again sees his former wife making love to the same man. The peacock tries to kill them both, but they wound him and get away. The dog (his former mother) sees the hurting peacock and kills it. King Yaśomati, annoyed that his dice game has been disturbed, hits the dog (his former grandmother) and kills it.

Yaśodhara is then born as a mongoose to a blind female and a lame male, who are unable to care for him. He survives by eating snakes. His mother, reborn as a cobra, engages him in battle. A hyena interrupts their fight and kills them both. Yaśodhara is reborn as a fish; his mother is born as a crocodile. The crocodile tries to eat the fish, but a woman falls into the river, allowing the fish to escape. The king orders the capture, slow torture, and killing of the crocodile, later reborn as a she-goat. The fish lives a while longer and then is caught and fed to his former wife, Queen Amṛtamatī, as a result of his former action or *karma*. He next takes birth as a goat and impregnates his former mother. At the moment of his climax, he is gored by another goat and killed, but enters her womb as his own son. His former son, King Yaśomati, hunts and kills the goat that had once been his grandmother, but releases and spares the baby goat from her womb. One day Yaśomati plans a big sacrifice to the goddess Kātyāyanī involving the killing of twenty buffaloes. His mother (Yaśodhara's former wife) doesn't want to eat buffalo meat that day and asks for goat instead. The cook slices some of the backside of the goat who was once Yaśodhara. His former mother had been reborn as a buffalo; both were roasted by the cooks of the court.

The last phase of their tale finds both reborn as chickens in a tribal village. Their untouchable keeper, Caṇḍakarmā, begins to learn about yoga and meditation. A yogi teaches him about the foundations of Jainism and, during the course of their discussions, tells Caṇḍakarmā about the past lives of the two chickens and how their adherence to princely *dharma* caused them repeated suffering. The chickens, having learned of their past tribulations, decide to accept the precepts of Jainism. In their joy, they utter a crowing sound. At that moment, Yaśodhara's son Yaśomati boasts to his wife that he could kill both chickens with a single arrow. Upon their death, Yaśodhara and his mother enter the womb of Yaśomati's wife and are eventually reborn as twins.

Yaśomati continues his cruel ways of hunting until one day he encounters a Jaina sage. Yaśomati urges his hounds to kill the sage, but they refuse. The king has a change of heart and spares the sage, who in turn tells him the amazing tale of his (Yaśomati's) twin children and how their misadventures were prompted by the sacrifice of a rooster made of flour. The king embraces the Jaina faith. The twins grow up to be great renouncers, and convince an entire kingdom to give up animal sacrifice. Eventually, having taken their final monastic vows, they fast to death and attain a heavenly state, further inspiring their host kingdom to widely embrace Jaina practices. The moral of the story, included in the final verses, states: "He who carelessly effects the killing of *one* living being will wander aimlessly on earth through many a rebirth."[6]

We have explored two genres of animal stories in the Jaina tradition. The first lauds animals for making correct moral decisions and explains how the adoption of the Jaina ethic leads to heavenly states of blessedness, or perhaps even liberation. Pārśvanatha's snake guardians reside in heaven; the lion who became Mahāvīra now dwells eternally in the state of liberation (*mukti* or *kevala*). The second genre shows the difficulty of animal life. Because of the initial intention to sacrifice a symbolic rooster, King

Yaśodhara and his mother had to endure six animal births before regaining human status. In none of these instances, except perhaps when they were chickens, did these animals rise above their basest instincts. They displayed none of the virtues exhibited in the snake and lion stories cited above. Their plight, while it reminds the hearer of the tale of the preciousness of human birth, in no way valorizes or sentimentalizes the animal realm. Instead it serves to underscore the inviolability of the law of *karma*.

The Symbology of Animals in Jaina Tradition

The first part of the *Ācārāṅga Sūtra* represents the earliest stratum of Jaina literature and can be dated to the fourth or fifth century BCE.[7] In this remarkable book we find an eloquent and detailed appeal for the benevolent treatment of animals:

> Some slay animals for sacrificial purposes, some slay animals for the sake of their skin, some kill them for the sake of their flesh, some kill them for the sake of their blood; others for the sake of their heart, their bile, the feathers of their tail, their tail, their big or small horns, their teeth, their tusks, their nails, their sinews, their bones; with a purpose and without a purpose. Some kill animals because they have been wounded by them, or are wounded, or will be wounded. He who injures these animals does not comprehend and renounce the sinful acts; he who does not injure these, comprehends and renounces the sinful acts. Knowing them, a wise man should not act sinfully towards animals, nor cause others to act so, nor allow others to act so.[8]

This respect for animals pervades Jaina literature and philosophy and has led to an array of distinctive lifestyle observances rooted in a concern to cause no harm to any animals.

Animal symbolism plays an important role in the story of Mahāvīra, the contemporary of the Buddha who widely promulgated the five primary vows of Jainism (nonviolence, truthfulness, not stealing, sexual restraint, nonpossession) and established the foundation for Jainism as we know it today. His birth was presaged by a series of auspicious dreams remembered by his mother Triśālā that include a variety of animals. The first dream included an elephant; the second, a beautiful bull; the third, a playful lion.[9]

In an account of his worldly renunciation given in the *Ācārāṅga Sūtra*, Mahāvīra is said to have been provided by the gods with a magnificent palanquin from which to descend as he entered the life of monkhood. In addition to being decorated with gems, bells, and banners, it also included pictures of "wolves, bulls, horses, men, dolphins, birds, monkeys, elephants, antelopes, *śarabhas* [fabled eight legged animals], yaks, tigers, [and] lions."[10] This reflects not only what we may presume to be the style of the times, but also a cultural consciousness of the nature and diversity of animals.

He then entered into twelve years of asceticism. During this time, not only was he described as "circumspect in his thought, circumspect in his words, circumspect in his acts ... guarding his senses, guarding his chastity; without wrath, without pride, without deceit, without greed; calm, tranquil, composed, liberated, free from temptations, without egoism, without property,"[11] he was also said to resemble or even replicate noble qualities associated with particular animals. The *Kalpa Sūtra* narrates,

> His senses were well protected like those of a tortoise; he was single and alone like the horn of a rhinoceros; he was free like a bird; he was always waking like the fabulous bird Bharunda; valorous like an elephant, strong like a bull, difficult to attack like a lion.[12]

These qualities enabled Mahāvīra to gain the state of *kevala,* after which he became a great teacher and religious leader.

The Jaina tradition additionally came to associate most of its twenty-four Tīrthaṅkaras with a particular animal. Although stories of each of these are not readily available in English translation, a listing of the names and their attendant animals conveys a sense of the centrality of these animals in the tradition:[13]

1. Ṛṣabha (bull)
2. Ajita (elephant)
3. Sambhava (horse)
4. Abhinanda (ape)
5. Sumati (partridge)
6. Padmaprabha (lotus [flower, not animal])
7. Supārśva (*nandyāvatara* figure)
8. Candraprabha (moon)
9. Suvidhi/Puspadanta (crocodile)
10. Śītala (*svastika*)
11. Śreyāṃsa (rhinoceros)
12. Vāsūpujya (water buffalo)
13. Vimala (boar)
14. Ananta (hawk or bear)
15. Dharma (thunderbolt)
16. Śānti (deer)
17. Kunthu (goat)
18. Ara (fish)
19. Malli (water jar)
20. Munisuvrata (tortoise)
21. Nami (blue lotus)
22. Nemi (conch shell)
23. Pārśva (snake)
24. Mahāvīra (lion)

In Jaina iconography, the symbol (usually an animal) plays a central role in identifying the specific Tīrthaṅkara. All Tīrthaṅkaras generally are portayed identically, either in a seated (*padmāsana*) or standing (*kāyotsarga*) meditative pose. For instance, Ṛṣabha is portrayed with a bull generally worked into the base of his statues. The art historians refer to these clues as "cognizances" and readily admit that without the specific animal or symbol, it is impossible to name a particular Jina image.[14]

The Tradition of Animal Protection

In order to enhance one's spiritual advancement and avoid negative karmic consequences, the Jaina religion advocates benevolent treatment of animals. The monks and nuns are not allowed even to lift their arms or point their fingers while wandering from village to village; according to the Jina, "This is the reason: the deer, cattle, birds, snakes, animals living in water, on land, in the air might be disturbed or frightened."[15] In passage after passage, the Jaina teachers exhort their students, particularly monks and nuns, to avoid all harm to living creatures. The speech, walking, eating, and eliminatory habits of the Jaina monks and nuns all revolve around a pervasive concern not to harm life in any form. Ultimately, the ideal death for a Jaina, lay or monastic, is to fast to death, consciously making the transition to the next birth while not creating any harm to living beings.

Manifestations of this concern for nonviolence can be found in the institutions of the *pinjrapole* or animal hospital and the *goshala*, or cow shelter. According to a 1955 survey, there were more than three thousand such animal homes at that time.[16] During the 1970s, Deryck Lodrick conducted a study of more than a hundred of these institutions, many of which were founded and maintained by members of the Jaina community. His study illuminates the ongoing tradition of animal protection in India and also investigates the economic support from community used to maintain these facilities.

Lodrick's description of perhaps the most famous *pinjrapole* follows:

In the heart of Old Delhi ... opposite the Red Fort and close to the bustle of Chandni Chowk, is a pinjrapole dedicated entirely to the welfare of birds. Founded in 1929 as an expression of the Jain community's concern for ahimsa, the Jain Charity Hospital for Birds' sole function is to treat sick and injured birds brought there from all over the city. Many Jain families have actually set up centers in their own homes in various parts of Delhi, to which sick and injured birds in need of treatment are taken and then sent on to the hospital by messenger.

The hospital, located inside the premises of a Digambara Jain temple and supported entirely by public donations administered through the temple committee, receives some thirty to thirty-five birds daily. Most of these are pigeons with wounds or fractures incurred in the city's heavy traffic, although diseases ranging from blindness to cancer are treated by the hospital's resident veterinarian. All birds, both wild and domestic, are accepted for treatment by the hospital with the exception of predators, which are refused on the grounds that they harm other creatures and thus violate the ahimsa principle. Incoming birds are treated in the dispensary on the second floor of the hospital (the first contains the staff quarters and grain store) and are placed in one of the numerous cages with which this level is lined. As birds improve they are taken to the third floor, where they convalesce in a large enclosure having access to the open sky. A special cage is provided on this floor for the weak, maimed, and paralyzed to separate them from the other birds. When birds die in the hospital, they are taken in procession to the nearby Jumna and are ceremoniously placed in the waters of that sacred river.[17]

Many of the *pinjrapoles*, particularly in the state of Gujarat, include insect rooms or *jīvat khan*. These rooms serve as receptacles for dust sweepings brought by Jainas. Knowing that these sweepings will include small insects, they will bring them to the *pinjrapole*, where they are placed in a closed room and sometimes given grain for sustenance. When the room is full, it is shuttered and locked for up to fifteen years. At the end of this waiting period, it is assumed that "all life will have come to its natural end" and the contents are sold as fertilizer.[18] This reflects the depth of concern that Jainas feel for preserving life forms.

The origins of the Jaina *pinjrapole* are somewhat difficult to trace. It could have developed in the early phases of Jainism (Aśoka's inscrip-

tions the third century BCE show similar concerns for animal welfare) or during the apex of Jainism, which lasted from fifth to the thirteenth centuries. In the state of Gujarat, a succession of kings gave state patronage to Jainism, such as Mandalika of Saurastra in the eleventh century, and Siddharāja Jayasimha, King of Gujarat, and his son and successor, Kumārapāla, in the twelfth century. Kumārapāla (1125–1159) declared Jainism the state religion of Gujarat and passed extensive animal welfare legislation.

We do know that the English merchant Ralph Fitch described *pinjrapoles* in 1583; he notes "They have hospitals for Sheepe, Goates, Dogs, Cats, Birds and for all other living creatures. When they be olde and lame, they keepe them until they die."[19] In Karnataka, where the Jainas have lived since 300 BCE, various kings have given support and patronage to the Jainas, particularly during the seven-hundred-year rule of the Ganga Dynasty beginning in 265 CE and its successor, the Hoysala Dynasty, which flourished until the fourteenth century.[20] However, Lodrick notes that there are nearly no animal shelters in this area, and surmises that the periodic droughts and floods and the general climactic uncertainties of northwestern India cause calamities at fairly regular intervals that have required large numbers of farmers to seek shelter for their cattle in particular.[21]

To give both an historical perspective and a modern view of the Jaina *pinjrapole*, Lodrick cites the Gazetteer of the Bombay Presidency as listing the following animals in the Ahmedabad Pinjrapole at the beginning of 1875: "265 cows and bullocks, 130 buffalo, 5 blind cattle, 894 goats, 20 horses, 7 cats, 2 monkeys, 274 fowl, 290 ducks, 2,000 pigeons, 50 parrots, 25 sparrows, 5 kites (hawks), and 33 miscellaneous birds."[22] Exactly one century later, he finds the situation little changed, with similar lists of animals and a board of directors (exclusively Jaina) continuing to employ the services of a bookkeeper to keep track of the accounts and seeking financial support from various prominent businessmen and trade organizations.

In one sense, this seems like a work of great benevolence. One French observer in 1875, Louis Rousselet, in his description of the *pinjrapole*, paints an almost Rousseauian tableau:

Aged crows that have committed all manners of crimes live out their lives peacefully in this paradise of beasts, in the company of bald vultures and buzzards that have lost their plumage. At the end of the court, a heron, proud of his wooden leg, struts about in the midst of blind ducks and lame fowl. All the domestic animals and those that dwell in the vicinity of mankind are represented here; rats are seen here in great numbers and display remarkable tameness; mice, sparrows, peacocks and jackals have their asylum in this hospital.[23]

However, while seemingly idyllic, this scene also disturbs the Frenchman. Although he notes that "Servants wash them, rub them down and bring the blind and the paralyzed their food," he also suggests that some of the animals would benefit from euthanasia. "Some of these animals appear to be so sick that I venture to tell my guide it would be more charitable to put an end to their suffering. 'But,' he replies, 'is that how you treat your invalids?'"[24]

In the movie *Frontiers of Peace* produced by Paul Kueperferle, one can witness directly the pain and suffering endured by some of the animals housed in Jaina shelters. Some are grotesquely misshapen by old injuries and others seem to writhe in anguish. By the standards of Western veterinary medicine, these animals should be "put down." However, for two reasons the practice of sparing animals more misery would be unacceptable from the perspective of the Jaina theory of *karma*. First, the person who would perform or approve of the killing would incur an influx of black, negative *karma*. This would bind to his or her life force (*jīva*) and further impede progress toward spiritual liberation (*kevala*), the state in which all karma is expelled. Second, it would do a disservice to the animal. As we saw above in the story of Yaśo-

dhara, each life force earns its status on the basis of its past actions. As cruel as it might sound, the present predicament, according to the karmic view, holds that the animal deserves its suffering. It is acceptable and meritorious for someone to alleviate the suffering, which helps counteract negative *karma* on the part of the helper. But if one has done all that can be done to make an animal comfortable, then one has no further obligation, and particularly must not prematurely kill the animal. If so, then the perpetrator of the killing will thicken and darken his or her karma, and the killed animal would necessarily have to endure an eventually torturous further life to finish the atonement process.

Another aspect of the *pinjrapole* that can be somewhat offputting to those who have not been involved with nonprofit organizations stems from the fact that this *pinjrapole* is a business enterprise. It must collect money, maintain buildings, provide food and medical care, hire staff, and so forth. Particularly in circumstances of family legacies, disputes between board members, and the often emotional realities of real estate values, one can only surmise that the maintenance of a *pinjrapole* presents great challenges to maintain the Jaina vows of nonviolence, truthfulness, not stealing, sensual restraint, and nonpossessiveness.

Conclusion

We have surveyed various aspects of the relationship between humans and animals in the Jaina religious tradition. Like other traditions of India, Jainism not only proclaims a biological and psychological continuity between the animal and human realm, but also sees insects, microorganisms, and life dwelling in the elements as part of the same continuum. The Jaina tradition developed a code of ethics that requires its adherents to avoid violence to all these life forms to the degree possible depending upon one's circumstance. All Jainas are expected to abstain from eating animal flesh. Jaina laypeople are expected to avoid professions that harm animals directly or indirectly. Jaina monks and nuns strive to minimize violence to even one-sensed beings and take vows to not brush against greenery or drink unfiltered water or light or extinguish fires. Perhaps more than any other religion in human history, the Jaina faith seeks to uphold and respect animals as being fundamentally in reality not different from ourselves.

But at the same time, Jainism, with few exceptions, avoids sentimentalizing animals. Ultimately, the reason one respects animals is not for the sake of the animal, but for the purpose of lightening the karmic burden that obscures the splendor of one's own soul. Seen positively, every act of kindness toward an animal releases a bit of karma. But the approach is more on the lines of a *via negativa:* by avoiding a potentially damaging entanglement with an animal, one can ward off a potential blot on one's core being. Hence, Jainas, as a general rule, do not own pets. To keep a cat or dog would engage one in the abetment of violent behavior. With rare exception, cats and dogs are carnivores, which is in direct contradiction with Jaina teachings.

The stories told of animals in the Jaina tradition reflect the somewhat ambivalent attitude taken toward animals. On the one hand, we can find inspirational tales of animals who have acted virtuously and gained for themselves the reward of a higher, even heavenly birth. On the other hand, we can look at stories that do not valorize animals but show their shortcomings and follies. The *Tattvārtha Sūtra* states "Deceitfulness leads to birth in animal realms,"[25] indicating that animals are born as animals because of their karmic impulses.

In conclusion, Jainism sees animals as former or potential human beings, paying for past sins yet capable of self-redemption. Human birth is considered to be the highest birth, as it is the only realm through which might enter final liberation or *kevala.* However, the best possible human life, that is, a life directed toward the highest spiritual ideal, takes the protection of animal life very seriously. The *Ācārāṅga Sūtra* (I.5.5) states that as soon as we intend to hurt or kill something, we ultimately do harm to ourselves by deepening and thickening the bonds of karma. According to Jainism, the best life pays attention to animals, not in a sentimental way, but in a way that gives them the freedom to pursue their own path, to fulfill their self-made destinies, and perhaps enter themselves into the path of virtue.

NOTES

1. *Tattvārtha Sūtra,* 2.33; Nathmal Tatia, translator. *Tattvartha Sūtra: That Which Is.* By Umasvati with the combined commentaries of Umasvati, Pujyapada and Siddhasenaguni. (San Francisco: HarperCollins, 1994), p. 53.

2. *Tattvārtha Sūtra,* 2.24, pp. 45–46.

3. Padmanabh S. Jaini, *The Jaina Path of Purification.* (Berkeley: University of California Press, 1979), p. 175. For additional stories, see "Indian Perspectives on the Spirituality of Animals," in Padmanabh S. Jaini, *Collected Papers on Jaina Studies* (Delhi: Motilal Banarsidass, 2000).

4. Ibid., p. 174.

5. Ibid., p. 176.

6. Verse 305 as translated by Adam Hardy in Phyllis Granoff, ed., *The Clever Adulteress and Other Stories: A Treasury of Jain Literature* (Oakville, Ontario: Mosaic Press, 1990), p. 132.

7. Paul Dundas, *The Jains* (London: Routledge, 1992), p. 20.

8. Hermann Jacobi, *Jaina Sūtras Translated from the Prakrit* (Oxford: Clarendon Press, 1884), p. 12.

9. Jacobi, *Jaina Sūtras,* pp. 231–32.

10. *Ācārāṅga Sūtra* in Jacobi, *Jaina Sūtras,* p. 197.

11. *Kalpa Sūtra* in Jacobi, *Jaina Sūtras,* p. 260.

12. Ibid., p. 261.

13. Padmanabh S. Jaini, *The Jaina Path of Purification* (Berkeley: University of California Press, 1979), p. 165.

14. Pratapaditya Pal, *The Peaceful Liberators: Jain Art from India.* (Los Angeles: Los Angeles County Museum of Art, 1994), pp. 126–67.

15. *Ācārāṅga Sūtra* in Jacobi, *Jaina Sūtras,* p. 145.

16. Deryck O. Lodrick, *Sacred Cows, Sacred Places: Origins and Survivals of Animal Homes in India* (Berkeley: University of California Press, 1981) p. 13.

17. Ibid., p. 17.

18. Ibid., p. 22.

19. Ibid., p. 68, quoting Samuel Purchas.

20. Jaini, *The Jaina Path,* pp. 279–82.

21. Lodrick, *Sacred Cows,* p. 31.

22. Ibid., p. 80.

23. Ibid., p. 69, quoting Rousselet.

24. Ibid., p. 69.

25. *Tattvārtha Sūtra* 6.27, p. 159.

Five-Sensed Animals in Jainism

KRISTI WILEY

According to Jain tradition, at certain times in our location of the universe, a series of twenty-four individuals are born who, in the course of their lives, are destined to attain enlightenment through their own efforts and to show others the path of salvation (*mokṣa*) from the cycle of birth and death (*saṃsāra*). These perfected human beings, called Jinas (Spiritual Victors) or Tīrthaṅkaras (Ford-Makers), share their knowledge of salvation with others by preaching in a specially constructed circular assembly hall (*samavasaraṇa*). Encircling the Jina on the first ring is the fourfold congregation of Jain monks, nuns, laymen, and laywomen. Behind them, on the second ring, is a congregation of five-sensed rational animals, including elephants, lions, tigers, and other four-legged animals, as well as snakes, birds, and aquatic animals.[1] Like humans, these animals have come here to be in the presence of the Jina, to partake in the sight of him (*darśana*), and to listen to his teachings.[2] It is believed that the sounds uttered by the Jina are in a form that each living being is

able to understand, in his or her own language. This truly constitutes a communion of subjects, humans and animals together experiencing the sight of the Jina and sharing in his sacred knowledge. Since both are thought to have the capacity to comprehend the discourse of the Jina, what differentiates human beings on the first ring in the assembly hall from the animals on the second? And what differentiates those animals on the second ring from those animals not present here?

I have chosen to use the words "humans" and "five-sensed rational animals" because these terms reflect the traditional classification system of the four states of existence (*gatis*) into which a soul may be born, either as a heavenly being, hell-being, human being (*manuṣya*), or as an animal, plant, or other form of organic life. These latter life-forms are grouped together in the state of existence called *tiryañca*, which often is translated as "animal" but literally means "going horizontally." Within this broad category, living beings are classified according to the number of modalities through which they experience the world. Among the one-sensed beings, those with only the sense of touch, are all types of plants or vegetation (*vanaspati*), as well as four forms of life in which the elements themselves serve as bodies: wind-bodied beings, fire-bodied beings, earth-bodied beings, and water-bodied beings. According to this traditional classification system, there are also two-sensed beings, having touch and taste, which include worms, leeches, mollusks, weevils, and so forth; three-sensed beings, with the sense of touch, taste, and smell, which include ants, fleas, termites, centipedes, and the like; and four-sensed beings (additionally, sight), which include wasps, flies, gnats, mosquitoes, butterflies, moths, scorpions, and so on. Five-sensed beings additionally have the ability to hear. Whether they are born from a womb or an egg, they have a mind with the ability to reason. Included among the five-sensed rational animals are various aquatic animals (such as fish, tortoises, and crocodiles), winged or aerial animals (birds), and terrestrials including quadrupeds (for instance, horses, cows, bulls, elephants, and lions) and reptiles (*parisarpa*).[3]

The state of existence into which one's soul is born in each life is determined by the residual effects of actions (*karma*) undertaken in one's past lives, with meritorious actions leading to meritorious (*puṇya*) births.[4] Birth as a heavenly being, human being, or five-sensed rational animal is considered meritorious either because there is a preponderance of pleasure or because there is a chance for significant spiritual progress. Birth as a hell-being or as a less-developed animal or plant is considered nonmeritorious because such births are characterized by a preponderance of suffering and there is very little chance for significant spiritual progress. Although one might think that all souls progress from the less developed forms of life to five-sensed animals and humans, this need not be the case. Given the laws of *karma*, it is quite possible that a soul currently embodied as a one-sensed being has been embodied as a human some time

in the past, and this soul may now be experiencing the effects of *karma* from actions undertaken as a human.

Although other life-forms in the *tiryañca*, or animal, category are not represented in the communion of subjects in the assembly hall, they are part of the larger communion of subjects living together in the universe, because they all have the same four basic instincts (*saṃjñās*) and therefore, at some level, share the same fundamental desire for life. Craving for food (*āhāra-saṃjñā*) is the most primary of these instincts. Other instincts include fear (*bhaya-saṃjñā*), the desire for reproduction (*maithuna-saṃjñā*), and the desire to accumulate things for future use (*parigraha-saṃjñā*).[5] Like five-sensed rational animals and humans, all living beings experience desire in the form of attraction (*rāga*) and aversion (*dveṣa*), which is expressed through the passions (*kaṣāyas*) of anger (*krodha*), pride (*māna*), deceit (*māyā*), and greed (*lobha*).[6]

In Jain texts, it is clearly stated that even one-sensed beings experience suffering through the sense of touch. It is said that an earth-bodied being experiences pain (*vedanā*) "as great as that of an old decrepit man whom a young strong man gives a blow on the head."[7] However, like other nonrational beings, they are distinguished from five-sensed rational animals in the way that this suffering is experienced. Indrabhūti Gautama, the chief mendicant-disciple (Gaṇadhara) of Mahāvīra, inquires of him, "Do all earth-bodied beings have an equal feeling of suffering (*samaveyaṇā* = Skt. *samavedanā*)?" Answer: "Yes, they have an equal feeling of suffering." Why? "All earth-bodied beings are devoid of a conscious mind (*asaṃjñī*) and so they experience pleasure and pain (*vedanā*) in an indeterminate way, or with the absence of positive knowledge (*aṇidāe*)."[8] A note on this verse states, "The indeterminateness of pain is signified by the word *aṇidāe*. This is so because of wrong outlook and absence of reasoning, for which, like one under the spell of a drug or drink, they do not know what they are suffering from, and how much is their suffering. They accept their suffering as *fait accompli* and are used to it. The same applies to the other one-sensed beings."[9]

These investigations into what constitutes a living being and how all living beings experience pleasure and pain were prompted by personal concerns for observing appropriate conduct and thereby avoiding karmic retribution from harming other beings. When we can equate the feelings of pleasure and pain experienced by other life-forms with our own feelings as humans, it becomes easier to practice a life of restraint from harming other living beings. Recognizing the commonality of desire and of suffering among all living beings, Mahāvīra has declared, "All beings are fond of life, like pleasure, hate pain, shun destruction, like life, long to live. To all life is dear."[10] "All breathing, existing, living, sentient creatures should not be slain, nor treated with violence, nor abused, nor tormented, nor driven away."[11] However, because less developed life-forms do not have the capacity for reasoning, they lack the ability to attain true spiritual insight (*samyak-darśana*), the first step toward salvation (*mokṣa*).

One might speculate that five-sensed rational animals might be distinguished from human beings by their lack of ability to act as "moral agents." But according to Jain textual sources, this is not the case. What separates these animals from all other beings in the category of "animals" is their ability to remember the past, to think about the future, and to make choices about the nature of their actions. It is believed that it is possible for both the humans and animals who are present in the assembly hall of the Jina to suddenly attain proper insight into the true nature of reality (*samyak-darśana*). They also may experience proper insight in other situations, for example, at the sight of an image of a Jina, while listening to the discourse of a Jain mendicant, or when hearing the sacred *pañca-namaskāra mantra*. Indeed, according to Digambara narratives, Mahāvīra, the twenty-fourth and final Tīrthaṅkara in our cycle of time, first attained proper insight in a previous birth as a lion when he was instructed by Jain mendicants.[12] This event marks a turning point in one's beginningless journey in the cycle of rebirth because all beings who attain this insight will eventually attain salvation.

It is said that animals who have attained proper insight can observe restraint with respect to killing, and so forth. Thus, they are able to follow a mode of conduct equivalent to that of a human who has formally accepted the vows of restraint (*vrata*s) that a Jain lay person may formally take to refrain from harmful actions (*ahiṃsā*), from telling lies (*satya*), from stealing (*asteya*), from inappropriate sexual activity (*brahmacarya*), and from possessiveness (*aparigraha*). Like laypeople, animals may undertake a fast ending in death (*sallekhanā*).

There are numerous accounts in the narrative literature about five-sensed rational animals attaining meritorious (*puṇya*) births as a result of behaving in a manner similar to humans who have formally assumed the lay vows (*aṇuvrata*s).

For example, in the *Triṣaṣṭiśalākāpuruṣacaritra* of Hemacandra, in the context of the stories of the twenty-third Tīrthaṅkara Pārśvanātha's previous births, there is the story of the elephant Marubhūti, the leader of an elephant herd, and Aravinda, the King of Potana (whose soul will be born as Pārśvanātha in a future birth), who had renounced the world and become a mendicant. In the course of his solitary wanderings, he converted a caravan leader. Marubhūti came to where the caravan was staying and frightened the people and animals by trumpeting and throwing water. Muni Aravinda, who knew by extrasensory knowledge (*avadhi-jñāna*) that the time for the elephant's enlightenment was near, remained motionless in the *kāyotsarga* posture. Seeing him, Marubhūti approached, and his anger was appeased by the power of the mendicant's penances.

The mendicant said to the elephant, "Do you not recognize me, [who prior to renunciation was] King Aravinda? Have you forgotten the *dharma* of the Arhats accepted in that [previous] birth? Remember everything." Immediately the elephant remembered his former birth and bowed respectfully to the mendicant, who said, "Accept again the layman *dharma* of your former birth." With gestures of his trunk, he agreed to the mendicant's speech.

It is said that the elephant-layman took care while walking, and so forth. He undertook various penances such as the two-day fast. Drinking water heated by the sun, breaking his fast with dried leaves, this elephant was averse to sporting with female elephants. Subsequently, the elephant Marubhūti, while drinking pure water heated by the sun, was bitten by a serpent. Mired in the mud, unable to get out because of emaciation from observing penances, he realized the time of his death was near. He rejected the four kinds of food, died engaged in concentrated meditation, and was born as a heavenly being in Sahasrāra (the eighth heaven).[13]

Being a "moral agent" can have negative consequences as well. There are narratives that tell of acts of cruelty and violence committed by five-sensed rational animals that lead to births in nonmeritorious states of existence. For example, the serpent in the above narrative that caused Marubhūti's death was reborn in the fifth hell.[14] In his last birth as a human before being born as a Tīrthaṅkara, Pārśvanātha was the Universal Emperor (*cakravartin*) Suvarṇabāhu. After becoming a mendicant, he was attacked by a hungry lion, who, on account of this action, went to the fourth hell and subsequently was born again and again in animal births.[15] Thus, both humans and five-sensed animals are understood to have the capacity to affect their destiny, positively or negatively, through the choices they make as manifested in the nature of their volitional actions.

As expressed by the elephant Marubhūti when he pondered his situation, "They are fortunate, who take the vow [i.e., the vows of a mendicant] as humans. The vow is the fruit of being human, like the gift of money in a dish. Alas! Being human then was wasted by me, like money by a rich man, as I did not take initiation. Now, what can I, an animal, do?"[16]

Five-sensed rational animals cannot informally take the more stringent vows of a Jain mendicant. Thus, they cannot accrue the spiritual benefits that follow from the observance of more severe restraints. Nor do they have the capacity to engage in the intense focused concentration that is undertaken in order to destroy *karma,* which binds one in the cycle of rebirth (*saṃsāra*). Thus, only human beings are capable of attaining the bliss of salvation and terminating their suffering in the cycle of rebirth. While the possibility of attaining salvation would have been an important distinction for the communion of subjects, human and animal, in the assembly hall of Mahāvīra, Jains believe that salvation is not possible at this time for anyone, human or animal, living here in our location of the universe because social conditions have deteriorated enough that Tīrthaṅkaras can no longer be born here.[17] Although attaining *mokṣa* in some future life is possible for five-sensed rational animals, as it is for all living beings, if they are reborn as humans, a human birth is still considered superior to birth as a five-sensed animal because greater spiritual progress can be made, especially for those who choose to take the mendicant vows.

In Jainism, the spiritual well-being of a human being is tied to the physical well-being of all forms of life. This consideration for the welfare of animals among Jains is demonstrated by their emphasis on vegetarianism, by their preference for those occupations that minimize harm to living beings, and by the establishment of special refuges for animals called *pinjrapole*s.[18] Throughout the ages, Jains have actively tried to dissuade others from killing animals, be it in the context of ritual sacrifice, for food, or merely for sport. For instance, Jain monks were influential in the Mughal emperor Akbar's issuing a decree to free caged birds and in his banning the slaughter of animals during the most sacred Jain festival of Paryūṣan.[19]

The recognition of the common feelings and experiences that humans share at some level with all living beings in the universe also finds expression in the confession of, and repentance for, faults that one has committed (*pratikramaṇa*). One of the commonly used formulas recited during this ritual, in which one asks for forgiveness from all living beings for any transgressions, reads as follows:

> I want to make *pratikramaṇa* for injury on the path of my movement, in coming and in going, in treading on living things, in treading on seeds, in treading on green plants, in treading on dew, on beetles, on mould, on moist earth, and on cobwebs; whatever living organisms with one or two or three or four or five senses have been injured by me or knocked over or crushed or squashed or touched or mangled or hurt or affrightened or removed from one place to another or deprived of life—may all that evil have been done in vain (*micchāmi dukkaḍam*).[20]

I ask pardon of all living creatures, may all of them pardon me, may I have friendship with all beings and enmity with none.[21]

NOTES

1. For an illustration, see Colette Caillat and Ravi Kumar, *The Jain Cosmology* (Basel, Paris, New Delhi: Ravi Kumar Publishers, 1981. English rendering by R. Norman), p. 44. The *samavasaraṇa* is sometimes depicted as square. See Caillat and Kumar, *The Jain Cosmology*, pp. 46–47. In Jain textual sources, all of these animals are classified as womb-born (*garbhaja*). This category includes animals born with an enveloping membrane (*jarāyu*), those born without an enveloping membrane (*potaja*), and those born from an egg (*andaja*). All animals that are born from a womb have the capacity for reasoning (*samjñī*). See *Tattvārtha-sūtra* 2.34, as translated by Nathmal Tatia, *That Which Is* (San Francisco and London: Harper Collins, 1994), p. 54. See also S. A. Jain, *Reality: English Translation of Pūjyapāda's Sarvārthasiddhi* (Madras: Jwalamalini, 1960; reprint, 1992), p. 74. In Jainism, there also is a category of five-sensed nonrational animals. They are not born from a womb but come into being through agglutination (*sammūrchana*). According to Tatia's notes on *Tattvārtha-sūtra* 2.36, animals in this category always are born outside the cosmic region inhabited by humans. Thus, they do not enter into our discussion here. See Tatia, *That Which Is*, p. 54.

2. There are two main sectarian traditions in Jainism, which are named after the appearance of their mendicants: Śvetāmbaras, whose mendicants wear white clothing, and Digambaras, whose male mendicants are sky-clad, or nude. I use the masculine here because according to Digambaras, all Tīrthaṅkaras are men. According to Śvetāmbaras, the nineteenth Tīrthaṅkara, Malli, was a woman, but this is considered to have been an extraordinary occurrence.

3. *Tattvārtha-sūtra* 2.22–2.24.

4. In other religious traditions of South Asia, *karma* is usually understood as mental traces or seeds that are left behind that someday will bear fruit. In Jainism, however, *karma* is classified as a subtle form of matter that clings to the soul. There are numerous varieties of *karma*, each of which produces a specific effect. Different varieties of karmic matter, for example, cause delusion about the true nature of reality and about proper conduct, give rise to desires or passions, and cause the formation of the physical body, which embodies the soul.

5. *Gommaṭasāra Jīvakāṇḍa of Nemicandra* 134–39, as translated by J. L. Jaini (Lucknow: The Central Jaina Publishing House, 1927; reprint, New Delhi: Today & Tomorrow's Printers & Publishers, 1990), pp. 93–95.

6. Technically, the various passions are produced by varieties of karmic matter called *cāritra mohanīya karma*s.

7. *Bhagavatī-sūtra*, *śataka* 19, *uddeśaka* 3, *sūtra* 33, p. 840 (766b), as translated by Jozef Deleu, *Viyāhapannatti (Bhagavaī): The Fifth Anga of the Jaina Canon* (Brugge: De Tempel, Tempelhof, 1970), p. 250.

8. *Bhagavatī-sūtra*, *śataka* 1, *uddeśaka* 2, *sūtra* 7.2,

p. 19 (39a) as translated by K. C. Lalwani, *Bhagavatī Sūtra*, vol. 1 (Calcutta: Jain Bhawan, 1973), pp. 39–40.

9. Ibid., 1:239–40. See also Deleu, *Viyāhapannatti*, p. 76.

10. *Ācārāṅga-sūtra* 1.2.3.4, as translated by Hermann Jacobi, *Jaina Sūtras Translated from the Prakrit*, pt. 1 (Oxford: Oxford University Press, 1884; reprint, Delhi: Motilal Banarsidass 1989), p. 19.

11. Ibid., 1.4.1.1, as translated by Jacobi, *Jaina Sūtras*, pt. 1, p. 36.

12. *Uttarapurāṇa of Guṇabhadra* 86.207–8, Pannalal Jain, ed. (Varanasi: Bhāratīya Jñānapīṭha, Sanskrit text with Hindi translation, 1954).

13. Helen Johnson, trans., *The Lives of Sixty-three Illustrious Persons* (trans. of *Triṣaṣṭiśalākāpuruṣacaritra of Hemacandra*), vol. 5 (Baroda: Oriental Institute, 1962), pp. 360–63. The elephant observed care in walking to avoid stepping on insects, and so forth, in keeping with the lay vow of not intentionally harming any being with two or more senses. Drinking water heated by the sun is the equivalent of a human drinking only boiled water to avoid harm to one-sensed water-bodied beings. Although this practice is obligatory for a Jain mendicant, who also vows not to intentionally harm any one-sensed beings, some observant laypeople choose to observe this restraint. Austerities such as fasting are thought to restrict the influx of new karmic matter to the soul and to remove large quantities of previously bound *karma*. Rejecting food at the approach of death is the equivalent to taking the vow of *sallekhanā*. Marubhūti's next birth as a heavenly being is consistent with the karmic law that it is possible, after accepting the lay vows, to bind the variety of *karma* that causes birth as a heavenly being (*deva-āyu karma*) but not those varieties that cause birth as a human being, animal, or hellbeing. For further details on *karma*, the lay and mendicant vows, and the practice of *sallekhanā*, see Padmanabh S. Jaini, *The Jaina Path of Purification* (Berkeley: University of California Press, 1979). For other such narratives in the religious traditions of South Asia, see Padmanabh S. Jaini, "Indian Perspectives on the Spirituality of Animals," in *Collected Papers on Jaina Studies*, ed. Padmanabh S. Jaini (Delhi: Motilal Banarsidass, 2000), pp. 253–66 (originally published in *Buddhist Philosophy and Culture: Essays in Honour of N. A. Jayawickrema*, David J. Kalupahana and W. G. Weeraratne [Viraratna], eds., Colombo, 1987, pp. 169–78).

14. Johnson, *The Lives of Sixty-three Illustrious Persons*, 5:364. In Jain cosmology, there are seven hells, located one above the other. According to the commentaries on *Tattvārtha-sūtra* 3.6, five-sensed rational reptiles with legs can be born no lower than the second hell, birds no lower than the third hell, terrestrial quadrupeds such as lions no lower than the fourth hell, legless reptiles such as snakes no lower than the fifth hell, while aquatic animals such as crocodiles and fish can be born as low as the seventh hell. I have found no discussion in the commentaries that would provide a rationale for these destinies.

15. Johnson, *The Lives of Sixty-three Illustrious Persons*, 5:377.

16. Ibid., pp. 362–63.

17. However, Jains believe that there are other locations in the universe that are not subject to cyclical time where Tīrthaṅkaras always are preaching.

18. For an examination of the institution of *pinjrapoles*, see D. O. Lodrick, *Sacred Cows, Sacred Places: The Origin and Survival of Animal Homes in India* (Berkeley: University of California Press, 1981).

19. Paul Dundas, *The Jains* (London and New York: Routledge, 2nd. ed., 2002), p. 146.

20. *Airyāpathikī-pratikramaṇa-sūtra*, in *Yoga Śāstra* iii. 124, as translated by R. Williams in *Jaina Yoga: A Survey of Mediaeval Śrāvakācāras* (London: Oxford University Press, 1963), pp. 203–4.

21. *Pratikramaṇa-sūtra* as translated in ibid., p. 207.

IV

ANIMALS IN CHINESE TRADITIONS

EARLY CHINESE RELIGION

"Of a tawny bull we make offering":

Animals in Early Chinese Religion

ROEL STERCKX

Historians and scholars of religion face one of their hardest tasks when trying to explicate and reconstruct "religion in practice" in ancient civilizations. Any attempt to resurrect a multifaceted and complex religious culture from fragmentary textual and material evidence remains subject to interpretative lacunae and ongoing revision. Although some ancient beliefs and practices survive their ritual practitioners and audiences through the collective memory in text, artifacts, and scripture, much of its antecedent religious lore shares a less enduring fate. Our understanding of ancient religious practice is further conditioned by the impossibility of direct witness and participation, a privilege reserved for the anthropologist. Describing the internal architecture of religious activity in archaic or ancient societies therefore requires a willingness to infer an approximate picture from fragmentary evidence while maintaining a critical measure of caution when matching thoughts to facts. To be sure, these methodological constraints apply to any study of the past. Yet, they are of special relevance to students of ancient Chinese religion, a field that for the past three decades has continued to be reshaped by an increasing number of newly found manuscripts and archaeological discoveries.[1]

Our current understanding of ancient Chinese religion and the role of animals in the religious culture of early China is based on a disparate corpus of source materials. These include tomb inventories, ritual codices, hemerological and medical texts, and received canonical literature (historiographical, literary, and philosophical writings). In addition to data preserved in bone and bronze inscriptions that document the use of animals in the late Shang 商 and early Zhou 周 periods (ca. 1200–771 BCE), most of our information is drawn from texts produced by elites during the period stretching from the sixth century BCE to the first century AD (i.e., pre-Buddhist China, an era that roughly coincides with the classical age of Plato, Aristotle, and Alexander the Great in ancient Greece, and ends at the time of the Late Republic and the dawn of the Augustan period in Rome). Despite the omnipresence of animal records in these texts, the identification of the social and ritual context in which some of the beliefs and practices involving animals described below were held remains tentative.[2] While animals no doubt played an important part in the religious culture of farmers, herdsmen, and commoners in ancient Chinese society, our information is preserved in texts generated by elites or is based on material evidence excavated from tombs that housed the souls and mortuary goods of members of the governing classes. Most transmitted texts describe the religious activities of kings and generals, feudal lords, or ritualists at the court. We may assume, however, that similar beliefs, or at least varieties thereof, were held by the lower elites and common folk who populated the manors and farms of ancient China and tilled the fields in the service of their superiors. Evidence suggests that differences in economic and social status did not play a determinative role in shaping religious beliefs and practices; rather, elites and commoners, in many ways, shared a common substrate of religious beliefs.[3]

In addition to (and partly as a consequence of) the limited nature of the source materials available for the study of so-called "popular religion" at the household level, our current insight into the role of animals in early Chinese religion also falls short of giving due account of regional variation. Local fauna varied substantially across the vast territory now referred to as China, with its climates ranging from the dry and windy steppes in the north to the tropical jungles of the south. We must assume that the perception of animals and their role in religious belief and practice also varied across these different regions, and indeed, the textual record provides some support for this view. The Han historian Sima Qian 司馬遷 (145?–86? BCE), for instance, notes that, more than the inhabitants of other regions, people in the southern states were preoccupied with beliefs in demons and engaged

in "unorthodox" practices such as divination by means of chicken bones (as opposed to the more widespread use of turtles [plastromancy] and yarrow stalks [achillomancy]).[4] Archaeological evidence increasingly bears out the impression of a diversity of religious worldviews among the main states in the Eastern Zhou period (ca. 771–221 BCE), and the record for the southern state of Chu 楚 is particularly informative in this regard.[5] The presence in Chu graves of "tomb-quelling animals" (zhen mu shou 鎮墓獸)—wooden figurines with horns and long, pendant tongues—provides another indication that religious perceptions of animals were marked by regional flavors.[6] No doubt new textual and material evidence will be unearthed in the years ahead that will enable us to trace the significance of these tomb objects and Sima Qian's comments with more precision, and to add pieces to an emerging puzzle of regional religious and ritual traditions.

Despite the inevitable gaps in our present understanding, there is sufficient evidence to show that animals figured in several ways as agents and objects in early Chinese religion. This dual function of animals as both mediums and objects of worship in Chinese religion deserves to be highlighted. Unlike the Greeks, who, as early as Pythagoras, engaged in philosophical deliberations that sought to define the ontological status of animals or trace the ethical communion that linked animals to human self-perception, the ancient Chinese largely refrained from theoretical speculation about the animal world. The Chinese did not perceive the demarcation of the human and animal realms as permanent; rather, animals were seen as part of an organic whole, a larger natural world of which humans themselves constituted but one unstable part.[7]

This worldview, in which the human-animal relationship was seen as contingent, continuous, and interdependent, also percolated into the realm of religious practice and was translated into a belief system in which animals figured as mediums as well as objects of worship. In what follows I distinguish three main functions associated with animals in the religious culture of pre-Buddhist China. First, animals and tutelary animal spirits were the recipients of ritual worship; second, animals functioned as intermediaries with the spirit world and as agents of demonic possession; third, and most importantly, animals were a central component in the sacrificial cuisine of early China.[8] Victim animals provided the blood and meats to be consumed by spirits and ritual participants. Furthermore, the breeding, management, and preparation of victim animals required the deployment of specialized officials and ritualists to serve the sacrificial needs of their communities. Underlying each of these areas of religious preoccupation with animals was the notion that the animal realm—in its various manifestations as a world of individuated species or a collective natural whole—was believed to facilitate and sanction human communication with the divine, and forge social, political, and ritual relationships in the world of humans.

Animals as Objects of Worship

Evidence confirming zoolatry is documented only sporadically in the received textual record of ancient China. According to a chronicle describing political events in the late seventh century BCE, people in the feudal state of Lu 魯 set out to organize sacrifices to worship an ominous sea bird that had perched on the city gates of its capital. While unusual appearances of animals near centers of human activity were regularly interpreted as signs portending pending political events, this particular occurrence was noteworthy to the scribes for another reason. In fact, the bird cult in Lu was criticized on the basis that the worship of birds had no place in the state's official ritual canons and therefore did not belong to the "orthodox sacrifices."[9] Given the paucity of comparable evidence, it is hard to tell whether this particular prohibition reflected a more general skepticism toward the

ritual worship of animals or animal spirits at the time or whether such taboos applied exclusively to the polity of Lu. The fact remains that, by the late third century BCE, when ritual scholars began to compile the systematizing ritual codices preserved today, prescriptions regarding the ritual worship of animals remained largely absent from these canons.

Zoomorphism appears to be less common in early Chinese religion than it was in ancient Egypt, Greece, Rome, or Gaul. To be sure, zoomorphic motifs abound on Shang and Zhou bronze vessels and artifacts. Yet while most scholars accept that such animal motifs must have been iconographically meaningful, there is no agreement as to how they should be interpreted in terms of the religious worldview or cosmology that inspired their production.[10] The textual record offers little help in this regard (only one text passage in a third-century BCE philosophical compendium contains a description of the enigmatic animal face or *taotie* 饕餮 often depicted on Shang bronzes as two dragons facing one another). Our currently preserved sources also indicate that Chinese deities did not systematically manifest themselves as animals and that the Chinese pantheon did not include many gods and spirits that were consistently identified with emblematic animals such as Dionysos with the bull, Zeus with the eagle, or Athena with the owl.

One notable exception perhaps was the lore and iconography associated with a goddess known as the Queen Mother of the West (*Xi wang mu* 西王母), who is sometimes described or depicted as a hybrid creature with the teeth of a tiger and the tail of a leopard. From Han times onward (ca. 200 BCE), when the Queen Mother became regularly associated with the paradisiacal quest for immortality, the hereafter, and the communication between the spirit world and the human realm, she appears in pictorial art surrounded by an array of animal acolytes, including a three-legged crow, a nine-tailed fox, a dancing toad, and a hare pounding the elixir of immortality. The nine-tailed fox was a creature of auspicious omen (nine symbolizing felicitous offspring); the three-legged crow resided in the sun and served as the goddess's messenger. Both the hare and the toad were believed to be lunar residents. The hare held the fungus that could grant immortality, and the toad symbolized the cycle of birth, death, and rebirth.[11] However, such references to alliances between gods and animals are rare and, with the exception of animal appearances interpreted as omens, divine epiphanies through the medium of animals are not widely documented.

Whether or not animals formed the object of officially approved religious devotion, it is clear that the ancient Chinese did engage in the cultic worship of several animal spirits related to agriculture and military affairs. Evidence of the sacrificial worship of such spirits can be traced back to the late Shang period. Oracle bone inscriptions indicate that the Shang people performed divinations concerning silkworms and the mulberry. Possibly they also performed incantations and sacrifices to tutelary silkworm spirits.[12] Texts dating to the Warring States, Qin, and Han periods confirm the sacrificial worship of horse, dragon, chicken, and cat and tiger spirits. The latter two were worshipped for their ability to catch mice and kill wild pigs.[13] Spirits related to the well-being of domestic animals included a number of horse spirits, reflecting the importance of the horse in transport and military affairs. By Han times, and possibly earlier, spirits known as the "horse traveler," "horse ancestor," "first herdsman," "first equestrian," and "horse walk demon" were the recipients of sacrificial offerings. The "horse walk demon" was a malign spirit that had to be propitiated to save horses from injury on the road.[14] A text fragment unearthed from a tomb in Shuihudi 睡虎 地 (Hubei) in 1975–76 suggests that a horse fertility spirit known as the "horse begetter" (*ma mei* 馬禖) was worshipped by elites in the late third century BCE. In an accompanying incantation this spirit is called upon to "make [the foals'] noses able to savor fragrances, their ears

sharp and sight clear, ... to make their stomachs become sacks for all kinds of grasses, and their four feet fit for walking."[15] During the Han, sheep and pigs were offered to a silkworm spirit prior to the ceremonial feeding of the imperial silkworms in the spring season.[16]

Occasionally the import or tribute of exotic animals from regions distant from the central court sparked the organization of cultic worship. It is recorded that Emperor Xuan 宣帝 (r. 74– 49 BCE) erected a shrine for the worship of a tributary gift consisting of the skin, teeth, and claws of a white tiger captured in the southern commanderies of the Han empire.[17] Early imperial sources further indicate that several non-Chinese tribes surrounding the Han Chinese heartland organized similar animal cults. Tigers were worshipped in the southern provinces, where they regularly plagued whole regions with savage attacks on human settlements.[18] The Ba 巴, who lived in the eastern part of present-day Sichuan, worshipped the white tiger with the sacrifice of human victims. Legend held that the Ba people descended from a king whose soul had transformed into a white tiger following his death.[19] Tigers were also worshipped as spirits among tribes living in northeast China near Chaoxian (Korea).[20] Snakes and reptiles occupied a prominent place in the religion of the southern Chu people. A recurring motif in Chu tomb art shows a shaman-like figure treading on one pair of snakes and grasping more of the creatures in his or her hands.[21]

In addition to invoking the spirit world to protect the fate of domestic animals and safeguard their fertility, the use of animals for farming and transport was also subject to mantic beliefs and cyclical divination procedures. Qin calendars record auspicious animal days and indicate that certain days were considered better than others for activities involving animals connected with the domestic sphere, including horses, cows, sheep, pigs, dogs, chickens, and silkworms.[22] Similar temporal taboos on the use and consumption of animals were incorporated in state calendars known as "monthly ordinances" (*yue ling* 月令). These calendars stipulated how the different stages in the breeding of animals were to be timed during the yearly cycle and prescribed how the ritual consumption of animals was to accord with the seasons. For instance, Han correlative schemes, based on five-phase theory, instructed that the emperor was to eat mutton in spring, chicken in summer, beef in midsummer, dog meat in autumn, and pork during the winter. According to one version of the monthly ordinances (under its instructions for the eighth month) the emperor or Son of Heaven was expected to "take a dog and (ritually) taste (its flesh, along with) hemp-seed, and then offer them as the first sacrificial offerings in the inner chamber of the (ancestral) temple." [23] While abstaining from advocating animal worship as such, these calendrical texts were organized following the premise that human activity had to be organized in harmony with the annual cycles that governed the workings of the animal world and nature at large.

Animals as Spirit Mediums

The use of animals as mediums of communication with the divine can be traced back to China's oldest known form of writing—namely, the inscriptions on Shang oracle bones. Shang plastromancy and scapulimancy were based on the idea that a priest or diviner could detect certain revealing patterns in the structure of an animal's bone tissue. The use of turtle plastrons possibly derived from the idea that the plastron enclosed a creature endowed with numinous powers. The priest's divinatory charges were communicated to the ancestors by cracking holes in the plastron; both the charges as well as the answers obtained from the ancestors were inscribed next to these cracks. The turtle itself was a creature associated with spirit powers; its shell was said to resemble the Shang vision of the cosmos with the under shell being flat and

roughly square like the earth, and the domed and round upper shell resembling heaven. As such the turtle carapace represented the universe in miniature. [24]

The turtle retained a special status as a spirit medium among early China's bestiary long after the Shang people had cracked turtle plastrons for divination. Because of its longevity, it became a symbol linked to physical immortality from the late Warring States period (third century BCE) onward. [25] Furthermore, Eastern Han apocryphal literature portrays the tortoise as a divine medium through which writing, in the form of trigrams, was revealed to humankind. According to legend, Fuxi 伏羲 based the composition of the trigrams on the patterns he observed on the back of a tortoise emerging from the river Luo. These designs allegedly inspired the composition of the famous Book of Changes (*Yijing* 易經). [26] Such origin tales established a close relationship between the observation of animal markings and the foundation of the Chinese script.

There were other animals that acted as spirit mediums in the religious world of pre-Buddhist China. Perhaps more than any other creature, the dog exemplified this mediating role. Dogs embodied familiarity and proximity between the human and animal world. They lived on the threshold of the realms of the living and the dead, and their mediating role between the domestic world and the world outside is well attested. In demonological literature we find dogs assuming human characteristics or displaying anomalous behavior:

> When a dog continually enters someone's house at night, seizes the men and sports with the women, and cannot be caught—this is the Spirit Dog who feigns to be a demon. Use mulberry bark to make . . . and . . . it. Steam and eat it. Then it will stop. [27]

A late Warring States manuscript excavated in 1986 from a tomb in Gansu province tells the story of a white dog operating as the agent of an underworld official known as the "Scribe of the Director of the Life-Mandate." In the account, a deceased man is released from the tomb by the underworld authorities to rejoin the world of the living. The underworld official orders a white dog to dig up the burial pit and let the man out.[28] The role of the dog as a guardian or mediator for the passage into different territory is further confirmed in the use of dog sacrifices to the road. During these sacrifices dogs were dismembered or crushed by chariots before travelers set out on a journey (the ritual was known as the "driving over" sacrifice). Sometimes such rituals involved the smearing of dog blood on the wheels of a chariot. Evidence also suggests that sheep were used in similar roadside sacrifices.[29] In addition to being sacrificed to the road, white dogs were also slaughtered in sacrifices at gates and paths close to human residences.[30]

The appropriation of the animal world as a means to communicate with the divine also figured prominently in shamanic rituals in which animal masks and animal hides were used as paraphernalia in imitative dances and incantatory prayers. A spirit medium known as the Exorcist (fangxiangshi 方相氏) covered his face with an animal mask and wore a bearskin hood during an annual festival known as the "Great Exorcism" (Nuo 儺) that was held at the beginning of the New Year during the Han. At the heart of the ceremony was a rite in which the shaman brandished a lance and shield to drive away noxious influences from the palace. Attendants disguised as spirit beasts wearing fur, feathers, and horns accompanied the spirit medium. A spell was chanted to urge these costumed actors to symbolically devour a host of evils and expel dreams. Various other officials put on wooden animal masks to participate in the exorcism. The identification with animal powers enacted by disguising the face with an animal mask or by wearing its skin reinforced the officiant's power to deter malign influences through the medium of a monstrous facial ex-

pression. An Eastern Han description from the hand of Zhang Heng 張衡 (78–139) gives a colorful account of the event:

> They (the expellers) batter the Chimei and chop to pieces the Jukuang. They decapitate the Wei serpents and brain the Fangliang. They imprison the Father of Cultivation in the Pure and Limpid River and drown the Drought Demoness in the Divine Waters. They kill the Kuei, the Xu and the Wangxiang. They destroy the Junior Brothers of the Wastelands and exterminate the Roving Lights. If the ghostly powers of all quarters quake with terror because of this, how much more the Qi, the Yu and the Bifang![31]

Animals also manifested themselves as agents of spirit power in the area of popular medicine. Animals were known as carriers of demonic diseases that had to be exorcised by means of magico-religious healing procedures. Since physiological and demonic conceptions of disease were not distinguished in separate pathologies, shamanic prayers and magico-religious rituals regularly accompanied healing procedures. The following passage from a late Warring States medical text, entitled *Recipes for Fifty-two Ailments* (*Wushier bingfang* 五十二病方), prescribes a curse followed by exorcistic beatings in order to rid a patient of fox possession:

> On a *xinsi* day utter this curse: "The day is *xinsi*" … three times. Say: "Spirit of Heaven send down the sickness-shield. Spirit Maids according to sequence hear the spirit pronouncement. A certain fox has seized a place where it does not belong. Desist. If you do not desist, I hack you with an ax." Immediately grasp a cloth and exorcistically beat the person twice seven times.[32]

Apart from causing disease through demonic intrusion, animals also provided a central ingredient in medicinal remedies to counter disease. The use of animal feces was widespread as a remedy for various ailments. The same *Recipes for Fifty-two Ailments* include a detailed prescription on how to treat epileptic fits with dog excrement and a chicken:

> First have ready a white chicken and dog feces. When (the seizure) occurs, use a knife to cut open (the patient's) head from the crown to the nape. Then moisten that with the dog feces and halve the chicken ... cover the place that was moistened with dog feces. Stop after three days. After stopping, cook the chicken that was used to cover and eat it ... desists.[33]

To obtain a cure for inguinal swelling, the same text prescribes the performance of a requital rite using a suckling pig. A demonic illness known as *gu* 蠱 poisoning (caused by a bug-infested concoction and possibly induced by female witchcraft) is treated with a potion obtained by boiling a black rooster and a snake.[34]

References to animals as disease-bearing agents or animals as medicinal ingredients or demonifuges are not limited to medical literature. A Qin calendar contains several entries describing how animals display demonic behavior. The remedies prescribed to counteract demonic intrusion are manifold and include the use of feces, whiskers, and hairs of various animals. The following examples illustrate the range of strange animal behavior that haunted households in third-century-BCE China:

> When killing legged and legless bugs, they are able to rejoin after having been broken in two. Spew ashes on them. Then they will not rejoin.
>
> When birds, beasts, and legged or legless bugs enter a person's house in great hordes or singly. Strike them with a bamboo whip. Then it will stop.
>
> When a wolf continually shouts at a person's door saying, "Open. I am not a demon." Kill it, boil it, and eat it. It has a fine taste.[35]

These daybooks paint a picture in which domestic and wild animals surrounding the fields and yards of ordinary households appear as creatures possessed with spirit powers that need to be propitiated to avoid harm. Anomalous animal behavior, such as birds and beasts that assume human characteristics, was interpreted as a warning sign from the spirit world. From the early Han onward, the analysis of omens increasingly preoccupied the minds of emperors and their entourage at the court, and scholars would engage in philosophical interpretations of strange animal appearances by linking such omens to past and present political events. For instance, creatures sprouting horns were interpreted as signs of pending military rebellion, and the appearances of snakes or other reptiles were associated with female "yin" forces usurping power in the inner courts. Hybrid and composite creatures showing physical deformities were interpreted as portents for social or political change.[36]

Animals as Sacrificial Victims

In early China, as in ancient Greece, sacrifice constituted the single most important act of organized religion and occupied a place at the heart of social and political life. The most frequent reference to the use of animals in early Chinese religion therefore occurs within the context of the ritual slaughter. From the wealth of preserved data on the sacrificial use of animals we can assume that the killing and cooking of animal victims was a most common sight around the sacrificial altars, tombs, and building sites of ancient China. Scenes in which ritually cleansed animal victims are paraded for slaughter, followed by the shock of the kill, the flow of blood, the subsequent roasting and boiling of meats and fat, and the communal consumption of the offerings, are omnipresent in the literature.

Specific animal victims as well as the occasions during which animals were to be killed are documented as far back as the divination records of the late Shang. Oracle bone inscriptions record ancestral offerings consisting primarily of such domestic animals as, sheep, cattle, and dogs. Domestic animals also figured prominently among offerings in Shang mortuary ritual.[37] It is clear from the oracle bone inscriptions that, very early on, the Shang people had developed an elaborate terminology for animal victims as well as for the techniques used to slaughter and offer them. A few examples:

Unto Ancestress Xin we will perform the slaughtering sacrifice. (The victim) should be a red-yellow ox. Auspicious (*Tunnan* 2710).

Crack-making on *yiwei* (day 32): To make a sacrifice to Ancestor ... (sacrifice) three penned sheep plus a white pig (*Heji* 2051).

We do not use black sheep, there will be no rain. It should be white sheep that are used for it, then there will be heavy rain (*Heji* 30552).

Crack-making on *xinsi* (day 18), divined: "On the coming *xinmao* (day 28), (we will) perform a *you*-cutting ritual (to) the (Yellow) River Power (with) ten bovines, split open ten penned bovines; (to) Wang Hai (we will) make burnt offering of ten bovines, split open ten penned bovines; (and to) Shang Jia (we will) make burnt offering of ten bovines, split open ten penned bovines" (*Heji* 32028).[38]

Data on the sacrificial use of animals are also recorded in Zhou bronze vessel inscriptions and texts datable to the early Zhou period. Bronze inscriptions mention the use of animal sacrifices in honor of ancestral kings, as gifts during exchanges and visits, and before or after military campaigns. An inscription on an early Western Zhou vessel known as the "Ling *yi*" 令彝 records how the son of the Duke of Zhou followed the promulgation of his administrative commands with animal sacrifices at temples dedicated to the deceased Kings Wu 武 and Kang 康:

... After he had completed the commands, (on) *jiashen* (day 210) Duke Ming used sacrificial animals at Jing *gong*; (on) *yiyou* (day 22) (he) used sacrificial animals at Kang *gong*. Completely having used sacrificial animals at Wang, Duke Ming returned from Wang. Duke Ming awarded Captain Kang fragrant-wine, metal, and a small ox saying, "Use them in ritual-entreaty." (He) awarded Ling fragrant-wine, metal, and a small ox, saying, "Use (them in) ritual-entreaty" ...[39]

Another famous inscription (inscribed on the "Shi Qiang *pan*" 史墻盤) praises the sacrificial oxen as "even-horned and redly gleaming."[40] The preparation and ritual cooking of animals also forms the subject of several early sacrificial liturgies preserved in China's oldest compilation of poetry, *The Book of Odes* (*Shijing* 詩經).

Of a tawny bull we make offering;
It is accepted, it is approved,
Many blessings are sent down.
The Duke of Zhou is a mighty ancestor;
Surely he will bless you.
In autumn we offer the first-fruits;
In summer we bind the thwart
Upon white bull and upon tawny.
In many a sacrificial vessel roast pork,
mince, and soup.[41]

Although oxen constituted the most important sacrificial victim, other domestic animals also provided the source of sacrificial meat throughout the late Zhou period. Sacrificial victims recorded in manuscripts excavated at Baoshan 包山 (Hubei; burial dated ca. 316 BCE) include horses, pigs, sheep, and dogs. These texts also contain a detailed terminology for specific victim animals within these main animal groups.[42]

What do we know about the practical organization of animal sacrifice? Ritual literature suggests that the breeding and preparation of sacrificial victims was the responsibility of specialized ritual officers, whose tasks are described in considerable detail. For instance "animal fatteners" were responsible for tethering sacrificial victims in their stables and feeding them. They also announced which victims were ready to be selected for various sacrifices.[43] Different standards had to be met depending on the nature of the sacrifice and the importance of the occasion. According to one ritual code an ox destined for sacrifice to the high god Di had to be kept in a cleansed stable for fattening for three months, while oxen destined for the spirit of the grain only needed to be perfect in parts.[44] According to another account, bull victims for the sacrifice to Heaven in Han times were fed over a five-year period until they reached a weight of 3000 *jin* (ca. 700 kg).[45]

Officiants such as the "animal fatteners" were only one part of a larger chain of officers charged with the care of animal victims. These included herdsmen, stable and park attendants, keepers of sacrificial meats, and many others. An "ox officer" was in charge of raising oxen for public use by the state, such as those used as offerings on the occasion of the reception of state guests or animals sacrificed at funerals. Another official was responsible for decorating sacrificial victims, placing vertical sticks on the horns to prevent them from goring, attaching a rope through the nose to lead them, and presenting water for ritual washing and wood for ritual cooking.[46] Before the actual sacrifice, both the choice of victim animal and the day of the sacrifice were determined by divination. Failure to obtain a favorable divination could result in the cancellation of the rite. For instance, in the year corresponding to 565 BCE, priests had failed to obtain an auspicious response after three divination sessions. As a result the sacrificial bull was set free.[47]

Since the offering of ill, wounded, or physically imperfect victims was thought to provoke an inauspicious response from the spirits, animals destined for sacrifice were subjected to careful periodic inspections. The cleansing and the ritual inspection of animal victims were deemed so important that on occasion it required the personal intervention or physical presence of the ruler. According to the "monthly ordinances" quoted above (under its rubric for the eighth month), the emperor

> commands those in charge of sacrifices and prayer to go to the sacrificial beasts and see to their fodder and grain, examine their fatness or leanness, and see that they are of uniform color. (The officials) check the sacrificial beasts for suitability and color, examine their quality and type, measure whether they are small or large, and see whether they are immature or fully-grown. When (they are sure that) none fail to meet the required standard, the Son of Heaven (sacrifices them) in an exorcism to lead in the autumn *qi* (vapors).[48]

As sacralized creatures, animals destined for ritual slaughter enjoyed a special status. A ruler was to descend from his chariot when passing a ritually cleansed sacrificial ox, and sacrificial victims were not to be sold at the market together with common animals.[49] Meats destined for sacrifice were not to be consumed as foodstuffs on secular occasions. Such sacrificial demands could, however, pose a serious economic burden on local communities that had to supply animals for religious ceremonies. A story from the mid-first century CE relates that the excessive use of cattle in sacrifices caused severe economic hardship among a local community that had been held ransom by local shamans. Rumor held that people who dared to eat ox meat destined to propitiate local spirits would die from disease and make a mooing sound before they passed away. The incident prompted the Han court to dispatch a new governor to the region in order to suppress the cult and put a halt to the excessive activities of the local shamans. Following the event, the unwarranted butchering of cattle was severely punished.[50] Wang Mang 王莽, the founding figure of the short-lived Xin dynasty (r. 9–23 CE), was also known for his prolific establishment of sacrificial cults. At more than 1,700 different cult centers he had more than 3,000 different kinds of birds and beasts to be used in sacrifice. When the provision of such animals turned out to be too expensive, Wang ordered that chickens be used instead of ducks and geese and dogs be used as substitutes for deer.[51]

Besides observing special procedures in the breeding, inspection, and ritual cleansing of animals prior to their use as victims in sacrifice, ritualists also used a special ritual nomenclature to refer to animal victims during rituals. Victim animals were given a "sacrificial appellation." Ritual prescription held that during sacrifices at the ancestral temple oxen were referred to as "creatures with a large foot," pigs were named "stiff bristles," sucking-pigs "fatlings," and sheep were called "soft hair." The sacrificial name for a cockerel was "red shriek," a dog was called the "broth offering," a pheasant "wide toes," and the hare was named "the clairvoyant."[52] Sacrificial appellations expressed a desire for the victims to be fat and glossy for sacrifice. Well-fed oxen would grow big feet and leave large footprints. Fat pigs would sprout hard hair and whiskers, and the distance between a pheasant's toes was taken as an indication that the bird had been well nourished. The eyes of a hare were believed to open when it was properly fattened, etc. Chickens and roosters were associated with the color red, the sun, and the south.

One example of a cockerel being praised by its sacrificial appellation is preserved in a prayer pronounced during suburban sacrifices in the state of Lu when red chickens were offered to the sun. The prayer invokes the apotropaic power of the color red as well as the sound of a rooster's cry that indicated the time and announced dawn: "By means of (this cockerel's) cry at dawn and its red feathers we ward off calamities for the duke of Lu."[53] Through the use of sacrificial names the status of the animal was transformed from profane to sacred. Sacrificial appellations were an act of word magic aimed at endowing the victim animal with special powers. The calling out of sacrificial appellations during ritual ceremonies must have been perceived by the participants as a gesture of ritual power and a token of respect toward the animals about to be slaughtered at the altar.

In addition to being used as victims in ancestral sacrifices, in sacrifices to various spirits and deities, and in rituals to consecrate or propitiate buildings and roads, animals were also used to seal covenants. Covenants were oaths in

which several parties made a pledge by slaughtering a sacrificial victim, smearing their lips with its blood, and burying the inscribed covenant tablets together with the victim in a pit. Victims used in covenants varied with the occasion or the rank of the covenanters and included sheep, oxen, pigs, dogs, horses, chickens, and cockerels. Covenant fields excavated at Houma 侯馬 (Shanxi, early fifth century BCE) and Wenxian 溫縣 (Henan, ca. 497 BCE) contained remains mostly of sheep with occasional oxen and horses.[54] Animal victims such as pigs, dogs, and fowl were also used to conjure a curse upon an enemy.[55]

That animal sacrifice was omnipresent in the daily lives of elites and commoners in early China is further reflected in the fact that even the masters of philosophy were inspired by the fate of animal victims when drawing moral analogies in support of their philosophical arguments. In the following parable Zhuangzi 莊子 (fourth century BCE?) suggests that upholding frugality and simplicity are a superior way to preserve one's life. Being well fed and dressed in ornaments only increases the likelihood of ending up on the sacrificial stands:

> The invocator of the ancestors wearing a ceremonial hat and robe was nearing the sacrificial animal corral and said to the pigs: "Why are you afraid of dying? I will fatten you with grain for three months (before the sacrifice), then I will fast for ten days and purify myself for three days. Next I will spread out white woolly grass on the ground and place your shoulders and rumps on the carved sacrificial stands. You'll go along with that, won't you?"[56]

Physical perfection, Zhuangzi suggests, leads to an unhappy (albeit ceremonious) end, an image reminiscent of another story, which tells of a cockerel performing self-mutilation by picking out its own tail feathers in order to avoid being selected as a sacrificial victim.[57] Elsewhere Zhuangzi uses the image of a sacrificial ox to refuse gifts presented by a ruler and turn down

an offer to serve in office. To Zhuangzi, serving in office is equivalent to being offered up in
sacrifice; it leaves no way back into an ordinary
existence:

Have you seen a sacrificial ox, sir? It is garbed
in patterned embroidery and fed with chopped
grass and legumes, but when the time comes
for it to be led into the great temple, though, it
wishes that it could once again be a solitary calf,
how could that be?[58]

The Book of Mencius (372?–289 BCE) contains a classic story in which King Xuan 宣 of
Qi 齊 (fourth century BCE) cancels the slaughter of a bull for the blood consecration of a
bell because he had seen the animal alive. Not
being able to bear its frightened appearance, and
moved by pity for the animal, the king orders
that the bull be replaced by a sheep. Sages and
gentlemen, the passage continues, ought to keep
a moral distance from the act of killing and
should not witness the killing of animals they
have personally seen alive. The analogy serves to
illustrate that true kingship requires a ruler to
show compassion for and protect the common
people.[59]

It may be clear from this brief survey that
animals played a significant role in the religious world of pre-Buddhist China. Despite the
absence in the literature of philosophical de-

bates on the fate of animals, their relationship
with humans, and the ethical justification for
the use of animals in the service of humans in
general, animal creatures—alive and dead—figured prominently in religious belief and practice both at the level of the household and in
institutionalized state cults. Animal spirits related to agriculture and sericulture were the recipients of sacrificial worship. The spirit world
was frequently called upon to ensure the fertility and well-being of animal stocks. As intermediaries between the world of the gods and
the human realm, animals appeared in various
demonic shapes and forms to the human observer. Finally, animals were slaughtered and
sacrificed to ancestors, deities, spirits, and demons in temples and shrines and on altars and
sacrificial mounds across China. The sight of
flowing blood and of fumes rising from sacrificial stands in which meats were cooked to
feed the spirits may have been as familiar to the
early Chinese as the bundles of smoldering incense sticks that grace temples and household
altars throughout the Chinese world are to modern eyes. When new Daoist religious movements
advocated the abolition of the blood sacrifice
during late Han times and shortly thereafter,
they were indeed calling for a reform of one of
the most commonly practiced acts of religious
devotion that had flourished in China over the
course of many centuries.[60]

NOTES

1. For a state of the field see the bibliographi-
cal surveys by Edward Shaughnessy, Constance A.
Cook, and Donald Harper in the *Journal of Asian
Studies* 54, no.1 (1995): 145–60.

2. For an assessment of the textual sources available for the study of animals in early China, see Roel
Sterckx, *The Animal and the Daemon in Early China*
(Albany: State University of New York Press, 2002),
pp. 21–38, 42–43.

3. As noted by Poo Mu-Chou in a critical assessment of the traditional model of "popular ver-

sus elite" religion in ancient China. See *In Search of
Personal Welfare. A View of Ancient Chinese Religion*
(Albany: State University of New York Press, 1998),
pp. 3–5, 7–14.

4. *Shiji* 史記 (Beijing: Zhonghua, 1959), 28.
1399–1400. See also *Hanshu* 漢書 (Beijing: Zhonghua, 1962), 25B.1241. On the superstitious nature of
southerners see Chen Qiyou 陳奇猷 ed., *Lüshi chunqiu jiaoshi* 呂氏春秋校釋 (Shanghai: Xuelin, 1995),
10.551; *Liezi* 列子 (*Sibu beiyao* ed.), 8.10a; Liu Wen-
dian 劉文典 ed., *Huainanzi honglie jijie* 淮南子鴻

烈集解 (Taipei: Wenshizhe, 1992), 18.589; and *Han-shu*, 63.2760.

5. See John S. Major, "Characteristics of Late Chu Religion," in Constance A. Cook and John S. Major, eds., *Defining Chu: Image and Reality in Ancient China* (Honolulu: University of Hawaii Press, 1999), pp. 121–43.

6. The exact meaning of these figurines remains subject to debate. These tomb guardian beasts often grasp and devour snakes. It is uncertain whether they were produced exclusively for tombs, or whether they were actual representations of regional deities. Some scholars have argued that they served as apotropaic psychopomps aimed at protecting the dead's spirit in the netherworld. Others argue that they were meant to ward off intruders from the world of the living or that the figurines should be connected with the earth spirit. A bibliography on the subject is included in Sterckx, *The Animal and the Daemon*, p. 247n. 30.

7. For a full treatment of the Greek debate, see Richard Sorabji, *Animal Minds and Human Morals: The Origins of the Western Debate* (London: Duckworth, 1993).

8. On the role of animals in sacrifice and dietary codes associated with China's main religious traditions, see the essays in Roel Sterckx, ed., *Of Tripod and Palate: Food, Religion and Politics in Traditional China* (New York: Palgrave, 2005).

9. *Guoyu* 国語 (Shanghai: Guji, 1978), 4.165–170; Guo Qingfan 郭慶藩 ed., *Zhuangzi jishi* 莊子集釋 (Taipei: Guanya, 1991), 18.621–22, 19.665–66; and Yang Bojun 楊伯峻, *Chunqiu Zuozhuan zhu* 春秋左傳注 (Beijing: Zhonghua, 1995), p. 526 (Lord Wen, year 2).

10. One explanation, proposed by Chang Kwang-chih, argues that offering animals in bronze vessels was a concrete means of achieving contact with the other world. If animals functioned as acolytes of shamanic powers, the possession of bronzes with zoomorphic decorations could symbolize the possession of the means to communicate with the spirit world. See Chang Kwang-chih, *Art, Myth, and Ritual: the Path to Political Authority in Ancient China* (Cambridge: Harvard University Press, 1983), pp. 44–80.

11. On the origins and development of the Queen Mother cult and its iconography see Michael Loewe, *Chinese Ideas of Life and Death: Faith, Myth and Reason in the Han Period (202 BC–AD 220)* (London: Allen & Unwin, 1982), pp. 31–34, 65–66, 119–120; Suzanne E. Cahill, *Transcendence and Divine Passion. The Queen Mother of the West in Medieval China* (Stanford: Stanford University Press, 1993), pp. 11–32.

12. Dieter Kuhn, *Science and Civilisation in China* (Cambridge: Cambridge University Press, 1988), vol. 5, part 9, "Textile Technology: Spinning and Reeling," pp. 250–52.

13. *Liji zhushu* 禮記注疏 (*Shisanjing zhushu*, ed.), 26.8b.

14. *Shiji*, 28.1386; *Hanshu*, 25A.1218; *Zhouli zhushu* 周禮注疏 (*Shisanjing zhushu*, ed.), 33.3b–4a.

15. See Roel Sterckx, "An Ancient Chinese Horse Ritual," *Early China* 21 (1996): 47–79; and *The Animal and the Daemon*, pp. 62–63.

16. *Han jiu yi* 漢舊儀 (*Sibu beiyao*, ed.), 2.1b ("bambix mori spirit"); *Hou Hanshu* 後漢書 (Beijing: Zhonghua, 1965), "zhi" 4.3110 ("silkworm ancestor").

17. *Hanshu*, 25B.1249–50.

18. For tiger plagues see *Hou Hanshu*, 38.1278, 41.1412–13, 76.2482; *Fengsu tongyi jiaoshi* 風俗通義校釋 (Tianjin: Renmin, 1980), 2.92–93; Liu Pansui 劉盼遂 ed., *Lunheng jiaoshi* 論衡校釋 (Beijing: Zhonghua shuju, 1990), ch. 48.

19. *Hou Hanshu*, 86.2840. Han emperor Gaozu 高祖 (r. 202–195 BCE) engaged a tribe known as the Board Shield Man-barbarians (Banshun Man) for shooting white tigers in exchange for tax exemptions. See *Hou Hanshu*, 86.2842–43; *Huayang guo zhi jiaozhu* 華陽国志校注 (Chengdu: Ba Shu shushe, 1984), 1.34–35.

20. *Hou Hanshu*, 85.2818.

21. Wu Rongzeng 吳榮曾, "Zhanguo, Handai de cao she shenguai ji youguan shenhua mixin de bianyi" 战国汉代的操蛇神怪及有关神话迷信的变异, *Wenwu* 10 (1989): 46–52; Major, "Characteristics of Late Chu Religion," pp. 129–131, 134.

22. Shuihudi Qin mu zhujian zhengli xiaozu, *Shuihudi Qin mu zhujian* 睡虎地秦墓竹簡 (Beijing: Wenwu, 1990), pp. 194, 235.

23. John S. Major, *Heaven and Earth in Early Han Thought* (Albany: State University of New York Press, 1993), p. 244.

24. On the principles of Shang scapulimancy, the use of animals in this process, and the turtle species used in divination see David N. Keightley, *Sources of Shang History* (Berkeley: University of California Press, 1985), ch.1, pp. 157–60; Léon Vandermeersch, *Wangdao ou La Voie Royale* (Paris: École Française d'Extrême-Orient, 1980), vol. 2, pp. 290–91; and Sarah Allan, *The Shape of the Turtle* (Albany: State University of New York Press, 1991), pp. 103–11.

25. *Shiji*, 128.3231; *Xin lun* 新論 (*Sibu beiyao* ed.), 8b, 24b; *Shuoyuan jiaozheng* 說苑校證 (Beijing: Zhonghua shuju, 1987), 18.456–57. See also Michael Loewe, "Shells, Bones and Stalks during the Han Period," *T'oung Pao* 74 (1988): 83–88.

26. See *Li han wen jia* 禮含文嘉 in Yasui Kôzan 安居香山 and Nakamura Shôhachi 中村璋八, eds., *Weishu jicheng* 緯書集成 (Shijiazhuang: Hebei renmin, 1994), p. 494. For the river chart see *Zhouyi zhengyi* 周易正義 (*Shisanjing zhushu* edition), 7.29b. For a thorough discussion of the Fuxi myth see Mark Edward Lewis, *Writing and Authority in Early China* (Albany: SUNY Press, 1999), pp. 197–209.

27. Donald Harper, "Spellbinding," in Donald S. Lopez Jr., ed., *Religions of China in Practice* (Princeton: Princeton University Press, 1996), pp. 241–50 (no. 9). The lacunae indicate missing or illegible graphs on the original bamboo slip manuscript.

28. Li Xueqin 李學勤, "Fangmatan jian zhong de zhiguai gushi" 放馬灘簡中的志怪故事, *Wenwu* 4 (1990): 43–47; and Li Xueqin, *Jianbo yiji yu xueshu shi* 簡帛佚籍與學術史 (Taipei: Shibao chuban, 1994), pp. 181–90. The story is translated in Donald Harper, "Resurrection in Warring States Popular Religion," *Taoist Resources* 5, no. 2 (1994): 13–28.

29. *Zhouli zhushu*, 32.15a, 36.10a; *Yili zhushu* 儀禮注疏 (*Shisanjing zhushu* ed.), 23.5a, 24.4b; Duan Yucai 斷玉裁 (1735–1815) ed., *Shuowen jiezi zhu* 說文解字注 (Taipei: Yiwen, 1965), 14A.51b; *Mao shi zhengyi* 毛詩正義 (*Shisanjing zhushu* ed.), 17A.16a (Mao 245).

30. Hubei sheng wenwu kaogu yanjiusuo, *Wangshan Chu jian* 望山楚簡 (Beijing: Zhonghua, 1995), p. 70, slip 28; p. 78, slip 119; Hubei sheng Jing-Sha tielu kaogudui eds., *Baoshan Chu jian* 包山楚簡 (Hubei: Wenwu, 1991), p. 33, slips 208, 210; p. 34, slip 219; p. 36, slip 233.

31. Derk Bodde, *Festivals in Classical China: New Year and Other Annual Observances During the Han Dynasty 206 B.C.–A.D. 220* (Princeton: Princeton University Press, 1975), p. 84. Bodde provides a thorough study of the Great Exorcism (pp. 75–138). For the *fangxiangshi* see *Zhouli zhushu*, 31.12a.

32. Donald Harper, *Early Chinese Medical Literature: The Mawangdui Medical Manuscripts* (London: Kegan Paul, 1998), p. 261 (no.124).

33. Harper, *Early Chinese Medical Literature*, p. 246 (no.71). For other examples see Harper, *Early Chinese Medical Literature*, p. 224 (no. 6), p. 289 (no. 211), p. 294 (nos. 233 and 235), p. 296 (no. 242).

34. Harper, *Early Chinese Medical Literature*, p. 268 (no.138), p. 301 (no.271).

35. These are excerpts from a Qin demonography reprinted in *Shuihudi Qin mu zhu jian*, pp. 212–19 and translated by Donald Harper as "Spellbinding" in Donald S. Lopez Jr., ed., *Religions of China in Practice*, pp. 241–50. The entries quoted here are nos. 17, 52, 66 in Harper's translation. For another example see no. 27 (a red pig with a horse tail and dog head causing the members of a household to be out of breath).

36. For a discussion see Roel Sterckx, "Debating the Strange: Records of Animal Anomalies in Early China," *Working Papers in Chinese Studies* (Center for Chinese Studies, National University of Singapore), 1 (1998); and Sterckx, *The Animal and the Daemon*, chapters 6 and 7.

37. See Chang Tsung-Tung, *Der Kult der Shangdynastie im Spiegel der Orakelinschriften* (Wiesbaden: Otto Harrassowitz, 1970), pp. 65–73.

38. Translations of the inscriptions are adapted from Wang Tao, "Colour Terms in Shang Oracle Bone Inscriptions," *Bulletin of the School of Oriental and African Studies* 59, no. 1 (1996): 63–101. The final inscription is translated in David N. Keightley, *The Ancestral Landscape. Time, Space, and Community in Late Shang China (ca. 1200–1045 B.C.)* (Berkeley: Center for Chinese Studies & Institute of East Asian Studies, 2000), p. 105.

39. Qin Yonglong 秦永龍, *Xi Zhou jinwen xuan zhu* 西周金文選注 (Beijing: Shifan daxue, 1992), p. 17; translated in Edward Shaughnessy, *Sources of Western Zhou History* (Berkeley: University of California Press, 1991), pp. 197–98.

40. Shaughnessy, *Sources of Western Zhou History*, pp. 4, 190.

41. *Mao shi zhengyi*, 20B.6a (Mao 300); tr. Arthur Waley, *The Book of Songs* (New York: Grove Press, rpt.1996), p. 315.

42. Chen Wei 陳偉, *Baoshan Chu jian chu tan* 包山楚簡初探 (Wuhan: Wuhan daxue, 1996), pp. 175–80; and Chen Wei, "Hubei Jingmen Baoshan bushi Chu jian suo jian shenqi xitong yu xiangji zhidu" 湖北荊門包山卜筮楚簡所見神祇系統與享祭制度, *Kaogu* 4 (1999): 57–59.

43. *Zhouli zhushu*, 13.5b–6b.

44. *Liji zhushu*, 26.6b. See also *Kongzi jia yu* 孔子家語 (*Sibu beiyao* ed.), 7.2b. For a detailed discussion of these ritual officiants and the criteria involved in the selection of animal victims see Sterckx, *The Animal and the Daemon*, pp. 47–50, 58–61, 76–78.

45. *Han jiu yi*, 2.2a; *Hanshu*, 25A.1231 n.5.

46. *Zhouli zhushu*, 13.3a–5b, 12.16a–18b.

47. *Zuozhuan zhu*, p. 950 (Lord Xiang, year 7). In 628 BCE a similar release had taken place after four divinations. See *Zuozhuan zhu*, p. 486 (Lord Xi, year 31).

48. Major, *Heaven and Earth in Early Han Thought*, p. 244.

49. *Liji zhushu*, 3.22b, 13.9b–10a; *Kongzi jia yu*, 7.6a.

50. *Hou Hanshu*, 41.1397; *Fengsu tongyi jiaoshi*, 9.339.

51. *Hanshu*, 25B.1270.

52. *Liji zhushu*, 5.19b; *Yili zhushu*, 43.4b.

53. *Fengsu tongyi jiaoshi*, 8.312; *Shuowen jiezi zhu*, 4A.55b.

54. For the use of a chicken in a covenant see *Shiji*, 39.1681; for the use of a white horse see *Shiji*, 69.2249. See also Kong Yingda's 孔穎達 (574–648 CE) commentary in *Liji zhushu*, 5.8b, and the discussion in Susan Weld, "The Covenant Texts from Houma and Wenxian," in Edward L. Shaughnessy, ed., *New Sources of Early Chinese History: An Introduction to the Reading of Inscriptions and Manuscripts* (Berkeley: The Society for the Study of Early China & The Institute of East Asian Studies, 1992), pp. 156–160. The role of oaths and covenants in the Warring States period is discussed in Mark Edward Lewis, *Sanctioned Violence in Early China* (Albany: State University of New York Press, 1990), pp. 45–46, 67–71, 264–65 nn. 129 ff. On the blood covenant in later times see Barend J. Ter Haar, *Ritual and Mythology of the Chinese Triads* (Leiden: E.J.Brill, 1998), pp. 151–179, 181–203.

55. *Zuozhuan zhu*, p. 76 (Lord Yin, year 11); *Mao shi zhengyi*, 12C.17a (Mao 199).

56. *Zhuangzi jishi*, 19.648; tr. Victor Mair, *Wandering the Way. Early Taoist Tales and Parables of Chuang Tzu* (Honolulu: University of Hawaii Press, 1998), p. 180 (modified).

57. *Zuozhuan zhu*, p. 1434 (Lord Zhao, year 22); *Guoyu*, 3.142–143; *Hanshu*, 27.1369; *Fengsu tongyi jiaoshi*, 8.312.

58. *Zhuangzi jishi*, 32.1062; tr. Mair, *Wandering the Way*, p. 332.

59. *Mengzi zhushu* 孟子注疏 (*Shisanjing zhushu* ed.), 1B.2b–3b (1A.7). The philosophical interpretation of this passage continues to spark debate. See, e.g., Shun Kwong-loi, *Mencius and Early Chinese Thought* (Stanford: Stanford University Press, 1997), pp. 141–44.

60. See Rolf A. Stein, "Religious Taoism and Popular Religion from the Second to Seventh Centuries," in Holmes Welch and Anna Seidel eds., *Facets of Taoism. Essays in Chinese Religion* (New Haven: Yale University Press, 1979), pp. 55–61.

DAOISM

Daoism and Animals

E. N. ANDERSON AND LISA RAPHALS

The Animal World of Ancient China

Ancient China was a world rich in animals. In dramatic contrast to the devastated modern landscape, China's biodiversity was the greatest of any temperate land. It was a land of vast lush forests, rich grasslands, fertile mountains, and enormous expanses of wetland-marsh, swamp, and river bottom. In these dwelt elephants, rhinoceri, pandas, apes, tigers, leopards, and countless smaller forms.

The earliest Chinese artifacts from the Shang dynasty (traditionally 1766–1122 BCE, actually somewhat later) include many representations of dragons and other imaginary creatures, but relatively few portrayals of real-world animals. Actual animals depicted include water buffaloes, tigers, sheep, and birds. Pigs, the most common animal found in archaeological remains, are conspicuously absent. In succeeding periods, more and more animals were portrayed, as were countless imaginary creatures, such as the nine-tailed fox, human-headed birds, the three-legged crow in the sun, and the humanoid owl.

The ancient Chinese knew their fauna intimately. The *Classic of Poetry* or *Shi jing* mentions at least ninety-three species, including twenty-one mammals (one mythical), thirty-five birds (one mythical, the phoenix), three reptiles (plus the mythical dragon), one amphibian, thirteen fish, and nineteen insects.[1] Here and elsewhere in Chinese literature, there is a striking awareness of insect life. The songs of the *Shi jing* reflect the fresh, direct vision of people who knew animals from daily experience. The wasp carries off the caterpillar to feed its young; the rats nibble the grain; the spider spins her web over abandoned doorways.

By the Warring States period (ca. 403–221 BCE), China's heartland—the North China Plain, the loess uplands west of it, and the Yangtze and Huai river valleys—had already been transformed by humans and biotically impoverished. Rhinos and elephants were exotic creatures, known from trade with non-Chinese groups on the margins. The common animals of daily experience were domestic: Horses, donkeys, cattle, goats, dogs, buffaloes, sheep, pigs, chickens. Of these, the last four were native, the others introduced (as domesticates—although some had local wild forms) but known for millennia. Pigs, then as now, were by far the most important meat source. Chickens and dogs were common, but horses were a luxury for the elite and cattle were uncommon beasts of the plow. Rulers kept large game parks, in which they hunted deer and other large animals. These were seen by many social critics as wasteful luxuries that tied up good land.

Animals per se are not a distinct category in most Chinese texts, Daoist or otherwise. More typically, texts that talk about animals at any length use the four or five distinct categories of beasts, birds, insects, and fish, with the occasional addition of dragons and snakes.

The term Daoism is equally problematic, because of the unclear affiliations of some of the texts and practices in which animals are most prevalent. Most textual accounts of animals come from the Six Dynasties period. While hagiographies from the *Dao zang* are unproblematically Daoist, the same cannot be said for the *Soushen ji* and other literature dealing with anomalies, which prominently features accounts of animals, both "normal" and anomalous.

In this essay we focus discussion on actual animals or on individual instances of animals that are described as anomalies for their kind. This approach largely omits the many accounts of mythological animals (the dragon, phoenix, unicorn, etc.) and the use of animals as purely directional symbols. We draw on both standard texts from the Warring States period and on recently excavated archaeological texts.

Early Daoism

The term "Daoism" as a specific body of thought is anachronistic when applied to ancient China.

Attributed to Sima Tan in the *Historical Records* or *Shi ji* (ca. 100 BCE), the term has been widely used to refer to mystical and quietistic interpretations of two texts: the *Dao de jing*, a collection of gnomic verses still wildly popular today, probably compiled abound 200 BCE, and *Zhuangzi*, attributed to the fourth-century BCE figure Zhuang Zhou. Recent archaeological finds and contemporary scholarship have brought about a reappraisal of the term as applied to pre-Han texts. Sima Tan's use of the term included a number of thinkers whose common ground was skepticism about active, interventionist government. Most of them talked about the need to find *dao*—the Way, the proper way of living, acting and governing—but so did most other Chinese philosophers.

Another important source was the *Chu ci* or *Songs of the South,* a collection of early poems by court officials of Han and immediately pre-Han times. Most of these invoke shamanistic and/or Daoistic images, and some are frankly Daoist. The *Chu ci* is incredibly rich in animal and plant images, mentioning at least eighty-eight animal species, many of which are imaginary. Its pages are rich with dragons, rainbow-serpents, wasps as big as gourds, and ants as big as elephants. Even the "real" animals are often completely unidentifiable.

The *Zhuangzi* is the most philosophically challenging, and the most rich and diverse, of the early sources. Like other early Chinese works, it was edited and supplemented in the Han dynasty, but it retained a solid core of early material—presumably by Zhuangzi himself—that have come to be called the "inner chapters." The *Zhuangzi* mentions approximately seventy-five animals, many of them mythical or unidentifiable. Like other early Chinese writers, Zhuangzi (and the other authors of the material that has accumulated around his name) were conscious of even the smallest insects. A pig louse becomes a symbol of foolish security, and insect transformations are recorded in exquisite, if biologically inaccurate, detail.[2]

Animals in Early Daoist Thought

Animals appear in many contexts in these writings. First, their practical value is immediately obvious. They provided food, clothing, and medicine. Meat, leather, silk, wool, and animal-derived medications are very frequently mentioned. In the early Daoist texts there is no indication that such uses were considered immoral. Excessive consumption of meat was identified with luxury and disparaged for that reason, but the general tendency of animals to eat each other was frequently and explicitly mentioned as a natural process, in harmony with Dao.

The horse probably is the most often mentioned animal in early Chinese texts. It was identified with wealth, power, and worldly glory, and it was an important source of energy for the elites. One of the most striking passages in the *Zhuangzi* attacks worldly power by contrasting the happiness and freedom of wild horses with the misery and bad behavior of captive ones:

> When they live out on the plains they eat grass
> and drink the water, when pleased they cross
> their necks and stroke each other, when angry
> swing round and kick at each other. ... If you put
> yokes on their necks and hold them level with a
> crossbar, the horses will know how to smash the
> crossbar, wriggle out of the yokes, butt the car-
> riage hood.[3]

Daoist texts also describe and depict human figures mounted on cranes, dragons, phoenixes, and other creatures.[4]

Second, animals were sacrificed to gods and ancestors, as they still are in traditional Chinese communities. Archaeologists have traced this practice back to highest antiquity. Among the animals mentioned are dogs, chickens, turtles, oxen, and sheep. There is little textual evidence that Daoists protested these practices. In one apocryphal anecdote, Zhuangzi, when asked to be minister of state, declined by comparing himself to a sacrificial tortoise, or ox, making the point that it is better to be a tortoise dragging its tail in the mud, free, safe, and unhonored than to live the stiff, artificial, and highly uncertain life of a courtier. In some cases, straw and pottery models were often substituted for the real animals, thus saving the latter. "Straw dogs" were also used as a metaphor for humans in the face of Heaven, which treats humans with the calm indifference of ritualists disposing of sacrificial straw dogs after the ceremony.

Finally, animals were also used as models for how to move in powerful, natural, spontaneous, and healthy ways. In a section of the *Zhuangzi* that probably dates from the Han dynasty, the anonymous commentator is a bit sarcastic about those who "huff and puff, exhale and inhale, ... do the 'bear-hang' and the 'bird-stretch.'"[5] As all of us know who have any acquaintance with Chinese martial arts and sexual yoga, the ways of the bear are still with us, along with the ways of the monkey, the crane, the snake, and many other animals whose motions offer salutary examples of how to move.

What Animals Did

Animals were not viewed simply as useful things. They had varying degrees of spiritual or numinous power. The most numinous were usually the most far from everyday experience—the dragons, phoenixes, and unicorns—but ordinary animals such as tortoises and snakes were also given numinous attributes. Cranes in particular were associated with magical and mystical experiences, and the image of a Daoist riding through the heavens on a crane eventually became an artistic cliché. Real-world Daoists kept tame cranes, until, alas, the birds became too rare to be available.[6] The crane retains its sacred status in Korea and Japan, where the few survivors are venerated and protected. However, significantly, the early Chinese texts devote very little attention to animal magic, except for purely imaginary creatures like dragons.

Real-world animals almost never have magical or spirit powers. This is in marked contrast to the shamanistic societies of North and Central Asia, whose animal cults were (and still are) spectacularly rich and complex.[7]

From the foregoing, it should already be clear that Daoist writers found animals especially important as a source of metaphors, similes, and subjects of teaching stories. However, we should not fall into the modern habit of reducing them to mere figures of speech. Zhuangzi's wild horses are not simply metaphors of freedom; real horses, like people, want freedom and do best when free. Zhuangzi presumably thought that the tortoise and ox really did appreciate their lives and really preferred them to an honored death. In perhaps the most famous animal story in Chinese literature, Zhuangzi dreams he is a butterfly, and wakes up uncertain whether he is a butterfly dreaming of being Zhuang Zhou.[8] A striking poetic image at the very least, it may also relate to shamanistic traditions in which the soul is a butterfly.[9] Similarly, the deer dream story in the later Daoist text Liezi, in which real and dreamed deer become one, has thought-provoking similarities to beliefs about deer as magical or spiritual quarry among the Mongols of north China.[10] These stories reflect a numinous aspect of the human-animal interface.

Analogy due to real homology is explicit in another famous Zhuangzi story, the happiness of fish. Standing on a bridge with his skeptical debate partner Huizi, Zhuangzi praises the free and easy action of the minnows. Huizi asks: "You are not a fish. Whence do you know that the fish are happy?" Zhuangzi replies that: "You aren't me, whence do you know that I don't know the fish are happy?" and adds that "you asked me the question already knowing that I knew."[11] Zhuangzi is saying that one intuitively knows the pleasure of fish. He implies that people and fish share enough basic similarity that humans can understand them.[12]

These stories often emphasize that animals live spontaneously and act according to their natures. This spontaneity and naturalness is also considered an ideal for human conduct. According to a comment in the wild-horses story: "In the age when Power [de, spiritual power or virtue] was at its utmost, men lived in sameness with the birds and animals, side by side as fellow clansmen with the myriad creatures."[13] Today, it adds, humans have lost the Way. They subject themselves to lords, to artificial habits, and to gratuitous and limiting mental constructs. There are countless variations on this theme — even individual thinkers like Zhuangzi were not always consistent. The question of whether (or how far) Zhuangzi and similarly minded Daoist philosophers were cultural relativists remains controversial. It does seem clear that the early Daoists criticized conventional ethical schemas of Benevolence, Duty, Ritual, and so forth, and their power to interfere with all the spontaneity and naturalness in life. Watching animals could help teach humans what really is and is not important and worthwhile. Some texts portray animals as able to detect humans. The Liezi describes how gulls came to play with a man but fled when he wanted to capture them.[14] (This became a poetic cliché in later dynasties, even more in Korea than in China.) Here again, freedom is seen as a basic desideratum for people and animals alike.

These texts also addressed cases where it was necessary to capture animals and remove them from their wild state; they make it clear that there was a right Way even to do that. These texts show how to focus on animals, understand exactly how they live and move, and enter into such harmony with them as to achieve anything. A fisherman catches a whale-sized fish with a single silk thread for a line and a wheat awn for a hook.[15] A cicada-catcher succeeds by concentrating his mind so much that there is nothing in all the universe for him except the cicada's wings.[16] The point of the story, of course, is to teach us how to live, not how to catch cicadas!

The early Daoists also recognized the importance of the food chain, and they had no illusions about that side of animal life. A beautiful teaching story, used today in many an ecology class, finds Zhuangzi in a game park, trying to poach a bit of dinner. He trains his bow on a strange bird that is itself about to eat a mantis about to eat a cicada. He becomes so absorbed in this instructive tableau that he himself is almost caught by the warden.[17] This is said to be the incident that turned his mind to Daoist philosophy—as well it might!

Transformation is another important aspect of animal life. The Chinese knew that caterpillars transformed into butterflies, grubs into wasps, and so forth. Zhuangzi provides a long string of transformations: the germ in a seed becomes the water-plantain, which turns into other plants and then to insects; eventually the horse is produced, and from the horse is born the human—a strange and still unexplained idea.[18] Liezi considerably expands this account, adding several truly uncanny transformations: "Sheep's liver changes into the goblin sheep underground. The blood of horses and men become[s] the will-o'-the-wisp."[19] Such change and evolution is part of nature. Everything changes; one can only resign oneself to the natural flow of things.

More seriously philosophical comments on death echo this account. A dying sage says his body may become a chariot and his spirit its horses.[20] Such passages say something real about the world. Even when animals are used for purely literary purposes, we are never far from actual comments on nature. Swallows symbolize humble domesticity because they nest under eaves. Lao Dan (the apocryphal Laozi) is a dragon in Zhuangzi's metaphor.[21] Daoist religious traditions developed moral charges that protected animal life, sometimes adopted verbatim from Confucian and Buddhist works.[22] The foundational Daoist texts are notably silent on these topics, beyond a general charter to leave animals in as natural a state as possible. The Daoists seem not to have conceived of a world in which animals were not used for food, clothing, traction, and medicine. They saw eating animals as a natural thing, and therefore appropriate for

humans. Tigers, and even mosquitoes, eat humans; why should not humans eat other animals? Moreover, sacrifice was and still is critically important to Daoist ritual. Today, Daoist ceremonies observed by E. N. Anderson involve sacrifice and consumption of chickens and pigs, and sometimes other animals. It is thus clear that Daoists differ from Buddhists in their tolerance of slaughter and consumption of animals.

The Zhuangzi and Animal Minds

The *Zhuangzi* uses animals in a new set of ways that reflect both observation of (and interest in) their actual behavior, and a keen sense of metaphor.

The first representation of the "great knowledge" (*da zhi* 大智) that preoccupies the Inner Chapters of the Zhuangzi is as an animal, or rather the transformation with which the work begins: the transformation of the Kun fish into the Peng bird in the first chapter of the *Zhuangzi*. It is the Peng bird, neither a human or a divinity, that first represents the greater perspective. The distinction between large and small perspective is elaborated first in the contrast between the perspectives of the Peng Bird and the turtledove that hops from branch to branch. That distinction is elaborated in human terms in the "Qiwu lun" chapter of Book 2. In these passages, the Zhuangzi uses a mélange of real and imaginary animals to comment on, and recommend, human choices.[23] Animal minds demonstrate the desirable attitudes of great perspective and detachment. This kind of metaphor extends to the political. In "Autumn Floods" (Zhuangzi 17), Zhuangzi himself uses the rhetorical example of the "turtle dragging its tail in the mud" to emphasize the priority of a natural and livable life over the demands and dangers of court life and high office.

The *Zhuangzi* also uses animal minds to show the limitations of attachment and loss of perspective. Zhuangzi's quarry in the hunting park (see above) is a "strange magpie" whose wings are huge but get it nowhere, and whose eyes are huge, but don't see. For all its "uselessness" —a theme of considerable importance in the *Zhuangzi*—it escapes his attentions, because he is distracted by the sight of the cicada stalked by the mantis stalked by the magpie stalked by Zhuangzi himself in *Zhuangzi* 20.

Animals, Gender, and Morality

The uses of animals in the arguments of the two "Classical Daoist" texts and in early medical literature is even more striking if we contrast the use of "birds and beasts" in the arguments of other Warring States thinkers, sometimes classed as "Huang-Lao" Daoism. The *Guanzi* contrasts animals negatively with the prehuman state before civilization. In this and other texts, the distinction between men and women (*nan-nü zhi bie* 男女之別) is taken as the defining feature of human, as opposed to animal, society. They ascribe the incorrect mingling of the sexes, among other things, to the prehuman behavior of animals and to the quasi-bestial practices of primitive society before the civilizing influence of the sage-kings.[24] According to the *Guanzi,* if ministers are allowed to indulge themselves,

> they will follow their desires and behave with reckless abandon. Men and women will not be kept separate, but revert to being animals. Consequently the rules of propriety, righteous conduct, integrity and a sense of shame will not be established and the prince of men will have nothing with which to protect himself.[25]

Part of the "protection" of the ruler is the order of human, as opposed to animal, society. The distinction between men and women is one of the defining features of human society. Beasts, by contrast, do not segregate males and females.[26]

The Shamanic Connection

An earlier generation of Sinologists often saw connections between Daoism and shamanism.[27] Shamanism, a form of religious and curing activity widespread in Asia, involves shamans who send their souls to other realms in order to search out the cause and cure of personal and social ills and misfortunes. There is every reason to pursue the issue, for the Han Chinese world is surrounded by shamanistic societies. The English word "shaman" is borrowed from the Tungus languages. Many Tungus groups live in China. One of the Tungus languages, Manchu, was the language of two Chinese dynasties (the Jin and Qing, both ruled by Tungus conquerors). It would be inconceivable that China would not be influenced by shamanism. Indeed, the Chinese word *wu* 巫, which now covers a range of spirit mediums, once clearly applied to shamans very similar in their practices to the Tungus and Mongol ones.[28] *Wu* and Daoist adepts could both send their souls to the heavens and to the lands of the immortals, as is clearly seen in the *Songs of the South* and in many later Daoist writings.[29] Daoist adepts live in a universe of meditation and inner travel, similar to the shamanic one.

A clear link with shamanic animal lore is the concern with transformations. The general texts on transformation, noted above, presaged a flood of animal tales in later literature. These often turn on the proneness of animals to take human shape, or vice versa; sometimes the transformation becomes complete, but at other times we are dealing with were-creatures. Statements in Daoist texts about the flux and transformation of all things may have roots in shamanistic traditions as well as Chinese cosmological knowledge and belief.

Another link between shamanism and Chinese folk religion is the concern with sacrifices and sacrificial animals. In modern Daoist practice, elaborate sacrifices involve special preparation and treatment of the animals; each ceremony has its own patterns, which vary from place to place. This is similar to the complex logic and structuring of sacrifice among the Daurs.[30] However, the shamanistic bond with animals is not very visible in the Daoist writings surveyed here. Animals are not the sources of spiritual power, nor are they companions or guides in supernatural travel, as they are in shamanism.[31] The nearest we come are the dragons and cranes used as mounts for travel to empyrean realms. This is, indeed, no doubt connected with shamanism; shamans ride spirit horses, and sometimes birds. But the connection is not obviously close. The whole complex of animal religion that reaches such incredible heights in central Asia seems absent from Daoism, except in so far as it is related to general Chinese beliefs about sacrifice and about the magical significance of dragons, turtles, and the like.[32] Even the tiger, so universally revered in folk cults throughout its range, gets no special treatment in Daoist texts. Nor does the fox, though we know that the incredibly rich folklore about foxes and fox spirits was already well established.[33] The huge, uncanny, and imaginary animals of Zhuangzi's and Liezi's stories, with their strange powers, might hark back a visionary shamanistic cosmology, but they give no obvious evidence of it. Conversely, the bizarre imaginary animals of the *Shan Hai Jing* ("Classic of Mountains and Seas") are almost certainly the visionary experiences of shamans traveling to the unreal "mountains and seas" in question, but the *Shan Hai Jing* never became a canonical Daoist text.

Most particularly, the early Daoist sources seem completely lacking in the strong moral component so prominent in shamanistic lore about hunting. Throughout most of northeast Asia and all of North America, myths, tales, and shamanic lore encode a very strong moral injunction not to take too many animals — usually, no more than one's family immediately needs. This view, shored up by spiritual beliefs about the animals themselves, is well documented for Altaic peoples on China's fringe.[34] Animals and animal parts are to be treated with reverence. This view may well be latent behind Liezi's deer story and several other Daoist stories, but it is not made explicit, nor do any such moral teachings occur in Daoist writings. Early Daoist teachings move us away from explicit moral rules, toward a meditative and aware state in which we can naturally act in an appropriate manner. Even shamanic moral rules may have smacked too much of propriety and self-righteousness for the early Daoists. Later Daoist religious communities adopted a variety of moral codes, including the animal-related ones noted above; but they came from Confucian and Buddhist teachings, not from shamanism.[35]

These texts contain an implicit and sometimes explicitly moral view of animals. Animals have their own natures, their own *dao,* and humans should not interfere unless necessary. Such an attitude contains an implicit conservation ethic; obviously, Daoists do not like to see lavish and conspicuous consumption, nor do they like to see animals used for any purpose unless real necessity is involved. Destructive uses clearly violate the animals' *dao.* Animals are spontaneous, able to live their good lives without worry about rites and ceremonies, morals and duties. They do all that they need to do, without thinking, and nothing more. We are better advised to learn from them than to kill or abuse them.

The Uses of Animals In Early Daoist Texts

THE WARRING STATES

Warring States quasi-Daoist accounts of animals vary widely, and they may contain a few surprises. Animals are almost completely absent from the *Dao de jing,* but, as we have seen, appear frequently in the *Zhuangzi,* as well as in the political rhetoric of the *Guanzi* and other Warring States texts associated with Huang-Lao

Daoism. In addition, they appear in recently excavated texts in contexts that range from recipes used to treat animal-inflicted injuries to metaphors for body movement in sexual arts literature.

DAO AS INANIMATE IN THE *DAO DE JING*

Animals are conspicuously absent from the many descriptions of *dao* in the *Dao de jing*. Its metaphors for *dao* are inanimate (water, the valley, the uncarved block) or not quite human (the unformed infant), and conspicuously do not include animals, either singly or collectively.

Animals are not used as positive metaphors for *dao*. Indeed, they are used as illustrations of the kind of negative happenstance that Daoist self-cultivation protects against. Verse 55 begins:

> One who embraces the fullness of Virtue
> Can be compared to a newborn babe.
> Wasps and scorpions, snakes and vipers do
> not sting him,
> Birds of prey and fierce beasts do not seize
> him.[36]

Here, animals are clearly viewed as sources of harm and injury. Early medical texts found in the same tomb as the oldest extant version of the *Dao de jing* "flesh out" this concern, and they also present a more positive and imaginative depiction of animals in metaphors for body movement.

Cures for Animal-inflicted Injuries

Before the second century, prevailing views (and methods of treatment) of disease treated illness as the invasive influence of external forces, including natural forces (wind, heat, cold), demonic entities and magical influence, and animal-inflicted injuries, including bites and the effects of parasites and insects.[37] Recent excavations of tombs from Mawangdui and elsewhere have yielded valuable medical documents that

provide new information about early Chinese medical theories. The premier medical document found at Mawangdui is the *Recipes for Fifty-two Ailments* (*Wushier bingfang* 吾十二病方). This late-third-century compendium is the oldest extant exemplar of a medical recipe manual, one of the oldest genres of medical literature. Its recipes are listed in fifty-two categories, which form the organizing principle of the text (each category contains up to thirty recipes). Animal bites and related injuries are included in several of these: recipes for mad dog bites (category 6), dog bites (category 7), crow's beak poisoning (category 10), scorpions (category 11), leech bites (category 12), lizards (category 13), grain borer ailment (category 18), maggots (category 19), chewing by bugs (category 46), and *gu* poisoning (category 49).[38]

ANIMALS AS METAPHORS FOR
WHOLE-BODY MOVEMENT

The Mawangdui texts also present us with an equally early, and much friendlier, view of animals: the use of animal movements as metaphors to describe whole-body movements that do not otherwise lend themselves to clear description. The same kinds of metaphors appear in the later literature of Daoist-inspired martial arts, where the modes of movement of cranes, mantises, and other creatures are taken as models for the defense and attack of martial artists. These late examples of the use of the movements of animals may be the Chinese "animal" imagery most familiar to the nonspecialist.

The first known uses of these metaphors are in Daoist sexual technique literature, of which the earliest examples extant come from the tomb excavations at Mawangdui and Jiangjiashan.[39] The Mawangdui texts "Uniting Yin and Yang" (*He yin yang* 和陰陽) and "Discussion of the Dao of Heaven" (*Tianxia zhi dao tan* 天下之道談) each contains a section that refer to the movements and postures of animals as whole-body metaphors for sexual techniques and postures:

一曰虎游，二曰蟬附，三曰尺蠖，四曰困桷，
五曰蟥礫，六曰爰 [猿] 據，七曰詹諸，八曰兔
驚，九曰蜻蛉，十曰魚嘬

The first is called roaming tiger, the second cicada clinging, the third inchworm, the fourth
roe deer butting, the fifth locust spreading,
the sixth monkey squat, the seventh toad in
the moon, the eighth rabbit startled, the ninth
dragonflies and the tenth fish gobbling.[40]

Similar exercises described in the "Pulling
Book" (Yinshu shiwen 引書釋文), a text found
at Zhangjiashan in Jiangling, describes exercises
that refer to or are named after animals, including: inchworms, snakes, mantises, wild ducks,
owls, tigers, chickens, bears, frogs, deer, and
dragons.[41]

Six Dynasties Daoism

Now let us turn to a few examples of the use of
animals in Six Dynasties and Tang Daoist texts.

HUMAN-ANIMAL INTERACTIONS IN
DAOIST HAGIOGRAPHIES

The Daoist hagiographies of the Six Dynasties
are equally sparing in their use of animals. What
marks the sages of the Liexianzhuan (列仙傳)
are interactions with immortals, longevity, immortality, distinct dietary habits, and receipt
of secret texts and techniques. In a few cases,
the remarkable qualities of the sage are shown
by visitation by animals. Every morning, yellow
birds would appear at the door of the Jin re-
cluse Jie Zitui (介子推) (LXZ 19). Zhu Qiweng
(祝雞翁) raised chickens and fish (LXZ 36); the
gardener Yuan Ke (公園客) was visited by five
colored butterflies (LXZ 47).

Some do interact, in various ways, with the
animal associated with immortality: the dragon.
Ma Shihuang (馬師皇) (Horse Master Huang),
the veterinarian of Huang Di, once cured a
dragon who took him away on its back (LXZ 3).

Shi Men (師門) lived on flowers, fish, and leaves,
and was a master of dragons (LXZ 14). In two of
these accounts, the human transforms into one
of the immortal animals. Huang Di (黃帝) is
described as "having the form of a dragon" (有
龍形, LXZ 5).[42] In other accounts, the appearance of the dragon is heralded by a more ordinary animal. A red bird appears over the forge
of the blacksmith Tao Angong (陶安公) to tell
him that a red dragon would come for him and
carry him away on its back (LXZ 60). In a similar story, Zi Ying (子英) catches a carp and feeds
it. It grows horns and wings; he mounts its back
and flies away (LXZ 55).

Even the story of Mao Nü (毛女), who grows
animal-like hair, involves no extended human-
animal interaction. Seen by hunters over several generations, the "Furry Woman" fled the
palace of Qin Shi Huang Di at the end of the
Qin dynasty. According to the hagiography, she
was taught by a Daoist to live on pine nuts, and
spontaneously grew a coat of hair (LXZ 54).

In summary, on the basis of this evidence, we
can make a few speculative observations about
the presence and absence of animals in so-called
Lao-Zhuang and Six Dynasties Daoist texts.

Despite the considerable prevalence of animals (like plants) in early Chinese texts, special interactions with animals are not an ingredient of the hagiographies of the Liexianzhuan—
the topos of the lifesaving nurture of abandoned
or refugee infants, children, or women by wild
animals. Even the "Furry Woman" of the Liexianzhuan learns to survive by the instruction
of a Daoist, not by imitating wild beasts. Animals do appear in these stories as vehicles for humans who cross the boundary between Heaven
and Earth, mortality and immortality, usually
by mounting to heaven on the back of a dragon.
But, as in earlier texts, animals seem largely to
be used as examples of living naturally.

"STRANGE" ANIMALS IN THE ZHIGUAI GENRE

Several texts within the genre of *zhiguai* (志怪), or "anomaly" literature, contain extensive accounts of animal anomalies, as well as contrasting accounts of animal "norms."[43] The *Bowuzhi* (博物志) or *Treatise on Curiosities of Zhang Hua* (張華) (232–300) is organized by thirty-nine subject headings, of which four concern animal anomalies. These are: Marvelous beasts (異獸 *yi shou*), Marvelous birds (異鳥 *yi niao*), Marvelous insects (異蟲 *yi chong*), and Marvelous fish (異魚 *yi yu*).

The *Soushen ji* (搜神記) or *Records of an Inquest into the Spirit Realm* by Gan Bao 干寶 (335–349) also contains five very different chapters that bear on animals: monstrous creatures, transformation of humans into plants and animals, spirits of mammals, snake and fish spirits, and accounts of rewards and retribution by animals. The third juan of the *Yi Yuan* (異苑) or *Garden of Marvels* by Liu Jingshu (敬叔) (fl. early 5c) is devoted to fifty-seven items of anomalies involving animals: birds (1–12), tigers (13–17), dragons and snakes (33–47), turtles and fish (48–52), and shellfish and insects (53–57). The *Soushen houji* (搜神後記), or *Further Records of an Inquest into the Spirit Realm* (late Song or early Qi), contains a section (10) of tales involving dragons, krakens, and large snakes. Of these, we explore the account in the *Soushen ji* at some length.

EXPLANATION FOR POSSESSIONS AND ANOMALIES

As Rob Campany as pointed out in his study of anomaly literature, the animal anomaly stories in the *Soushen ji* portray several different modes of anomaly, of which most involve crossing the animal-human boundary. These include: a variety of human-animal hybrids and a range of transformations among individual species, genders within species, humans, animals, and spirits, both human and animal.[44]

The sixth chapter of the *Soushen ji* begins by explaining the occurrence of possessions and anomalies:

> Possessions and anomalies (*yao guai*) prevail over a thing's essential qi (*jing qi*) and reconfigure it (妖怪者，蓋精氣之依物者也). Internally the qi is disordered; externally the thing is transformed.... if we rely on prognostication of good and malauspice (休咎之徵), in all these cases, it is possible to delimit and discuss them.[45]

Some cases are partial transformations, where an animal or human grows an extra or inappropriate body parts: a tortoise growing hair and a hare horns,[46] cows, horses or birds with extra legs,[47] and horses, dogs, and men growing horns.[48] In other cases the transformation is complete, and an animal (or human) changes entirely into another, for example, a horse to a fox,[49] or bears offspring of another species. Cases of cross-species matings and anomalous births include: a horse bearing a human child,[50] a dog mating with a pig,[51] swallows hatching sparrows,[52] falcons,[53] and the birth of two-headed children.[54] In one case, a cow bears a chicken with four feet.[55] Sometimes the transformation is of gender: a woman turning into a man, marrying and siring children,[56] a man turning into a woman, marrying and bearing children,[57] and a hen becoming a cock.[58] All these anomalies are ascribed to rulers of the Han and Later Han dynasties and the Three Kingdoms period. Again, the fascination with the bizarre and surreal continues from Warring States times and traditions. It and the longevity cult rather undercut the naturalistic side of Daoism, a point noted by Chinese scholars as well as modern readers.

NATURAL AND ANOMALOUS ANIMAL TRANSFORMATIONS

The nineteen items of Book 12 of the *Soushen ji* describe both "natural" and anomalous transformations of animals. The first item in Book 12 explains how the myriad creatures (*wan wu*) were formed from the five *qi* of heaven (wood, fire, metal, water and earth). Its premise is that animals made of one kind of *qi* will display similar forms and similar natures. Thus: eaters of grain (human society) have intelligence and culture; eaters of grass have great strength and little mind; creatures that eat mulberry leaves produce silk and become caterpillars; eaters of meat are courageous, fierce, and high-spirited; things that eat mud lack mind and breath. Now the passage returns to human beings; those that feed on primal energies become sages and enjoy long lives; those that do not eat at all do not die and become numinous immortals (*shen*).[59]

It goes on to classify the "natures" of animals in several other ways. One is "cock and hen mode" (雌雄 *ci xiong*), that is, to classify them by their "male" and "female" characteristics.[60] Creatures that lack "cock mode" must mate with other creatures to reproduce; creatures that lack "hen mode" need the nurturing of other creatures to reproduce. It proceeds to an account of how animals of one kind naturally transform one into another; the principle of these transformations is that "creatures of the heavenly sort have upward affinities; those with earthly origins list downwards. Each thing follows its kind" (各 從其類也).[61]

The text goes on to explain that transformations within category are normal and "too many to be counted."

> The movement of things in response to change follows constant ways, and it is only when things take a wrong direction that injurious anomalies appear.... If a human gives birth to a beast (*shou*) or a beast to a human it is case of *qi* in disorder (氣之亂者). When a man becomes a woman or a woman becomes a man, it is a case of transposition of *qi*.[62]

Other chapters go on to record animal and other anomalies without further explanation, including: transformations of humans into plants and animals (*SSJ* 14), accounts of the spirits

of mammals (*SSJ* 18), accounts of snake and fish spirits (*SSJ* 19), and accounts of reward and retribution by animals (*SSJ* 20). These human-animal transformations include: a horse into a silkworm,[63] women to birds,[64] and women into turtles (3 cases).[65] In the first of the seven fox or fox spirit stories in the eighteenth chapter of the *Soushen ji,* a man turns to a fox in the presence of the Han dynasty Confucian philosopher and anomaly specialist Dong Zhongshu.[66] Other stories in this chapter involve deer, sow, and dog spirits, and a rat. Chapter 19 contains six stories of snake, fish, and turtle spirits.

Chapter 20 presents a different kind of animal account, sixteen stories of rewards and retribution involving animals. In some cases, humans extend "human" compassion to animals, and are rewarded. Several of these stories specifically involve medical knowledge. One Sun Deng of Wei perceived that a dragon was ill; it transformed into a man, he cured it, and it rewarded the district with rains.[67] In another story, a tiger abducts a midwife named Su Yi to its lair, where she delivers the tigress of a breach birth. The tiger returns her home, and rewards her with gifts of game.[68] In other cases, a black crane, an oriole, a serpent, and a turtle return and reward the humans that cure and free them.[69] In other stories, humans show compassion to fish, ants, and a snake.[70] In one, a man is saved from false imprisonment and death by a mole cricket he feeds.[71] In these cases, humans extend the benefits of "human" morality to animals, who react in kind. In other cases, animals spontaneously act with human qualities. Two such stories involve dogs.[72] Other stories involve misbehaving humans and animals who act "humanely." A mother gibbon suicides when a man catches, and then kills, her baby.[73] A (talking) deer and a serpent bring retribution in the form of sudden illness on hunters who kill them.[74]

Animals and Traditional Chinese Medicine

This brief account has hardly touched on several other ways in which animals figure in Daoist and Daoist-influenced traditions. One of these is the sobering case of the use of animals in traditional Chinese medicine, which stands in utter contrast to these Han and Six dynasty accounts of human-animal moral reciprocity. Animals are the objects or means of cure in variety of medical texts. Animals, both living and dead, appear as elements in the treatment of disease. In some cases, live animals are used in ritual cures; in others, medications made from animal products are used as treatments. Suffice it here simply to mention the complex overlap of Daoism, alchemy, and medicine in the works of such figures as Ge Hong, (283–343), Tao Hong-jing (456–536) and Sun Simiao (581–682).[75] The use of animals in medicine is also of the greatest practical importance, since the (often illegal) killing of animals for medical products is a major factor in the depletion of many endangered animal species today. This problematic relation to animals dates from our earliest records of medical practice. Animal products as components of medical recipes go back as far as the *Fifty-two Ailments*.[76] The use of animal products in traditional Chinese medicine continues to the present day.

Conclusions

What can the contemporary world learn from early Daoist attitudes toward animals? First, the Daoists did not see a sharp barrier between people and animals, or, more generally, between humanity and nature.[77] In fact, they saw humans and animals as mutually dependent, and, indeed, regularly prone to change into each other. Change and transformation are seen in Daoism as universal and necessary; human beings can only adapt to the changes in the cosmos, and they do best by going along with them. In a deep and basic sense, *dao* unites humans and ani-mals, and teaches us to treat them with respect. On the other hand, Daoism is not a philosophy of animal rights in the modern sense. Daoists thought it natural to use animals for food, sacrifice, and service. However, they held that animals should not be used in ways that make them act contrary to their own natures.

Second, these early Daoist writings, especially the *Zhuangzi*, were centrally important for the development of a distinctive aesthetic among the educated elites, both scholarly and artistic. The impact of this style went far beyond Daoism in any sense of the term. Appreciation for the simple and natural led to a taste for flowering apricots (*meihua* 梅花), mountains, streams, and other beauties of nature. Recluses chanted poems or played the *qin* while admiring spectacular scenery. Tao Qian, one of the figures most associated with this style, made a cultural icon of the chrysanthemum, which he knew as a humble roadside weed. (Supposedly, it became a garden flower because of his love for it, so today's huge florist "mums" are a later innovation.) This distinctive way of looking at the world persisted through Chinese history and spread widely in eastern Asia. More recently, it has influenced the West, and through individuals such as the poet Gary Snyder it has materially influenced environmentalist thought. In this sense, Daoism implies a morality of respect for the inner nature of things, and for the place of all things in the vast, ever-changing cosmic flow.

Today, Daoist thinking might find its best use in ecosystem management. It could be the grounding philosophy for a view that does not separate humanity from nature; that looks at the whole, not just at segmented parts; and that focuses on the inevitable flow and change of things, not on static and frozen moments. Currently, environmental management suffers from the opposite tendencies. It usually separates "nature" or the "natural ecosystem" as a reified entity. It tends to look at one problem at a time: birds here, insects there, rather than the interrelationship of birds, insects, and the rest. It usually attempts to "preserve" an individual species or a local habitat, rather than seeing that change is inevitable and setting goals and policies accordingly. For example, when we preserve an endangered bird, we rarely preserve enough habitat to provide a safeguard in case of catastrophe. Ecologists and conservation biologists have criticized this, but the Endangered Species Act is still focused on the species, not the totality. Perhaps conservation biologists need more Daoist training.

NOTES

1. For translation see Bernhard Karlgren, *The Book of Odes* (Stockholm: Museum of Far Eastern Antiquities, 1950).

2. *Zhuangzi yinde* 莊子引得 [*A Concordance to the Zhuangzi*] (Shanghai: Guji chubanshe, 1982) 24/90–95. For translation see A.C. Graham, *Chuang-tzu: The Inner Chapters* (London: George Allen and Unwin 1981), p. 110.

3. *Zhuangzi* 9/14–16 (Graham, *Chuang-tzu*, p. 205).

4. Edward Schafer, *Pacing the Void* (Berkeley: University of California Press, 1977).

5. *Zhuangzi* 15/5–6 (Graham, *Chuang-tzu*, p. 265). These practices are discussed below.

6. Schafer, *Pacing the Void, passim.*

7. Caroline Humphrey, *Shamans and Elders* (Oxford: Oxford University Press, 1996); Jean Roux, *Faune et Flore sacrées dans les sociéétés altaïques* (Paris: Adien-Maisonneuve, 1966).

8. *Zhuangzi* 2/94–96 (Graham, Chuang-tzu, p. 61).

9. Humphrey, *Shamans.*

10. Ibid.

11. *Zhuangzi* 17/88–91 (Graham, Chuang-tzu, p. 123).

12. A possible example of the communion of subjects is discussed by Thomas Berry elsewhere in this volume. However, it should be noted that there is no indication in the story that animals understand humans.

13. *Zhuangzi* 9/9 (Graham, *Chuang-tzu*, p. 205).

14. *Liezi* 列子 2 p. 21 (Zhuzi jicheng edition). For translation see A.C. Graham, *The Book of Lieh-tzu* (London: John Murray, 1960), p. 45.

15. *Liezi* 5, pp. 58–59 (Graham, *Lieh-tzu*, p. 105).

16. *Zhuangzi* 19 (Graham, *Chuang-tzu*, p. 138).

The reader may be interested in why anyone would catch cicadas. E. N. Anderson has often observed the practice in China. Cicadas are used for chicken feed, and as noisy and active pets for young people. Small boys, especially, delight in the cicadas' loud songs, and sometimes torment proper young girls therewith. Naturally, such buyers are not affluent, and cicada-catching affords a very modest living. As he almost always does, Zhuangzi is picking his human exemplar from the most humble sectors of society.

17. *Zhuangzi* 20/61–68 (Graham, *Chuang-tzu*, p. 118).

18. *Zhuangzi* 18/40–45 (Graham, *Chuang-tzu*, p. 184).

19. *Liezi* 1, pp. 4–5 (Graham, *Lieh-tzu*, p. 21).

20. *Zhuangzi* 6/51–52 (Graham, *Chuang-tzu*, p. 88).

21. *Zhuangzi* 14/60–64 (Graham, *Chuang-tzu*, p. 214).

22. See Livia Kohn, *The Taoist Experience* (Albany: SUNY Press, 1993).

23. Lisa Raphals, "Skeptical Strategies in the Zhuangzi and Theaetetus." *Philosophy East and West* 44, no. 3 (July 1994): 501–26. Reprinted as chapter in *Zhuangzi and Skepticism*, eds., P.J. Ivanhoe and Paul Kjellberg. Albany: SUNY Press.

24. Lisa Raphals, *Sharing the Light: Representations of Women and Virtue in Early China* (Albany: SUNY Press, 1998), ch. 8.

25. *Guanzi* 管子 (Sibu beiyao edition) XXI 65:1b. For translation see W. Allyn Rickett, *Guanzi: Political, Economic and Philosophical Essays from Early China* (Princeton: Princeton University Press, 1985), vol. 1, pp. 110–11.

26. The definition of human society by the dis-

tinction between men and women also occurs at *Guanzi* XI 31:1a (Rickett, *Guanzi,* p. 412).

27. For example, see Arthur Waley, *The Nine Songs: A Study of Shamanism in Ancient China* (London: George Allen and Unwin, 1955).

28. See, e.g., ibid.

29. See: David Hawkes, Ch'u Tz'u, *The Songs of the South* (Oxford: Oxford University Press, 1959); Waley, *Nine Songs;* Schafer, *Pacing the Void.*

30. Humphrey, *Shamans.*

31. Mongush B. Kenin-Lopsan, *Shamanic Songs and Myths of Tuva.* (Budapest: Akademiai Kiado, 1997), Roux, *Faune;* and S.M. Shirokogoroff, *Psychomental Complex of the Tungus* (London: Kegan Paul, 1935), and Carmen Blacker, *The Catalpa Bow: A Study of Shamanistic Practices in Japan* (London: George Allen and Unwin, 1986), 2nd. ed. Judging from Blacker's work, Japanese shamanism is less concerned with animals than the Chinese texts considered here.

32. Roux, *Faune, passim.*

33. Han texts tell us, for instance, of the nine-tailed fox, a frightening supernatural being. In Chinese popular and literary traditions, fox spirits are often malevolent and inauspicious.

34. See, for instance, Kenin-Lopsan, *Shamanic Songs;* and also the famous tale of the Nisan Shaman; the conservation message is latent in the well-known Nowak and Durrant version (Margaret Nowak and Stephen Durrant, *The Tale of the Nisan Shamaness: A Manchu Folk Epic,* [Seattle: University of Washington Press, 1977]), but explicit in a version recorded by Caroline Humphrey (*Shamans,* p. 306). Still further is the complete prohibition on killing animals, at least in sacred localities, that characterizes Buddhism. Such prohibition came to China and added itself to mountain cults, as in Tibet (Toni Huber, *The Cult of Pure Crystal Mountain,* Oxford: Oxford University Press, 1999).

35. E.N. Anderson, "Flowering Apricot: Environment, Practice, Folk Religion and Taoism," in *Daoism and Ecology,* eds. N.J. Girardot, James Miller, and Liu Xiaogan (Cambridge: Harvard University Press for Center for the study of World Religions, 2001), pp. 157–84.

36. *Laozi dao de jing* 老子道德經 (Zhuzi jicheng edition), trans. Robert Henricks, *Lao-Tzu Te-Tao Ching: a New Translation Based on the Recently Discovered Ma-wang-tui Texts* (New York: Ballantine Books, 1989).

37. The Mawangdui medical corpus consists of eleven medical manuscripts written on three sheets of silk, recovered from Mawangdui Tomb 3 in 1973, a burial dating from 168 BCE. The individual manuscripts are untitled, but have been assigned titles by Chinese scholars on the basis of their contents. For discussion of the Mawangdui medical manuscripts see Donald Harper, *Early Chinese Medical Literature* (New York: Columbia University Press, 1999), pp. 22–30; for more general relevant discussions, Paul Unschuld, *Medicine in China: A History of Pharmaceutics. Comparative Studies of Health Systems and Medical Care* (Berkeley: University of California Press, 1986); Douglas Wile, *The Art of the Bedchamber: The Chinese Sexual Yoga Classics Including Women's Solo Meditation Techniques* (Albany: SUNY Press, 1992).

38. Harper, *Early Chinese Medical Literature,* pp. 221–22. Gu 蠱 poisoning, an affliction of demonic origins, was sometimes attributed to the pernicious activities of women, who were believed to cultivate gu, and pass it down for generations.

39. *Mawangdui hanmu boshu zhengli xiaozu* 馬王堆漢墓帛書正理小組 [The Official Editorial Board of the Silk Manuscripts of Mawangdui], Mawangdui hanmu boshu (BS) 馬王堆漢墓帛書 [The Han-Dynasty Silk Manuscripts of Mawangdui], (Beijing: Wenwu chubanshe, 1980, 1983), vols. 1–4.

40. *Mawangdui Hanmu boshu,* 4:155, 165; cf. Wile, *Art of the Bedchamber,* pp. 78–81. The differences in terminology between the two sections are minor. (This version is the *He Yin Yang.*) For discussion see Vivienne Lo, "Crossing the 'Inner Pass': An 'Inner/Outer' Distinction in Early Chinese Medicine." *East Asian Science, Technology and Medicine* 17 (2000): 15–65.

41. *Maishu shiwen* 脈書釋文 [Channel book], *Yinshu shiwen* 引書釋文 [Pulling book]. Reported in *Zhangjiashan Hanmu zhujian zhengli xiaozu, Jiangling Zhangjiashan Hanjian gaishu* 江陵張家山漢簡

概述 Wenwu 1 (1985): 9–16. Transcribed in *Zhang-jiashan Hanjian zhengli zu, Zhangjiashan Hanjian yinshu shiwen* 張家山漢 簡引書釋文, *Wenwu* 10 (1990): 82–86; analysis by Peng Hao 彭浩, *Zhangjiashan Hanjian yinshu chutan* 張家山漢簡引書初探, *Wenwu* 10 (1990): 87–91.

42. In a similar story abut the phoenix, Xiao Shi could imitate the sound of the phoenix with his flute. He married a princess, and later, with her, transformed into twin phoenixes and flew away (*LXZ* 35). Liu Xiang (attrib.), *Liexian zhuan* 列仙傳 [*Collected Life Stories of Immortals*], in *Dao zang* ["Treasury of Daoist Writings"—the complete encyclopedic collection], 138.

43. This literature is not specifically Daoist, but overlapped with the Daoist hagiographies described above, specifically in its treatment of animals. For a useful survey see Robert Ford Campany, *Strange Writing: Anomaly Accounts in Early Medieval China* (Albany: SUNY Press, 1996), pp. 52–79, especially 52, 58–59 and 79. References to what follows are from Gan Bao 干寶 (335–349), *Soushen ji* 搜神記 (*SSJ*) [*Records of an Inquest in to the Spirit Realm*], Congshu jicheng v. 2692–4. See also Tao Qian 陶潛 (Tao Yuanming 陶元 明 365–427, attrib.), *Soushen houji* 搜神後記 [*Further Records of an Inquest in to the Spirit Realm*], Congshu jicheng v. 2695; *Zhangjiashan Hanmu zhujian zhengli xiaozu* 張家山漢墓竹簡正理小組, ed. 1985–90.

44. Campany, *Strange Writing*, pp. 247–53.

45. *SSJ* 6:37.

46. *SSJ* 6:38.

47. *SSJ* 6:39, 40, 43 and 44.

48. *SSJ* 6:39–40 and 43.

49. *SSJ* 6:38.

50. *SSJ* 6:39.

51. *SSJ* 6:40.

52. *SSJ* 6:43.

53. *SSJ* 6:48.

54. *SSJ* 6: 46 and 47.

55. *SSJ* 6:45.

56. *SSJ* 6:39.

57. *SSJ* 6:43.

58. *SSJ* 6:41 and 46.

59. *SSJ* 12:81 cf. Kenneth J. DeWoskin and J.I. Crump, Jr. (ed. and trans.), *In Search of the Supernatural: The Written Record* (Stanford: Stanford University Press, 1996), pp. 142–44.

60. Somewhat misleadingly described by DeWoskin and Crump as "virility" and "mothering spirit." For more on cock and hen, see Raphals, *Sharing the Light*, ch. 6.

61. *SSJ* juan 12 p. 81.

62. *SSJ* juan 12 p. 81.

63. *SSJ* 14:93.

64. *SSJ* 14:94.

65. *SSJ* 14:94–95.

66. *SSJ* 18:121.

67. *SSJ* 20:133.

68. *SSJ* 20:133.

69. *SSJ* 20:133–34.

70. *SSJ* 20:134 and 136.

71. *SSJ* 20:135.

72. *SSJ* 20:134–35.

73. *SSJ* 20:135–36.

74. *SSJ* 20:136. For further discussion see Campany, *Strange Writings*, pp. 384–93.

75. The *Baopuzi neipian* [*Esoteric Chapters of the Book of the Preservation-of-Solidity Master*] Ge Hong describes the preparation of alchemical elixirs; the Daoist scholar Tao Hongjing also authored the *Shen Nong bencao* [*Collected Commentaries on Shen Nong's Classic of Materia Medica*]; the *Taiqing danjing yaojue* [*Taiqing Elixir Classic Oral Digest*] of Sun Simiao contains elixir recipes.

76. For example, one recipe for lizard bites includes the instruction to "Seal it with one *yang* sheaf of *jin*. Then incinerate deer antler. Drink it with urine." Harper, *Early Chinese Medical Literature*, p. 54.

77. In fact, taboos and restrictions, so characteristic of many religions, were and are sparse in Daoism. Unlike Judaism and Islam, it provides no list of taboo animals and animal uses (though some Daoist sects do have taboos). Unlike Hinduism and Buddhism, it does not enjoin nonviolence (though, again, some Daoist sects do, having probably picked up the idea from Buddhism). Unlike many religions (including early Judaism, most "animistic" traditions, and even Confucianism), it did not origi-

nally provide specific directions for animal conservation. Still less were animals worshiped as gods (as in Egypt) or as persons who were human in mythic time and still have human and divine attributes (as in most of Native America). Joseph Needham saw Daoism as the key ideology underlying early science in China, but only in medicine does Daoism take a scientific attitude toward animals, and here animals are considered only as sources for drugs. The animal management conspicuous in early Confucian and syncretist texts (Anderson, "Flowering Apricot"), based on empirical observation, finds no echo in Daoism (except in obvious borrowings).

CONFUCIANISM

Of Animals and Humans

The Confucian Perspective

RODNEY TAYLOR

Classical Confucianism: Heaven, Humans, and Moral Virtue

The classical Confucian tradition is distinctive in part because it emphasizes a specific set of moral relations within which the involved individuals are enjoined to develop appropriate moral virtues. This set of relations is usually described as the five human relationships: king-subject, father-son, husband-wife, elder brother-younger brother, and friend-friend.[1]

Conspicuous for their absence from this list are animals and other living things, a fact that goes some way toward explaining the prevailing tendency to classify the Confucian ethic as just another species of humanism. In its religious teachings, however, Confucianism does not restrict the realm of value or the scope of moral relations to human beings. *Tian* (Heaven) is the source of ultimate religious authority, and *Tianli* (the Principle of Heaven) permeates all living things, animals as well as humans, plants

as well as animals. The natural order, the Confucian *dao,* is a moral order. Though not identical, macrocosm and microcosm are similar because each is permeated by the principle of Heaven. Viewed in terms of the religious teachings of Confucianism, then, the religious agent (one who is guided by religious teachings) is simultaneously and inescapably a moral agent. Since the religious teachings of Confucianism involve ethical precepts, and since, as just noted, these teachings affirm the fundamental similarity of all living things, it is a mistake to assume that Confucianism is "just another form of humanism." How far this is from the truth will be clearer once we have examined representative passages from *Lunyu* (*Analects* of Confucius), *Mengzi* (works of Mencius), and *Xunzi* (works of Xunzi).

LUNYU, CONFUCIAN ANALECTS

The *Analects* are regarded as the primary source of the teachings of Confucius (551–479 BCE).

There are, of course, other writings that purport to represent Confucius, but for a variety of historical-critical reasons the *Analects* are considered our most historically authentic record. The work itself consists primarily of recorded conversations between Confucius and his disciples, but some passages deal mainly with the acts and character of Confucius. This is true of the first passage that concerns us, one of a small number that deal with human-animal relationships.

"The Master fished with a line but not with a net; when fowling he did not aim at a roosting bird."[2] Passages of this kind became for the later Confucian tradition descriptions of the wisdom of Confucius, and they instruct via example; since this is something that Confucius himself considered important, it is something we ought to take seriously and emulate. Personality characteristics of this kind were also considered to be part of the makeup of the general image of the sage (*sheng*) or, the phrase Confucius himself uses most frequently, of the *junzi* (the noble or moral human).

The point of this particular passage is not that Confucius refrains from taking life—such an attitude is not a major part of the early tradition—but rather that he does not take "unfair advantage" of the fish and the birds. There is, then, no judgment that catching fish and birds is morally culpable; culpability is restricted to the *methods* used to catch them. To take unfair advantage reflects poorly on the character of the agent; indeed, to do so, Confucius implies, would be to violate his own moral nature, particularly that aspect of the moral nature identified as *yi* (rightness). Rightness for Confucius is part of human nature, its function being to determine our moral relationships. Here he is suggesting that rightness also includes proper relations with fish and birds.

At a deeper level the authority of this moral system is *Tian* (Heaven). Within the framework of their religious ethic, Confucians will argue that humanity's moral nature is itself a reflection of *Tian*. The *junzi* reflects the religious authority of *Tian* in his way of life, and humaneness (*ren*) is action taken in conscious understanding of the relation of humanity to Heaven. Acting reasonably and sensitively toward other forms of life, such as Confucius does in the passage just quoted, is expressive of the relation between the moral nature of humans and that of Heaven. Thus sensitivity to animals is not only ethically suitable but also carries religious authority. However, though sensitivity to other forms of life is suitable, it is not unqualified. As other passages in the *Analects* show, such sensitivity to other forms of life does not override the special moral relations that obtain between human beings.

The clearest passage on this point is one that depicts the character of Confucius. "When the stables were burnt down, on returning from Court, he said, Was anyone hurt? He did not ask about the horses."[3] The passage shows Confucius' obvious concern with the potential loss of human life. As the disciple who recorded this incident appears to point out, Confucius could have asked about the horses but did not. Thus we may infer that he believed in the priority of human life.

This interpretation is consistent with the dominant tenor of Confucius' teachings. The traditional set of special moral relations focuses on the moral responsibilities human beings have to other human beings. However, we have also seen that moral relations to living things other than humans are not excluded; human life and relations are simply more important.

Another issue we must address, made more difficult than those considered up to now because it involves religious sources of authority, is that of animal sacrifice. "Zigong wanted to do away with the presentation of a sacrificial sheep at the Announcement of each New Moon. The Master said, 'Si! [Zigong's personal name] You grudge sheep, but I grudge ritual.'"[4]

The issue addressed in this passage is the maintenance of traditional sacrificial codes of state religion. In this particular ritual an announcement is made to the ancestors at the start

of each new month, accompanied by a sacrifice that includes a sheep. Zigong, one of Confucius' disciples, felt that the sacrifice of the sheep was an unnecessary part of the ceremony. Unfortunately we are not told why, although the tradition has tended to interpret Zigong's comments as suggesting his feeling for the life of the sheep. Confucius' response to Zigong emphasizes his view that it is far more important that the ritual (*li*) be maintained than that the sheep be spared. The explanation of Confucius' attitude is one that bears on his attitude toward the traditional state religion of China and the institutions of the ancient period. For Confucius, the primary task was to restore the moral order that prevailed in China during the reigns of the founding fathers of the Chou dynasty (1122–256 BCE). Confucius taught that the institutions, thought, and practices preserved in the Chinese Classics (*jing*) represented these early times. The term "state religion" applied to the religious practices associated with the maintenance of the authority of the ruler—a ruler who was seen as ruling by the authority of *Tianming* (the Mandate of Heaven) and who was viewed as an intermediary between humanity and Heaven, an *axis mundi,* as suggested by his title, *Tianzi* (Son of Heaven). At the center of this state religion was a strict ritual code, *li,* which, particularly to the Confucians, guaranteed the religious significance of ritual, its propriety for the individual and society, and its relation to Heaven itself. Confucius did not attempt to change this traditional religious point of view. He did just the reverse. He says of himself in an often-quoted phrase: "I am a transmitter and not a creator. I believe in and have a passion for the ancients."[5] Of course we know him to be a creator as well, but the passage is consistent with the importance he attached to the restoration of the ways of the ancients, including their elaborate ritual and ceremonial codes—even when, as ritual frequently required, a sacrifice of cooked meat (sheep, oxen, and pig) was made.[6]

In the passage quoted concerning the use of the sheep in sacrifice, the only significant question for Confucius is whether its use is required for the particular sacrifice. Feelings for the sheep are totally secondary and, indeed, quite irrelevant if ritual demands that a sheep be used. While in many contexts the *junzi* will show sensitivity to the feelings of other living things as part of the application of the general virtue of humaneness (*ren*), this sensitivity is not to exceed its proper place. When, as in this case, sensitivity toward animals conflicts with ritual, the maintenance of ritual prevails. Since the basis of ritual is to be found in the practices of the sages of antiquity, and since these sages represent the ultimate paradigm of moral reflection and activity, the details of ritual encapsulate their informed moral guidance and *must* be viewed as authoritive.[7]

Another passage from the *Analects* that bears on the classical Confucian's beliefs about humans and animals concerns those humans who withdraw from the world:

Under Heaven there is none that is not swept along by the same flood. Such is the world and who can change it? As for you, instead of following one who flees from this man and that, you would do better to follow one who shuns the whole generation of men. And with that he went on covering seed. Zilu went and told his master, who said ruefully, "One cannot herd with the birds and beasts. If I am not to be a man among other men, then what am I to be? If the Way prevailed under Heaven, I should not be trying to alter things."[8]

This passage is one of a series in which either Confucius or his disciples encounter individuals who have essentially given up on any reform efforts in the world. For them there is nothing that can be done other than to find some out-of-the-way place, settle down, and try to live out their years in a peaceful manner. To such individuals Confucius appeared as someone who was trying to do the impossible; his efforts were simply worthless. Confucius' attitude toward such individuals is obvious from the

passage. They are condemned for fleeing their moral responsibilities of serving and, when necessary, of reforming the world. Such individuals receive the wrath of Confucius, and he says of them that they differ little from the birds and the beasts.

Why are these individuals compared to the birds and the beasts? A person who withdraws from the human community thereby fails to act as a reasonable moral agent. The moral nature of such a person remains unfulfilled. As such he is not truly a moral agent and, by extension, given the degree to which our moral nature is itself definitive of human nature, such a person might very well be said to be something *less* than human. What does that make him like? The answer is clear: he has become as the birds and beasts.

We must, however, be certain not to be misled by this answer. The rustics who are the subject of this passage have *chosen* to ignore moral responsibilities that by nature they possess. Thus at one level they may be said to be little different from birds and beasts. By not employing their moral natures they function at the same level as those who, owing to their natural endowment, have only a rudimentary capacity to act morally. On the other hand, and this is where the analogy of birds and beasts can mislead, the rustics *do wrong* by choosing to ignore their moral responsibilities. Their conscious decision to ignore this responsibility is obviously *different in kind* from having only rudimentary capacities for reflection and action to begin with.

How then can we describe Confucius' position with regard to animals? At the heart of his teaching is the moral development of both the individual and society; responsibility for performing individual acts is determined by reference to these ends. At the level of individual moral development, Confucius teaches sensitivity to the life of animals. Such sensitivity may even be said to be characteristic of the *junzi* as a reflection of moral responsibility. It remains true, however, that the primary measure of those moral virtues we are to develop is tied largely to those special moral relations that bind members of the human species together—whether they are king-subject, father-son, elder brother-younger brother, husband-wife, or friend-friend. If these relations are fulfilled, *then* feelings can be extended outward to all people and, eventually, to all living things. But we are not to attempt to do the latter before we have successfully completed the former.

Mengzi, Mencius

Usually considered the second major Confucian thinker, Mencius (372–289 BCE) is now regarded as the primary interpreter of Confucius, a position he came to occupy as part of the Neo-Confucian movement beginning in the thirteenth century. It was at this point that his work was canonized as part of the collection of basic Confucian scripture. By developing and expanding upon basic themes represented only in the briefest of terms in the *Analects*, Mencius admirably clarifies the teaching of Confucius. His most basic teachings concern human nature. Confucius suggested, but never stated, that human nature was morally good. Mencius is explicit in making this idea basic to Confucian teaching. Mencius says of human nature, *xing:* it has the beginnings of moral goodness. He is specific about the nature of the beginnings, stating that it possesses the *siduan* or Four Beginnings—*ren* (humaneness), *yi* (rightness), *li* (propriety), and *zhi* (wisdom).[9] According to Mencius, these constitutive parts of human nature are endowed in us by Heaven at our birth. But they are merely beginnings; they are not yet fully developed. Such development is necessary before human beings can act morally to the fullest extent.

Mencius illustrates the universal nature of our natural goodness by referring to a child about to fall into a well.[10] To Mencius it is a plain matter of fact that humans possess moral goodness because any person who sees the peril of the child will spontaneously act to save him.

One's ability to develop one's moral nature will ultimately depend upon the use of the mind (*xin*). The learning and self-cultivation necessary to perfect the moral nature, Mencius seems to believe, will eventually yield a level of moral awareness that is all-encompassing. It is a state hinted at in Mencius' comment that all things are complete within him.[11] What are the moral implications of this kind of vision, especially as they relate to our relations with other living things?

Let me begin to answer this question by considering one of the classic discussions of animals in all of Confucian literature. The passage opens in the following way. While sitting in his hall, a king sees a man leading an ox. The king asks the man where he is taking the animal, and the man responds that he is on his way to consecrate a new bell with the blood of the ox. The king asks the man to let the ox go. The man in turn responds by asking the king whether the consecration of the bell is thereby to be omitted. The king responds that it was not his purpose to omit the consecration; rather, he ordered the release of the ox because "I cannot bear its frightened appearance, as if it were an innocent person going to the place of death."[12] In the place of the ox, the king orders that a sheep be used to consecrate the bell.

As he discusses the issue with Mencius, the king acknowledges the apparent arbitrariness of his choice. Was the sacrifice of a lesser order so that a smaller animal could be used? Was the sheep to suffer less than the ox? Was it less worthy of being reprieved from suffering than the ox? Was the king less culpable because he allowed the sacrifice of a sheep instead of an ox? Mencius gives the following response:

> Your conduct was an artifice of benevolence. You saw the ox, and had not seen the sheep. So is the superior man *affected* towards animals, that, having seen them alive, he cannot bear to see them die; having heard their dying cries, he cannot bear to eat their flesh. Therefore he keeps away from his cookroom.[13]

Mencius' response suggests that the king is a man of moral virtue and sensitivity and his behavior is an example of *ren,* here translated as benevolence. For the king acted in behalf of the ox, having seen its fright; the sheep, having had no direct contact with the king, remained an abstraction.

The discussion returns to the king's inability to bear the frightened appearance of the ox. The similarity between the king's reaction and the case of the child about to fall into the well is clear. In both cases it is said that by nature humans are unable to see others suffer, or, as it is stated at a later point in the text, "All men have a mind which cannot bear to see the sufferings of others."[14] This is the basic, quintessential ethical claim that is made about human nature. The goodness of human nature, described technically in terms of the four beginnings of goodness, must ultimately stand or fall on this claim. And in a formulation that parallels Bentham's plea for recognizing the suffering of others,[15] we have as basic a statement of Confucian ethics as will be found. The *junzi* cannot bear to see the suffering of others; moreover, the scope of this moral perception encompasses not only fellow humans but also the lives of other sentient creatures.

True to the classical Confucian tradition, however, the special moral relations between humans have priority over sensitivity to the suffering of animals and others. In particular, Mencius states that such feelings will be misplaced if they are not accompanied by a proper understanding of moral relations. For the king, for example, the most important moral relations are his obligations as ruler to his people. If these are overlooked, then the moral responsibility of the ruler is skewed. As Mencius says, "Now here is kindness sufficient to reach to animals, and no benefits are extended from it to the people —How is this?"[16] For Confucianism the first and foremost measure of the cultivation of the moral nature is the perfection of the classical set of special moral relations. If, as the philosopher Mozi (470–391 BCE) taught, one should

practice universal love, *jianai,* then according to the Confucians there would be no love. And there would be no love because it would have no beginning, no first special moral relations from which to develop. It would remain only an abstraction, nothing more. If, however, special moral relations are developed, then humanity's natural goodness will develop. And with the development of this goodness, the sphere of moral reflection and action will increase, including, for the *junzi,* all living things.

A later passage in Mencius' writings speaks directly to this point:

> In regard to inferior creatures, the superior man is kind to them, but not loving. In regard to people generally, he is loving to them but not affectionate. He is affectionate to his parents, and lovingly disposed to people generally. He is lovingly disposed to people generally and kind to creatures.[17]

The differences in this passage in terms of feelings toward animals, people in general, and people in special moral relations are expressed as the differences between *ai* (kindness), *ren* (humaneness or loving), and *jin* (affection). The *junzi's* moral nature has the capacity to act in all these ways. But there is a natural order to moral development, and natural feelings are associated with the different compartments of the moral life.

Mencius adds much to the discussion of Confucian ethics and the specific relationships of humans and animals. He defends the appropriateness of feelings of kindness toward animals in far more detail than Confucius and with a more clearly formulated basis. Ultimately he uses the same helping principle for animals as used for assisting human strangers—the inability to bear the suffering of others. But while it is appropriate to show kindness to animals, it is most inappropriate if in the process we fail to fulfill our special responsibilities to human beings, and, in particular, those in a special relationship.

XUNZI

In many ways Xunzi (fl. 298–238 BCE) is the most systematic of the early Confucian thinkers. His text is a model of the early method of argumentation. He is also more concerned than Mencius with the need for strict and unwavering attention to the process of learning. For Xunzi as well humans *can* perfect themselves, they *can* become sages, but a life-long commitment to learning is essential. As such, Xunzi makes a greater effort to distinguish human life from other forms of life. The distinction is drawn in terms of the uniquely human capacity to learn, with the implication that the goal of sagehood is obtainable only if one devotes one's life to learning.

Having drawn a sharp line between the realms of humans and animals, Xunzi nevertheless also displays an extraordinary sensitivity to animal behavior and urges that humans emulate it. He writes:

> All living creatures between heaven and earth which have blood and breath must possess consciousness, and nothing that possesses consciousness fails to love its own kind. If any of the animals or great birds happens to become separated from the herd or flocks, though a month or a season may pass, it will invariably return to its old haunts, and when it passes its former home, it will look about and cry, hesitate and drag its feet before it can bear to pass on. Even among tiny creatures the swallows and sparrows will cry with sorrow for a little while before they fly on. Among creatures of blood and breath, none has greater understanding than man; therefore man ought to love his parents until the day he dies.[18]

We still find the statement that man is the highest form of life, but the statement is qualified by pointing to the basic moral responses shared by animals. Though technically they would not be of the same order as human moral responses, they are nevertheless a *kind* of moral response. This reaffirms the Confucian teaching

that humans and animals differ in degree, not in kind. Even animals have a rudimentary common sense. This is an interesting perspective—all the more because it comes from the sternest of Confucian philosophers and portends something of the direction in which Confucian tradition moves in the hands of the Neo-Confucians. For though the Neo-Confucians still insist upon the superiority of humans in the scheme of things, they also insist, as we shall see shortly, on the unity of all living things.

The Neo-Confucian Ethical Vision

Neo-Confucianism refers to the form of Confucianism that arose during the Song dynasty (960–1269) and has continued until recent times. While there is much here that simply echoes the basic teachings of Confucianism, there is also a newfound interest in philosophical issues, in particular a metaphysical tendency that has as its goal the grounding of the Confucian moral virtues in a developed metaphysical system. There is also a new emphasis on the individual's religious quest for *sheng* (sagehood). These points will be explained as we proceed.

Neo-Confucianism functions in both the public and the private sector. In the former it is state orthodoxy, a role it plays in China, Korea, and Japan. In the latter, the instruction it gives to the individual is at the very center of the cultures of these countries. In its role as state orthodoxy it holds a prominent position as ideological authority, while its instructional role provides a profound religious and ethical orientation for the individual. It is hard to overestimate the importance of Neo-Confucianism in East Asia, where it continues to play a major role in sustaining the value systems of both individuals and groups.

MIND AND NATURE: METAPHYSICAL MODELS FOR MORAL ACTION

Within Neo-Confucianism there are two major schools of thought: the School of Principle (*lixue*), or the Cheng-Zhu School, named after its two major thinkers, Cheng Yi (1033–1107) and Zhu Xi (1130–1200), and the School of Mind (*xinxue*), or the Lu-Wang School, named after Lu Xiangshan (1139–1192) and Wang Yangming (1472–1529).

The School of Principle believes that principle (*li*), or the Principle of Heaven (*Tianli*), is to be found in all things, including human nature. Its thinkers follow a scheme of learning exemplified by the *Daxue* (Great Learning) that instructs the learner to investigate the principle in things (*gewu*). As this process of investigation is extended to a wider and wider circle of things and activities (*zhizhi*), the person who understands principle will develop his nature (*xing*) to the point of sagehood (*sheng*). The focus of much of this effort for the School of Principle is upon the meaning of *gewu,* the investigation of things, and how one discovers principle inherent in them.

Moral development also requires investigating "things" (*gewu*). But in addition it demands that the individual sincerely intend to internalize the principle as it exists in the particular case—for example, in *his* relation to *his* parents. Through this process the basic moral virtues, the Four Beginnings of Mencius, traditionally considered to be constitutive of human nature, are tied to a deeper metaphysic.

The School of Mind, on the other hand, finds principle to be inherent in the mind (*hsin*), not just in nature (*xing*), and as a result *the act of thinking* itself is a proper object of study of principle. The pedagogical schema changes dramatically as a result. Emphasis is placed not on the first two steps of the *Daxue, gewu* (the investigation of things) and *zhizhi* (the extension of knowledge), but on the third step, *chengyi* (sincerity of intention). The search for principle becomes thoroughly internalized.

The relevance of these differing models to the relationship of humans and animals can be over-estimated; there is a difference in emphasis, but little difference in the nature of how we should act. Like the classical Confucians before them, Neo-Confucianists continue to teach the superiority of humans over animals. Zhou Dunyi (1017–1073), for example, says that it is humans who receive material force (*qi*) in its highest form.[19] And Shao Yong (1011–1077) states that "man occupies the most honored position in the schema of things because he combines in him the principle of all species."[20] Though accounts of humans' superiority differ, it is clear that it has a metaphysical basis.

It is Zhu Xi, however, who puts the argument in its tightest form, and it is his teachings that may be viewed as the orthodox Neo-Confucian interpretation of the relation of man to animals. The argument is developed within the framework of a comparison of the nature of humans and the nature of animals. "The nature of man and the nature of things," it begins, "in some respects are the same and in other respects different."[21] First, as regards the creation of things, there is a similar aspect and a different aspect. In the basic Neo-Confucian cosmogony things are created from a beginning (or first) point, called the Great Ultimate (*Taiji*). The actual creation of things comes about through the intermingling of the two modes of material force (*qi*), the forces of *yin* and *yang*. Man and animals may be said to be similar, for they are both products of the intermingling of *yin* and *yang*. On the other hand, the intermingling of *yin, yang,* and the five elements (*wuxing*), another structure of metaphysical influences, produces inequalities in separate things. On the basis of the inequalities produced, humans and animals may be said to be unequal.

In this respect the issue of equality and inequality may be interpreted in terms of the distinction between the material force (*qi*) and the principle (*li*) of things: animals and humans are similar as regards their principle but different in

terms of material force. This point is made in the following passage:

> From the point of view of principle, all things have one source, and therefore man and things cannot be distinguished as higher and lower creatures. From the point of view of material force, man receives it in its perfection and unimpeded while things receive it partially and obstructed. Because of this they are unequal, man being higher and things lower.[22]

There is, however, a qualification to be noted. As the argument continues, we find that the human being is said to differ from animals even in terms of the principle that "constitute(s) nature."[23] In the case of humans, principle confers the capacity for moral reflection:

> Thus consciousness and movement proceed from material force while humanity, righteousness, decorum, and wisdom proceed from principle. Both humans and things are capable of consciousness and movement, but though things possess humanity, righteousness, decorum, and wisdom, they cannot have them completely.[24]

In this part of the argument we find the suggestion that animals do not differ from humans in material force, at least in terms of consciousness and movement, while they do differ in principle, humans possessing the capacity for moral reflection that animals lack.

If this line of reasoning has been followed, then it will appear that Zhu Xi has contradicted himself. Initially he argues that humans and animals are similar with regard to principle but differ in material force. In the end he argues that they are similar with regard to material force but differ in terms of principle. But there is no real contradiction. Zhu Xi is writing from two different perspectives. On the one hand, to say that animals and humans are similar in principle but differ in material force is to stress the Neo-Confucian cosmology, that places the Great Ultimate as the source of creation of all things. On the other hand, to say that animals and humans are similar in terms of material force but differ in terms of principle is to speak from the axiological perspective.

When one assesses the argument that is put forth by Zhu Xi, an argument expressed in the categories of Neo-Confucian metaphysics, the conclusion reminds one of something that Mencius said, though in far simpler terms. "That whereby humans differ from the lower animals is but small," he writes. "The mass of people cast it away, while *junzi* preserve it."[25] Is there a clear-cut distinction between humans and animals according to Zhu Xi? There seems to be little that one could point to that would justify saying that humans possess this but animals do not. As regards material force, for example, there is no categorical difference between humans and animals. The closest the argument comes to making a hard distinction is when it is said that humans receive material force in a clear form, while animals receive it in a turbid form. That, however, is not a distinction that is terribly meaningful, nor is it one that Neo-Confucians emphasized.

As far as principle is concerned, because both animals and humans share in it, they are similar. However, we are also told that principle is constitutive of human nature to a degree different from that of animals; humans have a full capacity for moral virtue as part of their nature. Does this mean that animals do not? Surprisingly, it does not mean this. Humans are said to have a *fuller* moral nature, but animals possess moral virtue too, even though it is not in a "complete" form. Humans are capable of thorough-going moral reflection, while animals are capable only of a rudimentary kind of moral reflection. The difference between humans and animals, again, is not a difference in kind, as we have seen in the earlier tradition as well, but, as always, a difference in degree. Thus we find Zhu Xi writing:

Heaven and earth reach all things with this mind. When humans receive it, it becomes the human mind. When things receive it, it becomes the mind of things (in general). And when grass, trees, birds, or animals receive it, it becomes the mind of grass, trees, birds and animals (in particular). All of these are simply the one mind of Heaven and Earth.[26]

A VISION OF UNITY

The fact that there is no difference in kind between humans and animals allows Neo-Confucianism to teach the unity of all forms of things. Cheng Hao (1032–1085) states that "the humane man forms one body with all things comprehensively.... All operations of the universe are our operations."[27] Cheng Yi said, "The humane man regards Heaven and earth and all things as one body. There is nothing which is not part of his self. Knowing that, where is the limit (of his humanity)?"[28] Lu Xiangshan said, "The universe never separates itself from man; man separates himself from the universe."[29] And the *Jinsilu* directs one to enlarge the mind in order to be able to enter into all things in the world: "Combine the internal and the external into one and regard things and self as equal. This is the way to see the fundamental point of the Way."[30]

Probably more than any other work, however, Zhang Zai's (1021–1077) *Ximing* (Western Inscription) has captured the imagination of Neo-Confucian ethical thought. The first few lines read:

Heaven is my father and earth is my mother, and even such a small creature as I finds an intimate place in their midst. Therefore that which extends throughout the universe I regard as my body and that which directs the universe I consider as my nature. All people are my brothers and sisters, and all things are my companions.[31]

The vision is clear: animals and humans share in the same material force and the same principle. Humans embody these in their highest or fullest form, but this only makes greater demands upon our ethical reflections and action. All living things, not just human beings, stand in *moral* relation to humans, and humans in turn fulfill their own moral nature by standing in moral relation to all living things.

The degree to which this was taken literally as a directive to moral action can be seen in several poignant examples. In a short biographical note about Zhou Dunyi (1017–1073), the *Jinsilu* states that he "did not cut the grass growing outside his window. When asked about it, he said, '[The feeling of the grass] and mine are the same.'"[32]

In the commentary to this passage a question is raised about the meaning of the statement that the feeling of the grass and Zhou Dunyi's feeling are the same. The first response simply states, "You can realize the matter yourself. You must see wherein one's feelings and that of the grass are the same."[33] A second response is recorded and gives more explanation.

> If we say that one's feelings and that of the grass are the same, shall we say that one's feeling and those of trees and leaves are not the same? And if we say that one's feeling toward the donkey's cry and one's own call are the same, shall we say that a horse's cry and one's own call are not the same?[34]

Once we recognize that we share the same material force and the same principle with all that lives so that we form one body together, we will grasp the moral need to see and listen for others in distress. Thus we return to the essential Confucian moral vision: The human being of moral insight cannot bear to see the suffering of others, and it is this inability to bear the suffering of others that culminates in moral action.

The great Neo-Confucian of the School of Mind, Wang Yangming, specifically ties this sense of moral responsibility to the basic ethical teaching of Mencius: the inability to bear the suffering of others. In his "Inquiry on the Great Learning," Wang Yangming makes the following statement:

> Therefore when he sees a child about to fall into a well, he cannot help a feeling of alarm and commiseration. This shows that his humanity forms one body with the child. It may be objected that the child belongs to the same species. Again, when he observes the pitiful cries and frightened appearance of birds and animals about to be slaughtered, he cannot help feeling an "inability to bear" their suffering. This shows that his humanity forms one body with birds and animals. It may be objected that birds and animals are sentient beings as he is. But when he sees plants broken and destroyed, he cannot help a feeling of pity. This shows that his humanity forms one body with plants.[35]

If this moral nature can be developed, then a person will have formed a true sense of "one body" with all things.

> Everything from ruler, minister, husband, wife, and friends to mountains, rivers, spiritual beings, birds, animals, and plants should be truly loved in order to realize my humanity that forms one body with them, and then my clear character will be completely manifested, and I will form one body with Heaven, Earth, and the myriad things.[36]

In Wang Yangming's view, these statements are of particular significance for specific moral action and culminate in one of the basic principles of his thought, the unity of knowledge and action — *zhixing heyi*. The two, knowledge and action, form a unity, because each is ultimately dependent upon the other. To speak of knowledge without action is empty talk, according to Wang Yangming, while to speak of action not motivated by knowledge is to speak of action of no consequence. Moral knowledge, the inherent or innate knowledge of the good (*liangzhi*), is inseparable from moral action. To know the good, as Socrates had taught, is to do it. Moral knowledge is not "abstract knowledge."

For the Neo-Confucian, ethics is a way of thinking that leads to a way of living, though Wang Yangming would suggest that the thought and the action are even more closely tied together. To stop with only the thought is to engage in empty and useless talk.

Kaibara Ekken (1630–1714), a Japanese Neo-Confucian of the Zhu Xi school, *Shushi-gaku*, perhaps more than any other figure, brought Confucian ethics to the forefront of discussion in the school and the home alike. This passage is from his *Shogaku-kun* (Precepts for Children) and stresses the ethics that flow naturally from the philosophical and religious position of the unity of all things.

> No living creatures such as birds, beasts, insects, and fish should be killed wantonly. Not even grass and trees should be cut down out of season. All of these are objects of nature's love, having been brought forth by her and nurtured by her. To cherish them and keep them is therefore the way to serve nature in accordance with the great heart of nature. Among human obligations there is first the duty to love our relatives, then to show sympathy for all other human beings, and then not to mistreat birds and beasts or any other living thing. That is the proper order for the practice of benevolence in accordance with the great heart of nature. Loving other people to the neglect of parents, or loving birds and beasts to the neglect of human beings, is not benevolence.[37]

Here, in a statement that builds upon the monism of *qi* (*ki* in Japanese), Kaibara Ekken identifies specific forms of ethical action. Nature itself is said to manifest loving kindness (*ren, jin* in Japanese), and we are to see that we are a part of the basic ethical goodness of nature. Thus our own actions must bear the quality of loving kindness. The loving kindness of nature is not a misplaced anthropomorphism but a manifestation of the moral nature shared by all. We in turn must recognize the moral obligations of being human—obligations that engage us in the lives of those closest to us in the most profound way but ultimately involve us in the lives of all living things. From the common perception of shared life comes the perception of shared moral feeling and the injunction not to cause suffering to others.

Such is the development of the Neo-Confucian tradition, its moral injunctions perpetuating the basic classical Confucian stance that humans possess a mind that is incapable of bearing the suffering of others. I want now to bring the tradition into a contemporary context and inquire into its implications for the use of animals in science.

A Neo-Confucian in Modern Japan

Virtually nothing has been written about the relation of Confucianism to the moral problems created by contemporary technological societies. Recognizing the large historical role the Confucian tradition has played in the creation of East Asian cultures, and yet knowing, too, how little its teachings are articulated in the affairs of contemporary Asia, it struck me that it would be appropriate to discuss its applications to these affairs with one of the last major Confucian thinkers in Japan. This I did during the summer of 1983, spending five weeks with Okada Takehiko in Fukuoka, Japan. Part of our conversation touched on the relation between humans and animals and, in particular, the use of animals in science. What follows is a record of our conversation on this topic.[38]

> TAYLOR: I want to turn now to the discussion of respect for life and the relation of respect for life to the development of science.

> OKADA: Since science has developed, it has reached a position where it has come to threaten the very existence of life itself.

Nevertheless, we can't stop the continued development of science because it appears necessary as the basis for the continued development of the human community. Science needs to be made aware of the degree to which it has to develop for the benefit of the human community. To make science develop in this way, both scientists and nonscientists have to come to understand the importance of the human community and human life itself. I think that Confucianism is the most suitable of teachings for this purpose because it emphasizes as a central idea the forming of one body with all things. One can live only by living with others. Confucian ethics are fundamental in this respect—one must consider the other person's heart. If we extend the concept, then we must consider nature itself as well, that is, all living things.

TAYLOR: You have talked about the extraordinary importance of respect for human life and the degree to which science, and for that matter humanity, if they are to survive, must reach toward the emergence of respect for human life. Therefore you have essentially said that science must be grounded in ethics if it is to be ultimately useful. I wonder to what degree you as a Confucian can speculate upon the importance of not just human life, but all life. Do we have ethical responsibilities to all forms of life, not just human life?

OKADA: Yes I think we do, and such an idea should be extended to all forms of life, animal life and plant life. The Confucian idea of forming one body with all things could be interpreted to mean one with animals and plants. ... All mankind has a mind that cannot bear to see the suffering of others and this is something that should be applied to all life.

TAYLOR: One of the issues that have become increasingly important in Western culture is what is called cruelty to animals. It refers primarily to the mistreatment of animals, and a large part of the question revolves around the issue of the use of animals in scientific research. I wonder the degree to which this mind that cannot bear to see the suffering of others, in being extended to all forms of life, does in fact provide a foundation for noncruelty and at least for not overusing animals in scientific research?

OKADA: Of course, according to the idea of the mind that cannot bear to see the suffering of others, we should not mistreat animals. As regards the overuse of animals in science, this is a very difficult problem. On the one hand, science seems to need such experiments in order to advance. In addition, at times benefits are brought to the animals as well, for example, new medicines or something of this kind. On the other hand, because animals are required, animals suffer. If, however, we truly have a mind that cannot bear to see the suffering of others, then perhaps the problem will be solved. Here in Japan we eat large quantities of fish from the rivers as well as the sea. At times we hold a memorial service in honor of the fish. Thus even when one kills animals or fish, there can still be a mind that cannot bear to see the suffering of others.

TAYLOR: In terms of these questions in America, and especially in Europe, where they are discussed at great length, there tend to be two extreme positions and, of course many shadings between, on the issue of the ethics of animal use. On the one hand are those who say that there should be no use of animals at all. On the other hand are those who feel that the use of animals is thoroughly justified and ought not to involve any ethical questions. It seems to me that what you are suggesting is a deep feeling of compassion through the mind that cannot bear to see the suffering of others, recognizing that for the advancement of humanity and the advancement of science animals must be used but that they must be used with care for their suffering, in as limited ways as possible, and always with respect.

OKADA: The idea of unlimited use of animals as well as the position that no animals may be used, both of these are extreme ideas. With the mind that cannot bear to see the suffering of others the problem will resolve itself. In some cases we need to differentiate man and animals, in other cases it is important to see man and animals as the same. Thus the cases themselves change and we need to be able to respond to such circumstances based upon the mind that cannot bear to see the suffering of others.

It would be helpful to be able to distinguish different types of uses of animals in science and their appropriateness or inappropriateness according to the religious ethics of Confucianism. The discussion with Okada is, however, as close as one can get to this at present. In East Asia issues of animal rights simply have not arisen to the degree that one finds in the West. While it is possible, therefore, that Confucianism can still be described as the primary mode of ethical thinking in much of East Asia, little can be seen in terms of concrete action directed toward animals. Much of the reason for this is simply that the questions themselves have not been posed. Okada himself was very surprised by my questions concerning animals, and he said repeatedly that these are not questions that are asked in Japan. Thus the kind of detailed study of uses of animals such as Ryder's *Victims of Science*[39] or Singer's more general statement in *Animal Liberation*[40] carries the issue much further than the present state of Confucian thinking. In many ways Confucianism has been in eclipse as a dominant voice in East Asia in recent times. There are signs, however, that this is changing, and with such change I would anticipate a greater correlation with the level of discussion of ethical responsibilities to animals in the West.

It is important to remember that the Confucian tradition remains committed to certain special moral relationships, relations that place the priority strongly with humans and only after with animals. The descriptions of sensitivity to animals have been reflective of one who has perfected his moral nature. Such people are able to extend their sensitivities to all life *after* they have perfected special moral relations. This bears upon the actual historical reality of treatment of animals in China, Korea, and Japan. Were animals treated with due respect for the mind that cannot bear to see the suffering of others? The answer is that for some it was an important consideration, while for others it was not. In this respect it is similar to the Confucian claim that anyone would rescue a child about to fall into a well. Certainly for some this was an informing ethical statement, but for others it would need to be adjudicated with the practice of infanticide.

Okada's position is representative of a contemporary Confucian response. It is extremely sensitive to the ramifications of the Confucian tradition for contemporary issues, even if it lacks the specific and detailed categorization of the problem as found in the West. Okada interprets the issue of the use of animals in science in terms of the very ideas that have been most basic to the development of Confucian and Neo-Confucian ethics. From Mencius he adopts the idea of the mind that cannot bear to see the suffering of others, and from the Neo-Confucians he adopts the idea of forming one body with all things. Combined, they form the foundation for arguing that sensitivity to all life is appropriate and, in fact, morally demanded. But like Confucians before him, he also suggests that the relation between humans and animals is a complex one. In his comments he suggests that there are times when humans and animals are to be viewed as the same and times when they are to be viewed as different. The criterion for such differentiations is the mind of compassion itself. Humans are morally bound to the plight of animals, and are morally bound to the suffering and plight of his fellow humans. There are times when these two obligations will come into conflict with each other. When they do, it is the mind that cannot bear to see the suffering of others that must adjudicate the proper moral course of action. The priority remains with the special moral relationships, but for the Confucian the mind of compassion feels all suffering and every loss of life as its own moral responsibility. As Okada himself said to me, there is so much suffering in this world that the man who cannot bear to see the suffering of others must bear it and try to reform human and animal alike.

Acknowledgments

Reprinted in revised form from Tom Regan, ed., *Animal Sacrifices: Religious Perspectives on the Use of Animals in Science* (Philadelphia: Temple University Press, 1986), pp. 237–63. My many thanks to Tom Regan for his initial insights and suggestions on my essay.

NOTES

1. While Confucius referred to several of the relationships (see, for example, *Lunyu*, 12:11), it was Mencius who first referred to the basic set of relationships (*Mengzi*, 3A:4).

2. *Lunyu*, 7:26, quoted in Arthur Waley, trans., *The Analects of Confucius* (New York: Vintage, 1938), p. 128. Hereafter cited as *Lunyu*, Waley.

3. *Lunyu*, 10:12, Waley, p. 150.

4. *Lunyu*, 3:17, Waley, p. 98.

5. *Lunyu*, 7:1, quoted in W. T. deBary, *Sources of Chinese Tradition* (New York, Columbia University Press, 1960), p. 25. Hereafter referred to as deBary, *Sources*.

6. The great sacrifice, *t'ai-lao*, was considered central to the maintenance of the state religion. It consisted in part of a cooked meat offering of all three animals, sheep, oxen, and pig. For a fuller description of the sacrifice and a discussion of its incorporation into Confucian practice, see R. L. Taylor, *The Way of Heaven: An Introduction to the Confucian Religious Life* (Leiden, E. J. Brill, 1985), and R. L. Taylor, *The Illustrated Encyclopedia of Confucianism* (New York: Rosen Publishing Group, 2005), vol. 2, pp. 578–80.

7. The nature of religious authority of the sages is closely related to the development of the idea of scripture and scriptural authority. For a discussion of Confucian scripture, see R. L. Taylor, "Scripture and the Sage: The Holy Book in Confucianism," in F. M. Denny and R. L. Taylor, eds., *The Holy Book in Comparative Perspective* (Columbia, University of South Carolina Press, 1984). Also included in R. L. Taylor, *Religious Dimensions of Confucianism* (Albany: SUNY Press, 1990), pp. 23–38.

8. *Lunyu*, 18:6, Waley, p. 220.

9. *Mengzi*, 2A:6.

10. Ibid.

11. *Mengzi*, 7A:4.

12. *Mengzi*, 1A:7, quoted in James Legge, *The Four Books* (Shanghai, Chinese Book Company, 1930), p. 450. Hereafter referred to as *Mengzi*, Legge.

13. *Mengzi*, 1A:7, Legge, p. 453.

14. *Mengzi*, 2A:6, Legge, p. 548.

15. See Tom Regan and Peter Singer, eds., *Animal Rights and Human Obligations* (New York, Prentice Hall, 1976), p. 130.

16. *Mengzi*, 1A:7, Legge, p. 454.

17. *Mengzi*, 7A:45, Legge, p. 974.

18. *Xunzi* 19:18, quoted in Burton Watson, *Hsün-tzu: Basic Writings* (New York, Columbia University Press, 1963), p. 106.

19. Zhou Dunyi, "Taijifu shuo," *Zhou Lianqi ji*, 1: 2a-b, quoted in deBary, *Sources*, p. 513.

20. Shao Yong, *Huangji jing-shh shu*, 8B: 16a-17b, quoted in deBary, *Sources*, p. 518.

21. *Zhu Zi quanshu*, 42:27b-30a, quoted in deBary, *Sources*, pp. 548–49.

22. Ibid.

23. Ibid.

24. Ibid.

25. *Mengzi,* 4B:19, quoted in Legge, n. 744.

26. *Zhu Zi quanshu,* 49:23b-24a, quoted in de-Bary, *Sources,* p. 542.

27. *Er Cheng yishu,* 2A:3a-b, quoted in deBary, *Sources,* pp. 559–60.

28. *Er Cheng yishu,* 1:7b, quoted in deBary, *Sources,* p. 530.

29. *Xiangshan quanji,* 34: 5b, quoted in deBary, *Sources,* p. 567.

30. *Jinsilu* 2:83, 105, quoted in W.T. Chan, trans., *Reflections on Things at Hand* (New York, Columbia University Press, 1967), pp. 74–75, 85. Hereafter referred to as *Jinsilu,* Chan, *Reflections.*

31. Zhang Zai, "Xi Ming," *Zhang Heng chu ji* 1:1a-5b, quoted in deBary, *Sources,* p. 525.

32. *Jinsilu,* 14:18, quoted in Chan, *Reflections,* p. 302.

33. Ibid.

34. Ibid.

35. *Wang Wencheng Gong quanshu,* 26:1b-5a, quoted in W.T. Chan, trans., *Instructions for Practical Living and Other Neo-Confucian Writings by Wang Yang-ming* (New York, Columbia University Press, 1963), p. 272. Hereafter referred to as *Wang Wencheng Gong quanshu,* Chan, *Instructions.*

36. *Wang Wencheng Gong quanshu,* 26:1b-5a, Chan, *Instructions, p.* 273.

37. Kaibara Ekken, Shogaku-kun, *Ekken zenshu* 3:2–3, quoted in R. Tsunoda and W.T. deBary, *Sources of Japanese Tradition* (New York, Columbia University Press, 1958), p. 377.

38. These passages, first published in this essay, were later published in my more complete study of Okada. See R.L. Taylor, *The Confucian Way of Contemplation: Okada Takehiko and the Tradition of Quiet-Sitting* (Columbia: University of South Carolina Press, 1988), pp. 165–212.

39. Richard Ryder, *Victims of Science* (London, Davis-Poynter, 1975).

40. Peter Singer, *Animal Liberation: A New Ethic for Our Treatment of Animals* (New York, Avon, 1975).

V

EAST MEETS WEST

ANIMALS IN PHILOSOPHY AND CULTURAL HISTORY

Human Exceptionalism versus Cultural Elitism

(Or *"Three in the morning, four at night"* 朝三暮四)

ROGER AMES

In classical Western thinking, from Aristotle and the Stoics through Aquinas and Descartes, down to the present day, the notion of "human exceptionalism"—human beings are an exception to nature, both in kind and quality—has been a persistent theme. The distinction between the human and the animal, when not assumed for religious reasons, has largely been argued for by equating thought with language: that is, animals don't talk, *ergo* they don't think.

In opposition to "human exceptionalism," there has been a countercurrent, which includes philosophers such as Rousseau, Hume, and certainly Nietzsche. Further, over the past century and a half, "chain-of-being" thinking and the pathetic fallacy that attends it has been challenged by the widespread acceptance of Darwin's theory of evolution that supports a "continuity across species" explanation of the animal world. Even so, the "sanctity of human life" is a contemporary expression of a world in which animals have been essentially defined, and rele-

gated to the down side of the familiar "means-end" dualism. The status of animals has quite simply not been a philosophical issue: they are for human use.

It is only very recently with Peter Singer and the animal rights movement that, over a relatively short period of time, the status of animals has not only sparked real philosophical debate but has become an issue of intense social activism as well. A rank "speciesism," which would justify painful laboratory experiments on monkeys but not on retarded human beings (the second group having much less claim to intelligence or social complexity than the former), has become the subject of serious moral concern.[1]

Turning to the sinitic cultures, there has been a "dharma bums" romanticism that, in contrast to "human exceptionalism," construes the mysterious East as an ecologically sophisticated world in which animals are accorded due respect. In this essay, I want to explore the worldview that gives context to classical Chinese literature and recover the philosophical assumptions that have influenced the sinitic narrative in locating animals in a fundamentally different natural cosmology. It is not all romanticism. There is much presupposed in the early Chinese tradition that, on comparison with "human exceptionalism" and "speciesism," would seem to be animal friendly and liberating. Against such an impression we will have to weigh a contemporary fact: to satisfy medicinal and culinary demand, the Chinese probably more than any other of the world's cultures are responsible for the decimation of endangered species.[2] How then do we reconcile this obvious tension between an inclusive natural cosmology and appallingly exclusive practices?

Qi 氣 as "Vital Energizing Field"

Most individual Western interpretations of the vital and spiritual character of things (*pneuma*) appeal to a physical/spiritual dichotomy, where the animating principle is largely distinguishable from the things it animates. In classical China, the animating fluid is conceptualized in terms of what today we might call an "energy field." This field not only pervades all things, but also in some sense is the means or process of the constitution of all things. As Judy Farquhar observes, "*qi* is both structural and functional, a unification of material and temporal forms that loses all coherence when reduced to one or the other 'aspect.'"[3] There is no reality/appearance distinction that typically privileges the "essential" and defining formal aspect of a thing as being more "real" than its changing aspect. That is to say, there are no separable "things" to be animated; there is only the field and its focal manifestations.

The energizing field as the "reality" of things precludes the existence of forms or ideas or categories or principles that allow for the existence of "natural kinds." Thus, discriminations in the field of *qi* are made in terms of observed and conventionalized classifications associated with diurnal and seasonal changes, directions, colors, body parts, and so forth. Such discriminations, far from being final in any sense, are processive and defusive. The diremption of the world into correlative "*yinyang*" 陰陽 categories, while arguably implicit in the natural cosmology of a proto-Chinese world that can be documented at least as far back as the Shang dynasty,[4] was in the course of time, formalized, systematized, and made explicit in the complex Han dynasty cosmological charts.[5]

Today we are most familiar with *qi* in its explanatory role in the areas of health, medicine, and exercises leading to bodily well-being. But in the classical correlative cosmology, the term "body," like any predication of *qi*, must of course be used advisedly; everything is a continuous field of *qi* manifesting itself as both "body" and "environs," as both "physical" and "spiritual" in aspect. In fact, the purpose of self-actualizing regimens, both physical and spiritual, has been to achieve an equanimity and balance that allows for a productively continuous flow of *qi* without stagnation or obstruction.

In the classical Daoistic literature we have sources such as the meditative "Inward Training" (*neiye* 內業) chapter of the *Guanzi* 管子, which contains techniques associated with correct posture, diet, and breath control aimed at bringing the internal landscape into harmony with its context, thereby allowing the practitioner to achieve health and long life.

The *Zhuangzi* 莊子 contains perhaps the most radical statement of what it terms "transformation-of-things" *wuhua* 物化 cosmology, in which erstwhile "things" dissolve into the flux and flow as porous, interpenetrating, and inclusive events and processes:

With the ancients, understanding had gotten somewhere. Where was that? At its height, at its extreme, that understanding to which no more could be added was this: some of them thought that there had never begun to be things. The next lot thought that there are things, but that there had never begun to be boundaries among them. The next lot thought that there are boundaries among things, but that there had never begun to be right and wrong among them.[6]

For Zhuangzi, the human being has no place of privilege. Like everything else, the human form is processive, and must yield deferentially to the ongoing, ineluctable propensity of transformation:

Not long thereafter, Ziyu fell ill, and Zisi went to ask after him. "Extraordinary!" said Ziyu, "The transformer of things continues to make me all gnarly and bent. He hunches me up so badly that my vital organs are above my head while my chin is buried in my bellybutton. My shoulders are higher than my crown, and my hunchback points to the heavens. Something has really gone haywire with the *yin* and *yang* vapors!" ...

"Do you resent this?" asked Zisi.

"Indeed no," replied Ziyu, "What's to resent? If in the course of things it transforms my left arm into a cock, I'll use it to tell the time of day. If it goes on to transform my right arm into a crossbow bolt, I'll use it to shoot me an owl for roasting. If it then transforms my buttocks into wheels and my spirit into a horse, I will ride about on them without need of further transportation. ... What's to resent?"

Before long, Master Lai fell ill. Wheezing and panting, he was on the brink of death. His wife and children gathered about him and wept. Master Li, having gone to inquire after him, scolded them, saying "Get away! Don't impede his transformations!"

Leaning against the door, Master Li talked with him, saying: "Extraordinary, these transformations! What are you going to be made into next? Where are you going to be sent? Will you be made into a rat's liver? Or will you be made into an insect's arm?"

Master Lai replied, "... Now if a great ironsmith were in the process of casting metal, and

the metal leapt about saying, 'I must be forged into a "Mo Ye" sword!' the great ironsmith would certainly consider it to be an inauspicious bit of metal. Now, if once having been cast in the human form, I were to whine: 'Make me into a human being! Make me into a human being!' the transformer of things would certainly take me to be an inauspicious person. Once we take the heavens and earth to be a giant forge and transformation to be the great ironsmith, where ever I go is just fine. Relaxed I nod off and happily I awake."[7]

The *Zhuangzi* locates the possibility of assuming a human form as an arbitrary and not especially welcome perturbation within the larger process of transformation. Zhuangzi's response to the misgivings one might have about "death" is that there is real comfort, and indeed even a religious awe, in the recognition that assuming the form of one kind of thing gives way to becoming another in a ceaseless adventure. Such a recognition presumably stimulates empathetic feelings and compassion for other creatures in a shared, continuous environment. It encourages an existential appreciation of the "very now" by relocating the "dying away" in every moment, and by redefining "life" itself as a reconciliation of "life-and-death." This is to realize "that living and dying, existing and perishing, are in fact the same thing."[8] Zhuangzi's counsel is simple: rather than wishing to be one thing as opposed to another, enjoy the ride.

It has been argued that the *Zhuangzi*'s famous butterfly story, informed as it is by the perceived liberation from rapacious, wormlike caterpillar to the happy dance of the strikingly colored butterfly, really has as its subtext Zhuang Zhou himself dying out of one kind of life only to be transformed into another.[9] This interpretation is certainly reinforced by another, lesser known, anecdote that tells a similar story of emergence and assimilation, but in much greater detail:

Liezi was having his lunch by the side of the road when he spied a hundred year old skull. Spreading back the reeds, he pointed at it and said: "Is it only you and I who know that we have never experienced either life or death? Should you then be anxious, and should I be glad?"

Within the seeds of things there is something that triggers them off. In water, seeds become amoebae, and at the water's edge they become a kind of seaweed. When they grow on a hillside, they become a hill-slipper grass, and when this grass is fertilized it becomes crowfoot grass. The roots of the crow-foot grass become beetle larva, and its blades become butterflies. Shortly the butterflies undergo a metamorphosis to become those insects which live under the stove and shed their skins—they are called house crickets. These house crickets after a thousand days become birds, and they are called "dried leftover bones" birds. The spittle of these birds becomes *simi* bugs which become vinegar flies. *Yilu* bugs are born from the vinegar flies, and *huangkuang* grubs are born from *jiuyou* insects. Gnats are born from fireflies, and when sheep's groom grass grows beside bamboo that has not sprouted for some time, it produces *chingning* bugs. *Chingning* bugs give birth to leopards which give birth to horses which in turn give birth to human beings. In due time, human beings revert to what triggered them off. All of the myriad things come out from what triggers them off and revert back to it.[10]

This passage uses everyday plants and beasties familiar in their own specific time and place to describe the animated process of transformation. Simply, one thing becomes something else, from gnats and "dried left-over bones" birds to human beings, and back again. Through the patterns of association that the reader brings to this everyday world, these various examples of living things provide a bottomless shared resource out of which all things in unceasing sequence emerge. The "something that triggers them off" *ji* 機 is the ever-present indeterminate

aspect that drives the ongoing self-reconstruing (*ziran* 自然) of the world around us.

But significantly, this "transformation-of-things" processual cosmology is not just Daoistic; it is pervasive in the tradition, and is the background against which the mainstream Confucian thinkers must also be understood. Even the practical Confucius has a cosmological moment in which he muses about the flux and flow of life: "The Master was standing on the riverbank, and observed, 'Isn't life's passing just like this, never ceasing day or night!'"[11]

Kwong-loi Shun, in the preamble to his discussion of the references to *qi* in the *Mencius*, rehearses passages from the *Zuozhuan* and *Guoyu* that expound upon *qi* as the vital energies making up and activating the natural world around us.[12] In the discourses in which Mencius invokes *qi,* he is not waxing mystical;[13] on the contrary, he is making explicit what for classical China is common sense. A *qi* world view might be considered the classical Chinese analogue of unannounced genetic and molecular assumptions that inform our everyday.

Mencius himself interprets the field of *qi* in terms of moral energy and offers advice on the attainment of human excellence. He speaks of his ability to nourish his "flood-like *qi* (*haoran zhi qi* 浩 然 之氣), describing this *qi* as that which is "most vast" (*zhida* 至 大) and "most firm" (*zhigang* 至 剛) (2A2). Restated in focus-field language, he is saying that his "flood-like *qi*" has the greatest "extensive" and "intensive" magnitude. This language of "extensive field" and "intensive focus" prompts us to understand Mencius as saying that one nourishes one's *qi* most successfully by making of oneself the most intense focus of the most extensive field of *qi*. In this manner, one gains greatest virtue (excellence, potency) in relation to the most far-reaching elements of one's environs:

Everything is here in me. There is no joy greater than to discover integrity (*cheng* 誠) in oneself and nothing easier in striving to be authoritative in one's conduct (*ren* 仁) than treating others as you would be treated yourself (7A4).

The meaning of this familiar passage from the *Mencius* is that "all things are in me and I am with, and in, all things." Integrity (*cheng* 誠) in a processual world, far from being discrete, is also integrative: what John Dewey might call the "doing and undergoing" within a radically situated experience. This sense of integration is reinforced explicitly by appeal to the correlative *ren* 仁 notion of "self." Recalling the meaning of *qi* as a continuous field, a better rendition might be "The field of *qi* is focused by me, and thus all *qi* is here in me."

THE PHILOSOPHICAL IMPLICATIONS OF A PROCESSUAL (*WUHUA*) COSMOLOGY

There is a coherence to the processual (*wuhua*) cosmology that can be captured in a series of mutually entailing summary propositions that are, for this world view, commonsensical, and which might serve us as a philosophical touchstone when interpreting the early literature.[14]

1. The priority of process and change over form and stasis: the "moving line" (*dao* 道) rather than "metaphysics."
2. The priority of situation over agency.
3. Paronomasia rather than literal language: definition by association (no strict, essential identity).
4. A way rather than the truth, "know-how" over "know-what": no final vocabulary.
5. Harmony and resonance rather than teleology and linear causation.
6. Events rather than things: overlapping radial centers rather than fixed boundaries.
7. Focus and field relations rather than part/ whole.
8. Intrinsic, constitutive relations rather than extrinsic, exclusive relations.
9. The underdeterminacy (*ji* 幾) and self-reconstruing (*ziran* 自然) of order.

10. "This world" inclusive correlativity rather than "two world" exclusive dualisms: no strict transcendence (*chaojue* 超絕): correlative clusters rather than essential categories.
11. Continuity between nurture and nature, between the human and the natural.
12. The uniqueness and omnipresence of particularity: no view from nowhere.
13. Cosmology rather than ontology: no reality/ appearance distinction.
14. A *wanwu* 萬物 "One-is-many" rather than a "One-many" cosmology: no reductionism.

Humans and Animals in the Transformation of Things

It is within this processual *wuhua* cosmology so defined that we have to locate the question of the status of animals in classical China. Roel Sterckx has been doing extensive research on the correlation between human society and the natural world, taking as his main focus the perceived relationship between humans and animals in ancient China. His insights are instructive and corroborative:

An important consequence of the incorporation of humans as a functional group within an overarching reality, rather than as an essential category that was ontologically differentiated from everything nonhuman, was the absence of a linear notion that perceived the living world as a hierarchy of more or less developed species. At least on the basis of biology, correlative models did not position human beings as the most developed specimens at the apex of an evolutionary progression; neither were humans differentiated on the basis of superior or inferior physical features or ontological properties innate or unique to their species. Instead the human animal was categorized by its functional properties in correlation with other creatures and the cosmos at large. Early Chinese categories, or "groups of beings that resemble each other" (*lei* 類), were rarely identified by appealing to "a shared essence or 'natural kinds,' but by a functional similarity or relationship that obtains among unique particulars." Herein lies a fundamental difference with the Aristotelian perception of animals for Aristotle saw animals as part of a hierarchy of existence in a scale of perfection with man at the top.[15]

As we might anticipate, given the processual *wuhua* cosmology and its *qi* fluidity, the line demarcating and separating out minerals, plants, animals, humans, cultural heroes, and local gods is porous and permeable. Sterckx's thesis is that early Chinese texts portray the animal realm as a constituent part of an organic whole in which the mutual relationships among the various species were characterized as contingent, continuous, and interdependent. Indeed, the conduct of one dimension of this integrated world has a direct influence on the well-being of the others. As a familiar example, in the *Huainanzi* we read that when the human world is able to effect proper order by operating in partnership with the forces of transformation, it stimulates a thriving natural environment:

> The two kings, the Tai Huang and the Gu Huang,
> Got hold of the handle of *dao*
> And stood at the center.
> In spirit they roamed together with the demiurge of transformation
> To bring peace to the world.

Hence (working the handles of *dao*), they can

> … Move like the heavens and stay still like the earth.
> Turning like a wheel without flagging,
> Flowing like water without cease,
> They begin and end at the same time as the myriad things.
> Just as when the wind rises, the clouds steam forth,

> There was nothing to which they did not respond;
> Just as when the thunder crashes, the rain falls,
> They are never at a loss in their response.
> Ghosts appear, gods disappear,
> Dragons fly away, phoenixes alight.
> Like the potter's wheel spinning, like the hub whirling,
> Going full circle they start going round again …
> Their *de* embraced the heavens and the earth
> and brought harmony to the *yin* and the *yang*,
> Ordered the four seasons and regulated the five phases.
> Brooding over things and nurturing them,
> The myriad things in all of their variety were produced.
> They provided moistening nourishment to the grasses and trees
> And penetrated the minerals and rocks.
> The birds and beasts grew large and tall
> With coats glossy and sleek,
> Wings sprouting out and horns growing,
> Animals did not miscarry and birds did not lay addled eggs,
> Fathers were spared the suffering of mourning their sons and elder brothers were spared the grief of weeping over the younger ones,
> Children were not orphaned
> Nor were wives widowed,
> Evil confluences of the *yin* and the *yang* did not appear
> Nor did ominous celestial portents occur.
> This all came of the *de* they harbored within.[16]

While this resonating interdependence (*ganying* 感應) among worlds is a much advertised feature of the early Chinese world view, it is the actual interpenetrating of these realms that makes the *wuhua* cosmology far more radical than simply synergy or symbiosis. Much of the mythological literature is populated with creatures in which human and animal identities are unstable, with one form assimilating elements from the other.[17]

For example, many of the figures of Chinese cultural mythology are depicted as being part animal and part human, and as defying any final distinction between humans and gods. Nu Wa 女媧 is human with a serpentine lower body, and Fu Xi 伏羲, her consort, is depicted with hybrid animalian features. The *Shanhaijing* 山海經 is a layered and agglomerated text that has been as difficult to classify as the plethora of miraculous beings that it locates across the landscape of the Chinese world.[18] Both the text and its contents are an object lesson in the blending of categories:

> In the mountains, there is a wild beast like the cow, except with a white tail, that makes a sound like a human shout. It is named the *nafu* 那父. A bird similar to the female ringed pheasant lives here, except it has a human face. When it sees a human being, it hops about. It is named the *songsi* 竦斯 ("be alarmed at this"), and its call is its own name.[19]

Perhaps emblematic of this fluid continuum that spans the animal, human, and spiritual realms is the *long* 龍, conventionally (but indeed unfortunately) translated "dragon."[20] John Hay has tallied the number of entries that begin with *long* in the *Chinese Comprehensive Dictionary* (*Zhongguo dazidian*) at 778, concluding that if we were to read and understand these entries, they would "take us on a remarkably comprehensive tour of Chinese thought and history."[21]

The *long* is one version of the "moving line" (*dao* 道) which, as an alternative to metaphysical sensibilities, sets the cultural horizons within the classical Chinese world view. Now undulating, sprawling, wriggling, coiling, spiraling, thrusting, and ultimately soaring through the clouds, this embodied moving line captures the notions of both center and unrestricted transformation across the axes of time, space, and light. Appearing as an object of reverence on the oracle bones, and as decoration on every kind of artifact from the earliest times, the *long* is an image that dominates Chinese cosmology: the ubiquitous moving line that frames cultural horizons. Over time, this snake-like figure, now swallowing creatures whole, now shedding its skin, has assimilated the features of "every animal" to become the generative and transformative symbol of Chinese culture.

In fact, an immediate correlation can be made between the *long* and "China" itself. While it is a commonplace in most introductory text books to translate *zhongguo* 中國 as "the Middle Kingdom," in fact this term is attested in pre-imperial literature to mean "the states of the central plains;" that is, *zhongguo* means centered diversity rather than unity. Tu Wei-ming sees this *long* as a symbol of the process of cultural accumulation and integration that reflects this diversity:

> The assumption that Chinese civilization began in a core area, the Wei valley of the Yellow River, and then radiated outward to cover the area of present-day China has been seriously challenged by recent archaeological discoveries. The thesis that China came into being through the gradual interaction of several comparable Neolithic civilizations (from Painted Pottery and Black Pottery to the Bronze Age) seems to have more persuasive power. ... As a composite totem, the dragon possesses at least the head of a tiger, the horns of a ram, the body of a snake, the claws of an eagle and the scales of a fish. Its ability to cross totemic boundaries and its lack of verisimilitude to any living creature strongly suggest that from the very beginning the dragon was a deliberate cultural construction. The danger of anachronism not withstanding, the modern Chinese ethnic self-definition as the "dragon race" indicates a deep-rooted sense that Chineseness may derive from many sources.[22]

There is some contemporary scholarship fortified by the accumulating archaeological evidence that disputes the "totemic" explanation of the *long* that was made popular in this century by Wen Yiduo 聞一多 and others. The argument is that, although the cumulative animal can be attested from the earliest finds, no evidence of the separate animal emblems has emerged to support the notion that independent tribes participated in a historical process of cultural convergence and assimilation.[23] Still, that this *long* creature, etched and sculpted everywhere and every way, is a pervasive symbol of the aggregation and diversity of China's early culture is compelling, and does not stand or fall with a totem theory that, while not yet proven, has not yet been disproven either. The *long* icon stretches back across history to represent fluidity, diversity, and inclusivity—the porousness and absorbency of the Chinese polity and its culture.

Again, the *long* cuts across the categories of animals, humans, and gods. There are several nonexclusive explanations of the meaning of *long* on the oracle bones: a posthumous name for the Shang ancestors, the name of a territory, the name of a particular spirit or god, and a symbol of pending disaster. It is a spiritual creature—an animalistic medium—to whom prayers are offered in the expectation that it will mediate the human realm and the forces of nature.[24]

Given the entrenched ambiguity that attends any attempt to separate out the animal and human worlds, and given the anticipation in the *wuhua* cosmology that one order of existence gives way to another in the ongoing flux and flow of transformation, the expectation is that human beings would treat their natural environs with compassion and respect. And, as we have seen, this does seem to be characteristic of the deferential Daoist sensibility that advocates an appreciation of the "parity obtaining among all things" (*qiwulun* 齊物論). But such a sense of parity is decidedly uncharacteristic of the Confucian sensibility. On the contrary, for the high-minded and sometimes sanctimonious Mencius:

> The attitude of exemplary persons (*junzi* 君子) to animals is this: having seen them alive, they cannot endure seeing them die; hearing their cries, they cannot bear eating their meat. It is for this reason that exemplary persons stay out of the kitchen.[25]

Cultural Elitism

As we have seen, for Mencius one nourishes one's moral *qi* most successfully by making of oneself the most intense focus of the most extensive field of *qi*. Most of the terms invoked to describe Confucian self-actualization connote this process of growth and extension explicitly. For example, as we have seen, productive familial relations are the "root" (*ben* 本) whence one's way (*dao* 道) advances.[26] The repeated contrast between exemplary persons (*junzi* 君子) and petty persons (*xiaoren* 小人), the inclusiveness of appropriateness (*yi* 義) as opposed to the exclusiveness of personal benefit (*li* 利), and the emergence of the relationally defined authoritative person (*ren* 仁) from individuated persons (*ren* 人) and from the common masses (*min* 民)—all of these expressions entail growth and extension through patterns of deference. Even the term "spirituality" *shen* (神) crosses the divide between "human spirituality" and "divinity," between "human clairvoyance" and the "mysteries."[27] *Shen* 神 is itself cognate with and defined paronomastically as "to extend, to prolong" (*shen* 申 and 伸); "exemplary person" (*jun* 君) is "to assemble" (*qun* 群); "excellence" (*de* 德) is "to get" (*de* 得); and so on.

The metaphors used to describe those ancestors and cultural heroes who have become "god-like" are frequently celestial—"the sun and moon," "the heavens," "the north star," and so on, expressing in a figurative way the familiar assumption that there is a "continuity between the human being and the ancestral realm (*tian-ren heyi* 天人合一)." For example,

> Zhongni (Confucius) ... is comparable to the heavens and the earth, sheltering and supporting everything that is. He is comparable to the progress of the four seasons, and the alternating brightness of the sun and moon.[28]

The intensity and influence of such personal growth is the measure of the human experience, and ultimately it is this creative elaboration of persons within a communal narrative that is productive of religious experience itself.

Elsewhere I have argued against the popular "essentialist" interpretation of Mencius' notion of *renxing* 人性 precisely because it overrides the processional natural cosmology in which the Chinese text is located.[29] The tendency of philosophy to reify human nature and assume it to be ready-made is challenged by a historicist understanding of human nature as a growth process, the ongoing aggregation of desirable human experience. The basis of community is not a metaphysically identical, ready-made mind, but rather a "functional" or "instrumental" inchoate heart-mind (*xin*) expressed in the language of initial relations (*siduan* 四端) which, through social transactions and communication, produces the aims, beliefs, aspirations, and knowledge necessary to establish the like-mindedness of effective community. Human realization is achieved not by whole-hearted participation in communal life forms, but by life in community that forms one whole-heartedly.

There is a correlate to this interpretation of Mencius in the pragmatist John Dewey who, on my reading, shares many philosophical assumptions that resonate with this processual *wuhua* cosmology. Rejecting supernaturalism, theism, absolutism, metaphysical idealism, and the psychologization of human nature, Dewey insists:

> Individuality is a distinctive way of feeling the impacts of the world and of showing a preferen-

tial bias in response to these impacts, it develops into shape and form only through interaction with actual conditions; it is no more complete in itself than is a painter's tube of paint without relations to a canvas.[30]

If a historicist and process interpretation of Mencius has to be argued for, such a reading of Xunzi does not. The idea that it is participation in community that forms one "wholeheartedly" is consistent with D.C. Lau's uncontroversial assessment of Xunzi in which he insists that the moral heart-mind is indeed a human artifact: "For Hsun Tzu [Xunzi] morality is purely an artificial way of behaviour.... Morality is a possible solution to the problem of human conflict but it forms no part of original human nature."[31]

Xunzi's account of the historical construction of the human heart-mind can be recounted rather simply: He begins from a concept of a nonpurposive natural world that is indifferent to human values. Within such a world, the initial conditions of the human being are basically self-regarding emotions and desires that are spontaneous and unlearned. It is specifically these spontaneous instincts that Xunzi chooses to call *renxing* 人性. Logically speaking, such instincts are neither good nor evil; they just are. It is only after human beings have transformed their experience through conscious activity that morality emerges, and it is only *post hoc* that what human beings "were" in their natural state can be deemed "unseemly" and "inefficacious" (*e* 惡).

While human beings do not have the moral heart-mind as standard issue, they do have the capacity to learn through effort and deliberation. This capacity to learn, articulated in terms of "appropriateness" (*yi* 義) and "social discrimination" (*fen*)," is what enables a person to be transformed.[32] While such a capacity is described as distinctively human and thus distinguishes the human from the animal, it is not a self-activating disposition, and thus on Xunzi's terms, is not *renxing*. In the absence of the stimulation of deliberate effort and accumulated education, this capacity would remain latent and undeveloped. An analogy might be that, in retrospect, we can say that the human being has the capacity to build contemporary modern cities with all of their technologies, but without the effort and accumulation of knowledge that made this possible, the human being is just a cave dweller.

Li Zehou and the "Sedimentation" of the Moral Mind

Perhaps a restatement of Xunzi's position in a more contemporary idiom might put a more persuasive spin on this understanding of both human beings and their creativity. I want to make two points here. First, there is enormous consonance between Li Zehou's position and that of Xunzi. Secondly, consistent with the Confucian tradition itself, it is the magnitude of the compounding human transformation that both Xunzi and Li Zehou (in spite of his concern about voluntarism) want to emphasize.

The Kantian scholar, Li Zehou, is one of China's most prominent social critics. Work being done by several contemporary interpretive scholars—particularly Woei Lien Chong (莊愛蓮) and Gu Xin (顧昕) at Leiden—is a recognition of Li Zehou's stature and the maturity of his thought. Woei Lien Chong demonstrates specifically how Li's commentary on Kant is an integral and foundational element in his rejection of Maoist voluntarism—the idea that the power of the human will can accomplish all things.[33] According to Li Zehou, Mao's voluntarism is not new, but emerges out of and is consistent with a traditional Confucian position that human realization lies with the transformative powers of the unmediated moral will. It is the unbridled confidence in the moral will—a belief that translates readily into ideologically driven mass mobilization campaigns—that has been responsible for China's contemporary crises, from Western colonialization down

to the Great Leap Forward and the Cultural Revolution.

The argument, simply put, is that Chinese philosophers from classical times have recognized a continuity between human beings and their natural environments. The nature of this continuity, however, has often been misunderstood, to the detriment of the natural sciences. Instead of being a continuity between subject and object, respecting both the ability of the collective human community to transform its environment productively, *and* the resistance of the natural world to this human transformation, it has been dominated by the belief that the moral subject holds absolute transformative powers over an infinitely malleable natural world. It violates its own premises in its tendency to become a kind of raw subjectivism, which discounts the need for collective human efforts in science and technology to "humanize" nature and establish a productive relationship between subject and object, a relationship that Li Zehou takes to be a precondition for human freedom.

Where does Kant come in? Li Zehou sees Kant as confronting a problem similar to contemporary Chinese intellectuals: how can "deterministic" scientific progress and its political expression, totalitarian socialism, be reconciled with human freedom? For Kant's world, it was the reconciliation of mechanistic Newtonian science, Church dogma, and Leibnizian rationalism on the one hand, and Rousseauean humanism on the other.

Kant's epistemic move is to claim that the forms and categories of science do not exist independently of the human being, but constitute an *active* structure of the human mind. This *a priori* structure of the mind acts to synthesize our experiences and to construct our world of scientific understanding. Hence, scientific understanding, far from contradicting the possibility of human freedom, is an expression of it.

Li Zehou appropriates this notion of "categories" of human understanding from Kant, but attempts to "sinocize" this structure by historicizing and particularizing it.[34] How so? First, China, *contra* the passive Marxian "mirror" conception of mind, has traditionally embraced a resolutely active notion of heart-mind (*xin* 心) as expressed in the performative force of knowledge. Li extends this assumption by offering a theory of "sedimentation" (*jidian* 積澱) — "the form of the human cultural psychology (*wenhua xinli jiegou* 文化心理結構) — that is synchronic, diachronic, and evolutionary. The structure of human understanding — Li Zehou actually prefers the more processional "formation" for *jiegou* — is not an *a priori* given, but dynamic — a function of shared human experience that is historically and culturally specific. As human beings have transformed their shared environment, the transformed environment has shaped their categories of understanding.

Sedimentation is the accumulation of a contingent social memory, underscoring the power of the collective community, through which each individual human being is socialized and enculturated. As Wei Lien Chong observes, it begins at the level of the human species through the designing and making of tools:

> The process of the "humanization of nature" (*ziran de renhua* 自然的人化) works in two ways: mankind humanizes external nature in the sense of making it a place fit for human beings to live in, and at the same time, by this very activity, it humanizes its own physical and mental constitution by becoming increasingly de-animalized and adapted to life in organized society.[35]

The argument moves from the human being as a species to specific cultural sites and experiences when Li Zehou insists that Chinese scholars must look to their own traditional resources in shaping a vision for China's future. Chong summarizes her conversations with Li Zehou in the following terms:

> When it comes to cultural regeneration, in Li's view, the Chinese should go back to their own

heritage rather than start from premises derived from Western worldviews, such as Christianity, liberalism, and Freudianism. ... These Western premises, Li holds, cannot take root in the collective Chinese consciousness, which is based on entirely different foundations.[36]

Jane Cauvel summarizes not two, but three dimensions of sedimentation in her examination of Li Zehou's philosophy of art:

> We all have what we might call a "species sedimentation," (those mental forms common to all human beings), and we also have a "cultural sedimentation," (those ways of thinking and feeling common to our culture), as well as a "subjective sedimentation," (those ways of looking at the world built up from our own individual life experiences).[37]

Li Zehou, with his theory of sedimentation, is, like Kant, able to reconcile causal science and human freedom, but in a way that, from the Chinese perspective, resists Kantian imperialism. What begins early in Li's career as Kantian commentary becomes a turn in Chinese philosophy consistent with underlying premises of the Confucian tradition, releasing the dragon and imbuing it with new energy to continue on, undeterred. The Kantian categories, far from providing a basis for discovering universal claims, becomes a dynamic process for formulating and respecting cultural differences. This is a signal of Li Zehou's continuing commitment to the aestheticism of the Confucian tradition in his belief that the highest form of cultural sedimentation is expressed as human creativity, as art.

The Human Being as a Member of the Triad

What is distinctive about the Confucian texts is that, while sharing a *wuhua* cosmology with the Daoistic literature, rather than embracing the notion of "the parity of all things," they promote a cosmic hierarchy in which a high premium is placed on the cultivated human experience. In the absence of some notion of transcendent deity as the creative source of truth, beauty, and goodness, the burden of creativity falls to the human world. Thus, the value invested in the human transformation effected through moral education and enculturation is enormous. Mencius states flatly that "what makes the human being different from the birds and beasts is ever so slight" (*jixi* 幾希).[38] But the magnitude of the transformation effected through education moves the human being up the ladder from erstwhile animal to god:

> The desirable is called "efficacious" (*shan* 善). Having this efficacy in oneself is called "being credible" (*xin* 信), and to have it in full proportion is called "beauty" (*mei* 美). To have it in full proportion and to radiate it all around is called being "extensive" (*da* 大). Being extensive and being transformed by it is called being "sagely" (*sheng* 聖). And being sagely, to be beyond the understanding of others is called "divine" (*shen* 神).[39]

The *Mencius* is not alone in its elevation of the human being to divine status. In the *Zhongyong*, human creativity expressed as "focusing the familiar in the ordinary affairs of the day" (*zhongyong* 中庸) gives the human being the status of becoming complement to the powers of nature (*pei tian* 配天):[40]

> only if one is able to get the most out of the natural tendencies of processes and events can one assist in the transforming and nourishing activities of heaven and earth; and only if one can assist in the transforming and nourishing activities of heaven and earth can one take one's place as a member of this triad.[41]

The *Xunzi* also sees the human capacity for "growth" and "extension" as lifting a person out of a very ordinary existence to become a cosmic partner with heaven and earth:

> Now were common persons on the street to take on these methods as the object of study, focus heart and soul on this one purpose, put thought and energy into the inquiry over an extended period of time, and were they to build up a record of effective conduct without respite, such persons could commune with the gods and spirits and take their place as a triad with heaven and earth.[42]

For the Confucian, and for Xunzi (and Li Zehou) in particular, enculturation transforms bird tracks and the markings on the backs of turtles into calligraphy and the *Book of Songs*, random copulation into love and family, feeding into fine dining and tea ceremony, raw sense data into inspiration and aesthetic feeling, and inchoate interpersonal relations into a flourishing community and the profound religious sensibilities that such communion fosters.

Such high expectations of the human experience have produced an a-theistic Confucian cultural elitism that elevates the *cultivated* human being to what Tu Wei-ming has called "anthropocosmic" proportions.[43] From such a lofty vantage, this human being, unconstrained by the limiting assumptions of religious transcendentalism and supernaturalism, becomes the meaning of the world. The downside, of course, is that life without cultivation, human or otherwise, is by contrast bestial, benighted, and base.

It is this elevation of the human being in Confucian "cultural elitism" that, on comparison with "human exceptionalism" prevalent in the West, makes the choice between them a case of "three in the morning, four at night."[44]

NOTES

1. See James Rachels' entry on "Animals and Ethics," in *Routledge Encyclopedia of Philosophy*, edited by Edward Craig (London: Routledge, 1998).

2. See Deanna Donovan, "Strapped for Cash, Asians Plunder their Forests and Endanger their Future," in *Asia Pacific Issues: Analysis from the East-West Center*, no. 39, April 1999.

3. Judith Farquhar, *Knowing Practice: The Clinical Encounter of Chinese Medicine* (Boulder, CO: Westview, 1994), p. 34.

4. David Keightley, "Shang Divination and Metaphysics," in *Philosophy East and West 38* (1988): 367–97.

5. John Major, *Heaven and Earth in Early Han Thought* (Albany: State University of New York Press, 1993).

6. *Chuang Tzu* [*Zhuangzi*] in Harvard-Yenching Institute Sinological Index Series, Supplement 20 (Peking: Harvard-Yenching, 1947), 5/2/40; cf. A.C. Graham (trans.) (1981), *Chuang-tzu: The Inner Chapters* (London: George Allen & Unwin, 1981), p. 54, and Burton Watson trans., *The Complete Works of Chuang Tzu* (New York: Columbia University Press, 1968), p. 40.

7. *Chuang Tzu* [*Zhuangzi*] 17/6/53; compare Graham *Chuang-tzu*, p. 88.

8. Ibid., 17/6/46; compare Graham *Chuang-tzu*, p. 87.

9. Kang Yunmei 康韻梅 *Zhongguo gudai siwangguan zhi tanjiu* 中國古代死亡觀之探究 (*An Exploration of the Ancient Chinese View of Death*), (Taipei: National Taiwan University History and Chinese Literature Series No. 85, 1994), pp. 21–22.

10. *Chuang Tzu* [*Zhuangzi*] 47/18/40; cf. Graham *Chuang-tzu*, p 184.

11. *Analects* 9.17.

12. Kwong-loi Shun, *Mencius and Early Chinese Thought* (Stanford: Stanford University Press, 1997), pp. 67–68.

13. Chad Hansen is familiar voice among commentators who would describe Mencius on *qi* as a "moral mysticism." See *A Daoist Theory of Chinese Thought* (Hong Kong: Oxford University Press, 1992), p. 175.

14. David Hall and I have elaborated upon many of these propositions in our interpretive studies of classical Chinese philosophy, especially *Thinking from the Han: Self, Truth, and Transcendence in Chinese and Western Culture* (Albany: SUNY Press, 1998) and *Anticipating China: Thinking through the Narratives of Chinese and Western Culture* (Albany: SUNY Press, 1995).

15. Roel Sterckx, *The Animal and the Daemon in Early China* (Albany: SUNY Press, 2000), p. 81, citing Hall and Ames, *Anticipating China*, p. 253.

16. D.C. Lau and Roger T. Ames, *Yuan Dao: Tracing Dao to Its Source* (New York: Ballantine, 1998), pp. 63–65.

17. The pervasiveness of this assumption is underscored by the fact that John Major finds an exception "unique in early Chinese literature" in the technical chapters of the *Huainanzi*, which contain systematic evolutionary schemes using the five phases as a model. See Major *Heaven and Earth in Early Han Thought*, pp. 210–12.

18. Ricardo Fracasso in his entry on "*Shan hai ching* [*jing*]" in Michael Loewe, ed., *Early Chinese Texts: A Bibliographical Guide* (Berkeley: The Institute of East Asian Studies, 1993), pp. 357–67, elaborates on the controversy surrounding this text. As we would expect in the early Han it is highly esteemed as "a handbook on prodigies," while in later Han it is regarded as "a reliable geographical text." "In recent times the work has been described variously as 'a traveller's guide' .. ; a 'geographical gazetteer' . . ; a 'record of exploration' .. ; a 'shamanic text' .. ; the 'secret records of Ch'in [Qin] and Han *fang shih* [shi] 方士 ..." (p. 358–59).

19. Zhang Yanyun 張艷云 and Qin Yun 秦云 (trans). *Baihua Shanhaijing* 白話山海經 (Xi'an: Sanqin Publishers, 1997), pp. 66–67.

20. A caution is needed here. To translate this icon as "dragon" as is conventionally done reflects the difficulties encountered in cultural translation, *long* needing as it does to be clearly distinguished from its Anglo-Saxon cousin that met a proper end "under the Christian foot of St. George." See John Hay, "The Persistent Dragon" in W. Peterson,

A. Plaks, and Y.S. Shih, eds., *The Power of Culture* (Hong Kong: Chinese University Press, 1994), p. 120.

21. Hay, "Persistent Dragon," p. 121.

22. "Chinese Philosophy: A Synopsis" in Eliot Deutsch and Ron Bontekoe, eds., *A Companion to World Philosophies* (Oxford: Blackwell, 1997), p. 4.

23. Liu Zhixiong 劉志雄 and Yang Jingrong 楊靜榮, *Long yu zhongguo wenhua* 龍與中國文化 (Peking: Peoples Press, 1992), pp. 1–6.

24. Ibid., pp. 8–10.

25. *Mencius* 1A7.

26. *Analects* 1.2; see also *Zhongyong* 1, 29, 32, and especially 17.

27. Many if not most definitions of *shen* proffered in classical corpus that preclude any severe distinction between humanity and divinity.

28. *Zhongyong* 30. See also *Analects* 2.1, 19.21, 23, 24, 25.

29. See "The Mencian Conception of *renxing* 人性: Does it Mean 'Human Nature'?" in Henry Rosemont, ed., *Chinese Texts and Philosophical Contexts: Essays Dedicated to Angus C. Graham* (La Salle: Open Court, 1991), and "Mencius and a Process Notion of Human Nature" in Alan K.L. Chan, ed., *Mencius: Contexts and Interpretations* (Honolulu: University of Hawaii Press 2002).

30. John Dewey, *The Political Writings,* eds. D. Morris and I. Shapiro (Indianapolis: Hackett, 1993), p. 87.

31. D. Lau, *Mencius* Volume One (Hong Kong: Chinese University Press, 1984), p. xx.

32. *Hsun Tzu* [*Xunzi*], Harvard-Yenching Institute Sinological Series, Supplement 22, (Peking: Harvard-Yenching, 1950), 28–29/9/69–73.

33. I am indebted here to Woei Lien Chong's article, "Mankind and Nature in Chinese Thought: Li Zehou on the Traditional Roots of Maoist Voluntarism" in *China Information* vol. 11, nos. 2/3 (Autumn/Winter, 1996), and also to the responses to Chong's work by Li Zehou and Jane Cauvel that have appeared in a special issue of *Philosophy East & West* vol. 49, no. 2 (April, 1999) guest edited by Tim Cheek. For a bibliography of recent scholarship on Li Zehou, see Chong (1996), pp. 142–43 note 12 and Chong (1999), pp. 148–49.

34. Li Zehou's reading calls to mind Clarence Irving Lewis's "pragmatic" reading of Kant. See his attempt to repudiate idealism with the notion of the "pragmatic" *a priori* in "The Given Element of Experience" in *Mind and the World Order* (reprint: New York: Dover, 1956; first published, 1929).

35. Chong, "Mankind and Nature," p. 150.

36. Ibid., p. 141.

37. Jane Cauvel, "The Transformative Power of Art: Li Zehou's Aesthetic Theory" in *Philosophy East and West* 49, no. 2 (1999): 158.

38. *Mencius* 4B19.

39. Ibid., 7B25.

40. *Zhongyong* 31.

41. Ibid., 22. See also 23 and 24.

42. *Hsun Tzu* [*Xunzi*] 89/23/69.

43. See Tu Wei-ming, *Centrality and Commonality: An Essay on Confucian Religiousness,* (Albany: State University of New York Press, 1989), pp. 106–7.

44. This saying in modern Chinese is an allusion to a story in the *Chuang Tzu* (*Zhuangzi*) 5/2/38 in which irate monkeys that have been told that they will receive three nuts in the morning and four at night are delighted when they are told that they will instead receive four nuts in the morning and three at night. In other words, "six of one, half a dozen of the other."

Humans and Animals

The History from a Religio-Ecological Perspective

JORDAN PAPER

Two essays in this volume—Roger T. Ames's "Human Exceptionalism versus Cultural Elitism: 'Three in the morning, four at night'" and Gary Steiner's "Descartes, Christianity, and Contemporary Speciesism"—in examining the ideological bases to the relationships between humans and animals, demonstrate considerable commonalities in classical Chinese and European philosophical and religious understandings. Ames discusses the Chinese conception of cultural elitism, which presumes that the achievement of culture provides humans with a privileged relationship vis-à-vis animals. Steiner examines the Greek and Classical influences on Descartes for the development of his influential understanding of animals as essentially machines, a view now termed "speciesism." For Descartes, humans have no moral obligations toward animals. Ames terms this understanding "human exceptionalism," a concept of animals that primarily perceives them as resources for human use.

The Chinese perception slightly differs from the above Western philosophical one in that animals are not understood as entirely devoid of feelings, nor is there an absolute ethical disjunction between humans relating to humans and humans relating to animals. For example, prior to the importation of New Zealand beef into Taiwan in the late 1960s, many Chinese there did not eat beef. The beef available was from water buffalo and oxen that were past their working years as draft animals, and there was a widespread feeling that it was unethical to kill the animals for food after they had devoted their lives working for humans. Besides, this beef was extremely tough. But many in the West also do not fully hold to the philosophical and religious disjunction between humans and animals and, as the Chinese, do impart some understanding of feelings to animals. Given that the similar, although not identical, understandings of the relationship between humans and animals in the West and China arise from radically different, in part diametrically opposed, religious and philosophical conceptions, detailed by Ames and Steiner in their essays, it seems that the causative factors for these perceived relationships must be found elsewhere.

Ritual studies and related recent modes of religious studies tend to understand formalized ideology to be informed by religious practices and behaviors rather than vice versa. From these methodological perspectives, cultural perceptions of the relationships between humans and animals are determined by nonideological factors. These cultural perceptions in turn influence developments in ideology to account for these cultural features. For this reason, common understandings and practices can be found in cultures with vastly different ideological underpinnings when the fundamental nonideological motivating factors are similar. In other words, cultures that share religio-ecological niches, as we shall see, tend to have a number of similarities, including the relationship between humans and animals, regardless of whether or not their ideologies are similar or differ.

For example, the seventeenth-century Europe of Descartes, the subject of Steiner's essay, and the sixth to third century BCE China of Kongzi (Confucius), Mengzi (Mencius), and Xunzi, whose views are analyzed by Ames, have a number of socioeconomic features in common.[1] Their economies were based on agriculture, although mercantilism was becoming of major importance. Their societies had been divided between a hereditary nobility and a farming peasantry, but an expanding lower middle class of artisans and upper middle class of wealthy merchants was beginning to complicate the social matrix. Both cultures were divided into nation-states ruled by kings in political situations that were becoming increasingly unstable. The multiple Chinese kingdoms would be replaced by a single imperial government, and Europe would be racked by attempts at military unification and changing modes of government. Of particular importance with regard to the common functional understandings of the relationship between humans and animals is agriculture. A brief outline of cultural evolution in this regard from a religio-ecological perspective can account for these commonalities. (It should be understood that evolution here simply means development, without any implication that what develops is better than what is replaced).

Religio-Ecological Paradigms

Among contemporary humans that still maintain gathering-hunting cultural traditions, the entire cosmos is understood to be numinous, including animals and plants, particularly those on which human life, in various ways, depends. These understandings may, to a degree, be read back into the earliest human cultures, as they accord with paleolithic art in their representation of animals and, rarely, humans. Such cultures understand that the world is a family in which humans are inferior members. Every encounter with a nonhuman being is with an entity that is simultaneously a natural being and a spiritual being.[2] Sought-after animals and plants, gifts of the Earth Mother, in various guises, must be supplicated to offer their individual lives so that pitiable humans may live.[3] Every act of hunting larger animals, as well as gathering plants, sea creatures, and smaller animals is ritualized. Predatory animals are spiritual models for the human hunters, and the dog is a hunting companion, whose sacrifice,[4] as well as that of the human-like bear,[5] is essentially a substitute for human self-sacrifice to the numinous realm. Hence, people in this religio-ecological situation understand a profound communion between themselves and animals, as well as plants.

As plants are domesticated, the gathering-hunting religious understanding of the cosmos continues, but the domesticated plants, understood as daughters of Earth,[6] gain ritual preeminence, as do the roles of females, who primarily carry out the gardening.[7] Those animals that are domesticated are no longer understood to be spiritual entities superior to humans, but are instead seen as members of the human community, ranging from quasi-children to pets, whose every slaughter is a ritual sacrifice.[8] Hunted animals continue to be supplicated and treated as in the gathering-hunting religio-ecological niche. But the shift from semi-nomadism to sedentary living-patterns leads to a closer relationship with the matrilineal-matrilocal family and clan dead, beginning a transition from theriomorphic and plant spirits to anthropomorphic spirits.[9]

Seminomadic gathering-hunting cultures that domesticate migratory herding animals, most recently occurring among reindeer hunters of northern Eurasia, undergo a major shift in the religious conception of the particular animal on which their economy depends. No longer individual numinous entities, the domesticated herds as a whole are understood to be a gift from their female numinous superior. Gifts of sacrificed animals from the herd are in turn offered to Her.[10] The communion is no longer between the humans and animals but between humans and the Mother of the domesticated species. The human hunter shifts to the role of the "good shepherd." Animal predators, no longer spiritual role models for human hunters, become enemies of the herded animals, for whose welfare humans are responsible. As hunting activities shift to herding, those ritual activities associated with shamanism are no longer generalized among the population as an essential aspect of hunting and gathering but become concentrated among ecstatic religious specialists.[11]

The horticultural-hunting religious understanding of animals and plants continues with the rise of agriculture, but there are significant socioeconomic transformations. The majority of males shift from hunting-raiding-trading roles to farming, while females continue their gardening-nurturing roles. With the average male no longer expert with hunting weapons, warrior specialists, supported by surplus agricultural productivity, tend to become the hereditary elite of a stratified social order, and the matrilineal-matrilocal pattern tends to shift toward a patrilineal-patrilocal pattern in consequence of the increased magnitude of the male roles. When warriors become the rulers, this patrifocal pattern tends towards patriarchy. Warriors also become ritual specialists, or a separate caste of female and male priests develops. The spirit realm now consists of ancestors, divinized ghosts, and/or anthropomorphic deities who were not previously human. These deities are understood in hierarchies modeled on the now-stratified human sociopolitical structures. An offshoot of this development, which occurred in one culture, becoming the basis for Western civilization, is for the male chief of the divinities to be considered the sole divinity of the culture, the "king of kings."

With a patrifocal social stratification between elite males who use weapons and the majority of males who wield farming implements, hunting of large animals becomes the prerogative of the elite as ritualized practice for warfare, also ritualized. Hence, undomesticated animals are treated as human enemies. The understanding of animals has become a construction based on political and military scenarios. Domesticated animals continue to be slaughtered solely in sacrificial rituals, but these rituals tend to be carried out by professional ritual specialists who are separated from the raising of the animals, no longer understood as quasi-children. Save for the Abrahamic religions, aristocrats play a major role in these sacrifices, but they distance themselves from the actual slaughtering. The pattern of ritualized slaughter continues in Western culture in the Jewish and Islamic traditions, where all animals to be eaten must be ritually killed by religious specialists.

The concentration of hunting activities among the elite as an avocation serves to create a disjunction among the general populace from the undomesticated world, leading to the concepts of wilderness and wild animals. Cultures now distinguish humans from animals, as well as humans of different cultures, who have come to be understood as "wild" humans or barbarians. Humans relate to wild animals no longer as numinous beings but as savage beasts to be tamed or killed. Spanish culture maintains a version of both these perspectives in the highly ritualized *corrida des toros,* although the modern ritual in itself is not of great antiquity.[12]

With agriculture, the relationship between humans and animals falls into four distinctive categories. For the elite, animals are pets, either playthings or facilitators for human hunting; working domesticants, particularly the horse, used for warfare and hunting, who become romanticized along with warriors toward the ends of these periods; domesticated animals for ritualized consumption; or wild beasts, often found in royal hunting parks, hunted with the same weapons used in warfare. The peasants raise the domesticated animals, ritually slaughtered and eaten by the elite, although peasants but rarely have the opportunity to eat these animals themselves. Peasants, responsible to the elite for the welfare of the domesticated animals, fear the predatory animals and kill them whenever possible. "Game" animals (it is important to notice our language in this regard), reserved for the pleasurable activities of the elite, are forbidden to the peasants, who are liable to be executed if caught hunting them. The middle classes fall somewhere in between, of course, depending on their status.

I have observed that when Italian immigrants in the Toronto area, often in the construction industry, achieve middle-class financial success, many purchase hunting dogs and luxury bird guns to use on private hunting preserves. They are engaging in an activity that remains the mark of elite status in Europe and in which, prior to emigrating, they could not take part.

In the transition from horticulture to agriculture, the understanding of plants changes from revered spiritual relatives to desired entities, whose sole purpose is the nourishment or other use of humans, or to undesired entities, such as weeds, which hinder the growth of the farmed plants. Similarly, animals also change from revered spiritual relatives to entities whose sole purpose is to feed or be of other use to humans, entities that threaten those animals, or entities that can be killed for practice in preparation for warfare. Of course, there are many cultural variations and moderate exceptions to this pattern.

In India, for example, cows became a special case, because of the unusual, virtually exclusive, dependence on them for animal protein (milk and milk products), edible oil (clarified butter), traction (draft animals), and fuel (dried dung). Hence, the concept of cows in India is closer to the understanding of animals in horticulture-hunting traditions than agricultural societies. But India still reserves hunting for the hereditary aristocracy or the new aristocracy modeled on the former British colonizers, save for remnant pockets of horticultural-hunting villages in the interior mountains.

Further changes in socioeconomic structures lead to increasing distance from the earlier human patterns in these relationships. As industrial manufacturing desacralized metals, clay, and wood, so the spread of industry to agriculture led to the desacralizing of Earth, plants, and animals in every regard. It is to be noted that this process begins in Christian culture, which had long since limited the numinous to Sky and understood Earth, as well as human females, to be the locus of evil (the opposite of Heaven is not Earth but Hell, and the doctrine of Original Sin relegates the origin of sin to women). Industrial manufacturing and the spread of industrial practices to agriculture also led to the increasing urbanization of the population, further distancing the average person from an intimacy with domesticated plants and animals, save for pets—who tend to be understood as quasi-humans rather than animals—and flowering plants. Thanks to agribusiness factory production of meat and grain, animals and grain plants are no longer understood as beings, let alone as relatives or gifts from the numinous realm. Undomesticated animals now are neither numinous entities nor respected enemies but anthropomorphized, desacralized fantasies: the "Bambi" syndrome.[13] Human characteristics and a human nature are projected onto animals; hunting and the slaughtering of animals for food can now be understood as murder.

Only among the anachronistic remnants of the European aristocracy or their industrial-era replacements (factory owners, etc.) does hunting continue combined with respect and acknowledgment of a special nature of hunted animals (who cannot be accorded numinous status in monotheistic traditions).[14] Nonurbanized Euroamericans, lacking a hereditary aristocracy, maintain hunting as a ritual of Americanism, which renews their connections with a mythic "pioneer" past and wilderness, upon which is projected a sacred aura of pristine purity.

In the postindustrial world, where virtual reality has replaced normative reality, the traditional real world itself becomes transformed into a realm of fantasy, and experience in nature *qua* nature is replaced by actual and vicarious thrills (e.g., dirt bikes and "personal water craft"). Animals become valued with no understanding of their life-cycles and ecological situations, and they are understood to be utterly divorced from food. Cellophane-wrapped meat tends not to be understood, from either the emotional or the religious standpoint, to come from living animals, just as factory-manufactured, cellophane-wrapped bread or pasta tends not to be understood as coming from living plants. The various traditional ritual relationships with animals and plants completely disappear, to be replaced by concepts of "cuteness"; wild animals are perceived no differently than nonworking pets. Hence, campaigns are mounted against hunting in general, regardless of potential disastrous consequences for noncompetitive herbivores in terrains where natural predators have been exterminated, and hunters can be perceived as the epitome of evil.

Just before the conference at which the initial version of this paper was presented, by chance,[15] I was at Neah Bay when the Makah undertook a whale hunt (May 17–19, 1999—the grey whales had been removed from the endangered species list and the hunt allowed by the International Whaling Commission). The hunt concluded with their taking of a whale, for noncommercial purposes, for the first time in seventy years. For the Makah, the hunt was absolutely essential for a revitalization of their rituals and conception of self-worth. Whale is their major deity, a spirit which offers itself to the Makah so that they may live, not just physically but spiritually.

From the contrary perspective of contemporary Western culture, the hunt was an unjustifiable and intolerable abomination; the Makah hunters had placed themselves outside the bounds of humaneness. Hence, protesters could comfortably shout: "Save the whales; kill the Indians," reminding one of the nineteenth-century Euroamerican adage that "The only good Indian is a dead Indian." Another protester was crying and mumbling that "Indian" culture had to disappear to save the animals. There was no indication that most of the protesters were vegetarians; rather, this was a religious clash between contemporary, secularized Western Christianity and indigenous American religions, continuing a long history of religious intolerance and attempted cultural genocide in the Americas.

The Makah were seeking to reestablish their traditional communion with their deity, Whale. The protestors seemed to have forgotten that Christianity too seeks a communion between humans and a sacrificed deity, a communion celebrated in the Eucharist. The difference is that for the Makah their primary deity is an animal and for Christians, it is a being that is both human and divine.

In a newspaper editorial published less than a week after the event, one finds the statement, "There may have been a time, oh, several hundred years ago, when the Makah needed to kill whales for food and fuel. But now there are alternatives—like McDonald's."[16] Obviously, the statement could not hold if prepackaged, frozen hamburgers were understood to come from living animals.

The distancing of humans from animals, plants, and Earth in postindustrial cultures becomes absolute. Theriomorphic and plant spirits, once replaced by anthropomorphic spirits, for an increasing number of contemporary Westerners in the New Age are now replaced by alien spirits from cosmically distant sacred realms.

Conclusions

For all of these religio-ecological transitions, philosophies and theologies develop to provide an intellectual justification for the slowly changing attitudes and behaviors. For example, we find in the fourth-century BCE *Mengzi*[17] the following passage from a dialogue with King Xuan of Qi on what a king requires in order to unify China under his sway:

[Mengzi said:] I heard [the following story]:

The King was sitting in the upper hall when someone leading a bull passed below. The King seeing this asked, "Where is the bull going?" "[The bull is to be sacrificed] to consecrate a bell." The King said, "Spare it. I cannot endure its trembling with fear, as if it were an innocent person nearing the execution grounds." "So should the consecration of the bell be abandoned?" "How can it be abandoned; replace it with a goat [or sheep]." I wonder if this really happened?

"It did." "Then the King's mind/heart is sufficient to be a king [over all of China]!" [Here follows discussion of the populace interpreting the preceding as a miserly act by the King, given a goat is worth far less than a bull. Mengzi continues,]

This is how benevolence works. You saw the bull but not the goat. The superior person, in regarding birds and animals, having seen them alive, cannot endure their cries, cannot bear to eat their flesh. This is why the superior person keeps away from the slaughterhouse and the kitchen.

Mengzi is politely chiding the king for misplacing an empathy properly belonging to humans to a domestic animal. Moreover, this was a useless gesture, since the sacrifice must take place and so an animal unseen by the king is sacrificed in its stead. Furthermore, being misunderstood by the populace, the act led to a loss of faith in the king's character by his subjects, a political liability. Should the king practically apply his natural empathy to his human subjects, and Mengzi provides in detail essential socioeconomic ramifications, including conservation measures, eventually the king could achieve his goal and conquer all of China.

Now King Xuan of Qi was not a vegetarian; he obviously did not neglect the sacrifices; and he undoubtedly had a royal hunting park. Mengzi clearly assumes a class division, with the lower classes slaughtering and cooking animals for the elite to eat in ritualized sacrificial banquets offered to the protecting ancestral spirits of the aristocratic clans.[18] Such a system distances elite humans from the animal realm, save for their hounds, hawks, and horses. Mengzi assumes a division, not an absolute distinction, between animals and humans, and he takes as a given that attitudes appropriate toward the two should not be confused. Mengzi would also have taken as a given that these elite warriors would hunt as a ritual killing of wild animals, an avocation directly related to their warrior profession. This is the pattern typical of the religio-ecological paradigm of an agricultural economy combined with the political order of kingship. The philosophies/theologies that develop in this paradigm reflect rather than cause the relationship between humans and animals.

Returning to our starting point, the commonalities of Chinese and Western philosophies in these regards, Aristotle and Mengzi, lived in the same century, although 7,500 kilometers apart, in similar religio-ecological circumstances. Aristotle's most famous student, Alexander, initiated a process that led to the eastern Mediterranean world having a degree of cultural homogeneity parallel to that of China from the century following Mengzi. Intellectual homogeneity in Western Europe begins with the introduction of Aristotle's writings into Europe, stimulated by its revival in the Islamic world. As would Descartes, two millennia later, Aristotle and Mengzi served as advisers and/or tutors to kings and other members of a hereditary aristocracy. All three were part of a middle-class intellectual meritocracy who theorized for their peers.

While all three philosophers left their imprint not only on their own time but on ours as well, the relationships between humans and animals were cultural givens which they but reflected. The convergence of their thought in these regards, therefore, is indicative of a profound religio-ecological similarity among their respective cultures. It is the religio-ecological similarity that leads to a common understanding of the relationship between humans and animals, which in turn influences the disparate philosophies of these cultures, leading to a similarity in these particular regards. Thus, we can understand the similar shift in the relationship between humans and animals in different parts of the world from a communion between related beings, to constructed notions of the inferiority, subservience, or enemy nature of animals, and then to the projection of an utterly unreal anthropomorphic personality onto animals. From my own personal perspective, this is not evolution but devolution.

NOTES

1. For China, see Hsü Cho-yun, *Ancient China in Transition: An Analysis of Social Mobility, 722–222 B.C.* (Stanford: Stanford University Press, 1965).

2. There is a long-held view in the scholarly literature that only a sovereign of animal species is numinous. But such an understanding is illogical, if not impossible, for egalitarian cultures, where temporary leadership for specific activities is only nominal and noncompulsive. See Jordan Paper, "The Post-Contact Origin of an American Indian High God: The Suppression of Feminine Spirituality," *American Indian Quarterly* 7, no. 4 (1983): 1–24.

3. For the hunting-gathering understanding of plants, see Kenn Pitawanakwat and Jordan Paper, "Communicating the Intangible: An Anishnaabeg Story," *American Indian Quarterly* 20 (1996): 451–65. The same attitudes and rituals here depicted for plants would apply to animals; see, for example, Joseph Epes Brown, *Animals of the Soul: Sacred Animals of the Oglala Sioux* (Rockport, MA: Element, 1992). For a rudimentary theology of animals in these regards, see Jordan Paper, *Offering Smoke: The Sacred Pipe and Native American Religion* (Moscow, ID: University of Idaho Press, 1988), pp. 57–63. A more developed theology will be found in Jordan Paper, *The Deities Are Many: A Polytheistic Theology* (Albany: State University of New York Press, 2005).

4. See Charles A. Eastman, *Indian Boyhood* (New York: McLuce, Phillips & Co., 1902), pp. 87–96.

5. See A. Irving Halowell, "Bear Ceremonialism in the Northern Hemisphere," *American Anthropologist* 28 (1926): 1–175.

6. Save for tobacco and other substances of non-subsistence but ritual use, which may be linked to Sky rather than Earth.

7. For example, see Michael F. Brown, *Tsewa's Gift: Magic and Meaning in Amazonian Society* (Washington, D.C.: Smithsonian Institution Press, 1985).

8. See Roy A. Rappaport, *Pigs For the Ancestors: Ritual And Ecology in a New Guinean People* (New Haven: Yale University Press, 1968).

9. In gathering-hunting traditions, the dead may be disposed of by burial away from residences or by exposure, but in horticultural-hunting traditions, the tendency is to bury the dead in the vicinity of residences, even under the floors of dwellings. For example, Iroquoian speaking cultures, in precontact times, took the bones of the dead with them when they periodically shifted their villages as the

fertility of their gardens was exhausted. See Bruce G. Trigger, *Natives and Newcomers: Canada's "Heroic Age" Reconsidered* (Montreal: McGill-Queen's Press, 1985).

10. Jordan Paper, *Through the Earth Darkly: Female Spirituality in Comparative Perspective* (New York: Continuum, 1997), p. 20.

11. That specialization, first observed among Siberian reindeer herders by Russian scholars, tends to be incorrectly read back into the gathering-hunting mode. See Jordan Paper, "Sweat Lodge": A Northern Native American Ritual for Communal Shamanic Ritual," *Temenos* 26 (1990): 85–94.

12. See Gary Marvin, *Bullfight* (Urbana: University of Illinois Press, 1994).

13. In the much later Disney animated feature-length film, *The Lion King,* lions seem not to be predators, let alone carnivores.

14. As an example, consider the present, respectful European practice of smoking a cigarette after shooting a game mammal before approaching it, in order to allow the animal time to die in dignified privacy. European elite thought on hunting will be found in José Ortega y Gasset, *Meditations on Hunting,* trans. by H. B. Wescote (New York: Scribner's, 1972).

15. "By chance" is from a Western mode of thinking. From a Native perspective, nothing takes place by chance. My being at Neah Bay, at the furthest northwest reach of the continental United States, before the conference to be able to bear witness at the conference to the Makah understanding was due to the influence of Whale, a powerful numinous being.

16. Paul Sullivan in the *Toronto Globe and Mail,* May 22, 1999.

17. IA7 (book 1, part A, section 7)—translation my own.

18. For a detailed description and analysis, see Jordan Paper, *The Spirits Are Drunk: Comparative Approaches to Chinese Religion* (Albany: State University of New York Press, 1995), ch. 2.

VI

ANIMALS IN MYTH

A Symbol in Search of an Object

The Mythology of Horses in India

WENDY DONIGER

Animals are good to think with, as Claude Lévi-Strauss noted long ago and famously. They become the objects of our thoughts as well as of our subjugation; but people who live with animals often pick up the mind-sets of their companions. Another anthropologist, E. E. Evans-Pritchard, warned that it was futile to try to imagine how it would feel "if I were a horse."[1] Radcliffe-Brown, in conversation with Max Gluckman, had nick-named James George Frazer's mode of reasoning the "If-I-were-a-horse" argument, from the story of the farmer in the Middle West whose horse had strayed from its paddock. The farmer went into the paddock, chewed some grass, and ruminated, "Now if *I* were a horse, which way would I go?"[2] Wittgenstein would have been skeptical of this enterprise; he argued that, "If a lion could talk, we could not understand him."[3] Working the other side of the street, as it were, Xenophanes said, "If cattle and horses or lions had hands, or could draw with their feet, horses would draw the

forms of god like horses."[4] This line of thinking not only gives subjectivity to animals, treats them as animals in their own rights, but also argues that we, too, can think like animals, can fit our subjectivity to them.[5] The history of the mythology of horses in India demonstrates the ways in which the people of India first identified horses with the people who invaded them on horseback and then identified themselves with the horses—in effect positioning themselves as their own exploiters.

Horses in Indian History

Most of the peoples who entered India did so on horseback, and after they arrived they continued to import horses into India.[6] Among them were the people formerly known as Indo-Europeans (who brought their horses with them), the Turkish people who became the Mughals (who imported Arabian horses from Central Asia and Persia, overland and by sea), and the British (who imported thoroughbreds and hunters from England at first, and then Walers from Australia). In the *Ṛg Veda*, composed in Northwest India in about 1,200 BCE, the horse represented the "Aryas," as they called themselves, against the indigenous inhabitants of India, the *dasyus* or "slaves," whom they associated with the serpent Vṛtra. This is a mythology in which (as in the icon of St. George, on horseback, killing the dragon) the horse that conquers the snake represents us against them.[7]

The political symbolism of the Vedic royal horse sacrifice is blatant: the king's men "set free" the consecrated white stallion to wander for a year before he was brought back to the king and killed. During that year, he was guarded by an army that "followed" him and claimed for the king any land on which he grazed. The king's army therefore drove the horse onward and guided him into the lands that the king intended to take over. Thus the ritual that presented itself as a casual equine stroll over the king's lands was in fact an orchestrated *Anschluss* of the lands on a king's border. No wonder the Sanskrit texts insist that a king had to be very powerful indeed before he could undertake a horse sacrifice.[8]

The horse is constantly in search of *Lebensraum,* eminent domain. Equines, unlike cows, pull up the roots of the grass or eat it right down to the ground so that it doesn't grow back. By doing so they quickly destroy grazing land, which may require some years to recover. And the ancient Indian horse-owners mimicked this behavior, as they responded to the need to provide grazing for their horses once they had captured them and kept them from their natural free-grazing habits. Like early American cowboys, these Indian cowboys (an oxymoron in Hollywood) rode over other peoples' land and took it for their own herds. This spirit was expressed in their very vocabulary; the word *aṃhas* ("constriction")—from which comes our "anxiety"—expressed the terror of

being hemmed in or trapped ("don't fence me in," as Cole Porter's musical cowboy warned); and the word *pṛthu* ("broad and wide"), as in, "Give me the wide open spaces," is the word for the earth (*pṛthivi,* the feminine form) as well as the name of the first king, the man whose job it was to widen the boundaries of his territory.[9]

It was not merely that the horse, thanks to the invention of the chariot, made possible conquest in war; the horse also came to symbolize conquest in war because of its own natural imperialism. But it is not easy for a stallion to find good grazing land in South Asia, for he is not well adapted to conditions in most of the area. He is uncomfortable in the humid heat of the Indian plains, and during the monsoon rains his hooves soften in the wet soil and pieces break off, resulting in painful, recurring sores. The Deccan Plateau and Central India provide suitable grazing land, but this becomes parched between May and September.[10] Though the Indian soil apparently has enough lime and calcium to support cattle, it is not good soil for horses; contemporary breeders now add calcium, manganese, iron, and salt to the horses' diet. After Independence, Indian breeders found some places suitable for breeding (though I have heard Hindu and Parsi stud owners still complain that Pakistan got the best grazing land). Today, in the Punjab, Maharashtra, and Karnataka there is some horse-breeding, and Pune, Mumbai, and Calcutta are breeding centers for thoroughbred horses. But the difficulties in breeding *large* horses are perennial. Kathiawar horses are good for long distances in the desert but are slightly built, not big or fast or strong enough for cavalry; the same is largely true of Arabian horses. And if no new stock is imported, the size of imported horses in India diminishes dramatically in just a few years. As one breeder told me, wistfully, "If we had pasturage all year round, the horses would be an inch taller."[11]

Marco Polo, in the thirteenth century, noted the sorry state of horses in Malabar:

No horses being bred in this country, the king and his three royal brothers expend large sums of money annually in the purchase of them. ... It is my opinion that the climate of the province is unfavourable to the race of horses, and that from hence arises the difficulty in breeding or preserving them. ... A mare, although of a large size, and covered by a handsome horse, produces only a small ill-made colt, with distorted legs, and unfit to be trained for riding.[12]

It is not strictly true that there were "no horses ... bred" in Marco Polo's time. Horses were bred successfully in North India long before the Turkish invasions in the tenth century, and they continued to be bred under the Mughals. The British established a stud in Bengal, bred some horses in the Punjab in Saranpur, and encouraged breeding in North India. At first they tried to establish a Bengal stud by importing "good thorough-bred English stallions together with a supply of big, bony, halfbred English hunting mares to serve as a breeding-stock," and a small "committee for the improvement of the breed of horses in India" was established in 1801.[13] But horses continued to be imported in large numbers, for several reasons.

The difficulties presented by the land and climate of India were compounded by the allegation, by people who may or may not have known what they were talking about, and who may or may not have wanted to slander the Hindus, that Indian kings and their servants simply did not know how to care for horses properly. Marco Polo said that "For food they give them flesh dressed with rice and other prepared meats, the country not producing any grain besides rice"; moreover, "in consequence, as it is supposed, of their not having persons properly qualified to take care of them or to administer the requisite medicines perhaps not three hundred of these [five thousand] remain alive, and thus the necessity is occasioned for replacing them annually."[14] Or, in another version of the text, only a hundred remain out of

two thousand; "they all die because, they say, they have no grooms to come to them in sickness and know how to give a remedy; nor do they know how to care for them, but they die from bad care and keeping."[15] Kipling expressed in *Kim* his scorn for "native" horse management: "They were camped on a piece of waste ground beside the railway, and, being natives, had not, of course, unloaded the two trucks in which Mahbub's animals stood among a consignment of country-breds bought by the Bombay tram-company."[16] Note here, too, the reference to country-breds, an acknowledged if inferior breed.

In addition to the difficulties of breeding, and possible mistakes in feeding, there was a third reason why horses failed to thrive in India. Marco Polo suggested that it was no accident that there were no "properly qualified" people to look after horses in India: "The merchants who bring these horses to sell do not allow to go there, nor do they bring there, grooms, because they wish the horses of these kings to die in numbers soon, on purpose that they may be able to sell their horses as they will; from which they make very great wealth each year."[17] South Indians well into the twentieth century continued to speak of the Arab trick of keeping not grooms but farriers out of India, so that the poor horses were simply ridden until their hooves wore down and they died, a kind of "planned military obsolescence [which] added to the popular notion of the horse as an ephemeral, semi-divine creature (and made for steady business at the Arab end)."[18] And this practice had important repercussions upon the history and mythology of the horse in India.

After each initial conquest, the rulers replenished their herds of horses with new stallions and mares imported from outside India, and this constant importing of new blood-lines made Indian horses extremely expensive. Ancient Sanskrit and Tamil sources (such as the *Arthaśāstra* and *Sangam* texts) observe that horses had to be imported, probably from Parthia. Ninth- and tenth-century Sanskrit inscriptions reveal the northern route,[19] which is also described in Kipling's *Kim*, set in Northwest India: through Kabul, Peshawar, Pindi, Kangra, Ambala, Delhi, and Gwalior. The Indo-Europeans, and later the Turks, entered India via this route.

But from the earliest recorded period in Indian history there was, in addition to the overland route from Central Asia, also a Southern route, by sea from Arabia. South Indians, particularly in the vicinity of Madurai, in recent decades have told stories about the Pandyan Kings' energetic importation of horses,[20] and there is much more information about the lust for horses among later dynasties such as the Nayakas and the Vijayanagar kings. When the Europeans arrived in India in the Mughal period, the horse was a very expensive animal indeed; the best ones sold for as much as $10,000.[21] Heavy losses at sea are the primary reason for their high cost. Since horses cannot throw up, sea-sickness is almost always fatal, and "shipping such fragile and valuable cargo in a pitching East Indiaman on a six-month journey halfway round the world" was a costly and risky venture.[22] British horses also became more scarce, and even more expensive, when so many of them were used, and killed, in the Napoleonic Wars.[23]

Since horses were so expensive, no native, village tradition of horses developed in India, as it did among the natives of Ireland or Egypt, where farmers kept horses, or even in Southeast Asia, where horses were and still are used in a number of ways. Stall feeding, essential during the dry months, is out of the question for subsistence farmers, and in any case, the horse is rarely used as a work animal in India. It does not pull a plow, it seldom carries a pack, and except in Sind and the Punjab, it is not ridden much either. The only common use for the horse in India was, formerly, for military purposes, and nowadays, for pulling carriages.[24] Throughout Indian history, horses have belonged only to people who were not merely economically "other" than the Hindu villagers—aristocrats

—but politically and religiously other. Though these people were often of low (or no) social status in the caste system, they had to have had superior political or economic powers to be able to afford the price of maintaining horses in India. The horse represented this political, military, or economic power; the tax-collector or the punitive military expedition rode into the village on horseback.

As a result of these historical and economic factors, the horse in India is a rare bird, as Stephen Inglis has remarked:

> The horse is still a semi-mythological animal for most rural people in present-day [Tamil Nadu] South Indian village life; those broken-down nags pulling carts at bus and train stations don't seem to link up [with the glorious ancient images]. Apparently a few landowners-who-would-be-kings still keep a few horses as symbols of prestige [in Konku Nadu], but in the heartland further south, most of the horses are clay (or stone, brick, or cement).[25]

In many parts of India, horses have never been useful at all, and nowhere in India have they thrived physically or been bred successfully. For most of India, the horse is *only* a mythical beast, like the unicorn. Yet horses remain centrally important to Indian mythology, historically associated with royalty, honor, and military might.[26] What is it about the *idea* of the horse that has survived among other people in India despite (or because of?) the absence of regular ownership or use of real horses?

Dalit Horses

There is, not surprisingly, a nexus of related folk traditions about horses among the separate aristocracies of each region—Rajasthan, Tamil Nadu, and so forth. But the equine folklore of Hindu India expresses the connection between horses and not only aliens or foreigners but also resident aliens, as it were, such as the Dalits (formerly called Untouchables or Scheduled Castes) and tribal peoples. A story that may well be a satire on the horse sacrifice was recorded in North India during the nineteenth century:

> There is a stock horse miracle story told in connection with Lal Beg, the patron saint of the sweepers [a Dalit caste]. The king of Delhi lost a valuable horse, and the sweepers were ordered to bury it, but as the animal was very fat, they proceeded to cut it up for themselves, giving one leg to the king's priest. ... The king, ... suspecting the state of the case, ordered the sweepers to produce the horse. They were in dismay at the order, but they laid what was left of the animal on a mound sacred to Lal Beg, and prayed to him to save them, whereupon the horse stood up, but only on three legs. So they went to the king and confessed how they had disposed of the fourth leg. The unlucky priest was executed, and the horse soon after died also.[27]

This is a horse sacrifice in the shadow world of the Dalits. The lost leg of the horse recapitulates Vedic themes such as the leg of the racing-mare Viśpalā, which was cut off and replaced by the Aśvins,[28] and the mutilated leg of Yama, the son of the solar horse and mare and half-brother of the equine Aśvins.[29] It may seem strange at first that stigmatized castes should be associated with this aristocratic animal, but a classical reason is provided to explain it: "Many low-castes, including Harijans [another name for Dalits], traded leather to the Portuguese in the 17th century in exchange for horses. This caused tremendous anger in high castes, since low castes were not supposed to ride on horses (or elephants or palanquins). Some of these horse-riding Harijans were killed and are now worshipped by [offerings of] images of horses."[30] In this way, the fact that there are *myths* about horse-riding Dalits is a direct result (and rationalization) of the fact that there once *were* but no longer *are* horse-riding Dalits. The Lal Beg myth follows the form of the many tales in which certain low castes claim to have fallen from a former Brah-

min status;[31] and we have evidence that some Brahmins, at least, were horse-traders.[32]

Tribal Horses

Dalits are closely associated with the tribal people, who also live on the blurred fringes of the pale of Hinduism. Many tribes have horse rituals and horse myths but no horses, which makes the cultural place of this animal in their societies a matter of some interest.[33] Across the tribal belt of India, from the Bhils, Bhilalas, and Kolis in the west to the Santals and Gonds in the east, clay representations of horses are used as votive objects.[34] Some Rajput Bhils worship a deity called Ghoradeva ("Horse God") or a stone horse; the Bhatiyas worship a clay horse at the Dasahra, and the Ojha Kumhars erect a clay horse on the sixth day after birth, and make the child worship it.[35] The Korkus of southern Madhya Pradesh carve tablets naming their dead and depicting them on horseback, placing them under a sacred tree.[36] In Orissa, terracotta horses are given to various gods and goddesses to protect the donor from inauspicious omens, to cure illness, or to guard the village.[37] In West Bengal, clay horses are offered to all the village gods, male or female, fierce or benign, though particularly to Dharma Thakur, the sun god. At Kenduli in Birbhum, clay horses are offered on the grave of a Tantric saint named Kangal Kshepa, and Bengali parents offer horses when a child first crawls steadily on its hands and feet like a horse.[38] In Tamil Nadu, as many as five hundred large clay horses may be prepared in one sanctuary, most of them standing between 15 and 25 feet tall (including a large base), and involving the use of several tons of stone, brick, and either clay, plaster, or cement.[39] They are a permanent part of the temple and may be renovated at ten- to twenty-year intervals; the construction of a massive figure usually takes between three and six months. In Balikondala, votive horses, or *thakuranis*, are provided as vehicles for the gods to ride at night to protect the fields and visit the infirm; and there are terracotta horses in the Śaivite temple on the edge of the village.[40] New horses are constantly set up, "while the old and broken ones are left to decay and return to the earth of which they were made."[41]

Some of these tribal horses are also associated with sacrifice—not the sacrifice *of* a horse (to a god) but the sacrifice *to* a horse, *of* a sheep or a goat. The Kunbis, who do have real horses, wash them on the day of the Dasahra, decorate them with flowers, sacrifice a sheep to them, and sprinkle the blood on them. But the Gonds, who do not have horses, have instead a horse deity named Kodapen, and at the opening of the rainy season they worship a stone in his honor outside the village: "A Gond priest offers a pottery image of the animal and a heifer, saying, 'Thou art our guardian! Protect our oxen and cows! Let us live in safety!' Rag horses are offered at the tombs of saints at Gujarat."[42] The heifer is then sacrificed and the meat eaten by the worshippers.[43] In sacrificing a goat or a heifer to a horse, these tribal people are doing what the Vedic Indians did when they killed a goat as part of the horse sacrifice, as well as what many race-horse owners do today, when they give their horses goats for stable companions: the goat carries away the evil from the horse.

Gods called Spirit Riders ride without stirrups, on saddled or unsaddled (invisible) horses, guarding villages all over India, and village potters make their equestrian images.[44] In Balikondala, as elsewhere, votive horses, or *thakuranis,* are provided as vehicles for the gods to ride at night to protect the fields.[45] Many of these riders are said to patrol the *borders* of the villages, a role that may echo both the role of the Vedic horse in pushing back the borders of the king's realm and the horse's association with liminal people on the borders of Hindu society. But the villagers do not express any explicit awareness of the association of the horses with foreigners; they think of the horses as their own. Perhaps this native tradition expresses the submerged memory of a time, somewhere along the line of history, when the horses of the others became their own.

Stella Kramrisch remarks that, in the absence of real horses, the village potters copy the images of horses that were made by people who *did* have horses, the Vijayanagar artisans:

> The potter-priest gives them basic shapes which he knows how to modify in keeping with the ardent naturalism of South Indian sculpture. He has seen the rearing stone horses supporting the roofs of the large halls of stone temples of the Vijayanagar style of the sixteenth century.[46]

The mythical horses, then, are not drawn from life; they are drawn from art, and from the imagination of horses.

People who have never had horses may have had or still have direct contact with other people who do have horses (people like Muslims, or in the case of the Bhils, Rajputs). And the myths of horses may be inspired by other peoples' myths of horses, or by pictures or sculptures of them. Even though the people of the tribes and villages did not usually *own* horses, they may well have been the people who were employed to *care* for the horses of the richer classes.[47] Such knowledge would still have been limited to a small part of these village or tribal cultures. And these people—who are the ones who tell many of the local stories, and made most of the local horse images—would not, perhaps, have ridden or even driven horses, let alone sacrificed them. But they may have fed them and groomed them and, indeed, spent more time with them than their owners did.

Moreover, people who do not have horses are not all the same in their equine deprivation. Some people who have horse mythologies may have no contact with horses at all. Technically, unless one believes (as I do not) that people are born with an archetypal horse in their heads, there can be no such group; people who have literally *no* contact with horses cannot invent them. But people who have no horses now may have had horses once. Megalithic remains of equines and riding equipment in India may represent the source of a pre-Indo-European equine tradition in some Indian tribes or villages. Some tribes in the Northwest of India are connected through their name with the horse (Sanskrit *aśva*), such as people called Aśmakas or Aśvakas, and the Assakenoi mentioned by historians who came to India with Alexander the Great;[48] there are also people called "horse-faced" (Aśvamukha, Turagānana).[49] Such names might be derived from the practice of wearing the skin and head of the sacrificed equine victims.[50] Cultural memory can be long.

Horses Taken from Tribals and for Tribals: Bhils and Rajputs

The Bhils, like the Gonds, may not own horses themselves, but, as Gunther Sontheimer put it, "at least their gods are made to ride horses."[51] The Bhils have horse rituals but no horses, while their neighbors on the north, the Hindu Rajputs ("Sons of Kings"), do have horses. The equestrian figure in Bhil art and legend links the tribal world with that of the feudal aristocracy. But which way do the horses run? It is often said that the Rajputs took from the Bhils their land and their right to have real horses. As Kramrisch tells it:

> Formerly [the Bhil] ruled over their own country ... prior to the arrival of the Rajputs. The Rajputs, the "sons of kings," invaded the country, subsequently Rajasthan, in about the sixth century A.D. ... The Rajputs are horse owners and riders. The Bhil use the image of the horseman; it is that of a Spirit Rider.[52]

Similarly, in nearby Maharashtra, real horses were used as an instrument of social mobility; people who came from low backgrounds managed, through the use of the horse, to rise in the social scale all across central and North India. Horsemanship conferred a higher status; a warrior who had his own horse to ride into battle grew in importance. Horses were valuable booty, given to the king. Thus the Rajputs increased their power through their monopolization of the horse in the land that became Rajasthan. Horse rituals and myths often persist among dynasties that have emerged from a tribal background.[53]

At the same time, the Bhils took their equine cult from the Rajputs:

> The Bhils and Kolis commemorate fallen heroes with stone slabs showing an engraved horse and rider, as do also the Korkus of Orissa. A possible explanation for both practices is that they are attempts by tribal peoples to assimilate into their own traditions an aspect of Rajput behavior; a step at Brahmanization as it were.[54]

More precisely, one might see this as Kṣatriyazation: through the symbolism of the horse, the Bhils seek and find a higher status. They have assimilated from their conquerors, the Hindu Rajputs, the values of horsemanship, without assimilating the actual use of the horse.

In some ways, the Bhils are *plus royaliste que le roi:* they use the Rajput horses in ways that the Rajputs did not. The Rajputs emphasized the qualities of the Vedic sacrificial stallion that symbolized power and fertility, playing down the closely related death symbolism. But the Bhils brought out the ancient power of the horse to symbolize death:

> The depiction of horse and rider in the memorial stones of the Bhils is not only an imitation of prestigious Rajput styles—in fact, in the Rajput memorials the horse is mostly not shown—but also reflects an incident of the death ritual.[55] The Bhils confer on their ancestors the nobility of the horseman, the chevalier, whereas the Rajputs do not particularly stress the equestrian form of their dead.[56]

The Bhils, however, generally appear in Hindu folklore not as people to whom the ownership of the land and the custom of riding horses were denied, but as people who steal other peoples' horses.[57] The projection of blame from the usurpers to the usurped in this way is a common feature of mythology everywhere: the people from whom one steals are themselves thieves from whom one is merely *retrieving* one's own treasure. Thus the *Ṛg Veda* tells us that Indra took *back* the cows of the Dāsas — the demonic natives of the India that his people in fact invaded, stealing *their* cows. In fact, there is historical evidence that the Bhils, at one time, *did* steal horses, though in time they ceased to do so and ceased to have any horses at all. But the fact of their original rustling was then augmented with the always at-hand mythology of the thieving natives, and the myth stuck where the horses did not.

Muslim Horses

Since the beginning of the invasions of India by the Turks, who were to become the Mughals, Muslims have played the role of good-and-evil foreigners in the horse mythologies of India. Hindus as well as Muslims worship at the shrines of Muslim "horse saints."[58] A trace of mystery, perhaps also of resentment, but also of glamour, hedges one of the best known South Indian stories about Muslim/Arab horses, a story often retold, in Tamil, Telugu, and other Dravidian languages.[59] This version is from a South Indian text composed in Sanskrit in the early sixteenth century:

Vāṭavur had spent on the worship of Śiva the money given him by the king to buy horses. Śiva appeared to Vāṭavur and said, "I will bring excellent horses; go to Madurai." Days passed and no horses arrived. The king imprisoned Vāṭavur, who prayed to Śiva. Then Śiva, transforming a whole pack of jackals into horses, himself put on the costume of a horse-dealer. Having taken the form of a supreme horseman, he himself chose a horse that was splitting open the earth with his hoof in order to adorn the form of him [i.e. of Śiva] with the snakes [that lived underground], and the dust on Śiva's face was blown away by the hissing of the snakes that he wore in his hair. The king had the horses brought to his palace.

He spent the whole day throwing to the horses food such as chickpeas [*canaka*]. Then the sun set. The horses went back to their jackalhood, gobbled up all the horses of the king, and went to the forests, like lions, their mouths smeared with blood. The grooms reported the various evil deeds of the horses.[60]

The false horses eat the other horses, as jackals would; but since they appear to be horses, they appear to be cannibals. The transformation into jackals might be regarded as a transformation from tame to wild, jackals being the untamed form of dogs; or from pure to impure, jackals, like other scavengers, being polluted and polluting, in contrast with the pure horse. Both of these categories would place the jackals with snakes as inversions of horses — and here we should note the presence of snakes in the metaphors describing these demonic, divine horses. Many Hindu myths depict Śiva as the ultimate other, a Dalit.[61] It is thus not really surprising to find him depicted here as a Muslim, or at least no more surprising than it is to find the god Dharma, the incarnation of Hindu religious law, incarnate as a dog (an animal that caste Hindus regard as an unclean scavenger) at the end of the great Sanskrit epic, the *Mahābhārata*.[62]

The statement that these horses eat other horses reveals this as a myth told by people who do not know horses, for such people generally fear the horse's mouth, with its big teeth. This is a dangerous misconception, for, as every horseman and horsewoman knows, though equines can indeed bite, it is the back hooves that pose the real danger; and horses are in any case strict vegetarians. The devouring equine mouth is a projection onto the horse of the violence that *we* inflict upon *it* in taming it, by putting a bit in its mouth.

A different sort of Indian horse-story, from North India, tells us that seventy-two riders, including one woman, came from the sea and landed in Kutch; these people, called Jakhs, saved the local villagers from the depredations of a demon; the horses were then sent to Delhi, and on the way they fertilized the local mares;[63] or, according to another variant, the riders themselves blessed childless women, including the queen, with children.[64] In most versions, the riders kill not a demon but a human, a tyrant named Punvro (or Punvaro), who had cut off the hands of the architect who had built the city of Patan (or Padhargadh) so that he might not construct anything like it for another prince.[65] To the end of the twentieth century, villagers in Kutch made statues of the seventy-two horses and offered sweet rice to the horsemen and asked them for boons.[66]

Most versions of this myth emphasize the skin-color of the invaders; they are "white-skinned foreigners said to have come in the thirteenth century from Anatolia and Syria,"[67] or "white-skinned, horse-riding foreigners from Central Asia," or Greeks, Romans, Scythians, or White Huns, "tall and of fair complexion, blue or grey-eyed."[68] According to Kramrisch, they stand for the Turks:

> Harking back to other, untold memories from Inner Asian horse-herding cultures, these apocalyptic horsemen transmute the fear generated by Muslim invasions into India into a liberating legend in which the evil power does not come from outside but is local, embodied in the tyrant Punvaro.[69]

These invaders are liberating Muslims; but another interpretation sees them as people liberated *from* Muslims, as "Zoroastrians from the northern parts of Iran, who, during the whole of this period, were emigrating to India in search of the religious toleration that Islamic persecutors denied them in their own country.[70]

Let us table for the moment the question of whether the invaders are liberating Muslims or liberated anti-Muslims, and ask, Who is Punvro? Onto an apparently historical ruler this myth may have grafted the myth of the tyrant who cuts off the hands of artists, calling upon not "untold memories" of Inner Asia but another, historically specific, myth about the British, who

treated the weavers in Bengal so cruelly (there is abundant testimony about this[71]) that they were widely believed, apparently on no evidence, to have cut off the weavers' thumbs, or, on the basis of one piece of dubious evidence, to have so persecuted the winders of silk that they cut off their own thumbs in protest.[72] The legend lives on today in a contemporary story about an artisan from Kutch, who made a diabolically clever box with a gun inside it; the gun fired when anyone opened the box. He gave it to Dalhousie, the Governor General of India, who gave it in turn to his adjutant (that is to say, his subaltern) to open; the adjutant was killed, and Dalhousie had the craftsman's hands cut off.[73] The myth of the weavers' thumbs may also have grown out of the famous *Mahābhārata* story of Ekalavya, a dark-skinned, low-caste boy whose skill at archery rivaled that of the noble heroes; to maintain their supremacy as archers, their teacher demanded that Ekalavya cut off his right thumb.[74]

The myth of Punvaro, in Kramrisch's gloss, turns history on its head, telling us that the Muslims save the good citizens of Kutch from the British, an inversion of the sentiment widely expressed in Chennai (Madras) today, that the British, especially the early East India Company, liberated Hindus in South India from Muslim control and played not merely a neutral but a positive role in establishing an even-handed attitude to all religions in its new territory. In discussing this argument, Joanne Waghorne invoked the equestrian metaphor, beginning with the title of her article: "Chariots of the God/s: Riding the Line between Hindu and Christian."[75]

Thus, different versions of the equestrian myth cast different actors as the native villain and the invading heroes. This Kutch tradition may or may not know the ancient Vedic myth of the hegemonic horse trampling the native/demonic serpent;[76] we have here the anthropomorphic, and quasi-historical, form of the mytheme, horsemen trampling natives. But the Vedic bias is maintained: the invading horse-

men are the heroes. The Vedic horsemen are replaced by Muslims or Anatolians, even by Dalits
and Tribal peoples in some variants,[77] while
the Dasyus, or Vedic Others, are replaced by a
demon, a Patan tyrant or, by implication, the
British. This plasticity kept the myth alive in
widely varying contexts,[78] which express, in very
different ways, the connection between horses
and aliens or foreigners.[79] The confusion of the
villains and the heroes in the story of Punvaro is
no accident; the myth is rife with obfuscation,
as well as a kind of inverted subversion, subversion from the top down: it speaks of the assimilation of the values of the conquerors by those
who are conquered, expressing, as it were, the
snake-eye view of horses, but in a positive light.
Certainly it is a myth about, and probably by,
invaders, which manipulates the native symbolism of horses and snakes in such a way as to
make the invaders the heroes, the natives the villains, in a myth that then took root within the
folklore of the natives. It's all done with mirrors,
which is to say, with myths.

We must take account of the people who
constructed this myth, who perpetuated it, recorded it, translated it, selected it. The popular
legends concerning these events were "first collected on the spot and written down by Major
(later Sir Alexander) Burnes in 1826; copied with
minor variations by Mrs. Postans (1839) and later
writers and finally embodied in the 'standard'
account of Kutch (otherwise a generally reliable
source) in Volume V of the *Gazetteer of the Bombay Presidency* in 1880."[80] It is not hard to guess
why the British might have wanted to preserve
this myth. But we are still hard pressed to explain the acceptance and perdurance in Hindu
India of other forms of this equine mythology,
such as the myth of the jackal horses, which has
been subject to far less British mediation and
still expresses a surprisingly positive attitude to
the equestrian conquerors of India.

Kipling's Kim

The myth of the liberating invader riding his
stallion continued to cast its old white magic
over the British. The white stallion was immortalized by Kipling in his novel *Kim*. In the very
first chapter, Kipling introduces a message about
a war, coded in horses: "the pedigree of the white
stallion." Ostensibly, it means that the Muslim
horse-trader Mahbub Ali, who is in the service
of the British spymaster Creighton, is able to
vouch for a valuable horse that the Colonel of
the Regiment may buy; and the coded message
on the second level is that a provocation has occurred that will justify a British attack. But the
idea of a pedigree implies that you know the
horse when you know its father and mother (or
dam and sire); the breeding of horses, of "blood-
stock," of thoroughbreds, was at the heart of a
theory of the breeding of humans, a theory of
race. Kim is even said to have "white blood,"
an oxymoron. I need not point out the significance of the color of the stallion in a book by
Kipling (who coined the phrase "the white man's
burden"). But we might recall that the Vedic
stallion of the ancient Hindus, the symbol of
expansionist political power, was also white, in
contrast with the Dasyus or Dāsas, the serpentine natives, who were said to come from "dark
wombs."[81]

The white stallion also implicitly represents
Kim's Irish father, in the metaphor that Creighton and Mahbub Ali apply to Kim, behind his
back: Kim is a colt who must be gentled into
British harness to play the game.[82] On the other
hand, to Kim's face Mahbub Ali uses horses as a
paradigm for multiculturalism *avant la lettre;* in
response to Kim's question about his own identity (he felt he was a Sahib among Sahibs, but
"among the folk of Hind ... What am I? Mussal-
man, Hindu, Jain, or Buddhist?"), Mahbub Ali
answers: "This matter of creeds is like horse-
flesh. ... the Faiths are like the horses. Each has
merit in its own country."[83]

In recorded British history, too, horse-
breeding, spying, and Orientalism combined in

the character of William Moorcroft, a famous equine veterinarian. In 1819, the British sent him to Northwest India, as far as Tibet and Afghanistan, on a Quixotic search for "suitable cavalry mounts."[84] Moorcroft had seen mares from Kutch that he thought might be suitable for the army,[85] and he was granted official permission "to proceed towards the North Western parts of Asia, for the purpose of there procuring by commercial intercourse, horses to improve the breed within the British Province or for military use."[86] But in addition he "collected information not only on military supplies but also on political and economic conditions obtaining at the peripheries of the Empire,"[87] and shortly before his mysterious final disappearance, he was briefly imprisoned in the Hindu Kush in 1824 on suspicion of being a spy.[88]

Moorcroft had delusions of Orientalism; he told a friend that he would have disguised himself "as a Fakeer" rather than give up his plan,[89] and after he was lost and presumed dead, in August of 1825, legends began to circulate about "a certain Englishman named Moorcroft who introduced himself into Lha-Ssa, under the pretence of being a Cashmerian," or who spoke fluent Persian "and dressed and behaved as a Muslim."[90] The final piece of Orientalism in his life was posthumous: from 1834 to 1841 his papers were edited by Horace Hayman Wilson, secretary of the Asiatic Society of Bengal and the Boden Professor of Sanskrit at Oxford.[91] According to his biographer, Moorcroft was thrilled by the stories he heard "from the north-western horse-traders — swarthy, bearded men like Kipling's Mahbub Ali."[92] But Kipling created Mahbub Ali fifty years after the publication of Moorcroft's papers, and aspects of the characters of Creighton, Mahbub Ali, and Kim himself may have been inspired by Moorcroft.

The Gift Horse

To this day, horses are worshipped all over India by people who do not have them and seldom even see one, in places where the horse has never been truly a part of the land. A Marxist might view the survival of the mythology of the aristocratic horse as an imposition of the lies of the rulers upon the people, an exploitation of the masses by saddling them with a mythology that never was theirs and never will be for their benefit, a foreign mythology that produces a false consciousness, distorting the native conceptual system, compounding the felony of the invasion itself. A Freudian, on the other hand, might see in the native acceptance of this foreign mythology the process of projection or identification by which one overcomes a feeling of anger or resentment or impotence toward another person by assimilating that person into oneself, *becoming* the other. Though there is much to be said for these interpretations, I would want to augment them by pointing out that myths about oppressive foreigners and their horses sometimes became a *positive* factor in the lives of those whom they conquered or dominated; and that the horse did not supplant but rather supplemented the continuing worship of other, more native animals — such as snakes.

The symbol of the horse became embedded in the folk traditions of India and then stayed there even after its referent, the horse, had vanished from the scene, even after the foreigners had folded their tents and gone away. The corpus of Hindu myths that depict the Turks and Arabs bringing horses into India seems to have assimilated the historical experience of the importation of horses not only to the lingering vestiges — the cultural hoofprints, as it were — of Vedic horse myths, but also to the more widespead theme of "magical horses brought from heaven or the underworld." The myth is, like the horse, a gift from the sea, or from the sky — from another world. And like all great symbols, the horse is often susceptible to inversion as well as subversion: the horse of the conquerors becomes the horse of the conquered. This mythology lends the horse, over and above its natural allure, all the glamour and pathos of the interior room as watched by the child outside, pressing her nose against the windowpane. This is an otherness not loathed but admired, not despised but coveted; it is an otherness that has been assimilated into the native system of values. The villagers who recognize that the horse belongs to those who have political power may be worshipping the horse in order to gain some of that power for themselves. But this is not all that is happening.

The myths of those who do and those who do not own horses differ not merely because one group knows horses better (and hence creates a mythology more accurate in horse-lore and, perhaps, more sympathetic toward the horse) but because many equine myths are inspired not merely by the horse itself but also by the *relationship* between the horse and humans, a relationship that may come to symbolize other human relationships — sexual, political, parental, or all of the above. And this interactive factor will clearly play different roles in the myths of people who have different sorts of contact with real horses.

The very earliest relationship between horse and humans was that of hunting; before the horse was domesticated, he was one of the many animals that were hunted, and doubtless participated in the more general mythology of hunting in the prehistoric period. But once domestication took place, the primary relationship between horse and humans became that of taming, and it is this metaphor that dominates the mythology of the horse in the historical period. Hunting and taming are therefore intrinsic to the mythology of the horse. To turn a wild horse into a domesticated horse is to move the animal from nature into culture. Non-horsey people tend to try to erase or destroy the wild, animal violence of the horse, often by overpowering it through their own human violence.

But where horses are known and loved, the metaphor of taming takes on a far more gentle and more mutual aspect. Horsemen and horsewomen speak of the "gentling" of the horse, the harnessing (yoking, *yoga*) of his violence for our good, but not necessarily for his ill. Humans can

never entirely succeed in taming the horse; this is the charm and the challenge of any intimate association with a wild animal — that he retains some measure of his wildness. The most basic power beyond manpower, horsepower, is what we still use as a touchstone, a basis for other sorts of mechanical power. But horses are not machines; people who work with them know that you are never in control, that you never entirely tame a horse, who remains at some level always wild. There is a cowboy saying about this: "Never was a horse that couldn't be rode; never was a rider who couldn't be throwed."

In the taming of a horse, force is used, but so is persuasion. At a certain moment, force becomes useless; there are some things that no one can make a horse do unless he wants to, unless he understands what is wanted of him and is willing to give up his freedom in exchange for something that he derives from his contact with humans. One might, perhaps, think of this in sacrificial terms, as a sacrificial exchange: the horse sacrifice is not merely a sacrifice *of* a horse, but a sacrifice *by* a horse. And it is this exchange that is mythologized in the narratives of people who have horses, narratives about horses that speak — that love their masters and willingly sacrifice their lives for them.

What is more, many myths testify to the other side of this transaction of taming, to the role of the horse in drawing humans from the tame into the wild. In the mythologies of India and Greece, as well as in medieval Europe and Britain, we read of princes who are lured by white stags or white hinds or white swans or white unicorns — or white horses — from the safe territory of the royal parks to the thick of the forest, to the Other World, where they may meet their princess or encounter their dragon, or both (or both in one female dragon), but where, in any case, they learn what they need to know. In many shamanistic myths of Central Asia and India, the initiate mounts a white horse and is suddenly carried off, out of control, into the world in which the initiation takes place.[93] The horse leads the human from the world of the tame into the world of the wild, which is the magic, supernatural world of the gods. Thus the horse in the ancient Indian ceremony of royal consecration is never tamed. On the contrary, he untames the human. He transfers to us some of his own wildness and freedom. And this other world may be cultural as well as mythological, the world of people of other religions, other languages, other powers over us.

For people who do not have horses, taming—particularly brutal taming—may appear as exploitation. And on another level, the relationship between horse-having people and horse have-nots may appear as exploitation. Several parallel power relationships are expressed through the symbolism of the horse in contrast with the serpent, on the one hand, and the rider, on the other. Rider is to horse as horse is to snake: power, and domination, travels down the line. First comes the power structure between humans and horses; then between people of power and people without such power; between foreigners and natives; and, specifically, between British and Muslims, on the one hand, and Muslims and Hindus, on the other. But who is represented by the horse, who by the serpent, and who is the rider? Though the village terracotta horse may express an implicit wish for the power of those who have horses, its worshippers seem to seek the power of the horse itself: fertility as well as political power.

For the horse is, after all, a contradictory symbol of human political power. It is an animal that invades other horses' territory but whose first instinct is always not to attack but to run away. Horses are prey rather than predators, as is evidenced by the fact that they have their eyes toward the back of their heads, the better to flee, rather than in the front, like the cats and other hunters. Like the villagers who worship him, the horse has been oppressed and robbed of his freedom by human beings who made up stories about horses. The fragility of the horse is well represented by the fragile, ephemeral medium in which villagers usually represent him: clay. The horse is thus both victim and victimizer, a ready-made natural/cultural symbol of political inversion. This tension, too, nourishes the image of the wild horse as predator and the tame horse as prey.

Some people have regarded the horse as nothing but a machine to pull a plow or to get you where you want to go; some as a useless symbol of wealth and elegance; some as a manifestation on earth of divine power. The Indian mythology of the horse is a testament to the vitality of the imagination and to the human drive to go on and on, responding merely to the memory, or to the view from afar, of an animal that uniquely embodies sacred beauty, royal nobility, and vital power. For, finally, the horse is a potent natural symbol of things other than power: fertility, yes, but also beauty, which people continue to care about even when it is clearly not in their best interests to do so. Horses are numinous; they captivate the eye, they inspire desire, they have magic. Their allure infects even people who know, on a rational level, that horses aren't good for them. And this allure is what Indian artisans try to capture in their religious images; it is what makes them treat horses like gods.

NOTES

1. E. E. Evans-Pritchard, *Theories of Primitive Religion* (Oxford: Oxford University Press, 1965), pp. 24, 43.

2. Cited by R. Angus Downie, *Frazer and the Golden Bough* (London: Weidenfeld and Nicolson, 1970), p. 42.

3. Ludwig Wittgenstein, *Philosophical Investigations*, 3rd ed., trans. G. E. M. Anscombe (New York: Random House, 1958), p. 223.

4. Xenophanes, *Die Fragmente,* ed. Ernst Heitsch (Munich: Insler Verlag, 1983), fr. 15.

5. Wendy Doniger O'Flaherty, *Other Peoples'*

Myths: The Cave of Echoes. (New York: Macmillan; Chicago: University of Chicago Press, 1995), ch. 4.

6. Parts of the following paragraphs formed a portion of an earlier article, Wendy Doniger, "Presidential Address: 'I Have Scinde': Flogging a Dead (White Male Orientalist) Horse," *Journal of Asian Studies* 58 (4): 940–60 (November, 1999).

7. Wendy Doniger O'Flaherty, "Horses and Snakes in the Adi Parvan of the *Mahābhārata*," in Margaret Case and N. Gerald Barrier, eds., *Aspects of India: Essays in Honor of Edward Cameron Dimock* (New Delhi: American Institute of Indian Studies and Manohar, 1986), pp. 16–44.

8. Wendy Doniger O'Flaherty, "The Tale of the Indo-European Horse Sacrifice," *Incognita* 1 (1990): 1–15.

9. Wendy Doniger O'Flaherty, *The Origins of Evil in Hindu Mythology* (Berkeley: University of California Press), pp. 321–48.

10. Lawrence S. Leshnik, "The Horse in India," in Franklin C. Southworth, ed., *Symbols, Subsistence and Social Structure: The Ecology of Man and Animal in South Asia* (Philadelphia: University of Pennsylvania, South Asia Regional Studies, 1977–78), pp. 56–57.

11. Personal communication from Dr. Faroukh Wadia at the Wadi Stud, Pune, January, 1996.

12. Marco Polo, *The Travels of Marco Polo* (New York: Dutton, 1908), pp. 356–57; *Marco Polo: The Description of the World*, eds. A.C. Moule and Paul Pelliot (London: George Routledge, 1938), p. 174.

13. Garry Alder, *Beyond Bokhara: The Life of William Moorcroft, Asian Explorer and Pioneer Veterinary Surgeon 1767–1825* (London: Century Publishing, 1985), pp. 50–51.

14. Polo, *The Travels*, p. 357.

15. Polo, *Description of the World*, p. 174.

16. Rudyard Kipling, *Kim*, ed. with an introduction and notes by Edward W. Said (Harmondsworth: Penguin Books, 1987), p. 185.

17. Polo, *Description of the World*, p. 174.

18. Stephen Robert Inglis, "Night Riders: Massive Temple Figures of Rural Tamilnadu," in M. Israel, et al., eds., *A Festschrift for Prof. M. Shanmugam Pillai* (Madurai: Madrai Kamaraj Univerity, Muttu Patippakam, 1980), pp. 297–307.

19. Georg Bühler, "The Peheva Inscription from the Temple of Garibnath," in *Epigraphica Indic,* vol. 1 (Calcutta: Thacker, Spink and Co. 1892), pp. 184–90.

20. Stephen Inglis, personal communication, March 26, 1985.

21. Simon Digby, *War Horse and Elephant in the Delhi Sultanate* (Oxford: Orient Monographs, 1971).

22. Leshnik, "The Horse," p. 56.

23. Alder, *Beyond Bokhara*, pp. 50–51.

24. Leshnik, "The Horse," p. 57.

25. Stephen Inglis, personal communication March 26, 1985.

26. Stephen P. Huyler, *Village India* (New York: Harry Abrams, 1985), p. 105.

27. William Crooke, *The Popular Religion and Folk-lore of Northern India* (2 vols. London: Archibald Constable 1896), 2:206; citing *Indian Antiquary*, xi.325 ff; *Panjab Notes and Queries* ii.2.

28. *Ṛgveda* 1.116.15, 1.117.6 (*Rig Veda*, with the commentary of Sayana, 6 vols. London: Oxford University Press 1890–92); Wendy Doniger O'Flaherty, *Women, Androgynes, and Other Mythical Beasts* (Chicago: University of Chicago Press, 1980) p. 179.

29. *Mārkaṇḍeya Purāṇa* 103–5; Doniger O'Flaherty, *Women*, pp. 175–76.

30. Personal communication from Stuart Blackburn, April 4, 1986.

31. Doniger O'Flaherty, *The Origins of Evil.*

32. The ninth- or tenth-century Pehova or Pṛthudah inscription in Sanskrit mentions four Brahmin horse-traders. Personal communication from Romila Thapar, Oxford, May 25, 1986.

33. Leshnik, "The Horse," pp. 56–57.

34. Ibid., p. 57.

35. Stephen Hislop, *Papers Relating to the Aboriginal Tribes of the Central Provinces*, ed. R. Temple, (Nagpur 1866), Appendix, i.iii.

36. Huyler, *Village India*, p. 226.

37. Ibid., p. 162.

38. Asutosh Bhattacarya, *Folklore of Bengal* (New Delhi: National Book Trust, 1978), pp. 48–49.

39. Inglis, "Night Riders," pp. 298, 302, 304.

40. Huyler, *Village India*, 105; "Folk Art in India

Today," in Basil Gray, ed., *The Arts of India*, (Oxford: Oxford University Press, 1981), p. 200.

41. Stella Kramrisch, *Unknown India: Ritual Art in Tribe and Village* (Philadelphia: Philadelphia Museum of Art, 1964), p. 57.

42. Hislop, *Papers,* Appendix, i.iii.

43. Crooke, *The Popular Religion,* vol. 2, p. 208.

44. Benoy Kumar Sarkar, *The Folk Element in Hindu Culture* (London, 1917; New Delhi: Oriental Books, 1972), p. 111.

45. Huyler, "Folk art in India today," p. 200.

46. Kramrisch, *Unknown India,* p. 57.

47. Romila Thapar, personal communication, May 25, 1986, Oxford.

48. K. K. Das Gupta, "The Asvakas: An Early Indian Tribe," *East and West,* n.s., 22:1–2 (1972), pp. 33–40.

49. Willibald Kirfel, *Die Kosmographie der Inder nach der Quellen dargestellt* (Bonn and Leipzig, 1920), pp. 88 ff.

50. Asko Parpola, "The Pre-Vedic Indian Background of the Srauta Rituals," in Frits Staal, ed., *Agni: The Vedic Ritual of the Fire Altar* (Berkeley: Asian Humanities Press, 1983, 2 vols.), 2:41–75.

51. Gunther D. Sontheimer, "The Mallari/ Khandoba Myth as Reflected In Folk Art and Ritual," in *Anthropos* 79 (1984): 155–70, fn. 18.

52. Kramrisch, *Unknown India,* p. 51.

53. Sontheimer, "The Mallari," p. 163.

54. Leshnik, "The Horse," p. 57.

55. Sontheimer, "The Mallari," p. 163.

56. Kramrisch, *Unknown India,* p. 51.

57. Om Prakash Joshi, *Painted Folklore and Folklore Painters of India* (Delhi: Motilal Banarsidass, 1976), p. 52.

58. Crooke, *Popular Religion,* 2.206.

59. This well-known story is told in several versions of Manikkavacakar's biography, in the *Tiruvātavurar Purāṇa* (a fifteenth-century hagiography) and the *Tiruvilaiyatal Puranam;* see also G. U. Pope, *Tiruvācagam* (London, Oxford: Oxford University Press, 1900), xx–xxvii, and Glenn E. Yocum, *Hymns to the Dancing Śiva: A Study of Manikkavcakar's Tiruvācakam* (New Delhi: Heritage Publishers, 1982), pp. 51–52, 62.

60. Mandalakavi, *Pāṇḍyakulodaya,* ed. K. V.

Sarma (Hoshiapur, Vishvesvaranand Visva Bandhu Institute of Sanskrit and Indological Studies, Panjab University, 1981), 7.1–48.

61. Doniger O'Flaherty, *The Origins of Evil,* pp. 272–320.

62. *Mahābhārata* (Poona: Bhandarkar Oriental Research Institute, 1933–69),17.2.26 17.3.7–23.

63. Jyotindra Jain, "Painted Myths of Creation: The Art and Ritual of an Indian tribe," in *The India Magazine* 5, no. 2 (January 1985): 24.

64. C. Rushbrook Williams, *The Black Hills: Kutch in History and Legend: A Study in Indian Local Loyalties* (London: Weidenfeld and Nicolson, 1958), p. 83.

65. Williams, *The Black Hills,* p. 83; Kramrisch, *Village India,* p. 55.

66. Kirin Narayan, personal communication, February 22, 1999.

67. Kramrisch, *Unknown,* p. 55.

68. Williams, *The Black Hills,* pp. 84–86.

69. Kramrisch, *Village India,* p. 55.

70. Williams, *Unknown,* p. 88.

71. Ramkrishna Mukherjee, *The Rise and Fall of the East India Company: A Sociological Appraisal* (New York and London: Monthly Review Press, 1974), pp. 300–303.

72. William Bolts, *Considerations on Indian Affairs; Particularly Respecting the Present State of Bengal Dependencies* (London 1772, repr. in *The East India Company: 1600 1858,* vol. 3, ed. Patrick Tuck [London and New York: Routledge, 1998]), p. 194. The thumb-cutting story is found only in contemporary British accounts from the 1770s, when there was fierce rivalry between various factions of the East India Company's servants in Bengal and their supporters in London. The silk-winders' incident, reported by Wilhelm Bolts, a highly disreputable and probably unreliable witness, writing against his rivals in the Company, found its way into Edmund Burke's attacks on Warren Hastings and then into Indian writings in English in the late nineteenth century. The weavers were caught between the rapacity of the Indian agents who served as middlemen and the young Englishmen for whom they worked. But no contemporary Bengali writers, Hindu or Muslim, seem to have mentioned it, per-

haps because they attached little importance to what happened to weavers, who were low caste Muslims and Hindus.

73. Kirin Narayan, personal communication, February 22, 1999.

74. *Mahābhārata* 1.123.

75. Joanne Waghorne, "Chariots of the God/s: Riding the Line between Hindu and Christian," *History of Religions* 39, no. 3 (November, 1999).

76. Wendy Doniger O'Flaherty, "The Deconstruction of Vedic Horselore in Indian Folklore," in A. W. van den Hoek, D. H. A. Kolff and M. S. Oort, eds., *Ritual, State and History in South Asia: Essays in Honor of J. C. Heesterman* (Leiden: E. J. Brill, 1992), pp. 76–101.

77. Crooke, *Popular Religion*, 2.206; Sontheimer, "The Mallari."

78. Doniger, "The Tale," pp. 79–108.

79. Near Banaras, at Fort Chunnar, people tell stories about a "Gun Major"—they use the English word; this name is explicitly regarded as a later British variant of the name of Janamejaya, a king who sponsors a notorious snake sacrifice in the *Mahābhārata*. Thus, through the association of the horse with foreign invaders, the ancient Sanskrit epic is updated and the British are folded back into ancient Indian history. Personal communication from Peter Kepfoerle.

80. Williams, *The Black Hills*, p. 83.

81. *Ṛgveda* 2.20.7.

82. Kipling, *Kim*, p. 161.

83. Ibid., p. 191.

84. Anand A. Yang, *Bazaar India: Markets, Society, and the Colonial State in Gangetic Bihar* (Berkeley: University of California Press, 1998), p. 116.

85. Alder, *Beyond Bokhara*, p. 105.

86. Ibid., p. 209.

87. Yang, *Bazaar India*, p. 116.

88. Alder, *Beyond Bokhara*, p. 341.

89. Ibid., p. 209.

90. Ibid., p. 357–58.

91. Ibid., p. 367.

92. Ibid., p. 107.

93. See the story of King Lavana, in Wendy Doniger O'Flaherty, *Dreams, Illusion, and Other Realities* (Chicago: University of Chicago Press, 1984), ch. 4.

Animals in African Mythology

KOFI OPOKU

Our African forbears regarded themselves as an inextricable part of the environment, and their lives were interconnected with all living things. They found themselves to be in a neighborly relationship with the created order of things, such as the earth, trees, animals and spirits, and this awareness expressed itself in numerous restrictions and taboos aimed at regulating human relationships with the world around them. These regulations suggest the conscious awareness that the environment was not dead or inert but was populated by beings, just like ourselves, and the existence of these beings presupposed relationships between us (humans) and them.

Animals are of particular importance in the category of beings, as they share the same environment, the same faculties, and the same experience of life and death. They constitute an indispensable source of wisdom without which our self-understanding would be incomplete and, even though animals in the real world may be used for food, clothing, transportation and medicine, they nevertheless remain our useful companions at a much deeper level of human experience. Even in such anti-social behavior as the practice of witchcraft, animal familiars— owls, hyenas, bats, frogs, and insects—accompany witches on their nocturnal missions. The extent of our involvement with animals is borne out in the multifarious roles they play in African mythology.

The mythology, or "sacred wisdom" of Africa, is the product of the ceaseless wonder of our African ancestors, who raised essentially fundamental and central questions of value and meaning about themselves, as humans in the world, and their relations to the world around them. This ceaseless wondering engendered, from an African perspective, a reflection on the fundamental aspects of human existence and experience that all human beings share.

The answers to the questions they posed came in the form of timeless stories, which were clearly distinguishable from "entertaining folktales," because they contained "universally recognizable symbols of psychological and spiritual significance."[1] These answers, which expressed profound and multidimensional truths, helped them to understand themselves and their place in the cosmos, in both its physical and spiritual dimensions, and enabled them to make the "past sensible, the present meaningful and the future possible,"[2] and their whole lives were constructed around the values in these stories. As Clyde Ford wrote: "Myths bring us into accord with the eternal mysteries of being, help us manage the inevitable passages of our lives, and give us templates for our relationship with the societies in which we live and for the relationship of these societies to the earth we share with all life."[3]

While these stories deal with the facts of human existence — that humans find themselves in the world; that humans are born and will die at one time or another; that humans experience pain and pleasure, anger and peace, cold and heat; that humans experience light and darkness; and that they are co-inhabitants in the world with animals and trees and other forms of life — the stories themselves are not factual. Rather they shape the way we think about these facts and help us in our apprehension and encounter with the real world of facts. But these stories do not stand alone; they are reinforced by the performance of rituals, which makes attitudes towards facts and reality acceptable.

A study of these stories reveals a keen awareness of the environment on the part of their originators; they also reveal their exuberant imagination, whose contribution to mythological insights, in general, is immense and can be overlooked, belittled or even ridiculed only by those who, in the name of scholarship, are unwilling to recognize universal truths in African cultures and continue to think of Africa as a blank space or a region brimming with "mumbo jumbo." Joseph Campbell, the acclaimed mythologist, wrote about listening "with aloof amusement to the dreamlike mumbo jumbo of some red-eyed witch doctor of the Congo,"[4]

and contrasted it with the "cultivated rapture" that one derives from reading the sonnets of Lao-Tze. It is clear that Campbell, as well as other Western scholars, operated on the assumption of the existence of "higher mythologies," as opposed to "lower mythologies." Campbell reserved the former for Western and Oriental mythologies, and did not endeavor to look for universal themes in African mythologies simply because they were to him "mumbo jumbo." But it is palpably clear that such denial of validity to African mythology is less than just in the face of the evidence that comes from a careful and unbiased study of African mythology.

Africa is, of course, a large continent with a multiplicity of languages and societies; and to speak of African mythology would appear to impose a uniformity that does not accord with the reality of diversity so characteristic of the continent and its peoples. But beneath the otherwise startling diversity lies a core of basic ideas and concepts that warrants the use of the adjective "African." Although there are wide differences in these ideas and concepts, they have all sprung from the African experience, and to speak of them as African is not to impose an unwarranted uniformity but rather to suggest their African provenance. This essay concerns itself with that part of Africa which lies below the Sahara.

All the myths from antiquity were passed down from generation to generation, not only by word of mouth (an Akan proverb says: *When a person dies, his/her tongue does not rot*—what a person says survives his/her death), but also through rituals, festivals, ceremonies, music and dance, symbols and art, as well as through certain social institutions in African societies. And while myths were not written down, that does not detract from their usefulness as sagacious insights into the human condition and reflections of human attitudes toward the existential facts of life. African myths therefore deserve our serious and considered attention.

Interconnectedness of All That Exists

One of the cardinal beliefs in the traditional religious heritage of Africa is the interconnectedness of all that exists, and African people who continue that tradition believe themselves to be interconnected with, and interdependent on, all that exists. Africans therefore do not consider themselves as separate beings, but rather as beings in relation with the world around them. Humans are not the only beings with life, and everything that has life is potentially sacred. For this reason certain objects in nature, such as some animals and trees, feature in the spirituality of traditional Africa and are treated with reverence. Human faculties of consciousness, will, and purpose are attributed to objects with life, and thus communication between humans and other forms of life is possible. Such objects are thus better described, and comprehended, as subjects.

ANIMALS IN TRADITIONAL CULTURES

African cultures reveal an absorbing and seemingly inexhaustible fascination with animals. Folk tales are replete with animals with human characteristics—behaving, talking, and thinking like humans. Much of African proverbial wisdom is acquired from meditating upon animals who are used as a means by which humans meditate upon themselves, and the animals who are portrayed in art perform the same function for humans. As Fernandez wrote:

> Meditation on animals and our relations with them must be very nearly the oldest and most persistent form of human pensiveness; it is doubtful that we could ever really adequately know our identity as humans if we did not have other animals as a frame for our own activity and reflectivity.[5]

Animals also feature prominently in African mythology as agents in creation and stories of the origin of things, companions of the first humans, and messengers of the spirits. Their fitting roles are based on their observable characteristics.

CREATION MYTHS

The answer to the question of the origin of the world and humankind is found in African myths that tell of the creation of the world by a Creator. The Yoruba, for example, narrate a myth in which *Olodumare,* the Almighty, decided to create the world.[6] And at that time, what is now the earth was a watery, marshy waste. *Olodumare* lived in the heavens with the *orishas*—agents and messengers of Divinity—who used to descend on spiders' webs, which connected the heavens with what is now the earth. The spiders' webs were a metaphor for the *axis mundi* that connects humanity with divinity.

Olodumare sent the arch-divinity, *Orishanla,* with some loose soil in a snail's shell, and a hen. The deputy's responsibility was to throw the soil on a spot on the surface of the watery waste, and the hen was to scatter and spread it. The hen scattered the soil over a significantly wide area, and the deputy went back to report the completion of the assignment. *Olodumare* then sent the chameleon to inspect the work. As Idowu describes it, the chameleon was "chosen on the merit of the extraordinary carefulness and delicacy with which it moves about, and the still more extraordinary way in which it can take in any situation immediately."[7] The chameleon made two trips: after the first, he reported that the earth was wide but not dry enough; and after the second, he reported that the earth was both wide and dry. And, according to the Yoruba, the place where creation began was Ife, which means "wide" or "that which is wide." Animals therefore play a crucial role as agents of the Creator in the creation of the world.

SEPARATION OF THE SKY FROM THE EARTH

A number of African myths tell of a time when the sky and the earth were connected by a rope, and when the rope was cut the sky was separated from the earth. The Fajulu of Sudan and Madi of Uganda both blame the hyena for biting off the cow-skin rope that once joined the earth to heaven, thus causing a separation between the two worlds.[8]

The separation of the two worlds in African mythology, often called "withdrawal stories" by scholars (in other versions of the story it is God who moves away from humankind),[9] must be understood metaphorically and not literally. The stories tell a universal truth about humans and their lack of self-sufficiency and their consequent need for fulfillment. The "separation" or "withdrawal" signifies the beginning of religion, for God or the heavens have to be at a distance, from the earth or from humankind, before communication can be possible. As Zahan explains it:

All African ritual practices concerning rainbows, clouds and rain are based on the "distance" which separates the sky and the earth. Similarly, all relations between the divinity and men can exist logically only if the space between the creator and created is acknowledged. Thus, far from representing an action which unfolds in two eras, paradisiac life and the fall, these themes contain the element which establishes the possibility of religion as communication: distance. In other words, in order to understand the significance of these mythical accounts it is necessary to reverse what they seem to suggest at first glance. The period of man's "religiousness" is not at all the "paradisiac" era when God lived in the "village" of men, but the period following, when God had lost his earthly and human qualities in order to live separately from mankind.[10]

But where the idea of "separation" is implied in these myths it is the otherness of God that is being alluded to and not God's physical separation. Divinity is above creation and at the same time is involved in creation, not only by upholding the universe—as the Igbo say in a proverb: "If *Chuku* removes *Chuku's* hand, the world will collapse"—but also by being involved in the life of humanity.[11]

ORIGIN OF FOOD

A Bantu myth about a contest between the Elephant and Lightning explains the origin of food:

Long ago Elephant came down to earth from heaven where he was born. One day he met Lightning, who had also come down from heaven. They agreed to hold a competition in noise making. Elephant trumpeted grandly, but Lightning let forth such a blast that Elephant dropped dead of fright on the spot. His body just lay there, and his bowels started fermenting. His stomach began to swell up until it burst, and out of it came all the seeds of all the good plants that Elephant had been eating in Heaven. That is how vegetables came to the Earth.[12]

THE COMING OF DEATH

In the Sudan, the Nuer myth of the origin of death begins with a rope that linked the sky with the earth, and when humans grew old they simply climbed up to the sky, became young again, and returned to the earth. The hyena and weaver bird climbed the rope to heaven but cut it on their return. The rope was drawn up to the sky and since then humans have died.[13]

On the West coast of Africa, the Mende say the Creator sent two messengers: a fast creature, the dog, with the message that humans would live forever; and a slow creature, the toad, with the message that humans would die. It makes sense to expect the faster creature to arrive at their destination first, but in the story it was the slower creature who got there first with the message of death, which is why, according to the Mende, humans die.

This myth, and others like it, is true to human experience because humans die, and since they are not immortal, the slower animals always win the race; and the rope that humans used to climb to the sky to be rejuvenated when they grew old had to be cut. And, of course, the stories are not factual but metaphorical.

THE SOCIOPOLITICAL MYTH OF THE KOM OF CAMEROON

The Kom, who live in the Bamenda Grassfields of northwest Cameroon, identify themselves as "people of the snake." This goes back to their myth of origin which states that a python, who was an incarnation of one of their rulers, led their ancestors on their journey to their present territory, and they have remained where the python stopped to this day.[14]

Snakes are regarded as representatives of the ancestors by the Kom, and a person who sees a snake in an area where people are buried sprinkles camwood on it as a blessing. Many Kom medicines contain dried snake, and altogether serpents are regarded as intermediaries between the dead ancestors and the living. The King of the Kom, as a representative of the Kom ancestors, cannot eat the meat of a python. Thus the myth serves as a canon for the social, political, and customary practices of the Kom.

THE BAMILEKE STORY OF THE HARE AND THE ELEPHANT

The elephant is a metaphor for the ruler in many African societies; as the elephant is the biggest animal in the forest, so is the ruler the most important and powerful person in the society. But the ruler's power must be tempered by the advice of the elders and the will of the people over whom he rules. In areas where the ruler takes an oath before he assumes office, such as among the Asante of Ghana, the ruler swears never to act without consulting the elders. The oath and other mechanisms place restraints on the authority and power of the ruler and ensure good government.

The Bamileke, as a justification for the checks and balances imposed on the authority of the ruler, narrated this story of the Hare and Elephant:

In fact, impressed by the size of the elephant, the hare went to ask him for his secrets. But by the law of the elders, such secrets are not revealed for nothing. The elephant gave hare three riddles to solve in order to become as big as he. At the appointed day, the elephant realized that the three riddles were perfectly solved. He therefore called an extraordinary assembly of all the animals in the forest. On the appointed day, every one was present, and the elephant standing before his throne started to speak:

"People of the forest, my citizens, the hare had asked me to teach him the secret to become as big as your majesty. To challenge his ambition, I proposed to him three difficult riddles—but, let me tell you the truth, all the truth. Thus, to make you or anyone as big as myself, I regret that I cannot do it. Only God can do that. We are all born according to the creator of the world. Nevertheless, because you deserve it, I can do one thing for you. By these words, I swear today that I will never do anything or henceforth take any decision concerning the kingdom without discussing with you or listening to your opinion."[15]

The ruler or king is chosen from among the members of the royal family that has the right to rule in a given society and the story legitimizes the rule of the royal family, which is accepted by the ruled. Just as the hare—or, for that matter, the other animals in the forest—have to accept the prodigious size of the elephant and the weighty authority that comes with it, the people of any given society have to accept the rule of the royal family. They may not have a choice in the selection of the ruler, but they do have a choice in how they will be governed; and this is where the will of the people and the counsel of the elders come in to place restraints on the authority of the ruler in order to ensure good government.

The Pangolin: King of the Beasts

The sheer extraordinariness of the pangolin has led to its being regarded in some African societies as the "King of the Beasts." While the pangolin looks like a lizard, with triangular scales on its body, it is a mammal which gives birth to a single baby that it carries at the base of its tail. The scales on its body make it look like a fish, and yet it shuns water. It has legs and often walks upright on its hind legs. It can live on the ground as well as in trees; and when it is attacked, it rolls its body into a ball and stays put until the imperilment passes away. More oddly still, the pangolin has no teeth and uses its extended and sticky tongue in hunting for food, mostly ants and termites, by sticking it into the ground.

The pangolin baffles human imagination by its inscrutable incomprehensibility and becomes therefore a suggestive metaphor for many. Allen Roberts clarifies the matter in this manner:

> The pangolin is so "good to think" because it is strangely "human." The pangolin has a single baby, walks upright, and shows "dignity" when attacked, almost as though it were turning the other cheek. Some Africans make the pangolin the central emblem of healing people who have been unable to bear children. The pangolin is so odd that its existence seems almost impossible. But it does exist. If a pangolin can really exist, perhaps *anything* is possible! The pangolin serves as a symbol of hope that even the unhappiness of not being able to have children may be overcome. Furthermore, just as a pangolin is protected by its scales, people may be shielded from difficulties. And in the same way that a pangolin rolls itself until adversity passes, perhaps people, too, can overcome their problems.[16]

And just as the scales on the pangolin cover the secrets buried in its body waiting to be discovered, healers in Zaire, for example, see a connection between their professional and social role in society and the wonderingly curious animal. The healers therefore wear beaded headbands with triangular designs called "pangolins," which cover and protect the secrets of their craft and make their practice possible and successful.[17]

MYTHOLOGY AND ROCK ART

Studies that have been made of rock art in Southern Africa[18] in which antelopes predominate have pointed out that the depiction of antelopes goes beyond the utilitarian considerations as a source of food, and that social and metaphysical realities account for their preponderance. Nearly 77 percent of San paintings are of antelopes,[19] and the relationship between the people and the antelopes is not characterized by opposition but by agreeable continuity, incessant interaction, and harmonious integration.[20]

The San, who are mainly hunters, regard the antelope as the "master animal," on whom they depend for their major source of food; but beyond that the antelope represents for them the presence of the sacred. In San mythology, the praying mantis is the incarnation of the Creator God, Kaggen. And at the beginning of time, Mantis sat in a half open white flower in the primeval ocean. As Ford points out: "This symbol of the godhead at the centre of a flower is well-known: in Christianity the rose encloses the Virgin in whose arms rests the child Christ, and in Hinduism and Buddhism, the Brahma or Buddha sits at the centre of the lotus."[21]

In San mythology, Mantis changes into other animals or even humans, but one of his favorite transfigurations is into an eland. The centrality of the eland in San mythology and life is seen in its uses in their rituals. Young San boys have to kill an eland with a bow and arrow, as their initiation into manhood, and the principal rituals take place with the boys sitting on eland skins. The cicatrizations made on the bodies of the young men to signify their change in status are made with eland fat. These rituals make a total identification of the young men with the eland possible.

But the San girls are not left out of this pivotal and fundamental identification with the eland. The young girls undergoing initiation rituals are referred to as elands, and the female initiation rite, performed after a girl's first menstruation, is called the Eland Bull Dance. A man who intends to marry a woman has to give to his future mother-in-law the heart of an eland, and at the wedding ceremony the bride is smeared with eland fat. And, here again, the identification with the eland is substantially total.

There is thus a sacred relationship between the eland and the San that is given meaning in ritual and myth. And, even when the San have to kill eland for food, it is believed that the animal willingly offers itself as food, while the hunter who kills it helps the animal on its spiritual journey so that it would come back again as food for humans.

ELANDS AND SHAMANIC VISIONS

San rock paintings show a dying eland as a metaphor for a shaman going into trance and entering the spiritual world. An eland struggling to die and a shaman entering into trance behave in the same way. Like the eland about to die, the shaman shakes violently, sweats superabundantly, bleeds from the nose, and ultimately collapses unconscious.[22] And these rock paintings, dating to 30,000 years, constitute not only the San record of the shaman's adventure into the spirit world, but also humanity's spiritual journey into the world of the spirit.[23]

ANIMALS AS LIVING EMBLEMS

The Akan of Ghana divide themselves into eight matrilineal clans and each clan has an animal or bird as its living emblem. The clan finds its own characteristics in the living emblems. The clans and their emblems are as follows:

1. Oyoko: hawk, patience
2. Aduana: dog, adroitness, skillful and adept under pressing conditions
3. Asona: crow, wisdom

4. Ekoona: buffalo, conscientiousness, thorough and painstaking, scrupulous
5. Asenee: bat, diplomacy, skill in dealing with people
6. Bretuo: leopard, tenacity, aggressiveness
7. Asakyiri: eagle, vigilance
8. Agona: parrot, eloquence

The kings of the Asante are selected from the Oyoko clan, which is charged with the responsibility of protecting the Golden Stool from capture and defilement. The guardians of the Sacred Golden Stool need the dogged patience, stern vigilance, and amazing celerity of a hawk that, high in the skies, focuses its sharp eyes on its prey and, with incredible speed, swoops down and captures it with its unsparingly sharp talons. The Oyoko clan and the Asante kings have kept the Golden Stool with hawk-like reputation to this day.

ANIMALS AND PROVERBIAL WISDOM

Much of African proverbial wisdom is based on the keen observation and philosophical reflection of animal characteristics. While the proverbs talk about animals, they are essentially about humans, for animal behavior is seen as a metaphor for human behavior. To cite a few of these proverbs:

1. *Short though the antelope's tail may be, it can flick away pests with it* (handicaps are no excuse for lack of effort).
2. *When the leopard is desperate, it eats grass* (the need to adapt oneself to changing circumstances).
3. *However poor (desperate) the crocodile becomes, it hunts in the river, not in the forest* (one must not do what is improper or undignified, however outrageous the circumstance).
4. *A horse has four legs, yet it often falls* (adversity may befall even the strong and powerful).
5. *The lizard does not eat pepper and make the frog suffer the burning heat* (each person must be responsible for his or her own actions).

6. *If you get hold of the snake's head, the rest of its body is a mere string* (controlling a person's mind is the most effective way to dominate him or her completely).

7. *With patience you can skin an ant and obtain its liver* (patience can accomplish the impossible).

8. *When the parrot eats, the toucan also eats* (an expression of egalitarianism—all people have equal political economic and social rights).

9. *When the cock becomes intoxicated, it forgets that it came from an egg* (power, influence, or wealth can blur our perspective and distort our vision to the extent that we forget that we are after all, human like everybody else).

10. *The snake does not bite for nothing* (provocation elicits violence).

Conclusion

In my study of African proverbs, I observed:

The … ancestors found wisdom everywhere—in the environment, in the human body, in trees,

birds and animals, in the skies etc. The originators of the proverbs were very keen observers of nature, and, in a sense, the whole environment was an open book from which they could read lessons to benefit human life, to make it meaningful, understandable, livable, and tolerable. And this tradition has been passed on from generation to generation.[24]

Lessons from animals, as the different mythologies mentioned above show, enabled our African ancestors to make sense of their circumstances of life. Animal life and behavior are not attributes humans gave to the animals; on the contrary, by observing animals and thinking about them, humans discovered an abundant source of wisdom that already existed. This wisdom is indispensable in the human quest for meaning, which has not been rendered obsolete by humanity's increasing technological advancement. The mythological wisdom in African stories continues to speak to the human condition.

NOTES

1. Clyde W. Ford, *The Hero with an African Face: Mythic Wisdom of Traditional Africa* (New York: Bantam Books, 1999), p. x.

2. Barbara Sproul, *Primal Myths: Creating the World* (San Francisco: Harper, 1979), p. 5.

3. Ford, *The Hero,* p. viii.

4. Joseph Campbell, *The Hero with a Thousand Faces* (Princeton: Princeton University Press, 1968), p. 3.

5. James W. F. Fernandez. "Meditation on Animals—Figuring Out Humans," in Allen Roberts, ed., *Animals in African Art* (New York: The Museum for African Art, 1995), p. 8.

6. E. Bolaji Idowu, *Olodumare: God in Yoruba Belief* (London: Longman, 1962).

7. Ibid., pp. 19–20.

8. John S. Mbiti, *African Religions and Philoso-*

phy, 2nd ed. (Oxford and Portsmouth: Heinemann, 1990), p. 51.

9. Kofi A. Opoku, "Ancient Wisdom in the African Heritage," *Christian-Jewish Relations* 20, no. 1 (Spring 1987): 45–61.

10. Dominique Zahan, *The Religion, Spirituality and Thought of Traditional Africa* (Chicago: University of Chicago Press, 1979), p. 16.

11. Opoku, "Ancient Wisdom," p. 52.

12. Donald J. Consentino, "Talking (Gray) Heads: Elephant as Metaphor in African Myth and Folklore," in Doran Ross, ed., *Elephant: The Animal and Its Ivory in African Culture* (Los Angeles: UCLA, Fowler Museum, 1992), p. 87.

13. Geoffrey Parrinder, "God in African Mythology," in J. M. Kitagawa and Charles Long, eds., *Myths and Symbols: Studies in Honour of M. Eliade*

(Chicago: University of Chicago Press, 1969), pp. 111–25.

14. Eugenia Shanklin, "In the Track of the Python: A West African Origin Story," in Roy Willis, ed., *Signifying Animals: Human Meaning in the Natural World* vol. 16, Proceedings of the World Archaeology Congress, Southampton, UK (London: Unwin Hyman, 1990), pp. 204–13.

15. Donald J. Consentino, "Talking (Gray) Heads," p. 92.

16. Allen Roberts, "An Unexpected King of Beasts," in *Faces: The Magazine About People* (New York: Express, January, 1995), p. 29.

17. Ibid.

18. M. Leakey, *Africa's Vanishing Art: The Rock Paintings of Tanzania* (London: Hamish Hamilton, 1983); J. D. Lewis-Williams, *Images of Power: Understanding Bushman Rock Art* (Johannesburg, South Africa: Southern Book Publishers, 1989); P. Vinnicombe, *People of the Eland* (Durban, South Africa: University of Natal Press, 1976).

19. Leakey, *Africa's Vanishing Art.*

20. Ford, *The Hero.*

21. Ibid., p. 103.

22. Ibid., p. 106.

23. Ibid., p. 109.

24. Kofi A. Opoku, *Hearing and Keeping: Akan Proverbs* (Pretoria: University of South Africa Press, 1997), p. xx.

"Why Umbulka Killed His Master"

Aboriginal Reconciliation and the
*Australian Wild Dog (*Canis lupus dingo*)*

IAN MCINTOSH

A Totem to Think With

During his voyages of exploration along Australia's east coast in 1770 Captain James Cook made mention in his diaries that Aborigines often ignored his presence, desired none of his many gifts, and would not give up anything of their own to him. This image of Aboriginal self-sufficiency and total uninterest in the new is characteristic of many stories of first contact. Although they are far removed in time and space from the Cook encounters, northern Australian Aboriginal narratives describing first contact with Macassan fisherman from Sulawesi in Indonesia—who visited northern Australia from as early as 1700 in search of beche de mer or trepang[1]—suggest a similar self-sufficiency and defiance.

Neither the Macassans' power and influence nor their relative wealth in relation to Aborigines could be dismissed. Unlike the fleeting appearances of explorers like Captain Cook, the Macassan presence was an annual occurrence and of up to three months' duration. And with prolonged contact came the growing problem of the encounter's diverse antisocial outcomes —greed, violence, and self-doubt. How could those Aborigines desirous of the new uphold the laws of old when the fabric of their society was being undermined as a direct consequence of contact? With imaginative flair the Arnhemland mythmaker chose the wild dog or dingo as the instrument with which to negotiate the encounter. Narratives featuring the dingo became the basis of trade routes for the transfer of introduced items such as iron, cloth, tobacco, and alcohol, from the coast to the interior, making all Aborigines beneficiaries of contact. These "outside," or public, narratives were an integral part of the Aboriginal "foreign policy" regarding these uninvited outsiders—a policy or "law" that enabled the narrator to ascribe a place for the intruders within Aboriginal cosmology without compromising the sanctity of cherished beliefs associated with the Wangarr or Dreaming.

One of the foundations of this "foreign policy" is the myth of the dingo's origins in this period of turmoil. It murders and partially consumes its Aboriginal masters and then retreats into the wilderness. According to variations of this "starter" myth, when "Macassans" first appeared all along the Arnhem Land coast, the wild dog was first on the scene to investigate. The meeting places are sacred sites, and the related narratives are celebrated in ceremony and song. Why? The "hidden" message of the "starter" and its many variations presents the listener not only with a commentary on the culture/nature, human/animal divide, but also a blueprint for future dealings with non-Aborigines. The mythmaker, while taking an uncompromising stand in relation to the Aborigines' rights, used the dog symbol in myth to lay a foundation for a reconciliation between ethnicities. Aborigines would not lose sight of essential truths, like the fact that they were traditional land owners, and the visitors were unceremonious exploiters of the land's resources; but they could be partners and share in the wealth of the land. Each would benefit from the other's presence, so long as they both acknowledged each other's humanity—rejecting those types of behavior more characteristic of the wild dog—a message as relevant today as during the unruly days of first encounter between Aborigines and others.

Canis lupus dingo

Dingo myths in Aboriginal Australia, at one level, reinforce a view of dogs prevalent in popular literature.[2] The dingo inhabits two worlds simultaneously—the natural and the supernatural, the culturally constructed cosmos and the untamed wilderness. Despite the potential for domestication when young, the dingo's natural inclination is to be wild and anarchic, and in myth, this "free agent" is seen as a threat to the social order.

While superficially recognizable as canine, the dingo (*Canis lupus dingo*) is biologically distinct. Similar in size to the German Shepherd, it has a short-haired coat that ranges in color from tan, to black with white spots, to white. The dingo has a bushy tail, strong claws, and an angular head with erect ears. It is an opportunistic carnivore, hunting mainly at night. While preferring to eat mammals, it is also known to feed on birds, reptiles, and insects. Dingoes have clearly defined home territories, though parts of this may be shared with other dogs. It breeds only once a year, the female giving birth to three or four pups.[3]

The dingo's origins are a mystery. About four thousand years ago, this relative of the semi-wild dogs of Indonesia and Papua New Guinea appeared in Australia. It eradicated the Thylacine—the zebra-striped native dog—and today is regarded as a pest of significant proportion. The world's largest fence keeps this merciless predator out of the "civilized" settled areas and away from the sheep stations of eastern Australia.

Unlike the domestic dog, the dingo appears to be a trickster. In Aboriginal myths and legends, it shares some of the characteristics of the Chinese monkey and the North American coyote and rabbit, but any other resemblance to the classical trickster figure is illusory. Jung saw tricksters as primordial figures transcending humankind's conceptual boundaries, moving freely between the worlds of gods and humans and playing tricks on both. But the dingo, in the words of one Aboriginal elder, is a "fully fledged lawman." It institutes Dreaming laws but also breaks them. In some parts of the continent it is considered the ultimate destroyer, disrupting the status quo and bringing disarray to human affairs.[4] At least one group credits it with the origin of death.

For Australia's indigenous peoples, the dingo is a totem of great import as it provides a reference point for Aboriginal customs and social structure. Somewhat like other tricksters, the dingo's behavior suggests alternate ways of being that, if implemented, would subvert the desired order of things. The dog mates indiscriminately, kills for pleasure, and does not share its food. It makes its own camp and follows its own rules —and yet, when young, the pup hankers for human company and is completely dependent upon its Aboriginal masters. Like a child, it is given a name, a kinship label (son, daughter, etc.), and a place in the family. But when the pup grows up it deserts its human family. In some areas of Aboriginal Australia, young men are referred to as wild dogs before they are initiated: during this period they know nothing of the sacred laws by which humans must live. To operate in society they must learn to act according to cultural expectations. The dingo is therefore a powerful symbol for moderation in behavior at both individual and group levels. According to anthropologist Debbie Bird Rose, "dingo makes us human."[5]

Dogs and the Moiety Framework of Trade

In northeast Arnhem Land, dualism defines the Aboriginal universe. Each person is born into a patrilineal and exogamous landowning clan, or Mala, that forms an integral part of one of two moieties, namely Dhuwa or Yirritja. The small subset of myths referred to here are drawn solely from the Yirritja moiety, as this was the moiety responsible for the development of policy in relation to outsiders and all things "new."[6]

Lany'tjun was the great ancestor of the Yirritja moiety and Djang'kawu of the Dhuwa moiety. They gave to their respective clans certain totems, which would be collectively owned and honored in moiety-wide celebrations, and others for which they were primary custodians.[7] Almost the entire natural world has been divided between the moieties and clans. The dingo, however, is somewhat of an anomaly. It is not moiety specific. It is Dhuwa in Dhuwa lands, and Yirritja in Yirritja lands—except of course in mythical episodes where it maintains a moiety association.

Moiety solidarity rests on the acknowledgement of the myriad of interrelationships established between the clans by Djan'kawu and Lany'tjun. These bonds emphasize the maintenance of often exclusive ties between groups of people and territory. As Turner[8] declares, clans' alliances imply communality, cooperation, and sexual inaccessibility, as well as the formation of compatible, cohesive work groups and the exchange of information, goods, and services. According to Williams,[9] one particular clan relationship stands out above all others. The maari-gutharra (maternal grandmother, grandchild) relationship that was instituted by both Lany'tjun and Djang'kawu is the backbone of Aboriginal society. The relationship is enshrined in numerous songs, dances, and narratives reflecting the movement of totems across the land and seascape at the "beginning of time." Gutharra clans have certain rights over their maari's sacred totemic designs, and they have the strongest claim to succession if their maari's clan becomes extinct.

Turner[10] argues that Aborigines have spread themselves over the landscape in such a way that their respective estates are, to a degree, resource specific, thereby ensuring the establishment of bonds with owners of other estates if their economic needs are to be met. And during the days of first contact, those Aboriginal groups in close contact with Macassan trepangers took on a very prominent role within the moiety. Inland clans established or reaffirmed ties with those coastal groups who had opened their lands to resource exploitation by outsiders so as to ensure access to additional highly desirable trade resources. And it was along these pathways formed between gutharra and maari clans that the dingo was to travel. In so doing, the dog was to facilitate the flow of trade goods from the coastline to the interior. And because Dhuwa and Yirritja are intermarrying moieties, all peoples had access to the trade that was opened up by the dingo.[11]

The "Starter" Myth

Three Wangurri "dog-men," Umbulka, Martingarr, and Djarrk, are hot and unhappy. There is no wind. They meet a Warramiri "dog-man," Bulunha, who invites them to his country at Cape Wilberforce where cool winds blow year round courtesy of their maari, the Golpa from the north in the Wessel Islands. On their return to Wangurri territory, the Wangurri "dog-men" eat rats until their stomachs are full and they begin to growl. A Wangurri man and woman, seeing the "dog-men," ask them why they are growling. Had they been to Warramiri lands, and seen the calamity unfolding there? The "dog-men" urinate on the feet of their masters, then bite them to death, burying their partially consumed bodies in a shallow grave creating a sacred totemic emblem. They then retreat to the hinterland, meeting up with a Dhalwangu "dog-man" called Lupana. Upon hearing the sound of a man chopping wood, they retreat further into the hinterland, shunning all contact with humanity, becoming the wild dingoes we know today.

In this "starter" myth, adapted from W. L. Warner's account,[12] the dog (and sometimes related totems)[13] was chosen by the mythmaker as the most appropriate symbol for describing the vast array of antisocial and other responses to first contact. But what does it mean, for example, for the wild dogs to eat raw meat, rats in this instance, urinate on the feet of their masters, then kill and bury them? Why are they bellicose, afraid of contact with humans, and unhappy with their lot? What did they see in Warramiri lands that changed their lives and that created the antisocial entity we know as the dingo?

An examination of other dingo narratives helps to draw out the underlying significance of the Umbulka narrative, providing some insight into the Aborigines' purpose in creating, telling, and retelling such a narrative both in the past and now. Take, for example, the following highlighted Yirritja moiety myths:

- A wild dog, of similar disposition to Umbulka, desires contact with the Macassan visitors, wanting them to stay in his country to bring to his people the benefits of contact, but as a dog he lacks the necessary social skills and is ineffectual in building an alliance. [Reflects the dingo's timidity and asociality.]

- Another dog lives a life of abundance and is prepared to share the bounty of its land with the outsiders if they are hungry. [Reflects the fact that the dingo will, on occasion, share its food.]

- Certain dogs are fed cooked whale meat by the visitors and they ravenously devour it. They want more—the entire raw whale carcass—a desire that leads to their demise. [Reflects the dingoes' greed, lack of self-control, and often "murderous" intent.]

- A pack of dogs live "traditionally," but in isolation, according to the laws of old, refusing to use any "modern" conveniences. Visitors to their land must abandon all the trappings of the new world. [The dingo is viewed as a culture bearer that is capable of the same loyalty to its origins as displayed by humans.]

- One dog travels aboard a visitor's boat, and the captain gives it the name of a sacred totem; the Aborigines kill the captain for this breach of etiquette, and the dog retreats into the wilderness to become a wild dog. [Paralleling the Umbulka origin narrative, it reminds us of how humans and dogs are interchangeable in narratives.]

- At the beginning of time, Aborigines are white and rich, Macassans black and poor. One dog refuses to parley with Macassans and speaks rudely to them, and consequently all Aborigines are now black and poor, while Macassans are white and rich. [Reflects upon the decisive nature of contact between the "dog" and Macassans for future generations.]

Reading "history" from these narratives, it is apparent that, within the Yirritja moiety, some Aborigines rejected the Macassans, some tried to live with them, and some attempts at alliance building were made but shattered by perceived antisocial behavior from one or both parties. Some acted as if Macassans did not exist, clinging to the life of old, while others were overcome with desire for the introduced goods and nearly self-destructed. None could ignore the visitor's presence. In a majority of cases, Aborigines (portraying themselves as dogs in myth) became thoroughly discontented with their lot in the wake of contact. How to account, cosmologically speaking, for their sudden great interest in, and dependency upon, all the new ideas and technologies (iron manufacture, pottery, cloth), and the concomitant threats to social cohesion and leadership?

In all the stories examined, even those focused on rejection or loss, there is a general movement of the dingo from the inland to the sea, and from its homeland to that of a maternal grandmother's clan (its *maari*). The simplest reading of the myths is that these were the very first trade routes. From out of the chaos, trading networks were established to facilitate the movement of trade goods from the sea to the interior along lines of established sacred alliances. But there is another message in these journeys that Aborigines call upon today in their dealings with outsiders, and the best narrative to describe this overall picture, this unfolding Aboriginal "foreign policy" in relation to visitors, is in the well-recorded narratives of a dingo called Djuranydjura.

The Transformation of Djuranydjura

The best developed of contact stories emerging from the Umbulka "starter" involves the meeting of Indonesian fishermen and the black male dog Djuranydjura. It goes thus:

When the Macassans arrived at Howard Island and started to build their houses, Djuranydjura came down to meet them. The dog had never seen white skin before and was curious, and walked right up to the visitor. The Macassan man said, "I will give you matches." The dog was excited with the ease by which he could make fire, but said, "I use fire sticks. It takes longer, but that's the way I do it."

The Macassan man offered the dog rice, but it got stuck in his teeth and he spat it out saying

that he had plenty of bush food to eat and didn't need any more.

The Macassan then offered to build the dog a house and lift him up off the ground so he could live on carpets, but the dog said that he was happy to live in the long grass and would continue to do so.

The Macassan offered the dog tobacco, tomahawks, and canoes, all the things that his people had, but the dog said, "No. I don't want them."

The Macassan said, "Why do you act like this? You could have everything that I have." The dog replied, "I want you to be a Macassan man. I am a black man. If I get these things I will become a Macassan and you will become an Aborigine."

So the Macassan packed up his house and went away, and the dog went back to the bushes. Today you can see the sacred rock that represents Djuranydjura. When people look at it they think about why blacks have so little and Macassans and whites so much. Djuranydjura had rejected these things so many years ago.[14]

The Djuranydjura narrative refers to the dingo as a representative of Aborigines, on an errand for Aborigines, or representing the "law" of the Aboriginal people. It is the wild dog that determines the nature of actual relations with overseas visitors, for in the area where this mythical rejection took place, the Indonesians did not fish for trepang (sea cucumber). The Macassans called that part of the Australian coastline Marege Siki—a dangerous area—and were careful to avoid it. One aged trepanger, reminiscing in the 1970s, said that if the Macassans tried to land at Marege Siki, the Aborigines would spear them.

But Djuranydjura's rebuff of the Macassans does not the end the story. When examining the variations of this myth, a fascinating pattern emerges, providing the answer to a puzzling question. For more than 200 years, Aborigines benefited materially from the presence of Macassans. Trade goods like cloth and knives had long since become indispensable. But how could this be the case if the dog's law, Aboriginal law, demanded the rejection of the visitors? In the vicinity of Howard Island, myth variations drawn from the vast Aboriginal repertoire provide clues: The Macassans see a fire burning in the direction of their homeland across the seas, and depart. The dog also sees smoke rising, but it is from the land of its *maari*—the Warramiri. Djuranydjura is worried, and sets out to investigate, but its canoe sinks as it tries to cross to the next island, a clear statement of the inferiority of its technology when compared to that of the Macassans.

In another variation, the dog travels along the beach, drawn by a strange smell, one it has never smelt before. As it gets closer to the source, it is transformed: its color changes from black to white, its sex from male to female, and its language to that of its Warramiri *maari*. According to the keepers of this narrative, the transformation was indicative of the newly established trading relationship between Aborigines and the Indonesian "whites" based on a body of Aboriginal law that viewed the presence of all outsiders as being a part of the plan of a Yirritja moiety ancestral entity known as Birrinydji to bring the Aborigines "up to date."[15] Djuranydjura had arrived at its *maari*'s camp in Warramiri land at the far north of Elcho Island to see a visitor cutting up and cooking a beached whale in the shallows. This was the source of the unfamiliar aroma. Djuranydjura was offered a piece of rotting whale meat, and she ate it, and in a repeat of the meeting with Macassans at her homeland, she was offered a necklace and a fishing line; this time she accepted it, but added, "I'm only taking this because you want me to. These things still belong to you."[16]

This interaction and sex change suggests that Aboriginal women were the medium of exchange—that trade between Macassans and Aborigines was through women, that is, that sexual favors were traded in return for highly desired trade goods. But today Aborigines merely say that this narrative was a mandate for the intermarriage of the parties. A deeper reading of the female dog's acceptance of gifts would be that while the women were being used by the men as items of barter—and "given" in the short term to the Macassans—they remained the "possession" of Aborigines—just as ownership of the Macassan gifts remained in the visitor's hands. It is a statement of "each to their own" as in the original Djuranydjura narrative.

The sacred alliance of *gutharra* and *maari* created by the moiety founder Lany'tjun is reaffirmed through the travels of the antisocial dog and a pathway is created for the movement of goods from the coast to the hinterland. The dog's Aborigines—even though they rejected the visitors—now had access to Macassan goods without compromising the decisions they had made about intercultural contact or their integrity as a people.

This pattern of local rejection and acceptance of the Other through the law of the *maari* (Birrinydji), and in the *maari* territory, repeats itself in at least three other Arnhem Land localities—although the narratives are not so well documented. In one case Macassans are rejected by honey bees in Gupapuyngu territory and a dog, Wananda, then travels to the land of its maari on Elcho Island, where it accepts dugong meat from the visitors. In another case, the Mildjingi dog Kurrumul travels from the interior to the sea, where it fails to engage successfully in trade relations with Macassans. Its alter ego, Gurarinja, however, undertakes the same journey and successfully enters into a partnership with its *maari*, the Warramiri. Finally, there is the story of the rejection by Aborigines of Macassans at Dholtji through the person of the insolent dog Bol'lili, but with the simultaneous acceptance of visitors by Bulunha at nearby Cape Wilberforce. There are also hints of this initial and public rejection of outsiders and, later, guarded acceptance of them, in other narratives (see appendix). Many appear to form the basis of trade routes.

Foreign goods, one might assume, had no place in the traditional system of Yolngu totemic allocations, but in a Yirritja-moiety–Warramiri-clan perspective, all these new possessions were associated with their ancestor Birrinydji, a powerful Dreaming figure inspired by the image a boat captain and blacksmith—a mighty being who drew all outsiders onto the Arnhem Land coast like a magnet by the strength of its *marr* or desire to "bring Aborigines into the modern world."[17] Through Birrinydji, all new things were understood to be associated with the Yirritja moiety. Consequently, they were the ones to develop the "foreign policy" in relation to outsiders.

In many of the dog stories, the Yirritja dingo journeys from the inland to the country of a related Yirritja clan associated with Birrinydji. It is drawn to the sea by a new smell—a fire burning (a reference to people in distress)—a desire for a cool breeze, etc. In some cases, a "road" is explicitly mentioned, or a "rope," or "line of vision" joining the clans from some high vantage point. While in several cases the threat posed by the presence of the visitors is of paramount significance, in a majority of cases, trade is the desired outcome of a renewed clan alliance between *maari* and *gutharra* clans. In some cases an alliance is formed directly with the Macassans, or a pathway is created for both Aborigines and non-Aborigines to travel upon. In others, a partnership is desired but not activated. In a few instances there is no contact with the visitors but an alliance is forged by the travel between an inland Yirritja clan and the Warramiri or another Birrinydji clan. In this latter case, the Macassans may be referred to in a metaphorical sense—as boats or sailing canoes, or even whales. The consumption of whale or dugong meat is the equivalent of acceptance of Macassan trade goods, or a mandate for a trading alliance, even intermarriage. A fundamental precondition of any partnership, however, is made clear in a number of the narratives. Aborigines, though dependent upon Macassans' goods for their livelihoods, would not accept a subservient or "dog" status in relation to these visitors. If treated in such a manner, they would become like Umbulka, and kill their "masters."

What Did Umbulka See in Warramiri Lands?

As mentioned earlier, the mythmaker used the dog symbol in myth to comment upon Aboriginal attempts to live in a world no longer in their control—one that entices them in with new things—but that fundamentally challenges their previous ways. And this challenge is as real and pressing today as it was at the time of first contact. A young Aboriginal boy or girl growing up at Elcho Island in northeast Arnem Land, for instance, knows from the earliest age the story of the defiant dog-hero Djuranydjura. While the land and seascape of the Aboriginal domain is ablaze with totemic significance (whale, crocodile, etc.), it is the dog story that many Aboriginal children first learn. It is an outside or public story, but its message is one and the same as the intricate, chilling, and profound sacred or inside narratives of Birrinydji that the young will come to understand only with experience of outsiders, when they know how the non-Aboriginal world had oppressed them, and still threatens their sovereign rights as a people. A child, however, knows only the story of Aboriginal defiance in the face of outside intrusion. And it is a story told with gusto—the children learn never to give up on what they have—they alone are the inheritors of the sacred land, their language, and culture.

Later on the chidlren will learn that at the beginning of time (and in the Macassan period) a sharp division was created by Umbulka between humans and animals, Aborigines and wild dogs. Aborigines are social beings, their "wild" nature concealed by the constraints of culture. It was the will of the ancestors that they might live in partnership with non-Aborigines. The Aborigines owned the land and its resources, but the visitors had the technology to transform these raw materials into highly prized items of trade. Here was the basis of a lasting alliance. And Umbulka's actions remind the listener of the need to be sociable, even under conditions that had threatened to undermine the whole fabric of Aboriginal society, as during first contact at Cape

Wilberforce in Warramiri country. What Um-bulka witnessed was the near total collapse of the Warramiri.[18] The Birrinydji narratives speak of how jealousy, greed, and violence followed the wholesale switch to dependence upon what they could not supply themselves, i.e., intro-duced goods. In a spate of unparalleled vicious-ness, the people turned on themselves and on the Macassans and were almost annihilated. The dog was infected with anger and resentment, and its Wangurri masters knew that it must have witnessed this terrible scene and in the Umbulka "starter" story, it came to personify that collec-tive madness of the period. It made a sacred em-blem of the human body, forever affirming the sacred truth of a human being's sociable nature. In so doing, Umbulka created a higher form of being—a human being—and called it "Mas-ter." "Humanity" is a sacred construct that is constantly under threat but can never be lost or forfeited if one affirms the sanctity of life. This is why the anti-social dog is so sacred to Aborigines.

Conclusion

The Umbulka narrative was the "starter" for a whole series of myths that would allow people to understand the proper place of outsiders in re-lation to Aborigines. Umbulka killed its master in order to remind everyone that Aborigines are human beings and would behave accordingly, even when challenged by the presence of out-siders whose behavior all too often resembled that of a wild dog. People recall, upon hearing these stories, that Aboriginal responses to en-counters were often dog-like, as they drove the visitors from the coast and into the sea. The mes-sage is a simple one. Umbulka created the social being known as the Aborigine. It makes humans sacred and itself profane in the process. This fundamental distinction between animality and humanity underlies all the dingo narratives and still guides Aboriginal thought regarding the na-ture of intercultural relations.

The implication is that in Arnhem Land, there was no wild dog—no dingo—until the "white man" Macassan came to Australian shores. There were no human beings either, just as there was no category for the liar, the thief, murderer, or double-crosser.[19] And Aboriginal groups like the Warramiri were not always "quick to temper" and so conflicted about rela-tions with the Other. This is now a clan charac-teristic, a direct legacy of contact with Macas-sans. In Warramiri territory, the dog Umbulka witnessed the sudden and dramatic breakdown of a society; the rapid destruction of a cul-ture tormented from within and without, and a people fleeing from the scene of chaos. The wild dog is a product of intercultural mayhem, and at night the Warramiri say you can hear the dingo cry for what the Aborigines had gone through and how their world was changed forever by its actions. The "white man" had become part of their lives. But so too had the wild dog, and the two became inseparable in myth.

Today, a great deal of emphasis is placed by Australian governments upon the concept of reconciliation between Aborigines and non-Aborigines. But Arnhemlanders often complain that they are being treated like dogs and not as human beings by federal and state bureaucrats. The antisocial behavior of non-Aborigines in trying to steal the land and its resources relegates them to the antisocial canine category. Recon-ciliation, from the perspective of this great to-temic legacy of the dingo—the many narratives of encounter between Macassans and Aborigi-nes—begins when each party treats the other as sacred entities—as human beings—and not as wild and "cultureless" animals. This is the essence of the Aboriginal "foreign policy." The trade that once flowed along the pathways cre-ated by the moiety ancestors and retraced by the wild dog no longer flows. But the "foreign policy" determined by Aboriginal thinkers dur-ing a time of great turmoil is as relevant today as in the first days of the often turbulent encoun-ters between Aborigines and others.

APPENDIX: NARRATIVE OVERVIEWS[20]

1. Umbulka, et al.

Wangurri "dog-men" travel to Warramiri land to find relief from the heat in the cool north wind. Upon their return, they hunt and eat uncooked rats, and then kill their Wangurri masters, making a sacred emblem of their bodies. They run away to Dhalwangu land and become wild dingoes. [The starter myth. The creation of the wild dog.][21]

2. Djuranydjura (male)

Dingo meets Macassans on the beach but rejects all offers of gifts and retreats to its homeland. The Macassans return to the west, into the sunset. [A message of self-sufficiency on the part of Aborigines.][22]

3. Djuranydjura (female)

Dingo sees a fire burning in the north and investigates. On the way, its canoe sinks. In the land of its *maari* it meets the Macassan, eats whale meat, and accepts gifts. [Dingo facilitates a lasting partnership between Aborigines and non-Aborigines.]

4. Kurrumul et al.

Dingo smells whale meat cooking and travels to the sea to be fed. It is greedy and in trying devour the entire raw stranded whale carcass, perishes with the incoming tide, and turns to stone, becoming a permanent threat to navigation. [A no-go area is created for visiting Macassans. This is a sacred place for Aborigines; Macassans must stay away.][23]

5. Gurarinja, et al.

Dingo smells "fish" being cooked in Warramiri lands and travels to the sea, plays in the water, and throws up water in the form of vapor, like a whale. [An alliance is formed between a "dingo" clan and a "whale" clan.][24]

6. Bulunha

Bulunha will share the produce of the sea with "black" people if they are hungry. All are equal under Aboriginal law. [An alliance is formed between clans and between Aborigines and Macassans.]

7. Bol'lili

Aborigines are white and rich and Macassans black and poor. The dingo is rude to the Macassans and henceforth the Macassans become rich white masters and Aborigines become black and poor servants. [To behave like a wild dingo precludes the possibility of any mutually beneficial partnerships between Aborigines and others.][25]

8. Bandhurrk, et al.

Dingoes make a traditional bark canoe so they can travel to other places. [A reminder of the value and importance of traditions in the face of change.]

9. Djirrwadjirrwa

This dingo is a land owner and leader but is shy of outsiders. It forms a road between Warramiri and other lands for all to travel upon and wants the Macassans to stay in his country. [An alliance is formed between clans.]

10. Namalia, et al.

Dingo travels from the inland to the sea to cool off. The whale instructs it to stay on the hilltop, but it disobeys, swims, only to be frightened back to its proper place on the hilltop by the snake. [The division reflected here is between land and sea clans—an alliance is built between groups who have a separate place in the cosmos.] [26]

11. Marmuru, et al.

Two dingoes—a brother and sister—attempt copulation on the beach but are frightened by the sound of breaking waves, becoming sand hills. [Dingo is a creational entity whose antics provide the basis for contemporary reflection upon social mores.] [27]

12. Kakmanmurru

Wangurri dingo travels to Warramiri land and returns, and now sits on the hilltop looking back there. [An alliance is formed between clans.]

13. Balkubalku

Dog travels from Lamamirri to Wangurri land—a rope now links the two clans. [An alliance is formed.]

14. Wananda, et al.

Dingoes travel from interior (where honey bees had rejected Macassans) to Elcho Island, where they eat dugong meat that was cut up and cooked on the beach. [An alliance is formed between clans.] [28]

15. Djalatung, et al.

Djalatung means "anchor." These dingoes will never run away in times of trouble, as in the era of first contact. [Many Aborigines fled their lands in the troubled times of early contact with the Macassans for fear of their life. They fled like "cowardly dingoes," but these dingoes instruct the listener to do the opposite.]

16. Ngalalwanga

Dingo "pet" is given a sacred whale's name by the captain. Aborigines kill the captain for this breach of etiquette and the dingo retreats inland to Wangurri territory. [Aborigines will not be subservient and expect outsiders to abide by Aboriginal law.]

NOTES

1. See C.C. Macknight, *The Voyage to Marege: Macassan Trepangers in Northern Australia* (Melbourne: Melbourne University Press, 1976).

2. For example, consider Jack London's *The Call of the Wild,* and Edward Albee's *A Zoo Story.*

3. As reported in, among other sources, R. Breckwoldt, *A Very Elegant Animal: The Dingo* (Melbourne: Angus and Robertson, 1988).

4. E. Kolig, "Aboriginal Dogmatics: Canines in Theory, Myth and Dogma," *Bijdragen Tot de Taal Land en Volenkunde* 134, no. 1 (1978): 106.

5. D.B. Rose, *Dingo Makes Us Human: Life and Land in an Australian Aboriginal Culture* (Cambridge: Cambridge University Press, 1992).

6. See R.M. Berndt, *An Adjustment Movement in Arnhem Land* (Paris and The Hague: Cahiers de L'Homme, Mouton, 1962) and later in this essay.

7. See I.S. McIntosh, "The Totemic Embrace: Belonging and Otherness in the Australian Bush" *Australian Folklore* 20 (2005): 30–39.

8. D.H. Turner, *Dialectics in Tradition: Myth and Social Structure in Two Hunter-Gatherer Societies,* Royal Anthropological Institute of Great Britain and Ireland, London: Occasional Paper no. 36, 1978.

9. N.M. Williams, *The Yolngu and Their Land: A System of Land Tenure and the Fight for Its Recognition* (Canberra: AIATSIS, 1986), p. 38.

10. See Turner, *Dialectics in Tradition.*

11. Donald Thomson describes an Arnhem Land economic exchange and ceremonial song cycle but does not identify the pivotal place of the dog in relation to Aboriginal–non-Aboriginal trade. See D. F. Thomson, *Economic Structure and the Ceremonial Exchange Cycle in Arnhem Land* (Melbourne: Macmillan, 1949).

12. In W. L. Warner, *A Black Civilization: A Social Study of an Australian Tribe* (Chicago: Harper and Row, 1958).

13. See I. S. McIntosh, "The Bricoleur at Work: Warrang (Dingo) Mythology in the Yirritja Moiety of North-East Arnhem Land," M.Litt. Thesis, University of New England, 1992.

14. Adapted from stories recorded in R. M. Berndt and C. H. Berndt, *The Speaking Land: Myth and Story in Aboriginal Australia* (Ringwood, Victoria, Australia, and New York: Penguin Books, 1989), p. 418; I. Keen, "Yolngu Sand Sculptures in Context," in P. Ucko, ed., *Form in Indigenous Art* (Canberra: AIATSIS, 1977), pp. 165–183; McIntosh, "The Bricoleur at Work"; Rraying (one name), "Macassan and Dingo Give Each Other Fire," trans. M. Christie (Milingimbi Literature Center, Milingimbi, Northern Territory, n.d.); and Warner, *A Black Civilization,* p. 536. In other localities along the Northern Territory coastline, myths highlight the ambivalence of Aborigines toward the newcomers, and it is not only the dingo that rejects them. In one case, the scrub fowl uses its powerful legs to kick down the Macassans' bamboo hut and sets fire to their provisions with their matches. In another area, honey bees sting the trepangers as they trek overland searching for fresh water, and drive them away. In yet another narrative, the trepang itself spurts out a huge torrent of water from its mouth, capsizing an Indonesian fishing craft. See also the discussions in I. Keen, *Knowledge and Secrecy in an Aboriginal Religion: Yolngu of North-East Arnhem Land,* Oxford Studies in Social and Cultural Anthropology (Oxford: Clarendon Press, 1994).

15. With their advanced technological skills, Macassans and others would draw wealth from Aboriginal land and sea resources, and Aborigines would learn from them.

16. See also J. Rudder, "Yolngu Cosmology: An Unchanging Cosmos Incorporating a Rapidly Changing World?" (Unpublished PhD Thesis, Australian National University, 1993).

17. For more details on this belief system, see I. S. McIntosh, *Aboriginal Reconciliation and the Dreaming: Warramiri Yolngu and the Quest for Equality,* Cultural Survival Series on Ethnicity and Change (Boston: Allyn and Bacon, 2000).

18. See I. S. McIntosh, "Islam and Australia's Aborigines? A Perspective from North-East Arnhem Land," *Journal of Religious History* 20, no. 1 (1996): 53–77.

19. Ibid.

20. For full details, see McIntosh, "The Bricoleur at Work."

21. Reported in Warner, *A Black Civilization,* p. 535.

22. Warner, *A Black Civilization,* p. 536; Berndt and Berndt, *The Speaking Land,* p. 418; Rraying, "Macassan and Dingo Give Each Other Fire."

23. D. F. Thomson, "Proof of the Indonesian Influence upon the Aborigines of North Australia: The Remarkable Dog Ngarra of the Mildjingi Clan," *The Illustrated London News,* August 12, 1939, p. 277.

24. H. M. Groger-Wurm, *Eastern Arnhem Land Australian Bark Paintings and Their Mythological Interpretation* (Canberra: AIATSIS, 1973), vol. 1, p. 98.

25. Warner, *A Black Civilization,* p. 537.

26. R. M. Berndt, "The Gove Dispute: The Question of Australian Aboriginal Land and the Preservation of Sacred Sites," *Anthropological Forum* 1, no. 2 (1964): 275.

27. Ibid.

28. R. M. Berndt, "Territoriality and the Problem of Demarcating Sociocultural Space," in N. Peterson, ed., *Tribes and Boundaries in Australia* (Canberra: AIATSIS, 1976), p. 154.

VII

ANIMALS IN RITUAL

Knowing and Being Known by Animals

Indigenous Perspectives on Personhood

JOHN GRIM

One of the least understood dimensions of indigenous thought from a Western intellectual perspective is the mutuality of knowing between humans and animals. That animals can be perceived directly or that animals can be skillfully tracked with very little physical evidence are not the issue. Rather, hunter-gatherers and small-scale agriculturists from many different regions of the globe speak of knowing and of being intimately known by animals. This knowing exchange with animals is often described by these individuals as an affective and transformational mode of knowing. This essay explores that intimacy of relations between indigenous peoples and animals through perspectives on personhood, perceptions of ecology, and reflections on cosmology.

In the rational economic model now dominant around the planet, animals are typically understood as objects of utilitarian use. From this standpoint, animals are seen as totally available to humans whether as food, entertainment, scientific research, or as pets. In an extreme version of such a perspective, the current massive extinction of species stirs little concern. A technofix solution holds to a fantasy that all extinct species can be ultimately re-created from their DNA, and their habitat re-created by means of restorative ecology. From an indigenous perspective, as well as other ethical standpoints, such a view has little or no understanding of the long-term interdependence of flourishing life. In his Prologue to this volume Thomas Berry uses the phrase "communion of subjects" to draw attention to an understanding of life that derives from "this primordial need that humans have for the natural world and its animal inhabitants." Indigenous peoples have responded to this need for an intimate experience of animals in their distinct cultural ways and historical times. Indigenous perspectives remind us that, even as we rely on animals for food or companionship, there are alternative ways to relate to and with animals as other than as utilitarian objects.

I provide examples from the North American Lakota and Cree traditions to illustrate animal relationships and personhood conceptualizations. Next, I briefly consider terms and methodological issues related to animal subjectivity. I conclude with an examination of two indigenous rituals, the Winter Dance of the Salish people of the interior Columbia River Plateau, and the Mask Festival of the Dogon people of sub-Saharan Africa. Therein, I explore the human-animal relationships fostered in those rituals. I propose that relationships with animals among different indigenous peoples are embedded in subsistence practices, affirmed by the depth values of mythic narratives, and celebrated in ritual performances. These cultural practices flow from and interact with local environments to mold human bodies that are sensually alert to animal presence. Social practices, rituals, and mythic narratives all manifest and validate cultural concepts of personhood that are intimately connected to ecological perception. That is, the work of knowing animals for survival purposes and evoking animal presence as cosmic power involves a somatic, sensual training, an intellectual effort, and a spiritual empathy with larger cosmological forces. In other words, the intricate weaving of traditional environmental knowledge of animals is not simply for subsistence purposes, such as the oft-cited mystical union of hunter and hunted in so-called "sympathetic magic." Knowing and being known by animals in indigenous lifeways fosters self-knowledge and social cohesion in the contexts of life in the local bioregion and spiritual movement in the broader cosmos.

Animals and Personhood: Introductory Examples

THE NURTURING BUFFALO AND THE VISIONARY HORSE IN LAKOTA TRADITION

The narration of Nicholas Black Elk from the Plains Lakota people of North America provides remarkable insight into the shaping of a healing personality (*wichasha wakan*) in conjunction with a visionary experience of animals. Black Elk's cosmological vision stands as one of the most significant religious statements of the twentieth century, both because of its continuity with Lakota cultural values and the insight it provides into the formation of a healer's ritual. Nicholas Black Elk himself contemplated and ritually performed his own visionary experiences throughout a long life, in which he no doubt revisited and reexperienced their eidetic vitality. Therefore, to attempt a total interpretive act as an outsider analyst is naïve. Nonetheless, Black Elk's vision provides a basis for thinking about the roles of animals in an individual Lakota's life and thought as descriptive also of his people's larger journey.

At one point in his youthful vision Black Elk describes a movement of horses in which they transform into animals of the four quarters participating in a cosmic dance:

> The bay horse said to me: "Behold them, your horses come dancing." I looked around and saw millions of horses circling around me—a sky full of horses. Then the bay horse said: "Make haste." The horse began to go beside me and the forty-eight horses followed us. I looked around and all the horses that were running changed into buffalo, elk, and all kinds of animals and fowls and they all went back to the four quarters.[1]

More than an impressive example of shape-shifting mythology, this visionary cosmic dance expresses the creative, animal-related power embedded in the Lakota concept of *wakan*. No abstract symbol, the horse surges through Lakota mind-body symbolism as a generative ideal not limited, but especially pertinent, to Lakota men. Introducing Black Elk himself to his own visionary role, the bay horse guides him to the numinous forces experienced as Grandfathers.

Before Black Elk can approach these powerful cosmological figures, the cosmic dance of the animals prepares him for the transition to the cosmic centers of his visionary world. The dance of the animals embraces the whole of reality in the symbol of the four quarters, and their movement establishes a relationship with Black Elk as a young male Lakota. The horse is the animal that mediates entry into the numinous world, just as the horse mediates the buffalo hunting skills and the warrior ethos of a Lakota male. Integrated into the symbolic power of this animal presence are the Lakota gender divisions of labor. Black Elk's experiential knowing of cosmic relatedness through these *wakan* animals brings him to deeper self-awareness after years of self-questioning. Moreover, with the assistance of elders, Black Elk came to understand that the ritual evocation of animal presences from his vision made present transformative, healing power not solely for himself but more importantly for his people.

His emergence as a healer among his people was a gradual learning process with distinct somatic, epistemological, and cosmological ripples across the flow of his life. The difficult passage of time during which Black Elk came to know and be known by the cosmological forces experienced in his vision is often characterized as a "wounding" in studies in shamanism. Healing emerges from the capacity of the shaman-in-training to endure and to learn from the somatic trauma of "wounding." Such a disturbing time is not an abstract time-out-of-time; rather, it is grounded in body-mind maturing. Nor is this the story simply of another maturing Lakota person; rather, it is the emergence of a particular Lakota male sensitized in distinctive ways to the depth values of his culture by means of personal visionary experiences.

"Epistemological" is not used here to convey an abstract, analytical knowing by Black Elk. Instead, the term "episteme" can be used to suggest a bodily knowing over a strictly mental act of knowing.[2] One way of understanding Black Elk's visionary episteme is found in his ritual practices; in them he reenacted the bay horse vision. The argument here is that Black Elk's vision of animals activated a relational epistemology, a way of knowing animals in his immediate world that was mutually responsive.[3] Relational episteme is expressed in diverse cultural forms among indigenous peoples

and this work suggests that this way of knowing often frames indigenous concepts of personhood. That is, in the Lakota Plains culture of the late nineteenth and into the twentieth century, a particular relational episteme disposed men and women to experience the world, at times through powerful animal presences that affirmed gender roles. This episteme in relationship with animals was not simply an isolated symbolic force; its deep affect was also based in the land, narrated in powerful myths, and capable of drawing on ancient historical experiences of the people.

The central imagery of the horse in Black Elk's vision is striking, because the horse had come back to the North American continent only with the Spanish invasion of the sixteenth century. Nonetheless, the horse quickly entered into Native American dreams and visions, especially as an archetypal expression of maleness. There are several points to be made that are significant for our discussion regarding this symbolic positioning of the horse. First, the complex symbology that centered on the horse continued ancient Lakota religious imagery associated with buffalo hunting. As the horse emerged with such central significance from the seventeenth century on, it transformed the generative symbolism associated with Lakota maleness. Subsistence practices and the sexual divisions of labor adjusted, as the Lakota moved onto the ecological realities of the Missouri River plains and away from mixed hunting and farming practices. Thus, when early ethnographers spoke of native hunters and warriors as one-body with their horse, they were inadvertently identifying deep somatic practices whose foundations were ancient and whose expressions were historically determined. These cultural adjustments, and the individual bodies that transmitted those changes, closely identified the horse as the symbolic entry for cosmological contact with the powerful animal beings.

Second, the bay horse of Black Elk's vision provides an interesting example of the horse as an image associated with masculinity in the collective psyche of a people undergoing intense transitions. The Lakota collectively had long celebrated the buffalo, which crossed gender divisions but had strong feminine associations in ancient Lakota culture. In their earlier, ancient transitions as a people emerging from the woodlands of what is now known as the state of Minnesota, it may have been that the buffalo for the Lakota was an ancient feminine symbol of nourishment. In the form of White Buffalo Calf Woman, she mediated between the deepest reflections on the wholeness of the sacred, *Wakan Tanka,* and the needs of the Lakota people. White Buffalo Calf Woman transmitted cultural life to the Lakota ostensibly in the form of seven major rituals that mediated across the sexual divisions of Lakota lifeway. Thus, Black Elk's vision of animals, especially the horse, reflects not only his transition from youth into early adulthood as a healer, but also transformations in the collective thinking of his people undergoing major cultural changes.

Third, and perhaps most importantly for our discussions here, Black Elk's knowing and being known by animals provides insight into Lakota cosmological views of shared personhood with the more-than-human world.[4] From a Western analytical perspective the horse of Black Elk's vision crossed ontological boundaries between sentient beings by speaking intelligently to a human. Similarly, Black Elk's visionary bay horse crossed cultural divides set in rational, Western thought between wild and domesticated animals. In a Lakota perspective, however, Black Elk's vision-horse bridges personhood, enabling significant human and animal dialogue that has personal and communal implications. No doubt, Lakota kinship concepts are a crucial field of inquiry for deepening insight in these relationships.

Black Elk's vision offers insight into Lakota views on the personhood of animal beings in which they are not necessarily crossing boundaries marked by intelligence or consciousness. Rather, the Lakota relational episteme ritualized experiences of communication with animals.

This episteme, embedded in Lakota bodies by means of these rituals and the whole of their cultural lifeway, attests to the possibility of a mutual responsiveness of sentient beings to one another. This embodied episteme opens the possibility for relationships with human persons to the cosmos as a whole by means of animal relatedness. We know from Black Elk's extensive interviews with John Neihardt and others that reenactment of his visionary experiences of animals was a major feature of his ritual healings.[5] A consideration of indigenous rituals, then, shows a close connection between vibrant, mature personhood and animal presences that evoke cosmic powers.

THE INTIMACY OF CREE HUNTING

Any discussion of animals from the diverse perspectives of indigenous peoples requires attention to differences. No one supposes that something as particular as human-animal relations are uniform among such strikingly different cultures. Thus, while cultural differences in human-animal relationships are evident, nonetheless, indigenous traditions consistently express ritual concerns for, and ecological attention to, animals. Moreover, the intimacy and immediacy of contact with animals by hunter-gatherers and small-scale agricultural societies has not been totally extinguished by the centuries of colonial contact and modernity. Though much diminished and changed by the forces of global colonialism, in many rural settings indigenous perspectives on animal personhood continue into the present.

One anthropologist described a novel transition among the Waswanipi Cree of the Canadian Subartic of Hudson Bay:

Thus, the changes occurring in the Waswanipi [Cree] world from 1925 to 1950 were interpreted by younger elders as a strengthening of the bonds between humans and animal spirits. This was manifested in an increase in the power of personal thought [*meteo,* personal thought in contrast to *mistapeo,* personalized spirit helpers]. For this generation, dreaming (and thinking) of animals was enough to link humans and spirits. This development did not mean that humans had conquered or gained mastery over the environment; indeed, they continued to depend on it. Because of a more intense relationship with the spirits, however, humans had become more secure and better able to predict the immediate future.[6]

These comments on cultural change from direct visionary experience of spirit-helpers to thoughtful attunement with local spirit-helpers also signal transitions in ecological perceptions among the Cree people. Changes in Cree relations with animals as well as continuities with the earlier traditions hinge on cultural experiences and embodiments of human-animal relations. Many indigenous societies have, in order to survive, somatically reimagined themselves as a people along with the lands they inhabit in terms of their relationships with animals.[7]

The explorations of indigenous concerns for animals consistently lead to concepts of personhood, perceptions of ecology, and reflections on cosmology. The thread of many fibers that weaves through indigenous cultures, then, is a differential way of knowing. This way of knowing derives from sense experiences shaped themselves by that way of knowing. Different ecosystems and the animal-plant-mineral beings of those bioregions interact with cultural dispositions to mold human bodies in direct relationships with animals. Embodied persons capable of knowledge and communication with animals become the cultural nexus for learning rather than simply teachers who convey an abstract knowledge. The thread of differences that unites indigenous perspectives provides further elaboration of what Thomas Berry calls a "communion of subjects."

This differential thread of "family resemblances" emphasizes cultural particularity and also acknowledges the widespread understanding among indigenous peoples that animals can be known, can be communicated with, and can themselves be knowing agents. For much of the twentieth century these ideas about knowing and being known by animals were framed by the term "animism," which attributed to indigenous people the view that the whole world was indiscriminately alive.

Reclaiming and reconfiguring the term animism acknowledges the colonialist past that typically denigrated indigenous peoples by using this term. The vitality that indigenous thought recognized in the world was overwhelmed by the ideological charge of vitalism, namely, the attribution of unseen forces acting on the world. Revisiting animism, as many anthropologists have suggested, rejuvenates a term that seeks to affirm and understand personhood from indigenous perspectives as participation in a living world of numinous, cosmic forces often imaged as animals. This participation involves a relational epistemology of "interagentivity" in which forces other than the human are understood as having will, intention, empathy, and intelligence.[8] Ritual practices interwoven with traditional environmental knowledge provide a penetrating lens for seeing the power of these ways of knowing in forming personal bodies, social groups, and worldviews. Thus, the linkage of ceremonial and subsistence activities requires a broader, wholistic view of native modes of knowing. This animism is at once interrelational and efficacious. A reconfiguration of animism calls for a reconsideration of the limits and usefulness of several terms such as "religion" and "lifeway."

Methodological Issues

DEFINING TERMS

The term "indigenous" is limited and at times ambiguous, as all humans descend from original peoples; but the term is useful in that it draws attention to the historical marginalization in the colonial period of small-scale societies sharing language, mythic narratives, kinship, and land-base. So also, the term "religion" carries baggage from Western usage such as named roles, institutional forms, or recognized architecture. However, the notion of religion can be useful in affirming the social complexes of symbol, ritual, and myth among small-scale hunting-gathering and agricultural societies. Religion in this study, then, drawing on the perspectives of indigenous peoples, indicates relatedness with a communion of subjects in the surrounding world as an ultimate concern. In many of the world's religions, the concept of religion is typically associated with a transcendent, creative being. However, religion in indigenous contexts typically refers to cosmological forces and beings that are more immanent, immediate, and plural. Broadly speaking, indigenous religions emphasize social and communal concerns for harmonious relations with local, ecological realities rather than redemptive salvation from this world or the liberation of individual souls.

In this sense the terms "lifeway" and "life-world" are useful to avoid misplaced dichotomizing tendencies that separate religion from other life activities such as economics, politics, and subsistence practices. Indigenous cultures present a more seamless weave between social, economic, ecological, and cosmological realms. This is not intended to portray indigenous traditions as timeless, ahistorical, or static cultures.[9] Rather, historical changes and personal life cycle changes are framed by indigenous traditions in conceptions of body development, and personhood, as well as in perceptions of ecology. Ritual performance mediates this conception-perception strategy by refocusing it in the realm of animals.

The terms lifeway and lifeworld describe an efficacious and seamless worldview that is evident, for example, in the ethnography of A. I. Hallowell. His studies among the Ojibwa of the Great Lakes region in North America have established personhood as a theoretical entry into studies of indigenous peoples. In this sense it is a metaphor for one of the fibers of the differential thread that ties together indigenous peoples. Hallowell describes the Ojibwa concept of the "good life," or *pimadaziwin* as "a long life and a life freed from illness and other misfortune." Hallowell stresses that *pimadaziwin* depends upon the experience of "dream visitors," who are often other-than-human animal spirits.[10] This term, *pimadaziwin,* then, frames the lifeway path in the Ojibwa context as intrinsically relational. Hallowell writes:

> pimadaziwin [can] only be achieved by individuals who seek and obtain ... the help of superhuman entities and who conduct ... themselves in a socially approved manneri. ... it is important to note that superhuman help [is] sought in solitude, that the "blessing" or "gift" [can] not be compelled, but [is] bestowed because the superhuman entities [take] pity upon the suppliant who, in effect, asks for Life (i.e. pimadaziwin).[11]

The lifeway activities of the Ojibwa, which flow from human efforts and normative social values, are not adequately described as simply human centered or "anthropocentric." Clearly they depend upon cosmological or extraordinary forces that in Ojibwa are called *manitou.* Stressing the cosmological and interactive character of this effort of humans to achieve *pimadaziwin,* Ojibwa lifeway is more appropriately described as "anthropocosmic."[12] This suggests an intricate interweaving of cosmological power, ecological processes, animal sentience, human reciprocity, and somatic sensitivity.

It is important to note that the relational character of achieving the "good life" does not eliminate the possibility of Ojibwa conceptualizations of an "individual" or "objectification." Often, in an effort to alert a reader to a worldview different than that formed by "individualism" and scientific objectivity, discussions of indigenous traditions assert wholly communal orientations and dramatically subjective interactions. For the Ojibwa a sense of individuals and of objects are qualified by a way of knowing that is experiential, relational, sensual, and mutual. This qualified individuality and objectification are explored in Hallowell's observations that the Ojibwa language has markers for animate and inanimate categories that are quite different from those in English. Seeking an explanation, Hallowell asked an elder Ojibwa "Are all the stones we see around us alive?" The man thought briefly and replied, "No, but *some* are."[13] The *some* that this Ojibwa elder described were those qualified by the experience of power, or *manitou*, whose ramifications resonate throughout one's life. The experience of *manitou*, then, results in movement toward *pimadaziwin*, which is a life lived in relational knowing with that power. Such close relationships have been described by the Ojibwa as occurring between animals and humans. More than simply casual encounters or simply pragmatic hunting relations between individuals, the relationships leading to *pimadaziwin* establish values at a deeper level. Theoretically, this level of "discourse" can be suggested as a tribal anthropology, a sociology, and a cosmology. Mythic narratives and ritual celebrations enact and invoke these relationships within small-scale indigenous hunter-gatherer and agricultural societies.

In this article the phrases, knowing animals and being known by animals, have been used to frame an investigation of indigenous peoples and animals as a reciprocal relationship, a way of knowing, and a quest for personhood. Interestingly, even framing the question with these phrases positions it within the epistemological concerns of Western thought. That is, a duality is presumed between knower and known similar to separations associated, for example, with mind, body, and soul. However, "knowing animals" and "being known by animals" are also used here as phenomenological referents that reflect the rich ethnographies on indigenous peoples.[14] Based on these diverse ethnographies, stories of experiential communication with animals can also be interpreted as indigenous metaphors for thinking about self, society, environment, and cosmology.

In their seminal work on metaphors, George Lakoff and Mark Johnson suggest that "Metaphor is one of our most important tools for trying to comprehend partially what cannot be comprehended totally: aesthetic experiences, moral practices, and spiritual awareness. These endeavors of the imagination are not devoid of rationality; since they use metaphor, they employ an imaginative rationality."[15] Moreover, if metaphors are "seeing one kind of thing in terms of another kind of thing," a salient distinction in indigenous thought emerges.[16] Namely, as an ethnographic metaphor, personhood suggests a mutual responsiveness between humans and animals that is established in mythic narratives, performed in rituals, and molded into bodies through cultural life.

RECONFIGURING ANIMISM

As suggested above, the question of animism shadows much of this investigation.[17] During the late nineteenth century, colonial-period interpretive studies described communication with animals among indigenous peoples as a failed epistemology. The assumption that only humans know, or at least that only humans report on their knowing, resulted in the long-standing critique of indigenous ways of knowing coded in the term animism. As a means of actually knowing the world, animism was dismissed as simply a delusion, or a projection of a deluded human subjectivity.

Many in the modern West have continued this critique of animism as a projection of souls or subjectivity into a world of objective, inert matter. From this critical, analytical perspective anything concerning the consciousness of animals cannot be known. Nor do we know, as this discourse asserts, how or if animals know humans. Moreover, from the standpoint of many colonialist psychologies, indigenous thought was compared to the immature reasoning of children. From some cultural evolutionary perspectives, indigenous thought generally was described as prelogical and inferior to scientific ways of knowing.[18]

By exploring human-animal relations in indigenous rituals, however, two different dimensions of animism emerge. One is a fuller concept of personhood and the other is a broader understanding of the lifeway transitions that persons undergo. From one perspective, then, personhood is cultivated in ritual by establishing bodily, sensuous connections to the surrounding world of animals, plants, and minerals. The self-reflective dynamics within ritual situate the human body and the natural world not simply as passive subjects but as active reciprocal agents that both embody ways of knowing. In an altered perspective, namely, one that assists in making lifeway transitions, the sense of a shared intelligence-as-power (e.g., *manitou*) experienced in the lifeway (e.g., *pimadaziwin*) is evoked at crucial times. These involve seasonal and ecological cycles in the natural world linked to significant bodily changes in human life. Thus, animism is descriptive of a dimension of indigenous thinking that is concerned with significant transitions in the personal life cycle as well as communal transitions involving nutrition, migrations, and subsistence practices.[19] This view of animism as a way of knowing that is insightful for understanding indigenous thought during times of transition is significantly different from an interpretation of animism that sees indigenous peoples as incoherently and indiscriminately scattering a vague soul-stuff across a horizon of being.

Moreover, a fuller understanding of personhood in the context of transitions refers to a dynamic mutual agency of persons that assists movement across lifeway transitions. "Intersubjectivity" has sometimes been used to describe the diverse modes of conceiving personhood that occur in small-scale, indigenous societies. However, intersubjectivity may itself be a reification of the individual as posited by Cartesian thought. Intersubjectivity suggests a Western paradigm of the communication of independent mind to mind, rather than an indigenous view of the mutual responsiveness of persons. The anthropologist Tim Ingold is critical of intersubjectivity as an accurate term for discussing indigenous ways of knowing. He writes that, "In the hunter-gatherer economy of knowledge … it is as entire persons not as disembodied minds, that human beings engage with one another and, moreover, with non-human beings as well. They do so as beings *in* a world, not as minds which, excluded from a given reality, find themselves in the common predicament of having to make sense of it."[20] Following from his critique Ingold proposes "interagentivity" as a term that conveys the constitutive quality of the indigenous world in which "intimate relations with nonhuman and human components of the environment is one and the same."[21] Agency, the capacity of movement and action, is linked, in his view of indigenous thought, with personhood in both humans and animals.

Marilyn Strathern, who uses the terms "individual" and "dividual," has discussed the difference in perceptions of relatedness between persons in indigenous societies.[22] In contrast to a Western notion of the irreducible character of the individual as separate person, the concept of "dividual" accentuates personhood as a composite of relationships. The concept of a dividual is not presented here as a mental construct necessarily articulated in indigenous thought. Dividual is an etic/outsider, interpretive category that can be useful for understanding what it is that indigenous peoples strive to embed in individual bodies by means of their rituals, namely, a relationality that is not only a given but also an achievement. The study of ritual in indigenous cultural contexts typically demonstrates how peoples work toward relatedness, especially in knowing animals. These rituals interweave symbols drawn from communal subsistence practices, knowledge acquired in personal exchanges with ecosystems, and ceremonial celebrations of cosmological forces. In ritual performances indigenous peoples affirm and celebrate the beauty, authority, and intimacy of these relational insights into the world around them. Moreover, they display "traditional environmental knowledge" in subsistence practices that reflects their empirical observations of animals and interactions in the local bioregions.

Nurit Bird-David draws on the writings of evolutionary psychologist James Gibson, who distinguishes the "meaning" concerns of Western thought from the "attention" work of indigenous peoples to acquire and pass on traditional environmental knowledge.[23] The more intellectual and abstract search for "meaning" dominant in the West is not primary in the work of acquiring skills about animals. About this knowing-as-work in the context of personhood and its value to the discipline of anthropology, Nurit Bird-David explains:

> "Meaning" is not "imposed" on things—it is not pre-given in consciousness—but "discovered" in the course of action; it is also both "physical and psychical, yet neither." There is endless "information" in the environment, by which Gibson means "the specification of the observer's environment, not ... of the observer's receptors or sense organs." People continuously "pick up" information in acting within the environment by means of "attention." Gibsonian "attention" is "a skill that can be educated" to pick up information that is more and more subtle, elaborate, and precise. Knowing is developing this skill; knowing is continuous with perceiving, of which it is an extension.[24]

Meaning in indigenous settings, then, results from cultivated bodily attention to the environment. Education is not a formal time set apart, but immersion in the lifeway itself. Giving attention to the relationships that parents and elders cultivate in skills of hunting, fishing, or plant-gathering brings children into the information they need to develop their own skills. A primary characteristic of knowledge acquired in

indigenous ecological attention, then, is of personhood in the lifeworld of animals.

In his studies with the Mistassini Cree of the eastern Subartic region of Hudson Bay, Adrian Tanner provides an example of this work to develop a mutual knowing with animals. He relates how the attention given to animals in the subsistence acts of hunting finds intellectual gravity in Cree concepts of personhood:

> The facts about particular animals are reinterpreted as if they had social relationships between themselves, and between them and the anthropomorphized natural forces, and furthermore the animals are thought of as if they had personal relations with the hunters. The idealized form of these latter relations is often that the hunter pays respect to an animal; that is he acknowledges the animal's superior position, and following this the animal "gives itself" to the hunter, that is allows itself to assume a position of equality, or even inferiority, with respect to the hunter.[25]

Here Tanner explores the triangulated relationships of animals among themselves, with natural forces, and with hunters. He situates ecological perception and personhood among the Cree as entering into those sets of relationships through ritualized respect. Thus, acquiring hunting skills requires an appropriate ethical response to those communal forces by relating to animals respectfully.[26] These rituals of respect are not simply detached actions of a hunter, but rather, complex cultural constructions that relate to ancient lineages of relational knowledge. The practice of these rituals of respect embodies a way of knowing in Cree bodies that enables the mutual reciprocity of traditional environmental knowledge that the rituals anticipate.

Indigenous rituals provide a strikingly different range of ways of knowing and being known by animals that are not verifiable by scientific experiment. This is not to denigrate scientific, empirical knowing, but to suggest that there are other ways of knowing that cannot be properly evaluated using the quantifiable approaches of science to understand personhood, ecology, and cosmology. The avoidance of subjectivity in a scientific worldview blocked the capacity for understanding the imaginative coherence of indigenous thought. One intriguing way of describing this knowing has been to label it as a "double vision" in which "hunting was experienced both from the perspective of the hunter and the animals that were hunted."[27] In this sense, "double vision" affirms personhood relationships embedded in both animal and human bodies. From this standpoint traditional environmental knowledge itself becomes more of a process than an acquired, fixed body of data. Yet, the suggestion of a "double" continues to imply a separation of the animal world of consciousness and sentience from that of the human. Such a separation is more characteristic of a Western worldview. It may not adequately describe the worldviews of a particular indigenous people. In the following section two indigenous ceremonials provide case studies in which animals and humans relate to each other both as individuals who mature by means of particular experiences and as individuals primarily constituted by social relationships.

THE SALISH WINTER DANCE

Since 1985, I have attended twelve Winter Dances with the permission of the Louie family of Inchelium, Washington.[28] The Winter Dance is a major ceremonial of Salish-speaking peoples of the Interior Plateau region of the Columbia River in North America. It involves, over four nights and three days, ritual activities such as the symbolic cleaning of a place in preparation for the arrival of spirit powers (*sumix*), singing vision songs, dancing around a center pole, celebrating sacred foods, feasting, sweatlodges, giveaways, stick-game gambling, and storytelling.

At the heart of the ceremonial is the individual guardian-spirit relationship made manifest in visionary songs sung at a centering pole in the Winter Dance house. The songs come from the animal-plant-mineral beings placed in the local land, according to Salish mythology, as a gift of *sumix* power for humans. With the acquisition of a song, a mature singer also takes on the burden of a spirit sickness that returns with each Winter Dance season. Thus, the Winter Dance encourages reflection on human-animal relations in the context of social celebration and physical sickness. Ethics in the Winter Dance refers to acquiring skills in relation to the numinous powers and bringing forward appropriate knowledge needed to sustain the village communities. Singers announce their personal spirit helpers in a communal, ritual setting. They reaffirm the values of Salish cosmological narratives and recall the sacred exchange of food.

The Interior Salish understand songs as a gift from the primal, mythic animal-plant-mineral beings who preceded humans in the stages of creation. In the traditional Salish lifeway, young boys and girls are sent out to fast in specific locations to acquire a song from a spirit guardian. Acquisition of a song not only announces a special relationship between that individual and an animal, plant, or place, but it also initiates the work of knowing and acquiring skills about the environment of the guardian spirit. Interestingly, the Salish are culturally disposed to forget their vision songs until they mature, in their late twenties, and begin to attend and sing at Winter Dances.[29] As in many societies, what is "forgotten" becomes the basis for establishing the deepest values of a society. For the Salish of the Columbia River, the acquisition of traditional environmental knowledge linked with the guardian spirit commences with the bestowal of the song, even as it is "forgotten," and deepens with maturity.

When mature singers in their thirties emerge at the Winter Dance, then, their songs announce to the community the personal spirit with whom that individual is related. Singing the spirit song transmits significant information about which beings in the environment the singer intimately knows, for example, salmon, bitterroot, or deer. This religious, environmental, and transactional knowledge was crucial for the shared tasks undertaken by the independent Salish villages in the days before contact, when foods were communally gathered. For example, singers with deer or salmon songs would lead those respective hunting and fishing activities. Even today knowledge of particular animals and plants announced by a singer at the Winter Dance are important for family and community subsistence.

A description of a Winter Dance from 1954 remains accurately descriptive of current dances. It reads:

> The dance is held in the largest room, usually the living room of a male or female shaman's house. In the centre of the room is a bare pole affixed to the ceiling and floor. This pole acts as the centre point for all activity during the dance. Only a shaman [or singer] may touch the pole. ...
>
> Before performing, a shaman [or singer] will begin humming a song softly while he [or she] sits or stands in some part of the room. As he sings louder he approaches the pole. He may walk around the pole singing to it or hold out his arms to the pole as he sings. When he grasps the pole in both hands he has become one with his [animal] guardian spirit. As long as he is holding the pole his words are not his own but those of his guardian spirit. Guardian spirits speak unintelligibly and in a low voice, and therefore, the guardian spirit's words must be transmitted to the audience by another person. For this purpose an interpreter stands by the shaman [or singer] and repeats the guardian spirit's speech in a loud voice. ... This pipeline from the guardian spirit via the shaman [or singer] and the interpreter continues for as long as the guardian spirit has something to say to the audience. As a rule the guardian spirit makes prognostications of the future, gives free advice, and makes comments on present events.[30]

The performance of the singer communicates the embodied reciprocity established with an animal spirit being. Personhood is embedded in bodies through the maturing years of acquiring the song and in the work of gathering traditional environmental knowledge about one's spirit guardian. Singing at the cosmological center pole also provides an occasion for ethical reflection on community events. Thus, singing signals the anthropocosmic character of the Winter Dance that interweaves personal growth, attention to the environment, reflection on the pragmatic activities of village life, and performance of the song of relatedness. Ritual singing at the Winter Dance manifests the deep relationality that is present in the myths of creation of the Interior Columbia River Salish peoples.

Two pervasive and dramatic values of Salish cosmology are manifested by the singer at the center pole, namely, giving and sacrifice. The singer gives to the people just as the cosmos so freely gives to sustain the people. By singing at the Winter Dance centering pole, a person manifests a relational epistemology in which *sumix* powers, personally known by the singer, are made present for the welfare of the community. Symbolically the center pole is the world around which all the participants dance as a singer sings his or her song. As the singer repeats the song in a faster mode, all the participants at the ceremonial perform a cosmic dance evocative of the animal beings who give their bodies to feed humans. Songs celebrate the giveaway of the cosmos. As the participants dance around the singer at the center pole they are said to be on the move like animals during the winter season. The agency of the spirit guardian and the relatedness established by the singer are celebrated by the community in the movement of symbolic beings around the cosmological center.

Singers relieve themselves of the burden of spirit sickness that descends upon them with the Winter Dance season. Disorienting loneliness and physical discomfort that comes over a dancer at the onset of the Winter Dance season is said to be directly linked to the cosmogonic giving of the primal beings. The spirit guardians are described in the mythic narratives both as having given themselves as food and as having established a moral force in songs and spirit sickness. Spirit sickness places singers in a bodily experience that directly relates them to the original and ongoing gifts of the animal-plant-mineral spirit beings. The underlying tension of the spirit-sickness also relates to widespread ideas among indigenous peoples of the need for a "second gift" of animals to humans.[31] The complexity of the gift of food, in this interpretation, requires the additional or second gift of suffering by the singers. Enduring the spirit-sickness and celebrating its release by singing at the center tree are modes of acknowledging the maturing exchange of personhood by animals and humans in the Winter Dance.[32]

This brief overview of the Winter Dance ceremonial gives some idea of the ways in which Salish peoples have ritually integrated the *knowing of animals* in the acquisition of songs, along with hunting and fishing skills, with *being known by animals* in ethical reflections upon food through spirit-sickness and giveaways. Attending to the environment in the context of the Winter Dance constitutes a religious path drawing together bodily maturation, social politics, economic activities, and ritual performance. According to the Salish, animals, along with other beings in the world, have a central role in sustaining humans and teaching them ethical limits and gifts of life. This reminder is fixed in the transitional process of acquiring and performing a spiritual song. For the Columbia River Salish peoples, animal beings facilitate the transition from youths who learn skills in the environment to adults who contribute to the flourishing life of the village community.

THE DOGON MASKED FESTIVAL

The Dogon are a Voltaic-speaking people who came in the fifteenth century to southwestern Mali in Africa. They have built their villages in the mountainous Bandiagara Cliffs overlooking nearby cultivated fields and the rugged bush beyond. In the last thirty years the Dogon have been the focus of increased Islamic and Christian conversion. However, the traditional Dogon lifeway is still intact with its distinct language, hierarchical village structures, agricultural and hunting practices, and religion based on sacrifice, speech, and a complex of animal-mask performances evoking the powers of the bush.[33]

A striking example of human and animal interaction occurs in the animal mask festival, or *dama,* among the Dogon.[34] The major concern of this Dogon ceremonial is to undertake the "second burial" of the dead. The *dama* may take place years after the first funeral (*nyu yana*) has been performed, in which the wrapped corpse of the deceased is interred in the cliffs above the village. At the mask festival the Dogon urge those who have died since the last *dama* to undertake their journey into the bush (*oru*) away from the human communities (*ana*). This concern derives from the view that the dead must leave this world or they might cause harm to the living. The dead must be urged to take up their appropriate roles as ancestors in the next world. *Dama* accomplishes its ritual tasks by mediating male creative animal power from the numinous bush and evoking the animals as masked presences. The Dogon remember the dead and name them as ancestors at *dama.*

The bush (*oru*) for the Dogon is a complex, dangerous, and auspicious reality associated with the feminine; whereas Dogon culture and villages are socciated with the male gender. *Jinu* and *yènèû* spirits from the bush may attack humans and invade or exchange body parts. Sorcery and witchcraft derive from individuals who secretly embody destructive forces from the bush. Yet, from the dangerous setting of the bush also came millet as food, millet beer whose fermentation process signals the presence of ancestors, and all the powerful forces that generate life, language, and wisdom. Male cultural leaders (*orubaru*) are initiated in a three-month period in the bush. From their seclusion they bring back understandings of pervasive Dogon attitudes toward the bush and culture, namely, respect (*bawa*) and work. Respect is the key, say the Dogon, to their hierarchical social order and village life. Respect is extended to elders, millet, beer and a range of sacred beings who stand in relationship with wealth, health, happiness, and children.

Work is understood as necessary to acquire the knowledge of the environment needed to sustain the villages. Work is attending to the world. Work joins with respect as the basic virtues of the Dogon with which one responds to the dynamic movements of the world. The bush is in constant movement and men enter into relationship with animals as mediators from the bush to exert control over death. "In the masks the men proclaim themselves able to control the sources of fertility, the sources of power, the sources of life."[35]

Along with the masked dance ceremonials, sacrifice is central to Dogon religion. Sacrifices are performed at all levels of social organization, namely, individual, family, lineage, clan, ward, and village. Distinct individual, group, and clan altars are used to guard against illness believed to come from the bush. Sacrifices at altars heal the sick, establish oaths, and advocate for village health and fertility. The blood-force of animals is joined with sacrificial speech and ritual action to creatively order Dogon life. Similarly, the animal mask performances, such as the *sigi* performed every sixty years, call animals from the bush to manage life forces, and creatively assist the movement of the dead so that they can become revered ancestors.

Before considering the events of the masked festival of *dama,* it is helpful to have an overview of Dogon views of the human body, especially its capacities for speech. Speech is the quintessential cosmogonic act for the Dogon. It bridges between and distinguishes the human world of the villages from the animal realm of the bush. The masked festivals, especially *dama,* present a relational epistemology in which the wild bush

is rationally imagined. *Dama* interweaves personhood concepts embedded in speech with gender roles in which men work to continue the cycle of Dogon life.

Speech occupies a central role in all Dogon activities, whether exchanges in the market, offering sacrifices at an altar, or praying to the dead at *dama.* For the Dogon the creator god, Amma, made the world in which everything is a bearer of "speech."[36] Spoken words define the human. Animals do not have the external speech of humans. Yet, all the animals of the bush have inner "speech" with which they communicate. *Animals also have foreknowledge of all events. Thus animal calls and other signs of their presence have divinatory power.*

The Dogon construe cause and effect in the world by hearing and viewing the speech of the bush as signs. Knowing animals is the work of acquiring traditional environmental knowledge of the bush and its many gifts. Because animals know the outcome of all activities, the Dogon hunter must equip himself with magical skills that mask his intentions from the animals being hunted. Being known by animals is covertly expressed in the hunt, and made overt in the mask festival when the animal persons knowingly allow the men to display their creative power to assist the dead in their final journey into the bush as ancestors.

Nothing occurs without form in the Dogon worldview; there are no accidents. The Dogon believe that speech is what forms the human body, and everything in the universe corresponds to the cosmological body pattern. Drawing on mathematical theory, it can be said that the Dogon see a self-similarity, a fractal logic, underlying the world in which even seeds are said to have discrete "body" parts. Similarly, the *sigi* stool, a simple "y" shaped stool, used in the *dama* to symbolize elders who have died since the last festival, is described as having body parts. Animal bodies thus have the same inner speech forms as human bodies. Dogon elders, or "experts in the word," sense the messages of the world and are able to respond as body to body.[37]

According to the Dogon, the body is composed of the four elements of the world—black for water, red for fire, white for air, and yellow for earth. The body is a setting of constant dialogue between the sustaining elements of creation. Speech reveals individual personality as one's awareness and relationship to the larger cosmological dialogue. The composite human, thus, flows from and stands in relation to the surrounding world. Distinct body parts are named by the Dogon and understood as connected by the joints. Significant transitions take place at the joints of the body as well as of space and time. *Dama* is such a joint where the living, the ancestors, and the animals of the bush meet to transact the deeper relationality of Dogon mythic thought.

Spiritual principles (*kikinu*) are embedded in the body by the creator god, Amma, and during dreams the images perceived are projections of particular aspects of the body. One's "animal *kikinu*" can manifest in one's eyes, and a skilled expert can determine one's animal, or totemic, ancestor. The interrelationships of inner ancestral and animal dimensions are principles of personhood important during the Dogon maturing process. Speech, as a projection into social space of one's inner personality, demonstrates one's awareness of these spiritual elements. Speech is sexed and may be seeded and fruitful if another responds, or barren and hollow if one's speech is disregarded. Thus, transmitted speech germinates in others. As the most cultivated act of intelligence, speech finds technical expression and accomplishes the skills of the Dogon such as weaving, farming, iron-crafting, hunting, healing, herding, governing, dancing, and praying at the altar during sacrifice.

At death the elements of a person scatter and may become harmful to the living. The rites for the dead, especially the *dama* mask festival, are to assist the spiritual principles in their after-death journeys to their respective locations as ancestors. The Dogon accomplish this transition for the numinous dead by bringing animal masks, *èmna,* into the village. The term *èmna* refers not simply to the carved and painted wooden masks with their plaited, red-and black-dyed fibers, but also to the full costume the dancers wear along with accessories that they carry, such as a stick horse, a rattle, or an axe. In short, *èmna* are the men themselves who make present the wild animal masks with dance, shouts, and exuberant performance.

At times during the opening days of *dama* women and children are expressly forbidden to come near or even see, the masked dancers. This prohibition regarding women is especially interesting in light of the myth of the masks' origin. This myth expressly states that the masks came from the *yènèû,* the spirits of the bush and its animals, and were given to the *kei,* the black ants, the first to dance them. Then a bird stole the masks and dropped them near the village of Yougo, where a woman found them. She put them on and scared her husband, but an old woman told him where the masks were in the cliffs. He then made himself into a mask and used the power to bend his wife's will to his own. Since that time the men have appropriated the masks and the fertilizing power they bring to ensure the crops and to assist the journey of the recent dead into the bush where they await rebirth as ancestors.

The *dama* begins after the harvest when permission has been secured from the fourteen oldest men living. Thirteen years is a typical interval between performances of the *dama.* The whole mask festival typically lasts four Dogon weeks of five days each. During the opening period the young men who have not danced and those who will personify different beings begin to carve their masks. All the dancers will prepare a *bèdyè* (pupil) mask, which is a simple cloth mask. They wear it during the opening weeks of fire or night masks. During this period the dancers choose to construct one or more masks of the rabbit, shaman-healer, stork, tree, antelope, stilt-dancers, the Dogon granary door, monkey, goiter, and more contemporary masks such as the Muslim and the tourist. All of these masks are beings associated with animals of the bush. The dance costumes also show a distinct tendency toward the female gender. The framing of the masks in red-dyed fibers typically enlivens them. This suggests the blood of menstruating women. Moreover, the dancers contrive pointed breasts, and they wear jewelry and skirts. When the time arrives for the masks to enter the village, they initially come from the direction of Yougo, where the masks originated. Later entries are made from different directions but all are related to the bush.

When the dancers "descend from the plains," the dancing begins in earnest. Then, a ritual leader greets them in the secret language (*sigi so*) given to men by the *dyinu,* another group of bush spirits. This is the only way to speak to the masks. The leader greets the masks saying:

God has seen you, has seen a good thing. Something big is there, something small, if anything is wrong, it is with God. This is not work for children. If you see a woman, beat her. Greeting, good heads, who came running, all the women are afraid, beat them.[38]

This ritualized hostility to women stands in marked contrast with male feminization evident in the costumed dress of the animal figures. Men assert their male creativity, against the fertility of women, and in relation to the bush animals that they dance.

The vigorous dances over the many days of *dama* establish male control over fertility associated with the bush. A complex of activities asserts the efficacy of male fertility. They include beer drinking in which the inebriated shout as the ancestors. There are elaborate speeches in *sigi so* by elders to the masks. The elders also smash the *sigi* stool symbolizing the final death of a deceased individual and their rebirth as an ancestor. From these events the villagers recognize the success of the *dama.* The relationships of animals and the masked performers bring the powers of the bush to effect the movement

of the dead. One interpretation, that of Walter van Beek, says:

Mask rituals usher in a new existence for the dead—that of ancestor—and thus contain some rites in which the individual's existence on this earth is ended. Characteristically, the *sigi* stool plays a central role here: the old men in charge of the *dama* smash the *sigi* stools of the deceased and discard the pieces in a mountain crevasse. The end of the *sigi* symbol signifies the end of the individual's life. While the *sigi* constitutes the rebirth of the human being through strictly male endeavors, negating in ritual the female monopoly on reproduction, the male powers to create life are its very destroyers. That only men participate in the *sigi,* as in the *dama,* is emblematic. Birth and *sigi* together stress the life and mortality of man, the fleeting male creation of himself against the continuing chain of life generated by the women. Meaningful existence has to be created by ephemeral beings, in this case men—at least once in their lifetime—playing a role in the origin of life."[39]

Complementarity is interwoven throughout the Dogon lifeway—bush and village culture, genders, animals and men, body parts, ancestors and the living. Underlying this complementarity are the respect and work required to maintain life and to know the movement of life. A relational epistemology underlies knowing and implementing the cosmogonic work of Amma who placed the spiritual principles within the bodies of all beings. The Dogon animal mask festival exemplifies the work of culture in mediating male fertility from the bush animals to assist the dead in their transition to becoming ancestors. Knowing and being known by animals, then, are directly related to transitions in the Dogon cycle of life and death. The transitions of the youthful dancers into mature men are marked by their gradual acquisition of the skills needed to perform the difficult dances of the major animals, such as antelope, stork, and stilt dancers. The association of animals with the transition at death enables ancestors to continue their work for the living. The anthropocosmic work of the Dogon mask festival accomplishes these significant transitions at the "knowing joints" of humans and animals.

Conclusion

From the discussions of concepts of personhood, perceptions of ecology, and reflections on cosmology several observations surface regarding indigenous perspectives on animals. First, epistemologies of relatedness are closely tied to personhood concepts among diverse indigenous peoples in which animals constitute a cosmo-logical link to a greater knowing of self. Second, personhood flows from being creatively attentive to the surrounding world of animals. Cosmological dispositions embedded in bodies through cultural practices and perceptions of the environment enable individuals and communities to attain spiritual maturity as they engage in lifeway activities. Finally, where indigenous peoples have maintained these anthropocosmic rituals focused on animals, sustainable bioregions are evident. These sustainable fields break down where historical events have brought invasions of peoples, ideas, and ways of interacting with the surrounding world that fragment indigenous knowing and being known by animals.

NOTES

1. Raymond DeMallie, ed., *The Sixth Grandfather: Black Elk's Teachings Given to John G. Neihardt* (Lincoln: University of Nebraska Press, 1984), p. 115.

2. See Lee Irwin, *The Dream Seekers: Native American Visionary Traditions of the Great Plains* (Norman: University of Oklahoma Press, 1996).

3. "Relational epistemology" is from Nurit Bird-David, "'Animism' Revisited." *Current Anthropology* 40 (Supplement, February 1999): S77–79.

4. The phrase "more-than-human world" comes from David Abrams, *The Spell of the Sensuous: Perception and Language in a More-Than-Human World* (New York: Vintage Books, 1997).

5. See DeMallie, *The Sixth Grandfather*, and Joseph E. Brown, recorder and ed., *The Sacred Pipe: Black Elk's Account of the Seven Rites of the Oglala Sioux* (Norman: University of Oklahoma Press, 1963; reprint New York: Penguin, 1973).

6. Harvey Feit, "Dreaming of Animals," in Takashi Irimoto and Takako Yamada, eds., *Circumpolar Religion and Ecology* (Tokyo: University of Tokyo Press, 1994), p. 309.

7. A striking example of a type of covenant made with animals is embedded in the Maasaum ceremony of the Tsistsistas/Cheyenne people. Space does not allow a full discussion here of the extensive animal dances and ritual activity that reenacts the agreement made between the Cheyenne and the animals of the Plains. See Karl H. Schlesier, *The Wolves of Heaven: Cheyenne Shamanism, Ceremonies, and Prehistoric Origins* (Norman: University of Oklahoma Press, 1987).

8. Tim Ingold, *The Perception of the Environment: Essays in Livelihood, Dwelling, and Skill* (London: Routledge, 2000), p. 47.

9. Nor is "lifeway" intended to imply that all indigenous societies mirror the type of soteriological fit between cosmological myth, subsistence practices, and ritual life attributed to the Dogon by Marcel Griaule. See Marcel Griaule, *Conversations with Ogotemmeli: An Introduction to Dogon Religious Ideas* (London: Oxford University Press for the International African Institute, 1965) [Original: *Dieu d'eau Entretiens aves Ogotemmeli* (Paris: Editions du Chêne, 1948)]).

10. A. I. Hallowell, *Culture and Experience* (Philadelphia: University of Pennsylvania Press, 1955), p. 121.

11. Ibid., p. 360.

12. See Weiming Tu, "Beyond the Enlightenment Mentality," in Mary Evelyn Tucker and John

A. Grim, eds., *Worldviews and Ecology: Religion, Philosophy, and the Environment*, eds. (6th edition, Maryknoll, NewYork: Orbis, 2002), pp. 19–29.

13. A. I. Hallowell, "Ojibwa Ontology, Behavior, and World View," in *Culture and History: Essays in Honor of Paul Radin* (New York: Octagon Books, 1960), p. 362.

14. Ethnographies themselves in some strident colonialist contexts may (and should) be questioned regarding their descriptive accuracy, but that is not an issue for this essay.

15. George Lakoff and Mark Johnson, eds., *Metaphors We Live By* (Chicago: The University of Chicago Press, 1980), p. 193.

16. Ibid., *seriatim*.

17. This section draws on the reinterpretation of animism undertaken in Bird-David, "'Animism' Revisited," and Ingold, *The Perception of the Environment*.

18. This critique is evident from the early work of Edward B. Tylor, *Primitive Culture* (1871; reprint Vol. 1 *Religion in Primitive Culture*, New York: Harper and Row, 1958); it is developed in the work of Lucien Levy-Bruhl, *The 'Soul' of the Primitive* (London: Allen & Unwin, 1966); and it is evident even in the empathetic discussions of Claude Lévi-Strauss, *The Savage Mind* (1962; repr. Chicago: The University of Chicago Press, 1966). For a novel perspective in the West speculating on the thoughts of animals see Max Weber, *The Theory of Social and Economic Organization*, ed. Talcott Parsons (New York: Free Press, 1947).

19. See Gary Urton, ed., *Animal Myths and Metaphors in South America* (Salt Lake City: University of Utah Press, 1985).

20. Ingold, *The Perception of the Environment*, p. 47.

21. Ibid.

22. See especially M. Strathern, *The Gender of the Gift: Problems with Women and Problems with Society in Melanesia*. (Berkeley: University of California Press, 1988), pp. 130–31.

23. See James Gibson, *The Ecological Approach to Visual Perception* (Boston: Houghton Mifflin, 1966).

24. Quote from Bird-David, "'Animism' Revisited." The citations are from Gibson, *The Ecological Approach to Visual Perception*, pp. 242 and 246.

25. Adrian Tanner, *Bringing Home Animals* (New York: St. Martin's Press, 1979), p. 136.

26. In using the term "anthropomophized" Tanner retains a divide between the cultural world of the Cree and the natural world of animals. What is argued here is that indigenous peoples may very well have terms for "bush" and "camp," but these are not metaphors for separated worlds. Rather they are worlds that can not only be distinguished but also provide metaphorical conceptions of one another.

27. Howard Harrod, *The Animals Came Dancing: Native American Sacred Ecology and Animal Kinship* (Tucson: University of Arizona Press, 2000), p. 102.

28. See John Grim, "Cosmogony and the Winter Dance: Native American Ethics in Transition," *The Journal of Religious Ethics* (Fall 1992).

29. The Salish author, Mourning Dove, described this unusual cultural feature in this manner, "When a man or woman had previously experienced the finding of a supernatural power to guide them, it usually left them alone in childhood. It came back when they were adults, appearing as a dream or vision to remind them of the contact saying, 'Sing my song and the world will shine for you.'" See Mourning Dove, *Mourning Dove: A Salishan Autobiography*, ed. Jay Miller (Lincoln: University of Nebraska Press, 1990), p. 125; also Walter Cline, "Religion and World View," in Leslie Spier, ed., *The Sinkaietk or Southern Okanagon of Washington*. (Menasha, Wisconsin: George Banta Publishing Company, 1938), p. 186, and Verne Ray, "The Sanpoil and Nespelem Salishan Peoples of Northeastern Washington," *University of Washington Publications in Anthropology* 5 (December 1932): 186.

30. Norman Lerman, "Fieldnotes collected at Riverside, Washington, February, 1954," in Jill A. Willmott, ed., *Indians of British Columbia* (Vancouver, B.C.: University of British Columbia Press, 1963), p. 35.

31. Harrod, *The Animals Came Dancing*, pp. 58–59.

32. Interestingly, current elders now understand the estrangement and anomie resulting from Salish

interactions over the centuries with dominant Euro-American cultures as a form of spirit sickness that can also be relieved at the Winter Dance. See Wolfgang Jilek, *Indian Healing: Shamanic Ceremonialism in the Pacific Northwest Today* (Blaine, Washington: Hancock House Publishers, 1982).

33. This broad claim should be nuanced by the development of tourist masked dances among the Dogon, for example, at Sanga. See Walter E. A. van Beek, "Enter the Bush: A Dogon Mask Festival," in Susan Vogel, ed., *Africa Explores: 20th Century African Art* (New York: The Center for African Art, 1991), p. 70.

34. Ethnography on the Dogon from the 1930s to the present has generated a lively controversy largely based on the post World War II fieldwork and publications of Marcel Griaule especially his work, *Dieu d'eau: Entretiens avec Ogotommêli* (Paris: Editions du Chene, 1948); published as *Conversations with Ogotemmeli: An Introduction to Dogon Religious Ideas* (London: Oxford University Press for the International African Institute, 1965). A critique of Griaule's method and resulting work in that period can be found in Walter E. A. van Beek, "Dogon Restudied: A Field Evaluation of the Work of Marcel Griaule," in *Current Anthropology* 32, no. 2 (April 1991): 139–67. While the arguments need not be repeated here it is important to note that van Beek seriously questions the cosmologies Griaule presents as unknown to Dogon with whom he studied, and that there is no overarching integral, coherent association between myth and institutions among the Dogon as described by Griaule.

35. Walter E. A. van Beek (text) and Stephanie Hollyman (photographs), *Dogon: Africa's People of the Cliffs* (New York: Harry N. Abrams, 2001), p. 169. The discussion of the bush is adapted from van Beek's text.

36. This discussion is based on Geneviève Calame-Griaule, *Words and the Dogon World* (Philadelphia: Institute for the Study of Human Issues, 1986).

37. Ibid., pp. 8 and 10.

38. Van Beek, "Enter the Bush," p. 59.

39. Van Beek and Hollyman, *Dogon: Africa's People of the Cliffs,* p. 171.

Animal Sacrifice

Metaphysics of the Sublimated Victim

KIMBERLEY PATTON

The ritual of sacrifice has proven perhaps the most susceptible to the label of socially enacted "strategy," a façade whose various "real" goals can be laid bare by the scholar of religion: the distribution of protein, for example, or the collective diversion of attention from internecine violence, or "the production of a political ideology in which the perspective of male nobles is elaborated as a transcendent divine truth."[1] This insistence on sacrifice as strategy is made because, as a ritual, sacrifice seems by the light of contemporary ethical sensibilities horrifying and senseless, "cruel" and "compulsive," or even, in the words of one recent essay, ethically "impossible."[2] Sacrifice artificially creates violence, when so much of the world is now convulsed with social violence and obsessed with the efforts to contain it. In other words, so the critique goes, it cannot possibly represent a metaphysical "good," and hence must be masking a social desideratum. In sacrifice, as Jill Robbins has recently argued, the validity of the other is annihilated, following Lévinas's question about

whether there is not "in sacrifices joyously consented to, heroically offered in the exaltation of faith, a necessary turning away from the sufferings violently imposed by that same exaltation[?]"[3] Sacrifice enacts apparently counterintuitive dynamics, ones that seem to do the opposite of what they claim to do. The recipient is invisible; worse, the gift, a living, unwilling other, is willfully destroyed. The source of all life is thus supposedly magnified, by the *loss,* not by the gain, of a life. And as the reinscription of social and gender structures is so starkly patent in the idiosyncratic determination of who can sacrifice, who can benefit from the sacrifice, and who can receive the hierarchically subdivided body of the victim—including the dead in every guise: ghosts, ancestors, saints—it is no wonder that the central action, which is ritual killing, is understood as a portal to the hypostasis of what Hubert and Mauss called, a century ago, "social things."[4] The victim must therefore surely be only instrumental. Or so most prevalent models would still have it.

Sacrifice is a tightly controlled dance whose very space, costume, implements, words, and even agonal cries are repetitively choreographed according to primordial paradigms, as in a sixteenth-century Aztec formula: "From [our ancestors] have we inherited / our pattern of life. / They taught us / all their rules of worship, / all their ways of honoring the gods. / Thus before them, do we prostrate ourselves; / in their names we bleed ourselves; / our oaths we keep, / incense we burn, and sacrifices we offer."[5] And it almost invariably points in one direction: while the ritual idiom and dénouement of sacrifice is death, its teleology is one of life—indeed, of outpouring abundance. This theme is the meditative focus of John Steinbeck in the often neglected novel *To a God Unknown,* its title taken from Hymn 10.121 of the *Rgveda*. In the book's final scene the hero, Joseph Wayne, worn down by a devastating drought in the early 1900s in the Salinas valley in California, climbs upon an altar-like rock at the center of his property and opens the vessels of his wrists. His blood runs onto the moss and into the dried up stream. "The grass will grow out of me in a little while," Joseph whispers as he dies. Steinbeck ends the penultimate chapter of his book with the biblical lyric: "And the storm thickened, and covered the world with darkness, and with the rush of waters."[6] Joseph believes that his self-offering has brought the rains at last. This is quintessential sacrificial logic. Far from being counterintuitive, it tends to unfold according to a very clear internal logic all its own. In order to understand —or at least to inhabit for a time long enough to begin to understand—the world of sacrifice, one must first rightly describe some of its starting premises, and honestly attempt to answer the question: "What is at stake?"

We do not need necessarily to accept these premises, nor even to suppress a view we may hold of sacrifice as the most barbaric or neurotic of religious reflexes, in order to take a closer look at the role played by animals in sacrifice, namely, that of the victim. If human sacrifice is unimaginable to modern sensibilities, animal sacrifice offends many as well. This plays out in ethical-critical contexts, whereby, for example, Tom Regan can entitle his edited volume on religious perspectives on the use of animals in science *Animal Sacrifices* without devoting any discussion to the semantic range of this traditional term or the meaning of its appropriation in his title—"sacrifice" being a standard term in laboratory experimentation for an animal that does not survive a given procedure.[7] It goes without saying, Regan seems to imply, that in the case of clinical trials, animals are *things* that are *used* in the service of some putative higher good; and this is the same as in religious sacrifice.[8] This unreflective analogical move on Regan's part allows him, of course, to undermine the morality of both sacrifice as well as the methodologies of laboratory science. Discomfort with sacrifice extends to religious spheres as well, even ones that once embraced it—the Reformation reinterpretation of the sacrificial nature of the Eucharist is a potent example—but the tension continues to this day. Through textual excision and modification, recent versions of some modern reform, reconstructionist and even conservative Jewish *siddurim* suppress the traditional Orthodox prayers, found in the seventeenth blessing of the *Amida,* for the rebuilding of the Temple and the renewal of the sacrificial cult.[9] Many modern Orthodox Jews, including rabbis, privately shudder at the thought of such a restoration, however farfetched, so thoroughgoing has been the historical, post-destruction replacement of the sacrificial ideal by communal prayer, *mitzvot,* lived tradition, and Torah study.

In the value schemeta of most traditional forms of sacrifice, in both literate and nonliterate societies, animals were (and are) far from being *things*. The metaphysical situation of the animal victim in the sacrificial context is far from simple. Rather than dismissing sacrifice as a manipulative burlesque and a cruel abrogation of animal rights, we might learn more by taking a closer look at its dynamics. Religious traditions are not, in fact, indifferent to the consciousness or rights of animals, treating them as objects in the context of sacrifice. Instead the opposite is true. Animals are seen as active subjects from start to finish in the sacrificial process, glorified mediators between realms, whose cooperation is essential to the efficacy of the ritual, whose forgiveness is often sought from kinship groups to avert vengeance. Animal victims' feelings can be appeased in elaborate speeches denying the ultimacy of death. Often, as in the case of human sacrifice, a luminous fate in the afterlife for the victims is guaranteed by their immolation on earth.

This is made clear in several features of animal sacrifice, a combination of which is shared by many traditions that practiced or continue to practice it. The sacrificial victim is not historically construed by traditional sacrificial systems as an object, a reified entity, but instead as a theophoric *subject* that has metaphysical standing in its own right. If one examines closely the public distaste professed on a sociological level, such as the Supreme Court case brought against the Santería sacrifice of chickens in Hialeah, Florida, one will see that the objection draws its rhetorical strength not mainly from "the death of innocent animals," for it ignores the daily slaughter in America of hundreds of thousands of food animals. Santería priests are usually quite skilled at killing a chicken thank-offering or a propitiatory sacrifice with dispatch, like their counterparts, the ancient *kohainim* of the Jerusalem Temple, who could decapitate a dove in *melika* with a flick of the thumbnail, or the contemporary Nuer leopard-skin priests of the Sudan, who can swiftly bleed a goat to death with one quick knife blow to the jugular vein in the *gar* ceremony. The issue in the Hialeah case was sacrifice itself, that it is somehow not an appropriate way or reason for an animal to die.

But sacrifice is not the same as ordinary killing, and has never been, even when sacrifice was deemed holier and better than ordinary murder—as in traditional societies—instead of worse, as in ours. Rather, the Hialeah case represents First World discomfort with the association of *animals*—those furry and feathered "others" that we sentimentalize, caricature, denature, and consume—with *religion*, namely, the collective entity that attempts to align self and society with higher moral or transcendent structures, and to reinscribe community values. Animals live in zoos; they live in Disney films; they are endangered species; they are how we relate most easily to our children. They do not "rightly" inhabit the realm of worship any longer. This is of course our European Christian legacy, the same that so consistently led scholars of religion to embrace developmentalist models that viewed the prominence of animals in a particular tradition as a reliable index of its theological sophistication: the more animal powers, the more theriomorphic gods, the more animal sacrifices, the less "evolved" the religion. By extension, the preservation of animal sacrifice, which still to a great extent divinizes the animal victim, often jars modern ethical (and, I would argue, aesthetic) sensibilities. Animal sacrifice is equated with atavistic cruelty and mindless ceremonialism.

Four of the features of animal sacrifice that we might examine in light of these polemics are:

- Required perfection and ritual beautification of the victim;
- Voluntary cooperation of the animal, or so-called "fiction of willingness," and its relationship to efficacy;
- Religious elevation and individuation of the animal victim as a consequence of consecrated destruction;
- Eschatological dimensions of the sacrificed animal.

As heuristic tools, these categories predictably overlap and interlock.

Required Perfection and Ritual Beautification of the Victim

It is typical of many sacrificial systems that animals offered for sacrifice must be "perfect" according to certain ideologically determined categories: male, unblemished, and whole; they must be in the prime of life. Their bones may not be broken. The last is familiar to Western and other biblically fluent scholars in the New Testament passion narratives that identify Jesus with the Paschal lamb of Exodus: "Then the soldiers came and broke the legs of the first and of the other who had been crucified with him. But when they came to Jesus and saw he was already dead, they did not break his legs. Instead, one of the soldiers pierced his side with a spear, and at once blood and water came out. . . . These things occurred so that scripture might be fulfilled, 'None of his bones shall be broken.'" (John 19:33–34, 36; cf. Exodus 12:46, of the lamb for the qorban). But the significance of unbroken bones is by no means limited to the biblical tradition, and surfaces in startling ways in unrelated religious worlds. For example, in Buriat Mongol animal sacrifice, "a deep concern is to protect the bones of the sacrificial animal. For if the bones of the offerings are broken, the soul would be injured and the sacrifice would be rejected by the deity to whom it was offered."[10]

The more perfect the animal (or human being, for that matter), the less it belongs to this death-dealing, corrugated mortal world, and the more susceptible it is to election as a sacrificial offering. Further gilding the lily, sacrificial victims were and are often elaborately adorned. Indeed, the tragic confusion of human and animal sacrifices might be said to be the heart-breaking engine of stories like the aqedah ("Father! . . . where is the lamb for a burnt offering?" [Genesis 22:7]) and the sacrifice of the virginal Iphigenia, who in Aeschylus's Agamemnon is pointedly called adaitos, "untasted," highlighting her resemblance yet horrible difference from the normal Olympian sacrifice that always culminated in a feast. The aqedah plays on the required per-

fection, beauty, and youth of the qorban, in the innocence and specialness of Isaac. He is the yaḥid, the only son of the only legitimate wife of Abraham, and as such is fair game for the divine claim of Exodus: "whatever is the first to open the womb among the Israelites, of humans and animals, is mine" [13:1]). Euripides' Iphigenia at Aulis dramatically exploits these sacrificial features, and then goes on to dwell on the way in which the Iphigenia, deceived into thinking that she has been summoned to Aulis to be Achilles' bride, is adorned in festive splendor like an animal walking to the sacrificial altar. In ancient Greece, the trappings of marriage and those of sacrifice, from flutes to flowers, were virtually the same.

> So the gods sang this wedding hymn
> Blessing the marriage
> Of Peleus, noble in birth,
> And of the most favored
> Of Nereus' daughters.
> But you, Iphigenia, upon your head
> And on your lovely hair
> Will the Argives wreathe a crown
> For sacrifice.
> You will be brought down from the hill
>   caves
> Like a heifer, white, unblemished,
> And like a bloody victim
> They will slash your throat.
>   (Iphigenia at Aulis 1076–84)[11]

The required perfection of sacrificial animals, as well as their beautification, is often understood as the elaboration of a gift. This is not an incorrect hermeneutic, but it is a superficial one. The operant deep structure theology is that the animal's perfection is a microcosmic reflection, mirroring the perfection of the god to which it is offered. As well as representing a perfect gift or offering to God ("fit for a king"), at a deeper but related level, the animal is like God, expressing through its own form God's perfection. In addition to "standing in" for any number of things —the first-born child of the sacrificer, for example, in the Exodus substitution model, or the life force of the sacrificer himself, in Nuer offerings—the animal simultaneously *belongs to,* and is supremely *like*—thus, in some sense, "*is*" the god who receives it as a gift through immolation, suffocation, or drowning. The thundering words that begin the holiness code, Leviticus 19:1, are the paradigm: "Be ye therefore holy as I am holy." In miniature, perishable form, the animal victim manifests God's own vast and immortal perfection. Its return to its source via sacrifice is therefore of a supremely reflexive nature. "Like knows like" or better, "Like yearns for like; like must be returned to Like." There can be no question that this idea, although sublimated and secularized, drives the wistful saying, "only the good die young." The gods have a habit of gathering back to themselves the very best of what they have brought into being, as though such god-like beings cannot stay away from home too long. Sacrifice or violent death are the quickest paths to such a divine reclamation; this is why in so many societies the premature deaths of the young, beautiful, or supernaturally gifted are often spoken of in covertly sacrificial terms.

As John Carman expresses it in his study of divine polarity, *Majesty and Meekness,*[12] "It is a striking feature of sacrifice in many religious traditions that what is offered in sacrifice to a deity represents something not only vital to the sacrifice but something appropriate to, belonging to, even part of the deity who receives the sacrifice." That this involves a profound paradox is unmistakable: how can one *give* to the Lord what has always belonged to the Lord? And yet this principle of sacrifice as a kind of return of something to the originating source is repeatedly demonstrated throughout the history of religions, and not just the "classical," highly scriptural traditions. Because Nuer cattle come from Kwoth and are a gift of Kwoth, sacrifice is a return of the life force to Kwoth. It is entirely in keeping with classical sacrificial logic that the Nuer are profoundly and specifically identified with their own cattle, knowing them individu-

ally from birth, being identified with them at (male) puberty, and continually praising their beauty in the composition of song; thus the sacrifice of a cow is also understood as a kind of intentional offering of the owner's very self to Kwoth. Just as the Psalmist, Jeremiah, and Isaiah called Israelite sacrifices to account, for the Nuer if the quality of the intentionality is in question, the sacrifice may not be acceptable. This underscores the point: it is *not* that the sacrificed cow is a thing given as gift or even that it is a vehicle for human religious communication with God. The schema of Hubert and Mauss here does not go far enough. The cow instead is literally both identified with Kwoth as well as with the human who loves it. Sacrifice is therefore nothing less than a visible ratification of the existential symbiosis of Nuer theology.[13]

God takes back what already belongs to God, as the Eucharistic liturgy of John Chrysostom used in the Eastern Orthodox church makes clear: Τὰ Σὰ ἐκ τῶν Σῶν Σοὶ προσφέρομεν— "We offer you these gifts, *which are your own.*"[14] Through the ritual destruction of sacrifice God or the gods receive that which homologically evokes or even constitutes divine essence, most often understood as the life force. This, in turn, is often located explicitly in the entity of blood, endlessly circulating, whose metaphysical potency is unleashed when it is spilled out of the individual body it animates and into the collective ritual sphere and hence the entire cosmos. "For the life of the flesh is in the blood," says God in Leviticus 17:11, "and I have given it for you upon the altar to make atonement for your souls; for it is the blood that makes atonement, by reason of the life." It is through the shedding of blood that the animal can "stand for" and represent the one who offers it, the one who seeks expiation or aid. The blood of the animal is so numinous a substance that it is splashed on the sides of the altar of the Holy of Holies, as it is similarly used in ancient Greek sacrifice.[15] Blood is life, and life must be returned to Life. A similarly circular cosmogram charts the flow of *ch'ul,* the Mayan life force, from the divinized sun to flourishing maize to the hungry human being to ritual blood-letting, in both lethal and nonlethal forms, by way of offering life back to the sun.[16]

The sacrificial animal is special, even unique; it is perfect; it is ritually adorned and beautified for its death. It has a special relationship to God and in sacrifice is given back to Him. If we want to understand animal sacrifice in a given religious context, and if human sacrifice existed in the culture as a parallel phenomenon, we can always look there to begin the process of extrapolation. Rather than being sharply differentiated, as we, subtly influenced by monotheistic thought, might like to see, human and animal sacrifice are usually two modalities of the same dynamic. The ritual slaughter of human beings either intensifies established forms of animal oblation (as in time of crisis), or else serves as the default category, not the exception. Hence, in Aztec society, where animal sacrifice was rare but human sacrifice was extremely prevalent—at the height of the cult at the Templo Mayor at Tenochtitlan, as many as 20,000 warriors per year are estimated to have been killed by cardiac evisceration—we can look to the *teotl ixiptla*, the sacrificial victim who splendidly impersonated the god to whom he (or she, in the case of The Great Festival of the Lords) was to be sacrificed and treated with divine honors for a year—recalling the year of absolute, vast, and godlike freedom accorded the stallion to be sacrificed for the Vedic *aśvamedha* as it roamed the grasslands.[17]

Voluntary Cooperation and its Relationship to Efficacy

"But the animal has no choice in the matter!" runs the exposé. The sacrificial theater of action, whether it be circle in the grass with stake, altar, or temple steps, appears to be a place of appalling coercion. One of the oddest features of sacrifice, however, is that without the idea (often called the "pretext," itself a term that affirms the rubric of masquerade, discussed above, and

hence is far from neutral) of the animal's cooperation in every step of proceedings, the sacrifice cannot work. The animal is virtually never divested of agency or free will. Instead, it is understood to assent to its own demise; this "voluntary" self-offering by the animal is nonnegotiable. This was accomplished, for example, by the sprinkling of water upon the animal's head in both the ancient Greek *thusia* and ancient Israelite *qorban 'olah* so that it appeared to nod its assent. In the wider sphere of hunting ritual, one encounters over and again the necessity of the decision of the prey animal, fully ensouled, to allow itself to be hunted and killed. Without this assent severe retaliation is exacted upon the transgressor.[18]

Rather than simply killing the restrained sacrificial victim, which the sacrificing priest could easily do, the ritual requires that the animal first "assent" to its own destruction—that it appear to be an active, even self-conscious ritual participant, not a passively manipulated "sacred thing." On first blush this action appears so patently a charade, so supremely exploitative of a simple act of mammalian behavior, as to render the notion of voluntary animal "participation" a mockery. Scholars of ancient Greek sacrifice such as Walter Burkert, drawing from the earlier work of Karl Meuli, have argued that this is part of a great scheme of denial on the part of Greek society, what is called "la comédie d'innocence."[19] This denial reflected the discomfort of the Greeks with the violence, however dressed up, of sacrifice, and evidence for the comedy of innocence range from the chronic Greek aversion to depicting the actual moment of killing in vase-painting scenes of sacrifice to the ancient Attic mock trial at the Bouphonia, whereby after the annual slaughter of an ox to Zeus, each party to the sacrifice is tried and acquitted of murder, the sacrificial knife (*machaira*) itself is found guilty and flung into the sea. But strong parallels exist in nonliterate sacrificing societies; consider Malinowski's celebrated take on animal sacrifice among the Trobriand Islanders:

For the act they were about to commit elaborate excuses were offered; they shuddered at the prospect of the sheep's death, they wept over it as though they were its parents. Before the blow was struck, they implored the beast's forgiveness. They then addressed themselves to the species to which the beast belonged, as if addressing a large family clan, beseeching it not to seek vengeance for the act that was about to be inflicted on one of its members. In the same vein the actual murderer was punished in the same manner, either beaten or sent into exile.[20]

This is what Girard refers to as "the paradox —not without its comic aspects on occasion— of the frequent references to vengeance in the course of sacrificial rites, the veritable obsession with vengeance when no chance of vengeance exists,"[21] playing a key role in his controversial idea of sacrifice as a kind of "shunt" of eruptive internal violence. Girard's assertion that "no chance of vengeance exists" is in and of itself both patronizing and misleading, running as it does counter to entrenched traditional interpretations of the animal realm as a place of both power and punitive capabilities against human beings. In other words, in a world where animals are independent subjects (not objects), there is real (not pretend) dread involved in both sacrifice and the hunt of reprisal, as the complex of Inuit taboos indicate: the angry souls of coerced seals will haunt the hunter. This dread is neither "comic" nor superficial among sacrificing communities; the required assent of the animal victim is not an incidental matter, and the elaborate mechanisms reported throughout the history of religions for neutralizing the destabilizing guilt of murder are not farces.

Led "like a sheep to the shambles," where it is robbed instantly of life, sentience, and future, the animal victim undertakes through the sacrificial process a role that is far from passive. Instead it is one of theurgic and social agency, accomplishing a whole, rich range of religious ends: world-making, consecration, thanksgiving, expiation, and catharsis, to name a few. *Pace*

the reductionist sociological view that wants to see sacrifice as nothing more than a theologized opportunity to consume meat in protein-deprived societies, these ends obtain and are kept in clear view even when the entire animal is consumed, usually in an hierarchical distribution that reflects sacerdotal authority.

Elevation and Individuation of the Victim: The Consequences of Consecrated Destruction

In traditional sacrifice, the voluntary participation of the unblemished animal that is singled out for sacrifice removes it from a life among countless other domesticated animals. In a sense, it is thereby "rescued" from inconsequentiality as one of a multitudinous herd; it is given ritual, and therefore, ontological standing, thus also acquiring special cultural status. In their acclaimed and still important study, *Sacrifice: Its Nature and Functions,* Henri Hubert and Marcel Mauss posited that the victim serves as a divinized bridge between the divine and human realms, or as they expressed it, as a form of "communication" between the worlds.[22] What we may plainly see as senseless death is construed quite differently in sacrificial traditions. Sacrifice results from start to finish in a kind of magnification of what had been quite ordinary: an animal, a "typical" member of a domesticated species, becomes atypical, a player in a sacred drama. Sacrifice *singles out* the otherwise anonymous animal—or in some cases, a special group of animals, as in the patrilineally owned "holy herd" of the Mbanderu in Namibia, set apart from the alimentary herd and "directly under the blessing of the ancestors."[23] By the force of that which it channels, the victim thus gains a kind of highly charged individuality. It is an individuality with some personal but mostly transpersonal elements. It is individuality nonetheless, in keeping with the animal's uniqueness.

This elevation results in supreme efficacy. In Numbers 19:1–21, in order to ritually purify anyone who has suffered proximity to a corpse or a grave, a red heifer is slaughtered outside the camp, and its blood is sprinkled seven times before the *mishkan*. Cedarwood, hyssop, and scarlet stuff are cast into the midst of the burning holocaust. A clean man, not the one who sacrificed the heifer, gathers up the ashes of the heifer and deposits them outside the camp in a clean place, "and they shall be kept for the congregation of the people of Israel, for the water of impurity, for the removal of sin." (Numbers 19:9). Whether theses ashes, or any sacrificial offerings, are efficacious in and of themselves is a debate stretching back to the prophetic critique of the Jerusalemite cultus. Even now, scholars struggle with the apparently magico-religious nature of the remains of the animal. Note, for example, the use by Elijah Judah Schochet of the rationalizing language of signification: "Did the ceremony of the red heifer symbolize the atoning power of blood, or did its red color represent the eradication of sin from the Israelite camp? In either event, the crucial aspect here is Israel's relationship with God and the rectification of her uncleanliness. The red heifer is merely the vehicle for the removal of uncleanliness."[24] Notably, Schochet does not confront the parallel issue of the ancient Israelite concept of uncleanliness itself, which is so clearly a matter of material holiness or lack thereof—not unrelated to moral categories but ultimately unanchored in them. In the eyes of the deity, then, as well as those of the corollary community, the sacrificial animal is both elevated and individuated. It is "seen" by God (or smelled, or eaten, or encompassed, as in the Hawaiian case). We may reject this cultic logic on humane or even epistemological grounds. But we cannot ignore it. Through sacrifice the animal becomes "somebody"; it has religious and therefore social identity. In a sense, sacrifice makes the victim "real."

The occasional drama of "singling out" in the secular, public context occurs when the tables of fate are turned and an individual animal somehow escapes the slaughterhouse. This theme is the poignant crux of the children's classic *Char-*

lotte's Web by E. B. White. Through her tears and pleas, the young girl Fern rescues the runt of a litter of pigs from her father, a farmer, whom she discovers one morning carrying piglet in one hand and axe in the other. Fern's choice transforms Wilbur into more than a pet; he becomes, arguably, a person; later, through the web-weaving alchemy of Charlotte the spider at the state fair, Wilbur is further exalted as "RADIANT"—"SOME PIG." Or we might mention the case of the 500-pound cow in Queens who in 2000 escaped her holding pen, where she was awaiting butchery at Astoria Live Poultry. She was cheered as she eluded capture on New York City streets. In response to hundreds of calls made to The Center for Animal Care and Control and Astoria Live Poultry, "urging both the agency and the slaughterhouse owner to release the animal to a sanctuary where she could live out the remainder of her life," she was ultimately adopted by an organization called Farm Sanctuary. Importantly, she was also given a name: Queenie.[25] Interestingly, Astoria Live Poultry is a *halal* slaughterhouse. Aladdin El-Sayed, the owner, said, "God was willing to give it a new life, so why wouldn't I?"[26] In both of these cases, fictional and true, Wilbur and Queenie respectively avoid the collective, routinized anonymity of the meat lockers by virtue of somehow staying alive against all odds. By avoiding slaughter, they become creatures worth naming instead of numbering. Their destinies thus mirror the fate of the sacrificial animal, but in reverse; the principle of elevation and individuation, however, is the same.

The Talmud tells the extraordinary story of the encounter of Rabbi Judah the Prince, redactor of the Mishnah, with a calf on its way to kosher slaughter. "When it broke away, [it] hid his head under Rabbi's skirts, and lowed [in terror]. Judah haNasi remained unmoved by the little creature's plight, and said, "Go, for this you were created." The Gemara tells us that the angels heard this: "Thereupon they said [in Heaven], 'Since he has no pity, let us bring suffering upon him.'"

Judah haNasi was then afflicted for thirteen years with excruciating bodily suffering. He was only freed when, as the story in *Baba Metzia* continues, "One day Rabbi's maidservant was sweeping the house; [seeing] some young weasels there, she made to sweep them away. 'Let them be,' he said to her; 'It is written, and his tender mercies are over all his works.' [Psalms 145:9]. Said they [in Heaven], 'Since he is compassionate, let us be compassionate to him.'"

The calf is bolting from its normal socially prescribed fate, namely to be killed in a kosher manner to be eaten. This is what lies behind Judah the Prince's calmly heartless statement to the calf: "Go, for this you were created." But here the story takes an utterly unexpected twist. The calf's breaking away from restraint and seeking refuge under the skirts of a great religious authority transforms it from an anonymous food source into an individual. The calf becomes a religious "person," specifically, a supplicant, in relationship with another religious person—an arbiter, a potential source of mercy. In this situation, Rabbi Judah is called upon to make the choice made daily by God Himself in *Berakhot* 7a, when He prays that His mercy might overcome His justice and all His other attributes. Judah cannot brook the exception to what is expected, and invokes religious justification to overrule compassion, sending the little calf to its doom. For this failure the great rabbi is cruelly, even disproportionately, punished by the angels. *Nothing can reverse his sentence but his later redemptive act of compassion toward animals—and, unlike the edible calf, socially useless ones at that.*[27]

We said earlier that the principle of sacrifice is one of elevation and individuation of the victim. Why then is the victim ostensibly destroyed? How does this apparently counterintuitive piece of sacrificial logic "work"? "Like mirrors Like"; "like belongs to Like." Forms of ritual killing— throat-cutting, burning, hanging, and suffocating—apparent negations of the vitality of life, are in fact ways of mimicking the gods' undying, unchanging state. Sacrifice changes the animal not into a state of death but into a state of deathlessness. The final piece drops into place: this likeness, this belonging requires a metamorphosis. The sacrificial victim must become "like the gods": in other words, not normal, not everyday, not perishable. Death is the most "other" state known; the most uncanny. In the case of the slaughtered animal that accompanies the deceased head of the household to the realm of the ancestors, there is an even more direct translation. The ancestors, the source of authority par excellence, are eternal, and the animal is made "like" them, just as its owner passes from the changing to the unchanging realm. And so to that weird, hallowed realm the sacrificial victim is consigned once and for all, joining in its power and efficacy.

This kind of thinking seems to have animated Celto-Germanic ritual immersions: the bog sacrifice of the Gundestrup cauldron in Denmark, for example, and other beautifully worked metal vessels, as well as "beautifully hanged" and decapitated persons, given to Odin. Utter and complete remoteness—transformation into another existential state, which is the province of the divine, or at least most closely resembles it—is necessary. Hence the metamorphosis took the form of the ritualized killing of the living thing, the holocaust of the whole thing, the irretrievable submersion of the priceless thing. This is an exigency of sacrifice, not an option: what is surrendered must be extremely precious, and it must ultimately be completely ruined or lost, without hope of retrieval.

Through this metamorphosis, it is thought that destruction will generate new life. Sacrificial death is usually structurally bound up with notions of extreme generativity, vital forces that cannot be released unless there is a death. And if there is to be a resurrection, a memorial to that ideal, quite often sacrifice has as its strange goal a kind of divinized reconstitution of the animal. The ancient Greeks, for example, had a custom of rebuilding the animal, using its bones upon the altar after sacrifice, almost as a way of re-presenting it. This was part of their larger practice of *anatithenai*—of "setting up" votive gifts in or outside the sanctuary. However, it is a special form of the practice. The hanging of the *boukranion,* or ox skull, above the sacrificial altar or even carving it as a motif onto the altar is a common iconographic device in ancient Greek vase-painting. The dead animal lives again, presiding over future sacrifices like the one in which it died. When the Mbanderu master of the house in buried, every single cow of the "holy herd" that he received "as a gift from his father when he was a boy" is "sympathetically" killed, accompanying the dead man to the next world.[28] "During the whole mourning period the cows of the holy herd are slaughtered and eaten," segmented and distributed according to precise socio-religious rules. (One Herero elder told Sundermeier that the distribution of the meat "is fixed like on a map.")[29] However, [a]t the end of the mourning period, at the latest after one year, the skulls with the horns are piled up on the father's tomb, an obvious sign of the importance of the man who is buried here. The skulls are a sign of remembrance, a "memorial."[30]

In other words, the resurrection of the sacrificial victim can only be symbolic, not literal: the set divisions of the sacrificial feast, the reassembling of bones and their display in a funerary setting, or the institution of cultic memory, regularly celebrated (as for example, in the case of the daughter of Jephtha). But it is nevertheless a potent statement, with both visual and rhetorical aspects, of a paradoxical idea: because of the "special" manner of its death, the victim lives on, in stronger form, now assimilated to a sphere of power beyond the human.

The ancient Vedic sacrificial imagination, however, went even further, reconstituting the horse in heaven. The Ṛgvedic hymn to the sacrificial stallion, so often interchangeable with fire and the sun, is marked by an elaborate concern for the horse's well-being. The hymn prays for his freedom from pain during the process of the sacrifice, and for his resurrection in heaven, including the retention of all that belongs to him: his territory, his entire body, and even the sacrificial instruments that are used ritually to dismember him. Above all note that the *bodily integrity* of the horse is understood to be uncompromised, even as it is ritually killed, chopped up, cooked, and consumed. The singer of the hymn addresses the horse directly, and this form of direct address to the sacrificial victim is the prevalent voice throughout the rest of the hymn. The horse is not only the subject of religious thought and action, but also a divinized subject at that; the hortatory tone concerns itself with nothing less than his bodily resurrection after death, down to the most apparently gruesome details:

The charger's rope and halter, the reins and bridle on his head, even the grass that has been brought up to his mouth—let all of that stay with you even among the gods.

Whatever of the horse's flesh the fly has eaten, or whatever stays stuck to the stake or to the axe, or to the hands or to the nails of the slaughterers— let all that stay with you even among the gods. . . .

Whatever runs off your body when it has been placed on the spit and roasted by the fire, let it not lie there in the earth or on the grass, but let it be given to the gods who long for it. . . .

The place where he walks, where he rests, where he rolls, and the fetters on the horse's feet, and what he has drunk and the fodder he has eaten— let all of that stay with you even among the gods.

Let not the fire that reeks of smoke darken you, nor the red-hot cauldron split into pieces. The gods receive the horse who has been sacrificed, worshipped, consecrated, and sanctified with the cry of "Vaṣat!"

The cloth that they spread beneath the horse, the upper covering, the golden trappings on him, the halter and the fetters on his feet—let these things that are his own bind the horse among the gods.

If someone riding you has struck you too hard with heel or whip when you shied, I make all these things well again for you in prayer, as they do with the oblation's ladle in sacrifices.

The axe cuts through the thirty-four ribs of the racehorse who is the companion of the gods. Keep the limbs undamaged and place them in proper pattern. Cut them apart, calling out piece by piece.

(*Ṛgveda* 1.162, 8–18 *passim*)[31]

Seen from within a traditional lens, then, the sacrificial destruction of an animal is not what it seems. There is no question that sacrificial traditions honor and even exaggerate the tension between appearance and theological claim; they are acutely aware that in sacrifice, a life is violently taken—that the act seems like a horrible fragmentation of what once was alive, whole, and in some sense, free (although, as Jonathan Z. Smith has pointed out, the sacrificial animal is nearly always the domestic animal and almost never the wild, randomly entrapped animal).[32] But in various ways, sacrificial logic then defiantly points to dedicated ruin as a kind of redemption. In fact, from an emic perspective, the tension between appearance and theological claim is more like the relationship between appearance and reality.

Eschatological Dimensions of the Sacrificed Animal

The scripted, lethal drama of sacrifice catalyzes enormous transformations; we have outlined briefly what it does for deity and community. But it also does something for the sacrificial victim, too; its temporary divinized state, effected from the moment of selection for sacrifice and emphasized by the ritual killing itself, is often rendered permanent, and its eschatologi-

cal future assured in a kind of glistering light. This is a persistent idea across any number of traditions; again, the example of human sacrifice renders the animal version intelligible. One thinks of the later rabbinical celebration, elaborating on the Torah account, of Isaac's willing autosacrifice,[33] or the glorious afterlife imagined for sacrificed Aztec warriors, who, changed into hummingbirds, travel celestially with the sun-god Huitzilopochtli. It has remained a key idea in the religious imagination of India, in the outlawed practice of *sati,* the "voluntary" self-burning of widows upon their husbands' pyres; the autosacrifice, commemorated throughout India in carved stone monuments, brings enormous honor to the family and supreme glory after death.[34]

To return to the Vedic horse sacrifice, the sacrificer's prayer is for the horse's ultimate bodily integrity and his exaltation in an afterlife, one that very much resembles his present sphere of life and capabilities, only more glorious. The horse will dwell among the gods. He will tread upon the roads of the sky in the same kind of royal freedom that marked his last year on earth. Sacrifice will accomplish many things, as the last verse says: "good cattle and good horses, male children and all-nourishing wealth." But most striking for our inquiry, it will bring about spectacular apotheosis of the horse himself.[35] The Ṛgvedic hymn continues:

Let not your dear soul burn you as you go away. Let not the axe do lasting harm to your body. Let no greedy, clumsy slaughterer hack in the wrong place and damage your limbs with his knife.

You do not really die through this, nor are you harmed. You go to the gods on paths pleasant to go on. The two bay stallions, the two roan mares are now your chariot mates.

(*Ṛgveda* 1.162, 20–21)[36]

We can surely read the Vedic phrase "You do not really die," sung to the dismembered horse, as a kind of cruel self-deception, one that seeks to clothe in transcendental language what Hubert and Mauss, following Durkheim, would call "social facts." "You do not really die" would then represent the formulaic assuaging of guilt for instigating the destruction of a magnificent animal, one whose identifications with royalty perdured for millenia throughout Indo-European civilizations.[37] But increasingly I wonder whether Meuli's notion of "the comedy of innocence," extensively deployed by Walter Burkert in the case of ancient Greek sacrifice, is as useful as it seems on first blush. To read "You do not really die" as an expression of wish contrary-to-fact may be heuristically unhelpful; instead, perhaps, we ought to read it more as the proclamation of a central eschatological tenet. The horse's soul is immortal, and remains uncompromised by the act of ritual killing; in fact it is enhanced. The belief is that the horse will have a far better afterlife than he would have otherwise *because* he has been sacrificed; in fact, the process is one of apotheosis.

The principle of *samsara* teaches that what goes around comes around; everything is ultimately impermanent, including the oscillating roles of sacrificer and victim. The most dramatic illustration of the metaphysical standing of the sacrificial animal I know comes by way of ethnographic note from Kathmandu. There, Eric Mortensen told me he observed a domestic sacrifice of multiple goats to Kali in front of a home near Bodhanath in Nepal. The priest whispered something in the ear of each goat that he slaughtered. After much gentle persistence on Eric's part, the priest finally divulged what he was saying. "Next life you kill me."

Conclusion

It is not my goal here to "rehabilitate" animal sacrifice in the eyes of its ethical detractors. It is one thing to parse sacrificial logic; it is quite another to see Wilhelm Radloff's ghastly diagram of a horse sacrifice to the god Ülgön by an Altai tribe in southern Siberia that he watched

in the early 1880's, a type of celestial equine sacrifice that may date back to similar practices among the Huns or even earlier. The body of a blond horse, whose soul was delivered to the god by a shaman (*kam*) leading it through multiple heavens after snaring it, is suspended high in the air, impaled on a great wooden pole extending diagonally to the sky, its nose and head forced heavenward.[38] Among the many underlying metaphysical ideas in this arrangement are death, ecstatic flight, and divine propitiation. Yet the eyewitness drawing of the physical rite and its apparatus is almost unbearable to look at.

The point I am making is a specific, even a technical one, which in my view must be addressed before credible ethical analysis can begin. The exegesis of any sacrificial system, whether historical or contemporary, obsolete or viable, calls for a complex, internally informed understanding of its premises and ideologies. When this is undertaken with care and without presuppositions, I would argue that it is often the case that far from objectifying animal victims, "the logic of sacrifice," *on the terms of its own self-presentation,* hallows and empowers them. This logic is almost always dependent on some form of visionary construction of the animal. In many types of sacrifice, far from appropriately occupying the semantic field of our modern word "victim," the immolated animal has instead agency, purpose, identity, and metaphysical standing. Rather than a death-sustaining object, an expendable resource, a reified and destroyed "thing" without hope or future, the sacrificial animal instead is seen as a life-dealing subject, a sanctified mediator between realms on behalf of the sacrificing community, and a divinized entity of eternal, powerful, and unassailable immortal status.

Whether this is "false logic," a masquerade hiding violence through the transcendental mechanism of the scapegoat, a strategy to maintain patriarchal domination, or a choreographed expression of collective anxieties about death and its control, remains open to question. But then one finds oneself in the uncomfortable arena of asking why secular paradigms, particular those that assume that animals have *only* physical and instinctual nature, ought to be accorded the mantle of "objectivity" over and against religious models. The "cruelty" of sacrifice is debatable, as is the usually unquestioned idea that it inherently reifies and debases animals. Perhaps animal sacrifice can be challenged on other grounds, but, I would argue, not on these ones.

NOTES

1. Nancy Jay, *Throughout Your Generations Forever: Sacrifice, Religion, and Paternity* (Chicago: The University of Chicago Press, 1992), p. 146.

2. Jill Robbins, "Sacrifice," in Mark C. Taylor, ed., *Critical Terms for Religious Studies* (Chicago: The University of Chicago Press), p. 296: "Sacrifice is ... impossible in ethical terms, insofar as it is abhorrent ..." See also Nancy Jay's remarks about Aztec and African sacrificial practices, "Only the Aztecs outdid the Dahomeans in volume, compulsiveness, and cruelty of sacrificing." (Jay, *Throughout Your Generations Forever*, p. 39).

3. Emmanuel Lévinas, "Lévy-Bruhl and Contemporary Philosophy," in *Entre nous: Essais sûr le penser-à-l'autre* (Paris: Grasset, 1991), p. 48.

4. Henri H. Hubert and Marcel Mauss, *Sacrifice: Its Nature and Function,* trans. W. D. Walls (Chicago: University of Chicago Press, 1964), p. 101: "Religious ideas, because they are believed, exist; they exist objectively, as social facts. The sacred things in relation to which sacrifice functions, are social things. And this is enough to explain sacrifice."

5. From the sources collected in Miguel León-Portilla, *Aztec Thought and Culture: A Study of the Ancient Nahuatl Mind,* trans. J. E. Davis (Norman: University of Oklahoma Press, 1971 [1963]), p. 64.

6. John Steinbeck, *To a God Unknown* (New York, Penguin, 1995 [1933], p. 184.

7. Tom Regan, ed., *Animal Sacrifices: Religious Perspectives on the Use of Animals in Science* (Philadelphia: Temple University, 1986). Regan's ironical use of the laboratory term "sacrifice," with its (undefended) implications that medical experimenters who use animal subjects are unaware of the older religious meanings of sacrifice, can be challenged more eloquently than I am able to do by those who actually work with animals in these contexts.

In December 2004, a memorial stone was unveiled at the Animal Research Institute in Beijing honoring the mice, guinea pigs, rabbits, and rhesus monkeys who died in the race to develop a vaccine for the SARS (severe acute respiratory) virus, the deadly flu-like illness that first emerged in southern China in late 2002, killing 349 in mainland China and sickening thousands elsewhere. China has been working on a vaccine since 2003. Wan Zijun, administrator of the China Academy of Medical Sciences, said that the number of animals killed in the development of the vaccine, now in clinical trials, was unknown. The stone slab in the institute courtyard is etched with three Chinese characters that read, "A stone to comfort the departed souls" (http://www.sciencemag.org/cgi/content/summary/306/5704/2184b).

8. For discussions of the deployment of the language of sacrifice in these contexts, see A. Arluke, "Sacrificial Symbolism in Animal Experimentation," *Anthrozoos* 2, 2 (1988): 98–117 and M. Lynch, "Sacrifice and the Transformation of the Animal Body into a Scientific Object," *Social Studies of Science* 18 (1988): 265–89.

9. See *Sharei Tefilla, Kol Haneshama,* and *Sim Shalom.*

10. Eric Mortensen, Inner Asian Studies and Study of Religion, Guilford College, personal correspondence.

11. Euripides, *Iphigenia in Aulis,* trans. Charles R. Walker, in Euripides IV, *The Complete Greek Tragedies,* eds. David Grene and Richmond Lattimore (Chicago: University of Chicago Press, 1958).

12. John B. Carman, *Majesty and Meekness: A Comparative Study of Contrast and Harmony in the Concept of God* (Grand Rapids: Eerdman, 1994).

13. For the most detailed theoretical discussion

of this, see the chapter on "Sacrifice" in E. E. Evans-Pritchard, *Nuer Religion* (Oxford: Oxford University Press, 1956). Dramatic ethnographic evidence of it lies in the recorded interview and footage of sacrifice in the film *The Nuer,* made in Eastern Ethiopia in 1970. That animals that are ritually killed are often intimately known and even loved by those who kill them is, again, more often the exception than the rule. Mary MacDonald, a scholar of the religions of Oceania, reveals that the pigs who die in the ancestrally linked "pig kills" of the people of the Erave area of the Southern Highlands Province of Papua New Guinea, held every six to eight years, are those who survived the previous pig kill by being breast-fed from infancy by human women in the household. (Mary N. MacDonald, "Pigs in Rituals of Healing and Renewal in Highlands New Guinea," unpublished paper and discussion afterwards for the panel "Animals and Religious Ritual: Spanning the Globe," American Academy of Religion, Annual Meeting, November 2004, San Antonio, Texas).

14. St. John Chrysostom, The Divine Liturgy (Η ΘΕΙΑ ΛΕΙΤΟΥΡΓΙΑ). *The Divine Liturgy, The Sunday Epistles & Gospels* (Ecumenical Publications, 1975), p. 52. Italics mine.

15. The Levitical divine claim would seem to challenge Jacob Milgrom's rejection of the notion of ancient Israelite sacrifice as an assimilation by the deity of the life-force of the animal; see his discussion in his *Leviticus 1–16: A New Translation with Commentary* (New York: Doubleday, 1991). Milgrom attempts here consistently to distance ancient Israelite sacrifice from the principles of other Ancient Near Eastern sacrificial cults, whereby the god was clearly "fed" and thus pacified, cajoled, or induced to grant favors). One can observe similar tensions among interpreters of Zoroastrian animal sacrifice, which despite the strong palimpsest of "spiritualized" worship retroactively overlaid on the history of the tradition, particularly among Parsi intellectuals, was practiced along with the Haoma sacrifice until the tenth century: the Avesta testifies to the idea that sacrifices were thought to strengthen the gods (*Yt.* 8; *Yt.* 14), although "the main idea has always been that prayer, worship and

belief strengthen the good gods in their fight against evil." (A. de Jong, "Animal Sacrifice in Zoroastrianism," in Albert I. Baumgarten, ed., *Sacrifice in Religious Experience,* [Leiden: Brill, 2002], p. 144).

16. See Linda Schele and Mary Ellen Miller, *The Blood of Kings: Dynasty and Ritual in Maya Art* (New York: George Braziller, 1986), esp. chs. 4–8.

17. For the most energetic and thorough analysis of the Aztec *teotl ixiptla,* see Davíd Carrasco, *City of Sacrifice: The Aztec Empire and the Role of Violence in Civilization* (Boston: Beacon Press, 1999), esp. pp. 81–82 117–21, and 140–47.

18. See, for example, the discussion of Inuit hunting taboos and animal-human relationships in David Pelly, *Sacred Hunt: A Portrait of the Relationship Between Seals and Inuit* (Vancouver: Greystone Books; Seattle: The University of Washington Press, 2001), esp. pp. 11 ff.

19. See Karl Meuli, "Griechische Opferbräuche" in Olof Gigon and Karl Meuli, eds., *Phyllobolia: Festschrift Peter von der Mühll,* (Basel, 1946), pp. 185–288; reprinted in K. Meuli, *Gesammelte Schriften,* vol. 2, ed. Thomas Gelzer (Basel: Schwabe and Co., 1975), pp. 907–1021; Walter Burkert, *Homo Necans: The Anthropology of Ancient Greek Sacrificial Ritual and Myth,* trans. Peter Bing (Berkeley: University of California Press, 1983), esp. pp. 12–14. In his recent essay "Sacrifice in African Traditional Religions," Theo Sundermeier problematizes, point by point, Burkert's analysis of the elements of sacrifice as a kind of "fraud of the gods," which Sundermeir calls a "deep misunderstanding." He posits that Burkert is partially influenced by Hesiod's account of the Promethean deception of Zeus at Mecone: "A sheep or an ox, for example, never groans when its carotid artery is cut. Therefore the cries of the women do not drown out its groaning, but they are—if I see this right—the normal 'hallel' shouts, which are made with a stroke of the tongue at the palate as we know them from the Mediterranean up to the south of Africa. They are always given at special, festive occasions. They show and increase the joy. The slaughtering of an animal does not make the participants shudder, but it produces joy, as now they will have meat. ... When we are dealing with the traditions of the early epoch, much could be said

about the symbolical meaning of the bones and the gall bladder and why they are burnt. One thing however is certain, that in matters of sacrificing, the law "pars pro toto" is applied. It is a basic law of all rites. … Without this law no communication would be possible. Therefore 'fraud' is out of the question." Theo Sundermeier, "Sacrifice in African Traditional Religions," in Baumgarten, ed., *Sacrifice in Religious Experience,* pp. 5–6.

20. Bronislaw Malinowksi, *Crime and Custom in Savage Society* (Totowa, New Jersey: Littlefield, Adams, 1966 [1926]), p. 94.

21. René Girard, *Violence and the Sacred* (Baltimore: The Johns Hopkins University Press, 1977), esp. pp. 1–38, e.g., "the function of sacrifice is to quell violence within the community and to prevent conflicts from erupting."

22. Hubert and Mauss, *Sacrifice: Its Nature and Function,* and the critical reassessment of the book at its centennial in Ivan Strenski, *Theology and the First Theory of Sacrifice* (Leiden: Koninklijke Brill, 2003).

23. Sundermeir, "Sacrifice in African Tribal Traditions," pp. 6–7.

24. Elijah Judah Schochet, *Animal Life in Jewish Tradition: Attitudes and Relationships* (New York, Ktav, 1984), pp. 30–31.

25. See the Farm Sanctuary version of the story at http://www.farmsanctuary.org/about/index.htm. El-sayed also stated to *Newsday* that he had paid $500 for the cow, had been fined $1,000 for causing an "animal nuisance," and faced an additional $2000 fine. El-sayed claimed he "lost a lot of money," but that it didn't matter because, in his own words, "There is something with this cow."

26. Ibid.

27. See Schochet's discussion at pp. 164–65.

28. Sundermeir, "Sacrifice in African Tribal Traditions," p. 9.

29. Ibid, p. 8.

30. Ibid, p. 9.

31. Wendy Doniger O'Flaherty, trans. and ed., *The Rig Veda* (Harmondsworth: Penguin, 1981), "The Sacrifice of the Horse," p. 91.

32. Jonathan Z. Smith, "The Domestication of Sacrifice," in Robert G. Hamerton-Kelley, ed., *Violent Origins: Walter Burkert, René Girard and Jonathan Z. Smith on Ritual Killing and Cultural Formation* (Stanford: Stanford University Press, 1987), 191–205, esp. pp. 196–203.

33. For a comprehensive history of the interpretive permutations of the aqedah, see Shalom Spiegel's unparalleled *The Last Trial. On the Legends and Lore of the Command of Abraham to Offer Isaac as a Sacrifice: The Akedah* (Woodstock, Vermont: Jewish Lights, 1993 [1967]).

34. See the essays in John Stratton Hawley, ed., *Sati, the Blessing and the Curse: The Burning of Wives in India* (New York: Oxford University Press, 1994), especially essays on the *sati* of Roop Kanwar by Lindsey Harlan and Veena Talwar Oldenburg.

35. *Ṛgveda* 1.162.

36. O'Flaherty, *The Rig Veda,* "The Sacrifice of the Horse," p. 91–92.

37. As developed in Wendy Doniger O'Flaherty, *Women, Androgynes, and Other Beasts* (Chicago: University of Chicago Press, 1980).

38. Wilhelm Radloff, *Aus Siberien. Lose Blätter aus einem Tagebuche eines reisenden Linguisten,* (Leipzig: T. O. Weigel 1884), 2:18, and description on pp. 20 ff.; reproduced and discussed in Marianne Görman, "Influences from the Huns," in Tore Ahlbäck, ed., *The Problem of Ritual: Based on Papers Read at the Symposium on Religious Rites Held at Åbo, Finland, on the 13th-16th of August, 1991, Scripta Instituti Donneriani Aboensis XV,* (Åbo, Finland: The Donner Institute for Research in Religious and Cultural History, 1993), pp. 292–93.

Hunting the Wren

A Sacred Bird in Ritual

ELIZABETH LAWRENCE

My study of the wren-hunt ritual began with a tantalizing question: Why in certain areas of Britain and Europe would the little brown wren, a familiar and beloved bird, be hunted and killed on a certain day of the year? In recent times answers to this riddle have sprung out of people's consciousness and experience, and those answers have been added to the lore of the wren ceremony as rationalizations of a custom whose meanings have been obscured by time and changing ideologies. Evidence points to the origin of the wren hunt as an ancient winter sacrificial rite that involved killing a sacred bird in order to ensure the continuance of life.

The creature that was persecuted once a year, typically on St. Stephen's Day, December 26, is a tiny, plump-appearing, russet-brown songbird with an extremely short tail that is often held upward at a sharp angle to its body. The volume, length, variety of notes, and richness of the wren's song are in direct contrast to the bird's minuscule size (3.5 to 4 inches). Its scientific name, *Troglodytes troglodytes*, signifies cave-dweller or creeper into holes, referring to its cavernous nest as well as its behavior. Denoting affection, the bird is commonly known as "Jenny Wren." Other local names such as "Bird of God" celebrate the belief that at the Nativity the wren made a nest for the holy child and covered him with feathers. But the wren also has a masculine image. Names for the wren in many languages denote "king," attesting to its image as a royal monarch. Wren hunt customs occurred most commonly in places where Celtic tradition was firmly established, and although no indisputable evidence connects the wren to the Druids, Celtic priests, long-standing tradition upholds that linkage. The Druids revered the wren and designated it "king of all birds." By interpreting the wren's musical voice and actions Druids could foretell the future.

An old deeply entrenched narrative relates to the tiny bird's paradoxical kingly status. Long ago a contest among the birds was held to determine which one could fly the highest and thus earn the title of king. The eagle, as expected, outdistanced its competitors and announced its victory. But suddenly, a wren who had secreted itself in the eagle's feathers emerged, flew a few inches upward, and declared itself winner of the race and king of all birds. Every version of the tale expresses the idea that through cunning and strategy the smallest and most unpromising contestant defeated the largest and most powerful creature. Plutarch derived moral lessons from the wren-eagle story, indicating that a brave or talented but humble person can rise in status and obtain honor equal to those of superior rank, and the same encoded message persists through the present day.

Victory over the eagle was said to account for the wren's audacity and impudence, which seem inconsistent with its tiny form. Ambivalence toward the bird results from contrasting interpretations of its behavior: the wren's cleverness in taking advantage of the eagle's strength to accomplish its goal may glorify its achievement, but the dishonesty of using such a ruse to win also can be used to vilify the wren. The duality represented by the eagle and the wren exemplifies the idea of oppositional pairs (such as large/small, powerful/weak, and sky/earth) that, along with the wren's contradictory traits (such as female/male, hardy/frail, familiar/aloof, and wild/tame), allow the cognitive framework underlying the ritual to incorporate evil and death along with goodness and life into a unified pattern.

Throughout its range in Britain and Europe the tiny wren has been esteemed and even revered, associated with good fortune, and protected by prohibitions that warn of dire punishments such as disfigurement, illness, and death meted out to perpetrators of harm to the bird, its eggs, or its nest. Such powers of retribution evoked by injury to the wren illustrate belief in reciprocity between humans and nature—a concept once taken for granted that is generally absent from Western culture today. As a sacrosanct species, the wren was often coupled with the robin, both being objects of taboo, expressed in "Kill a robin or a wren,/Never prosper, boy or man." At the time of the solstice, the pairing of these two familiar birds takes on special significance that explains their frequent depiction on Christmas and New Year's cards. The robin redbreast, representing the New Year, is said to stain itself with blood during an annual sacrifice in which it kills the wren, who symbolizes the Old Year. Thus the cycle of seasons is perpetuated.

In areas where the ritual thrived, on "wren day" groups of men and boys, armed with sticks, clubs, or stones, hunted and killed their quarry. Once the wren had been slaughtered, it was displayed in prescribed ways and carried through the neighborhood. Sometimes the wren's body was fixed to the top of a long pole, often with wings outstretched. Manx tradition dictated that the bird was suspended by one leg from the junction-point of two crossed willow hoops at the top of the pole. Ribbons were attached and greenery was fixed around the hoops to form a "wren-bush." In other areas the wren was displayed in a wooden "wren house" with doors and windows, or with glass ends through which the corpse could be viewed.

Participants, known as "Wren Boys," paraded with the dead wren and went to people's homes soliciting money, food, or drink. On the Isle of Man the wren's feathers were sold as good-luck talismans which, when taken to sea, would ensure successful fishing and protect against shipwreck for a year. In some versions of the ceremony, celebrants buried the dead wren with solemnity at the end of the day while singing dirges, and then held elaborate dances in its honor. In France, wren customs were generally associated with homage to high-ranking civil or religious authorities. In a few instances, such as the Scottish practice of the "Deckan' o' the Wren," hunters did not kill the bird they caught, but released it during their rites. Singing was an integral part of wren hunt ceremonies, and the words of surviving versions of ancient wren songs express concepts and themes embedded in the ritual. Wren songs are still sung in vestiges of the ceremony on the Isle of Man, in which participants carry artificial wrens in "bushes," perform traditional dances, and collect money for charitable and civic causes. Over the centuries, the wren hunt was gradually transformed from a sacred ritual to a folk custom without religious significance, and rites that were once the domain of adult men were relegated to adolescents and children.

As the seasonal persecution of the wren, handed down through generations, lost its original meaning, people searched, consciously and unconsciously, for reasons underlying such illogical behavior. Various surface explanations arose to rationalize puzzling actions. These elaborations reveal that people who have inherited inexplicable traditions feel a need to fit them into their own belief systems, legends, and social contexts. By means of such explanations, human moral values were thrust upon hunted creatures who could then be judged and punished for their purported sins. Outdated customs that were still enjoyable and entertaining were justified at the expense of a tiny bird that was no longer sacred.

Superimposed explanations have been created with ingenuity and fused upon the old rituals. The most commonly repeated rationale for the wren hunt was that because the wren was sacred to the Druids, early Christian missionaries hated the bird and encouraged people to hunt and kill it at Christmas time to demonstrate rejection of pagan connections. Thus any lingering perceptions of the hunt as a sacrificial ceremony were eliminated, and the event was changed to a secular campaign against a creature that must be hated in order to make its killing intelligible. Vengeance was invoked as the motive for a misunderstood rite. It was alleged that the wren had a drop of the devil's blood and thus deserved to be killed. Another explanation for its persecution was that the Druids presided over courts of justice, and when a verdict was questioned they relied upon the wren to disclose the truth. Thus people grew to hate the wren for its influence on their fate. Guilt was laid upon the bird in connection with various

religious figures. It was blamed for disclosing Christ's whereabouts to the soldiers who arrested him. In the same way, the wren was alleged to have prevented the escape from captivity of the first Christian martyr, St. Stephen, by alerting his guards or by revealing his hiding place to his pursuers. Another explanation for the bird's slaughter relates that when St. Paul was converted to Christianity, the evil side of his character went into the wren. The wren has been identified as Judas, the disciple who betrayed Christ. A different legend asserts that St. Moling cursed the wren and condemned it to be hunted because it ate his pet fly. The Irish were said to hunt the wren because it was a witch. Patriotic motives projected treachery upon the bird, as when the Irish claim they persecute the wren because its pecking on a drum once alerted the enemy forces, preventing a surprise attack on the Vikings when they were invading Ireland.

On the Isle of Man, where the wren hunt may represent the oldest surviving custom in existence, a legend involving a siren-like fairy and centering on seafaring was grafted on to the wren tradition to account for the killing of the bird that has been carried out since time immemorial. The tale relates that for long ages a beautiful fairy used her charm and sweet voice to lure men into the sea, where they drowned. Finally, when the male population had been seriously depleted, a knight devised a plan to counteract her powers and destroy her. The fairy, however, escaped annihilation by being transformed into a wren. But a spell was cast upon her, by which she would take that bird's form every New Year's Day, when she would be killed. Thus on that date each year men and boys on the Island pursued the wren as the embodiment of an evil spirit and destroyed it without mercy.

The goldcrest (erroneously called goldcrested wren), a bird somewhat resembling the wren except for the gold feathers on its head suggesting a king's crown, may have been the forerunner of the wren as victim of the winter sacrifice.

The bird was commonly addressed as "king," and the ceremony can be interpreted as exemplifying the phenomenon of the periodic sacrifice of the divine king. According to that ancient practice, the king, as the incarnated god upon whom the welfare of his people depended, was ceremonially killed at the height of his power so that the divine principle could be released and transferred to his successor. During the time of his reign the king was inviolable, but on a certain date he had to be sacrificed to avoid disaster to his kingdom. His health and spirit, which were intimately bound to the well-being and productivity of the whole country, must never be allowed to wane. The role of the Sacred King was not that of a forced victim; rather he was a willing contributor to the pattern of earthly life—the cycle of death and rebirth. The reigning divine king represented the faltering forces of nature in winter that would perish with the coming of spring. Just as the winter would lose the battle against spring, so the old king would lose the ritual struggle with the new divinity. Thus he was sacrificed to redeem the community. His death signaled the end of winter and the transfer of his power to his successor represented springtime's rebirth and renewal of the cosmos.

At some indeterminable time, the ritual killing of the divine king came to be symbolized by the execution of the wren, the little king whose revered status, analogous to the sacred king's inviolable period of rule, protected the bird against persecution except for the annual sanctioned slaughter. The wren, referred to as king in the hunt and in its attendant ceremonies held around the time of the winter solstice, became a substitute for a human sacrificial victim. Not only was the bird called king, but also in many instances the man who was the first to strike the wren or who caught or killed it was given the title of king during the ensuing rites.

The killing of the wren represents a sacrifice of pre-Christian origin in which the virtue of the victim could be bestowed upon those taking part in the rites. Sacrifice rested on the principle that there must be death in order to have life. Killing the bird—a part of creation—released a force that brought invigoration of the whole. In sacrifice, supernatural powers were expected to give something great in return for something small, and communication was established between the sacred and profane worlds through the mediation of the victim. The killing of the wren was believed to bring fertility to the land and good fortune to people. Often the wren's feathers and bones were buried following the sacrificial eating of the carcass. Just as the hair or skin of a sacrificed animal was often preserved as a token containing part of the divine, feathers from the wren had magical qualities to protect against evil. In numerous wren songs, the minuscule bird was transformed by gross exaggeration into a huge creature that constituted an infinitely bountiful sacrificial meal for the whole community.

Sacrifice relates to marking boundaries in social time. The sacred wren was killed at the darkest period of the year, the winter solstice, when the celebrants attempted, by means of ritual, to influence the seasonal change in the cycle of the sun to ensure the return of warmth and light. The wren hunt is comparable to other rites held at the time of the New Year involving the chasing, killing, and carrying in procession of an animal who takes the role of scapegoat, atoning for the anxieties and sins of the community. As a species that habitually creeps along the ground rather than flying, and frequents dark recesses in the earth, the wren represented opposition to the sun and symbolized the weak sun that must be eliminated to make way for the returning strong sun of spring. Involving the persecution of a creature protected at other times of the year, the wren hunt also is a rite of reversal—sanctioning behavior contrary to the norm that is tolerated only at the time of the solstice, as during Saturnalia.

With the rise of Christianity, the wren became identified with St. Stephen. Just as the first

Christian martyr was executed by stoning, so the little wren was often killed in that manner. Because the hunt took place around the time of the Nativity, the wren was also closely associated with Christ. This connection is related not only to the juxtaposition of death and rebirth in the hunt ritual, but also through the maiming and crucifixion of the wren and its display on a cross. The identification of both Jesus and the wren as divine kings is another point in common. There is folkloric evidence, too, of a link between "Jenny Wren," the feminine form of the bird, and Mary, mother of Christ.

The wren is a striking example of a living creature that was changed by the human mind into a construct mingling biology with perceptions based on preconceived notions. The symbolic process created a new entity that originated from the characteristics of the species but incorporated the nature-to-culture transition. Thus the wren was endowed with metaphoric significance that made people regard it in highly eccentric ways. Although the wren may live in proximity to human habitation, it often remains hidden, indicating its presence only by its distinctive song. Special magic was attributed to the secretive singer whose voluminous voice is such a marked contrast to its small size. Its habit of vanishing into undergrowth or crevices made the bird seem mysterious. Except in the breeding season, the wren is generally observed alone, a solitary creature. This reclusive character led to its image as a sage, thinker, or shaman. Its brown plumage afforded the bird a serious, contemplative aspect, like a cleric or prophet dressed in a somber robe. Its piercing eye gave the aspect of a seer, and its perpetual movements made the wren seem to be under the influence of an unseen force. It is spirited and restless, and constantly bobs its head, teeters, and flicks its tail. Its seeming preoccupation with some inner mental state suggested the possession of occult knowledge. Thus it is understandable that the wren was seen as a mystical being, a mediator between humankind and nature, and a prognosticator of future events. Unlike most other birds

within its range, the wren continues to sing in winter, often late into the evening, even in snowstorms. The ability of such a minute creature to appear cheerful even in the harsh weather and darkness of the solstice makes it a symbol of endurance and hope for renewal.

The wren became axiomatic for the concept of tiny, and the sharp contrast between its diminutive size and its audacity, alertness, quick movements, and exuberant song commands attention. It is a bold, feisty, creature, aggressive in defense of its territory and offspring. Its legendary parental devotion and large number of offspring also seem out of proportion to its size. The wren hunt songs that magnify the bird's miniature carcass into huge proportions highlight its size and denote miraculous transformation. The inexplicable vitality emanating from so diminutive a form suggests supernatural qualities. The wren's elusiveness led to the idea that it could be the source of hidden knowledge, and its ground-dwelling habits associate it with caves and the Underworld where wisdom is found. Because the dead allegedly pass into the earth in order to be reborn, the bird who stayed close to the ground and disappeared into fissures was associated with resurrection and renewal. Observation of the species' well-camouflaged dome-shaped nest led to the concept of the wren in the Western mystery tradition as representing the word of God concealed within the human heart.

The wren's role in ritual depended upon the symbolic power generated by certain striking and idiosyncratic traits. I believe that the wren's sacredness derived from its distinctive role in human cognition. The bird's rich complex of natural and humanly conferred attributes made it a spiritual rather than a material being. The wren's outward, observable traits were felt to be indicative of extraordinary invisible, inner qualities. Out of metaphor was created the "king of all birds," who must die to ensure fertility in the land. In the same manner was fashioned "Jenny Wren"—symbol for rebirth and the regeneration of life. Wrens were sacrificed to cause the sun to return, to make green the living universe, to find a kernel of wisdom, discern the will of the gods, to unlock eternal things, and achieve everlasting life. Images of the king and Jenny represent the transformed biological bird—a small thing made magnificent—part living creature and part imaginary figure whose varied meanings, as expressed in the ritual of the wren hunt, represent an aspect of the cosmic dialogue between people and the natural world.

REFERENCES

Aarne, Antti, and Stith Thompson. 1928. *The Types of the Folktale: A Classification and Bibliography.* Folklore Fellows Communications, no. 74. Helsinki: Suomalainen Tiedeakatemia.

Abercromby, John. 1884. "Irish Bird-Lore." *Folk-Lore Journal* 2:65–67.

"Ancient Game Revived as Hunt the Wren Continues." 1991. *Isle of Man Examiner,* January 1, p. 11.

Armstrong, Edward A. 1958. *The Folklore of Birds.* London: Collins.

Armstrong, Edward A. 1992. *The Wren.* Haverfordwest: C. I. Thomas and Sons.

Carr-Gomm, Philip, and Stephanie Carr-Gomm. 1994. *The Druid Animal Oracle.* New York: Simon and Schuster.

Crippen, T. G. 1923. *Christmas and Christmas Lore.* London: Blackie and Son Ltd.

Deane, Tony, and Tony Shaw. 1975. *The Folklore of Cornwall.* Totawa, New Jersey: Rowman and Littlefield.

Douglas, Mary. 1976. *Purity and Danger.* London: Routledge and Kegan Paul.

Douglas, Mona. 1963. "It's Just an Old Manx Custom." *The Isle of Man Weekly Times,* December, 27, p. 2.

Drummond, William H. 1838. *The Rights of Animals, and Man's Obligation to Treat Them with Humanity.* London: John Marden.

Dyer's British Popular Customs. 1876. *The Saturday Review* (London) 41:313–14.

Eliade, Mircea. 1975. *Myth and Reality.* New York: Harper and Row.

Fargher's Sixpenny Edition of the Master Mariner's Pocket Book. 1853. Douglas: Robert Fargher.

Garai, Jana. 1973. *The Book of Symbols.* New York: Simon and Schuster.

Geertz, Clifford. 1973. *The Interpretation of Cultures.* New York: Basic Books.

Gill, W. Walter. 1932. *A Second Manx Scrapbook.* London: Arrowsmith.

Glassie, Henry. 1983. *All Silver and No Brass.* Philadelphia: University of Pennsylvania Press.

Greenoak, Francesca. 1979. *All the Birds of the Air.* London: Andre Deutsch.

Hare, C. E. 1952. *Bird Lore.* London: Country Life Limited.

Hartley, Christine. 1986. *The Western Mystery Tradition.* Wellingborough, Northamptonshire: The Aquarian Press.

Heinberg, Richard. 1995. *Memories and Vision of Paradise: Exploring the Universal Myth of A Lost Golden Age.* Wheaton, Illinois: Quest Books.

Hubert, Henri, and Marcel Mauss. 1964. *Sacrifice: Its Nature and Functions.* Chicago: University of Chicago Press.

"Hunt the Wren on Boxing Day." 1987. *Isle of Man Examiner,* December, 12, p. 19.

Ingersoll, Ernest. 1923. *Birds in Legend, Fable and Folklore.* New York: Longmans, Green.

Killip, Margaret. 1975. *The Folklore of the Isle of Man.* London: B. T. Batsford.

Lawrence, Elizabeth Atwood. 1997. *Hunting the Wren: Transformation of Bird to Symbol.* Knoxville: University of Tennessee Press.

Leach, Edmund. 1976. *Culture and Communication.* New York: Cambridge University Press.

Lévi-Strauss, Claude. 1966. *The Savage Mind.* Chicago: University of Chicago Press.

Lewis, H. Durbin. 1926. "The Wren." *Word-Lore* 1, no. 2:76–78.

Lockley, R. M., ed. 1960. *The Bird-Lover's Bedside Book.* London: The Country Book Club.

Mathews, F. Schuyler. 1936. *Field Book of Wild Birds and Their Music*. New York: Putnam's.

Matthews, Caitlin. 1989. *The Celtic Tradition*. Longmead, Shaftesbury, Dorset: Element Books.

Morris, F. O. n.d. *British Birds*. London: Groomsbridge and Sons.

Ó Cuív, Brian. 1980. "Some Gaelic Traditions About the Wren." *Éigse* 18:43–66.

O'Curry, Eugene. 1991. "Druids and Druidism in Ancient Ireland." In John Matthews, ed., *A Celtic Reader*. Wellingborough, Northamptonshire: Aquarian Press.

O'Leary, Sean C. 1988. *Christmas Wonder*. Dublin: O'Brien Press.

Owen, Trefor M. 1959. *Welsh Folk Customs*. Cardiff: National Museum of Wales.

Paton, C. I. 1942. *Manx Calendar Customs*. London: Folk-Lore Society.

"Peel Keeps 'Hunt the Wren' Tradition." 1973. *Manx Star*, December 31, p. 1.

Roheim, Géza. 1930. *Animism, Magic, and the Divine King*. London: Kegan Paul.

Rothery, Guy Cadogan. n.d. *Armorial Insignia of the Princes of Wales*. London: Newberry and Pickering.

Rowland, Beryl. 1978. *Birds with Human Souls*. Knoxville: University of Tennessee Press.

Stewart, Bob. 1977. *Where Is Saint George?: Pagan Imagery in English Folklore*. Bradford-on-Avon, Wiltshire: Moonraker Press.

Stewart, Susan. 1989. *Nonsense: Aspects of Intertextuality in Folklore and Literature*. Baltimore: The Johns Hopkins University Press.

Stewart, R. J. 1991. *Celtic Gods, Celtic Goddesses*. London: Blandford.

Swainson, Charles. 1886. *The Folk Lore and Provincial Names of British Birds*. London: Elliot Stock.

Tegid, Llew. 1911. "Hunting the Wren." *Journal of the Welsh Folk-Song Society* 1:99–113.

Terres, John K. 1980. *The Audubon Society Encyclopedia of North American Birds*. New York: Knopf.

Thomas, N. W. 1906. "The Scapegoat in European Folklore." *Folk-Lore* 17, no. 3:258–87.

Thompson, C. K. S. 1989. *The Hand of Destiny: Folklore and Superstition for Everyday Life*. New York: Bell Publishing Co.

Train, Joseph. 1845. *An Historical and Statistical Account of the Isle of Man*. 2 vols. Douglas, Scotland: Mary A. Quiggin.

Woodward, Marcus. 1928. *How To Enjoy Birds*. London: Hodder and Stoughton.

Zeleny, Robert O., ed. 1985. *Christmas in Ireland*. Chicago: World Book Encyclopedia, Inc.

Ridiculus Mus:

Of Mice and Men in Roman Thought

CHRISTOPHER MCDONOUGH

Montes parturient, nascetur ridiculus mus.
"The mountains will labor, a ridiculous mouse will be born."

–Horace

In 208 BCE, in the very midst of the Second Punic War, Roman military operations were brought to a complete halt because it was announced that several mice had nibbled gold in a temple of Jupiter (Livy 27.23.1–4). Remarkable as it may seem, Roman authorities did not reject out of hand this report of "church mice" scrounging about for a most unlikely bite to eat, but instead treated it as a very dire prodigy. As an omen, it was not alone in the annals of Roman religious lore: similar instances are recorded in the years 203, 179, and 90 BCE.[1] According to Pliny the Elder's *Natural History* (8.221), mice were creatures of the highest significance in public omens, and they were labeled by another naturalist "the most mantic of creatures" (Aelian, *Varia Historia* 1.11).

That the mouse was so reckoned is clear, but somewhat harder to ascertain is why. Not much help is forthcoming from what the anthropologist Victor Turner calls "the native exegesis," which consisted of little more than ridi-

cule. Commenting on the ominous mice of 208, the historian Livy scoffs, "How far does superstition bring the gods into even the littlest things!" (27.23.2). When asked whether it was an omen if mice chewed shoes, the statesman Cato is reported to have said, "It would be ominous if the mice were chewed by the shoes instead" (cited by Augustine, *On Christian Doctrine* 2.31). In *On Divination* (2.59), Cicero responds to all such omens of mice with the mocking question, "So if we follow this line of thinking, I suppose I should be afraid for the state, because mice recently nibbled my copy of Plato's *Republic?*" (The mice seem to have augured accurately, however: shortly after he wrote this sentence in 44 BCE, Cicero was murdered in the final phase of the civil wars that brought the Roman Republic to an end.) Remarks of this sort, amusing as they are, only underscore the chasm between rational understanding and lived belief. Though the logic of these omens eluded Livy, Cato, and Cicero, nonetheless, such omens continued to be reported. Reading beneath the ridicule, it is fair to ask, what to a Roman was so foreboding about a mouse?

While a great deal of interest in ancient mice has been lavished on the Greek cult of Apollo Smintheus,[2] most scholars of Roman culture have been loath to express any opinion on the topic at all. To be sure, there are some half-hearted attempts to explain why mice are featured in omens: Franklin B. Krauss wonders whether the mouse's "secret and prying activity" could be responsible for its ominous status,[3] while Otto Keller, after noting that the mouse "alle Frauen nervös macht" ("makes all women nervous"), wonders whether the mice accused of gnawing gold in temples were in fact innocent, and "daß vielleicht die Priester selbst die Gold- und Silbersachen abgefeilt haben könnten" ("that perhaps the priests themselves have filed off the gold and silver items").[4] Most scholars have less to say: E. Steier, in his Pauly-Wissowa article, provides no explication for the mouse superstitions,[5] while A. S. Pease, uncharacteristically laconic, states only that mice were "chthonic animals."[6] Perhaps most honestly, Raymond Bloch can only bring himself to exclaim, "Que de phénomènes naturels passaient aux yeux des Romains pour des prodiges!" ("How many natural phenomena passed in the eyes of the Romans for prodigies!").[7]

The historian working with questions about ancient mice is thwarted by, among other things, a lack of physical data. The question of even which species of rodent existed in classical times is difficult to answer, according to the archaeozoologist D. S. Reese.[8] The variance between the many sorts of rodents can be gauged only by reference to their molars which, because of their small size, are usually not listed among the faunal remains in archaeological site reports. But while there were surely many different species living in ancient Italy, the Romans referred to this large group of rodents by the single word *mus,* an even less precise word than the English "mouse."[9] This paucity of information has led to some studies that are more imaginative than useful, as, for instance, Josef Grohmann's argument "that [the] lightning was originally regarded by the Aryan race as the 'flashing tooth of a beast,' especially a mouse."[10] In a similarly creative vein, Freudian psychoanalytical explanations, though fascinating, are anachronistic and therefore out of place in this discussion.[11]

In the face of this scantiness of evidence, and the lack of a respectable scholarly tradition, we should probably return to the remarks of the Romans themselves. To get a fuller picture of the mouse in Roman popular thought, we should start with the belief that the mouse's origin was terrestrial in nature. This idea, held by much of the ancient Mediterranean world, is found among the Egyptians, for example, who thought that mice grew up out of the mud of the Nile (Pliny, *Natural History* 9.179). Likewise, in Cicero's *On the Republic* (3.25), Furius Philus likens the autochthonous Athenians and Arcadians to the mice that spring up out of the fields. When in the seventh century Isidore of Seville derived the word *mus,* "mouse," itself from *humus,* "ground" (*Etymologies* 12.3.1), it was not just a fortuitous etymology but the capstone to a longstanding tradition.

Such beliefs were based, of course, in the simple observation that mice live beneath the ground or close above it. As Vergil writes, in a famous passage from the *Georgics* (1.181), "often the little mouse makes his home underground." Such subterranean existence gave the mouse an otherworldly character, for beneath the ground, philosophers held, were worlds like our own with pools, caverns, and the like (as discussed, for instance, by Lucretius in *On the Nature of Things,* 6.536–42). In these regions, Seneca writes, lived underground mice, born blind because they had no need for sight (*Natural Questions* 3.16.5). Such subterranean mice were not simply the product of philosophical musing: mice were reportedly to be found in goldmines, where they frequently had to be cut open in order to retrieve whatever metal they had eaten (Pliny, *Natural History* 8.222). Thus, concludes a Hellenistic epigram on this topic,

"Even among dumb animals, gold, are you a cause of evil" (*Greek Anthology* 9.310). But mice also lived closer to the surface, living in—and within—the fields; Robert Burns' famous poem, "To a Mouse," for example, was occasioned by his plowing up of one such unfortunate creature. Mice might at times be discovered in the harvested grain itself: on the reverse of several fourth-century BCE coins from the wheat-producing city of Metapontum, in fact, a mouse can be seen nibbling away at an ear of barley.[12] One brand of barley was even called *hordeum murinum,* "mouse's barley," another name for *lolium perenne,* or English raygrass (Pliny, *Natural History* 22.135). Living beneath the ground in the mines as well as amid the grain in the fields, the mouse seemed to pass easily between the underworld and the upper.

The mouse's ability to cross such boundaries was a fundamental aspect of its nature. Yet, precisely because of this capacity for passing between the worlds, the mouse belonged simultaneously to neither realm but somehow to both. As a creature caught "betwixt and between," in the anthropologist Victor Turner's phrase, the mouse was a liminal entity existing on the cusp between categories. It embodied opposites, and so possessed an essential ambiguity at once powerful and upsetting.

The association of opposites in the mouse's nature was not limited simply to its location above or below, but extended to considerations of size as well. This can be seen, for instance, in a story told by the lyric poet Callinus (*apud* Strabo 13.1.48), in which an army is attacked by mice, thus fulfilling the prophecy that they would encounter enemies that were *gegeneis,* "earthborn," an adjective used more normally of the Titans (whom we call in English "giants," a word derived from *gegeneis*). Still more telling is the maxim cited by Horace (*Poetic Art* 139), *Montes parturient, nascetur ridiculus mus,* "The mountains will labor, a ridiculous mouse will be born." Lurking in the background of this proverb is the belief in the mouse's spontaneous generation from the earth; as a commentary on deflated expectations, however, the adage draws its force from the ironic juxtaposition of large and small. The differences in sizes between mountains or giants, on the one hand, and mice, on the other, is emphasized by each poet for the sake of ridicule. Yet in neither instance is there anything particularly amusing in this relationship: Callinus' tale is one of ambuscade, while the belief informing the proverb, if not an *adynaton,* is at least somewhat unsettling. Behind these images is an upsetting incongruity at odds with the natural order of things, a situation that, for all its irony, is far from laughable.

Symbolic inversions of this sort often point to more deeply buried cultural anxieties, and in this case the anxiety is rooted in agricultural reality. A mouse or two in the fields is harmless, of course, but in larger numbers, owing to their unbelievable fertility, they become a serious scourge. Mice were and are a constant nuisance of the fields, in this respect mimicking the earth from which they derived. The speed with which rodents reproduce was noted in antiquity by Aristotle, who reported that a single pregnant mouse shut up in a jar would yield 120 mice (*History of Animals* 6.580b). His estimate seems to be low, for, according to modern researchers, the female of a pair of mice that gives birth to six offspring per litter will produce more than 2,500 mice at the end of six months.[13] This irrepressible capacity for reproduction suggested to the ancients a certain lasciviousness of nature, a trait noted as early as Old Comedy and finding currency throughout later Western tradition.[14] But the reproductive behavior of mice is not so much a product of lust as it is a necessity of evolution. As they are preyed upon by many carnivorous species, mice have a high mortality rate.

While this high death rate normally keeps the rodent population in check, any disturbance in the ecological balance can radically alter the situation. During such times the numbers of mice can reach truly staggering proportions: some fourteen million mice, for example, were killed in Monterey, California, in 1968.[15] Over thirty-two million mice were captured *in a single town* in Australia in 1917,[16] during which time, according to one source, "one farmer put down poisoned bait and next morning found 28,000 dead mice on his veranda."[17] The ancients were certainly familiar with swarms of field-mice of the same magnitude.[18] In many parts of the ancient world such fluctuations in murine population are recorded. Theophrastus (cited in Pliny, *Natural History* 8.104) claims, for example, that the island of Gyara was so overrun by field-mice that the inhabitants were forced to flee. Similar stories are told of the island of Elymnium (Aristotle fragment 611), Spain (Strabo 3. 4.18), Caspia (Aelian, *On the Nature of Animals* 17.17), and elsewhere. Italy too was subject to such mouse-infestations in antiquity (Diodorus Siculus 3.30.3), even as it is periodically in modern times.[19]

In such numbers, of course, mice were nothing short of a disaster. The voracity with which they devoured crops, for example, was a matter of some concern to the ancients. Aristotle describes a typical infestation thus (*History of Animals* 6.37 580b):

> It is mysterious the way that mice appear in enormous numbers in the countryside and then disappear. In many places an innumerable multitude of field mice appears regularly, with the result that very little of the grain crop is left. They go to work with such speed that owners of small farms notice one day that it is time to start reaping, and the next day early in the morning, go out with the reapers only to discover that the entire crop has been devoured! Their disappearance too defies logic: in a few days they are completely gone.[20]

An entire season's worth of labor could be consumed in a few hours by a horde of rodents, resulting in famine for the human population, and worse. Because rodents carry fleas, which are pestilent, widespread epidemic disease also accompanied such outbreaks in the mouse population. Yet the association of plague and outbreaks of mice did not go unnoticed by the ancients. The Achaeans of *Iliad* Book One as well as the Philistines of the Old Testament (1 Samuel 6:4–5) seemed to recognize some connection. It should be stressed, however, that the ancients did not understand this association to be causal. The appearance of a large number of mice was taken as a harbinger of illness, according to Strabo (3.4.18); as Christopher Faraone has noted, the relationship between the appearance of mice and the outbreak of disease was interpreted in terms of omen.[21] While the mouse was considered not the agent but rather the index of epidemic, it was in any event associated with death.

Against this background, it is not surprising, then, to discover that the mouse is featured in the symbolism of the tomb.[22] The tomb is a liminal space in two senses: it is poised between the underworld and the upper, and it is likewise lodged between the living and the dead. In a number of Etruscan tombs, images of mice figure prominently.[23] We find in the Tomba del Topolino, for example, a small gray mouse, painted on the rear wall, apparently awaiting his eventual Etruscan cellmate.[24] More evocative is the painting in the Tomba delle Olimpiadi, which shows three mice crawling over a reclining male reveler—one mouse even seems to be nibbling at his back.[25] Perhaps this can be explained by the propensity of mice to chew on human skeletal remains, a matter frequently confronted by many an archaeologist.[26] In fact, there is a simple zoological explanation for this behavior: "Because of the continual growth of their incisors, rodents have an unusually heavy need for calcium, which, together with a need for abrasion of the incisors, explains the frequency with which rodents gnaw bones."[27]

For the ancients, however, this activity suggested something supernatural. In Thessaly, Apuleius notes, witches would sneak into tombs in the form of mice, among other creatures, in hopes of taking a bite from the corpses' faces (*Golden Ass* 2.22.9). In a striking illustration of *edax tempus rerum,* "time, the consumer of things" (Ovid, *Metamorphoses* 15.354), the mice that nibble away at our belongings in life eventually will gnaw on our bones and bodies in death.

Like the earth from which it was thought to derive, the mouse was associated both with the fertility of life and the finality of death. In the abundance of its life, of course, the mouse was at its most deadly, turned from a tiny, insignificant creature into an agent of enormous destruction. In its subterranean existence, meanwhile, the mouse dwelled in the place where crops and corpses shared quarters. Unsettling and ambivalent, the mouse can thus be seen as a liminal creature that fluctuated between categories, while simultaneously occupying the uneasy space between them.

As a liminal entity, the mouse straddled yet another important line, that between rural and urban, or, more generally, between Nature and Culture. The Romans, like most ancient peoples, thought of animals as being divided into two broad groups, wild and domesticated. Cicero, for example, speaks axiomatically of *varia genera bestiarum vel cicurum vel ferarum,* "the various sorts of animals, either tame or wild," referring later in the same paragraph to *pecuda,* "flocks (or herds)," and *silvestria,* "animals living in the woods" (*On the Nature of the Gods* 2.99). This distinction is one of both demeanor and location: such location, of course, is defined by human boundaries, for the domesticated animal lives within man-made confines while the wild animal, by contrast, lives outside them. The mouse, however, was a problematic creature, being found in both the wilderness and the city. As we now know, of course, there are various species of mice, some of which live in the wild and some of which are commensal with man, but in antiquity, only the slightest difference seems to have been recognized. To the casual observer in both modern and ancient times, the difference between the house mouse and field mouse was not an intrinsic but rather a geographic one, a simple matter of location.

As Aelian notes, the mice are either *hoi kata tēn oikian,* "those of the house," or *hoi arourai,* "those of the field" (*On the Nature of Animals* 9.41). The only distinction between the town mouse and the country mouse (or, if you will, the house mouse and the field mouse) was its location on either side of the dividing line between town and country: the ease with which this line is transgressed is illustrated by Horace, who writes in his famous satire that the Country Mouse and the City Mouse "crept beneath the walls at night" (*Satires* 2.6.100) to enter the city.

The intrinsic nature of the mouse, then, was uncertain. As Pliny writes (*Natural History* 8.220–21): "There are numerous creatures that are neither tame nor wild, but rather of a middle character between the two. ... In this group many would number even those inhabitants of our homes, the mice."

This description of mice as inhabitants of our houses leads us to consider further the association of mouse and house, of *mus* and *domus.* In a literal sense, the *domus* is an architectural space circumscribed by a series of defining walls, with a similar set of walls inside marking off the rooms from each other. It is a recognized facet of zoological behavior that, because mice prefer confined areas, they tend to stay close to and live within walls. The degree to which this is so has been demonstrated by the scientist Peter Crowcroft who, conducting research for the Ministry of Agriculture and Fisheries, chose to observe mice not in the artificial atmosphere of the laboratory but rather in dark, quiet rooms like grain storage areas. He writes of a mouse named Arthur, released into such a room, thus:

This is what happened when Arthur's cage was opened, and it was to be the same with mouse after mouse, whether male or female. After only a few seconds he slowly climbed to the floor, ran a few steps, and retraced his path to the cage. He turned about at once, followed his first path, but this time went a little farther. This brought him to one wall of the room. After taking a few steps along the wall he turned and again retraced his path to the release cage.

More excursions followed, each one bolder than the last, until after fifteen minutes Arthur was running around the entire periphery of the room, and beginning to make little short-cuts across the corners. Then there came a moment when he turned away from the now familiar wall, and began to explore the unknown interior.[28]

Here we see that the mouse's instinct is to remain by the periphery of a room, running alongside its walls. They also like to run *inside* the walls; such behavior was noted by the ancients, as, for example, Plautus who writes, "then you shall live, you rogue, in the middle of the wall, like a mouse" (*Casina* 140). Ovid too knew of the liminal mouse, writing: "beneath the threshold ... where the little mouse makes its hidden journey" (*Fasti* 2.573–74). The mouse dwells within the actual defining spaces of domestic architecture, thus raising the problematic issue of whether it belongs within the *domus* or not.

A mouse's appearance in the house was not in itself a particularly ominous matter, unlike the appearance of a snake, a difference Cicero explains thus (*On Divination* 2.62): "Why are snakes more ominous than lizards or mice? Because these latter are everyday creatures, while snakes are not."

The presence of a mouse within the house was nothing out of the ordinary. The departure of mice from a house, however, was a particularly disturbing sight, as found in an old superstition cited by Cicero in a letter to Atticus, "thus the inhabitants fled even as the mice" (*Letters to Atticus* 14. 9.1). This folk belief, found in numerous authors (cf. Pliny, *Natural History* 8.103 and Aelian *Varia Historia* 6.41), recalls to modern readers the proverb of rats deserting a sinking ship. It is worth pointing out here a more elaborate version of this same motif told of the seer Melampus, who had been given the power to understand animal language. The seer had been placed in prison, and overheard some worms conversing in the walls about how they had almost eaten through the entire beam of the cell. In reaction to this, Melampus successfully demanded to be transferred to another building, and thus was spared when the roof collapsed.[29] (With this story we should perhaps compare Bdelycleon's remarks at *Wasps* 204, suggesting to Xanthias that a mouse in the ceiling has caused a bit of debris to fall on him from above). Because marginal animals like Melampus' worms and the mice of the Roman superstition possess an intimate knowledge of a building's structure, they were considered a reliable index of its well-being. But, as the story of Melampus' worms also suggests, the existence of creatures within the walls could also be instrumental in the weakening of a building's structure. This destruction of borders is, of course, more than figurative, for mice quite literally pierce the walls of the buildings which they enter. Against this background, it is easy to see why the siege instrument used by Roman armies for undermining walls was called the *musculus*, "little mouse."[30]

In general, the Romans were uncomfortable with undefined space; along with this goes a certain anxiety about broken walls. From the time of Romulus, Roman walls were endowed with a particularly sacred nature, which consecratory rites hallowed and legal sanctions preserved. As Plutarch notes in the *Roman Questions* (27), "they consider every wall inviolable and holy." A breach in a wall was thus a cause for great apprehension, representing not just a threat to defense but, more important, a rupture of religion. Vergil's depiction of the breaking of Troy's walls for the entrance of the Trojan Horse, for example, has been plausibly explicated by W. F. Jackson Knight as an expression of this apprehension.[31] Such anxiety was not confined to matters of state. It is surely a premonition of the doom awaiting Pyramus and Thisbe that their love first transpires through a crack in a prohibitive wall.[32] In this respect, too, the law also recognized the *sanctitas murorum*: the crime of theft was as much a matter of penetrating the walls as intending to steal. One of the regular Latin expressions for "thief" was *per-fossor parietum*, "one who digs through walls," a phrase found as early as Plautus and as late as the Vulgate.[33]

In both a literal and figurative sense, the mouse, too, is a disrupter of the boundaries marking a *domus*. In this way, it is an animal counterpart to the thief, as can be seen in the following passage of Cicero (*On the Nature of the Gods* 2.157): "Neither do men produce grain for the sake of mice and ants but for that of their spouses, children and family; so what the beasts enjoy by theft, as I have stated, the masters enjoy openly and freely."

The ambivalent relationship of *mus* to *domus* is expressed most acutely by Babrius' description of the mouse as *ho oikotrips klōps*, "the house-bred thief" (107). It is worth contrasting the mouse with other household animals, the dog and the cat (or, more commonly in antiquity, the weasel). Although these animals were kept as pets, each served a distinct purpose within the household: the dog's principal duty was to guard a house to catch and ward away thieves, even as the duty of the cat and weasel was to catch and ward away mice. A certain equivalency between mice and thieves can be expressed almost mathematically:

weasel/cat: mouse: : dog: thief
mouse = thief

In this we see an elaboration of the well-established principle of structural anthropology that animal categories frequently have equivalent categories defining human relationships. Thus, just as we find the mouse is considered to be neither within nor outside of the household, there are human beings who stand in similar, "isomorphic" relationships.

An investigation of such borrowed analogies is worthwhile. In addition to the thief, we find a number of such relationships that correspond to the mouse's liminal position: according to Artemidorus (*On Dreams* 3.28), for instance, the mouse is associated with domestic servants in dreams. Like a domestic servant, the mouse is intimately connected with the household but is at the same time strangely disassociated from it.[34] The most obvious manifestation of the servant's estrangement from the *paterfamilias* and his family proper is expressed architecturally. Andrew Wallace-Hadrill makes particular mention of the distinction between servile and "seigniorial" spaces in his treatment of the Roman house as a social structure: "An important architectural feature of the houses is the way in which service areas are marginalised, thrust out to the edge of the imposing and often symmetrical 'master's' quarters."[35] In the extravagant House of Menander at Pompeii, for example, he notes that the slaves' quarters are situated far from the main living area, accessible only by long, narrow corridors. One gets a distinct image of the slaves' mouselike existence in such mansions, scurrying to their hidden habitations through cramped passageways resembling walls.[36]

Like both the parasite and the domestic servant, the mouse is neither a complete stranger to the household nor a true member of it, but rather, like them, occupies an uneasy marginal location. As in the case of the thief, this association of mouse and house is sometimes considered to be of an adversarial nature. In this respect, the mouse stands in antithetical relationship to the *dominus*, the owner and protector of the household. In Cicero's *On the Nature of the Gods*, for example, contrasts the mice and masters represent opposite ends of the domestic spectrum (3.26): "If there is a beautiful house, let us understand that is was built for the masters and not for the mice," he said.

As the least significant occupant of the household, the mouse is a symbolic inversion of the master, who is the house's proprietor and central tenant. With respect to the *domus*, the contrast here is between significance and insignificance, but on a larger scale the distinction is more generally between powerful and weak.

Again, the domestic servants also resemble mice in the procurement of their meals, which

Figure 1. Early Christian epitaph from Rome for a girl named Ilara, alongside whose name is depicted a crudely drawn mouse. From *Inscriptiones Christianae urbis Romae septimo saeculo antiquories* n.s. 9.25250.

were in both cases made up of leftovers from dinner parties.[37] Like the mouse who nibbles the remains of a banquet depicted on the Unswept Floor mosaic (from the Lateran Collection, now in the Vatican Museum), the slave had to wait until afterward to eat his meal.[38] This prandial situation is still more pronounced in the case of the parasites of Roman comedy, who often introduce themselves, as does Ergasilus in *The Captives*, thus: "like mice we always eat someone else's food" (77). The relationship of parasite to host is problematic, defined as it is by food rather than friendship, and seemingly more animal than social in character. Furthermore, the parasite freely admits that in his quest for dinner, he also transgresses another all-important line, that between what belongs to one person and what belongs to another. Small wonder, then, that it is the parasite who, in David Konstan's phrase, "bends the rules and softens the lines that define the social structure."[39]

The manner in which the powerful relates to weak, of course, varies from contempt to indulgence, a range which, in respect to the topic under study, is reflected in the usage of *mus* as a term of both opprobrium and endearment. On the one hand, *mus* is also used as a diminutive expressing affection, as found in Martial and numerous inscriptions.[40] The fondness in this sense of the term perhaps is most touchingly represented in an early Christian epitaph for a girl named Ilara, alongside whose name is depicted a crudely drawn mouse (see figure 1).[41] Yet, *mus* can be used as a rebuff that is, quite literally, belittling: at Trimalchio's feast, for instance, a freedman, having excoriated Giton with references to the Saturnalia and unpaid manumission taxes, at length calls him *mus* (*Satyricon* 58.4), later amplifying the insult to *mus in matella*, "mouse in a piss-pot" (*Satyricon* 58.9), in order to point out the difference in their social status. In any event, we see that the colloquial usage of *mus*, in either a positive or negative sense, is an implicit recognition of inequality in social relations.

In the Roman popular imagination, the mouse occupied a place "betwixt and between" several important categories of thought: as creatures of the earth, mice inhabited the region where grain grew and bodies were buried, and so were poised on the brink of life and death. Likewise, in the fields, their presence was small and insignificant, unless by awful chance their numbers should suddenly swarm to a truly staggering size. Whether they even belonged exclusively to the fields was uncertain, for mice were a common part of every household, so ordinary that they were often the source of metaphors both comforting and unsettling. Difficult to define precisely because of its thoroughgoing marginality, the Roman mouse is best conceptualized in the very terms of its ambiguity. In general, such cultural ambiguity breeds cultural anxiety, and the mouse, as a taxonomically problematic entity, was just such a source of discomfiture. From this we can begin to understand why the mouse was a creature of great ominous status for the Romans, as its anomalous character raised unsettling issues of disorder in the natural world. As Robert Burns wrote, "The best-laid plans o' mice an' men / Gang aft a-gley"; and that is not a ridiculous matter at all.

NOTES

1. Franklin B. Krauss, "An Interpretation of the Omens, Portents, and Prodigies Recorded by Livy, Tacitus, and Suetonius" (Dissertation, University of Pennsylvania, 1930), pp. 117–18.

2. Lewis R. Farnell, *The Cults of the Greek States* (Oxford: Clarendon Press, 1896–1909), vol. 4, pp. 346, 448–449.

3. Krauss, "Interpretation of the Omens," p. 117.

4. Otto Keller, *Die Antike Tierwelt* (Leipzig: W. Engelmann, 1909–1913), vol. 1, p. 196. There does not appear to be any ancient evidence, however, for women's fear of mice.

5. E. Steier, *Paulys Realencyclopädie der classischen Altertumswissenschaft* (Munich: A. Druckenmüller, 1845–1972), vol. 14, pp. 2405–8, s.v. "Maus."

6. Arthur Stanley Pease, ed., *M. Tulli Ciceronis De Divinatione Libri Duo* (Urbana: University of Illinois Press, 1920–1923), p. 276.

7. Raymond Bloch, *Les Prodiges dans l'Antiquité Classique* (Paris: Presses Universitaires de France, 1963), p. 114. See p. 118 for mention of mice, with incorrect footnote ("Tite-Live, XL, 39, 8." should read "XL, 59, 8.")

8. Personal communication, February 25, 1995.

9. Keller, *Antike Tierwelt*, vol. 1, pp. 203–4.

10. Cited dismissively by Andrew Lang, *Custom and Myth* (New York: Harper & Brothers, 1885), pp. 116–17.

11. See discussion of Leo Shengold, "The Effects of Overstimulation: Rat People," *International Journal of Psycho-Analysis* 48 (1967): 403–15.

12. Sydney P. Noe, *Coinage of Metapontum, with additions and corrections by Ann Johnston* (New York: The American Numismatic Society, 1984–1990), p. 12, catalogue AB nos. 7–28.

13. R. Conniff, "Shall We Clap for the Enduring Mus Musculus?" *Smithsonian* 19, no. 7 (1988): 72–83.

14. Beryl Rowland, *Animals with Human Faces: A Guide to Animal Symbolism* (Knoxville: University of Tennessee Press, 1973), pp. 127–29.

15. Charles T. Gregg, *Plague: An Ancient Disease in the Twentieth Century* (Albuquerque: University of New Mexico Press, 1985), p. 65.

16. Conniff, "Shall We Clap," p. 81.

17. Peter W. Hanney, *Rodents: Their Lives and Habits* (Newton Abbot, England: David and Charles, 1975), p. 112, though one can doubt that he counted them.

18. On mouse plagues in general, see Charles S. Elton, *Voles, Mice and Lemmings* (Oxford: The Clarendon Press, 1942), pp. 1–125, especially pp. 1–12 for the ancient world.

19. Elton, *Voles, Mice and Lemmings*, pp. 61–64.

20. Cf. Elton, *Voles, Mice and Lemmings*, p. 3, who, as a zoologist, says this is a textbook account of the vole's destructive behavior.

21. Christopher A. Faraone, *Talismans and Trojan Horses: Guardian Statues in Greek Myth and Ritual* (New York: Oxford University Press, 1992), p. 42.

22. The image of the mouse as psychopompos is found, for example, in the Egyptian Book of the Dead, where a mouse-headed god seems to beckon to the souls of the newly deceased, on which see B. Brentjes, "Zur 'Beulen'-Epidemie bei den Philisten in 1 Samuel 5–6," *Das Altertum* 15 (1969): 67 fig. 1.

23. See Erwin Panofsky, "The Mouse that Michelangelo Failed to Carve," in L.F. Sandler, ed., *Essays in Memory of Karl Lehmann* (New York: Institute of Fine Arts, New York University, 1964), pp.

242–51, who, in a brilliantly argued essay, shows that Michelangelo had intended to carve a mouse in the Medici Chapel as the result of a visit to Etruscan tombs.

24. Stephan Steingräber, *Etruscan Painting: Catalogue Raisonné of Etruscan Wall Paintings* (New York: Harcourt Brace Jovanovich, 1985) p. 349, no. 119.

25. Ibid., p. 328–29, no. 92.

26. Alan McWhirr, et al., *Romano-British Cemeteries at Cirencester* (Cirencester: Cirencester Excavation Committee, Corinium Museum, 1982), pp. 194–95. This has been particularly noted in the Romano-British burial sites of Cirencester, where the skulls and tibias show clear evidence of rodent chewing activity.

27. *The New Encyclopaedia Britannica,* 15th ed. (Chicago, 1993), vol. 23, p. 408b, s.v. "Mammals."

28. Peter Crowcroft, *Mice All Over* (Chester Springs, PA: Dufour Editions, 1966), p. 13. See too p. 44, where Crowcroft notes, after he had added some boxes to the room, "The mice liked the boxes. They liked to climb up and sit near a corner, peering down and sniffing up. But most of all they liked to run along the extra wall area provided."

29. See Apollodorus 1.9.12 for fuller discussion.

30. See Julius Caesar, *Civil War* 2.10 for description and use. Other siege weapons named after animals include the *testudo, scorpio* and *aries* (whence English "battering ram.").

31. W. F. Jackson Knight, *Vergil, Epic and Anthropology* (New York: Barnes & Noble, 1967), pp. 103–27.

32. Ovid, *Metamorphoses* 4.65–66. Shakespeare too makes use of this same wall motif in *Romeo and Juliet* 2.2.66–7: "With love's light wings did I o'erperch these walls, / For stony limits cannot hold love out."

33. Famously in the Vulgate translation of Matthew 24.43.

34. On the relationship of *domus* and *familia,* see Richard P. Saller, "Familia, Domus, and the Roman Conception of Family," *Phoenix* 38 (1984): 344.

35. Andrew Wallace-Hadrill, "The Social Structure of the Roman House," *Papers of the British School at Rome* 56 (1988): 79.

36. For a modern example, cf. Robertson Davies's novel, *What's Bred in the Bone* (New York: Viking, 1985), p. 299: "That's one of the interesting things about these old castles. Dividing all the main rooms are terribly narrow passages—not more than eighteen inches wide, some of them, and as dark as night—and through those corridors creep servants in soft slippers who poke firewood into these stoves from the back. Unseen by us, and usually unheard. … They are the hidden life of the house."

37. Cf. Juvenal 9.5 and 11.142–143. In general, see Keith Bradley, *Slavery and Society at Rome* (Cambridge: Cambridge University Press, 1994), p. 83.

38. Jocelyn M. C. Toynbee, *Animals in Roman Life and Art* (Ithaca: Cornell University Press, 1973), p. 232, pl. 101.

39. David Konstan, *Roman Comedy* (Ithaca: Cornell University Press, 1983), p. 129, writing particularly about Terence's Phormio.

40. Martial 11.29.3, *Corpus Inscriptionum Latinarum* 6.16771a, 6.26407, 6.35887.

41. *Inscriptiones Christianae* n.s. 9.25250. *Inscriptiones Christianae urbis Romae septimo saeculo antiquiores,* n.s., Iohannes Baptista de Rossi and Angelus Silvagni, eds. Auspiciis Pont. Collegii a Sacra Archaeologia at R. Societatis Romanae ab Historia Patria. (Rome: Ex Officina Libraria Doct. Befani, 1922–).

Raven Augury from Tibet to Alaska

Dialects, Divine Agency, and the Bird's-Eye View

ERIC MORTENSEN

He flies swiftly—
The flute sounds piercingly.
On his wings is an inscription,
On his tail is drawn an ornament,
He flies to where the beast with red blood
    dwells,
He ascends to the zenith,
Such thou art, my slender, my black raven.
You are carried easily through the air,
My black raven, hungry raven!
You are my black scout, you are my white
    scout.
I beg you to come to me, to come nigh![1]

Ravens (*Corvus corax*), through their speech and behavior, serve as divinatory messengers in the folk traditions of people throughout Eurasia. The raven is a bird of augury in Tibet and Mongolia, and among other Asian religious cultures as diverse as the Naxi and the Tuvans. Along the coast of Arctic Asia and across the Bering Strait in Alaska and the Pacific Northwest of North America the raven is a deity, a mischievous creator, a transformer. How and why and when did the raven come to be seen and heard, religiously, in such differing ways? Historical migration of peoples, transmission of folklore, and the diffusion of diverse religious traditions all conspire to complicate a lucid analysis of the changing role of the raven. Nevertheless, upon close scrutiny of textual and oral evidence, we find that the distinction between medium and divinity is itself inexact and malleable. Ravens, themselves, seem to be able to play a variety of religious roles simultaneously, depending upon their mood.

This essay will raise some questions regarding the methodology of comparative religion in the context of animal divination, with an eye to the extent to which prehistoric religious complexes can be reconstructed utilizing textual and ethnographic evidence from more recent times. To date, most studies of ravens and raven augury have focused on specific geographical locales or specific cultural traditions; projects of synthesis, of comparative analysis of the religious role of the raven across ethnic, linguistic, and religious traditions, are rare.[2]

We will begin with a scientific look at the raven and its corvid kin. Textual evidence of raven augury in Tibet and Yunnan will then be presented alongside ethnographic data from oral traditions in Central Asia and Siberia. Following this we cross to North America in order to address the religious role of the mercurial raven in a different context. Attention will then be turned to a few specific issues of theoretical importance including issues of diffusions of peoples versus diffusion of ideas, the relationship between notions of the raven as a medium versus the raven as a divinity, and religion as a product of human agency versus religion as the product of divine agency.

By divine agency, I mean religion as created by the god or gods, as opposed to religion as a product purely of human behavior, belief, social practices, or imagination. Fundamental in this project is the raven itself, for although the symbolic religious meaning of the raven to any specific folk tradition may lead us to view the bird as purely a culturally constructed archetypal myth, or a set of variations upon an archetype, the ornithological reality of the lives of these intelligent birds can illuminate much in the way of why humans understand the raven as a religious *agent*.

The common raven, *C. corax*, is a large ebony bird with a wingspan that can be more than a meter, and a life span up to fifty years.[3] Prevalent throughout much of the northern hemisphere, the raven is more widespread and adaptable than any other bird. They are imposing birds, well known for their intelligence and their association with food, which they acquire either through hunting or scavenging. This scavaging consists of either stealing or consuming the remains of a kill left by other carnivores, such as eagles, wolves, bears, wolverines, and humans, and it is this role as a carrion bird that often identifies the raven as a bird of infamy. Ravens typically hunt small creatures such as lizards, voles, and some small birds, although occasion-

ally they have been known to prey on larger animals.[4] They are brave, seemingly unafraid of humans and wolves, and do in fact know where the caribou are. They follow herds in hopes of scavenging from other predators' kills.

Ravens are capable of producing a surprising variety of sounds, arguably more than any animal other than humans. The biologist Bernd Heinrich has gone so far as to postulate that ravens of different regions speak different dialects.[5] Many biologists, ornithologists, and raven-watchers have attempted to attach specific meanings to specific vocalizations in order to decipher potential meanings.[6] Heinrich writes:

> There is probably nothing about the raven, *Corvus corax* (the Latin name comes from the Greek *Korax,* a croaker), that has been more commented on, studied, and written about than its voice. But I'm convinced that there is nothing that we know less about. Indeed, what we know is minuscule at best.[7]

The notion that vocalizations of nonhuman animals can be matched with behavior in order to locate a particular "meaning" has been highlighted by numerous scientists as an endeavor worthy of intense skepticism.[8]

Heinrich notes:

> I hear distinctly different calls in every area outside New England where I've been. There are tremendous variations of intonation and dialect, and I'm not at all sure that what I perceive as one call type is not really many, or vice versa. But what are the meanings? Peter [Enggist-Düblin] concludes from his work that ravens' calls do not all have the same meaning. Rather, some calls' meaning are context-dependent and established by convention. They are then culturally transmitted.[9]

Notice that the very same claim, albeit from an altogether different perspective, could be made about the diffusion and transmission of folk beliefs about the raven. The meaning of the raven (not just their calls) changes from people to people, and this meaning is context dependent, established by convention, and culturally transmitted. However, the question is begged: what is the dependent "context" in this instance? In part, it is the sum total of influences of fluid and moving folk stories, myths, and rituals, diffusing over geographic areas and through the intellectual histories of different local peoples.

In essence, Heinrich has covered all of the bases, and has briefly mentioned in his works the folkloric significance of ravens in the western world, from the Mediterranean to northern Europe, from Alaska to Maine. In any event, the Asian raven is absent from his studies, likely because extremely little has been published in Western languages on the raven in the Asian world. In fact, the raven is very prevalent and culturally important in Asia. There are many raven augury manuals extant in Asia, including manuscripts in Sanskrit, Naxi, Yi, Tibetan, and other languages.[10] A number of crucial questions must be asked: if we were to compare the copious material on the meaning of raven speech and behavior from Western sources to the meanings of raven speech and behavior from Asian sources (both written and oral), would we be able to decipher any patterns? Further, would we be able to better demonstrate the differences between the ways ravens are understood religiously from a comparison of this material? If we then also include North American data, does the picture change? Can we fruitfully compare North American and European empirical scientific data about ravens to the Asian texts and folklore?

Ravens have been known as birds of augury from Rome to the Celtic world, from Arabia to Scandinavia.[11] The term augury refers to divination through the interpretation of the flight and speech of birds.[12] In Europe the raven has a decidedly mixed reputation, and although conflation with the symbolic meaning of the ominous crow (*Corvus brachyrhynchos*) is prevalent in both Asia and Europe,[13] the further northeast we move in Asia, the more the raven becomes

a more neutral or positive messenger. The raven is often a more predominant bird in the North than is the crow. The lives of the real birds largely inform and determine the way they fit into the context of human religious perspectives.

As we move to the study of the religious and folkloric meanings of the soothsaying raven in Asia, we find that the bird appears to play the role of an active medium between the human and divine world, or the human and the "spirit" world in the case of more shamanic traditions. In Tibet and the eastern Himalayas, ravens are mediums of prescience, messengers relating otherwise unknowable information, usually temporal in nature, to the humans who pointedly endeavor to understand them.

Scholarship to date has illuminated that the practice of bird divination existed among the Tibetans.[14] Textual evidence demonstrates, in detail, the future signified via the speech and behavior of ravens. In 1914, Berthold Laufer penned a pioneering work on bird divination among the Tibetans.[15] In this essay, Laufer discusses two Tibetan texts. The first carries the Sanskrit title *Kākajariti,* and the Tibetan *bya rog gi skad brtag par bya ba,* which Laufer appropriately translates as "Examination of the Sounds of the Raven." Located in the Sūtra section of the Narthang edition of the canonical Buddhist Tanjur, this text lists prognostications based on the direction of raven speech and the time of day. It further explains the prescient meanings of raven speech when the oracular birds are heard by the traveler, the prophetic meaning of particular nesting locales, as well as the providential or inauspicious implications of certain types of cry. Norbu Chophel, in 1983, also translated this text, though it seems doubtful that he read Laufer's essay before he published his translation. Chophel's source-text was itself a translation from Sanskrit by Dānashila at Tangboche.[16] We know of Sanskrit texts from the middle of the sixth century which mention, specifically, raven (or crow) augury.[17] It appears possible that the Sanskrit original of the *Kākajariti,* (no longer extant, as far as I know) contained a number of gaps.[18] Both translations are excellent, and only differ in a few instances of terminology. In his exhaustive footnotes, Laufer investigates the Indic origin of Tibetan bird divination, and in doing so provides a broad and unprecedented list of sources for the field of Tibetan divination in general.

The text includes examples of the meaning of particular cries of the raven:

When in the second period [mid-morning through mid-day], [if] a raven speaks in the east, a relative will come.

When it speaks in the south, praise and a raise in status will occur.

When it speaks in the northwest, it is an omen of the king being replaced.

When it speaks in the northeast, a quarrel will break out.

When, while traveling, a raven in a thorn bush speaks, an enemy is about to attack.

When a raven makes its nest on the east side of a tree, it will be a very good year with a lot of rain.

When a raven makes the sound *ta ta* [you will] find clothing.

When a raven makes the sound *gha gha* [your] wishes will be fulfilled.[19]

A second Tibetan text examined by Laufer is the pre-eleventh-century parchment known to Western academia as the *Document Pelliot no. 3530,* which was exhumed from the Cave of a Thousand Buddhas in Dunhuang. This manuscript contains a table of divination as well as a *préambule* that offers insight into how the act of soliciting a prophecy is done. This text was first addressed by Bacot, who proffered a translation much ameliorated by Laufer in his erudite 1914 *T'oung Pao* article.[20] The divination table, as was lucidly demonstrated by Laufer, was undeniably influenced by the text of the *Kākajariti.* Now, above and beyond the intriguing colloquial language, the twenty-one lines of the *préambule* explicate much about the decidedly Tibetan perspective on augury:

The raven is the protector of men

And the officiating priest [carries out] the orders of the divinities

[Sending the raven] into the middle of the land

Where he [the raven] has occasion for eating yak flesh in the distant pastures

The venerable of the divinities convey [their wishes] by means of the language [of the ravens]

When in the eight quarters [directions], making nine with the addition of the zenith

He [the raven] sounds his cry, the three means [to be observed] are explicated as follows:

The offering must be presented to the bird [the raven], and it should be a complete feeding in each instance

[In such a fashion, the offering] is given into the hands of the divinities

The omens are not derived only from the cries [of the ravens]

However, in the pronouncement of the omens, there is a difference between the auspicious and inauspicious speech

The officiating priest possesses the knowledge of the divinities

He teaches [the wishes of] the divinities, and the bird [raven] is his helper

The remedies for protecting from demons are announced by the helpers

Full of veracity, he is to be trusted

The raven is a divine bird

He has six wings and six pinions

Because of his journeys in the high realm of the divinities

His eyesight is sharp, as is his hearing

He can teach the wishes of the divinities

For humans, there is only a single method for investigating [the speech of ravens]

[You] can therefore trust and have confidence [in the omens from the ravens]

In the eight quarters [directions], making nine with the addition of the zenith, [the raven speaks as follows:]

The sound *lhong lhong* heralds a beneficial omen

The sound *thag thag* heralds a mediocre omen

The sound *krag krag* heralds the arrival of someone from afar

The sound *krog krog* heralds the coming of a friend

The sound *iu iu* is an omen of any event in the future [as listed on a following table].[21]

Ravens (Tibetan: *bya rog, pho rog,* and sometimes *bya ro, ag rog,* or *ka ka*) are found in the context of augury in many other places in Tibetan writings, folklore, the re-performative *Ge sar* epic, as well as in scholarly accounts of Tibetan and Himalayan religion.[22] The calls and behavior of many other birds are divinatory, but it is the extensive vocabulary of raven speech, coupled with the religious significance of the raven, that deserves special attention.[23] Yet, in Bhutan, north of Bumthang, in November of 1991, I witnessed a raven with a golden pendant tied around its neck. Upon asking, I was told by Nima Gyaltsen, a translator from Thimphu, that ravens, if they are caught stealing from crops, are captured (if possible) with a net. The family that caught the raven would then invest a substantial sum of money to commission a golden pendant of a jeweler, then tie it around the neck of the bird securely, so that in the future the particular bird could be identified as a thief. This demonstrates, among other things, that to the folks of Bumthang, ravens are treated with respect (not killed), and that although some are thieves, they certainly are not all so mischievous as to warrant capture and bedecking with gold

In an area adjacent to Tibet, many different ethnic groups of northwest Yunnan, including the Yi (Nuosu), Moso, Naxi, Lisu, Pumi, and Bai, used to perform divinatory rituals in which the raven played a central role. The literate Naxi ritual experts, *dto-mba,* composed pictographic texts beginning in the 1870s.[24] A select few divination handbooks, *dso-la,* show the raven (Naxi: *lee ar*) to be an agent (a medium) of prescience.[25] Ravens are also mentioned in passing in many Naxi ritual books, *ddu-mun,* as the ritual feeding of sacrificed meat to birds following various ceremonies resulted in auspicious

or inauspicious prognostications, depending on the amount of sacrificial meat consumed by the birds. The meat was usually placed in the crook of one of the trees in the ritual grounds or a tree higher on a mountainside, though special offering stones were sometimes used for this purpose. Such stones are still present, for example, in the small valley due east of the town of Daju, in north-central Lijiang County, Yunnan.

An excerpt from one of the pictographic texts reads as follows:

On the eighth, eighteenth, or twenty eighth day of the Rabbit, Dragon, or Tiger month of Spring [if one were to hear the raven speak] the raven is speaking from the west to the east.

On the ninth, nineteenth, or twenty ninth day of the mouse, pig, or ox month of winter [if one were to hear the raven speak] the raven is speaking from the east to the west.

On the first, eleventh, or twenty-first day of the monkey, rooster, or dog month of autumn [if one were to hear the raven speak] the raven is speaking from the north to the south.

On the fifth, fifteenth, or twenty-fifth day of the snake, horse, or duck month of summer [if one were to hear the raven speak] the raven is speaking from the south to the north.[26]

Why does the direction of the raven's speech matter? The pictographic frames, alone, do not give any indication as to their divinatory use. Yet seen in the light of other texts (particularly dozens of other *dso-la* divination texts), it seems fair to hypothesize that the direction is important for the sake of interpreting the prognostic nature of raven speech.[27] This is either a textual fragment, or, quite likely, the *dto-mba* would note the direction indicated by the text, then either consult a second text, or rely on orally transmitted knowledge about the significance of the direction of the bird's utterances. These texts were the exclusive manuals of literate ritual specialists, *dto-mba;* no one else knew how to read them, no one else had no access to the texts. Today, the general extent of knowledge of this tradition amongst lay people is simply that the *dto-mba* can divine through raven speech. The manner of this divination is unknown to the general population, although Naxi hunters searching for birds will not shoot ravens. I spoke at length with two Naxi hunting parties on high eastern ridges of Haba Snow Mountain (in the southern reaches of Zhongdian County, recently renamed Shanggalila County, Yunnan Province) in the autumn of 1995, and again with bird hunters from the village of Haba in February, 2001. I was assured by the hunters that they would never shoot a raven, and that if they were to "inadvertently" do so, they would be obliged to seek out a *dto-mba* (ritual expert) in order to mitigate the ill effects of such an inauspicious act. Every hunter with whom I spoke was adamant about the sacrosanct nature of ravens (or possibly crows, for the two birds, both *lee ar* in Naxi, manifest overlapping folkloric significances in Naxi oral and pictographic traditions).[28] It is generally believed that anyone who has killed a raven will, following his or her own death, encounter a malevolent rooster-headed demon impeding passage on a bridge along the path to heaven. Pictographic texts illustrate the propitiatory rituals necessary to satiate the demon.

Ravens are also birds of augury throughout central Asia and Siberia.[29] Many ethnographic studies have been made over the past century in Mongolia and Siberia, and the literature is saturated with mentions of the raven. Ravens have played prominent roles in shamanic practices throughout the entirety of the region of eastern Russia, Tuva, and Siberia, though the religious vigor of the area has been in decline for most of the past century. With the exception of some Mongols, Manchus, and the Russians, the people who inhabited this immense area were generally illiterate. Thus, as is the case in North America, the predominance of our data must come from oral traditions, and folklore.

The identification of the raven as a prescient messenger changes as our inquiry crosses to the northwestern reaches of North America. How-

ever, upon closer scrutiny, the distinction between medium and divinity becomes tenuous and problematic. Though Raven (and here we may begin to capitalize the archetype) is a creator *god* in many local songs and stories, he is often also a *messenger,* bringing tidings previously unknown.[30]

Among the Haida and Tlingit, Raven is certainly not to be trusted.[31] The ambiance of many folktales is firmly rooted in the duplicity of Raven, in whichever form he chooses to appear. For the peoples of the Pacific Northwest of North America, Raven is a divinity *par extraordinaire,* capable of doing just about anything he wishes, but although clever, he is constantly bumbling, deceiving, and getting caught (and often horribly smashed). Along the northern coast of the Pacific, among the Haida for example, Raven is the creator, and often a mischievous trickster figure. The Athapaskan people of Alaska, however, see Raven both as a creator as well as a messenger.

Among the Koyukon it is forbidden to kill a raven. Heinrich (1989) quotes Koyukon hunters: "If a raven sees people hunting, it will occasionally help find them game. It flies ahead, toward an animal that is visible from above, calling ggaagga-ggaagga (animal animal)."[32] Heinrich also notes an article for *International Wildlife* by Fred Bruemmer wherein two ravens in Alaska are described as croaking while flying. Bruemmer turned to his companion, an old Inuk asking, "What are they saying?" The Inuk smiled, *"Tuktu tavani! Tuktu tavani!"* (The caribou are there! The caribou are there!).[33]

It seems clear that there is a circumpolar cultural continuity of sorts, although the specifics remain elusive. Numerous acute questions complicate any attempt to do truly comparative studies of divinatory religious practices across this enormous area. If we compare adjacent cultural traditions, we need to be wary of two distinct factors: first, there is the historical diffusion of peoples, and second, there is the historical diffusion of ideas through text, and oral interaction. Both types of diffusion, of peoples and ideas, are ongoing. It is easier to trace the diffusion of texts; we can often get some sort of sense of dates, or at the very least (when the ultimate target subject of the search is for a time period many thousands of years ago) determine a limiting date, the date writing and literacy first entered into a cultural locale. However, it is vastly more difficult to determine dates for the diffusion of oral traditions, folkloric elements, let alone religious notions. For how do we determine what was religious, what local humans perceived as sacred, and, more crucial for our purposes, what was exchanged or appropriated intentionally?

We do, in fact, have some sense about the general patterns and time lines of the migrations and diffusions of peoples. We know of such things from linguistics, material culture through the lens of archaeology (mostly comparative dental studies), and increasingly so through DNA analysis. Asian hunters migrated across to what is now Alaska over a span of many thousands of years.[34] The last ice age provides a clue. At that time, there was a land bridge where the Bering Strait now is, which connected Asia and North America. We surmise that migrants to the Americas followed game—caribou, whales, oxen, or seals—yet we also suspect that the animals predated humans in the Americas. Migrant hunters would follow their prey. People would follow the big game, and would find their targets either by skill, luck, or with the assistance of ebony guides from the avian world. We know that ravens follow wolves and other carnivores, including human beings. However, we do not know with certainty whether or not the religious significance of the raven came over land, nor whether the people in the Americas themselves, thousands of years ago, granted the raven religious significance at all.

Phenomenologically speaking, it can be argued that a divine view of ravens developed independently in both continents. However, this theory of independent origination seems doubtful upon close examination of the (at least partially) maritime circumpolar cultures that span the gap between the continents. It is doubtful, in that there had been hundreds, if not thousands, of years of ongoing cultural contact between Asia and North America before the first ethnographic record of the presence of raven mythology amongst the peoples of northwestern North America.[35] Phenomenology allows for the study of a subject in and of itself, cross-culturally, though possibly from diverse geographic locales. Thus the archetypical Raven could be addressed. The notion of divine agency, complicated by dialect, could go a long way in support of such theory. If we entertain the notion of Raven as a real god (divinity) we can better account for the trans-historical cross-cultural similarity in its religious function. However, philologists and biologists are allergic to such methods and notions, and quite rightly demand a more responsible and rigorous investigation of all available (even cultural) data before such phenomenological (and theological) hypotheses can be even rudimentarily entertained. There is a conundrum at hand: unless we, as scholars of animals and religion, are willing to discount and dismiss as necessarily incorrect the religious claims and beliefs of the various peoples whose traditions we study, we must find a way to add to the equation the *possibility* of augury. How can scientific inquiry incorporate nonempirical possibility into its investigative discourse?

In essence, in terms of methodology, we must check all extant data from every culture, diachronically adjacent from the Pacific Northwest through to Tibet. When human beings from disparate regions share enough salient aspects of the specific practice, yet the temporal issues and means of transmission remain speculative, it seems more productive to revert to a Boasian method of collecting ethnographic, literary, oral, and archaeological examples *en masse*, then to take an Eliadean approach and speculate that the existence of similar phenomena in disparate cultures can *mean* something.[36] As the noted evolutionary biologist Stephen J. Gould observed, "[y]ou have to sneak up on generalities, not assault them head-on."[37] But in our case, the goal is to avoid generalities altogether. The dichotomy of ravens as messengers/oracles in Asia and Raven as creator/divinity in the Americas is one with little viability. If we can break down the dichotomy, we can go a long way toward disproving notions that diffusion did not occur.

Among the central questions and issues within the theoretical framework of this project is the extent to which a comparative pattern of a set of particular religious practices, such as augury, informs the patterns of the diffusion and history of other similar religious practices, such as scapulamancy. If close and meticulous mappings and studies of the shift in the forms of practice show demonstrable overlap, to what extent can a correlation of these different practices across wide geographical areas tell us anything about larger issues regarding divination in general, animal divination in particular, understandings of time and divinity, and the diffusion patterns of people, ideas, and texts throughout the prehistoric Northern Hemisphere? The primary counter-argument for such a methodology reads as follows: because we cannot know empirically what people were doing religiously prior to any archaeological or written record, and because contemporary written or oral records cannot definitively demonstrate with any certainty the practices of earlier times, then we can say nothing definitive; nothing can be proven; and we are left with speculation, however appealing. There is theoretical danger here, for when comparativists trace connections between the practices of different people, based upon a conceptual pattern or similarity, the honesty and logic of the method collapse under the onslaught of biased constructions of archetypes. Thus, to back up a bit, calling into question the very project of perceiving patterns in comparative analysis—questioning any attribution of a sense of causality to seeming "similarities"—must lie at the root of a careful comparative methodology.[38]

Any given compendium of folklore contains, among other things, a partial record of extant truth claims as well as ghosts of archaic religious beliefs. Thus, a broad analysis of instances of augural practices and beliefs will paint a correspondingly broad yet vague canvas of the widespread continuity of the religious significance of the raven.

Crucial, in this regard, is the methodology that one uses to approach the project of comparative analysis. Generalized and hypercontextual claims of "similarity" may erroneously lead one to believe that European raven augury can tell us anything about seemingly "similar" practices in Asia and North America. Vladimir Propp wrote that, "[a]t present one hardly needs to offer special proof that every art, including folklore, is derived from reality and reflects it. Difficulties arise when we attempt to interpret the historical process and to decide how history has been reflected."[39] To take this a step further, contemporary folklore offers "living proof" of archaic religious reality, but a reconstruction of the transmission of folklore through time and across vast distances requires meticulousness and a refusal to interpret patterns as facts.

Jonathan Z. Smith, the master of raising the hurdles on the scholar of comparative religion's methodological racetrack, provides a litmus test for the comparative project in his epilogue to Patton and Ray's 2000 work, *A Magic Still Dwells*. His formula for what might constitute a successful project of comparison includes the criteria that: "first, the comparative enterprise is related to strong theoretical interests; second, the data for comparisons form an unusually thick dossier in which micro-distinctions prevail; and third, as a consequence of the first two preconditions, the genealogical comparison has been able to provide rules of *difference*."[40]

Now, this is of course, in part, a call to repair to the bastion of a Boasian meticulousness, though Smith distinctly hinges the validity of a comparative process on an orientation toward explicit illumination of conceptual differences, and *not* similarities. Folklorist Albert Lord said: "The poet was sorcerer and seer before he became 'artist.' His structures were not abstract art, or art for its own sake. The roots of oral traditional narrative are not artistic but religious in the broadest sense."[41]

Another set of factors in the discussion of the idea of the Raven's prescient powers could be identified as the possibility of epistemic, psychological, or behavioral biological explanations. Bernd Heinrich would likely argue for the biological perspective: ravens are simply remarkably vocal and imposing long-lived corvids. Any prophetic notions associated with the bird must have scientific explanations. There may be a raven language at work, and any specific cry *may*, in fact, carry a meaning within a biological intraspecies context. Hunters, further, may subconsciously follow a raven to caribou under the understanding that the raven "told" them that the caribou were there. The term "subconsciously" leads us into the realm of psychology, according to which religious experience, to simplify, can be explained as delusion, a need to make sense of phenomena not comprehensible scientifically (the ramifications of this perspective become of paramount importance when, for example, we consider the many psychologically-based etic studies of oracles and of shamans). Attempting to *affect* the future, after all, is importantly different from attempting to know what will occur in the future. Is it the attempt to divine that matters, or the efficacy of the prognostication? Further, the *spontaneous* interpretation of a raven's flight by a Koyukon hunter as diagnostic of foul weather is, for example, different from an elaborate and complex scientific examination of the blubber of a beached minky whale by Japanese whalers in attempting to determine the health and thus the estimated population of whales next season. Both rely on knowledge garnered by other hunters in their region, oral histories (to greater and lesser extents), and past causal relations. Yet, the importance placed on efficacy differs. And, although people act in ways often determined by the message given by an oracle, a raven, or a scientist, how much do these issues of efficacy and spontaneity

have to do with religiosity? In other words, does a decrease in prioritization of divinatory efficacy equate, to any extent, with a ratio increase in religiosity?

Finally, there is the possibility that ravens are indeed oracles. Perhaps ravens can, in fact, see and/or affect the future. If they can, then our mystery is solved, and phenomenology deserves its due. Does myth drive reality, or does reality drive myth? Does myth reshape reality? Ritual, with a syntax, can reactivate myth.

Let us return for a moment to the definition of divine agency offered earlier in the essay: religion as created by the god or gods, as opposed to religion as a product of human behavior, belief, social practices, or imagination. The fact remains that the people whose religious traditions we have addressed in this essay believed that the raven itself could see the future, and could report this future to humans. The issue of whether or not ravens can see the future is, of course, a different issue than the question of who believes that they can or cannot. "The fact that animals can think, that they are not Cartesian machines, is no longer disputed. But what about animal consciousness? Do animals have spiritual awareness? Can they pray? Do they know God?"[42]

Heinrich notes that in the 1988 book *Moose*, by Michio Hoshino, the author quotes Catherine Attla, an Athapaskan Indian, regarding moose hunting:

> Sometimes people call on raven for help. One of the things we say to raven while we hunt is "Tseek'aal, sita'a nohaaltee'ogh," which means "Grandpa, drop a pack to me." If the bird caws and rolls, it is a sign of good luck. ... They talk to Raven the same way we pray to God.[43]

The point may be that epistemic commitments necessary for beliefs, when placed in the context of ritual, myth, and their culture-drenched memory, allow for religiosity and subjective truth. We know that throughout the Northern Hemisphere humans consider ravens to be sacred, even divine, but the extent to which the birds themselves could possibly have a religious world outside the context of humans remains a pressing question. As Heinrich puts it, "[w]e have hardly begun to decipher the language of the raven. Its dictionary so far contains but a few 'words.'"[44] We nevertheless are more prone to believe that ravens might be able to understand each other, even if we, as humans, have trouble understanding the charismatic birds. Yet we can accept that ravens may misrepresent meaning, or "lie." Furthermore, Heinrich has scrupu-

lously documented that individual ravens have distinct calls, "names" for each other, as well as supremely distinct personalities. It is well known that ravens will play games with wolves in Canada, and with road-builders (mimicking explosions) in Yunnan. Yet how far do we need to shift our human logic to allow for the unthinkable possibility that ravens create their own myths, their own religions? When we hear the ravens cry, are we (to paraphrase the great George Steiner) eavesdropping on the gossip of gods?

NOTES

1. This poem is found in Mongush B. Kenin-Lopsan, "Tuvan Shamanic Folklore," in M. M. Balzer, ed., *Shamanic Worlds* (New York: M.E. Sharpe, 1997), p. 271. The poem was told to Kenin-Lopsan by his informant Aleksei Bair. Note the variant of this poem found in Nikolai A. Alekseev, "Shamanism among the Turkic Peoples of Siberia: Shamans and their Religious Practices," in M.M. Balzer, ed., *Shamanism: Soviet Studies of Traditional Religion in Siberia and Central Asia* (New York: M.E. Sharpe, 1990), p. 74.

2. For the best area-specific accounts of augural practices with regard to ravens see Berthold Laufer, "Bird Divination among the Tibetans," *T'oung Pao* 15, (1914): 1–110; and E.M. Meletinsky, "Typological Analysis of the Paleo-Asiatic Raven Myths" *Acta Ethnographica* 22, no. 1–2 (1973): 107–55. For more information on the comparative study of augury, see Eric D. Mortensen, "Raven Augury in Tibet, Northwest Yunnan, Inner Asia, and Circumpolar Regions: A Study in Comparative Folklore and Religion" (Ph.D. Thesis, Harvard University, 2003).

3. There are numerous textual resources available to those who wish to study the raven. In the realm of behavioral biology, the most salient materials include those by Heinrich. See Bernd Heinrich, *Ravens in Winter* (New York: Vintage Books, 1989); and Bernd Heinrich, *Mind of the Raven: Investigations and Adventures with Wolf-Birds* (New York: Cliff Street Books, 1999). The bibliography in Hein-

rich, *Ravens,* pp. 357–71, is particularly thorough and extensive. For a general survey on the raven see also Derek Ratcliffe, *The Raven* (London: T., & A.D. Poyser, 1997).

4. See, for example, the bibliography at the end of Heinrich, *Mind of the Raven,* pp. 362–63. On the intriguing subject of tool-use by a related corvid, the New Caledonian crow (*C. moneduloides*), see Nathan J. Emery and Nicola S. Clayton, "The Mentality of Crows: Convergent Evolution of Intelligence in Corvids and Apes," *Science* 306 (Dec. 2004): 1903–7. See also Gavin R. Hunt, "Manufacture and use of hook-tools by New Caledonian crows," *Nature* 379 (1996): 249–51.

5. Heinrich, *Ravens,* p. 247. He writes: "Could it be that there are strong local raven dialects? Or do the birds have only a few standard calls and improvise the rest of the time? It is one thing to recognize the different vocalizations, still another to decipher their meaning. So far we have not made much progress even on the first." See also Heinrich, *Mind of the Raven,* pp. 191–205.

6. Most notably Heinrich, *Ravens,* 1989; Heinrich, *Mind of the Raven,* 1999; as well as many others. Note Heinrich, *Mind of the Raven,* p. 195, wherein he makes reference to Peter Enggist-Düblin's having "made 64,000 additional recordings of raven calls". Regarding the variety of vocalizations, many individual calls have been classified by different observers. Some of the more common include *rapp* or

krapp, ruh, kra, kaah, kruk, kwulkulkul, ko-pick, woo-oo, awk-up, quork, percussive sounds, and hollow metallic bell-like sounds. In the recounting of a variant of the Haida tale of Raven stealing light, Reid and Bringhurst write that Raven "had a cry that contained all the noises of a spoiled child and an angry raven—yet he could sometimes speak as softly as the wind in the hemlock boughs, with an echo of that beautiful other sound, like an organic bell, which is also part of every raven's speech." Bill Reid and Robert Bringhurst, *The Raven Steals the Light* (Seattle: University of Washington Press, 1996), p. 21. "Yells" are also commonly identified and have been a particular subject of study. Heinrich read the graphs R.N. Brown made for each of 30 Alaskan call categories, yet concluded, "to my eye, there is sometimes more variation within the sound categories than between them. I recognize few of these calls and have difficulty matching them either to my sonographs of Maine ravens or others' sonograms." Heinrich, *Ravens,* p. 248. These calls have often been matched with a behavior, lending them meanings like "place-indicating," "aggressive," "intimate," "defensive," "antagonistic," or "alarming."

7. Heinrich, *Ravens,* p. 246.

8. This problem is certainly not something about which Heinrich, a careful scientist, is unaware. He even goes so far as to address the question of whether or not ravens can themselves apply meaning to a sound they have learned. Heinrich, *Mind of the Raven,* p. 198., writes: "it may be the methods of studying animal communication systems which are limited, rather than the communication systems themselves." For an excellent discussion regarding the dated notion that any move by an ethologist to attribute a mental state to a non-human animal necessarily denies the possibility of its subjectivity, see Kenneth J. Shapiro, "A Phenomenological Approach to the Study of Nonhuman Animals," in R.W. Mitchell, *et al.,* eds., *Anthropomorphism, Anecdotes, and Animals,* p. 277 (Albany: State University of New York Press, 1997). Further, see Judith Kiriazis and Con N. Slobodchikoff, "Anthropocentrism and the Study of Animal Language," in R.W. Mitchell, *et al.,* eds., *Anthropomorphism, Anecdotes,*

and Animals, p. 366 (Albany: State University of New York Press, 1997), note that "... many researchers attempt to define one single meaning of a particular animal signal by studying all the behavioral situations in which it occurs, and assigning a meaning based on something common to all these situations." They also note that: "While a calling animal might indeed produce something comparable to a sentence, its syntax and grammar might be unrecognizable to us because it evolved along a totally different pathway. ... Testing for these ideas can be very difficult because, once again, we work from our own anthropocentric need for a lexicon, or meanings encoded into discrete entities called words. Isolating such a lexicon in other animals might be impossible if we are not aware that their perceptions of their world, how they receive sensory information and interpret it, may be beyond the grasp of our senses." Kiriazis and Slobodchikoff, "Anthropocentrism and the Study of Animal Language," pp. 367–68. Nevertheless, scientists have indeed spent tremendous energy scrutinizing the mechanisms of birdsong. Despite what we might wish to believe about "consciousness" in bird speech, "birds don't rely on their brains as much as was thought to generate the complex acoustic patterns characteristic of birdsong." Franz Goller, "Vocal Gymnastics and the Bird Brain," *Nature* 395, no. 6697 (September 1998): 11.

9. Heinrich, *Mind of the Raven,* p. 196.

10. For information relating to augury manuscripts in Naxi and Tibetan languages, see Mortensen, "Raven Augury in Tibet," pp. 45–124.

11. Few large studies of raven augury have been published. For the most comprehensive work on Roman augury see J. Linderski, "The Augurial Law," *Aufstieg und Niedergang der Römischen Welt* II 16, no. 3 (1986): 2146–312. See also J. Linderski, "Watching the Birds: Cicero the Augur and the Augural Templa," *Classical Philology* 81 (1986): 330–40. My thanks to Christopher McDonough for calling these invaluable works to my attention. The folkloric literature is vast indeed, and it would require dozens of pages of bibliography to dent the surface of the literature in which ravens appear as the harbingers of tidings, pleasant or ill. Odin's ravens

Hugin and Munin (thought and memory) are well known, as are Noah's and Elijah's ravens. Edgar Allan Poe immortalized the raven as a fell and vocal bird, and the raven appears in Irish battles, Icelandic sagas, and folksongs across Europe and northern Africa. Faust, Lorenz, and Shakespeare were all studied of the raven.

12. The term "augury" likely stems from the Latin *avis*, "bird," and *gerere,* "perform." The term "auspice," in a similar vein, may have developed from *avi-s*, "bird" (related to synonymous Greek and Indo-Iranian words), and the hypothesized *spic-,* "to look." See C. T. Onions, ed., *The Oxford Dictionary of English Etymology* (Oxford: Clarendon Press, 1996), pp. 62–63.

13. For example, in literary Tibetan, the term *bya rog* can refer to both crows and ravens, though distinctions are sometimes made in particular local areas.

14. There is a spotty record of the raven in literature on Tibet and the Himalayas. Most often, mention of ravens is brief. Few purely augural texts are extant. For local Tibetan texts reported in this paper, see Laufer, "Bird Divination Among the Tibetans"; Norbu Chophel, *Folk Culture of Tibet* (Dharamsala: Library of Tibetan Works and Archives, 1983), pp. 69–72; and Mortensen, "Raven Augury in Tibet," pp. 54–86.

15. Laufer, "Bird Divination among the Tibetans," pp. 1–110.

16. Laufer, "Bird Divination among the Tibetans," p. 19, mistakenly identifies Dānashila as a ninth-century figure. His correct dates are sometime in the thirteenth century, as we know, for example, that he came to Tibet in the year 1204.

17. See David Gordon White, "Predicting the Future with Dogs," in D. S. Lopez, Jr., ed., *Religions of India in Practice* (Princeton: Princeton University Press, 1995), p. 288; and Mortensen, "Raven Augury in Tibet," pp. 133–41.

18. It is interesting to note the structural parallels of this divination text with other divination manuscripts from India. See, for example, the translation of a text on dog divination in White, "Predicting the Future with Dogs." Of particular curiosity here is the classification of dogs into various castes in

White's article, a direct parallel to raven castes in the Kākajariti.

19. These examples are compiled from Laufer, "Bird Divination among the Tibetans," pp. 1–7, and 31–51.

20. M. J. Bacot, "La table des présages signifés par l'éclair," *Journal Asiatique,* (March–April 1913), pp. 445–49. Bacot's work is accosted in polished detail in Laufer, "Bird Divination among the Tibetans."

21. This translation is a compilation of Laufer, "Bird Divination among the Tibetans," pp. 32–35; and my own work with the original.

22. For further examples of divination practices (Buddhist or otherwise) in Tibet, and Tibetan language raven augury manuscripts including a two-folio raven augury manuscript in Tibetan filmed by the author in Tuva, provisionally titled the *Kyzyl Manuscript,* and a Tibetan xylograph of excerpts from the collected works of *Klong rdol bla ma ngag dbang blo bzang* (1719–1794) titled *The Perfectly Clear Mirror,* see Mortensen, "Raven Augury in Tibet," pp. 56–86; and for a discussion of the layering of folk religion in Tibet see Eric D. Mortensen, "Pasum Tso: The Tributaries of Tibet's Religious Folklore," *Harvard Asia Quarterly* 3, no. 2 (1999): 36–42.

23. For example, the Eurasian Cuckoo (*Cuculus canorus*) in Tibet, as elsewhere, presages the onset of spring. For an intriguing mention of birdsong as mantric in southeast Tibet, see Ian Baker, *The Heart of the World* (New York: The Penguin Press, 2004), p. 327. For more on general interpretation of birdsong, see the remarkable work of Charles Hartshorne, *Born to Sing: An Interpretation and World Survey of Bird Song* (Bloomington: Indiana University Press, 1973).

24. For more on the translation and dating of Naxi *dso-la,* see Pan Anshi, "The Translation of Naxi Religious Texts," in Michael Oppitz and Elizabeth Hsu, eds., *Naxi and Moso Ethnography* (Zürich: Völkerkundemuseum der Universität Zürich, 1998), p. 275; and Anthony Jackson and Pan Anshi, "The Authors of Naxi Ritual Books, Index Books and Books of Divination," in *Naxi and Moso Ethnography,* p. 237. It is worth noting the singular failure of

the majority of Chinese (both Han and Naxi) scholars to take note of or entertain this crucial theory of the relatively recent genesis of the Naxi pictographic script. For a summary of the dating debate, albeit also ultimately disagreeing with Jackson and Pan, see Christine Mathieu, *A History and Anthropological Study of the Ancient Kingdoms of the Sino-Tibetan Borderland— Naxi and Mosuo* (Lewiston: The Edwin Mellen Press, 2003), pp. 149–77.

25. These texts include two untitled manuscripts filmed by the author in June, 2001, from the personal collection of He Zhiben, of Sanba village by Baishuitai in Zhongdian County, Yunnan Province, People's Republic of China. An additional text can be found in Zhu's catalog as entry "L-70." Zhu Baotian, *Annotated Catalog of Naxi Pictographic Manuscripts in the Harvard-Yenching Library, Harvard University* (Cambridge: Harvard-Yenching Library Harvard University, 1997), pp. 785–86.

26. An original translation of this text into Chinese was made by Zhu Baotian, and translated into English by the author, Li Ruohong, and Huang Pochi. For notes on the original Naxi text, see: Zhu Baotian, *Annotated Catalog,* pp. 785–86. I am indebted to Li Ruohong and Huang Pochi for their generous assistance with translation from Chinese to English in numerous personal conversations with Zhu Baotian at the Harvard Yenching Library in 1997. Without their help this project would never have begun.

27. I have had the opportunity to study the collections of *dso-la* at the Harvard Yenching Library, the Dongba Culture Research Institute (*Dongba Wenhua Yanjiusuo*) at Black Dragon Pool (*Heilongtang*) in Lijiang, Yunnan, as well as the manuscripts in the collections of He Zhiben in Sanba, He Xuewen in Lijiang, and of Ge Agan (He Chongren) in Kunming. My thanks to these three tutors for their patience and generosity. Given the typical association of directional speech (or signs/omens) with prognosticatory meaning, we can suppose a corollary dynamic implied in this manuscript; it seems plausible to claim that this text outlining the direction and timing of bird speech should somehow correspond with augural intent.

28. For more on the overlapping folkloric and religious aspects of ravens and crows, see John Marzluff and Tony Angell, *In the Company of Crows and Ravens* (New Haven: Yale University Press, 2005). Lisu hunters, less than 100 miles due west of Haba Mountain (as the crow flies) practice a similar prohibition on shooting ravens.

29. For mention of ravens as birds of augury in Mongolia, Tuva, and Siberia, see, among many others, Kenin-Lopsan, "Tuvan Shamanic Folklore;" C. Bawden, *Confronting the Supernatural: Mongolian Traditional Ways and Means* (Wiesbaden: Harrassowitz, 1994); V. Diószegi, ed., *Popular Beliefs and Folklore Tradition in Siberia* (Bloomington: Indiana University Press, 1968); Walther Heissig, *The Religions of Mongolia* (Berkeley: University of California Press, 1970); Meletinsky, "Typological Analysis of the Paleo-Asiatic Raven Myths"; Marian W. Smith, ed., *Asia and North America: Transpacific Contacts* (Salt Lake City: Society for American Archaeology, 1953); and S.M. Shirkogoroff, *Psychomental Complex of the Tungus* (London: Kegan Paul, 1935), p. 7.

30. But perhaps it would be helpful to question the range of this notion of knowledge, for if Raven as a messenger is a bird of augury, does this idea of divination come loaded from Asia with a significance of temporal knowledge? Is divination, after all, necessarily concerned with the future? To answer this question, we must take care to be specific about the cultural location of the inquiry.

31. Ravens, we know, do steal. Note Heinrich, *Ravens;* Heinrich, *Mind of the Raven;* and Douglas H. Chadwick, "Ravens" *National Geographic* 195, no. 1 (January 1999): 100–115. The Athapaskan regard the raven as lazy, unwilling to do any work (or hunting) of his own. Richard K. Nelson, *Make Prayers to the Raven* (Chicago: The University of Chicago Press, 1983). The Haida and Tlingit agree. See, for just the tip of the iceberg, Tom Lowenstein, *Ancient Land: Sacred Whale; The Inuit Hunt and Its Rituals* (New York: Farrar, Straus and Giroux, 1993); Bill Reid and Robert Bringhurst, *The Raven Steals the Light;* Robert Bringhurst, *Story as Sharp as a Knife* (Vancouver: Douglas & McIntyre, 1999). Regarding the relationship between divination and tricksters, see Mortensen, "Raven Augury in Tibet,"

pp. 113–24. See also the many discussions of ravens in Paul Radin, *The Trickster: A Study in American Indian Mythology* (New York: Schocken Books, 1956).

32. Heinrich, *Ravens in Winter,* pp. 250–51. Heinrich, in turn, is borrowing this quote from Nelson, *Make Prayers to Raven,* p. 83. For more on the religious role of ravens among the Koyukon people of Alaska, see Nelson, *Make Prayers to Raven,* pp. 17, 19, 27–31, 56–57, 79–84, and 96–97.

33. Heinrich, *Ravens in Winter,* p. 246. For the original quotation, see Fred Bruemmer, "Ravens," *International Wildlife* 14 (1984): 33–35.

34. We can also postulate that the groups from which these migrating peoples split, the proto-Dene, themselves divided into various migratory waves of settlement in the Himalayas through Inner Asia to Siberia. The Athapaskan-speaking peoples, for example, seem to have split off from what are now Eastern Tibetans somewhere in Central Asia some time before 9,000 BCE. Both groups migrated, some much further than others. However, much in the way of specifics lies beyond the current conclusive domain of scientific inquiry. In the years to come, we will doubtless have relatively advanced maps and dates for the migrations of peoples across Asia and North America. However, it seems less likely that we will witness a correlative increase in our knowledge of the details of the transmission of ideas for preliterate periods of ancient prehistory. For more on Trans-Pacific history, see the somewhat problematic work by Charles Graves, *Proto-Religions in Central Asia* (Bochum: Universitätsverlag, 1994), pp. 189–91; and the much more valuable, though somewhat dated works by Waldemar Bogoras, "Early Migrations of the Eskimo Between Asia and America," *Proceedings of the 21st International Congress of Americanists* (1924): 216–35; Waldemar Bogoras, "Elements of the Culture of the Circumpolar Zone" *American Anthropologist* 31, no. 4 (1929): 579–601. See also Elaine Dewar, *Bones: Discovering the First Americans* (New York: Random House, 2001); Brian M. Fagan, *Ancient North America* (London: Thames and Hudson, 1991), pp. 69–90, and 159–220; and Stewart J. Fiedel, *Prehistory of the Americas* (Cambridge: Cambridge University Press, 1996), pp. 1–38.

35. Wendy Doniger is quite right when she writes that "there are no Galapagos Islands for myths." Wendy Doniger, *The Implied Spider: Politics and Theology in Myth* (New York: Columbia University Press, 1998), p. 139.

36. I am following what I believe to be an important methodological claim pioneered by Franz Boas. See, for a solid explication of Boas' scholarly method, Franz Boas, *A Franz Boas Reader,* ed. George W. Stocking (Chicago: The University of Chicago Press, 1989). Boas purported a view of the word "culture" as plural to such a subjective extent that categorizations should best be avoided until the data has been sufficiently gathered. Only then could the data be even generally and (even then only) speculatively interpreted.

37. Stephen J. Gould, *The Mismeasure of Man* (New York: Norton, 1996), p. 20.

38. Jonathan Z. Smith, "In Comparison a Magic Dwells," in Kimberley C. Patton and Benjamin C. Ray, eds., *A Magic Still Dwells* (Berkeley: University of California Press, 2000), pp. 25–26, and 40–41. The article was originally published as the second chapter (pp. 19–35) of Jonathan Z. Smith, *Imagining Religion: From Babylon to Jonestown* (Chicago: The University of Chicago Press, 1982).

39. Vladimir Propp, *Theory and History of Folklore,* A. Liberman, ed., A. Y. and R. P. Martin, trans. (Minneapolis: University of Minnesota Press, 1984), p. 48.

40. Jonathan Z. Smith, "The 'End' of Comparison: Redescription and Rectification," in Patton and Ray, eds. *A Magic Still Dwells,* p. 238. Emphasis added.

41. Albert B. Lord, *The Singer of Tales* (Cambridge: Harvard University Press, 1960), p. 67.

42. Kimberley C. Patton, "'He who sits in the heavens laughs': Recovering Animal Theology in the Abrahamic Traditions," *Harvard Theological Review* 93, no. 4 (2000): 422.

43. Heinrich, *Ravens,* pp. 24–25. Heinrich's reference is to the work: Michio Hoshino, *Moose* (San Francisco: Chronicle Books, 1988).

44. Ibid., p. 252.

VIII

ANIMALS IN ART

On the *Dynamis* of Animals,
or How *Animalium* Became *Anthropos*

DIANE APOSTOLOS-CAPPADONA

We picture our deepest emotions and our loftiest ideals as animals:
courage as a lion, wisdom as an elephant, power as a bull, gentleness as a doe, majesty as an eagle.

—Otto von Simson[1]

After the death of the renowned French Minister of Culture, and avowed agnostic, André Malraux (1901–1976), a memorial ceremony celebrating his life and works was held at the Palais du Louvre in Paris.[2] There, in the institution so well known to him and to other aesthetes, Malraux was remembered for his singular achievements in redefining French culture and cultural institutions, his role in the French resistance in World War II, and his extraordinary commitment to the idea of the arts as a form of spiritual transcendence. Yet, he was not to be imaged or even imagined in the form of a photograph or a collection of his publications, but in the form of a cat—by an ancient Egyptian sculpture of the feline deity, Bastet (figure 1).

According to Egyptian tradition, Bastet was the guardian and benefactress of human beings. A tutelary deity, she was invoked to overcome hidden enemies and obstacles. Malraux communed regularly with this exact feline image on his visits to the Musée du Louvre. The nature of their conversations is left open to specula-

tion, while the reality of them is recorded fact. The Egyptian *Book of the Dead* invokes Bastet: "Engage your powers of enchanting mystery and waylay all cruel masters, keep the betrayers away from the children of the light and from the darkness of our hearts."

Is it a curiosity or a propriety that the leading aesthetician and cultural thinker of twentieth-century France requested that he be re-presenced at his own memorial ceremony simply by this wondrous statue of the Egyptian feline deity? A work of art fashioned before *animalium* became *anthropos*—a time when animals and their images evoked a sacred *dynamis,* and when works of art were simultaneously vehicles and vessels of The Sacred.

For *animalium,* from the Latin for animal, is invested with the sacral qualities of integrity, dignity, and vitality fundamental to the essence of an "animal" as opposed to a "beast." *Dynamis* is the Greek word for energy and/or dynamism, specifically for those energies of beauty, grace, and power which the Eastern Church Fathers

Figure 1. *The cat-goddess Bastet,* Egyptian. Period of Pharaoh Psammetich I, 664-610 BCE. (Musée du Louvre, Paris.) Photo credit: Erich Lessing/Art Resource, N.Y.

understood as divine and yet accessible to believers. The Greek word *anthropos* is normally translated as "man," but in fact it has the inclusive sense of "human."

Therefore, what I am suggesting here is that the foundational concepts of *animalium, dynamis,* and *anthropos* are charged with moral and religious overtones. *Animalium* was a mediator between The Sacred and nature; and this mediation was expressed in the *dynamis* of animals. However, once the natural order is realigned and the "roles" of *animalium* and *anthropos* are redefined, the diminishment of the fundamental integrity and nature of animals becomes apparent. The anthropomorphism of *animalium* signals a transvaluation of religious and cultural values evidenced in the linguistic move from sentiment to sentimentality, and in the presence of animals in religious art.

Every world religion has had from its beginnings an attitude(s) toward the visual modality, i.e., the arts. The fundamental relationship between art and religion is premised upon the unconscious preference for image or word as the means through which universal truths are presenced. Visual art expresses truth, especially religious truth, through its intuitive ability to communicate the invisible, the abstract, and the intangible. Even in contemporary culture, children see and draw before they learn to read and write. The process of *seeing* is primary to human development, and the primacy of the visual modality needs to be respected not negated.

The art historian David Freedberg reaffirmed the primacy of the visual modality in his groundbreaking text, *The Power of Images.*[3] The quest for meaning is predicated upon the fact that the fundamental human realities of sensitivity and sensuality are communicated through the image. Thereby, a visual culture provides as the initial source of religious meaning art as a primary locus for the encounter with The Sacred. Creative works afford the artist and the viewer the tangibility of sensuous and perceptible insights toward religious experience.

Just as Western culture has sought to deny the "reality" of nature and animals, so too has it deviated from the centrality of the visual modality. The post-Enlightenment emphasis on the authority of "the text" as reasoned, logical, and unchanging needs to be reexamined, not simply in terms of the fundamental role of the visual in human development but also in recognition that the arts, as forms of historical documentation, are as "factual" as any written text. The reality may well be that history has been written in images. The dancer-choreographer Martha Graham was fond of employing the example of what she identified as a long-lost civilization whose existence is known to us only from an undocumented fragment which reads, "They had no poet and so they died for the history of man is written in the arts."[4]

As the historian of religion Mircea Eliade opined, the primary nature of the human person is that of *homo religiosus.* The philosopher Ernst Cassirer has suggested that fundamental to being human is the ability to create and communicate through symbols. Thereby, Eliade's *homo religiosus* become simultaneously Cassirer's *homo symbolicus.* I want to expand this "united" category to signify that the mode through which *homo religiosus* merges with *homo symbolicus* is as *homo aestheticus*—that is, not simply, through the arts but because of our natural and primary aesthetic sensibilities. It is through these that we can distinguish icon from image, myth from story, *animalium* from *anthropos.* Herein lies, it seems to me, the initial answer to the epistemological question: we come to know through the visualization of concepts, ideas, and truth, through the imaging energies of the imagination.

There are two traditional epistemological models: the rational and the intuitive. Rational learning is premised upon human reason and the empirical experience of self and world. This, I would suggest, is the modality of *anthropos,* of image, of a sign, and most important, of word. Rational learning is predicated upon the authority and clarity of "the word" and thereby of the written text, whereas intuitive learning is authenticated by human intuition and the "felt" experience of self and word. This, then, is the modality of *animalium,* of icon, of symbol, the visual, and most important, of the arts. Intuitive learning is evidenced by the fundamental human experience of the process of *seeing* and thereby of the arts as primary documents for human history.

Contemporary scholarship on the role of the arts, the concept of visual culture, and the redefinition of gender has acknowledged the category of "*the* Gaze." Not simply a protracted or intensified mode of looking, the conceptual basis for "*the* Gaze" presumes that there is a right and a wrong way to look: cultured, cultivated, and/or engendered. Thereby, the lens through which we look and come to know what we have looked at is partial and conforms to fashion. Looking in this manner is not the process of *seeing,* which advocates impartiality and truth. *Seeing* expands beyond the traditional boundaries of looking and involves more than vision and the visual. The meaning of *seeing* can be expanded based on the Greek root of *aesthetic,* which signified the ability to perceive, to come to know, through the senses. Thus, the human imagination, sensitivities, and intuition fused together in the experience of *seeing,* which was an experience predicated upon the ability to *see* without preconditions, conformity, or prejudice. *Seeing* is a fundamental human activity that can be enhanced but not achieved simply by intellectual training or study. It may well be the situation that in the modern world it is as impossible for us to *see* and to come to know in the act of *seeing* as it is for us to distinguish *animalium* from *anthropos.*

Crucial to this distinction is the recognition that the progress of domestication has become synonymous with the act of "taming." Etymologically the roots of these words are distinct from each other; domestication comes from the Latin for house, home; so that "to domesticate" intends "to accustom for home use/life." In so doing, however, the domesticator retains an awareness of the dignity and integrity of the

(about-to-be-) domesticated. Whereas "taming" comes from the Old English for "without spirit," so that "to tame" an animal was to take away its indigenous spirit. Think simply of the oft-used phrase in relation to a horse which "must be broken" or the puppy which requires "a handler, controller." Thereby, the act of taming implies the impingement upon the essential dignity and integrity of *animalium.*

Further attention needs to be drawn to the language employed in the ensuing discussion of animals in religious art, as the issue of power arises from the historical transfer from animal dominion over humans to human domination over animals. The question of power—what is it? who has it?—is central to this process of domestication, which becomes synonymous with the process of domination. The primal reverence for animals is replaced by human "ownership" and "control" of animals. In some mysterious manner, the human awareness of the *dynamis* of *animalium* was simultaneously an awareness of "otherness." This recognition awoke the fundamental human need to identify with "the other" by controlling and dominating "the other." Ironically, central to this otherness of *animalium* was its embodiment of sacred energy, power, and beauty. As Marcel Brion advised, "The sacred mission of the animal, the power to make a single living creature the bearer of a religious idea, evident since prehistoric times, is found in old religions."[5]

In his introduction to the collection entitled *Man and Animal,* the magisterial medievalist Otto von Simson identified a series of questions pertinent to the object of my present inquiry: the iconology of the animal, or more specifically of animals, in religious art. For von Simson, the significance of animals led to their becoming a subject of art. Ranging from the cultural matrixes that undergird the evolution of animal imagery in Western religious art from the transformation of the divinity of the animal to its use as an emblem of human spirituality, his comments support my thesis that the viewing of the animal in religious art and culture is symptomatic of the religious condition of humanity. "We have stepped out of the Garden of Eden and its gates closed behind us."[6]

A chronological analysis of the iconography of animals or more specifically of one species, like the horse or the dog, in religious art might be the efficient method by which to initiate the discussion of the visualization of the relations between religion and animals. However, I am not convinced it would be a method sufficiently comprehensive to discern the meaning of this singular relationship. Further, the selectivity of one species would place geographic and religious limitations that would prove inappropriate for the nature of both interdisciplinary study and this encyclopedic theme. Therefore, I turned initially to those foundational resources which prove normally dependable in the formation of my thesis statements. When I turned to *The Dictionary of Art,* I found the following introductory paragraph to the entry entitled "Animal subjects:"

> Although animals have been represented in the art of almost all cultures from prehistoric times, the depiction of animal subjects in painting and the graphic arts became a particularly well-established tradition in Western art following the Renaissance, as European explorers discovered a new species, as the demand for illustrated books increased and as the traditional Christian interpretation of the relation between humanity and the rest of creation began to be reappraised. Moreover, while hunting, falconry, and similar pursuits continued to provide artists with subjects, animals came to have a more complex relation to society, as curiosities, status symbols or in a domesticated role. Animals continued to occupy an ambiguous role in 19th and 20th century Western art, as the subjects of human science, as opportunities to demonstrate technique, and as the instinctive, unrestrained vehicles for a range of Romantic and post-Romantic symbolic possibilities.[7]

Once I learned that this was not exactly the most helpful source with which to begin my ap-

proach to the encyclopedic question of the role of animals in the arts of world religions, I turned to the *Encyclopedia of Comparative Iconography,* in which I found no individualized entry on animal(s). Rather, there was the following note in the "Index of Other Names and Terms": that animals were treated in more than fifty entries as wide-ranging as beheading/decapitation to luxury to madness to pregnancy to virgin/virginity.[8] As true as both of these statements from major reference publications may be, they offered no insights for this study, except that they became the impetus by which I asked myself what did I *see* when I looked at animals in religious art: signs, symbols, emblems, attributes, types, topoi, motifs, something more, or something less?

I proceeded to search for information in the normative research texts in art history and religious studies, despaired in the aisles of books dedicated to anthropology and archaeology, and realized that "the canon" of traditional knowledge was neither as normative nor as comprehensive as I wanted it to be. So I reversed myself and turned away from rational learning toward intuitive learning. I looked at the images I had collected. I had reasoned that the easiest solution to my problem would be to prepare a historical and iconographical investigative survey of one species of animal in religious art. As visually pleasing, probably even stimulating, as such a study would be, I voiced my otherwise silent concern that the "heart of the matter" was wider than one species of animal, and that the more I looked at the images I had collected I began to *see* that there was much more to these images than what was on the *surface.*

My focus shifted from iconography to iconology as my concerns were refocused on the uncultured meaning of the image, so that what happened to the animal in each image and what these depictions of animals attempted to communicate became the critical issues. Exactly what is the difference between the two images of a primal rendering of a bull (figure 2) and the cultivated presentation of a little terrier dog (figure 3)?

Figure 2. *Bull from the Hall of the Bulls.* (Paleolithic: Lascaux, Dordogne.) Photo credit: Bridgeman-Giraudon/Art Resource, N.Y.

The paleolithic mural of the second bull from the Hall of the Bulls is an emotive rendering of the energy and power of *animalium* made present through the minimal use of details. The expressive black outline of the bull's form promotes, through the alternating thickness and thinness of line, a rhythmic cadence of its fundamental *dynamis*. The black bull is superimposed over a series of smaller ochre bulls, and projects an aura of vitality and presence through the optical illusion of depth and volume created by the muralist's use of varied coloration and scale. There are no careful or even tentative lines in either the second bull itself or the surrounding environment. There are no human figures either as dominators, tamers, partners, or companions visible in this segment of the mural. In a word, the muralist calls our attention to one, and only one, reality—that of the bull.

Conversely, C. D. Weldon paints a charming domestic scene in which two little girls appropriately attired in white pinafores "take tea" with each other, their dolls, and their special guest—a cairn terrier who is postured carefully on a chair. As the little girl in the red dress "pours" and the little girl in the blue dress delicately sips her tea, the little dog engages the viewer's attention by staring outward beyond the painting's frame. Before the dog rests an ostensibly filled tea cup sitting on its saucer, and a little white cookie is seen on the edge of the table. Weldon presented a carefully detailed domestic setting for this special tea party from the vase of flowers, framed painting, and decorated screen in the

Figure 3. Chromolithograph published by Louis Prang and Company of Boston in 1889 after C. D. Weldon, *Five O'Clock Tea*. Courtesy of the Hallmark Archives, Hallmark Cards Inc.

background to the patterned rug strewn with an open book, pillows, dolls, and other toys to the delicately patterned white tablecloth. Perhaps the only accommodations to the cairn terrier's fundamental "terrier nature" are her frontal engagement with the viewer and her sitting directly upon the chair's hard surface—the rejected comfort of the plump blue pillow having been tossed underneath her chair.

As charming as *Five O'Clock Tea* is as a painting, what fates have doomed this little dog to the position in which she finds herself? How exactly has the *dynamis* of the extraordinary animal become anthropomorphized into this little furry doll? Perhaps von Simson's discussion of his identified "three interrelated ideas"[9] that undergird the varied artistic motifs of animals provides some insight into the transformation from *animalium* into *anthropos*. His first idea is

the recognition of the significance of animals both within the natural world of created beings and the constructed world of modern humanity. The significance of animals is a multifaceted reality even into the twenty-first century. Animals have been integral to the transformation from primal societies to modern civilizations. They have been the source of food, clothing, and other necessities for human existence. They have provided companionship as well as a labor force. They have been a source of entertainment and athletic prowess. They offer engagement as "wonders of nature"—untamed and free in their indigenous natural environments *or* dominated and confined in zoos and aquaria. They can be the enemies of human beings as a powerful force wreaking havoc and destruction to property, as well as to human and other animal life. They can be legendary and fabulous, exotic and elegant, awesome and sublime, profane and dangerous, and spiritual and sacred. The significance of animals cannot be diminished as they continue to offer us a model for humane behavior within the natural order as communicators of Thomas Berry's categories of *communio* and *compassio*.

Secondly, von Simson notes the established role of animals as subjects of art from the very beginnings of primal art into the contemporary arts. Given their continuing significance in our daily life, the reality of our recognition of "animal" has found them as artistic topics in their own right from the caves at Lascaux to the photographs of William Wegman. Animals are included as artistic or essential elements in the narrative themes of works of art. They may be employed as symbols, signs, emblems, or attributes. Animals may garner artistic interest as the empowering presence in the work of art, such as the depiction of the horse and rider or the hunter and the hunted.

Thirdly, von Simson suggests the idea of the "crises moments in human and animal relations." During those peak times, the precious balance within the boundaries of animal-human relations is shifted, expanded, constricted, and/or redefined. As a result, the ways in which we *see* and know animals are transformed. Clearly, different interpreters will offer alternate crises. For myself, the great crises are the advents of human domination over animals, the invention of the machine, and the modern glorification of the domestic pet. For all interpreters, of course, there is that initial paradisiac ideal when all of creation coexisted in harmony and balance in a state of innocence. Unfortunately, this innocence was lost, stolen, or disappeared so that the *dynamis* of *animalium* was recognized not simply as the "natural state" but as a source of energy, beauty, and power that humans characterized as divine.

Primal peoples were in awe of animals. They recognized simultaneously a kinship with animals and the singularity of *animalium*. The evidence for these facts is so overwhelming that it is recognized across academic boundaries from an-

thropology to art history to religious studies and to the sciences, as witnessed in the varied contributions to this volume. With specific reference to the animals in religious art, the foundational reality is evident throughout prehistoric art as a reflection of the deep bond(s) between animals and humans as a result of the reverence for the *dynamis* of *animalium* even into the hunt where speed and power prevailed. The art historian Marcel Brion wrote:

> Prehistoric art is full of harmony, nobility and greatness, firstly because it is essentially based on truth, on that knowledge which comes from a sense of unity with its subject; perhaps also on a sort of spiritual brotherhood between man and animal. This is what makes it supremely religious.[10]

Further, he affirmed that "Never perhaps in the whole history of animal art, even in China, has the animal appeared so magnified, so sublimated, without ever losing its reality or naturalness, than in Paleolithic art."[11] My questions became clarified: Is there something overtly or qualitatively distinctive in the paleolithic perception of animal(s) that is absent from the modern? If so, when and how was this perception transformed?

As Western culture evolved through the varied stages of hunter-gatherers to farmer-herdsmen into the classical empires of Egypt, Greece, and Rome, we witness alterations in the delicate balance between humans and animals, and these have been documented in the arts. The presentations of animals as vehicles or vessels of divinity became transformed into the human-animal deities and then into the anthropomorphic deities, as human beings came to dominate animals. The architectural historian Siegfried Giedion wrote of this evolution:

> Up till then, man had considered himself a minor creature, less powerful and less beautiful than his revered fellow creature, the animal. With the domestication of some animals. ...

the animal was dethroned. From then on man was to consider himself the chosen master of creation.[12]

In my *seeing* of animals in religious art, I recognize here a major crisis in which the *dynamis* of *animalium* is redefined. Artists from the Imperial Roman into the Reformation periods provided us with animals owned, controlled, directed, or otherwise dominated by the persons present within the work of art. *Animalium* has become domesticated and tamed in that etymological root of being "without spirit," as evidenced in the visual move from riderless horse to horse and rider.

My second crisis is the advent of the machine and hence of industrialization. The earlier dependence upon animals for physical work diminished as machines were created to complete agrarian tasks more efficiently. As evidenced in the arts, this crisis further devalued the essential dignity and integrity of animals, as visually documented in the distinctively different depictions of the monumental horse-and-riders of Imperial Roman and Italian Renaissance art as juxtaposed to the racehorse paintings of nineteenth-century Impressionism. Animals were not merely subject to human domination but also specifically "valued" as objects for amusement, entertainment, and sport, in the worst sense of the term.

My third crisis is a natural extension of the devaluation of animals with the advent of the machine. I refer to this as the glorification, in the sense of an apotheosis, of domestic pets, ranging from birds, fish, hamsters, gerbils, pot-bellied pigs, bunnies, and ferrets to dogs and cats, and even in some instances to miniature horses. Without doubt, this is the elevation of *animalium* to the highest definition of *anthropos* as their "owners" provide adoration, glorification, and humanization to "their pets." We see the initial reality of this humanizing tendency in the cairn terrier who sits so prim and proper in *Five O'Clock Tea*. We recognize the negativity of it in the very contemporary reality of the eleva-

tion of pet food stores into "boutiques" and of pet grooming centers into "salons." This trans-valuation of values, if you will, has damaged not simply the dignity of animals but also that of humans, as we have lost the lessons of humane behavior possible only in a state of *communio* and *compassio*.

I returned to von Simson's essay and reviewed his claim that there was a chronology which explained the depiction of animals in western art and that this chronology rested firmly upon what he identified as the "two decisive turning points in human history."[13] The first turning point is the move from prehistory to the dawn of civilization. Von Simson characterizes this as the "end of human innocence" and as the period signified by the establishment of "civilization," which he characterizes as "mastery over the animal." His second turning point is the replacement of the animal by the machine and the societal, political, religious, and economic transformations that ensued.

A critical key to von Simson's chronology is how we understand not simply the animal but the human and the machine as well. His schema may be "read" as developmental, as this transformation of both *animalium* into *anthropos* and of *anthropos* into *machina* is a move from intuitive learning to rational learning. The fundamental human need for the intuitive modality has been subjugated by the rational methodologies of analyses as human history unfolded. Similarly, these same progressive periods rejected the spiritual value which recognized that what was once identified as "sympathetic magic"—that is, becoming one in spirit and energy with "the other," specifically when that other was an animal, occurred through the process of a religious ritual or ceremonial action—is not simply an illusion of the "the primitive mind," but rather a more fundamental human need, as recognized in the early twentieth century by artists like Pablo Picasso and Martha Graham who sought out *"le primitif."*[14]

Thus, *animalium,* whether real or imaginary, was sought after by human beings. This "spiritual" quest was made manifest in the imagery found on everyday and sacred items such as screens, decorative objects, sacred protectors, food vessels, and even clothing. The human became one with the animal spirit either by assimilation, osmosis, mimesis, digestion, gesture, and/or appropriation. Eventually even the qualities human beings admired most in animals—loyalty, strength, grace, beauty, majesty, and "sacredness"—were translated into human virtues; they became "our own" through these religious rituals and daily ceremonies. Sympathetic magic became a transformation not simply of matter into energy but of *animalium* into *anthropos*.

Even a cursory survey of the visual history of animals in Western religious art suggests the transformation from the primal depiction of pure admiration and worship present in paleolithic art into the Egyptian deification referencing the mutuality of the sacral dignity of the animal with that of the human. The eventual fusion of the animal with the human image of sacrality in the classical Greek spiritualization of animals is evidenced in the ethereal elegance of the horses on the friezes and tympani of the Parthenon. It is the characteristic Roman pragmatism through which the animal becomes sign as the sacral becomes anthropomorphized and the visual universe anthropocentric. Thus, we decipher the rational move from image to sign and the intuitive move from icon to symbol as signifiers of the transformation of Western culture from primal society to civilization.

The Western Christian assimilation, the "baptism" if you will, of classical animal symbols turned them into signs of Christ, such as the lost lamb rescued by the *Good Shepherd* and the wild beasts charmed by the music of *Orpheus*. The Western Christian employment of animals as images of good and evil is evidenced in the visual motif of a lamb caught between wolves for the narrative of *Susanna and the Elders* on early Christian sarcophagi or the topos of Lilith in the form of the serpent tempting Eve popularized in medieval Christian art. The Western Christian classification of animals as emblems is attested

to by the lion, the ox, and the eagle, which signify three of the Four Evangelists found on the tympani of medieval cathedrals or on the pages of medieval manuscript illuminations such as those in the *Book of Kells*. The common Western Christian form of animal as attribute prevails in Albrecht Dürer's popular engravings such as the *Fall of Man* (fig. 4) and *Knight, Death and the Devil* in which the cat and the parrot identify the fallible acts of humanity while the horse and the dog represent human virtues.

As *animalium* was transformed visually from image to sign and from icon to symbol, animals became *anthropos,* and thus the secularization of religious art became further documentation of the cultural evolution from theocentric to anthropocentric world views. The eventual secularization of the animal in Western art, such as the pet dog found in either Titian's *Venus of Urbino* or Diego Velasquez's *Las Meninas,* raises the further question of the relationship between animals and women in Western art, and thereby in Western culture. The indigenous energy and power of a horse can be "read" as qualities transferred to its rider in Francisco Goya's *Second of May 1808,* Jacques Louis David's *Napoleon Crossing the St. Bernard Pass,* or Éugene Délacroix's *The Lion Hunt.* The reduction of the animal into an abstracted idea may be found in Franz Marc's paintings of the *Yellow Cow* and *Blue Horses,* Paul Klee's *Around the Fish,* or Morris Graves' *Blind Bird.* Pablo Picasso may be singular among modern artists in his iconic presencing of the *dynamis* of the horse and the bull in many of his now classic works such as *Guernica* or the Minotaur and bullfight series.

Some commentators on this otherwise named developmental (or evolutionary) scenario indicate that this move from animal sacrality to animal-human sacrality to human sacrality works in a tandem with the developmentalist theory of Western religious history. Therefore, such a visual religious symbolization documents the process of the advancement of *man*.[15] But what *if* this scenario is wrong? What *if* this style of analysis is rooted in a rational learning cate-

Figure 4. Albrecht Dürer, *Fall of Man* (*Adam and Eve*), 1504. Photo credit: Foto Marburg/Art Resource, N.Y.

gory mistake? What if this isn't developmental or evolutionary at all? Reverse it, like Alice slipping through the looking glass, and ask yourself what if we have been looking but not *seeing* what art and the images of animals are about? What if we weren't supposed to assert ourselves as the dominators of animals but rather were to be like Francis of Assisi, who strove to be their partner in a cohabitation of the earth or, to invoke Berry's vocabulary, to live "in a state of *communio?*"

Animals and art have a great deal more in common than we normally think. There is "the rub"—that word "think," that act of thinking, which removes us from the reality of feeling, of being, of living. Recall that our word *aesthetic* comes from a Greek root that signifies not beauty or thought or "taste," but rather the ability or gift to perceive through the senses—through the fullness of humanity: body, mind, spirit, soul, and senses. Simply put, when you are given an anaesthetic you don't *feel* a thing —the anaesthetized person doesn't feel anything, hear with clarity, move with stability, or *see* clearly. Further, we must consider the implications of Berry's term "*communio*" given my premise of how *animalium* became *anthropos,* and the qualitative difference between *feeling* and *sentimentality.*

The *power of images,* as Freedberg has argued so eloquently, is predicated upon the response of the viewer.[16] So as an example of the *power of images* and the relationship between animals and humans, let us consider two masterpieces by the Italian renaissance sculptor, Donatello: his *Judith and Holofernes* (figure 5) and his *Gattamelata* (figure 6). The historic leader known as *Gattamelata,* or "honeyed cat," sits astride his powerful horse in a classic military monument to honor his prowess and brilliance as a leader of men in battle. His horse is massive in stature but controlled in movement. He does not have the *dynamis* of the Second Bull (figure 2) but rather is the image of tamed energy and strength. His tamer is ostensibly also his controller, the great condottiere, Erasmo di Narni. Following a classic visual metaphoric tradition, the depiction of the victorious general astride his powerful horse signifies the extraordinary ability of this man to direct and control the animal's greater weight and strength. As he is able to handle his horse, so too is he able to handle an army of men whose united weight and strength are greater than his own. The gestural sign of his authority is the way that he controls the reins in his left hand and the horse's mid-section with his knees. Donatello's *Gattamelata,* then, is more than an equestrian statue dedicated to a heroic leader, it is a visual metaphor for his authority as he controls the power of the horse.

The bronze sculpture of the Hebrew Scriptural heroine, Judith, in the act of decapitating the enemy general Holofernes does not initially reveal the presence of an animal(s). Rather Donatello presents his viewers with an extraordinary rendering of the slumping figure of an adult male general beneath the trunk of the adult female figure of a widow. The artist knows that our normal understanding of the male and female bodies must be defied—that is, hers as smaller and more delicate than his masculine power—in order for the decapitation to "work." However he recognizes that the scriptural action is a wondrous act, as God has chosen a woman to perform a man's job to defend the city and its citizens. So Donatello creates an extraordinary posturing as Judith stands astride the shoulders of the drunken general.

As we circumambulate the sculpture, we come to recognize that the heroine's legs are bent at the knee and her back is positioned like that of a mounted rider. Like Gattamelata, Judith holds her weapon in her right hand and the "reins" of her mount's hair in her left hand. The visual parody of the reversal of maleness and femaleness to create the vision of the horse and rider is confirmed when the viewer *sees* the medallion hanging on Holofernes' back and positioned near Judith's bent left knee. This medallion would be recognized by any contemporary citizen of Florence as the award given to the "champion rider."

Figure 5. Donatello, *Judith and Holofernes* (1495)
Piazza della Signoria, Florence. Photo credit:
Alinari/Art Resource, N.Y.

Figure 6. *Monument to General Gattamelata* (Erasmo
da Narni, 1445–53: Piazza del Santo, Padua.) Photo
credit: Alinari/Art Resource, N.Y.

I know that the ordinary and the extraordinary references to a horse were not immediately obvious in the sculpture of *Judith and Holofernes*. However if one becomes engaged in the act of *seeing* this sculpture, then my premises that *animalium* becomes *anthropos* and that the aesthetic is predicated upon the senses become gateways into a participative encounter. The horse(s) is neither sympathetic magic nor an emblem. Rather, it is a heuristic symbol whose multivalent qualities open up a new "world" to be experienced and known.

The more mundane domestic situation depicted in that well-known painting from just about every introductory Art History course Jan van Eyck's *Arnolfini Wedding Portrait* (figure 7) provides recognition that the dog as animal is more than sign, emblem, or attribute.[17] Situated carefully in the foreground, this sturdy little terrier positions herself between bride and bridegroom *and* the viewer. Her frontal engagement with the viewer extends the limitations of the traditional figure of an interlocutor. Further, she is a symbol of fidelity, integrity, and loyalty[18] as she extends our limited distinctions between feeling and sentimentality. The initial "cuteness" of the terrier is an enchanting addition to the couple whose matrimonial vows are reaffirmed if not accentuated by the symbolic qualities of the dog. The process of *seeing* permits the recognition that the canine life force combines *élan vital* with *joie de vivre* to dominate the foreground of the canvas. Thus, we move from sentiment to feeling as we experience the aesthetic reality in this frame.

For the arts, the primary modality is the ability to perceive through the senses: to *see* is to look, to *see* is to hear, to *see* is to move, to *see* is to touch, to *see* is to intuit, to *see* is to come to know. Image, form, color, sound, and gesture — these are fundaments of the arts. Throughout human history we recognize that the majority of persons have learned by *seeing*, by drawing, by imitation of what they have *seen*, *not* by reading. The image may be the natural and foundational

form of the human quest for meaning. What we *see* is the tangible attempt to express the otherwise inexpressible or to use the poetic language of the nineteenth-century theologian Samuel Taylor Coleridge a *mediated immediacy*.[19]

The animal is the primary visual expression of that *dynamis* understood as primal energy, grace, and power identified by Mircea Eliade as characteristic of The Sacred.[20] Animals provided simultaneously a sense of vitality infused with sacred energy and power, an intimate contact with the natural and cosmic orders, a sacramental meditation of mundane events, and a means of transformation. Rather than recognizing and respecting this reality, human beings have sought to empower themselves as representatives of The Sacred, as transformers of matter into spirit, and as the visualization of *dynamis*. So the animal(s) has been desecrated, degraded, and denatured. They have been transformed in the arts from *animalium* into *anthropos* as evidenced in the photographs by William Wegman who poses his beloved Weimaraner, Fay Wray, in every day human situations such as *Ray and Mrs. Lubner in Bed watching TV* or in a parody of western art classics such as *Le Dounaier Fay* in contrast to Diego Velasquez's *Rokeby Venus*. Now consider whether or not these post-Renaissance depictions are comparable examples to the primal admiration for the beauty and strength, for the *dynamis* of animals found in the caves of Lascaux, the lions at Luxor, the great sphinx of Giza, or the horses on the Parthenon.

Most of all we need to ask ourselves what have we sacrificed in this transformation of *animalium* into *anthropos*? Is Kenneth Clark right when he concludes his essay on "Sacred and Symbolic Animals": "Men had ceased to think symbolically, and their feelings about animals had changed from veneration to curiosity. It was a loss to the human imagination. Whether it will ultimately be a gain to the understanding of animals remains to be seen."[21]

We may come to recognize that perhaps, just perhaps, art and animals are in our lives as fun-

Figure 7. Jan van Eyck, *The Arnolfini Wedding Portrait (Giovanni Arnolfini and his wife)*, 1434. (The National Gallery, London.) Photo credit: Alinari/ Art Resource, N.Y.

Figure 8. Giotto di Bondone, *Saint Francis Preaching to the Birds*, 1295–1300. (Church of Saint Francis, Assisi.) Photo credit: Alinari/Art Resource, N.Y.

damental and necessary elements of what Mircea Eliade identified as "the nostalgia for Paradise."[22] Restoring our fundamental relationship with animals was integral to the radical message of Francis of Assisi whose own communion with animals was captured so eloquently in the art of Giotto (figure 8). This connection between animals, art, and religion is not simply a foundational element in our quest for The Sacred but in the rediscovery of our humanness, or perhaps more appropriately to Berry's category of our *compassion*. As Clark noted in his eloquent book-length essay on animals and art:

We can never recapture the Golden Age; but we can regain that feeling of kinship which will help us establish a feeling of the unity of creation. It is a faith we all share.[23]

Acknowledgments

This text was originally presented at a special session of the conference, *Religion and Animals*, sponsored by the Yenching Institute, Harvard University, in May 1999. I am grateful to the conveners of that conference, Kimberley C. Patton and Paul Waldau, for that opportunity. Further, I am pleased to acknowledge Professor Patton's editorial support in the revision of my slide-illustrated lecture into a written essay.

NOTES

1. Otto von Simson, "Introduction," in Anil da Silva, Otto von Simson, and Philip Troutman, eds., *Man and Animal*. (Greenwich: The New York Graphic Society, 1965), p. 9. (Hereafter cited as von Simson, "Introduction.")

2. This discussion of André Malraux's memorial ceremony is derived from Ferit Egdü, "Homo Sapiens and the Animal Kingdom" in the special issue of *P Art and Culture Magazine* dedicated to the theme of *Animals in Art* 6:5 (Spring–Summer 2002). This interpretation of Malraux's motivation for his request and its meaning are mine.

3. David Freedberg, *The Power of Images* (Chicago: The University of Chicago Press, 1989).

4. Most often quoted from her testimony to the Senate Appropriations Subcommittee during NEA Appropriations in March 1979. As cited by Diane Apostolos-Cappadona, "Introduction: Mircea Eliade, The Scholar as Artist, Critic, and Poet" in Mircea Eliade, *Symbolism, The Sacred, and the Arts*, ed. Diane Apostolos-Cappadona (New York: Crossroad Publishing, 1986), p. xvi, n. 23.

5. Marcel Brion, *Animals in Art* (London: George C. Harrap and Co., 1959), p. 22.

6. von Simson, "Introduction," p. 11.

7. Edward Nygren, "Animal subjects" in *The Dictionary of Art*, ed. Jane Shoaf Turner, 34 vols. (London: Macmillan, 1996), vol. 2, p. 102.

8. *Encyclopedia of Comparative Iconography*, ed. Helene Roberts, 2 vols. (Chicago: Fitzroy Dearborn, 1997), vol. 2, p. 1067. The reader should note that there is no description of the entries related to animals; rather there is simply a list.

9. von Simson, "Introduction," p. 9. This interpretation and expansion of von Simson's "three interrelated ideas" is mine.

10. Brion, *Animals in Art*, p. 15.

11. Ibid., 15.

12. As quoted in von Simson, "Introduction," p. 10.

13. Ibid., p. 9 . This interpretation of his decisive turning points and their implications is my own interpretation of von Simson's text.

14. Diane Apostolos-Cappadona, "Toward a Spirituality of *Seeing*: O'Keeffe's *Black Cross, New Mexico* and Graham's *Primitive Mysteries*," *Journal of Women and Religion* 11(1992): 6–17.

15. I use the term *man* as distinct from human very carefully here. The italics and underlining are for emphasis and are mine.

16. Freedberg, *Power of Images*, esp. pp. 1–26.

17. See, for example, Robert Rosenblum, *The*

Dog in Art: From Rococo to Postmodernism (London: Murray, 1989), or Apostolos-Cappadona, *Dictionary of Christian Art* (New York: Continuum Publshing, 1986), p. 107.

18. Apostolos-Cappadona, *Dictionary of Christian Art,* p. 107.

19. Samuel Taylor Coleridge, *Biographia Literaria* (London: J.M. Dent, 1975 [1817]). See especially book I, chs. IV and XIII.

20. Mircea Eliade, *The Sacred and the Profane* (New York: Harcourt Brace, 1959), esp. pp. 9–16.

21. Kenneth Clark, *Animals and Men: Their Relationship as Reflected in Western Art from Prehistory to the Present Day* (New York: William Morrow, 1977), p. 22.

22. Eliade's concept of the "nostalgia for paradise" was a common theme in much of his writings. Concrete examples with special relationship to animals in religious art is found in Mircea Eliade, "Survivals and Camouflages of Myths," and "Beauty and Faith," in his *Symbolism, The Sacred, and the Arts,* pp. 38, 92 respectively.

23. Clark, *Animals and Men,* p. 61.

IX

ANIMALS AS SUBJECTS

ETHICAL IMPLICATIONS FOR SCIENCE

Wild Justice, Social Cognition, Fairness, and Morality

A Deep Appreciation for the Subjective Lives of Animals

MARC BEKOFF

Social Cognition and Virtuous Nature

I have known many dogs, and many a story I could tell of their wisdom and devotion; but to none do I owe so much as to Stickeen. At first the least promising and least known of my dog-friends, he suddenly became the best known of them all. Our storm-battle for life brought him to light, and through him as through a window I have ever since been looking with deeper sympathy into all my fellow mortals.

(Muir 1990:69–70).

Nonhuman animals (hereafter "animals") are subjects, not objects. They have their own lives and are not to be viewed or treated as backpacks, couches, or bicycles. This, to me, is an undebatable claim. So, when one examines the nitty-gritty details of their lives or how they spend their time, when one observes who they interact with, where they do what they do and how

they do it, or when one studies their intellectual and cognitive abilities and their deep emotional lives, one gainsnot only a full appreciation of *their* lives, but also a full appreciation of human spirituality and what it is to be human (Bekoff 2001a). I hope, in this brief essay, to provide a window—an entry—through which you can view the subjective worlds of other animals and come away with a greater understanding and heightened feeling for who these wonderful beings are.

Thomas Berry's prologue to this volume speaks to this theme when he suggests: "we cannot be truly ourselves in any adequate manner without all our companion beings throughout the earth. This larger community constitutes our greater self." It takes only a little familiarity with modern scientific literature to realize that many of the grounds traditionally cited for claims about human uniqueness—tool use, language use, self-awareness and self-consciousness, culture, art, and rationality—are no longer defensible given the enormous growth in our knowledge of our animal kin with whom we share Earth.

Minding Animals and Deepening Ethology

The study of animals' minds is extremely exciting, challenging, and frustrating. There are innumerable dimensions to their cognitive and emotional capacities (Bekoff 2002a–2006; Bekoff, Allen, and Burghardt 2002). In my own research on social behavior and behavioral ecology, I stress evolutionary, ecological, and developmental (ontogenetic) perspectives, and I try to understand individual differences within species and variations among them. Variation is not noise to be dispensed with but rather information that highlights just how different individuals, even closely related individuals, can be. My approach is called the "comparative approach to the study of behavior" (Allen and Bekoff 1997) and if I am to be labeled at all, then call me a "cognitive ethologist." I have done much interdisciplinary work, and I consider myself a pluralist.

I also work at different levels of analysis, for I am an interdisciplinary holist at heart. I prefer to tackle "big" questions. I also do not shy away from conducting detailed statistical analyses, but never do the animals I am studying get thrown aside as numbers, unnamed variables in an equation, or points on a graph. It is important that the "protective membrane of statistics" (Randour 2000:xvii) not shield us from the worlds of other animals—their joys and pains, their wisdom, their otherness.

When I study animals I try to "mind" them. Basically, the phrase "minding animals" means two things. First, it refers to caring for other animal beings, respecting them for who they are, appreciating their own world views, and wondering what and how they feel and why. Second, it refers to the fact that many animals have very active and thoughtful minds.

I also call myself a deep ethologist. I, as the "see-er," try to become the "seen." When I observe animals I become coyote, I become penguin (I also become tree, and often I become rock). I name my animal friends and try to step into their sensory and motor worlds to discover what they might be like, how they sense their surroundings, and how they move about and behave in certain situations. The worlds of other animals are laden with magic and wonder. Just as we exclaim "Wow" when we marvel over the mysterious lives of other animals, I would not be surprised if they say "Wow" in their own ways as they experience the ups and downs of their daily lives and the grandeur and magic of the environs in which they live.

On Being a Dogocentrist

My research and that of others begins with the question, "What is it like to be a specific animal?" So, when I study dogs, for example, I try to be a dogocentrist and practice dogomorphism. Thus, when I claim that a dog is happily playing, I call it dog-joy, and that dog-joy may be different from chimpanzee-joy. There are important species and individual differences in behavior, cognitive capacities, and emotions, and so it is wrong and simplistic to claim that if animal joy is not like our joy then they do not have it. Perhaps we are the ones who do not have it.

What it basically comes down to is that, as humans studying other animals, we cannot totally lose our anthropocentric perspective. But we must try as hard as possible to blend in the animals' viewpoints to the ways in which we study, describe, interpret, and explain their behavior.

The Necessity for Biocentric Anthropomorphism

We are obliged to acknowledge that *all psychic interpretation of animal behavior must be on the analogy of human experience.* ... Whether we will or no, we must be anthropomorphic in the notions we form of what takes place in the mind of an animal.

(Washburn 1909:13)

Let me say a few words about anthropomorphism (for more detailed discussion see Bekoff 2002a, 2004, 2006). Anthropomorphism is inevitable. Unfortunately, many researchers have ignored what is so very obvious: We are humans, and we have by necessity a human view of the world. The way we describe and explain the behavior of other animals is limited by the language we use to talk about things in general. By engaging in anthropomorphism—using human terms to explain animals' emotions or feelings—we are making other animals' worlds accessible to ourselves. But this is not to say that other animals are happy or sad in the same ways in which humans (or even others of their species) are happy or sad. Using anthropomorphic language does not have to discount the animals' point of view. Anthropomorphism allows other animals' behavior and emotions to be accessible to us. Thus, I maintain that we can be *biocentrically anthropomorphic* and do rigorous science; in fact, our anthropomorphism can be a tool rather than an obstacle to such rigor.

The Use of Animals by Humans and the Activist Response

I am deeply concerned with the nature and asymmetry of human-animal interactions from theoretical and practical perspectives (Bekoff 1998a, b, c, 2002a, 2006; Goodall and Bekoff 2002), specifically the anthropocentric use of animals that usually is justified by some form of a utilitarian calculus in which human benefits are traded off against costs to the animal. When the benefits outweigh the costs, animal use is justified. I also want to stress that indifference about animals is deadly, not only for them

but also for us. Activism for animals has helped me tap into my own spirituality, for there are numerous costs to activism—harassment, intimidation, humiliation, and frustration—that often become personal. Compassionate people who push the envelope can easily engender the wrath of others.

Science and the Presumption of Omniscience

Often scientists discount possibilities in the absence of data, but a clear distinction should be made between what is *not* found by science and what is found to be *non-existent* by science. What science finds to be non-existent, we must accept as non-existent; but what science merely does not find is a completely different matter. ... It is quite clear that there are many, many mysterious things.

(His Holiness the Dalai Lama 1999:9)

While science has much to offer, science does not have a monopoly on truth. There are many ways of knowing. Scientists sometimes parade about as know-it-alls, afraid to utter "I don't know." The presumption of omniscience not only precludes learning about much of the mystery and awe of the natural world, but it also presents the big business of science as an arrogant and authoritarian enterprise that offends nonscientists.

There needs to be a new social contract between science and society that is characterized by two-way dialogue (Gibbons 1999). Science will continually have to be legitimized. Thus the dialogue will have to go two ways—science to society and society to science. Scientists have numerous and deep social responsibilities that can no longer be ignored (Mackey 1999; Bekoff 2000a, 2002a; Bradshaw and Bekoff 2001).

Many are also concerned with the politics, economics (rush for patents, financial gains), and arrogance of science. While we are certainly making some progress in living in harmony with other animals and inanimate landscapes, we are nowhere near to achieving a high grade in these encounters.

The Importance of Interdisciplinary Cooperation: The Evolution of Social Morality and Wild Justice

There are many areas in which we scientists can pursue interesting and important questions that center on human spirituality and the place of humans in the world. One such area concerns the evolution of social morality. People often wonder if some animals have codes of social conduct that regulate their behavior in terms of what is permissible and what is not permissible during social encounters. They want to know just what are the moral capacities of animals—are they moral agents with a moral sense who are able to live in moral communities? In a recent issue of *Journal of Consciousness Studies* (vol. 7, no. 1/2, 2000), researchers from many different disciplines debated the evolutionary origins of morality. These scholars were interested in discussing animal roots on which human morality might be built, even if it is not identical to animal morality. Charles Darwin's (1859; [1872] 1998) ideas about evolutionary continuity, that behavioral, cognitive, emotional, and moral variations among different species are differences in degree rather than in kind, are often invoked in such exercises. This view argues that there are shades of gray among different animals as well as between nonhumans and humans, that the differences among species are not black and white, with no transition stages or inexplicable jumps. There is not a void in the evolution of moral capacity or agency. Current work in evolutionary biology and anthropology suggests that linear scales of evolution, in which there are large gaps between humans and at least some animals, are simplistic views of the evolutionary process.

The study of the evolution of morality, specifically cooperation and fairness, is closely linked to science, religion, theology, spirituality, and perhaps even different notions of God, in that ideas about continuity and discontinuity (the possible uniqueness of humans and other species), individuality, and freedom need to be considered in detail. Furthermore, it is important to discuss relationships among science, religion, and God, because spirituality and the notion of one form of God or another had strong influences on the evolution of our ancestors and their cognitive, emotional, and moral lives.

Recently, Gregory Peterson (2000; see also Peterson 1999) has pondered the evolutionary roots of morality (stages that he refers to as "quasi-morality" and "proto-morality" in animals) and religion in relation to the roles played by cognition and culture. He also has stressed the importance of recognizing continuities and discontinuities with other animals, arguing ultimately (and speciesistically) that while some animals might possess proto-morality (they are able "to rationally deliberate actions and their consequences" [2000:475]), none other than humans is "genuinely moral," because to be able to be genuinely moral requires higher emergent levels of cognition as well as culture and the world view that culture provides, namely, religion. Peterson claims that "Quasi-moral and proto-moral systems do not require a global framework that guides decision making. They are always proximate and pragmatic. In these systems, there is no long-term goal or ideal state to be achieved. Yet, genuine morality is virtually inconceivable without such conceptions" (2000:478).

But if one views stages of moral evolution as Peterson does, it looks like quasi-morality and proto-morality are less than genuine morality. It is also an understatement to note that it is extremely difficult to study the evolution of morality in any animal species, and the very notion of animal morality itself often makes for heated discussions. When animals are studied in their own worlds they may indeed be found to have their own form of genuine morality, and there might indeed be long-term goals and ideal states to be achieved. Our anthropocentric view of other animals, in which humans are so taken with themselves, is far too narrow. The worlds and lives of other animals are not identical to those of humans and may vary from species to species and even within species. The same problems arise in the study of emotions if we believe that emotions in animals are going to be identical to or even recognizably similar among different species. While Irwin Bernstein's concern that "morality in animals might lie outside of the realm of measurement techniques available to science" (2000:34) needs to be taken seriously, nonetheless, it seems clear that detailed comparative analyses of social behavior in animals can indeed provide insights into the evolution of social morality. Peterson also claims that any sociobiological account (based on selfishness or combativeness) of human morality is incomplete. I agree, and I also argue that this is so for some nonhuman animals as well. Elsewhere (Bekoff 2001b, 2002a, 2002b, 2004) I discuss comparative data on social play behavior in hope of broadening the array of species in which researchers attempt to study animal morality. Of great interest is the notion of "behaving fairly." By "behaving fairly" I mean the idea that when they engage in various sorts of social encounters animals often have social expectations, which, if violated, constitutes being treated unfairly because of a lapse in social etiquette.

In some nonhuman animals, as in humans, it is through social cooperation that groups (communities) are built from individuals agreeing to work in harmony with other individuals. Whether or not individuals lose various freedoms when balanced against the benefits that accrue when they work for the good of a group is unknown and needs to be studied more carefully in various species.

In my view, cooperation is not always merely a byproduct of tempering aggressive and selfish tendencies (combating Richard Dawkins's selfish genes; Dawkins 1976) and attempts at reconciliation. Rather, cooperation and fairness can evolve on their own because they are important

in the formation and maintenance of social relationships. The combative Hobbesian world in which individuals are constantly at one another's throats is not the natural state of affairs, nature is not always "red in tooth and claw," and altruism is not always simply selfishness disguised. Dawkins (2001) himself has been quoted as saying "A pretty good definition of the kind of society in which I don't want to live is a society founded on the principles of Darwinism."

Does It Feel Good to Be Fair?

Are some animals capable of the emotions and empathy that underlie morality? To skeptically dismiss animals as nothing but nonsentient automatons is a dead end. Skeptics need to share the burden of proof with those who claim that some animals have highly evolved, passionate natures. While one cannot prove without doubt that some animals have rich emotional lives, it also is impossible to prove that they do not.

Watching animals in action has convinced many researchers, including myself, that they possess various emotions upon which a moral sense is built. We know that in humans the amygdala and hypothalamus are important in emotional experiences and that they are mediated by neurotransmitters such as dopamine, serotonin and oxytocin. We also know that many animals, especially mammals, share with humans the same neurological structures and chemicals (Panksepp 1998; Bekoff 2002a). Of course, this does not necessarily mean animals share our feelings, but careful observation of individuals during social encounters suggests that at least some of them do. While their feelings are not necessarily identical to ours, there is no reason why they should be. Indeed, it is unlikely that any two humans share precisely the same feelings when a given emotion is expressed.

Empathy is also important to consider. Preston and de Waal (2002) argue that empathy it is more widespread among animals than has previously been recognized (see also Kuczaj, et al. 2001). In one classic study, Wechlin, Masserman, and Terris (1964) showed that a hungry rhesus monkey would not take food if doing so subjected another monkey to an electric shock. In similar situations rats will also hold back when they know their actions would cause pain to another individual. In another study, Diana monkeys were trained to insert a token into a slot to obtain food (Markowitz 1982). A male was observed helping the oldest female, who had failed to learn the task. On three occasions he picked up the tokens she had dropped, put them into the machine, and allowed her to have the food. His behavior seemed to have no benefits for him at all; there did not seem to be any hidden agenda.

Along these lines, de Waal observed Kuni, a captive female bonobo, capture a starling and take the bird outside and place it on its feet (Preston and de Waal 2002). When the bird did not move Kuni tossed it in the air. When the starling did not fly Kuni took it to the highest point in her enclosure, carefully unfolded its wings and threw it in the air. The starling still did not fly and Kuni then guarded and protected it from a curious juvenile.

Elephants also may show concern for others. Joyce Poole (1998), who has studied African elephants for decades, was told a story about a teenage female who was suffering from a withered leg on which she could put no weight. When a young male from another group began attacking the injured female, a large adult female chased the attacking male, returned to the young female, and touched her crippled leg with her trunk. Poole argues that the adult female was showing empathy and sympathy.

While good stories are not enough to make a compelling argument, there are so many such anecdotes that can be used to provide a solid basis for further detailed empirical research. Ignoring them is to ignore a rich data base. I have argued elsewhere (Bekoff 2002a) that "the plural of anecdote is data."

It is important to consider the possibility that it feels good to be fair to others, to cooperate with them and to treat them fairly, to forgive them for their mistakes and shortcomings. Recent neural imaging research on humans by Rilling and his colleagues (Rilling et al. 2002) has shown that the brain's pleasure centers are strongly activated when people cooperate with one another, that we might be wired to be fair or nice to one another. (I do not want to argue here that "being fair" always means "being nice.") This is extremely significant research, for it posits that there is a strong neural basis for human cooperation and that it feels good to cooperate, so that being nice is rewarding in social interactions and might be a stimulus for fostering cooperation and fairness. This sort of noninvasive research is precisely what is needed on other animals. Studies of the evolution of social morality need to consider seriously the rich cognitive ("intellectual") and deep emotional lives of other animals (Bekoff 2000b, 2002a, 2002b, 2006) and how these capacities and a sense of self figure into a moral sensibility and the ability to make moral judgments. Truth be told, we really do not know much about these capacities even in our primate relatives despite claims that we do (Bekoff 2002c, 2002d, 2003a, 2004; Peterson 2003; Bekoff and Sherman 2004). Do some animals say "Wow, that's me!" when they look into a mirror? We really do not know.

Speciesism and the Taxonomic Distribution of Moral Capacity: The Importance of Studying Social Carnivores

Currently we simply do not have enough data to make hard and fast claims about the taxonomic distribution among different species of the cognitive skills and emotional capacities necessary for being able to empathize with others, to behave fairly, or to be moral agents. Peter Marler (1996:22) concluded his review of social cognition in nonhuman primates and birds as follows:

"I am driven to conclude, at least provisionally, that there are more similarities than differences between birds and primates. Each taxon has significant advantages that the other lacks." Michael Tomasello and Josep Call (1997:399–400) summarized their comprehensive review of primate cognition by noting that "[t]he experimental foundation for claims that apes are 'more intelligent' than monkeys is not a solid one, and there are few if any naturalistic observations that would substantiate such broad based, species-general claims." While Flack and de Waal's (2000) and others' focus is on nonhuman primates as the most likely animals to show precursors to human morality, others have argued that we might learn as much or more about the evolution of human social behavior by studying social carnivores (Schaller and Lowther 1969; Tinbergen 1972; Thompson 1975), species whose social behavior and organization resemble that of early hominids in a number of ways—of labor, food sharing, care of young, and inter- and intrasexual dominance hierarchies. What we really need are long-term field studies of social animals for which it would be reasonable to hypothesize that emotions and morality have played a role in the evolution of sociality, and that emotions and morality are important in the development and maintenance of social bonds that allow individuals to work together for the benefit of all group members. Stories about wild animals are also important for informing us about what they do in the course of their life cycles (Bekoff 2002a). Naturalistic studies, often thought to be "soft science," need not be casualties of "hard" science.

Animal Play: Lessons in Cooperation, Fairness, and Spirit

Animal play is obvious (for definitions of social play see Bekoff and Byers 1981, 1998; Fagen 1981; Power 2000; Burghardt 2005). Indeed, social play in animals is an exhilarating activity in which to engage and to observe. The rhythm, dance, and spirit of animals at play is incredibly contagious.

I think of play as being characterized by what I call the "Five S's of Play," its Spirit, Symmetry, Synchrony, Sacredness, and Soulfulness. The Spirit of play is laid bare for all to see as animals run about, wrestle, and knock one another over. The Symmetry and Synchrony of play are reflected in the harmony of the mutual agreements to trust one another—individuals seem to share intentions to cooperate with one another to prevent play from spilling over into fighting. This trust is Sacred. Finally, there is a deepness to animal play in that the players are so immersed in play that they are the play. Play is thus a Soulful activity, perhaps the essence of individuals' being at the moment as they play from deep in their hearts.

Play is about being; there are no whys in play. There also is a feeling of incredible freedom and creativity in the flow of play. So it is important also to keep in mind the six F's of play: Flexibility, Freedom, Friendship, Frolic, Fun, and Flow. As they run about, jump on one another, somersault, and bite one another, animals create confusing scenarios. Behavior patterns that are observed in mating are intermixed in flexible kaleidoscopic sequences with actions that are used during fighting, looking for prey, and avoiding being eaten.

Studies of the chemistry of play support the claim that play is fun. Dopamine (and perhaps serotonin and norepinephrine) are important in the regulation of play. Rats show an increase in dopamine activity when anticipating the opportunity to play (Siviy 1998), and they enjoy being playfully tickled (Panksepp 2000). There is also a close association between opiates and play (Panksepp 1998). Neurobiological data are essential for learning more about whether play truly is a subjectively pleasurable activity for animals as it seems to be for humans. Siviy's and Panksepp's findings suggest that it is. In light of these neurobiological (hard) data concerning possible neurochemical bases for various moods, in this case joy and pleasure, skeptics who claim that animals do not feel emotions might be more likely to accept the idea that enjoyment could well be a motivator for play behavior.

Fine-Tuning Play: Why Cooperate and Play Fairly?

In a long-term and continuing study of social play I also found that play signals in infant canids (domestic dogs, wolves, and coyotes) were not used at random, especially when biting accompanied by rapid side-to-side shaking of the head was performed (Bekoff 1995). Biting accompanied by rapid side-to-side shaking of the head is performed during serious aggressive and predatory encounters and can easily be misinterpreted if its meaning is not modified by a play signal.

Play signals are an example of what ethologists call "honest signals." There is little evidence that social play is a manipulative or "Machiavellian" activity. Play signals are rarely used to deceive others in canids or other species. There are no studies of which I am aware that actually look at the relative frequencies of the occurrence of honest and deceptive play signaling, but my own long-term observations indicate that deceptive signaling is so rare that I cannot remember more than a few occurrences in thousands of play sequences. Cheaters are unlikely to be chosen as play partners, because others can simply refuse to play with them and choose others. Limited data from my personal observations of infant coyotes show that cheaters have difficulty getting other young coyotes to play. It is not known if individuals select play partners based on what they have observed during play by others.

Domestic dogs have little tolerance for cheaters, who may be avoided or chased from play groups. There seems to a sense of what is right, wrong, and fair. While studying dog play on a beach in San Diego, Alexandra Horowitz (2002) observed a dog she called Up-ears enter into a play group and interrupt the play of two other dogs, Blackie and Roxy. Up-ears was chased out of the group, and when she returned Blackie and Roxy stopped playing and looked off in the direction from which they had heard a distant sound. Roxy began moving in that direction, and Up-ears ran off following their line of sight. Roxy and Blackie immediately began playing once again.

Even in rats fairness and trust are important in the dynamics of playful interactions. Sergio Pellis (2002), a psychologist at the University of Lethbridge in Canada, discovered that sequences of rat play consist of individuals assessing and monitoring one another and then fine-tuning and changing their own behavior to maintain the play mood. When the rules of play are violated, when fairness breaks down, so does play.

Why do animals carefully use play signals to tell others that they really want to play and not try to dominate them? There is a premium on playing fairly and trusting others to do so as well. There are codes of social conduct that regulate actions that are and are not permissible, and the existence of these codes likely speaks to the evolution of social morality. There can be no better atmosphere in which to learn social skills than during social play, where there are few penalties for transgressions. Individuals might also generalize codes of conduct learned in playing with specific individuals to other group members and to other situations such as sharing food, defending resources, grooming, and giving care. Social morality does not mean other animals are behaving unfairly when they kill for food, for example, for they have evolved to do this.

Can Animals Forgive?

Even for the behavior of forgiving, which is often attributed solely to humans, the renowned evolutionary biologist David Sloan Wilson (2002) shows that forgiveness is a complex biological adaptation. In his book *Darwin's Cathedral: Evo-*

lution, Religion, and the Nature of Society, Wilson concludes that "forgiveness has a biological foundation that extends throughout the animal kingdom." And further, "Forgiveness has many faces—*and needs to*—in order to function adaptively in so many different contexts." While Wilson concentrates mainly on human societies his views can easily be extended—and responsibly so—to nonhuman animals. Indeed, Wilson points out that adaptive traits such as forgiveness might not require as much brain power as once thought. This is not to say that animals aren't smart but rather that forgiveness might be a trait that is basic to many animals, even if they don't have especially big and active brains. Perhaps if we try to learn more about forgiveness in animals and how it functions in play we will also learn to live more compassionately and cooperatively with one another.

Playtime generally is safe time—transgressions and mistakes are forgiven and apologies are accepted by others, especially when one player is a youngster who is not yet a competitor for social status, food, or mates. There is a certain innocence or ingenuousness in play. Individuals must cooperate with one another when they play—they must negotiate agreements to play (Bekoff 1995). The highly cooperative nature of play has evolved in many other species (Fagen 1981; Bekoff 1995, 2002a, 2004; Bekoff and Allen 1998; Power 2000; Burghardt 2004).

During early development there is a small time window when individuals can play without being responsible for their own well-being. This time period is generally referred to as the socialization period, for this is when species-typical social skills are learned most rapidly. It is important for all individuals to engage in at least *some* play, and there is a premium for playing fairly if one is to be able to play at all. If individuals do not play fairly they may not be able to find willing play partners. In many species individuals also show play-partner preferences and it is possible that these preferences are based on the trust that individuals place in one another.

Wild Justice, Social Play, and Social Morality: Doing What Comes Naturally

Justice presumes a personal concern for others. It is first of all a sense, not a rational or social construction, and I want to argue that this sense is, in an important sense, natural.

(Solomon 1995:102).

It is not difficult to imagine the emergence of justice and honor out of the practices of cooperation.

(Damasio, 2003:162).

To stimulate further comparative research (and the development of models) on a wider array of species than has previously been studied, I offer the hypothesis that social morality, in this case behaving fairly, is an adaptation that is shared by many mammals, rather than being confined to the primates. Behaving fairly evolved because it helped young animals acquire social (and other) skills needed as they mature into adults. A focus on social cooperation is needed to balance the plethora of research that is devoted to social competition and selfishness (for further discussion see Boehm 1999; Singer 1999; Wilson 2002).

I also wonder if our view of the world would have been different had Charles Darwin been a female, if some or many of the instances in which competition is invoked were viewed as cooperation. Women tend to "see" more cooperation in nature than do men. Adams and Burnett (1991) discovered that female ethologists working in East Africa use a substantially different descriptive vocabulary than do their male colleagues. Of the nine variables they studied, those concerning cooperation and female gender were the most important distinguishing between women's and men's word use. They concluded that "The variable COOPERATION demonstrates the appropriateness of feminist claims to connection and cooperation as women's models for behaviour, as divergent from the traditional competitive model." Why women and men approach the same subject from a different perspective remains largely unanswered. Perhaps there is more cooperation than meets the eye.

Group-living animals may provide many insights into animal morality. In many social groups individuals develop and maintain tight social bonds that help to regulate social behavior. Individuals coordinate their behavior—some mate, some hunt, some defend resources, some accept subordinate status—to achieve common goals and to maintain social stability. Consider pack-living wolves. For a long time researchers thought pack size was regulated by available food resources. Wolves typically feed on such prey as elk and moose, each of which is larger than an individual wolf. Successfully hunting such large ungulates takes more than one wolf, so it made sense to postulate that wolf packs evolved because of the size of wolves' prey. Defending food might also be associated with pack-living. However, long-term research by David Mech (1970) showed that pack size in wolves was regulated by social, not food-related, factors. Mech discovered that the number of wolves who could live together in a coordinated pack was governed by the number of wolves with whom individuals could closely bond ("social attraction factor") balanced against the number of individuals from whom an individual could tolerate competition ("social competition factor"). Codes of conduct and packs broke down when there were too many wolves. Whether or not the dissolution of packs was due to individuals behaving unfairly is unknown, but this would be a valuable topic for future research in wolves and other social animals. Solomon (1995:143) contends that "[a] wolf who is generous can expect generosity in return. A wolf who violates another's ownership zone can expect to be punished, perhaps ferociously, by others." These claims can easily be studied empirically. (For interesting studies of the "social complexity hypothesis" that claims "that animals living in large social groups should display enhanced cognitive abilities" when com-

pared to those who do not (see Bond, Kamil, and Balda 2003:479; Drea and Frank 2003).

In social groups, individuals often learn what they can and cannot do, and the group's integrity depends upon individuals agreeing that certain rules regulate their behavior. At any given moment individuals know their place or role and that of other group members. As a result of lessons in social cognition and empathy that are offered in social play, individuals learn what is "right" or "wrong"—what is acceptable to others—the result of which is the development and maintenance of a social group that operates efficiently. The absence of social structure and boundaries can produce gaps in morality that lead to the dissolution of a group (Bruce Gottlieb, personal communication).

To sum up, I argue that mammalian social play is a useful behavioral phenotype on which to concentrate in order to learn more about the evolution of fairness and social morality. In the absence of adequate information, it is premature to dismiss the possibility that social play has some role in the evolution of fairness and social morality, or to assert that animals other than primates are unable to choose to behave fairly because they lack the necessary cognitive skills or emotional capacities. Mark Ridley (1996) points out that humans seem to be inordinately upset about unfairness, but we do not know much about other animals' reaction to unfairness. He suggests that perhaps behaving fairly pays off in the long run. Dugatkin's and my model of the development and evolution of cooperation and fairness (Dugatkin and Bekoff 2003) suggests it might. These are empirical questions for which the comparative data base is scant. Hauser (2000) concluded that there is no evidence that animals can evaluate whether an act of reciprocation is fair. However, he did not consider social play in his discussion of animal morality and moral agency. De Waal (1996) remains skeptical about the widespread taxonomic distribution of cognitive empathy after briefly considering social play, but he remains open to the possibility that cognitive empathy might be found in animals other than the great apes (see Preston and de Wall 2002). Let me also stress that I am not arguing that there is a gene for fair or moral behavior. As with any behavioral trait, the underlying genetics is bound to be complex, and environmental influences may be large and difficult to pin down. Nonetheless, provided there is variation in levels of morality among individuals, and provided virtue is rewarded by a greater number of offspring, then genes associated with good behavior are likely to accumulate in subsequent generations. The observation that play is rarely unfair or uncooperative is surely an indication that natural selection acts to weed out those individuals who do not play by the rules.

Future comparative research that considers the nature and details of the social exchanges that are needed for animals to engage in play —reciprocity and cooperation—will undoubtedly produce data that bear on the questions that I raise here and also help to "operationalize" the notion of behaving fairly by informing us about what sorts of evidence confirm that animals are behaving with some sense of fairness. In the absence of this information it is premature to dismiss the possibility that social play plays some role in the evolution of fairness and social morality or that animals other than primates are unable to choose to behave fairly because they lack the necessary cognitive skills or emotional capacities. These are empirical questions for which the comparative data base is scant.

Play may be a unique category of behavior in that asymmetries are tolerated more than in other social contexts. Play cannot occur if the individuals choose not to engage in the activity, and the equality (or symmetry) needed for play to continue makes it different from other forms of seemingly cooperative behavior (e.g., hunting and care giving). This sort of egalitarianism is thought to be a precondition for the evolution of social morality in humans. From whence did it arise? We really do not know much about the origins of egalitarianism. Armchair discussions, while important, will do little in compari-

son to our having direct experiences with other animals. In my view, studies of the evolution of social morality are among the most exciting and challenging projects that behavioral scientists (ethologists, geneticists, evolutionary biologists, neurobiologists, psychologists, anthropologists), theologians, and religious scholars face. We need to rise to the task before us rather than dismiss in a speciesistic manner the moral lives of other animals.

I have no doubt that studying and learning about animal play can teach us to live more compassionately with heart and love. Keep in mind the Spirit, Symmetry, Synchrony, Sacredness, and Soul of play. Learning about the evolution of cooperation, fairness, trust, and social morality goes well beyond traditional science and can be linked to religion, theology, and perhaps even to different notions of God, because ideas about continuity and discontinuity (the possible uniqueness of humans and other species) and individuality have to be taken into account.

The importance of interdisciplinary collaboration and cooperation in studies of animal cognition, cooperation, and moral behavior cannot be emphasized too strongly. It is clear that morality and virtue didn't suddenly appear in the evolutionary epic with the advent of humans. While fair play in animals may be a rudimentary form of social morality, it still could be a forerunner of more complex and more sophisticated human moral systems. It is self-serving anthropocentric speciesism to claim that we are the *only* moral beings in the animal kingdom. It is also a simplistic and misleading view to assume that humans are merely naked apes.

The origins of virtue, egalitarianism, and morality are more ancient that our own species. Humans also aren't necessarily morally superior to other animals. Indeed, it might just be that animal morality is purer than human morality because animals likely don't have as sophisticated notions of right and wrong. Wouldn't that be something? But, we will never learn about animal morality if we close the door on the possibility that it exists. It is still far too early to draw the uncompromising conclusion that human morality is different in kind from animal morality and walk away in victory.

Animal Emotions: Exploring Passionate Nature

> It is hard to watch elephants' remarkable behavior during a family or bond group greeting ceremony, the birth of a new family member, a playful interaction, the mating of a relative, the rescue of a family member, or the arrival of a musth male, and not imagine that they feel very strong emotions which could be best described by words such as joy, happiness, love, feelings of friendship, exuberance, amusement, pleasure, compassion, relief, and respect.
>
> (Poole 1998: 90–91)

To me, the major question in the study of animal emotions is *not* "Do some animals experience a range of deep emotions?" but rather "Why have emotions evolved?"

If indeed the experienced researcher is right that elephants feel joy, might it not also be true that chimpanzees feel grief and depression, and dogs happiness and dejection? People disagree about the nature of animal emotions, especially concerning the question of whether any animals other than humans can feel emotions. Joyce Poole, who has studied elephants for more than two decades, believes that elephants have highly evolved emotional lives, and the ancient Greeks believed that many animals experience the same range of emotions as humans. Current research, especially in ethology, neurobiology, endocrinology, psychology, and philosophy, is providing compelling evidence that at least some animals likely feel a full range of emotions, including fear, joy, happiness, shame, embarrassment, resentment, jealousy, rage, anger, love, pleasure, compassion, respect, relief, disgust, sadness, despair, and grief (for detailed discussions and long lists of references see Panksepp 1998; Bekoff 2000b, 2000c, 2002a, 2006).

In my book, *The Smile of a Dolphin: Remarkable Accounts of Animal Emotions* (2000b), many world-famous researchers who have spent their lives with a wide variety of animals shared their stories about the emotional lives of the animals they know best. Their stories, supported by copious amounts of data, leave no doubt as to whether many animals experience the deepest of emotions ranging from joyful glee when playing to bereavement, grief, and depression over the loss of a mate, child, or other friend. Animals may even fall in love. So, writes Bernd Heinrich in his book, *Mind of the Raven* (1999:341): "Since ravens have long-term mates, I suspect that they fall in love like us, simply because some internal reward is required to maintain a long-term pair bond." Heinrich has studied and lived with ravens for many years and knows these wonderful birds well.

The study of animal emotions is an important endeavor, because not only will it allow us to achieve an understanding and appreciation of the lives of many of the animal beings with whom we share this splendid planet, it also will help us come to terms with how we "mind them"—especially how we treat our animal kin. One reason that many animals can form tight and reciprocal social bonds with one another and with humans is because of shared emotions. Emotions are the glue for the development and maintenance of these bonds.

Clearly, an understanding of behavior and neurobiology is necessary if we are ever to understand how emotions and cognition are linked. It is essential that we learn as much as we can about individuals' private experiences, feelings, and mental states. If and how animals' emotions are experienced is a challenge for future research. Consider two preeminent researchers' comments about whether any nonhuman animals display grief at the loss or absence of another.

The following vivid description is offered by Jane Goodall after she observed Flint, an eight-and-a-half year old chimpanzee, withdraw from his group, stop feeding, and finally die after his mother, Flo, died.

> Never shall I forget watching as, three days after Flo's death, Flint climbed slowly into a tall tree near the stream. He walked along one of the branches, then stopped and stood motionless, staring down at an empty nest. After about two minutes he turned away and, with the movements of an old man, climbed down, walked a few steps, then lay, wide eyes staring ahead. The nest was one which he and Flo had shared a short while before Flo died. ... In the presence of his big brother [Figan], [Flint] had seemed to shake off a little of his depression. But then he suddenly left the group and raced back to the place where Flo had died and there sank into ever deeper depression. ... Flint became increasingly lethargic, refused food and, with his immune system thus weakened, fell sick. The last time I saw him alive, he was hollow-eyed, gaunt and utterly depressed, huddled in the vegetation close to where Flo had died. ... The last short journey he made, pausing to rest every few feet, was to the very place where Flo's body had lain. There he stayed for several hours, sometimes staring and staring into the water. He struggled on a little further, then curled up—and never moved again.
>
> (Goodall 1990:196–97)

The Nobel laureate Konrad Lorenz observed grief in geese that was similar to grief in young children. He provided the following account:

> A greylag goose that has lost its partner shows all the symptoms that John Bowlby has described in young human children in his famous book *Infant Grief*. ... the eyes sink deep into their sockets, and the individual has an overall drooping experience, literally letting the head hang.
>
> (Lorenz 1991:251)

Other examples of grief are offered in *The Smile of a Dolphin* (2000b). Sea lion mothers, watching their babies being eaten by killer whales, squeal eerily and wail pitifully in the anguish of their loss. Dolphins have been observed struggling to save a dead infant. Elephants have stood guard over a stillborn baby for days with their head and ears hung down, quiet and moving slowly. Orphaned elephants who saw their mothers being killed often wake up screaming. Joyce Pool claims that grief and depression in orphan elephants is a real phenomenon. It has also been noted of traumatized orphaned gorillas: "The light in their eyes simply goes out, and they die" (McRae 2000:86). Comparative research in neurobiology, endocrinology, and behavior is needed to learn more about the subjective nature of animal grief.

Studying Animal Emotions: Where to From Here?

The best way to learn about the emotional lives of animals is to conduct noninvasive comparative and evolutionary ethological, neurobiological, and endocrinological research and to resist critics' claims that anthropomorphism has no place in these efforts. To claim that we cannot understand elephants, dolphins, or other animals unless "we are one of them" gets us nowhere. It is important to try to learn how animals live in their own worlds, to understand their own perspectives. Animals evolved in specific and unique situations, and it discounts their lives if we try to understand them only from our own perspective. Certainly, gaining this kind of knowledge is difficult, but it is not impossible.

There is much disagreement about the emotional lives of other animals, but we are learning more and more each day as researchers from different disciplines tackle the difficult questions that I have laid out elsewhere (Bekoff 2002a, 2004, 2006). The following questions can be used to set the stage for learning more about the evolution and expression of animal emotions: Our moods move us, so why not other animals?

Emotions help us to manage and regulate our relationships with others, so why not for other animals? Emotions are important for humans to adapt to specific circumstances, so why not for other animals? Emotions are an integral part of human life, so why not for other animals?

Current research suggests that no one single theory of emotions can explain all of the psychological phenomena that are called emotions. There is no doubt that there is continuity between the neurobehavioral systems that underlie human and nonhuman emotions, and that the differences between human and animal emotions are, in many instances, differences in degree rather than differences in kind.

In remaining open to the idea that many animals have rich emotional lives, even if we are wrong in some cases, little truly is lost. If we close the door on the possibility that many animals have rich emotional lives, even if they are very different from our own or from those of animals with whom we are most familiar, we will lose great opportunities to learn about the lives of animals with whom we share this wondrous planet.

The future holds many challenges and perhaps surprises for those who want to learn more about animal emotions. The rigorous study of animal emotions will require harnessing the best possible resources. These resources include researchers in various scientific disciplines who provide hard data and anecdotes, other scholars who study animals, nonacademics who observe animals and tell stories, and the animals themselves. There is ample room for hard and soft science in the study of animal emotions. There are many worlds beyond human experience. There are no substitutes for listening to and having *direct* experiences with other animals. We truly can ask such questions as, Do animals love one another? Do they mourn the loss of friends and loved ones? Do they resent others? Can they be embarrassed? Certainly our own lives will be richer for the effort we make to gain this knowledge, and the lives of other animals will be better

understood, more appreciated, and more highly respected. This knowledge can also be used to fuel activism for the benefit of animals.

Giving Thanks to Kindred Spirits

Our animal companions are spiritual beings abounding in generosity and love. We can learn much from them about compassion, kindness, generosity, devotion, respect, spirituality, and love. For example, by honoring a dog's trust we can tap into our own spirituality and humanness.

The pioneering and courageous holistic veterinarian, Allen Schoen, has recently written a wonderful and inspirational book titled *Kindred Spirits: How the Remarkable Bond between Humans and Animals Can Change the Way We Live* (2001). Schoen suggests that we "go forth and make a conscious, active effort to rejoice in the interconnectedness of all of life, every day. Love yourself by extending love to all other living beings … do something special to support the beauty of life on our one and only planet, Mother Earth" (p. 200). This is good, heartfelt advice, coming from a traditionally trained veterinarian who has gone beyond the narrow confines of scientific autonomy, authority, and presumed objectivity.

Let us make every effort to understand and to appreciate the essence of our companions. Let us praise them openly and thank them for who they are as we embrace their lessons in compassion, devotion, respect, spirituality, and love. Their lives and ours will be richer, more fulfilled, complete, and radiant. Love will abound, and the awe-inspiring universe as a whole will become a better place—a soulscape—in which to live in harmony with all of our kin, other life, and inanimate landscapes. Surely, a more compassionate world will be a better place in which to raise our children and theirs with grace and humility.

The Importance of Ethological Studies

I study foxes because I am still awed by their extraordinary beauty, because they outwit me, because they keep the wind and the rain on my face
... because it is fun.

(Macdonald 1987:15)

In my view, we need much more than traditional science—science that is not socially responsible, science that is autonomous and authoritarian, science that fragments the universe
and disembodies and alienates humans and
other animals—to make headway into understanding other animals and the world at large.
We need to broaden science to incorporate feeling, heart, spirit, soul, and love (for a recent and
compelling discussion, see Dalai Lama 2005).
Scientists need to exit their heads and go to their
hearts, and science needs to open its arms to
people who love the world and who have a reverence for all life. We need a science of unity, a
science of reconciliation.

How we view ourselves and other animals informs how we interact with and treat our animal kin. There are many lessons to be learned.
Open discussions about science, spirituality, religion, love, and God will enable us better to
come to terms with who we are in this splendid, awe-inspiring universe. Ethological studies
motivated by compassion, respect, understanding, appreciation, and love are needed. Some
lines from a poem by Thich Nhat Hanh with
which Schoen ends his book are important to
consider: "We are the shared emotions of all our
brethren, We are truly a kindred spirit with all
of life" (Schoen 2001:257). I feel that I am a
better scientist by being open rather than (ideologically, in the dogma of science) closing the
door on such rich and deep experiences. As I
wrote above, when I study coyotes I am coyote; when I study birds I am bird. Often when I
stare at a tree, I am tree. There is a strong sense
of oneness. We are all part of the same deeply
interconnected and interdependent community

in which I, the seer, am the seen, woven into a
seamless tapestry of unity with interconnecting
and reciprocal bonds."

Minding Animals, Loving Animals: Do Animals Exclaim "Wow!"?

My own spirituality is based on a deep drive for a
seamless unity that is motivated by compassion,
respect, and love. During my brief tenure on
this wondrous planet, I am more than happy to
open the door of my heart to all beings. I dream
of and envision a unified, peaceable kingdom—
a peaceful kinship—based on respect, compassion, forgiveness, and love. Animals are truly a
source of deep wisdom.

(Bekoff 2003b)

We can love animals more without loving people
less. We need to be motivated by love and not by
fear of what it will mean if we come to love animals for who they are. They need to be understood in their own worlds. As we learn about
other animals and how important they are to us,
we will learn more about ourselves. This knowledge and the intense feelings they bring forth
will help make us better to one another and to
the planet as whole. We need to do this now and
be proactive, for we have limited time. Time is
not on our side mainly because we are so powerful and ubiquitous. Cooperation among representatives from different disciplines combined
with holism and pluralism will surely help us
learn that science and religion are not incompatible. The study of animal behavior can help us
immensely.

If we forget that humans and other animals
are all part of the same interdependent world—
the more-than-human world (Abram 1996)—
and if we forget that humans and animals are
deeply interconnected at many different levels
—when things go amiss in our interactions with
animals (as they surely will), and animals are
set apart from and inevitably "below" humans,

I feel certain that we will miss the animals more than the animal survivors will miss us. The interconnectivity and spirit of the world will be lost, and these losses will make for a severely impoverished universe.

In the end, it boils down to love. The power of love must not be underestimated as we try to reconnect with nature and other animals (Ehrenfeld 1981; Goodall 1999; Sewall 1999; Bekoff 2001a, 2002a; Goodall and Bekoff 2002). We must love the Earth and the universe and all of their inhabitants, animate and inanimate.

In the grand scheme of things, individuals receive what they give. If love is poured out in abundance, it will be returned in abundance, and there is no fear of exhausting the potent self-reinforcing feeling that serves as a powerful stimulant for generating compassion, respect, and more love for all life. It is important to recognize that each individual plays an essential role and that each individual's spirit and love are intertwined with the spirit and love of others. These emergent interrelationships, which transcend individuals' embodied selves, foster a sense of oneness and can work in harmony to make this a better and more compassionate world for all beings.

So, as I have argued before and will continue to argue, when animals and other wild nature lose, we all lose. We must "stroll with our kin" and not leave them in our tumultuous wake of rampant destruction (Bekoff 2000d). Holism and universal compassion and love need to replace impersonal, objective reductionism that alienates and disembodies individuals, and dispenses with or fragments their hearts, their spirits, and their souls.

By stepping lightly into the lives of other animals, humans can enjoy the company of other animals without making them pay for our interest. I find myself continually exclaiming "Wow!" when I am immersed in Nature (Bekoff 2003b). But some might think that the question "Do animals say 'Wow!' as they experience the ups and downs of their daily lives?" is a frivolous one, one that is not tractable scientifically. I do not

think this is so. They likely have a sense of wonder about where they live and who they are and in the right circumstances many animals might look around and say "Wow!" We know that humans and other animals share the neural apparatus and neurochemicals that underlie the expression and experience of a wide variety of emotions. We know that many animals experience rich and deep emotional lives. We know that they can be happy and sad, that they can experience joy and grief.

I think that many animals exclaim "Wow!" in their own ways—when they are experiencing the panoply of joy and happiness associated with delighting in life's pleasures or when they are experiencing the agonizing depths of pain and suffering when their well-being and spirit are compromised, when we breach the trust they have in us. Surely we owe it to all animals to offer them the best life we can. Surely all beings benefit when we treat other animals with the dignity, compassion, respect, and love they deserve.

Animals are at once within us and without us. In many ways we need them more than they need us. In our absence most animals will go on to live quite contentedly. But, our hearts and spirits erode when we abuse other animals because they are an essential part of who we are. We must step lightly with respect, caring, compassion, humility, generosity, kindness, grace, and love when we trespass into animals' lives. We owe it to the animals, and we owe it to ourselves and especially to our children and theirs, to stop ravaging Earth. Love must rule.

When we pillage Earth we destroy the deep and reciprocal interconnections that define all life, the interrelationships that resonate in all beings and all things. It chills my heart to imagine being severed from the Earth community. Surely, we do not want to be remembered—if there's anyone around to recall—as the generation that killed nature.

When we desecrate Earth an eerie coldness prevails, for in slaying nature we kill ourselves, other animals, tree beings, landscapes, and the ubiquitous universal spirit that connects us all.

We destroy our and Nature's integrity. Let us honor other animals for who they are in their words, not for what they are in our own—often narrow—minds. Our curiosity about other animals need not harm them.

It is essential that we do better than our ancestors, and we surely have the resources to do so. The big question is whether we will choose to make the proactive commitment to making this a better world, a more compassionate world in which love is plentiful and shared, before it is too late. It is important to move forward and step lightly with kindness, compassion, generosity, respect, grace, and love. I believe we have already embarked on this pilgrimage. My optimism leads me in no other direction.

As we come to live more in harmony with Nature we can restore, rekindle, and re-create ourselves, and our psyches, which have been fragmented because of our alienation from animals and other Nature.

We need animals, Nature, and wildness. We need their spirit.

Acknowledgments

I thank Paul Waldau for going way beyond the call of duty for his help with this essay. Much of this chapter is excerpted from some of my other essays (mainly Bekoff 2001a, b, 2002a, 2004).

REFERENCES

Abram, D. 1996. *The Spell of the Sensuous: Perception and Language in a More-Than-Human World.* New York: Pantheon.

Adams, E. R. and G. W. Burnett. 1991. "Scientific Vocabulary Divergence Among Female Primatologists Working in East Africa. *Social Studies of Science* 21:547–60.

Allen, C., and M. Bekoff. 1997. *Species of Mind: The Philosophy and Biology of Cognitive Ethology.* Cambridge: M.I.T. Press.

Aureli, F., and F. B. M. de Waal. 2000. *Natural Conflict Resolution.* Berkeley: University of California Press.

Bekoff, M. 1975. "The Communication of Play Intention: Are Play Signals Functional?" *Semiotica* 15:231–39.

———. 1977a. "Social Communication in Canids: Evidence for the Evolution of a Stereotyped Mammalian Display." *Science* 197:1097–99.

———. 1977b. "Mammalian Dispersal and the Ontogeny of Individual Behavioral Phenotypes." *American Naturalist* 111:715–32.

———. 1995. "Play Signals as Punctuation: The Structure of Social Play in Canids." *Behaviour* 132:419–29.

———. 1998a. "Minding Animals." L. Hart, ed. *In*

Responsible Conduct of Research in Animal Behavior. New York: Oxford University Press, pp. 96–116.

———. 1998b. "Deep Ethology, Animal Rights, and the Great Ape/Animal Project: Resisting Speciesism and Expanding the Community of Equals." *Journal of Agricultural and Environmental Ethics* 10:269–96.

———, ed. 1998c. *Encyclopedia of Animal Rights and Animal Welfare.* Westport, CT: Greenwood Publishers.

———. 1998d. "Intentional Communication and Social Play: How and Why Animals Negotiate and Agree to Play." In M. Bekoff and J. A. Byers, eds., *Animal Play: Evolutionary, Comparative, and Ecological Perspectives.* New York: Cambridge University Press, pp. 97–114.

———. 2000a. "Redecorating Nature: Reflections on Science, Holism, Humility, Community, Reconciliation, Spirit, Compassion, and Love." *Human Ecology Review* 7:59–67.

———, ed. 2000b. *The Smile of a Dolphin: Remarkable Accounts of Animal Emotions.* New York: Random House, Discovery Books.

———. 2000c. "Animal Emotions: Exploring Passionate Natures." *BioScience* 50:861–70.

———. 2000d. *Strolling with Our Kin: Speaking for and Respecting Voiceless Animals*. New York: Lantern Books.

———. 2001a. "The Evolution of Animal Play, Emotions, and Social Morality: On Science, Theology, Spirituality, Personhood, and Love." *Zygon: Journal of Religion and Science* 36: 615–55.

———. 2001b. "Social Play Behaviour, Cooperation, Fairness, Trust and the Evolution of Morality." *Journal of Consciousness Studies* 8:81–90.

———. 2002a. *Minding Animals: Awareness, Emotions, and Heart*. New York: Oxford University Press.

———. 2002b. "Virtuous Nature." *New Scientist* 13 (July): 34–37.

———. 2002c. "Self-awareness." *Nature* 419:255.

———. 2002d. "Empathy: Common Sense, Science Sense, Wolves, and Well-being." *Behavioral and Brain Sciences* 25: 26–27.

———. 2003a. "Consciousness and Self in Animals: Some Reflections." *Zygon: Journal of Religion and Science* 38:229–45.

———. 2003b. "Minding Animals, Minding Earth: Science, Nature, Kinship, and Heart." *Human Ecology Review* 10:56–76.

———. 2004, *Wild Justice and Fair Play: Cooperation, Forgiveness and Morality in Animals, Biology and Philosophy* 19:489–520.

———. 2006. *Animal Passions and Beastly Virtues: Reflections on Redecorating Nature*. Philadelphia: Temple University Press.

Bekoff, M., C. Allen, and G.M. Burghardt, eds. 2002. *The Cognitive Animals*. Cambridge: M.I.T. Press.

Bekoff, M., and J.A. Byers. 1981. "A Critical Reanalysis of the Ontogeny of Mammalian Social and Locomotor Play: An Ethological Hornet's Nest." In K. Immelmann, G.W. Barlow, L. Petrinovich, and M. Main, eds., *Behavioral Development: The Bielefeld Interdisciplinary Project*. New York: Cambridge University Press pp., 296–337.

———. eds. 1998. *Animal Play: Evolutionary, Comparative, and Ecological Perspectives*. New York: Cambridge University Press.

Bekoff, M. and P.M. Sherman. 2004. *The Self-awareness Continuum. Trends in Ecology and Evolution*, vol. 19, 176–80.

Bernstein, Irwin S. 2000. "The Law of Parsimony Prevails: Missing Premises Allow Any Conclusion." *Journal of Consciousness Studies* 7:31–34.

Boehm, C. 1999. *Hierarchy in the Forest: The Evolution of Egalitarian Behavior*. Cambridge, Harvard University Press.

Bond, A., A.C. Kamil, and R.P. Balda. 2003. "Social Complexity and Transitive Inference in Corvids." *Animal Behaviour* 65:479–87.

Bradshaw, I.G.A. and M. Bekoff. 2001. "Ecology and Social Responsibility: The Re-Embodiment of Science." *Trends in Ecology and Evolution* 8, 460–465.

Burghardt, G.M. 2005. *The Genesis of Play*. Cambridge: MIT Press.

Dalai Lama. 1999 (His Holiness The). *The Path to Tranquility: Daily Wisdom*. New York: Viking Arkana.

———. *The Universe in a Single Atom: The Convergence of Science and Spirituality*. New York: Morgan Road Books.

Damasio, A. 1999a. *The Feeling of What Happens: Body and Emotion in the Making of Consciousness*. New York: Harcourt Brace.

———. 1999b. "How the Brain Creates the Mind." *Scientific American* 281:112–17.

———. 2003. *Looking for Spinoza: Joy, Sorrow, and the Feeling Brain*. New York: Harcourt.

Darwin, C. 1859. *On the Origin of Species By Means of Natural Selection*. London: Murray.

———. [1871] 1936. *The Descent of Man and Selection in Relation to Sex*. New York: Random House.

———. [1872] 1998. *The Expression of the Emotions in Man and Animals*. 3d ed. Introduction, Afterword, and Commentaries by Paul Ekman. New York: Oxford University Press.

Dawkins, R. 1976. *The Selfish Gene*. New York, Oxford University Press.

Dawkins, R. 2001. *Sustainability Doesn't Come Naturally: A Darwinian Perspective on Values*. www.environmentfoundation.net/richard-dawkins.htm

de Waal, F. 1996. *Good Natured*. Cambridge: Harvard University Press.

Drea, C.M. and L.G. Frank. 2003. "The Social Complexity of Spotted Hyenas." In F. de Waal and P.L. Tyack, eds., *Animal Social Complexity: Intelligence, Culture, and Individualized Societies*. Cambridge: Harvard University Press, pp. 121–48.

Dugatkin, L.A. and M. Bekoff, M. 2003. "Play and the Evolution of Fairness: A Game Theory Model." *Behavioural Processes* 60:209–14.

Ehrenfeld, D. 1981. *The Arrogance of Humanism*. New York: Oxford University Press.

Fagen, R. 1981. *Animal Play Behavior*. New York: Oxford University Press.

———. 1993. "Primate Juveniles and Primate Play." In M.E. Pereira and L.A. Fairbanks, eds. *Juvenile Primates: Life History, Development, and Behavior*. New York: Oxford University Press, pp. 183–96.

Flack, J.C., and Frans de Waal. 2000. "Any Animal Whatever: Darwinian Building Blocks of Morality in Monkeys and Apes." *Journal of Consciousness Studies* 7:1–29.

Gibbons, M. 1999. "Science's New Social Contract with Society." *Nature* 402:C81–C84.

Goodall, J. 1990. *Through a Window*. Boston: Houghton Mifflin.

———. 1999. *Reason for Hope: A Spiritual Journey*. New York: Warner Books.

Goodall, J. and M. Bekoff. 2002. *The Ten Trusts: What We Must Do to Care for the Animals We Love*. San Francisco: HarperCollins.

Hauser, Marc. 2000. *Wild Minds*. New York: Holt.

Heinrich, Bernd. 1999. *Mind of the Raven: Investigations and Adventures with Wolf-Birds*. New York: Cliff Street Books.

Horowitz, A.C. 2002. "The Behaviors of Theories of Mind, and a Case Study of Dogs at Play." Ph.D. dissertation, University of California, San Diego.

Kuczaj, S., K. Tranel, M. Trone, and H. Hill. 2001. "Are Animals Capable of Deception or Empathy? Implications for Animal Consciousness and Animal Welfare." *Animal Welfare* 10: S161–173.

Lorenz, K.Z. 1991. *Here I Am — Where Are You?* New York: Harcourt Brace Jovanovich.

Macdonald, D. 1987. *Running with the Fox*. New York: Facts on File.

Mackey, B.G. 1999. "Environmental Scientists, Advocacy, and the Future of Earth." *Environmental Conservation* 26:245–49.

Markowitz, H. 1982. *Behavioral Enrichment in the Zoo*. New York, Van Reinhold.

Marler, P. 1996. "Social Cognition: Are Primates Smarter than Birds?" In V. Nolan Jr. and E.D. Ketterson, eds. *Current Ornithology* 13:1–32. New York: Plenum Press.

McRae, M. 2000. "Central Africa's Orphaned Gorillas: Will They Survive the Wild?" *National Geographic* 197:84–97.

Mech, D. 1970. *The Wolf*. Garden City, N.Y.: Doubleday.

Muir, J. 1990. *Stickeen*. Berkeley: Heyday Books.

Panksepp, Jaak. 1998. *Affective Neuroscience*. New York: Oxford University Press.

———. 2000. "The Rat Will Play." In M. Bekoff, ed. (2003), pp. 146–47.

Pellis, S. 2002. "Keeping in Touch: Play Fighting and Social Knowledge." In Bekoff, Allen, and Burghardt (2002).

Peterson, G.R. 1999. "The Evolution of Consciousness and the Theology of Nature." *Zygon: Journal of Religion and Science* 34:283–306.

———. 2000. "God, Genes, and Cognizing Agents." *Zygon: Journal of Religion and Science* 35: 69–80.

———. 2003. "Being Conscious of Marc Bekoff: Thinking of Animal Self-consciousness." *Zygon: Journal of Religion and Science* 38:247–256.

Poole, J. 1998. "An Exploration of a Commonality Between Ourselves and Elephants." *Etica & Animali* 9:85–110.

Power, T.G. 2000. *Play and Exploration in Children and Animals*. Hillsdale, N.J.: Lawrence Erlbaum Associates.

Preston, S.D., and F.B.M. de Waal. 2002. "Empathy: Its Ultimate and Proximate Bases." *Behavioral and Brain Sciences*. 25:1–72.

Randour, M.L. 2000. *Animal Grace: Entering Spiri-

tual Relationship with Our Fellow Creatures. Novato, CA: New World Library.

Ridley, M. 1996. *The Origins of Virtue: Human Instincts and the Evolution of Cooperation.* New York: Viking.

Rilling, J. K., D. A. Gutman, T. R. Zeh, G. Pagnoni, G. S. Berns, and C. D. Kitts. 2002. "A Neural Basis for Cooperation." *Neuron* 36:395–405.

Schaller, G. B., and G. R. Lowther. 1969. "The Relevance of Carnivore Behavior to the Study of Early Hominids." *Southwestern Journal of Anthropology* 25:307–41.

Schoen, A. 2001. *Kindred Spirits: How the Remarkable Bond between Humans and Animals Can Change the Way We Live.* New York: Broadway Books.

Sewall, L. 1999. *Sight and Sensibility: The Ecopsychology of Perception.* New York: Jeremy P. Tarcher/Putnam.

Singer, P. 1999. *A Darwinian Left: Politics, Evolution, and Cooperation.* New Haven: Yale University Press.

Siviy, S. 1998. "Neurobiological Substrates of Play Behavior: Glimpses into the Structure and Function of Mammalian Playfulness." In M. Bekoff and J. A. Byers, eds. (1998), pp. 221–42.

Skyrms, B. 1996. *Evolution of the Social Contract.* New York: Cambridge University Press.

Smith, H. 2001. *Why Religion Matters.* San Francisco: Harper.

Sober, E. and D. S. Wilson. 1998. *Unto Others: The Evolution and Psychology of Unselfish Behavior.* Cambridge: Harvard University Press.

———. 2000. "Summary of: Unto Others: The Evolution and Psychology of Unselfish Behavior." *Journal of Consciousness Studies* 7:185–206.

Solomon, R. 1995. *A Passion for Justice: Emotions and the Origins of the Social Contract.* Lanham, MD: Rowman & Littlefield.

Thompson, P. R. 1975. "A Cross-Species Analysis of Carnivore, Primate, and Hominid Behavior." *Journal of Human Evolution* 4:113–24.

Tinbergen, N. [1951] 1989. *The Study of Instinct.* New York: Oxford University Press.

———. 1963. "On Aims and Methods of Ethology." *Zeitschrift für Tierpsychologie* 20:410–33.

———. 1972. Introduction to Hans Kruuk, *The Spotted Hyena.* Chicago: University of Chicago Press.

Tomasello, M. and J. Call. 1997. *Primate Cognition.* New York: Oxford University Press.

Washburn, M. F. 1909. *The Animal Mind: A Textbook of Comparative Psychology.* London: Macmillan.

Wechlin, S., J. H. Masserman, and W. Terris Jr. 1964. "Shock to a Conspecific as an Aversive Stimulus." *Psychonomic Science* 1:17–18.

Wilson, D. S. 2002. *Darwin's Cathedral: Evolution, Religion, and the Nature of Society.* Chicago: University of Chicago Press.

Würsig, B. 2000. "Leviathan Lust and Love." In M. Bekoff, ed. (2000), pp. 62–65.

From Cognition to Consciousness

DONALD GRIFFIN

Most people take it for granted that animals want to get such things as food, shelter, and companionship, and that they try to avoid unpleasant experiences. Certainly much of their behavior is consistent with this commonsense view. But convincing scientific demonstrations that these assumptions are valid have been very difficult to achieve. Nevertheless, recent observations and experiments have tended to increase the likelihood that animals do think consciously, albeit in very simple terms, and make sensible choices about what they do. This essay will review these developments, which are still in an early and tentative stage, and attempt to reflect the wide range of strongly held views of scientists who have been concerned with these difficult but fundamentally important questions. Behaviorism in psychology and reductionism in biology were so dominant from roughly the 1920s to the 1960s that scientists were reluctant even to consider the possibility that there was such a thing as animal cognition,

let alone animal consciousness. However, scientific investigations have revealed so much complexity and flexible versatility in animal behavior that scientific students of animal behavior have greatly expanded their conceptual horizons since the 1970s, and this process is continuing.

The first step was a "cognitive revolution," which led psychologists to relax the inhibitions of behaviorism in favor of a cognitive psychology in which internal processes such as memory and decision making are analyzed as principal factors necessary to understand behavior. An influential early contribution to this development was the book *Plans and the Structure of Behavior* (Miller et al. 1960). The history of this cognitive revolution has been reviewed by Baars (1986), Gardner (1985), and Johnson-Laird (1988), and the volume edited by Johnson and Erneling (1997) discusses its development and future.

Another important development has been the impressive renaissance of scientific investigations of consciousness, not only by neuroscientists, philosophers, and psychologists, but also by distinguished molecular biologists such as Edelman (1989, 1992) and Crick (1994). Recently there have been several international conferences and symposia devoted to consciousness and related topics. One of the most inclusive of these was edited by Hammeroff et al. (1996). General reviews of what is known about human consciousness have been published by Baars (1988, 1997), Flanagan (1992), Searle (1992), and Chalmers (1996).

Initially both the cognitive revolution in psychology and the renaissance of scientific concern with consciousness emphasized primarily human mentality, but by the late 1970s the cognitive revolution began to include nonhuman animals as well. This development has the significant potential of adding a truly comparative basis from which to explore the philosophical question of other minds. This extension of the cognitive revolution to animal psychology was greatly stimulated by a symposium at Dalhousie University leading to a book edited by Hulse et al. (1978). This included chapters by R.A. Rescorla on cognitive aspects of Pavlovian conditioning, by A.R. Wagner on expectancies, on working memory by W.K. Honig, selective attention in pigeons by D.A. Riley and H.L. Roitblat, spatial memory by D.S. Olton, and cognitive mapping in chimpanzees by E.W. Menzel.

Another important symposium volume (Roitblat et al. 1984) reviewed evidence of serial learning, representations in pigeon working memory, rehearsal, expectancies, order competencies, categories and concepts, spatial memory, memory of food caches. These symposia are representative of a large literature in which the emphasis is on cognition, this term being used to mean information processing in animal nervous systems, by which an animal learns, recognizes, competes, chooses, decides, or controls its behavior in ways based on more than direct reactions to concurrent stimulation. What have been added to simple stimulus-response analyses of behavior are internal cognitive processes. General reviews of animal cognition

have been provided by Roitblat (1987), Vauclair (1996) and Allen and Bekoff (1997).

Beginning at about the same time, Burghardt (1985) and I attempted to stimulate a further broadening of perspective (Griffin 1976, 1978, 1984, 1991, 1992), hoping to encourage the development of a cognitive ethology that would include not only neural information processing, but also subjective mental experiences, including conscious mental states and processes. My approach has emphasized the value of animal communication as a source of evidence (figuratively speaking a "window") that can provide investigators with information about what animals are thinking and feeling. For ethologists have discovered such a surprising versatility of communicative behavior in such a wide variety of animals, as reviewed by Hauser (1996), Owings et al. (1997), and Bradbury and Vehrencamp (1998), that interpretation of animal communication can provide fairly direct evidence about some of their thoughts and feelings, just as human communicative behavior is our chief basis for inferring what our human companions think and feel.

A growing number of students of animal behavior are now tending to agree with Burghardt (1997) that

> We now do seem to be at the stage where we can say that how animals perceive, experience, and comprehend their world is an important question.
>
> (p. 271)

> It is important to maintain a balanced perspective that does not dismiss the potential role of individual personal experience. in studying behavior. In the past this dismissal has occurred by treating such phenomena as outside science, by explaining them away as something else and thus effectively ignoring them.
>
> (p. 276)

A basic and very challenging question for cognitive ethologists is whether it is desirable and feasible to investigate the extent to which animal cognition is accompanied or influenced by conscious experiences. Although some behavioral scientists argue that it is not possible to learn anything at all about nonhuman conscious experiences, others have begun to try. In view of the difficulty of this subject, and its neglect by scientists studying animal behavior, it is necessary to begin with exploratory "pre-science." This entails considering a wide range of views and attempting to evaluate them, and exploring how the subject could be investigated more effectively in the future.

Konrad Lorenz (1958) and H. Hediger (1947, 1976) believed that at least birds and mammals have subjective experiences. But Niko Tinbergen (1951) advocated that ethologists should not attempt to investigate private subjective states in the animals they study, not because he denied their existence, but because he could see no valid way to obtain verifiable objective evidence about them. This development has been most helpfully reviewed by Richard W. Burkhardt Jr. (1997) with special reference to the longstanding debate between Tinbergen and Julian Huxley, who argued that animals do have mental experiences.

Tinbergen's advice has been almost universally followed, but there were a few exceptions, notably the psychologist E. C. Tolman (1932, 1959) and the ethologist W. H. Thorpe (1963, 1974). Tolman advocated what he called "purposive behaviorism," and his experiments led him to conclude that rats could experience "expectancies." Thorpe was "thinking all the time of the possibility of the existence of consciousness in animals. ... I do indeed find it essential to assume something very similar to consciousness and conscious choice in many of the highest animals." (1974:320). But the general climate of scientific opinion was much closer to the behavioristic position expressed by B. F. Skinner (1988): "Complex repertoires of behavior are shaped and maintained in strength with appropriate contingencies of reinforcement. Behavior once attributed to feelings and states of

mind can then be explained in a simpler way." Recently, however, it has come to seem less obvious that specifying all the contingencies of reinforcement necessary to explain the versatility of animal behavior is more parsimonious than postulating that animals employ simple but rational conscious thinking.

Because the majority of ethologists continue to follow Tinbergen's admonition to avoid considering questions of animal subjectivity, one rarely finds in the scientific literature any mention of the possibility that animals do things intentionally or know what the results of their behavior are likely to be. Like Tinbergen, most scientists studying animal behavior do not deny the possibility of animal consciousness but instead justify their avoidance of the issue by emphasizing the great difficulty, some say the impossibility, of learning anything at all about the mental experiences of animals. One reason for this skepticism is a reaction against overenthusiastic nineteenth-century ascriptions of complex cognition to animals on the basis of anecdotal reports relied upon by G. J. Romanes (1884) that were later shown to be questionable. Charles Darwin had no doubt that some animals had simple mental experiences, as reviewed by Crist (1996). But, perhaps because we all admire his major contributions so greatly, contemporary criticisms are ordinarily deflected to Romanes. A century of active investigation of animal behavior in both field and laboratory has revealed so much versatility that we can now draw on a much extensive and reliable data base than was available to Darwin and Romanes.

In view of the similarity of neurons and synapses, and the flexible versatility of many animals' behavior, it seems unlikely that the difference between human and animal minds is an absolute dichotomy, with no animal ever conscious. Instead, the principal difference is probably the *content* of consciousness. Thanks in large measure to the scope and versatility of human language, we think about a vastly wider range of objects and events. Animals are probably conscious of a different and more limited range of subject matter, appropriate for their ways of life rather than ours. Recognizing this distinction enables us to avoid the sorts of unjustified ascription of complex mental abilities to animals that have turned scientists away from the whole subject. Simple conscious thinking about available alternatives may well permit animals to make appropriate choices of behavior that is both desirable from the animal's point of view and also adaptive in the evolutionary biologist's sense of increasing the likelihood of survival and successful reproduction.

One important consideration, emphasized by Karl Popper (1978), is the practical advantage of thinking about possible actions, and trying them out in one's head rather than the real world where, for many animals, mistakes can easily be fatal. This in turn allows the selection of those actions that seem most likely to get what one wants or avoid what one dislikes or fears. Although Popper was concerned with human mentality, the economy and efficiency of simple conscious thinking may well have led to its evolutionary selection in a wide variety of animals. Animals often select certain patterns of behavior over others of which they are quite capable, and these choices seem to be based on simple beliefs that the selected action will obtain some desired object or outcome. Having outgrown behaviorism there is no longer any compelling reason why ethologists should neglect the possibility that many animals choose what to do on the basis of their conscious recognition that some actions are likely to have a favorable result while others are likely to have undesirable consequences.

Human consciousness is a heterogeneous ensemble of mental states, and many behavioristically inclined scientists claim that it cannot be defined adequately for scientific analysis. As emphasized by Crick (1994) and Allen and Bekoff (1997) we know too little about consciousness to formulate precise definitions, but since we all have a general idea what it is, we can profitably investigate it without bogging down in struggles to provide a definition that satisfies everyone. As Crick points out, precise definitions of the term "gene" are difficult to set down rigorously, and behavioral scientists could say the same about such terms as motivation, or even learning, which can nevertheless be investigated effectively.

Animal and human consciousness probably differ primarily in the greatly restricted *content* of the former. This essay will concentrate on perceptual consciousness, and its use in making simple but rational choices based on an animal's belief that a certain action will get something it wants or avoid something it dislikes or fears. The psychologist T. Natsoulas (1978:910–11) defined perceptual consciousness as "the state or faculty of being mentally conscious or aware of anything." He considered this "our most basic concept of consciousness, for it is implied in all the other senses [of the term]." Farthing (1992) uses the term "primary consciousness ... the direct experience of percepts and feelings, and thoughts and memories arising in direct response to them" for approximately the same type of simple-conscious awareness.

A more challenging question is whether animals experience reflective consciousness, which Natsoulas called "being aware of, or being in a position to be aware of, one's own perception, thought or other occurrent mental episode." Many scientists tend to believe that only reflective consciousness is "the real thing," and that a creature is not truly conscious unless it can think about its own thoughts, as argued explicitly by Bermond (1997) and Mahner and Bunge (1997). A related question is whether nonhuman animals can think about the mental states of others, and this ability is often claimed to be possible only for animals capable of reflective consciousness. But because it is prudent to attack challenging scientific problems one step at a time, I will not consider nonhuman introspection or ascription of mental states to others, a topic that has been discussed in detail by Premack and Woodruff (1978), Povinelli (1993), Povinelli and Preuss (1995), Hauser (1996), de Waal (1991, 1996), Savage-Rumbaugh (1997) and Seyfarth and Cheney (1997).

An Appreciative Perspective on Animals

In an attempt to make sense of the thicket of scientific puzzles that have entangled the subject of animal consciousness, I will outline below a speculative alternative to the generally prevailing view that animal cognition is an appropriate subject for scientific analysis but that animal consciousness is not. I will begin with nine statements that I believe are more likely than not to be correct, although most of them cannot yet be rigorously evaluated, and then discuss the evidence and arguments that have been advanced to bolster or dispute them. I hope that critical evaluation of these speculations will constructively stimulate future inquiries.

I. It is self-evident that we sometimes think about our situation and about the probable results of various actions that we might take; that is, we plan and choose what to do. This sort of conscious subjective mental experience is significant and useful because it often helps us select appropriate behavior; thus mental experiences are "local causes" of behavior, although of course they, in turn, are influenced by prior events.

II. Animals are actors who choose what to do, although their choices are often constrained within quite narrow limits. Thus it is more realistic to view them as selective doers rather than as objects totally dependent on outside influences.

III. When animals attempt to solve newly arisen challenges and adjust their behavior in versatile ways to solve problems, their choices are sometimes guided by simple conscious thoughts, such as fear of dangers, a desire to get something good to eat, or a belief that food can be obtained in a certain place or by a particular activity.

IV. These difficult but important questions about animal mentality can best be approached from the viewpoint of a materialist who assumes that mental experiences result from physiological processes occurring in central nervous systems. These processes, and relationships among them, are neither tangible objects nor immaterial essences, as emphasized by Mahner and Bunge (1997). They appear to be roughly analogous in this respect to homeostasis, which is an important physiological process but one that cannot be pinned down to a specific structure. In the scientific investigation of animal minds there is no need to call on immaterial factors, vitalism or divine intervention.

V. Communicative behavior of animals can serve the same basic function as human verbal and nonverbal communication by expressing at least some of an animal's private experiences. Therefore cognitive ethologists can gather verifiable, objective data about some of the private experiences of communicating animals by interpreting the messages that they convey to others. It is often claimed that although language allows us to obtain significant (though imperfect and incomplete) evidence about the thoughts of our human companions, animals lack language and therefore this source of information is not available. But animal communication is much richer than we used to believe, and this supposed barrier crumbles once we are prepared to listen.

VI. As far as we know, there is no special neuroanatomical "packaging" that is essential for conscious as opposed to nonconscious thinking. Of course some parts of our nervous systems are more closely involved in conscious thinking than others —the reticular formation, Wernicke's area, and the prefrontal cortex are more important for our conscious thinking than the spinal cord. But locating *where* in a brain some function occurs tells us almost nothing about how human or other brains generate conscious as opposed to nonconscious thinking, as emphasized by Chalmers (1996) and Block (1996).

VII. The need for numerous relatively specific rules of behavior may be what requires large volumes of central nervous tissue. If so, large brains may be needed for voluminous unconscious mechanisms. On the other hand, simple perceptual consciousness and thinking about alternatives and selecting ones judged favorable may be a basic core function of central nervous systems. Therefore it may be especially important for animals with small nervous systems.

VIII. Given our basic ignorance of the neural mechanisms producing conscious rather than nonconscious information processing, and the general assumption that neural structure and function are strongly affected by genetic influences, there is no reason why those neural processes that lead to conscious experience may not be affected by genetic instructions. This calls into serious question the widespread belief that if some behavior has a strong genetic basis it cannot, for that reason, be accompanied or influenced by conscious thinking. Recognizing that genetic influences on behavior are rarely, if ever, totally rigid prescriptions immune from environmental influences, it becomes quite possible that genetic heritage can affect conscious thoughts and feelings.

IX. C. Lloyd Morgan, J. B. Watson, and most of their contemporaries considered associative learning to be an indication of consciousness, and we still feel that it is more likely that behavior entails conscious thinking if it is learned. But in many discussions of animal cognition and mentality learning is considered to be an *alternative* to consciousness. This is a curious historical anomaly, which probably results from a deep-seated aversion to the idea that nonhuman animals might sometimes be conscious.

These nine statements differ so greatly from the current climate of scientific opinion that they will be disputed to varying degrees by many scientists concerned with animal behavior. But on close analysis the customary objections turn out to be based on questionable evidence or unjustified prior convictions. I will first review evidence that tends to support at least some of the conclusions outlined above, and then turn to the contrary views.

Evidence and Arguments in Favor of Animal Consciousness

The great range of versatile and flexible behavior of many animals provides strong suggestive evidence that they are consciously thinking about their actions. Effective coping with novel challenges is especially suggestive, because fixed or stereotyped reactions to stimuli that occur often in the evolutionary history of a species or in the experiences of an individual seem more likely to result from nonconscious information processing. An appealing analogy is to complex motor behavior, which is accompanied and guided by conscious thinking while we are learning to perform it, but after it is mastered we carry it out rapidly and efficiently without conscious thought, as emphasized by Baars (1988, 1997). It seems reasonable to infer that similar changes occur when an animal learn new skills. But when the challenges faced by an animal vary significantly from time to time, as they often do, or when wholly new problems arise, it seems more likely that simple conscious thinking in "if, then" terms takes place. Yet many scientists who gather such data are reluctant to draw this conclusion.

Walker (1983) reviewed extensive experimental evidence concerning animal learning and problem solving, and summarized his conclusions in the following two passages:

Some kind of mental activity is being attributed to the animals: that is, there is considered to be some internal sifting and selection of information rather than simply the release of responses by a certain set of environmental conditions. Knowledge of goals, knowledge of space, and knowledge of actions that may lead to goals seem to be independent, but can be fitted together by animals when the need arises.

(p. 81)

Our organ of thought may be superior, and we may play it better, but it is surely vain to believe that other possessors of similar instruments leave them quite untouched.

(p. 388)

Marian Dawkins (1993) has developed procedures by which an animal's preferences can be evaluated by allowing it to choose between different environments. She has also critically analyzed evidence for animal consciousness and the difficulties of determining whether animals have conscious experiences. Her basic conclusion is that at least mammals and birds are probably conscious at times, but that there are many pitfalls that must be carefully avoided in scientific attempts to determine the existence and content of animal consciousness. She sums up the balance of evidence as she sees it as follows:

Our near-certainty about (human) shared experiences is based, amongst other things, on a mixture of the complexity of their behavior, their ability to "think" intelligently and on their being able to demonstrate to us that they have a point of view in which what happens to them *matters* to them. We now know that these three attributes—complexity, thinking and minding about the world—are also present in other species. The conclusion that they, too, are consciously aware is therefore compelling. The balance of evidence (using Occam's razor to cut us down to the simplest hypothesis) is that they are and it seems positively unscientific to deny it.

(1993:177)

In a book titled *How Monkeys See the World: Inside the Mind of Another Species,* Cheney and Seyfarth (1990) reviewed extensive evidence that monkeys understand many facts about important aspects of the world they inhabit, and can communicate some of their knowledge, especially through alarm calls that designate different categories of predator. They have also reported evidence that baboons and monkeys do not seem to think about the mental states of their companions (Seyfarth and Cheney 1997). Although they use the term consciousness to mean self-awareness, Seyfarth and Cheney conclude that nonhuman primates know and understand a great deal about their physical, and especially their social, environment, but that they do not "know that they know."

Gordon Burghardt (1997) recommends that scientific ethology should be expanded to include the private experiences of animals, and that this be recognized as a fifth basic objective in addition to the four that Tinbergen advocated, proximal mechanisms of causation and control, ontogeny, evolutionary history, and survival value. Private experiences include subjective feelings as well as cognition, and Burghardt therefore feels that "cognitive ethology" is not a sufficiently inclusive term. Twenty years ago it seemed appropriate to emphasize that animal behavior could not be adequately understood without considering animal cognition. But we have now begun to appreciate the likelihood that animals make conscious choices about their actions, deciding to do what they perceive as helpful in achieving desired goals. Subjective private experiences are certainly an important part of cognitive ethology. The attempt to limit cognitive ethology to information processing is an obsolete relict of behaviorism.

Three contributors to a symposium volume (Dol et al. 1997) have argued that many animals have conscious experiences of some sort, although other contributors disagree. Van der Steen (1997) considers consciousness a heterogeneous "umbrella concept," but concludes that although the subject is a difficult one it can be studied scientifically and that some animals are probably conscious at times. Meijsing (1997:57) reviews the diverse views of scientists and philosophers and concludes: "From an evolutionary point of view, as soon as there is locomotion there is perceptual awareness and as soon as there is perceptual awareness there is self-awareness (meaning awareness of an animal's own body)." Wemelsfelder (1997:79) argues that subjective experience is not "hidden," but is expressed in behavior: "Attention is not a by-product of the ability to process information, it forms the very condition for that ability, enabling the animal to evaluate and apply acquired information in flexible and adaptive manner." Recognizing that we cannot be certain which animals are conscious, Bradshaw (1998) recommends that when issues of animal welfare are concerned it is best to "assume animals do have consciousness in case they do; if they do not it does not matter."

Allen and Bekoff (1997) have reviewed the extensive recent discussions of cognitive ethology, which they agree is an important scientific field of inquiry. They advocate a broad, multidisciplinary approach that should include

... remaining open to the possibility of surprising findings about animals' cognitive abilities ... concentrating on comparative, evolutionary, and ecological questions ... naturalizing the methods of study by taking the animals' points of view (communicating with them on their terms) ... using all sorts of data, ranging from anecdotes to large data sets

(Allen and Bekoff 1997:xx)

In a final chapter they discuss the difficulties of determining whether animals are conscious,

and clearly prefer to emphasize other aspects of animal cognition, partly perhaps because they feel that other scientists will look more favorably on cognitive ethology if it avoids involvement with subjective experiences. Here they differ from Gordon Burghardt's advocacy of extending ethology to include analysis of private experiences.

Skutch (1996) has reviewed his life-long studies of birds with emphasis on observations that lead him to conclude that

... birds' mental capacities have been grossly underestimated. ... In courtship and rearing young, birds give indications of emotions and affection that imply conscious ness. ... Many birds resort to dissimulation to lure potential predators from their nests or fledged young, mainly by injury feigning. Whether they are aware that they are using deception is not known; but numerous observations leave no doubt that they are in full control of their movements and aware of what they do.

(Skutch 1996:161–62)

Ristau (1991) describes experiments showing that plovers often selectively use displays to distract predators and that their performance is adjusted to the immediate situation, including changes depending on the resulting behavior of the intruding predator. She concludes, tentatively, that a plover "engaged in injury feigning wants to lead an intruder away from its offspring and acts as needed (within limits) to achieve that end" (Ristau 1991:91). Marler and Evans (1996) have shown experimentally that in domestic chickens "calling is not completely impulsive, but can be controlled. ... Although emotion is undoubtedly involved in bird calling, ... simple emotion-based models of bird calls are inadequate as the sole basis for explaining the vocal behavior of birds."

Heinrich (1995) investigated the degree to which hungry ravens could understand the totally novel problem presented by food suspended from a string, when they had had no previous experience with strings or string-like objects. After some time spent trying ineffective ways to get the food, some of the ravens suddenly performed a complex series of actions without any preliminary practice or reinforcement. These consisted of standing on a horizontal pole from which the food was suspended, grasping the string with the bill, pulling it up as far as possible, then holding the string with one foot and repeating the process five or six times until the food could be reached with the bill. It was demonstrated long ago that birds can learn to pull strings to get food, but this has always before required a long process of gradual learning in which each step in the process serves as reinforcement. But the ravens received no reinforcement until the whole sequence was completed.

Even more significant was a second phase of Heinrich's experiments. Almost every time a hungry raven succeeded in grasping the food after the pull-and-hold procedure Heinrich frightened it so that it flew off to another perch. Hungry ravens that have just obtained a morsel of food ordinarily fly off with it held firmly in the bill; but the birds that had just obtained food by the pull-and-hold procedure dropped it before flying away. Other ravens that had obtained pieces of food that one of their companions had pulled up *did* fly off with the string still attached so that the food was pulled from their bills. Heinrich concluded, reasonably enough, that the ravens understood the nature of the string and its attachment to the food.

One of the difficulties encountered by cognitive ethologists is that many examples of versatile behavior are by their very nature unique events that cannot be replicated precisely. This is especially true of deceptive behavior, because its effectiveness wanes rapidly if it is repeated, and it has been customary for ethologists to dismiss as anecdotes occurrences of what appears to be deception. However, Byrne and Whiten (1988) reviewed numerous reports of what looked like deceptive behavior by monkeys and apes in the journal *Behavioral and Brain Sciences*. Most of these reports would not, in isolation, have been considered valid enough to warrant publication in a scientific journal. But their cumulative effect is to cast doubt on the rigid, behavioristic, attitude that no animal can possibly engage in conscious attempts to deceive its companions. The numerous commentaries published with this paper demonstrate the wide range of opinion about what kinds of evidence, if any, can convincingly demonstrate conscious intent on the part of a nonhuman animal.

Although several philosophers have considered animal consciousness, space does not permit a complete review of their widely varying conclusions. Radner and Radner (1989) have examined in detail both the evidence that some animals are conscious at times, and the deficiencies in the arguments that deny that this is possible. Their basic conclusion is that in scientific investigation, "There is room for consciousness if one is willing to make room for it" (Radner and Radner 1989:208). Lindahl (1997) has critically discussed the possibility that consciousness is an adaptive trait that has been favored in natural selection. On balance he favors "the interactionist theory [which] asserts that neural events may bring about and influence conscious mental events and vice versa" (Lindahl 1997:613). More recently Brown (1996) has discussed in detail the inconsistencies in arguments that attempt to rule out the possibility of simple conscious thinking on the part of birds and mammals.

A further and very significant body of evidence that some animals think consciously about simple matters that are important to them has come from successful efforts to teach modifications of human communicative procedures to apes, dolphins, sea lions, and parrots. The first successes were reported by the Gardners (Gardner and Gardner 1969; Gardner et al. 1989) who trained chimpanzees to communicate by means of gestures modeled after those used by the human deaf. This approach and subsequent extensions of it have recently been reviewed by Fouts (1997) who describes how extensively these chimpanzees use the communicative gestures they have been taught to communicate to each other. Very influential criticisms of these experiments by Terrace et al. (1979) and by Sebeok and Rosenthal (1981) led to their dismissal by many behavioral scientists. But these criticisms have since been convincingly rebutted by Lieberman (1984, 1998), Savage-Rumbaugh and Lewin (1994), and Savage-Rumbaugh (1997). In recent years E. S. Savage-Rumbaugh and her colleagues have developed modified computer keyboards by which apes communicate with human experimenters and with each other. By this type of communicative behavior they identify familiar objects and persons from their photographs, ask for things they want, including trips to specified destinations, answer questions, and request specific tools needed for particular activities.

Dolphins have also been trained to respond appropriately to both acoustic and gestural signals from human trainers, as reviewed by Herman (1986, 1987, 1988), and they can also respond correctly to sequences of signals where the order of signals determines the correct response. Herman interprets this as mastering of a very simple type of syntax, but Schusterman and Gisiner (1989) prefer to interpret the behavior of dolphins and sea lions in these types of experiments in terms of learning a few rules. Yet stating these rules required four lines of text, so that it is difficult to believe they could be mastered without some conscious understanding. Finally, and most impressively in many ways, Pepperberg (1981, 1991, 1994) has trained African gray parrots to use their imitations of spoken English words in a meaningful fashion to request desired objects or activities, and to answer simple questions about shapes, colors, number of objects, and whether two objects are the same or different in color or shape. These are clear examples that the animals concerned can communicate their simple thoughts and feelings.

In all these cases animals have been trained to use communication systems modeled to varying degrees on human language. But even their most ardent admirers do not claim that the apes, dolphins, or parrots have mastered anything remotely approaching the power and versatility of human language. One of the most obvious differences is the almost total lack of what George Miller (1967) aptly called combinatorial productivity—our ability to recombine words or syllables in new ways to derive entirely new meanings. And none of these communication systems have more than minuscule amounts of syntax, whereas grammatical rules of one sort or another are universal in human languages. But syntax and combinatorial productivity are not needed to communicate simple feelings and thoughts, and their absence does not diminish the value of communicative signals as evidence about the mental experiences that they express.

Huysmans (1992) has reviewed in detail the evidence of conscious thinking provided by animal communication. Although she recognizes the limited nature of this evidence and the many uncertainties affecting its interpretation, she concludes that the complex communication systems of certain animals demonstrate the existence of mental processes no less than does human communication: "les systèmes de communication complexes de certains animaux ... ne démontrent pas moins (comme chez l'homme) l'existence de processus mentaux chez les animaux" (Huysmans 1992:121).

Evidence and Arguments Against Animal Consciousness

One type of objection to statement I, that we sometimes consciously decide what to do, comes from the philosophers Stephen Stich (1983) and Patricia Churchland (1986), who argue that even such basic mental concepts as belief and desire are obsolete and will, eventually, be replaced by neurophysiological mechanisms. But this is far from actually happening, and other philosophers have strongly disputed such eliminativist claims, as reviewed in detail by Baker (1995) and several others cited in Griffin (1992:245).

If and when neural mechanisms that generate beliefs and desires are actually discovered, this will be a magnificent scientific accomplishment, comparable to the discovery that DNA and RNA are the chemical basis of heredity. But even that monumental discovery has not eliminated heredity as a highly significant concept, nor will anticipated, but still remote, discoveries of neural bases for mental experiences eliminate them from existence or significance. In short, no Copernicus has yet provided any convincing alternative to the commonsense view that conscious mental experiences exist and have at least some effect on behavior.

A frequently stated reason for denying that conscious thoughts or feelings are important and influence behavior is the enormous preponderance of nonconscious information processing in our brains (Velmans 1991; Kennedy 1992; Gopnik 1993). But there is an unstated assumption hidden from view here, namely that the proportion of conscious to unconscious activity must be even smaller in animal than in human brains. It is not at all clear what evidence supports this implicit assumption. Insofar as simple conscious thinking is effective and adaptive, it may be one of the most important functions of a central nervous system. In the absence of any definitive explanation of the neurophysiological basis for consciousness, we have come to assume that it is uniquely human, and then rely on this prejudgment to reinforce the palatable belief in our superiority.

Statement II, that animals are conscious actors, has been vigorously disputed by Kennedy (1992) who concluded that "[a]lthough we cannot be certain that no animals are conscious, we can say that it is most unlikely that any of them are" (p. 31). Many other psychologists and ethologists have expressed more cautious opinions while strongly resisting the idea that conscious experiences occur in nonhuman animals, or that they have any effect on their behavior if they do occur. A clear example is provided by the work of E. A. Wasserman, whose ingenious experiments (Wasserman et al. 1988) have demonstrated that pigeons can learn to make quite elaborate discriminations between categories of pictures, leading to the conclusion that

> ... these results suggest that many words in our language denote clusters of related visual stimuli which pigeons also see as highly similar. To the degree that reinforcement contingencies correlate with these human language groupings, pigeons' discrimination learning is hastened and generalization to new and altered examples is enhanced.
>
> (Wasserman et al. 1988:235)

Yet Wasserman stated that

> I, for one, have tried to steer clear of the possibility of subjective experience in my animal subjects; the more prudent of my professional colleagues have as well; ... cognitive psychology need not be construed as mentalistic. Those cognitive processes that are said to mediate behavioral relationships are the public behaviors of scientists, not the private experiences of their subjects (1983:10–11) ... No statement concerning consciousness in animals is open to verification and experiment.
>
> (Wasserman 1985)

Blumberg and Wasserman (1995) extend this line of argument by likening the suggestion that animals make conscious choices about their behavior to invoking divine intervention to account for biological complexity. These views represent contemporary expressions of the basic behavioristic conviction that mental experiences should be banned from science.

A similar opinion has been expressed recently by G. C. Williams (1997):

> Ultimately the only mind you can really know is your own, not those of computers or animals or friends. I think that this removes the domain of the mental from biology and from material science in general.
>
> (Williams 1997:65)

My inclination is to purge all biological discussion of mentalistic interpretation.

(Williams 1997:70)

Williams holds that:

Supernatural agencies are banished not only from explanation of the development of biological mechanisms but also from modern attempts to understand their operation ... The alternative is vitalism, which assumes that the workings of an organism, human or other, require something more than physical machinery.

(Williams 1997:63–66)

Many scientists concur with Williams in disputing statements I and II indirectly by relying on the "privacy argument" that conscious experiences can be known only by the one who has them, and that no statements about them can be independently verified.

The privacy argument holds that we can never know for certain whether a particular animal is conscious. This means that it is just as impossible to prove it is not conscious as to prove that it is. We might define P_a as the probability that a given animal is consciously aware in a particular situation, or that the content of its consciousness includes a particular item, for example being aware that a large predator is approaching. If we were absolutely certain that this animal is conscious, P_a would be 1.0; and conversely if we are completely sure it is not, P_a would be 0. According to the privacy argument we can never know anything about this matter, and therefore we must always assume that $P_a =$ 0.500. But we can really do better than that, for it seems almost certain that some animals are conscious of simple facts of their lives, so that we can reasonably infer that P_a lies somewhere between 0.5 and 1.0. Granting that we can never assume that P_a is either 0 or 1, it does seem quite plausible to infer values either above or below 0.5.

Williams also appears to disagree with statement IV, that mental experiences can be investigated effectively by considering them to be processes produced by the functioning of central nervous systems. He and many others tend to consider conscious experience as something immaterial. Yet this view implies that they do not result from the functioning of central nervous systems, for if they do, they could be characterized and analyzed by studying their effects, as we do with processes such as inhibition or homeostasis.

Objections to statement III often take the form of arguing that *all* animal behavior takes place without any conscious awareness whatever. For example Terrace (1984:8) asserted that

Just as the modern rationale for using human cognitive terms is not based upon arguments that appeal to consciousness or introspective reports the rationale for the study of cognitive processes in animals requires no reference to animal consciousness. Both in human and animal cognition it is assumed that the normal state of affairs is unconscious activity and thought.

This is a clear statement of the behavioristic position that no matter how versatile an animal's behavior may be, even when it successfully copes with novel challenges, its cognition should be analyzed without considering the possibility that it consciously thinks about what it is doing.

Galef (1995) quotes the conclusion of Jennings (1906) that "the problem as to the actual existence of consciousness outside of the self is an indeterminate one; no increase in objective knowledge can ever solve it." It is difficult to surmise what Jennings might conclude with the advantage of ninety years of progress in ethology and comparative psychology. But extreme skepticism rules out any recognition of consciousness in our human companions. Thus the aggravation that Galef expresses seems to be based on a deep-seated aversion to the idea that consciousness can be studied scientifically. Those who believe that something cannot be studied are obviously unlikely to learn much about it.

Lijmbach (1997) argues that "An animal's experiential ability is bound to its experiential body and experienced environment, while humans are able to reflect on their own body and environment. ... But I do not agree that ... animals are not able to have meaningful experiences and expressions at all." But if animals do reflect on their own bodies, how would we detect that they do so? They certainly pay abundant attention to their bodies, cleaning and grooming them, for example; but Lijmbach presumably means that animals do not engage in metacognitive reflection.

Van Rooijen (1997) denies that mental entities have any causal effect on behavior, that is, they are epiphenomena, and states that "The main reason for the exclusion of mental entities from ethology is not their fundamental vagueness, but the fear of vitalism." This implies a dualistic view that conscious mental experiences are something lying outside the physical universe, and thus departs from the customary materialistic assumptions of science.

Bermond (1997) concludes, largely on the basis of data from human brain lesions, that "to experience suffering, a well developed prefrontal cortex and right neocortex are necessary." This implies that whatever neural processes cause suffering can occur only in anthropoid apes and possibly dolphins, but no supporting evidence for this sweeping conclusion is provided other than the results of damage to human brains. This overlooks the distinct possibility that similar processes could occur in other brains composed of very similar elements.

The psychologist Robert Boakes (1992) asserts that

Attributing conscious thought to animals should be strenuously avoided in any serious attempt to understand their behavior, since it is untestable, empty, obstructionist and based on a false dichotomy. ... By the age of three years most children can describe in detail some arbitrary event or scene in the objective world that the listener cannot directly perceive. No such ability has been found in any other species. ... This uniquely human ability can then be used to report on a subjective world. In its absence there is no way of knowing what this might be like for a non-human creature.

Savage-Rumbaugh's apes satisfy this requirement, however, when they use the computer keyboard to convey new information to other apes or to human companions. The waggle dances of honeybees, also, inform the dancer's sisters about important things they cannot perceive directly.

Boakes continues:

For many psychological students their first, and only, contact with animal psychology is a practical class in which they shape a rat to press a lever. Their almost universal way of explaining what happens is to talk in terms of the rat's beliefs, expectations, intention or boredom when it stops doing very much. In past years this was strenuously discouraged. Recently such talk has become more acceptable as long as imaginary quotation marks are placed around the mentalistic terms. Griffin would have us all remove the quotation marks. His book left me with the resolution to go back to abolishing such talk the next time I run such a practical. It clearly produces a false sense of complacency and gets in the way of looking carefully at what the animal is actually doing and thinking hard about what may be going on in its brain.

Here we have a clear and explicit statement of the anti-mentalistic indoctrination to which students have been exposed. Thinking hard about brain function is impeded rather than facilitated by adamantly ignoring some of the most important processes that occur in central nervous systems.

Statement V expresses a positive proposal for overcoming the alleged barrier that is held to exclude private conscious experiences from the reach of objective investigation and the testing of hypotheses by gathering objective evidence. Interpretation of human communication, both verbal and nonverbal, is our chief means of judging what our companions are thinking and feeling.

But the prevailing view of ethologists appears to be that animal communication is inherently different and incapable of playing this role. It is important to distinguish two basic attributes of animal consciousness, its *content* and its *causation*. The question of content is whether an animal is conscious at all, and if so what is the nature of its conscious experience. The question of causation is what caused the animal to have a conscious experience with a particular content. Interpreting communicative behavior has great potential for answering the first question but not the second.

Because a great majority of the information processing in human brains occurs without our conscious awareness, because animals are much simpler that we are, and because their communication has only a negligible degree of syntax or combinatorial productivity, most ethologists feel it is more conservative to assume that *all* animal communication results from nonconscious information processing. Yet consistency would require that we apply the same criteria to our human companions, as emphasized by Brown (1996). In the case of human nonverbal communication there is no syntax or combinatorial productivity; but we feel free to make inferences about the conscious experiences of our companions on the basis of flinching, scowling, blushing, smiling, trembling, or changes in vocal intonation.

Ascribing conscious experiences to animals is often held to be misguided and unscientific because it is anthropomorphic. In scientific usage anthropomorphism means ascribing to a nonhuman organism some attribute that is in fact uniquely human. A book entitled *Anthropomorphism, Anecdotes, and Animals* (Mitchell et al. 1997) grew out of a symposium held at the 1989 meeting of the Animal Behavior Society in reaction to the symposium at the previous meet-

ing that led to the book *Cognitive Ethology: The Minds of Other Animals* (Ristau 1991). Twenty-nine chapters present a wide range of views about the uses and alleged abuses of anthropomorphic thinking, ranging from Burghardt's advocacy of private mental experiences as an important aspect of ethology to the argument advanced by Hank Davis (1997:327) "that even human conscious thinking is epiphenomenal and that it is premature to assume that there is 'a continuum of mental life that includes both humans and animals.'"

The customary view of anthropomorphism as a serious error suffers from circular reasoning. Consciousness is assumed in advance to be uniquely human, and any suggestion to the contrary is then dismissed as anthropomorphic. This is merely reiterating a prejudgment that consciousness is uniquely human, as pointed out by Bennett (1964), Radner and Radner (1989), and especially by Fisher (1990) who concludes: "The idea that anthropomorphism names a widespread fallacy in commonsense thinking about animals is largely a myth ... and the use of the term as a critical cudgel ought to be given up. It cannot stand for what it is supposed to."

Under certain circumstances conscious awareness, rather than preceding one of our actions, appears to follow after a fraction of a second (Libet 1993). This has been taken as supporting epiphenomenalism, the claim that conscious experiences have no effect on behavior (Hamad 1982). But the fact that some neural processing occurs before human subjects report verbally that they are experiencing a certain *thought* does not mean that the conscious thinking and decision reaching is ineffective or insignificant. The epiphenomenalist argument is that whatever unconscious processes occur before verbal report might themselves be the important influences on subsequent behavior. But there is no reason that conscious thoughts cannot affect behavior and other experiences at a slightly later time, even though they were generated by prior unconscious processes.

In many recent discussions of the possibility that animals sometimes have conscious experiences it is tacitly assumed that these would have to be simplified versions of ours. This implies that human experiences are the only conceivable kind. But to the extent that animals do have mental experiences, these may be quite different from any human *thoughts* or feelings, so that it is a needless limitation of our imaginations to assume otherwise. Because consciousness probably differs widely among species, it will take enterprising imagination to generate and evaluate hypotheses about its nature and content in various animals. Are animals so different from us that we are inherently incapable of understanding any conscious thoughts they might experience, because all our ideas about consciousness are so closely linked to human consciousness that we simply cannot imagine what subjective experiences might occur in other species—especially those distantly related to us? Some philosophers such as Nagel (1974) and Dennett (1996) are at a loss even to imagine what life is like for a bat, a vulture, or an insect. But let's not underestimate our own mental capabilities. We can guess, and then seek to devise ways of testing the correctness, of our speculations. This is scientific exploration, and it is therefore unrealistic to hope for logical rigor or neat and tidy data until we evaluate a variety of plausible hypotheses based on knowledge of the animals concerned.

It is often held that animal behavior that seems to suggest conscious thinking is better explained as genetically programmed responses that occur without any awareness on the animal's part. This view has been vigorously advocated in the criticism by Helena Cronin (1992) of my book *Animal Minds* including:

All that Mr. Griffin's animal stories illustrate is the immense power of information-processing machinery to produce versatile behavior. But information processing need not involve consciousness. ... My computer had to be programmed. So did the animals. Their programmer is natural selection, which writes in the language of genes.

Cronin is relying on the almost universal assumption that if some behavior pattern is under genetic control, it cannot be influenced by conscious thinking.

It is generally assumed by scientists that conscious experiences result from physiological processes taking place in brains, or perhaps more generally in central nervous systems, even though neurophysiologists cannot yet determine just *what* these consciousness-generating processes are (Milner 1998). Furthermore, we assume that genetic instructions determine how neurons develop and establish appropriate connections. Interactions among neurons, synapses, and possibly glial cells are also assumed to generate conscious experience. Given these assumptions, how can we be certain that genetic influences do not also guide or even determine some of the conscious experiences to which these nervous systems give rise?

If genetic influences can account for everything that animals do, including their most versatile actions in solving novel problems, it would seem possible that they could also lead to simple conscious thinking. For instance, one might postulate the existence of genetic instructions to represent and evaluate the likely results of actions and perform the one thus projected to produce desired results. Gould and Gould (1994) point out that genetically programmed motor patterns are often *used* selectively and that "Perhaps animals ... can consciously weigh which innate behavioral unit to bring to bear in a difficult situation" (Gould and Gould 1994:87).

Another common implicit assumption in the behavioral sciences is that if behavior is learned it does not involve conscious awareness of the relationship, or contingency, that has been learned. This is a curious historical anomaly, for Lloyd Morgan, Watson and their contemporaries considered associative learning an indication of conscious understanding, rather than an alternative explanation. But when experiments showed that animals more and more distantly related to ourselves did actually learn, there came to be a subtle shift from considering learning to be evidence of consciousness to seeing it as an alternative to awareness on the animal's part of what it had learned. Perhaps this resulted from a prior conviction that only (say) birds and mammals were capable of consciousness *and* learning. When at least simple kinds of learning were demonstrated in insects and cephalopods, the climate of scientific opinion appears to have reversed itself, so that learning to do something came to be taken as an alternative explanation to conscious understanding.

As a result of this implicit assumption, many examples of animal behavior that suggest conscious thinking are often dismissed as "merely" learning of one sort or another. This tendency may be a relict of the behaviorists' endeavor to liken as much behavior as possible to Pavlovian conditioning. It is ironic that even classical or Pavlovian conditioning, often considered to be the simplest form of learning, has turned out to be more complex and cognitive than Pavlov assumed, as reviewed by Rescorla (1988). Dawson and Furedy (1976) demonstrated that classical conditioning of the galvanic skin response in human subjects often does not occur unless the subjects are aware of the relationship between the stimuli. More recent investigations and analyses by Shanks and St. John (1994), Ohman et al. (1995), and others support the conclusion of Baars (1988) that "only conscious functions seem to have the relational capacity to bring together two arbitrarily related stimuli" (Baars 1988:78–79). Although some kinds of conditioning of human subjects is possible without their explicit awareness, as reviewed by Schacter et al. (1993), the fact that in many cases conscious awareness is required for successful classical conditioning means that learning and consciousness are often closely linked. Therefore learning is an indication of consciousness rather than an alternative.

Discussion

The tendency to demand absolute certainty before accepting any evidence about mental experiences of animals reflects a sort of double standard. For in other scientific subjects we are accustomed to make the best of incomplete and often ambiguous evidence. Indeed, demanding absolute perfection of evidence before reaching even tentative conclusions would have seriously impeded progress in almost every area of science, especially in the early stages of investigation. For example, should the biologists of the early twentieth century have refused to study chromosomes because they could not see how to determine the exact nature of genes? This demand for perfection appears to be a subtle and probably unconscious way of avoiding the issue, and it is thus an insidious barrier to scientific investigation. It can be called "paralytic perfectionism," when it is taken as an excuse to deny that any conceivable evidence about conscious experiences is scientifically significant.

The antagonism of many scientists to suggestions that animals may have conscious experiences is so intense that it suggests a deeper, philosophical aversion that can reasonably be termed "mentophobia." The taboo against scientific consideration of private, conscious, mental experiences is more prevalent when nonhuman animals are concerned; but some scientists tend to minimize the significance of even human consciousness. This mentophobic taboo has become a serious obstacle to scientific progress. Conscious experiences obviously exist in at least one species; and they are clearly important, though of course they are not the only factor influencing our behavior.

A central component of all these objections is the claim that no effective procedures have been proposed (some would say none can ever be proposed) to determine whether a given animal is thinking consciously. If we refrain from relying on paralytic perfectionism as an excuse for neglecting the whole question, it is quite reasonable to ask how significant evidence can be gathered that will at least reduce our ignorance about this important question. As Crick (1994:20–21) has emphasized, the ideal solution would be to identify whatever neural process produces conscious awareness and then determine whether this process occurs in nonhuman brains. But although some parts of human brains are more directly involved in conscious thinking than others, neuroscientists are not yet able to specify just *what processes* correlate uniquely with consciousness.

When inquiring about the neural basis of consciousness it is quite natural to start with the human brain because it obviously gives rise to our consciousness. Evidence from brain lesions, from electrical measures of brain activity such as event-related potentials, together with recently developed methods of noninvasive imaging, show that what Newman (1997) terms the "extended reticular activating system," including the prefrontal cortex, is heavily involved in conscious thinking. Then, when the question of nonhuman consciousness is raised, it is natural to look for similar structures and to find it more likely that consciousness occurs in animals whose brains have the same basic anatomy as ours.

But when we inquire just what processes taking place in the extended reticular activating system give rise to consciousness, none of the suggested functions depend on these particular features of gross neuroanatomy. Consider for example three possibilities that have been recently suggested as neural correlates of conscious awareness: (1) the concept of a "global workspace" formulated by Baars (1988, 1997); (2) the idea that consciousness depends upon coordinated activity in widely dispersed areas of the brain (perhaps involving neurons firing synchronously at roughly 40Hz) as tentatively suggested by Crick (1994); and (3) the hypothesis advanced by Woolf (1997) that "cholinergic afferents to the cerebral cortex ... enhance activity at specific cortical circuits and determine the content of a conscious moment by activat-

ing certain combinations of postsynaptic sites in select cortical modules."

None of these, or other serious candidates for neural correlates of consciousness, appear to require any particular pattern of gross anatomy. Therefore it is quite possible, in principle, that similar interactions among neurons, synapses, and possibly glia can occur in any central nervous systems. A global workspace is quite possible within any central nervous system; as is coordinated activity in widely dispersed areas; and cholinergic afferents are found in almost every central nervous system.

Scientific investigation has often achieved substantial progress long before ideally convincing data became available, and in the case of animal consciousness the accumulation of suggestive evidence can serve to shift P_a, the likelihood that particular animals are conscious, upward from 0.5, even though for the foreseeable future we cannot expect perfectly conclusive proofs of consciousness so that P_a would be 1.0. When we learn that the bonobo named Kanzi has used his keyboard to ask to go to the tree house, and then leads his companions there while resisting efforts to persuade him to go elsewhere, we might estimate that P_a for his thinking consciously about this destination was well above 0.5.

It also seems quite reasonable to infer values of P_a exceeding 0.5 when animals display versatile modifications of their behavior that help them cope with novel challenges. And P_a would be given a further nudge toward higher values if the animal communicates what it is appears to be thinking, as for example when vervet monkeys employ the appropriate type of alarm call to warn their companions of particular kinds of danger, as described by Cheney and Seyfarth (1990). Of course determined behaviorists can always postulate that whatever an animal does, or no matter how specific its communication signals may be, this *could* result from unconscious information processing, so that we have no basis for moving P_a away from 0.5. But the probability that a behavioristic explanation is correct does seem to be shifted downward from

0.5 by the accumulated evidence provided by the recent advances in cognitive ethology.

A common theme articulated explicitly by Yoerg and Kamil (1991) and by Vauclair (1992, 1996, 1997) is the strongly held opinion that animal cognition, in the sense of information processing, is an appropriate, and indeed a significant, area of scientific investigation; but that subjective mental experience of animals is not. Yet even if one holds that mental experiences are epiphenomena without any causal effects on behavior, our feelings and thoughts are obviously important to us, and insofar as animals have any mental experiences these are probably important to them as well. Therefore our understanding of animals will never be adequate until we are able to evaluate and appreciate what life is like to them.

Evolutionary continuity does not by any means imply identity. Animals have diversified enormously in the course of biological evolution, and the magnitude of the differences between the mentality of our species and others is astronomical. As A. N. Whitehead (1938) put it "The distinction between men and animals is in one sense only a difference in degree. But the extent of the degree makes all the difference." A question of major significance is whether the difference is absolute, with conscious thinking totally limited to our species, or whether simple forms of perceptual consciousness and rational choice occur in other animals, that is, whether we differ from other species primarily in the content of our consciousness.

The mentophobic baggage inherited from behaviorism has seriously inhibited scientific investigation of whatever conscious, private mental experiences may occur in other species. But this barrier to progress has begun to crumble, and scientists are now devoting their imaginations and experimental ingenuity to these questions. This renewed freedom of inquiry can eventually lead to a significant understanding of what life is really like for animals. Most of Darwin's basic ideas about evolution are now generally accepted by scientists, but the notion that there has been evolutionary continuity with respect to conscious experiences is still strongly resisted. Overcoming this resistance may be the final, crowning chapter of the Darwinian revolution.

Acknowledgment

Reprinted by permission from *Animal Cognition* (1998): 1:3–16, Springer-Verlag, with some modification of critical apparatus.

REFERENCES AND AN ADDENDUM

Allen. C., and M. Bekoff. *Species of Mind: the Philosophy and Biology of Cognitive Ethology*. Cambridge: MIT Press.

Baars, B. J. 1986. *The Cognitive Revolution in Psychology*. New York: Guilford.

———. 1988. *A Cognitive Theory of Consciousness*. New York: Cambridge University Press.

———. 1997. *In the Theatre of Consciousness, the Workspace of the Mind*. New York: Oxford University Press.

Baker, L. R. 1995. *Explaining Attitudes, a Practical Approach to the Mind*. New York: Cambridge University Press.

Bennett, J. 1964. *Rationality: An Essay Towards an Analysis*. London: Routledge and Kegan Paul.

Bermond, B. 1997. "The Myth of Animal Suffering." In Dol, et al. (1997): 125–43.

Block, N. 1996. "How Can We Find the Neural Correlates of Consciousness." *Trends in Neurosciences* 19:456–59.

Blumberg, M. S. and E. A. Wasserman. 1995. "Animal Mind and the Argument from Design." *Am Psychol* 50:133–44.

Boakes, R. 1992. "Subjective Experience." *Times Higher Education Supplement*, November 29, 1992, p. 22.

Bradbury, J. W. and S. L. Vehrencamp. 1998. *Principles of Animal Communication*. Sunderland: Sinauer.

Bradshaw, R. H. 1998. "Consciousness in Nonhuman animals: Adopting the Precautionary Principle." *J Consciousness Stud* 5:108–14.

Brown, A. 1996. "The Minds of Animals: Theoretical Foundations of Comparative Psychology." PhD thesis, University of Colorado, Boulder.

Burghardt, G. M. 1985. "Animal Awareness: Current Perceptions, and Historical Perspective." *Am Psychol* 40:905–19.

———. 1997. "Amending Tinbergen: A Fifth Aim for Ethology." In Mitchell, Thompson, and Miles, eds. (1997): 254–76.

Burkhardt, R. W., Jr. 1997. "The Founders of Ethology and the Problem of Animal Subjective Experience." In Dol, et al. (1997): 1–13.

Byrne, R. and A. Whiten. 1988. "Tactical Deception in Primates." *Behav Brain Sci* 11:233–44.

Chalmers, D. J. 1996. "The Conscious Mind: In Search of a Fundamental Theory." New York: Oxford University Press.

Cheney, D. L. and R. M. Seyfarth. 1990. *How Monkeys See the World: Inside the Mind of Another Species*. Chicago: University of Chicago Press.

Churchland, P. S. 1986. *Neuropsychology: Toward a Unified Science of the Mind-Brain*. Cambridge: MIT Press.

Crick, F. 1994. *The Astonishing Hypothesis: The Scientific Search for the Soul*. New York: Simon and Schuster.

Crist, E. 1996. "Darwin's Anthropomorphism: An Argument for Animal-Human Continuity." *Adv Hum Ecol* 5:33–83.

Cronin, H. 1992. "What Do Animals Want?" *New York Times Book Review,* November 1, 1992, p. 14.

Davis, H. 1997. "Animal Cognition Versus Animal Thinking: the Anthropomorphic Error." In Mitchell, Thompson, and Miles, eds. (1997): 335–47.

Dawkins, M. S. 1993. *Through Our Eyes Only? The Search for Animal Consciousness*. New York: Freeman.

Dawson, M. E. and J. J. Furedy. 1976. "The Role of Awareness in Human Differential Autonomic Classical Conditioning: The Necessary-Gate Hypothesis." *Psychophysiology,* pp. 150–53.

Dennett, D. C. 1996. *Kinds of Minds*. New York: Basic.

Dol, M., S. Kasanmoentalib, S. Lijmbach, E. Rivas, and R. van den Bos, eds. 1997. *Animal Consciousness and Animal Ethics*. Assen, The Netherlands: Van Gorcum, pp. 1–13.

Edelman, G. M. 1989. *The Remembered Present: A Biological Theory of Consciousness*. New York: Basic.

———. 1992. *Bright Air, Brilliant Fire*. New York: Basic.

Farthing, G. W. 1992. *The Psychology of Consciousness*. Englewood Cliffs: Prentice-Hall.

Fisher, J. A. 1990. "The Myth of Anthropomorphism." In M. Bekoff, and D. Jamieson, eds., *Interpretation and Explanation in the Study of Animal Behavior*. Boulder: Westview.

Flanagan, O. 1992. *Consciousness Reconsidered*. Cambridge: MIT Press.

Fouts, R. and S. T. Mills. 1997. *Next of Kin: What Chimpanzees Have Taught Me About Who We Are*. New York: William Morrow.

Galef, B. G., Jr. 1995. "Review of Animal Minds." *Animal Behavior* 49:1133–34.

Gardner, H. 1985. *The Mind's New Science: a History of the Cognitive Revolution*. New York: Basic.

Gardner, R. A. and B. T. Gardner. 1969. "Teaching Sign Language to a Chimpanzee." *Science.* 165:664–72.

Gardner, R. A., B. T. Gardner, and T. E. Van Cantfort. 1989. *Teaching Sign Language to Chimpanzees*. New York: Basic.

Gopnik, A. 1993. "How We Know Our Minds: The Illusion of First-Person Knowledge of Intentionality." *Behav Brain Sci* 16:1–14.

Gould, J. L. and C. G. Gould. 1994. *The Animal Mind*. New York: Freeman.

Griffin, D. R. 1976. *The Question of Animal Awareness: Evolutionary Continuity of Mental Experience*. New York: Rockefeller University Press.

———. 1978. "Prospects for a Cognitive Ethology." *Behav Brain Sci* 1:527–38.

———. 1984. *Animal Thinking*. Cambridge: Harvard University Press.

———. 1991. "Progress Toward a Cognitive Ethology." In: Ristau, ed. (1991): 3–17.

———. 1992. *Animal Minds*. Chicago: University of Chicago Press.

Hammeroff, S. R., A. W. Kaszniak, and A. C. Scott, eds. 1996. *Toward a Science of Consciousness: The First Tucson Discussions and Debates*. Cambridge: MIT Press.

Hamad, S. 1982. "Consciousness: An Afterthought." *Cogn Brain Theory* 5:29–47.

Hauser, M. D. 1996. *Evolution of Communication*. Cambridge: MIT Press.

Hediger, H. 1947. "Ist das tierliche Bewusstsein unerforschbar?" *Behaviour* 1:130–37.

———. 1976. "Proper Names in the Animal Kingdom." *Experientia* 32:1357–64.

Heinrich, B. 1995. "An Experimental Investigation of Insight in Common Ravens (*Corvus corax*)." *Auk* 112:994–1003.

Herman, L. M. 1986. "Cognition and Language Competencies of Bottlenosed Dolphins." In: R. J. Schusterman, A. J., Thomas, and F. G. Wood, F. G., eds., *Dolphin Cognition and Behavior: A Comparative Approach*. Hillsdale: Erlbaum, pp. 221–52.

Herman, L. M. 1987. "Receptive Competencies of Language-trained Animals." *Advances in the Study of Behavior,* vol. 17. New York: Academic Press.

———. 1988. "The Language of Animal Language Research: A Reply to Schusterman and Gisiner." *Psycho Rec* 38:349–62.

Hulse, S. H., H. Fowler, H., and W. K. Honig, eds. 1978. *Cognitive Processes in Animal Behavior*. Hillsdale: Erlbaum.

Huysmans, A. 1992. "La communication: un accès á la conscience animale?" *Cah Ethol* 12:1–126.

Jennings, H. S. 1906. *Behavior of Lower Organisms*. New York: Columbia University Press,.

Johnson, D. M., and C. E. Erneling, C. E., eds. 1997. *The Future of the Cognitive Revolution*. New York: Oxford University Press.

Johnson-Laird, P. N. 1988. "A Computational Model of Consciousness." In A. J. Marcel and E. Bisach, eds., *Consciousness in Contemporary Science*. New York: Oxford University Press, pp. 357–65.

Kennedy, J. S. 1992. *The New Anthropomorphism*. New York: Cambridge University Press.

Libet, B. 1993. *Neurophysiology of Consciousness*. Boston: Birkhauser.

Lieberman, P. 1984. *The Biology and Evolution of Language*. Cambridge: Harvard University Press.

Lieberman, P. 1998. *Eve Spoke: Human Language and Human Evolution*. New York: Norton.

Lijmbach S. 1997. "Less Is Different: Discontinuity Between Animal and Human Consciousness." In Dol et al., eds. (1997): 62–72.

Lindahl, B. I. B. 1997. "Consciousness and Biological Evolution." *J Theor Biol* 187:613–29.

Lorenz, K. 1958. *The Evolution of Behavior*. San Francisco: Freeman.

———. 1971. *Studies in Animal and Human Behavior,* vol 2. Cambridge: Harvard University Press.

Mahner, H. and M. Bunge. 1997. *Foundations of Biophilosophy*. Berlin: Springer.

Marler, P. and C. Evans. 1996. "Bird Calls: Just Emotional Displays or Something More?" *Ibis* 138:26–33.

Meijsing, M. 1997. "Awareness, Self-Awareness and Perception: An Essay on Animal Consciousness." In Dol et al., eds. (1997): 48–61.

Miller, G. A. 1967. *The Psychology of Communication*. New York: Basic.

Miller, G. A., E. Galanter, and K. H. Pribram. 1960. *Plans and the Structure of Behavior*. New York: Holt Rinehart and Winston.

Milner, D. A. 1998. "Streams of Consciousness: Visual Awareness and the Brain." *Trends Cogn Sci* 2:25–30.

Mitchell, R. W., N. S. Thompson, and l. Miles, eds. 1997. *Anthropomorphism, Anecdotes and Animals*. Albany: SUNY Press.

Nagel, T. 1974. "What Is It Like to Be a Bat?" *Philos Rev* 83:435–50.

Natsoulas, T. 1978. "Consciousness." *Am Psychol* 33:906–14.

Newman, J. 1997. "Putting the Puzzle Together: Towards a General Theory of Consciousness, Parts I and II." *J Consciousness Stud* 4:47–66, 100–121.

Ohman, A., F. Estebves, and J. J. F. Soares. 1995. "Preparedness and Preattentive Associative

Learning: Electrodermal Conditioning To Masked Stimuli." *J Psychophysiol* 9:99–108.

Owings, D.H., M.D. Beecher, M.D., and N.S. Thompson, eds. 1997. "Communication." *Perspectives in Ethology,* vol. 12). New York: Plenum.

Pepperberg, I.M. 1981. "Functional Vocalization by an African Grey Parrot (Psivacus *erithacus)."* *Z Tierpsychol* 55:139–60.

———. "A Communicative Approach to Animal Cognition: A Study of Conceptual Abilities of an African Grey Parrot." In Ristau, ed. (1991): 153–86.

———. 1994. "Vocal Learning in Grey Parrots (*Psittacus Erithacus*): Effects of Social Interaction, Reference, and Context." *Auk* 111:300–313.

Popper, K.R. 1978. "Natural Selection and the Emergence of Mind." In G. Radnitzky, W.W. Bartley III, eds., *Evolutionary Epistemology, Rationality, and the Sociology of Knowledge*. LaSalle: Open Court, pp. 139–56.

Povinelli, D.J. 1993. "Reconstructing the Evolution of Mind." *Am Psychol* 48:493–509.

Povinelli, D.J. and T.M. Preuss. 1995. "Theory of Mind: Evolutionary History of a Cognitive Specialization." *Trends Neurosci* 18:418–24.

Premack, D. and G. Woodruff. 1978. "Does the Chimpanzee Have a Theory of Mind?" *Behav Brain Sci* 1:515–26.

Radner, D. and M. Radner. 1989. *Animal Consciousness*. Buffalo: Prometheus.

Rescorla, R.A. 1988. "Behavioral Studies of Pavlovian Conditioning." *Annu Rev Neurosc* 11:329–52.

Ristau, C.A. 1991. "Aspects of the Cognitive Ethology of an Injury-Feigning Bird, the Piping Plover." In C.A. Ristau, ed., *Cognitive Ethology: The Minds of Other Animals*. Hillsdale: Erlbaum, pp. 91–126.

Roitblat, H.L. 1987. *Introduction to Comparative Cognition*. New York: Freeman.

Roitblat, H.L., T.O. Bever, and H.S. Terrace, eds. 1984. *Animal Cognition*. Hillsdale: Erlbaum.

Romanes, G.I. 1969 [1884]. *Mental Evolution in Animals*. New York: ABS Press.

Savage-Rumbaugh, E.S. 1997. "Why Are We Afraid of Apes with Language?" In A.B. Scheibel and J.W. Schopf, eds., *The Origin and Evolution of Intelligence*. Sudbury: Jones and Bartlett, pp. 43–69.

Savage-Rumbaugh, E.S. and R. Lewin, R. 1994. *Kanzi, the Ape at the Brink of the Human Mind*. New York: Wiley.

Schacter, D.L., C-Y.P. Chiu, and K.N. Ochsner. 1993. "Implicit Memory: A Selective Review." *Annu Rev Neurosci* 16:159–82.

Schusterman, R.J. and R. Gisiner. 1989. "Please Parse the Sentence: Animal Cognition in the Procrustean Bed of Linguistics." *Psychol Rec* 39:3–18.

Searle, J.R. 1992. *The Rediscovery of the Mind*. Cambridge: MIT Press.

Sebeok, T.A. and R. Rosenthal, eds. 1981. "The Clever Hans Phenomenon: Communication With Horses, Whales, Apes and People." *Ann N Y Acad Sci* 364:1–311.

Seyfarth, R.M. and D.L. Cheney. 1997. "Behavioral Mechanisms Underlying Vocal Communication in Nonhuman Primates." *Anim Learn Behav* 25:249–67.

Shanks, D.R. and M.F. St. John.1994. "Characteristics of Dissociable Human Learning Systems." *Behav Brain Sci* 17:367–95.

Skinner, B.F. 1988. "Genes and Behavior." In G. Greenberg and E, Tobach, eds., *Evolution of Social Behavior and Integrative Levels*. Hillsdale: Erlbaum, pp. 77–83.

Skutch, A.F. 1996. *The Minds of Birds*. College Station: Texas A&M University Press,.

Stich, S.P. 1983. *From Folk Psychology to Cognitive Science: the Case Against Belief*. Cambridge: MIT Press.

Terrace, H.S. 1984. "Animal Cognition." In H.L. Roitblat, T.O. Bever, and H.S. Terrace, eds. (1984): 7–28.

Terrace, H.S., L.A. Petitto, and T.G. Bever. 1979. "Can an Ape Create a Sentence?" *Science* 206: 891–902.

Thorpe, W.H. 1963. *Learning and Instinct in Animals*. Cambridge: Harvard University Press.

———. *Animal Nature and Human Nature*. Garden City: Doubleday.

Tinbergen, N. 1951. *The Study of Instinct.* Oxford: Oxford University Press.

Tolman, E.C. 1932. *Purposive Behavior in Animals and Men.* New York: Appleton-Century.

———. 1959. "Principles of Purposive Behavior." In S. Koch, ed., *Psychology: A Study of a Science. Study I. Conceptual and Systematic, Vol. 2, General Systematic Foundations: Learning and Special Processes.* New York: McGraw-Hill, pp. 92–157.

Van den Steen, W.J. 1997. "Fighting Against Umbrellas: An Essay on Consciousness." Dol et al., eds. (1997): 17–31.

Van Rooijen, J. 1997. "Suffering and Well-Being and the Study of Behaviour." In Dol et al., eds. (1997): 114–24.

Vauclair, J. 1992. Psychologie cognitive et représentations animales. In L Gervet, P Livet, and A Tete, eds. *La Représentation animale, représentation de la représentation.* Nancy: Presses Universitaires, pp. 127–42.

———. *Animal Cognition: An Introduction to Modern Comparative Psychology.* Cambridge: Harvard University Press.

———. 1997. "Mental States in Animals: Cognitive Ethology." *Trends Cogn Sci* 1:35–39.

Velmans, M. 1991. "Is Human Information Processing Conscious?" *Behav Brain Sci* 14:651–726.

Waal, F.M.B. de. 1991. "Complementary Methods and Convergent Evidence in the Study of Primate Social Cognition." *Behaviour* 118:297–320.

———. *Good Natured: The Origins of Right and Wrong in Humans and Other Animals.* Cambridge: Harvard University Press.

Walker, S. 1983. *Animal Thought.* London: Routledge and Kegan Paul.

Wasserman, E.A. 1983. "Is Cognitive Psychology Behavioral?" *Psychol Rec* 33:6–11.

———. 1985. "Comments on Animal Thinking." *Am Sci* 73:6.

Wasserman, E.A., R.R. Kiedinger, and R.S. Bhatt. 1988. "Conceptual Behavior in Pigeons: Categories, Subcategories, and Pseudocategories." *J Exp Psychol Anim Behav Proc* 14:235–46.

Wemelsfelder, F. 1997. "Investigating the Animal's Point of View. An Enquiry Into a Subject-Based Method of Measurement in the Field of Animal Welfare." In Dol et al., eds. (1997): 73–89.

Whitehead, A.N. 1938. *Modes of Thought.* New York: MacMillan.

Williams, G.C. 1997. *The Pony Fish's Glow, and Other Cues to Plan and Purpose in Nature.* New York: Basic.

Woolf, N.J. 1997. "A Possible Role for Cholinergic Neurons of the Basal Forebrain and Pontomesencephalon in Consciousness." *Consciousness Cogn* 6:574–96.

Yoerg, S.I. and A.C. Kamil. 1991. "Prospects for a More Cognitive Ethology." In Ristau, ed. (1991): 273–89.

Although the authors do not discuss this possibility, two recent books review many examples of versatile animal behavior that may well involve simple conscious thinking:

Dugatkin, L.A. 1997. *Cooperation Among Animals. An Evolutionary Perspective.* Oxford: Oxford University Press.

Dukas, R., ed. 1998. *Cognitive Ecology. The Evolutionary Ecology of Information Processing and Decision Making.* Chicago: University of Chicago Press.

Addendum: The Maturation (or Growing Pains?) of Cognitive Ethology

Editors' note: In late 2001, a little over two years before his death in 2004, Donald Griffin wrote, at our request and expressly for this volume, this addendum to his famous article, "From Cognition to Consciousness," which we have reprinted. The text follows.

Since this article was first published in 1998 a veritable flood of books and scientific papers has strengthened the evidence that some sort of conscious awareness is widespread among animals with central nervous systems. Living animals are coming to be recognized as not only physical objects but also subjects and actors, who have at least limited levels of conscious awareness. The content of their thoughts and feelings must vary widely by species and situation, and some of their subjective experiences may be quite different from any of ours. Even in the months since I completed a revised edition of *Animal Minds* (Griffin 2001), so much has been published that it is difficult to review it adequately. The recent publications listed below are especially relevant to the questions discussed in the present volume.

Three multi-authored collections review the overwhelming evidence of animal *cognition,* although most authors use this term to mean information processing and avoid any discussion of subjective experience. But the versatility of the cognition is strongly suggestive of conscious thinking.

Balda, R. P., I. M. Pepperberg, and A. C. Kamil, eds. 1998. *Animal Cognition in Nature: The Convergence of Psychology and Biology in Laboratory and Field.* San Diego: Academic Press.

Hauser, M. D., and M. Konishi, M., eds. 1999. *The Design of Animal Communication.* Cambridge: MIT Press.

Heyes, C. and L. Huber, eds. 2000. *The Evolution of Cognition.* Cambridge: MIT Press.

The active search by neuroscientists for the neural correlates of consciousness is exemplified by three books and two technical papers in addition to earlier investigations reviewed in Griffin (2001):

Edelman, G. and G. Tononi, G. 2000. *A Universe of Consciousness: How Matter Becomes Imagination.* New York: Basic Books.

Hampton, R. R. 2001. "Rhesus Monkeys Know When They Know." *Proceedings of the National Academy of Sciences* 98:5359–62 and comments 5833–34.

Menzel, R. and Giurfa, M. 2001. "Cognitive Architecture of a Mini-Brain: The Honeybee." *Trends in Cognitive Science* 5:62–71.

Searle, J. R. 2000. "Consciousness." *Annual Review of Neuroscience* 23:557–78.

Taylor, J. G. 1999. *The Race for Consciousness.* Cambridge: MIT Press.

Finally, the adaptive versatility and revealing communication of animals have been well reviewed in the following four books and three papers:

Call, J. 2001. "Chimpanzee Social Cognition." *Trends in Cognitive Science* 5:192–97.

Cartmill, M., ed. 2000. "Animal Consciousness: Historical, Theoretical, and Empirical Perspectives." *American Zoologist* 40:835–46.

Griffin, D. R. 2001. *Animal Minds: From Cognition to Consciousness.* Chicago: University of Chicago Press.

Heinrich, B. 1999. *The Mind of the Raven: Investigations and Adventures with Wolf-Birds.* New York: Cliff Street Books.

Matsuzawa, T. ed. 2001. *Primate Origins of Human Cognition and Behavior.* New York: Springer.

Pepperberg, I. M. 1999. *The Alex Studies: Cognitive and Communicative Abilities of Grey Parrots.* Cambridge: Harvard University Press.

Seeley, T. D. and Buhrman, S. C. 1999. "Group Decision Making in Swarms of Honeybees." *Behavioral Ecology and Sociobiology* 31:375–83.

Waal, F. M. B. de. 2001. *The Ape and the Sushi Master: Cultural Reflections of a Primatologist.* New York: Basic Books.

Scientists have tended to assume that any conscious experiences of animals would necessarily be direct results of external stimulation, either contemporary events or memories of previous stimulation. But we know far too little to rule out the possibility that nonhuman experiences are not always tightly linked to *any* external stimulation. Subjective experiences must have causes, but in addition to immediate external stimulation, such causes might include at least three other general categories:

1. Reorganized memories of prior external stimulation. Sifting and rearranging memories, especially those that are especially important in the animal's life, may yield experiences that are so remote from the initial stimulation that tracing their causal ancestry becomes impossible.

2. Genetic influence, probably honed by na-

tural selection to be adaptively useful to the animal.

3. Spontaneous generation of new thoughts and feelings—anticipations, hopes, or worries about what might happen next.

At present we know far too little to do more than speculate about such endogenously generated experiences, but future theoretical and empirical inquiries should keep this possibility in mind.

Are Animals Moral Agents?

Evolutionary Building Blocks of Morality

MARC HAUSER

Once upon a time, a serpent seduced a young woman to eat a piece of fruit from a forbidden tree. Having tasted this delectable fruit, this woman suggested that her lover taste the fruit as well. He did, faithfully. She couldn't resist the serpent's offer, and he couldn't resist hers. Both were weak. Both lacked control. Both fell victim to temptation, to a cunning serpent and a piece of fruit. The Bible and other religious narratives provide one story about the relationship between temptation and control. Here, I would like to provide another story—one motivated by a history that I suggest is deeper and older, and informed by scientific facts, and by an appreciation of our evolutionary legacies.

For animals living in nature, and with nature, temptations abound. Not only must animals choose when to give in to temptation and when to fight it, but they also must learn from experience, attempting to overcome passions that might prove destructive. Humans are no different. The story I wish to tell, however, predates the evolution of our species, while raising important moral questions about how we live our life. It is a story that lays out the biological facts, steers clear of assuming that "*is* equals *ought*," and then makes the point that what *is* should guide how we think about what *ought* to be.

I start with an exploration of the kinds of problems that require inhibitory control, and how animals fare when it comes to engaging such systems in order to avoid temptation. I then discuss how our increasing knowledge of the mental lives of animals should move center stage with respect to our treatment of them. Finally, I conclude with an argument concerning how humans evolved a unique trick, one that provided them with a degree of control over their passions that no animal has or ever could exert. With this trick in hand, humans must nonetheless remain vigilant of the *is* handed down from biology and use this knowledge to guide the *ought* associated with an ethical life.

A Topographic View of Control

In the psychological and neuroscientific literature, it is not uncommon to hear scientists referring to "problems of inhibitory control" as if this
were a homogeneous process. And yet, there is
not a single problem of inhibition, but an entire
landscape of problems, each involving potentially different neurobiological, emotional, and
mental processes.

Consider first the problem that Descartes
thought was at the center of the distinction between humans and other animals. The Cartesian view says that whereas animals are driven
by instinct and passion, humans are motivated
by rational thought, and act by carefully weighing the issues and then making an emotionally cool choice. This view is wrong on several
counts. First, and as recent studies have made
clear, all animals, humans included, are guided
by instincts (Hauser 2000:25; Pinker 1997:33).
Instincts make learning possible. The genetic
mechanisms that enable animals to learn, and in
some cases, to learn different things, are essential to survival. The instinct to learn provides a
filter on the nature and timing of the experiential input. Thus, in the same way that a songbird
must be exposed to species-typical song during a sensitive period of development in order
to acquire the correct phrasing and sound, so
must a child acquiring language. If the input is
other than the species-typical material or input,
neither the bird nor the child will develop normally. Similarly, if the input is correct, but is
provided too late in development, then abnormalities will emerge. What keeps the young bird
and child on track is an instinct to learn, song
for birds and language for children.

A second error associated with Descartes' position is that it dichotomizes decision-making
into rational and emotional components. And
yet, when one looks carefully at decision-
making, the rational and emotional are so clearly
intertwined that it doesn't make much sense
to separate them (Damasio 1994:2; Damasio
2000:3; Rolls 1999:34). More precisely, when

individuals make any decision, they use both
good sense and good emotions. Emotions are a
guide to which of the various options are best.
Sometimes, the rational overwhelms the emotional, and sometimes the emotional overrides
the rational. These are precisely the cases where
inhibitory control is most important, and where
nonhuman animals often falter. Let me illustrate by discussing several examples from different peaks within the landscape of control.

Critical to any theory of moral or ethical behavior is an understanding of why an individual
repeats or perseveres with a particular response.
If someone repeatedly steals, it is important to
figure out whether this is because they are incapable of inhibiting their desires or whether
they lack an understanding of the legal and
moral consequences associated with stealing.
Damasio and his colleagues (Anderson 1999,
et al.:1; Bechara et al., 1997:4; Damasio 1994:2;
Damasio 2000:3) have explored this problem
by looking at patients with damage to orbitofrontal cortex, a region of the brain that appears
to be critically involved in inhibitory control.
In cases where the damage occurred in adulthood, subjects were able to understand moral
dilemmas and moral explanations for behavior, but had difficulty making decisions because
they lacked appropriate emotional responses;
this makes sense when one considers that the
orbitofrontal cortex has significant connections
to the amygdala, an area involved in processing emotions. As a result of their deficit, these
patients might persevere with an inappropriate response because they lack the requisite
emotional input that enables normal adults to
properly evaluate a decision. In contrast, when
damage to orbitofrontal cortex occurs in infancy, a more dramatic, conceptual deficit arises
(Anderson, et al. 1999:1). Specifically, when such
patients were tested on Kohlberg's battery of
moral problems (Colby and Kohlberg 1987:13),
they scored in the range of a very young child.
These patients failed to understand why something was wrong, and why they should feel bad
or good about their actions. Their performance

on these verbal tests matched their behavior in real life, as evidenced by repeated convictions for the same petty crimes.

No one has yet developed an animal-friendly battery of moral dilemmas that might reveal how animals make such choices. There are, however, two experiments that reveal how repetitive errors of judgment might be explored. In an ingenious, yet simple experiment, Boysen (Boysen, 1995:14; Boysen and Berntson, 1996:15) presented two chimpanzees—a selector and a receiver—with a task about choice of food. On each trial, one of two containers (food wells) always was stocked with more food. The selector's task was to point to one of them. The receiver chimp obtained the food from the container pointed to, while the selector received the food in the other one. Thus, if chimpanzees are greedy—a reasonable assumption—then they should point to the container with less food. Over the course of dozens of trials, where selector and receiver changed roles and partners, no selector ever pointed to the smaller container with any consistency. That is, selectors most often pointed to the container with more food, and thus obtained less food. One interpretation of this finding is that chimpanzees are the ultimate altruists. An alternative interpretation is that chimpanzees lack the capacity to inhibit their desire to obtain the larger quantity of food.

To test between these alternative explanations, Boysen covered the food wells with cards associated with an Arabic numeral. Since the chimpanzees playing this game knew the meaning of the Arabic numerals, they understood that a card with the number "4" on it represented four pieces of food, while a card with "1" on it represented one piece of food. On the first trial of this transfer test, chimpanzees pointed to the card with the lower number, and thereby obtained the larger amount of food. This shows that chimpanzees are greedy, and that they can comprehend the rules of this game: Pick the one you don't want to get the one you want. It also shows that when the food is directly in view, they are incapable of inhibiting their greed.

Moreover, and somewhat surprisingly, Boysen (Boysen, Mukobi, and Berntson 1999:16) has repeatedly tested the chimps on the original, no-card task, and the results are the same: they continue to point to the larger quantity of food. Thus, even though they clearly understand the rules of this game, they are incapable of applying their understanding from one context to another. The chimpanzees' error shows that when it comes to inhibiting their emotions or motivational drives, they are weak.

To evaluate the claim that chimpanzees lack inhibitory control on the original "pick the one you don't want" task, Silberberg and Fujita (1996:17) ran a modified version of this task with Japanese macaques. The experiment was motivated by the fact that whichever well the chimpanzees select, they are always rewarded, sometimes with the larger quantity and sometimes with the smaller. Given that Boysen's chimpanzees are not food-deprived, it is possible that the costs of picking the larger quantity are relatively trivial. This argument can't account for the chimps' success with the Arabic number cards, but could account for their failure without them. In Silberberg and Fujita's experiment, they first ran the macaques on Boysen's original design, and replicated the results exactly: the macaques consistently picked the well with more food. In a second condition, they changed the contingencies. Now, when subjects selected the larger food quantity, they received no food at all. Under these conditions, the macaques switched strategies and consistently picked the well with less food. What this shows is that Japanese macaques, and presumably chimpanzees as well, can inhibit their desire to point to the well with more food if the costs of doing so are high. This does not negate the importance of Boysen's original finding, but does point out how the problem of inhibition is a subtle one, and that it requires a careful investigation of an animal's motivational state. It also shows that within the landscape of control, there are problems associated with both learning a rule and controlling a natural motivation, the desire to eat more food. Chimpanzees appear to be able to learn the rule, but have difficulty applying it when their hunger levels get in the way.

In a second experiment, designed to disentangle problems of rule learning from problems of motivational control, cotton-top tamarins were presented with a means-end task involving the use of a tool to gain access to a piece of food (Hauser 1999:18). In the original training condition, subjects were presented with two potential tools. On one side of a tray was a piece of food on top of a piece of cloth. On the other side of the tray was an identical piece of food positioned next to the cloth, but not on top. To gain access to the food, the subject was required to pull the piece of cloth with food on top; pulling the other cloth resulted in the cloth advancing but without the food. The tamarins readily learned this problem, and then generalized (on the first trial of each new condition) to a wide variety of novel conditions involving different cloths of different color, texture, shape, and size, as well as connected as opposed to disconnected pieces of cloth. These transfer trials show that the tamarins understand the means-end task.

However, two additional conditions show how an animal's conceptual knowledge can interact with its motivational state. In one condition, an experimenter presented a subject with two identical pieces of cloth. On one side, a small piece of food was placed on top of the cloth, while on the other side a large piece of food was placed off to the side of the cloth. Although the tamarins clearly understood the means-end task as demonstrated on hundreds of trials, on this condition they consistently reached for the cloth associated with the large piece of food; as a result; they persevered with a response bias that failed to yield food. Apparently, the desire to obtain a large piece of food overwhelmed their problem-solving abilities. A second condition revealed, however, the subtlety of the inhibitory problem. Here, an experimenter presented the subject with two pieces of cloth and food located off both pieces.

Thus, neither side of the tray provided the tamarins with an opportunity to gain food. On these trials, several tamarins looked at the tray, and refrained from pulling either cloth. This shows that tamarins can inhibit cloth-pulling even when there is food in view. Together, these studies show that animals have difficulty inhibiting some impulses but not others. Overall, when the temptation to gain access to more over less food strikes, animals fall victim. The inhibitory mechanism is simply insufficient to overwhelm this temptation.

Rules can be arbitrary (the traffic light's designation of red for stop and green for go) or nonarbitary (objects lacking support fall down due to gravity). Neither arbitrary nor nonarbitrary rules hold under all circumstances, and an intelligent creature adapts to both the consistent and inconsistent cases. For example, although red indicates "stop" in the domain of traffic, it indicates "approach" in the domain of Christmas (think children awaiting Santa Claus and Rudolf leading the way); although an unobstructed falling object drops straight down to the lowest point of support, an obstructed falling object will be deflected by the obstruction. What do animals make of such arbitrary and nonarbitrary rules? More important, having acquired them through experience or as part of their innate endowment, can they acquire an understanding that under some circumstances, rules are made to be broken? Can they inhibit the old to bring in the new?

Teach an animal that pressing a red button leads to a food reward whereas pressing a green button does not. All animals will rapidly learn to press red but not green. Once they have this rule down, switch the association: pressing green yields food, pressing red does not. Most animals have a terrible time with this task, maintaining their old bias and pressing red. Eventually, animals will switch. But if you switch again, back to the old red = food, their performance will plummet again. There is some indication that the bigger-brained primates do better on these switches than do either

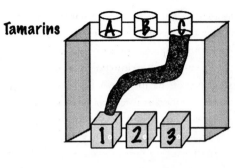

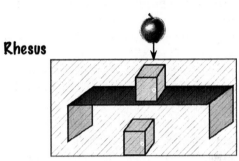

(Top). Tubes task used to assess cotton-top tamarin's ability to understand the movement of an invisibly displaced piece of food (black circle) through an opaque tube. (Bottom). Shelf task designed to assess where rhesus monkeys search for the apple when it has fallen out of view behind an opaque screen (stippled rectangle in front of table with boxes on top and bottom).

the smaller-brained primates or other animals. Overall, animals have difficulty with this one class of inhibitory problems.

Given gravity's tenure on earth, one would expect animals to have some kind of understanding about how objects move in relation to the forces of gravity. One would expect them to have some kind of a theory of falling objects. Before I say what I mean by having a "theory," consider the following experiments with cotton-top tamarins (Hood 1999:22) and rhesus monkeys (Hauser 2001:23).

An experimenter presented tamarins with a vertical frame, open in the middle, and with three short pipes (A, B, and C) on top and three boxes (1, 2, and 3) lined up below (see figure 1, top). While the subjects watched, the experimenter attached an opaque S-shaped tube from pipe-C to box 1 and dropped a piece of food down the C-pipe. Where did the tamarins search? On their first try they looked, in vain, in box 3, the box directly beneath the release point. Since there is no connection between pipe-C and box 3, and since the tamarins never saw food drop into this open space, noth-

ing about their perceptual experiences would have led them to this result. After they opened box 3, the experimenter closed the door and gave them another chance. Sometimes they reopened the door to box 3 and again found nothing; usually, they next opened box 2, and finally box 1, where they found the food. When the experimenter played this game again, keeping the tube in the same C-1 configuration, the tamarins typically repeated the same error, searching first in box 3, then 2, then 1. Some individuals repeated this error twenty or thirty times! After several failures, however, some tamarins did select box 1 on the first try. At this point, the experimenter moved the tube, attaching it from pipe-B to box-3. Where did the tamarins search? Box 2, the box beneath the release point. This extraordinary error was repeated over and over and over again. But when the experimenter replaced the opaque tube with a transparent one, allowing the tamarins to see the food fall, they searched in the correct box, and did so consistently. However, when the experimenter put the opaque tube back in, placing it in the same position as the transparent tube on the previous trial, the tamarins bounced back to their original error, searching in the box beneath the release point.

Newton would have been proud of the tamarins' error. Darwin would have been embarrassed. The tamarins appear to have a remarkable gravity bias, one that causes search-error after search-error. Why don't they use their failed attempts to find food beneath the release point to try some other strategy? Why don't they try the most obvious solution to this problem and pick the box *associated* with the tube? Without even looking at the food's release point, the answer on every trial is always the box associated with the tube. Since we know that animals as genetically distant as worms and humans use associations to solve problems in the world, why don't the tamarins fall back on this simple strategy? Perhaps tamarins, unlike their distant relatives the worms, are too smart for their own good. Instead of using the simplest strategy for finding food, they are overthinking the problem. Or perhaps this kind of gravity bias pays off most of the time, falling victim to the exceptional cases when a warped experimental mind sets up some tortuous contraption.

To show that there is not just something odd about the apparatus with the tubes, or about tamarins, consider two additional experiments. If gravity is the primary source of their difficulty, as opposed to some other factor such as the artificiality of the experiment or the fact that there are no tubes in the real world, then removing gravity should change the patterns of search. An experimenter presented the tamarins with the same apparatus, but set it up horizontally as opposed to vertically. When the experimenter rolled the food down the tube, the tamarins showed a marked improvement in their search patterns; critically, they did not show the equivalent of the gravity bias. This shows that when there is no effect of gravity, tamarins can find a piece of food that has been invisibly displaced within a tube. Tubes are not the problem.

But perhaps, since the same tamarins were run on the horizontal test after they were run on the vertical test, they finally figured out what was going on. To examine this possibility, and to look at the idea that tubes are just odd things, an experimenter tested the tamarins on a vertical setup that was identical to the original experiment, but replaced the tube with a hidden ramp —a flat piece of plastic concealed by a screen. Although these animals had hundreds of trials with the vertical tubes, and hundreds of trials on the horizontal tubes, they once again failed on the vertical ramps, and with the same comical errors, picking the box beneath the release point, then the middle, and then the correct box, and starting all over again on consecutive trials.

Tamarins are not the only species with a rigid Newtonian mind. Show a rhesus monkey a table, place one box on top and one box directly below (see figure 34.1, bottom). Hide the boxes and table from view with a screen, drop an apple over the two aligned boxes so that it falls out of view, remove the screen and allow the subject to approach. As if the tamarins passed on their secret to the rhesus, individuals search in the box below the table, and consistently, fail to find the apple. It can't be there. Apples can't travel through the top box, then through the table and into the bottom box. The fact that boxes are containers and that tables are solid are, well, facts of the physical world. In parallel with the tamarins, if the experimenter now turns the problem on its side, removing gravity, and then rolling an apple toward two concealed boxes placed in a straight line, rhesus always pick the near box. Here, they seem to *know* that when you roll an apple toward two boxes, that the closest box will stop or contain the apple. Rhesus monkeys know that an apple can't roll *through* a box. But they somehow think that an apple can drop through a box and then a table and into a box below.

Tamarins, rhesus, and many other animals have some understanding of physical principles. The fact that they are absolutely pathetic when it comes to searching for invisibly displaced falling objects is actually more, rather than less, evidence for what they know or understand. What is striking about their error with falling objects is how consistent it is, how immune it appears to be to counter-evidence. This kind of immunity is precisely what is expected if the animal has a theory (Carey 1985:24; Hauser 2000:25). Like scientists with an idée fixe, both tamarins and rhesus appear to hold a theory of falling objects, one that they adhere to even in the face of evidence that the theory is wrong and requires modification. We can say that it is a theory about falling objects rather than objects or moving objects in general, because both tamarins and rhesus have the right theory when it comes to making predictions about objects that move along the horizontal plane. And what gives this story even greater support is the fact that the searching pattern for tamarins and rhesus are similar even though each species lives in a different environment and has been designed to solve somewhat different ecological and social problems. Importantly, tamarins are highly arboreal animals, spending most of their time high up in the canopy. Rhesus monkeys, in contrast, are largely terrestrial, spending most of their time on the ground. Tamarins have therefore had little experience watching objects roll on a flat surface, and although they have presumably seen objects falling (e.g., fruit), they are unlikely to track and search for such objects on the ground. Rhesus monkeys have presumably seen numerous objects moving on the ground and falling from trees, and most likely have searched for falling objects, since they spend more time on the ground than do tamarins. Nonetheless, both species showed a strong gravity bias.

Although tamarins and rhesus monkeys may be like scientists in terms of holding a theory about falling objects, they differ in at least one critical way. Most scientists eventually give in, admitting that their own theory no longer accounts for the data, and that a new theory is necessary. It is possible, of course, that if an experimenter were willing to test the tamarins for a year they would eventually cave in and pick the correct box. But then it would be necessary to distinguish between theory change and mere training or shaping. The main point here is that conceptual change doesn't appear to be a strong point among animal minds, at least when the expectations or theories that underlie their behavior represent statistical regularities of the world. Gravity is one such regularity.

With the exception of Boysen's food choice experiments, all of the work reviewed thus far has focused on inhibitory problems that are related to inanimate objects, as opposed to animate or living objects—such as other animals. Are there any studies that speak to the problem of temptation and control, but that pose a social challenge? To my knowledge, there are only a handful. Of those studies that do speak to this problem, most date back approximately fifty years, and some would be considered unethical by most current standards for animal testing. As I and others have discussed elsewhere (Hauser 2000:25; Preston and de Waal 2002:26), these studies deserve some attention because they shed light on the question of temptation and control, and raise some of the more difficult questions concerning evolutionary changes in the mind that led to the capacity for empathy and attributing beliefs and desires to others.

An experimenter taught a rat to press a lever for food (Church 1959:11). The experimenter then introduced a second rat into an adjacent cage and switched the wiring to the lever. When the rat with access to the lever pressed it, he delivered a strong shock to his neighbor. This shock not only had a direct effect on the recipient, but also on the actor rat in control of the levers, in that the actor actually stopped pressing for a while and thereby forfeited access to food. In so doing, the actor incurred the cost associated with hunger while relieving the recipient of the shock, his neighbor, of pain. Definitionally, this is altruistic. Definitionally, it also shows that rats can control their immediate desire for food to block an action that would cause pain to another. Although rats initially curtail their pressing, ultimately they go back to pressing, a release from control that makes sense given that they will starve if they don't press the levers. Even though it may be wrong to shock another, and even though the rat is directly responsible for the shock, individual survival carries the moment.

In a follow-up study, an experimenter taught a group of rats to press a lever to lower a suspended block of Styrofoam to the ground; if a rat failed to press the lever, the experimenter delivered a shock (Rice and Gainer 1962:12). Once the rats learned to press the lever, the shock was eliminated, and gradually, so was their tendency to press the lever; in the absence of either punishment or reward, there is no motivation to press. For half of the rats, the study continued with a Styrofoam block suspended by a harness and the lever available for pressing. For the other rats, the experimenter replaced the Styrofoam with a live rat suspended by a harness, a stressful position that leads to wriggling and squealing. Rats presented with suspended Styrofoam blocks do nothing at all. Rats presented with suspended rats in their immediate environment immediately start pressing the lever. Although the experimenter would not have shocked these rats for apathy, nor rewarded them with food for pressing, they nonetheless pressed the lever and thereby lowered their compatriots, relieving them of the stress associated with suspension. Definitionally, this is altruistic in that the actor incurs the cost of pressing and thereby benefits the suspended individual by lowering him to safety. Definitionally, it also shows that rats can control the temptation to sit still as an innocent bystander and watch another rat in distress. Unlike residents who turn the other cheek as an unknown victim is attacked in their neighborhood, these are *carpe diem* rats, seizing the moment and helping an unrelated rat in need. At least this is one interpretation.

What do these results tell us about control and temptation? Perhaps seeing another in distress triggers an emotional response in the actor that blocks the route to temptation. There is no control problem because there is no alternative choice. Seeing another rat in pain or distress is sufficient to cause a sympathetic or empathetic response. Alternatively, perhaps seeing another in distress is aversive. When rats experience something that is aversive, they do what they can to stop it. What would the rats have done if they witnessed another rat suspended from the harness or in the process of receiving shock, but without access to a lever? Would they have attempted a rescue mission, using their crafty minds to find a solution? Lastly, perhaps the rats in control of the lever pressed because they thought they were in some kind of reciprocation game. If they press now and relieve another of pain, then when the roles switch, they too might benefit from an actor who presses and relieves them of pain—the Golden Rule rules. Although this game was never played, the rats may well have perceived the set up in precisely this way. Given that there were no follow up experiments to these early studies, we can't distinguish between these alternative explanations. Parallel studies of rhesus monkeys (Masserman, Wechkin, and Terris 1964:27; Miller, Banks, and Ogawa 1963:7; Miller, Banks, and Kuwahara 1966:8; Miller 1967:9; Wechkin, Masserman, and Terris 1964:10), however, provide additional insights.

An experimenter trained a rhesus monkey to pull one of two chains for food; if the subject failed to pull, then it would obtain no food on that day. Consequently, the experimenter placed the rhesus monkeys in a self-service, work-for-your-food setup. Subjects readily complied and fed themselves. Next, the experimenter introduced another rhesus monkey into the adjacent cage, and in parallel with the studies on rats, hooked up one of the chains to a machine that would deliver a shock to the newly introduced neighbor. Mirroring the rats' behavior, rhesus also stopped pulling the chains. But in contrast with the rats, most of the rhesus monkeys showed far greater restraint—far greater inhibitory control. Some individuals stopped pulling for five to twelve days, functionally starving themselves. The extent to which rhesus refrained from pulling was related to three important factors: experience with shock, familiarity, and species identity. If the actor had previously been on the receiving end, and had been shocked, then the actor withheld pulling the chains for longer. If the actor was paired with a familiar group member as opposed to an unfamiliar member of another group, then the actor withheld pulling for longer. If the actor was paired with another rhesus monkey as opposed to a rabbit, then the actor withheld pulling for longer. Definitionally, these rhesus monkeys are acting altruistically in that they incur the costs of food deprivation but provide a benefit to another who avoids shock. Definitionally, these rhesus monkeys are also exhibiting control over temptation, and in some cases, quite extraordinary levels of control because as the days go by and the desire to eat increases, the temptation to pull increases as well.

The experiments on rats and rhesus are unambiguous problems of motivational control. Whether they are also problems of control over emotions and feelings is unclear. If empathy is defined as a kind of mirrored emotion, where one animal's emotional state triggers a comparable emotion in another, then both rats and rhesus are likely to be empathetic (Preston and de Waal 2002:26). If, in contrast, empathy is defined as knowing what it is like to experience what another is emotionally experiencing, then a different capacity is necessary. Knowing what it is like to have someone else's emotions takes us from emotion to feeling and from a straightforward triggering system to having a theory of mind. Although some recent studies suggest that chimpanzees and rhesus monkeys have a theory of mind, recognizing the correspondence between seeing and knowing (Hare et al. 2000:28; Hare, Call, and Tomasello 2001:29; Hare et al. 2003; Flombaum and Santos 2005), there are conflicting reports for chimpanzees (Heyes 1998:32; Povinelli and Eddy 1996:30; Tomasello and Call 1997:31), as well as monkeys. Although these experiments leave us with many unanswered questions, they do show that in the context of social interactions with others,

individuals can control the temptation to eat when it will save someone else's hide.

Putting this altogether, I draw the following conclusions. Overall, animals exhibit weak inhibitory control. When motivational challenges are at stake, animals readily fall victim to temptation. When conceptual change is required because of an environmentally imposed switch in the effectiveness of a rule, most animals are incapable of such change, persevering with the old action patterns even though they fail to achieve the target goal. No value judgments should be placed on these patterns of behavior. Rather, they indicate what animals do under different conditions, and what constraints operate on their ability to cope with novel situations. Importantly for the next section they begin to reveal what animals want, desire, and expect —psychological processes that are at the heart of most ethical theories and of philosophical reflections on human responsibilities to other living creatures.

What Animals Want and Deserve

For several years now, applied ethologists have been making an economic argument concerning animal welfare. The basic idea is that if one wants to know what animals want or need, then one needs to see what they will pay to obtain such commodities. If I am starving, I will pay more for a banana then if I am stuffed. Although one might argue about the logic of this work, what I particularly like about it is that it provides recommendations for animal welfare that are grounded in careful experimentation and observation, and supported by good natural history. These are the two most important ingredients in working out what it is like to be another creature.

The ethologist Marianne Dawkins was one of the first to take this approach seriously, starting with an experiment designed to address whether the British government was justified in changing their policies concerning battery hens. In particular, was it the case, as the government had suggested, that battery hens could be kept in cages without chipped wood? The government's position was that chipped wood was expensive, and that they could save money by getting rid of it. If hens do as well without chipped wood as with, then of course they are right. The question is: what does it mean to do "as well?" Of course, this is one of the central questions underlying animal welfare, as it is for current discussions of human welfare. What are the basic rights? What are the basic conditions for satisfying such rights?

Dawkins designed a simple, yet elegant experiment, based on the fact that in nature, chickens frequently scratch the earth beneath them, a species-typical behavior. She created a two-chambered box with a transparent door separating each side. On one side of the cage she placed chipped wood on the floor, leaving the other side bare. When Dawkins put the hen into one of the compartments, the hen stayed if the starting cage contained chipped wood, but immediately moved if it did not. To see what the hen would pay to have chipped wood, Dawkins increased the tension on the latch of the door, making it harder for her to open. Remarkably, hens leaned into the door like a middle linebacker charging the line, pushing with all their might merely to enter the compartment with chipped wood. Do hens want chipped wood? I leave it to the reader to decide. Perhaps another example will help you make up your mind about animal needs and desires.

Most farmers think that mink live in satisfactory conditions. "Satisfactory" means something like: has all of the essential commodities for living a healthy life. "Healthy" means something like: has water and food and a roof over its head. Those who disagree with this view suggest that there is more to having a life than eating, drinking, and sleeping. To test between these two positions, the ethologist Georgia Mason and her colleagues set up mink in individual cages, replicating the conditions of mink farms: one nest box, drinking water, and food. Based

on the assumption that all animals are hedonists, designed to obtain good things and avoid bad, each mink was offered a choice between seven alternative compartments, each associated with some unique property: a water-filled pool, a raised platform, novel objects, a second nest site, a tunnel, toys, and extra space. To access these compartments, the mink pushed open a door; and like the chicken studies, Mason and colleagues increased the difficulty of opening the doors by attaching weights. The experiment therefore simulated a closed economy whereby individuals were required to pay for what they wanted.

When the experimenters released the mink from their home cage, they consistently chose the compartment with the water pool, spent the most time in this compartment, and paid the greatest costs (i.e., pushed open the most heavily weighted door) to do so. Moreover, when a stress hormone known as cortisol was measured, levels were highest when mink were deprived of food and equally high when deprived of the water pool. What do mink want? Water pools. Why? Because in their natural habitat, they spend a considerable amount of time in the water, swimming and hunting for aquatic prey. These results clearly suggest that mink farmers should spend the pittance it costs to buy small water pools to provide mink with a "healthy life." Mink without water pools are stressed as much as food-deprived mink. And since no humane farmer would ever think of depriving them of food, why deprive them of a water pool? Such a decision simply makes no economic or ethical sense.

These studies highlight the importance of understanding animal behavior and cognition so that we can properly coexist with them on this planet. In many ways, animals are extremely different from us. But such differences should not cloud our ability to think about their needs and to design facilities that at least meet those needs. Although one can question, as many have, whether we should have animals in captivity at all, I suggest here that there is a compromise position. Given that animals are likely to be in captivity for many years to come, including wildlife reserves, zoos, and laboratory facilities, we should at least take advantage of what we know about their species-typical behavior and habitats to design better conditions.

Using the Is *to Constrain the* Ought

Humans are part of a community of living creatures, what Thomas Berry calls "a communion of subjects." Many of our characteristics have been shaped by three histories: evolutionary, developmental, and historical. All three of these histories reflect the *is,* the biology that was handed down over the years to constrain what we do. History, the history of *Homo sapiens,* tells us that biology isn't the end of the line. The *is* of biology provides a set of limitations, but it does not dictate what is possible, permissible, or *ought* to be. Like other animals, our species has also fallen prey to temptation. This is not surprising, given that we share with other animals some of the same desires and needs, to eat, to have sex, to acquire wealth, and to recruit allies. In fact, when one looks at the world in which we live, especially that part of the world we have created, it is surprising that we haven't been eliminated by the predatory tentacles of temptation.

Unlike animals, however, we invented a trick, one that has allowed us to survive in a world where the range of temptations evolves at an exponential pace thanks to our creativity and desire for change. When humans discovered mind-altering drugs, they didn't stop with the first plant or alcoholic beverage; they invented thousands of varieties, each with its own signature style of alteration and seduction. When humans discovered their sweet tooth, they invented new sugars and new desserts, from the pure sugar of cotton candy to the technically challenging but delicious soufflé. Similarly, the extraordinarily diverse ways that the timeless drive to copulate is marketed through magazines, strip tease, prostitutes of both sexes, and pornographic movies

reveal how this human trick continues to evolve temptations that challenge all sorts of traditional constraints.

Our unique trick for combating such temptations has taken the form of physical constraints, mental commitments, religious strictures, and legal documents. It is a trick that most likely saved our species from self-destruction by allowing us to live like Ulysses, constrained by ropes while simultaneously holding the Siren's hand. Our laws lay out what is permissible and what is not, thereby providing constraints on some of our more selfish desires. However, when legal systems explore and then recognize the limits of human nature—our foibles—they often shift the severity of punishment. In several countries, for example, "crimes of passion" are often given more lenient sentences, because the courts recognize that to control one's passions under such circumstances is beyond the call of duty. Interestingly, but unfortunately, many countries that recognize crimes of passion do so in a sexist way, pardoning men but not women.

For many, religions perform comparable functions, providing guidance for how to live a life that resists temptations. Calvinism provides a particularly extreme version in that it tells people that they were inherently weak and vulnerable to temptation and that in order to combat such evil ways, they should submit to the catechisms that Calvin proposed. Of course, this "eschatology of temptation and control" is not new with Calvin, and can be found throughout religious history; Manichaeanism provides a spectacular example, as do a number of practices and sects found on the Indian subcontinent.

If we step outside of the explicit rules and regulations that are part and parcel of our legal and religious systems, we find other tricks for combating temptation. We remove temptations when we know that we are vulnerable, cutting up credit cards to avoid rash shopping sprees, throwing away alcohol bottles and taking Antabuse as punishment for sneaking a nip here and there, and joining Weight Watchers in order to have someone else regulate the desire for one more ice cream sundae. The many studies of addiction, of course, reveal that addicts lack an ability to make such self-regulatory behaviors "stick" permanently to change the overall pattern of excess; far stronger interventions are usually required.

Nevertheless, these attempted tricks, whether successful or not, reflect the fact that as a species, we recognize the *is* of temptation, the biology that drives us to eat, have sex, acquire wealth, and so on. They also reflect the fact that what *is* does not dictate what *ought* to be. By recognizing the *is* of temptation, we can temper the outcome, deciding instead what *ought* to be. This is a view of ethics that is sharpened by biology rather than being determined by it. In other words, by understanding the *is,* of what biology both sets in play and also constrains with respect to our behavior, we will be in a better position to evaluate how realistic or likely our prescriptive ethical claims will be to work. Take, for example, the biblical commandment, "Thou shalt not covet thy neighbor's wife": Reasonable *ought,* but the chances of this being a stable global social principle is close to nil. The proportion of cultures with promiscuous or polygamous mating systems far outnumber the monogamous ones. The temptation to do more and more for our own species by developing technologies that potentially do less and less for other species, in some cases injuring them, is a temptation we should avoid. We must find a way to balance what is possible with what is permissible, recognizing that we cannot always anticipate how an action today could have catastrophic consequences for the future. I would like to conclude, therefore, with an example that showcases both the excitement associated with recent understandings of animal brains and the need for concern about the consequences of such findings.

The experiments on rats, rhesus monkeys, chickens, and mink demonstrate how science can provide a better understanding of what animals feel and want, and how such information can be applied to issues of animal welfare. But the techniques described are quite crude, especially given recent developments in genetics and the brain sciences. Scientists are tempted by these techniques because they have the potential to uncover an understanding of the brain that has thus far never been contemplated, and could have dramatic implications for clinical and therapeutic applications to humans. Consider the recent creation of smart or "Doogie" mice, after the precocious young doctor star of the sitcom *Doogie Howser*. Tang and colleagues (Tang 1999:336) created these genetically engineered mice by inserting extra copies of a gene called NR2B, which plays an important role in memory formation. Experiments suggested that mice with extra copies of these genes were smarter than controls because they rapidly learned to discriminate between objects, acquire a fear response to an aversive stimulus, and to find a concealed ramp. For those interested in the genetics of higher cognitive functioning, such results are stunning. They not only reveal the power of this technological advance, but also showcase the kinds of genetic engineering that might be used for applied purposes, especially the treatment of human medical disorders. For example, by changing the number of memory-related receptors, one might be able to reverse the devastating memory losses of Alzheimer's patients. But the excitement associated with the findings on Doogie mice must be tempered by the results of another experiment that reveals the potential dangers of both gene and brain manipulations, and the consequences for animal welfare.

Two years after members of the scientific community were introduced to Doogie mice, they were presented with an unanticipated consequence of being a "smarter mouse." In contrast to their normal counterparts, Doogie mice turn out to have an increased awareness of acute pain for longer periods of time (Wei 2001:35). This result has significant ramifications. Practically, we must avoid drawing naïve conclusions about the causal relationship between genes and behavior (ditto for the relationship between specific parts of the brain and specific mental functions), failing to appreciate the complex genomic and environmental contexts in which genes live. When one gene is removed, another replaced or duplicated, we can only make educated (statistical) guesses about the kinds of consequences it will have. The implication is not that genetic or brain manipulations are worthless. On the contrary, such technologies are likely to open up a range of novel discoveries and insights. Along with such findings, however, we must be prepared to uncover unpredicted complications and difficulties, some of which will certainly carry significant moral weight and force difficult ethical decisions. It is thus important to recognize that for science to profit from

the creative energy of its contributors, the intellectual climate must support radical and even risky explorations. But scientists must also realize the potential ethical consequences of their actions, and this includes studies of nonhuman animals.

For the near future at least, we will continue to use animals in biomedical research. I support much of this work. But I also support the position that we should work as hard as possible to use our understanding of animal thought and emotion to guide our understanding of animal welfare. This will allow us to advance science, and to do so in a way that is consistent with a view that respects the community of living organisms.

REFERENCES

Anderson, S.W., A. Bechara, H. Damasio, D. Tranel, and A.R. Damasio. 1999. "Impairment of Social and Moral Behavior Related to Early Damage in Human Prefrontal Cortex." *Nature Neuroscience* 2:1032–37.

Bechara, A., H. Damasio, D. Tranel, and A.R. Damasio. 1997. "Deciding Advantageously Before Knowing the Advantageous Strategy." *Science* 275:1293–94.

Boysen, S.T. 1996. "'More Is Less': the Distribution of Rule-Governed Resource Distribution in Chimpanzees." In A.E. Russon, K.A. Bard, and S.T. Parker, eds., *Reaching into Thought: the Minds of the Great Apes.* Cambridge: Cambridge University Press, pp. 177–89.

Boysen, S.T. and G.G. Berntson. 1995. "Responses to Quantity: Perceptual Versus Cognitive Mechanisms in Chimpanzees (*Pan troglodytes*)." *Journal of Comparative Psychology* 21:82–86.

Boysen, S.T., K. Mukobi, and G.G. Berntson. 1999. "Overcoming Response Bias Using Symbolic Representations of Number by Chimpanzees (*Pan troglodytes*)." *Animal Learning and Behavior* 27:229–35.

Carey, S. 1985. *Conceptual Change in Childhood.* Cambridge: MIT Press.

Church, R.M. 1959. "Emotional Reactions of Rats to the Pain of Others." *Journal of Comparative and Physiological Psychology* 52:132–34.

Colby, A., and L. Kohlberg. 1987. *The Measurement of Moral Judgment.* New York: Cambridge University Press.

Damasio, A. 1994. *Descartes' Error.* Boston, MA: Norton.

Damasio, A. 2000. The *Feeling of What Happens.* New York: Basic Books.

Dawkins, M.S. 1983. "Battery Hens Name Their Price: Consumer Demand Theory and the Measurement of Ethological 'Needs'." *Animal Behaviour* 31:1195–1205.

Flombaum, J. and L.R. Santos. 2005. "Rhesus Monkeys Attribute Perceptions to Others." *Current Biology* 15:1–20.

Hare, B., J. Call, B. Agnetta, and M. Tomasello, M. 2000. "Chimpanzees Know What Conspecifics Do and Do Not See." *Animal Behaviour* 59:771–85.

Hare, B., J. Call, and M. Tomasello, M. 2001. "Do Chimpanzees Know What Conspecifics Know?" *Animal Behaviour* 61:139–51.

Hare, B., E. Addess, J. Call, M. Tomasello, and E. Visalbergh. 2003. "Do Capuchin Monkeys

Know What Conspecifics Do and Do Not See?" *Animal Behaviour* 65:131–42.

Hauser, M. D. 1999. "Perseveration, Inhibition, and the Prefrontal Cortex: A New Look?" *Current Opinions in Neurobiology* 9:214–22.

———. 2000. *Wild Minds: What Animals Really Think.* New York: Henry Holt.

———. 2001. "Searching for Food in the Wild: A Nonhuman Primate's Expectations About Invisible Displacement." *Developmental Science* 4:84–93.

Hauser, M. D., J. Kralik, and C. Botto-Mahan. 1999. "Problem Solving and Functional Design Features: Experiments with Cotton-Top Tamarins." *Animal Behaviour* 57:565–82.

Heyes, C. M. 1998. "Theory of Mind in Nonhuman Primates." *Behavioral and Brain Sciences* 21:101–14.

Hood, B. 1995. "Gravity Rules for 2–4 Year Olds?" *Cognitive Development* 10:577–98.

———. 1998. "Gravity Does Rule for Falling Objects." *Developmental Science* 1:59–64.

Hood, B., M. D. Hauser, L. Anderson, and L. Santos. 1999. "Gravity Biases in a Nonhuman Primate?" *Developmental Science* 2:35–41.

Mason, G. J., J. Cooper, and C. Clarebrough. 2001. "Frustrations of Fur-Farmed Mink." *Nature* 410:35–36.

Masserman, J. H., S. Wechkin, and W. Terris. 1964. "'Altruistic' Behavior in Rhesus Monkeys." *American Journal of Psychiatry* 121:584–85.

Miller, R. E. 1967. "Experimental Approaches to the Physiological and Behavioral Concomitants of Affective Communication in Rhesus Monkeys." In S. A. Altmann, ed., *Social Communication Among Primates.* Chicago: University of Chicago Press.

Miller, R. E., J. Banks, and H. Kuwahara, H. 1966. "The Communication of Affects in Monkeys: Cooperative Conditioning." *Journal of Genetic Psychology* 108:121–34.

Miller, R. E., J. Banks, and N. Ogawa. 1963. "The Role of Facial Expression in 'Cooperative-Avoidance' Conditioning in Monkeys." *Journal of Abnormal Social Psychology* 67:24–30.

Pinker, S. 1997. *How the Mind Works.* New York: Norton.

Povinelli, D. J., and T. J. Eddy. 1996. "What Young Chimpanzees Know About Seeing." *Monographs of the Society for Research in Child Development,* no. 247.

Preston, S. D., and F. B. M. de Waal. 2002. "Empathy: Its Ultimate and Proximate Bases." *Behavioral and Brain Sciences* 25:1–72.

Rice, G. E., and P. Gainer, P. 1962. "'Altruism' in the Albino Rat." *Journal of Comparative and Physiological Psychology* 55:123–25.

Rolls, E. T. 1999. *Brain and Emotion.* Oxford: Oxford University Press.

Silberberg, A., and K. Fujita. 1996. "Pointing At Smaller Food Amounts in An Analogue of Boysen and Bernston's (1995) Procedure." *Quarterly Journal of Experimental Psychology* 66:143–147.

Tang, Y. P., E. Shimizu, G. R. Dube, C. Rampon, G. A. Kercher, M. Zuo, G. Liu, and J. Z. Tsien. 1999. "Genetic Enhancement of Learning and Memory in Mice." *Nature* 401:63–69.

Tomasello, M., and Call, J. 1997. *Primate Cognition.* Oxford: Oxford University Press.

Wechkin, S., J. H. Masserman, J. H., and W. Terris. 1964. "Shock to a Conspecific as an Aversive Stimulus." *Psychonomic Science* 1:47–48.

Wei, F., G.-D. Wang, G. A. Kerchner, J. J. Kim, X.-M. Xu, Z.-F. Chen, and M. Zhuo. 2001. "Genetic Enhancement of Inflammatory Pain by Forebrain NR3B Overexpression." *Nature Neuroscience* 4:164–69.

Ethics, Biotechnology, and Animals

BERNARD ROLLIN

I.

Any new technology, of whatever form, will create a lacuna in social ethical thought. To put it simply, powerful new devices and tools, when first introduced, cause us to wonder about the positive and negative effects and implications they will have on our lives. For example, with the introduction of the automobile, people immediately worried (and rightly so) about the possible dangers cars posed to pedestrians and to horses. On the other hand, less obvious concerns probably did not get discussed, for example, the proliferation of respiratory disease or the growth of suburbs or the decline of close, nuclear families. The more esoteric the technology, the less its nature is understood; and the less experts in the area articulate socio-ethical implications of the technology, the more likely it is that the lacuna in social ethical questions will be replaced by lurid, ill-defined concerns. Thus, for example, when computers were first introduced, experts

such as Norbert Wiener saw no downside at all, and predicted only that computers would accelerate, as one of his book titles put it, *The Human Use of Human Beings*. Ordinary people, however, were suspicious; they expressed concern about computers "making people obsolete," or "taking over the world." As a result, serious issues such as privacy, child pornography, the increasing elimination of literacy, and the decline in the reading of books by young people were never envisioned until they became acute problems.

The lesson here is simple. In the absence of good, reflective, careful ethical thinking about technology initiated by those who introduce a technology, and who should (in principle) understand it well enough to think through its implications, the social-ethical lacuna created by the technology will be filled by sensationalistic, simplistic, emotionally based slogans that dominate social thought and whose intuitive appeal make them difficult to dislodge. I have called this phenomenon a "Gresham's Law for Ethics," for it describes a state of affairs quite analogous to what Thomas Gresham noted in economic life; to wit, that "bad money" (e.g., hugely inflated paper money such as what was found in post–World War I Germany, with low intrinsic value) will drive "good money" (e.g., gold coins with high intrinsic value) out of circulation. Clearly if one owes a million dollars, one would be wise to pay it off with money that possesses no inherent value, and the gold will be hoarded.

Similarly, this is precisely and manifestly what has taken place in the area of biotechnology. Virtually no ethical discussion of animal cloning was forthcoming from the scientist who had effected the cloning of the sheep Dolly; in fact, he specifically affirmed that, as a scientist, socio-ethical discussion of this achievement was outside of his bailiwick. He did, however, opine that cloning humans was morally unacceptable. Period. Nor did other people in the field leap to fill the ethical lacuna, since most scientists have typically been raised in what I have elsewhere called "scientific ideology," a view which affirms that science is value-free, hence ethics free, and thus it is society's job (if anyone's) to articulate the ethical implications of science and technology (Rollin 1995b; Rollin 1998; Rollin 2006). What quickly filled the vacuum turned out to be in large measure classic examples of bad ethical thinking, based on the philosophically problematic, but psychologically powerful, principle that whatever clashes with one's cherished basic assumptions tends to be seen as violating the moral order, and thus as ethically wrong. Dr. Hwang Woo-suk, who recently cloned the first puppy in South Korea, did not forbear an attempt at cloning humans, but was nevertheless equally cavalier in failing to raise, let alone address, any ethical issues attendant upon cloning animals.

In earlier writings on biotechnology (including genetic engineering and animal cloning), I used the Frankenstein story to differentiate the three types of issues that may possibly emerge from new techniques for manipulating life. The relevance of this story is patent, as it is clearly a myth that pervades attempts to wrestle with breathtaking—yet ever-emerging—new technologies. The Mary Shelley novel, unreadable and dense though it may be, has nonetheless appeared in numerous editions (145 by 1984), and inspired thousand of other novels, stories, poems, films, cartoons, etc., painstakingly enumerated in the extraordinary *Frankenstein Catalogue,* appropriately edited by one Donald Glut (Glut 1984).

The Frankenstein story has been used to articulate social concerns about the full range of new scientific discoveries, from nuclear power (*Time* Magazine, at the fortieth anniversary of the Hiroshima bombing) to human cloning (Willard Gaylin in 1972) and continues to flourish. In order to explain the pervasiveness of this myth, one can discern three distinct themes pertaining to ethics in the story (see Rollin 1995b:Pt. I).

II.

The first aspect of the myth can be characterized as "there are certain things humans were not meant to know or do," a line familiar to aficionados of horror movies, and one ideally delivered by Maria Ouspenskaya. This proposition expresses the idea that, in and of themselves, certain scientific activities are inherently wrong, regardless of ensuing consequences. The theme of forbidden knowledge (pure or applied) and human *hubristic* attempts to attain it, is an ancient one, and is vividly epitomized throughout the ages in the stories of the Garden of Eden, the Tower of Babel, Daedalus and Icarus, the four great rabbis who, the Talmud relates, "entered the garden" of forbidden mystical knowledge (only one of whom emerged unscathed), the Golem, the Sorcerer's apprentice, and of course, Dr. Frankenstein himself, who, despite his noble

intentions, has transgressed against limits on hu
man knowledge and thus on the moral order.

I would venture the claim that it is the abov
theme that underlies most of the horrified r
actions to cloning and to genetic engineeri
and the notions that these are "just wrong"
"inherently wrong." The proliferation of co
ments affirming that these technologies
"against God" (affirmed by three-fourths of
American public [CNN/Time 1997]), or inv
"playing God," or "violating natural barriers
"failing to respect species boundaries," or
ing to be God," are all examples of the firs
pect of the Frankenstein story. Yet despite the
genuine horror, fear, and rage that they clearly
encompass, in my view they do not represent
defensible moral claims. In fact, they are quite
the opposite—examples of bad ethics seizing
center stage when rationally based moral discussion is not forthcoming. For it is difficult to see
what would count as making any piece of pure
or applied knowledge intrinsically wrong, rather
than wrong in virtue of its likely consequences
and results. Perhaps the consequences of some
knowledge are so likely to be harmful as to be
virtually inexorable; but that does not prove the
knowledge in itself to be inherently wrong, only
its consequences, effects being, as Hume taught
us, logically separable from causes.

Defending the inherent wrongness of cloning, for example, requires an argument showing
some *logical* connection between the knowledge
and some harm or evil. As soon as one moves
to affirm such wrongness on the basis of possible, or even probable, consequences of possessing such knowledge, one has moved away
from a position of intrinsic wrongness to a consequentialist one. One can, of course, argue that
good consequentialist reasons warrant the claim
that humans should not achieve knowledge of
cloning. That is a reasonably arguable point,
but one that is quite different from saying that
such knowledge is *inherently* wrong, regardless
of what consequences—even good ones—do in
fact result. And it is clear that many critics are

clearly a logical fallacy. Unfort
amples of bad ethics come
spectives. Here, for examp
"playing God" objecti
as it appears in the
Commission re

This sl
sign

worlds,
world that God (or nature) intends. The form
is of course indefensible without innumerable
ad hoc hypotheses. The latter requires that we
know God's (or nature's) will or design. Further,
even if we did "know" God's will (as if we were
all to believe cloning was forbidden explicitly
by a sacred text we all shared), it is not obvious
why violating it is immoral—at best, as Russell
pointed out, such disobedience is imprudent,
since God is stronger than we are, not intrinsically immoral, unless we add the ancillary premise that (God's) might makes right, vitiating morality as we know it! In the case of nature rather
than God, one obviously must show why cloning is unnatural and Caesarian sections are not,
and why the unnatural is necessarily immoral.
Obviously, the same logic holds vis-à-vis genetic
engineering.

In sum, our inability to provide a rational interpretation to the claim that cloning is inherently wrong, makes the first aspect of the Frankenstein story morally meaningless in a secular
society, however widely held it may be.

Other examples of bad ethics encapsulated in
this vision of the Frankenstein story are readily
apparent. For example, Jeremy Rifkin has, in
essence, argued throughout his career that the
Nazis were interested in human genetic improvement, that genetic engineers have a similar
orientation, so that genetic engineering therefore represents a Nazistic worldview. This is

nately, most ex-
from religious per-
ple, is a summary of the
on we mentioned earlier
National Bioethics Advisory
ort on cloning.

gan is usually invoked as a moral stop
to some scientific research or medical prac-
ce on the basis of one or more of the following
distinctions between human beings and God:

• Human beings should not probe the fundamental secrets or mysteries of life, which belong
to God.

• Human beings lack the authority to make
certain decisions about the beginning or ending
of life. Such decisions are reserved to divine sovereignty.

• Human beings are fallible and also tend to
evaluate actions according to their narrow, partial, and frequently self-interested perspectives.

• Human beings do not have the knowledge,
especially knowledge of outcomes of actions, attributed to divine omniscience.

• Human beings do not have the power to
control the outcomes of actions or processes that
is a mark of divine omnipotence.

• The warning against "playing God" serves
to remind human beings of their finiteness and
fallibility. By not recognizing appropriate limits
and constraints on scientific aspirations, humans
reenact the Promethean assertion of pride or hu-
bris. In the initial theological discussions of cloning humans, Ramsey summarized his objections
by asserting: "Men ought not to play God before
they learn to be men, and after they have learned
to be men, they will not play God." (National
Bioethics Advisory Commission [NBAC]:1997)

While such an account presumably makes
sense within the theological context or universe
of discourse of Judaeo-Christianity (but not,
notably, of Hinduism or Buddhism), it is difficult to extract secular moral sense from it, save
by seeing it as an admonishment against human
"arrogance." As the NBAC summary puts it:

"If making people in your laboratory isn't playing God, the phrase has no meaning." (NBAC
"Summary":2)

There is a serious point to such warnings,
but it is not restricted or special to cloning or
biotechnology, nor does it justify the intrinsic
wrongness of cloning; it only stresses the possibility of unanticipated risks that may emerge
from it. The theme of humans sawing off tree
limbs on which they are seated, painting themselves resolutely into corners, or being left up the
creek without a paddle, is an ancient one. The
aforementioned chutzpah stories of the Tower of
Babel, Daedalus and Icarus, the Golem, Frankenstein, and the Sorcerer's Apprentice, all warn
of excessive optimism by humans in deploying
new knowledge or *technē*. "Oops" should be the
logo for humanity, not only in the realm of
the religious or literary imagination, but just as
manifestly in the real world.

As implied by our discussion so far, one can
extract a moral issue in any new technology
or area of knowledge from the claim that it is
just wrong only by modifying that claim to one
which affirms that the area in question is wrong
because of the likely negative consequences or
harms likely or highly likely to emerge from it.
To do this, however, is to give up the claim of
inherent wrongness. As noted, there is a major
conceptual gap separating the claim that cloning
will inevitably cause bad results from the claim
that cloning is intrinsically wrong, regardless of
consequences.

III.

Thus, we encounter a second aspect of the
Frankenstein story, namely that some scientific activity is wrong because it will produce
bad consequences for nature or society. The
Frankenstein story is quite explicit on this. Despite Dr. Frankenstein's noble goals in undertaking his experiments (or those of the Rabbi
of Prague who creates the Golem), the creation
runs amok. I call this aspect of the story "ram-

paging monsters," and it is the view that a given piece of science or technology will cause disastrous results in virtue of our imperfect understanding of all of its causal ramifications. Such an argument must rely heavily on past history, and invoke such examples as the Chernobyl catastrophe, Three Mile Island, killer bee escapes, the space shuttle disasters, introduction of non-native, invasive species such as the mongoose into Hawaii or the Australian possum into New Zealand, and so forth. A common argument to this effect affirms that science can never possibly anticipate all glitches, and when we are dealing with powerful technologies, like biotechnology, glitches are equivalent to disasters.

"Rampaging monsters" is the image of the human creation run amok. This concern is more prudential than ethical—*no one* benefits from biotechnology run amok—and can be cashed out as the demand for public education as to the dangers of genetic engineering, and as to the safeguards for managing them. I have argued that the public will never accept genetic engineering until it has been so educated and until it feels it has been party to deciding the *ethical question* of what risks are justified by what benefits. These risks are far from negligible (Rollin 1995b). In the area of genetic engineering of animals they include environmental despoliation or catastrophe occasioned by release of transgenic animals; risk of new disease growing out of changing animals in both immunological and nonimmunological ways and unwittingly selecting for new pathogens dangerous to humans and/or other animals; risk of genetically engineered animals such as the SCID mouse, designed to be susceptible to infection by the AIDS virus, either infecting humans or having the endogenous mouse viruses interact with the AIDS virus to produce pathogens with unpredictable characteristics (Lusso 1990); risk of developing weaponry by way of genetic engineering; risk of increasing our unfortunate tendency in agriculture toward monoculture; risks of sociocultural disruptions, for example further elimination of small farms in favor of large cor-

porate industrialized agribusiness. While scientists may deploy one set of values in weighing heavily, for example, the benefits of the SCID mouse, and correlatively minimize the importance of the risks associated with creating such a mouse and emphasize their ability to control these risks, ordinary citizens may well be unwilling either to suffer any risks in order to create a mouse model for AIDS, or to place their own security in the hands of scientists' assurances about the certainty of containment. Fairly weighing these competing values and interests represents the key ethical issue in aspect two of the myth.

What are the risks of cloning animals? The most significant risk seems to me to arise from the potential use of cloning to narrow the gene pool of animals, particularly in agriculture. With the advent in the mid-twentieth century of an agriculture based in a business model, and emphasizing efficiency and productivity rather than husbandry and way of life as supreme values, it is now evident that sustainability has suffered at the hands of productivity—we have sacrificed water quality to pesticides, herbicides, and animal wastes; soil quality to sodbusting and high tillage; energy resources to production; air quality to efficiency (as in swine barns and chicken houses); and rural ways of life and small farms to large, industrialized production techniques. What is less recognized but equally significant is that we have also sacrificed genetic diversity on the same altar.

A lecture I once attended by one of the founders of battery cage systems for laying hens provides an excellent example of how this works. He explained that, with the rise of highly mechanized egg factories, the trait most valued in chickens was high production —i.e., numbers of sellable eggs laid. Laying-hen genetics focused with great skill and success on productivity. Inevitably, the production horse race was won by a few strains of chicken, with other traits deemed of lesser significance. Given the efficiency of artificial selection and rapid generational turnover in chickens, the laying chicken genome grew significantly narrower. Thus today's laying hens are far more genetically uniform than those extant in the 1930s. In fact, said the speaker, such selection has so significantly narrowed the gene pool that, had he known this consequence, he would never have developed these systems!

Why not? Because the narrowing of the gene pool in essence involves, pardon the execrable pun, putting all our eggs in one basket, and reduces the potential of the species to respond to challenges from the environment. Given the advent of a new pathogen or other dramatic changes, the laying hens could all be decimated or even permanently destroyed because of our inability to manage the pathogen. The presence of genetically diverse chickens, on the other hand, increases the likelihood of finding some strains of animals able to weather the challenge.

Cloning will almost inevitably augment modern agriculture's tendency toward *monoculture,* i.e., cultivation and propagation only of genomes that promise, or deliver, maximal productivity at the expense of genetic diversity. Thus, for example, given a highly productive dairy cow, there will be a strong and inevitable tendency for dairy farmers to clone her, and stock one's herd with such clones. And such cloning could surely accelerate monoculture in all branches of animal agriculture. Cloning could also accelerate our faddish tendency to proliferate what we think are exemplary animals, rather than animals we might really need. For example, very high production milk cows for which we have selected have very short productive lives and significant reproductive problems; very lean pigs are highly responsive to stress, etc.

At the moment, agriculture's only safety net against ravaged monocultures are hobby fanciers and breeders. Although commercial egg production disdains all but productive strains, chicken fanciers, hobby breeders, and showmen perpetuate many exotic strains of chickens. Given a catastrophe, it would surely be difficult to diversify commercial flocks beginning with

hobby animals as seed stock, but at least some genetic diversity has been preserved.

IV.

The final, and in my view, most morally significant aspect of the myth is "the plight of the creature," eloquently captured in Mary Shelley's novel and in the Kenneth Branagh film. This is the aspect of the myth most directly relevant to a pure moral issue, namely, the well-being of animals. Unlike controlling the dangers of genetic engineering, dealing with this issue is not patently a matter of self-interest, for concern for the animals can limit, constrain, and even nullify some of the economic and human benefit emerging from genetic engineering and cloning. What makes this third concern about biotechnology especially dramatic is that the technology is emerging at precisely the same historical moment that the traditional social ethic for animal treatment is undergoing rapid and dramatic change.

What is the nature of this new ethic for animals and how does it differ from the traditional ethic?

Although society has paid formal attention to limiting human behavior regarding animals for more than two thousand years, such attention was restricted to the prohibition of overt, intentional, willful, extraordinary, malicious, or unnecessary cruelty, or deviant or outrageous neglect—for example, not providing food or water. This ethic can be found even in the Bible —for example in the injunction not to yoke the ox and the ass to a plow together, or in the restriction against muzzling the ox when he is being used to mill grain.

This minimalistic, lowest-common-denominator ethic was formally encapsulated in the anticruelty laws enacted during the nineteenth century. These laws were as much designed to ferret out sadists and psychopaths who might begin with animals and, if left unchecked, move to venting their twisted urges upon human beings, as to protect the animals for themselves. The same view of prohibiting animal cruelty can be found in Catholic theology where, although animals do not in themselves count morally, animal cruelty is forbidden for its potential consequences for people, since people who are cruel to animals will "graduate" to abusing people. Interestingly enough, contemporary research has buttressed this insight.

Within the purview of this traditional ethic, any suffering inflicted on animals for "acceptable," "normal," "necessary" reasons, such as economic benefit, food production, pursuit of scientific knowledge, cures for disease, or, as one law puts it, otherwise "ministering to the necessities of man," was morally and legally invisible, shrouded by the all-encompassing cloak of "necessity." By and large, therefore, the "normal" use of animals for human benefit in research, agriculture, hunting, trapping, rodeo, and the like was not the concern of social moral thought about animals.

During the past two decades society has begun to move beyond the overly simplistic ethic of cruelty and kindness and to reach for a more adequate set of moral categories for guiding, assessing, and constraining our treatment of other animals. Perhaps the key insight behind this change is the realization that the overwhelming majority of animal suffering at human hands is not the result of cruelty, but rather, the animals suffer because of normal animal use and socially acceptable motives. To prove this, I ask the reader to perform a thought experiment. Imagine a pie chart representing the total amount of suffering that animals experience at human hands. Then ask yourself, what percentage of that suffering is the result of intentional, sadistic, useless, deliberate infliction of pain or suffering on the animals for no purpose? Interestingly enough, all of my lecture audiences, be they Montana rodeo people or San Francisco animal rights activists, say the same thing—well under one percent. Most animal suffering comes from reasonable human motives and goals. Scientists may be motivated by benevolence, high ideals,

and noble goals, yet far more animal suffering is occasioned by people acting in pursuit of these motives than by the actions of overt sadists. Confinement agriculturalists may be motivated by the quest for efficiency, profit, productivity, low-cost food, and other putatively acceptable goals, yet again, their activities occasion animal suffering in orders of magnitude traditionally unimaginable.

As mentioned, the old ethic opposing cruelty doesn't apply to these normal, nondeviant uses of animals. This is true not only conceptually, but practically. The limitations of the ethic and the laws based in it were dramatically illustrated when the Animal Legal Defense Fund, a group of attorneys whose *raison d'être* is raising the moral status of animals in society by use of the legal system, attempted to extend the scope of the anti-cruelty laws by a test case. As animal advocates, they generate many fascinating lawsuits that test, press, and expose the limits of the legal system's control over the treatment of animals. In 1985, they brought suit against the New York State Department of Environmental Conservation, that branch of New York State government charged with administering the use of public lands. Specifically, they charged the department with violating the anti-cruelty laws by permitting trapping on public lands by means of the steel-jawed trap. Since there are no laws regulating how often a trapper must check his trap line, an injured animal could be trapped without food, water, medical care or euthanasia for long periods of time. That, according to the plaintiffs, constituted unnecessary cruelty. They were thus seeking an end to such trapping (*Animal Legal Defense Fund v. The Department of Environmental Conservation of the State of New York* 1985).

Given the laws, the judge made a very wise decision. He opined that the steel-jawed trap was, in his view, an unacceptable device. But given the way the anti-cruelty laws have been written and interpreted, the actions of the agency in question did not constitute cruelty. After all, steel-jawed trapping is widely done as a means to achieving pest control, supplying fur, and providing a recreational pastime. Thus the activity of trapping is a legitimate one from a legal point of view, and does not fit either the intent, judicial history, or statutory language of the anti-cruelty laws. If one wishes to change the status of the steel-jawed trap, he asserted, one should therefore go not to the judiciary, but to the legislature. In other words, one must change the laws, i.e., the social ethic.

This case neatly illustrates some important features of what is happening in social thought: First of all, social thought is moving "beyond cruelty." Second, society is attempting to create new social rules and laws to protect animals. The best illustration of this point is the passage in the United States in 1985 and in Britain in 1986 of new laws to protect laboratory animals after society realized that the research community was not regulating itself. Third, society is moving beyond concern about traditional cute and cuddly animals to concern about all animals who can suffer.

Why is society suddenly concerned about the 99 percent of animal suffering that is not the result of deliberate cruelty? One can speculate as to why the demand for such an ethic has emerged only recently. First, society has just lately focused its concern on disenfranchised human individuals and groups, such as women, blacks, the handicapped, and the Third World. This same emphasis on moral obligation rather than patronizing benevolence toward the powerless has led to a new look at animal treatment. Second, the urbanization of society makes the companion animal, not the food animal, the paradigm for animals in the social mind. Third, graphic media portrayal of animal exploitation fuels social concern. As one reporter said to me, "animals sell papers."

Fourth, numerous rational voices have been raised to spearhead the articulation of a new ethic for animals. Although concern for animals was traditionally seen (with much justice) as largely a matter of inchoate emotion, such a charge cannot be leveled against the numerous scientists, philosophers, and other intellectuals of today, who eloquently and forcefully nudge the social mind in the direction of increasing moral awareness of our obligations to animals.

Fifth, and by far most important, the nature of animal use has changed significantly. The major use of animals in society was and is, of course, agricultural. Before the mid-twentieth century, the essence of agriculture was husbandry. People who used animals placed them in environments for which they were evolved and adapted and then augmented their natural ability to cope with additional food, shelter, protection from predators, etc. The biblical shepherd who leads the animals to green pastures, evoked by Jonathan Klawans in this volume, is the lovely paradigm case of this approach. Producers did well if and only if animals did well. This is what has been aptly called "the ancient contract"—"we take care of the animals and they take care of us," as U.S. Western ranchers say. No producer could, for example, have attempted to raise 100,000 egg-laying chickens in one building—he would have had all his animals succumb to disease in weeks.

In contrast, when "animal husbandry" departments in the U.S. symbolically became "animal science" departments in the 1940s and 1950s, industry replaced husbandry, and the values of efficiency and productivity above all else entered agricultural thinking and practice. Whereas traditional agriculture was about putting square pegs in square holes, round pegs in round holes, and creating as little friction as possible while doing so, "technological sanders" such as antibiotics and vaccines allowed us to produce animals in environments that didn't suit their natures but were convenient for us. For example, now we could indeed raise 100,000 chickens in one building.

Similarly, the rise of significant amounts of research and toxicity testing on animals in the mid-twentieth century also differed from the ancient contract—we inflict disease on animals, wound, burn, and poison them for our benefit, with no benefit to them.

These, then, are the reasons society seeks a new ethic for animals. We have no room here to explain the form the new ethic is taking—I have done this in detail elsewhere (Rollin 1993; Rollin 1995a)—but the conclusion is clear. While society wants to continue to use animals, it wants to make sure they live happy lives, or at least that they don't live miserable lives. U.S. society felt so strongly about this that, despite years of laissez faire and dire threats from the research community about endangering human health, it passed two major federal laws regulating the use of animals in biomedicine and aimed at limiting pain and suffering.

V.

Thus there is a significant onus on those who genetically engineer or clone animals to attend to the suffering of these animals.

In research on creating these animals, this is relatively easy to deal with. Indeed, in the United States and Britain laws militate in this direction by specifying proper use of anesthesia, analgesia, and early euthanasia. For example, one of my colleagues was attempting to genetically engineer cattle for double muscling, and in fact succeeded in producing what I believe was the first transgenic calf. Though the calf was born showing no apparent problems, within a month it could not stand up on its own, for reasons not yet clear. To the researcher's credit, the calf was immediately euthanized at the first sign of problems.

In agriculture, attempts to engineer animals have been largely based on increasing animal efficiency and productivity. Based on the history and the development of confinement systems in industrialized agriculture, it is clear that if the pain, suffering, and disease of the animal do not interfere with economic productivity, the condition is ignored. (Hence the existence of the so-called "production diseases" endemic to confinement agriculture.)

Most important, there are in the United States no legal or regulatory constraints on what can be done to animals in pursuit of increasing agricultural productivity, either in agricultural research or in industry. Given the absence of such constraints, and the historical willingness of industrialized agriculture to sacrifice animal welfare for productivity, the moral problem inherent in genetically engineering animals for production agriculture is obvious.

Many of the attempts thus far made to genetically engineer farm animals have generated serious welfare problems. For example, attempts to increase the size of pigs, chickens, and sheep by insertion of modified genes to control growth, while achieving that result, have engendered significant suffering (Pursel et al. 1989). The desired results were to increase growth rates and weight gain in farm animals, reduce carcass fat, and increase feed efficiency. While certain of these goals were achieved—in pigs, rate of gain increased by 15 percent, feed efficiency by 18 percent, and carcass fat was reduced by 80 percent—unanticipated effects, with significantly negative impact on animals' well-being, also occurred. Life-shortening pathogenic changes in pigs, including kidney and liver problems, were noted in many of the animals. The animals also exhibited a wide variety of diseases and symptoms, including lethargy, lameness, uncoordinated gait, bulging eyes, thickened skin, gastric ulcers, severe synovitis, degenerative joint disease, heart disease of various kinds, nephritis, and pneumonia. Sexual behavior was anomalous—females were anestrous and boars lacked libido. Other problems included tendencies toward diabetes and compromised immune function. The sheep fared better for the first six months, but then became unhealthy.

There are certain lessons to be learned from these experiments. In the first place, although similar experiments had been done earlier in mice, they did not show many of the undesirable side effects. Thus it is difficult to extrapolate in a linear way from species to species when it comes to genetic engineering even when, on the surface, the same sort of genetic manipulation is being attempted.

Second, as we mentioned, it is impossible to effect simple one-to-one correspondence between gene transfer and the appearance of desired phenotypic traits. Genes may have multiple effects; traits may be under the control of multiple genes. The relevance of this point to welfare is obvious: one should be extremely circumspect in one's engineering until one has a good grasp of the physiological mechanisms affected by a gene or set of genes. A good example of the welfare pitfalls is provided by attempts to genetically engineer mice to produce greater amounts of interleukin 4, in order to study certain aspects of the immune system (Lewis et al. 1993). This, in fact, surprisingly resulted in these animals experiencing osteoporosis, a disease resulting in bone fragility, clearly a welfare problem. Yet another bizarre instance of totally unanticipated welfare problems can be found in the situation where leglessness and cranio-facial malformations resulted from the insertion of an apparently totally unrelated gene into mice.

Thus welfare issues arise both in research on genetically engineered agricultural animals and, more drastically, in potential commercial production. As we said, the research animal issues can best be handled with judicious use of anesthesia, analgesia, and, above all, early end points for euthanasia if there is any suffering. The issues associated with mass production of suffering genetically engineered animals must be dealt with in a different way. For this reason, I have proposed "the Principle of Conservation of Welfare" to guide the agricultural industry (Rollin 1995b). This principle states that *genetically engineered animals should be no worse off than the parent stock would be if they were not so engineered, and ideally should be better off.* Genetically engineering disease resistance, e.g., for Marek's disease in chickens, is a good example of the latter case.

What of cloning animals? The first such possible negative welfare consequence arises out of the possibility that cloning per se can have unexpected and deleterious effects on the animals. Although one is putatively creating an organism that ought to end up indistinguishable from a naturally derived animal, it is conceivable that the process of cloning could itself have deleterious effects that emerge at some stage in the life of the organism. This phenomenon has already been manifested in cattle clones created by splitting embryos by nuclear transfer. According to veterinarians working with these animals, they have been oversized and thus difficult to birth, had difficulty surviving, and have also been behaviorally retarded, requiring a good deal more care at birth than normal calves (Garry et al. 1996). (Indeed there also seem to be problems in non-cloned animals created by in-vitro fertilization.) The cause of this is not known, and it is quite possible that clones could "crash" later in life by virtue of some unknown mechanism. At this point, there is no evidence for this concern—it is an empirically testable possibility that will be verified or falsified as our experience with cloned animals develops. If it turns out that there are in fact unanticipated welfare problems for animals that are cloned, this should and likely will abort the technology until the problems are solved.

There is a more subtle sense in which cloning can conceivably create problems for animal welfare and thus give rise to genuine socio-moral concerns. Many people believe that cloning will contribute to the mind-set of "commodification" of animals that underlies industrialized agriculture. In such an agriculture, animals are products, pounds of pork, eggs per cage, commodities. The ability to clone them, one might argue, augments and reinforces this view. After all, cloned animals are manufactured, and, like cars or soup cans coming off an assembly line, are "identical."

I have some sympathy with this concern, the same concern that informs animal advocates' vigorous opposition to patenting animals. But the issue here is far more basic than cloning —it is the industrialization of animal agriculture and the correlative loss of the ethic of husbandry. On traditional hog farms, for example, sows had *names* and received individual attention. In today's huge production units, they do not. Cloning per se is perhaps a reflection of this industrialization, but there is no necessary connection between the two. After all, one can imagine a strongly husbandry-based agriculturalist caring a great deal for his herd of cloned pigs. Although cloning has emerged from a questionable mind-set, that does not mean that it could not thrive in a highly morally acceptable agriculture. Admittedly cloning is far likelier to be developed and employed in an industrial mind set, but it does not follow that there could not be a use for it in a softer, more morally concerned agriculture. Just because cloning has been spun off from industrialized agriculture does not mean that it is conceptually incongruous with sustainable husbandry. Western ranchers—the last large group of husbandry agriculturalists—will continue to provide husbandry for their animals whether they are produced by artificial insemination, cloning, or natural breeding; after all, they are still animals under our care.

It could perhaps be claimed that cloning will accelerate public apathy about the treatment of farm animals, based on the psychological fact that the more of something we encounter, the more we see the units as interchangeable, the less we care about each unit. I doubt that cloning will worsen the situation we already have— though it won't improve it either. Phenotypically all non-cloned laying hens, all broilers, all black cattle, all white sheep or pink pigs or white laboratory rodents look alike to the average urban citizen. But this has not served to diminish social concern about their treatment—concern for the treatment of these uniform animals in the laboratory or on the farm has continued to grow, not diminish, as evidenced by legislation in the in the United States, Britain, Sweden, and the European Union.

ANIMAL MODELS FOR HUMAN DISEASE

The most vexatious issue regarding the welfare of genetically engineered animals arises out of the potential for creating transgenic models for human disease that were historically unresearchable in animals. (Cloning is relevant here as a potentially rapid modality for proliferating such animals.)

A chapter in a book devoted to transgenic animals helps to focus the concern:

> There are over 3,000 known genetic diseases. The medical costs as well as the social and emotional costs of genetic disease are enormous. Monogenic diseases account for 10% of all admissions to pediatric hospitals in North America … and 8.5% of all pediatric deaths. … They affect 1% of all liveborn infants … and they cause 7% of stillbirths and neonatal deaths. … Those survivors with genetic diseases frequently have significant physical, developmental, or social impairment. … At present, medical intervention provides complete relief in only about 12% of Mendelian single-gene diseases; in nearly half of all cases, attempts at therapy provide no help at all. (Karson 1991:189–90).

This is the context in which one needs to think about the animal welfare issues growing out of a dilemma associated with transgenic animals in biomedical research. On the one hand, it is clear that researchers will embrace the creation of animal models of human genetic disease as soon as it is technically feasible to do so. Such models, which introduce the defective human genetic machinery into the animal genome, appear to researchers to provide convenient, inexpensive, and, what is most important, high fidelity models for the study of the gruesome panoply of human genetic diseases outlined in the more than three thousand pages of text constituting the sixth edition of the standard work on genetic disease, *The Metabolic Basis of Inherited Disease* (Scriver et al. 1989). On the other hand, such animals will live lives of considerable suffering, since they would be used for long-term studies, and we cannot control such suffering occasioned by these diseases in the humans these animals model.

The very first attempt to produce an animal "model" for human genetic disease by transgenic means was the development, by embryonic stem cell technology, of a mouse designed to replicate Lesch-Nyhan's disease, a particularly horrible genetic disease, leading to a "devastating and untreatable neurologic and behavioral disorder." (Kelley and Wyngaarden 1983: 1137). Patients rarely live beyond their third decade, and suffer from spasticity, mental retardation, and choreoathetosis (uncontrollable random body movements). The most unforgettable and striking aspect of the disease, however, is an irresistible compulsion to self-mutilate, usually manifested as biting fingers and lips. This disease is so dramatic that I predicted in 1985 that it would probably be the first disease for which genetic researchers would attempt to create a model by genetic engineering.

Though the asymptomatic mouse is still a useful research animal, clearly a symptomatic animal would, as a matter of logic, represent a higher fidelity model of human disease, assuming the relevant metabolic pathways have been replicated. This case provides us with an interesting context for our animal welfare discussion. Although the animals were in fact asymptomatic, presumably at some point in the future researchers will be able to generate a symptomatic model transgenically. Let us at least assume that this can occur—if it cannot, there is no animal welfare issue to concern us! Cloning is relevant here since it can be used to rapidly proliferate such animals once they are produced, assuming the technology were perfected.

The creation of such animals can generate inestimable amounts of pain and suffering for them, since genetic diseases, as mentioned above, often involve symptoms of great severity. The obvious question then becomes the following: Given that such animals will surely be developed wherever possible for the full range of human genetic disease, how can one assure that vast numbers of these animals do not live lives of constant pain and distress? Such a concern is directly in keeping with the emerging social ethic for the treatment of animals; one can plausibly argue that minimizing pain and distress is the core of recent U.S. and British legislation concerning animal use in research. I have argued elsewhere that this is the major reason that a recent survey shows Europeans rejecting animal model biotechnology for ethical reasons (Rollin 2000).

To my knowledge, no one in the research community is addressing this issue.

VI.

Fascinating work by George Gaskell (Gaskell et al. 1997) has exploded the "truism" that Europeans have by and large rejected biotechnology—BST, cloning, patenting of animals, genetically engineered animals—because they are more "risk aversive" than Americans. In fact, Gaskell's work indisputably shows that it is not *risk* that is decisive in leading people to reject biotechnology, but rather it is *ethics*. Indeed, Gaskell shows that people are willing to accept risk in areas of biotechnology they consider ethical if they see a benefit to society, but reject other areas that provide great benefit and less risk, but are considered unethical (e.g., as just discussed, creation of defective animals to model human disease). The inescapable conclusion, then, is that society needs to be as clear about the ethics of biotechnology as it needs to be about the nature of biotechnology, lest we accept bad aspects of biotechnology and reject good ones. Yet who will lead public education in the ethics of this technology unparalleled in power in human history? Not the scientific community, because it is neither comfortable talking to lay people, nor has it comprehended and accepted the role of ethics in science.

We saw earlier that much of the bad ethical thought about biotechnology comes from religious quarters. Yet, in my view, this need not be the case. Long ago, John Dewey pointed out that the role of religion in a scientifically based society is not to tell competing stories about nature (Dewey 1934). As one might express Dewey's insight today, religion will assuredly lose such a "pissing contest." Rather, argued Dewey, religious institutions need to be a locus for the discussion and explanation of emerging ethical issues in society. And the churches have, I believe, done an excellent job in this regard in some areas—race issues, for example. Yet in the area of illuminating ethical issues emerging from developments in science, particularly biomedical science, churches have failed, as evidenced by a good deal of the nonsense they have disseminated regarding biotechnology. If churches are to be more than quaint and archaic institutions selling insurance for the afterlife, they must lead in defining and articulating what is morally obscure and problematic, yet of profound importance to human and animal life,

and to the well–being of the planet. Biotechnology is an excellent place to begin such education and dialogue.

Our religious institutions cannot ignore the pressing socio-ethical concerns about genetic engineering and cloning of animals. By meeting the issues head on, they can first of all separate good ethical coin from bad and avoid the pernicious consequences of our "Gresham's Law for Ethics." Second, they can listen to and orchestrate dialogue with the public, engage their concerns about risk, and thereby bridge the gulf of fear and ignorance distancing ordinary people from this new technology. Finally, they can help assure that the unfortunate tendencies in modern agriculture to place emphasis on productivity and efficiency above genetic diversity and animal well-being can be checked in this new technology, and that biomedical advances not come at the expense of inestimable animal suffering.

REFERENCES

Animal Legal Defense Fund v. The Department of Environmental Conservation of the State of New York. 1985. Index # 6670/85.

CNN/*Time* Poll. 1997. "Most Americans Say Cloning is Wrong." March 1.

Dewey, John. 1934. *A Common Faith.* New Haven: Yale University Press.

Garry, F., R. Adams, J. P. McCann, and K. G. Odde. 1996. "Post-Natal Characteristics of Calves Produced by Nuclear Transfer Cloning." *Theriogenology* 45:141–52.

Gaskell G., et al. 1997. "Europe Ambivalent on Biotechnology." *Nature* 387:845–46.

Glut, D. 1984. *The Frankenstein Catalogue.* Jefferson, N.C.: McFarland, 1984.

Karson, E. M. 1991. "Principles of Gene Transfer and the Treatment of Disease." In N. First and F. P. Haseltine, eds. *Transgenic Animals.* Boston: Butterworth-Heinemann, ch. 16.

Kelley, W. N., and J. B. Wyngaarden. 1983. "Clinical Syndromes Associated with Hypoxanthine-Guanine Phosphororibosyltransferase Deficiency." In J. B. Stanbury et al., eds., *The Metabolic Basis of Inherited Disease,* 5th ed. New York: McGraw-Hill, 1983, ch. 51.

Lewis, D. B., et al. 1993. "Osteoporosis Induced in Mice by Overproduction of Interleukin-4," *Proceedings of the National Academy of Sciences* 90, no. 24, pp. 1618–22.

Lusso, P., et al. 1990. "Expanded HIV-1 Cellular Tropism by Phenotypic Mixing with Murine Endogenous Retroviruses." *Science* 247:848–51.

National Bioethics Advisory Commission (NBAC). 1997. *Cloning Human Beings.* Rockville, MD. June.

———. "Summary of Arguments Against Cloning." *http://vvww.al.org/clontxol.htm:* 2.

Pursel V., et al. 1989. "Genetic Engineering of Livestock," *Science* 244:1281–88.

Rollin, B. E. 1993. *Animal Rights and Human Moral-ity*, 2nd ed. Buffalo: Prometheus Books.

———. 1995a. *Farm Animal Welfare*. Ames, Iowa: Iowa State University Press.

———. 1995b. *The Frankenstein Syndrome: Ethical and Social Issues in the Genetic Engineering of Animals*. New York: Cambridge University Press.

———. 1998. *The Unheeded Cry: Animal Consciousness, Animal Pain and Science*. Revised edition. Ames. Iowa: Iowa State University Press.

———. 2000. "Social Ethics, Animal Suffering, and the Creation of Transgenic Animal Models of Human Genetic Disease." In A. Lanny Kraus and David Renquist, eds. *Bioethics and the Use of Laboratory Animals: Ethics in Theory and Practice*. ACLAM (American College of Laboratory Animal Medicine). Dubuque, IA: Benoit, 2000.

Scriver, C. R. et al., eds. 1989. *The Metabolic Basis of Inherited Disease*. 6th ed., vols. 1 and 2. New York: McGraw-Hill.

Animal Experimentation

KENNETH SHAPIRO

As a psychologist who is also an animal advocate, I am perforce interested in ethics, which I take to be central to the project of religion. In fact, the current debate over our treatment and use of animals in the laboratory invokes both science- and ethics-based discourses. Here, I largely bracket ethical considerations to present a critique of animal research that originates in the scientific enterprise itself. I present a case built on scientific methods of assessing animal research and offer illustrative findings of their application (Shapiro 1998). I welcome this opportunity for I see it as part of a larger project to which I have contributed. The development of a field of animal studies comparable to women's studies and African-American studies will, I hope, provide an intellectual infrastructure for the animal rights movement as they do for the feminism and the civil rights movement (Shapiro 1993). Thomas Berry's fortuitous phrase, "communion of subjects," could serve as the cornerstone of that project. Through animal studies, each of the various disciplines, whether in the humanities, social sciences, or natural sciences, in its own way can move to a more respectful study of animals other than humans, through understanding them not as models of us, or as protein on the hoof or commodities or therapeutic aids, or even as symbols or cultural artifacts, but as beings with their own forms of subjectivity.

In this discussion of animal experimentation, I will undertake two tasks. The first is to describe nonhuman animals in the laboratory—how they got there and how they live there. The second task is to describe the primary strategy underlying animal research, the use of animals as models of human phenomena. For each of these two segments, I raise questions relevant to the relationships among religion, science, and ethics. Hopefully, doing so will help us all come out of our houses, to use Kofi Opoku's metaphor.

Science and Religion

As a bridge to the discussion of animal experimentation, let me offer a few reflections on differences and similarities between science and religion. In the received view, at the time of the Enlightenment science displaced religion, as faith, intuition, and subjective participation gave way to empiricism, reason, and objective detachment. In its earliest accounts, the philosophy of science argued that this modernist enterprise grounded itself in a rigorous, systematic, rationalist set of procedures. Contemporary philosophy of science, influenced by recent literature in critical theory and the sociology of science, offers different, more shifting grounds that, so it would seem, return the enterprise closer to the region of its original rebellion. Science, in common with religion, has its own ideological presuppositions and commitments. Further, examination of its praxis reveals a helter-skelter process in which the attribution, "a scientific fact," is more intelligible as a social construction than an ineluctable product of a rule-bound protocol (Latour 1987). Like other complex human enterprises, scientific findings are partially determined by social context and individual motivation. Science, like religion, is messier in practice than in theory.

Another comparison between science and religion: although ethics occupies a clear and robust position in religion, its place in science is more ambiguous. I discovered this personally in the early 1980s when, as a young psychologist, I first began trying out the wings of my newly acquired commitment to animal advocacy. At that time I organized a symposium at Bates College on the issue of the ethics of the use of animals in research. I approached many of my colleagues in both academic and applied psychology with a straightforward inquiry about their views on the issue. Fresh from my own initial reading of Peter Singer (1975), the seminal philosopher of the animal rights movement, I framed my question in terms of the ethical rather than the scientific issues raised by the practice. I quickly discovered

that the majority of psychologists had peculiar notions of what is meant by ethics. Many relegated ethics to a purely subjective region of personal judgment outside of the objectivity and rationality of science. Ethics is up to an individual's personal choice for it is reducible to personal preference and there are no ethical truths beyond personal opinion. Ethics is precisely *not* science, for it is part of those subjective and speculative ways of thinking from which science historically had carefully sought to distinguish itself.

Other psychologists confused ethics with science itself. They believed that acting scientifically, that is, according to the scientific method, is itself acting right or good. The rules of good science are an ethic, and following them assures the goodness of an act. To make objective observations and to form and test hypotheses is to impartially and fairly arrive at the truth of the matter—and to do that is to do good. Psychologists who are scientifically rigorous act ethically.

Both of these notions are conversation stoppers; no further discussion is constructive. Leaving aside these patently self-serving and scientistic views, scientific practices have ethical implications, and scientific findings are often useful in arguing ethical positions. If nonhuman animals are beings that require moral consideration, then the practice of animal research raises ethical issues. If scientific findings demonstrate the sophistication of nonhuman animal being, then those findings must be imported into the ethical debate.

Science is often considered the modern replacement of traditional religion—again, reason displaced faith as the proper grounding of an individual's relation to the world. In another sense, critics of science argue that science has taken on the trappings of a religion, such as the language of sacrifice and truth; the importance of transcendent values and ends that, in the final analysis, are maintained through faith and personal commitment; the valorization of abstractions often in the face of common sense.

How the Rat Turned White

As an illustration of the latter, consider the strategy of using non-human animals in a laboratory setting as models of human phenomena. The history of the adoption of rats as the most common nonhuman subject of psychological research suggests a denial of their commonly accepted nature. The commonsense view of those furry, scavengers of the night is replaced by a complex abstraction.

In the spirit of Kofi Opoku, I present this account of the social construction of rats in the laboratory in the form of a parable, "How the Rat Turned White." The thesis is that rats, like other animals in the laboratory, are a construction fitted, if you will, to the philosophy of science underlying psychology, positivism; rats are fitted to the laboratory, the architecture of which is itself an embodiment of that philosophy. That construction deconstructed rats through a process of deindividuation, despeciation, and deanimalization, to use deliberately ugly terms.

In 1898, only a few decades after the first recorded use of them in modern science, rats were used for the first time in psychological research (Lockard 1968). Before this period laboratory animals did not exist. They had to be created for the purpose. In the case of rats, the process of "laboratization," as Lockard puts it, was accelerated by selectively breeding albino forms of the Norway rat.

The differences between these lab rats and the Norway rats found in nature are striking; they clearly show how psychologists intentionally created breeds that would fit the requirements of their emerging experimental laboratory-based science. As compared to a "wild" or even a first-generation captive Norway rat, an albino rat is more quiet, tractable, manageable, handleable—and controllable.

The experimental method values the reduction of individual variation in the objects of study. Animals are bred to produce genetic homogeneity. Housing conditions and experimental manipulations also promote that individual invariability. Those individual differences that are observed are understood as results of the experimental manipulation, while any residual differences are attributed to errors in measurement or age or species.

To further effect this process of deindividuation the animals are typically not named, and any one animal may be substituted for another with no experimental loss. Animals are members of a "population," not unique individuals (see figure 1).

But if there are no genuine individuals in the lab, surely there are different species, and there are then differences among animals based on species-specific behavior. However, psychologists and other scientists using lab animals commonly refer to them not as "the rats" but as "animals." In more formal settings, such as publications, "organism" might be used instead. Another term used for an animal is a "preparation" (Devereux 1967)—that is, a generic animal rather than a member of a particular species. These terms express a prevalent attitude that an animal under study is an organic process, a physiological and behavioral system. Beyond deindividuation, an animal in the laboratory is reduced to a general process that overrides species-specific physiology and behavior.

Housing conditions, such as caging an animal for much of his or her life and without the company of other animals, further strips away species-specific behavior. Wemelsfelder (1993) describes the profound effects of chronic caging: the behavior of a chronically caged animal is largely limited to bored behavior. At the extreme, behavior is reduced to repeated stereotypical movements and postures that are similar for animals across species. Species-specific identity is lost as a bored animal no longer demonstrates much of his or her species-specific behavior.

As we journey from individual to species to organism, and then on to preparation, we encounter one more feature in this deconstructive process. Again, emulating other natural sciences, the fledgling field was preoccupied

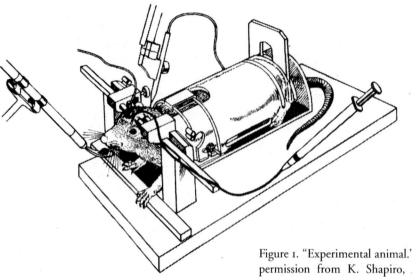

Figure 1. "Experimental animal." Reproduced with permission from K. Shapiro, *Animal Models of Human Psychology* (Hogrefe & Huber Publishers), Fig. 1, p. 162.

with technology, for through the development of apparatus and instrumentation experimental effects could be produced and measured (Capshew 1992). Psychologists became engineers for whom the laboratory provided an ideal site in which technology to enhance and extend the limits of observation could be innovated. The new science's preoccupation with instrumentation and technology was built around laboratory animals. The tiers of animal cages, the mazes, the automated food dispensers, the Skinner box, the controlled environment (lighting, temperature, noise, and bacteria), the electronic recorders, the stereotaxic devices, the plastic restraining tubes—all were designed to snugly fit the laboratory animal. As described, this fit was met in the other direction, as psychologists constructed "wild" rats to fit an increasingly instrumentalized laboratory life.

The emphasis on technology blurred the boundary between instrument and object of measurement. Consider a rat that is chronically implanted with an electrode in his or her brain and is connected by a tether to a machine that sends stimuli and receives and records responses. The rat is more a part of the instrumentation

than a discrete object of study. The animal is a conduit, a vehicle, for the study of certain relations between brain function, external stimuli, and movement. The animal has lost his or her integrity in that only certain parts of the animal are the focus of interest. The rats are "*laboratory* animals" in the sense that they are *part* of the laboratory; they are part of this complex of sophisticated apparati, instrumentation, and recording devices that constitutes the site and object of psychological scientific study. Far from communing subjects, they are perceived and treated as "highly specialized scientific instruments" (Phillips 1994) (see figure 2).

They are precisely not themselves—subjects of their own world—for they are bereft of their natural habitat, confined in an artificial, boring, yet stressful cage, stripped of autonomy, individuality, species-specific behavior, and, in a sense, of their generic animality. These reductions of animals in the laboratory have important negative effects on their care by humans and on human attitudes toward them generally.

The animal in the laboratory, finally, is not him or herself for he/she is a stand-in for us, as I shall describe more fully below. The descrip-

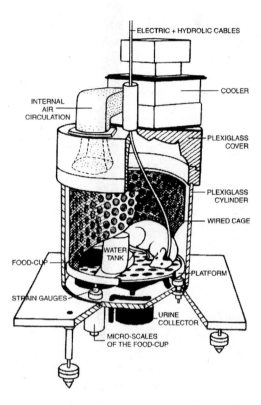

Figure 2. "A freely moving rat in a metabolic chamber." Reproduced with permission from Stylianos Nicolaidis and Patrick Even, "Metabolic Rate and Feeding Behavior," in *The Psychobiology of Human Eating Disorders: Preclinical and Clinical Perspectives,* in Annals of the New York Academy of Sciences 575 (1989): 89, Fig. 1'. Copyright 1989 New York Academy of Sciences, U.S.A.

tion of the social construction of animal in the lab is, to this point, abbreviated, simplified, and somewhat caricatured. Lab rats, for example, although more docile than their wild forebears, still latently retain much of their species-specific behavioral repertoire and can revert back to it given the chance—they will build burrows and survive a winter outside (Wyers 1994). However, the construction does embody the philosophy of science and, although ambivalently, does describe the implicit attitude of animal investigators—how they live—toward rats in the lab.

Reduction or Amplification of Animal Being

What is the relation of social construction, as exemplified in the construction by science of the lab animal, to the symbolism of animals in religion? The present account keys on the reduction, from individual to instrument. Another account could emphasize its inflation, as science

has borrowed the language of sacrifice and positioned itself as a secular religion with its own transcendent ends (Lynch 1988). Does the lab animal as constructed largely reduce the being of animals while that of religion largely amplifies it? or is the symbolism of animals in religion also reductionistic?

In my view, any amplification of animals in religious imagery is intended to elevate us, not the animals themselves. Neither the reduction of animals in the lab nor this symbolic use in religious texts tells us much about the animals as such, about them as subjectivities whom we can know and with whom we can commune. In fact, in both enterprises, the work of reduction or amplification gets in the way of such knowledge and relationship.

When you, my readers, and I, here, as amateur sociologist of science, unpack the constructions and symbols, we learn about ourselves rather than the animals. While the unpacking is a necessary first step to the illumination of the animals, both the construction and the symbolism obscure them more than they illuminate them. Of course, in the case of the animal as a model in science, the intention is to make the animal into a human—a stand-in for us. Can this reduced being illuminate us?

Animal-based Psychological Research

We explore this question by returning more directly to the scientific project. While a minority of psychologists study nonhuman animals to learn about them at least as exemplars of different species (comparative psychology), most use animals as models of human psychology and, particularly, psychological disorders. Many such disorders are indistinguishable from medical disorders. In practice, there is little distinction between psychological and biomedical research as the former heavily emphasizes physiology, particularly neurology. We need to examine this approach, the use of models of the actual object of study, first conceptually, that is as a strategy, for there are misconceptions on both sides of the current debate over animal research.

What is a model, what is the relation of a model to the modeled, how can we evaluate a particular model? It is important to understand that a model, whether animal or nonanimal, is not intended to be and, by definition, is not identical with the entity modeled. A model is an analogy. But why do scientists use this indirect method instead of directly investigating the object of study? Is not direct observation a foundational desideratum of objective science? Scientists turn to the construction of analogies when the object of study is inaccessible (stars) or too complex (the human brain) or too uncontrollable, or when there are ethical constraints on direct study of the object under investigation.

A model is only an analogy. Even a model of a relatively simple physical entity (a small-scale glider in a wind-tunnel) cannot perfectly re-create either the actual glider or the environment within which it actually functions. It follows that for any model there is a set of similarities to and differences from the actual object of study. When we consider animal models of human disorders, scientific considerations support the logic of this definition. Both evolutionary theory and systems analysis hold that there necessarily are significant differences between two different species (LaFollette and Shanks 1996). Even when there are similarities in certain subsystems or processes, the fact that these occur in a more complex system ensures differences as well.

Evaluating Animal Model Research

In the positivist tradition a model is evaluated through validation, which refers to a formal testing of the hypothesis that there are significant similarities between the model and the modeled. Validation assures that the model is really getting at the target phenomenon. While critical to the scientific basis of the animal research enterprise, such testing against the original does not imply either a gain in understanding or a treatment advance. Obviously, any feature found to be similar in the model and modeled and thus validated may not be a new understanding. Conversely, any feature found to be different in the model and modeled and thus, as it were, invalidated may yet generate new understanding and/or effective treatment. For example, a difference may provide an insight into the process or mechanism that protects an individual of one species from contracting a disorder while one of another species becomes ill. One of the reasons we have comparative anatomy, history, linguistics, and religions is that exposure to systematic differences helps reveal underlying organizing principles and determinative variables.

It follows that a critique of animal model research that is limited to the specification of differences between the model and the original is a preliminary and weak critique. On the other hand, it also follows that any defense of a model that is limited to the specification of similarities is a preliminary and weak defense. Unfortunately, animal rights advocates and animal researchers, respectively emphasizing differences and similarities, too often rely exclusively on these two forms of argument. The debate takes on the character of the eternal question whether the bottle is half empty or half full.

Validation by testing similarities in the model/modeled is, then, not the bottom-line consideration. A high-fidelity model is not necessarily a useful one. The critical issue is whether either the similarities or the differences in the animal model are productive of new insights into, and effective treatments of, the human disorder being modeled. We term this broader evaluative frame "productive generativity."

Although issues of the validity, beneficiality, extrapolability, and efficiency of animal research have been raised in the current debate over animal research, they are typically done so polemically, without provision of empirical evidence. It is important to understand that animal model research itself rarely addresses these issues. The great majority of animal model studies are not validation studies even in the narrow sense: they do not formally test the hypothesis of similarity.

Rather, in practice, the development of a model proceeds largely through recursive and duplicative investigation of other already studied variables and other models. "Validation" is limited to this insular testing within the lab enterprise. Going back to the target phenomenon for mid-course correction or validation is rare. Arguably, the absence of systematic, scientific evaluation of animal research is one reason that the debate over animal research is often polarized, with exaggerated claims and defensive posturing on both sides.

A Method of Evaluation and its Application

How can the broader evaluation of productive generativity be effected? We turn to a description of relevant methods and their application to selected animal models. Through their application we can furnish evidence that goes beyond the mere assertion of similarity and the related assertions, without evidence, of benefits by pro-research scientists and of dissimilarity and cruelty by animal rights advocates.

While only a small percentage of psychologists conduct research using nonhuman animal subjects, psychologists have attempted to develop an animal model for virtually every problem in the human condition that has a psychological component (Overmeier and Burke 1992). The scope of the procedures devised to create the models is as broad as the conditions to be modeled. In general, the procedures involve manipulations of genes, the nervous system, other parts of the body, behavior, or the environment. Many of the manipulations involve invasive surgical and other physically and psychologically painful, distressing, and harmful procedures.

There are a number of analytic tools available that are useful in the evaluation of animal models. The evaluative methods include outcome study, citation analysis, survey, and a measure of pain, stress, and harm to animal subjects. These familiar quantitative methods are supplemented by informal historical inquiry, which is useful in order to disentangle the specific contribution of animal research and, as well, to clarify the source of an animal model—for example, is the model based on direct observation of the target phenomenon?

To illustrate the method, I have evaluated three animal models of eating disorders: the sham feeding and tail pinch models of bulimia and the activity wheel model of anorexia. Bulimia involves recurrent episodes of bingeing and purging; self-starvation characterizes anorexia. In both instances, the client typically is a female adolescent or young adult who is preoccupied with her body-shape and weight. In sham feeding, the investigator surgically inserts a hole in the wall of the stomach of a rat, dog, or nonhuman primate. This allows the investigator to feed the animal through the mouth and siphon off the food before it is fully digested. In this way, analogous to bingeing-purging, the individual "eats without calories" (Hoebel et al. 1989). In the tail pinch model, the investigators clamp the rat's tail to induce stress to explore the role of stress in inducing bulimia (Vaswani, Tejwani, and Shaker 1983). In the activity wheel model, they study the role of excessive exercise in the production of anorexia (Lambert 1993).

A review of treatment outcome studies shows that eating disorders remain relatively intransigent to intervention (Mitchell and Raymond 1992). Treatments are only modestly and temporarily effective. Although there are some initial gains from treatment, these are limited to a reduction in the frequency of symptoms, such as bingeing-purging, and relapse rates are high. To the limited degree that they are effective, the most common psychotherapy employed, cognitive-behavioral therapy, does not derive from animal models of these disorders.

While emphasizing investigation of physiological mechanisms and the search for pharmacological treatments, the research involving these models has yielded no effective drug treatment to date. Fenfluramine, a drug earlier explored in research on obesity, was found to be ineffective in the treatment of bulimia, and was recently pulled off the market because it produced abnormalities in heart valves. Antidepressant drugs are effective within the limits described, but they do not derive from these animal models.

Citation analysis provides a measure of the frequency that published studies are mentioned in subsequent publications (Garfield 1979). Studies published on these three animal models by nine investigators were cited .69 times per year during the nine-year period considered (1986–1994). By comparison, the average annual frequency of all the references in the *Science Citation Index* is 1.87, or more than two and a half times the rate of those examined in the present study. When only those citations judged significant are tallied (compared to those cited only in a generalized introduction), the overall

annual frequency drops to .31. Therefore seven of ten studies receive no significant citation in a given year.

A survey of clinicians specializing in the treatment of eating disorders found that 60 percent did not know animal models of ED existed; 67 percent could not name or describe any model; 87 percent could not identify or describe the sham feeding model; and 87 percent indicated that these models did not influence their treatment approach. There was no overlap in the list of journals these specialists indicated they found "most helpful" in their work and those in which the nine investigators' studies were cited. Results of a survey of psychologists are related to these findings. Plous (1996) found that more than 90 percent of psychologists who are primarily practitioners indicated that they rarely, never, or only occasionally used findings from animal research.

Application of the Invasiveness Scale (Shapiro and Field 1987) found that these animal studies typically involve considerable pain, distress, and harm. The scale rates common experimental procedures on a 6 point scale, ranging from 0 to 5 (highest level). While it was developed to score psychological research, the scale correlates significantly with other more general pain scales, The models studied scored in the 3 and 4 range, which is consistent with the levels of invasiveness found in the field of psychology as a whole. For example, in the sham feeding model animals are subjected to surgery, the distress of recovery, and harm and distress of a permanent fistula, which produces chronic indigestion. Further, many of the additional variables tested add to the level of invasiveness—brain lesioning, implanting electrodes into muscles involved in ingestion, and depriving the animals of food.

Informal historical inquiry reveals that these models already existed in the lab as models of other disorders and as experimental procedures. They do not derive from direct observation of the clinical phenomenon under study. For example, sham feeding has been used in the study of digestive physiology since the late nineteenth century (Wolff 1943). The activity wheel was originally used as a model of ulcers (Lambert 1993). Tail-pinching has been used to induce stress and was explored, at one time, as a model of schizophrenia (Vaswani, Tejwani, and Mousa 1983).

The analogy between the model and the actual disorder is coarse, being based on only limited similarity. Sham feeding is only roughly analogous to binge-purge behavior, as is the activity wheel to the inclination to overexercise in anorexics. Tail-pinching produces stress, a generalized precursor to many, if not most, psychological disorders.

The eating disorder animal model research emphasizes physiological process and the search for pharmacological treatment, although strong evidence points to a cultural basis for the disorders (the "slimming culture"). Finally, there is a preoccupation with developing technology and instrumentation. Investigators report on the development of metabolic chambers, tethering devices, wire implants, micro-lesioning, and computer-based recording of neural and metabolic events, but they provide little description of features of the disorders based on direct observation in their clinical setting.

The methods used in the study briefly reviewed evaluate the degree of productive generativity of selected animal models in psychology and find it minimal. What is the generality of the findings? Although limited to one area of research, I evaluated three families of models, as each of the three has variations. Further, I informally evaluated a second area of psychological research, models of human aggression, and found comparable results.

The results of the evaluation are a function of the limited time that has elapsed since this research was conducted—mostly late 1980s and early 1990s. However, I did select three models, the development of which peaked at different times within that period. As a final issue of generality, it is debatable whether or not these evaluative methods are more power-ful for applied research as against basic research. The survey targets a population of practitioners, although it contains items assaying both applied (treatment innovations) and basic (further understanding) research.

What is the scope of applicability of this evaluative method? Although the models evaluated were psychological research, the two areas of inquiry, biomedicine and behavior, increasingly, are closely related. Much research in both is framed as brain/behavior relations. The analytic tools used in the present study are equally applicable to both fields of research. Undoubtedly, some animal models in biomedicine will be evaluated positively with these analytic tools. However, on the basis of the similarities between the two enterprises, I predict that evaluation of much biomedical animal model research will produce negative results comparable to those reviewed here. In any case, I suggest that the current stalemate over animal research might be broken if both sides grounded their claims regarding costs and benefits in empirical and historical analyses such as those reported here.

Science and Ethics

There are two discourses in the current debate over the use of animals in research—science- and ethics-based arguments. The latter are relatively highly developed, and there is a lively and fruitful literature centered on the several proposed ethics—Regan's rights theory, Singer's utilitarianism, a feminist ethic of caring, and humane, communitarian, and contractarian theories. As indicated, to this point I have purposely bracketed the ethics argument to sketch the arguments within the science enterprise itself. I conclude by setting these arguments into the setting of contemporary ethics.

When properly understood, a model is an analogy to the actual object of interest. It is not the thing itself. It functions as a heuristic or generative device. As such it is either productive or it is not, and we have provided suggested methods to rigorously evaluate that productivity. Their application indicates that some, perhaps most, animal models—this remains an empirical question—are not productive. If they are not, then when we apply a utilitarian ethic the strategy of developing animal models of human disorders is wrong, and we should desist. If some are productive, then there is the problem of prescreening those likely to be productive. Some of the methods described would be relevant in a proposal or pilot study context.

From a broader perspective but still within a utilitarian frame, there is the possibility that there are other more productive strategies. If like all others, animal models have the limited function of helping us to think by providing other contexts within which to view variations of the actual object of interest, perhaps there are better heuristics available. Or more radically, perhaps advances in technology that allow us directly to observe phenomena formerly hidden from view (e.g., brain-imaging techniques) will undercut

any advantage of their indirect observation as seen in the merely analogous setting provided by models. In this case also, we are ethically obliged to move away from the strategy of using animal models.

I have not mentioned a rights-based ethic to this point, although it is an ethic that I espouse. In accordance with a theme of this edited volume, rights theory builds on the fact that some nonhuman animals are "subjects of a life" (Regan 1983). They are gendered individuals each of whom is aware, although not reflectively, of his or her own interests, intentions, and needs. Unfortunately, with respect to nonhuman animals, in judiciary, legislative, and regulatory contexts, the language of rights is not even on the map. Utilitarian language, along with language from a humane ethic, is used but really only given lip-service as no cost-benefit analyses are actually undertaken. Perhaps the methods as applied here will help to change that.

REFERENCES

American Medical Association. 1988. *Use of Animals in Biomedical Research: The Challenge and Response.* Chicago: AMA.

Capshew, James H. 1992. "Psychologists on Site: A Reconnaissance of the Historiography of the Laboratory." *American Psychologist* 47:132–42.

Devereux, George. 1967. *From Anxiety to Method in the Behavioral Sciences.* The Hague: Mouton.

Garfield, Eugene. 1979. "Is Citation Analysis a Legitimate Evaluation Tool?" *Scientometrics* 1:359–75.

Hoebel, Bartley G., L. Hernandez, D. H. Schwartz, G. P., Mark, and G. A. Hunter. 1989. "Orasensory Stimulation by Sucrose Involves Brain Dopaminergic Mechanisms." In Linda H. Schneider, S. J. Cooper, and Katherine A. Halmi, eds., *The Psychobiology of Human Eating Disorders: Preclinical and Clinical Perspectives* New York: The New York Academy of Sciences, pp. 171–93.

LaFollette, Hugh and Niall Shanks. 1996. *Brute Science: Dilemmas of Animal Experimentation.* London: Routledge.

Lambert, Kelly G. 1993. "The Activity-stress Paradigm: Possible Mechanisms and Applications." *The Journal of General Psychology* 120:21–32.

Latour, Bruno. 1987. *Science in Action.* Milton Keynes, England: Open University Press.

Lockard, Robert B. 1968 "The Albino Rat: A Defensible Choice or a Bad Habit?" *American Psychologist* 23:724–34.

Lynch, Michael. E. 1988. "Sacrifice and the Transformation of the Animal Body into a Scientific Object: Laboratory Culture and Ritual Practice in the Neurosciences." *Social Studies of Science* 18:265–89.

Mitchell, James, and Nancy Raymond. 1992. "Cognitive-Behavioral Therapy in Treatment of Bulimia Nervosa." In Katherine Halmi, ed.,

Psychobiology and Treatment of Anorexia Nervosa and Bulimia Nervosa, Washington D.C.: American Psychiatric Press, pp. 307–28.

Overmier, J. Bruce. and P. D. Burke, eds. 1992. *Animal Models of Human Pathology: A Bibliography of a Quarter Century of Behavioral Research, 1967–1992.* Washington, D.C.: American Psychological Association, 1992.

Phillips, Mary. 1994. "Proper Names and the Social Construction of Biography: The Negative Case of Laboratory Animals." *Qualitative Sociology* 17:119–43.

Plous, Scott. 1996. "Attitudes Toward the Use of Animals in Psychological Research and Education: Results from a National Survey of Psychologists." *American Psychologist* 51:1167–80.

Regan, Tom. 1983. *The Case for Animal Rights.* Berkeley: University of California Press.

Shapiro, Kenneth. 1993. "Editor's Introduction to Society and Animals." *Society and Animals* 1:1–4.

——. 1998. *Animal Models of Human Psychology: Critique of Science, Ethics, and Policy.* Seattle: Hogrefe and Huber.

Shapiro, Kenneth. J. and Peter Field. 1987. "A New Scale of Invasiveness in Animal Experimentation." *PSYETA Bulletin* 7:5–8.

Singer, Peter. 1975. "Animal Liberation: A New Ethic for Our Treatment of Animals." New York: Avon.

Van Vort, Walter B. 1987. "Is Sham Feeding an Animal Model of Bulimia?" *International Journal of Eating Disorders* 7:97–806.

Vaswani,. Kuldeep, Gopi A. Tejwani, and Shaker Mousa. 1983. "Stress Induced Differential Intake of Various Diets and Water by Rat: The Role of the Opiate System. *Life Sciences* 32:1983–1996.

Wemelsfelder, Françoise. 1993. *Animal Boredom: Toward an Empirical Approach of Animal Subjectivity.* Utrecht: Elinkwijk.

Wolff, H. 1943. *Human Gastric Functioning: An Experimental Study of Man and His Stomach.* New York: Oxford.

Wyers, Everett. 1994. "Comments on Behavioral Research in Naturalistic Settings." In Edward Gibbons, Everett Wyers, Everett Waters, and Emil Menzel, eds., *Naturalistic Environments in Captivity for Animal Behavior Research.* Albany: State University of New York Press, pp. 19–36.

X

ARE ANIMALS "FOR" HUMANS? THE ISSUES OF FACTORY FARMING

Caring for Farm Animals

Pastoralist Ideals in an Industrialized World

DAVID FRASER

When one of my students began doing scientific research on the welfare of farm animals, he mentioned this eccentric new interest to his grandmother. The grandmother had been raised in rural Poland in the early 1900s, and recalled an argument that had arisen in her family when she was a child. At that time the family and their farm animals lived in the same dwelling, but some family members wanted to build a wall to separate the humans from the other species. Those who wanted the wall argued that it would be more pleasant and hygienic to be removed from the intrusion and smells of the animals. Opponents were concerned that the animals would not receive such attentive care on the other side of a wall, and they were rather sad at the idea of banishing their four-legged friends to separate quarters. The wall won out; but the anecdote reminds us of the strong sense of community that has often existed between farming people and their animals, of the profound changes that have occurred in that sense of community during a short historical period, and of

the persistent nature of debate about the proper relationship between people and farm animals.

In this essay I briefly examine traditional animal care values in Western culture, the challenges to those values in modern agriculture, the resulting concerns that have arisen over the treatment of farm animals, and how we can begin to address those concerns.

The Ethics of Pastoralism

In a now famous essay, the American medievalist Lynn White (1967) claimed that the historical roots of today's environmental crisis lie in the Jewish and Christian scriptures. Our misuse of the environment, according to White, stems from "the Christian dogma of man's transcendence of and rightful mastery over nature." According to this view, animals, being part of nature, had been created "explicitly for man's benefit and rule," and were available for humans to dominate and use as they saw fit.

This interpretation of biblical texts has been criticized on many grounds (e.g., Moncrief 1970; Dobel 1977; Bratton 1984; Linzey 1991), but for my purposes its key failing is that it does not acknowledge the pastoralist ethic inherent in the biblical view of our relationship to animals. The pastoralist economy of the Hebrew people required that domestic animals be owned, traded, and used for human purposes (Schochet 1984). At the same time, human prosperity required that animals be given appropriate care: in biblical terms they had to be rested in green pastures, led beside still waters, and protected from danger. With this mixture of demands, the Bible placed animals in a special moral category, whereby they were not seen as equal to humans, nor yet as mere objects. Instead, they were viewed as beings—or "subjects" as Thomas Berry puts it—created by God and assigned to people for appropriate use and care (Schochet 1984, Preece and Fraser 2000). The relationship was called *rada* or "dominion," a term that was sometimes used to describe the relationship of God to the world (Psalms 72:8) and of conquering people to conquered people (Judges 14:4). It was a relationship of unequal status, but it did not imply the lesser party to be of no moral worth.

The pastoralist ethic included at least two elements that guided how people should deal with animals. First, it allowed animals to be used for certain purposes as long as appropriate conventions were observed. Domestic animals could be eaten, but they were to be slaughtered and prepared in a ritually correct manner (Deuteronomy, chapters 12–14). Animals could be used for labor, but they, like human servants, were to be given the customary day of rest (Exodus 20:10), and certain inappropriate muzzling and harnessing practices were expressly forbidden (Deuteronomy 25:4). Second, the pastoralist ethic attached high value to the diligent care of animals. Rescuing or caring for animals, like healing sick humans, was one of the few tasks permitted on the Sabbath (Luke 13:15). When God selected Rebecca as the wife of Isaac and the mother of her nation, the sign that she had been chosen was her volunteering, when asked for water by a thirsty stranger, to water his camels as well (Genesis 24:19). David's care and courage in protecting his father's sheep were the earliest indications that he was suited to become king (1 Samuel 17:35). Indeed, a conscientious shepherd protecting his sheep was such a positive image that it served as a common metaphor for divine goodness (e.g., Psalms 23:1–4). At times, descriptions of divine love were hard to distinguish from lessons in animal husbandry.

> For these are the words of the Lord God: Now I myself will ask after my sheep and go in search of them. As a shepherd goes in search of his sheep when his flock is dispersed all around him, so will I go in search of my sheep and rescue them no matter where they were scattered. ... I myself will tend my flock, I myself pen them in their fold, says the Lord God. I will search for the lost, recover the straggler, bandage the hurt, strengthen the sick, leave the healthy and strong to play, and give them their proper food.
>
> Ezekiel 34:11–16 (The New English Bible)

The pastoralist ethic of the Bible has been misunderstood by many modern writers (Lynn White being only one example), perhaps because it does not fall into the categories commonly used in modern animal ethics. It was not an ethic based specifically on kindness and avoidance of cruelty, although within such a complex tradition that idea was occasionally expressed (Proverbs 12:10). Nor did it espouse a fundamental kinship between humans and other species, although that idea, too, was heard on occasion (Ecclesiastes 3:18–20). And it certainly did not espouse equality between humans and other species. Rather, the biblical approach defined a relationship between humans and animals involving a mixture of legitimate use combined with, and occasioning, diligent care. This is treated elsewhere in this volume, in Jonathan Klawans's essay on biblical pastoralism and its relationship to sacrifice.

When we look at statements by conscientious animal producers today, we often see much the same combination of use and care. As one Canadian dairy farmer expressed it (Davidson 1995):

> Our life's work is to make the life of our cows the best possible. ... Our animals are never hungry, thirsty, homeless and never really at a loss for company. ... I feel that they live a full, productive and useful life. Ultimately I have to feel responsible for them for I was responsible for their arrival. And when my old cows complete their life here I have to think that it was better for them to have lived the life I helped provide for them, rather than not to have lived at all.

But let us consider the difficulties faced today by animal producers who adhere to this pastoralist ethic.

The Reshaping of Animal Agriculture

Until about 1950, farm animals in the industrialized countries were raised using fairly traditional methods that relied on labor to accomplish routine tasks such as feeding and removal of manure, and that often involved keeping animals partly outdoors. After the Second World War, there emerged a new generation of technology, which is often called "confinement" or "intensive" animal production. These systems used hardware and automation instead of labor for many routine tasks, and the animals were generally kept in specialized indoor environments. The more restrictive practices include keeping hens in cages with automated feeding and egg collection, and housing pregnant sows in individual stalls where the animals can be fed individually but have too little space to walk or turn around. (For more details see Fraser et al. 2001).

At the same time as the technology was changing, farm size was gradually increasing (Fraser et al. 2001). Larger farms had certain economies of scale such as greater bargaining power in purchasing feed, and they were able to sell animal products at lower prices. To remain competitive, other producers had to expand their operations, often by taking on more debt and responsibility, and the newer, more automated production systems helped to make this feasible. Eventually, for certain commodities in certain regions, family-sized units ceased to be economically viable at all.

It would take careful analysis to identify why those changes occurred when they did. Some of the reasons may have been cultural: the use of hardware to automate repetitive manual tasks must have seemed modern and progressive in the 1950s and 60s; the production of low-priced food from larger, more cost-effective units was encouraged by government policy in certain countries; and more industrial methods of production were seen as a way to improve the lot of low-income farmers (Thompson 2001). Another factor was undoubtedly the difficulty in retaining a reliable agricultural workforce as people, drawn by employment opportunities in more mechanized sectors of the economy, shifted from rural to urban living. Especially as farm size increased, automation provided a way to keep farm labor requirements within the capability of the individual farmer or farm family, and farmers were willing to invest capital in order to reduce their dependence on hired labor. A further reason was that confinement systems reduced some of the major animal care problems and production losses of the older systems. For example, death by predation and exposure was largely eliminated, and feed costs could be lowered by protecting animals from cold weather. Therefore, despite their greater capital cost, confinement methods were often seen as more feasible, more profitable, and, within the culture of the day, as newer and better ways of raising animals.

Underlying the changes in animal agriculture was an economic development driven by two forms of twentieth-century technology: refrigeration and transportation. A century earlier, many animal products, being highly perishable, were produced and sold locally. The supply chain generally involved primary production on local farms, processing at local slaughterhouses and dairies, and sale through local butcher shops and retailers. During the twentieth century, improvements in refrigeration, fast freezing, and transportation technology made it possible for animal products to be kept longer, transported farther, and sold into increasingly larger markets. This, in effect, meant that producers found themselves competing against thousands of other producers, sometimes in different parts of the world. Under these conditions price competition became intense, and the need to reduce production costs became more severe.

Expanding markets and shrinking profits undoubtedly played a role in the reshaping of animal agriculture. As long as competition was not too severe and profits per animal were sufficiently high, producers could earn a modest but acceptable living by keeping smaller herds and flocks; with severe competition, they had little choice but to increase herd and flock size in order to generate adequate income. With ample profit margins, producers were free to choose among different production systems; with severe competition, many felt more or less obliged to switch to confinement systems in order to avoid the losses, higher costs, and labor requirements common to the older systems. Thus, expanding markets and shrinking profits helped drive the move toward larger units and confinement technology.

In addition to these macro-level effects, shrinking profits also had important micro-level effects on animal rearing methods. With adequate profit per animal, producers could provide animals with space and bedding designed to promote comfort, even at levels that were not cost-effective; at low profit levels, these amenities had to be severely constrained. With adequate profit per animal, producers could spend time caring for individuals, attending births, and nursing the sick; with severe economic competition, staff time per animal had to be kept to cost-effective levels. Thus, the shift toward confinement technology and larger farm size oc-

curred at the same time as cost-cutting measures such as minimal space allowances and limited staff time per animal. Indeed, as discussed below, critics have sometimes blamed confinement systems and large farm size for animal welfare problems that might more accurately be attributed to the cost-cutting measures that became the norm at the time when confinement and large farms were becoming established.

The Standard Critique

Perhaps it was merely a coincidence of timing, but during the same half century when these changes were taking place in agriculture, a major shift was also underway in attitudes toward animals in Western society. To a degree, this was a continuation of a long historical trend, dating roughly to 1700 in England and perhaps earlier on the European continent, for animals to receive increasing amounts of attention and sympathy in literature, the visual arts, and philosophy (Harwood 1928). The change in attitudes may also have reflected the growing scientific knowledge of animals, which has tended to narrow the gap that people perceive between themselves and other species (Fraser 2001b). It may also have resulted from changes in human exposure to animals in the twentieth century, especially the trend for urban people to be exposed to pets rather than farm animals, and the role of television and other media in making the lives of wild animals accessible to people as never before. Whatever the causes, the latter half of the twentieth century saw a profound increase in attention to animal issues, and in concern over the treatment of animals in zoos, laboratories, wildlife management and, of course, agriculture. As a result, animal agriculture found itself under intense scrutiny from critics who claimed, among other things, that standards of animal welfare are unacceptably low in modern animal production (Fraser 2001a).

Much of the writing has pinned the blame on three factors. The first is confinement technology itself, the argument being that restrictive, indoor systems are so inappropriate for animals that they result in widespread suffering. For example, in *The Price of Meat,* author Danny Penman (1996) states:

> Whether they are battery chickens in their cages or pigs in sow stalls, all experience the same mental anguish that would drive many humans to suicide. (p. 25)

And Edward Dolan (1986), in *Animal Rights,* states:

> In all, the natures, welfare, and comfort of the animals are totally ignored for the sake of production methods that seek the greatest profit possible at the least possible cost in housing and care. (p. 67)

A second factor, more emphasized in North America than elsewhere, is corporate ownership of farms, with critics often creating the impression that corporately owned units have largely replaced individually or family owned farms, and that corporate ownership accounts for the negative effects on animal welfare.

For example, in *Vegan: The New Ethics of Eating,* author Erik Marcus (1998) writes:

> In the 1980s, big corporations stepped in and took over the pig industry with the same large-scale systems applied to poultry. (p. 115)

and:

> With the decline of the family farm, animals that used to be cared for with kindness and a general regard for their welfare now live and die in unconscionable conditions. (p. 89)

A third factor is an alleged erosion of animal care values, whereby producers are said to have callously abandoned humane treatment of animals in favor of greater profit. In *Old Mac-Donald's Factory Farm,* C. D. Coats (1989) states:

> Now humane treatment is seen as unnecessary, irrelevant, and in conflict with the maximization of profit (p. 21).

Again, corporate ownership of farms is often blamed for this change in values. For example, John Robbins (1987) in *Diet for a New America,* writes:

> The problem is that the behemoths of modern agribusiness seek profit without reference to any ethical sensitivity to the animals in their keeping (p. 97).

As some of these quotations indicate, the critics, as well as identifying these three factors, often create the impression that the three go together as a package whereby corporate ownership is accompanied by confinement housing and the disappearance of animal care values, in contrast to the older package of family ownership, older rearing methods, and animal care values, all of which lead to happier animals. Writers adopting this standard critique of modern animal production appear to offer only two solutions: either a return to the type of agriculture that preceded the recent revolution or, since that is unlikely to happen, for consumers to boycott animal products altogether.

Problems with the Standard Critique

The issues raised by the standard critique deserve attention and analysis, but the package, as it is commonly presented, does not correspond to the complex realities of animal agriculture, nor adequately identify the major causes of farm animal welfare problems. Let us consider some of the ways the standard critique leads us astray.

First, does confinement technology necessarily lead to reduced animal welfare? This is a complex question which needs careful analysis, some of which has been provided by Fox (1984), Webster (1994), Rollin (1995) and others. Confinement systems have sometimes made disease transmission more problematic because of the large number of animals housed together, but they have sometimes helped to prevent disease because pathogens can often be excluded from enclosed herds and flocks. Indoor environments often increase the stress caused by hot, humid weather because of inadequate ventilation, but they tend to reduce the stress caused by cold, wet weather because they provide better shelter. Animals confined in indoor pens may have difficulty escaping from aggressive pen-mates, but they are protected from predators. In short, the move to confinement housing created or exacerbated certain animal welfare problems, but helped to solve others.

A second problem with the standard critique is the portrayal of animal agriculture as having fallen into corporate ownership. In reality, corporate ownership of animal agriculture has become the norm only for certain commodities in certain countries. In the United States, most egg and poultry production is now controlled by a handful of corporations, but in Canada the individual producer remains the dominant player. The last two decades have seen the appearance of huge, corporately owned swine units in the United States, but these are viewed as an aberration in many other industrialized swine-producing countries. In fact, the wholesale replacement of family-owned farms by large, corporately controlled units has occurred mainly in two areas of the world—parts of the United States and certain former Soviet countries—where socioeconomic goals (the market economy in the United States; collectivism in the former Soviet Union) were pursued with such vigor that traditional agricultural norms were displaced. Ultimately we need sound empirical investigation of the trends in farm ownership, but we can safely say that in many countries and many commodities, much of the increase in farm size to date consists of owner-operated units becoming progressively larger, rather than corporate ownership replacing individual or family ownership. Moreover, confinement methods are

by no means the invention of corporately owned farming. Most of the confinement methods in use today were becoming the standard technology of family- and individually-owned farms during the 1950s, 1960s and 1970s, before large, corporately owned units became common; and confinement methods continue to be staunchly defended by many producers operating individually- and family-owned enterprises.

Third, is it true that animal producers have undergone a major shift away from traditional animal care values? This, too, is an empirical question that critics have answered more with rhetoric than with real investigation. For example, Singer (1990), in *Animal Liberation*, reproduced a number of quotations indicating extreme callousness on the part of animal producers. He quoted an egg producer who said: "The object of producing eggs is to make money. When we forget this objective, we have forgotten what it is all about," and a pig producer who justified selling crippled pigs with the comment: "We don't get paid for producing animals with good posture around here. We get paid by the pound."

Obviously these quotations were selected to illustrate callous attitudes, and Singer did not provide counterbalancing quotations from the other end of the moral spectrum. Instead he tended to extrapolate to animal agriculture in general with the conclusion: "The fact is that the meat available from butchers and supermarkets comes from animals who were not treated with any real consideration at all while being reared" (p. 160).

But is this an empirically accurate portrayal of the values of animal producers, or is it mere condemnatory stereotyping? We need empirical research to identify how and whether modern methods, farm size, and ownership have influenced the values of animal producers; however, the small amount of evidence suggests that the situation is not as simple as critics imply. Philosopher Bernard Rollin (1995), after talking about animal ethics with cattle ranchers in the western United States, reported finding a strong sense of moral responsibility for proper animal care, linked to the view that proper care of animals is essential for the ranchers' own prosperity. My own impression is that producers' attitudes toward animals range from the very callous to the very caring, as they probably always have, and that many producers today continue to espouse fairly traditional animal-care values, although they experience serious constraints on their ability to act on those values in today's world.

A fourth problem of the standard critique is that it has tended to overlook the key role played by economic constraints influencing animal welfare through the micro-level factors noted above. Whether animals are kept in confinement or nonconfinement systems, a crucial element in animal welfare is the skill and care provided by farm workers (Hemsworth and Coleman 1998); hence, animals are likely to suffer if low wages lead to inappropriate or poorly trained staff, high staff turnover, and insufficient staff time per animal. Similarly, cost-cutting in areas such as space, bedding, veterinary care, and feed quality can exert profound effects on animal welfare, perhaps far more important than any negative effects of indoor rearing and large farm size, yet the economic constraints facing animal producers are rarely cited as critical factors in animal welfare.

Finally, in blaming the problems on declining animal care values among producers, the standard critique has tended to miss the important role played by the values of consumers. Specifically, as long as consumers use (or are perceived by retailers to use) low cost as the main criterion for purchasing animal products, they are, in effect, driving producers to minimize space, amenities, staff time, and other factors that play a key role in animal welfare.

To summarize, the standard critique of animal agriculture has tended to misconstrue the factors affecting farm animal welfare. It has tended to focus on macro-level factors—confinement technology and ownership structure —whose influence on animal welfare is some-

what mixed. It has tended to miss the micro-level factors that influence farm animal welfare more directly and that are driven at least in part by market competition. It has also tended to focus on producer values rather than consumer values, thus underemphasizing the role of consumers and society at large in allowing market economics to dictate standards of farm animal care.

The Pastoralist Ethic as a Solution?

To properly address farm animal welfare problems, I believe we need a new consensus between consumers and producers on appropriate use and care of animals, based on a value system commanding strong enough support to counteract some of the pressure of market economics. Could the pastoralist ethic, with its emphasis on appropriate use and diligent care of animals, provide such a value system?

For various reasons, including perhaps its religious roots and its origins in a lifestyle that is largely extinct in the West, the pastoralist ethic has been largely ignored by most of the philosophers and social critics who have contributed to modern animal ethics. It finds some resonance in contemporary writing about humans and animals forming communities as proposed, for example, by Thomas Berry (2002) and Mary Midgley (1983). It is reflected most strongly in the animal husbandry ethic of Bernard Rollin (1995) and in the ideas of stewardship and *agapē* toward nature found in some Christian theology (Dobel 1977; Hall 1982; Bratton 1992; Bruce and Bruce 2000). It is also reflected in some feminist writings about care and responsibility for others (Donovan and Adams 1996; Campbell 1994). But despite these links, the pastoralist ethic has played little explicit role in the contemporary philosophical debate about animal ethics.

Instead, much of this philosophical debate has gone in quite different directions. For one thing, many contributors to the debate have invoked the principle of equality between humans and nonhumans in some manner. Most famously, Singer (1990) argued for equal consideration of human and animal interests, and Regan (1983) claimed that those (humans and animals) who possess inherent value possess it equally. In such systems, as Midgley (1983:65) points out, we are presented with two options: give animals equality or consign them to "outer darkness." Moreover, much of the debate has focused on the most general questions of whether we should use animals for human purposes at all, rather than on specific questions about appropriate animal care practices. Philosophical debate about whether to eat animals has attracted the attention of reflective people over the millennia (Sorabji 1993), but it has consistently been a byway of Western ethics, with most people finding some use of animals to be acceptable; and the burgeoning worldwide industry of animal production allows us to plausibly predict that the current iteration of the debate will, like its predecessors, not bring animal agriculture to an end. Indeed, instead of helping to resolve practical conflicts about the welfare of farm animals, much of the philosophical debate has tended to create two solitudes: a minority of people who accept equality-based thinking and thus reject the commercial use of animals; and the vast majority who may perceive that all is not right with farm animals but see no practical way forward. Worse yet, the people who most closely influence farm-animal welfare—the producers themselves—often feel alienated and vilified by the debate rather than being engaged in it.

In contrast, the pastoralist ethic, emphasizing appropriate use of animals combined with diligent care, could potentially provide an alternative philosophy that would give practical guidance on farm animal welfare. For this to occur, a number of questions need to be answered. Does the pastoralist ethic continue to have widespread support among animal producers? In a secular and multicultural world, would consumers recognize it as a legitimate philosophy of animal use, to the point of allowing animal-care standards to trump some of the effects of market economics? More fundamentally, could a given community (a country, region, faith community, or the like) develop a consensus to support certain forms of animal use combined with certain standards of animal care? These questions require the attention of agriculturalists, ethicists, scientists, and theologians. With appropriate thought, dialogue, and moral leadership, the pastoralist ethic might form the basis of a new and badly needed social consensus in modern animal ethics, as it appears to have done in biblical times.

Acknowledgments

I am grateful to Rod Preece for helpful comments and for allowing me to use some of our joint work in this essay, to Edmond Pajor for the introductory anecdote, and to Raymond Anthony, Helena Röcklinsberg, and Vonne Lund for reading the manuscript.

REFERENCES

Berry, T. 2006. "Prologue." This volume.

Bratton, S. P. 1984. "Christian Ecotheology and the Old Testament." *Environmental Ethics* 6:195–209.

———. 1992. "Loving Nature: Eros or Agape?" *Environmental Ethics* 14:3–25.

Bruce, D. M. and A. Bruce. 2000. "Animal Welfare and Use." In J. Hodges and I. K. Han eds., *Livestock, Ethics and Quality of Life.* Wallingford, UK: CABI Publishing, pp. 53–77.

Campbell, M. 1994. "Beyond the Terms of the Contract: Mothers and Farmers." *Journal of Agricultural and Environmental Ethics* 7:205–20.

Coats, C. David. 1989. *Old MacDonald's Factory*

Farm: The Myth of the Traditional Farm and the Shocking Truth About Animal Suffering in Today's Agribusiness. New York: Continuum.

Davidson, A. B. 1995. "It Isn't All Black and White." In K. B. Beesley, S. Burns, M. Campbell and P. Sanger, eds. *Decision Making and Agriculture: The Role of Ethics.* Truro, Canada: Rural Research Centre, pp. 25–30.

Dobel, P. 1977. "The Judeo-Christian Stewardship Attitude Toward Nature." In L. Pojman, ed. *Environmental Ethics: Readings in Theory and Application, Second edition,* 1998. Belmont, CA: Wadsworth Publishing, pp. 26–30.

Dolan, E. F. Jr. 1986. *Animal Rights.* New York: Franklin Watts.

Donovan, J. and C. J. Adams, eds. 1996. *Beyond Animal Rights: A Feminist Caring Ethic for the Treatment of Animals.* New York: Continuum.

Fox, M. W. 1984. *Farm Animals: Husbandry, Behavior and Veterinary Practice.* Baltimore: University Park Press.

Fraser, D. 1995. "Science, Values and Animal Welfare: Exploring the 'Inextricable Connection.'" *Animal Welfare* 4:103–17.

———. 2001a. "The 'New Perception' of Animal Agriculture: Legless Cows, Featherless Chickens, and a Need for Genuine Analysis." *Journal of Animal Science* 79:634–41.

———. 2001b. "Farm Animal Production: Changing Agriculture in a Changing Culture." *Journal of Applied Animal Welfare Science* 4:175–90.

Fraser, D., J. Mench, and S. Millman. 2001. "Farm Animals and Their Welfare in 2000." In D. J. Salem and A. N. Rowan, eds. *State of the Animals 2001.* Washington, D.C.: Humane Society Press, pp. 87–99.

Hall, D. J. 1982. *The Steward: A Biblical Symbol Come of Age.* New York: Friendship Press.

Harwood, D. 2003 [1928]. *Love for Animals and How It Developed in Great Britain.* Lampeter, U.K.: Edwin Mellen Press.

Hemsworth, P. H. and G. J. Coleman. 1998. *Human-Livestock Interactions: The Stockperson and the Productivity and Welfare of Intensively Farmed Animals.* Wallingford, U.K.: CABI Publishing.

Linzey, A. 1991. *Christianity and the Rights of Animals.* New York: Crossroad.

Marcus, E. 1998. *Vegan: The New Ethics of Eating.* Ithaca: McBooks Press.

Midgley, M. 1983. *Animals and Why They Matter.* Athens: University of Georgia Press.

Moncrief, L. W. 1970. "The Cultural Basis of Our Environmental Crisis." *Science* 170:508–12.

Penman, D. 1996. *The Price of Meat.* London: Victor Gollancz.

Preece, R. and D. Fraser. 2000. "The Status of Animals in Biblical and Christian Thought: A Study in Colliding Values." *Society and Animals* 8:245–63.

Regan, T. 1983. *The Case for Animal Rights.* Berkeley: University of California Press.

Robbins, J. 1987. *Diet for a New America.* Walpole, NH: Stillpoint Publishing.

Rollin, B. E. 1993. "Animal Production and the New Social Ethic for Animals." In *Food Animal Well-Being 1993 — Conference Proceedings and Deliberations.* West Lafayette, IN: USDA and Purdue University Office of Agricultural Research Programs, pp. 3–13.

———. 1995. *Farm Animal Welfare: Social, Bioethical, and Research Issues.* Ames: Iowa State University Press.

Schochet, E. J. 1984. *Animal Life in Jewish Tradition: Attitudes and Relationships.* New York: KTAV.

Singer, P. 1990. *Animal Liberation, Revised Edition.* New York: Avon.

Sorabji, R. 1993. *Animal Minds and Human Morals: The Origins of the Western Debate.* Ithaca: Cornell University Press.

Thompson, P. B. 2001. "The Reshaping of Conventional Farming: A North American Perspective." *Journal of Agricultural and Environmental Ethics* 14:217–29.

Webster, J. 1994. *Animal Welfare: A Cool Eye Towards Eden.* Oxford: Blackwell Science.

White, L. 1967. "The Historical Roots of Our Ecological Crisis." *Science* 155:1203–7.

Agriculture, Livestock, and Biotechnology

Values, Profits, and Ethics

MICHAEL FOX

Compassion is a boundless ethic, drawing all living beings into the circle of our moral community, which is a reflection of our ecological community as well as our ecocentric or ecospiritual perception and perspective. All beings are interrelated, interdependent, and of the same origin. This has all been scientifically verified; it provides the objective basis for a creation-centered or cosmocentric spirituality that is essentially panentheistic and moves us from compassion to communion and a reverential respect for the life and beauty of Earth.

As Thomas Berry has opined, the cosmos is a communion of subjects, not a collection of objects created for our own use. Only that which we regard as sacred is secure; and our reverence must be total, or it is not at all.

Bringing Bioethics to Life

The "big three" bioethical principles—compassion, reverential respect, and *ahiṃsā* (nonharm-

ing)—can lead us to discover a diversity of hitherto unaddressed issues, as in endeavoring to farm without harm. Other more specific ethical, socioeconomic, and related issues and concerns are brought to the surface by the holistic or multifactorial scope of bioethical evaluation.

A combination of economic, ecological, and ethical considerations enable us to more clearly delineate what kinds of animal usage are acceptable, which should be prohibited, and which should be reformed. Ecological, economic, and ethical considerations should be given equal and fair consideration, and all vested human interests, especially those of a pecuniary nature, should be tempered by the absolute bioethical principles mentioned above.

A holistic or multifactorial paradigm is needed in the many areas of animal protection where consideration of animals from an economic perspective is acceptable. By way of illustration, the benefits of humane farm animal husbandry and of ecological agriculture are embedded in a complex multifactorial matrix of interdependent bioethical criteria that converge on sustainable "eco-nomics." A full cost accounting of the benefits of treating animals humanely moves us away from an exclusive focus on compassion (or animals' rights) as a moralistic "ought" or duty to reveal the unequivocal societal benefits of a symbiotic relationship of reciprocity with our fellow creatures.

Economics as a Factor

Until the advent of conventional, industrial agriculture, livestock played a diversity of roles in the economy of rural communities. They were not raised just for their meat. In less developed countries like India, Central and South America, and parts of Africa, livestock continue to be valued for these multiple purposes. These include draft power; fuel and fertilizer (from manure); companionship; clothing (from wool) and leather products from hides; a banking system of capital "stock" that has the potential to double in value annually (as each animal produces one or more offspring per year); and a sustainable source of fat and protein from milk, meat, blood, and various internal organs. This food source is sustainable, since the animals are fed agricultural byproducts, surpluses, and forages. Livestock also provide a safe and efficient way of controlling weeds and various pests, and of improving soil and forage quality, especially via "mixed" and rotational grazing practices. The biological and ecological attributes of different animals, like geese, pigs, sheep, goats, cattle, and equines and cameloids, are thus fully utilized.

In a speech at the Oregon Tilth twentieth anniversary meeting in the fall of 1995, farmer-philosopher Wendell Berry said, "If animals are an integral part of the ecology in which you live, then you have a responsibility to eat meat ... even if it kills you." Rhetoric aside, Berry's words are worth some reflection and have different connotations in different cultures and contexts. In developed countries, animals raised in intensive "factory farming" bioconcentration camps are not an integral part of the farming system, since feed is imported and there is insufficient acreage to properly recycle animal waste.

Currently, vegetarianism is justified by many in the West as a healthy choice and as an ethical decision in protest against inhumane, intensive industrialized livestock production methods that break the ecological connections among animals, soil, and crops. In countries like India, where religion and caste influence dietary choices, lacto-vegetarianism and cow-slaughter taboos combine to result in much animal suffering. Berry misses a major point: we humans also need to become part of the ecology or bioregional food-shed that sustains us by composting our own manure instead of wasting it (and a lot of water) via flush toilets. But this is not to discount the other important ecological roles of livestock detailed above.

Bioethical Travesties of the Livestock Industry

For those not familiar with the bioethical travesties of conventional livestock production, the following concerns will provide a brief introduction. Extreme confinement and animal suffering: veal calves and sows unable to walk or turn around; laying hens confined to "battery" cages, four or five birds living in a space too small for even one to stretch her wings; dairy cows and beef cattle confined to dirty feedlots with no access to pasture and often no shade or shelter. These conditions cause animals distress and stress and create an ideal environment for the spread of so-called production or husbandry-related diseases that cause animals further suffering.

- Widespread use of antibiotics and other drugs to control stress-related diseases and to stimulate growth, egg and milk production means significant consumer health risks from drug residues and the development of antibiotic resistant strains of bacteria responsible for epidemics of food poisoning.

- Squandering of natural resources—notably arable land and water to raise corn and soybeans results in inefficient conversion into animal fat and protein as livestock feed, along with fish industry and food and beverage industry byproducts. Even animal wastes (poultry manure fed to cattle) and the condemned and unused remains of slaughtered livestock (44 billion pounds per year in the United States) are included in livestock feed, as well as the rendered remains of euthanized cats and dogs and road kills. The presence of such wastes is believed to have caused the epidemic of bovine spongiform encephalopathy in cattle in Europe, which in turn affects humans, cats, and other animals. The feeding of diseased, dying, and dead animals to livestock and to companion animals is an economically rationalized parody of ecologically sound recycling.

- The billions of livestock in the United States and other industrialized countries produce vast quantities of urine and feces, too much for the surrounding farmland to recycle. The net result is surface and groundwater pollution, fish kills, bacterial and drug contamination of drinking water, and a contribution to global warming.

- Animal wastes, including diseased offal, dumped at sea, cause ecological damage and account for epidemic diseases in marine wildlife and pelagic avifauna.

- Herbicides, insecticides, synthetic fertilizers, fungicides, and new genetically engineered crops used by the livestock feed industry cause environmental and genetic pollution, endangering wild plants and animals, and contiguous organic farming systems.

- Predaticides, from poison baits to cyanide guns and trapping to eliminate wild predators, coupled with overstocking and overgrazing by livestock, decimate natural ecosystems where cattle are bred and raised prior to going to feedlots to be "finished" for human consumption.

The above activities are encouraged by the government-agribusiness system through loans, subsidized tax-writeoffs, all at taxpayers' expense, and are a significant cost to public health, which itself is to the benefit of the biomedical animal research and pharmaceutical-medical industrial complex that now calls itself the "life science" industry.

The bioconcentration camps of the animal industry have ruined the sustainable economy and livelihoods of family farms and rural communities through market monopoly and the economy of scale. In developing countries they have had a similar impact, first by co-opting land owners to produce livestock feed for export, second by encouraging and subsidizing the adoption of intensive poultry, pig, beef, and dairy production systems, and third by "dumping" their surplus livestock and other agricultural produce on third world countries—legalized via GATT and the WTO and promoted by the World Bank and IMF. This puts local producers out of business, because their production costs are higher than the market price of these "dumped" imports—like U.S. powdered milk and chicken parts in Jamaica. Indigenous peasant farmers in some developing countries have even been forced off their land at gun point by the military, whose governments want their land to raise soybeans for export to the U.S. livestock industry.

The net consequences of colonial agribusiness are manifold: indigenous farmers are bankrupted or disenfranchised; indigenous knowledge and indigenous seed-stocks and sustainable agricultural practices—the keystones of biocultural diversity—are lost; rural communities are impoverished and malnourished and rely on food imports, often of inferior quality; many emigrate to urban slums to seek employment, while others degrade marginal lands and encroach on wildlife preserves to graze livestock and raise food crops, and poach bushmeat and various forest products, practices often encouraged by corrupt authorities and donor agencies.

People in developing countries who can afford to adopt the Western diet high in animal fat and protein soon develop Western diseases associated with such a diet, notably arteriosclerosis, osteoporosis, and various forms of cancer. In the process they unwittingly support one of the most harmful and costly industries in the world — the livestock industry, which, along with agri-biotechnology and fast-food franchises like McDonald's and Kentucky Fried Chicken, are encouraged by the State Department through their embassies around the world.

Hidden Costs of Industrial Agriculture

Rather than utilizing the biological and ecological attributes of a diversity of animal and plant species as in sustainable and traditional farming systems, industrial agriculture specializes in a few varieties of plants and livestock. These are valued on the basis of their biomass productivity potential and as commodities. Finite resources — water, top soil, and fossil fuels — are squandered in the process.

This commodification and specialization in conventional agriculture has led to market concentration, commodity monopolies, and vertical integration, with farmers becoming the contract-peons of corporate feudalism. The hegemony of transnational agribusiness corporations is leading to global control of food and fiber production. The sale of costly farming and food processing equipment, petrochemicals, and new creations or biotechnology (from genetically engineered drugs and food additives to patented super pigs and wonder corn) displaces traditional farming systems and marginalizes small producers. This is not agriculture. It is agro-industrialism that is as divorced from culture, from traditional ways of farming and food preparation, as it is from the biological realism of ecologically sound, socially just, and sustainable land cultivation and animal husbandry. Cultivation and good husbandry are traditional

terms and practices embodying a more reverential relationship with the Earth, and a more sacramental attitude toward Nature, life, and food.

Through the newly established World Trade Organization (WTO) and the Codex Alimentarius international agreements on food quality and safety codes, the prevailing values and practices of industrial agriculture, notably deficient in social justice and humane and environmental ethics, may well become the global norm. U.S. agribusiness corporations, facing international competition, will understandably resist environmental and farm animal protection legislation so long as it is illegal under WTO rules for the United States to protect its own farmers from imports from other countries that have inadequate or no environmental and animal protection legislation, and so long as increased costs might weaken their competitive edge. But in the absence of international harmonization of sound environmental and farm animal protection laws and regulations, and protection of the rights and interests of indigenous peoples, international agreements and standards for food quality and safety are ethically unacceptable.

When there are no ethical and moral constraints on the twin goals of maximizing (rather than optimizing) productivity and profitability, the commoditization and industrialization of Nature, life, and food becomes a nemesis to agriculture. I have termed this process "Agricide," after my book of the same title (Fox 1996). In the absence of ethical and moral constraints, laws and costly regulatory compliance and enforcement procedures must be established to protect consumers and the environment. The agribusiness livestock sector has continued to deflect public efforts to establish ethical criteria for animal rearing practices, for their transportation and slaughter, and for the handling of injured and sick animals. This sector's preference for self-regulation, ostensibly to relieve the burden on government and to save public tax dollars, amounts to lip service, since there is ample evidence that a fox cannot be trusted to guard the hen house. While the livestock sector ponders in an ethical vacuum the scientific criteria for proper animal care, it is being called upon by an increasingly concerned public to be accountable for the humane treatment of animals and for the environmental impact and public health consequences of producing meat, milk, and eggs as dietary staples.

The advent of genetic engineering biotechnology and its applications in livestock and crop production and food processing have raised yet more questions and concerns, especially since the U.S. government has essentially deregulated this new industry to ostensibly give U.S.-based multinationals a competitive edge in the world market.

Consumers' Rights and Costs

If food is not labeled as to country of origin and method of production (like free range, organic, or genetically modified), U.S. consumers will have no choice in the marketplace and no opportunity to support either U.S. farmers or particular farming methods, which, for ethical and other reasons, they should have a constitutional right to decide upon for themselves. The recently established federal organic food standards have actually set a lower standard than many U.S. organic farmers have achieved, which sets up unfair competition and misleads consumers.

Agribusiness claims that the public will not pay more for food that is of similar nutritive value but has been produced without harm to the land, to animals, and to the environment, but this assumption is unfounded. When the public is made more fully aware of the harms caused by conventional agriculture, including the harms to human health, to the land, to rural communities and culture, and knows about the unnecessary but economically rationalized suffering of farm animals in bioconcentration camps, most consumers would surely be willing to pay more.

But in reality they would probably have to pay less for food from humane, sustainable, and organic farming and ranching systems. A full cost-benefit analysis of conventional agriculture would show that the costs far outweigh the benefits, in which we should include: up to $60 billion annually in public health costs (Barnard, et al. 1995) related to nutrient-deficient soils and foods, harmful agrochemicals, and from consuming too much animal fat, protein, and refined denatured and processed foods; and annual subsidies of animal agriculture of $50–60 billion. Some costs and losses, like biodiversity, wildlife habitat, and the decline of our rural communities, crafts and cultures, cannot be given a dollar value. Nor can the physical and emotional suffering of farm animals from stress and diseases, as indicated in an annual loss of profits at an estimated $17 billion.[1]

We are surely morally bound, as reasonable and responsible planetary tenants and not owners, to find less harmful ways to feed, clothe, shelter, and convey ourselves. Are we not wise enough to develop the bioethical principles of a more humane and sustainable global community and put those principles into practice? We surely care for the generations to come, if not for Nature, and for the beauty, diversity, and functional integrity of Earth's Creation. If we care for the fate of our children's children, then we must also care for the fate of the Earth and not allow the nonsustainable petrochemical-based food industry, and the nascent life science industry that is developing genetic engineering biotechnology, to limit the options of future generations by squandering nonrenewable resources and polluting our food, air, water, and the environment.

There is no real profit in such pointless and unethical activity. But it will continue so long as government continues to serve the interests of the industrial technocracy; and so long as consumers do not vote with their dollars and establish community-supported agriculture to keep local producers in business, purchase produce from local marketing cooperatives, and support those nongovernmental organizations that are protecting consumers' right to know by demanding proper food-labeling and encouraging the adoption of more humane, sustainable, and organic farming methods.

Certainly more research and development is needed in alternative agriculture, and its adoption by farmers should not be discouraged or penalized by government policies, programs, and price supports that favor the adoption and perpetuation of conventional, nonsustainable agricultural practices. Academia, especially in the land-grant colleges, could provide additional support by developing courses in agricultural and veterinary bioethics that encourage students to impartially examine the values, costs, and benefits of conventional and alternative agricultural systems. The university-industrial-political complex may then become something of the past.

Feeding a Hungry World

Now agribusiness advocates like Dennis T. Avery would contest these criticisms of industrial agriculture, which he calls "high yield" agriculture (Avery 1993). Its proponents, who are promoting biotechnology as a way to further enhance agricultural productivity and monopolistic control, claim that it will help save wildlife species and biodiversity, and that it is the only way to feed a rising human population.

The agribusiness view is that because the human population is expanding and needs food, the risks and costs of intensive "high yield" agriculture are justified (or insignificant). There's no alternative, like organic farming, according to Avery, because it is so low yield that it will mean global famine if more wildlife habitat isn't taken over to make up for the deficit per acre. Thus, organic farming is seen as a major threat to conservation and biodiversity and to the human good.

People who live by such truths structure reality in such a way that they do not know when they are deceiving themselves or others. The new

agribusiness myth that Avery promotes is that industrial agriculture is the best way to protect the environment and biodiversity. Its absurdity has been well documented in a report by the Henry A. Wallace Institute for Alternative Agriculture (Hewitt and Smith 1995).

This report details how chemically based, intensive crop production (especially questionable as a livestock feed-source) harms both terrestrial and aquatic ecosystems; and confirms that a range of alternatives to the chemically based production model can achieve equivalent or higher yields per unit area of land with less harmful consequences.

Avery goes on in one of his epistles for agribusiness to suggest that industrial agriculture, with its agrochemicals, agrobiotechnology, and patented hybrid seeds will not only alleviate world hunger, but also help reduce population growth because people who have a better income and can afford more meat and other animal produce have fewer children.

This is an overly simplistic correlative inference. These smaller affluent families are, per capita, as much, if not more, of a drain on the environmental economy and energy budget as poorer families who eat little or no meat and who sustain themselves on a low-input, labor-intensive agriculture.

It is education and access to family-planning programs and the development of local self-sufficiency and sustainable enterprises, especially agricultural, not agribusiness "high yield" farming (that put small farmers in debt for life), that will help control human population growth and alleviate world hunger.

Agribusiness has much to contribute to help alleviate such problems as human hunger, poverty, and malnutrition; and it has a major role to play in conservation and the protection of wildlife and biodiversity. But it must be less focused on selling products, investing in, researching, and developing ever more farm inputs, since the Achilles heel of Avery's "high yield" farming is its dependence on high inputs from chemical fertilizers and genetically engineered and patented seeds to mega-farm machinery that small farm operators cannot afford. Instead, agribusiness industry should focus more on process rather than on productivity, which is the end-point of an extremely complex, biodynamic system that does not fit within the narrow industrial paradigm of conventional agricultural economists.

Regenerative Agriculture

By "focusing on process," I mean paying attention to the economic and health benefits of maintaining a living soil, the primary resource, as well as pure water, air quality, and normal solar radiation of agriculture. There is much money to be made in helping to restore and maintain the quality of soil, air, and water, as well as the quality of livestock and seedstock (without having to resort to genetic engineering). Let agribusiness find its profits in helping farmers restore agriculture and rural life rather than selling more products and processes that simply increase farm inputs, lower farmers' profits, and increase market profits for the life science industry. A science, economy, and ethics of regenerative agricultural inputs and practices that lead to healthier soils, crops, livestock, and food should be on the corporate agenda and the mission of land-grant colleges of agriculture "food science" and veterinary medicine.

The same must be said for human medicine, which needs to establish a closer linkage via nutrition with remedial innovations in agriculture and in consumer eating habits. It is absurd that the pharmaceutical and medical industries should continue to profit by selling many products and treatments that would not be needed if our soils were healthy and our food were safe and nutritious, and that at the same time cause animals to suffer in biomedical and product testing laboratories.

Recent developments in agricultural biotechnology illustrate clearly how the decision-making processes of corporations and government are framed within an outmoded anthropocentric paradigm[2] that is purportedly "science-based," but actually precludes such bioethical considerations as socioeconomic, ecological, and moral consequences. While approval of genetically engineered bovine growth hormone (rBGH), for use in dairy cows, and the patenting of genetically engineered animals and plants have been put on hold by the European Parliament, precisely because of these bioethical concerns, the U.S. government has approved both.

Current risk-benefit analyses and scientific studies to determine the safety and effectiveness of new biotechnology products and processes, like potatoes and corn that produce their own pesticides, virus-resistant squash, herbicide-resistant soybeans, porcine growth hormone, and transgenic salmon and catfish are too simplistic. Without a paradigm shift that makes the science base broader and more relevant, and also includes bioethics, the real benefits of biotechnology may never be fully realized.

The public interest is not being served by conventional agriculture with its emphasis on maximizing the production of specialized and publicly subsidized commodities, much of which are for export, in a highly competitive world market. There are many hidden costs, including the environmental and health risks of agrichemicals and antibiotic feed additives, and diet-related health problems and public health costs that are a significant drain on the national economy. A sustainable, regenerative agriculture is the cornerstone of a viable economy and of every nation's ultimate security.

Restore Humus, Recover Humanity

In using agrochemicals to boost food production for profit and to ostensibly meet the demands of an ever-expanding human population, agriculture has become chemically addicted.

Many of the chemicals used have adversely affected not only the living organisms and elements of the soil but also the trophic processes of transmutation and energy flow at the molecular and subatomic levels. As we are killing our soils, we are doing no less to ourselves and to our air, food, and water. At the molecular level of soil management and crop and livestock health and productivity, trace minerals are of especial concern; they are being disrupted by industrial agriculture. Vitamin and trace mineral imbalances and deficiencies are at the root of many crop, livestock and human diseases, since they play such a vital role in cellular metabolism, most enzyme processes, and all organ-system functions —especially of the immune, circulatory, nervous, and reproductive systems. The decline and demise of past civilizations was almost invariably linked with the devitalization of the soil and consequent malnutrition. Today is no different, and this problem is being compounded by variously denatured, deficient, refined, processed, and adulterated foods as well as by the specter of genetic pollution (see Fox 2004).[3] We human beings tend to forget that we are humus beings. From the earth we are born; to the earth we return, and by the earth we are sustained.

Humility, humanity, and humus are words that connect and ground us in the reality of our being. But the mayhem of unbridled self-interest separates us from biological reality, and out of arrogance and ignorance, coupled with rationalization and denial, we demean, neglect, and abuse Earth. The commodification of life leads to contempt for life. Caught in the delusional realm of anthropocentrism we fail to realize that when we harm the earth we harm ourselves. When the humus is depleted of microorganisms, the soil becomes nutrient deficient and toxic with agrichemicals, so become our crops, farm animals, and the food we consume: And so become our bodies, minds, and spirits. In harming the soil we soil; ourselves physically, mentally, morally, and spiritually. Such retributive justice—Nature's Nemesis—was rec-

ognized as the law of karma in more enlightened times.

When we recover our humanity and humility we rediscover the wisdom of living in harmony with Earth. Through the sacraments and communion of seed and soil, of toil and food, our health and well-being and the vitality of the earth are mutually enhanced. As we enter the deep communion of a reverential symbiosis with Earth, human purpose and fulfillment gain greater meaning and significance. And we are secure in the knowledge that we are part of that which is forever being renewed, as the self is forever sustained, transfigured, transformed, and reborn. Through the intercommunion of reverential symbiosis we come to understand and respect, as the laws of Nature, all the relationships and processes that maintain and sustain the life community. Obedience to these laws enables us to participate in a creative and mutually enhancing way and by so doing avoid causing harm to ourselves and to other sentient beings that are not commodities but are "ours" only in sacred trust.

Our scientific understanding of ecology and evolutionary biology provides a rational, ethical basis for what we regard spiritually as our sacred connections and shared origins, since we are part of the same Creation as all other sentient beings. This spiritual kinship leads us to acknowledge the intrinsic value and inherently divine aspect of every being. We neither rob animals of their dignity nor their sanctity and right to be themselves and fulfill their cosmic purpose. The livestock bioconcentration camps of industrial agriculture, and the vast monocultures of commodity crops, are anathema to this worldview.

A rigorous bioethical evaluation of the risks and benefits of some new product or process, for example, like synthetic bovine growth hormone (rBGH) or irradiation of meat (to help prevent bacterial food poisoning), includes a wide spectrum of ethical questions that go beyond simplistic "science-based" determinations of efficiency and consumer risk. These are as follows:

1. Necessity. Is the new technology, product, or service really necessary?
2. What is the public demand, or need, and acceptance?
3. What are the possible environmental impacts, short- and long-term?
4. What is the public health impact, short- and long-term?
5. What are the economic impacts; who will benefit, and who might be harmed in the short- and long-term?
6. Animal welfare. Will the new product or service enhance or be detrimental to advances in the health and overall well-being of farm animals?
7. Social and cultural consequences, e.g., what impact may there be on the structure of agriculture, nationally and internationally, and on more sustainable traditional and alternative agricultural practices at home and abroad?
8. Oversight and compliance. Can the new technology, product, or service be effectively regulated to maximize benefits and minimize risks, and at what cost to society?

I developed the following alternative way of framing these concerns (NDSA 1994) for the U.S. National Dialogue on Sustainable Agriculture, Marketing and Organics Issue Committee, in preparing documentation for the 1995 U.S. Farm Bill:

All new agricultural products, processes and policies should be subject to rigorous bioethical evaluation prior to approval and adoption in order to promote the farm-without-harm ideal of sustainability. The criteria for bioethical evaluation include safety and effectiveness; social justice, equity, farmworker and farm animal well-being; environmental impact, including harm to wildlife, loss of ecosystems and biodiversity; socioeconomic and cultural impacts especially harm to established sustainable practices and communities, and violations of Native American rights; accord with established organic

and other humane sustainable agriculture practices, standards and production claims.

The following three stipulations for appropriate labeling of food were also identified:

A. Require labeling of all genetically engineered foods.
B. Require labeling of all processed irradiated foods.
C. Require point-of-origin labeling.

From a narrow economic perspective, rBGH and food irradiation are acceptable, but from a purely animal welfare perspective they are not, because rBGH can subject cows to production-related stress and disease, and because humane rearing, transportation, handling, and slaughter methods reduce bacterial contamination and negate the need for irradiation. Following further evaluation on the basis of the above bioethical criteria, reasonable solutions can be found that will ultimately be in the best interests of society.

These three bioethical principles—compassion, reverence for life, and *ahimsā*—can inspire us to live the way we feel is right, but unless we abandon living in the modern world they must first become the key criteria for determining the policies and goals of community, government, and multinational corporations. These principles are not included in the GATT for adoption by the World Trade Organization. All efforts to create a sustainable global economy are likely to fail if these basic bioethical principles and evaluation of all forms of animal exploitation, as in "factory farming," are excluded from the agenda. This is because these basic bioethical principles essentially determine our chosen role on Earth by identifying the cardinal virtues that make us human in relation to the entire Earth community: Not just the global marketplace. These principles and concerns were excluded from the 1992 Rio Earth Summit conference on sustainable development. To help insure their future inclusion, it is incumbent upon us all to establish an Animal Bioethics Council (UNABC) within the UN and to initiate an International Animal Welfare and Protection Fund to help support this council. The United Nations' acceptance of an Animal Bill of Rights would be a significant step toward a more humane and sustainable world community, along with an amendment to the U.S. Constitution that addresses citizens' duties to ensure the well-being of all animals and to protect the natural environment.

A major flaw of this Earth Summit was the evident lack of any spiritual vision and values, or recognition of basic bioethics, all of which embody universal and universalizing principles that transcend cultural, religious, and political differences, and take us beyond the shallow materialistic and deterministic paradigms of scientism and economism on which this important global conference was primarily based and upon which no firm future for humanity and the Earth could surely ever be made. In the absence of a universal bioethics for the people and by the people there can be little hope. The presence of a unifying bioethics has been shown by Daryll Macer to be transcultural and integral to our human and humane sensibility (Macer 1994).

We should be mindful of the distinction that theologian John B. Cobb Jr. and economist Herman C. Daly make in their seminal book *For the Common Good* (Daly and Cobb 1994), namely that between economism and planetism. To value animals and other life forms and ecosystems primarily, if not exclusively, in economic terms, and to label them as "living resources," is a backward step into rationalized anthropocentrism, self-serving dominion, and unbridled exploitation in the name of progress and necessity. We should, therefore, be mindful also of the Orwellian "newspeak" rhetoric of "industrial growth," or "science-based" sustainable development, policies, and goals. The latter concept is an oxymoron—human "development," especially industrial and popula-

tion growth, must be contained, since it can no longer be sustained at nature's expense. A planetary dimension—planetism—is needed to replace the limited and ultimately nihilistic paradigm of economism, which regards industrial expansion and economic growth as the *ethos* and *telos* of *Homo sapiens*. In the process of transforming the *ecos* into a bioindustrialized wasteland, and forcing the *telos* of animals to serve our own ends, we will unwittingly transform ourselves into something less than human—something that does not recognize contempt and indifference toward life as a disease of the soul.

In the final analysis, the highest value of animals and nature to us humans is transcendental insofar as they can imbue humanity with a sense of the sacred, adding depth and meaning as well as mystery and wonder to our lives. It is through humane education, awakening our innate biophilia and capacity to empathize, that animals and nature will be respected and protected, and in the process of becoming more humane we become more human and worthy of the title *Homo sapiens*.

Restoring Our Organic Connections

As we humans come to see that our arrogance and alienation arise when we forget our origins and that most evil in the world comes from our self-centeredness and denial, we may, with Nature's help, mature into a Creation-centered being. Our pathological and evolution-arresting anthropocentrism has pervaded our major religious and cultural institutions and caused great harm for millennia. The recovery of humanity and civilization lies in the anthropocosmic transformation of our consciousness, which will herald a new epoch in human evolution and in the refinement and metamorphosis of the human spirit. An auspicious beginning is to respect the living soil as a primary life-giver and sustainer, and to farm accordingly, with less harm and greater care, harmony and veneration.

To be a good gatherer, hunter, farmer, or natural scientist, you must have feelings for plants, animals, and the land: to have respect, even reverence, and a degree of empathic understanding as well as practical, biological knowledge.[4] This feeling and wisdom is being lost as the last of the gatherers-hunters, and now increasingly, indigenous and sustainable farmers around the world, are being colonized by the dominant cult and culture of materialism and industrialism.

I have found that organic farmers are enthusiastic because they feel that what they are doing is biologically, scientifically, and ethically sound. To be enthusiastic means to be inspired by en-theos, the God within. Organic farmers see the light, if not the God, in all. The bioethics of humane, organic, sustainable agriculture are the seeds of a new civilization that does not seek to dominate and exploit—one that does not need latter-day agribusiness missionaries promoting the colonization of industrialism with the dogma and catechisms of agrichemicals and genetically engineered seeds. It seeks to establish a mutually enhancing symbiosis with the land and all who dwell therein.

Thomas Berry contends that the "Great Work" for all of us in this age is to facilitate the social evolution of a reverential attitude toward all life that enables each of us to establish a mutually enhancing earth-human relationship. Organic agriculture epitomizes the spirit and praxis of Great Work. The needs of the many and the greed of the few are surmountable obstacles. It is enlightened self-interest to not just live for today regardless of the consequences. To be virtuous is to be mindful of the precepts of sustainable self-reliance—what I call "spiritual anarchy"[5]—of the frugal and equitable use of natural resources; and of the protection of the environment, animals, and biocultural diversity. The development of a moral ecology and the awakening of empathic and ethical consciousness are integral to the commencement of the Great Work. We are all spiritually challenged in this age of increasing ecological and socioeconomic chaos (Fox 2001).

Our social evolution calls for a new sensibility based upon a more empathic and compassionate relationship with all beings, as exemplified by organic agriculture. It calls for an ethically consistent attitude and set of values that give equal and fair consideration to all beings, reflecting an attitude of reverential respect for life. Conscience and compassion are the antidotes to selfishness and ecological illiteracy. As we humans become more empathic, organically connected, and thus ethical beings, our quality of life will be enhanced, and the integrity and future of Creation will be better assured.

NOTES

1. According to a 1986 report by the Office of Technology Assessment, in *Feedstuffs*, March 14, 1994.

2. For further discussion, see Kuhn (1970). Note: a paradigm is a set of fundamental assumptions concerning the nature of reality.

3. Genetic pollution resulting from the transfer of alien genes from genetically modified crops to conventional crops, wild plant relatives, etc.

4. Some of this material is from an audio tape of a presentation I made at a 1995 Acres U.S.A. conference in St. Louis.

5. This begins with "eating with conscience," kitchen anarchists being mindful of what and whom they put on the ends of their forks, and who say "fork you" to the food and drug industries that continue to profit royally from promoting and marketing unhealthy diets and costly, and potentially harmful medicines to "cure" the adverse health consequences of the Western diet.

REFERENCES

Avery, Dennis T. 1993. *Biodiversity: Saving Species with Biotechnology.* Indianapolis: Hudson Institute, 1993.

Barnard, Neal D. et al. 1995. "The Medical Costs Attributable to Meat Consumption." *Preventive Medicine* 24:1–10.

Daly, Herman E., and John B. Cobb, Jr. 1994. *For the Common Good: Redirecting the Economy Toward Community, the Environment, and a Sustainable Future.* 2nd ed. Boston: Beacon Press.

Fox, Michael W. 1996. *Agricide: The Hidden Farm and Food Crisis That Affects Us All.* 2nd ed. Malabar, FL: R. E. Krieger Publishing Company.

———. 2001. *Bringing Life to Ethics: Global Bioethics for a Humane Society.* Albany: State University of New York Press.

———. 2004. *Killer Foods: When Scientists Manipulate Genes, Better Is Not Always Best.* New York: Lyons Press.

Hewitt, T. I., and K. R. Smith. 1995. *Intensive Agriculture and Environmental Quality: Examining the Newest Agricultural Myth.* Greenbelt, MD: Henry A. Wallace Institute for Alternative Agriculture.

Kuhn, Thomas S. 1970. *The Structure of Scientific Revolutions.* Chicago: The University of Chicago Press.

Macer, Daryll R. J. 1994. *Bioethics for the People by the People.* Christchurch, New Zealand: Eubios Ethics Institute.

National Dialogue on Sustainable Agriculture (NDSA). 1994. Alexandria, VA.

Agribusiness

Farming Without Culture

GARY VALEN

Agriculture is an ancient relationship between humans and nature that provides sustenance and livelihood for all the generations we call civilization. The foundations of human organizations from family units to empires are based on the ability to produce food. Through most of history, interrelationships between animals and humans along with soils and climate have formed the cornerstones of agriculture.

The industrialization of food production and the emergence of agribusiness are ending the delicate balance among humans, other animals, and nature in modern farming systems. Machines, technologies, and the use of animals as commodities now produce incredible profits for a few powerful conglomerates. One half of the United States' favorable balance of trade comes from the sale of agricultural products, technology, and services. If we measure success as financial, then farming and farm businesses as well as food processing and distribution are highly profitable enterprises.

The Value of Agriculture is the Export Potential

Farm animals contribute to the remarkable expansion of U.S. agribusiness in the second half of the twentieth century. Pointing to the record $60 billion of farm exports in 1996, U.S. Deputy Agriculture Secretary, Richard Rominger, declared: "In our most recent comparisons among 11 major industries, agriculture ranked number 1 as the leading positive contributor to the U.S. merchandise trade balance" (Rominger 1997). Farm animals traditionally represent half of U.S. farm exports.

Agriculture's role in the U.S. favorable balance of trade has its downside. The record exports of 1996 have not kept pace with the predictions as the USDA reports the 1998 export number at $49 billion. In addition, the U.S. expected to increase its farm exports to $63 billion in 2000 and $84 billion by 2007 (USDA 1999). The basis for this anticipated increase was the expansion of trade to developing countries.

In fact, the United States experienced its first trade deficit since the 1980s in agricultural products in August 2004. Exports in 2004 were $57.7 billion, far below the projected increases predicted in 1996. The export of red meat products was down 30 percent, while the import of poultry was up 40 percent from the previous year. (USDA Trade Update 2004). The long-anticipated economic benefits of agricultural trade surpluses that stimulated the development of animal-confinement systems has not materialized in the past ten years.

Anticipating record windfalls, agribusinesses are pushing a rapid expansion of the food production capacity in the United States, especially in the growth of intensive confinement livestock and poultry systems. When exports fell flat in 1998, hog prices dropped to record lows because there were too many hogs in the market. Poultry and cattle prices were also lower. Many smaller farmers closed their operations, causing several states to declare a farm crisis. The federal government provided some financial relief to farmers, but the payments were seldom enough to compensate for the full losses.

The farm crisis of 1998 underscored a basic flaw in contemporary agricultural policy. Agribusinesses, which specialize in animal confinement systems, are profitable when they sell buildings, equipment, feed, feeder pigs, and even provide financing to the farmers for installation costs. These businesses make money for their investors when they sell systems, no matter how low livestock and poultry prices go. Farmers and investors are lured to factory farm systems because the anticipated lucrative export markets seem to offer rich financial rewards. If exports are limited when other countries want to feed themselves or to ban U.S. food because they do not approve of our production methods, agribusinesses and the U.S. government spring into action to do whatever it takes to reopen the markets.

When food is viewed merely as an export commodity, many decisions are made that influence trade policy, agricultural methods, and the lives of many people. As an example, the World Food Summit in 1996 identified almost 800 million people, many in developing countries, who go hungry every day. Many of these developing countries want help from the developed nations so that they can become more self-sufficient in food production. Self-sufficiency is an evil concept among U.S. agribusinesses and is rejected by U.S. foreign policy.

A spokesperson for Cargill, Inc. articulated the business and government position: "What promotes food security? A combination of maximizing a country's efficient food production potential while developing its other economic capabilities to generate the income that allows it to buy food from the global market" (Thrane 1999).

In other words, countries will have food security when they earn enough income each year to buy U.S. food or they purchase U.S. manufactured industrial farming systems such as intensive-confinement livestock and poultry facilities.

The control of world food markets is a major prize in upcoming trade negotiations and in the race to use technology and industry-like production systems to create so-called cheap food for exports. One result is what is now termed a trade war between the United States and the European Union over Europe's ban on U.S. beef treated with growth-promoting hormones (Schuff 1999). The Europeans believe that hormones are not good for the animals and are not thoroughly tested for food safety concerns. The U.S. claims that sound science has not demonstrated any food safety problems with the use of hormones and declares that the animal well-being issues are irrelevant according to WTO rules.

The trade wars between the U.S. and Europe illustrate two conflicting views of food production. If the Europeans are successful in banning a U.S. product for any reasons other than the absolute scientific proof that food is not safe, other issues such as environmental degradation or farm animal well-being can reduce U.S. agribusinesses' trade advantages. This view was reflected by former U.S. Trade Representative and Secretary of Agriculture, Clayton Yeutter, in a speech to the International Poultry Exposition, where he warned the poultry industry that the Europeans will attempt to make "social issues" a permissible part of trade rules in the future. If the Europeans are successful, he declared, U.S. exports are in jeopardy (Thornton 1999).

Gary Thornton, editor of *Broiler Industry,* warns the poultry industry that a "new world order" with traces of "New Age" leanings may impose the discussion of environmental matters into trade negotiations. He writes: "We need to keep reminding our leaders that the interests of U.S. agricultural producers should not be sacrificed through treaties that favor producers in other economies—not even on the altar of the world environment" (Thornton 1999).

Agribusinesses and their allied organizations push the opening of world markets with few restrictions through the auspices of the WTO. The April 6, 1999, issue of *Inside US Trade* quoted a letter to then-President Bill Clinton from fifty-nine major agricultural corporations and organizations pleading for trade negotiators to provide agribusinesses with access to the 96 percent of the world's consumers who live outside the United States. Clearly, U.S. agriculture is focused on export markets.

Should we celebrate the lucrative export of U.S. products or services? The promotion of agricultural practices and food systems that will provide U.S. agribusinesses trade advantages, especially in developing countries, is a natural activity in a free market society. The agricultural contributions to a favorable balance of trade and the expansion of export markets should be good news for farmers and their rural communities. Problems develop when production techniques, industry-like technology, and corporation control eliminates small-scale farmers, ignores the environment, and treats animals as mere commodities, all because the United States has such a vital stake in dominating global markets.

Broader Vision of Agriculture Production

It is clear that something is wrong with our present vision of agriculture. If we accept corporate profits from exports as the only basis by which to judge the success of our food and fiber production systems, then we lose the opportunity to consider other factors that may be just as important. Here are a few examples.

Do we really want to lose our small-scale and community-based farmers and the rural communities that support them? Are we comfortable losing farming as a valid opportunity for young people? Is it important that farmers have an adequate livelihood? Does the industrialization of agriculture match our values and our principles about food production?

Should the protection of the environment be left out of agricultural management strategies? Is water and air pollution from excess animal waste the price we must pay to maintain the economic advantages of our farm exports? Can we accept the loss of farm lands to urban sprawl knowing that future generations will need the land to produce food and fiber?

Does it matter how animals are treated in intensive-confinement livestock and poultry systems? Should laying hens be condemned to tiny battery cages where they are unable to even spread their wings? Are we comfortable knowing that factory farm sows spend their lives in tiny crates on concrete-or metal-slatted floors where they must eat, sleep, eliminate, give birth and nurse their babies in the same small space?

Should farm workers have the protections enjoyed by workers in other industrial systems?

Do we have good reasons to examine public health and safety concerns associated with factory farm system? Is the ability of our future generations to grow or raise food important to us?

Do we agree that our agricultural science institutions should be primarily concerned with technology that will improve U.S. trade advantages or should we be looking for more ecologically based production methods? Do consumers have a right to ask if their food is safe without the threat of lawsuits?

The answer to these questions and others is that food production must be viewed from a wider perspective than simply the profits that can be earned. Food is more than just the bargaining chip in a series of trade wars; it is an essential ingredient for life. We must look, therefore, at food production through a new lens that establishes a vision based on ethics, not just the bottom line.

Soul of Agriculture — The Process

The Soul of Agriculture: A Production Ethic for the 21st Century is a project that intends to widen our perspectives about the role and impact of agriculture in our society. Created in 1996 by The Center for Respect of Life and Environment (CRLE) and The Humane Society of the United States (The HSUS), the Soul of Agriculture is a vehicle to open an ethics-based dialogue on food and fiber production in the United States.

The Soul of Agriculture was first suggested by Fred Kirschenmann, a North Dakota organic farmer, at a CRLE board meeting in 1996. Kirschenmann based his proposal on *The Spirit of the Soil,* a book written by Paul Thompson about the need for a new production ethic in agriculture. Kirschenmann was struck with Thompson's observations that there is a polarity between farmers and environmentalists about meeting society's production needs while at the same time enhancing the natural world (Kirschenmann 1996).

The dilemma that Kirschenmann highlighted in his proposal for an agricultural ethics project is one of the major questions facing our society, although it is doubtful that few people ever think about it. If we employ farming methods that use industrial techniques without concern for the environment, social issues, people, and animals; our agricultural business sector will be highly profitable and, therefore, successful. As pointed out above, this is what the industry is calling for in our trade negotiations/trade wars.

On the other hand, if we adopt farming methods that insure the ability of future generations to have access to food, protect the environment, treat animals with respect, and establish social justice for farmers and farm workers, we may have to trade immediate financial gains for the long-term goal of a more sustainable and hospitable Earth in the next millennium. This is not an easy choice, as illustrated by U.S. agribusinesses' pleas to U.S. trade negotiators to be tough on all efforts to restrict the trade of agricultural products for any reason.

Agricultural products, services and technologies are the great hopes as the U.S. corporate world increasingly competes with emerging societies in Europe, Africa, South America, and Asia. The scientific development of synthetic agricultural chemicals, intensive livestock and poultry systems, genetically engineered organisms (GMOs), and seed stock that cannot be reproduced will give U.S. agribusinesses a clear comparative advantage in world markets. That means more money in the stock market, more funds for baby boomer retirement funds, more money to endow universities, museums, animal protection organizations, and, in fact, more funds for most of the nonprofit world. Do we give up these revenues for our social and environmental values and principles?

In 1996, Kirschenmann believed that many people would opt for such a change. He pointed to a growing movement that some call an Ecological Revolution (intent on cooperating with the interconnected whole of nature) that will be replace the Copernican Revolution (preoccupied with dominating nature) (Kirschenmann 1996). His proposal to the CRLE board was the bold suggestion that the time was right for the social evolution of a new production ethic.

One of the first problems with Kirschenmann's proposal was the sponsorship of CRLE, an affiliate of The Humane Society of the United States. It is clear that CRLE and The HSUS have specific agendas. As the largest animal protection organization in the United States, The HSUS urges its members and other consumers to eat with conscience by: reducing the number of foods they eat that come from animals; refining their diet by choosing foods that come from animals raised more humanely and fruit and vegetables grown organically, sustainably, and locally; replacing animal-based foods with foods that don't come from animals (*Choosing a Humane Diet* 1998).

CRLE promotes The HSUS animal protection goals and sponsors a number of environmental education programs and projects on its own. The creation of a new agricultural ethics would require participation by many individuals and organizations who do not necessarily agree with The HSUS and CRLE, and yet Kirschenmann's proposal for an agricultural ethics project needed to be funded and administered. A compromise solution was the separation of the funding and administrative work from the drafting process to write a production ethic statement.

A planning group began work in the fall of 1996 to organize the Soul of Agriculture process. Consisting of CRLE and HSUS staff and board members, and a few others who expressed an interest in the organizing work, the planning group created the structure for the Soul of Agriculture process. Roger Blobaum, a former candidate for Congress from Iowa and a longterm agricultural consultant, was hired to monitor and nurture the project.

The planning group determined both the strategy and the desired outcome of the project. The end goal would be an agricultural production ethics statement that would guide farming practices and techniques in the twenty-first century. After much debate the planners agreed that the discussion would focus on production techniques "to the farm gate" with marginal attention given to markets and other agricultural matters. As the members expressed their

individual concerns about contemporary farming methods in relation to social, environmental, and animal issues, it was clear that Soul of Agriculture should be about farming (*Committee Minutes* 1996).

The planning group agreed to a process format that would begin in 1997. A panel of twenty agricultural spokespersons who reflected a broad perspective of agricultural production would meet for three days to write the first draft of a Soul of Agriculture statement. A small committee headed by Kirschenmann nominated the twenty-person Drafting Committee.

The Drafting Committee intensely labored over a three day weekend in March of 1997 to create the base document for the Soul of Agriculture process. Each member of the committee brought a paper to the table that outlined what they hoped would be in the document. The diversity of perspectives established a broad and sometimes contentious series of questions that guided the group in the final statement.

Perhaps the most interesting exercise came when the participants wrote questions they wanted to ask others about agricultural production. Farmers stated what they wanted environmentalists to understand about their work, and environmentalists countered with what they hoped farmers would do to protect the natural world. By the end of the weekend there were a series of questions for farmers, community leaders, environmentalists, faith community members, and sustainable agriculture advocates. Then the entire group established an action agenda for each subgroup that would form the basis for a new set of ethics in agricultural production.

Brad DeVries of the Sustainable Action Coalition collected all of the notes, recordings, flip charts, and conclusions of the Drafting Committee and wrote a draft statement that reflected the weekend deliberations. The document, *Vision Statement/Call to Action: Building a New Ethic of Production in Agriculture* was submitted to the Drafting Committee for individual comment and editing in the summer of

1997. The edited version was then sent to more than two hundred people, who provided further suggestions.

The next step in the process was a national conference held in Minneapolis on November 14–16, 1997, to discuss the draft document and to establish a plan of action for the Soul of Agriculture process. Approximately two hundred people attended the event and heard a series of speakers and panel discussions about various aspect of the document, the U.S. agricultural situation, and the need to view agricultural production through a series of widely accepted ethical guidelines.

One of the key moments in the conference came when the group broke into small discussion groups and seriously examined each section of the draft, *Vision Statement/Call to Action*. The final round of small-group discussions provided recommendations for the future of the Soul of Agriculture project. One of the clearest messages from the conference participants was that the search for agricultural production ethics is an ongoing process that will never reach a final conclusion because farming methods change every year. There was almost unanimous consent that "ethics matter" when it comes to growing and raising food in contemporary agricultural production systems.

The notes, suggestions, and written comments from the national conference were given to Stan Dundon of the Sustainable Agriculture and Research Program at the University of California at Davis for another editing process. Stan used the first draft as a guide and added the inputs from the conference participants to write a new Soul of Agriculture statement entitled: *Creating a New Vision of Farming*. The new document was printed and distributed to the conference participants along with the people who worked on the first draft.

It is interesting to note that few commentators questioned the need for ethics in agriculture. Most clarified statements or suggested clearer text. When most of the comments had been collected and incorporated into the document, a third version of the production ethics statement was published in October 1998.

Soul of Agriculture: Creating a New Vision of Farming

The word agriculture implies relationships among people and the soil, animals, and nature. Agribusiness is an entirely different concept that views the use of soil, animals, and nature as way to make money. These rather simplistic definitions have created the biggest dilemma for most of the participants in the Soul of Agriculture process. It is difficult to build a case for a vision of farming that is not simply a way to make money when so many farmers are going broke and their rural communities are in decline.

One of the first principles that gained universal acceptance by the participants in the Soul of Agriculture process is that farmers must be able to achieve an adequate livelihood in a healthy agricultural system. It is a subtle yet vital distinction. A new vision of agriculture based on ethics does understand that farmers must make money. When advocates call for ethical guidelines for farming methods, they understand that the well-being of farmers is the only way to ensure that the guidelines will be put into practice. On the other side, the need for profits under the agribusiness model is never an excuse to ignore people, animals, and the environment.

Creating a New Vision of Farming acknowledges its origins to Paul Thompson's *Spirit of Soil* on its first page. It offers Thompson's observations that industrial agriculture believes it operates on a set of ethical and religious ideals and traditional values. These are hardwork, practicality, efficiency, and prosperity as evidence of God's favor. The tension between these noble ideals and traditional values, and the evidence that our farm communities are in trouble, the environment is threatened, and animals are being mistreated, leads us to experience a "fractured soul" about contemporary agriculture. The Soul of Agriculture process questions the widely accepted view that industrial farming is based on ethics because it seems that agribusiness removes the cultural characteristics of agriculture.

If we define culture as relationships based on cohesive connections, then industrial farming cannot be called an *agriculture* as stated above. The objective of agribusiness is the accumulation of financial rewards for stockholders and managers. This is why farm corporation spokespersons argue that the "environment" and "social issues" have no relevance in decisions about the trade of farm products. In this model it is not even important that farm workers, including contract farmers, make an adequate livelihood or that their communities are supported. A rural culture is not important in the industrial model for farming.

The Soul of Agriculture identifies values that are required for even the most modest definition of farm production ethics. It is interesting that some of these same values, as among them hard work, practicality, efficiency, and prosperity, are also found in industrial agriculture. The disparity is explained by the wide variety of opinions about why we farm. Are we growing or raising food and fiber to benefit people, or are we simply producing a steady revenue stream from the sale of commodities that are required by all peoples and animals? Industrial agriculture spokespersons argue that the demands of the market place and the fierce competition for global food markets take precedence over other values or concerns such as the "environment" or "social issues."

Another way to look at agriculture is to accept food production as a special and perhaps even sacred aspect of life on this Earth. Guided by a process that uses our basic values to identify ethical guidelines for farming, we could stipulate that production methods must protect the environment, ensure the well-being of farm animals, and enhance human life. We might even agree that we will hold sacred the ability of future generations to have access to good food. At the same time we could stipulate that farm-

ers can adopt ethical standards and still have adequate livelihoods. Specifically, we will compensate farmers for whatever it costs to produce food in ways that meet our ethical standards. The financial promises of producing so-called industrial "cheap food" without concerns for the "environment" or "social issues" would then be irrelevant to farmers because their income would depend, in part, on their adoption of publicly supported ethical standards.

An ethically based agriculture is often ridiculed by commentators who say the majority of consumers demand "cheap food" and would balk at spending more than the national average of 11 percent of their annual incomes for food (Marbery 1999). Many consumers, however, are increasingly shopping at markets that feature foods that they consider healthier and, in many cases, closer to their personal values.

Here are three examples of how ethical considerations can be a part of the agricultural marketplace. (1) There is an increasing demand for organic food by consumers who want to support ecologically based farming methods. (2) The humane treatment of farm animals has led to a growing market for free-range or pasture-raised livestock and poultry. (3) Local food systems such as farmers' markets and community supported agriculture (CSA) projects are springing up all over the country, because consumers want to use their food-buying dollars to benefit their neighbors and communities. A new ethical vision of agriculture can be achieved.

Soul of Agriculture: Establishing Ethics

A new vision of farming based on widely held ethical standards requires a great amount of work on the part of many people. The Soul of Agriculture is a process to identify and clarify ethics based on carefully structured steps designed to solicit inputs from people of all backgrounds and opinions. There are four tasks assigned to anyone who participates in the Soul of Agriculture process.

1. Attain clarity and consensus on the goal-values of farming and on the values involved in the means used in farming.
2. Clearly state and attain consensus on the ethical principles which can protect those values.
3. Depict attractive real and potential examples of model, institution, and practices that put those principles into action and make a better agriculture.
4. Face the painful questions that are obstacles to relevant groups and proposed actions to restore trust and cultivate active learning between groups (Dundon 1998).

FIRST TASK: VALUES

There are several types of values in agriculture. A basic value is what agriculture is all about, the production of sufficient, sustainable and healthy food and fiber. Other basic values refer to the tools of agriculture such as human dignity of labor, farmer well-being, beauty of the environment, and animal well-being. Goal values refer to the products of agriculture while tool values refer to the impact of farming tools or methods.

Goal values connect farming with the maintenance of life and health for people on our Earth. Soul of Agriculture participants defined "sufficient" to mean accessible and affordable to all humans, and to all generations of humans. "Healthy" refers to food that is nutritious and also delightful so that people will want to eat it. It also refers to food that is nontoxic and safe. "Sustainable" food means perpetual continuation of the healthy and sufficient food.

Tool values are identified as the farmers' use of tools, practices, and institutions that are "efficient in the use of resources, sustainable and safe" (Dundon 1998). While tool values may vary according to custom and locality, they are fundamental in creating an agriculture based on ethics. As an example, the term "efficiency" is often used to describe highly technical and synthetic chemically based cropping systems. These systems are not efficient, however, if they create serious environmental problems, or they elimi-

nate the use of crop ground by future generations of farmers. Most people acknowledge the basic values for agriculture to produce food and fiber; the debates center on the tools, methods and institutions.

The Soul of Agriculture participants have a lot to say about the tools of agriculture. Most people are concerned about the role of the principal farming tool—the labor of farmers and farm workers. While all humans have a basic need to achieve a livelihood, there are other needs that are essential to the well-being of farmers or farm workers. People engaged in agriculture have their own values that will come first no matter how much they are tied to a community or business association.

Farmers and farm workers need an adequate family income, income security, health, and bearable levels of stress. Other needs are more local or individual, such as a relationship with a specific religious belief or the identification with a specific community or nationality. If these values are not met, farmers or farm workers refuse to work and find a more meaningful life in another situation.

Another set of values concern farmers' knowledge and caring that allow them to achieve excellence in their work. As an example, a farmer's long-term knowledge about the specific soils and weather conditions on a farm is essential not only to excellent crop production but also the wise use of the land. Farmers' caring saves wetlands or wildlife habitat that is beneficial in the control of unwanted insects or enhances the beauty of the community.

Farmers' knowledge and caring about their communities may be essential to securing a market for their products and maintaining a healthy place to live for their families. Other values such as long-term and secure lives in places of safety, beauty, and productive environments are all secured through a farmer's knowledge and caring. The traditional family farm is usually envisioned as a place where the long-term caring and understanding have created a home place for a successful and healthy agricultural enterprise.

A major place where tool values have an impact is the well-being of animals and other living species. Animals once were farmers' partners in agricultural production, but today many farmers raise animals for food. Farmers know that knowledge and caring are the best ways to work with animals. In the last sixty years machines have mostly replaced animals as the essential source of power in agricultural production. At the same time farm animals are raised increasingly in massive intensive-confinement systems where appropriate care is limited to crowded shelter and unnatural food. Farmers have no opportunity to exhibit their long-term knowledge and care in these industry-like systems that are operated under agribusiness rules and often by nonfarmer laborers.

Other living creatures also are a part of an agricultural value system. Insects, plants, and even species that live in the soil are all crucial to farming. Whether a farmer grows crops or raises animals, the remarkable diversity of a healthy ecological system is crucial for long-term success. It is a value for all of us to protect the ongoing vitality of nature in our agricultural landscape. It is useful in our farming practices. "But it is above all beautiful and it calls for a response of caring from the human heart" (Dundon 1998).

The values we cherish in our relations with animals and other living creatures are seriously degraded by industrial agricultural systems. This should not be a permanent situation. If we reevaluate our beliefs in terms of an expanded recognition of our values, we will recognize that the production of food can be done in harmony with what we hold both useful and sacred.

A third value identified by the Soul of Agriculture process is the farmer to farmer relationships. Friendships are sacred values that are both useful and good in their own right. Love thy neighbor is a cherished belief in many religions. The collaborators recognize the importance of improving the cohesiveness among farmers if we are to achieve a new vision of farming.

Farmer-to-farmer relationships are another victim of industrial agriculture. Factory farms are often operated from corporate headquarters where the managers do not know their neighbors. Many intensive confinement operators antagonize their neighbors with the intense odors of confined animals and the inevitable environmental damage of too much manure polluting waterways. The value of farmer to farmer cooperation and friendship is made less important by machines and technical systems on a factory farm.

The final value identified so far by Soul of Agriculture collaborators is the relationships between food producers and their customers. Participants identified the "human pleasure in being appreciated for a good product, the outcome of one's intelligence, labor and caring." It is also a useful value in that consumers can be more confident about the quality of their food and the protection of their environment if they have a personal and good relationship with their farmer neighbors. This is even true in a city where farmers become acquainted with their customers through CSAs or farmers' markets.

Our values form the basic building blocks to construct a new vision of farming. The next step is to use our values to establish principles that lead to ethics.

SECOND TASK: PRINCIPLES

We establish ethics by using our values to create principles that guide our visions and plans. It is natural for advocates of sustainable farming, environmentalists, and academics to articulate principles that spring from our reasoned dialogues and intellectual pursuits. Farmers have principles that must be translated to profitable enterprises in their pastures, crop fields, and orchards. The task for the Soul of Agriculture process is to envision new farming practices that work while meeting our values for people, animals, and the Earth.

Many collaborators comment that institutions and technologies of industrial agriculture have a crushing impact on farm families, rural communities, and the natural world. These structures often evolve as a way to ease labor or provide more profit for an individual farmer or company rather than meet a widely accepted standard for farm practices. In these cases the values are saving labor and making money. The principles that guide these practices seem like good ideas, but they are short-sighted when the total picture is in focus.

A new vision of farming based on conscious principles will require new institutions and technologies. These new structures will be consciously based on social and environmental as well as economic principles, the very concepts that agribusiness spokespersons warn us about. It is certainly possible that agricultural corporations can be a part of the new vision if they are willing to build new structures and methods based on broad ethical principles.

The Soul of Agriculture process consistently identifies local decision making as the best way to achieve a new vision of farming. In spite of the best efforts of corporations to ignore local differences with the same fast food outlets, shopping malls, and entertainments, we all live in unique places. Carefully structured farming decisions will vary in all parts of the country.

Our vision of new farming assumes local inputs based on the ethical principles we all agree are good for people, animals and the Earth.

Creating a New Vision of Farming outlines the thinking of the Soul of Agriculture collaborators to date. While it is not possible to list them all in this paper, here are some examples of principles that illustrate how ethics should guide agriculture.

What are the principles that secure the ends of agriculture? Dedicating critical land, water, and other resources to farming is fitting in nature unless there are special ethical reasons not to farm at that location. Fertile places for agriculture should be permanent, as human needs will always have need for them. The conditions for farmers and farm workers must be rewarding and healthy. Economic conditions of farming must encourage the preservation of agricultural resources. Soils and the safety of crops must be protected.

What principles guide the means of agriculture? Farmers and farm workers should reap the rewards of their work according to their time, efforts, and responsibility; and in consideration of the needs of a decent human living. Continuity of time and place for farmers must be preserved and encouraged to secure the knowledge and caring needed for good farming. Whenever possible, local farm ownership and local owner management is a good moral policy. Social needs of farmers such as community, church, and schools must be preserved and protected. Farmers and their communities must be able to act ethically without retribution. "Futile individual heroism is not a moral principle" (Dundon 1998).

"Animals and other living systems are sacred gifts of Creation, given for our use, not abuse. They are worthy in themselves of being treated with respect." This sentiment is endorsed by most of the collaborators in the Soul of Agriculture process, including farmers who raise animals for food. Other statements include:

Any form of animal agriculture about whose animals we must say: 'They would, from their birth on, have been better off dead' is morally shameful.

It is morally unacceptable to cause serious suffering to animals for trivial reasons. Freedom from inhumane pain and pathological stress should be sought for animals.

Serious and long term suppression of animals' freedom to express natural functions and movements is not justified by non-essential economic advantage.

(Dundon 1998)

Soul of Agriculture participants acknowledge that farms are living systems in themselves that are also crucial to the local community. One principle boldly asserts that the public should share the cost of farmers' efforts to preserve nature's balance, variety, and elements of wildness. Farmers have a moral obligation to share knowledge about production methods that are least harmful to nature. Solar, bio-intensive, and other regenerative technologies enjoy an ethical superiority due to their gentleness on the environment and their sustainability.

Principles applied to farmer to farmer relationships call for friendship rather than competition. Collaboration in shared information, experience, and labor should be cultivated. Farmers have a moral obligation to build communities of support for benign production alternatives such as organic, biological, ecological, and regenerative systems. Collaborative efforts by farmers to return the power of ethical decision making to farmers must be cultivated.

Farmer-Community relations should be promoted by making decisions from the community rather than outside corporations. Collaborations within a community about environmental protection are more acceptable than coercive and distant mandates. Community policy should be adopted based on the needs of the urban center and the farms that surround it. Agricultural production should benefit the community first with benefits, economic gain, and employment possibilities.

Two key principles address the tensions that often exist between environmentalists and farmers. The first stipulates that a moral obligation exists to reduce harmful side effects of farming on the community. On the other hand, environmental policy makers must recognize that poverty and economic hardships to farmers are often the cause of environmental damage. Economic justice for farmers is a way to protect the environment.

The farmer-consumer relationships are receiving considerable attention from the Soul of Agriculture process because this appears to be an area of great weakness in the contemporary agricultural structure. The principles identified by the collaborators include the use of forms of marketing and purchasing to restore a friendship-like relationship between farmers and consumers. Institutions and practices that enhance consumer awareness of the nature and needs of farming and farmer awareness of consumer needs should be encouraged.

> Free market forces as a means to produce and market food must be frequently guided and limited by the moral demands of justice and basic human needs as well as other values of the means and ends of farming. The free market must be kept as an instrument of human good. It is morally appropriate to guide free market forces by the communally determined needs of local consumers and local farmers.
>
> (Dundon 1998)

The identification of principles based on values is an ongoing process for the Soul of Agriculture. Individuals and organizations are encouraged to contribute and to write their own principles. The next task is the identification of models that embrace the values and principles that become ethics of agricultural production.

THIRD TASK: MODELS

A new vision of farming based on widely held ethics must work for farmers and consumers. As a principle, the collaborators agreed that new institutions will be needed to form a new agriculture. As one person stated, "If we try to simply fix the present system, it is like putting new wine in old skins. What is needed is new wine in new skins." Participants in the Soul of Agriculture process are asked to list the characteristics of a new agriculture based on the ethics identified by the first two tasks. Some of these lists are presented here for examples and potential models. The third task is the creative step that allows all of us to explore a new vision of agriculture based on our values and principles.

What will farms look like in our new vision of agriculture? The general response to this question can be organized into five general topics. The first is that the hallmark of the "new" farm will be diversity in crop selection, enterprises, cultures, and markets. The farms will use long-range planning to integrate a variety of products that complement each other in closed nutrient cycles and increasing independence from off-farm sources of energy and nutrients. The farmers will increasingly use alternative energy sources such as solar in the place of diesel fuel and chemical inputs.

Second, animals on the new farm will be seen as helpers. Farm animals' nutritional needs, natural activities, and manure will be an integral part of a farming operation. Waste products will become assets in other parts of the farm operation. Managed grazing will replace fossil-fuel-consuming grain-feeding programs. The new farm will allow animals to live natural lives, not just because the care of animals is a good business decision, but because it the right and respectful way to treat another living creature.

The third characteristic of the new farm is a new generation of farmers who know and care. The participants strongly recommend that farms be controlled largely by owner operators or farmers who live on the land they manage. If farming is to become more diversified, then each aspect of the operation must be carefully monitored and managed by the person with the knowledge, ability, and care to do excellent work. These farmers will succeed because they cooperate with nature rather than spend a lot of time and money trying to overcome it.

Fourth, farms will be places of beauty. A surprising conclusion of the Soul of Agriculture colleagues is the call for farms that are places of beauty that fit into the local landscape. "They will reflect the pride, hard work, and consciousness of nature of their owners, because they will be both homes and the public face of a family to the local community" (Dundon 1998). Every farm will have a place for nature as homes for wild plants and animals and for farm families to enjoy. The economic returns from farming must allow the preservation of places for nature.

Finally, the new farms will increasingly use ecological and biological farming methods. These methods will serve an increasingly supportive consumer market because they reflect good farming practices. This will be especially true when farmers and consumers establish face-to-face relationships in the market and in the community.

What will markets and communities look like in the new vision of farming? Two basic themes have emerged so far from the process. Markets will reflect the diversity and variety of farms that are liberated from the massive production of mono crops for agribusiness exports or factory farm systems. Farmers and consumers will increasingly share a common bond in food-related political, social, and economic issues. The process has listed eight general categories as models for markets and communities in the new ethically based agriculture.

The first category is the consumer-sensitive niche market. The new farms will produce goods that meet consumer expectations and demands based on the diversity of people and place. The price of food will be based on what the consumer can spend and what the producer needs, including the costs of caring for the environment, animals, and people's health.

Direct marketing is a second category of concern for our Soul of Agriculture colleagues. Direct marketing is beneficial to the new farm for several reasons. Producers and consumers will set the price based on mutually agreed upon goals such as quality, farmer livelihood, environmental and animal well-being concerns, and consumer income. The CSA movement is the present model for direct marketing that meets the needs and the ethics of farmers and consumers.

A third characteristic is the increasing growth of community focused farming. Production, processing, and control will be more local because consumers will want food from places they can visit or know about. Food choices will reflect regional preferences and growing conditions. Consumers will support their own communities by keeping their food buying dollars at home.

The fourth vision is community-owned farms. The models for this exist in some cohousing projects and community cooperatives. It is good public policy to make land available for food production in place of urban sprawl as a way to ensure food security for future residents.

The fifth category, called "local delights," deserves a direct quotation:

> Markets, restaurants and retail establishments will reflect the renaissance in local food as a pleasurable, central part of daily life. There will be a blossoming of "slow food" restaurants where food is not simply a way to fuel up the body at a drive-in window, but instead nourishes people, families, and neighborhoods. Such restaurants will become vital centers of neighborhoods and communities featuring the prize food produced by farmers known as friends and neighbors. Markets will do the same and respond to the health concerns of consumers.
>
> (Dundon 1998)

Sixth, farming will become more collaborative. Farmers will work together to share costs, labor, and expertise. While there will be some competitiveness in a free market economy, farmers will join to form community processing facilities, brokerage operations, and distribution systems. Community farmers will also make certain that young people have the ability to enter the noble profession of agriculture.

The seventh recommendation from the Soul of Agriculture process is a network of communities as a support for the new farms. Community networks can trade products that are unique to a special area and form associations for an export marketing approach that benefits both the home producer and the international buyer. Environmental, animal, and health concerns can be shared by a web of linked communities. Food security is enhanced when one region of the country helps others during times of disaster.

Finally, the Soul of Agriculture participants call for vigorous educational components in a new vision of farming. Schools' curriculums will include specific information about where their food comes from, how farming is done and what consumers should know about food systems. Consumers will have the opportunity to visit farms, not as tourists, but as vital links in an agricultural system that is the pride of our communities and nation.

FOURTH TASK: HARD QUESTIONS
AND ACTIONS

The Soul of Agriculture process engages people with diverse backgrounds and perspectives. Just like nature, this diversity brings strength to the whole. Our efforts to write an agricultural production ethics statement obviously have not brought unanimous agreements on everything; this is why it must be an ongoing process.

The identification of values, principles, and models provides common ground for interested people to begin the dialogue. As an example mentioned above, environmental organizations are now taking a close look at farming practices, and especially alternatives to any systems that may lead to the degradation of water, land, and air. At the same time the environmentalists acknowledge that farmers need to achieve a livelihood and want to help farmers adopt ecologically sensitive practices. Many farmers acknowledge their responsibilities to the environment as stewards of the land and seek production methods that are in harmony with nature. The key element is that farmers and environmentalists are communicating with each other and asking vital questions.

The Soul of Agriculture project urges everyone to engage in the search for an ethical basis for agriculture. Some of this dialogue will happen by design at future conferences and collaborations. Most of the discussion and the examination of our own values about agricultural production and the food we eat should happen in our daily lives. As stated above, the choices we make with our food purchasers, our investments, our community developments, and many other aspects of our lives directly impact the type of agriculture we have now and will have in the future.

Adopting an ethical vision of food production is shared by some of the nation's leading agricultural leaders. Richard Rominger, Former USDA Deputy Secretary, urged participants of the National Town Meeting for a Sustainable America to support sustainable agriculture. He wrote:

> You may not live on a farm. But we share this planet. You have the power to put your knowledge to work to protect it through the choices you make. The choices that you the consumer make to purchase sustainable agricultural products are a conscious one. This choice shows a commitment to and an investment in the environment, the community, and the future.
>
> (Rominger 1999)

As vital components of our national economy, agribusinesses should also be expected to adopt broader ethics in agricultural production. As stated above, the export of food, farm technology, and agricultural services is a large factor in our trade policies. Unfortunately, the benefits of this export agriculture and the industrial methods engineered to drive it are destroying a way of life. In his important study of the consolidation of food and agricultural systems, Dr. William Heffernan of the Department of Rural Sociology at the University of Missouri, details the most profound shift imaginable in the countryside. He writes: "Today, most rural economic development specialists discount agriculture as a contributor to rural development" (Heffernan 1999). Heffernan concludes with this statement:

> The centralized food system that continues to emerge was never voted on by the people of this country, or for that matter, the people of the world. It is the product of deliberate decisions made by a very few powerful human actors. This is not the only system that could emerge. Is it not time to ask some critical questions about our food system and about what is in the best interest of this and future generations?
>
> (Heffernan 1999)

The Soul of Agriculture process urges all people to ask the essential questions about agriculture and food systems after careful examinations of their personal values and principles. It is time to adopt ethical standards for the structures and institutions that provide us food, clearly a vital element of our lives. It is time for all of us to restore culture to the practices of agriculture.

REFERENCES

Agriculture Outlook Forum. 1999. U.S. Department of Agriculture.

Choosing a Humane Diet: How to Get Started. 1998. The Humane Society of the United States

Dundon, Stan. 1998. *Creating a New Vision of Farming.* Washington, D.C.: The Humane Society of the United States, pp. 3–12.

Heffernan, William. 1999. *Consolidation in the Food and Agriculture System.* National Farmers Union, p. 13.

Kirschenman, Fred. 1996. "Toward a New Food and Farming Ethic: From a Copernican to an Ecological Agriculture." Unpublished paper delivered to the Center for Respect of Life and Environment Board of Directors, November 7, 1996.

Marbury, Steve. 1999. "Pork Sector Struggles with Structural Changes." *Feedstuffs* 4:12.

Rominger, Richard. 1997. Unpublished speech presented to the February 28, 1997 National Center for Food and Agricultural Policy meeting in Washington, D.C.

———. 1999. Unpublished letter to participants of the April 1999 National Town Meeting in Detroit.

Schuff, Sally. 1999. "Beef Battle with Europe Moves Closer to War." *Feedstuffs* 4:21.

Thrane, Linda. 1999. The Cargill Bulletin Editorial. *Feedstuffs* 3:2.

Thornton, Gary. 1999a. "Poultry's Place in a 'New World Order." *Broiler Industry* 2:13.

———. 1999b. "One if by Treaty, Two if by Codex." *Broiler Industry* 4:5.

U.S. Agriculture Trade Update. October 15, 2004. Washington, D.C.: U.S. Department of Agriculture.

XI

CONTEMPORARY CHALLENGES: LAW, SOCIAL JUSTICE, AND THE ENVIRONMENT

ANIMALS AND THE LAW

Animal Law and Animal Sacrifice

Analysis of the U.S. Supreme Court Ruling on
Santería Animal Sacrifice in Hialeah

STEVEN WISE

Editors' Note: "Animal Law" has recently emerged as a subject taught in dozens of American law schools, including Harvard Law School. It was taught at Harvard first by Steven M. Wise in 2000 and then in 2002 and in 2006 by Paul Waldau. Such courses now are beginning to appear in some European law programs as well. In some legal systems, the killing of food animals using traditional methods of slaughter is explicitly protected, as in the United States, which officially recognizes Jewish and other forms of traditional religious slaughter through 1958 legislation known as the "Humane Slaughter Act." In other legal systems, however, religious slaughter based on traditional methods is outlawed (for example, in 2002 Holland became the sixth country in Europe to ban kosher slaughter). What follows is a brief description of a well-known case that is often cited to support the claim that the practice of ritual animal sacrifice, as opposed to killing for food purposes, is a protected form of religious expression in the United States.

In 1993, the United States Supreme Court voided ordinances enacted by the City Council for Hialeah, Florida, because they violated the Free Exercise Clause of the First Amendment to the United States Constitution (*Church of the Lukumi Babalu Aye, Inc. v. Hialeah,* 508 U.S. 520 [1993]). A series of actions by the Hialeah City Council had impinged the ability of followers of the Santería religion to engage in the ritual sacrifice of nonhuman animals (Id., at 526–28). As a result, the Santeríans remained free to engage in this practice.

Many erroneously believe the Court ruled that the ritual sacrifice of nonhuman animals was protected by the First Amendment, but the Court did not so rule. It voided the ordinances on the grounds that the Santeríans had been invidiously singled out solely for their religious practices. Here it followed the rule of Employment Division, Department of Human Resources of *Oregon v. Smith,* 494 U.S. 872 (1990). Justice Blackmun, concurring, thought Smith had been wrongly decided precisely "because it ignored the value of religious freedom and treated the Free Exercise Clause as no more than an antidiscrimination principle (*Church of the Lukumi Babalu Aye, Inc.*, supra at 578 [Blackmun, J., concurring]).

Here is the background. The City Council first passed a resolution noting the "concern" many residents expressed "that certain religions may propose to engage in practices which are inconsistent with public morals, peace, or safety." This resolution reiterated a commitment to prohibit "any and all acts of any and all religious groups which are inconsistent with public morals, peace or safety." The City next, by ordinance, incorporated the Florida anti-cruelty law, which prohibited the unnecessary killing of any animal, and obtained an opinion from the Florida Attorney General that the ritual sacrifice of animals for purposes other than food was not a necessary killing, as it was done without any useful motive and would violate the anti-cruelty law.

The City Council then declared its policy to oppose the ritual sacrifices of animals within Hialeah and announced that anyone who did so would be prosecuted. The Council followed up with three ordinances. The first defined "sacrifice" as "to unnecessarily kill, torment, torture, or mutilate an animal in a public or private ritual or ceremony not for the primary purpose of food consumption." Everyone who "kills, slaughters, or sacrifices animals for any type of ritual, regardless of whether or not the flesh of blood of the animal is to be consumed" was prohibited from owning or possessing a nonhuman animal for that purpose. An exemption was carved out for slaughtering performed by licensed establishments of nonhuman animals raised for food.

The second ordinance made it unlawful "to sacrifice any animal" within Hialeah. The third defined "slaughter" as "the killing of animals for food," and prohibited it outside of areas zoned for slaughterhouse use. It contained an exemption for the slaughter and processing for sale of "small numbers of hogs and/or cattle per week in accordance with an exemption provided by state law."

The ordinances were enacted in a highly charged anti-Santería environment. One City Councilman recalled that Santeríans had been jailed in Cuba for practicing their religion. Another claimed that the religion violated everything the United States stood for. A third expressed hostility to the sacrifice of nonhuman animals, distinguishing kosher slaughter because it had a real purpose. The chaplain of the Hialeah police department testified that Santería was a sin, foolishness, an abomination to the Lord, and the worship of demons. The Santeríans needed, he said, to be sharing the truth of Jesus Christ. Both the city attorney and assistant city attorney said that one of the resolutions indicated that Hialeah would not tolerate religious practices abhorrent to its citizens (Id., at 541–42). After the Santeríans filed suit, Hialeah claimed that the animal sacrifices presented a substantial health risk to the participants and the public, that it emotionally injured children who witnessed it, that it allowed for the killing of nonhuman animals cruelly and unnecessarily, and that such actions should be limited to areas zoned as slaughterhouses (Id., at 529–530).

The Court said that laws targeting religious beliefs are never permissible (Id., at 33). If the object of a law is to infringe upon religiously motivated practices, it will be struck down unless it can be justified by a compelling state interest and is narrowly tailored to advance just that interest (Id.). The Court found that "[t]he record in this case compels the conclusion that suppression of the central element of the Santería worship service was the exclusive object of the ordinances" (Id., at 534, 536).

The Free Exercise Clause, the Court said, "protect[s] religious observers against unequal treatment" (Id., at 542, quoting *Hobbie v. Unemployment Appeals Commission of Florida*, 380 U.S. 136, 148 [Stevens, J., concurring]). Such inequality "results when a legislature decides that the governmental interests it seeks to advance are worthy of being pursued only against conduct with a religious motivation" (Id., at 542–

43). Thus the government may not "in a selective manner impose burdens only on conduct motivated by religious belief (Id., at 543). The ordinances used the words "sacrifice" and "ritual." One resolution said that Hialeah residents had expressed concern that certain religions proposed to engage in practices that are inconsistent with public morals, peace, or safety. The city was committed to prohibiting "any and all (such) acts of any and all religious groups" (Id., at 534–35). Yet, the only conduct prohibited, however, was Santería animal sacrifice (Id., at 535).

That the ordinances prohibited virtually no other killings of nonhuman animals, even those that were arguably less necessary and less humane than was Santería animal sacrifice was damning (Id, at 536). They actually failed either to protect the public health or prevent cruelty to animals because they failed to prohibit nonreligious conduct that infringed those interests to a similar or greater degree than Santería animal sacrifice (Id.). One might still hunt and fish for sport in Hialeah, slaughter nonhuman animals for food, kill pests, euthanize stray companion animals, and inflict pain and suffering upon nonhuman animals being used in biomedical research (Id. at 536, 537, 543–44, 546). The state interest alleged could have been furthered by restrictions less onerous than a prohibition of animal sacrifice, for instance by regulating the treatment of nonhuman animals and the conditions in which they are kept across the board, regardless of why the animal was being kept (Id., at 539). Similarly, if Hialeah was genuinely interested in protecting public health from the threat of the improper disposal of carcasses and the consumption of uninspected meat, why did it still permit hunters and fishermen to bring the nonhuman animals they kill home, eat them, and dispose of their remains as they saw fit (Id., at 544, 545)?

The Court concluded that legislators "may not devise mechanisms, overt or disguised, designed to persecute or oppress a religion or its practices. The laws here in question were enacted contrary to those constitutional principles, and they are void" (Id. at 547). These principles explain why some religious practices might be, and have been, constitutionally suppressed. Polygamy might be prohibited because a law making it illegal would truly be neutral and of general applicability. (*Mormon Church v. United States,* 136 U.S. 1 [1990]). Had polygamy been as common as monogamy, a legislature could not have suppressed just Mormon polygamy. Similarly, a religion that insists upon human sacrifice could legitimately find its practices suppressed and be unable to complain that the prohibition was neither neutral nor general.

In his concurrence, Justice Blackman noted that laws such as those enacted by the City of Hialeah, which directly burdened religious practice as such, were rare (*Church of the Lukumi Babalu Aye, Inc.,* supra at 577–578, 580 [Blackmun, J., concurring]). The Hialeah case, he thought, "is an easy one to decide" (Id. at 580). "A harder case would be presented if petitioners were requesting an exemption from a generally applicable anti-cruelty law (Id.). In such a case, given the pervasiveness and of the law that protects nonhuman animals from cruelty, this request would probably be denied.

ANIMALS AND SOCIAL JUSTICE

"A very rare and difficult thing"

Ecofeminism, Attention to Animal Suffering

and the Disappearance of the Subject

CAROL ADAMS

"The capacity to give one's attention to a sufferer is a very rare and difficult thing; it is almost a miracle; it *is* a miracle."

— Simone Weil

This essay is an ecofeminist exploration of two out-of-place cows and what they teach us about several interrelated issues regarding the religious imagination and human relations with nonhumans. The first cow was fashioned by filmmaker David Lynch for the "Cow Parade," a collection of artily painted sculptured bovines scattered throughout New York City in 2000. Lynch's painted cow had "Eat My Fear" written across its hacked, decapitated, and disemboweled body. This cow appeared in the cow parade for two and a half hours, but caused children to cry and subsequently was kept under wraps in a warehouse. The other cow, an actual cow, jumped a six-foot fence in Cincinnati in the winter of 2002 to escape a meatpacking plant and then, until she was captured, ran free in a city park for ten days. The day after Easter, she appeared in a parade that celebrated the start of the baseball season. Now called, "Cinci Freedom," she received a key to the city as part of the city's festivities. She was then transported to an animal sanctuary to live out her natural life

unmolested by meat packers, while many of the humans who celebrated her freedom headed to the ballpark to watch baseball and chomp down on some hot dogs. Ecofeminist insights offer assistance in unraveling the paradoxes concerning nonhuman suffering inherent in these stories.

Through the lens of ecofeminism, a celebrated escapee from the clutches of meatpackers, a banished reminder of what meat eating is, and quotidian hot dogs teach us about structures that enable suffering. If humans want to talk about human-nonhuman relationships, they must bring attention to the 95 percent of the nonhumans whose suffering is caused by humans — *terminal animals,* that is, the nonhumans used in the food industry to produce milk, eggs, and flesh (the cows that Cinci Freedom left behind at the meat packers for instance). Every day good people participate in activities that cause the suffering of these terminal animals. Why do they seem to care so little about this suffering? They care so little because of the cultivated disappearance of the subject.

Not only does the *subject of suffering* disappear, especially when the issue is reframed as being about "existence" rather than suffering, but also the subject who is suffering disappears, like the "Eat My Fear" cow locked in a warehouse. The suffering remains invisible. Further, the subject (the individual human who eats nonhumans) who is *causing* the suffering disappears, the agential role of requiring the existence of terminal animals is hard to pinpoint during the enjoyable pastime of watching a ball game and eating a hot dog or hamburger. Finally, the issue of suffering disappears because, religiously speaking, knowledge of suffering requires attention; the process of following attention can lead to grief, and how we experience grief is messy—bodily—and humans have been socialized to fear the body.

Following Weil's thought, the religious imagination, I would submit, is the capacity to recognize the possibility of relationships and bring attention to suffering: "Not only does the love of God have attention for its substance; the love of our neighbour, which we know to be the same love, is made of this same substance" (Weil 1971:75). Cinci Freedom, safe at an animal sanctuary in upstate New York, became a "neighbor." Ecofeminist theory helps us identify why it is that nonhumans have not usually been included in our conception of "neighbors." Ecofeminism, while bringing awareness of our culture's failure in certain areas of relationships, reminds us how much humans are truly in community with all living beings. It therefore aids in understanding humans' relationship to the disappearance of the subject of nonhuman suffering.

Ecofeminist Frameworks

Ecofeminism posits that the domination of the rest of nature is linked to the domination of women and that both dominations must be eradicated. To the issues of sexism, racism, classism, and heterosexism that concern feminists, ecofeminists add naturism—the oppression of the rest of nature. Many ecofeminist writers have demonstrated how the exploitation of nonhuman animals is an aspect of naturism, incorporating specific attention to the status of the other animals into a larger critique of the maltreatment of the natural world.[1]

Ecofeminist philosopher Karen Warren (1987, 1990) identifies three significant features of an oppressive or patriarchal conceptual framework: dualistic thinking, value-hierarchical thinking, and "the glue that holds it all together" (personal communication)—a logic of domination. "Up-down" or *"value-hierarchical thinking"* places higher value, status, or prestige on what is up rather than what is down. Elisabeth Schüssler-Fiorenza calls this "kyriarchal" (i.e., rule of the master or lord) in which elite propertied men have power over those subordinate and dependent on them. In such hierarchies, men are "up," women are "down"; culture is "up," nature is "down." Species is theorized hierarchically, so that humans are "up," the other animals are "down"; hot dog eaters, for instance, are "up" and cows are "down." Humans are not only seen as above the other animals, but also as opposed to them in terms of interests and abilities. This is an aspect of *dualistic thinking.* Warren continues, "Patriarchal value-hierarchical thinking supports the sort of 'either-or' thinking which generates *normative dualisms,* i.e., thinking in which the disjunctive terms (or sides of the dualism) are seen as exclusive (rather than inclusive) and oppositional (rather than complementary), and where higher value or superiority is attributed to one disjunct (or, side of the dualism) than the other" (Warren 1987:6).

Dualisms reduce diversity to two categories: A or Not A. They convey the impression that everything can then be appropriately categorized: *either it is A or Not A.* Ecofeminist philosopher Val Plumwood calls dualism "the logic of colonisation" (Plumwood 1993:41). Plumwood (1993:43) identifies the key elements in the dualistic structure of Western thought as:

culture / nature
reason / nature
male / female
mind / body (nature)
master / slave
reason / matter (physicality)
rationality / animality (nature)
reason / emotion (nature)
mind/spirit / nature
freedom / nature
universal / particular
human / nature (nonhuman)
civilised / primitive (nature)
production / reproduction (nature)
public / private
subject / object
self / other

Through dualistic thinking, humans are conceptualized both as "not animals" and as "better than animals." In a similar manner, dualisms give higher value or status to that which has historically been identified as "mind," "reason," and "male" than to that which has historically been identified as "body," "emotion," and "female" (Warren 1987:20). As Plumwood points out, the mind or "reason" is constructed to exclude nature, so nature (and nonhuman animals) is constructed as mindless (Plumwood 1993:107). Such radical exclusiveness positions nature as oppositional and alien to humans. The result is that differences are "naturalized," so much so that construction of humans' notion of themselves is based on "hyperseparation." We look at nature and nonhuman animals and there is no neighbor there.

Historically, men positioned themselves as being morally superior to women and a male-identified humanity similarly positioned itself as being morally superior to animals (with whom women are often equated). Together value hierarchical thinking and dualistic structures are entangled within a logic of domination "which explains, justifies, and maintains the subordination of an 'inferior' group by a 'superior' group

on the grounds of the (alleged) inferiority or superiority of the respective group" (Warren 1987:6). So superiority justifies subordination.

Justification for the consumption of animals intertwines dualistic thinking, value-hierarchical thinking, and the logic of domination: Human beings are different from animals. Human beings are superior to animals. By virtue of that difference and concomitant superiority, humans have the right to eat animals. But to reduce any guilt, or other potent feelings (see Luke 1992, 1995), that might exist about eating animals, humans are also told the lie that because humans are a kind and caring species, the animals live comfortable lives until they are humanely slaughtered. We need not be attentive to suffering because no suffering exists, or so those on the "up" side propose.[2]

Transcending the Animal

Because of dualistic thinking, descriptions of human beings exclude the animal or animal-like. Humans are intelligent, nonhumans are instinctive; humans love, nonhumans mate; humans cultivate friendships, nonhumans have "affiliative behavior;" humans are humane, refined, nonhumans are beasts, brutal.[3] Like the "animal"—cut off from any association with the "human"—the animal-like, especially the body, is disowned.

As feminist philosophers have pointed out, the Western definition of the man of reason was that he could overcome body, history, social situations, and thereby gain knowledge of others he examined as objects. "Western philosophers have for the most part assigned a lower ontological status to the body than to whatever must hold this body, with its propensity of moral and epistemological error, in check: *nous;* spirit; soul; rational intuition" (Bartky 1989:78). Disembodied rationality proclaims that the body is an "organ of the deceptive senses" (Bordo 1987:450). The idea of the "man of reason" draws upon "men's gender-specific criteria" (Harding 1986:48) and more highly values activities identified as male or "masculine." Reason is defined as the antithesis of what is thought to be female. "[T]he feminine has been associated with what rational knowledge transcends, dominates or simply leaves behind" (Lloyd 1984:2)—emotions, feelings, and body.

Consequently, emotions have been denigrated as untrustworthy and unreliable, as invalid sources of knowledge. Feminist philosopher Elizabeth Spelman refers to this as *somatophobia*: hostility to the body. The legacy of the soul/body distinction, Spelman believes, is that it is used to denigrate women, children, animals, and "the natural" who are guilty by association with one another and with the body (Spelman 1982:120, 127). The body, identified with animals, is what must be transcended. A rational, objective knowing person is one who esteems autonomy over relationship, hyperseparation over attention.

The rational/feeling dualism follows the fault line of a culture in which white, upper-class men have shaped the philosophical and religious discussions for centuries, a fault line that adheres to gender, class, race, and species assumptions. According to feminist and ecofeminist insights, modern epistemology and its suspicion of emotions, its dualistic ontologies, its rationalist bias, its concern for achieving objectivity, and its avoidance of sympathy as a basis for ethical treatment—these all may represent not some universal response, but a very specific one: the response to the experience of being an elite human male.

Constituting the Subject

The most efficient way to ensure that humans are not reminded of animals' suffering and our role in it is to transform nonhuman subjects into nonhuman objects. Some*one* becomes some*thing,* a *who* becomes a *that,* ultimately, the living are made (as) dead, and the process of reification triumphs. Who is suffering? No one.

What we think of as a one-directional process, the disappearance of the nonhuman subject, is in fact bi-directional—related to the construction of the human (male-identified, body-denying) subject. Subjectivity is constructed hierarchically and dualistically. Subjectivity for the "up" side of a value hierarchical dualistic world exists in relationship to the object status of those on the "down" side. While our species is capable of a great range of behavior, the cultural relationship paradigmatic in the West is one of subject to object, in fact, subject *over* object. As dualistic apprehensions of the world take on the appearance of reality, our notions of human subjectivity depend, in part, on the presumed object status of nonhumans. The process of subjectification is thus dependent on depriving subject-status to another subject. This is how, in cultures of dominance and subordination, a subject knows he (or she) is a subject—through relationship to an object. Val Plumwood explains, "In the egoist-instrumentalist model (the master model of self), the self erases the other as part of the ethical domain" (Plumwood 1993:145). The other is seen as interchangeable and is experienced only in terms of the dominant self's need for gratification. The dualistic subject is trained to remain untransformed by the other, the objectified subject. No real interaction can occur because it is too threatening to the dominant self's private desire. (This is the reason Weil sees attention as so miraculous, the self is able to overcome the very desires that require the suffering of another.) Attention is further discouraged by constructs that hide the subject-status of terminal animals.

The Disappearance of the Nonhuman Subject

What if Cinci Freedom had not leapt over the six-foot fence at the meatpackers? What structurally oppressive frameworks would have butchered any concern for her just as the meat packers were set to butcher her literal body?

Behind every meal of meat is an absence: the death of the nonhuman whose place the product takes. The *absent referent* is that which separates the consumer from the animal and the animal from the end product. If nonhumans are alive they cannot be meat. Thus a dead body replaces the live nonhuman and nonhumans are conceptually absent from the act of eating flesh because they have been transformed into food.

The function of the absent referent is to keep our "meat" separated from any idea that she or he was once an animal, to keep the "moo" or "cluck" or "baa" away from the meat, to keep some*thing* from being seen as having been some*one*. Cow becomes "beef," pig becomes "pork." In cases in which slaughtered nonhumans carry the same name before and after their deaths, e.g., "chicken," "duck," "turkey," the absent referent is still at work. Their body parts are labeled without any possessiveness attributed to the nonhuman, that is, a lamb's leg becomes "leg of lamb," many chickens' wings become chicken wings. Once the existence of flesh is disconnected from the existence of a nonhuman who was killed to become that product, "meat" becomes unanchored by its original referent (the animal), becoming instead a free-floating image, a metaphor, unbloodied by suffering. David Lynch's Cow Parade entry, "Eat My Fear" disturbed the structure of the absent referent. It was too graphic a reminder that someone is suffering as she or he becomes something.

Had Cinci Freedom not leapt over the wall, she would have been interchangeable with the cows who were killed that day. In our culture, "meat" operates as a mass term (see Quine 1960: 99), defining entire species of nonhumans. Mass terms refer to things like water or colors; no matter how much you have of it, or what type of container it is in, it is still water. You can add a bucket of water to a pool of water without changing it at all. Objects referred to by mass terms have no individuality, no uniqueness, no specificity, no particularity. When humans turn a nonhuman into "meat," someone who has a very particular, situated life, a unique being, our neighbor, is converted into something that has no distinctiveness, no uniqueness, no individuality. When one adds five pounds of hamburger to a plate of hamburger, it is more of the same thing, nothing is changed. But to have a living cow, Cinci Freedom for instance, and then kill that cow, and butcher that cow, and grind up her flesh, you have not added a mass term to a mass term and ended up with more of the same. You have destroyed an individual. You have injured a neighbor. What is on the table in front of us is not devoid of specificity. It is the dead flesh of what was once a living, feeling being. The crucial point here is that humans make someone who is a unique being and therefore not the appropriate referent of a mass term into something that is the appropriate referent of a mass term. Humans make a subject into an object. Humans do so by removing any associations that might make it difficult to accept the activity of rendering a unique individual into a consumable thing. Not wanting to be aware of this activity, humans accept this disassociation, this distancing device of the mass term "meat."

The majority of nonhumans dominated by humans have been so devalued they no longer appear to be a part of nature, so thoroughly trivialized by their mass term status that it seems impossible to find meaning in their individual lives. A dualistic understanding of nonhumans who are eaten—conventionally termed either "wild" or "domesticated" nonhumans—then evolves. This dualistic approach has lifted up the "wild" nonhuman and denigrated enslaved nonhumans, who become seen as separate from rather than as a part of "nature." The noncaptive "wild" animal becomes the bearer of the dignity and personal values that humans cherish—and which they themselves may feel they have lost in the urbanized, business world, specifically, freedom and independence—while the majority of nonhumans consumed are seen as the negation of the "wild" and then apparently despised for their enslaved and powerless status.

Removing terminal animals from "nature" as it is conceptualized results not only in the trivialization of their lives, but also in a linguistic structure that uses their names to express contempt: consider the derisory sense of "chicken," "turkey," "pig," and "cow." This process of circular reasoning, noted by Catharine MacKinnon (1989) in regard to women's status (that women's devalued status becomes proof of why women are devalued), results in an ethical stance that harm to a now-degraded individual does not require a human's attention. Terminal animals are seen as "creatures whose lives appear too slavishly, too boringly, too stupidly female, too 'cowlike'" to deserve caring about (Davis 1995:196). They become so devalued that mere existence is considered a blessing, thus confirming the legitimacy of their degraded status.

Disembodied suffering is easier to ignore than the direct experience of someone's suffering. The very size of the problem—nine billion terminal animals (excluding sea animals) in the United States alone—favors objectification of the suffering because the numbers involved are inconceivable. The implications of flesh-eating are simply too big to be comprehended. Innumeracy—mathematical illiteracy—works in favor of the dominant subjectivity. Greek mathematician Archimedes pointed out that a group of small numbers when added together will exceed any large number, no matter how great it is. This "additivity" of small numbers explains how 200 pounds of flesh per person per year translates into more than nine billion land animals. If one doesn't grasp the additivity of small numbers, he or she won't see how his or her individual role as a meat eater contributes to the suffering of terminal animals. And so, individual nonhuman bodies disappear as the locus of suffering, the locus of experience, the locus of being a subject.

Becoming a (Male-Identified) Subject

If we prefer definitions of human beings that establish the idea that the human transcends animality, then anything associated with animality or animal-like behavior will be denied, feared, avoided, or destroyed. A clear example of this is the way in which grief is responded to. We encounter an anxious stance that distrusts the body and sees emotions as faulty. Yet, we do everything through our bodies, and sometimes it is grief that reminds us of this.

When we mourn, we experience the physicality of grief. We know this because we feel "truly stricken and stripped."[4] Grief, C. S. Lewis reminds us, is agonizingly bodily. After his wife's death, his journal recorded stomach flutters, yawning, swallowing: "like being mildly drunk, or concussed," "faint nausea," "feelings, and feelings, and feelings" (Lewis 1961:31). Grief is not one feeling, but a group of feelings that spiral around—anger, depression, guilt, acceptance, anger, depression, guilt ... feelings, feelings, feelings. Yet, because both the body and emotions are distrusted, our culture finds grief troubling. The unruly nature of grieving, thus, threatens our sense of how we constitute ourselves as "human."

Structurally, our culture does not really allow grieving at all: one week if one loses a spouse, two weeks if one loses a child. Then one is supposed to be fully functional. The message is "finish grieving and get back to living." Yet grief does not work that way. Grief needs acceptance. Often what is substituted for grief is judgment. "I shouldn't be feeling this way." "Why are you feeling this way? Over this?" In the face of the powerlessness of grief, judgment provides the reassurance of control.

In a culture that is very human oriented, grieving for other humans is barely allowed. Grieving for nonhumans remains largely incomprehensible. Yet, we can't live fully if we don't grieve fully, or to put it affirmatively: if we are allowed to grieve fully, we can live fully. To be attentive to terminal animals involves encountering grief for what they are experiencing. We cannot acknowledge terminal animals as neighbors if we do not allow grief to have a place in our lives.

Each and every day, human beings acknowledge the subject status of the nonhumans with whom they live. And when a certain nonhuman dies, one who was loved deeply, humans find themselves stricken and stripped. Yet when one is grieving for a nonhuman, one is encouraged even more to "get over it"; "it" was "just an animal"; "we'll get another one." Again, judgment is interposed where grief should be. In their relationship with a specific animal, humans' experience a nonhuman's loyalty, love, companionship, nonjudgmentalism, and individuality. They have experienced the nonhuman as a subject, a very specific who. That is why the death of a nonhuman friend (a "neighbor" in Weil's terms) is so devastating and the ineptness in responding to it so damaging.[5]

Of all the experiences of childhood that haunt one's adult years, one in particular is noted in memoirs, interviews, biographies: the death of a "pet."[6] Dick Cavett, a talk show host and comedian Joan Rivers, whose husband had committed suicide, once had a discussion on his show about grief. Each of the two celebrities had suffered losses, but the death that had devastated each of them the most, the loss that caused them to be truly stricken and stripped, was the death of a nonhuman animal.

Feeling grief over the death of a nonhuman reveals one's potential to respond to the suffering of nonhuman animals. In fact, this response is assumed to be so intense that human beings are protected from them. Steve Baker reports, "In 1990 the RSPCA [Royal Society for Prevention of Cruelty to Animals] found itself requested by the Advertising Standards Authority [ASA] to withdraw a press advertisement featuring a photograph of a dead horse suspended from a meat hook in an abattoir, as the ASA thought it likely to cause 'distress and revulsion' to the public." Anti-bullfighting posters were seen as too disturbing as well, so they were

not allowed in British airports (Baker 2001: 222, 224). The responses to individual cases of nonhuman animal suffering that receive media attention, the outpouring of offers of assistance, the ongoing concern, the anger at perpetrators who have harmed specific nonhumans reveal how intense awareness and action on behalf of an individual nonhuman's suffering can be. How intense and, yet, how feared.

If awareness of nonhuman suffering occurs in our bodies and if these feelings are uncomfortable, and if the body is devalued, then we are blocked from exploring what it means to be aware of nonhuman suffering. Humans are eminently animal because of our grieving. Lots of animals grieve. Humans are the only ones who try to repress, ignore, or minimize this grieving. Consequently, animals are disowned in two ways—humans disown their own animal bodies, and this allows humans to disown the other animals.

Several animal rights leaders have described to me how the mind/body dualism and the untrustworthy view of emotional responses to suffering influenced their lives. They spent years insisting they did not care for other animals because they did not feel caring would be seen as an appropriate response. They needed to appear rational, "in control," distanced from nonhuman animals. With the appearance of ecofeminist writings on nonhumans, they felt such relief because they now had a language that legitimated the idea that one might care for nonhumans and that this was an appropriate motivation for activism.

"Be a Man" Subjectivity

When a child grieves the death of a beloved nonhuman friend, when a sobbing 4-H teenager watches his prizewinning nonhuman companion sold to become flesh, when an adolescent resists learning how to hunt, the response is often "be a man." The lesson is that subjectification and adulthood occur at the expense of another's subject status as well as that one's own bodily responses are unreliable and must be conquered. I am going to call this "Be a Man" subjectivity. It involves a demand to ignore feelings, to distrust the body, and shoulder the responsibility of disengagement. The "man of reason," in this case the flesh eater, must deny his (or her) own body and its sensations of unease, concern, sadness, revulsion, etc. to pursue the cultural privilege of treating nonhumans as objects. Through "be a man" subjectivity, something else happens as well, something with religious implications regarding a suffering caused by dominance over others. To avoid recognizing such suffering, an individual is taught to identify with those causing the suffering, with those in power, not with those who are suffering and powerless, to accept the consciousness of the dominant not the dominated.[7]

Consequently, one identifies with the consumer not the consumed, the subject not the object. Engaging with the suffering of nonhumans requires, in most cases, acknowledging a suffering that humans themselves are causing. This is not comfortable. The agential role of the dominant subject must disappear as well as any reminders of the dominated animal subject. We encounter the triumph of phallic discourse that assumes sacrifice needs to be made (by others). Thus we hear about giving thanks to terminal animals for sacrificing themselves. The only volition apparently granted nonhumans is the desire to die for humans. If nonhumans really wanted to sacrifice themselves for us, why, when Cinci Freedom was given the choice between life or death, did she leap over the six-foot fence? And if we are truly comfortable with the idea that nonhumans make this ultimate sacrifice for us, why was she not sent back to the meat packers after her escape, so that we could, as David Lynch called it, "Eat Her Fear"? Perhaps this is why the use of pornographic constructs in meat advertisements exist: the animals' imputed desire to die for humans takes on sexualized overtones. The individual pig, cow, chicken, is transformed not only into the mass

term, "pork," "beef," "chicken," but further into being depicted as a "hooker" awaiting not just consumption, but consummation. They "want it."[8] The result is the "heroic" meal of a dead nonhuman which situates the eater as active and virile, the conqueror of his emotions. The pragmatic legacy of male subjectivity is the ability to dismiss nonhumans' suffering.

This movement away from engaging with a subject occurs through denial. First, something happens—a personal experience of reading, talking, seeing something, feeling something, a hint of discomfort. Something makes us aware that we are not eating just "food." This initial thought may be momentary, a glimpse of another's subjectivity: "I am eating a once-living cow." Such awareness can easily be dismissed. "This doesn't matter" or "I can't bear to think about nonhuman's suffering" and awareness is moved elsewhere. Or one can accept awareness as a gift of the religious imagination. The question becomes, "What am I going to do with awareness?" And the answer can be: "I need to engage with it." Following awareness leads to attention.

Attention is when one can respond to the insights awareness raises within without fear, rejection, or control. For example: "Dairy. Oh, it comes from cows. Cows suffer. But I want a cheese pizza." If the cheese pizza is more important and immediate than this awareness, attention to what happens to cows will be resisted. The cow becomes an absent referent, a mass term, so trivialized that her fate is immaterial.

Awareness interrupted, deflected, or denied can lead to guilt and defensiveness. Though it is thought that becoming a vegan requires energy, in fact, *not* becoming a vegan requires energy too. The difference is that vegans can follow awareness about terminal animals' suffering, rather than using their energy constantly to derail attention or subdue guilt. Nonvegans must block or redirect awareness of their neighbors. When awareness leads to attention, and attention to engagement, feelings about nonhumans' suffering are not frightening. The individual's agential role in causing suffering has ended. "I want the pizza. But if I eat the pizza, I am compromising my own commitment to not causing nonhumans' suffering. How can I keep this commitment? I could have a non-cheese pizza."

If one knows one is being inconsistent, the response may be to defend oneself against this knowledge, rather than to acknowledge that one is being inconsistent. "What I am doing cannot survive close scrutiny, it does not accord with my idea of my own—and others—humanity. It clashes with the values I believe I have. So, I am going to distort this action, split it apart from everything else, and do everything to defend myself against the realization."[9] The more people are uncomfortable with what they are doing, the more they will have to defend it. Because discomfort, too, is a feeling, and feelings are viewed as untrustworthy, subjects who require objects to complete their subjectivity will find ways to continue disowning any animal-identified feeling.

In this culture, women are supposed to do the emotional work for heterosexual intimate relationships: "a man will come to expect that a woman's role in his life is to take care of his feelings and alleviate the discomfort involved in feeling" (Bathrick et al 1987:39). This could be one reason women outnumber men in the animal rights movement. Even at the cultural level, women may be doing the emotional work of responding to the other animals as our neighbors. Whether men or women, animal activists, it could be argued, are doing the unvalued emotional work of our culture: They are attentive.

While the process of objectifying someone is an essential aspect of the "master" or dominant subjectivity, we are actually taught a myth about the construction of the subject—that it occurs autonomously. The idea of the construction of a separate and individual self directly reflects the masculinist predilection to make invisible the context and interconnections between people and all living things (Kaschak 1992:136, 150). In fact, we become subjects in re-lationship to other subjects. Each "man of reason" became one through relationships. Feminist philosopher Lorraine Code (1991) points out, drawing upon the work of Annette Baier, we do not begin as autonomous, unlocatable knowers of the world, we begin as "second persons." We are the second-person "you" to others who feed us, teach us to walk, instruct us on the dangers of a hot stove. This is how we initially acquire our knowledge. As opposed to the idea of the atomistic individual gaining knowledge of the world by oneself, we become persons through our dependence upon other persons from whom we "acquire the essential arts of personhood." Code explains that the concept of second persons demonstrates "the communal basis of moral and mental activity. ... A human being could not become a person, in any of the diverse senses of the term, were she or he *not* in 'second person' contact from earliest infancy."[10] (Code 1991:82) Lives begin in communality and interdependence; thus our acquisition of knowledge is not atomistically individualistic or "self-made" (Code 1991).

We learn in and through relationships with others, and, importantly, these relationships are not only among other humans, but also include nonhumans. Children, especially, constitute a self that relates to other beings as peers. Gail Melson (2001) proposes that children form what could be called a naïve biology. She argues that developmental psychologists have ignored this aspect of a child's growth. A central problem in acknowledging other animals as neighbors, therefore, is that the relationships that were formative to us as children become disowned or "outgrown" as we move into the framework of the "adult" world; the "second person" nature of the relationships that obtained for many in childhood—relationships that included respect for and learning from other animals—is buried within "be a man" subjectivity that maintains a fiction of autonomy and an autonomous education. Indeed, the relationship between the adult world and the child's world is recapitulated in the relationship between the dominant culture and the animal rights movement. Animal activists are told to "get a life" ("grow up") as though activism on behalf of animals is not a life, or at least not a mature one. People who care about nonhumans' suffering are seen as caring "too much." They are called "Bambi vegetarians"—i.e., they never got over their childhood experience of the movie Bambi and the shock of the death of Bambi's mother. Weil observes that attention to a sufferer "is a very rare and difficult thing." Attention to a nonhuman sufferer is an even more rare and difficult thing.

The God Trick and Terminal Animals' Existence

Those who cause nonhuman suffering by eating terminal animals and their products must maintain a "be a man" subjectivity, remaining dispassionate, detached, objectifying. Their position must be distanced and aloof, not intertwined and "second person." Their pleasure that results from oppression becomes instead a privilege that results from entitlement. They disappear as agents who cause harm. In Donna Haraway's terms, "those occupying the positions of the dominators are self-identical, unmarked, disembodied, unmediated, transcendent, born again" (Haraway 1988:586). Rendered invisible are the structures of oppression that enable such positioning. Haraway argues that knowledge arising from a place where one has the illusion of a view of infinite vision produces unlocatable and thus irresponsible—that is, unable to be called into account—knowledge claims. The result of such epistemologies is to release the knower from any accountability for the claims that emanate from this distanced, apprehensive position. Haraway calls this "the god trick." Claims about terminal animals that deny them subject status or dispute whether they suffer or are conscious of suffering—these claims are evidence of a god trick. Such arguments require distance. Staying unlocatable and unaccountable makes one much more able to accept the suffering of terminal animals because one is less likely to en-counter nonhuman subjects or their suffering. One who is unlocatable and unaccountable has no neighbors.

The tension between responding as a neighbor or enlisting the "god trick" to escape accountability is exemplified in the debate about suffering versus existence. Those who are distanced from suffering, who are unlocatable, often claim that "at least the animals were born." To those who benefit from oppression, the simple fact of terminal animals' existence mitigates the suffering inherent to that state of existence. Because the victims have been trivialized, the issue of their suffering can be trivialized as well. Queries about nonhumans that pose the question, "why else are they here?" position humans in their relationship to nonhuman animals as akin to God's relationship to humans. Humans become the reason for terminal animals' existence. The question, "What would happen to the cows if we didn't eat them?" implies that terminal animals are the only oppressed group for whom the elimination of their oppression appears to eliminate them. This allows for the comforting belief that God-like, we have been beneficent in granting life and so we can take it when we desire. What of the suffering in between? It disappears. By claiming the credit for the existence of terminal animals, (and so it is the meat eaters' need to eat meat that allows for the existence of animals who become "meat"), nonvegans commit an error in logic, (terminal animals were born because we wish to objectify them, so since they are born, we can use them as objects). At the same time, nonvegans create a belief system that implicitly forgives themselves for what they cause nonhumans to experience.

All of this is based on fallacious reasoning: One who is not born cannot actually regret one's nonexistence.[11] In fact, there is no state of nonexistence from which existence can be judged. Once one exists, the issue becomes the quality of that individual's life, and the ethical issue for humans must be one of attention to our neighbors, the farmed animals.

When the ethical issue is framed so that it appears the only option for terminal animals is existence with suffering *or* nonexistence, the either/or thinking that is an aspect of an oppressive worldview is evident. Such either/or thinking conveniently eliminates the ethical perspective that existence *without* suffering is a possibility. But it is only a possibility if humans take responsibility for the suffering they cause terminal animals. Instead, through the "god trick," persons who establish such an either/or framework for a debate about meat eating, situate themselves as unlocatable in relationship to the suffering of nonhumans. They cannot and will not be neighbors in Weil's sense of the word. The belief that existence is good in and of itself arises from a disembodied rationalized position. Although their subjectivity depends on the erasure of the other, this position makes a suspect epistemological claim—that despite their role in dominating animals, they believe they can speak for what the animals experience. The nonhuman other who exists to become "meat" is needed for the dominator's gratification.

Bernard Rollin (1990) asserts that "to be morally responsive to pain in animals, one must ideally know animals in their individuality." This is precisely what the god trick precludes. Instead, someone who is "up" dismisses the issue of suffering as immaterial or nonexistent precisely because they have experienced its materiality only in regards to their own narcissistic pleasures and not in relationship to the other individual's experience of suffering. As Simone Weil reminds us, "Those who are unhappy have no need for anything in this world but people capable of giving them attention" (Weil 1971:75). Weil herself understood that such attention is transformative and miraculous.

Changing the Subject

Fearing that we care too much, we create structures that enable us to care too little. It could be argued that this value hierarchical structure creates a narcissistic need *not* to know. As a result, human self-definition evolves split off from acknowledging relationships in which we are the cause of nonhumans' suffering.

Attention to suffering makes us ethically responsible.[12] Only those who are "up" can deny the ethical implications of suffering for those who are "down." Simone Weil suggests that love of our neighbor, in its fullness, means being able to ask, "What are you going through?" and to be able to be attentive to the answer. The question, Weil says, "is a recognition that the sufferer exists, not only as a unit in a collection," but as an individual. To be able to ask of nonhumans, "What are you going through?" requires a sense of the self that is related and interdependent, involved with others. Val Plumwood calls this the "ecological self": "one which includes the goal of the flourishing of earth others and the earth community among its own primary ends, and hence respects or cares for these others for their own sake" (Plumwood 1993:154). Seeing ourselves as born into relationships rather than as atomistic, self-made individuals, and recognizing that these valued relationships include other animals, can challenge the boundary between the presumably "self-made (hu)man" and the presumably "nature-made animal," between the subject and the putative object, between "doer" and the "done to." This requires that subjectivity be redefined—freed from its death dance with an objectified other.

It is the quality of relationship that we have with each other, human and nonhuman, that matters. Attention to others, as Weil states, involves being able to ask "what are you going through?" and being able to acknowledge that we can, in relationship with animals, understand their answers. Attention to another's suffering means that we may feel pain, alarm, anguish, and guilt. We may encounter deep grief, both for what they are going through, and what we caused them to experience.

For those who care about the suffering of nonhumans, the stages of grief Elisabeth Kubler Ross enumerated are configured somewhat differently. The final stage is not "acceptance." Nonhuman suffering is not inevitable. The "ecological self," the interdependent self, the second-person subject need not make peace with the inevitability of the (human-willed) death of terminal animals. Instead, we will understand that grief will be a daily presence. Because of the extensive ways in which humans are harming nonhumans, grief will be the companion to attention. Attention allows human beings to be fully human as they acknowledge how humans and nonhumans are interrelated.

Changing the object status of nonhumans involves changing the subjectification process of humans. What is needed is a theology of relinquishment in which subjectivity does not arise from the object status of others. Instead, each subject, each ecological self, is able to acknowledge the grieving/feeling aspect of one's own self. An ethic of attention to others is actively embodied—acknowledging the other's body and its capacity for suffering and one's own body and its capacity to feel grief. Then one can become a good neighbor, and transform one's own body from being a locus of oppression through consumption of dead animal bodies to being a locus of change—one that survives on plant food instead.

We require a self-in-relationship that is not bound by species-identification. Many people report that they could not eat a nonhuman after looking into her or his eyes. They realized there was a "who" there, as desirous of living as Cinci Freedom. Redemption, it could be claimed, is related to bodily integrity, to trusting our bodies, our bodies' authority. What we need is not "I" language, from a separate, autonomous subject, but "eye," "hand," and "ear" language, able to acknowledge the many ways that nonhumans answer the question, "What are you going through?"

Acknowledgments

Thanks to Paul Waldau, friend and scholar, for patience, persistence, supportive presence and vision, and to Josephine Donovan for being both catalyst and friend.

NOTES

1. For ecofeminist work generally see Plumwood (1993), Adams (1993), Gray (1982), Warren (1987), Ruether (1991), and Diamond and Orenstein (1990). For ecofeminist approaches to animals see Adams (1990, 1994), Gaard, Adams and Donovan (1995), Donovan and Adams (1996). A comprehensive bibliography of works that deal specifically with women and animals and/or feminism and animal defense theory can be found in Adams and Donovan (1995:353–61).

2. I take as a given that terminal animals—those animals who are raised to become humans' "meat" —suffer. Space does not allow the defense of this claim, but since the literature on the subject is plentiful, I direct any reader who doubts this claim to the following: Coats (1989), Dunayer (2001), Eis-entz (1997), Mason and Singer (1980), Rollin (1990), Singer (1990).

3. See Dunayer (2001) for a persuasive analysis of the problem of language in *Animal Equality*.

4. Insight of Martha Murphy Hall, Dallas, spring 2001.

5. In *Prayers for Animals* (2004) and *God Listens When You're Sad: Prayers When Your Animal Friend Is Sick or Dies* (2005), I have created prayers to acknowledge grief at the death of animal friends.

6. On the failure of psychological theory to address children's relationship to nonhumans, see Melson (2001).

7. Thanks to Gus Kaufman, Jr. for suggesting this as a response to suffering.

8. On this see Adams (2003).

9. Kovel (1971:19) summarizes this thought process, "Since this set of ideas is inconsistent and will stand neither the test of reason nor of my better values, I am going to distort it, split it up, and otherwise defend myself against the realization."

10. Code (1991) is quoting Annette Baier, "Cartesian Persons," in *Postures of the Mind: Essays*

on Mind and Morals (Minneapolis: University of Minnesota Press).

11. See my discussion of this issue in Adams (1994:69–70).

12. Donovan's work (1990, 1994) has been extremely influential in the formulation of my own position.

REFERENCES

Adams, Carol J. 1990. *The Sexual Politics of Meat: A Feminist-Vegetarian Critical Theory.* New York: Continuum.

———, ed. 1993. *Ecofeminism and the Sacred.* New York: Continuum.

———. 1994. *Neither Man nor Beast: Feminism and the Defense of Animals.* New York: Continuum.

———. 2003. *The Pornography of Meat.* New York: Continuum.

———. 2004. *Prayers for Animals.* New York: Continuum.

———. 2005. *God Listens When You're Sad: Prayers When Your Animal Friend is Sick or Dies.* Cleveland: Pilgrim Press.

Adams, Carol J., and Josephine Donovan, eds. 1995. *Animals and Women: Feminist Theoretical Explorations.* Durham: Duke University Press.

Baker, Steve. 2001. *Picturing the Beast: Animals, Identity, and Representation.* Urbana and Chicago: University of Illinois Press.

Bartky, Sandra. 1989. "Women, Bodies and Power: A Research Agenda for Philosophy." *APA Newsletter on Philosophy and Feminism* 89, no. 1:78–81.

Bathrick, Dick, Kathleen Carlin, Gus Kaufman, Jr., and Rich Vodde. 1987. *Men Stopping Violence: A Program for Change.* Atlanta: Men Stopping Violence.

Bordo, Susan. 1987. *The Flight to Objectivity: Essays on Cartesianism and Culture.* Albany: State University of New York Press.

Coats, C. David. 1989. *Old MacDonald's Factory Farm: The Myth of the Traditional Farm and the Shocking Truth about Animal Suffering in Today's Agribusiness.* New York: Continuum.

Code, Lorraine. 1991. *What Can She Know? Feminist Theory and the Construction of Knowledge.* Ithaca: Cornell University Press.

Davis, Karen. 1995. "Thinking Like a Chicken: Farm Animals and the Feminine Connection." In Adams and Donovan, eds. (1995): 192–212.

Diamond, Irene and Gloria Feman Orenstein. 1990. *Reweaving the World: The Emergence of Ecofeminism.* San Francisco: Sierra Club.

Donovan, Josephine. 1990. "Animal Rights and Feminist Theory." In Donovan and Adams, eds. (1996): 34–59.

———. 1994. "Attention to Suffering: Sympathy as a Basis for Ethical Treatment of Animals." In Donovan and Adams, eds. (1996): 145–69.

Donovan, Josephine and Carol J. Adams, eds. 1996. *Beyond Animal Rights: A Feminist Caring Ethic for the Treatment of Animals.* New York: Continuum.

Dunayer, Joan. 2001. *Animal Equality: Language and Liberation.* Derwood, Maryland: Ryce Publishing.

Eisentz, Gail A. 1997. *Slaughterhouse: The Shocking Story of Greed, Neglect and Inhumane Treatment Inside the U.S. Meat Industry.* Amherst, N.Y.: Prometheus Books.

Fiorenza, Elisabeth Schüssler. 1992. *But She Said: Feminist Practices of Biblical Interpretation.* Boston: Beacon Press.

Gaard, Greta, ed. 1993. *Ecofeminism: Women, Animals, Nature.* Philadelphia: Temple University Press.

Gray, Elizabeth Dodson. 1982. *Patriarchy as a Conceptual Trap.* Wellesley, MA: Roundtable Press.

Haraway, Donna. 1988. "Situated Knowledges: The Science Question in Feminism and the Privilege of Partial Perspective," *Feminist Studies* 14, no. 3: 575–99.

Harding, Sandra. 1983. "Is Gender a Variable in Conceptions of Rationality? A Survey of Issues." In Carol C. Gould, ed., *Beyond Domination: New Perspectives on Women and Philosophy*. Totowa, N.J.: Rowman and Littlefield.

———. 1986. *The Science Question in Feminism*. Ithaca: Cornell University Press.

Kaschak, Ellyn. 1992. *Engendered Lives: A New Psychology of Women's Experience*. New York: Basic Books.

Kovel, Joel. 1971. *White Racism: A Psychohistory*. New York: Vintage Books.

Lewis, C. S. 1961. *A Grief Observed*. New York: The Seabury Press.

Lloyd, Genevieve. 1984. *The Man of Reason: "Male" and "Female" in Western Philosophy*. Minneapolis: University of Minnesota Press.

Luke, Brian. 1995. "Justice, Caring, and Animal Liberation." In Donovan and Adams, eds. (1995): 77–102.

———. 1995. "Taming Ourselves or Going Feral? Toward a Nonpatriarchal Metaethic for Animal Liberation." In Adams and Donovan, eds. (1995): 290–319.

MacKinnon, Catharine A. 1989. *Toward a Feminist Theory of the State*. Cambridge: Harvard University Press.

Mason, Jim, and Peter Singer. 1980. *Animal Factories*. New York: Crown.

Melson, Gail. 2001. *Why the Wild Things Are: Animals in the Lives of Children*. Cambridge: Harvard University Press.

Plumwood, Val. 1993. *Feminism and the Mastery of Nature*. London and New York: Routledge.

Quine, Willard Van Orman. 1960. *Word and Object*. Cambridge: MIT Press.

Rollin, Bernard E. 1990. *The Unheeded Cry: Animal Consciousness, Animal Pain, and Science*. New York: Oxford University Press.

Ruether, Rosemary R. 1991. *Gaia and God*. San Francisco: Harper.

Singer, Peter. 1975. 1990. *Animal Liberation*. 2nd ed. New York: New York Review Book.

Spelman, Elizabeth V. 1982. "Woman as Body: Ancient and Contemporary Views." *Feminist Studies* 8, no. 1: 109–31.

Warren, Karen J. 1987. "Feminism and Ecology: Making Connections." *Environmental Ethics* 9, no. 1: 3–20.

———. 1990. The Power and the Promise of Ecological Feminism. *Environmental Ethics* 12, no. 2: 125–46.

Weil, Simone. 1971. "Reflections on the Right Use of School Studies with a View to the Love of God," in *Waiting on God*. London: Fontana Books.

Interlocking Oppressions

The Nature of Cruelty to Nonhuman Animals and its

Relationship to Violence Toward Humans

KIM ROBERTS

This volume explores the concept of the world as a "communion of subjects, not a collection of objects." Tragically, many in our world community are treated as objects, and the ideal of communion is lost in the effort to oppress and subjugate others. Subjects become objects. This objectification can be seen, for example, in the abuse of nonhuman animals, as well as the abuse of children, spouses, and elders. The oppressors view many nonhuman animals as "tools" to be used to further efforts to dominate others. To address oppression, we must explore and understand the interconnectedness of these many forms of oppression.

Sadly, ours is a society consumed by violence and oppression. The U.S. Bureau of Justice Statistics reported that in 1996 there were 9.1 million violent crimes in the United States. On an average day more than 65 people die from homicide, another 18,000 are violently victimized, and more than 6,000 of these victims suffer physical injuries (Dobrin, et al. 1996). In 1991, the United States Board on Child Abuse

and Neglect reported that more than 2.5 million American children suffered from abuse and neglect. Every 15 seconds a woman is beaten by her partner (Harlow 1991). Violence and oppression are interconnected. Often where you find one, you will find the other. Violence, or the threat of violence, is used to oppress, and oppression is used to rationalize violence to maintain the status quo. For example, women are beaten to keep them oppressed, and because they are oppressed society tacitly condones their beating.

The belief that the treatment of nonhuman animals is closely related to the treatment of humans is a concept that is gaining interest as a source of insight into the dynamic of violence. Although this concept has a long history in popular culture, scientific and scholarly attention to the issue has been minimal. Closer examination of animal cruelty within the framework of family and community violence offers an opportunity to explore violence in a societal context, no longer isolated from other forms of violence.

The development of a general theory of animal cruelty must go beyond narrow psychological and sociological models to include the social meaning of violence. In order to fully understand the ecology of animal cruelty and human violence, we must also consider the powerful influence of religious teachings throughout history and the religious communities' role in addressing violence and oppression. The power of the religious community is not just an untapped resource; it may actually be exerting a negative influence on efforts to address the abuses of human and nonhuman animals.

Religious Teachings and the Violence Connection

For centuries civilized societies have known that people's treatment of nonhuman animals mirrors their treatment of fellow human beings. This knowledge did little to stem the tide of violence against human and nonhuman victims. As noted elsewhere in this volume, religious figures were often among those speaking out about the need for compassionate treatment of nonhuman animals. Many also understood the connection between animal abuse and the abuse of humans. Ironically, much of this abuse could be directly or indirectly linked to religion.

The Middle Ages in Europe were known for the ritualistic abuse inflicted on many human and nonhuman victims. These abuses were often carried out in the name of religion and assisted in one way or another by the church or its officials. According to Regenstein (1991), with the advent of the Renaissance in the fourteenth century the lot of animals, human and nonhuman, deteriorated. Justifications for persecuting nonhuman animals, often religious ones, were also used to rationalize abuse of humans, many of whom suffered along with the animals. A few prominent figures showed enlightenment beyond the arts and literature of the day. The essayist Michel de Montaigne was a Roman Catholic who served as mayor of Bordeaux and championed the cause of compassion and

tolerance. Montaigne understood the connection between violence against nonhuman animals and violence against humans, and its deleterious effect on the abuser's character. He wrote in his *Essays* (1575, 1952 edition) that those who took pleasure from "spectacles of the slaughter of animals ... proceeded to those of the slaughter of men."

By the sixteenth century people were becoming less tolerant of the public displays of cruelty. A few courageous individuals began to speak out. Sir Thomas More, who served as an archbishop and a Carthusian monk, was one of the earliest British leaders to publicly advocate kindness to animals. Sir Thomas thought the ideal society would include religious tolerance, education of women as well as men, and common ownership of land. He also condemned cruelty to nonhuman animals, saying that it would lead to cruelty to humans. Despite his position, More was also known for his skill at cock-throwing, a contradiction that seems obvious today.

A movement for social reform gained momentum in the eighteenth century. Demands for the abolition of slavery and the prevention of cruelty to children and nonhuman animals were growing. John Welsey, the founder of Methodism, and his brother Charles were key to this movement. Wesley traveled on horseback evangelizing and calling for fair treatment for the lower classes and nonhuman animals (Regenstein 1991). By the end of the eighteenth century the concept of kindness and compassion to others was catching on, due in part to the influence of individuals within the church. In a 1776 book entitled *A Dissertation on the Duty of Mercy and Sin of Cruelty to Brute Animals*, Dr. Humphrey Primatt, noted that violence knows no species boundary: "If all barbarous customs and practices still subsisting amongst us were decreed to be as illegal as they are sinful, we should not hear of so many shocking murders and acts of inhumanity as we now do."

The animal protection movement continued to grow in the nineteenth century, when it became part of series of reform movements to improve the treatment of women, children, the poor, and the mentally ill. In the United States and England, organizations for the protection of children grew out of animal protection groups. The founder of the Royal Society for the Prevention of Cruelty to Animals (RSPCA), the first organization of its kind, was the Reverend Arthur Broome, an Anglican priest. It was originally founded as a Christian society "based on Christian principles." In the United States, many of those involved with the animal and child protection movements in the 1800s and early 1900s were woman from the religious community. In fact, the famous 1874 child-abuse case involving Mary Ellen Wilson and prosecuted by the American Society for the Prevention of Cruelty to Animals (ASPCA), was initiated by Etta Wheeler, a Methodist social worker (Costain 1991).

Gender and Violence

In the United States, the movement to address violence against women also involved many women from the religious community. From 1850–1900, the Women's Christian Temperance Union (WCTU), along with the suffragists, protested the brutality of "drunken husbands" and fought for changes in divorce laws so that women could divorce for "mental cruelty" (Maine Coalition to End Domestic Violence 2000).

Many different methods have been devised to oppress women and keep them subordinate to men in patriarchal societies. For more than a thousand years, the Chinese used foot binding to cripple women. Purdah is a practice of keeping women secluded from all men except members of the immediate family. It is still in use among some Muslim populations of the Middle East, Asia, and North Africa, with the effect of making women prisoners in their own homes. Rape and assault, both within and outside of the family, are two of the most brutal and devastating ways that the oppression of women continues in patriarchal societies (Maine Coalition to End Domestic Violence 2000).

The role of gender in violence is an issue that must be considered when developing comprehensive strategies to address the problem. Male violence against women comes from an imbalance and misuse of power, from a desire for dominance and control over another. Men are the most likely offenders in acts of intimate as well as non-intimate violence (Chalk and King 1998). Males are more than nine times more likely than females to commit murder (Fox and Zawitz 1999). Ninety-five percent of juvenile homicides are committed by boys (Dalton 1999). White adolescent males have been the perpetrators of the rash of shootings at U.S. schools. It is tempting to look at these individual acts of violence as manifestations of individual pathology and seek to treat only the individual while ignoring the broader context of the violence. This approach allows us to distance ourselves from the problem as well as the perceived solution: the "you are broken, you need fixing" mind set. This is a shortsighted approach, as it overlooks the social and cultural environment in which these acts occur. Looking at violence as gender-neutral keeps us trapped in an endless cycle of treating the symptoms while ignoring the disease.

Carol Adams (1994:75) stated:

Among the features of an oppressive conceptual framework is value-hierarchical thinking or "up-down thinking" that places higher value, status, or prestige on what is up rather than what is down. Abuse enacts a value hierarchy—through abusive behavior a person establishes control, becoming "up" rather than "down"—while originating in value hierarchies: those who are "down" in terms of (public) status—women, children, nondominant men, and animals are more likely to be victimized.

This framework allows those who are "up" to rationalize the domination, oppression, and victimization of those viewed as inferior. A common theme in the recent school shootings was a desire by the perpetrators to be "up." This framework is tragically reflected in some religions. Although most of the major religions of the world include teachings of respect for nature and kindness to nonhuman animals, some of the most enlightened perspectives on the treatment of nonhuman animals come from the most abusive, patriarchal traditions. Many followers rely heavily on the framework of "tradition," which is frequently misinterpreted as "religion." These traditions are often selectively implemented independent of the fundamental principles of the religion. For example, some Hindus celebrate the Goddess and yet engage in dowry-related murders and other violent acts against women and girls. It is important to note that the caretakers of religion and tradition are primarily men.

Violence, power, and control are all part of our cultural definition of manhood or masculinity. One strategy to address violence and oppression must lie in a new shared value that redefines concepts such as masculinity and power in a way that nurtures empathy and compassion for all life on this planet. According to Carol Adams (1995:80): "Recognizing harm to animals as interconnected to controlling behavior by violent men is one aspect of recognizing the interrelatedness of all violence in a gender hierarchical world. The challenge now, as it has been for quite some time, is to stop it."

This is a challenge we all must face, including those in the religious community who seek to develop a new ethic for an increasingly alienated society.

Animal Cruelty: An Overview

Animal cruelty encompasses a wide range of behaviors that are harmful to nonhuman animals, from neglect to malicious killing. The most common form of animal cruelty is unintentional neglect that can often be resolved through education. Intentional cruelty or abuse is know-

ingly depriving an animal of food, water, shelter, socialization, or veterinary care, or maliciously torturing, maiming, mutilating, or killing an animal.

According to a 1997 study by the Massachusetts Society for the Prevention of Cruelty to Animals (MSPCA) and Northeastern University (Arluke, et al. 1997) the perpetrators of animal cruelty are typically adolescent to young adult males. Although other research data also indicates that the typical abuser is an adolescent, it is possible that the number of adult male perpetrators is much higher than reported. Juveniles often abuse nonhuman animals in a group, in a public or semipublic setting and brag about their abuses to others. This behavior would increase the likelihood that the abuse would be reported. Adult males are more likely to abuse nonhuman animals at their home, often behind closed doors, in an effort to terrorize and control family members. Since the violence and abuse in the family is often a secret, he and the family members are less likely to discuss the abuse with others. Therefore it often goes unreported.

Nonhuman animals are often targeted for violence because they are physically weaker, therefore easier to control, and may be more accessible. Given the low social and legal status of nonhuman animals, they are often seen as less deserving of humane treatment. The abuse of a nonhuman animal presents less risk to the abuser because of their status as property and the weakness of the law. Nonhuman animals are often dependent on the abuser for care and therefore more vulnerable to abuse and neglect.

People abuse nonhuman animals for many reasons. Animal cruelty, like other forms of violence, is often committed by someone who feels powerless, has low self-esteem, poor interpersonal skills, and feels under the control of others. The motive for the abuse may be to shock, offend, threaten, or intimidate others. Abusers may imitate their own abuse or abuse they have witnessed. Others may abuse as a way to control or retaliate against the nonhuman animal. One element common to most violent abusers of humans and nonhumans is a lack of empathy. Empathy connects us to other living beings and nurtures and preserves our feelings of communion with the world and all those who inhabit it. Lack of empathy, whether as result of "nature or nurture" or some combination of both, results in isolation and alienation. These individuals view other living beings as having no intrinsic value.

When we lack empathy, we lack security; and we seek the destructive path of power. When we lack empathy, we lack the sensitivity and wisdom to use knowledge creatively (Fox 1989). Jeremy Rifkin (1985) said:

> The great challenge that lies before our generation is to recognize the path to our own freedom. We will need to understand that to renounce power is not to give up.... It is to let go.... Some will wonder loud as to whether an empathetic consciousness can succeed in a world still largely dominated by a power-seeking mind. They fail to see that the very act of repudiating the old consciousness and embracing the new is victory, the most impressive victory one could ever hope to claim.

Community Violence

In the early 1970s the U.S. Federal Bureau of Investigation began a retrospective study of serial killers, mass murderers, serial rapists, and perpetrators of sexual homicide to gain insight into the histories of violent offenders. The study found that 36 percent of these violent criminals described incidents of participating in the mutilation and torture of nonhuman animals as children, and 46 percent described such activities in adolescence (Ressler et al. 1986). Prevalence rates of early nonhuman animal cruelty of 25 to 50 percent have been described in studies of aggressive prison inmates, offenders who assaulted women, convicted rapists, and convicted child molesters (Tingle et al. 1986). The 1997 study of convicted animal abusers by the MSPCA and Northeastern University found 70 percent had

committed at least one additional serious criminal offense, compared with 22 percent of the control group. The additional offenses were not restricted to violent crimes. While 38 percent of the abusers had been convicted of a violent crime, they were also convicted of three times as many property crimes, drug offenses, and disorderly-conduct charges. The research clearly shows a connection between violence to nonhuman animals and humans.

Anecdotal case histories also provide some insight into this connection. Notorious cases of American serial killers who tortured nonhuman animals prior to killings humans are common. Examples include Jeffrey Dahmer, Ted Bundy, David Berkowitz, Henry Lee Lucas, and the "Boston Strangler," all of whom tortured animals during childhood and/or adolescence. The recent rash of school shootings by young boys provides other examples of the connection between animal cruelty and human violence. They highlight the importance of taking cruelty seriously as predictor and indicator of future violence. Luke Woodham of Pearl, Mississippi, who killed his mother prior to opening fire on his classmates, describes in a diary his first "kill," his own dog Sparkle. This heinous act, committed with one or more accomplices and apparently witnessed by at least one adult, went unreported. Allegations of animal cruelty have also been reported in the cases of several other "school shooters," including Kip Kinkel of Springfield, Oregon; Andrew Golden of Jonesboro, Arkansas; Michael Carneal of West Paducah, Kentucky; and notoriously, Eric Harris and Dylan Klebold of Columbine, Colorado. These incidents repeatedly point out the importance of acts of cruelty as warning signs of potential for future violence.

Why do young boys start on the path to animal cruelty? There is no simple answer. It is likely a combination of the influence of the individual, the family, the community, and society. Some have suggested that these boys lack the capacity to connect to others, human and nonhuman, or have denied those feelings to protect themselves from the pain of loss. Some may imitate the violence they have experienced or witnessed in their family on the one being less powerful than themselves. Others feel helpless and may abuse in order to gain a sense of power and control, or they may act out the anger they feel against their parents, peers, or society as a whole. Finally, some of these young abusers simply seem to have never learned to value the lives of others.

Family Violence

Nonhuman animals are part of more than half of all American households, and part of three-fourths of households with school-age children. How a family treats their nonhuman members often reflects the health of the family. A family with a skinny, diseased dog who is left tied to a tree in the backyard without food or shelter is unlikely to provide its other vulnerable human members with sterling care. The man who throws the family cat against the wall is unlikely to be a warm, loving husband and a caring, nurturing father. Likewise, the little dog who sleeps with the child, is included on family outings, and is healthy and happy, probably lives a household where everyone is treated with love and respect.

Research looking at the family dynamics in violent households supports this idea. In the 1980s, interest in animal cruelty as an integral part of the dynamic of family violence was gaining momentum. A study in 1981 by the RSPCA in England found that 83 percent of families with a history of animal cruelty had also been identified by social service agencies as at-risk for child abuse or neglect. A 1983 survey of New Jersey families reported for child abuse found that in 88 percent of the families reported for physical abuse at least one person had abused animals. In two-thirds of the cases the abuser was the abusive parent, and in one-third of the cases the abuser was a child (DeViney, Dickert, and Lockwood 1983).

This cruelty connection can take many forms. Nonhuman animals may be abused by the parent in an effort to punish the child, to force the child to keep the family violence a secret, to terrorize and control family members, or to retaliate against the nonhuman animal for perceived wrongs. Animal cruelty rarely involves a single act of cruelty against a single victim. It is part of a tangled web of disturbed relationships. Within this web, an abused child may become violent to others, including nonhuman animals. It is also possible that, without intervention, he will become an abusive parent who may produce another generation of violent children. This is the cycle of violence.

It is not just child abuse and animal cruelty that are interconnected; violence against women also plays a strong role in this violent dynamic. According to the National Clearinghouse on Child Abuse and Neglect Information (1998) there is a 30 to 60 percent overlap between violence against children and violence against women. The connection doesn't end with the women and children; it also includes nonhuman animals as well. The 1990s saw interest in the connection between domestic violence and animal cruelty increase. As a result of the growing interest, new data, case reports, and anecdotal evidence came to light that provided substance to the gut instinct that where one is found, so is the other. Surveys in women's shelters in the mid- to late 1990s found an average of 74 percent of "pet-owning" women reported that the animals had been threatened, injured or killed by their abuser (Ascione 1995, 1997).

Contrary to what most batterers would like us to believe, when a man batters a woman he has not lost control; he has gained it. According to Adams (1995) he is also reminding the woman of her subordinate status in the world. Men who batter believe that they have the right to use violence. The primary goal of batterers who abuse nonhuman animals is to gain or maintain power and control over their victims. The nonhuman animals are used as living weapons against their human victims. The batterer may also threaten, injure, or abuse the nonhuman animal to force the family to keep the battering a secret or to retaliate against acts of independence. The abuse helps the batterer to perpetuate the context of terror. A batterer's abuse of nonhuman animals exposes the deliberateness of battering. He may try to convince his victim that he only hits her because he is out of control, but threatening to kill the dog if she doesn't return from the store on time or nailing the cat to the door is hardly the act of someone "out of control." It is the act of someone in complete control and trying to maintain that control. Reports from some batterers' intervention groups indicate that the men are more reluctant to discuss the abuse of nonhuman animals than the abuse of their human victims, not because they are ashamed, but because it contradicts their rationalization for the violence. "I couldn't help myself; I was out of control" is no longer believable. They would then have to accept responsibility for their actions.

The abuse can also be used to prevent a woman from leaving, coerce her to return, or punish her for ending the relationship. One battered women's advocate told the story of a woman whose husband would dangle her dog outside their twelfth story apartment window by his ears and threaten to drop him anytime she threatened to leave or disobeyed him. In addition to the horror of hearing the dog yelp in pain and fear, she knew he would drop the dog to his death if she didn't do as he demanded. Another woman left her batterer during a particularly violent episode and left her beloved dog behind. After entering the women's shelter she received a letter from her husband forwarded to her from her mother. Enclosed was a note saying that if she did not return right away he would kill her dog. The envelope included a picture of her dog with his ears cut off. Knowing he would carry out the threat, she returned in fear, and the shelter never heard from her again (personal and confidential communication).

Two parallel cases involved women who ended the relationship with the batterer. In one case the dog was left behind because the woman did not yet have a place to keep him and was staying with friends. Her husband called her and told her if she did not return to him her puppy would die. Although she feared for her puppy, she refused to return. The next day he arrived at the door, hat in hand. Tragically, the hat contained her puppy's severed head. In a similar case, the batterer was forced to leave the home and began to stalk his estranged wife. On her birthday she found a threatening note on the front seat of her car, held down by the severed head of her cat. In both of these cases the batterer no longer needed the animal as a living weapon. To the batterer, the usefulness of the dog or cat was to punish the woman for leaving (personal and confidential communication).

To ensure total control and domination over the family, the batterer will try to isolate the woman from family and friends. He may not allow her to have money of her own; he may not let her leave the house without him; he may make her account for every minute she is gone. Because of this isolation, her companion becomes even more important. Nonhuman animals are often the only source of comfort and unconditional love for victims of abuse. The batterer uses that love against his human victims. Sadly, the closer the bond, the more he may use it against them.

Many women will stay in the violent relationship out of fear that their animal companion will be harmed if they leave. Most battered women's shelters are unable to accommodate nonhuman animals in their facilities, and rather than leave them behind many women will delay leaving the situation. One study found that nearly 20 percent of women reported that they delayed leaving their abuser out of fear that a "pet" would be harmed (Ascione 1997). Data collected in Canada found that 43 percent of women reported that concerns over the safety of their "pet" prevented them from leaving sooner (Arkow 2001).

If women are to leave these violent relationships, we must understand and address their very real concerns. A woman is most likely to be seriously injured or killed by her abuser when she threatens to leave or has already left the relationship. It is also a very dangerous time for her nonhuman companions as well. To remove this barrier to leaving, we must work together to educate and assist battered women in how they can protect themselves, their children and their nonhuman companions.

Intervention Strategies

When we hear stories of abusers decapitating puppies or cats to threaten and terrorize women and children we may feel an emotional need for revenge. But we must temper that need with reason and compassion. But how do we hold people accountable for such cruelty in a way that is reasonable and compassionate? Our modern justice system serves three needs: punishing wrongdoing, providing supervision and/or treatment when appropriate, and protecting the public. We cannot expect to put an end to animal cruelty by putting all abusers in jail. According to the National Institute of Justice our jails are at 97 percent capacity, and offenders convicted of violent acts against humans are routinely granted early release to ease crowding. One of our best hopes lies in the early identification of violent individuals. We must identify them at the earliest possible stage in the escalation of violence. That is when intervention is most effective.

Prosecution of abusers is the key to getting abusers into the criminal justice system where we can mandate intervention. Intervention should be based on the individual case. There is no "one size fits all" answer for what to do with animal abusers. The courts should have a "menu" of options that provide the most effective response. But we must make sure that our communities have the resources to carry out an appropriate sentence. In addition to incarceration, communities should design and evaluate options that include diversion programs, community service, counseling for individuals and families, education, and a variety of support services for victims of violence.

Community Collaborations in Detecting, Preventing, and Intervening in Violence

It not only "takes a village to raise a child"; it will take a village to end violence. Yet our current systems for responding to violence are often fragmented. There are several factors that contribute to this fragmentation: animal protection, child protection, domestic violence, and other related services are at different points in their development; they have different mandates and philosophies; they use different professional terminology; and they typically see themselves as having different missions. Lack of attention to animal cruelty issues among professionals does not appear to be a result of rejection of its importance, but rather, of unfamiliarity with the evidence of an association with other violence or competition with other concerns.

A number of new initiatives across the United States, Great Britain, and Canada are providing a coordinated community response to violence that includes animal protection professionals as key players. The resources and expertise of each profession is increasingly being blended to ensure the safety of all family members affected by violence and to provide comprehensive services. Cross-training and cross-reporting initiatives are being developed in many communities. Cross-training of professionals in fields such as child protection, domestic violence, elder abuse, animal protection, education, and law enforcement about the violence connection allows us to overcome the barriers that have kept our responses to violence fragmented. It helps us define a common language and a common goal. In a violent household there are many victims. Cross-reporting enables us to share information about violent individuals so that we can identify and assist all members of the family, and track and monitor offenders. For example, an animal control officer investigating a case of animal cruelty enters a home to interview the family and sees a child who appears frightened and bruised. If the officer has been cross-trained she will know what to look for and whom to contact to report the suspected abuse.

Another popular program that is gaining attention was developed to address the needs of battered women with nonhuman companions. These programs, sometimes called "Safepet," "Safehaven," or emergency housing programs, provide temporary shelter for the nonhuman companions of women leaving a violent relationship. These programs are often cooperative ventures between the local animal shelter and battered women's shelter. Some include a broader network of veterinarians, foster homes, boarding kennels and stables, and farms. This service allows women to enter a safehouse and have the time to make permanent housing arrangements without worrying that her nonhuman companion will be neglected, injured, or killed by her partner.

A comprehensive program in Colorado Springs, Colorado called DVERT (Domestic Violence Enhanced Response Team) includes cross-training, cross-reporting, and emergency housing for nonhuman animals. DVERT is one of several models across the country developing truly coordinated community responses to violence. The members of the DVERT team include professionals from the local humane society, law enforcement, child protection, adult services, and domestic violence agency. Weekly meetings are held to discuss cases and share information and resources. The program is designed to identify high-risk cases and provide comprehensive services to all members of the family, human and nonhuman. In addition to the positive benefits for the families who receive services, it also benefits the agencies. Many of these agencies are working together for the first time. The benefits of the new partnerships go beyond the program and provide an important tool in the creation of a nonviolent society.

Role of the Religious Community in Addressing Violence

Forty percent of Americans attend church or synagogue. Worldwide there are an estimated 1.75 billion Christians, a third of the world's population. Conservationist Russell Train sees an invigorated church role as crucial to the survival of our civilization. He said "The church has the credibility and the historic mission of articulating and teaching values to society" (Regenstein 1991).

Organized religion has tremendous potential to shape people's behaviors and values. Yet it is important to note that a study at the Yale Forestry School found that the more often a person attended church or participated in religious services, the more likely she or he would feel negative or hostile toward the natural environment, and the less likely she or he would have a concern for nature. Dr. Stephen Kellert also found that those who were less involved in a formal worship had a greater concern for ecological values (Regenstein 1991).

Religious teachings can serve as either a roadblock or a resource in addressing violence and oppression. There are religious teachings that can be misused or distorted to suggest that violence and oppression is acceptable or even necessary. When these teachings or interpretations of teachings are misused, they become substantial roadblocks to ending violence.

Members of the religious community play a vital role in addressing violence. They must become better informed and more proactive. By assisting their community in identifying resources, by publicly and privately speaking out, members of the religious community can help victims and begin to change our cultural acceptance of violence and oppression. A proactive, informed religious community can serve as a powerful reminder that "the universe is composed of subjects to be communed with, not of objects to be exploited."

If the religious community is to stem the tide of negative sentiment toward the earth and all its inhabitants, a new shared vision must be developed—a vision that addresses not only environmental concerns but also the oppression and victimization of all vulnerable members of our world community, human and nonhuman. The Earth Charter Preamble says "we urgently need a shared vision of basic values to provide an ethical foundation for the emerging world community." This is a beginning, but we must recognize that the "shared vision" must truly be shared. It must include every living being; otherwise we run the risk of alienating those who would seek to improve the lot of oppressed humans. Until we come together, our efforts are doomed to failure, as the fragmentation prevents the unified voice needed to overcome centuries of vio-lence, oppression, and disconnectedness to our world.

The following excerpt from a sermon given by the Reverend James Morton in the Cathedral of St. John the Divine, New York City, on the Feast Day of St. Francis in 1986 provides a vision that would hold *all* life sacred, including women, children, and nonhuman animals.

We don't own animals, any more than we own trees or own mountains or seas, or indeed, each other. We don't own our wives or our husbands or our friends or our lovers. We respect and behold and we celebrate trees and mountains and seas and husbands and wives and lovers and children and friends and animals.

BIBLIOGRAPHY

Adams, Carol J. 1994. "Bringing Peace Home: A Feminist Philosophical Perspective on the Abuse of Women, Children, and Pet Animals." *Hypatia* 9, no. 2, p. 75.

———. 1995. "Women-battering and Harm to Animals." In Carol G. Adams and Josephine Donovan, eds. *Animals and Women: Feminist Theoretical Exploration.* Durham: Duke University Press.

Arluke, A., J. Levin, and C. Luke. 1997. *Cruelty to Animals and Other Crimes.* A study by the MSPCA and Northeastern University. Boston, Massachusetts.

Arkow, P. 2001. "Putting the 'Link' All Together: Ontario SPCA's Violence Prevention Initiative." *The Latham Letter,* Spring, pp. 16–17.

Ascione, F. R. 1995. "Domestic Violence and Cruelty to Animals." Paper presented at the 4th International Conference on Family Violence. Durham, N.C., July 24.

———. 1997. "The Abuse of Animals and Domestic Violence: A National Survey of Shelters for Women Who Are Battered." *Society and Animals.* 5, no. 3:205–18.

Chalk, R., and P. King, eds. 1998. *Violence in Fami-lies: Assessing Prevention and Treatment Programs.* Washington, DC: National Academy Press.

Costain, Lela, B. 1991. "Unraveling the Mary Ellen Legend: Origins of the Cruelty Movement." *Social Service Review.* June 1991, pp. 203–23.

Dalton, P. "When Did We Lose Sight of Boys?" *The Washington Post,* May 9, 1999.

De Montaigne, M. 1575, 1952. *Essays. Encyclopedia Britannica Great Books* 25:206. Chicago.

DeViney, E., J. Dickert, and R. Lockwood. 1983. "The Care of Pets Within Child Abusing Families." *International Journal for the Study of Animal Problems* 4, no. 4: 226–46.

Dobrin, A., B. Wiersema, C. Loftin, and D. Mc-Dowal. 1996. *Statistical Handbook on Violence in America.* Phoenix: Oryx Press.

Downes, D. 1982. "The Language of Violence: Sociological Perspectives on Adolescent Aggression." In P. March and A. Campbell, eds. *Aggression and Violence.* New York: St. Martin's, pp. 27–45.

Fox, J., and Zawitz, M. 1999. "Homicide Trends in the United States." *Bureau of Justice Statistics Crime Data Brief.*

Fox, M. 1989. *St. Francis of Assisi, Animals, and Nature*. Washington, D.C.: Center for Respect of Life and Environment.

Harlow, Caroline Wolf. 1991. "Female Victims of Violent Crime." *Bureau of Justice Statistics* 5.

Maine Coalition to End Domestic Violence. 2000. *Domestic Violence Crisis Advocates Training Manual*.

Nash, J. 1996. *The Meaning of Social Interaction*. Dix Hills, N.Y.: General Hall.

Regenstein, L. 1991. *Replenish the Earth*. New York: Crossroads.

Ressler, R.K., C.R. Burgess, J.E. Hartman, and A. McCormack, A. 1986. "Murderers Who Rape and Mutilate." *Journal of Interpersonal Violence*, pp. 273–87.

Rifkin, J. 1985. *Declaration of a Heretic*. London: Routledge and Kegan Paul.

Tingle, D., G. Barnard, L., Robbins, G., Newman, and D. Hutchinson. 1986. "Childhood and Adolescent Characteristics of Pedophiles and Rapists." *International Journal of Law and Psychiatry*. 9:103–16.

Animal Protection and the Problem of Religion

An Interview with Peter Singer

PETER SINGER

An interview with ethicist Peter Singer in 2004 by co-editor Paul Waldau of the Tufts School of Veterinary Medicine.

PAUL WALDAU: Your ground-breaking *Animal Liberation,* sometimes referred to as "the Bible" of the animal protection movement, includes in chapter 5 extensive observations and claims about the relationship of religion to attitudes toward nonhuman lives. Do you still hold substantially the same attitudes on the subject "religion and animals" that you held when you wrote that book in 1975?

PETER SINGER: Substantially, yes, but not in every detail. First, as I said in that chapter, I was writing for Western readers, and therefore focusing on the Jewish and Christian religious traditions. Now that the animal movement has spread to non-Western cultures, it would be better to include more discussion of non-Western religions. Moreover, within the Christian tradition, some animal advocates have pointed out

that there is more diversity than I had suggested in *Animal Liberation.* By focusing on Paul, Augustine, and Aquinas—whose views about animals are truly dismal—they thought, I had neglected figures more sympathetic to animals, like Basil and John Chrysostom. That's a reasonable point, for those seeking sources in their own tradition to use as a basis for a more favorable view toward animals. But in terms of the history of Christian attitudes and their impact upon Western attitudes to animals, the men that I focused on were far more influential than those who had more positive attitudes to animals.

PW: In your experience, is it true that many animal activists regard organized religion as an ideological opponent?

PS: I think that depends what country you are talking about. It's not true of the United States, in my experience. That may be because hostility to religion is rather rare in the United States, almost a taboo. On the other hand in, say, Italy, where "organized religion" basically means the Roman Catholic Church, and there is a long tradition of anticlericalism on the left, then yes, many animal activists do regard organized religion as an ideological opponent. In other countries, like Australia or Britain, where organized religion is relatively weak, I think people differentiate between different religions, seeing some as an obstacle to progress, and others as more helpful.

PW: Assuming for the sake of argument that religion in its mainline institutions and best-known forms has not been a friend of nonhuman animals, do you see that historical phenomenon as precluding the development of nonhuman-centered forms of the religions most familiar to Westerners—Christianity, Judaism, Islam? In other words, do you think "animal-friendly" subtraditions might be developed in these religions?

PS: Anything is possible, I suppose, but it would take a very dramatic change for any of those religions to cease to be human-centered. People within these religions are still struggling for equality for women, gays, and lesbians. If a religion won't accept women as equals, what chance is there that it will drop the idea that humans, and only humans, were made in the image of God, and have immortal souls? And unless those ideas are dropped, religions will still be saying that human beings are more significant than nonhuman animals, irrespective of the particular capacities or characteristics of the humans or the animals.

On the other hand, there is much positive work that could be done short of these religions ceasing to be human-centered. For example, a strong argument can be made within the Jewish tradition that animals reared in conditions that cause extensive suffering—as modern factory farming does—cannot be considered "kosher" and so should not be eaten by observant Jews. Christians too can argue—as Matt Scully does very powerfully in *Dominion*

—that there is a Christian duty of mercy to animals, which is violated by factory farming and by many other ways in which we routinely abuse them. No less a religious authority than Pope Benedict XVI has stated that human "dominion" over animals does not justify factory farming. When head of the Sacred Congregation for the Doctrine of the Faith, the future pope condemned the "industrial use of creatures, so that geese are fed in such a way as to produce as large a liver as possible, or hens live so packed together that they become just caricatures of birds." This "degrading of living creatures to a commodity" he said, was contrary to "the relationship of mutuality that comes across in the Bible." I'd like to see more Jews and Christians moving their religions in these directions.

PW: You have observed from time to time (for example, in your 1993 book *How are We to Live,* at 221) that some religions have been kinder to nonhuman animals than others. Do you think there is any role in the animal movement to be played by those religions commonly said to more "animal friendly" around the world?

PS: Definitely. The best book written about animals by a significant contemporary religious figure, to my knowledge, is Philip Kapleau's *To Cherish All Life.* Kapleau, a Zen roshi, makes a strong case that compassion for all sentient beings is at the core of Buddhist teachings, and that all Buddhists living in normal conditions in modern societies should follow a vegetarian diet. Buddhists, in particular, should therefore be playing an important role in the animal movement. I'd like to see Kapleau's position become more influential among Buddhists, and I'd like to see similar arguments developed within, say, the Hindu tradition.

PW: Can religion play a part in helping humanity develop a relationship with nonhuman animals that would meet your sense of ethics?

PS: Consistently with the answers I've given above, it is possible, but in many religions, it's an uphill task.

PW: Do you think that the present cultural crisis regarding nonhuman animals can be solved without the help of churches, synagogues, mosques, and other communities of faith?

PS: Yes, it certainly can be. Historically, at least in the West, many of the most important teachers who were advocates for animals —Plutarch, Montaigne, Hume, Bentham, Mill, Henry Salt, George Bernard Shaw—have been skeptical about religion. The same is largely true in recent times—Henry Spira, Ingrid Newkirk, and I can include myself as well. The organizations that have done most for animals have also been independent of religion. There are exceptions, but you couldn't say that communities of faith have been especially prominent in the modern animal movement.

PW: If we assume, again, for the sake of argument that religion could become a less harmful force regarding other living beings, how might it do so? Would you focus on attempts to turn the dominion concept from Genesis into a notion of stewardship or non-domination caretaking? Do you see any particular features of religion that might have animal protection and ecological implications?

PS: I'd focus on traditions of compassion and mercy. If properly understood, how can they exclude nonhuman animals? The idea of stewardship might be useful in some traditions, but it presupposes knowing what God would want us to do with his creation. I'm not sure how we would know that. Certainly the texts in Genesis are not very helpful. They portray God as drowning virtually every living thing on earth, just because humans had behaved badly. What kind of an example does that set?

PW: What is your view of animal activists' use of references to the Holocaust to illustrate features of contemporary treatment of nonhuman animals?

PS: That's a very tricky subject. The great Jewish writer Isaac Bashevis Singer pointed to some parallels between the Nazis' attitude to Jews and our contemporary human attitudes toward animals. We have power over them, we regard them as inferior, we kill them en masse, and most people prefer to avert their gaze from the details of how this killing takes place. But at the same time there are differences. As I've argued at length in other places (*Practical Ethics, Rethinking Life and Death, Writings on an Ethical Life*), there are sound, nonspeciesist reasons for thinking that it is much worse to kill a self-aware being, who wants to go on living, than to kill an animal who is not capable of having plans or long-term desires about the future. So it would be a mistake to go beyond the parallels I have described above, and equate the slaughter of animals with the Holocaust, or regard them as evil in exactly the same way.

NOTE

1. Joseph Ratzinger, *God and the World: Believing and Living in Our Time. A Conversation with Peter Seewald.* San Francisco: St. Ignatius Press, 2002, p. 78.

ANIMALS AND
GLOBAL STEWARDSHIP

Earth Charter Ethics and Animals

STEVEN ROCKEFELLER

The Earth Charter, a product of the 1990s global ethics movement, is receiving growing support internationally. The worldview expressed in the Earth Charter is in many respects a variation on the theme of Thomas Berry's statement that the universe is "a communion of subjects, not a collection of objects" (Berry and Swimme 1992; "Prologue," this volume). Consistent with this outlook, at the heart of the Earth Charter is an ethic of respect and care for Earth and all life. This essay explores how this document views animals and how its ethic of respect and care is applied to them. In the discussion of the various Earth Charter principles relevant to relations between people and animals, an effort is made to provide brief accounts of some of the debates that influenced the wording of these principles.

The mission of the Earth Charter initiative is to help establish a sound ethical foundation for the emerging global community. The document contains a declaration of fundamental principles for building a just, sustainable, and peaceful world. (For the text of the Earth

Charter and information about the Earth Charter Initiative, see the Earth Charter website, www.earthcharter.org.)

The Preamble introduces the principles "as a common standard by which the conduct of all individuals, organizations, businesses, governments, and transnational institutions is to be guided and assessed." The principles are divided into four parts:

    I. Respect and Care for the Community of Life
    II. Ecological Integrity
    III. Social and Economic Justice
    IV. Democracy, Nonviolence, and Peace

Each part has four main principles and many supporting principles. The inclusive ethical vision presented in the Earth Charter recognizes that the well-being of people and the integrity of Earth's ecological systems are interdependent.

The drafting of the Earth Charter was part of the unfinished business of the 1992 United

Nations Earth Summit held in Rio de Janeiro. In 1994, Maurice Strong, secretary general of the Rio Earth Summit, and Mikhail Gorbachev, president of Green Cross International, organized a worldwide civil society initiative to undertake the drafting of the Earth Charter. The Dutch government helped to launch the project and provided the initial financial support. A secretariat was established at the Earth Council in Costa Rica, and an Earth Charter Commission with representatives from all regions of the world was formed to oversee the project.

The creation of the Earth Charter involved the most open and participatory process ever undertaken in an effort to draft an international declaration. Thousands of individuals and hundreds of organizations from Africa, the Americas, Asia and the Pacific, Europe, and the Middle East became engaged in the process. Contributions from representatives of grass-roots communities and indigenous peoples and from experts in international law, science, philosophy, religion, and sustainable development helped to shape the document. Only ideas and principles that generated wide support remained in the evolving draft. The final text, which was approved by the Earth Charter Commission in March 2000, reflects a consensus on common goals and shared values taking form in the emerging global civil society.

A major objective of the Earth Charter is to promote a fundamental change in the attitudes toward nature that have been predominant in industrial-technological civilization, leading to a transformation in the way people interact with Earth's ecological systems, animals, and other nonhuman species. Humanity must, of course, use natural resources in order to survive and develop. However, the Earth Charter rejects the widespread modern view that the larger natural world is merely a collection of resources that exists to be exploited by human beings. It endeavors to inspire in all peoples commitment to a new ethic of respect and care for the community of life. The document seeks to promote this new ethic in a variety of ways.

First of all, the planets in our solar system all have names, and when the Earth Charter refers to our home planet, it spells its name, Earth, with a capital E, and without the definite article. The recommendation to use Earth rather than "the earth" came from an astrophysicist, and this proposal immediately received especially strong support from indigenous peoples. The astrophysicist pointed out that referring to the planet as Earth was common practice among scientists and that when his colleagues speak of "the earth," they are referring to dirt.[1]

The drafting committee accepted this recommendation because it came to realize that the language we use to refer to the planet influences the way we perceive the natural world and our attitudes toward other life forms. On the one hand, when "Earth" is employed, it tends to evoke the image, provided by the astronauts, of the planet floating in space—the image of an extraordinarily beautiful, fragile, living whole upon which we are utterly dependent and which deserves our respect, love, and care. On the other hand, talking and writing about "the earth" tends to objectify the planet in a problematical way. It reinforces old habits of thinking about culture and nature as radically separate and the planet as merely an object that can be taken for granted and one that has no purpose in being other than to provide living space, food, and materials for people. This anthropocentric attitude toward the planet extends to animals and plants as well as ecosystems. It is one major factor contributing to humanity's ongoing degradation of the environment. The Earth Charter has been written in the conviction that this way of thinking must be changed if humanity is to care wisely and compassionately for the greater community of life and achieve sustainable patterns of production, consumption, and reproduction.

In developing a worldview consistent with these concerns, the Earth Charter Preamble emphasizes the concept of global interdependence and the idea of a community of life. It affirms that "in the midst of a magnificent diversity of cultures and life forms we are one human family and one Earth community with a common destiny." The Earth community is the greater community of life on Earth together with the whole biosphere that sustains it. The concept of "one Earth community with a common destiny" involves the view that people are part of nature and all beings are interdependent. In addition, by using terms like "Earth community" and "the community of life" along with more scientific terms such as "biosphere" or "ecosystem," the Earth Charter indicates that being part of nature has moral implications. Just as membership in a human community entails moral obligations and duties in relation to its members, so human membership in the greater community of life involves responsibilities in relation to other species and the community as a whole. Other life forms are not just objects, mere means to human ends, but also subjects, ends-in-themselves. In this regard, the Preamble of the Earth Charter affirms that people have responsibilities "to" as well as "for" other species and the larger living world.

These ideas are brought sharply into focus in the first two principles of the Earth Charter:

1. Respect Earth and life in all its diversity.
2. Care for the community of life with understanding, compassion, and love.

These two principles provide a solid foundation on which to build the new global ethics. All the other principles in the Earth Charter follow from and clarify the meaning of Principles 1 and 2.[2]

Fundamental to humanity's moral consciousness is an attitude of respect. Respect involves recognition and appreciation. What is worthy of respect deserves moral consideration. People only feel morally responsible to and for what they respect. The Earth Charter challenges us to expand our moral awareness and to respect and value all life, including ourselves, other people, other cultures, animals and plants, and nature as a whole.

Before the wonder and awesome mystery of life, respect can become a reverence for life. Reverence may be defined as deep respect tinged with awe and a sense of the sacred. Religious traditions that view life as sacred, such as the Jain and Hindu traditions, often employ the language of reverence for life.[3] Albert Schweitzer's life and thought provide a compelling twentieth-century expression of reverence for life as the supreme ethical guideline (Schweitzer 1933, 1987). In a final summons to spiritual and ethical transformation and social action, the Earth Charter adopts this language: "Let ours be a time remembered for the awakening to a new reverence for life, the firm resolve to achieve sustainability, the quickening of the struggle for justice and peace, and the joyful celebration of life."

As stated in Earth Charter Principle 1.a, the principle of respect for all life is founded on a recognition "that all beings are interdependent and every form of life has value regardless of its worth to human beings." That affirmation is another way of asserting that nonhuman species are subjects, ends-in-themselves, and not just objects that exist only as a means to human ends. It is significant that Principle 1.a affirms this idea together with recognition of the interdependence of all beings. All life forms and all living beings are to be valued and respected both as interrelated members of the community of life and for themselves.

Some philosophers and some international law documents use the concept of the intrinsic value of all species to express the belief that all life forms warrant respect quite apart from whatever instrumental or utilitarian value they may or may not have from a human perspective. Early drafts of the Earth Charter did employ the concept of intrinsic value, asserting that "all beings are interdependent and have intrinsic value." However, alternative language was eventually adopted ("every form of life has value regardless of its worth to human beings"), primarily because many Buddhist philosophers object to the statement that all beings have intrinsic value.[4] They argue that it implies the existence of an independent, fixed self, which Buddhism denies. Buddhism does fully endorse the principle of respect for all life, and Buddhist philosophers find support for this principle primarily in the realization that all beings are interdependent. The emphasis on interdependence in Principle 1.a reflects the influence of Buddhism as well as contemporary physics, ecology, and new currents of thought like process philosophy.

Only when respect develops into a deep sense of caring for the other does the ethical life assume concrete form. Respect and care are both fundamental to the development of an ethically responsible human being and community. Caring involves a person's whole being—feeling, thought, and will. It springs from a sense of being related, and it involves respect, affection, and concern for the other. Caring means preventing harm and helping others. The practice of caring includes safeguarding, tending, nourishing, nurturing, and healing. Caring builds and sustains community.

The second principle of the Earth Charter affirms that everyone has a shared responsibility to care for the community of life as a whole—each individual according to his or her situation and capacity. This second principle also emphasizes that caring, if it is to be fully effective, requires "understanding, compassion, and love." Understanding in this context means knowledge, intelligence, wisdom. However, knowledge, by itself, lacks the power to motivate and generate action. There must also be compassion and love, two related virtues that are of central importance in the ethical teachings of the world's great religious traditions. An integration of the head and the heart, science and compassion, wisdom and love is the ideal.

The meaning of the Earth Charter ethic of care for animals and other nonhuman species is spelled out more fully in Principles 5 and 6 in Part II on Ecological Integrity and Principle 15 in Part IV on Democracy, Nonviolence, and Peace. However, it is important to understand that the Earth Charter contains only general ethical principles and strategic guidelines. It does not attempt to set forth all the practical implications of these principles or to identify the mechanisms and instruments required to implement them. This would require a very lengthy, complex document. Furthermore, this work is being undertaken by many organizations, governments, and UN agencies, and different cultures will develop their own distinct approaches.

Principle 5 calls for the preservation of the diversity of animal species and the habitat required to sustain this diversity. The principle is also concerned with biodiversity in general. It states: "Protect and restore the integrity of Earth's ecological systems, with special concern for biological diversity and the natural processes that sustain life." Principle 5 is followed by six supporting principles that identify major strategies for achieving this goal. The first of these supporting principles emphasizes the importance of making "environmental conservation and rehabilitation integral to all development initiatives." The other supporting principles address the need for viable nature and biosphere reserves, the recovery of endangered species, the control of nonnative species, and the environmentally responsible use of renewable and nonrenewable resources.

Principle 5 should be read together with all the other principles in Part II. Principle 6 is especially important. It combines in an innovative way the principle of prevention and the precautionary principle: "Prevent harm as the best method of environmental protection and when knowledge is limited, apply a precautionary approach." This is the basic ethical guideline that industry, business, and government, including the military, should use in order to maintain a healthy environment and protect biodiversity. Prevention of harm is always better than trying to clean up pollution, restore habitat, or reestablish an endangered species. Precaution is the way to ensure prevention. The six supporting principles that follow Principle 6 clarify its meaning.

a. Take action to avoid the possibility of serious or irreversible environmental harm even when scientific knowledge is incomplete or inconclusive.

b. Place the burden of proof on those who argue that a proposed activity will not cause significant harm, and make the responsible parties liable for environmental harm.

c. Ensure that decision making addresses the cumulative, long-term, indirect, long distance, and global consequences of human activities.

d. Prevent pollution of any part of the environment and allow no buildup of radioactive, toxic, or other hazardous substances.

e. Avoid military activities damaging to the environment.

A number of international law declarations and treaties, such as the World Charter for Nature (1982), the Convention on International Trade in Endangered Species (CITES) (1975), and the Convention on Biological Diversity (1992), call for the protection of biological diversity and express special concern for endangered species. These documents are primarily concerned about the preservation of species and not with the abuse and suffering of individual animals. This is the general orientation of international law that deals with animals. The CITES treaty does assert that states should endeavor "to minimize the risk of injury, damage to health or cruel treatment" of "any specimen of a species" covered by the treaty, but in this case the only individuals protected are those belonging to endangered species or others in a recognized special category.[5] Legislation in many nations, however, does make the cruel treatment and abuse of individual animals a punishable offense quite apart from whether they belong to an endangered species. The Earth Charter in Principle 15 seeks to make respect for individual living beings as well as all species part of the new global ethics.

Principle 15 states: "Treat all living beings with respect and consideration." It explicitly affirms that Principles 1 and 2 on respect and care

for the community of life apply to individual animals and to other individual living beings. This principle acknowledges that the individual animal as an individual has moral standing. The three supporting principles clarify the meaning of "respect and consideration" for animals:

a. Prevent cruelty to animals kept in human societies and protect them from suffering.

b. Protect wild animals from methods of hunting, trapping, and fishing that cause extreme, prolonged, or avoidable suffering.

c. Avoid or eliminate to the full extent possible the taking or destruction of non-targeted species.

These Earth Charter principles do not explicitly address practices like factory farming, the use of animals in experimental research, trade in wild animal species, and the exhibiting of animals in circuses and zoos. However, they set forth general ethical guidelines that can be helpful in the moral evaluation and legal regulation of such activities. The reference to "non-targeted species" in Principle 15.c refers, for example, to the huge quantity of fish that are considered useless by-catch and destroyed by the fishing industry, or to the fish and birds unintentionally killed by the use of some agricultural pesticides. Principle 15.c is concerned with both the suffering inflicted by procedures such as these and with the threat they pose to the survival of some species.

The drafting of Principle 15 involved a debate over its wording that took over two years to resolve. In early drafts the principle was worded to read: "Treat all living beings with compassion and protect them from cruelty and wanton destruction." The Inuit, who live in the circumpolar North and are largely dependent on hunting for their food, opposed inclusion of the word "compassion" in this principle and asserted they could not support the Earth Charter if it were not deleted. They maintained that one can and should hunt with respect for animals, but one cannot hunt with compassion for them. One

Inuit leader asked the drafting committee: "Do you know what is involved in killing a whale?" Some tribal groups in sub-Saharan Africa agreed with the Inuit, but other indigenous peoples, including some North American Indians, argued that one can hunt with compassion. The principle of treating all living beings with compassion was strongly supported by Jains, Hindus, and Buddhists as well as animal rights groups and others. However, some Jains and Hindus objected to the language about protecting living beings from "wanton destruction," because they argued this implied that other forms of destruction were acceptable. This contradicted their understanding of reverence for life.

Over time common ground was found. The breakthrough came when it was proposed that the word "compassion" be moved to Principle 2 on caring for the community of life. The Jains, Hindus, and Buddhists and groups like the Humane Society supported this change, because it gives the principle of compassion a more prominent place in the Earth Charter and applies it to the community of life as a whole, including the human family. The general guideline of caring for the community of life with compassion was acceptable to the Inuit. All parties also agreed to a rewording of the principle in question along the lines proposed by the Inuit. They recommended that it read: "Treat all living beings with respect." The Inuit also agreed to the addition of the word "consideration," which strengthens the principle and which can be understood to mean moral consideration. The reference to "wanton destruction" was deleted. All participants in this lengthy negotiation expressed their satisfaction with the outcome, and the Inuit were among the first to endorse the Earth Charter and to translate it into their own language.

Another debate over the wording in Principle 15 involved Christian groups, who strongly recommended that the Earth Charter include an explicit reference to the Creator and refer to "creatures" rather than "living beings" because this would imply a Creator. Because Buddhists do not believe in a Creator and do not use God-language, and because such language is controversial among other groups as well, the Earth Charter could not adopt this approach. The Earth Charter Preamble does, however, make a reference to "reverence for the mystery of being," and "the mystery of being" can be given a theological as well as a naturalistic interpretation. In addition to the possible philosophical controversy that the word "creature" might engender, there was another reason why "living beings" rather than "creatures" is used in Principle 15. The term "living beings" is widely used in Eastern traditions, and it is also readily understandable in a Western context, and there was a concern to draw on the traditions of many regions in the process of finding common language.

Some representatives of the animal rights movement and those concerned with the humane treatment of animals wanted rights language used in Principle 15 and additional supporting principles. The Earth Charter Commission made the decision not to use language about the rights of nature and animal rights in the Earth Charter, because there is no international consensus on the matter and the Commission was concerned that the use of rights language would mire the Earth Charter in an unproductive controversy. However, it is important to recognize that the Earth Charter does affirm the ethical principle upon which the use of rights language with regard to animals is based. It affirms that all animals are worthy of respect and warrant moral consideration. This is the most critical issue involved in changing human attitudes and behavior in relation to animals. Furthermore, the principles of the Earth Charter can be used to provide support for the concept of animal rights as one of several ways of articulating what humanity's moral responsibilities are with regard to animals. Rights language is especially useful in legal and judicial contexts.

One example of how some groups would have liked to expand Principle 15 and its supporting principles was a proposal to include a principle on animal experimentation. It had considerable support, and at one point the following principle was included in a draft of the Earth Charter: "Limit animal experimentation to research required to meet basic human needs and to situations where alternative forms of research are not possible." Very strong objections from representatives from India with ties to Hinduism and Gandhi led to deletion of the principle. They opposed any principle suggesting that animal experimentation in any form is morally acceptable. Representatives from China pointed out that a principle on animal experimentation is very much needed in their country and in other developing nations where animal experimentation is beginning to expand in a significant way. In support of this view, others pointed out that the proposed principle recognized the reality of animal experimentation and would do far more good than harm. However, those opposed to the draft principle felt they could not support the Earth Charter if it remained in the text. Even though the Earth Charter does not explicitly refer to animal experimentation, Principles 15 and 15.a do make clear that there are significant moral constraints on how animals may be used in medical and other research programs.

It is significant that Principle 15 on respect for all living beings appears within the framework of a section of the Earth Charter principles entitled "Democracy, Nonviolence, and Peace." One can interpret this placement as implying that treating animals with respect and consideration means ensuring that their voice is heard in the councils of government. Representatives of the interests of the larger community of life should be included in decision-making processes that have significant consequences for the well-being of other species, especially animals. This is part of the meaning of democracy in an era of sustainable living and environmental ethics. In addition, one aspect of the task of building a culture of nonviolence and peace involves promoting respect for animals and stopping their cruel treatment and abuse by humans. The animals with whom we share this planet

deserve no less. In addition, it has long been recognized that insensitivity to the suffering of animals and toleration of their cruel treatment breeds a callousness that easily leads to indifference to human suffering and to the cruel treatment of human beings. Peace on Earth will not be realized if humanity fails to establish just relations with other species.

The Earth Charter recognizes that education, and especially the education of children, is fundamental to social transformation. Education is the focus of Principle 14: "Integrate into formal education and life-long learning the knowledge, values, and skills needed for a sustainable way of life." The educational programs envisioned in this principle include teaching the knowledge, values, and skills required to implement an ethic of respect and care for individual animals and animal biological diversity. Principle 14.b highlights "the importance of moral and spiritual education," recognizing the critical role that the religions among others can play in shaping attitudes and values. The Earth Charter identifies several widely shared spiritual values that can deepen commitment to an ethic of respect and care. More specifically, in addition to reverence for the mystery of being and reverence for life, the Preamble mentions a sense of belonging to the universe, gratitude for the gift of life, humility regarding the human place in nature, a realization "that when basic needs have been met, human development is primarily about being more, not having more," and the spirit of human solidarity and kinship with all life.

The Earth Charter has been constructed as an inclusive and integrated ethical framework, and the Preamble asserts that all its principles are interdependent. It is important for those concerned with the ethical treatment of animals and other species to recognize that realization of their agenda of justice for animals is interconnected with the realization of other Earth Charter goals, including the eradication of poverty, economic justice for all, human rights, gender equality, and democracy. As noted above, it is also critical to recognize that peace and justice among people will not be fully realized as long as society persists in abusing animals.

The articulation of the Earth Charter principles culminates with a vision of peace in Principle 16 and its six supporting principles. All the principles of the Earth Charter can be read as an endeavor to identify the fundamental con-ditions of peace. The very last principle, 16.f, states: "Recognize that peace is the wholeness created by right relationships with oneself, other persons, other cultures, other life, Earth, and the larger whole of which all are a part." Right relations with animals are a fundamental aspect of the vision of sustainable living and of wholeness and peace set forth in the Earth Charter.

NOTES

1. Professor Eric Chaisson of Tufts University made this recommendation at an Earth Charter drafting committee meeting in 1997.

2. In addition to Principles 1 and 2, there are two other main principles in Part I of the Earth Charter. Part I includes Principle 3 on building just, participatory, sustainable, and peaceful societies, and Principle 4 on protecting Earth's bounty and beauty for future generations. Principles 3 and 4 elaborate the meaning of Principles 1 and 2, making it clear that the Earth Charter is concerned about the well-being of people, including future generations, within the framework of respect and care for the community of life. All four principles in Part I are very broad in scope, and their meaning is clarified by the principles that follow in Parts II, III, and IV.

3. For a further discussion of the ethical and spiritual meaning of reverence for life, see Steven C. Rockefeller, "The Wisdom of Reverence for Life," in Paul Brockelman and John Carroll, eds., *The Greening of Faith: God, the Environment and the Good Life* (New York: University Press of New England 1996), pp. 44–61.

4. The wording used in Principle 1.a is derived in part from the Preamble of the United Nations World Charter for Nature (1982), which states: "Every form of life is unique, warranting respect regardless of its worth to man, and, to accord other organisms such recognition, man must be guided by a moral code of action."

5. See, for example, Articles III, IV, and V in the Convention on International Trade in Endangered Species of Wild Fauna and Flora.

BIBLIOGRAPHY

Berry, Thomas and B. Swimme. 1992. *The Universe Story*. San Francisco: Harper.

Rockefeller, Steven. 1996. "The Wisdom of Reverence for Life." In P. Brockelman and J. Carroll, eds., *God, the Environment and the Good Life* New York: University Press of New England, pp. 44–61.

Schweitzer, Albert. 1933. *Out of My Life and Thought: An Autobiography*. Trans. C. T. Campion. New York: Holt, ch. 13 and Epilogue.

——. *The Philosophy of Civilization*. 1987. Trans. C. T. Campion. Buffalo, N.Y. Prometheus Books, pt. 2, Preface, chs. 6, 22–27.

Pushing Environmental Justice to a Natural Limit

PAUL WALDAU

The Chartists were mid-nineteenth-century English reformers who fought for the rights of all men. They fell silent when they were confronted with the fact that their campaign, allegedly based on equality, failed to include *women*.[1] As Cora Diamond notes, John Stuart Mill was one of the few who pointed out that the Chartists' silence on the larger issue reflected the possibility that they were not really concerned with equality, as they professed to be, but with a lesser vision.[2] Today it is easy to see that while from some vantage points the Chartists promoted an important set of reforms, from other vantage points what they sought actually perpetuated any number of vicious oppressions and exclusions.

Claiming that a broad, altogether appealing principle, such as equality, undergirds a narrower, exclusivist agenda is not, of course, uncommon. One finds it, for example, in political systems that the ruling elites profess to be "democratic" but which are, upon examination,

plagued by profound exclusions and different levels of access to real power. Appealing to language that masks an underlying exclusion is also a common feature of propaganda emanating from overtly dictatorial and fascist political systems. In fact, such an appeal is characteristic of claims to represent "the people," as the Chartists misleadingly claimed, when, in reality, what is represented is but a favored minority among a larger human populace.

For the purpose of pushing the positive, affirming notion of "environmental justice" to its fullest and, as it were, most natural limit, query whether this kind of problem—broad claims masking a narrower agenda—exists in contemporary calls for "environmental justice." The following paragraphs examine the important additional notion of "environmental racism" in order to raise both this query and this volume's general themes, but the same general ideas could be advanced using thematically similar, though far less common, terms like "environmental classism," "environmental sexism," or even "environmental ageism."

The Extraordinary Problem of Environmental Racism

Environmental racism is a distinct component of modern societies and a vicious phenomenon that affects the lives of many humans. A common theme used to illustrate the nature of the problem is the siting of a disproportionate percentage of waste sites in communities of color whose inhabitants have little political power to oppose such decisions. Since factors of skin color or ethnic identity, integrally related to the political marginalization of the affected group, have nothing to do with the ability of the affected humans to tolerate the debilitating effects of nearby environmentally sensitive waste sites, the term "environmental racism" works well as a description of this widespread phenomenon.

There are grounds other than *explicit* racism, of course, for this kind of oppression. Sometimes it is argued that there is a *rational* basis, and even one dictated by economic theory, for locating waste sites or other economically and personally harmful industries in poor areas. For example, Lawrence Summers, recently past president of Harvard University but at the time chief economist of the World Bank, argued in 1991 that a rigorously applied cost-benefit analysis suggests that it is more rational for a society to locate certain practices and industries among the poorest people because doing so creates the lowest "cost" by some theoretical measures.[3]

The term "environmental racism" continues to work well even when it includes certain practices that are promoted by those who do not explicitly advocate racism but who nonetheless promote effects that are indistinguishable from those who do. The term, even when it is employed in this broad sense, turns out to be a helpful tool for describing ways in which the politically and economically dominant elites of a pluralistic society cause their own waste to "disappear" into adversely affected communities.[4]

Dividing the Labor

It is not uncommon to find scholars or activists who use terms such as "environmental justice" or "global justice" either as a synonym for "environmental racism" or in a manner that connects the two closely. One prominent example connecting environmental racism closely with global justice is the title of one of the leading essay collections, *Faces of Environmental Racism: Confronting Issues of Global Justice*. One can also see the obvious connections of the terms "environmental racism" and "environmental justice" in the titles of Robert Bullard's works:

> *Dumping in Dixie: Race, Class, and Environmental Quality*[5]
> *Confronting Environmental Racism: Voices From the Grassroots*[6]
> "Race and environmental justice in the United States"[7]
> *Unequal Protection: Environmental Justice and Communities of Color*[8]

The themes treated throughout this volume suggests that there will be a valuable insight available if we distinguish the work that can be done by the term "environmental racism," which is, of course, a negative and value-laden description of an important phenomenon, from broader uses of the terms "environmental justice" and "global justice." The latter terms are, to be sure, representative of altogether positive ideals, and they share the justice-orientation of the environmental racism critique. But a division of labor, based on a number of important conceptual and ethical distinctions made in this volume, would result in terms like "environmental racism" doing clearly different work than that allocated to terms like "environmental justice" and "global justice." Indeed, there will be serious problems and confusions if these two groups of terms are not carefully distinguished at important junctures.

Work in the budding field of "Religion and Animals" helps make it clear that the underlying concepts of these related groups of terms are, so to speak, not identical twins—the positive, constructive features of "environmental justice" and "global justice" make them paradigmatic notions that have extraordinary range, while the negative, condemnatory features of "environmental racism" make it ideally suited to the vitally important task of describing a world plagued by racism and other oppressions advanced by some humans. To be sure, "environmental racism" can also be described as "paradigmatic" in some contexts, for two major reasons—race bias continues to have pernicious effects in modern societies, and the moral insights driving critiques of environmental racism are truly foundational.

Yet the underlying problems addressed by the term "environmental racism" give the term negative, descriptive functions that are radically different from the paradigmatic work being done by the broader notions of "environmental justice" and "global justice." The latter include a wide range of problems and ideals, such as those that drive critiques of environmental sexism, environmental classism, and environmental ageism, *as well as,* this essay argues, some of the central problems driving inquiries about religion and animals.

The relationship of the terms "environmental racism" and "environmental justice," then, is best understood as that of species and genus. In other words, "environmental racism" (or other terms geared to describe any of the many "human versus human" problems manifested in environmentally sensitive ways) is most helpfully understood as one important species of the much larger "environmental justice" genus or category. In effect, the term "environmental racism" and its powerful critique comprise an individual member of the multifaceted vision that is "environmental/global justice."

The problems that the environmental racism critique has identified are, of course, negative in nature, but the critique either implicitly or explicitly calls upon the positive ideal of choosing a world that refuses to indulge in the harmful, race-based discriminations that comprise the injustices created by environmental racism. As will be suggested below, those who condemn environmentally racist decisions have not always called upon the entire range of broad ideals found in the environmental justice genus. In fact, ideals driving calls for "environmental justice" or "global justice" are, upon close examination, diverse in some interesting ways. They include not only a world free of injustices based on race, but also the concerns for women, the elderly, and marginalized socioeconomic classes that inform, respectively, environmental sexism, environmental ageism, and environmental classism—the latter reflect important insights that may not be reflected in environmental racism analyses. Most pertinent to this volume's themes, the ideals motivating calls for "environmental justice" can also include important *nonhuman* interests—for example, the range of issues raised by this volume is sufficiently diverse to make it clear that "environmental justice" fairly describes not only the set of issues driving criticisms of discriminations based on race, sex, age or class, but also commitments to go beyond human groups alone when developing notions of justice.

As set out below, the ideal that is most commonly expressed in environmental racism critiques is that *all humans matter.* This is the same ideal that drives the sex, age, class critiques as well, for there is no doubt whatsoever that race, sex, age, and class are completely irrelevant to forcing negative environmental consequences upon living beings.

Concerns to protect all humans can be expressed in many ways, though. There are, for example, calls for humans' protection expressed in inclusivist terms along the lines of Berry's insight that "we cannot be truly ourselves in any adequate manner without all our companion beings throughout the earth." The insight suggests that effective protection of humans' fullest selves and possibilities will naturally include protection of nonhumans as well.

In contrast to this inclusivist approach, there are far more exclusivist approaches that invoke environmental notions. These are not uncommon, and they include, for example, approaches characterized by a radical human-centeredness that excludes all nonhuman animals. These remain prevalent today, and some have been so pernicious in their effects that they have generated the debate over "speciesism."[9] As this volume attests over and over again, there are other ideals, other visions grounded in concerns for those who are not members of the human species. Historically, these have motivated any number of humans to challenge justice problems that are both environmental and global. As a conceptual matter, concerns for nonhuman issues can sit as squarely in the center of environmental justice critiques as can concerns for oppressed humans. The genus "environmental justice," then, need not be exclusively human-centered, although some of the species within the genus could well be (and, of course, historically have been and presently are).

This broad, inclusivist claim for the meaning of "environmental justice" will seem odd, even alienating, to some ears because of the long history of human-centeredness in the Western intellectual and ethical traditions. Indeed, the dominance of ethical anthropocentrism in philosophical, theological, and ecological thinking has been so extreme that one might characterize much that has passed as "environmentalism" as, instead, environmental speciesism.

Note that the ideals of the environmental justice genus are, in a manner of speaking, a compass point toward which we travel as we aspire to a more just world. If, as Berry suggests, "the larger community constitutes our greater self," then it is clear that justice-based concerns can reach beyond the species line.[10] This can be argued in several ways—we might frame, for example, an ethical argument that we

and other, nonhuman lives are so integrally related and interconnected that "justice denied" a nonhuman group is tantamount to justice denied for our human group. More radically, we might treat some nonhumans as equals who are entitled to the important protections of "just" laws.[11] Alternatively, using more human-centered criteria and concentrating solely on our children, we might identify an injustice to our heirs whenever our actions today demonstrably harm other animals in their habitats and thereby unjustly impoverish the ecological integrity or biodiversity of our children's future world.

Such considerations suggest that the category "environmental justice" cannot be automatically equated with concerns that are solely human-centered. Rather, the category has a truly broad, life-affirming genius that can orient us to both humans and nonhumans—it can readily focus on concerns ranging from individuals to the entire Earth.

The many voices in this volume make it clear that countless humans have imagined, and then engaged, such broad possibilities of "justice." In myriad ways, many humans have already acted on notions like "fairness," "dignity," "seeing honestly," and "compassion"—all of which are components of any conception of justice—when dealing with multiple species and even ecosystems as well.

There are some significant benefits if the work that narrower terms like "environmental racism" are asked to do is explicitly differentiated from the work that other, broader terms like "environmental justice" are asked to do. Special negative descriptions like "environmental racism" (or, again, some term for another form of intrahuman discrimination, such as "environmental classism" or "environmental sexism") work best for acts that have racist effects (or, again, classist, sexist, etc., effects). Importantly, these are so significant that they need careful description if we are to rectify the important injustices they describe.

Further, cautious and sensitive employment of the most applicable terms preserves the possibility of seeing the actual agenda that is driving any particular analysis—is the advocate concerned with race alone, with sex and gender solely, with nonhuman animals primarily, or with all living beings? Identifying the agenda will allow, in turn, the specifics of the oppression to be seen clearly and in detail. Thus, use of terms like "environmental racism" in the conservative manner here proposed—that is, as a primary tool describing intrahuman exclusions along the lines of race, etc.—maintains the possibility of identifying as fully as possible the precise form of injustice that animates our ethical concerns.

With an appropriate division of labor among terms that reveal different justice concerns— "environmental racism" being allocated the important role of describing racist effects of many environmentally charged decisions made within our human community, and "environmental justice" being allocated the larger role of identifying the ideals that help us critique environmental racism and other problems—we thus discern important differences and avoid debilitating confusions that arise when terms such as "environmental justice" are used in ways that mask some of the complicated problems, such as radical human-centeredness, addressed by this volume. In the end, taking care to use these words and concepts with specific purpose will foster our ability to identify distinctly varied motivations and actions that impact our ability to create a truly just world. If our species can achieve that, then perhaps it can say, with Meister Eckhart, "the person who understands what I say about justice understands everything I have to say."[12]

Engaging Narrow Species of
"Environmental Justice"

Consider some of the simplest, often invisible assumptions that provide background for many current demands for "justice." Following the Stoics, who suggested that the only beings to which we owe justice are the members of our human society because only they can speak (thereby eliminating nonhuman animals from our moral circle), the Western intellectual tradition has increasingly assumed that the precious commodity "justice" is *obviously* not relevant to nonhuman animals.[13] As a result, demands for justice within the Western intellectual tradition have characteristically gone forward on a speciesist platform, although this has rarely been noticed in the Western ethical tradition because of the distinct anthropocentric bias of its moral philosophies.[14]

This bias of the best-known analyses of justice is noticeable, however, if we move outside the mainstream of the Western philosophical and theological traditions. If we measure calls for "justice" by a criterion drawn from certain non-Western societies or from any of dozens of non-mainline thinkers in the occidental tradition, such as St. Francis of Assisi, the traditional emphasis of westernized ethics on universalism *among humans alone* no longer has the decidedly inclusive cast such "universalism" seems to have when the only measuring stick is the Western intellectual tradition's mainline political and moral philosophies. Consider, for example, the analysis suggested by the theologian James Cone, a landmark in Western societies where racism has been an integral part of the cultural tradition. Cone opposed racism in Christian churches by referring to any minister who backs racism as "inhuman. He is an animal. ... We need men who refuse to be animals and are resolved to pay the price, so that all men can be something more than animals."[15]

Cone's analysis was directed to contexts where racism had long reigned as an extraordinarily vicious problem. But if Cone's specific language here is measured by some non-Western standards, such as the ethical assumptions of the Indian subcontinent or those implicit in many indigenous peoples' cosmologies, his approach of deriding nonhuman animals might seem altogether shrill. This isn't because Cone has no point to make, for his overall analysis is a powerful, even a landmark, indictment of the Christian establishment's racism. But his powerful point about the exclusion of black humans relies on another exclusion (and an indictment), namely, that of nonhuman animals.

Helpful insights about how repudiation of one oppression can implicitly advance other oppressions come from some feminists' observation of other feminists' arguments:

Metaphoric comparisons to treatment of animals—that a violent man treats a woman like a dog, or pornography treats a woman like meat, etc.—actually validate the oppression of animals, implying that while these things should not be done to women, they *may* be done to animals.[16]

Historically, explicit and implicit disparagement of all other animals as a way of enhancing the status of all humans has been, unfortunately, a common occurrence.[17]

Arguments against racism and sexism can, however, go forward on a non-speciesist platform. Examples include certain indigenous-nation advocates' talk of nonhuman animals, or certain religious leaders' or scholars' assessment of what constitutes violence.[18] Similarly, environmental discussions generally, including those about "sustainable development," need not foreground human considerations *alone* when proposing how to measure an environmentally responsible lifestyle. The interests of nonhuman individuals or populations, and even those of entire ecosystems, can be, and in fact often have been, of concern to some human communities when assessing how they should solve the inevitable problems that arise because we live in a world populated by many different kinds of beings with competing interests.

There are, then, potentially serious problems that loom when we label narrowly drawn, human-centered interests as the only interests raising "justice" issues. Moreover, unconsciously equating highly anthropocentric notions with broad environmental concepts can

be highly insensitive to the views of other humans. It is form of cultural imperialism to equate the answer of the dominant European intellectual tradition, namely, human-centered ethics, to all humans' answer to the question "who are the others for whose benefit I will use my considerable ethical abilities?" The prevailing answer now found within the industrialized world's dominant institutions of law, business, politics, and religion has by no means been the answer of most peoples or cultures. To assume that *our modern answer,* dominated as it is by our cultural assumptions that "the others" we should care about are humans alone (and perhaps as well, these days, our "companion animals" though certainly not the tens of billions of food animals, wild animals, or research animals killed annually in industrialized societies of the twenty-first century), is to be needlessly insensitive to the many points of view expressed across time and place by other humans.

One can see a similar tension in Western societies' insistence on an extension of "rights" to previously marginalized indigenous peoples—these extensions are, of course, politically and functionally of the utmost importance, but vital protections have often been framed under a *humanocentric* formulation of what "rights" are (only human individuals *can* have rights because they are the only animals that *really* matter as individuals). Such a framing of this otherwise laudable development has often ignored the *non-humanocentric values* of marginalized humans.

In the end, any use of broad-sounding terms for inherently narrow and human-centered concerns is precisely the hypocrisy we easily recognize in the Chartists' claim to speak for "the people" and for "equality" even as they excluded women. But hypocrisy is inevitable if we treat an overtly speciesist resolution of an environmental problem as the heart and soul of *all* "environmental justice." Intrahuman problems are desperate for solutions, to be sure, but that undeniable fact cannot alone justify a repudiation or dismissal of all nonhuman interests. Indeed, as suggested below, repudiations of one kind of interest, whether human or nonhuman, may simply condition us to accept more readily an unjust abridgment of other interests.

We have an important balance to strike, then —environmental racism has extremely important justice features that must be acknowledged at every turn, even as we refuse to convert that salient ethical insight into an exhaustive account of *all* dimensions of the idea of justice.

Environmental Speciesism?

It will, after this analysis, surprise no one that much environmental talk, and even talk about other species, is not talk about nonhuman animals, even if they are sometimes mentioned in such discourse. Suppose, for example, that in the debates occurring in the council chambers of a rich suburban municipality we hear the question, "What kind of a world are we going to leave for our children?" In such a scenario, it can be obvious that talk about the extinction of species and biodiversity amounts to, as it were, code words for a narrow, selfish, and potentially racist, classist, or otherwise exclusivist position. When elites in an exclusivist community ask, "What are we leaving for *our* children?," that can be altogether different from someone asking "What are we leaving for the *whole* human race?"

The insight that inclusivist-sounding language sometimes masks self-interest leads even further when assessing discussions about "the environment." Asking "What are we leaving for the whole human race?" can be, in light of Berry's insight that "the larger community constitutes our greater self," altogether different from asking "What is the right thing to do for the community of all living beings?" As implied above, the question "Are we sharing fairly with the marginalized humans in the world?," even though it has justice dimensions of the utmost importance, does not exhaust the entire range of questions and concerns that rely on the intu-

itions that lead humans to seek justice. For example, the concept of justice has recently been employed to ask about chimpanzees and bonobos (pygmy chimpanzees)[19] echoing the concerns of, among others, those ancient Greeks who disagreed with the Stoics that the "natural" extent of justice is the human community alone.[20] Modern instances of such questions are of a piece with the questions asked by many other humans around the earth for millennia.

The persistence of such inquiries across time and place raises the question of whether exclusivist, arguably speciesist formulations of what constitutes "justice" fail our human spirit in crucial respects. Framing our search for "justice" in ways that are responsive to all that we are and can be is, of course, an important task. Formulations of justice that do not countenance humans' ability to apply justice considerations beyond the human species risk the loss of a central human dimension. As the contributions to this volume reveal, reaching out to "others" beyond the human species line has been a recurring reality for many humans and cultures. The possibility of continuing to do so clearly begs many questions about the breadth and depth of humans' working out of our ethical natures.[21]

Shared Margins—Interlocking Oppressions

As noted above, when the practices of some individuals and groups in a society marginalize many kinds of living beings, there is a serious risk that thereby all individuals, human and nonhuman alike, will suffer greatly. Historically, it was work on behalf of marginalized humans that first brought to light the connection between the humans and nonhumans who have been marginalized by the established elite in the developed world. Historians of human/nonhuman relations now regularly describe the interrelatedness of these oppressions:

The obsession with ostentatious dominance and supremacy that characterizes post-Neolithic civilizations was not confined to their treatment of wilderness and other life forms. ... Throughout history, antipathy for wilderness, gratuitous cruelty to animals, and brutality toward people have walked hand in hand.[22]

If one considers some general features of the oppressed and marginalized in industrialized societies — namely, those out of power being subject to decisions of the humans who hold and use power over others — one sees that the tendency of humans to seek power over others is no respecter of species lines. In fact, framing the issue in this way permits one to understand the *interlocking* features of oppressions, whether the victims be human or not.

Interlocking oppressions come in many forms, but for the sake of understanding how they are interlocked, consider the nature of the following three major categories.

(1) As discussed in the essay "Interlocking Oppressions" by Kim Roberts in this volume, links in contemporary societies between the specific harms perpetrated against nonhuman individuals and those committed against human individuals have repeatedly been confirmed. Indeed, the correlations among child abuse, domestic violence, and abuse of nonhuman animals are such that the occurrence of one is often seen as a diagnostic tool for discovering the others in this tragic trio.[23]

(2) Cultural imperialism affecting both humans and nonhuman animals comes in many forms. The well-known examples of human/human imperialism in the Americas, Australia, Asia, and Africa are punctuated by many instances in which the dominated culture's access to the nonhuman world was limited by the imperialist culture. For example, just as access to resources and land by native Namibians in southwest Africa was limited by European colonizers, white settlers excluded the natives from hunting the very species that the white settlers had depleted through trophy hunting, land use, and trade development.[24]

(3) Modern production processes for food animals obviously disadvantage the nonhuman animals involved, but they also have extraordinarily debilitating effects on humans as well.[25] These effects include hunger that is, ironically, produced by an insatiable appetite for meat and milk, since a people relying on legumes and cereals for protein needs far less grain than a people eating creatures fed by these same plants. Countless tragic stories from North, South, and Central America and from Africa and Asia testify to the displacement of native peoples and the attendant environmental degradation resulting from promotion of large-scale cattle farming and the related marginalizing of classic pastoralists, who used traditional grazing systems closely adapted to varying environments.[26]

Speaking of Animals

A second, related historical development is recognition of the power of language or discourse traditions as shapers of worldviews. In the twentieth century, critical thinkers such as ethicists, theologians and philosophers emphasized that human abilities to comprehend our own oppressive behaviors are enhanced dramatically when we become more aware of the ways we talk about particular subjects. In general, how one is trained to speak about the world affects dramatically how one sees the world.

Several sources already cited document well that our ordinary discourse includes many ways of talking that still betray serious prejudices and unjustifiable assumptions. In large part, our ability to see these features of our language is the product of those liberation movements that challenged slavery, racism, and patriarchy by pushing us to speak more clearly about the exclusivist claims that we had inherited. Insensitive ways of viewing other living beings, backed by social values and deprecating language, remain integral parts of large institutions. Here, again, oppressions are interlocked, for greed, selfishness, caricature, and lack of sympathy worsen the oppression of whichever disfavored humans and nonhuman animals happen to be nearby.

In sum, not only is our ability to oppress non-discriminatory—that is, we can oppress any animal, human or otherwise—but the very exercise of power over others can desensitize and thereby exacerbate ignorance and myopia. The perpetrator, insensitive to one group, facilely oppresses other groups as well. The capacity for tyranny is increased by the very act of tyranny, just as the regular exercise of compassion develops character and virtue.

Note, then, how concerns for social justice and concerns for seeing other, nonhuman individuals dovetail. Identify one oppression, and you are likely to find others nearby. Social-justice movements, then, including those that identify and oppose the many forms of environmental racism and those that oppose other forms of environmental injustice perpetrated on humans, have much in common with the animal-protection movement. Both invoke a profound sense of humans' moral abilities when they oppose oppression in any of its myriad forms.

Ethics—Who Are the Others?

Consider that ethics can be helpfully framed as a set of questions that derive from this simple inquiry—*Who are the others?* This central question isn't always noticed in its simplicity because it is, upon examination, a complex of inquiries that usually receive silent answers within one's inherited cultural background. The question can be broken down into these fundamental inquiries.

The consequentialist's question: *Who are the others my actions affect?*

The philosopher's question: *Which of these others* can *I care about?*

The realist's question: *Which of these others* do *I care about?*

The moralist's question: *Which of these others* should *I care about?*

To these natural, basic inquiries, there have been many answers across human cultures. It is imperative that we acknowledge that the narrow, human-centered answer now dominating our educational institutions not be played out as either the only or the most common human answer. Educational institutions today in the matter of nonhumans are inclined to follow, rather than lead, other cultural authorities such as courts and legislatures, businesses, government, industrialized scientific research, and religious institutions.

To pretend that industrialized society's prevailing answer to "Who are the others?" has been the response of all people at all times would be both misleading and, as suggested above, a form of cultural imperialism foisted on the rest of the world because, across cultures and time, answers to these basic questions have always been, as this volume reveals, richly varied. Ranging from exclusivist egotism to inclusivist biophilia, answers to "Who are the others?" have been so personal and so obviously a part of humans' capabilities that, as a practical matter, the question is inevitably posed again and again as young humans develop into responsible moral agents.[27] The renewed interest within the industrialized West and East toward issues of animal protection is but one manifestation of a long-standing concern, which is also being manifested in the growing religion and ecology movement.[28] Hence, one should expect that today and tomorrow the question "Who are the others?" will constantly be posed anew.

Environmental Justice and the Study of Religion and Animals

Consider the relevance of "interlocking oppressions" to the issues discussed under the broad name "Religion and Animals," speaking carefully of other animals, the importance of affirming human moral abilities, and the relevance of ecological insights. Seeing the interlocked nature of oppressions, one learns that seeing one kind of oppression can help one see other kinds of oppression. In fact, it may be that the general phenomenon of oppression *cannot* be well seen, or at least well understood, *unless* one sees the wide range of oppressions that are practiced on marginalized individuals, human or not. If this is true, a broad understanding of the phenomenon of oppression will be needed in order to understand suffering well, and to oppose each form of oppression. This implies that those who are committed to the importance of applying humans' religious and ethical abilities beyond the human sphere, whether at the ecosystem level or for individual nonhuman animals on the basis of justice concerns, *must* see the relevance of social justice concerns to nonhuman animal and ecological issues.

Second, if one pays careful attention to one's own patterns of speech regarding (1) justice, (2) other humans, (3) one's own and surrounding communities, and (4) the unknown parts of the world, such self-consciousness, or self-archeology, as it were, will reveal a great deal about one's own (cultural or religious) tradition's images and claims about nonhuman animals, positive and negative. This kind of self-exploration helps immensely in seeing the shortcomings of traditional ways of speaking about other animals, including religious discourse that has often marginalized nonhuman animals.

Third, for the individual who wants to be a compassionate, moral being, considering the widest range of manifestations of oppression has some very distinct advantages which pertain to religious traditions' investments in humans' moral abilities. Without knowledge of a wide range of oppressions, each of us *cannot* achieve one of the hallmarks of all morality, namely, taking full responsibility for the consequences of our actions. This has relevance not only to social justice and opposing environmental racism (for it is only with an informed view of the relevant facts that one can oppose existing oppressions), but also to any of the broadest senses of environmental justice. One needs good information in order to know the consequences of one's acts. If one has been enjoined by one's own religious tradition to be compassionate, then one *must* know what effects one is creating by one's acts. Further, if one believes that creation is sacred because it was divinely created, then the effects of one's acts on the surrounding created entities is a *religious* matter.

Finally, if one advances the importance of ecological sensibilities to the religious life, then one must know the impacts one has on one's econiche or bioregion. Being responsible in this way requires *specific* knowledge, such as the impact of one's consumerism, a meat-based or plant-based diet, or patronizing of or investment in industrialized manufacturing processes. Such practices surely marginalize many kinds of living beings. Since other beings suffer in *their* world, one must understand something of the impacted animals' realities in order to know whether one has created consequences for *them* that are in violation of one's own ethical and religious principles. Engaging other living beings in *their* context is a fundamentally ecological enterprise, and the impacts of such an inquiry on human-centeredness are no doubt one of the reasons that ecology has been referred to as "the subversive science."[29]

Getting Beyond Our Own Limitations—Expanding the Circle

It has been said that one pattern across the history of human ethics is that of an expanding circle.[30] This has a certain appeal following the rise of one social justice movement after another in some countries, and it surely has distinct implications for going beyond the horizons of the views and values one inherits. The insights of the environmental racism critique, for example, provide insights into how we can bring marginalized humans as fully as possible into the moral circle.

Getting beyond our own heritage, including our own society's patterns of environmental discrimination against the politically and economically powerless, is an implication of Mill's challenge to the Chartists' hypocrisy—equality as a goal requires honesty about those who use prized words like "equality" but in fact have profoundly limited agendas. In retrospect, we can easily see that many movements that sought some form of liberation from an existing regime of oppression sought only a limited liberation for some humans. Seeking the cause of this phenomenon is no easy matter, and it is certainly beyond the scope of this essay. The most general cause of this may well be nothing less than the obvious fact that humans, as primates, have limited abilities and thus live finite lives in which they can accomplish only a few basic tasks.

To be sure, the image of an expanding circle suggests both that we can expect new possibilities *and* that we should be prepared to encounter some prejudices against and resistance to including those *not* now within our moral circle. The expanding circle image may also suggest the humbling reality that shortcomings in existing systems may be seen only incrementally and then dismantled only one or a few at a time. But it is possible to see that we can push the broad, powerful notion of environmental justice to a natural holism, as it were.

If we avoid uses of the term "environmental justice" that are radically anthropocentric, and thus in tension with both the "environmental" theme and the broader implications of the "justice" notion, we lose no prospects or opportunities to challenge all sorts of environmental discrimination, including the debilitating phenomena of environmental racism. We gain, from such careful use of ideas, the chance to see the entire range of oppressions much better. What is encouraging in this is that concerns for the oppression of environmental racism can, if handled in their broader context of the ideals of environmental justice, open minds to the breadth and depth of many other exclusions, including those beyond the species line.

Conclusion—Holistic Environmental Justice Today

It has been noted that, "Our understanding of the world is achieved more effectively by conceptual improvements than by the discovery of new facts, even though the two are not mutually exclusive."[31] Expanding our concerns beyond the human species, and even using the prized notion of "justice" in connection with larger, extra-human ecological realities (whether individual animals, particular populations, entire species, or whole groups of animals, ecosystems or the Earth itself) is an ancient concern of religious traditions that has close affinities with the best of the modern animal-protection and environmental movements. Elsewhere in this volume it has been suggested that particularly holistic ways of thought include ecofeminism,[32] deep ecologies, and various creationist and sacramental theologies.[33] Sensitive advocates from paradigmatic human liberation movements have also reached beyond the human species line to problems created by our treatment of nonhumans. From the black liberation movement come examples from Dick Gregory and Alice Walker, who work positively with a comparison between, on the one hand, the abuse of humans and, on the other hand, abuses of nonhuman animals.[34] Isaac Bashevis Singer used the sacred Holocaust image to illuminate his view of the human/nonhuman animal connection, stating that "in their behavior toward creatures all men were Nazis" and that "for the animals it is an eternal Treblinka."[35] These are controversial connections, viewed by some as demeaning the oppressed humans, and yet viewed by others as helpful, though obviously limited, analogies that increase our understanding of the horrific realities of different oppressions.

What can make any human/nonhuman comparisons seem "radical" or "irreligious" is the extraordinary emphases in industrialized cultures and their mainline religious institutions on *human-centered* notions of ethics, justice, and suffering. Yet the long history of religious and other ethical traditions reaching out to nonhumans and beyond remains a simple fact and a continuing resource for humans today when we address the breadth and depth of our own ethical natures.

For these reasons and for our posterity, it is respectfully suggested that we will see issues better if we reserve the term "environmental justice" for the broadest range of issues, including those not confined solely to the human species, and continue to employ the term "environmental racism" to describe race-based injustices arising out of our environmental decisions.

NOTES

1. Chartism, which flourished between 1838 and 1848, derived its name from "the People's Charter," a popular name for a legislative program submitted to Parliament in 1837 by the London Working Men's Association. The demands of the People's Charter included suffrage for all male citizens past their twenty-first birthday and elections by secret ballot.

2. Cora Diamond, "Eating Meat and Eating People," *Philosophy* 53 (1978): 465–79, at 466. This essay can also be found in her book entitled *The Realistic Spirit: Wittgenstein, Philosophy, and the Mind* (London: Bradford, 1991), pp. 319–34.

3. In Laura Westra, and Peter S. Wenz, eds., *Faces of Environmental Racism: Confronting Issues of Global Justice,* Studies in Social, Political, and Legal Philosophy (Lanham, MD: Rowman and Littlefield, 1995), Summers' reasoning is discussed in Westra's introduction, at page xvii, and by Segun Gbadegesin's "Multinational Corporations, Developed Nations, and Environmental Racism: Toxic Waste, Exploration, and Eco-Catastrophe," pp. 187–202, at 192; Peter Wenz's essay "Just Garbage," pp. 57–71, at 67, also addresses this kind of reasoning.

4. Howard McCurdy's "Africaville: Environmental Racism" in Westra and Wenz eds., pp. 75–92, addresses a Canadian community whose treatment exemplifies well some of these problems.

5. Boulder: Westview Press, 1990.

6. Boston,: South End Press, 1993.

7. *The Yale Journal of International Law,* 18, no. 1, (Winter 1993): 319–35.

8. San Francisco: Sierra Club, 1994.

9. The history and logic of the term, as well as many other terms meant to provide a similar critique, are set out in Paul Waldau, *The Specter of Speciesism: Buddhist and Christian Views of Animals* (New York: Oxford University Press, 2001).

10. Richard Sorabji in his *Animal Minds and Human Morals: The Origins of the Western Debate* (Ithaca: Cornell University Press, 1993) lists many in the ancient Greek and Roman worlds who proposed that notions of justice could be extended to nonhuman animals. Examples of specific changes can be found in the transcript of the 2002 symposium at Harvard Law School entitled "The Evolving Legal Status of Chimpanzees," *Animal Law* 9 (2003): 1–95. More generalized considerations both from legal and nonlegal scholars can be found in Cass R. Sunstein and Martha Nussbaum, eds., *Animal Rights: Current Debates and New Directions* (New York: Oxford University Press, 2004).

11. Although this suggestion will, against the backdrop of much modern jurisprudential thought, seem heretical to some, more than seventy law schools in the United States, including those of Harvard and Yale, now include an "animal law" component in their curriculum. Many relevant de-

velopments in this history are described in Steven W. Wise, *Rattling the Cage: Toward Legal Rights for Animals* (Cambridge, MA: Merloyd Lawrence/ Perseus, 2000) and Paul Waldau and Sarah Whitman, "The Animal Invitation," *Global Dialogue* 4, no. 1 (Spring 2002): 125–37.

12. Matthew Fox, *Creation Spirituality: Liberating Gifts for the Peoples of the Earth* (San Francisco: HarperCollins, 1991), p. 102.

13. The early debates are described well by Sorabji, *Animal Minds and Human Morals*. Sorabji summarizes, "According to the Stoics, justice depends on a process (*oikeiôsis*) of extending fellow feeling, a process which can naturally reach only as far as beings who are rational like ourselves" (p. 8). Sorabji also notes that "The Aristotelian and Stoic denial of rationality to animals proved all too congenial to Jews and Christians" (p. 8). Sorabji later argues (at pp. 130ff.) that Augustine played a critical role in making this denial the established position of the Western intellectual tradition.

14. The issue has not been denied altogether, even if routinely ignored—for example, John Rawls returned three different times in his seminal *Theory of Justice* to the notion that some senses of "justice" can reasonably be extended to other animals. See John Rawls, *A Theory of Justice* (New York: Oxford University Press, 1972), pp. 17, 504, and 512.

15. James H. Cone, *Black Theology and Black Power* (New York: Seabury Press, 1980), p. 80.

16. Susanne Kappeler, "Speciesism, Racism, Nationalism ... or the Power of Scientific Subjectivity," in Carol J. Adams and Josephine Donovan, eds., *Animals and Women: Feminist Theoretical Explorations* (Durham: Duke University Press, 1995), pp. 320–52, at 320. For examples and a summary of this argument, see Adams and Donovan, "Introduction," pp. 1–8, and Joan Dunayer, "Sexist Words, Speciesist Roots," pp. 11–31, 19.

17. This argument is made about both early Buddhist and Christian sources in Waldau, *The Specter of Speciesism*.

18. On the first point, consider the way Thom White Wolf Fassett talks about nonhuman animals in "Where Do We Go From Here?," in Jace Weaver, ed., *Defending Mother Earth: Native American Perspectives on Environmental Justice* (Maryknoll, New York: Orbis, 1996), pp. 177–91. On the second point, consider the differences about what constitutes "violence" between, on the one hand, the mainline Abrahamic traditions and, on the other, the Indian subcontinent's religious traditions. The latter consider violence against nonhuman animals a far more central part of religious ethics than do the former—see the following three articles discussing these differences: "On Breadth and Exclusion in Concepts of Nonviolence," *Philosophy East and West* 50, no. 3 (July 2000); "The Question of Nonviolence in Hinduism and Other Traditions," *International Journal of Hindu Studies,* 1999 (at www.clas.ufl.edu/users/gthursby/ijhs/); "On Peace and the Extent of Community," *The Journal of Buddhist Ethics* 6 (1999): 223–27.

19. Wise, *Rattling the Cage*.

20. Sorabji, in *Animal Minds and Human Morals* provides the details of the Stoics' many opponents on this point.

21. Relevant to the expressions of concerns for other animals, though not necessarily the Earth generally, is the biophilia hypothesis proposed by E. O. Wilson, *Biophilia* (Cambridge: Harvard University Press, 1984).

22. James Serpell, *In the Company of Animals: A Study in Human-Animal Relationships* (Cambridge: Cambridge University Press, 1996), pp. 225–26.

23. One detailed collection of papers dealing with this disturbing, complex phenomenon is Frank R. Ascione and Phil Arkow, eds., *Child Abuse, Domestic Violence, and Animal Abuse: Linking the Circles of Compassion for Prevention and Intervention* (West Lafayette, Indiana: Purdue University Press, 1999). See also, Randall Lockwood and Frank R. Ascione, Frank R., eds., *Cruelty to Animals and Interpersonal Violence: Readings in Research and Application* (West Lafayette, Indiana: Purdue University Press, 1998).

24. See, J. S. Adams and T. O. McShane, *The Myth of Wild Africa* (New York: Norton, 1992), and J. M. MacKenzie, *The Empire of Nature: Hunting, Conservation and British Imperialism* (Manchester, U.K: Manchester University Press, 1988).

25. One of the best known studies is Gail Eisnitz, *Slaughterhouse: The Shocking Story of Greed, Neglect, and Inhumane Treatment Inside the U.S. Meat Industry* (Amherst, New York: Prometheus Books, 1998). Consider also the important problem of the environmental effects of factory farming—see, for example, Richard P. Horwitz, *Hog Ties: Pigs, Manure, and Mortality in American Culture* (New York: St. Martin's Press, 1998).

26. For example, Jeremy Rifkin, *Beyond Beef: The Rise and Fall of the Cattle Culture* (New York: Dutton, 1992).

27. Much new work has been done on children's interation with nonhumans—see, for example, Gail F. Melson, *Why the Wild Things Are: Animals in the Lives of Children* (Cambridge: Harvard University Press, 2001).

28. Details are at the website of the Forum on Religion and Ecology—http://environment.harvard .edu/religion/.

29. This is Paul Sears' comment, the history of which is set out in Donald Worster, *Nature's Economy: A History of Ecological Ideas,* 2nd ed. (Cambridge: Cambridge University Press, 1994), p. 23.

30. This is the theme of William Edward Hartpole Lecky's oft-revised *History of European Morals: From Augustus to Charlemagne,* 2 vols. (London: Longman's Green, 1869), and Peter Singer, *The Expanding Circle: Ethics and Sociobiology* (Oxford: Clarendon, 1981).

31. Enst Mayr, *The Growth of Biological Thought: Diversity, Evolution, and Inheritance* (Cambridge: Belknap Press of Harvard University Press, 1982), p. 23.

32. See, for example, Greta Claire Gaard, ed., *Ecofeminism: Women, Animals, Nature* (Philadelphia: Temple University Press, 1993).

33. See, for example, Andrew Linzey, *Animal Theology* (Urbana and Chicago: University of Illinois Press, 1994); John Habgood, "A Sacramental Approach to Environmental Issues," in Charles Birch, William Eakin, Jay B. McDaniel, eds., *Liberating Life: Contemporary Approaches to Ecological Theology* (Markyknoll, New York: Orbis Books, 1990), pp. 46–53, and ecological visions out of the Indian subcontinent's religious traditions.

34. Cited in Mark Gold, *Animal Rights: Extending the Circle of Compassion* (Oxford: Jon Carpenter, 1995), p. 26.

35. Ibid, pp. 25–26. Footnote 9 indicates that the first cite is from *Enemies, A Love Story,* and Footnote 10 indicates that the second cite is from *The Letter Writer,* in *The Séance and Other Stories.*

CONCLUSION

A Communion of Subjects and a Multiplicity of Intelligences

MARY EVELYN TUCKER

Thomas Berry has observed that there are three key principles that have shaped the evolutionary process of the universe, namely, differentiation, subjectivity, and communion. By differentiation he suggests that from the primordial flaring forth of the universe differentiated particles arose and over time were forged into enormously varied galaxies. Our own solar system is a highly differentiated group of planets with Earth emerging as the most abundant expression of life forms we know. Each plant, insect, and animal is different from every other. No two red oaks or white pines are exactly the same, no two daffodils or tomato plants, no two lions or baboons, no two grasshoppers or dragonflies. This remarkable fact of uniqueness is expressed in the spectacular variety and biodiversity of the natural world.

The second principle is that of subjectivity, that everything has an inner unifying component, a depth dimension that increases with greater complexification of being. The subjective dimension might be seen in certain religious traditions as the animated depths of interiority in things or the ensouled element of things. It is the numinous quality of reality comparable to the inner ordering principle of *logos* in Greek thought, *li* in Chinese thought, or *ṛta* in Indian Vedic thought.

Finally, by "communion," Berry speaks of that which draws things together, like gravitation in the physical sphere or love in the human sphere. Communion is the bonding force of reality that makes possible the exchange of energy among humans and other species. Communion is the expression of a deeply felt relationality. This shared sense of life reflects the profound interconnection of everything to everything else. From this perspective the universe is experienced as "a single if multiform, energy event."[1]

When Berry speaks of "the communion of subjects," he is drawing on these larger principles governing the universe. In identifying these three principles of differentiation, subjectivity, and communion he observes that they must be activated in our consciousness and experience if the human venture is to continue. Activating communion and subjectivity means seeing that the universe is far from dead inert matter simply to be manipulated by humans. Nor does it consist of a collection of objects that can be used or abused by humans engaged in exploiting or quantifying the world. Instead, Berry makes it abundantly clear that the future flourishing of life will depend on a new understanding of reciprocity, reverence, and respect for the vast diversity of flora and fauna that graces our planet. This will require a shift from an anthropocentric sense of domination to an anthropocosmic sense of communion with all life forms. The human needs to recover a sense of being part of, and not apart from, the Earth community. Thus the human is being called to live within the vastness of the cosmos in the context of local life—to dwell in intimate immensities. This implies awakening to the multiplicity of intelligences in other species.

This book, *A Communion of Subjects,* is a testimony to that deepening awareness in the human community that we live amidst a multiplicity of intelligences, among them hunting and foraging intelligences, courting and mating intelligences, flying and swimming intelligences, migrating and molting intelligences, communicating and playing intelligences. These are displayed in particular and differentiated forms throughout the enormous array of species with whom we share our planet. These intelligences are qualitatively different and species-specific.

An appreciation of these intelligences was perhaps more apparent to earlier peoples less entangled in the circumscribed anthropocentric perspectives of urban and industrialized societies. Now, the range and shape of these intelligences are revealing themselves anew under the scrutiny of scientific research and the ancient disciplines of patient watching and silent waiting in the presence of other species, both wild and domesticated.

We might then speak of the reawakening to these various intelligences as our participation in the collective wisdom of the Earth community. How we describe this wisdom—as inherited instinct, innate knowledge, genetic coding, or learned behavior—may be debated, but the fact of its presence and continuity is irrefutable. These multiple intelligences are part of survival strategies, but they also partake of what the poet and essayist Gary Snyder has called "the grand old culture of nature." In other words, the subtle and not-so-subtle exchanges of life energies are based on intricate patterns and principles analogous to our cultural habits and social codes. The complex patterning and apparently random interaction we see in the life around us, while not fully understood, evokes wonder and awe as well as further questions for exploration and study. For just as the wisdom traditions of the human community are studied and passed on, so too we are beginning to see how the more-than-human world[2] has its own wisdom for survival and for play, which is apparently both inherited and learned.

Such wisdom is evident, for example, in migratory intelligences. The knowledge of various species to move from place to place in search of food, mates, or breeding grounds is nothing short of remarkable. This applies across species —the massive movements of porcupine caribou herds over northern tundra, of timber wolf packs passing through taiga wilderness and temperate forests, of Canadian geese and sand hill cranes streaming from cool northern climates in summer to warm southern regions in winter, of gray whales swimming from Alaska to Mexico and back again, of Pacific and Atlantic salmon returning to spawning grounds in the inland reaches of stone-strewn rivers, of monarch butterflies journeying from eastern North America seeking wintering grounds in the Mexican highlands.

Are these not processes to be cherished and protected? Are these not numinous markings on the landscape, seascape, skyscape that we need to understand for survival—not only physically, but also psychically and spiritually as well? For as our religious and cultural traditions demonstrate, animals have been guides and teachers embodying patterned knowledge that draws us out of our self-enclosed human egos and into the numinous world of nature in which we live and move and share a deeper being. This is why the movements of animals and birds, fish and insects were so carefully observed by earlier peoples who recognized their dependence on these creatures and celebrated their closeness to them in song and painting, myth and dance. The right relationship to the world at large could be encouraged, evoked, and maintained by rituals that respected the animals as a source of food, clothing, and celebration.

In our preoccupation to identify the ways in which we as humans are distinctive among the myriad species of life, we have forgotten to highlight the ways in which we are related. In our earlier desire to establish a hierarchy of species over which we had dominion we ignored the inherent relationship of the subjectivity of other species to human subjectivity. And in our concern to underscore our own reflexive consciousness we lost sight of the multiplicity of intelligences that surround us.

We have thus become like a species that has lost its familiar migratory route. We are now trying to find our way back home as we discover the journey of our evolutionary past and our interrelated future. In our attempt to de-center and re-center ourselves in an unfolding evolutionary universe, we are recognizing, as if for the first time, that we are primates amidst other primates. What does this awareness awaken in us of our evolutionary lineage as we seek our place as a species in a cosmos vaster than our ancestors actually knew?

We are recovering a profound sense of kinship to the more than human world that shares the planet with us. And this realization of kinship is not simply a romantic or idealized vision. It is, rather, a complex prismatic appreciation for the intricate and subtle transformations of life for life. The condition of life is the exchange of energy marked by food—whether plant or animal. The growth, survival, diminishment, and sacrifice of one form of life for another are all the inevitable lineage of life. The plant and animal world are our ancestors in every sense of the word. To be a member of the food chain is to participate also in a communion of subjects. In the end, we are all part of what Gary Snyder calls "the shimmering food-chain. The food web is the scary, beautiful condition of the biosphere." With some humility, then, we may be able to participate again in the patterned and transformative life of the animal world that we share. In doing so we may still find our way back into this "grand old culture of nature."

NOTES

1. Thomas Berry, *The Dream of the Earth* (San Francisco: Sierra Club Books, 1988), pp. 45–46.

2. As referenced in "Heritage of the Volume" at the start of this book, this is David Abram's phrase.

EPILOGUE

The Dance of Awe

JANE GOODALL

An interview with Dr. Jane Goodall on April 9, 2001, in Boston, Massachusetts, on the occasion of of the annual conference of The Great Apes Project by co-editors Kimberley Patton, Harvard Divinity School, and Paul Waldau, Tufts School of Veterinary Medicine.

KCP: Jane, I have read your work in the context of teaching my course on animals and religion at Harvard, and I want to start by asking you to reflect on the fact that when you went into the field in Tanzania, you weren't trained at that time to see animals as numbers, or as objects, or as things, but rather from your own experience automatically treated them as individuals. It seems in a way that you were therefore more open to the possibility of observing in them a wider range of behavior, emotion, and cognition than you would have been had you [first] been classically, "scientifically" trained.

JG: I think it was so incredible that Louis Leakey had the foresight to deliberately pick someone whose mind was unbiased by the very reductionist thinking of the ethologists of the sixties. And I think that, like anyone who's ever grown up with a dog or with any kind of animal, I knew—absolutely knew—that animals had personalities, and that they could think, and definitely that they had feelings. I don't think you'd find any child who would question that. And if they were to come into contact with rigorous scientific method, particularly in those days, you were told, well, "You can't *know* that animals have emotions like ours, we don't even *know* that other humans have emotions like ours, how can we *know* that animals do. And even if they do we can't possibly learn anything about them, so it's best not to think about them." It was the same with personality and individuality—I was actually told that although such things might be, they were best pushed under the carpet.

KCP: [In other words, to think] such a thing would actually be an obstacle to [scientific] investigation ...

JG: [The idea was that] these things were totally confined to humans. Only *we* had personalities, only *we* had rational minds, and only *we* had emotions. And everything that animals did that looked like happiness, sadness, fear, etc., was just looking like it. It couldn't possibly *be* like it. What was lucky is that by the time I got to Cambridge and was subjected to what seemed like an attempt at brainwashing, I was already pretty set [in my ideas]. I was fairly tough-minded. I was taught to be that way by my dominant mother and grandmother, you know, who taught me to stick to my convictions, the courage of my convictions, at the same time keeping an open mind.

The scientific experience at Cambridge helped me to present my intuitive understanding in such a way that I could publish it without being told I was wrong.

KCP: You had to learn …

JG: … for example, I remember how one professor told me, "You cannot say that Fifi was 'jealous,'" to which I replied, "But she *was,* so what do I say?" He said, "Well, you say, Fifi behaved in such a way that had she been a human child we would have said that she was jealous."

KCP: And did you actually put things in those terms? Because you don't any more …

JG: I did then … because that was a groundbreaking time. You know, I suppose even then I was so passionately sure I was right that I wanted acceptance.

KCP: You wanted a forum.

JG: I think I realized that it would help animals.

KCP: You wanted a place to stand so that your voice would be heard; you wanted to be credible within the scientific community.

JG: It was an unconscious way of thinking, looking back on it …

PW: Were there others at Cambridge who were more resistant than your advisor with regard to even giving that sort of accommodation, [i.e.,] "if this were a human child, she would have been jealous"—were there others who were really unwilling [to even go that far]?

JG: Oh there were, faculty and some of the students, too. Because most of the students I'd come into contact with and most of the professors were actually doing [animal] experimentation. So obviously you don't want to hear such ideas. *But they must have known.* I mean, this is what I wrestled with then, and still do today. To what extent do these people who maintain that animals are just machines, to what extent do they *really* believe it—*can* they really believe it? Very honestly, truly, can they really believe that animals are just machines? Maybe they never had anything to do with animals? Really and truly if they had a dog, or a cat, could they honestly believe what they were saying?

KCP: There must be some kind of disconnect between the heart and the mind—

JG: Yes, they're just blinkering it—

KCP: I remember reading about your first meeting at SEMA[1] that you felt, "how should I begin to speak about what I've just seen?"—and you started out by appealing to what they already knew …

JG: … what they already knew.

KCP: You wrote of that moment, "What on earth could I say? And then, as so often happens when my mind goes blank, words came." You said to them, "'I think you all know what I felt in there. … And since you are all decent, compassionate people, I assume you feel much the same.'"

JG: That was so clever. I don't know *how* I thought of it—the lab visit had left me in shock.

KCP: But it must have disarmed them.

JG: Well, there was silence. I mean how could anybody say, "No, I'm not a caring, compassionate person."

KCP: Which is a form of saying [if you acknowledge that] *you see what I see,* you'd do something different here.

JG: And you know that led to a big success story.[2]

KCP: Let's talk about the waterfall. I have been struck by your account of the chimpanzees' dance of awe at the waterfall at Kakombe. In *Reason for Hope,* you write [reading]:

The chimpanzees, I believe, know feelings akin to awe. In the Kakombe valley is a magnificent waterfall. There is a great roar as the water cascades down through the soft green air from the stream bed above. Over countless aeons the water has worn a perpendicular groove in the sheer rock. Ferns move ceaselessly in the wind created by the falling water, and vines hang down on either side. For me it is a magical place, and a spiritual one. And sometimes, as they approach, the chimpanzees display in slow, rhythmic motion along the river-bed. They pick up and throw great rocks and branches. They leap to seize the hanging vines, and swing out over the stream in the spray-drenched wind until it seems the slender stems must snap or be torn from their lofty moorings.

For ten minutes or more they may perform this magnificent "dance." Why? Is it not possible that the chimpanzees are responding to some feeling like awe? A feeling generated by the mystery of water; water that seems alive, always rushing past yet never going, always the same yet ever different. Was it perhaps similar feelings of awe that gave rise to the first animistic religions, the worship of the elements and the mysteries of nature over which there was no control? Only when our prehistoric ancestors developed language would it have been possible to discuss such internal feelings and create a shared religion.

KCP [continues]: I find myself fascinated by the waterfall. And the dance ... the way you describe the dance ... It reminds me of what [the late Harvard comparative zoologist] Donald Griffin said about consciousness in animals: that if consciousness is important to us, it is probably important to them too. I asked him once whether he thought animals think about God and he responded by saying, "I'm enough of a scientist to be an agnostic, but if there is a God, then I have no doubt that animals think about Him too."

JG: When you spend time in the wild with chimpanzees in freedom, it's so noticeable how they are sometimes amazed by things around them. And of course they have these big liquid eyes that draw attention to what they're looking at. They're fascinated by an insect crawling along or they're fascinated by a dewdrop falling off the tip of a leaf; they're fascinated by so much around them—it seems over and above just play; over and above mere curiosity.

KCP: It's [something] like wonder?

JG: It's like wonder. And then they perform a wild "dance." These performances really are like a kind of primitive dance, because they're very rhythmic, very different from the normal display. In a typical charging display, a male races across the ground, slapping and stamping, hurling rocks, standing up and swaying the vegetation. His hair bristles. He tries to make himself as big and dangerous as possible, trying to intimidate rivals.

KCP: Trying to send a message?

JG: He's sending him a message that "I'm a big tough guy." Trying to make himself look as big and dangerous as possible. But at the sudden onset of heavy, heavy rain or arrival at a big waterfall the display is completely different. It's very rhythmic. Imagine that you're sitting on one side of a valley. You can see the grey clouds and you can hear the rain coming across the forest towards you with this loud noise. The rain is getting closer and closer and closer. At this moment you feel a sort of heaviness. Then the first great drops come, and the downpour is upon you. Then one or more of the adult males start this rhythmic display, much of which is in an upright movement. Very, very slow—slapping and slapping and slapping—and stamping and stamping and stamping—and standing up, and swaying and swaying and swaying—and moving rhythmically from foot to foot to foot.

KCP: Like at the waterfall.

JG: Like at the waterfall.

KCP: They are both forms of falling water.

JG: The sound of falling water, but also maybe the magic of it. Where does it come from? And these displays can last twenty minutes. And it is such a marvelous display. The waterfall display can involve climbing the slender vines that hang down the sides of the rocks and push out over the stream into the spray. The amazing thing is that afterwards they occasionally stamp in the water, whereas normally they hate getting their feet wet. Sometimes after a waterfall display one of the males will sit on a rock. If you are close enough you will see his eyes watching the falling water. Are they not questioning, "*What is it? It's always coming; it's always going.*"

PW: What was the first time you ever saw the rain display?

JG: The first time I ever saw the rain display was the most spectacular rain display that had ever been seen and there was I; it was the first rainy season, four months into the study and you can see it in my book of letters. I wrote a letter home after seeing this incredible sight—when I very first saw it. There were—there were seven adult males. I remember the sky over the

slope opposite got darker and darker. The trees were dark green and there were areas of yellow-green grass. Then the rain arrived, the thunder crashed and rumbled from the purple-black clouds. Suddenly, opposite me, the chimpanzees climbed into low trees at the top of the very narrow valley. And then, one by one, the big males charged down the grassy, tree-studded slope, dragging branches in the drenching rain. One or two stood upright, holding onto low branches, swaying rhythmically from foot to foot. After his display, each one walked back up the slope, then started his display, his dancing, all over again. It was amazing.

KCP: And you had no experience of this? No idea what it meant?

JG: No. I could only say that it was like primitive man defying the elements with a display of power. With the waterfall; it's always there, so it's different; they know it's going to be there; they hear it as they approach … and then they put on this display. It's usually more than one male, but it has been at times a single individual …

KCP: What is so amazing to me about what you describe; what I love is that so often theorists and scientists, particularly sociobiologists, will try to reduce human religious ritual, saying, "Well, it's like animal ritual; animals have ritual too." But what you suggest to me is that *maybe we're thinking about it backwards*. It's rather that ritual action is a natural response to living in a world of mystery and beauty and divinity. It is a response that is shared by animals with human beings. So it's not that we can reduce human ritual behavior to instinct "because animals do it too," but rather that animals need to be brought conceptually into the sphere of human religious experience; animal ritual action might be "elevated" to the world of human ritual action.

JG: What I saw was an expression of what I think is a spiritual reality.

PW: In the Great Ape Project there is a description of two chimpanzees who go out to a sunset, who enjoy a sunset. Are there any other experiences that you think reflect awe, other than the rain dance and the dance around the waterfall, that would reflect somehow their fascination of the mystery of the world around them?

JG: There is the amazing photo in *Reason for Hope,* which I suppose you have seen? In which a male chimpanzee, sitting in heavy rain, holds out his hand and watches as the raindrops splash off it. Is he feeling a sense of wonder? Of awe? These are the feelings aroused in us by the beauty or majesty of nature, [or by] the beauty of some manmade creations. I think chimpanzees know similar emotions.

PW: Kimberley's done some nice work demonstrating that religious traditions at different times have held that other animals have an awareness of the divine. It is surprisingly frequent. Pliny wrote about how elephants pray, and it's interesting to read your book and to think of how that's a modern manifestation of what appears in many other places and times many different times.

KCP: And in these historical traditions where animals pray and so forth, people aren't in the middle mediating, but the animals have a direct connection with the divine. It's unmediated, and it's sometimes actually even stronger, more powerful than that of humans—that's why Balaam's ass [in the Book of Numbers] could see the obstructing angel, even when Balaam couldn't. You find this even in the most orthodox traditions.

JG: I know an account of a Buddhist monk; he decided to go into the forest and when he got there, he discovered another monk, who was obviously meditating. An elephant stood there before the monk and bowed.

PW: This is a very long tradition in Buddhism. There are many forest monks in the Buddhist world, throughout history, who tell of animals joining them in meditation or fasting.

KCP: In one legend from his life, St. Francis hears the birds singing in the thicket and says to his fellow monks as they walk along the countryside, "Our sisters are praising God; let us go and join them." But then the birds make such a terrific racket that the monks cannot hear themselves chanting the divine office, and so St. Francis says, "Please, my sisters. Could you cease praising God just for a few minutes so that we may hear ourselves sing?" And the birds stop, and are still, and only when he gives them leave do they resume their joyous noise in the brambles.

Jane, you allow a collapse of the distinction between the world of nature and the world of culture in the forest epiphany of ultimate unity —and boldly say that for you, there was no difference between the living music of God as you heard it filling Nôtre Dame and that mystical experience in the forest ...

PW: Have you had many people react to your comments about the waterfall?

JG: What I find really fascinating is the way in which people's questions about the inner lives of animals have changed over the years. After lectures people used to be totally fascinated with the question of *what do they do about death?* More recently, as we've gradually broken down the barriers, again and again, I am asked, *do they have souls?* This reflects, I think, a change in the way people are thinking.

PW: Do you find that this pretty much happens around the world, this question?

KCP: I would think that in the Far East where the doctrine of *samsāra* holds that the soul can be born again and again in many incarnations, both animal and human, the question would be less pressing, or the idea that animals have souls less startling ...

JG: We're all just brothers and sisters.

KCP: The question of animal soul is interesting in that traditional Christian theology, reflecting the monotheistic beliefs about human exceptionalism, has taught for centuries that animals have no immortal souls.

JG: The soul is the last bastion [of difference between animals and us].

KCP: But it sounds from what you're saying that people are very curious about that; they wonder if perhaps that last "difference" can also be questioned.

PW: I remember Andrew Linzey[3] saying "people want permission to care." What Kimberley's research into animals' religious response does is actually to give people a chance to think and to match up their desire to care with the dignity and complexity animals manifest. So it's nice to have your work, Jane, suggesting that animals may experience religious feelings, the same awe and connection to mystery that we feel. I'm not so sure we think very clearly about this ... but we seem to have begun to do so ...

JG: And after this book, even more.

NOTES

1. SEMA, Inc., is a federally funded laboratory in Maryland conducting medical research on viral diseases such as hepatitis, HIV, and others using infant chimpanzees in isolated, confining cages, whose facility Jane Goodall toured in March 1987. See Jane Goodall, with Phillip Berman, *Reason for Hope: A Spiritual Journey* (New York: Warner Books, 1999), p. 213.

2. This refers to the new standards regarding minimum requirements for cage size, social, life and mental stimulation for lab chimpanzees generated by a later interdisciplinary workshop that was sug-

gested by Jane Goodall at SEMA that day. The document, which included the views of lab scientists themselves and not only animal rights advocates, was refined in three later meetings, and has had great influence on lab standards thereafter, despite the failure of the National Institute of Health to participate in its creation or the United States Department of Agriculture to adopt it.

3. The British Christian theologian at Oxford University, author of *Animal Theology* (Urbana and Chicago: University of Illinois Press, 1994).

Contributors

CAROL ADAMS is the author of the pioneering *The Sexual Politics of Meat: A Feminist-Vegetarian Critical Theory; Living Among Meat Eaters: The Vegetarian's Survival Guide; Neither Man nor Beast: Feminism and the Defense of Animals; Woman-Battering; The Inner Art of Vegetarianism* series on the spirituality of vegetarianism; *The Pornography of Meat; Help! My Child Has Stopped Eating Meat: The A-Z Guide to Surviving a Conflict in Diets; Prayers for Animals;* and a series of books for children of prayers for animals. She has edited four collections: *Ecofeminism and the Sacred; Violence Against Women and Children: A Christian Theological Sourcebook* (with Marie Fortune); *Animals and Women: Feminist Theoretical Explorations,* and *Beyond Animal Rights: A Feminist Caring Ethic for the Treatment of Animals* (both edited with Josephine Donovan). She was instrumental in bringing back into publication the great nineteenth-century book *The Ethics of Diet: A Catena of Authorities Deprecatory of Flesh Eating* by Howard Williams. She has shown her *The Sexual Politics of Meat* slide show on campuses throughout the United States, and in Canada and Great Britain as well.

ROGER AMES is professor of philosophy and editor of *Philosophy East & West.* His recent publications include translations of Chinese classics: *Suntzu: The Art of Warfare* (1993); *Sun Pin: The Art of Warfare* (1996), and *Tracing Dao to its Source* (1997) (both with D.C. Lau); the *Confucian Analects* (with H. Rosemont) (1998); *Focusing the Familiar: A Translation and Philosophical Interpretation of the Zhongyong;* and *A Philosophical Translation of the Daodejing: Making This Life Significant* (with D.L. Hall) (2001). He has also written many interpretative studies of Chinese philosophy and culture: *Thinking Through Confucius* (1987); *Anticipating China: Thinking Through the Narratives of Chinese and Western Culture* (1995); and *Thinking From the Han: Self, Truth, and Transcendence in Chinese and Western Culture* (1997) (all with D.L. Hall). Recently he has undertaken several projects that entail the intersection of contemporary issues and cultural understanding. His *Democracy of the Dead: Dewey, Confucius, and the Hope for Democracy in China* (with D. L. Hall) (1999) is a product of this effort.

E. N. ANDERSON received his BA from Harvard College and his PhD from the University of California, Berkeley. He has been teaching at the University of California, Riverside from 1966 to the present. His major works include *The Food of China* (Yale University Press, 1988) and *Ecologies of the Heart* (Oxford University Press, 1996). His professional focus is on cultural ecology and ethnobiology. His principal areas of field work have been Hong Kong (1965–66 and 1974–75), Malaysia and Singapore (1970–71), British Columbia (1984–85), and the Yucatan Peninsula of Mexico (1991, 1996).

DIANE APOSTOLOS-CAPPADONA is Adjunct Professor of Religious Art and Cultural History in the Prince Alwaleed bin Talal Center for Muslim-Christian Understanding and Adjunct Professor in Art and Culture in the Liberal Studies Program at Georgetown University. She is the author of *Encyclopedia of Women in Religious Art* (1996); *Dictionary of Christian Art* (1994); and *The Spirit and the Vision: The Influence of Christian Romanticism on the Development of 19th-century American Art* (1995). She is also the editor of, and a contributor to, numerous collections addressing a wide range of subjects in religion and art, and a co-translator of *A History of Religious Ideas, Volume III* by Mircea Eliade (1985). At present, she is completing the foreword to the reprint edition of *Sacred and Profane Beauty: The Holy in Art,* by Gerardus van der Leeuw (2005), and several edited volumes, including *Sources and Documents in the History of Christian Art.* She is Area Editor for the Visual Arts for the thirty-volume *Encyclopedia of the Bible and Its Reception* (2008–20).

ALI ASANI, born in Nairobi, Kenya, is currently Professor of the Practice of Indo-Muslim Languages and Culture at Harvard University, where he provides instruction on Islam in India, Pakistan, and Bangladesh; Islamic mysticism; and Islamic civilizations around the world, including a popular course in the undergraduate core curriculum program, "Understanding Islam and Contemporary Muslim Societies." He also offers instruction in various South Asian and African languages. He is the author of many scholarly articles and several books on the devotional literatures of Muslim communities in South Asia, including the *Bujh Niranjan: An Ismaili Mystical Poem; The Harvard Collection of Ismaili Literature in Indic Languages: A Descriptive Catalog and Finding Aid; Celebrating Muhammad: Images of the Prophet in Popular Muslim Poetry* (with Kamal Abdul Malek); *Ecstasy and Enlightenment: The Ismaili Devotional Literatures of South Asia;* and more recently, *Aaiye Urdu Parhe: Let's Study Urdu.* He has contributed chapters to various books as well as articles to *The Encylopedia of Religion, The Oxford Encylopedia of the Modern Islamic World, Encyclopedia of South Asian Folklore,* and *The Muslim Almanac.* He has been particularly active post–September 11 in conducting workshops for high school and college educators on teaching about Islam. In 2002, he was awarded the Harvard Foundation medal for his outstanding contributions to improving intercultural and race relations by promoting a better understanding of Islam.

MARC BEKOFF is Professor of Biology at the University of Colorado, Boulder, and is a Fellow of the Animal Behavior Society and a former Guggenheim Fellow. In 2000 he was awarded the Exemplar Award from the Animal Behavior Society for major long-term contributions to the field. Marc is also regional coordinator for Jane Goodall's Roots & Shoots program, in which he works with students of all ages, senior citizens, and prisoners, and a member of the Ethics Committee of the Jane Goodall Institute. He and Jane co-founded the organization Ethologists for the Ethical Treatment of Animals: Citizens for Responsible Animal Behavior Studies in 2000 (www.ethologicalethics.org). Marc also is on the Board of Directors of the Fauna Sanctuary and of the Cougar Fund, and is an honorary member of Animalisti Italiani and Fundacion Altarriba. In 2005 he was presented with the Bank One Faculty Community Service Award for the work he has done with children, senior citizens, and prisoners.

His main areas of research include animal behavior, cognitive ethology (the study of animal minds), and behavioral ecology, and he has also published extensively on animal issues. He is a prolific writer with more than 200 articles as well as two encyclopedias to his credit, and is the author or editor of numerous books, including *The Enclycopedia of Animal Rights and Animal Welfare; The Cognitive Animal* (co-edited with C. Allen and G. M. Burghardt); *The Ten Trusts: What We Must Do to Care for the Animals We Love* (co-written with Jane Goodall); and *The Enclypedia of Animal Behavior.* His most recent books include *The Smile of a Dolphin: Minding Animals* and *Animal Passions and Beastly Virtues: Reflections on Redecorating Nature.* His home page is http://literati.net/Bekoff.

THOMAS BERRY received his PhD from The Catholic University of America in European intellectual history with a thesis on Giambattista Vico. Widely read in Western history and theology, he also spent many years studying and teaching the cultures and religions of Asia. He has lived in China and traveled to other parts of Asia. He has written two books on Asian religions, *Buddhism* and *Religions of India,* both of which are distributed by Columbia University Press. For twenty-five years, he directed the Riverdale Center of Religious Research along the Hudson River. During this period he taught at Fordham University, where he chaired the history of religions program and directed twenty-five doctoral theses. His major contributions to the discussions on the environment and ecological thought are in his books *The Dream of the Earth* (Sierra Club Books, 1988) and, with Brian Swimme, *The Universe Story* (Harper San Francisco, 1992); and *The Great Work: Our Way Into the Future* (Bell Tower/Random House, 1999). His newest book is *Evening Thoughts: Reflecting on Earth as Sacred Community* (Sierra Club Books and University of Califronia), edited by Mary Evelyn Tucker.

EDWIN BRYANT received his PhD from Columbia University in 1997 and is presently Associate Professor of Hinduism at Rutgers University. His primary areas of teaching and research are Hindu philosophies, the Krishna Tradition, and Indian proto-history. His publications and edited volumes include *In Quest of the Origins of Vedic Culture: The Indo-Aryan Invasion Debate* (Oxford, 2001); *Krishna: The Srimad Bhagavat Purana, 10th Canto* (Penguin, 2003); *The Hare Krishna Movement: The Post-Charismatic Fate of a Religious Transplant* (Columbia, 2004); *The Indo-Aryan Controversy: Evidence and Inference in Indian History* (Routledge Curzon, 2005); and *Krishna: A Sourcebook* (Oxford, in press). He is currently working on a number of projects including a recently completed translation of *The Yoga Sutras of Patanjali* with notes from the Traditional Commentators.

CHRISTOPHER CHAPPLE is Professor of Theological Studies and Associate Academic Vice Present at Loyola Marymount University, where he teaches religions of India and comparative theology. He has published several books, including *Karma and Creativity; Nonviolence to Animals, Earth, and Self in Asian Traditions; Reconciling Yogas: Haribhadra's Collection of Views on Yoga;* a co-translation of Patanjali's *Yoga Sutra;* and several edited collections of essays, including *Ecological Prospects: Scientific, Aesthetic, and Religious Perspectives; Hinduism and Ecology: The Intersection of Earth, Sky, and Water;* and *Jainism and Ecology: Nonviolence in the Web of Life.*

DAN COHN-SHERBOK was born in Denver, educated at Williams College, and ordained a rabbi at the Hebrew Union College. He received a PhD from Cambridge University, and taught Jewish theology at the University of Kent at Canterbury from 1975. He has been a Professor of Interfaith Dialogue at Middlesex University and is currently Professor of Judaism at the University of Wales. He is the author or editor of more than seventy books including (with Andrew Linzey): *After Noah: Animals and the Liberation of Theology.* He and his wife and their two cats live in an old coach house in Wales, and also in London.

WENDY DONIGER is the Mircea Eliade Distinguished Service Professor of the History of Religions at the University of Chicago. Among her many books are *Śiva the Erotic Ascetic* (Oxford, 1973, 1981); *The Origins of Evil in Hindu Mythology* (Berkeley, 1976); *Dreams, Illusion, and Other Realities; Other Peoples' Myths: The Cave of Echoes* (Chicago, 1995); *The Implied Spider: Politics and Theology in Myth; Splitting the Difference: Gender and Myth in Ancient Greece and India* (Chicago, 1998); *The Bedtrick: Myths of Sex and Masquerade* (Chicago, 2000); and *The Woman Who Pretended to Be Who She Was* (Oxford, 2005). In progress is a novel, *Horses for Lovers, Dogs for Husbands.*

RICHARD FOLTZ is Associate Professor of Religion at Concordia University, Montreal. He holds a PhD in history and Middle Eastern studies from Harvard University. He is author or editor of eight books, including *Animals in Islamic Tradition and Muslim Cultures* (Oneworld, 2005); *Spirituality in the Land of the Noble: How Iran Shaped the World's Religions* (Oneworld, 2004); *Religions of the Silk Road: Overland Trade and Cultural Exchange from Antiquity to the Fifteenth Century* (Palgrave, 1999); and *Islam and Ecology: A Bestowed Trust,* co-edited with Frederick M. Denny and Azizan Baharuddin (Harvard, 2003).

MICHAEL FOX is a veterinarian and syndicated newspaper columnist with doctoral degrees in medical science and ethology/animal behavior. He served as Senior Scholar, Bioethics with The Humane Society of the United States. His most recent books are *The Boundless Circle: Caring for Creatures and Creation* and *Bringing Life to Ethics: Global Bioethics for a Humane Society..*

DAVID FRASER is Professor of Animal Welfare at the University of British Columbia, cross-appointed between the Faculty of Land and Food Systems and the W. Maurice Young Centre for Applied Ethics. After studying ethology in Canada and the United Kingdom, he has pursued a research career on the behavior, management, and welfare of animals. His research has spanned a wide range of topics, from designing better pigpens to exploring the role of values in science.

JANE GOODALL is most commonly known for her groundbreaking study of chimpanzees, although currently she works primarily as an advocate for animals and the environment. She is founder of the Jane Goodall Institute, with headquarters in Silver Spring, Maryland and branch operations in fourteen countries worldwide. She was recently appointed United Nations Messenger of Peace. Dr. Goodall's publications list is extensive, including two overviews of her work at Gombe, *In the Shadow of Man* and *Through a Window,* as well as two autobiographies in letters, the spiritual autobiography *Reason for Hope,* and many children's books such as *The Chimpanzees I Love* and *The Eagle and the Wren. The Chimpanzees of Gombe: Patterns of Behavior* is recognized as the definitive work on chimpanzees and is the culmination of Dr. Goodall's career.

DONALD GRIFFIN was Professor Emeritus at The Rockefeller University and Associate Professor of Zoology at Harvard University. During his years as a student, Junior Fellow at Harvard, and professor at Cornell, Harvard, and Rockefeller, he investigated the orientation behavior of animals, especially the echolocation or sonar of bats. He rekindled the scientific investigation of comparative ethology through *The Question of Animal Awareness* (1976, 1981), *Animal Thinking* (1984), and *Animal Minds* (1992, revised as *Animal Minds: Beyond Cognition to Consciousness,* 2001). His basic theme was that animal communication provides scientists with objective evidence of nonhuman thoughts and feelings. Donald Griffin died on November 7, 2003.

JOHN GRIM is co-coordinator of the Forum on Religion and Ecology. Formerly a professor of religion at Bucknell University, he is now a Research Fellow at Yale University. As a historian of religions, he undertakes annual field studies in American Indian lifeways among the Apsaalooke/Crow peoples of Montana and the Swy-ahl-puh/Salish peoples of the Columbia River Plateau in eastern Washington. He published *The Shaman: Patterns of Religious Healing Among the Ojibway Indians,* a study of Anishinaabe/Ojibway healing practitioners (Oklahoma, 1983). With his wife, Mary Evelyn Tucker, he has co-edited *Worldviews and Ecology* (1994), and a *Daedalus* volume (2001) discussing perspectives on the environmental crisis from world religions and contemporary philosophy. Tucker and Grim organized the series of ten conferences on Religions of the World and Ecology held at Harvard University's Center for the Study of World Religions, and they now direct the Forum on Religion and Ecology as a continuation of that project. He edited *Indigenous Traditions and Ecology* (Harvard, 2001) from this conference series. He is also president of the American Teilhard Association.

IAN HARRIS was educated at the Universities of Cambridge and Lancaster. He is Senior Scholar at the Becket Institute, St. Hugh's College, University of Oxford, Professor of Buddhist Studies in the Division of Religion and Philosophy, University College of St. Martin, Lancaster, and author of *The Continuity of Madhyamaka and Yogacara in Early Indian Mahayana Buddhism* (1991) and *Buddhism and Politics in Twentieth Century Asia* (1999). He is co-founder of the UK Association for Buddhist Studies and has written widely on aspects of Buddhist ethics. He is currently responsible for a research project on Buddhism and Cambodian Communism at the Documentation Center of Cambodia, Phnom Penh. His most recent book is *Cambodian Buddhism: History and Practice* (Hawaii, 2005).

MARC HAUSER received a BS from Bucknell University and a PhD from UCLA. Currently, he is a Harvard College Professor and professor in the departments of psychology, organismic and evolutionary biology, and biological anthropology. He is co-director of the Mind, Brain, and Behavior Program at Harvard, and a recipient of the National Science Foundation Young Investigator Award. He is the author of *The Evolution of Communication* (MIT Press, 1996) and *Wild Minds: How Animals Think* (Henry Holt, 2000) and the forthcoming *Moral Minds: How Nature Designed a Universal Sense of Right and Wrong* (HarperCollins). His research sits at the interface between evolutionary biology

and cognitive neuroscience and is aimed at understanding the processes and consequences of cognitive evolution. His observations and experiments focus on captive and wild primates, human infants and adults, incorporating methodological procedures from ethology, infant cognitive development, cognitive neuroscience, and neurobiology. Current foci include studies of the evolution and development of aesthetics, mathematics, language, and morality.

ROBERTA KALECHOFSKY is a widely published and translated author of both fiction and nonfiction works. She graduated from Brooklyn College and received a doctorate in English literature in 1970 from New York University. A critical essay on her work can be found in *The Dictionary of Literary Biographies*, vol. 28: *Jewish Fiction Writers*. In 1975 she founded Micah Publications (www.micahbooks.com) and has received publishing grants from the National Endowment for the Arts and the Massachusetts Council on the Arts, in addition to her literary fellowships. As a publisher, she created The Echad Series, which includes five anthologies of Jewish writing from around the world, and she has published forty different titles in poetry, fiction, scholarship, vegetarianism, and animal rights. She is active in the animal rights and vegetarian movements and began the organization, Jews for Animal Rights, in 1985, and coordinates publishing projects with this organization.

ZAYN KASSAM is Associate Professor of Religious Studies at Pomona College, Claremont, California, and is also on the faculty at Claremont Graduate University, Claremont, California. A graduate of McGill University (PhD 1995), she teaches courses in Islamic philosophy, mysticism, gender, and literature as well as a course on philosophical and mystical texts from a comparative perspective. She has been twice honored with a Wig Award for Distinguished Teaching at Pomona College, and a national Teacher of the Year award by the American Academy of Religion (2005). She has lectured widely on Muslim gender issues as well as medieval Islamic philosophy in the United States, Canada, and Britain. Her published articles include: "Politicizing Gender and Religion"; "Muslim Women Writers in South Asia"; "Our Worlds and His: Naguib Mahfouz's *Palace Walk*"; "Mindfield or Minefield: Teaching Religion in a Multicultural Classroom"; "The Individual and Notions of Community"; and others dealing with ethics and gender. She is currently working on two books, one on aspects of Qur'anic interpretation in medieval Islamic philosophy, and one on gender issues in the Islamic world.

BEVERLY KIENZLE is John H. Morison Professor of the Practice in Latin and Romance Languages at Harvard Divinity School, and former President of the International Medieval Sermon Studies Society. A scholar of medieval Christian preaching, hagiography, and heresy, her publications include: *The Sermon. Typologie des sources du moyen âge occidental*, (Brepols, 2000); *Cistercians, Heresy and Crusade (1145–1229): Preaching in the Lord's Vineyard* (Boydell and Brewer, 2001); and *Women Preachers and Prophets Through Two Millennia of Christianity*, co-edited with Pamela J. Walker (Berkeley, 1998).

JONATHAN KLAWANS is Associate Professor of Religion at Boston University, where he teaches courses in Western Religion, Hebrew Bible, Dead Sea Scrolls, ancient Jewish history, and Rabbinic literature. His first book, *Impurity and Sin in Ancient Judaism* (Oxford University Press, 2000), won awards as a best first book for 2000 from the American Academy of Religion and the American Academy for Jewish Research. He has recently completed his second book, *Purity, Sacrifice, and the Temple: Symbolism and Supersessionism in the Study of Ancient Judaism* (Oxford University Press, 2005).

ELIZABETH LAWRENCE, VMD, PHD, a veterinarian as well as a cultural anthropologist, was Professor of Environmental and Population Health at Tufts University School of Veterinary Medicine, where she taught and carried out research in the field of human–animal relationships. She was the author of four scholarly books and numerous book chap-

ters and journal articles in that field. Among the honors for her work are the Elsie Clews Parsons Award of the American Ethnological Society, the James Mooney Award of the Southern Anthropological Association, and the International Distinguished Scholar Award of the International Association of Human–Animal Interaction Organizations. Elizabeth Lawrence died on November 12, 2003.

JAY MCDANIEL is the author of three books on ecotheology, including *Of God and Pelicans: A Theology of Reverence for Life* (Westminster/John Knox, 1989). He is also co-editor of *Good News for Animals? Contemporary Christian Approaches to Animal Well-Being* (Orbis Press). He teaches world religions and contemporary religious thought at Hendrix College in Conway, Arkansas, where he is Director of the Steel Center for the Study of Religion and Philosophy. He is a member of the board of directors of the Center for Respect of Life and Environment (Washington DC) and is currently organizing a Center for Spirituality and Sustainability, in conjunction with Heifer Project International Development Agency (Little Rock).

CHRISTOPHER MCDONOUGH received his PhD from the University of North Carolina at Chapel Hill in 1996, having written his dissertation on animals in Roman culture with Jerzy Linderski. He has taught in the classics departments of the University of North Carolina at Greensboro, Princeton University, Boston College, and The University of the South (Sewanee). He is the co-author of the annotated translation *Servius' Commentary on Vergil's Aeneid, Book Four* (Bolchazy-Carducci, 2004). His articles on matters of ancient religion and folklore have appeared in numerous classical journals. He is currently at work on a primer to Roman religion of the Republic for Blackwell (London).

IAN MCINTOSH received his PhD in anthropology at Charles Darwin University in northern Australia. He is the Director of International Partnerships and Adjunct Professor of Anthropology at Indiana University-Purdue University at Indianapolis (IUPUI). From 1988 to 2003 he was managing director of the international indigenous human rights group, Cultural Survival Inc. In 2003, he also held the post of Deputy Executive Director of the Armenia Tree Project. Ian has more than twenty years experience working with Australia's indigenous peoples and has written numerous books and articles on the subject of Aboriginal reconciliation and cosmology.

ERIC MORTENSEN is Assistant Professor of East Asian Religion in the Religious Studies Department at Guilford College in Greensboro, North Carolina. He received his PhD in Tibetan and Himalayan Studies from Harvard University's Committee on Inner Asian and Altaic Studies. He is currently researching the roles of animals in the religious traditions of the Eastern Himalayas (Yunnan and Tibet), as well as scapulamancy, augury, divination, and comparative religious theory. He combines textual study with regular fieldwork in Northwest Yunnan.

LANCE NELSON is Professor of Theology and Religious Studies at the University of San Diego. He received his PhD from McMaster University. His writings on Advaita Vedānta and other aspects of South Asian religion have appeared in books and scholarly journals in the United States and India. He has published several articles on Hinduism and ecology and edited the volume *Purifying the Earthly Body of God: Religion and Ecology in Hindu India* (SUNY, 1998).

KOFI OPOKU, formerly Associate Professor of Religion and Ethics, Institute of African Studies, University of Ghana, Legon, is currently Visiting Professor of Religion at Lafayette College, Easton, Pennsylvania. He was educated at the University of Ghana, Yale University Divinity School, and the University of Bonn, Germany. He has taught at Queens College, New York; the University of Calabar, Nigeria; the University of Northern Iowa, Cedar Falls, and North Carolina State University, Raleigh. His publications include, *Speak to the Winds: Proverbs from Africa* (1975); *West African Traditional Religion* (1978); *Healing for God's World: Remedies from Three Continents* (1991), co-written

with Kim Yong Bock and Antoinette Wire; and *Hearing and Keeping: Akan Proverbs* (1997).

JORDAN PAPER is Professor Emeritus at York University in Toronto (East Asian, Environmental, Religious and Women's Studies). He is also an Associate Fellow at the Centre for Studies in Religion and Society and Adjunct Professor in the Indigenous Governance Program at the University of Victoria (British Columbia). He has written books on Chinese religion, northern Native American religions, and female spirituality. His latest books are *The Mystic Experience: A Descriptive and Comparative Analysis* (2004) and *The Deities Are Many: A Polytheistic Theology* (2005), both published by the State University of New York Press.

KIMBERLEY PATTON is Professor of the Comparative and Historical Study of Religion at Harvard Divinity School, where she teaches a course entitled "Realms of Power: Animals in Religion." She is co-editor of, and contributing author to, *A Magic Still Dwells: Comparative Religion in the Postmodern Age* (Berkeley, 2000) as well as *Holy Tears: Weeping in the Religious Imagination* (Princeton, 2005). She is also the author of two books, *Religion of the Gods: Ritual, Paradox, and Reflexivity* (Oxford, 2008); and *The Sea Can Wash Away All Evils: Modern Marine Pollution and the Ancient Cathartic Ocean* (Columbia, 2006).

LISA RAPHALS is Professor of Comparative Literature at the University of California, Riverside, and Book Review Editor of the journal *Philosophy East & West*. Trained in Classics and Chinese, she has used a comparative perspective to investigate a wide range of problems in comparative philosophy, cultural studies, and history of science that fall between the cracks of contemporary academic disciplines. She is author of *Knowing Words: Wisdom and Cunning in the Classical Traditions of China and Greece* (Cornell, 1982); *Sharing the Light: Representations of Women and Virtue in Early China* (SUNY, 1998); and articles on comparative philosophy, history of science and Taoism. Publications include: "Skeptical Strategies in the Zhuangzi and Theaetetus"

(*Philosophy East & West* 1994); "The Treatment of Women in a Second-Century Medical Casebook" (*Chinese Science* 1998); "Arguments by Women in Early Chinese Sources" (*Nan Nu* 2002); and "Gender and Virtue in Greece and China" (*Journal of Chinese Philosophy* 2002).

KIM ROBERTS served the Humane Society of the United States for six years, was Manager of the First Strike Campaign, and is currently Director of the Maine Coalition to End Domestic Violence. She received a Master's degree in Social Work from the University of Kentucky in 1987. She has more than eighteen years' experience in the animal protection and social service fields. Before joining the HSUS, she was a Cruelty Caseworker for People for the Ethical Treatment of Animals where she worked with local and national animal protection organizations, government agencies, law enforcement, prosecutors, legislators and the media. She served as Executive Director of a humane society in Maryland, and she was also founder and president of a local animal rights organization, and cofounder and board member of a humane society in Kentucky. Ms. Roberts' social service experience includes work as a researcher, grant writer, trainer and curriculum development specialist with a state child protection agency, a national probation and parole organization, and a county mental health agency. Her articles have appeared in numerous criminal justice publications.

STEVEN ROCKEFELLER is Professor Emeritus of Religion at Middlebury College, where he served as dean of the college. He received his master of divinity degree from Union Theological Seminary in New York City and his PhD in the philosophy of religion from Columbia University. He is the author of *John Dewey: Religious Faith and Democratic Humanism* (1991) and co-editor of *The Christ and the Bodhisattva* (1987) and *Spirit and Nature: Why the Environment Is a Religious Issue* (1992). He chaired the Earth Charter international drafting committee and serves as a member of the Earth Charter Commission. He is also the chair of the Rockefeller Brothers Fund, an international grant-making insti-

tution, and he serves as a trustee of the Asian Cultural Council.

BERNARD ROLLIN is University Distinguished Professor of Philosophy, Biomedical Sciences, and Animal Sciences at Colorado State University, where he is also University Bioethicist. Rollin is the author of fourteen books and more than three hundred papers and has given more than nine hundred invited lectures in twenty countries. His books include *Animal Rights and Human Morality* (third edition, 2006); *The Unheeded Cry: Animal Consciousness Animal Pain and Science* (1989, 1999); *Farm Animal Welfare* (1995); *The Frankenstein Syndrome: Ethical and Social Issues in the Genetic Engineering of Animals* (1995); *The Well-Being of Farm Animals: Challenges and Solutions* (with G. John Benson, 2004); and *Science and Ethics* (2006). He was a principal architect of 1985 United States federal legislation protecting laboratory animals.

KENNETH SHAPIRO is Co-Executive Director of the Animals and Society Institute. His educational background includes a BA in intellectual history from Harvard University and a PhD in clinical and personality psychology from Duke University. He has published scholarly work in the areas of phenomenological psychology and animal welfare. He is founding editor of *Society and Animals* and cofounding editor of *Journal of Applied Animal Welfare Science*. He is the author of *Animal Models of Human Psychology: Critique of Science, Ethics, and Policy* (Hogrefe and Huber, 1997).

PETER SINGER is DeCamp Professor of Bioethics in the University Center for Human Values at Princeton University, and Laureate Professor in the Centre for Applied Philosophy and Public Ethics at the University of Melbourne. He first became well-known internationally after the publication of *Animal Liberation*. His other books include: *Democracy and Disobedience; Practical Ethics; The Expanding Circle; Marx; Hegel; How Are We to Live?; Rethinking Life and Death; Ethics into Action; One World;* and *Pushing Time Away.* He is the author of the major article on Ethics in the current edition of the *En-*

cylopaedia Britannica. Two collections of his work have been published: *Writings on an Ethical Life,* which he edited himself, and *Unsanctifying Human Life,* edited by Helga Kuhse. His most recent book, co-authored with Jim Mason, is *The Way We Eat: Why Our Food Choices Matter.* Peter Singer was the founding president of the International Association of Bioethics and, with Helga Kuhse, founding co-editor of the journal *Bioethics.* Outside academic life, he is president of Animal Rights International, and Chair of the Board of Directors of The Great Ape Project.

GARY STEINER has BA degrees from UCLA (economics, 1977) and U.C. Berkeley (philosophy, 1981), and a PhD in philosophy from Yale (1992). He is currently John Howard Harris Professor of Philosophy at Bucknell University. He specializes in German philosophy from Kant to Heidegger, and also in Descartes and early modern philosophy. He is the author of *Descartes as Moral Thinker: Christianity, Technology, Nihilism* (Journal of the History of Philosophy Book Series, Prometheus/Humanity Books, 2004), and *Anthropocentrism and Its Discontents: The Moral Status of Animals in the History of Western Philosophy* (Pittsburgh, 2005). He has translated Karl Löwith's *Martin Heidegger and European Nihilism* (Columbia, 1995, paperback 1998), and co-translated Gerold Prauss's *Knowing and Doing in Heidegger's "Being and Time"* (Humanity Press/Prometheus Books, 1999). He has also published articles on Heidegger, Descartes, and Derrida.

ROEL STERCKX is University Lecturer in Classical Chinese and Director of Studies at the Faculty of Oriental Studies in the University of Cambridge. He is the author of *The Animal and the Daemon in Early China* (SUNY, 2002) and contributing editor of *Of Tripod and Palate: Food, Politics and Religion in Traditional China* (Palgrave, 2005).

RODNEY TAYLOR is Professor and Chair of Religious Studies, University of Colorado at Boulder. He is the author of the following books: *The Cultivation of Sagehood as a Religious Goal in Neo-Confucianism:*

A Study of Selected Writings of Kao P'an-lung (1562–1626) (1978); ed. (with F.M. Denny) *The Holy Book in Comparative Perspective* (1985); *The Way of Heaven: An Introduction to the Confucian Religious Life* (1986); *The Confucian Way of Contemplation: Okada Takehiko and the Tradition of Quiet-Sitting* (1988); ed. (with J. Watson) *They Shall Not Hurt: Human Suffering and Human Caring* (1989); *The Religious Dimensions of Confucianism* (1990); *Confucianism* (2004); and *The Illustrated Encyclopedia of Confucianism* (2 vols., 2005).

MARY EVELYN TUCKER is co-director with her husband John Grim of the Forum on Religion and Ecology. Together they directed ten conferences on World Religions and Ecology at the Center for the Study of World Religions at Havard Divinity School. They were editors for the book series that resulted from the conferences. She is the author of *The Philosophy of Qi: The Record of Great Doubts* (Columbia, 2007) *Worldly Wonder: Religions Enter Their Ecological Phase* (Open Court 2004), and *Moral and Spiritual Cultivation in Japanese Neo-Confucianism* (SUNY 1989). She also edited two volumes on Confucian Spirituality with Tu Weiming. She received her PhD from Columbia University in East Asian religions. During 1993–1996 she was a National Endowment for the Humanities Chair at Bucknell University and until 2005 was a professor of religion at Bucknell. She is a visiting professor at Yale in the Institution for Social and Public Policy.

GARY VALEN serves as a consultant on sustainable agriculture and local food systems from his home in the agricultural preserve near Poolesville, Maryland. He is the former Director of Operations of Glynwood Center in New York and the former Director of Sustainable Agriculture for the Humane Society of the United States. He is the Chariman of the Board of Directors of Meadowcreek, Inc., a sustainable community in the Arkansas Ozark Mountains. Gary founded the first in the nation institutional local food project at Hendrix College in Conway, Arkansas in 1986. He was the first coordinator for the secretariat of the Soul of Agriculture Project for the Human Society and its affiliate, The Center for Respect of Life and the Environment.

IVETTE VARGAS received a PhD in Buddhist Studies from Harvard University and is Assistant Professor in Asian Religious Traditions at Austin College, Texas. Her dissertation, entitled "Falling to Pieces, Emerging Whole: Suffering Illness & Healing Renunciation in the Dge slong ma Dpal mo Tradition," focused on illness and renunciation in Tibetan biographical literature and fasting practices. Her recent and forthcoming publications and research include: "The Life of dGe slong ma dPal mo: The Experiences of a Leper, Founder of a Fasting Ritual, and Transmitter of Buddhist Teachings on Suffering and Renunciation in Tibetan Religious History" (*Journal for the International Association of Buddhist Studies,* 2001); "Tibetan Medicine: The Interface of Religion, Medicine, and the West" in *Religious Healing in Boston: Reports from the Field* (Center for the Study of World Religions Publications, Harvard University Divinity School, 2004); "Keeping It All in Balance: Teaching Asian Religions Through Illness and Healing," *Teaching Religion and Healing* (Oxford, 2006); and "Nun Palmo: A Legend Across Tibetan Communities" (Delhi, 2006). Her interests include illness, medicine, and religious development in Buddhist and Hindu traditions; animals in religion; religious imagery and healing; and the role of women in fasting.

PAUL WALDAU is Director of the Center for Animals and Public Policy at Tufts University's Cummings School of Veterinary Medicine. He holds a PhD from University of Oxford, a JD from UCLA Law School, and an MA from Stanford University in Religious Studies. He is the author of *The Specter of Speciesism: Buddhist and Christian Views of Animals* (Oxford, 2001). Paul has taught courses in animal law at Harvard University, Yale University, and Boston College law schools, and is the Vice President of the Great Ape Project. He is also co-chair of the Animals and Religion Consultation at the American Academy of Religion and the president of the Religion and Animals Institute.

KRISTI WILEY received her PhD from the University of California at Berkeley, where she is a visiting lecturer in the Department of South and Southeast Asian Studies. She has taught Sanskrit and courses on religions of India and religion and ecology. She is the author of the *Historical Dictionary of Jainism* (Scarecrow Press, 2004). She is also a contributor to collections addressing a range of subjects in Jainism, including *Jainism and Ecology* (Harvard, 2002).

STEVEN WISE is President of the Center for the Expansion of Fundamental Law Rights, Inc. He has been a lecturer at Harvard Law School and is an adjunct professor teaching animal rights law at the Vermont and St. Thomas Law Schools. a past president of the Animal Legal Defense Fund. A lawyer whose private practices focuses on animal-related litigation, he is the author of several groundbreaking books, including the widely discussed *Rattling the Cage: Toward Legal Rights for Animals* (Perseus, 2000).

Index

Aborigines (Australia)
  children and Birrinydji narratives, 366–367
  dingo narratives, overviews of, 368–369
  dingos and, 360–370
  intercultural relations, guiding principals of, 367
  maari–gutharra relationship, 362, 363, 364, 365
  Macassans and: benefits of Aborigines' trade with, 364–366; changing characteristics, compared with Aborigines, 363; in Djuranydjura narrative, 364; importance to Yolngu, 362; Yirritja moiety members' relationship with, 363–364
  myths, trade routes in, 364, 365–366
  starter myth, 362–363
Abraham Ibn Ezra, 83
Abrahamic traditions. *See* monotheistic traditions
Abram, David, 475, 646
Abramtzi, Rabbi, 84–85
absent referent, 595
abuse. *See* violence (*hiṃsā*) and oppression
Ācārāṅga Sūtra (Jaina text), 244, 248
accidents, Dogon views of, 385
Adam and Eve (Dürer), 449i
Adams, Carol J.: biography of, 657; chapter

authored by, 591–604; cited, 553, 607, 608, 610
adolescence, 31
adults, loss of animal spirituality, 31
Aelian (Roman naturalist), 413, 417
Aeschylus, 394
affection (*jin*), 298
Africa
  diversity of, 352
  mythology, 351–359; animals and proverbial wisdom, 353, 357–358; animals as living emblems, 357; animals in traditional cultures, 353; of Bamileke people, 355; creation myths, 353; on death, 354–355; elands and shamanic visions, 357; food, origins of, 354; of Kom people, 355; pangolin, 356; rock art and, 356–357; separation of sky from earth, 353–354
  proverbial wisdom, 357–358
  traditional cultures, animals in, 353
After Noah: Animals and the Liberation of Theology (Linzey and Cohn-Sherbok), 89, 136–137
Agamemnon (Aeschylus), 394
agency, 380
aggadic tradition (Judaism), 91
agribusiness. *See* agriculture; animal agriculture; factory farming

Agricide: The Hidden Farm and Food Crisis That Affects Us All (Fox), 559
agriculture: biotechnology, anthropocentrism of, 562; biotechnology, influence on natural ecosystems, 558, 562–563; economic, social, and regulatory concerns, 559–560, 564, 569–570; as export commodity, 568–570; genetic pollution, 563, 566n3; markets and trade wars, 569–570, 571; organic vs. conventional, 560–561, 562, 566; production, ethical and social issues, 570–571, 573–581; production, industrialization of, 568–570; productivity, biotechnological enhancement of, 561–562. *See also* animal agriculture; Earth Charter; factory farming
agro-industrialism. *See* agriculture; factory farming
ahiṃsā. *See* nonviolence
ai (kindness), 298
Ajanta cave-temple, 223–224
Akan people, 357
Akbar (Moghal emperor), 253
Akṣobya Vyūha Sūtra (Buddhist text), 220
al-Damiri (scientist), 155
al-Ghazali, Abu Hamid Muhammad ibn Muhammad, 172
al-Jahiz (scientist), 155
al-Ma'arri (poet), 153

Illustrations are indicated by an "i" after the page number. Notes are indicated by an "n" after the page number.

Alain of Lille, 105, 107, 109

'alam-i mirthal (world of symbols), 172

Alaska, 423, 428, 429, 433

Albigensian crusade, 104

All Ceylon Buddhist Congress, 215n13

Allegoriae in universam Scriptoram Sacram (Rabanus Maurus), 111

Allen, Colin, 462, 469, 482, 484, 488

Altaic peoples, 281

alternative agriculture. See organic agriculture

Ambrose of Milan, 106, 111

American Society for the Prevention of Cruelty to Animals (ASPCA), 607

Americas, religious intolerance in, 329

Ames, Roger T.: biography of, 657–658; chapter authored by, 311–324; cited, 325

Amitābha (Buddha), 221

amphibians, frogs, 165, 224, 237n72

Analects (Lunyu, Confucianist text), 293–296

anatithenai (setting up votive gifts), 400

ancient Chinese religion, 259–272; animals as objects of worship in, 261–263; animals as sacrificial victims, 265–269; animals as spirit mediums in, 263–265; problems of reconstruction of, 259–260; Queen Mother of the West, 261–262; regionalism in, 260

ancient Israel, 65–80

imitatio Dei: domestication and, 69–70; ritual purity and, 67–69; sacrificial process and, 70–72

sacrifices: animal vs. plant, 74; meaning of, 74–75; metaphor and, 72–74; vegetarianism and, 73–74

andalib. See nightingales

Anderson, E. N.: biography of, 658; chapter authored by, 275–290

Anderson, S. W., 506

Androphy, Ronald L., 86

anima (soul, psyche), 8–9

animal, as term, 9

animal agriculture: colonial agribusiness, 558–559; livestock roles in traditional rural economy, 557; market-economic constraints in, 549–550, 553, 558–560; modern methods and policies, 550–553, 557–561; shift from husbandry to industry, 526–527, 549–551, 552, 557, 561, 636. See also factory farming

animal care values. See animal welfare; environmental ethics

animal cults, 32

animal encyclopedias, 103

animal experience, Descartes on, 118–123

animal experimentation: on choices and inhibitory controls, 507–513; Descartes on, 123; on empathy, capacity for, 466, 511–513; on errors of judgment, 507; ethics and techniques, 516, 533, 539–542, 652; on gravity bias, 509–511; on inhibitory controls, 507; Judaism on, 88; Masri on, 155; memorial to animals used in, 403n7; on motivational control, 508, 513; Muslim views on, 155–156;

religious authorities' ignoring of, 53; on rule learning, 508–509; sacrifice and, 392; welfare experiments, 514

animal fatteners (Chinese ritual officers), 266–267

animal-headed female deities, 229

animal law. See animal rights; U.S. legal system

Animal Legal Defense Fund v. The Department of Environmental Conservation of the State of New York (1985), 525–526

Animal Liberation (Singer), 552, 616

animal literature, 104. See also narratives

animal-loss counselors, 28

Animal Minds (Griffin), 495

animal names, 150, 357

animal protection movement, 55

Animal Research Institute (Beijing), 403n7

animal rights: in American legal system, 533, 542, 585–587; animal rights movement, 533, 542, 617–618; anthropocentrism of contemporary debates on, 126, 542, 565; Descartes's influence on modern discussions of, 123–127; in East Asia, 305; increase of attention to, 550; in India, campaigners for, 193n43; in Islamic legal tradition, 152–153; in Jewish tradition, 92; physis-based views of, 126–127; Regan on, 130n46

Animal Rights (Dolan), 551

animal studies, communion of subjects and, 533

animal testing. See animal experimentation

animal welfare: biomedical research and, 516–517, 526–527; cloning and, 520–522, 527–530; economic argument for, 513–514, 552; environmental ethics and, 135–136; genetic engineering and, 516–517, 521–522, 523, 527–530; in modern animal agriculture, 549–552; in new ethics, 525–527, 530–531, 550–551; in traditional ethics, 21, 524–525, 547–549, 554, xvi

animalium: anthropomorphism of, 441; industrialization and, 447; intuitive learning and, 441–442; as mediator, 441; as object of spiritual quest, 447–448; as term, 439; transformation to anthropos, 439–457

animals: antelopes, 356; bats, 357; buffalo, 357, 376; bulls, 443–444; crocodiles, 187; deer, 219, 278; dragons, 283, 317–318; fallow deer, 116n58; frogs, 165, 224, 237n72; goats, 340, 402; griffins, 165; mink, 514; orca, 33; oxen, 448; pangolin, 356; pigs, 70, 164–165; rats, 182, 511–512, 535; sea lions, 490; sheep, 295; squirrels, 32; tigers, 262, 281; veal calves, 87, 96; weasels, 419. See also birds; cows; dingos; dogs; elephants; foxes; horses; insects; lions; mice; monkeys; snakes; wolves

animals, in general

behavior, neurobiological data on, 467–468, 472, 476, 497

consciousness: awareness of the divine

and, 653–656; behavioristic position on, 481, 483–484, 487, 489, 491–493, 496–498; as conscious awareness, 484, 492, 494–497, 502–503, 653–654; Griffin on, 485–490; human consciousness vs., 483–484, 487, 491; nature of, 484, 485, 486–488; philosophers' views on, 489; physiological process, comparison with, 485, 491; possibility of, 481; pre-science's exploration of, 483; privacy argument, 492; probability of, calculated, 492, 497

hospitals and shelters for (pinjrapoles), 245–247

humans' rebirth as, 182, 185, 197

McDaniel's definition of, 133, 139–140

as mediums, 263–265

minds of, in Zhuangzi, 279–280

perceptual encounter with world, 126

problem of diversity of, 13

relationships of, as isomorphic with human relationships, 419

religious vs. secular views of, 42

reverence for, in religions, 2

significance of, 445–446

skins, use of, 152

subject/object views of, 67, 594–597

subjective lives, 461, 483, 493, 653–654

as subjects, 13, 74, 461, 485, 548

suffering of (See suffering)

in the wild, perceptions of, 7–8

wild animals, 143–144, 277, 278, 327–328, 417

See also animal experimentation; cognition (animals); cruelty to animals; domesticated animals; factory farming; human–animal relationships; pets; play; sacrifices; social morality (animals); use relationship; violence (hiṃsā) and oppression

animals' viewpoints. See anthropocentrism, difficulty of avoiding

animism, 377, 379–382

anomaly (zhiguai) literature, 284–285

antelopes, 356

anthropocentric use of animals. See use relationship (human–animal)

anthropocentrism: of agricultural biotechnology, 562; of Christianity, 135, 547, 617; of contemporary animal rights debates, 126, 542, 565; difficulty of avoiding, 57, 462, 634; in Hinduism, 181, 184; Jewish lack of commitment to vegetarianism as, 97; speciesism and, 632, 633, 634; of views on animal morality, 464–465. See also Earth Charter

anthropomorphism: of animalium, 441; biocentric, 462–463; review of criticism, 494; use of, in children's literature, 31–32; in wheel of saṃsāra, 219

Anthropomorphism, Anecdotes, and Animals (Mitchell et al.), 494 *anthropos* (human), transformation from *animalium*, 439–457

anti-heretical literature, 103–116

antinomianism, 32, 189

antitype, type and prototype, 104

anxieties, cultural, 415

Āpastamba (Vedic author), 196, 197

apes. *See* monkeys

Apostolos-Cappadona, Diane: biography of, 658; chapter authored by, 439–457

apotheosis, in sacrifices, 402

appreciation of animals, role in human spirituality, 461, 474, 475–476

Apuleius (writer), 416

aqedah (binding, as part of sacrificial ceremony), 394

Aquinas, Thomas, 5, 9, 120–121, 122–123, 137

Arabian horses, 335

Arabic language, terms for animals and humans, 150

Arabs, in pre-Islamic times, 150

Āranyakas (Vedic texts), 195

Aravinda (king of Potana), 252–253

Arbeitman, Yoel, 93–94, 96

archetypes, 36

Arianism, 106

Aristotle: on animals' souls, 120–121; on animals' use relationship, 122; great chain of being, 154; hierarchical views, 316; *Historia animalium*, 153; on imagination, 120–121; influence of, 330–331; on mice, 415, 416; on slaves, 52

Arius (the Great Heretic), 111

Arkow, Phil, 611

Arluke, A., 608

Arnhem Land, Australia, 362

Arnold of Brescia, 107

Arnolfini Wedding Portrait (van Eyck), 453, 454i

art
    animals in, 439–457; *Arnolfini Wedding Portrait*, 453, 454i; cat-goddess Bastet, 440i; *Five O'Clock Tea*, 445i, 447; *Judith and Holofernes*, 450, 451i, 453; Malraux and, 439; *Monument to General Gattamelata*, 450, 452i; Paleolithic art, 446; problems of analysis of, 443–445; von Simson on, 442, 446; von Simson's chronology of, 447
    Muslim representational, 155
    prehistoric, explanations of, 29
    religion, relationship to, 441
    rock art and African myths, 356–357

Artemidorus (diviner and author), 419

Aryas, 336

Asani, Ali S.: biography of, 658; chapter authored by, 170–175

Asante people, 357

ascetics, 182

Ascione, Frank R., 610, 611

Ashkelon, canine burials at, 27

Asia: ravens in, 425. *See also* Buddhism; China; Confucianism; Daoism; India; Jainism; Tibet

Aśoka (Indian Buddhist king), 210

ASPCA. *See* American Society for the Prevention of Cruelty to Animals (ASPCA)

ASPCA (American Society for the Prevention of Cruelty to Animals), 607

associative learning, 486, 487, 495–496

Astoria Live Poultry, 398

aśvamedha (horse sacrifice), 195

asymmetry of human-animal interactions. *See* use relationship (human-animal)

Athapaskan people, 428

Athapaskan-speaking peoples, 436n34

Athar, Shahid, 159n62

ātman (soul): embodiments of, 189–192; identicalness in all beings, 181; nature of, 189

'Attar, Farid ad-Din, 153, 154, 172–174

attention, Gibson on, 381

Attla, Catherine, 431

augury. *See* divination

Augustine, Saint, 122, 123, 129n30

Augustine of Hippo, 105

Australia: mice in, 415–416. *See also* Aborigines (Australia)

Australian Walers (horses), 336

autonomy of animals, 32–33, 36

Avalokiteśvara (*bodhisattva* of compassion), 231

Avery, Dennis T., 561

Avicenna (Abu 'Ali al-Husayn ibn 'Abd Allah ibn Sina), 172

axis mundi, 353

Aztecs, 392, 396, 401

Ba people (China), 262

Baars, B. J., 481, 482, 486, 496, 497

Babrius (Roman author), 419

Bahn, Paul, 29–30

Baier, Annette, 599

Baker, L. R., 490

Baker, Steve, 597

Balda, R. P., 470

Balikondala (Asian Indian tribe), 339–340, 340

Balkubalku (mythological dingo), 369

Bambi syndrome, 328

Bamileke people, 355

Bandhurrk (mythological dingo), 368

Banks, J., 512

Bantu people, 354

Bartky, Sandra, 593

Bashevis Singer, Isaac, 618, 639

Bastet (Egyptian cat deity), 439, 440i

Bathrick, Dick, 599

bats, 357

Baudhāyana Dharmasūtras (Vedic texts), 197

bawa (respect), 385

Bde kun las byang (*Union of Blissful Manual*), 229

bear altar, in Chauvet Cave, 29–30

Bear with White Paw (Sioux), 34

Bechara, A., 506

Beer, Robert, 227

bees, 166, 493

behaviors: antisocial, 363, 367; commonsense view of, 481; comparative approach to study of, 462, 464–465; flexible versatility, investigation of, 483–484, 486, 489, 498; genetic programming of, 495. *See* associative learning; violence (*himsā*) and oppression

Bekoff, Marc: biography of, 658–659; chapter authored by, 461–480; cited, 482, 484, 488

belief systems, inexplicable traditions and, 408

Bengal, British in, 343

Bennett, J., 494

Bentham, Jeremy, 297

Berekiah, Rabbi, 83–84

Berkman, John, 56–57

Bermond, B., 484, 493

Bernard of Clairvaux, 104, 107, 111

Bernstein, Irwin S., 465

Berntson, G. G., 507

Berry, Thomas: biography of, 659; chapter authored by, 5–10; on evolutionary principals, 645; on the greater community, 515; on human's place in the universe, 160–161, 566, 631–632; on natural world, 2–3, 13, 548; on the world, 134, 645–647. *See also* communion of subjects

Berry, Wendell, 557

Berthold of Regensburg, 109

bestiaries of heretics, 106–112

Beston, Henry, 32

bête-machine hypothesis, 120

Bhagavad Gītā (Hindu text), 181

Bhāgavata Purāṇa (Hindu text), 184, 186–187, 200–201

bhājanaloka (receptacle world), 214n7

Bhils (Indian tribe), 339, 341–342

Bhiṣma (character in *Mahābhārata*), 198–199

Bhutan, 427

Bible: animal-friendly themes in, 137–138, 548–549; Biblical references (*See specific books of the Bible*)

Bible moralisée, 109

bioconcentration camps. *See* animal agriculture, modern methods and policies

biodiversity, in ancient China, 275

bioethics: anthropocosmic transformation, 565–566, 646; Earth Charter and, 621–628; initiatives for, 565, 571–581; multiplicity of intelligences, 646–647; in official policies, 564–565; planetism, 565; regenerative agriculture, 562–565, 574–580; social historical reforms and, 629; sustainable global community and, 560–561. *See also* ecofeminism; environmental ethics; use relationship (human-animal)

biomedical experimentation. *See* animal experimentation

Bird-Davis, Murit, 381

Bird of God, 406

birds: cranes, 277; crows, 357; 406–407, 448; falcons, 1...

birds (*continued*)
  garudas, 225, 226–227; geese, 87; gold-
    crest, 408–409; hawks, 357; hens, 514;
    hummingbirds, 401; nightingales, 171–
    172, 173, 174; parrots, 357; Peng birds,
    279; pigeons, 171, 491; robins, 407;
    wren-hunt ritual, 407–411. *See also*
    ravens (*Corvus corax*)
birds, in general: bird cult in ancient China,
    261; communication and birdsong,
    433n8; Deuteronomy on, 82; Dosto-
    evsky on, 7; hospitals for, 245–246;
    in Islamic mystical poetry, 170–175;
    language of, 171; mental capacity ob-
    served, 488–489, 491; as oracles, 35–36;
    primates, comparison with, 466–467;
    response to Krishna's beauty, 186, 189;
    as sacrificial animals, 70; symbolism of,
    170; taught to communicate, 489–490
Birrinydji (Dreaming figure), 366–367
bla (life force), 232
Black Elk (Nicholas Black Elk, Oglala
    Sioux), 33, 374–376
Blackmun, Harry A., 585, 587
Blobaum, Roger, 572
Bloch, Raymond, 414
Block, N., 486
blood: God and, 71; sacrifices and, 395
Bloss, Lowell W., 222
Blumberg, M. S., 491
Board Shield Man-barbarians (Banshee
    Man), 270n19
Boas, Franc, 436n35
bodhisattvas, 221
bodies: Descartes's conception of, 119;
    Dogon views on, 385–386
Bohemia, C., 469
Bol'lili (mythological dingo), 368
Bolts, William, 349n72
Bond, A., 470
Book of Animals (*Kitāb al-hayawān*, al-Jahiz),
    155
Book of Changes (*Shijing*), 263
Book of Mencius (*Mencius, Mengzi*), 269,
    330
The Book of Odes (*Shijing, Classic of Poetry*),
    18, 266, 275
Book of the Border-keeper (*Marzbā-nāma,
    Warawini*), 155
Book of the Dead, 439
Bookies, Robert, 493
borders, 340, 415, 417, 419, 420–421
Bordo, Susan, 594
Bousquet, G. H., 152
Bowuzhi (*Treatise on Curiosities of Zhang
    Hua*), 284
Boysen, S. T., 507
BPNP (Buddhist Perception of Nature
    Project), 212–213
Bradbury, J. W., 482
Bradshaw, I. G. A., 463
Bradshaw, R. H., 488
Brāhmaṇa texts, 195
Brahmavaivarta Purāṇa (Hindu text), 199
brahmavihāra (divine-abidings), 211
Brahminism, 190

Brahmins (priests), 339
brain and neuroanatomy: consciousness
    and, 466, 485–486, 491, 493, 494, 495,
    497; emotional behaviors and, 469, 506;
    imaging of, 466, 497, 542; nonhumans,
    possible similar structures in, 469, 493,
    497
Bratton, S. P., 548, 553
Brethren of Purity, Pure Brethren (Ikhwān
    al-Ṣafā), 153, 161–162, 168n3
Breuil, Henri, 29
Bṛhadāraṇyaka Upaniṣad (Vedic text), 196
Bringhurst, Robert, 433n6
Brion, Marcel, 442, 446
British, 336, 337, 343
Broome, Arthur, 607
Brother Lawrence, xix
The Brothers Karamazov (Dostoevsky), 7
Brown, A., 489, 494
Brown, Joseph Epes, 36
Brown, R. N., 433n6
Bruce, A., 553
Bruce, D. M., 553
Brueggemann, Walter, 135
Bruemmer, Fred, 28, 428
Bryant, Edwin: biography of, 659; chapter
    authored by, 194–203
Bstan ma bcu gnyis (Tenma Chunyi,
    mountain deities), 226
Buddha. *See* Gautama
Buddha families, 220
Buddhaghosa (Buddhist scholar), 218, 232n2
Buddhism, 207–237; animal-headed female
    deities, 229; on animals, 208; animals
    and Buddhist cosmos, 207–217; ani-
    mals as transmitters and transformers
    in, 218–237; Buddhist modernism,
    212–213; communion of subjects,
    variation on, 209; culture/nature dis-
    tinction in, 211–212; ethical issues,
    animals and, 209–211; five destinies
    in, 208; human-animal distinctions
    in, 35; loving-kindness (*mettā*), 211;
    modern, and animal protection, 212–
    213, 617; monks, restrictions on, 210;
    Theravādan, 207
Buddhist Perception of Nature Project
    (BPNP), 212–213
buffalo, 357, 376
buildings, animals' destruction of, 418
Bull from the Hall of the Bulls (Paleolithic
    art), 444i
Bullard, Robert, 630
bullfighting (*corrida des toros*), 328
bulls, 443–444
Bulunha (mythological dingo), 368
Bunge, M., 484, 485
Burghardt, Gordon M., cited, 462, 467,
    469, 482, 487, 494
Buriat Mongols, 394
Burke, P. D., 539
Burkert, Walter, 69, 396, 402
Burkhardt, Richard W. Jr., 483
Burma, 213
Burnes, Alexander, 344
Burnett, G. W., 469

Burns, Robert, 415
butterflies, 278
bya rog gi skad brtag par bya ba (*Kākajariti*,
    "Examination of the Sounds of the
    Raven"), 425–426
Byers, J. A., 467
Byrne, R., 489

Caitanya (Bengali saint), 188
Caitanyacaritāmṛta (Hindu text), 188
Cakravartin, Viśvanātha, 186
calculative imagination, 120–121
California, mice in, 415
Call, Josep, 467, 513
Callinus (Roman poet), 415
Cameroon, 355
Campany, Rob, 284
Campbell, Joseph, 352
Campbell, M., 553
Canada, Italian immigrants and hunting,
    328
canines. *See* dogs
Cantor, Aviva, 89
Capshew, James H., 536
The Captives (Plautus?), 420
Carey, S., 511
caricatures, 53
Carman, John, 395
carnivores, social behavior and organization
    of, 467
carrion birds, 424
Carrithers, Michael, 232
*The Case of the Animals versus Man Before
    the King of the Jinn* (Basra), 163–168; on
    animals as property, 164; bees in, 166;
    on bodily forms, 163–164; on epochal
    cycles, 165; on eternal life, 167; on
    food, 166; on Greeks, 166; on human
    superiority, 167; location of text, 161;
    mentioned, 153; on pigs, 164–165; pur-
    pose of, 168; rational discourse in, 163;
    on swarming creatures, 166
Casina (Plautus), 418
Cassirer, Ernst, 441
caste system: animal symbolism and, 186;
    dog classification in, 434n18
castles, 422n36
Cathars, 104, 109
Catholic Catechism, on humans' use of
    animals, 54
Cato (Roman statesman), 413
cats, 109, 110, 439, 440i. *See also* lions; tigers
cattle. *See* cows
Cauvel, Jane, 321
Cavett, Dick, 597
Celtic traditions, 406
Center for Respect of Life and Environment
    (CRLE), 571–572, 581
Center for the Study of World Religions,
    Harvard Divinity School, 1
central nervous system. *See* brain and
    neuroanatomy
Ceylon, 220
Chāndogya Upaniṣad, 185
chain of being, 154, 162, 311
Chaisson, Eric, 628n1

Chalk, R., 607
Chalmers, D. J., 482, 486
'cham (dance performances), 227–228
chance, 332n15
Chāndogya Upaniṣad (Vedic text), 196
Chang Kwang-chih, 270n10
change. See metamorphosis; transformations
Chapple, Christopher Key: biography of, 659; chapter authored by, 241–249
chapter authored by, 11–23
Charlotte's Web (White), 398
Chartism, 629, 640n1
Chatsumarn Kabilsingh, 216n35
Chauvet Cave, 29, 30
Cheney, D. L., 485, 487, 497
Cheng Hao, 301
Cheng Yi, 301
Cheng-Zhu School (School of Principle, Neo-Confucianism), 299
chengyi (sincerity of intention), 299
Chenu, Marie-Dominique, 105
Chesterton, G. K., 51
chi (qi), 284, 285, 300, 312–315
chickens, factory farming of, 86–87
child abuse, 605, 607, 610, 636
children: animal naming by, 37n16; animals, changing understanding of, 38n20; animals' importance to, 30–31, 599, 637; communication with, 5
children's literature, 31–32
chimpanzees. See monkeys
China: beef eating in, 325; classical, status of animals in, 315–318; Confucianism, 293–307; Daoism, 275–290; dragon thrones, 220–221; early religion in, 259–272; Europe in seventeenth century, comparison with, 326; human exceptionalism vs. cultural elitism in, 311–324; origins, 317–318; state religion, 295; translation of Chinese term for, 317
Chong, Wei Lien, 320, 321
Choosing a Humane Diet: How to Get Started, 572, 581
Chophel, Norbu, 425
Christ, 104, 408, 410, 448
Christianity, 103–145; animals as emblems in, 448; anthropocentrism of, 135, 547; as becoming good news for animals, 132–145; Descartes and contemporary speciesism and, 117–131; diverging paths within, 136–139; early noncanonical texts, 138; exegetical typology (medieval), 104; Franciscan alternative, 138–139; heresy, medieval animal images of, 103–116; heterodoxy in, 129n24; Instrumentalist tradition, 138; letter/spirit dichotomy, 104–105; McDaniel's definition of, 133, 139; medieval animal lore, sources for, 106; negative traditions, 136–137; positive traditions, 137–138; sacrifices and, 65–66; spiritual depth, 143–144; theological understanding, 142; theory of significance, 105
Chryssipus, 121
Chu ci (Songs of the South), 276, 280
ch'ul (Mayan life force), 395–396

Chulin 84a, 97
Church, R. M., 511
Church of the Lukumi Babalu Aye, Inc. v. Hialeah, 508 U.S. (1993), 585–587
Churchland, Patricia S., 490
cicadas, 287n16
Cicero (Roman orator), 413, 414, 417, 418, 419
Cinci Freedom (cow), 591, 592, 594–595, 598
Cirencester, 422n26
CITES. See Convention on International Trade in Endangered Species
The City of God (Augustine), 122
Clark, Kenneth, 453, 456
Clark, Stephen R. L., 51, 56
Classic of Poetry (Shijing, The Book of Odes), 18, 266, 275
classificatory models, 207
clay horses (thakuranis), 339–340
cloning, 520–524; defense of wrongness of, 521; ethical discussions of, 520; Frankenstein story and, 520; of humans, 520; monoculture and, 524; National Bioethics Advisory Commission report on, 522; negative welfare consequences of, 528–529; reactions to, 521; risks of, 523
Coats, C. David, 551
Cobb, John, 132, 135
Cobb, John B., Jr., 132, 135, 144n1, 145n9, 565
Code, Lorraine, 599
Code of Jewish Law, 83
Codex Alimentarius Commission, 559
cognition (animals): in Hindu tradition, 189; as information processing in nervous systems, 482, 486, 491, 494, 495, 498, 503; recent literature on, 503; reluctantly considered, 481; social, 461, 466–467
cognitive ethology: animal communication, emphasis on, 482, 485; consciousness, question of, 494; human-animal differences and, 498; importance of, 475; methodologies for, 462; as term, criticism of, 487–488
Cognitive Ethology: The Minds of Other Animals (Ristau), 494
cognitive language, animals as, 30
cognitive mapping, 31
Cohen, Noah, 91–92, 95
Cohen, Richard, 223–224
Cohn-Sherbok, Dan: After Noah: Animals and the Liberation of Theology, 136–137; biography of, 659; chapter authored by, 81–90
coins, 415
Colby, A., 506
Coleman, G. J., 553
Coleridge, Samuel Taylor, 7, 453
Collectanea rerum mirabilium (Solinus), 106
comedy of innocence, 402
commoditization of nature, life, and food. See animal agriculture; factory farming
common sense, 299
communal inquiry, 49–50
communication (animals): content and

causation, 494; as evidence of mental experiences, 490; Heinrich on, 433n8; in ravens, 424, 433n8; as scientific data, 482, 485; teaching animals to communicate, 489–490. See also language; speech
communion, as evolutionary principal, 645
communion of subjects: animal studies and, 533; Berry's use of term, 2; Buddhist variation on, 209; as challenge to human–animal relationship, 11; Earth Charter and, 621; food chain and, 647; indigenous peoples and, 373, 377, 378; in Jainism, 250, 251; in Judaism, 90; as model for human–animal relationships, 160–161; physis and, 126–127; significance of animals and, 446; Tucker on, 645–647
community, basis of, 319
companion animals. See pets
compassion, 41, 84, 96, 181–182
complementarity, in Dogon lifeway, 387
Cone, James H., 633–634
The Conference of the Birds (Mantiq al-tayr, 'Attar), 153, 172–174
confinement in animal production, 549–552, 557–558, 569. See also factory farming
Confronting Environmental Racism: Voices from the Grassroots (Bullard), 630
Confucianism, 293–307; Analects (Lunyu), 293–296; cosmic hierarchy in, 321–322; five human relationships, 293; on hermits, 295–296; on human nature (xing), 296–297; Mencius, 296–298; Neo-Confucianism, 299–306; on sacrifices, 294–295, 297; sages, religious authority of, 306n7; Xunzi, 298–299
Confucius: character of, 294; on rituals, 294–295
conscious mental experiences, 490–491
conscious thinking, 481–504
consciousness: absence of neuroanatomical packaging for, 485–486; differences among species, 495, 498; privacy argument, 492; Xunzi on, 298. See also animals, in general, consciousness; mental experiences
consecrated destruction, 396–397
consecration rituals, Tibetan, 230
conservation, 212, 281, 330, 561, 624
Conservative Judaism, on sacrifices, 66
consumerism, 134–135
contemplation of nature, 143–144
contemplative seeing, 133–134
Convention on Biological Diversity (1975), 625
Convention on International Trade in Endangered Species (CITES, 1975), 625
Cook, James, 360
cooperation, 396–397, 469–470. See also social morality
Corbin, Henry, 169n3
corporeal souls, 120
corpses, purification of, 77n21
Corpus Hermeticum (Macrobius), 161
corrida des toros (bullfighting), 328

cosmogony, of Neo-Confucianism, 300
cosmology: Buddhist, 207–217; of Jainism,
    241–244, 255n14; processual (wuhua),
    312–313, 316–317
Costain, Lela, 607
covenants, sacrifices and, 268
Cow Parade, 591
Cow Protection Movement, 180
cowboys, 346
cows: attainment of spiritual liberation,
    187, 188, 189; caste associations of, 186;
    Cinci Freedom, 591, 592, 594–595,
    598; holy, 179–180; in India, 328; of
    Mganderu holy herd, 400; Nuer people
    and, 395; Queenie, 398; ritual killing of,
    195; slaughter of, Vedic texts on, 196;
    three-legged, 261, 262
cranes, 277
creation myths, African, 353
Cree, sub-Arctic, 376–377, 381
Crick, F., 482, 484, 497
Crist, E., 483
CRLE (Center for Respect of Life and
    Environment), 571–572, 581
crocodiles, 187
Cronin, Helena, 495
cross-species matings, 284
Crowcroft, Peter, 417–418
crows, 357, 428
cruelty to animals: animal protection move-
    ment, 606–607; intervention and
    prevention, 612–613; maliciousness,
    range and degrees of, 608–609; motives
    and reasons, 608–610; Okada on, 304–
    305; perpetrators of, 608–610; power
    and control vs. empathy, 608–609;
    religious teachings and, 606–607, 613–
    614; violence to humans, relation to,
    605–606, 608, 609–610, 610–612, 635–
    636. See also suffering; violence (himsā)
    and oppression
Crusades, 41
Cukoo, Eurasian (Cuculus canorus), 434n23
cultural anxieties mice and, 415
cultural elitism, 311–324, 325
cultural sedimentation, 321
curses, rebirth as animals and, 187–188
cuteness, 329
Cyavana (Hindu sage), 198

dabba (nonhuman animals, Arabic), 150
Dalai Lama, 213, 216n38, 463, 475
Dalits (Harijans, Untouchables), 338–339
Dalton, P., 607
Daly, Herman C., 565
dama (Dogon animal mask festival),
    384–388
Damasio, A., 469, 506
dance performances ('cham), 227–228
Dao de jing (Chinese text), 276, 282
Daoism, 275–290; blood sacrifices, call for
    end to, 269; early, 276–279; Huang-Lao
    Daoism, 280; shamanism, connections
    with, 280–281; Six Dynasties texts, 283;
    zhiguai (anomaly) literature, 284–285
Darwin, Charles Robert, 464, 483

Darwin's Cathedral: Evolution, Religion, and
    the Nature of Society (Wilson), 468–469
David, Jacques Louis, 448
Davis, Dick, 174
Davis, Hank, 494
Davis, Karen, 596
Dawkins, Marian S., 487, 513–514
Dawkins, Richard, 465
Dawson, M. E., 496
De bestiis (Hugh of Folieto), 106
De doctrina christiana (Augustine of Hippo),
    105
De nugis curialium (Courtier's Trifles, Map),
    109
de Waal, Frans, cited, 465, 466, 467,
    470–471, 485, 511, 513
death: African myths on, 354–355; burial
    of the dead, 331n9; horses as symbols
    of, 341; human caretakers, effects on,
    28–29; life after, 133; Lucretius on, 124;
    nature of, in sacrifices, 68–69; ritual
    purity systems and, 67–68; sacrificial,
    metamorphosis and, 399–400; sex,
    relationship with, 68; transformation
    and, 279; of the young, 395
decay, Buddha on, 213
Deckan' o' the Wren, 407
DeCleer, Hubert, 234n27
deer, 116n58, 219, 278
Délacroix, Éugene, 448
Delhi, monkeys in, 191n2
demonifuges, 265
Dennett, D. C., 495
Descartes, Rene: on animal experience,
    nature of, 118–123; on immortal souls,
    animals' lack of, 120–121; influence of,
    123–127, 331; on killing animals, 123;
    mythologizing of, 127n2; on pain in
    animals, 121, 122; response to Gassendi,
    119–120; on sight in animals, 121–122;
    Steiner on, 325
Description of the Human Body (Descartes),
    123
Deuteronomy: 5:15, 92; 12:21, 85; 12:23,
    120; 14, 70; 14:2, 83; 22:1–3, 82; 22:4,
    82; 22:6–7, 82; 22:10, 82; 25:4, 95, 548;
    32:14, 104; 32:39, 69; 12–14, 548
developmentalism, 32
Devereux, George, 535
DeViney, E., 610
DeVries, Brad, 572
Dewey, John, 315, 319, 531
Dge slong ma Palmo (Indian Buddhist
    nun), 225–226
dharma (duty, correct ritual behavior), 184
Dharma Sū, 196
Dharmarakṣita (Indian teacher), 221
Dhuwa moiety, 362
Dickert, J., 610
The Dictionary of Art (Turner), 443
Didascalion (Hugh of St. Victor), 105
Diet for a New America (Robbins), 551
differentiation, as evolutionary principal,
    645
diffusion of people and ideas, problematics
    of, 428–429

dingos (Canis lupus dingo, Australian
    dogs), 360–370; description of, 361;
    Djuranydjura, transformation of, 364–
    366; narratives of, overview of, 368–369;
    origin myths, 360–361; symbolic use
    in myth, purpose of, 366; Umbulka,
    362–363, 366–367
directions, of raven speech, 427
discipleship, 140
Discourse on Method (Descartes), 118–119
"Discussion of the Dao of Heaven" (Tianxia
    zhi dao tan), 282–283
diseases and illnesses: The Case of the Ani-
    mals versus Man Before the King of the
    Jinn on, 166; genetic research, 516–517,
    521–523, 527–530; mice infestations
    and, 416; modeling of human, valida-
    tion issues in, 538–539; nāgas and, 225;
    psychological disorders, 538–542; of
    Winter Dance season (Salish), 383–384
A Dissertation on the Duty of Mercy and Sin
    of Cruelty to Brute Animals (Primatt),
    93, 606
distance, religion and, 354
dividual, concept of, 380
divination: Cicero on omens of mice, 413,
    418; raven augury, 423–436; Shang
    oracle bones and, 263; in southern
    China, 260; temporal nature of, 435n30.
    See also omens
divine-abidings (brahmavihāra), 211
divine agency, 424, 429
divine kings, 409
divine world, animals' awareness of, 230
divinity, 35–36, 354. See also God
Diwald, Susanne, 168n3
Djalatung (mythological dingo), 369
Djang'kawu (Aboriginal mythical ancestor),
    362
Djirrwadjirrwa (mythological dingo), 368
Djuranydjura (mythological dingo),
    364–366, 368
Dobel, P., 548, 553
Dobrin, A., 605
Document Pelliot no. 3530 (Tibetan text), 426
Dogon peoples, 384–388
dogs: canine burials, 27; caste associations
    of, 186; Dharma as, 342; dingos, 360–
    370; divination with, 434n18; Muslim
    views on, 157; in Rangoon, Burma,
    215n18; sacrifices of, 264; as spirit me-
    diums, 263–264; spiritual liberation,
    attainment of, 188, 189; symbolism of,
    357; terriers, in art, 445i, 453, 454i
Dol, M., 488
Dolan, Edward, 551
dolphins, 490
domestic architecture, 418
domestic servants, 419–420
domestic violence. See violence (himsā) and
    oppression
Domestic Violence Enhanced Response
    Team (DVERT), 613
domesticated animals: in agricultural
    religio-ecologic contexts, 327, 328; in
    early China, 276; mantic beliefs about,

262–263; as metaphor for ancient
Israelites, 69; mice as, 417; in religio-
ecologies, 326–327; ritual slaughter of,
265–266; as sacrificial victims, 69, 70;
spirits related to well-being of, 262. *See
also* wild animals
domesticated plants, 326
domestication, 69–70, 442
"The Domestication of Sacrifice" (Smith),
69
Dominic (Dominican founder), 109
Dominicans, 109
dominion, as concept, 93–94, 95
*Dominion: The Power of Men, the Suffer-
ing of Animals, and the Call to Mercy*
(Scully), 617
Donatello (artist), 450, 451i, 452i, 453
Doniger, Wendy: biography of, 659–660;
chapter authored by, 335–350; cited,
186, 436n35
Donovan, Josephine, 553
Doogie mice, 516
Dostoevsky, Fyodor, 7
double vision (knowing and being known),
382
dragon thrones, 220–221
dragons, 283, 317–318
dream visitors, 378
drugs, mind-altering, 515
Druids, 406
dso-la (Naxi divination handbooks),
427–428
dto-mba (Naxi ritual experts), 427–428
Du Bois, W. E. B., 55
dualism: in Arnhem Land, Australia, 362;
in Christian thought, 135; of mice, 415;
soul-body dualism, Descartes's, 120; of
Yolngu (Aboriginal people), 362
ducks, 87, 173–174
Dugatkin, L. A., 470
*Dumping in Dixie: Race, Class, and Environ-
mental Quality* (Bullard), 630
Dundon, Stan, 572, 575–580
Dürer, Albrecht, 448, 449i
DVERT. *See* Domestic Violence Enhanced
Response Team (DVERT)
dwelling in the earth, human vocation of,
127
dynamis (energy): of animals, 439–457;
animals as primary visual expression of,
453; domestication and, 442; as term,
439, 441

eagles, 357, 406–407, 448
early Chinese sacrificial religion. *See* ancient
Chinese religion
earth, separation from sky, 353–354
Earth Charter: on animal protection, 623,
624, 625, 626–628; communion of
subjects and, 621; founders of, 622;
mentioned, 134; mission of, 621, 622;
name of our planet and, 622; origin,
worldview, and vision of, 621–623;
Preamble and Principles explained, 621,
623–625, 628n2; related documents,
624, 625; support for, 621–622, 624;

web site, 621; wording, 621, 623–624,
625–626, 628n4
earthist movement, 134–135
East India Company, 343
Eastern Orthodoxy, 395
Eat My Fear (Lynch), 591, 595, 598
Ecclesiastes: 43:13, 111; 3:18–20, 548
Eckhart, Johannes (Meister Eckhart), 633
ecofeminism: absent referent, 595; and animal suffering, problem of, 591, 592, 593,
594–596, 597; "be a man" subjectivity,
597–600; frameworks of, 592–594;
god trick, 600–601; grief, perspective
on, 596–598, 601–602; on the individual and acquisition of knowledge,
599; mass term, 595; objectification of
animal subjects and, 594–597; sexist
language, implications of, 634, 640n.16;
social historical reforms and, 629;
somatophobia, 594; terminal animals,
591, 596, 600; value-hierarchical thinking, 592; vocabulary of devaluation of
women and, 596
eco-justice movement, 133, 140–142
ecological contemplation, 133
ecological theologians, 132
ecology, 638
economic status, 260
economism, 135
ecosystem management, 286–287
eculturation, 322
Eddy, T. J., 513
Edelman, G. M., 482
Egypt, ancient, 77n21
Ehrenfeld, D., 476
Eid al-Adha (Feast of Sacrifice), 150
Eiseley, Loren, 7
Ekalavya (fict.), 343
Ekken, Kaibara, 303
elands, 356–357
Eldredge, Niles, 6
elephants: in Buddhist traditions, 207–
208, 220; lightening, contest with,
354; Marubhūti, 252–253; as metaphor
for rulers, 355; observed behaviors,
466, 472, 473; spiritual liberation,
attainment of, 187–188, 189; white,
214n4
El-Fadl, Khaled Abou, 157
Eliade, Mircea, 441, 453
Eliezer ha-Kapar, 88
elitism. *See* human elitism
El-Sayed, Aladdin, 398
emblems, 448
èmna (animal mask), 386
emotions and empathy (animals): altruism
in rats, 511–512; altruism in rhesus monkeys, 512–513; grief, 472–473; need for
further research on, 466, 467, 471, 473–
474; neurological structures for, 465. *See
also* social morality (animals)
empathy, of ancient Israelites for domesticated animals, 75
empathy (animals). *See* emotions and
empathy (animals)
The Encyclopedia Judaica, 93

Encyclopedia of Comparative Iconography
(Roberts), 443
endangered species, 286, 312
Endangered Species Act, 287
Enggist-Düblin, Peter, 424
The Environmental Dimensions of Islam (Izzi
Dien), 156
environmental ethics: education in animal
protection and, 637; lacunae in social
ethical thought and, 519–520, 526–
527, 531, 629, 638–639. *See also* animal
welfare; bioethics; Earth Charter; environmental justice; science, Frankenstein
myth
environmental justice, 629–642; discourse, exclusivist modes of and,
636–638; ecofeminism and, on sexist
language, 634; environmental racism
and, 630, 631, 636; expansion of, 639–
640; failure to address, 629, 633–635;
human-centeredness, 632, 640n10;
marginalized humans and, 633–636;
scope of field of, 631–633; terminology,
analysis of, 630–631, 633, 639
environmentalism, 212, 286–287
epics, 189, 195
epilepsy, 265
epiphenomenalism of mental experiences,
493, 494, 498
Episcopal Church, 59n35
epistemé (bodily knowing), 375
epochal cycles, 165
Erneling, C. E., 481
eschatology, 515
Essays (Montaigne), 606
eternalism, Buddhism and, 232n2
ethics: anthropocentric framing of, 54;
Buddhist, animals and, 209–211; ethical
values and others, need to understand,
46; of inquiry, 54; in Winter Dance,
382. *See also* morals and morality
ethnography, 429–431
ethological studies, importance of, 475
Etruscan tombs, 416
Etymologiae (Isadore of Seville), 106, 414
Eurasian Cukoo (*Cuculus canorus*), 434n23
Euripides, 394
Europe: ravens in, 425; in seventeenth
century, comparison of China with,
326
Evans, C., 488
Evans-Pritchard, Edward E., 35, 335
Evervin of Steinfeld, 107, 109
evolutionary continuity, and roots of
morality, 464, 498
"Examination of the Sounds of the Raven"
(*bya rog gi skad brtag par bya ba*,
Kākajariti), 425–426
exclusivism, 48
Exodus: 12, 71; 12:46, 394; 13:1, 394; 20:10,
92, 548; 23:4–5, 82; 23:19, 83; 23:26, 83;
25:5, 95–96; 29:38–42, 74
Exorcist (*fangxiangshi*), 264
experiences. *See* mental experiences
experiments. *See* animal experimentation
extinction, 2, 6, 373

eyes, placement of, 347
Ezekiel: 34:11–16, 548; 34:15–16, 75; 37, 73

Faces of Environmental Racism: Confronting Issues of Global Justice (Westra and Wenz), 630
factory farming, 547–582; Christian duty of mercy to animals, violation of, 617; eco-justice movement and, 141; in India, 193n43; influence on human–animal relationships, 328; Jewish views on, 86–87, 617; Masri on, 155; religious authorities' ignoring of, 53; technology of, 549–550; where animals are not integral to ecology, 557. *See also* animal agriculture
Fagen, R., 467, 469
Fajulu people, 354
falcons, 172, 174–175
fallow deer, 116n58
familiars (of witches), 351
Faraone, Christopher, 416
farm animals. *See* factory farming
farm exports, 568–570
Farquhar, Judy, 312
Fasti (Ovid), 418
fatteners, animal (Chinese ritual officers), 266–267
Feast of Sacrifice (Eid al-Adha), 150
feces, as remedy, 264–265
fecundity, of mice, 415–416
feeling, thinking vs., 450
feelings in animals. *See* emotions and empathy (animals)
Feinberg, Joel, 125
Feinstein, Moishe, 96
feminism. *See* ecofeminism
feminist theology, 133, 142
Fernandez, James W. F., 353
fertility, Dogon mask festival and, 386, 387
Fielding, H., 213
Filch, Ralph, 246
1 Peter 5:8, 105, 106
first precept of Buddhism, 209
1 Samuel 2:6, 69
First Time, 28
fish, happiness of, 278
Fisher, J. R., 494
five human relationships (Confucianism), 293
Five O'Clock Tea (Weld), 445i, 447
Five Point Plan for Tibet, 213
five products of the cow (*pañcagavya*), 180
five-sensed rational animals, 250–255
Flack, J. C., 467
Flanagan, O., 482
flies, 156
Flombaum, J., 513
flour-animals (animal effigies), 184
flowers, godhead and, 356
folk taxonomies, in Buddhist texts, 207
Foltz, Richard C.: biography of, 660; chapter authored by, 149–159
food: *The Case of the Animals versus Man Before the King of the Jinn* on, 166; food

chain, 278–279, 647; God and, 72; origins of, in African myth, 354; pate de foi gras, 87; ritual uses of, 196. *See also* meat, eating of; vegetarianism
For the Common Good (Daly and Cobb)., 565
Ford, Clyde W., 352, 356
foreign policy, of Yolngu, 360–361
forests as metaphor, 216n27
forgiveness as a biological adaptation, 468–469
forms human vs. animal, 163–164
Forum on Religion and Ecology, 3n11
Four Beginnings (*siduan*), 296, 299
four-sensed beings, 251
Fouts, R., 489–490
Fox, J., 607
Fox, Michael W.: biography of, 660; chapter authored by, 556–567; cited, 551, 559, 609
foxes: in Daoist texts, 281; Eiseley and, 7; medieval symbolism of, 106, 108; nine-tailed, 261–262; transformations and, 285
France, Anatole, 27
France, wren customs in, 407
Francis of Assisi, Saint, 103, 453
Frankfurt, Henry, 8
Fraser, David: biography of, 660; chapter authored by, 547–555; cited, 548, 549, 550
Frazer, James George, 335
Freedberg, David, 441
Freud, Sigmund, 32
friendship relation, 5
frogs, 165, 224, 237n72
Frontiers of Peace (Kueperferle), 247
Frymer-Kensky, Tikva, 68
Fujita, K., 507
fur, Judaism on wearing of, 96
Furedy, J. J., 496
Fürer-Haimendorff, Christoph von, 228
Furius Philus (Roman consul), 414
"Furry Woman," 283
Further Records of an Inquest into the Spirit Realm (Soushen houji), 284
Fuxi (mythical Chinese sovereign), 263

Gaffney, James, 93, 96
Gainer, P., 512
Gajendra (elephant), 187–188, 189
Galef, B. G., 492
game animals. *See* hunting
Gandhi, Mahatma, 56
Gandhi, Maneka, 193n43
garbhaja (womb-born animals), 254n1
Garden of Eden, 87
Garden of Marvels (Yi Yua), 284
Gardner, B. T., 489
Gardner, H., 481
Gardner, R. A., 489
Garfield, Eugene, 540
Garry, F., 528
garudas (mythical bird-like creatures), 225, 226–227

Gaskell, George, 530
Gassendi, Pierre, 119
gathering-hunting cultures, 326
gati (destinies), 208
GATT. *See* General Agreement on Tariffs and Trade (GATT)
Gautama (Buddha): animal incarnations of, 208; *Jātakas* (birth stories of his previous lives), 212; as a lion, 220; on meat eating, 196; *nāgas* and, 223; on sacrifices, 209; on vegetarianism, 209, 210
Gaylin, Willard, 520
the Gaze, 442
gdon (evil spirit), 225
geese, 87
gender, 280, 284, 375
General Agreement on Tariffs and Trade (GATT), 558, 564
Genesis: 1:20–28, 38n27; 1:26, 162; 1:26–28, 81–82; 1:29, 87; 1:29–31, 74; 3:17–19, 74; 4:1–5, 74; 4:1–8, 74; 8:20, 74; 9:1–3, 74; 9:1–11, 74; 9:2, 162; 9:3, 137; 9:9–10, 92; 22:7, 394; 24:19, 548; problem of interpretation of, 93
genetic diversity, 523–524
genetic engineering: animal suffering and, 527–530, 533, 538–542; compromised ethics of, 521–522, 560; grounds for concern, 560–564, 569; regulatory issues, 560, 562; risks of, 523–524; smart mice, 516–517
genetic influences and consciousness, 486, 503–504, 506
geologians, 11
Georgics (Vergil), 414
gewu (principle in things), 299
Gibbons, Michael, 463
Gibson, James, 381
Giedion, Siegfried, 446
Giotto di Bondone, 455i, 456
Girard, René, 69, 397
Gisiner, R., 490
Glimpses of Paradise: The Marvel of Massed Animals (Bruemmer), 28
global justice. *See* environmental justice
global stewardship, animals and, 621–642
Glut, Donald, 520
go-pūjā (cow worship), 180
goats, 340, 402
God: blood and, 71; as consuming, 72; *Olodumare* (Almighty), 353; sacrificial victims as, 394–395
God-stories (*hari-kathā*), 190
goldcrest (bird), 408–409
Golden Ass (Apuleius), 416
Gombrich, R., 209
good. *See* morals and morality
good news: for animals, Christianity as, 132–145; McDaniel's definition of, 133, 140
Goodall, Jane: cited, 463, 472–473, 476; interview with, 651–656
Goodman, Lenn Evan, 168n3
Gopnik, A., 491

Gorbachev, Mikhail, 622
gosálas (aging and enfeebled cattle), 180
goshala (cow shelter), 245
Gottlieb, Bruce, 470
Gould, C. G., 495
Gould, J. L., 495
Gould, Stephen J., 429–430
Govindacharya, Bannanje, 179
Graham, Martha, 441
Graves, Morris, 448
great chain of being, 154
Great Exorcism (annual festival), 264
great knowledge (*da zhi*), 279
Great Learning (*Zhong-yong*), 322
great sacrifice (*t'ai-lao*), 306n6
Great Ultimate (*Taiji*), 300
Greeks, sacrifices, victim's cooperation in,
     396
Green, Arthur, 97
Gregory IX, 109
Gregory the Great, 106, 111
Grhya Sūtra, 196
Griaule, Marcel, 390n34
grief, 28–29, 186, 596–597, 601–602
Griffin, Donald R.: biography of, 660; chap-
     ter authored by, 481–504; cited, 481,
     482, 490, 493, 495; on consciousness in
     animals, 653
griffins, 165
Griffiths, Paul, 232n2
Grim, John A.: biography of, 660–661;
     chapter authored by, 373–390
Grohmann, Josef, 414
gu poisoning, 265, 288n38
Gu Xin, 320
Guanzi (Daoist text), 280
Guide for the Perplexed (Maimonides), 84
Gujarat, India, 246
gulls, 278
gunas, theory of, 185
Gurarinja (mythological dingo), 368
Gyanendra, King Bir Kibram Shah (of
     Nepal), 180
'gyur ba (transformation), 221

Ha-Levy, David, 96
Haarh, Erik, 231
Hafiz (Persian poet), 170
Haida, Raven and, 428, 433n6
halachic material (Judaism), 91
halaf (instrument of slaughter), 85
Hall, D. J., 553
Hallowell, A. I., 378
Hamad, S., 494
Hammeroff, S. R., 482
Hanafi school of law, 159n64
Hanina, Rabbi, 95
Hanumān (monkey god), 179, 187, 189
haqq al-shurb (law of the right of thirst), 153
Haraway, Donna, 600
Harding, Sandra, 594
Hare, B., 513
hares, 261, 262, 355
hari-kathā (God-stories), 190
Harijans (Dalits, Untouchables), 339

Harlow, Caroline Wolf, 605
Harris, Ian: biography of, 661; chapter
     authored by, 207–217
Harvard Conference on Christianity and
     Ecology, 136
Harvard University, 1, 56
Harwood, D., 550
Hauser, Marc D.: biography of, 661; chapter
     authored by, 505–518; cited, 470, 482,
     485, 506, 508, 509, 511
Havel, Václav, 29
hawks, 357
Hay, John, 21, 23n5
Hayat al-hayawān al-kubra (al-Damiri), 155
hayawān (animals, Arabic), 150
hayawān al-nātiq (speaking animals,
     Arabic), 150
He yin yang ("Uniting Yin and Yang"),
     282–283
healers. *See* shamanism
healing personality (*wichasha wakan*), 374
health. *See* diseases
heart-mind, human, 319, 321
heaven, separation from earth, 353–354
Heaven (*Tian*), 294
Hediger, H., 483
Heffernan, William, 581
Heidegger, Martin, 127
Heinrich, Bernd: on perspectives on Raven's
     prescient powers, 431; on raven speech,
     424, 432, 432n5, 433n6; on ravens,
     folkloric significance of, 425; on ravens,
     learning in, 488–489; on ravens, love in,
     472; on ravens and Koyukon, 428; on
     ravens and moose hunting, 431
Hélinand of Froidmont, 105–106
hell, 214n11, 242, 255n14
Hemacandra (Jaina scholar), 252
Hemsworth, P. H., 553
Henry A. Wallace Institute for Alternative
     Agriculture, 561
Henry of Clairvaux, 109, 111–112
hens. *See* birds
herding, art of, 70
heresy, 104
heretics, bestiary of, 106–112
Herman, L. M., 490
Hermanns, Matthias, 237n71
hermits, moral agency of, 295
heroes, animal, 186–189
Hertzberg, Arthur, 97–98
Herzog, Harold A., Jr., 55
Hessel, Dieter, 141
Hewitt, T. I., 561
Hexameron (Ambrose of Milan), 106
Heyes, C. M., 513
Hialeah, Florida, Santería in, 393, 585–587
Hicks, Edward, 38n21
hierarchies, 94, 184–186, 185, 241–242
high yield farming, 561–562. *See also* animal
     agriculture; factory farming
Hildegard of Bingen, 107
Hillman, James, 30, 36
himsā. *See* violence

Hinduism, 179–203; animal heroes, 186–
     189; anthropocentrism of, 181, 184;
     Brahmin elite, Sanskiritic orthodoxy
     of, 181; hierarchical universe in, 185;
     non-dualist (*advaitin*) theologians, 181;
     nonviolence and vegetarianism in, 184;
     theists, 181; theological disputes in,
     181; vegetarianism in post-Vedic India,
     194–203
Hirsch, Samson Raphael, 94
Historia animalium (Aristotle), 153, 415, 416
Historia Naturalis (Pliny the Elder), 106
Historia Scholastica (Petrus Comestor), 106
Hitopadeśa (Hindu text), 184, 186
*Hobbie v. Unemployment Appeals Commission
     of Florida*, 380 U.S., 586
Hoebel, Bartley G., 540
holistic ecology. *See* environmental justice
holistic view of the world. *See* environmental
     justice
holy cows. *See* cows, holy
Holy Crusades, 41
Honig, W. K., 482
Hood, B., 509
hoopoe bird, 172–174
hope, 124, 125
Horace (Roman poet), 415, 417
Horowitz, Alexandra C., 468
horse-headed figures (Tibetan traditions),
     229
horses
     Arabians, 335
     in art, 450, 451i, 452i, 453
     in Black Elk's visions, 374–376
     clay representations of, 339
     eating habits, 336
     eyes, placement of, 347
     goats and, 340
     horse saints, 342
     in India, 335–350; Bhils and Rajputs
          and, 341–342; breeding of, 336–337;
          cost of, 338; Dalits and, 338–339;
          Freudian views on, 345; gift horses,
          345–347; health problems, 336;
          Marxist views on, 345; Muslim
          horses, 342–344; native tradition
          of, 338; necessity for importation,
          337–338; pre-Indo-European tra-
          ditions, 340–341; sacrifices of,
          400–402; symbolism of, 341; tribal
          horses, 339–341; as work animals,
          338
     lost legs of, 339
     as Native American archetype, 375
     as sacrificial victims, 400–401, 402
     spirits, in ancient Chinese religion, 262
     symbolism, in early Chinese texts, 277
     taming of, 346
     tantric significance of, 229
     Walers, 336
     war, uses in, 336
horticulture, 328
Hosea: 1, 2, 73; 5:12, 111
Hoshino, Michio, 431
Hosiah 2:20, 92

House of Menander, Pompeii, 419
householders (Hindu): *ahiṃsā* and, 183–184
How Are We to Live (Singer), 617
How Monkeys See the World: Inside the Mind of Another Species (Cheney and Seyfarth), 487
HSUS (Humane Society of the United States), 133, 140, 142, 145, 571–572
Huainanzi (*The Masters of Huainan*), 316, 323n17
Huang, Pochi, 435n26
Huang-Lao Daoism, 280
Hubert, Henri H., 66, 391, 395, 397, 402
Hugh of Folieto, 106
Hugh of St. Victor, 105
Hulse, S. H., 482
human–animal forms. *See* therianthropic figures
human–animal relationships: in agricultural religio-ecologic contexts, 328; in ancient Chinese religion, 260–261; animal deaths' effects on, 28–29; benefits of, 8; Black Elk's, 374–376; communion of subjects as model for, 160–161; in Cree, 376–377; crisis moments in, 446; diversity of religious views on, 43; horse-man relationships, 346, 347; human-bird identification, 174; in industrial religio-cultural contexts, 328–329; knowing and being known, 373–390; Patton on, 27–28; societal benefits of, 556–557. *See also* use relationship (human–animal)
human–divine mediation, 35–36
human elitism, 330
human exceptionalism: classical China, 315–318, 318–320; Confucian cosmic hierarchy, 321–322; Li Zehou and, 320–321; moral mind, sedimentation of, 320–321; *qi* as vital energizing field, 312–315. *See also* anthropocentrism; speciesism
human innocence, end of, 447
human nature (*xing*), 296–297, 319
Humane Society of the United States (HSUS), 133, 140, 142, 145, 571–572
humanism, Confucianism as, 293
humans
 animals as metamorphosed, 34
 biology as evolutionary history of, 515
 conscious information processing, 485, 494
 consciousness: awareness of multiplicity of intelligences, 646–647; compared to animal consciousness, 483–484; as ensemble of mental states, 484; renaissance of scientific investigations of, 481–482
 as reference for good and evil, 6
 sacrifices of, in Hindu tradition, 192n27
 self-regulatory behaviors, 515–516
 temptation, activities used against, 515
 uniqueness, claims of, 461
Hume, David, 124, 617–618
hummingbirds, 401
hunger, 94–95

hunting: in agricultural religio-ecologic contexts, 328; Daoist texts on, 278; of horses, 346; in India, 328; indigenous people's approach to, 381; in industrial religio-cultural contexts, 329; moral injunctions on, 281; for pleasure, 88, 152
hunting-gathering cultures, 326
Huxley, Julian, 483
Huysmans, A., 490
Hwang, Woo-suk (South Korean scientist), 520
hyper-separation, 593, 594

ibn 'Abd al-salam, 'Izz al-din, 152–153
Ibn al-Muqaffa, 155
Ibrahim ibn Adham, 154
iconography: chronological analysis, 443; Jaina, 245; of Queen Mother of the West, 261. *See also* art, animals in
icons, 133–134, 135
identification: with animal powers, in Great Exorcism, 264; human-bird, 174; of Jesus and wrens as divine kings, 410; raven as messenger, 428; San boy-eland, 356–357
ideology, religion and, 326
Idowu, E. Bolaji, 353
Idradyumna (king), 188
Igbo people, 354
ignorance, self-inflicted, 52–53
Ikhwān al-Ṣafā (Brethren of Purity, Pure Brethren), xviii, 16, 153, 161–162, 168n3
illnesses. *See* diseases and illnesses
images, 29, 41–42, 450. *See also* art, animals in
imaginary/mythological animals, 165, 224–226, 275, 283, 317–318
imagination, Aristotle on, 120–121
IMF. *See* International Monetary Fund (IMF)
imitatio Dei, 67–70, 71, 72, 95, 98
immortal souls, Descartes on animals' lack of, 120
The Imperative of Responsibility (Jonas), 126–127
impermanence, 216n27
impurity. *See* rituals, ritual purity and impurity
India
 Ajanta cave-temple, 223–224
 animal rights campaigners in, 193n43
 Buddhist traditions, 207–224
 cows in, 328
 Hindu traditions, 179–203
 horses in, 335–350; breeding of, 336–337; cost of, 338; Dalits and, 338–339; Freudian views on, 345; gift horses, 345–347; health problems, 336; Marxist views on, 345; native tradition of, 338; pre-Indo-European equine tradition, 340–341; tribal horses, 339–341; white stallion in *Kim*, 344–345
 Jaina traditions, 241–255
 meat exports, 193n43
 sati (self-burning by widows), 401

indifference, religious, 54–55
indigenous, use of term, 377–378
indigenous peoples: communion of subjects and, 373, 377, 378; knowing and being known, 373–390; spirit of non-living world and, 9; universe, perceptions of, 8
individuals: Dewey on, 319; interrelatedness and, 45–46; in Ojibwa worldview, 378–379
Indrabhūti Gautama, 251
industrial cultures, religio-ecology of, 328–329
industrialization, effects on *animalium*, 447
Inglish, Stephen, 338
Ingold, Tim, 380
inherited preconceptions, 14, 46–47
injuries, animal-inflicted, cures for, 282
inner form of non-living world, 9
insects: bees, 166, 493; butterflies, 278; in Chinese literature, 275; Jaina respect for, 246; Lausch on, 6; moths, 109, 111; in *Zhuangzi*, 276
instincts, four basic, in Jainism, 251
Instrumentalist tradition, 138
integrity, 315
intelligence: differing meanings of, 58n22; multiplicity of, 646; nonhuman, awareness of, 646–647. *See also* cognition (animals)
intentional acts, 210
interagentivity, 377, 380
interconnection of all existence, African belief in, 353
interdisciplinary viewpoints, 44–45, 462, 464
interests and rights. *See* animal rights
interlocking oppressions, 54–55
International Monetary Fund (IMF), 558
intersubjectivity, 380
intimacy, Berry on, 6, 8
intuitive learning, 441–442, 447
inua (animals' human essence), 35
Inuit, 34, 35, 397
Iphigenia at Aulis (Euripides), 394
Iqbal, Muhammad, 174–175
Ireland, wren hunts in, 408
Irenaeus of Lyons, 107
Isaac (Biblical), 394
Isadore of Seville, 106
Isaiah: 2:20, 112; 11:6–7, 9, 85; 14:11, 111; 40:11, 72, 75; 50:9, 111; 51:8, 111; 63:1–6, 71; 63:6–7, 71
Isidore of Seville, 107, 109, 112, 414
Islam, 150–175; animal rights in, 152–153; *The Case of the Animals versus Man Before the King of the Jinn*, 160–168; description of, 149–150; dietary laws, 151–152; meat-eating and slaughter, 151–152; Muslim literature and art, 154–155; Muslims scientists, 155; mystical poetry, birds in, 170–175; philosophy and mysticism, animals in, 153–154; texts of, animals in, 149–151; vs. Muslim, 149. *See also* Qur'ān
Isle of Man, 407–408, 408

Israel: seven sacred foods of, 97. *See also* ancient Israel; Judaism
Israel Museum, 27
Isserles, Moses, 88
Izzi Dien, Mawil, 156

Jackson Knight, W. F., 418
Jacobson, Dorane, 179–180
jaguars, 36
Jaini, Padmanabh S., 189, 242
Jainism, 241–255; animal lives, regard for, 47; animal protection in, 245–247; animal symbolism in, 244–245; communion of subjects in, 250, 251; cosmology of, 241–244, 255n14; five-sensed animals in, 250–255; on injuring animals, 214n12; primary vows of, 244; sectarian traditions in, 254n2
Jājali (Hindu sage), 198
James 5:2, 111
Japan, Neo-Confucianism in, 303–306
Jasper, James M., 55
Jātakas (birth stories of Buddha's previous lives), 35, 212, 218
Jaṭāyu (vulture-king), 187
Jennings, H. S., 492
Jenny Wren, 406, 410
Jeremiah: 11:19, 68; 11:20, 72, 73
Jerstad, Luther, 228, 230
Jewish tradition. *See* Judaism
jin (affection), 298
Jinas (Tīrthaṅkaras, enlightened ones), 244, 250
Jinsilu (Reflections on Things at Hand, Zhu Xi), 301, 302
jīva (life force), 241
Job: 4:19, 111; 13:28, 111; 27:18, 111; 39,40, 164
John: 10:12, 107; 19:33–34, 36, 394; 10:12a, 107; 10:12b, 107
Johnson, D. M., 481
Johnson, Elizabeth, 133, 142, 143
Johnson, Mark, 379
Johnson-Laird, P.N., 481
Jonas, Hans, 126–127
Judah ha-Hasid, 83
Judah the Prince, Rabbi (Judah haNasi), 398–399
Judaism, 65–99; on animal experimentation, 88; on animal welfare, 82–83, 83–85; Bible translations, problems of, 96; Code of Jewish Law, 83; communion of subjects in, 90; compassion in, 84, 96; diversity of voices in, 89; on fur, wearing of, 96; on hunting for pleasure, 88; justice for animals, 95; on lost animals, 82; modern society, animal welfare in, 86–89; moral life, vision of, 81; on pain, 83; on pets, 88–89; religious slaughter, 85–86, 96–97; retributive justice, application to animals, 92; Sabbatical years, treatment of animals during, 83; sacrifices, 65–80, 392; *tsa'ar ba'alei chayim* (kindness to animals), 85, 86, 87, 88, 91; on veal calves, 96; vegetarianism and, 87–88, 97–98

Judaism and Animal Rights (Androphy), 86
Judas, wrens as, 408
Judges (Biblical text): 14:4, 548; 15:4–5, 107
Judith and Holofernes (Donatello), 450, 451i, 453
Jung, Carl, 361
junzi (moral human), 294
justice, 95, 399

Kaiser, Rudolph, 9n1
Kākajariti (*bya rog gi skad brtag par bya ba,* "Examination of the Sounds of the Raven"), 425–426
Kakmanmurru (mythological dingo), 369
Kalechofsky, Roberta: biography of, 661; chapter authored by, 91–99
Kālidāsa (playwright), 186
Kalila and Dinma (fable collection), 155
Kalpa Sūtra, 244
Kāmadhenu, 180
Kamil, A. C., 470, 498
Kant, Immanuel, 59n33, 320–321
Kapleau, Philip, 617
karma, 247, 251, 254n4
Karṇī Mātā, 182
Karson, E. M., 529
kashrut (Jewish dietary laws), 97, 617
Kassam, Zayn: biography of, 661–662; chapter authored by, 160–169
Kathiawar horses, 336–337
Katz, Eric, 97
Kaufman, Gus, 598
Keduli (Asian Indian tribe), 339
Keller, Otto, 414
Kellert, Stephen, 613
Kelley, W. N., 530
Kennedy, J. S., 491
Khamene'i, Ayatollah Ali, 157
Kienzle, Beverly Mayne: biography of, 662; chapter authored by, 103–116
kikinu (spiritual principles), 386
killing of animals: Aquinas on, 122–123; Augustine on, 122, 129n30; Descartes on, 123; Plutarch on, 128n11; Santería animal sacrifice, 585–587. *See also* meat, eating of; ritual slaughter; sacrifices
Kim (Kipling), 337, 338, 344–345
kindness (*ai*), 298
Kindred Spirits: How the Remarkable Bond Between Humans and Animals Can Change the Way We Live (Schoen), 474
King, P., 607
king of kings, development of, 327
King of the Beasts (pangolin), 356
kings, 222, 409
kingship, and agricultural religio-ecology, 330
kinship: of dingo pups, 362; Earth Charter on, 627; in Judaism, 91–99; Lakota concepts of, 376; of primal peoples with animals, 446; regaining sense of, 647
Kipling, Rudyard, 337, 344–345
Kiriazis, Judith, 433n8
Kirschenmann, Fred, 571
Kitāb al-hayawān (*Book of Animals,* al-Jahiz), 155

Klawans, Jonathan: biography of, 662; chapter authored by, 65–80; cited, 548
Klee, Paul, 448
klu khang (Tibetan temple), 224
klu (snake-like entities), 224–226
knowing and being known: Gibson on, 381; indigenous perspectives on, 373–390; scientific knowledge vs., 381–382
knowledge: of animals, limitations on, 44, 465; art and, 441; nature of, 278
Kodapen (Asian Indian tribe), 340
Kohlberg, L., 506
Kom people, 355
Komal Rajya Laxmi, Queen (of Nepal), 180
Korkus (Asian Indian tribe), 339
Koyukon people, 428
Kramrisch, Stella, 340, 341, 343
Krauss, Franklin B., 414
Kṣatriyas (warriors), 184, 198
Kṣatriyazation, 341
Kuczaj, S., 466
Kueperferle, Paul, 247
Kuk, Avraham, 93, 95, 97, 98
Kunbis (Asian Indian tribe), 340
Kūrma Purāṇa (Hindu text), 200
Kurrumul (mythological dingo), 368
Kusher, Howard, 55
Kutch (India), 343, 344
Kuwahara, H., 512
Kwoth (Nuer god), 395

LaFollette, Hugh, 538
Lakoff, George, 379
Lakota tradition, 374–376
Lakshmi (cow), 187, 188, 189
Lakṣmī (Hindu goddess), 180
Lal Beg myth, 339
Lambert, Kelly, 540, 541
The Lament of the Nightingale (*Nala-yi-Andalib,* Nasir), 174
Landau, Yehezkel, 88
land ethic, 7
language: of animals, 119, 150, 156, 385, 433n8; assumptions in, 164; Ojibwa, 379; Tungus, 280. *See also* communication (animals); speech
Language of the Birds. See Conference of the Birds
Lany'tjun (Aboriginal mythical ancestor), 362
Lao Dan (Laozi), 279
Latour, Bruno, 534
Lau, D. C., 319
Laufer, Berthold, 425–426
Lausch, Joanne, 6
law of the right of thirst (*haqq al-shurb*), 153
Lawrence, Elizabeth A.: biography of, 662; chapter authored by, 406–412
The Laws of Manu, 184, 185
LCA (Life Conservationist Association), 212
Leahy, Michael P. T., 123–124
learning, Xunzi on, 298
legal standing. *See* animal rights
leopards, 116n58, 357
Leopold, Aldo, 6–7, 8
leprosy, 225

letter/spirit dichotomy, 104–105
Letters to Atticus (Cicero), 418
Levenson, Jon D., 70–71
Levi, Rabbi, 83–84
Lévi-Strauss, Claude, 30, 335
Lévinas, Emmanuel, 391
Leviticus: 1, 2, 74; 1:2, 65; 1:3, 71; 10:10, 71;
    11, 70; 11:7, 69; 11:46–7, 71; 17:10–14,
    67; 17:11, 395; 19:1, 395; 22:16–28, 71;
    22:17–28, 71; 22:19–20, 70; 22:28, 83;
    24:5–9, 74; 25:6–7, 83; on *imitatio Dei*,
    68; on ritual impurity, 67
Lewin, R., 490
Lewis, C. S., 596
Lewis, D. B., 528
li (principle of things), 300–301
li (rituals), 294–295, 296
Li Ruohong, 435n26
Li Zehou, 320–321
Liber divinorum operum (*Book of Divine
    Works*, Hildegard of Bingen), 107
liberal theory, 126
liberation (*moksa, mukti*), 185, 187, 253
Libet, B., 494
Lieberman, P., 490
Liexianzhuan (Daoist text), 283
Liezi (Daoist text), 278
life, 133, 184–186, 351
life force (*bla*), 232
life force (*jiva*), 241
life projects, 124, 125, 126
life sciences, 57n9
lifeway (lifework), 378–379
Lijmbach, S., 493
Lindahl, B. I. B., 489
Linnaeus, 51
Linzey, Andrew, 89, 133, 136–137, 142, 548
The Lion King (Disney), 332n13
lions: in Buddhist traditions, 220; as Chris-
    tian emblem, 448; in Jaina stories,
    242; lion figures, 155; in *The Lion
    King*, 332n13; lion of Judah, 106; as
    representatives of evil, 105
livestock industry. *See* animal agriculture,
    modern methods and policies
Livy (Roman historian), 413
Lloyd, Genevieve, 594
Lockard, Robert B., 535
Lockwood, Randall, 610
Lodrick, Deryck, 245, 246
logos (reason), 119
long (dragons), 317–318
Lord, Albert, 430–431
Lorenz, Konrad Z., 473, 483
lost animals, 82
love for animals, importance of. *See*
    spirituality
loving-kindness (*mettā*), 211
lovingness, 298
Lowther, G. R., 467
Lu, China, bird cult in, 261
Lucretius (Roman poet and philosopher),
    124, 414
Luke: 12:33, 111; 13:15, 548
Lunyu (*Analects*, Confucianist text),
    293–296

Lusso, P., 523
Luther, Martin, 137
Lu Xiangshan, 299, 301
Luzzatto, Samuel David, 84
Lynch, David, 591, 595
Lynch, Michael E., 537

maari-gutharra relationship, 362, 363, 364,
    365, 366
Macassans (traders): Aborigines' trade with,
    benefits of, 364–366; changing char-
    acteristics, compared with Aborigines,
    363; in Djuranydjura narrative, 364;
    importance to Yolngu, 362; Yirritja
    moiety members' relationship with,
    363–364
Macdonald, D., 475
MacDonald, Mary, 404n13
Macer, Daryll R. J., 565
machines, animals as. *See* Descartes, Rene;
    speciesism
Mackey, B. G., 463
MacKinnon, Catharine A., 596
Macrobius (writer), 161
Madhva (Madhvacharya), 184
Madi people, 354
magic, 410, 447–448
A Magic Still Dwells (Patton and Ray), 430
Mahā Kassapa (Buddhist saint), 212
Mahābhārata (Hindu text), 182, 188,
    198–199
Māhābhārata, 195
Maharashtra, India, 341
Mahāvīra, 242, 244, 252
Mahner, H., 484, 485
Maimonides, Moses, 83, 84
Maine Coalition to End Domestic Violence,
    607
Majesty and Meekness (Carman), 395
Major, John, 323n17
Makah tribe, 329
Malaba, India, 336–337
Mali, 384–388
Malinowsky, Bronislaw, 396–397
Malraux, André, 439
Man and Animal (de Silva, von Simson and
    Hinks), 442
Manchu language, 280
Mani Rimdu rituals, 228–230
manitou (cosmological forces), 378
Mantiq al-Tayr (*Conference of the Birds,
    'Attar), 153, 172–174
Mantiq ut-Tayr ('Attar), 172
Manu, 184, 185, 197–198
Maoist volunteerism, 320
Map, Walter, 109
Maqamat-i-tuyur. *See Conference of the Birds*
Marbury, Steve, 574
Marc, Franz, 448
Marco Polo, 336–337
Marcus, Erik, 551
marginality. *See* anthropocentrism; envi-
    ronmental justice; speciesism; violence
    (*himsā*) and oppression
market forces, 550, 578
Markowitz, Hal, 466

Marler, Peter, 466–467, 488
Marmuru (mythological dingo), 369
Marshack, Alexander, 30
martial arts, 282
Marubhūti (elephant), 252–253
Mary (mother of Christ), 410
Marzbā-nāma (*Book of the Border-keeper,
    Warawini*), 155
masks, 227, 228, 264, 384–388
Mason, Georgia J., 514
Masri, Basheer Ahmad, 155
mass term. *See* ecofeminism, objectification
    of animal subjects and
Massachusetts Society for the Prevention of
    Cruelty to Animals (MSPCA), 608
massed animals, 28
Masserman, J. H., 466, 512
Mathnawī al-ma'anawī (Rumi), 153–154
matrilineal cultures, 326
Matsya Purāṇa (Hindu text), 200
Matthew: 6:19, 111; 7:15, 107; 8:20, 107;
    10:7, 107
mausya-loka (middle world), 242
Mauss, Marcel, 66, 391, 395, 397, 402
Mawangdui medical corpus, 288n37
Maya, *ch'ul* (life force), 395–396
Mayr, Ernst, 639
Mbanderu people, 397, 400
McCloskey, H. J., 125
McDaniel, Jay: biography of, 662; chapter
    authored by, 132–145; cited, 112
McDonough, Christopher Michael: biog-
    raphy of, 662; chapter authored by,
    413–422
McFague, Sallie, 133, 143, 144
McIntosh, Ian S.: biography of, 662–663;
    chapter authored by, 360–370
McRae, M., 473
meaning: in animal communication, 433n8;
    indigenous environmental knowledge
    vs., 381
meat, eating of: in China, 263, 325; India's
    meat exports and, 193n43; Islam on,
    151–152; Izzi Dien on, 156; Judaism on,
    96–97; Luther on, 137; *Mahābhārata*
    on, 198–199; Manu on, 197–198; in
    modern world, 557, 591, 595–596, 598–
    599, 636; Vedic texts on, 195. *See also*
    vegetarianism
Mech, David, 470
mechanism. *See* Descartes, Rene; speciesism
medicine, 264, 282, 285, 286
medieval heresy, animal images of, 103–116
meditation, 211–212, 213, 353
mediums, animals as, 263–265. *See also*
    divination
Meijsing, M., 488
Melampus (mythical Greek seer), 418
Melson, Gail F., 31, 599
Mencius (Meng Zi, Confucian thinker),
    296–298, 314–315, 318, 321, 330–331
Mende people, 354
Meng Zi. *See* Mencius
mental concepts, replacement by neuro-
    physiological mechanisms, 490–491
mental experiences: conscious vs. neural-

based, 490–491; differences among species, 495, 503; as domain to be removed from science, 491–492, 493, 498; epiphenomenalism of, 493, 494, 498; limits in animals, 490–493, 498; as local causes of behavior, 485; origins of, 485, 492. *See also* animals, subjective lives; consciousness

mentality. *See* consciousness; mental experiences

Menzel, E. W., 482

mercy, justice vs., 399

messengers, ravens as, 425, 434n11

messianism, Jewish, 97

The Metabolic Basis of Inherited Disease (Scriver), 529

metacognitive reflection. *See under* animals, subjective lives

metamorphosis, 32, 111–112, 374, 399–400. *See also* transformations

metaphors: in African proverbial wisdom, 357; of ancient Israelites and domesticated animals, 69; animals as, in Buddhist narratives, 218, 219–220; in *Dao de jing*, 282; Lakoff and Johnson on, 379; sacrifice and, 72–74

metempsychosis (*tanasukh*), 35, 150

meto (personal thought), 376–377

mettā (loving-kindness), 211

Meuli, Karl, 396, 402

Mi g.yo glang bzang ma (Tibetan goddess), 230

mice, 413–422; alleged terrestrial origins, 414; calcium, need for, 416; confined spaces, liking for, 417–418; domestic servants, association with, 419–420; houses, relationship with, 418, 419; infestations of, 415–416; life and death, associations with, 417; liminal nature, 415, 417, 419, 420–421; as omens, 413–414, 416, 417; reproductive rates, 415–416; Romans and, 413–422; smart mice ("Doogie" mice), 516; species in Roman era, 414; as thieves, 418–419

Michaelangelo, 422n23

Middle Ages. *See* medieval heresy, animal images of

Midgley, Mary, 52, 553, 554

migration, of Asian hunters, 429, 436n34

migratory herding animals, 327

Milgrom, Jacob, 67, 404n15

Mill, John Stuart, 617

Miller, George A., 481, 490

Miller, R. E., 512

mind. *See* entries beginning "mental"

Mind of the Raven: Investigations and Adventures with Wolf-Birds (Heinrich), 472

mindful attention, 143

minding animals. *See* cognitive ethology

mink, 514

mirror (of God, *speculum*), 105

mistapeo (personalized spirit helpers), 377

Mistassini Cree, 381

Mitchell, James, 540

Mitchell, R. W., 494

The Modern Ark: The Story of Zoos: Past, Present and Future (Croke), 55

modern societies, 135

Moghuls, 335

moieties, of Yolngu, 362

mokṣa (*mukti*, liberation), 185, 187, 253

moles (animals), 111–112

Moling, St., 408

Moncrief, L. W., 548

money, mice on, 415

Mongolia, 428

Mongols, 394

monkeys: in Buddhist texts, 207; in Delhi, 191n2; observed behaviors and experiments, 466, 472–473, 489–490, 507–513, 653–654; status in India, 179; taught to communicate, 489–490, 493, 497

monks, Buddhist, 210, 211–212

monotheistic traditions, 33–34. *See also* Christianity; Islam; Judaism

Montaigne, Michel de, 606, 617–618

monthly ordinances (Chinese state calendars), 263, 267

Monument to General Gattamelata (Donatello), 450, 452i

Moorcroft, William, 344–345

moral human (*junzi*), 294

The Moral Status of Animals (Clark), 56

Moralia in Job (Gregory the Great), 111

morals and morality

    moral agents: animals as, 242; in Confucianism, 293; hermits as, 296; human category applied to animals, 464, 466, 505; negative consequences of, 253

    moral behavior, 506–507

    moral capacity, taxonomic distribution of, 466, 467

    moral codes of Daoist religious communities, 281

    moral communities, 123

    moral life, Judaism's vision of, 81

    moral nature, Confucianism on, 302

    moral obligations, animals' lack of, 121

    moral qualities of animals, didactic use of, 103

    moral reflection, Neo-Confucianism on, 300–301

    moral relations, Confucianism on, 294, 297–298, 305

    moral responsibility for proper animal care, 552–553, 600–602

    Xunzi on morality, 319

    See also bioethics; ethics; social morality (animals)

More, Henry, 118

More, Thomas, 606

Morgan, C. Lloyd, 486, 495

Mormon Church v. United States, 136 U.S. (1990), 587

Mortensen, Eric D.: biography of, 663; chapter authored by, 423–436; cited, 402

Morton, James, 614

moths, medieval symbolism of, 109, 111

Mourning Dove (Salish author), 389n29

Mousa, Shaker, 540, 541

mouse. *See* mice

movement, animals as models for, 277, 282–283

Mozi (philosopher), 297–298

MSPCA (Massachusetts Society for the Prevention of Cruelty to Animals), 608

Mudaliar, A. D., 187

Muhaiyadeen, M. R. Bawa, 156

Muhammad (prophet), 152, 156

Muir, John, 54, 461

Mukobi, K., 507

mukti. See mokṣa

mukti (liberation, *mokṣa*), 185, 187, 253

mus (mouse), as term, 420

Muslim horses in India, 342–344

Muslims, 149, 150. *See also* Islam

Myers, Norman, 6

mythological animals. *See* imaginary/mythological animals

myths and mythology: Aboriginal starter myth, 362–363; African (*See under* Africa); animals in, 335–370; blame, projection from usurpers to usurped, 341–342; Chinese, therianthropic figures in, 317; complexity of animal images in, 33; dingos symbolic use in, purpose of, 366; Ford on, 352; mythology of horses in India, 335–350; white horses in, 346

Myths of the Dog-Man (White), 30

Nafs-i Kull (Universal Soul), 167

Nagarajan, Vijaya Rettakudi, 189

Nāgārjuna (Indian Buddhist scholar), 224

nāgas (snake-like entities), 222–224, 225

Nagel, Thomas, 126, 131, 495

Nakhshabi (writer), 155

Nala-yi Andalib ("The Lament of the Nightingale," Nasir), 174

Namalia (mythological dingo), 368–369

naming of animals, 37n16, 94, 268

Narni, Erasmo di, 450, 452i

narratives: Buddhist, 218–237; Daoist, 278; dingo, overview of, 368–369; Djuranydjura narrative, 364–366; on wrens, 406–407. *See also* myths and mythology; stories

Nash, James, 452

Nasir, Muhammad, 174

Nasr, Seyyed Hossein, 162, 168n3

National Bioethics Advisory Commission, 522

National Clearinghouse on Child Abuse and Neglect Information, 610

National Dialogue on Sustainable Agriculture, Marketing and Organics Issue Committee (NDSA), 564

Native Americans: Black Elk (Oglala Sioux), 33, 374–376; Cree, sub-arctic, 376–377, 381; Lakota tradition, 374–376; northern, visionary traditions of, 32–33

Natsoulas, T., 484

Natural History (Pliny the Elder), 413, 414, 415, 417

Natural Questions (Seneca), 414

nature (natural world): Berry on, 2–3; contemplation of, 143–144; human need for, 5; human reciprocity with, 407; loving kindness of, 303; quiet listening to, 143–144; traditional Western view of, 126

Naxi, 427–428

NDSA (National Dialogue on Sustainable Agriculture, Marketing and Organics Issue Committee), 564

Nebesky-Wojkowitz, René de, 228, 230, 232

Needham, Joseph, 290n77

Nelkin, Dorothy, 55

Nelson, Lace, 33

Nelson, Lance E., 33; biography of, 663; chapter authored by, 179–193

Neo-Confucianism, 299–306; cosmogony of, 300; in Japan, 303–306; Mencius and, 296; metaphysical models, 299–301; things, unity of, 301–303

Nepal, 225, 228–230

Netton, I. R., 161, 168n3

neural-based mental experiences, 490–491

neuroanatomy. See brain and neuroanatomy

New Year rites, 409

Newar tradition, 225

Newkirk, Ingrid, 617–618

Newman, J., 497

Ngag dbang bstan 'dzin nor bu 'gyur med chos gyis blo gros (author), 229

Ngalalwanga (mythological dingo), 369

Niehardt, John, 376

nightingales, 171–172, 173, 174

nigoda (micro-organism), 241

non-living world, inner form of, 9

nonconscious information processing, 491

nonhuman animals. See animals

noninjury. See nonviolence

nonviolence (ahimsā), 181, 182–184, 198–199, 245, 289n77. See also violence (himsā) and oppression

Nuer people, 35, 354, 395, 404n13

Numbers: 19:1–21, 397–398; 19:8, 67; 19:10–22, 67; 22:32, 83; 28:1–8, 74

numinousness, 277, 326, 331n2, 347

Nursi, Bediuzzaman Said, 155–156

oaths, 268

objectification of animals, 105, 112, 261–263. See also pets

observations of animal lives, 461, 466, 472–473, 488–489. See also specific animals

Ogawa, N., 512

Ohman, A., 496

oikeiosis (community), 121

Ojha Kumhars (Asian Indian tribe), 339

Ojibwa, 378–379

Okada Takehiko, 303–305

Old MacDonald's Factory Farm (Coats), 551, 554

Olodumare (Almighty), 353

Olton, D. S., 482

omens: mice as, 413–414, 416, 417. See also divination

On Divination (Cicero), 413, 418

On Dreams (Artemidorus), 419

On the Nature of Animals (Aelian), 417

On the Nature of the Gods (Cicero), 417, 419

On the Nature of Things (Lucretius), 414

On the Republic (Cicero), 414

one-sensed beings, 251

Opoku, Kofi Asare: biography of, 663; chapter authored by, 351–359; cited, 533, 535

oppression. See violence (himsā) and oppression

oracles. See divination

Oracles and Demons of Tibet (Nebesky-Wojkowitz), 232

orca, 33

order in Buddhist traditions, 222–223

Oregon v. Smith, 494 U.S. 872 (1990), 585–586

organic agriculture vs. conventional agriculture, 560–561, 562, 566

Orientalism, 344–345

Origen, 105

Orissa (Asian Indian tribe), 339

Orthodox Judaism, 76n8

The Orthodox Way (Ware), 143

oru (bushland), 384–385

orubaru (Dogon male cultural leaders), 384–385

others: animals as, 41–42, 126; assimilation of, 345; dynamis of animalium as, 442; religions and, 14–15; religious significance of animals as, 43. See also objectification of animals

The Others: How Animals Made Us Human (Shepard), 14, 28

Overmeier, J. Bruce, 539

Ovid (Roman poet), 418

Owings, D. H., 482

ownership, beauty and, 7

ox-names of Nuer people, 35

ox officers (Chinese ritual officers), 267

oxen, as Christian emblem, 448

Pad ma gling pa (Tibetan visionary), 227–228

Padma Thang Yig (biography), 226

Padmasambhava (tantric meditation master), 224, 231

pain, 83, 121, 122. See also suffering

Paleolithic art, 446

Paley, William, 52

Pāli canon (Theravāda Buddhism), 207

Palmo, Dge slong ma (Indian Buddhist nun), 225–226

pañcabali (sacrificial offering), 180

pañcagavya (five products of the cow), 180

Pañcatantra (Hindu text), 186

pangolin (King of the Beasts), 356

Panksepp, Jaak, 465, 467, 472

Paper, Jordan: biography of, 663; chapter authored by, 325–332

parasites (humans as), 420

Pāraskara (Vedic author), 196

Parrot Book (Tūtī-nāma, Nakhshabi), 155

parrots, 357

paśu-badha (animal-binding), 183–184

Passmore, John, 128n18

pastoralist ethics, 21. See also environmental ethics

Patañjali (Hindu writer), 182

pate de foi gras, 87

paths, constraints on traveling, 43–44

patrilineal cultures, 327

Patton, Kimberley C.: biography of, 663; chapters authored by, 11–23, 27–39, 391–405; cited, 230; interview with Jane Goodall, 651–656

Paul, Robert A., 237n71

Paul, Saint, 95, 96

"The Peaceable Kingdom" (Hicks), 38n21

peacock thrones, 221

Pease, A. S., 414

Pellis, Sergio, 468

Peng birds, 279

Penman, Danny, 551

People for Animals, 193n43

Pepperberg, I. M., 490

perceptual consciousness. See animals, in general, consciousness

Persia, 171–172, 174

personal archeology, 43

personhood, indigenous perspectives on, 373–390

Peterson, Gregory R., 464, 465, 466

Petrus Comestor, 106

pets: animalium as anthropos, 447; in antiquity, 419; care of, 144; dogs as, 157; Hillman on, 36; Jainas and, 248; Judaism on, 88–89; McDaniel on, 134

Phillips, Mary, 536

Philo (Jewish historian), 41

Philo of Alexandria, 97

Photinus (heretic), 111

phra men ma (female figures), 229

Physiologus, 106

physis (nature), 118, 126–127

Picasso Pablo, 448

pigeons, 171, 491

pigs, 70, 164–165

pimadaziwin (good life), 378–379

pinjrapoles. See animals, in general, hospitals and shelters

pinjrapoles (animal hospitals and shelters), 245–247

Pinker, S., 506

piṣṭa-paśu (animal effigies), 184

Plans and the Structure of Behavior (Miller et al.), 481

plants: in agricultural religio-ecologic contexts, 328; in Buddhist traditions, 214n7; Confucianism on, 302; domesticated plants, 326; Ekken on, 303; flowers and the godhead, 356; Hinduism on, 184; roses, 171–172. See also vegetarianism

plastromancy, 263

Plautus (Roman playwright), 418

play (animals), 467–469, 470, 471, 653–654. See also social morality (animals)

Pliny the Elder, 106, 413, 414, 415, 417

Plous, Scott, 540

Plumwood, Val, 592, 593, 594, 601

pluralism, 48

Plutarch, 119, 128n11, 407, 418, 617–618

pneuma (vital and spiritual character of things), 312

Poetic Art (Horace), 415

poetry: Islamic mystical, birds in, 170–175; Muslim, 154–155, 174; Persian mystical, nightingale-rose images in, 171–172

poisons (venial sins), 219

Pompeii, House of Menander, 419

Poole, Joyce, 472, 473

Popper, Karl R., 484

popular medicine, 264

possessions (spiritual dominations), 284

Postans, Mrs., 344

postindustrial cultures, religio-ecology of, 329

Povinelli, D. J., 484–485, 513

Power, T. G., 467, 469

power of images, 450

The Power of Images (Freedberg), 441

power relationships, 347. *See also dynamis* (energy)

Prabhupada, A. C. Bhaktivedanta Swami, 188

practical action, 133, 140–142

Prajñāpāramitā ("Perfection of Wisdom") texts, 224

pratikramaṇa (repentance), 254

prayers, by animals, 171

praying mantis, 356

Precepts for Children (*Shogaku-kun*, Ekken), 303

predators, 326, 327

Preece, R., 548

prehistoric art, 29, 446

Premack, D., 484

Preston, Stephanie D., 465, 466, 471, 511, 513

Preuss, T. M., 485

The Price of Meat (Penman), 551

Primatt, Humphrey, 93, 606

principle in things (*gewu*), 299

private sector, Neo-Confucianism in, 299

process theology, 133, 142

processual (*wuhua*) cosmology, 312–313, 316–317

proof, Descartes' preoccupation with, 118

prophetic imagination, 135

Propp, Vladimir, 430

proto-morality. *See* social morality (animals)

prototype, type and antitype, 104

proverbial wisdom, African, 353, 357–358

Proverbs 12:10, 84, 548

Psalms: 23:1, 69; 23:1–2, 75; 39:11, 111; 50:12–13, 72; 95:7, 70; 145:9, 399; 23:1–4, 548; 72–8, 548

Pseudo-Dionysius the Areopagite, 5

psyche (*anima*, soul), 8–9

psychic space, 9

psychology: animal-based research on, 538–542; cognitive revolution in, 481, 482, 498; on religious experience, 431

psychopompos, 421n22

public sector, Neo-Confucianism in, 299

Puerto Rico, 237n72

"Pulling Book" (*Yinshu shiwen*), 283

punar-bhāva. See rebirth

punctuation, in Persian, 174

Punvro (Punvaro), 343

Purāṇas (Hindu texts), 195, 199–201

"Pure Brethren" (*Ikhwān al-safā*), 153

Pursel, V., 527

Qawā'id al-ahkām fī masālih al-anām (*Rules for Judgment in the Cases of Living Beings*, ibn 'Abd al-salam), 152–153

qi (chi), 284, 285, 300, 312–315

quasi-morality. *See* social morality (animals)

Queen Mother of the West (*Xi wang mu*), 261–262

Quine, Willard Van Orman, 595

Qur'ān
on animal communities, 33
on animals, 150–151
chapters named for animals, 150
on humans' responsibility to animals, 150
references to: 6:38, 167, 170–171; 16:5–6, 163; 16:8, 163; 16:68, 166; 16:68–69, 169n19; 20:52, 164; 22:36, 162; 23:22, 163; 24:41, 171; 27:16, 171; 27:18, 171; 89:27, 172
on use relationship, 163

Qushayri, 'Abd al-Karim al-, 154

Rabanus Maurus, 106, 107, 109, 111, 112

rabbinic views on animal welfare, 83–85

Rabi'a of Basra, 154

"Race and Environmental Justice in the United States" (Bullard), 630

Radcliffe-Brown, Alfred R., 335

Radloff, Wilhelm, 402

Radner, D., 489, 494

Radner, M., 489, 494

Rainbow Serpent, 33

Raining Bird (Cree), 36

rainmakers, 223

rajas (energy), 185

Rajputs (Asian Indian tribes), 341–342

Ramana Maharishi (Bhagavan, the Blessed One), 183, 190

Rāmāyaṇa, 195

Randour, Mary Lou, 462

Raphals, Lisa: biography of, 663–664; chapter authored by, 275–290

Rasbih ut-Tuyur ("The Rosary of the Birds" Sanai), 172

Rashbam (Rabbi Shmuel the son of Meir), 83

rational learning, 441, 447

rational souls, 119, 120–121

Ratnasambhava (Buddha), 220

rats, 182, 511–512, 535

The Raven Steals the Light (Reid and Bringhurst), 433n6

ravens (*Corvus corax*): in Asia, 425; augury and, 423–436; augury and, methodological problems of studying, 429–431; folk beliefs about, 424–425; folklore of, in northwest North America, 428; as messengers, 428, 434n11; as oracles, 431; physical description of,

424; speech of, 424, 426, 427, 432, 432n5, 432n6–433n6; Tibetan texts on, 425–427

Raymond, Nancy, 540

realities of animals, importance of, 44

reason, meaning of term, 58n22

Reason for Hope: A Spiritual Journey (Goodall), 653

rebirth (*saṃsāra*): animal images of, 219; in Buddhist tradition, 208–209, 213; cycles of (*saṃsāra*), 182; divine kings and, 409; human-animal distinctions and, 35; of humans as animals, 17, 187–188; implications of, 185; in Jaina tradition, 241; karma and, 251; in late Vedic period, 194; negative consequences of moral agency and, 253; in Nuer myth, 354; *punar-bhāva*, 182; sacrifices and, 402; wrens and, 410

Recipes for Fifty-two Ailments (*Wushier bingfang*), 264–265, 282

The Recognition of Śakuntalā (Kālidāsa), 186

Reconstructionist Judaism, 66

Records of an Inquest into the Spirit Realm (*Soushen ji*, Gan Bao), 284–285

reduplication of animal features, in Paleolithic sites, 30

Reese, D. S., 414

Reform Judaism, 66

Regan, Tom: on animal interests, 125; on animal rights, 124, 130n46, 541, 542; cited, 392; sacrifice, use of term, 541; on speciesism, 127n3; on values, equality of, 553

Regenstein, L., 606, 613

Reid, Bill, 433n6

reincarnation. *See* rebirth

relational epistemé, Lakotan, 375, 376

relational souls, animals as, 136

religio-ecology, 325–332; agricultural, role of animals in, 328; of gathering-hunting cultures, 326; paradigms of, 326–330; of postindustrial cultures, 329; rise of agriculture and, 327–328; of seminomadic gathering-hunting cultures, 327

religion(s)
Abrahamic, theocentric nature, 17
ancient, problem of reconstructing, 259–260
animal activists' views on, 616–617
animal engagement, role in, 42–43
animal-friendly subtraditions, possibility of developing, 617
animal movement and, 617–618
animal symbolism in, 537
animals and: core questions of, 40–42; corollary questions, 42–43; goals of studying, 47–50
animals in, 393
art, relationship to, 441
Brahminism, 190
definition of, 30
diversity in, 134
diversity of, 134
environmental ethics and, 2, 638 (*See also* Earth Charter)

religion(s) (*continued*)
    evaluative role for status of animals, 42
    function against temptation, 515
    goals of studying, 638
    in indigenous contexts, 378
    intolerance in, 329
    others and, 14–15
    place in Western intellectual world, 11
    Santería, 393, 585–587
    scepticism of, by animal advocates,
        617–618
    science, comparison with, 534, 537
    totems, 28–29, 30
    See also ancient Chinese religion; Bud-
        dhism; Christianity; Confucianism;
        Daoism; hell; Hinduism; Islam;
        Jainism; Judaism; morals and
        morality; shamanism; souls; Sufism
Religions of the World and Ecology
    conferences, 1, 56
Religions of the World and Ecology series, 11
religious art, animals in. *See* art, animals in
religious imagination, on attention to
    animal suffering, 592, 638
religious slaughter (Judaism), 85–86
ren (humaneness), 295, 296, 298
Renfrew, Colin, 30
Report to the World Council of Churches
    (1998), 138–139
Rescorla, R. A., 482, 496
resources, animals as. *See* use relationship
    (human-animal)
Ressler, R. K., 609
resurrection of sacrificial victims, 399–400
retributive justice, application to animals, 92
Revelation 5:5, 106
Ṛgveda, 195, 336, 342, 400–401
Rgyud bzhi (Tibetan medical text), 225
Rice, G. E., 512
Ridley, Mark, 470
Rifkin, Jeremy, 609
rightness (*yi*), 294, 296
rights and interests, in speciesism debates,
    124–125. *See also* animal rights
Riley, D. A., 482
Rilling, J. K., 466
Rim, John A., 1
Rime of the Ancient Mariner (Coleridge), 7
Risalat at-tayr (Avicenna), 172
Ristau, C. A., 488, 494
rites. *See* rituals
ritual immersions, 399
ritual sacrifice. *See* ritual slaughter; sacrifices
ritual slaughter: in agricultural religio-
    ecologic contexts, 327; in ancient
    China, 265–269; in Islam, 151; Santería
    animal sacrifice, 585–587; *shechitah*,
    85–86, 96–97. *See also* sacrifices
rituals: in agricultural religio-ecologic
    contexts, 327; animals in, 373–436;
    Confucius on, 294–295; in indige-
    nous cultural contexts, 380–381; *Mani
    Rimdu*, 228–230; personhood and, 380;
    of reversal, 409; ritual purity and im-
    purity, 67–69; stories and, 352; Tibetan
    consecration, 230; as ways of knowing

and being known, 381–382. *See also*
    sacrifices
Rivers, Joan, 596
Robbins, Jill, 391
Robbins, John, 551
Roberts, Allen, 356
Roberts, Kim: biography of, 664; chapter
    authored by, 605–615
robins, 407
rock art, 356–357
Rockefeller, Steven C.: biography of, 664;
    chapter authored by, 621–628
rodents: calcium, need for, 416. *See also* mice
Roitblat, H. L., 482
Rollin, Bernard E.: biography of, 664; chap-
    ter authored by, 519–532; cited, 520,
    527, 528, 551, 553, 601
Rolls, E. ., 506
Roman Questions (Plutarch), 418
Romanes, G. J., 483
Romans 8:12, 103
Romans (historical civilization): houses
    as social structures, 419; mice and,
    413–422; theft, views on, 418–419; un-
    defined spaces, uncomfortability with,
    418
Rominger, Richard, 568, 581
Rosary of the Birds (*Rasbih ut-Tuyur*, Sanai),
    171, 172
Rose, Debbie Bird, 362
Rosen, David, 97
Rosenthal, R., 490
roses, 171–172
Ross, Elisabeth Kubler, 601–602
Rouselet, Louis, 247
royal families, African, legitimacy of, 355
Royal Society for the Prevention of Cruelty
    to Animals (RSPCA), 607
Rta mgrin (horse-headed deity), 229
*Rules for Judgment in the Cases of Living
    Beings* (*Qawā'id al-ahkām fī masālih
    al-anām*, ibn 'Abd al-salam), 152–153
Rumi, Jalal ad-Din, 153–154, 172
Russia, raven augury in Siberia, 428
rustics, moral agency of, 296

Sabbath law, on animal welfare, 82–83, 92
Sabbatical years, 83
sacralization, process of, 68
sacramental consciousness, 143
The Sacred, 453
"Sacred and Symbolic Animals" (Clark), 453
Sacred Kings, 409
Sacrifice: Its Nature and Functions (Hubert
    and Mauss), 397
"Sacrifice in African Traditional Religions"
    (Sundermeier), 404n19
sacrifices
    animals as human substitutes, 35
    animals as subjects of, 393
    Bhāgavata Purāṇa on, 184
    as boundaries in social time, 409
    cults for, 267
    of deities, 329
    of dogs, 264
    domesticated animals, 327

    effigies for, 184
    great sacrifice (*t'ai-lao*), 306n6
    to horses, 340
    human, vs. animal, 396
    killing vs., 393
    The Laws of Manu on, 184
    Linzey and Cohn-Sherbok on, 137
    meanings of, 42
    Mencius on, 330
    metaphors and, 72–74
    metaphysics of, 391–405
    nature of death in, 68–69
    pañcabali (sacrificial offering), 180
    in religious traditions: ancient Chinese,
        265–269; ancient Israel, 65–80;
        Aztec formula for, 392; bibli-
        cal, context for, 66; Buddha on,
        209; Confucianism on, 294–295,
        297; Daoism, 277, 279, 280–
        281; Dogon, 385; Hindu human
        sacrifice, 192n27; Hinduism, 180;
        Jesus on, 137; pre-Christian, prin-
        ciples of, 409; pre-Islamic blood
        sacrifices, 150; Santería, 393, 585–
        587; Vedic, 183–184, 195–197, 336,
        400–401; Zoroastrianism, 404n15
    sacrificial appellations, 267
    sacrificial exchanges, 346
    selection of animals for, 71
    victims of: elevation and individuation
        of, 397–401; eschatological dimen-
        sions of, 401–402; metaphysics
        of, 391–405; required perfection
        and ritual beautification of, 394–
        396; special status, 267; voluntary
        cooperation of, 396–397
    violence, relationship with, 65
    of wrens, 406, 410–411
    See also wrens, wren-hunt ritual
sādhu-sanga (association with holy persons),
    188
sage (*sheng*), 294
St. Moling, 408
St. Stephen, 408, 409–410
Saint Francis Preaching to the Birds, 455i, 456
St. Francis of Assisi, 103, 453, 455i, 456
Śākyanumi (Buddha), 223
Salenter, Israel, 84
Salisbury, Joyce, 109
Salish peoples, Columbia River Plateau,
    382–384
Salt, Henry S., 125, 617–618
salvation. *See moksa* (*mukti*, liberation)
Sāma Jātaka, 212
Sāmaveda (Vedic text), 196
samjñās, 251
samsāra. See rebirth
Samuel: 11,12:1–4, 92; 17:35, 548
San people, 356
Sanai, Hakim, 171
sanctitas murorum (sanctity of the walls),
    418–419
sanctity of human life, 311
Śaṇkara, 181–182, 185–186
Santería (religion), 393, 585–587
Santos, L. R., 513

Sardis, 27, 37n1

Sarvodaya movement, 215n13

Śatapatha Brāhmaṇa (Vedic text), 196

sati (self-burning by widows), 401

Satires (Horace), 417

sattva (goodness), 185

Saturnalia (Macrobius), 161

Satyricon (Arbiter), 420

Savage-Rumbaugh, E. S., 51, 485, 490, 493

scapulimancy, 263

Schacter, D. L., 496

Schaller, G. B., 467

Schmithausen, Lambert, 213

Schochet, Elijah Judah, 89, 92, 398, 548

Schoen, Allen, 474, 475

School of Mind (*xinxue*) (Lu-Wang School), 299

School of Principle (Cheng-Zhu School, Neo-Confucianism), 299

Schopenhauer, Arthur, 131n53

Schrempf, Mona, 224

Schuff, Sally, 569, 582

Schüssler-Fiorenza, Elisabeth, 592

Schusterman, R. J., 490

Schwartz, Richard, 88

Schweitzer, Albert, 623

science

    distanced from ethics, 530, 534, 536, 538, xxiii

    ethical implications for, 461–543, 561

    Frankenstein myth, 520–521, 522–524, 524–527

    Kant on, 320

    limitations of, 45, 463, 466–467, 475, 482, 651; animal communication and, 485, 493–494; anthropocentric, 465, 495, 538, 652; lack of objective evidence, 483, 496–497; mentophobia, 496, 498; paralytic perfectionism, 496

    Okada on, 303–304

    presumption of omniscience and, 463, 492

    religion and, 534, 537

    technology, preoccupation with, 535–536

    of unity and reconciliation, need for, 475, 554, 561

    vocabulary divergence, 469–470, 477

    See also animal experimentation; Earth Charter

scientific knowledge, 381–382

scientists, Muslim, 155

Scivias (Hildegard of Bingen), 107

Scotland: Deckan' o' the Wren, 407

Scriver, C. R., 529

Scully, Matthew, 617

sea lions, 490

Searle, J. R., 482

Sears, Paul, 638

seasonal transformations, 6

Seattle, Chief (Suquamish tribe), 5, 9n1

Sebeok, T. A., 490

2 Corinthians 3:6, 104

2 Peter 2:1, 107

sedimentation (*jidian*), 321

seeing, 143, 441, 442, 453

Seethl (Squamish chief), 9n1

SEMA, Inc. (laboratory), 652

Seneca (Roman philosopher), 414

senses, differing natures of, 44

sensitive imagination, 120–121

sensitive souls, 120–121, 128n18

separation: earth-heaven, 354; Freud on, 32; of human and animal worlds, 382; in ritual purification, 72

serpents. *See* snakes

servants, domestic, 419–420, 422n36

Sewall, L., 476

sexual technique literature, 282–283

Seyfarth, R. M., 485, 487, 497

shahin (falcon or eagle), 174–175

Shakespeare, William, 422n32

shamanism, 280–281, 327, 357, 375

Shan Hai Jing ("Classic of Mountains and Seas"), 281, 317, 323n18

Shang period China, 262

Shanks, D. R, 496

Shanks, Niall, 538

Shao Yong, 300

shape shifting. *See* metamorphosis

Shapiro, Kenneth Joel: biography of, 664; chapter authored by, 533–543; cited, 534

shari'a (Islamic code of life), 149

Shaw, George Bernard, 617–618

shechitah (ritual slaughter), 85–86, 96–97

sheep, 295

shen (spirituality), 318

Shepard, Paul, 14, 28, 30–31

Sherira Gaon, 87

Sherman, P.M., 466

Shi'ites, 149

Shijing (*The Book of Odes, Classic of Poetry*), 18, 266, 275

Shmuel the son of Meir, Rabbi (Rashbam), 83

shochet (slaughterer), 85, 86

Shogaku-kun (Precepts for Children, Ekken), 303

Shun, Kwong-loi, 314

Siberia, 428

siduan (Four Beginnings), 296, 299

siege weapons, 418

sight, in animals, Descartes on, 121–122

significance, theory of, 105

signs, in medieval Christian exegesis, 105

Sikkim, 237n66

Silberberg, A., 507

silkworms, 262

Sima Qian, 260

Sima Tan, 276

Simurgh (mythical bird), 172, 173, 174

sincerity of intention (*chengyi*), 299

Singer, Peter, 158n40; on animal interests, 130n49; biography of, 664–665; cited, 469, 534, 541, 552, 553; interview with, 616–618; mentioned, 311; scepticism of religion's role in animal protection, 617–618; speciesism, definition of, 158n40

singing. *See* songs and singing

sins, moths as representative of, 111

Siviy, S., 467

Six Dynasties texts, 283

Skandha Purāṇa (Hindu text), 200

skin color, 61n54

Skinner, B. F., 483

Skutch, A. F., 488

sky, separation from earth, 353–354

slaughter. *See* ritual slaughter

slavery, 52

Slobodchikoff, Con N., 433n8

The Smile of a Dolphin: Remarkable Accounts of Animal Emotions (Bekoff), 472, 473, 477

Smith, Bruce D., 69

Smith, Huston, 11

Smith, Jonathan Z., 69, 401, 430

Smith, K. R., 561

Smith, Norman Kemp, 118

snakes: in ancient Chinese religion, 262, 265; as inversions of horses, 342; in Jaina stories, 242; in Kom origin myths, 355; *nāgas*, 222–224, 225; rebirth, links to, 226; snake charmers and, 223

Snyder, Gary, 46, 647

social complexity hypothesis, 470

social construction, 47–48, 638

social contract between science and society, 463–464

social cooperation vs. freedom. *See* social morality (animals)

social facts, 402

social justice, animals and, 591–618

social morality (animals): cooperation and fairness, 469–471; coordinated and regulated behavior, 470; evolution of, 464–465, 471; inhibitory controls, lack of, 505, 507–513. *See also* emotions and empathy (animals); play

social play. *See* play

social structures, houses as, 419

social time, 409

Solinus, 106

Solomon, R., 469, 470

Solomon (Jewish king), 171

Song of Songs: 2:15, 104, 107

songs and singing, 382–383, 407, 409, 410

Songs of the South (*Chu ci*), 276, 280

Sorabji, Richard, 554

soul (*anima, psyche*), 8–9

Soul of Agriculture project, 571–581

souls: of animals, 35, 120–121, 151; *ātman*, 179–192; birds as symbols for, 170; degrees of, 145n15; relational, animals as, 136; sensitive, Passmore on, 128n18; soul-body dualism, Descartes's, 120; soul travel, 280; universal, 167

The Souls of Black Folk (Du Bois), 55

Soushen houji (*Further Records of an Inquest into the Spirit Realm*), 284

Soushen ji (*Records of an Inquest into the Spirit Realm*, Gan Bao), 284–285

speaking animals, 150. *See also* language, of animals

species extinction, 373

species line, problem of, 55

species sedimentation, 321

speciesism: definition of, 117; Descartes and, 117–131; environmental justice and, 633–636; Regan on, 127n3; self-inflicted ignorance and, 52–53; Singer's definition of, 158n40. *See also* anthropocentrism

speculum (world as mirror of God), 105

speech: Dogon views of, 385–386; of ravens, 424, 426, 427, 432, 432n6–433n6, 433n5. *See also* communication (animals); language, of animals

Spelman, Elizabeth V., 594

Spira, Henry, 617–618

spirit mediums, animals as, 263–265

The Spirit of the Soil (Thompson), 571, 573

Spirit Riders, 340, 341

spirit sickness, 383–384

spirit songs, 382–383

spirits, 9, 269

spiritual depth, 133, 143–144

spiritual liberation. *See moksa (mukti, liberation)*

spirituality: animal activism and, 463, 475, 550, 551, 599–600, 616–617; animal appreciation and, 461, 474, 475–477, 537–538, 565; evolution of social morality and, 464–465; *shen*, 318. *See also* religion(s)

Spiro, Melford E., 211

spontaneity, 278

squirrels, 32

Sri Lanka, 215n13, 220

St. John, M. F., 496

starter myth, 362–363

state religions, 295, 299

Stations of the Birds. See Conference of the Birds

Steier, E., 414

Stein, R. A., 228

Steinbeck, John, 392

Steiner, Gary: biography of, 665; chapter authored by, 117–131; cited, 325

Stephen, St., 408, 409–410

Stephen of Bourbon, 109

Sterckx, Roel: biography of, 665; chapter authored by, 259–272; mentioned, 315, 316

Stich, Stephen P., 490

stories: religious, variety of animals in, 41; withdrawal stories, 354. *See also* myths and mythology; narratives; proverbial wisdom, African

Strabo (Greek historian), 416

Strathern, Marilyn, 380

straw dogs, 277

Strong, Maurice, 622

subjectification of animals, in Vedic traditions, 194

subjective experiences. *See* animals, in general subjective lives

subjective sedimentation, 321

subjectivities (animal), 12

subjectivity, as evolutionary principal, 645

suchness, 143

suffering: animal use and, 525–527, 535–537, 551, 560, 591; brain processes and, 493;

captivity and, 514–515, 535–537, 557–558; Confucianism on, 302, 304–305; deconstruction of animal being and, 535–538, 594–602; ecofeminist frameworks of, 592–602; experience of, in Jain texts, 251–252; genetic engineering and, 527–530; human nature and, 297; invisibility of, 592; Mencius on, 298, 318; modeling of eating disorders and, 539–541. *See also* cruelty to animals; use relationship (human-animal); violence (*himsā*) and oppression

Sufism: bird symbolism in, 170; historical vegetarians in, 154; poetry, 170, 172, 174; treatises, 153–154

sumix (spirit powers), 382

Summa contra hereticos (Alan of Lille), 109

Summers, Lawrence, 630

Sundermeier, Theo, 404n19

sunna (life of Prophet Muhammad), 149

Sunnis, 149

Surabhi, 180

survival, human focus on, 6

sutras: *Ācārāṅga Sūtra* (Jaina text), 244, 248; *Sutra of the Remembrance of the Good Law*, 209; *Tattvārtha Sūtra* (Jaina text), 248; Vedic texts, 195; *Yogasūtras* (Patañjali), 182

swallows, 279

swarming, 27–28

symbols and symbolism: of animals in Christianity, 448; caste system and, 186; dingos, symbolism of, 361–362; ecological situatedness and, 33; horns, animals with, 265; of horses, 277, 345–347; in Jainism, 244–245; of robins and wrens, 407; of snakes, in ancient China, 265; symbolist mentality of medieval Christian exegetes, 105; of tombs, mice and, 416; understanding human's use of, 50; of wolves, 106, 107, 108; of wrens, 409, 410

taboos, 208, 289n77

t'ai-lao (great sacrifice), 306n6

Taiji (Great Ultimate), 300

Taittirīya Āraṇyaka (Vedic text), 196

Talmud, 97

tamas (darkness), 185

Tamil Nadu (Asian Indian tribe), 339

taming, domestication vs., 442

Tang, Y. P., 516

Tanner, Adrian, 381

Tao Qian, 286

Targum Yanatan, 83

Tasbih at-tuyur ("The Rosary of the Birds," Sanai), 171

Tasmanian Tiger (thylacine), 361

Taylor, Rodney L.: biography of, 665; chapter authored by, 293–307

Tejwani, Gopi A., 540, 541

Temple of Rats, 182

Terrace, H. S., 490, 492

terriers, in art, 445i, 453, 454i

Terris, W., Jr., 466, 512

Thailand, 216n31, 216n35

thakuranis (clay horses), 339–340

theft, Roman views on, 418–419

theological understanding, 133, 142

theophany, dream animals as, 36

Theophrastus (Greek philosopher), 416

theory of significance, 105

Theravāda Buddhism, 207

therianthropic figures, 227, 228, 229, 317

thinking, 450. *See also* cognition (animals); *entries beginning "mental"*

Third Lateran Council, 109, 111

Thompson, P. R., 467

Thompson, Paul B., 549, 571

Thoreau, Henry David, 7

Thornton, Gary, 570

Thorpe, W. H., 483

Thrane, Linda, 569

three-sensed beings, 251

throne images, in Buddhist texts, 220–221

thylacine (Tasmanian Tiger), 361

Tian (Heaven), 294

Tianxia zhi dao tan ("Discussion of the Dao of Heaven"), 282–283

Tibet: animals in rituals in, 230–232; exiles, in India, 212–213; *garudas*, symbolism of, 227; *klu* (snake-like entities), 224–226; life power, animals as seat of, 232; peacocks as transformative, 221; raven augury in, 425–427; religious dances, 228; temples in, 224; therianthropic figures in, 227–228, 229; Yarlung dynasty, 231

Tibetan Religious Dances (Nebesky-Wjkowitz), 228

tigers, 262, 281

time, social, sacrifices as boundaries in, 409

Tinbergen, Niko, 467, 483

Tingle, D., 609

tiracchānakathā (animal talk, low conversation), 208

Tīrthaṅkaras (Jinas, enlightened ones), 244, 250

Titian, 448

Tlingit, Raven and, 428

To a God Unknown (Steinbeck), 392

"To a Mouse" (Burns), 415

To Cherish All Life (Kapleau), 617

toads, 261, 262

Tolman, E. C., 483

Tomasello, Michael, 467, 513

Tomba del Topolino, 416

Tomba della Olimpiadi, 416

tombs, 270n6, 416

Torah, 81–83

Toronto, Canada, 328

Totemism (Lévi-Strauss), 30

totems, 28–29, 30

trade routes, in Aboriginal myth, 364, 365–366

traditional animal care values. *See* animal welfare; environmental ethics

traditional Chinese medicine, 286

Train, Russell, 613

transformations: anomalies and, 284; *'cham* and, 227–228; consecration rituals and, 230; Daoist views on, 286; dragons and,

283; in Inuit belief system, 34; jackals into horses, 342; Leizi on, 279; natural and anomalous, 284–285; in San mythology, 356; shamanic animal lore and, 280; in Tibetan Buddhist traditions, 221; *wuhua* cosmology and, 312–315; Zhuangzi on, 279, 313–314

transitions, animism and understanding of, 380

translations, problems of, 96

transmigration. *See* rebirth

transport, animals as, 283

Treatise of Man (Descartes), 119

Treatise on Curiosities of Zhang Hua (*Bowuzhi*), 284

trees, 212, 223

tricksters, 361, 428

Triṣaṣṭiśalākāpuruṣacaritra, 252

Trobriand Islanders, 396–397

tsa'ar ba'alei chayim (kindness to animals), 85, 86, 87, 88, 91

tsunamis, animal response to, 32

Tu Wei-ming, 317, 322

Tucker, Mary Evelyn: biography of, 665; essay in this volume, 1–3, 645–647

Turner, D. H., 362

Turner, Victor, 66, 228, 413, 415

turtles, 263

Tūtī-nāma (*Parrot Book,* Nakhshabi), 155

Tuva (Russian federated republic), 428

Twelfth-Century Renaissance, 104

two-sensed beings, 251

typology, as used by medieval exegetes, 104

Umbulka (mythological dingo), 362, 366–367, 368

uncleanliness, ancient Israelite concept of, 398

Unequal Protection: Environmental Justice and Communities of Color (Bullard), 630

"Uniting Yin and Yang" (*He yin yang*), 282–283

unity, in Confucianism, 301–303, 304

universal empathy, 181

Universal Soul (*Nafs-i Kull*), 167

universe, 5–6, 8, 224, 645–646

Untouchables (Harijans, Dalits), 338–339

Upāli Sutta, 212

Upaniṣads (Vedic texts), 195

urbanization, 328

U.S. Agriculture Trade Update (USDA), 569

U.S. legal system, 585–587, 632, 640–641n11

U.S. Supreme Court, ruling on Santería, 585–587

use relationship (human-animal): activist response and, 463; Aquinas on, 137; Aristotle on, 122; Berry on, 8; Catholic Catechism on, 54; in Daoism, 279, 281–282; eating animals, debate on, 554, 591; of horses, 336, 338; in Jewish tradition, 81–90, 548; in modern society, 526–527, 535, 539–541, 550, 554; pastoralist, 547–549, 554; pastoralist, and problems of modern animal producers, 549–550, 552–553, 554; in Qur'ān, 162.

See also bioethics; meat, eating of; vegetarianism

Vairocana (Buddha), 220

Vaiṣṇava, Gauḍīya, 186

Vaitaraṇī (river), 180

Vajravārāhī (female Buddha form), 229–230

Valen, Gary L.: biography of, 665–666; chapter authored by, 568–582

van Beek, Walter E. A., 387

Van der Steen, W. J., 488

van Eyck, Jan, 453, 454i

Van Rooijen, J., 493

Vargas, Ivette M.: biography of, 666; chapter authored by, 218–237

Varia Historia (Aelian), 413

Vasiṣṭha (Vedic sage), 196, 197, 202n20

Vaswani, Kuldeep, 540, 541

Vauclair, J., 482

Vayikra Rabba, 83–84

veal calves, factory farming of, 87, 96

Vedas, 180, 195

Vedic period, 183–184, 195, 336, 400–402

Vegan: The New Ethics of Eating (Marcus), 551

vegetarianism: *ātman*s and, 194; animal sacrifice and, 73–74; Bhīṣma on, 199; of early Sufis, 154; health benefits of, 159n62; Izzi Dien on, 156; Jainism and, 253; Judaism on, 87–88, 97–98; in modern world, 557, 598–599; Muhaiyadeen on, 156; Muslim views on, 155, 156–157; nonviolence in Hinduism and, 184; parallels with religious commitment, 55; in post-Vedic India, 194–203; in Sri Lanka, 215n13. *See also* meat, eating of

vehicles, animals used as, 226–227

Vehrencamp, S. L., 482

Velmans, M., 491

vengeance, 397, 408

Vergil (Roman poet), 414

Vessantara, Prince (fict.), 210

Vijayanagar (Asian indian tribe), 340

Vinaya (Theravādan text), 209

vineyards, ravaged, symbolism of, 107, 109

violence (*himsā*) and oppression: abuse's connection with other forms of, 141; child victims, 605, 607, 610; crime statistics, 605, 610; gender roles, 607–608, 609; of humans, link with animal oppression, 15; pervasive in modern society, 605, 635–636; power and control vs. empathy in, 608–609; protective organizations for children and women, 606–607, 610, 613; religious teachings and, 606–607, 608, 634, 641n18; serial killings and school shootings, 609–610; species line problem and, 55; women victims, 605, 607–608, 610, 611–613; Yoga on, 182–183. *See also* cruelty to animals; environmental justice; nonviolence; sacrifices; suffering

virtual reality, 329

Vischer, Lukas, 138

vision in animals, Descartes on, 121–122

vitalism, 377, 485, 492, 493

vivisection, 123

vocalizations, behavior and, 424

The Voice of the Infinite in the Small (Lausch), 6

Voltaire (François Marie Arouet), 92–93

volunteerism, Maoist, 320

von Simson, Otto, 442, 445–446, 447

votive objects, 339–340

Vyāsa (Hindu commentator), 182–183

Waghorne, Joanne, 343

Wagner, A.R., 482

wakan (sacredness, Lakota concept), 374

Waldau, Paul: biography of, 666; chapters authored by, 11–23, 40–61, 629–642; cited, 585; interview with Jane Goodall, 651–656; interview with Peter Singer, 616–618

Waldensians, 104, 107, 109

Walens, Stanley, 30, 33

Walers (horses), 336

Walker, S., 487

Wallace-Hadrill, Andrew, 419

walls, 417–418

Wan Zi-jun, 403n7

Wananda (mythological dingo), 369

Wang Mang (emperor, China), 267

Wang Yangming (Confucian philosopher), 302–303

Warawini (writer), 155

Ware, Kallistos, 133, 138, 143

Warner, W. L., 363

Warramiri (Aboriginals), 367

Warren, Karen J., 592, 593

Warring States (China), texts of. *See* Guanzi; Zhuangzi

warriors in agricultural-based communities, 327

Washburn, Margaret Floy, 463

Wasserman, E. A., 491

Waswanipi Cree, 376–377

water rights, 153

Watson, J. B., 486, 495

Way (*dao*), 276

WCTU. *See* Women's Christian Temperance Union (WCTU)

weapons, 418

weasels, 419

weavers, in Bengal, 343, 349n72

Webster, J., 551

Wechlin, S., 466, 512

Wegman, William, 453

Wei, F., 516

Weil, Simone, 591, 592, 594, 601

Weldon, C. D., 444–445

Wemelsfelder, Françoise, 488, 535

Wen Yiduo, 318

Wesley, Charles and John, 606

Wesley, John, 138

West: art history, *animalium* vs. *anthropos* and, 439–457; civilization of, 446; intellectual tradition, 629, 633–635; interior communion, loss of, 9; religious history, developmentalist theory of, 448, 450; Western tradition, exclusivism of, 50. *See also* anthropocentrism; speciesism

West Bengal, India, 339
whaling, 329
Wheeler, Etta, 607
White, David Gordon, 30
White, E. B., 398
White, Lynn, 129n24, 547, 548
white, symbolism of, 344–345
White Buffalo Calf Woman, 376
white elephants, 214n4
white tigers, 262
Whiten, A., 489
Why the Wild Things Are: Animals in the Lives of Children (Melson), 31, 599
wichasha wakan (healing personality), 374
Widengren, Geo, 168n3
wild animals, 143–144, 277, 278, 327–328, 417. See also domesticated animals
wild justice, 464–465, 469–472
wilderness, development of concept of, 327
Wiley, Kristi L.: biography of, 666; chapter authored by, 250–255
Williams, Bernard, 122
Williams, G. C., 491–492
Williams, N. M., 362
Wilson, David Sloan, 468–469
Wilson, Horace Hayman, 345
Wilson, Mary Ellen, 607
Winkler, Jakob, 224
Winter Dances (Salish-speaking peoples), 382–384
wisdom (zhi), 296
Wise, Steven M.: biography of, 666; chapter authored by, 585–587
witches, animal familiars and, 351
withdrawal stories, 354
Wittgenstein, Ludwig, 124, 125, 335
Woei Lie Chong, 320
Wolff, H., 541
wolves: as group-living animals, 470; illustrations of, 108; Leopold and, 6–7, 8; medieval symbolism of, 106, 107, 108; Midgley on, 52
womb-born animals (garbhaja), 254n1
women: Dogon mask festival and, 386, 387; ecofeminism and vocabulary of devaluation, 596; gu poisoning and, 288n38; protective organizations for, 606–607, 610, 613; as victims of violence and oppression, 605, 607–608, 610. See also ecofeminism

Women's Christian Temperance Union (WCTU), 607
Woodruff, G., 484
Woolf, N. J., 497
word magic, 268
work, Dogon understanding of, 385
world, animals' perceptual encounter with, 126
World Charter for Nature (1982), 625
World Food Summit (Rome 1996), 569
world of symbols ('alam-i mirthal), 172
World Religions and Animals conference, 1–2
World Trade Organization (WTO), 558, 559, 570
wounding, in shamanism, 375
Wren Boys, 407
wrens (Troglodytes troglodytes): Christ and, 408, 410; Deckan' o' the Wren, 407; Druids' reverence for, 406; French customs concerning, 407; as Judas, 408; magic of, 410; narratives on, 406–407; rebirth and, 410; symbolism of, 409, 410; wren-hunt ritual, 407–411; wren songs, 407, 409, 410
Wright, David P., 68
writing, Chinese, origins of, 263
WTO. See World Trade Organization (WTO)
wu (spirit mediums), 280
Wu Ti (Chinese Emperor), 210
wuhua (processual) cosmology, 312–313, 316–317
Wushier bingfang ("Recipes for Fifty-two Ailments"), 264–265, 282
Wyers, Everett, 537
Wyngaarden, J. B., 530

Xenophanes, 335
Ximing (Western Inscription), 301
Xin dynasty, China, 267
xing (human nature), 296–297, 319
Xuan, Emperor (China), 262
Xunzi (Confucian thinker), 298–299, 319
Xunzi (Confucian text), 322

Yajñavalkya Smṛti (Vedic text), 197
yaks, 228, 230–231
Yarlung Dynasty (Tibet), 231
Yaśodhara, 242–244

Yehudah, Rabbi, 88
Yeshodei ha-Torah (Luzzatto), 84
Yeutter, Clayton, 570
yi (rightness), 294, 296
Yijing (Book of Changes), 263
yin-yang, 300
Yinshu shiwen ("Pulling Book"), 283
Yirritja moiety, 362, 363–364
Yi Yua (Garden of Marvels), 284
Yoga, 182–183
Yogasūtras (Patañjali), 182
Yogavāsiṣṭha, 182
Yolngu (Aboriginal people), 360, 362
Yoruba, 353
young, premature deaths of, 395
Ysengrinus, 113n4
Yudhiṣṭhira (son of Dharma), 188, 198–199
Yunnan China, 427, 428

Zaban-i murghan. See Conference of the Birds
Zahan, Dominique, 354
Zawitz, M., 607
Zaynab (early Sufi), 154
Zhang Heng, 264
Zhang Zai, 301
zhi (wisdom), 296
zhiguai (anomaly) literature, 284–285
zhixing heyi (unity of knowledge and action), 302–303
Zhong-yong (Great Learning), 322
Zhou Dunyi, 300, 302
Zhou period (China), 266
Zhu Baotian, 435n26
Zhu Xi, 300–301
Zhuangzi (Chinese text), 276, 279–280, 312–313
Zhuangzi (Zhuang Zhou, Chinese philosopher), 268–269, 276, 277–279, 313
Zigong (disciple of Confucius), 294–295
zoolatry. See ancient Chinese religion; animals as objects of worship; objectification of animals
zoology, Muslim scientists, 155
zoomorphism, 261. See also therianthropic figures
zoos, 55
Zusya, Rabbi, 84